The Douglas DC-1/DC-2/DC-3 The First Seventy Years

Volume 1

Jennifer M Gradidge
in collaboration with Douglas D Olson,
David W Lucabaugh, Allan Bovelt,
John M Davis and John A Whittle

AN AIR-BRITAIN PUBLICATION

The Douglas DC-1 / DC-2 / DC-3
The First Seventy Years

Copyright © 2006
Jennifer M Gradidge
and Air-Britain (Historians) Ltd

Published in the United Kingdom by:

Air-Britain (Historians) Ltd

Sales Dept:
41 Penshurst Road, Leigh,
Tonbridge, Kent TN11 8HL, England

Website: www.air-britain.com

Correspondence regarding this publication to:

Jennifer M Gradidge
32 Meadow Way, Rickmansworth,
Herts WD3 7PA, England

or to our dedicated email address: **dc3@air-britain.co.uk**

Registered Office address:

Victoria House, Stanbridge Park,
Staplefield Lane, Staplefield,
West Sussex RH17 6AS, England

All rights reserved. No part of the contents of this publication may be reproduced, stored in a retrieval system or transmitted in any form by any means, electronic, mechanical, photocopying, recording or otherwise without the prior permission of the author and Air-Britain (Historians) Ltd.

ISBN 0 85130 332 3
     978 085130 332 1

Second impression: 2010

Printed and bound by:
www.polskabook.pl

Origination by Howard Marks, Winchelsea

Front cover photograph:

NC21745 c/n 2103 American Airlines. A posed shot taken just pre-war while loading.   [American A/l via A Pearcy]

Rear cover photograph:

A DC-2 and DC-3 fly together over the Los Angeles basin in June 1990. In the foreground is DC-2 c/n 1368 NC1934D which was originally delivered to Pan American as NC14296 in March 1935. Behind it is DC-3 c/n 34370 N541GA, delivered after the end of WW2 as C-47B 45-1100. Since this photograph was taken the DC-2 has been repainted in TWA colours and the DC-3 to represent a United Air Lines aircraft.
    [Douglas Historical Foundation/Harry Gann]

Contents

Volume 1

Dedication 4

Preface 4

Tributes to the DC-3 6

Chapter 1
Development History 7

    US Production 9

    Russian Production 19

    Japanese Production 20

    Production Figures 20

Chapter 2
Technical Data 21

    Approved Type Certificates 22

    Civil Customer Model Variants 23

    Military DC-2, Air Force and
    Navy DC-3 Variants 32

    Airframe Modifications 34

    Technical Description and
    Performance Tables 34

    Drawings 36

Chapter 3
Military Operators 43

Chapter 4
Commercial Operators 155

    Index to Commercial Operators 258

Volume 2

Dedication 292

Preface 292

Chapter 5
Production History 295

    The DC-1 and DC-2 299

    The DST and DC-3 pre-War 304

    C-47 and C-53 commencing c/n 4200 321

    C-47A and C-53 commencing c/n 9150 362

    C-47B commencing c/n 20599 507

    DC-3D, DC-3C and Super DC-3
    commencing c/n 42954 632

    R4D-8 and C-117D commencing c/n 43301 634

Chapter 6
Turboprop Conversions 673

Chapter 7
Lisunov Li-2 681

Chapter 8
Survivors 695

Chapter 9
Preserved, Museum and Collection Exhibits 697

Chapter 10
Fictitious Markings 703

Chapter 11:
Civil Registration – C/n cross-reference 705

Chapter 12
Bibliography 741

Dedication

This volume is dedicated to the memory of two DC-3 enthusiasts who are no longer with us.

Roger Caratini, recently of Noumea, New Caledonia, who died in November 1998. Many of his photographs appear later. He was also known as Roger Colin, founder of Air Outre-Mer in Indo-China.

Peter Keating who passed away on 9 August 1998 and whose photographs of DC-3s will be found throughout the pages of this book.

Preface

It is impossible to write about the Douglas DC-3 without using superlatives. Simply, it has probably had a greater impact on the aviation scene than any other type of aircraft. It became the background of America's airline fleets soon after it was introduced in 1936, allowing many to make a profit for the first time, without relying on mail subsidies. When war came it was soon adapted for military use as the C-47 or Dakota, and became as important as any other single type used by the Allies. Bombers and fighters were vital in defence and to take the war into enemy territory, but without the support provided by the C-47 no invasion of Europe would have been possible, China would have remained under Japanese domination and the island hopping campaign through the Pacific could not have been undertaken.

Post-war, the DC-3 immediately became an essential piece of equipment for existing airlines and in the formation of new operators. The C-47 was also the transport mainstay of almost every post-war air force and continues in use to this day in significant numbers, some fitted with turboprops to allow the tough airframe to go on working. It is hardly surprising that the type has so many battle honours, for if one includes the DC-2, it saw active service in every war theatre from the Spanish Civil War in 1938 until the civil wars still simmering in Latin America, spanning over 60 years. In the recent Gulf War Turkish C-47s were used for ECM work. Who would have thought to see DC-3s equipped with turboprop engines and infra-red detectors helping in the war against drug barons in Colombia, where one was lost on operations during 2001.

Even in 2006 there remain approaching 1,000 DC-3s in existence, of which some 249 are believed to be active and about 300 preserved. An increasing proportion now languish out of use for lack of spares or engines, or simply because they have been replaced by more economical types. Even in Russia and other ex-Communist countries many Li-2s are preserved and one remains flying. How much longer the DC-3 will go on flying is a matter of conjecture, but the shortage of Avgas coupled with its high price in some parts of the World have reduced drastically the numbers in use.

However much research is done into the lives of individual DC-3s and C-47s it is clear that it will never be possible to compile a complete history of every one of the 10,000 plus built. Records of many no longer exist or are in store and inaccessible because of the cost of retrieving the files. It has become difficult in some cases to separate fact from fiction (or guesswork). Even official sources are not foolproof, being compiled by clerical staff who either had no interest in the data they were handling, or who made errors under wartime pressures which were never corrected. They certainly never had a thought for the historians of later years. Because of this, any history must contain some informed guesses or re-interpretations of what has been published before, and there will always remain disagreement between the various experts, depending on their source material. It is to be hoped that most of the mysteries have now been solved, and where they have not this is stated in this volume.

The production list given later is the result of some fifty years of observation and recording by a dedicated band of enthusiasts. Amongst the earliest of these must be mentioned the late Flt Lt Don MacKay and Jack (AJ) Jackson. These two, with John Bagley and many others, stimulated the author of this volume to delve more deeply. Since then, there has been a veritable flood of researchers who will be mentioned later. John Davis and John Whittle contributed massively to the earlier Air-Britain volume on the DC-3 and have provided the essential stimulus to keep the work moving. Both have made immense contributions by delving into original files, microfilm and by correspondence with many American and other enthusiasts. Dave Lucabaugh has added considerably to the history of USAAF C-47s, adding flesh to the bare bones in official records. Doug Olson has undertaken the massive and tedious task of transcribing the more recent USAF microfilm so that the full life of the many aircraft used by that air arm are recorded. Al Bovelt has been a vital link with the Australian scene, and the 5th Air Force/ADAT in particular. The authors of "*More than Half a Century of Soviet Transports*" have supplied a comprehensive list of Li-2 production in Russia, showing that many more were built, well into the fifties, than had been thought originally. Apart from these the data have been drawn from published and unpublished official registers, official files in the archives of sundry departments of civil aviation, examination of individual aircraft data plates, log books, squadron histories and so on, as well as from countless personal notes.

To all those individuals listed below we also offer our sincere thanks and ask that any whose name has been omitted forgive us. We also thank the many photographers who have supplied the illustrations, both from official sources and private collections. Every attempt has been made to replace the photos used in the earlier book, but one or two may have had to be re-used because no other was available. Apologies are due to some photographers whose work may not be credited to them, but negatives have been traded around so much over the years that attribution has become difficult. Also, some forget to put their names on the backs of prints!

Colour and black and white photographs have been used. The colour photographs have been arranged in c/n order, and appear in four blocks of sixteen pages each, placed at intervals in both volumes. Black and white photographs have been arranged to illustrate the chapters to which they relate; eg, appearing in both Military and Commercial Operators chapters in country order, and in the Production History chapter in c/n order.

The drawings are the work of Air-Britain artists Cliff Minney and Mike Zoeller. Many colour slides were transferred to CD-Rom by Janeen Willis.

Lastly, let us thank those who designed and built the DC-3 and its derivatives at the Douglas Aircraft Corp., without whom there would be nothing to write about, nor it is certain, would the World be quite the same. We should remember Arthur Raymond, who helped design the DC-3 and whose death was announced recently. Also, Harry Gann, who sadly passed away on October 30, 2000. He supplied many McDonnell Douglas photos which have been used in this book. At the time of his death he was a Vice-President of the American Aviation Historical Society. Harry was also Director of Information for Douglas Aircraft and later Company Historian.

It would be invidious to place contributors who have helped in order of merit, so an alphabetical list is fairest:

Carlos Abella, Harry Adams, R S Allen, Adolfo Alonzo, Geoff Ambrose, Michael Andersen, Kjell Anderson, Lennart Andersson, John Andrade, John Appleton, Tony Arbon, L Attenoux, Alexandre Avrane, Carlos Ay (Argentina), K Baff, Steve Bailey, Colin Ballantine*, P I o Bao, John Barowski, Jose de Barros* (Brazil), Ken Bates, J Baugher, Dave Becker, Dave Benfield, Peter Berry, Roger Besecker, John Bessette, Martin Best, Rene Biber, John Bigley, Bruce Blanche, Jacques Bodecot, Ulf Boie, Peter C Boisseau (LAAHS), Herman Bosman, Winston Brent, Trevor Broughton (Australia), David Buck, Ian Burnett, Phil Butler, Mick Butt, Herman Buttigieg, Bernard Canovan, Guy Cassiman (Belgium), Vladimiro Cettolo (Argentina), Peter Chamberlain, Chris Chatfield, Harrison Chen (Taiwan), Jacques Chillon (France), Mike Clayton, Paul Compton, Bob Cooper, Colman Corcoran, Keith Cruttenden, Ron Cuskelly, Antoine Daltun, Ron Cuskelly, Ted Damick, Peter Danby, Steve Darke (Thailand), Peter Davies, Peter Davis, Nigel Daw, E C Deanesly, Ray Deerness, Herman Dekker, Marco Dijkshoorn, Lew Dodgson, Barry Dowsett, Michael Draper, Jean-Pierre Dubois, Carlos Dufriche (Brazil), John Ellis (Canada), Gunter Endres, Jaime Escobar (Colombia), C Feather, Bill Feeny, Dave Fidler, Malcolm Fillmore, Bill Fisher, Eric Fleming, Jackson Flores, Clarence Fu, Harry

Preface

Gann* (McDonnell Douglas), Paddy Gardiner, Brian Gates, Peter Gerhardt (Germany), Joop Gerritsma, Tommy Gjerling, Claudio Caceres Godoy, Benno Goethals, Barry Goldsack, Christoph Haag, Dan Hagedorn, Don Hannah, Francisco Halbritter (Argentina), Jim Halley (RAF Units), Tony Hancock, Graham Hardman, Brian Harris, Alan Hartley, Noam Hartoch (Israel), Ronald Harrison, John Havers (Middle East), Karl Hayes, Andy Heape, Leif Hellstrom, Guy van Herbruggen, Bob Hickox, Mike Hollick, John Hopton, Lee Howard, Paul Howard, Alan Howell*, Bruce Hoy, Sergio Hulaczuk (Argentina), Paul Jackson, Milan Janac, Stig Jarlevic, Vojislav Jereb, Lennart Johnsson, Malm Jones, Terry Judge, Ron Killick (New Zealand), Fred Kirby, Hans Kofoed (Denmark), Jan Koppen, Alfred Kruger (Germany), Fredric Lagerquist, J Laneiro, Bill Larkins, Rolf Larsson, Dave Lawrence, Peter Layne, Ruud Leeuw, Bob Livingstone, Mario Canongia Lopes, Fleming Lovenvig, S J Ludman, Lars Lundin, Brian Lusk, Clive Lynch, Robert Lynn, Tom Macfadyen, Ian MacFarlane, Iain C MacKay, John MacMaster, Gerald Manning, C L Manship, Andy Marden, Atilio Marino (Argentina), Peter Marson, Bernard Martin, P T McCulloch, Ian McGarrigle, Neil McKinnon, Frank McMieken, Jack McNulty*, H W McOwan, Sean Meagher, David Menard, Andras Meszaros (Hungary), Matt Miller, Marcelo Miranda (Argentina), Bjorn Mojord, Coert Munk, Terry Murphy, Nicolai Musante, J Mutin, Aad Neeven, Geoff Negus, Dick Neumann, D J Newell, Barbu Nicolescu, Bjorn Nordbo, Ole Nordbo, Joel Norman, Peter Norris, Martin Novak, Mike Ody, Bob Ogden (Museums), Donald Orcutt, A J Osborne, Gunther Ott, Jorge Nunez Padin (Argentina), J Parfitt, Charles Parker, Bob Parmerter, Neville Parnell (Australia), Dave Partington, Kyösti Partonen (Finland), Roger Pattenden, Dave Paull, Arthur Pearcy Jr* (Russia and Japan), Jerry Penwarden, Stephen Piercey*, Leonardo Pinzauti, John Plunkett, James Pollack, Marc Portengen, Ivan Prince, Sakpinip Promthep, Michael Prophet, W Reddan, Dan Reid, Gordon Reid, Robbie Robinson, Michael Robson, Michael Roch, Matt Rodina Jr, Bob Rongé, Douglas Rough, Chris Rudge, Bob Ruffle (Russia), Lawrence Safir (turboprop conversions), Keith Sanders, Fons Schafers, Don Schofield, R A Scholefield, Edwin Shackleton, M J Sheather, Harry Sievers, Antonio Sapienza (Paraguay), Rod Simpson, Stephen Simms, P E Skinner, Graham Slack, Andy Smith, Anne Smith, Colin M Smith - Market Harborough, Colin R Smith (S Vietnam), Terry Smith, Tony Smith, Ken Smy, Timothy Staats, Bill Steeneck*, Malcolm Stride, Jan Stroomenbergh, Bas Stubert, Ray Sturtivant, Robert Swan, Roger Syratt, Luis Tavares, Ken Tilley, Barrie Towey, Charles Trask, Paul Trask, Jack Travers, Paul Treweek, Bart van der Klauuw (Netherlands), Jokke Vallikari, Ad Vercruijsse, José Vilhena, Hans Van Der Vlist, Luis Vosloo (South Africa), Jimmy Wadia (India), Eric Wagner, Dacre Watson, G Warren, Pete Webber, John Wegg, Tom Weihe, Liang-yen Wen, Klaus Wernicke, Micky West, Ron Wheatman, Tony Wheeler, Maurice Wickstead, Paul Wigley, John Wilkinson, Stan Wilkinson, Nick Williams, Martin Willing, C Wilson, Gerry Wilson, David Wilton, Luc Wittemans, Edward Woods, John & Maureen Woods and Peter de Zeeuw.

Where the above have helped particularly with a section this is given in brackets. Some*, alas, are no longer with us but we remember their contributions.

The early part of this work owes much to the original Douglas Commercial Story edited by Peter Berry in 1971, which was overseen in its production by many of Air-Britain's present Publishing Committee, to whom grateful thanks are acknowledged for their considerable efforts in respect of the present volume. This volume started as a new edition to the 1984 volume compiled by this author, but so much has been added that it has now become a new work using some of the text from the 1984 volume. Peter Dance kindly transferred the 1984 text to disk so that the tedious job of copying it out again was by-passed!

Particular thanks must go to Chris Chatfield and Dave Partington, who have made outstanding contributions to the final work over the last two years.

Many airlines have made considerable contributions through their public relations departments by answering endless enquiries from the Editor. They are: Aero O/y (Finnair), Aerolineas Argentinas, Aeronaves de Mexico, Aerovias Reforma, Air India Ltd, ALI Flotte Riunite, Arab Airways (Jerusalem) Ltd, AVENSA, AVIANCA, AVIATECA, Bharat Airways, Bonanza Airlines, Braniff Airways, Capital Airlines, Caribbean Atlantic Airlines, Central Airlines Inc, Chicago & Southern Air Lines, Civil Air Transport, Colonial Airlines, Cia Mexicana de Aviacion, Continental Air Lines, Corps d'Aviation de l'Armee d'Haiti, Deccan Airways, Delta Air Lines, DHY, DETA, Ethiopian Air Lines, Flugfelag, Fred Olsen, Garuda Indonesian, Hawaiian Airlines, Indian National Airways, Indian Overseas Airlines, Iranian Airways Co, JAT, Kar Air, KLM, LACSA, LAN Chile, Linea Aeropostal Venezolana, Linee Aeree Italiane, Lloyd Aereo Boliviano, Loftleidir, Maritime Central Airlines, Middle East Airlines, Mohawk Airlines, New Zealand National, Northeast Airlines, Northern Consolidated Airlines, Northwest Airlines, Ozark Airlines, Pacific Northern, Pakistan International, Pan American Airways, Panair do Brasil, Philippine Air Lines, Piedmont Airlines, Pioneer Air Lines, PLUNA, Qantas, Quebecair Ltd, Robinson Airlines, Southern Airways, Southwest Airways, TAE National Greek, Thai Airways, Trans Texas, Transportes Aereos Nacional, TAP, Trans World, United Airlines, Western Air Lines, and Wien Alaska Airlines.

The Royal Air Force Museum, Hendon, provided microfilm of the RAF Dakota cards for the 1984 volume and this has been amplified with the aid of later work by Jim Halley and Ray Sturtivant. Steve Payne of the CAF Museum has kindly provided copies of the record cards of Dakotas that served with the RCAF/CAF, filling a huge gap in the records. Bob Murray contributed considerably to this work. Colin R Smith has contributed in similar measure to a number of European and Far East air force sections.

I would also like to express my special thanks to two individuals, namely Eduardo Amores Oliver of the Depto Investigaciones Historicos of the Fuerza Aerea Argentina and Sergio Barriga Kreft, Presidente del Instituto de Investigaciones Historico Aeronauticas de Chile, who have added considerably to our knowledge of DC-3 use in these two countries.

We are also most indebted to the authors of 'More Than Half A Century of Soviet Transports' (Adrian Morgan, Peter Hillman, Stuart Jessop, Tony Morris, Guus Ottenhof and Michael Roch) for permission to include their data on Li-2s, and data on C-47s operated in the Soviet Union.

Finally, if any readers can add to the contents of this work the Editor would like to hear from them, or news can be posted on Air-Britain's dedicated DC-3 update website at **dc3@air-britain.co.uk**.

Jennifer M Gradidge　　　　　　　　　　　　　　　30th September 2006
32 Meadow Way
Rickmansworth
Herts WD3 7PA
England

Tributes To The DC-3

Many aircrew owe their lives to the Dakota/C-47/Skytrain, call her what you will, but perhaps the following edited report on a ditched aircraft, dated 18Sep44, says more than most that has been written about the aircraft.

From: 36th Troop Carrier Squadron, Office of the Intelligence Officer, APO 133, US Army, to 316th Troop Carrier Group.

SUBJECT: Ditched Aircraft

1. C-47 42-100517, Chalk No 74, took off from RAF Cottesmore at 1050 hrs on 17 September 1944. The pilot was 1st Lt John H Fulton, Co-pilot 2nd Lt Thomas J Flanigan, Crewchief Henry J Young T/Sgt and Radio operator Sgt John D Mead. The mission was MARKET Serial A-9 and the load consisted of twelve paratroops and four parapacks. [The DZ was north of Eindhoven]

2. About 30 miles out a paratrooper became ill and the aircraft was landed at Feltwell at 1150 hours, the paratrooper being removed to hospital.

3. Lt Fulton then took off at 1201 hrs and tacked onto a formation whose Squadron identification letters were Z4. He fell in behind an aircraft with the tail number '353' and followed to the IP without incident, where he left the formation for his proper DZ.

4. He dropped his troops on the DZ just south of the woods and made a turn. In order not to cause jamming he pulled slightly off course and then returned to course where he followed a formation of ships whose squadron identification letter was X, but the number was not known.

5. Near Tilburg, C-47 42-100965 crashed into the rear of this ship from approximately five o'clock. It tore off the right propeller and gear case, tore the roof off the fuselage from the pilot's bulkhead to the cabin bulkhead, crushed in the side of the fuselage from the cabin bulkhead to the tail and knocked out the hydraulic system, VHF equipment, and damaged other radio equipment. The pilot managed to maintain flight on one engine.

6. 42-100965 was seen to go off to the left with its left engine smoking and one parachute was seen to open.

7. Near Bergen op Zoom heavy machine gun fire, intense and accurate, was encountered. The pilot took evasive action and descended to a low altitude while two P-51s, which had been covering him, pulled off to attack the flak sites.

8. In order to avoid fire over land Lt Fulton began to fly through the Scheldt Estuary, at very low altitude. More heavy flak was encountered from the southern tip of Zuid Beveland. It was accurate 20 or 40mm, and numerous hits were suffered on the right side of the aircraft.

9. Opposite Flushing 88 mm flak was encountered and a heavy burst on the right side knocked out the co-pilot's controls, splintering the windshield and demolishing the vertical fin. At the same time lighter machine gun fire was directed at the ship from the town of Breskens on the opposite bank.

10. The pilot still maintained control although most instruments no longer worked and the right wingtip was knocked off and the right aileron was knocked loose at the tip end. At this point a P-47 of the 82nd Fighter Squadron, 78th Group, pulled in front of the aircraft and following the fighter's directions Lt Fulton altered course from about 330 degrees to 280 degrees.

11. Vibration then became pronounced in the tail assembly and after flying about thirty miles in this heading an Air Sea Rescue Launch was sighted and the pilot decided to ditch.

12. He flew low over the launch, made a left turn, returned to the launch and fired a red flare. The crew took up crash stations and the pilot landed into the wind at about 90 mph IAS, hitting the sea tail first. It settled nose low and the left propeller was torn off, about 100 yards from the launch at 51 degrees 54 min N, 02 degrees 47 min E.

13. The crewchief and radiooperator left by the cargo door where they inflated a dinghy. The pilot and co-pilot used the pilot's escape hatch and stayed on the wing until the launch drew alongside and pulled them in. The aircraft sank at 1503 hrs, having floated for ten minutes.

14. The launch RML 550 gave first aid and an hour later transferred the men to another launch which took them to Felixstowe at 2100 hrs. The crew suffered minor injuries and returned to Cottesmore the following day.

Is it any wonder that C-47/Dakota crews had such affection for an aircraft which saved so many of their lives?

A typical example of the problems that beset the aviation historian is illustrated by the following story, gleaned from a USAAF B-17 pilot, stationed in Italy at the end of World War II. On his way to a job in Rome with a case of bourbon, he encountered a US Army major who told him that he had been a C-47 squadron commander during the war. The major put a deal to the pilot; he had a C-47 near Naples, which he had put together with the wings off two different aircraft. He offered to check the pilot out on the C-47 in exchange for the case of bourbon. So they both went down to the Naples area and took the C-47 up for a couple of circuits. The major declared the pilot checked out on the C-47, took the case of bourbon, and was never seen again.

Now the plot learned shortly after that there were 39 brand-new C-47s at the Pomigliano depot near Naples, waiting to be delivered to Russia for twenty thousand dollars each. So he flew his newly-acquired composite C-47 across to Pomigliano, where he put a deal to the captain in charge of the C-47s, suggesting that he put his C-47 at the end of the line of brand-new aircraft and fly the one at the other end of the line away. So they changed over the serial numbers and parked the old C-47 next to the others. The pilot departed in his brand-new aircraft, which he flew around Italy for the rest of the year.

When he came to have to return to the United States, there was no-one to give his plane back to, as it didn't officially exist. So it was donated to the Italian Air Force, likely to become one of their four as-yet-unidentified examples. With these kind of activities, it is no wonder that there remain so many problem examples of the ubiquitous DC-3/C-47!

Chapter 1

Development History

X223Y DC-1-109 c/n 1137 - The original DC-1 flew for the first time on 01Jul33, but a moment of forgetfulness led to this gear-up landing at Mines Field, CA on the third flight, when the flight engineer was not told that it was his task to lower the gear. Fortunately, the wheels had been designed to take the shock of such a malfunction and the only damage was bent props and shock-loaded engines. Mechanical failure caused a repeat on 18Dec33, and it happened again a little later, after which latches were fitted! [via John Underwood]

NC223Y DC-1A-109 c/n 1137 - By now certificated and named 'City of Los Angeles', NC223Y was used on TWA services between Apr34 and 1936. It is seen here taxying in at Glendale, CA. [Gordon Williams]

R223Y DC-1 c/n 1137 - Taken after Howard Hughes' 11 hour 5 minutes' record flight between Los Angeles, CA and New York City, NY on 30Apr35. The significance of the underwing stripes remains uncertain, as does the wording 'General Air Express' just behind the cockpit. [via John Underwood]

CHAPTER 1: DEVELOPMENT HISTORY

US PRODUCTION

HOW THE DC-3 BEGAN

When Boeing began work on their model 247 twin-engined all-metal cantilever winged monoplane transport in 1932 and United Airlines placed an order covering the first 60 aircraft, both Transcontinental and Western (TWA) and American Airways (AA) realised the effect this would have on their competitive position. The 247 used recent developments in construction, for example engine nacelles in the wing, a retractable undercarriage and the latest flight systems, which resulted in a transport aircraft which could carry ten passengers in some comfort, at 161 mph (260 kph) over a range of 485 miles (775 km). This performance would put an end to the trimotors then in use.

The first reaction came from TWA on 2 August 1932 when Jack Frye, Vice President and Chief of Operations, issued a specification for a three-engined transport to the Douglas Aircraft Company of Santa Monica, California. Douglas assigned Chief Designer Kindelberger and assistant A E Raymond to the task. The result was the Douglas Commercial One or DC-1 outline, which was presented to TWA President Richard Robins, Jack Frye and Charles Lindbergh. Power was to be supplied by only two 700 hp Wright Cyclones to give the low-wing all-metal monoplane a speed of 190 mph (305 kph) and to carry 12 passengers over a range of 1000 miles (1600 km). Split trailing-edge flaps assisted take-off and landing and a safe single-engined performance was guaranteed.

Design work began on 20 September 1932 under Jack Northrop who took charge of structural design and Drs Millikan and Klein who handled aerodynamic research. When the Boeing 247 flew for the first time on 8 February 1933 and United introduced the type on coast-to-coast services in June of that year, the pressure on Douglas increased until on 1 July 1933 the DC-1 prototype, registered X233Y, was taken into the air for the first time from Clover Field, Santa Monica, in the hands of Chief Test Pilot Carl Cover with engineer-observer Herman. The twelve minute flight almost ended in disaster as the engines lost power in the climb. The aircraft was brought down successfully and it was found that the arrangement of the carburettor floats was causing fuel starvation, a problem quickly put right. If disaster had occurred the whole of air transport history might have changed. Another later mishap was a wheels-up landing, due to human error. Damage, however, was confined to the propellers as the partly exposed main wheels protected the underside of the aircraft.

Test flying continued for five months while the first complete cruise control charts were developed and single-engined performance was demonstrated. Pratt & Whitney Hornets were then installed and CAA approval was granted on 8 November 1933 for the DC-1A, as this variant was designated. This approval was amended on 13 February 1934, when Cyclones were re-installed.

The prototype was delivered to TWA as fleet no. 300 and set up a new two-stop coast-to-coast commercial record of 13 hrs 4 mins on 19 February 1934, carrying the last load of mail before the Air Corps took over for a disastrous period. In April the DC-1 was put on the New York to Pittsburgh run, taking 1 hr 45 mins for the daily service. Eight new World records and 11 US records for speed and endurance were set up. The DC-1 continued to be used by TWA until it was retired from passenger service in 1936 to be used on high-altitude research work. Wright GR-1820-F55s with two-speed blowers were fitted, driving Hamilton Standard constant speed propellers. The crew was supplied with oxygen and an autopilot was fitted to allow research at over 20,000 ft (6000 m). In September the aircraft passed to Howard Hughes who planned to use it for a round-the-world flight in 1938. However he used a Lockheed 14 instead and in May of that year the DC-1 was shipped across the Atlantic to the United Kingdom for Earl Forbes. After a few months' use he sold it in France, whence it went to Spain in October 1938 for use in various roles in the Civil War, eventually joining Iberia's fleet in July 1940 and ending its days in December of that year in a take-off accident at Malaga, Spain. Rumour has it that parts were used as an altar table at a local monastery for some time thereafter.

The DOUGLAS DC-2

The DC-2 was an improved version of the DC-1, and 20 were ordered by TWA on 4 September 1933. The cabin was lengthened by two feet (0.61 m) to allow an extra row of seats and 1740 lb (790 kg) more freight. There were slight improvements in performance as well and a new rudder and wheel brakes were also fitted.

The first DC-2 was rolled out at Santa Monica in May 1934 and flew on the 11th, delivery to TWA as '301' following only three days later. Proving flights were started almost immediately on the Columbus - Newark - Pittsburgh route and on 28 June 1934 ATC 540 was granted; such was the pace of trials in those far-off days. By this time 75 DC-2s had been ordered.

TWA took delivery of their first DC-2 in May 1934, started services on the over-night New York to Los Angeles run in August, and at the end of that month the first DC-2 was delivered to Pan American for Pan American Grace, for use around the Caribbean and to South America. General, Eastern's predecessor was next, taking delivery at the end of September and putting the DC-2 into service between New York and Miami before the end of the year. American Airlines followed in November 1934, replacing their Curtiss Condor biplanes on the coast-to-coast run.

Subsequent deliveries were made to overseas operators, including Pan American's China subsidiary, and to Japan and Australia. Fokker acquired a licence to build the DC-2 in Europe in 1934, but in the event only undertook assembly work for KLM and other European customers, early aircraft being shipped over as deck cargo. Airspeed Ltd of Portsmouth, England, also took out a licence and proceeded as far as allotting design number A.S.23 and registration mark G-ADHO, but nothing came of this project.

The first European DC-2 was KLM's "Uiver" (PH-AJU) which was flown by Parmentier and Moll in the 1934 MacRobertson Air Race, gaining second place overall to the much smaller DH.88 Comet racer and winning the transport section with three passengers and 30,000 letters in a time of 90 hrs 17 mins, beating Turner and Pangborn's Boeing 247D into second place. During the Spanish Civil War the Republicans used four DC-2s taken from LAPE. One was captured by the Nationalists, but the others were used for a time as bombers, during August and September 1936, before returning to transport duties.

Back in the USA, with the DC-2s very much in the forefront of airline operation, they were also adapted for executive use by Swiflite, Standard Oil (one of only two with P&W Hornets) and by Capt. George Whittell. That owned by Swiflite was entered in the 1936 Bendix Air Race from New York to Los Angeles, coming fourth to the Beech C17R of Thaden and Noyes, Ingalls' Lockheed Orion and Gulick and Warner's Vultee V-1A.

The first military variants were five R2D-1s supplied to the US Navy in 1934-35, two for use by the Marines. The US Army Air Corps followed in 1936 with an order for a development model known as the XC-32 for use by General Andrews. Later in the year the first of eleven C-33s followed. These had cargo doors and the larger fin and rudder found necessary for single-engined flight, and already in use on the DC-3. Two C-34s with the standard DC-2 tail were bought for use by the US Army Secretary and his staff. The first C-33 was modified in 1937 with improvements to the undercarriage, brakes, tailplane and dorsal fin to bring the tail up to DC-3 standards, resulting in the C-38. The production model became the C-39 and 35 were built, some surviving to be used by post-war airlines, particularly in South America. The C-42 was the final military variant and had the cargo door bolted closed and 1200 hp P&W R-1830-55s. The last DC-2 derivative was delivered in 1937.

While the DC-2 gave good service, expanding many civil air routes, the war put an end to its commercial use in most parts of the World. The German invasion of Holland destroyed many of KLM's DC-2s when they were bombed at Schiphol in May 1940, though a few survived in the East Indies to be destroyed by the Japanese invaders or to be taken into the Allied war effort. Many US DC-2s were taken over by the USAAC to supplement their limited numbers of C-33s and C-39s, and others were bought by the British Purchasing Commission from TWA and American. They found their way to the Middle East where 31 Squadron used them to help put down Rashid Ali's rebellion in Iraq and then to India where they helped in the evacuation of Burma. Spares shortages and hard usage soon took their toll and few survived more than a year or so. Many of Eastern's DC-2s were bought by the Royal Australian Air Force to supplement those taken over from Australian National and for use in navigational and parachute training. Several survived the war and after being used as a source for spares for VH-CDZ, one is now on display in KLM colours as PH-AJU, and another has returned to Holland for rebuild. Ex R2D-1 N39165, painted as PH-AJU, was purchased by Holland for the Aviodrome.

Swissair kept two of their DC-2s airworthy until they were sold post-war in South Africa in 1952. One later returned to Europe and was used in France by Airnautic until scrapped after 1961. In the USA another served with Johnson Flying Services for dropping forest fire fighters by parachute, and is now preserved airworthy in TWA colours by the Donald Douglas Museum.

Top: DC-2 PH-AJU c/n 1317 at Amsterdam, Netherlands probably before the MacRobertson Australia Race, so likely to be Aug/Sep34, before the aircraft crashed in December that year. [KLM]

Above left: The first DC-3 was built as a DST or Douglas Sleeper Transport X14988 c/n 1494, flying for the first time on 17Dec35. Taken soon after the first flight, there was no dorsal fin. This was added in Mar36. Because American Airlines favoured the starboard cabin door, an extra window was fitted, giving eight on the port side and only seven on the starboard side. Smaller overhead windows were fitted for the bunks, but these were all removed in later life. [William T Larkins]

Above right: PH-AKK DC-2-115E c/n 1357 was delivered on 17Apr35, but whether this meant at the factory, at the quayside or at Schiphol, Netherlands is not known. Whichever way, it was shipped as deck cargo from New York City, NY with the wings, tailplane and rudder removed. PH-AKK was test-flown by Douglas before shipment, and re-assembled as Fokker no.17. It was destroyed by bombing at Schiphol in May40. [via David Lucabaugh]

Left: DC-2 VH-USY c/n 1580 'Bungana' was delivered to Holyman's Airways in Apr36. Fitted with Wright R-1820s, the nose-mounted landing lights are clear. Later, on the DC-3, they were moved to the wings. Holyman's became Australian National in Nov36, and VH-USY lasted a further ten years in ANA service. [via John Hopton]

CHAPTER 1: DEVELOPMENT HISTORY

THE FINAL EVOLUTION

While the DC-2 was a substantial improvement on all its predecessors, it was still underpowered and too small to carry an economic load over an adequate distance. Its controls were heavy and its handling left something to be desired, causing several accidents due to poor single-engined performance. This was cured by fitting a wider chord fin. However, when the new Wright Cyclone G2 was offered with an extra 300 hp and 1000 hp for take-off, American Airlines drew up a specification to make use of this extra power. The first ideas suggested using 85% of DC-2 parts, and eventually led to the DST or Douglas Sleeper Transport, and to the DC-3 (for daytime use) which only used 10% of DC-2 assemblies.

Initial doubts by Donald Douglas as to American's ability to raise the necessary finance, and also as to the market for an aircraft bigger than the DC-2, were soon dispelled when American's president C R Smith obtained a loan from the Reconstruction Finance Corp and made a verbal commitment to order 20 aircraft during a two hour telephone call to Douglas. Donald Douglas put his design staff to work on the new model following an assessment by American's Chief Engineer Bill Littlewood, and an order was placed formally on 8 July 1935 at $79,500 per aircraft.

The new model was slightly larger overall than the DC-2, with a longer, wider fuselage, rounded in section to take sleeper berths or an extra row of seats (four abreast in later years). The centre section remained unchanged but the wing span and area were increased to keep the wing loading to DC-2 levels. The 920 hp Wright GR-1820-G5 Cyclone gave a cruising speed of 184 mph (295 kph) at 70% power and a range of 1100 miles (1800 km) with 16 sleeper or 24 day passengers. A larger tail unit was fitted to balance the increased power and the gross weight increased by 6000 lbs (2700 kg) to 24,000 lb (10,750 kg).

The DST had a 55 cu ft (1.56 m3) forward mail hold and eight sleeper compartments, each with two berths, upper and lower. The upper berth had its own slit window, distinguishing this model externally from the DC-3. There were separate men's and women's dressing rooms installed in the rear of the aircraft. The DC-3 had a larger forward baggage hold of 150 cu ft (4.27 m3) capacity and another holding 156 cu ft (4.45 m3) at the rear to cater for the larger passenger load. Each hold had a separate external door. Other improvements over the DC-2 can be summarised best as follows:-

1. Mechanical down latches on the main landing gear to prevent retraction on the ground.
2. Electro-hydraulic pumps for landing gear and flaps to speed operation in case of engine failure on take-off.
3. Extra carburettor heat to cope with severe icing conditions.
4. Leading edge landing lights to replace those in the nose, thus improving visibility during night landings.
5. Better instrument lighting.
6. Ice protection on the rudder counter-balance.

THE DC-3 FLIES

The first flight of the DST X14988 was also in the hands of Carl Cover and took place on 17 December 1935. By this time American had ordered ten DSTs and DC-3s and then doubled the order to eight DSTs and 12 DC-3s. Following initial tests, the only modifications needed were a dorsal fin-fillet to improve directional stability (added in March 1936) and some engine adjustments to restore full take-off power. During early tests in January 1936 the prototype could not meet the unstick distance of 1000 ft (310 m) at gross weight. This deficiency was serious enough to cause TWA to postpone their order but the problem was solved by releasing pressurised oil in the crankcase and 970 ft (300 m) was achieved to unstick. Further trouble during test flying was caused by a brake actuating cylinder bursting on touch-down so that one brake locked. A pilot-induced ground loop prevented the aircraft hitting a hangar by two feet!

On 21 May 1936 ATC 607 was granted to the DST powered by Wright Cyclone G5s and the greatest airliner of all time had passed its first hurdle. American's DSTs and DC-3s were all fitted with right-hand side passenger doors to standardise apron operations with their Ford Trimotors and other airlines followed this precedent. Their first DST 'American Eagle' service on the New York to Chicago route was flown on 25 June 1936 and transcontinental services began on 18 September taking 17 hrs 45 mins. westbound. The DC-3 'dayplane' followed, entering service on 18 August 1936, two days after its first flight. By then the DC-3A with Pratt & Whitney R-1830 Twin Wasps had been ordered by United who found they could no longer compete using their smaller Boeing 247Ds. The DC-3A entered service to Chicago on 19 January 1937.

On the other side of the Atlantic, Fokker extended their agency to include the DC-3 and eventually sold 63 to European customers, KLM once again being the first to place an order. By the end of 1936 31 DSTs and DC-3s had been delivered, including 20 for American, 7 for United, 2 to Eastern and one each to KLM and Russia. TWA ordered the more powerful DC-3B with Wright Cyclone G-102s at an all-up weight of 24,800 lb (11,200 kg). This was a half-sleeper, half-day plane with 8 bunks and 9 seats. It had roof windows over the berths above the third and fourth main windows. A steady stream of orders continued to flow in over the next five years including Pan American, Western, Australian National, Swissair, Sabena, ABA-Sweden, Air France, CLS (Czechoslovakia), Aer Lingus and LARES (Romania). These orders confirmed the popularity of the type which resulted from its remarkable economics. An increase of 3% in operating costs was offset by a 50% increase in capacity over the DC-2, allowing owners to make a profit without government mail contracts, while at the same time providing safe and reliable all-weather transport.

USAAC PROCUREMENT

As the various military models of the DC-2 had already proved the basic design, so the DC-3 was ordered by the services in a continuous programme of military transport development. The C-41 was the first, ordered as a single example with Pratt & Whitney engines and 14 seats, combining some features of the C-39 and DC-3. It was followed by the C-41A with somewhat more luxurious seating for ten. War clouds in Europe were already looming on the horizon as the 200th DC-3 came off the line and development of further military variants was wisely started.

The DC-3 was the only medium range transport available and tested, and plans were soon made to acquire more. The first USAAC DC-3s came from two sources, those taken over on the production line from existing commercial orders, and soon after the outbreak of war the compulsory purchase of aircraft from airline fleets. On 6 May 1942, President Roosevelt directed that 200 DC-3s be retained within the USA as an emergency air transportation reserve and that any excess should be commandeered by the Army. Those taken over before delivery were to many different specifications, according to the customer layout, engines and interior, and were duly designated C-48, C-49, C-50, C-51, C-52 and C-68 (see later Air Force DC-3 variants table for individual differences). The bulk of military DC-3s were ordered specially as the DC-3-360 and eventually delivered in huge numbers and in a variety of models developed for various military and Navy uses. The first USAAC order was for 545 C-47 Skytrains and was placed on 16 September 1940 and was followed by a US Navy order for 30 R4D-1s. For troop transport the C-53 Skytrooper, basically similar to the DC-3A, was ordered in June 1941, the first of 150 being delivered in August. Further contracts were placed later for the C-53C and C-53D.

At the time of Pearl Harbor in December 1941, US airlines had 289 DC-3s and DSTs in use and in the following May, 92 of these were purchased for use by the USAAF (as it had just become) for troop carrying and VIP duties. These were designated as sub-types of those taken over on the line, namely C-48B, C-48C, C-49D, C-49E, C-49F, C-49G, C-49H and C-84 and are tabulated in more detail later. Many were operated by the airlines for the USAAF but on 29 April 1944 the President agreed to raising the limit of the domestic military reserve and 57 DC-3s were returned to them as they were non-standard. Some were leased back for use on routes assigned by the government, though not all DC-3s returned to their original owners. Few saw service overseas because they were non-standard and a spares problem would have resulted. Attrition was relatively low, and many survived into post-war service.

A small number of DC-3s was allotted to the Royal Air Force in April 1941 to supplement the DC-2s with 31 Sq in India and also with 267 Sq. These were known as DC-3s and later Dakotas, but never had a mark number. Most were flown out by Pan American-Africa in civil markings, and some operated in NC numbers but with RAF roundels until the paper work caught up with them.

Meanwhile work on the C-47 was progressing. This version had double cargo doors on the left-hand side, a strengthened floor to take heavy loads and a utility interior devoid of soundproofing. Grommets were fitted in the middle of each window to allow a rifle to be fired for defence and to help ventilation in hot countries. Nine 100 gallon fuel tanks could be fitted within the fuselage for ferrying. Suspension points were fitted under the centre section for carrying cargo externally and for supply dropping. The tail cone was omitted so that the C-47 and the C-53 could have a towing cleat for gliders. The first C-47 came off the line in January 1942 and deliveries to the USAAC started soon after. Operational use is described under the various air force sections later in the book, these operations often dictating various modifications to the original airframe.

TWA's first DC-3 NC17312 c/n 1922 was listed as a DC-3B-202, but was inscribed 'Luxury Sky-Sleeper' and had bunk windows over two forward main windows. This photograph was taken on 09Apr37, before delivery. [Harry Gann/Douglas]

Although DC-3 production for the airline industry exceeded anything previously experienced, military needs dictated an even greater effort, and 16 C-47A-DLs can be seen here on the Long Beach, CA flight line on 04Apr44, undergoing final checking and test flights. The line numbers are still visible, 43-15563 in the foreground being l/n 3416. Behind it are 43-15539/45/46/50/51/55, all delivered by 11Apr44. [Harry Gann/Douglas]

The C-53 was built in some numbers as a stop-gap while C-47 production got under way. They were used for paratroop training, but the door was not really large enough for comfort (though much better than the Whitley used by the RAF). Most were sold surplus from January 1945 to US airlines. As early as January 1941 Douglas had been asked to convert the DC-3 to a cargo model, but had concluded that this would delay production of the C-47 because the DC-3s and C-53s would need new floor beams, new floors, some reskinning and a reinforced forward cabin bulkhead for winch tie-down. Special tooling or jigs would be needed, and these proposals were not progressed.

NEW PLANTS BUILT

It was clear that the Santa Monica plant, from which all DC-2s and DC-3s came, would not be able to meet the new delivery schedules, and to assist manufacturers the US government started the Emergency Plant Facilities programme. This provided for the manufacturer to finance the construction of new plants and the government to reimburse the cost over five years, at which time the title passed to them and the manufacturer was not left with excess plant. Douglas formed Western Land Improvement Co to build a new plant at Long Beach, California, adjacent to the municipal airport and the first C-47-DL came off this line at the end of December 1941. This plant went on to build A-20s, A-26s and B-17s as well, and was acquired by Douglas in 1946. Santa Monica, meanwhile, was turned over to C-54 and A-20 production.

The original programme was supplanted by the Reconstruction Finance Corp (RFC) and its subsidiary the Defense Plant Corp (DPC) which built a series of factories. One of these was at Oklahoma City and was used only for the C-47-DK and C-117-DK until the lease expired and all orders were cancelled with the end of the war.

MILITARY VARIANTS

The earliest C-47s were the C-47-DLs which had a 12-volt electrical system. These were followed by 2954 C-47A-DLs which had a 24-volt system to cope with the greater electrical demand. Block numbers were allocated as improvements were incorporated within the basic C-47A airframe. These included minor equipment changes and some modifications incorporated in the field. With further orders 2300 more C-47A-DKs came off the Oklahoma City line. These were virtually identical to the Long Beach models though block numbers do not coincide. The C-47A was followed by the C-47B from both plants, though Long Beach production ceased after 300 had been built and the remaining 3064 were built at Oklahoma City. The C-47B was designed for high altitude operation over the "hump" into China on the India-China sector and had the more powerful R-1830-90C supercharged engine, cabin fuel tanks, hot air heating and a greater all-up weight of 30,000 lb (13,600 kg). The first was delivered in June 1944. The superchargers were often removed post-war to make the C-47D, although the intakes usually remained, and some were re-fitted by the USAF as C-47Bs for use in the Andes, in South America.

In anticipation of the need for transports capable of operating from Pacific Islands devoid of airstrips, an amphibian floatplane conversion was built in July 1942. The first of these, designated the XC-47C-DL, had an all-up weight of 34,162 lb (15,320 kg), but a reduced payload. A contract for 150 sets of Edo 78 floats was placed, but it seems that only five sets were fitted. A few C-47Cs reached India and others were used in New Guinea and the Aleutians, but the ability of the Marines to cut airstrips out of the jungle soon reduced the need for the floatplane. Apart from this the model was difficult to operate in a cross-wind or from any but smooth water. Most C-47Cs were re-fitted with wheels, and one was re-fitted with floats in the 1990s.

Various C-47 sub-types were produced. Some, like the TC-47B adapted for navigational training and fitted with three astro-domes in the cabin roof, were built as such, but others were modified from existing aircraft, mostly post-war. The AC-47D was adapted by Hayes for airways checks by the Airways and Air Communication Service (AACS) of the Military Air Transport Service (MATS) during the late forties and early fifties. This had a radome in the nose and other radio aids and 26 are known to have been modified. They were later re-designated EC-47D and the designation AC-47 was re-assigned to the armed version used in Vietnam for ground strafing. This had a trio of Vulcan miniguns firing through the windows on the port side and was flown in banked circles to concentrate the fire using special sights. 56 are believed to have been converted.

The SC-47A was a conversion of the C-47 for search and rescue and could (but probably never did) carry an airborne lifeboat. It was fitted with bulged windows for use by observers to scan the sea. In 1962 these were re-designated HC-47A. The RC-47A and RC-47D were further conversions fitted with cameras for reconnaissance work and flare dropping at night to aid bombing in Korea. For VIP transport the VC-47 was given an airline interior with soundproofing and was used by senior staff and air attaches around the World. There were VC-47A, B and D versions. Somewhat similar to the VC-47, but built on the line, was the C-117. This had a single airline type door, but only 17 had been completed by VJ-day and the bulk of the order was cancelled. Some were C-117Bs with the blowers removed, and the C-117Cs were C-47s bought by Pioneer Airlines and converted by them to C-117 standard and then re-designated C-117C after resale to the USAF when it was realised that there was a shortage of C-47s at the time of the Korean war.

The first C-47E was to have been fitted with R-1830-80s, but this was cancelled in 1951 and the designation re-used for a modification by Pan American with R-2000-4s for airways checking. Only eight were converted and most of these later went to the US Army for various special duties. Of the remaining C-47 modifications, the YC-47F was a test model of the Super DC-3 which started USAF use as the YC-129 and was later transferred to the Navy. The C-47G was never built and the C-47H, C-47J and C-47K were US Navy R4Ds re-designated in 1962. No C-47L was built and the remainder were special electronics aircraft. The EC-47M was ex-Navy and the EC-47N was an electronic counter-measures version of the C-47A. The EC-47P was a similar conversion of the C-47D, while the last or EC-47Q had R-2000-4 engines and classified ECM equipment.

GLIDER MODEL

When glider towing was being developed actively, a need was felt for a heavier glider than the wooden CG-4A. Initially a C-54 was used to tow a C-47 using partial power on the latter and landing dead-stick. Later the C-47 had its engines removed and the nacelles faired over, thus becoming the XCG-17. This proved to perform better than the CG-4A and to have a flatter gliding angle. It could be towed by two C-47s but was only used for research and, after storage regained its powerplants and was sold surplus. A C-47 was converted to a CG-17 in the Philippines and towed by a C-54 to Tachikawa, Japan with one stop and after storage it was broken up. Quite why this was done remains a mystery!

NAVAL DEVELOPMENTS

The US Navy, it should be remembered, ordered the DC-2 before the USAAC. However, they did not follow this up until the C-47 appeared and the identical R4D-1 was ordered on a Navy contract. These were followed by two R4D-2s taken over from Eastern AL (equivalent to the C-49). R4D-3s were ex-USAAF C-53Cs and the R4D-4s were DC-3s taken over before delivery to Pan American. All subsequent R4Ds were supplied from USAAF contracts. The R4D-5 was the C-47A, the R4D-6 the C-47B and the R4D-7 was the trainer TC-47B. Various suffix letters were applied subsequently to denote sub-types for specific purposes. These were E for special electronic equipment, L with skis for snow operation, R fitted with seats as a passenger transport, S with a radar nose for air-sea warfare training, T as a navigational trainer and Z as an executive or VIP transport. These were all re-designated in 1962 under the tri-service system (see later).

LEND-LEASE DELIVERIES

Many C-47s were delivered off the line direct to Allied forces under the lend-lease agreement. These came from USAAF contracts, and all the initial paper-work was completed by the USAAF after which they were handed over to the air forces concerned at various depots, whereafter the USAAF ceased to keep any record of them unless they were returned later. Most C-47s were then delivered by ferry pilots via, for example, Montreal or Nassau for RAF aircraft or Fairbanks, Alaska for Russia. By far the largest number went to the Royal Air Force which adopted the name Dakota (for Douglas Aircraft KO Transport Aircraft). The Dakota I was the C-47-DL, while the Mk II was the C-53 which was used only in very small numbers.

The C-47A and C-47B became the Dakota III and IV. These two models were also used by the RCAF, RAAF and RNZAF who took delivery of most aircraft direct. Dakotas for Britain generally went by the northern route, via Montreal while those destined for Africa and the East used the South Atlantic route, staging through Nassau, where they were taken on charge officially. Some of the latter were diverted south to South Africa, though unlike those for the RCAF, RAAF and RNZAF, all had RAF serial numbers prior to transfer. Both Canada and South Africa received further Dakotas when squadrons serving in the European or Mediterranean

XC-47C 42-5671 c/n 7365 - One of five fitted with EDO amphibious float gear, this aircraft first flew in Jul42 and was delivered to the USAAF on 26Jan43, so the photograph may have been taken after that date. The aircraft crashed in Jamaica Bay, NY on 13Nov43. This model was not too easy to handle, and the need for it had expired by the time it could have become available. [Harry Gann/Douglas]

C-41 38-502 c/n 2053 - This is in Air Corps colours, the photograph being taken during 1941. Built as a DC-3-253 for the USAAC, this aircraft eventually passed to the CAA as N12. In USAAC service, it was a staff transport for a two-star general, hence '1S'. The '2' is the last digit of the USAAC serial. It has been flying recently as NC41HQ in USAAC colours. [Peter Bowers]

C-49 41-7689 c/n 3274 - This photograph, taken on 24Feb41, shows a DC-3-384 originally ordered by TWA but delivered direct as 41-7689 on 16Feb41. It went to the 6th AF in Panama, serving with 20 Transport Sq and was later sold surplus to Eastern as NC88872, crashing on 12Jan47. [Harry Gann/Douglas]

theatres were transferred. All Dakotas were taken from USAAF orders and USAAF serial numbers were allotted and may be found on USAAF data plates internally. Some aircraft intended for the RAF never reached them as they were re-allotted before delivery, no doubt to allow for urgent requirements in the USAAF. Russia received 700 C-47s but unlike other lend-lease customers did not take delivery until they got to Alaska. These appear to have retained their USAAF serial numbers. Further lend-lease deliveries went to China (via Miami for CNAC), Brazil and France.

ANNUAL SUMMARY OF DELIVERIES OF C-47s AND C-53s to US AND LEND-LEASE USERS

Customer	1941	1942	1943	1944	1945
USAAF					
C-47-DK	-	-	96	1761	579
C-47-DL	-	690	2333	1314	-
C-53	32	152	158	-	-
US Navy	2	97	133	259	42
RAF	-	2	398	818	559
RAAF	-	2	26	36	56
RCAF	-	-	32	33	9
SAAF	-	-	24	18	6
RNZAF	-	-	6	15	29
Russia	-	6	154	257	241
China	-	22	16	27	9
NEIAF	-	1	3	6	6
France	-	-	-	25	28
Brazil	-	-	-	11	-
Annual					
Total	34	962	2389	4853	1563

POST-WAR PRODUCTION AND CONVERSION

When the war came to an end and the last C-47 deliveries had been made, Douglas was left with some uncompleted airframes on the line. These were completed as airliners, with single passenger doors and delivered to a few customers as DC-3Ds. They were followed by a number of C-47s rebuilt to the same standard, and designated DC-3C, again for airline and executive use. However, the flood of surplus C-47s so affected the market that orders soon ceased. Further C-47 conversions were made by a variety of concerns from surplus airframes and these have been generally known as the DC-3C which seems to have been applied broadly to any C-47 conversion. Amongst companies carrying out large numbers of conversions were Canadair Ltd (400 known as CL.01), Fokker NV and Scottish Aviation Ltd.

SUPER DC-3

At one time the CAA considered withdrawing the type certificate for the DC-3 as no longer satisfying the latest ICAO safety regulations relating to single-engined operation. Although this threat did not materialise, Douglas decided that there might be a market for a modernised version, with more power and greater load. This led to the Super DC-3 or DC-3S which appeared in 1950. It had a new nose and tail sections and the outer wing panels were slightly swept back outboard of the centre section, and had square cut tips. The fuselage was lengthened by the insertion of a 3ft 4in section forward of the wings. Engines were the more powerful Wright R-1820-C9HE. It was hoped that many airlines would have their DC-3 fleets modernised, but in the end only Capital had three aircraft converted and these were not used on airline service for long, before lease as executive aircraft to US Steel.

One of the Super DC-3 prototypes was evaluated by the USAF, initially as the YC-129, but this was changed to YC-47F. It was transferred to the US Navy and after further evaluation 100 R4D-8 conversions from existing R4D-5 and R4D-6 airframes were ordered, using the 1475 hp Wright R-1820-80. These were re-designated C-117D in 1962 and the last was retired to storage at Davis Monthan in 1983. Apart from the Wright-powered model, the second prototype was fitted with P&W R-2000-D7 engines, and this eventually went to an executive customer. The Super DC-3 failed to gain favour and lost out to the newer Convair 240 or larger aircraft and, of course, the original DC-3 continued to operate without safety restrictions with many of the smaller airlines. One was fitted with Rolls-Royce Darts by Pilgrim Airlines but never used commercially. Basler Turbo Conversions also has plans to convert C-117D airframes which already had the fuselage extensions built in, but none had flown by 2001.

FURTHER DEVELOPMENTS

In addition to efforts by Douglas to prolong the life of the DC-3 after the war, there were many other variants over the next thirty or more years, and the aircraft has been put to uses which the designers never dreamed of. It is impossible to deal with all these. Some were simple improvements in the interior or in radar etc and had no effect on the performance. Many were modernised by fitting a single passenger door in place of the double cargo doors. These new doors usually had integral steps exposed when the door was let down so speeding up airport turnround. Some USAF C-47s had the passenger door set in the forward cargo door similarly modified.

One well-known British example was the "Pionair" modified for British European Airways by **Scottish Aviation**. Others were rebuilt to luxury standards for executive use. The number of seats was usually reduced and in their place were installed cocktail cabinets, television and facilities for in-flight board meetings or "office work". **Remmert Werner** produced a model with panoramic windows by combining two adjacent windows on each side, and sometimes known as the "Viewmaster". These were popular on scenic flights and saw some airline use. Radar was fitted extensively in the late fifties and experiments in storm detection were carried out by United and Qantas in the late forties. Cross-wind landing gear was fitted experimentally by Goodyear for use by the CAA.

Improvements in take-off performance and cruising speed were achieved by faster undercarriage retraction and by fitting doors to enclose the wheels. The Dakota 6 was a similar UK version. An uprated version intended for operation from high altitude fields was the Hi-per DC-3, re-engineered at Miami by **Pan American** for Panagra and Avianca. R-2000 engines were installed, with new propellers, improved exhaust systems, air intakes and fire extinguishers. Some had a slightly increased wing span with squared tips, some were modified for the USAF as the C-47E.

Airtech Canada successfully replaced the existing P&W engines with 1,000hp PZL asz-621R radial engines driving PZL 4-bladed propellers, modified by Airtech to give full feathering capability. An ex-Spanish AF C-47 c/n 20721 was used and the prototype DC-3/2000 first flew on 06 March 1987, registered C-GJDM. The aircraft was found to be underpowered and plans to re-engine with 1,200hp PZL engines did not reach fruition.

TURBOPROP POWER

Various trial engine installations were made for test-bed purposes or with a view to commercial certification. In Britain, Rolls-Royce fitted the **Dart** turboprop to Dakota KJ829 in 1949. Various models were tested and in tropical trials at Dakar with the marking G-AOXI, it had one Dart 510 and one 526. BEA had two Dart-Dakotas modified by Field Aircraft Services in 1951, and used them for 18 months to gain experience in the operation of turboprops prior to the introduction of the Viscount. They were used only on cargo work, often flying at higher altitude than was normal for a Dakota, much to the surprise of other aircrews. Standard engines were re-fitted when the trials ended. One further British trial was with the Armstrong Siddeley **Mamba** which was fitted to KJ839 and flew for the first time on 27 August 1949. Both Mamba Mk 3s and Mk 6s were tested.

In the USA prop-jet trials did not begin until twenty years later, when the **Conroy** Turbo-Three N4700C with Dart 510s from ex-United Viscounts first flew on 13 May 1969. These engines were torque-rated to 1350 hp and had four blade Rotol propellers. No further aircraft were modified due to lack of interest, though a Super DC-3 was fitted with two Darts and was to have been used by Pilgrim Airlines (N156WC). There would have been problems in gaining a licence for passenger use. The next conversion was carried out by **Aircraft Technical Services Corp**, Van Nuys, CA for **Specialised Aircraft Inc**, and N23SA (earlier N4700C) was fitted with three United Aircraft PT-6A-45s, flying in this form for the first time on 2 November 1977. With lighter engines the payload was increased by 2,500 lb (1135 kg) to 12,000 lb (5443 kg) and the cruising speed went up to 230 mph (368 kph) at 10,000 ft (3280 m). The aircraft was fitted later with skis and radar for demonstration purposes, appearing as such at the 1979 Paris Salon, but no more came of this. A 1980 proposal to fit PT-7s in place of the R-1830s and thus give a higher take-off power and increased cargo capacity was likewise still-born. The next turboprop conversion was by **United States Aircraft Corp** who fitted two 1254 ehp PT-6A-45Rs, driving five-blade Hartzell propellers. As these are much lighter than the old piston engines the CG position was maintained by the insertion of a 3 ft 4 in (1.02 m) plug in the fuselage forward of the wings (just as used in the Super DC-3) and the cockpit bulkhead was moved forward 60 in (1.52 m), resulting in 35% more cabin volume. The

XCG-17 41-18496 c/n 4588 - Delivered as a C-47 in 1942, this aircraft was converted to a glider in Jun44, trials showing it to be superior to the gliders then being used. However, it was no longer needed and eventually the airframe was sold surplus and refitted with engines as N69030.
[Harry Gann/Douglas]

Super DC-3 N30000 c/n 43159 (ex 6017) - This photograph was taken on 24Mar49, before its first flight on 26Jun49, the area of darker skin showing the fuselage stretch. This was the same stretch used much later for the Basler BT-67 conversions.
[Harry Gann/Douglas]

KJ839 Mamba-Dakota c/n 25623 - Mamba turboprops were fitted to KJ839 in Jun49 as a test-bed. The aircraft did not enter service and was sold eventually to Skyways in Jun58 as G-APNK, when R-1830s were refitted. It was stored in Florida as late as 1977.
[via P J Marson]

Chapter 1: Development History

G-ALXN Dart-Dakota c/n 26106 - one of two Dakotas fitted in 1950 with Dart turboprops by Rolls-Royce for British European Airways, and initially flown as G-37-1. Both aircraft were used by BEA on cargo services to gain turboprop experience before the introduction of the Vickers Viscount. R-1830s were refitted later. [A J Jackson collection]

Judged by the background, this photograph of a C-47 fitted with a single Turbomeca Palas turbojet under the fuselage must have been taken at the Paris Salon at Le Bourget, France, probably in 1953. [Flight]

349881 C-47A-DL c/n 27142 - This photograph was taken at Le Bourget, France on 19Jun59, and shows two Turbomeca Palas fitted to the outer wing hard points. It is not known if this was the same aircraft as that fitted with the single Palas. [Jennifer Gradidge]

46 DC-3-294A c/n 2148 - This photograph illustrates the strength of the DC-3 airframe, as the aircraft was bombed by the Japanese on 20May41 and the starboard wing was destroyed outboard of the centre section. Lacking a DC-3 outer wing panel, a DC-2 wing was fitted and after craters on the airfield had been filled, the aircraft was flown out to Hong Kong. It force-landed eventually in the Yangtze River, China on 13Feb43. [CNAC?]

ZS-JMP DC-3-209B c/n 2119 - DC-3s have been modified in a variety of ways, but ZS-JMP has more modifications than usual. Fitted with a magnetometer tail boom, roof sensors and a trailing 'bomb' under the centre-section for mineral survey work, all the windows have been changed to either square or panoramic. This photograph was taken in 1971, when the aircraft was owned by Avex Air; more recently it has been used for aerial spraying. [Paul Tomlin]

N300BF Basler BT-67 c/n 26744 - The prototype BT-67 originally flew as the Turbo Express but was certificated eventually with further modifications. The wing tips are more angular as is the tailplane - though the latter was not adopted for later conversions. Straps between the centre section and the wing panel have been fitted, to counter the risk of cracking. [Jennifer Gradidge]

CHAPTER 1: DEVELOPMENT HISTORY

prototype Turbo Express N300TX first flew on 28 July 1982. Two aircraft were converted initially and were operated in Alaska by Harolds Air Service. USAC ran out of cash and Basler Flight Service, Oshkosh, WI finished the project.

Basler leased the technology from USAC, now a defunct company. Harolds Air also had problems and Basler then bought both aircraft and modified them to satisfy mainland US needs with radar, cockpit voice recorder, data recorder and a ground proximity unit to satisfy the latest FARs. The cargo doors were enlarged and a flap above the main door fitted so that five standard LD-3 containers could be loaded. The floor was altered to allow the containers to be latched down on the roller floor. Other changes have included an entirely new electrical system. The gross weight went up from 26,900 lbs to 28,750 lbs with optional metal control surfaces and extra fuel tanks in the outer wings. The centre-section and outer wings were strengthened to allow for the increased stresses due to higher cruising speed and the change in twisting moment because lighter engines are used. Round windows replace the square ones in some conversions, mainly to change the image. The engines were upgraded from PT-6A-45R of 1198 hp to PT-6A-67R of 1424 hp. This resulted in an increase in the cruising speed from 160 knots for the DC-3 to 196 knots (or 226mph) with turboprop power. The result was an aircraft marketed as the Basler Turbo-67 (BT-67). Certification was applied for on 18 April 1988 and the new Supplemental Type Certificate issued on 27 February 1990 was amended subsequently on 11 December 1990 and 27 March 1992. By 2006, almost 50 conversions had been completed of which almost 40 were for military customers in South America, Africa and Asia, with Colombia, Guatemala and Thailand the principal recipients. The prototype N300BF ex N300TX was not given a conversion number.

Schafer Aircraft Modification, in conjunction with **Aero Modifications International** of Fort Worth, TX were also engaged on PT-6 conversion work. Their version was known as the DC-3-65TP and was fitted with the PT-6A-65AR of 1424 hp. The prototype (N70BF) flew for the first time on 1 August 1986, and other conversions are known to have been made. However Schafer dropped out of the conversion work and AMI are no longer in business. At the end of 1987 six conversion kits were flown to **South Africa** and Wonderair rebuilt several at Wonderboom. The SAAF began converting their Dakota fleet planning to refit 40 airframes and by 1995 many were back in service. Professional Aviation of South Africa were marketing the conversions but there has been no recent work. Cracks were found in the centre-section and tailplane on the -65TP conversion, so that strengthening in this area was required. In addition one of their conversions suffered engine failure on take-off and was destroyed. By 1996 only the SAAF were converting aircraft, with the occasional conversion undertaken by Wonderair. Political changes in South Africa reduced the need for transports and many were sold to Dodson Aviation in the USA in 1997-2000. In late 2001 two Zimbabwean Dakotas arrived at Wonderboom for conversion.

Of those converted for the SAAF 18 remained on charge in 2000, including one stored and two in maritime configuration. Twenty have been sold. Auxiliary powerplants were tested in **France**, where initially a Turbomeca Palas was fitted under the centre section of a C-47. Later two 362 lb (160 kg) thrust Turbomeca Palas jets were fitted under the wings of French Air Force C-47 349881. Commercial use was made of C-47 F-BFGC similarly equipped. A similar conversion was performed in **Argentina**.

Rocket power has been much used to shorten take-off runs. JATO (RATOG) bottles have been fitted under the belly in various numbers for military and commercial use, and from carrier decks to reach the Antarctic, off snow and from high altitude fields.

AERIAL WORK

The DC-3 has been used for a wide variety of aerial tasks. Aerial spraying has been prominent amongst these and DC-3s fitted with spray booms along the wings have often been used for anti-mosquito larviciding, particularly in the southern USA. The US Forestry Service had a fleet of suitably equipped aircraft for applying pesticides over forested areas against the ravages of the budworm. In New Zealand the "Manure-Master" was an adaptation for aerial top-dressing over the hill sheep grazing areas. Loading was through a hatch in the top of the fuselage. Despite their name such aircraft were usually kept immaculately, a necessity when corrosive chemicals have to be used.

In 1982 a number of DC-3s were modified in the United Kingdom with spray booms under the tailplane for the application of chemical dispersants to be used by Harvest Air against oil slicks off the coast of England, such work being taken over by Air Atlantique. Other more mundane modifications have included geophysical survey equipment, aerial mapping cameras, fire bombing and very widespread navigational aid checking.

ROBUST AIRFRAME

The longevity of the DC-3 is a phenomenon that has often been remarked upon. It has come about as much because of the robust structure which allows it to survive accidents which would cause other types to be written off, as to its ease of maintenance and its adaptability. It was, of course, designed in the days when stress levels were kept low and it has proved to be a far stronger airframe than would have resulted to-day. The ability of the C-47 to keep flying despite battle damage was shown many times during World War II. Many anecdotes have been told of aircraft repaired on site after serious damage and flown out for more permanent repair.

Perhaps the best known was a Chinese CNAC DC-3 which lost a wing to Japanese air attacks. Because no spare DC-3 wing was available that from a DC-2 was fitted and the aircraft was flown out with no apparent effect on its handling. Two C-47s survived mid-air collisions with Japanese fighters or suicide attacks, to land safely despite large holes in their fuselages. Spare wings were carried regularly in wartime under the fuselage of a C-47 for field repair in New Guinea and North East Africa and one C-47 was equipped as a flying workshop to assist such recoveries. In peace-time there have been a number of forced landings in out of the way places from which aircraft have been salvaged, repaired and flown or brought out by various means for repair. Others have been repaired after total immersion in lakes or rivers or from the Canadian northern tundra, such was the value of the airframe at the time.

The production list which appears later cannot record all the minor accidents that have afflicted DC-3s, but of these a few were insurance write-offs and sometimes, despite loss of life, the aircraft was later salvaged and rebuilt. In some cases it must be suspected that very little of the damaged aircraft was used, but it provided an identity for parts of several aircraft so that the "new" aircraft could be licensed. There have also been cases where DC-3s have been stolen and others have been used for drug smuggling or other criminal activities, the value of such cargoes being such that it was worthwhile using an old aircraft for just one flight.

THE FUTURE

Having survived 70 years since first entering service, how much longer the DC-3 will remain in service depends very much on the availability of suitable grades of aviation fuel. The DC-3's ease of maintenance and low price are in its favour, but as supplies fall, so turboprop types take over. Another problem is that of spare parts, particularly for the engines. The R-1830 is no longer in production and there is a limit to the number of times an engine can be overhauled. It is now, unfortunately, commonplace to see DC-3s out to grass, devoid of engines, and with little hope that they will fly again, unless converted to turboprop power. A rough estimate would put the number of surviving airframes at about 9% of those built. How many of these are airworthy at any one time is impossible to tell, but the number in museums or preserved in public places is on the increase, so the DC-3 should be around for some time yet and some will certainly be flying well into the 21st century. In 1999 Fortune magazine cited the DC-3 as the greatest invention of the century in its Travel category (alongside the paper clip, safety razor, photocopier etc in their categories).

RUSSIAN PRODUCTION

The USSR bought 21 DC-3s direct from Douglas, through various trading companies, between November 1936 and March 1939. These comprised DC-3-196s c/n 1589, 2031 to 2035, 2042 to 2047 and 2112 to 2117, plus DC-3-227s c/n 1974, 1987 and 1988. At least two of these were delivered unassembled to serve as patterns for licence production. Vladimir Myasischev headed up the adaptation work until he was imprisoned in 1938, and Boris Lisunov took over, spending two years at the Santa Monica plant to study Douglas production methods and was put in charge of adapting the design to Soviet methods on his return home. Production was undertaken initially at State Aircraft Plant No 84, near Moscow and started there in 1940. At first the type was designated PS-84 (Passazhirskii Samolet = Passenger Aeroplane - Plant 84) and early aircraft were powered by the 900 hp Shvetsov M-62 - a developed version of the licence-built Wright SGR-1820F which powered the DC-2 and gave the PS-84 engine nacelles a narrower chord than the R-1830s fitted to later DC-3s. Later the ASh-62 was used and the power increased to 1200 hp, but the nacelle shape remained much the same.

As mentioned above, production began at the Khimki (Moscow) plant 84 but German advances forced the transfer of production to Tashkent (Plant 18) in 1941, and on 17 September 1942 the designation was changed to Lisunov Li-2. By 1945 2,258 aircraft had been built, but when production ceased in 1954 Russian sources quote 4,937 Li-2s having been built. This includes 353 Li-2Ts built between 1946 and 1950 at plant 126, Komsomolsk, before production was switched to the MiG-15 in 1950, and ten built at Kazan's plant 124. The total production of 4,937 was far in excess of earlier estimates, although German World War II sources quote 5,207 (1,017 at Khimki, 3,827 at Tashkent, 353 at Komsomolsk and 10 at Kazan). Only one aircraft remains airworthy, Hungarian HA-LIX c/n 18433209 restored in 2001.

Apart from the engines, various other modifications were applied to military and civil variants, as follows :-

Li-2P (Passazhirskii) - This was the basic passenger model built for Aeroflot pre-war. It had the starboard passenger door inherited from the DC-3 and the baggage doors remained on the port side.

Li-2G (Grazhdansky) - The "Civil" freighter built for Aeroflot.

Li-2T (Transportny) - The military freighter built for the V-VS (Voeunovozdushnyesily) or Military Air Force.

Li-2PG - A combined passenger/cargo model.

Li-2R (Razvdihih) - The photo-reconnaissance model which had various glazed observation blisters for camera work. Known as Li-2F by the Czechs.

Li-2D - The pathfinder version fitted with glazed panels in the cockpit entry door to locate dropping zones and observe parachute drops.

Li-2V - Ski-equipped model fitted with the TK-19 turbo compressor on the M-611R engines for post-war use in the far North at high altitudes. Cold weather baffle plates were used to restrict airflow over the engines in the cowl fronts on this and other models used in cold weather.

Li-2(B) - Fitted with centre section bomb racks to carry 1500 kg bombs.

Li-3 - A local designation used for a Jugoslav variant fitted with Wright Cyclones.

Both the Li-2T and Li-2G retained the starboard passenger door but had a port cargo door further forward than in the C-47 and in place of the two aft cabin windows. A further window was fitted behind the cockpit, but the front cabin window was omitted on that side. Military Li-2Ts had a dorsal VUC-1 gun turret with either a 12.7 mm UBT or a 7.62 mm SHYAS machine gun for self defence.

The Li-2 has not lasted as well as the DC-3, probably because spares did not remain in production for as long. Some were still flying in China during 1987 with CAAC, and others had been seen in Vietnam during the 1980s.

Li-2 serial numbers (s/n) give more information than Douglas c/ns. They give the plant number, batch number and position in each batch (out of ten). For example, 184 240 07 was the seventh aircraft in batch 240, built at plant 84. Despite some confusion, it now seems that the plant number was changed from 84 to 34 in 1952, the digit "2" being added as a prefix to indicate 1952. Thus 3 34 445 06 means year, factory code, batch number and place in the batch. A list of known aircraft by s/n is given in Chapter 7.

JAPANESE PRODUCTION

When the DC-2 was launched, Japan was looking for a replacement for the licence-built Fokker Super Universals and Trimotors which formed the backbone of their airline fleets at that time. In March 1934 Nakajima Hikoki KK bought the licence rights to build and sell the DC-2 in Japan and Manchuria. A single complete DC-2, J-BBOI, was delivered on 22 November 1934, via Great Northern Airways (a Canadian subsidiary set up for the purpose) and major components for five more were bought. These were assembled at Koizumi, not far from Tokyo, using some Japanese components, instruments etc and imported Cyclone engines. These DC-2s were used first by Japan Air Transport Co (later Japan Air Lines) in 1936 to start the Fukuoka-Taipei service. These were taken over later by the Army for use in French Indo-China in September 1938. No more DC-2s were built as the DC-3 showed greater promise.

The DC-3 was first ordered by Japan through two trading companies, Mitsui Trading Co and Far Eastern Fur Trading Co, who, between them bought 21 of the type. Many of these were used by Dai Nippon Koku KK. Mitsui purchased the production rights for the DC-3 in February 1938, but unknown to Douglas, this was at the instigation of the Japanese Navy, who needed the type to support the planned invasions of the East Indies. Production was handled by the Mitsui-owned Showa Airplane Co, again based near Tokyo, and American engineers continued to assist with production plans until April 1939. The first aircraft assembled from American components emerged in September for Japan Air Transport Co, but the 2nd and 5th went to the Navy. Japanese production built up slowly and by July 1941 only one a month was coming off the line. A year later the situation was much improved and Nakajima was sharing production of components. They had set up a parallel DC-3 line in 1940 mostly for the airlines, but this ceased assembly by 1942. Thereafter production was concentrated on the military version from the Showa line, and by 1945 a total of 416 had been built. Modifications to suit military use included a wide cargo door similar to that on the C-47, though it may have been designed before the C-47. The imported DC-3s were known as the D1 (D for Douglas) and Japanese production as the D2, later the L2D, but to the Allies it was "Tabby" - and a source of much confusion.

There were two prototype L2D1s delivered in October 1939 and April 1940, followed by the first production model or L2D2, which had the 1000 hp Mitsubishi Kinsei 43. The cargo model had, in addition to large doors, reinforced floors. They were designated L2D2-1. Later, the L2D2-2 was fitted with extended windows behind the flight deck. This basic model was the main production version which was built in four further variants:-

L2D-3 with 1300 hp Kinsei 51s, was a personnel transport.

L2D-3G with Kinsei 53s.

L2D3-1 and 1a were cargo versions with the Kinsei 51 and 53 respectively.

L2D4 and 4-1 were personnel and cargo models respectively, fitted with defensive positions. A glazed blister was fitted over the forward cabin to carry a 13 mm flexibly-mounted machine gun. A 7.7 mm gun was also fitted in the rear window on each side of the fuselage.

These versions of the basic DC-3 were lighter and more powerful and hence had a better performance. Some parts, including control surfaces, etc, were made of wood, to get round the metal shortages. This led to one final version, the L2D-5, which was in mock-up form at the end of the war, and was to have been made almost entirely of wood, and powered by 1500 hp Kinsei 62s. A total of 487 L2Ds were built, including DC-3s. The Imperial Navy operated most of the Japanese-built examples with Southern Philippines Kokutai squadrons attached to various Air Fleets responsible to the Combined Fleet and to the China Area and Southeast Area Fleets. About 20 went to the Japanese Army. By the end of the war many had been destroyed. One survived to fly briefly with the French Air Force in Indo-China. It is only identified as "4265". Another has been reported flying in China post-war.

Production figures by year are:-

	1939	1940	1941	1942	1943	1944	1945	Total
Showa	1	1	22	87	61	157	87	416
Nakajima	-	10	49	12	-	-	-	71

PRODUCTION FIGURES

Many attempts have been made to determine the total number of DC-3s produced, but the results have not always tallied. This is accounted for partly by the allocation of new c/ns to airframes that were rebuilt by Douglas post-war to DC-3C and Super DC-3. The following would appear to account for all aircraft produced:-

Santa Monica Civil DC-3	579
Santa Monica Military	382 (C-41, C-41A, C-53, C-53D, R4D-2)
Long Beach Military	4285 (C-47, C-47A, C-47B, R4D-1)
Oklahoma City Military	5381 (C-47A, C-47B, C-117A & R4Ds)
Oklahoma City Civil DC-3D	28
US Grand Total	**10,655**
Japanese L2D	487
Russian Li-2	4937
World total	**16,079**

Chapter 2

Technical Data

APPROVED TYPE CERTIFICATES

The Approved Type Certificate (ATC) is the stamp of approval for a production aircraft type built for the civil market and is granted by the Department of Commerce (later the Civil Aeronautics Administration) in the United States. Such certificates were first issued in 1927 and by the time the DC-2 was approved 539 types and variants had been certificated. Those types which satisfied the requirements but which were not intended for production or commercial use were given Memo numbers.

Model	ATC No	Date	Powerplant	All-up weight
DC-1A	Memo 2-460	08Nov33	700 hp P&W R-1690-SDG	
DC-1		13Feb34	710 hp Wright SGR-1820-F3	17,500 lb (8000 kg)
DC-2	540	28Jun34	710 hp Wright SGR-1820-F3	
DC-2-115	555	28Aug34	750 hp Wright SGR-1820-F2	18,000 lb (8200 kg)
DC-2-115H	570	20May35	720 hp P&W R-1690-S8EG	
DC-2-115F	Memo 2-507	09Jul35	690 hp Bristol Pegasus 6	
DC-2A	Memo 2-495	07Dec34	700 hp P&W R-1690-SDG	

All-up weights were increased to 18,200 lb (8300 kg) with a stronger undercarriage upper structure and to 18,560 lb (8450 kg) with strengthened main and tail wheel structures, fuselage and centre sections and with fuel dumping installation. A further increase to 19,000 lb (8650 kg) was allowed with the above changes and series F-2B, F-3B, F-52 and F-53 engines geared 16:11 with fully feathering propellers and using 87 octane fuel.

Specifications for ATCs granted to DC-3 and DST models were as follows. When a number is given in brackets beside the ATC number that model was also eligible under the alternative ATC number. Most military variants had ATC equivalents (see page 29) and these are obtained by reference to the c/ns quoted.

Model	ATC No	Date	Powerplant	All-up weight
DST	607	21May36	1000 hp Wright GR-1820-G2	24,000 lb (10,900 kg)
c/n 1949 up	607	01Mar39	1000 hp Wright GR-1820-G2E	24,000 lb (10,900 kg)
	(607)	24Sep37	1100 hp Wright GR-1820-G102	25,000 lb (11,350 kg)
		25Feb38	1000 hp Wright GR-1820-G103	24,000 lb (10,900 kg)
	(607)	31May40	1200 hp Wright GR-1820-G202A	25,000 lb (11,350 kg)
DST-A	647	30Jun37	1000 hp P&W R-1830-SBG	24,000 lb (10,900 kg)
c/n 1951 up	647	30Jun37	1000 hp P&W R-1830-SB3G	24,000 lb (10,900 kg)
DST-A	671 (669)	26Mar38	1200 hp P&W R-1830-S1CG	25,200 lb (11,440 kg)
c/n 1900 up	671	01May39	1200 hp P&W R-1830-S1C3G	25,200 lb (11,440 kg)
	671	01May39	1050 hp P&W R-1830-SCG	25,200 lb (11,440 kg)
	671	09Feb40	1050 hp P&W R-1830-SC3G	25,200 lb (11,440 kg)
	671	18Feb42	1200 hp P&W R-1830-S4C4G	25,200 lb (11,440 kg)
DC-3	618	27Aug36	1000 hp Wright GR-1820-G2	24,000 lb (10,900 kg)
c/n 1545 up	618	20Sep37	1100 hp Wright GR-1820-G102	25,200 lb (11,440 kg)
	618	04Nov37	1000 hp Wright GR-1820-G103	24,000 lb (10,900 kg)
	618	01Mar39	1100 hp Wright GR-1820-G102A	25,200 lb (11,440 kg)
	618	01Mar39	1000 hp Wright GR-1820-G2E	24,000 lb (10,900 kg)
	618	01Aug39	1000 hp Wright GR-1820-G103A	24,000 lb (10,900 kg)
	618	31May40	1200 hp Wright GR-1820-G202A	25,200 lb (11,440 kg)
DC-3A	619	28Nov36	1000 hp P&W R-1830-SB3G	24,000 lb (10,900 kg)
c/n 1900 up	619	02Jul37	1000 hp P&W R-1830-SBG	24,000 lb (10,900 kg)
DC-3A	669	31Oct37	1200 hp P&W R-1830-S1CG	25,200 lb (11,440 kg)
c/n 1900 up	669	01May39	1200 hp P&W R-1830-S1C3G	25,200 lb (11,440 kg)
	669	01May39	1050 hp P&W R-1830-SCG	25,200 lb (11,440 kg)
	669	09Feb40	1050 hp P&W R-1830-SC3G	25,200 lb (11,440 kg)
	669	18Feb42	1200 hp P&W R-1830-S4C4G	25,200 lb (11,440 kg)
DC-3B	635	03May37	1100 hp Wright GR-1820-G102	25,200 lb (11,440 kg)
c/n 1922 up	635	31Mar41	1200 hp Wright GR-1820-G202A	25,200 lb (11,440 kg)
DC-3C	669	10Jul44	1050 hp P&W R-1830-SC3G	25,200 lb (11,440 kg)
c/n 4200 up	669	10Jul44	1200 hp P&W R-1830-S1C3G	25,200 lb (11,440 kg)
(all C-47s)	669	16Jan48	1200 hp P&W R-1830-S4C4G	25,200 lb (11,440 kg)
	669	13Nov45	1200 hp P&W R-1830-90C	25,200 lb (11,440 kg)
DC-3D	669	15Jan46	1200 hp P&W R-1830-90C	25,200 lb (11,440 kg)
c/n 18548 up (C-117A) and c/n 42954 to 42981				
DC-3S	6A.2	24Jul50	1475 hp Wright R-1820-C9-HE2	31,900 lb (14,470 kg)
c/n 43159 and 43191 to 43193 plus all R4D-8/C-117Ds				

CHAPTER 2: TECHNICAL DATA

CIVIL CUSTOMER MODEL NUMBERS

The following table lists the model number suffixes allocated to different customers for the DC-2 and for civil customers only for the DC-3 together with the number of each model built and the c/ns applicable. First registration or delivery/customer registration is then quoted. DC-3s diverted from civil customers fo military use without first entering commercial service are shown as 'not delivered'.

DC-2 models

Model No.	Customer	No. built	C/ns	Initial Registrations
DC-2-112	TWA	20	1237 - 1256	NC13711 - NC13730
		8	1293 - 1300	NC13783 - NC13790
DC-2-112	General Air Lines	4	1257 - 1260	NC13731 - NC13734
DC-2-112	Eastern Air Lines	8	1261, 1286 - 1290, 1291, 1292	NC13735 - NC13740 NC13781, NC13782
DC-2-115A	Fokker (for KLM)	1	1317	NC14284/PH-AJU
DC-2-115B	Fokker (for ALI)	1	1319	PH-AKF/I-EROS
	Swissair	2	1321, 1322, 1329	HB-ITI, HB-ITE, HB-ITA
	French Government	1	1333	F-AKHD
	LAPE	1	1334	EC-AAY
DC-2-115D	Fokker (for Lufthansa)	1	1318	PH-AKF/D-ABEQ
	Austrian Government	1	1320	A-500
	LAPE	1	1330	EC-XAX
DC-2-115D/F	Swissair	2	1331, 1332	HB-ISI, HB-ITO
DC-2-115E	KLM	1	1335	PH-AKG
		12	1354 - 1365	PH-AKI - PH-AKS
DC-2-115F	LOT	2	1374 - 1376	SP-ASK, SP-ASL
DC-2-115G	KNILM	3	1374 - 1376	PK-AFJ - PK-AFL
DC-2-115H	KLM	1	1366	PH-AKT
DC-2-115J	LAPE	1	1417, 1521	EC-EBB, EC-BBE
DC-2-115K	CLS	2	1581, 1582	OK-AIA, OK-AIB
DC-2-115L	KLM	3	1583 - 1585	PH-ALD - PH-ALF
DC-2-115M	Fokker (for LAPE)	1	1527	?
DC-2-118A/B	Pan American/Panagra	6	1301 - 1306	NC14268 - NC14273
		3	1350 - 1352	NC14290 - NC14292
		4	1367 - 1370	NC14295 - NC14390
		1	1371	NC14950
		1	1600	Parts only, for CNAC
DC-2-120	American Airlines	10	1307 - 1316	NC14274 - NC14283
		3	1401 - 1403	NC14921 - NC14923
		1	1406	NC14966
		2	1410, 1411	NC14924, NC14925
		2	1407, 1412	Unregistered, (parts only)
DC-2-123	Nakajima	1	1323	NC14284
DC-2-124	Swiftlite Corp	1	1324	NC1000
DC-2-125	US Navy (R2D-1)	3	1325 - 1327	9620 - 9622
DC-2-127	Standard Oil	1	1328	NC14285
DC-2-142	US Navy (R2D-1)	2	1404, 1405	9993, 9994
DC-2-145	US AAC (C-33)	18	1503 - 1520	36-70 - 36-87
DC-2-152	Amtorg	1	1413	NC14949/URSS-M25
DC-2-153	US AAC (XC-32)	1	1414	36-1
DC-2-171	Eastern Air Lines	2	1372, 1373	NC14969, NC14790
DC-2-172	TWA	2	1408, 1409	NC14978, NC14979
		1	1599	NC16049
DC-2-173	US AAC (YC-34)	2	1415, 1416	36-345, 36-346
DC-2-185	Holyman's Airways	1	1580	VH-USY
DC-2-190	Capt G Whittell	1	1586	NC16048
DC-2-192	Nanking Government	1	1560	?
DC-2-193	Canton	1	1598	?
DC-2-199	Holyman's Airways	1	1561	VH-UXJ
DC-2-200	CLS	1	1562	OK-AIC
DC-2-210	ANA	2	1563, 1566	VH-UYB, VH-UYC
DC-2-211	Fokker (for CLS)	1	1564	PH-ALZ/OK-AIZ
	CLS	1	1565	OK-AID
DC-2-221	PAA (for CNAC)	2	1567, 1568	?

Model No.	Customer	No. built	C/ns	Initial Registrations
DC-2-243	US AAC (C-39)	35	2057 - 2059 2061 - 2092	38-499 - 38-501 38-504 - 38-535
DC-2-253	US AAC (C-41)	1	2053	38-502
DC-2-267	US AAC (C-42)	1	2060	38-503
DC-2- ?	Nakajima	5	1418 - 1422	Parts for assembly in Japan

DST & DC-3 models

Model No.	Customer	No. built	C/ns	Initial Registrations
DST-144	American	1	1494	NX14988
		6	1495 - 1500, 1549	NC16001 - NC16007
DC-3-178	American	4	1545 - 1548	NC16009, NC16030, NC16011, NC16012
		8	1551 - 1557, 1588	NC16013 - NC16019, NC16008
		5	1917 - 1921	NC17331 - NC17335
DC-3A-191	United	10	1900 - 1909	NC16060 - NC16069
DC-3A-191B	United	1	2018	NC18945
DC-3-194	KLM	1	1590	PH-ALI
DC-3-194B	KLM	10	1935 - 1944	PH-ALH, ALN, ALO, ALR - ALW
		5	1965, 2019 - 2022	PH-ALP, PH-ARW - ARZ
DC-3-194C	KLM	3	1980 - 1982	PH-ARB, ARE, ARG
DC-3-194E	KLM	1	2036	PH-ASK
DC-3-194F	KLM	3	2109 - 2111	PH-ASP, PH-ASR, PH-AST
DC-3-194G	KLM	1	2142	PH-ASM
DC-3-194H	KLM	1	2147	PH-AXH
DC-3-196	Amtorg, USSR	1	1589	NC15995
DC-3-196A	Fokker, USSR	5	2031 - 2035	URSS-....
		6	2042 - 2047	URSS-.... / Sov AF
DC-3-196B	Fokker, USSR	6	2031 - 2035	URSS-.... / Sov AF
DC-3A-197	United	5	1910 - 1914	NC16070 - NC16074
		5	1925 - 1929	NC16086 - NC16090
		2	1983 - 1984	NC18611, NC18612
DC-3A-197B	United	7	2004 - 2008, 2010, 2017	NC18938 - NC18944
DC-3A-197C	United	4	2174 - 2177	NC25677 - NC25680
		1	2221	NC25681
DC-3A-197D	United	7	3255, 3257 - 3262	NC25611. NC25613 - NC25618
	United (not delivered)	1	3256	(NC25612) *to C-48*
	United (not delivered)	1	4112	(NC34999) *to DC-3A-398 / C-52*
DC-3A-197E	United	3	4123, 4125, 4126	NC33644, NC33646, NC33647
	United (not delivered)	2	4127, 4128	(NC33648, NC33649) *to DC-3-395 / C-52B*
DC-3-201	Eastern	2	1915, 1916	NC16094, NC16095
		3	1948, 1949, 1971	NC16081 - NC16083
		5	1996 - 2000	NC18120 - NC18124
DC-3-201A	Eastern	2	2102, 2108	NC21743, NC21744
DC-3-201B	Eastern	3	2141, 2143 - 2144	NC21729, NC21727, NC21728
DC-3-201C	Eastern	3	2234 - 2236	NC25646 - NC25648
DC-3-201D	Eastern	2	2246 - 2247	NC15595, NC15596
		4	2257 - 2260	NC15597 - NC15599, NC19963
DC-3-201E	Eastern	2	2268 - 2269	NC28391, NC28392
		3	3252 - 3254	NC19968 - NC19970
DC-3-201F	Eastern	5	4089 - 4093	NC28381 - NC28385
	Eastern (not delivered)	3	4094 - 4096	(NC28386 - NC28388) *to DC-3-387 / C-49B*
DC-3-201G	Eastern (not delivered)	1	4136	(NC33630) *to DC-3-402/ C-52C*
	Eastern	4	4137 - 4140	NC33631 - NC33634
	Eastern (not delivered)	5	4141 - 4145	(NC33635 - NC33639) *to DC-3-389/ C-49D*
DC-3B-202	TWA	8	1922 - 1924	NC17312 - NC17314
		5	1930 - 1934	NC17315 - NC17319
DC-3B-202A	TWA	2	2027, 2028	NC18953, NC18954
DST-A-207	United	8	1951 - 1958	NC18103 - NC18110
		2	1977, 1978	NC18145, NC18146
	Western	2	1959, 1960	NC18101, NC18102
DST-A-207B	United	2	2222 - 2223	NC25682, NC25683
DST-A-207C	United	2	3263 - 3264	NC25619, NC25620
DST-A-207D	United	3	3265, 4113 - 4114	NC25621, NC33641, NC33642
DC-3-208	American	4	1961 - 1964	NC17326 - NC17329
DC-3-208A	American	5	2103 - 2107	NC21745 - NC21749
DC-3-209	TWA	5	1966 - 1970	NC17320 - NC17324
DC-3-209A	TWA	4	2013 - 2016	NC18949 - NC18952
DC-3-209B	TWA	3	2118 - 2120	NC14931 - NC14933
DC-3A-214	ABA	3	1947, 1972, 1975	SE-BAA - SE-BAC
DC-3-216	Swissair	2	1945, 1946	HB-IRA, HB-IRI
DC-3-217	American	1	1976	NC18144
DST-217A	American	2	2149, 2165	NC21769, NC21752
		2	2263, 2264	NC28325, NC28350

Chapter 2: Technical Data

Model	Operator	Qty	MSN	Registration
DST-217B	American	2	2216 - 2217	NC25685, NC25686
DC-3-220	CLS	1	1973	OK-AIH
DC-3-220A	CLS	2	2023, 2024	OK-AIE, OK-AIF
DC-3-220B	CLS	1	2095	OK-AIG
DC-3-227	Fokker (USSR)	3	1974, 1987 - 1988	Sov AF
	LARES	2	1985, 1986	YR-PIF, YR-PAF
DC-3-227A	Swissair	1	2054	HB-IRO
DC-3-227B	Sabena	2	2093, 2094	OO-AUH, OO-AUI
DC-3-228	PAA	7	1989 - 1994, 2012	NC18113 - NC18118, NC18937
DC-3-228A	PAA	1	2128	NC21717
DC-3-228B	CNAC	1	2135	41
DC-3A-228C	PAA	5	2193 - 2197	NC25653 - NC25657
		5	2228 - 2232	NC25641 - NC25645
DC-3A-228D	PAA	4	3290 - 3293	NC28301 - NC28304
		4	4085 - 4088	NC28305 - NC28308
DC-3A-228F	PAA	6	4100 - 4105	NC33609 - NC33614
DC-3-229	Panagra	2	1995, 2011	NC18119, NC18936
DC-3-232	Airlines of Australia	2	2002, 2003	VH-UZJ, VH-UZK
DC-3-232A	Airlines of Australia	2	2029, 2030	VH-ABR, VH-ACB
DC-3-237A	Mitsui	1	1979	(PH-ARA)
		1	2009	J-B . . .
		2	2025, 2026	J-B . . .
DC-3A-237B	Mitsui	5	2037 - 2041	J-B . . .
DC-3-237C	Mitsui	4	2049 - 2052	J-B . . .
DC-3A-237D	Mitsui	3	2048, 2055 - 2056	J-B . . .
DC-3A-253A	Northwest	1	2146	NC21777
DC-3-260	Nakajima (USSR)	6	2096 - 2101	URSS- . . . . / Sov AF
DC-3-268	Swissair	1	2132	HB-IRU
	ABA	1	2133	SE-BAF
DC-3-268B	Aer Lingus	1	2178	EI-ACA
DC-3-268C	Fokker (Aer Lingus)	1	2261	(EI-ACB)
DC-3A-269	Northwest	3	2123 - 2125	NC21711 - NC21713
		3	2129 - 2131	NC21714 - NC21716
DC-3A-269B	Northwest	3	2183 - 2185	NC25608 - NC25610
		1	2227	NC25621
DC-3A-269C	Northwest	2	2270, 3276	NC25622, NC25623
DC-3-270	Canadian Colonial	2	2126, 2127	NC21750, NC21751
DC-3-270A	Canadian Colonial	2	2237, 2238	NC21758, NC21759
DC-3-270B	Canadian Colonial	2	2271, 2272	NC28360, NC25694
DC-3-270C	Canadian Colonial (not del.)	1	3289	(NC34962) to C-51
DC-3-276	Swissair	1	2121	HB-IRE
DC-3-277	American	5	2136 - 2140	NC16096, NC18141 - NC18143, NC17340
DC-3-277A	American	2	2166, 2167	NC21767, NC21768
DC-3-277B	American	18	2198 - 2215	NC21793 - NC21795, NC21797 - NC21799, NC25658, NC25660, NC25661, NC25663 - NC25665, NC25670 - NC25673, NC25676, NC25684
DC-3-277C	American	3	2243 - 2245	NC15589 - NC15591
		7	2248 - 2254	NC15592, NC15629, NC19974, NC28310, NC28321, NC28323, NC28324
DC-3-277D	American	4	4115 - 4118	NC33651, NC33653 - NC33655
		2	4802, 4803	NC33656, NC33657
	American (not delivered)	4	4119 - 4122	(NC33656, NC33657, NC33659, N33662) to DC-3-396 / C-50
DC-3-279	Panagra	1	2134	NC21718
DC-3A-279A	Panagra	3	2190 - 2192	NC14967, NC14966, NC25652
DC-3A-279B	Panagra	2	4800 - 4801	NC28334 - NC28335
DC-3-294	Air France	1	2122	F-ARQJ
DC-3-294A	CNAC	1	2148	46
DC-3-310D	Penn. Central (not delivered)	1	4130	(NC33675) to C-49H
DC-3-313	Pennsylvania Central	6	2168 - 2173	NC21780 - NC21785
		4	2186 - 2189	NC21787 - NC21790
DC-3-313A	Pennsylvania Central	2	2256, 2262	NC25691, NC25692
		2	2266, 2267	NC25693, NC28343
DC-3-313B	Pennsylvania Central	2	4081, 4082	NC25696, NC25697
	Penn. Central (not delivered)	1	4083	(NC25697) to DC-3-391 / C-50C
	Penn. Central (not delivered)	1	4084	(NC25698) to DC-3-392 / C-50D
DC-3-313C	Pennsylvania Central	1	4099	NC25689
DC-3-313D	Pennsylvania Central	2	4132, 4133	NC33677, NC33678
	Penn. Central (not delivered)	1	4131	(NC33676) to DC-3-392 / C-50D
	Penn. Central (not delivered)	2	4134, 4135	(NC33679, NC33680) to DC-3-392 / C-50D
DC-3-314	Braniff	4	2179 - 2182	NC21773 - NC21776

Model	Operator	Qty	Construction Numbers	Registrations
DC-3-314A	Braniff	4	2239 - 2242	NC25666 - NC25669
DC-3-314B	Braniff	3	4106 - 4108	NC28362 - NC28364
	Braniff (not delivered)	3	4109 - 4111	(NC28370 - NC28372) *to DC-3-397 / C-50B*
DST-318	Eastern	3	2224 - 2226	NC25649 - NC25651
DST-318A	Eastern	2	3250, 3251	NC28394, NC28393
DC-3-322	Chicago & Southern	3	2218 -2220	NC25625 - NC25627
		1	2233	NC25628
DC-3-322A	Chicago & Southern	1	2255	NC19977
DC-3-322B	Chicago & Southern	1	3285	NC28378
DC-3A-343	Western	1	2265	NC19964
DC-3A-343A	Western	1	3283	NC28379
DC-3A-343B	Western	2	4811, 4812	NC33670, NC33671
DC-3A-345	Douglas / PAA	1	4957	NC34925
DC-3-348	CAA	1	4080	NC14
DC-3A-349	Western (not delivered)	1	4813	(NC33672) *to C-52A*
DC-3-357	Delta	3	3277 - 3279	NC28340 - NC28342
		2	3280, 3281	NC28343, NC28344
DC-3-357A	Delta (not delivered)	2	4814, 4815	(NC28346, NC28347) *to C-49C*
DC-3-362	TWA	4	3266 - 3269	NC1941 - NC1944
		3	3294 - 3296	NC1945 - NC1947
		2	3298 - 3299	NC1948 - NC1949
	unknown (not delivered)	1	3297	(NC1953) *to C-49*
DC-3A-367	Northeast	3	3286 - 3288	NC33621 - NC33623
DC-3A-363	Swiflite	1	3275	NC1000
DC-3A-375	Inter Island A/L	3	4806 - 4808	NC33606 - NC33608
DC-3-384	unknown (not delivered)	5	3270 - 3274	(NC1945 - NC1949) *to C-49*
DC-3-385	Delta (not delivered)	1	3282	(NC28345) *to C-49A*
DC-3-387	see DC-3-201F			
DC-3-388	Eastern (not delivered)	2	4097, 4098	(NC28389, NC28390) *to R4D-2*
DC-3-389	see DC-3-201G			
DC-3-392	see DC-3-313D			
DC-3A-393	Panagra	1	3284	NC28380
DC-3-395	see DC-3-197E			
DC-3-396	see DC-3-277D			
DC-3-397	see DC-3-314B			
DC-3-398	see DC-3-197D			
DC-3A-399	Panagra	1	4124	NC33645
DC-3-401	American (not delivered)	2	4804, 4805	(NC33627, NC33628) *to C-50A*
DC-3-402	see DC-3-201G			
DST-406	Eastern	1	4129	NC33643
DC-3A-408	Douglas	1	4809	NC30000
DC-3A-414	DSC / Panagra	2	4177, 4183	NC30008, NC30014
	DSC / PAA	3	4179 - 4181	NC30010 - NC30012
DC-3A-414A	PAA	1	4959	NC34948
	DSC / Cruzeiro	2	4963, 4968	NC33684/PP-CBS, NC33689/PP-CBT
		2	4977, 4981	NC30024/PP-CBV, NC33659/PP-CBU
DC-3A-438	DSC / PAA	1	4958	NC34947
DC-3A-447	PAA (not delivered)	3	4960 - 4962	(NC34949 - NC34951) *to R4D-4*
DC-3A-453	United (not delivered)	4	4964 - 4967	(NC33685 - NC33688) *to C-53C*
		8	4969 - 4976	(NC33690 - NC33697) *to C-53C*
	Northwest (not delivered)	3	4978 - 4980	(NC30025 - NC30027) *to C-53C*
DC-3-454	American (not delivered)	6	4987 - 4992	(NC14277 - NC14282) *to C-49J*
	Braniff (not delivered)	3	4993 - 4995	(NC34970 - NC34972) *to C-49J*
DC-3-455	TWA (not delivered)	5	4982 - 4986	(NC34973 - NC34977) *to C-49K*

CHAPTER 2: TECHNICAL DATA

The interiors of Douglas Commercials have changed considerably. The top photograph shows the cabin of the DC-1 as it was in TWA service in Jan34. It is interesting that some seats are in facing pairs. Emphasizing the extra width of the DC-3, the lower photograph shows the interior of a cargo C-47 with a Jeep and a light field gun, as well as a rather disinterested gun crew. [both Harry Gann/Douglas]

C-51 41-7702 c/n 3289 - Delivered on 28Jun41 and coded '2 10T' (for 41-7702 and 10 Transport Sq) this aircraft was ordered originally by Canadian Colonial as DC-3-390 NC34962. The bars across the windows indicate that it was used for cargo work, and it has a right-side passenger door.
[Harry Gann/Douglas]

C-47-DL 41-38614 c/n 4642 - Assigned to the USAAF 5th AF and 13 TCS in Aug42, this C-47 had double cargo doors and a strengthened floor to take heavy loads, such as the grader in this photograph. To aid loading, the rear door has been removed. Such loading tasks were time-consuming at first, but the men soon got it to a fine art. Post-war, this aircraft became NC90627 and it survived until it was destroyed in an accident in Jul71. *[USAF]*

C-53-DO 41-20046 c/n 4816 - Although this is a C-53 according to the serial number, and should have a single passenger door, it has been modified in the field with C-47-type double cargo doors, serving with the Pacific Wing ATC. It is unlikely that the floor has been reinforced, although what looks like a heavy generator has been loaded. This photograph was taken in Mar44 at Kwajalein in the Marshall Islands and the aircraft went on to serve with Hawaiian Airlines as NC62046 in 1946.
[via David Lucabaugh]

CHAPTER 2: TECHNICAL DATA

Douglas DC-1 cockpit (upper photograph) as it was on 23Aug33. This can be compared with the better-equipped DC-2 cockpit of Lufthansa's D-ABEQ (lower photograph) delivered in Feb35. The co-pilot's panels are reasonably similar. [Harry Gann/Douglas and Lufthansa]

When the flight deck of a fairly standard C-47 (VP-LVH) is compared with that of a Basler BT-67 turboprop conversion (facing page) it is not difficult to see the dramatic changes that have taken place over forty or more years.
[Austin Brown and Basler Turbo Conversions]

Chapter 2: Technical Data

MILITARY DC-2 VARIANTS

Model	No. built (conv)	Powerplant	All-up weight	Remarks
XC-32	1	750 hp Wright R-1820-25	18,200lb (8300 kg)	DC-2-153 c/n 1414 for General Andrews
C-32A	(24)	740 hp Wright R-1820-33	18,200lb (8300 kg)	DC-2s impressed from airlines
C-33	18	750 hp Wright R-1820-25	18,500lb (8400 kg)	DC-2-145 with DC-3 fin and rudder plus cargo floor.
C-33A	(1)	930 hp Wright R-1820-45	18,500lb (8400 kg)	DC-3 tailplane, nacelles, and undercarriage
C-34	2	750 hp Wright R-1820-25	18,500lb (8400 kg)	DC-2-173 for US Army Secretary
C-38	(1)			C-33A re-designated
C-39	35	975 hp Wright R-1820-55	21,000lb (9600 kg)	DC-2-243 production version of C-38
C-41	1	1200 hp P&W R-1830-21	25,000lb (11,350 kg)	DC-2-253 with 14 seats
C-42	1	1200 hp Wright R-1820-53	23,624lb (10,750 kg)	C-39 as VIP transport, Cargo door bolted up
R2D-1	5	750 hp Wright R-1820-12	18,200lb (8300 kg)	As XC-32 for US Navy and US Marines

AIR FORCE DC-3 VARIANTS

Model	No.built (conv)	Powerplant	All-up weight	Remarks
C-41A	1	1200 hp P&W R-1830-21	26,300 lb (11,950 kg)	DC-3-253A with 10 seats
C-47-DL	965	1200 hp P&W R-1830-92	29,300 lb (13,320 kg)	DC-3A-360 for cargo, 12-volt system & steam heating 27 seats
C-47A-DL	2954	1200 hp P&W R-1830-92	29,300 lb (13,320 kg)	DC-3A-456 with 24-volt system and hot-air heating
C-47A-DK	2300	1200 hp P&W R-1830-92	29,300 lb (13,320 kg)	As C-47A-DL but steam or hot-air heating

There were many derivative models of the C-47, some documented better than others. Reference to later sections will provide more precise details of individual conversions, but it should be recognised that some modifications were not recorded on record cards and care should be taken when making assumptions about the quantities involved. Some modification programmes were only recognised retrospectively on record cards and the 1962 rationalisation of US military designations added further complexity.

AC-47A	(1?)	A single C-47A modified by Hayes (with C-47Ds) for airways checking (it was destroyed prior to potential re-designation as 'EC-47A')
EC-47A	(10+)	C-47A of various commands (but typically AMC, ARDC) granted 'exempt' status from otherwise mandatory modifications due to the nature of their work. From Dec55 these aircraft became JC-47A, releasing the 'E' prefix for electronic use
HC-47A	(20+)	The 1962 re-designation of surviving SC-47A (qv). Includes one JHC-47A
JC-47A	(10+)	The 1955 re-designation of the EC-47A (qv)
NC-47A	(1?)	At least one JC-47A recognised as modified to permanent test status in 1968
RC-47A	(3+)	At least three unrelated uses. One 9th AF aircraft between 1944 and 1947, mission unknown. One used by MATS/APCS for photo-mapping from 1952. Brief allocation to single aircraft later to become RC-47N (qv)
SC-47A	(41+)	C-47A modified for search, rescue and recovery work, some with rafts and viewing windows. At least 20 survivors became HC-47A in 1962 re-designation
TC-47A	(11+)	C-47A re-designated for use with ATC (including seven in Oct47). Last aircraft reverted to C-47A in 1957
VC-47A	(many)	C-47A modified for VIP transport with airline seats and soundproofing. Designations frequently used casually and sometimes 'suspended' to disguise the use of the aircraft
C-47B-DL	300	1200 hp P&W R-1830-90C 30,000 lb (13,000 kg) DC-3A with cabin tanks, engine superchargers and hot-air heating
C-47B-DK	3064	1200 hp P&W R-1830-90C 30,000 lb (13,000 kg) Built by Oklahoma City plant
EC-47B	(2+)	At least two early 'exempt' aircraft. Both became EC-47D
NC-47B	(1?)	One former SC-47D used by Army 1960-1976 (later 'NC-47J')
RC-47B	(1+)	One aircraft used by ATC from Aug49 until re-designated RC-47D Jan52
TC-47B-DK	(133)	C-47B modified for training with three astrodomes and aft DF loop. At least 39 direct to USN as R4D-6/7. Most USAAF aircraft modified to TC-47D when superchargers removed
VC-47B	(?)	C-47B modified for VIP use (see VC-47A)
XC-47C-DL	(6?)	1200 hp P&W R-1830-92 34,162 lb (15,470 kg) Model 78 Edo floats fitted to C-47. 600 gallons of fuel in floats. Some field conversions
C-47D		1200 hp P&W R-1830-90 30,000 lb (13,600 kg) C-47B with superchargers removed post-war
AC-47D	(25)	C-47D modified by Hayes for use by MATS/AACS for navigational aids checking. Designation became effective 1953 (at least two were briefly referred to previously as RC-47D - qv). 23 survivors became EC-47D in 1962/63
AC-47D	(53)	Jan66 re-designation of 24 FC-47D gunships (qv). Conversion programme was underway and balance of 29 aircraft came from C-47D status. Total is exclusive of proof-of-concept C-47D and early field conversions (at least 2 C-47D) that did not receive designation
EC-47D	(16+)	'Exempt' C-47D including at least two former EC-47B. All to JC-47D in 1955 or returned to C-47D
EC-47D	(23)	All surviving MATS/AFCS AC-47D became EC-47D in 1962
EC-47D	(1)	Prototype EC-47Q (qv). So designated 1967-1968
FC-47D	(24)	Conversion of C-47D with three 7.7 mm side-mounted Vulcan miniguns for ground attack work in Vietnam theatre. Designation instigated in Sep65 but replaced by AC-47D in Jan66. All FC-47D survived to become AC-47D
GC-47D	(2?)	Two C-47D used for ground instructional purposes at Albrook AFB, Panama. Designation created in 1962 but apparently not used in records until Nov73
HC-47D	(7+)	The 1962 re-designation of surviving SC-47D (qv)
JC-47D	(14+)	The 1955 re-designation of the EC-47D (qv)
RC-47D	(8+)	Three unrelated uses in late 'forties and 'fifties. One intelligence gathering aircraft based in West Germany from 1949, five MATS/APCS photo-mapping conversions (including one from RC-47B) and two MATS/AACS aircraft briefly so-designated 1952-53 prior to re-designation as AC-47D in mid-1953. A fourth use (unrecorded on record cards) involved three PACAF C-47Ds, referred to as 'RC-47', used as communications-relay aircraft over Laos 1966-69
SC-47D	(50+)	C-47D modified as per SC-47A (qv). Survivors became HC-47D in 1962
TC-47D	(102+)	USAF TC-47B with superchargers removed
VC-47D	(many)	C-47D fitted with VIP interior. See VC-47A notes
C-47E	canc	1475 hp Wright R-1820-80. Not built.
C-47E	(9)	1290 hp P&W R-2000-4. Re-engined by Pan American for airways checks. Later to US Army
YC-47F	(1)	1475 hp Wright R-1820-80. Originally YC-129/Super DC-3. To R4D-8
C-47H to C-47M		US Navy models redesignated in 1962 under triservice system. See later for details

Designation	Qty	Details
EC-47N	(25)	The 1967 re-designation of the RC-47N (qv)
RC-47N	(25)	Electronic reconnaissance version of C-47A for use in Vietnam theatre. 25 aircraft delivered in 1966 and all survived to be re-designated EC-47N in May67
EC-47P	(26)	The 1967 re-designation of all surviving RC-47P (qv)
RC-47P	(28)	Electronic reconnaissance version of C-47D for use in Vietnam theatre, internally identical to RC-47N. 28 aircraft delivered in 1966. 26 survivors became EC-47P in May67
EC-47Q	(16)	1290 hp P&W R-2000-4. Electronic reconnaissance version of C-47A/D for use in Vietnam theatre. 12 conversions in 1967 received EC-47Q designation in Mar68 after one aircraft was briefly designated EC-47D. A second batch of 4 was delivered in 1970
C-48-DO	1	1200 hp P&W R-1830-82 25,200 lb (11,440 kg) DC-3A-377 for UAL
C-48A	3	1200 hp P&W R-1830-82 25,200 lb (11,440 kg) DC-3A-368 with 10 seats
C-48B	(16)	1200 hp P&W R-1830-51 24,390 lb (10,975 kg) DST-As impressed
C-48C	7 & (9)	1200 hp P&W R-1830-51 24,390 lb (10,975 kg) DC-3A-414 for airlines and impressed
C-49	6	1200 hp Wright R-1820-71 25,200 lb (11,440 kg) DC-3-384 for TWA
C-49A	1	1200 hp Wright R-1820-71 25,200 lb (11,440 kg) DC-3-385 for Delta
C-49B	3	1200 hp Wright R-1820-71 25,200 lb (11,440 kg) DC-3-387 for Eastern
C-49C	2	1200 hp Wright R-1820-71 25,200 lb (11,440 kg) DC-3-386 for Delta
C-49D	6 & (5)	1200 hp Wright R-1820-71 25,200 lb (11,440 kg) DC-3-389 for Eastern and impressed
C-49E	(22)	1100 hp Wright R-1820-79 23,400 lb (10,625 kg) Impressed DST and DC-3 (ATC-618)
C-49F	(9)	1200 hp Wright R-1820-71 25,200 lb (11,440 kg) Impressed DST and DC-3
C-49G	(8)	1200 hp Wright R-1820-97 23,400 lb (10,625 kg) Impressed DC-3s
C-49H	(19)	1200 hp Wright R-1820-97 25,200 lb (11,440 kg) Impressed DC-3s
C-49J	34	1200 hp Wright R-1820-71 29,000 lb (13,200 kg) DC-3-454 with 28 seats and 30" LH door
C-49K	23	1200 hp Wright R-1820-71 29,000 lb (13,200 kg) DC-3-455 as trooper
C-50	4	1100 hp Wright R-1820-85 29,300 lb (13,320 kg) DC-3-396 for American. RH door. ATC-618
C-50A	2	1100 hp Wright R-1820-85 29,300 lb (13,320 kg) DC-3-401 for American
C-50B	3	1100 hp Wright R-1820-81 29,000 lb (13,200 kg) DC-3-397 for Braniff. LH door
C-50C	1	1100 hp Wright R-1820-79 29,000 lb (13,200 kg) DC-3-391 for PCA. LH door
C-50D	4	1100 hp Wright R-1820-79 29,300 lb (13,400 kg) DC-3-392 for PCA. LH door
C-51	1	1100 hp Wright R-1820-83 29,500 lb (13,400 kg) DC-3-390 for Can. Colonial. RH door
C-52	1	1200 hp P&W R-1830-51 27,700 lb (12,600 kg) DC-3A-398 for UAL. RH door, 28 seats
C-52A	1	1200 hp P&W R-1830-51 27,700 lb (12,600 kg) DC-3A-394 for WAL. RH door, 28 seat
C-52B	2	1200 hp P&W R-1830-51 27,700 lb (12,600 kg) DC-3A-395 for UAL RH door, 28 seats
C-52C	1	1200 hp P&W R-1830-51 27,700 lb (12,600 kg) DC-3A-402 for EAL LH door, 29 seats
C-52D	(1)	1200 hp P&W R-1830-51 26,850 lb (12,200 kg) DC-3A-48. ex C-48C c/n 3275
C-53-DO	219	1200 hp P&W R-1830-92 29,300 lb (13,320 kg) Skytrooper DC-3A-405 for 28 troops with 26" LH door. 12-volt system
"C-53"	(1)	1200 hp P&W R-1830-S1C3G 25,200 lb (11,440 kg) c/n 4800 used by Douglas on bailment
XC-53A	(1)	1200 hp P&W R-1830-92 29,300 lb (13,320 kg) c/n 4932 with full-span slotted flaps
C-53B	(9)	1200 hp P&W R-1830-92 29,300 lb (13,320 kg) Winterised for use in arctic, extra fuel and astrodome
C-53C	17	1200 hp P&W R-1830-92 29,300 lb (13,320 kg) DC-3A-453 with 28 seats and 30" LH door
C-53D	159	1200 hp P&W R-1830-92 29,300 lb (13,320 kg) DC-3A-457 as C-53C but 24-volt system
C-68	2	1200 hp P&W R-1830-92 26,720 lb (12,150 kg) DC-3A-440 with 21 seats
C-84	(4)	1200 hp Wright R-1820-71 25,200 lb (11,440 kg) DC-3B with 25 seats, impressed
C-117A-DK	17	1200 hp P&W R-1830-90C 30,000 lb (13,600 kg) DC-3A-1003. C-47B with 21 seats and integral stairs
C-117B-DK	(10)	1200 hp P&W R-1830-90D 30,000 lb (13,600 kg) C-117A with superchargers deleted
C-117C-DO	(10+)	1200 hp P&W R-1830-92. Bought from Pioneer A/L and re-designated on return
YC-129-DO	(1)	Re-designated YC-47F
Un-designated	12	1200 hp P&W R-1830-92 29,300 lb (13,320 kg) DC-3A-414 from Defense Supply Corp for PAA and Panagra
XCG-17	(2)	Glider conversion from C-47

NAVAL DC-3 VARIANTS

Designation	Qty	Details
R4D-1	66 (+33)	As C-47-DL for Navy. 33 ex USAAF, rest on Navy contract
R4D-2	2	1200 hp Wr R-1820-71 25,200 lb (11,440 kg) DC-3-388 for Navy
R4D-3	(20)	C-53Cs transferred from USAAF order
R4D-4	12	1200 hp P&W R-1830-92 29,300 lb (13,320 kg) DC-3A-447 for PAA
R4D-5	(238)	C-47A-DL transferred to Navy ex USAAF order. Became C-47H in 1962
R4D-5E	-	C-47A for special electronics operations
R4D-5Q	-	C-47A with special ECM gear for training. 3 crew, 11 trainees and one instructor. Re-designated EC-47H in 1962
R4D-5L	-	Modified for use in Antarctica. Extra fuel and higher gross weight. Re-designated LC-47H. One converted to LC-47M with ECM gear
R4D-5S	-	Fitted with anti-submarine detection equipment for training, with space for nine students and one instructor. Re-designated SC-47H
R4D-5R	-	Military personnel transport with 21 passengers, became TC-47H
R4D-5T	-	Navigational trainer
R4D-5Z	-	Equipped as staff transport. Re-designated VC-47H in 1962
R4D-6	(157)	C-47B-DLs transferred to Navy from USAAF orders
R4D-6E	-	Equipped as R4D-5E
R4D-6Q	-	Equipped as R4D-5Q, became EC-47J in 1962
R4D-6L	-	Equipped as R4D-5L, became LC-47J in 1962
R4D-6S	-	Equipped as R4D-5S, became SC-47J in 1962
R4D-6R	-	Equipped as R4D-5R, became TC-47J in 1962
R4D-6T	-	Equipped as R4D-5T
R4D-6Z	-	Equipped as R4D-5Z. For 15 to 17 passengers, became VC-47J in 1962
R4D-7	(43)	TC-47B-DKs transferred from USAAF orders. Used for navigational training, taking 12 students. Re-designated TC-47K in 1962. Some converted to R4D-6Q

How many of the R4D series re-designated in 1962 under the Tri-service system actually survived to carry the new designations is uncertain. From photographic evidence it is known that C-47H, LC-47H, C-47J and NC-47K were used, the last by the US Army for special test work.

Designation	Qty	Details
R4D-8	(101)	1475 hp Wright R-1820-80 31,000 lb (14,100 kg) First aircraft was YC-47F transferred
R4D-8T		Modified as navigational trainers for eight students. Re-designated TC-117D
R4D-8L		Fitted with skis and other cold weather equipment for Arctic and Antarctic use. Extra fuel tanks and higher all-up weight, became LC-117D
R4D-8Z		Equipped as staff transport for 16 passengers, VC-117D

Various military and Navy models were eligible for ATC Certification, as follows :-

ATC-618	-	C-49E, C-50, C-50A, C-50B, C-50C, C-50D, C-51 with Wright G-102A
ATC-618	-	C-49, C-49A, C-49B, C-49C, C-49D, C-49J, C-49K, R4D-2 with Wright G-202A
ATC-669	-	C-48, C-48A, C-52, C-52A, C-52B, C-52C, C-53, C-53B, C-53C, C-53D, C-68, R4D-1, R4D-3 with P&W R-1830-S1C3G
ATC-669	-	C-47, C-47A, R4D-1. R4D-5 as DC-3C with P&W R-1830-S4C4G
ATC-669	-	C-47B and R4D-6 as DC-3C with P&W R-1830-90C
ATC-669	-	C-117A as DC-3D

AIRFRAME MODIFICATIONS

Various modifications of existing airframes have been made either experimentally or for commercial use, by fitting non-standard engines. Brief details are given here:-

Hi-Per DC-3	Modified by Pan American for use by Panagra and Avianca with 1450 hp P&W R-2000-D5 (see also C-47E), and various airframe modifications to improve single-engined performance.
Mamba-Dakota	Test-bed used by Armstrong Siddeley fitted with the 1425 hp Mamba ASMa.3 and later the 1590 hp Mamba ASMa.6.
Dart-Dakota	Test-bed modified by Rolls-Royce, with 1540 hp Dart 504 and later 1640 hp Dart 510 and 526 (one in each nacelle).
Dart-Dakota	Modified by Field Aircraft Services for BEA trials before Viscount deliveries. 1540 hp Dart 505s fitted. AUW 28,200 lb (12,900 kg).
Dart-R4D-8	Rolls-Royce Darts were fitted to N156WC for Pilgrim Airlines.
USAC DC-3 Turbo Express	In addition to fitting two PT-6A-45R, various airframe changes were made, eg. the tailplanes had square-tips. New generators, electric, fuel and hydraulic systems and fire protection were fitted. The payload is 13,128 lb (5,955 kg).
Basler BT-67	When Basler took over development of the Turbo Express further changes were made, as outlined earlier. PT-6A-67R fitted giving 1424 hp. payload 13,000 lb (5,897 kg).
AMI DC-3-65TP	The AMI conversion has the PT-6A-65AR of 1424 hp and a payload of 11,100 lbs (5,000 kg).
Airtech	R-1830s replaced by WSK ASz-621Rs, a variant of the Wright Cyclone R-1820.

TECHNICAL DESCRIPTION

The basic structure of the DC-1, DC-2 and DC-3 variants was almost identical, differing only in dimensions, as the design developed.

Fuselage The fuselage was of semi-monocoque construction with transverse frames of formed sheet and longitudinal formed stringers which were covered with smooth, mushroom riveted, "Alclad" sheet. The sides of the DC-1 and DC-2 fuselage were flat, while that of the DC-3 was rounded in cross-section to allow an extra row of seats. The normal crew complement was three, two pilots and a radio operator, though later two crew operation was normal. Passenger seating was 12 in the DC-1, 14 in the DC-2, 14 berths in the DST and 21 initially in the DC-3. This was later increased to 28, or 32 in troop-carrying configuration and some post-war passenger models. Channel Airways in the UK even had 38 seats on their DC-3s.

Up to 4,500 lb (2,050 kg) of cargo could be carried in the C-47 but when lighter turbine engines were fitted this could be increased. Accommodation varied with customer requirements, but the DC-1 and DC-2 had one seat either side of the aisle and the original DC-3 two seats to the left and one to the right of the aisle. Later lightweight seats in pairs were used to allow two seats either side of the aisle. Reduced spacing allowed an extra row of seats. The DST could be flown with 16 seats. These seats were converted into bunks and further bunks were lowered from the roof for night flights. No aircraft is now in this configuration and the roof windows originally fitted have all been deleted. Access to the cabin was by passenger doors which could be on either side of the fuselage according to customer requirements. This was dictated by the customer's previous equipment, so that no change in ramp handling was needed. Left-hand doors are now standard and some of the earlier aircraft have had right-hand doors replaced by left-hand doors. All military variants had the left-hand door or double cargo doors with a passenger door set into the forward door. The C-47 had a strengthened metal floor and undercarriage to take heavier loads. Folding bench-type seats were fitted along the fuselage sides to allow quick access for loading equipment, one of the earliest "quick-change" installations. Post-war, some USAF VC-47s were refurbished for VIP use with standard airline seats and soundproofing.

Wings and engines The wings were fully cantilever, of Northrop multi-cellular construction and in three sections. The centre-section was 23'8" (7.35 m) wide and was set into the under side of the fuselage. It carried the engine nacelles and the main undercarriage. The outer wing panels were attached to the centre-section using multi-bolt flange joints. The entire trailing edge of the wings inboard of the ailerons and including the portion under the fuselage incorporated hydraulically-operated split flaps to reduce speed during landing. The ailerons were metal-framed and fabric-covered, the right-hand one having a trim tab. The DC-2 and DC-3 used the same NACA-2215 aerofoil section at the root, but at the tip the DC-2 used the NACA-2209 and the DC-3 the NACA-2206 section. The whole was built up of a high tensile strength aluminium alloy known as "Alclad" which was developed at the time the DC-1 was designed. This material possesses a very high resistance to fatigue - which has allowed very high flying hours in many airframes.

The engines were mounted with all accessories forward of the fireproof bulkhead on the nacelles and were supplied with oil from tanks behind the firewall. Tanks varied in capacity from 38 (US) gallons in the DC-2 up to 66.5 gallons in some DC-3s. The engines could be detached quickly and interchanged. The engine nacelles present one way of distinguishing models. The Wright Cyclone had narrow chord cowlings, as had the Russian Li-2s, whereas the Twin Wasp R-1830 and R-2000 powered models had much broader nacelles. The R-2000 was indistinguishable apart from longer propeller shaft which can sometimes be detected because the propeller warning strips are further forward than normal. Early C-47s and C-53s fitted with R-1830s had a carburettor intake on top of the nacelles just behind the cowling, as on commercial DC-3As. When the tropical filter was added the fairing was extended to the front lip of the cowling on later C-47s and C-47As. C-47Bs and C-117As had the filter but because of the two stage supercharger the intake was further aft, behind the cowl, the fairing extending to the rear of the nacelle. When the blowers were deleted on the C-47D and C-117B there was no change to the fairing. Hence, the engine nacelle cannot be used to identify later C-47 models exactly.

Tail unit The tailplane and fin were attached to the fuselage and were of similar construction to the wings, covered with "Alclad". The elevators and rudder were, like the ailerons, fabric-covered.

Undercarriage The main undercarriage retracts forward into the engine nacelles, leaving about a third of each wheel exposed as a precaution in case of a wheels-up landing. Each unit has a twin air-oil shock absorber and hydraulic brakes, the latter controlled through the rudder pedals for steering and still effective when retracted. In recent years, various modifications to the nacelles have included doors which enclose the wheels, thus improving streamlining. Retraction time has also been reduced, making engine failure on take-off less risky. The tail wheel is fully swivelling, but not retractable.

Fuel system The main fuel tanks were carried in the centre section, 510 (US) gallons in the DC-1 and DC-2 and up to 822 gallons in the DC-3. For ferrying purposes the range could be increased by installing extra tanks in the fuselage, and the C-47 could take up to nine 100 gallon (378.5 litres) tanks. The XC-47C floatplane could also take 300 gallons (1136 litres) in each float. The Basler BT-67 could have extra fuel tanks in the outer wing panels.

DIMENSIONS, FUEL RATINGS & PROPELLERS

Span	DC-1 85'0" (26 m) DC-2 85'0" (26 m) DST/DC-3 95'0" (29 m) C-47A 95'6" (29.20 m) Super DC-3 90'0" (27.5 m)
Length	DC-1 60'0" (18.40 m) DC-2 62'0" (19 m) DST-DC-3 64'6" (19.75 m) Super DC-3 67'9" (20.7 m) C-47A 63'9" (19.5 m) Turbo Express 67'9.5" (20.65 m)
Height	16'11" (5.2 m) - all models except DC-3S 18'3" (5.56 m)
Wing area	DC-1 942 sq ft (87.52 sq m) DC-2 939 sq ft (87.2 sq m) DC-3/C-47 987 sq ft (91.7 sq m) Super DC-3 969 sq ft (90.0 sq m)
Fuel rating	90 Octane was used in the DC-3-G102 91 Octane was used in the DC-3-G102A, G103A, DC-3A SCG, SC3G, DC-3A S1CG, S1C3G, and all DC-3C and C-47A, B and C-117A models 100 Octane was required for the DC-3-G202A 100/130 Octane was required for the Super DC-3
Propellers	The standard DC-3/C-47 prop was the three blade 11'6.375" Hamilton Standard 3E50 driven by 16:9 reduction gear on all piston engines The Conroy Turbo-Three was fitted with four-blade Rotol propellers The Tri-Turbo-3 and Turbo Express both have five-blade Hartzell propellers

DC-1, DC-2 & DC-3 PERFORMANCE

Model	Powerplant	Take-off Power, hp	Cruise Power, hp	All-up weight lb/kg	Cruising speed mph, km/h	Range miles/km
DC-1	SGR-1820-F3	710		17,500 lb 8,000 kg	190 mph 306 km/h	1000 miles 1600 km
DC-2	SGR-1820-F52	875	550	18,000 lb 8,200 kg	200 mph 320 km/h	1060 miles 1600 km
DST	GR-1820-G2	1000	850	24,000 lb 10,900 kg	192 mph 310 km/h	1790 miles 2875 km
DC-3	GR-1820-G102	1000	900	25,200 lb 11,440 kg	-	-
DC-3	GR-1820-G102A	1100	900	25,200 lb 11,440 kg	191 mph 307 km/h	2125 miles 3420 km
DST-A	R-1830-SBG R-1830-SB3G	1000	850	24,000 lb 10,886 kg	-	-
DC-3A	R-1830-SCG/SC3G	1050	900	25,200 lb 11,440 kg	198 mph 316 km/h	2000 miles 3200 km
DC-3A	R-1820-S1CG/S1C3G	1200	1050	25,200 lb 11,440 kg	207 mph 331 km/h	2125 miles 3420 km
DC-3B	GR-1820-G202A	1200	1000	25,200 lb 11,440 kg	194 mph 310 km/h	2125 miles 3420 km
DC-3C	R-1830-SC3G	1050	900	25,200 lb 11,440 kg	170 mph 274 km/h	1025 miles 1650 km
C-47/A	R-1830-S1C3G/92C	1200	1050	26,900 lb 12,203 kg 31,000 lb max 14,100 kg max	170 mph 274 km/h	3800 miles 6115 km
C-47B	R-1830-90C	1200	1050	26,000 lb 11,793 kg	160 mph 257 km/h	1600 miles 2575 km
C-47C	R-1830-92	1200	1050	26,000 lb 11,805 kg	185 mph 296 km/h	1500 miles 2400 km
DC-3D/C-117C	R-1830-90C	1200	1050	25,200 lb 11,440 kg	-	-
DC-3S/R4D-8	R-1820-C9-HE2	1475	1275	31,900 lb 14,470 kg	251 mph 401 km/h	2200 miles 3520 km
Conroy Turbo-Three	Rolls-Royce Dart 510	1350	torque limited	26,900 lb 12,203 kg	215 mph 335 km/h	940 miles 1510 km 2250 miles 3620 km max
Specialised Aircraft Tri-Turbo-3	3 x P&W PT-6A-45	1174	-	-	220 mph 354 km/h	1135 miles 2700 miles 1820 km std 4350 km max
USAC DC-3 Turbo Express	P&W PT-6A-45R	1254	-	-	215 mph 346 km/h	-
Basler BT-67		1281	-	28,750 lb	176 kts	2,177 nm

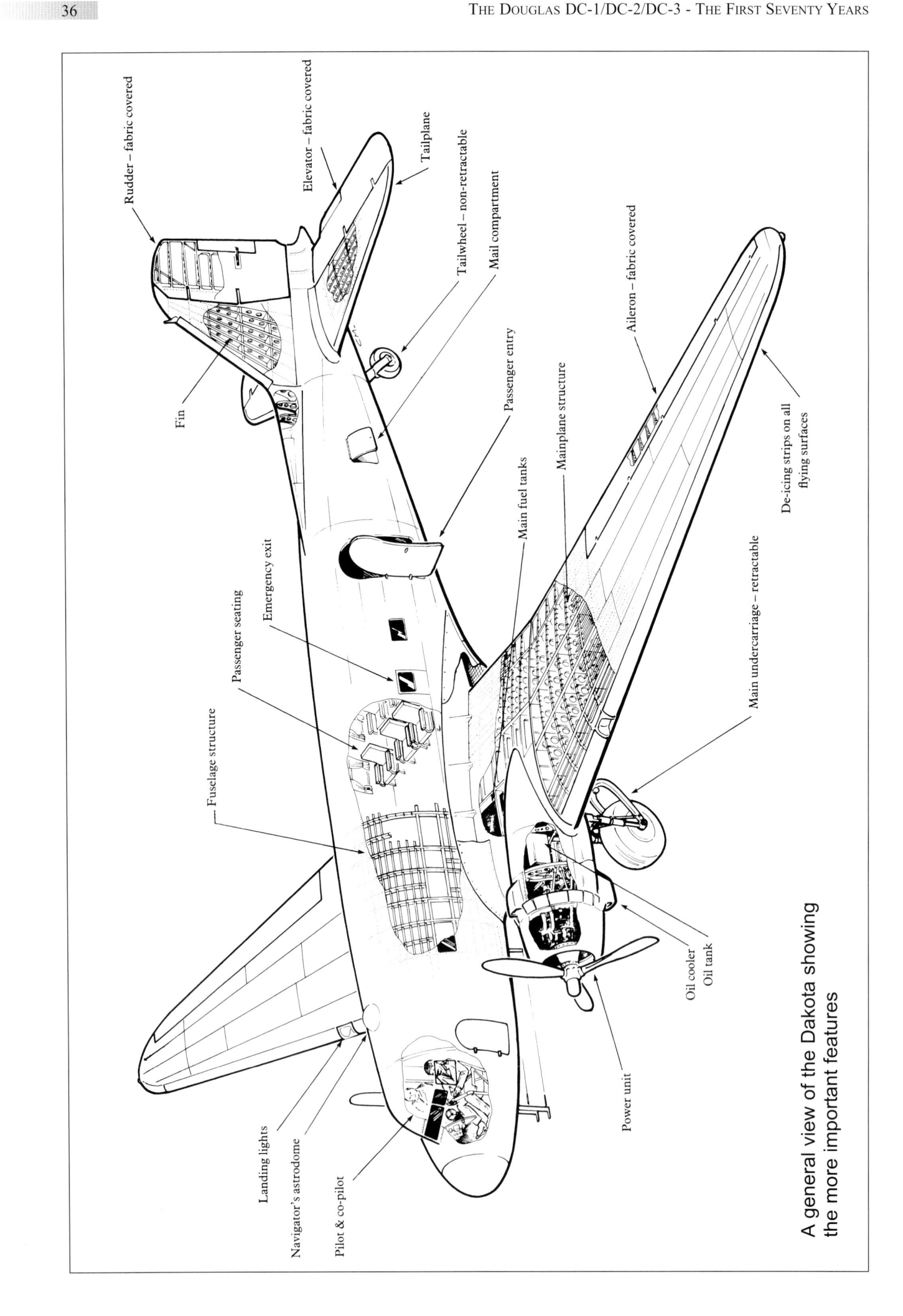

A general view of the Dakota showing the more important features

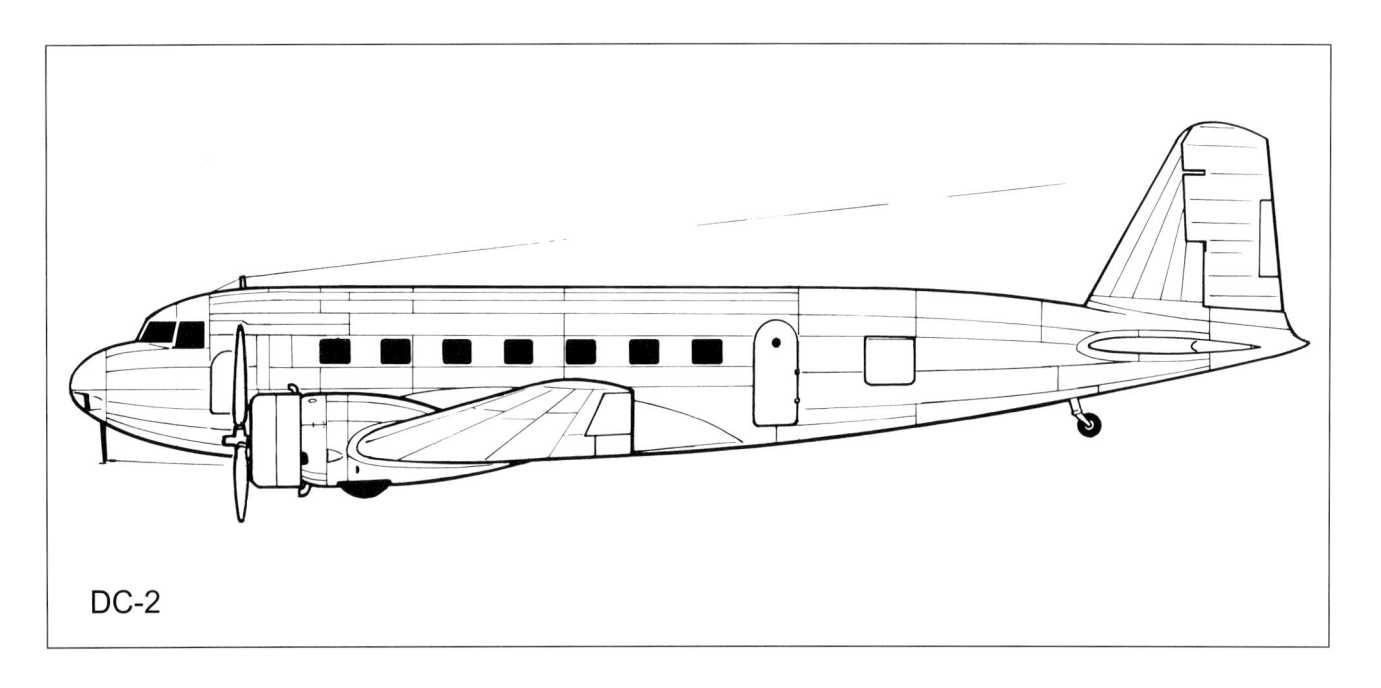

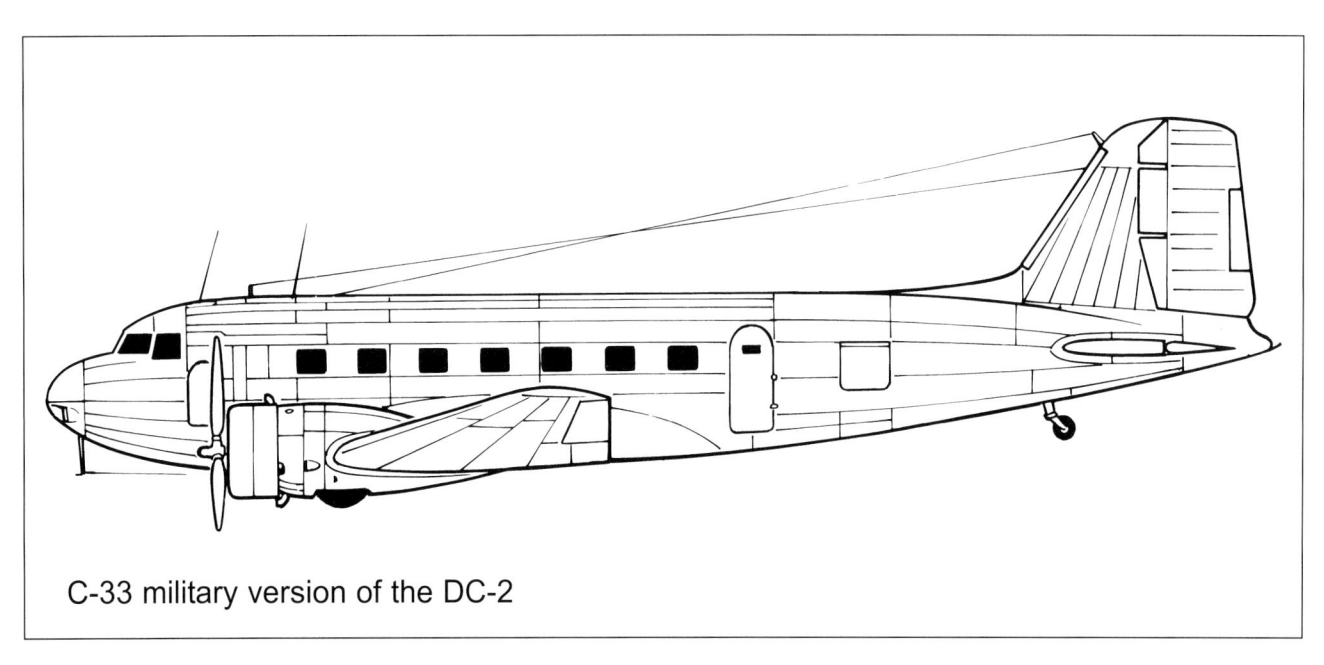

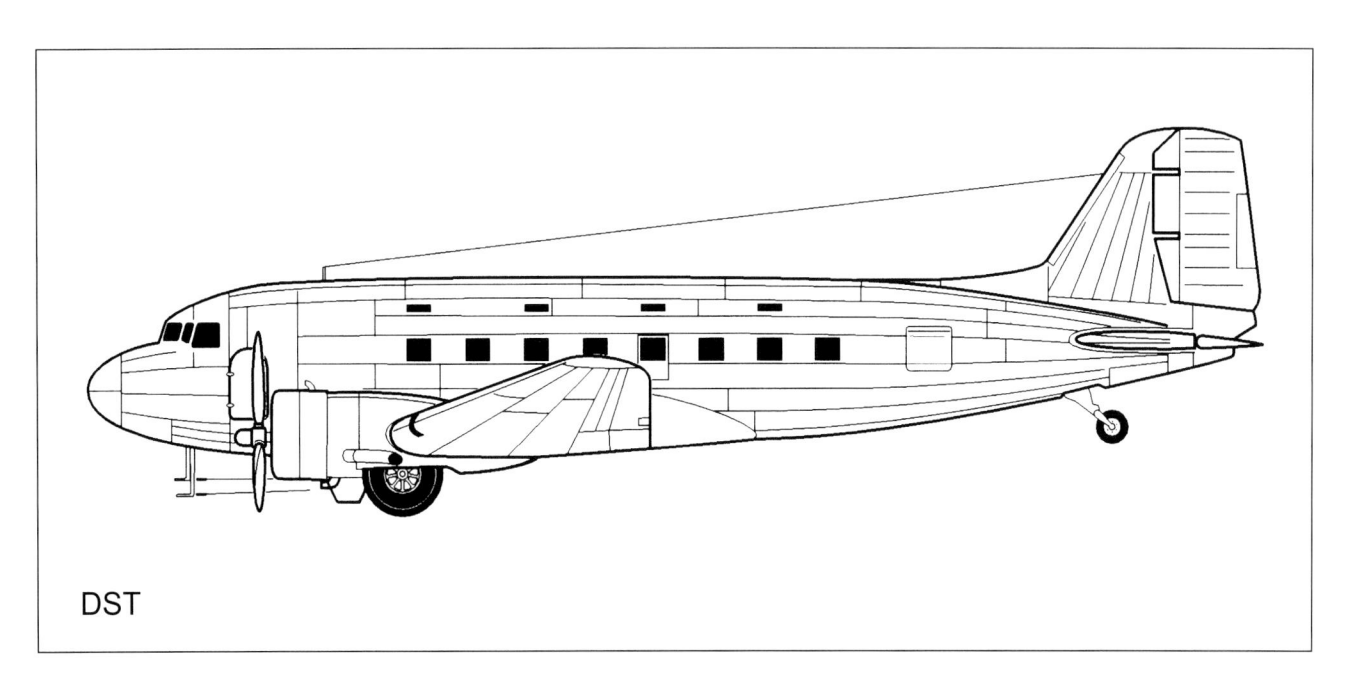

Chapter 2: Technical Data

DC-2

C-33 military version of the DC-2

DST

C-47B / Dakota IV

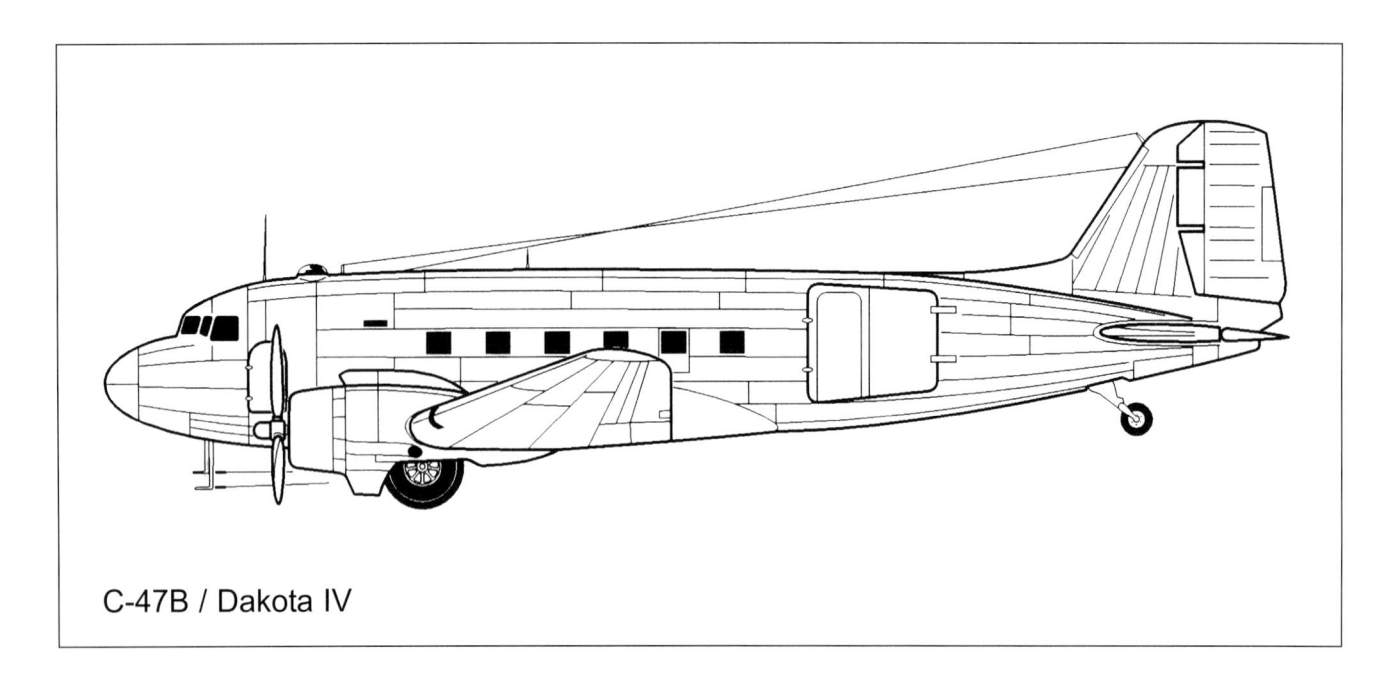

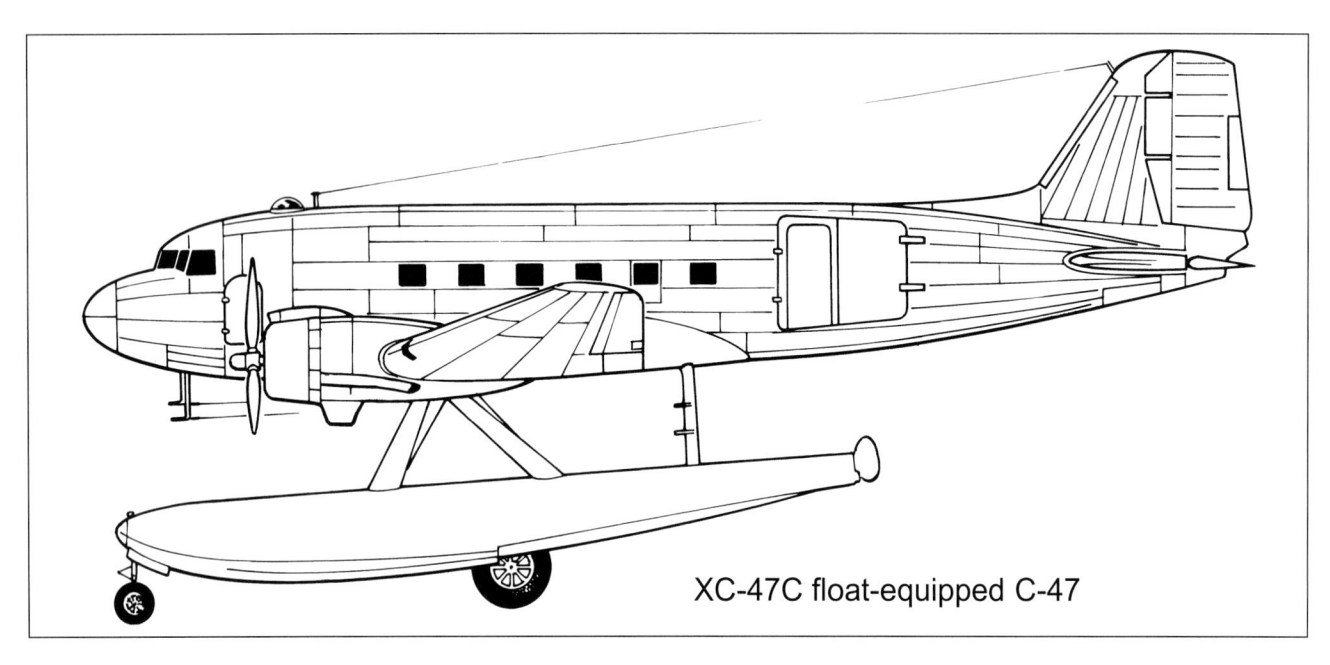

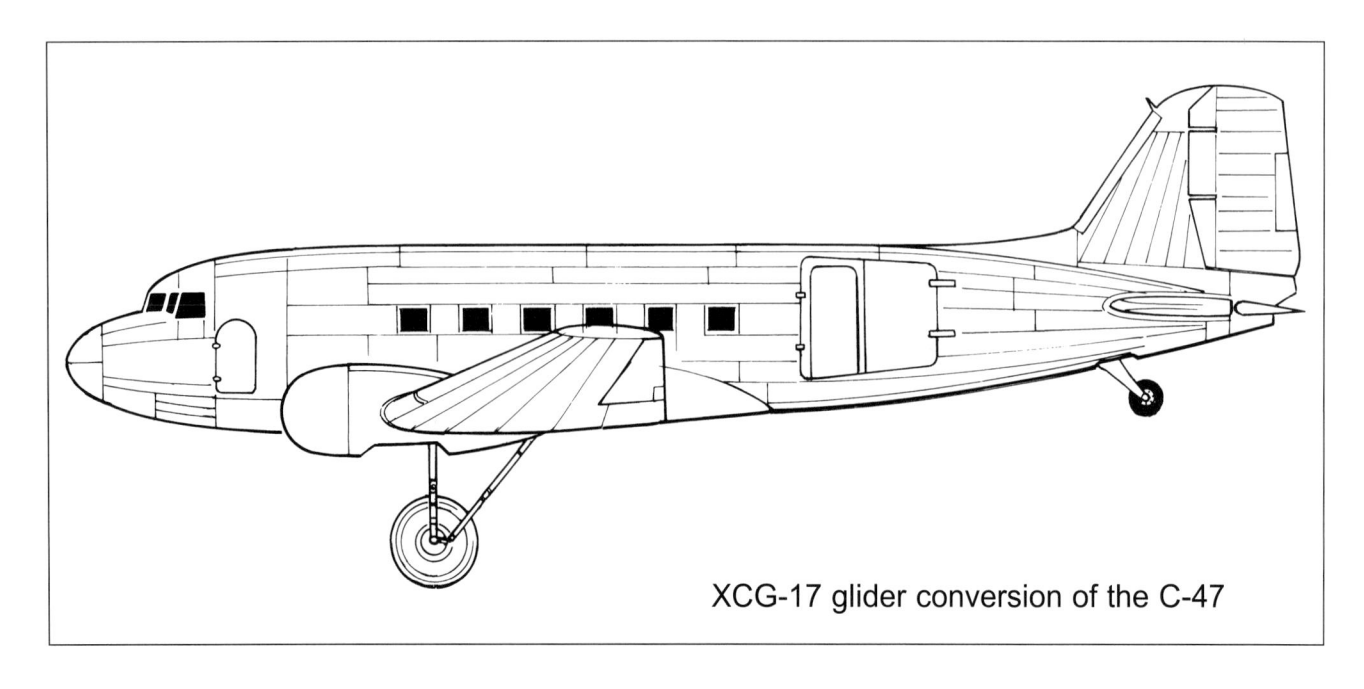

XC-47C float-equipped C-47

XCG-17 glider conversion of the C-47

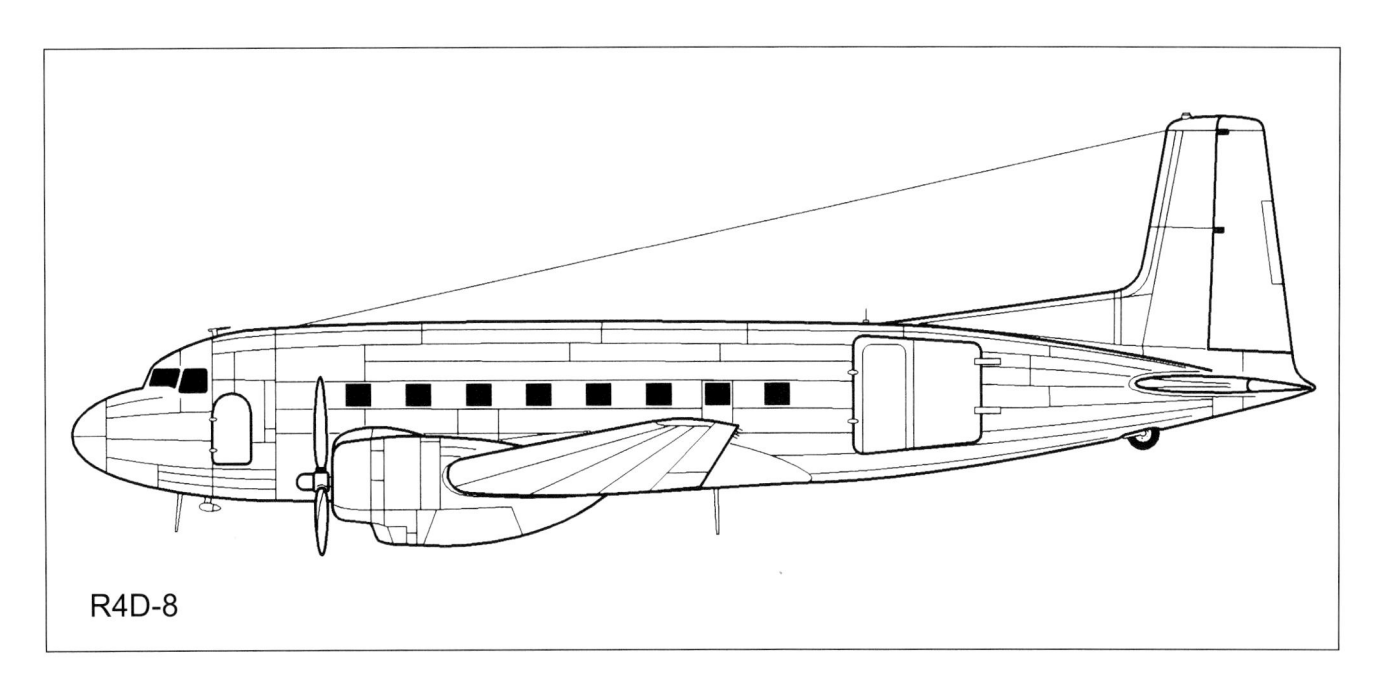

Chapter 2: Technical Data

R4D-8

Basler BT-67

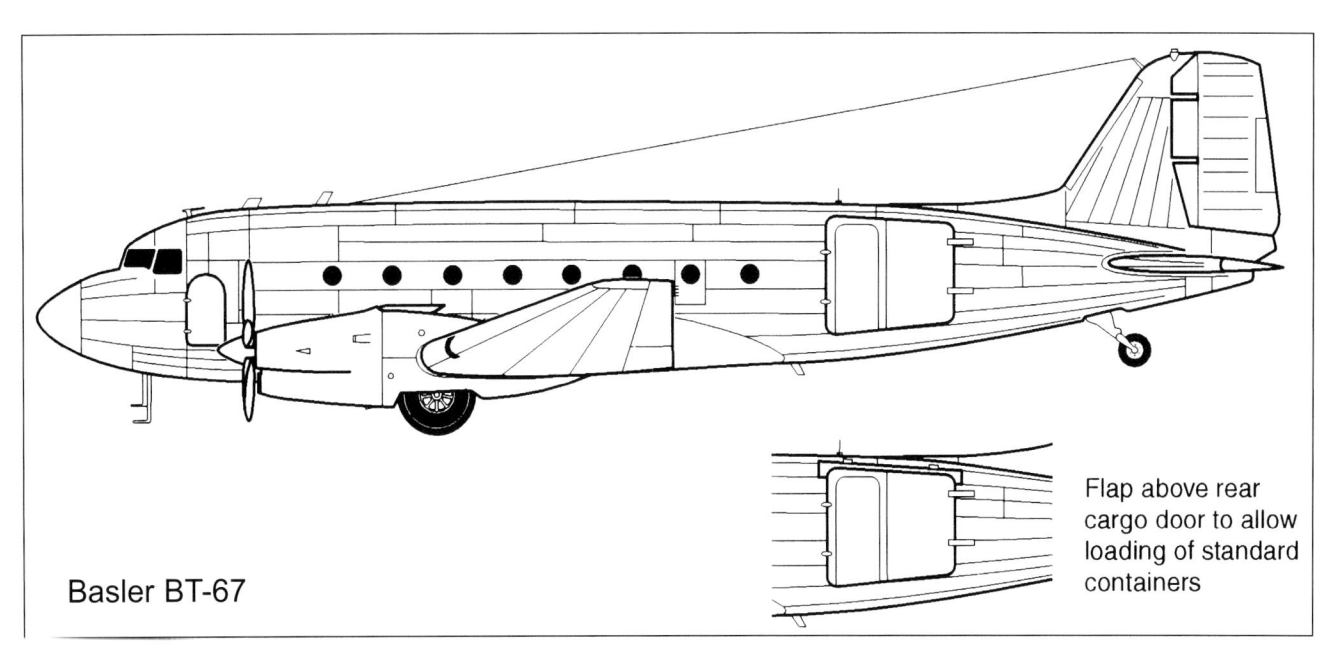

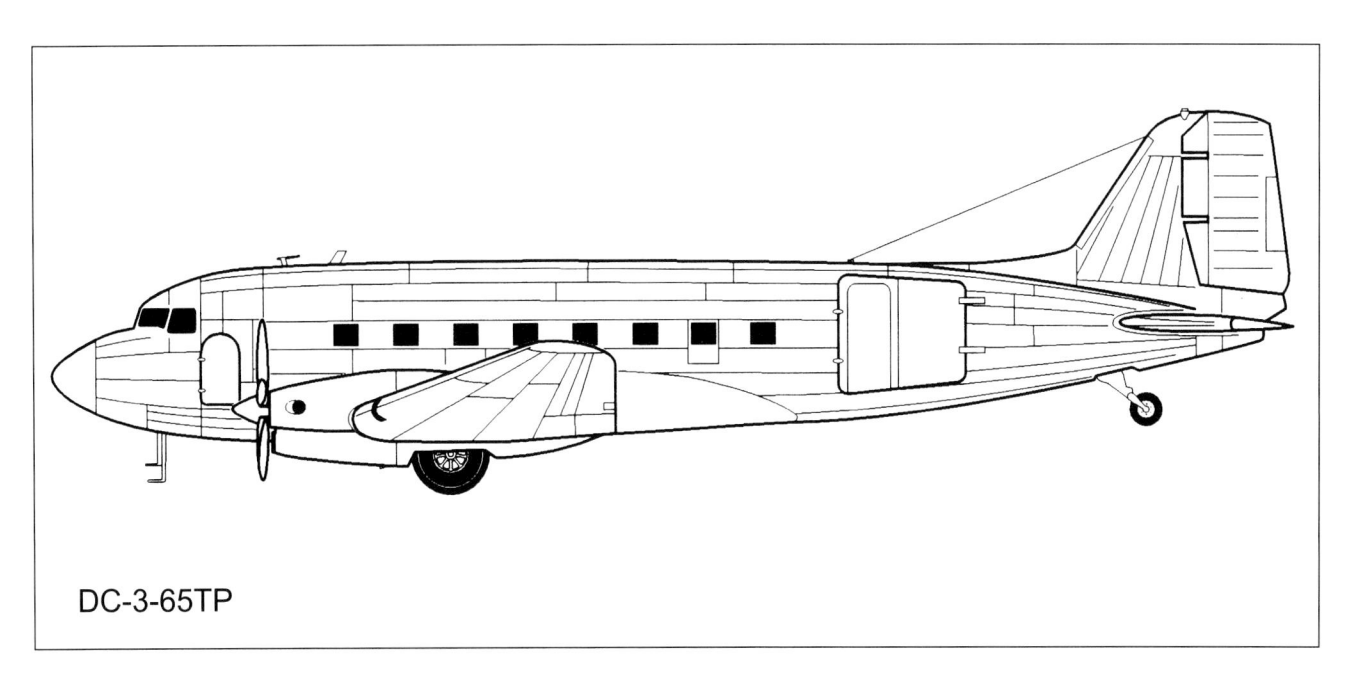

Flap above rear cargo door to allow loading of standard containers

DC-3-65TP

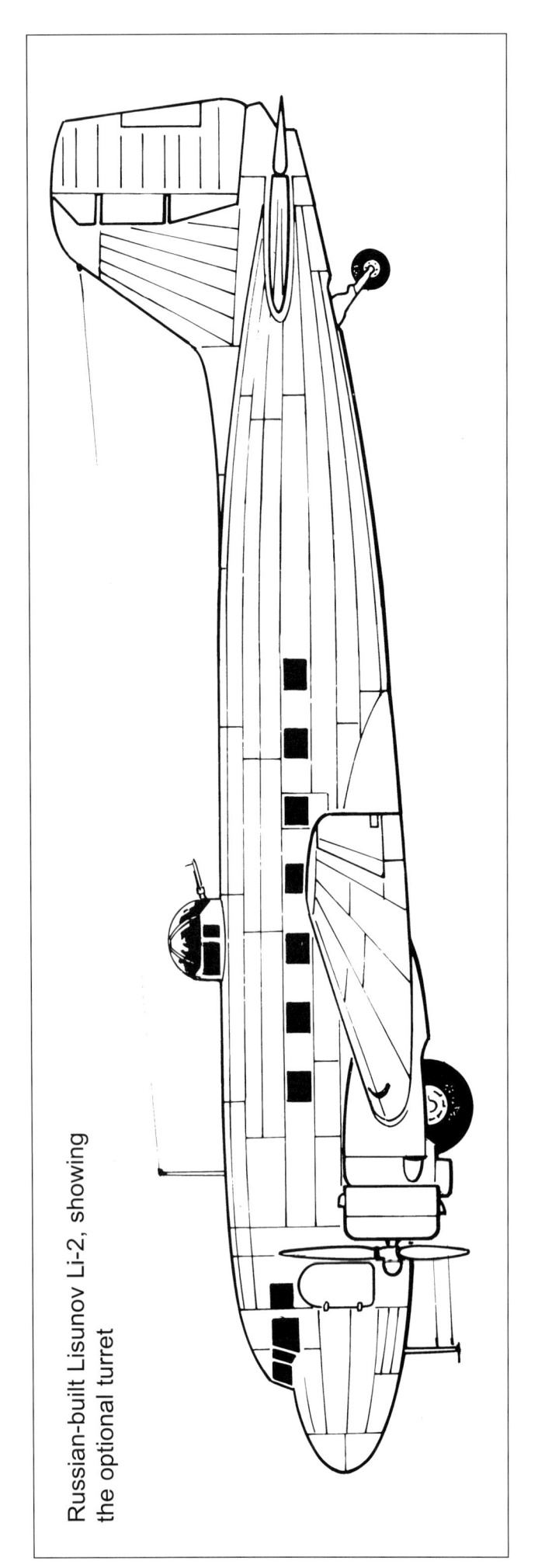

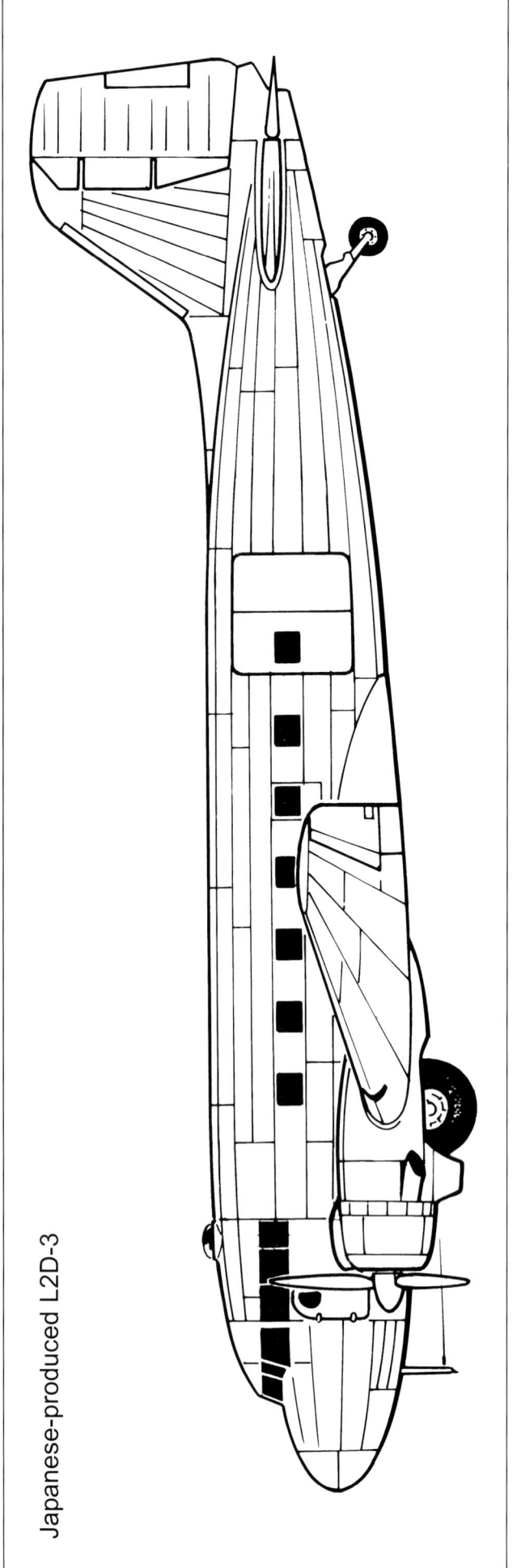

Russian-built Lisunov Li-2, showing the optional turret

Japanese-produced L2D-3

Chapter 2: Technical Data 41

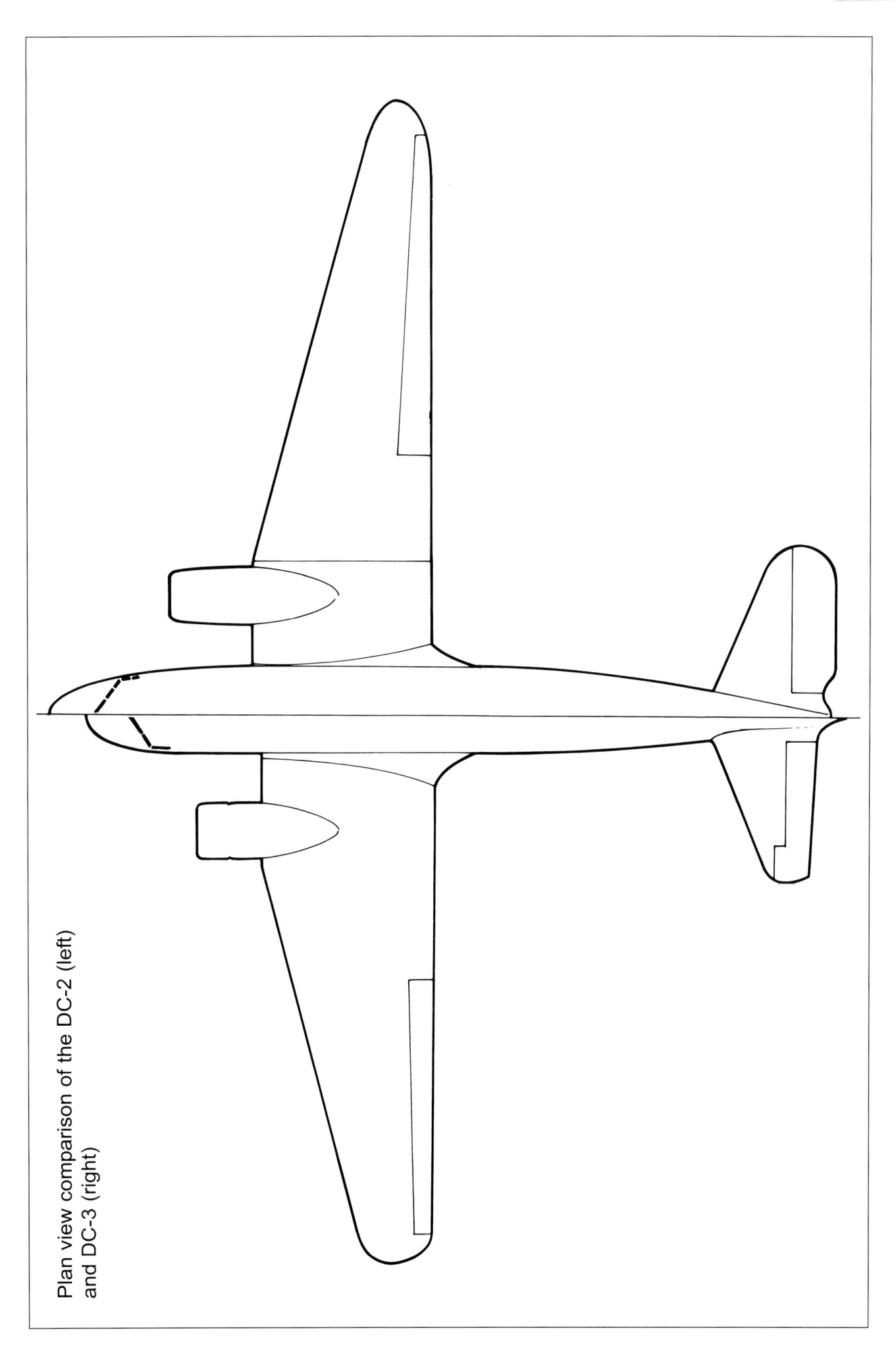

Plan view comparison of the DC-2 (left) and DC-3 (right)

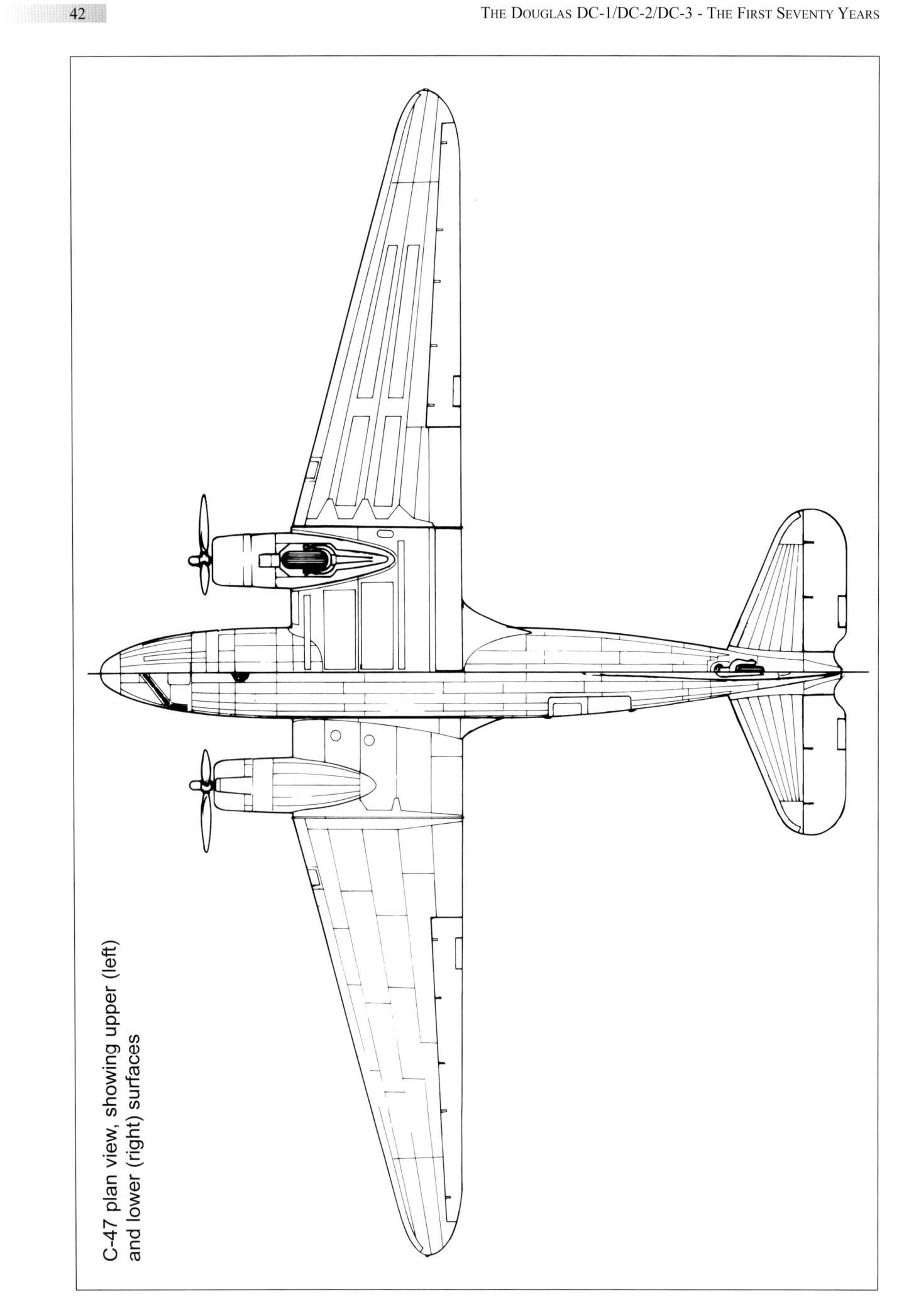

C-47 plan view, showing upper (left) and lower (right) surfaces

Chapter 3

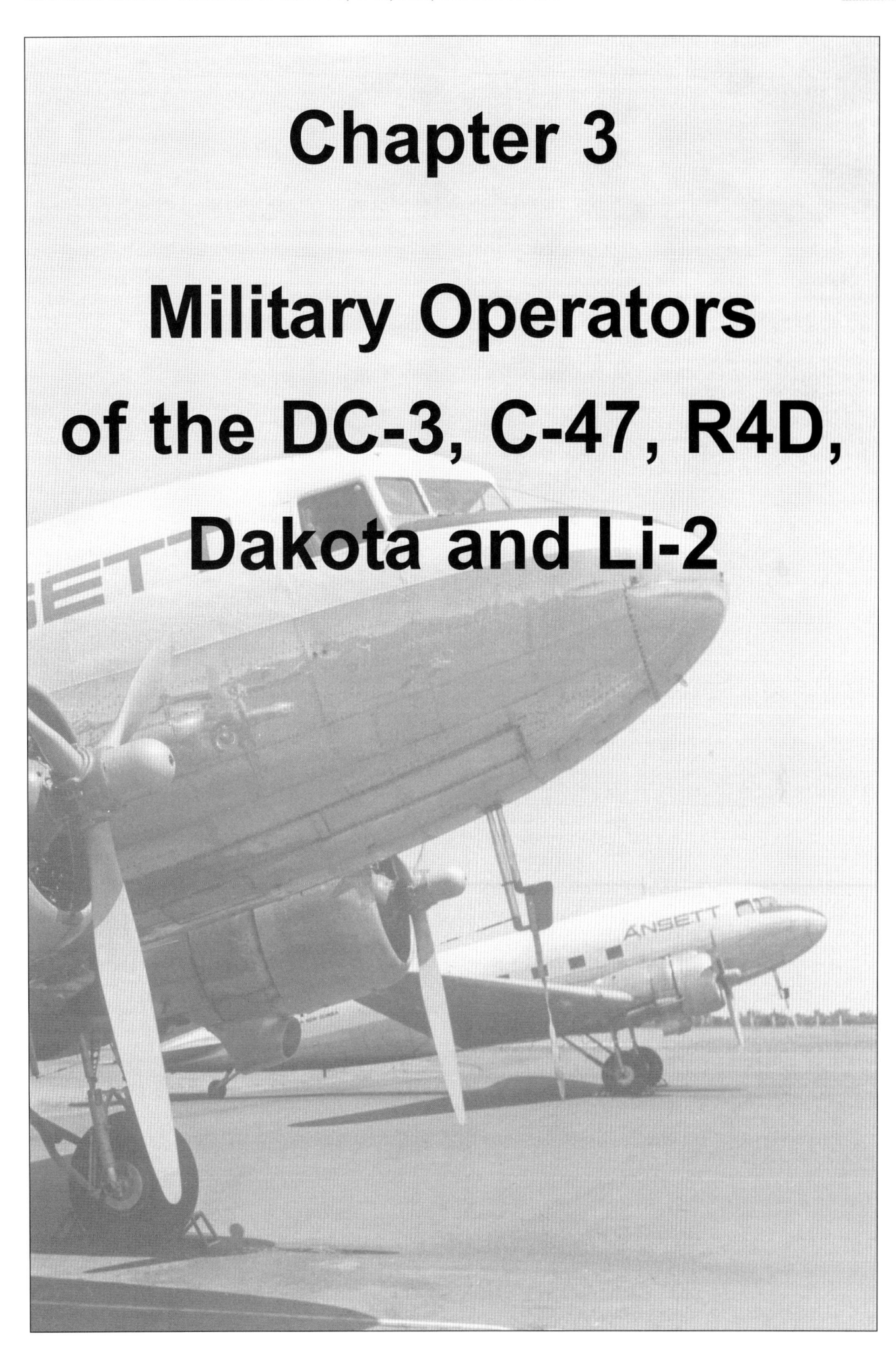

Military Operators of the DC-3, C-47, R4D, Dakota and Li-2

Variants of the DC-3 have been used on transport and other duties by almost every air force worthy of that term. In fact, so far as can be ascertained, there are only six that did not, and of the nearly 100 to have used the type it now probably remains in use with less than 10. Reports of numbers remaining in use vary, but there are up to 75 on charge, with further aircraft in store and only fit for use as a source of spares. The earliest military DC-2s and C-39s entered service in the United States in the mid-thirties, followed by C-47s in 1941. Prior to this, and before the Lend-Lease programme had got into its stride, the British Purchasing Commission had bought some DC-2s from US airlines to be used by the RAF in India and the Middle East. Some DC-3s followed shortly, and then the flood of Dakotas started to cross the Atlantic in early 1943.

The Dakota, as the C-47 was named by the RAF, rather than Skytrain in USAAF use, was also supplied to Canada, Australia, South Africa and New Zealand between 1943 to 1945. Of these, only South Africa remains a user, the latter having rebuilt theirs with Pratt & Whitney PT-6A-65ARs. A large number of C-47s went to Russia via Alaska between 1943 and 1945, supplementing their own Li-2 production. China also received some C-47s to help supply their armies in the battle to drive out the Japanese invaders. Some of these were delivered direct to CNAC and later COAA and others transferred from stocks in India. Other Lend-Lease C-47s went to France, Brazil and Bolivia in 1944/45.

Post-war many air forces benefitted from various US assistance programmes. With the formation of NATO in 1949 and under the Mutual Defense Assistance Program (MDAP) various European nations were supplied with C-47s, and France received large numbers to help in their campaigns in Indo-China and North Africa. Belgium, Denmark, the Netherlands, Norway and Turkey had all acquired C-47s or Dakotas from USAAF stocks at Oberpfaffenhofen, Germany at the end of the war and from RAF stocks. Greece, Jugoslavia, Portugal and Spain later gained C-47s from the USAF, some being ex-RAF aircraft overhauled after storage. Germany was also supplied with a batch from this source. In South and Central America a small, but steady, supply of surplus C-47s was delivered, some under the American Republic Program (ARP), and later under the Military Air Program (MAP) and deliveries continued from time to time until stocks were used up.

In Asia various countries equipped their air forces from the huge stocks of C-47s and Dakotas left behind at the end of the war. India, in particular, received a large fleet and the Philippine Republic also benefitted from the storage depots at Manila and Tacloban. Pakistan acquired stocks from India, while Indonesia took over the Dutch transport squadrons already supplied during the latter part of the war from the US. Burma's DC-3s came mainly from airline sources, but a few were bought from Britain. As communist activity built up in Indo-China, Korea and the China Sea, Cambodia, Laos, Korea, Taiwan and Thailand all received C-47s in varying numbers from various sources. None now remain airworthy in Taiwan (some originally supplied under lease-lend to China) while Thailand has nine Basler BT-67s delivered by 2004. The last C-47 in Turkey was replaced by a CN.235 early in 1998.

Many smaller air forces acquired their C-47s in a variety of ways other than from surplus stocks: from their country's airlines, sometimes bankrupt, from commercial sources and from time to time by clandestine means. Early Israeli DC-3s came by devious means, though later aircraft had more orthodox origins. Many other forces, including most French colonial territories, were given C-47s on independence. In many instances, such air forces used the C-47 only for routine transport duties. Papua-New Guinea was one of the last to acquire the C-47 when they were given five by the Australian government and another was Sri Lanka which took over two from the bankrupt Air Ceylon in 1979/80 to operate social service routes.

Basler BT-67s have been supplied to South American air forces via USAF contracts. El Salvador received four, converted to gunships, Bolivia received two, Guatemala six and Colombia seven, fitted with Forward Looking Infra Red (FLIR). In addition the Colombian Police had received five for internal security by the end of 2004. The Royal Thai Air Force have nine converted, and the Mali and Mauritania Air Forces both have two examples in service.

The layout for the Military Operators section which follows is a simple alphabetical one in country name order, with cross-references where names have changed. So far as possible a brief history of the type's use is given, listing units, aircraft serial numbers and constructor's numbers, from the last of which the individual aircraft's history can be found by reference to the Production History chapter. Where no c/n is known, dates are given when the aircraft was known to be in service (i/s) as well as fates. Dates should not be taken to be the full extent of an aircraft's use by that air arm. When countries such as the United Kingdom, United States and France - all large-scale users whose operations are well-documented - are concerned, considerable detail is given, and, as in many other cases, the information has come from a variety of sources, often unofficial and by observation. Commonplace abbreviations are decoded by reference to the introduction of Chapter 5, Production History.

ANGOLA

The **Força Aérea Popular de Angola** (FAPA) or Angolan People's Air Force is known to have used at least four C-47s in the late seventies. These were taken over from the Portuguese Air Force when independence was gained, but fell into disuse, the last two still with Portuguese Air Force serial numbers.

FP-501*	c/n
6164	26468
6178	12066

* possibly Mozambican as FP-502 derelict at Maputo.

ARGENTINA

The **Fuerza Aérea Argentina** (FAA) acquired its first DC-3 in 1941 when 169 was taken over from Air France. So far as is known no more were added until Jun46 when two ex-USAAF C-47s were ferried from Miami. The three flew with the 1st Transport Group at El Palomar, alongside Vickers Vikings. T-169 became T-16 for use by LADE (it was originally an airliner). The principal task of the Group was the carriage of men and materials to various mainland bases. Further C-47s were obtained between 1947 and 1952, by which time the Group had 22 C-47s on strength. A further 12 C-47s were bought from REAL, Brazil, via the Argentine Army, between Oct60 and Nov61. At the same time the FAA was reorganised and C-47s were used by I Brigada Aérea (El Palomar), IV Brigada Aérea (El Plumerillo) and V Brigada Aérea (Gral. Pringles). They continued to support mainland bases, but four C-47s were used from time to time to supply bases in Antartica, fitted with RATOG and skis.

In 1966 Aerolineas Argentinas transferred their social service routes to Linea Aerea del Estado (LADE), a unit of the FAA. With the transfer went 14 C-47s and these aircraft were used on the full LADE network, replacing the Vikings on other FAA scheduled services. The C-47s themselves were only replaced when F.27s were delivered from 1968. Other uses have included radio aid calibration and VIP government transport, particularly the Secretaria de Aeronautica. Many C-47s survived through the seventies and some further redeployed to organizations such as Area de Material Rio IV and to government agencies (see later). Three were donated to the Bolivian Air Force for use by TAM in Jul69, and two to Paraguay for air force use.

Recent research by individuals of the Argentine Air Force has allowed the publication of a nearly complete list of C-47s used by all three services. The full history of each aircraft is given in the Production History chapter with an 'index' provided in this section.

Initially all transport serials had a T- prefix for 'Transporte de Pasajeros'. This later developed to include TA- for 'Transporte Antartico' and TC- for 'Transporte de Pasajeros y Carga'. 'S' and 'TS' indicates 'Transporte Sanitario' and 'VR' for calibration aircraft ('Verificacion de Radioayudas'). Finally, 'E' indicates Entrenamiento or training.

The serial 'number' is not permanent and although some remained when the prefix changed, others did not, and the number may be re-used.

169	c/n 2122	T-20(1)		(Note 1)
T-01	19395	T-20(2)	2012	
T-02	18968	T-21	9936	
T-03		T-22(1)	19479	
T-04(2)	9162	T-22(2)	12190	
T-05	19965	T-23	19997	
T-08	12850	T-24	19642	(Note 2)
T-09	13150	T-25	19026	
T-10	13336	T-26	19344	
T-11	12246	T-27	13621	
T-12	11920	T-28	25228	
T-16	2122	T-29	4825	
T-17(1)	20093	T-30	25871	
T-17(2)	20160	T-31	20093	
T-18(1)	19659	T-32(1)		
T-18(2)	20388	T-32(2)	4365	
T-19(1)	33538	T-33	9254	
T-19(2)	4754	T-34	12792	

CHAPTER 3: MILITARY OPERATORS OF THE DC-3, C-47, R4D, DAKOTA AND LI-2

T-35	26794		T-89	19965
T-36	12025		T-101	25455
T-37	4957		T-102	2012/"2003"
T-38	4280		T-103	26114
T-39(1)	19438		T-104	13373
T-39(2)	4754		T-151	20093
T-40	19395		T-169	2122
T-48	19395		T-172	19659
T-49	18968		T-174	20093
T-50	(Note 3)		T-175	19659
T-51	(Note 4)			6176
T-52	(Note 5)			13473
T-53	(Note 6)			20541
T-67	"20013"			

Note 1: This was delivered on 27Feb47 and in Nov51 was flown to Alaska for installation of skis and other equipment for Antarctic service, though it was never used there. It was w/o on 19Mar56 at Curuzu Cuatia, Corrientes.

Note 2: Reported erroneously as 19542.

Note 3: Delivered to FAA in May47. Transferred to Army after accident, probably for ground instruction.

Note 4: Delivered to FAA in May47. SOC between 1953 and 1956.

Note 5: Delivered to FAA in Jun47. Rn T-03 in 1959 and still in service in Apr67. Probably wfu.

Note 6: Delivered to FAA in Jun47. W/o 28Jul59. T-32(1) allotted but ntu.

'TA-05'	4365		TA-07	20007
TA-05	19965		TA-33	9254
TA-06	26614			
TC-04	"20013"		TC-32	4365
TC-05	19965		TC-33(1)	9254
TC-11	13150		TC-33(2)	"20013"
TC-15	19796		TC-34	12792
TC-17	20160		TC-35	26794
TC-18	20388		TC-36(1)	12025
TC-19	25277		TC-36(2)	26614
TC-20	20158		TC-37(1)	4957
TC-21	19961		TC-37(2)	20007
TC-27	4280		TC-38	4280
TC-28	25228		TC-39	19438
TC-31	20093			
TS-03	25455		TS-04	26114
E-301	26114		E-304	"20013"
S-3	25455		S-4	26114
VR-10	4556		VR-12	2012/"2003"
VR-11	25775		VR-14	13373

Three C-47s were acquired by the **Comando de Aviación del Ejercito Argentina** (Army) in Dec54. These were ETA-101 c/n 20160, Rn ME-1T in 1956 and MG-1T in Mar58, ETA-102 c/n 20817, Rn ME-2T, MG-2T in Mar58, then AE-12E and AE-100, before sale in Sep68 as LV-JIG. ETA-103 c/n 20388 became ME-3T by Nov56 and MG-3T by Mar58. ETA-101 and ETA-103 went to the Air Force as T-17 and T-18 in 1960. Twelve DC-3s were bought from REAL, Brazil in October 1960, though they were passed to the Air Force in 1961. EA-1T to EA-12T served with Escuela de Tropas Aerotransportadores (Airborne Troop School). They are known to be c/ns 2012, 4280, 4365, 4754, 4825, 4957, 12025, 12190, 13621, 19438, 25228 and 25871, though tie-ups are unknown.

The **Aviación Naval Argentina** bought five C-39s from AVENSA, Venezuela, in Aug46. A sixth may not have entered service. They were used by a unit coded 3-O (O = Observacion) from Aug46 eventually ending with Comando de Transportes Aeronavales in 1956 (CTA), three being based at Comandante Espora and two at Puerta Indio, for general transport duties. They were sold in 1958. In 1946 C-47s were bought and more followed. One remained as late as 1989. Aviación Naval operated in Antarctica and U.T.78 Unidad de Exploracion y Reconocimento Aerofotografico of the Grupo Aeronaval Antarctico had C-47s CTA-12 and CTA-15. The former was the first Argentine aircraft to land at the South Pole and CTA-15 has been preserved at Ezeiza, Buenos Aires. The C-47 was used at first by the 2nd (1946 on) and 3rd (1947 on) Naval Air Force General Transport Units (Codes 2-Gt- and 3-Gt-). These units were reorganised and C-47s more recently saw service with the 3rd Naval Air Transport Sq (Code 3-T-), the 4th Sq from 1952 (Code 4-T-) and the 5th Sq from 1963 (Code 5-T-). Naval aircraft have a sequence number, starting at 0001, which remains with the aircraft despite unit code changes.

0103 (C-39)	2083	3-O-1	
0104 (C-39)		3-O-2, 3-T-31 Cr Jul48 Coronel Pringles, BA	
0105 (C-39)		3-O-3, 3-T-32, 1-E-302 (1953) and CTA-38 1956, Wfu and scr 1957. [E = Escuela]	
0106 (C-39)	2074	3-O-4	
0107 (C-39)	2060	3-O-5	
0108 (C-39)		[Missing c/ns are 2057, 2063, 2085]	
0117 (C-47)	19124	0264 (C-47)	12908
0171 (C-47)	4680	0278 (C-47)	13469
0172 (C-47)	9578	0281 (C-47)	12732
0187 (C-47)	20030	0282 (C-47)	4571
0188 (C-47)	9356	0296 (C-47)	4664
0220 (C-47)	12678	0490 (C-47)	26114
0232 (C-47)	9171	0652 (C-47)	33160
0260 (C-47)	9899		

Unit codes used and corresponding serials were:- Gt = General, transporte; T = Transporte

2-Gt-7	0117		2-Gt-15	0172
2-Gt-8	0171		2-Gt-16	0188
2-Gt-9	0172		2-Gt-17	0187
2-Gt-10	0187		2-Gt-18	0232
2-Gt-12	0296		2-Gt-19	0260
2-Gt-13	0117		2-Gt-20	0278
2-Gt-14	0171			
3-Gt-1	0220		3-Gt-5	0278
3-Gt-2	0264		3-Gt-9	0264
3-Gt-3	0232		3-Gt-12	0281
3-Gt-4	0188		3-Gt-13	0282
3-T-20	0117		3-T-23	0187
3-T-21	0171		3-T-25	0232
4-T-10	0220		4-T-22	0172
4-T-11	0264		4-T-23	0278
4-T-12	0281		4-T-24	0296
4-T-13	0282		4-T-25	0232
4-T-20	0117		4-T-26	0188
4-T-21	0171			
CTA-10	0220		CTA-22	0172
CTA-11	0264		CTA-23	0232
CTA-12	0281		CTA-24	0188
CTA-13	0282		CTA-25	0490
CTA-14	0278		CTA-37	0103
CTA-15	0296		CTA-38	0105
CTA-20	0117		CTA-39	0106
CTA-21	0171		CTA-40	0107
5-T-10	0220 & 0652		5-T-22	0172
5-T-11	0264		5-T-23	0117
5-T-12	0282		5-T-24	0188
5-T-13	0652		5-T-25	0296
5-T-21	0171		5-T-26	0278

The **Prefectura Nacional Maritime**, later known as the **Prefectura Naval Argentina** is also under the control of the Secretaria de Marina. It carries out coast guard duties. Two ex-Aerolineas DC-3s were delivered late in 1962; initially numbered PM-15 and PM-16 they became PA-15 and PA-16 in 1966 (c/ns 33430 and 12057, respectively). They were sold and replaced by Short Skyvans in 1972.

AUSTRALIA

At the outbreak of war in 1939 the **Royal Australian Air Force** (RAAF) was in the process of re-equipping with operational types and transports had low priority. Four airline DC-3s were therefore chartered in September to make good the gap. They were operated as A30-1 to A30-4 until 1940, equipping No 8 Sq at Canberra. Ten DC-2s were bought via the British Purchasing Commission from Eastern Air Lines, initially for use by 8 Sq on parachute training, but later with 1 and 2 Wireless Air Gunner Schools. They were replaced by Hudsons.

When Japan entered the war there was a major build-up of American forces in Australia from 1942 onwards. The first RAAF C-53s came from the USAAF and were loaned initially for use by 36 Sq in May43, being returned in 1944. These were followed by 124 C-47As and C-47Bs, supplied under Lend-Lease. They operated in the South West Pacific area, including Papua-New Guinea, the Netherlands E Indies and later in the Philippines.

Apart from those used by the RAAF, many other C-53s and C-47s were operated with Australian call signs under the American component of the Australian Directorate of Air Transport (ADAT), as part of Air Transport Command (ATC). This was formed as ADAT on 28Jan42 at Amberley. Call signs in the blocks VHCBA to VHCDZ and VHCKA onwards were allotted and used in place of USAAF serials. Many call signs were used several times over and individual aircraft often used several different call signs at various times, so these cannot be used as a means of identifying individual aircraft. They are listed later in this section and also in the production list with more detail. Ex-KLM aircraft were given call signs in the series VHCXA onwards. RAAF C-47s had similarly applied call signs during WWII in several series. These were allocated shortly after entering RAAF service, so are not always in sequence with the RAAF serials. They remained with the aircraft until 1946 when they changed several times post-war. Instructions were given that they be deleted in May47 at the next major inspection. In Aug47 the last three of the call sign were to be reinstated, but in Aug48 they were no longer a 'service requirement' and were again to be deleted! Then there were three nationality marks in use at various times, VH-, VJ- and VM-, according to the unit, the VMYxx series being applied to 300Wg RAF.

Post-war the RAAF transport squadrons were run down as needs were reduced, and several squadrons disbanded. Operations continued in New Guinea and Papua and 36 and 38 Squadrons also operated to Japan. The latter service was replaced by Qantas Lancastrians in 1947. Four RAAF C-47s operated in China with the UNRRA in 1946/47.

In 1948/49 40 RAAF crews flew RAF Dakotas on the Berlin Airlift; today commemorated by the gift of A65-69 to the Berlin Airlift Museum. In 1950 at least five C-47s of 36 Sq served in Korea as part of 91 (Composite) Wing. They were withdrawn in 1953. 38 Sq operated in Malaya from Jun50.

C-47s continued to serve the RAAF until 1980, though some were replaced earlier. The School of Air Navigation, Sale, Vic, took delivery of HS.748s in 1968 and in other units they gave way to C-130s and Caribous. However, the ARDU continued to use them until their retirement in 1999. Two were in use at the Technical Training School, Wagga Wagga (A65-64 and 98). The C-47 served for 56 years with the RAAF. The last three aircraft were sold by auction in 2000 to private buyers.

Units using DC-2s and Dakotas were:-

No 8 Sq Formed at Canberra, ACT, on 11Sep39, code 'H'. DC-2s and DC-3s used until 1940 when Hudsons replaced them.

No 33 Sq Formed at Townsville. Qld, on 16Feb42, code 'BT'. Disbanded 13May46. C-47s used were:- A65-11, 15 to 20, 28, 32, 35, 36, 38, 43, 44, 45, 47, 48, 53, 54, 56 to 61.

No 34 Sq Formed at Darwin, NT on 23Feb42, code 'FD'. Disbanded at Richmond, NSW on 06Jun46. Reformed on 01Mar48 from No 2 (Comm) Unit at Mallaia, SA. Disbanded 28Oct55. Renamed 34(VIP) Flight ex RAAF VIP Flight on 12Mar55. Became 34(ST) Sq in July 1959 and 34 Sq on 13Jun63. HS.748s replaced the C-47s in the late 1960s. DC-2 A30-11 was used as well as the following C-47s: A65-6 to 13, 17, 22 to 26, 29, 41, 42, 49, 52, 63, 65, 69, 84, 85, 90, 91, 92, 98, 103, 104, 105, 108, 118, 119, 122, 123, 124.

No 35 Sq Formed at Pearce, WA on 11Mar42, code 'BK'. Disbanded at Townsville, Qld, on 10Jun46. C-47s used were:- A65-15 to 22, 24 to 29, 40, 45, 51, 81, 82, 83, 85, 86, 88, 89, 90, 96 to 100, 107, 115.

No 36 Sq Formed at Laverton, Vic on 11Mar42, code 'RE'. Disbanded at Richmond, NSW on 26May53. Reformed on 01Mar53 ex 30 Comm Unit at Iwakuni, Japan, for Korean operations. Reduced to 36 Flt on 13Mar55 at end of Korean war. Reconstituted as 36 Sq on 01May55 at Canberra, ACT and moved to Richmond. Re-equipped with C-130As in 1958.

The following DC-2s were used: A30-5, 6, 9, 10 to 14; impressed DC-3s loaned by the USAAF were 41-7686, 7687, 7690, 7691, 7693, 7694, 7697, 7698, 7733, 41-1941, 1944, as well as C-53s 41-20053, 20054, 20070 and C-47s loaned were 41-7732, 18646, 18649, 42-23481, 92804, 92806, 92809, 92810, 100726 and 100727, and others by call sign only, VHCKC, CKD, CKI, CKJ, CKK, CKL and CKM (these all being leased in April 1944). Owned aircraft were A65-1 to 8, 10, 14, 22, 26, 27, 31 to 36, 39, 40, 46, 48 to 51, 55, 63, 64, 65, 84, 88, 94, 96 to 99, 103, 104, 109, 111, 113, 115 to 123.

No 37 Sq Formed at Laverton, Vic on 15Jul43, code 'OM'. Disbanded 24Feb48. Reformed on 21Feb66 at Richmond, NSW. One DC-2 A30-12 was on the roster and the following C-47s:- A65-21, 22, 26, 35, 41, 44, 48, 64, 65, 67, 69, 70 to 77, 82, 85, 87, 93, 94, 101, 102, 105, 106, 111, 112.

No 38 Sq Formed at Richmond, NSW on 15Sep43, code 'PK'. Re-equipped with Caribous in 1964. C-47s issued were:- A65-18, 22, 32, 36, 39, 42 to 45, 48 to 52, 56, 58 to 69, 71, 74, 76, 78, 79, 80, 90, 91, 92, 94, 95, 96, 98, 100, 102, 105, 108, 112, 114, 122, 124.

Other units
1 (Comm) Unit - Operated 01Nov39 to 30Jul48 with DC-2s and C-47s.
2 (Comm) Unit - Operated 02Dec40 to 31Jul44.
9 Local Air Support Unit.
1, 2 and 3 Wireless Air Gunner Schools - All used DC-2s initially. 1 WAGS had A30-5, 6, 7, 9, 10, 11; 2 WAGS used A30-7, 8, 9, 13, 14 and 3 WAGS had A30-5 and 9.
Signals School used DC-2s initially, A30-6, 8 and 9 being recorded.
1 Service Flying Training School. Used DC-2 A30-11 initially.
1 Aircraft Performance Unit - became Service Development & Performance Flight and then Aircraft Research & Development Unit (ARDU), at Laverton, Vic and later Edinburgh, SA. Five C-47s, A65-78, A65-86, A65-94, A65-95 and A65-114 remained until Jun85, when A65-114 was retired, but the rest survived until replaced in 1999 by a Fokker F.27 and a Beech 200 KingAir.
2 Air Trials Unit, Woomera.
Antarctic Flight.
Transport Support Flight, Butterworth, Malaya.
Paratroop Training Unit. Used DC-2s initially.
Royal Australian Engineers Training Centre, Wagga Wagga. Used a DC-2.
The Australian War Museum has VHCIN A65-71 which is loaned to 34 Sq and kept airworthy at RAAF Richmond. VH-JXD A65-98 joined the RAAF Historic Flight at Point Cook in July 1989.

Only four C-47s were used by the **Royal Australian Navy**, two (A65-23 and 43) received from 1949/50 and another two (N2-90 and 123) in 1968. The first two were used for training and transport, and the others for transport only. The A65 prefix was altered to N2- in 1965. All were replaced by HS.748s in 1973/74. N2-43 operates with the RAN Historic Flight.

Units were:-
723 Sq - 1952 to 1956 Fleet support (A65-23 and 43)
724 Sq - 1961 to 1968 Operational Flying School (N2-23, 43, 90 and 123)
725 Sq - 1958 to 1961 Fleet support and later anti-submarine training (A65-23 and 43).
851 Sq - 1954 to 1958 Training Firefly observers, code 'NW' Nowra (A65-23, 90 and 123). 1968 to 1974 Support duties.

A65-43 had a Sea Venom nose fitted while with 851 Sq, and A65-23 and 43 had Fairey Gannet retractable radomes for training. 821 Sq also used N2-43.

Serials and call signs are given below:

A30-1	c/n 2002		A30-10*	1372	VHCRD
A30-2	2003		A30-11*	1286	VHCRE
A30-3	2029		A30-12*	1257	VHCRF
A30-4	2030		A30-13*	1373	VHCRG
A30-5*	1287	VHCRA/CRI	A30-14*	1288	VHCRH
A30-6*	1259	VHCRB/CRJ	A30-15	6172	VHCCH/DAA
A30-7*	1290		A30-16	6149	VHDAB
A30-8*	1291		A30-17	9012	VHDAC
A30-9*	1292	VHCRK	A30-18	9107	
A65-1	6172	VHCTA	A65-17	9999	VHCTQ
A65-2	6149	VHCTB(1)	A65-18	10000	VHCTR
A65-3	9012	VHCTC(1)	A65-19	10001	VHCTS
A65-4	9107	VHCTD	A65-20	11967	VHCTU
A65-5	9285	VHCTE	A65-21	11970	VHCTC(2)
A65-6	9287	VHCTF	A65-22	11971	VHCTV
A65-7	9288	VHCTG	A65-23**	11973	VHCTB(2)
A65-8	9289	VHCTH	A65-24	11974	VHCTW
A65-9	9286	VHCTI	A65-25	12035	VHCTX
A65-10	9590	VHCTK	A65-26	12037	VHCTT
A65-11	9591	VHCTJ	A65-27	12051	VHCTY
A65-12	9592	VHCTN	A65-28	12045	VHCUA
A65-13	9593	VHCTL	A65-29	12056	VHCTZ
A65-14	9594	VHCTM	A65-30	12076	VHCUB
A65-15	9997	VHCTO(1)	A65-31	12285	VHCUC
A65-16	9998	VHCTP	A65-32	12360	VHCUD

Chapter 3: Military Operators of the DC-3, C-47, R4D, Dakota and Li-2

A65-33	12359	VHCUE	A65-78	32677	VHCIU	VHCCH	C-39 38-532, C-47 41-38713	
A65-34	12250	VHCUF	A65-79	32669	VHCIV	VHCCI	41-18560, 41-18682	
A65-35	12252	VHCUI	A65-80	32672	VHCIW	VHCCJ	41-18498	
A65-36	12248	VHCUJ	A65-81	32673	VHCIX	VHCCK	41-18538	
A65-37	12349	VHCUG	A65-82	27128	VHCIY	VHCCL	41-18539	
A65-38	12249	VHCUH	A65-83	32875	VHCIZ	VHCCM	41-18568	
A65-39	12361	VHCIG	A65-84	32877	VHRFA	VHCCN	41-18571	
A65-40	12539	VHCUM	A65-85	32878	VHRFB	VHCCO	41-18577	
A65-41	12540	VHCUK	A65-86	32879	VHRFC	VHCCP	41-18583	
A65-42	12541	VHCUL	A65-87	32876	VHRFD	VHCCQ	41-18584	
A65-43**	12542	VHCUN(1)	A65-88	32880	VHRFE	VHCCR	41-18586	
A65-44	12873	VHCIA	A65-89	32881	VHRFF	VHCCS	41-18601, 41-18585	
A65-45	12872	VHCIB	A65-90**	32883	VHRFG	VHCCT	41-18602, 41-18615	
A65-46	12874	VHCIC	A65-91	32884	VHRFH	VHCCU	41-18564, 41-18606	
A65-47	12875	VHCUO	A65-92	32887	VHRFI	VHCCV	41-18588	
A65-48	13083	VHCID	A65-93	33093	VHRFJ	VHCCW	41-18595	
A65-49	13084	VHCIE	A65-94	33106	VHRFK	VHCCX	41-18597	
A65-50	13082	VHCIF	A65-95	33096	VHRFL	VHCCY	41-38601, 41-38676	
A65-51	13085	VHCIH	A65-96	33097	VHRFM	VHCCZ	41-38631, 41-38662	
A65-52	13338	VHCII	A65-97	33099	VHRFN			
A65-53	13341	VHCTO(2)	A65-98	33102	VHRFO	VHCDA	41-7685	
A65-54	13339	VHCUP	A65-99	33103	VHRFP	VHCDB	41-7687, 43-16199	
A65-55	13340	VHCUQ	A65-100	33109	VHRFQ	VHCDC	41-7690, 42-24044, 43-16203	
A65-56	25365	VHCIJ	A65-101	33112	VHRFR	VHCDD	41-7691	
A65-57	25367	VHCUR	A65-102	33113	VHRFS	VHCDE	41-7693, 43-49755, 43-49905	
A65-58	25366	VHCUN(2)/	A65-103	33294	VHRFT	VHCDF	41-7694, 42-100481	
		VHCIK	A65-104	33295	VHRFU	VHCDG	41-7686, 43-16239	
A65-59	25364	VHCUT(1)/	A65-105	33300	VHRFV	VHCDH	41-7694, 41-7702, 41-7732, 41-18649	
		VHCIL	A65-106	33290	VHRFW	VHCDI	41-7695, 41-7733	
A65-60	25998	VHCUS	A65-107	33302	VHRFX	VHCDJ	41-7698, 42-23535	
A65-61	25999	VHCUJ/	A65-108	33297	VHRGZ	VHCDK	41-7697, 43-16297	
		VHCUT(2)	A65-109	33301	VHRGX	VHCDL	41-7732, 43-15454	
A65-62	26000	VHCKO	A65-110	33292	VHRGY	VHCDM	41-7688, 41-7733, 43-15436	
A65-63	26001	VHCKN	A65-111	33304	VHRFY	VHCDN	41-38647	
A65-64	26640	VHCUU	A65-112	33303	VHRFZ	VHCDO	41-18585, 41-18628	
A65-65	26637	VHCUV	A65-113	33459	VHRGA	VHCDP	41-18587, 42-23955	
A65-66	26639	VHCUW	A65-114	33460	VHRGB	VHCDQ	41-38629	
A65-67	26638	VHCUX	A65-115	33464	VHRGC	VHCDR	41-38630	
A65-68	27130	VHCUY	A65-116	33453	VHRGD	VHCDS	41-18598	
A65-69	27127	VHCUZ	A65-117	33456	VHRGE	VHCDT	41-38634	
A65-70	27129	VHCIM	A65-118	33457	VHRGF	VHCDU	41-18601, 43-15438	
A65-71	27131	VHCIN	A65-119	33463	VHRGG	VHCDV	41-20070, 43-15441	
A65-72	32668	VHCIO	A65-120	33461	VHRGH	VHCDW	41-20066	
A65-73	32671	VHCIP	A65-121	33452	VHRGI	VHCDX	41-20051, 42-23500	
A65-74	32680	VHCIQ	A65-122	33455	VHRGJ	VHCDY	41-18573, 42-23437	
A65-75	32667	VHCIR	A65-123**	34221	VHRGK	VHCDZ	C-39 38-501, 42-23856, 44-83227	
A65-76	32675	VHCIS	A65-124	34220	VHRGL			
A65-77	32679	VHCIT				VHCFA	41-7703, 41-18431, 41-18682	

* A30-5 to 14 were DC-2s
** R Australian Navy, later prefixed N2-

The **Directorate of Air Transport** came into being in 1942 to control the many transport aircraft operated by the USAAF 5th AF in Australia, as well as the RAAF. The USAAF serial numbers were overpainted with large registration-like call signs on the fin and rudder. These are quoted in this volume without any hyphen to distinguish them from civil marks. The change is believed to have been for security reasons as the aircraft operated into Australian commercial airports. The list given here is by no means complete and has been compiled from various sources including radio call sign lists and personal observations. Some call signs have been used two or three times over. The USAAF also used 'field' numbers and many aircraft had individual names. The former are a guide to the units which appear to have been allotted in blocks, eg 1 to 25 were 39 TCS and have no connection with the call signs. See the USAAF part for a listing of unit allocations. The ADAT ceased to operate on 03Oct44 and the RAAF took over these duties on 16Oct44.

An index of known ADAT call signs follows:-

VHCBF	C-33 36-77
VHCBG	C-33 36-83
VHCBP	C-53
VHCBZ	C-47 42-23887

Some Douglas B-18s also exist in this block

VHCCA	C-39 38-505, C-47 41-7732
VHCCB	B-18, C-47 41-20053
VHCCC	C-47 41-20054
VHCCD	C-39 38-527, C-47 41-7732, 42-24220
VHCCE	C-39 38-535, C-47 41-7733
VHCCF	C-39 38-530
VHCCG	C-39 38-519

VHCFB	41-18498, 41-18646
VHCFC	41-18538
VHCFD	41-18539
VHCFE	41-18667
VHCFF	41-38674, 42-23697
VHCFG	41-18577, 41-18668
VHCFH	41-18583
VHCFI	41-18584, 41-38666
VHCFJ	41-18585
VHCFK	41-18586
VHCFL	41-18585, 41-38601, 41-38680
VHCFM	[Cr 05Nov42]
VHCFN	41-18431
VHCFO	41-18588
VHCFP	41-18595
VHCFQ	41-18597
VHCFR	41-18602
VHCFS	?
VHCFT	41-18606, 41-38628
VHCFU	41-38629
VHCFV	41-38630
VHCFW	41-38634
VHCFX	[Cr 1943], 41-18601
VHCFY	41-18612
VHCFZ	41-38647
VHCGA	41-18642, 42-23418
VHCGB	41-18645, 42-23489
VHCGC	41-18648, 42-23485, 42-23490
VHCGD	41-18651, 42-23486, 43-15432
VHCGE	41-18656, 42-23491
VHCGF	41-18658, 42-23488, 42-100481
VHCGG	41-18671
VHCGH	41-38658, 42-23581, 41-19467

VHCGI	42-23590		VHCKJ		
VHCGJ	42-23583		VHCKK		
VHCGK	42-23589		VHCKL		
VHCGL	42-23584, 42-23953		VHCKM	42-100460	
VHCGM	42-23585, 42-23949		VHCKN	A65-63	
VHCGN	42-23586		VHCKO	A65-62	
VHCGO	42-23587				
VHCGP	42-23588, 43-30743		VHCNA	Bu 39067	
VHCGQ	42-23582		VHCNB	Bu 39068	
VHCGR	42-23651		VHCNC	Bu 39072	
VHCGS	42-23653		VHCND	Bu 17229	
VHCGT	42-23657, 43-30752				
VHCGU	42-23656		VHCWA	41-7698, 41-20070	
VHCGV	42-23660				
VHCGW	42-23662		VHCXA	DC-5 PK-ADB [44-83231]	
VHCGX	42-23659		VHCXB	DC-5 PK-ADD [44-83232]	
VHCGY	42-23658, 42-92805		VHCXC	DC-5 PK-ADC [44-83230]	
VHCGZ	42-23698, 42-92824		VHCXD	DC-3 PK-ALT,[11941],[44-83228]	
			VHCXE	DC-3 PK-ALW,[11944],[44-83229], 42-23421	
VHCHA	41-18646, 42-23664		VHCXF	DC-2 PK-AFJ?	
VHCHB	41-18649, 42-23599, 43-16297		VHCXG	DC-2 PK-AFK [44-83227]	
VHCHC	42-23598		VHCXH	DC-2 PK-AFL [44-83226]	
VHCHD	42-23654		VHCXL	DC-3 41-1944, 43-15484	
VHCHE	42-23655 [Also C-39]		VHCXM	DC-3 43-15427	
VHCHF	41-38668, 42-23661				
VHCHG	42-23952				
VHCHH	42-23954				
VHCHI	41-38664, 42-23955				
VHCHJ	41-38668, 42-23958				
VHCHK	42-23959				
VHCHL	42-23960				
VHCHM	42-23961				
VHCHN	42-23964				
VHCHO	43-30751				
VHCHP	43-30752				
VHCHQ	43-30753				
VHCHR	42-93683				
VHCHS					
VHCHT	43-30755				
VHCHU					
VHCHV	43-				
VHCHW	43-30759				
VHCHX					
VHCHY					
VHCHZ	42-92827, 42-92817				
VHCJA	41-18653				
VHCJB	41-38661, 41-18431				
VHCJC					
VHCJD					
VHCJE					
VHCJF	42-92790				
VHCJG	42-92791				
VHCJH	42-92792				
VHCJI	42-92793				
VHCJJ	42-92794				
VHCJK	42-92795				
VHCJL	42-92796				
VHCJM	42-92797				
VHCJN					
VHCJO	42-92798				
VHCJP	43-30744				
VHCJQ					
VHCJR					
VHCJS					
VHCJT	42-92802				
VHCJU	42-92803				
VHCJV					
VHCJW	42-92806				
VHCJX					
VHCJY					
VHCJZ					
VHCKA	42-100726				
VHCKB	42-100727				
VHCKC	42-100728?				
VHCKD	42-100729?				
VHCKE	42-92809				
VHCKF	42-92804				
VHCKG	42-92806				
VHCKH	42-92810				
VHCKI					

See also NEIAF for VHRCx, VHRDx and VHRE x series; Dutch Navy for VHPAx series, and United Kingdom for VMYAx series.

BELGIUM

Belgian pilots were flying Dakotas before the end of WWII, particularly with 525 Squadron, RAF Transport Command. Military flying started in Belgium on 01Oct46, when the **Aviation Militaire Belge** was formed and some C-47s were delivered from American stocks. The 169e Wing Transport was formed officially on 01Apr47, of which 366e Squadron was equipped with C-47s.

Operations included flights to various parts of Europe, for example Hendon, Prestwick, Wahn, Villacoublay and further afield to the Belgian Congo. In 1948 the air force was renamed **Force Aérienne Belge** and this was accompanied by an internal reorganisation. No 15e Transport Wing took over on 01Feb48, with two escadrilles. These were 20e (ex 366e) and 21e (ex 367e), both with C-47s. Further aircraft came from RAF stocks, and in the main these were overhauled by Scottish Aviation. A total of 41 aircraft was delivered to the 15e Wing at Evere, those with the 20e Smaldeele being given radio codes in the range OTCNA etc and those with the 21e OTCWA etc. These codes were retained throughout their lives. In 1952 the 15e Wing moved to Melsbroek (Brussels) but the arrival of the C-119 saw the progressive return to MDAP of 24 C-47s in 1952-53 (several went to France and Holland). The surviving aircraft were re-grouped within the 21e Smaldeele where they remained, irrespective of use, until final retirement. Fourteen remained in service, some for a considerable length of time, with some being used in civil marks by Sabena or by the Ministry of Communications. Others were operated in the Congo after it became independent on 30Jun60. A few were fitted with the long NASRR nose for F-104G training and the last was retired from service on 23Jul76. One is preserved in the Brussels War Museum.

Serial numbers ran from K-1 to 41, but various letter suffixes were used to denote their use. KFC indicated reconnaissance, KN navigational training, KP photography and KR VIP use. Known examples are given below, although all aircraft eventually reverted to the single 'K' prefix. The radio call signs were painted on the side. At first these were in the series A-CW to Z-CW. In 1949 the OTCNx series was used by No 20e and OTCWx by No 21e. Unfortunately there is no known connection between the two series and in the later series it has not proved possible to identify all the aircraft by c/n. Where there is doubt this is indicated by a query in the list which follows:-

K-1	OTCWA	c/n 26501	K-10/	OTCWE	25851
KP-2/	OTCWB	20741	KP-10		
KT-2			K-11	OTCWF	25869
K-3	OTCNA	25567	K-12	OTCNF	25880
K-4/KP-4	OTCNB	20864	KP-13/	OTCNG	26046
K-5	OTCWC	20879	KN-13		
K-6/KP-6	OTCNW	20884	K-14	OTCNH	26157
K-7	OTCWD	25745	K-15	OTCNF ?	25657
KP-8/	OTCND	25756	K-16	OTCWG	20823
KN-8/KFC-8			K-17	OTCNJ	26050
K-9	OTCNE	25846	K-18	OTCWH	26048

CHAPTER 3: MILITARY OPERATORS OF THE DC-3, C-47, R4D, DAKOTA AND LI-2

K-19	OTCWI	32557	K-31/	OTCNR	32812	
K-20	OTCNJ	26869	KP-31			
K-21	OTCWJ	32558	K-32	OTCNS	33323	
K-22	OTCNK	26865	K-33	OTCNT	33403	
K-23	OTCNL/M	26251	K-34	OTCNU	33167	
K-24	OTCNN	27085	K-35	OTCWN	33433	
K-25	OTCWK		K-36	OTCWO	33448	
K-26	OTCWL	32632	K-37	OTCWP	33401	
K-27	OTCWM	26996	K-38	OTCWQ	25816	
K-28	OTCNO	32664	K-39	OTCWR	32755	
K-29	OTCNP	33049	K-40	OTCWS	33244	
KP-30	OTCNQ	27211	K-41	OTCWT	25931	

Two aircraft are known to have been supplied which do not appear in the above list. These are c/ns 26159 on 17Feb47 and 26192. The former because of its early delivery date should be one of the low K- series, so it is possible that it was supplied for spares use, or that there is an undetected error.

BENIN/DAHOMEY

The **Force Aérienne du Benin** (Dahomey until 1977) was given a single C-47 in 1961, as were most ex-French colonial territories. At least a further four were supplied up to 1973, and three may still have been in use in 1997. Call signs and serial numbers are used:-

TYAAB	76307	c/n 32639	TYAAF	789	26050
TYAAC(1)	349881	27142	TYAAC(2)		4775
TYAAE	AE-164	20777			

BIAFRA

The Governor of Eastern Nigeria announced a Declaration of Independence on 30May67 and the region was known from that date as Biafra. The **Biafran Air Force** was formed in Jun67. Three ex-Luftwaffe C-47s were bought in clandestine circumstances in Sep68 and are known to have passed through W Africa in Mar69. Two reached Biafra. The third was abandoned at Faro, Portugal and was later rebuilt and sold in the USA. The aircraft were officially US registered, but while on delivery registrations N10801, N10802 and N10803 were partly painted out to read only 801, 802 and 803 respectively.

N10801 c/n 33238; N10802 c/n 32739; N10803 c/n 32725.

The Government of Zambia recognised Biafra and donated two DC-3s 9J-RIF (c/n 4235 quoted in error) and 9J-RIG. 9J-RIF was abandoned after the war at Libreville, Gabon, having been used mainly for ferrying fuel from Libreville to Uli. 9J-RIG may have been used for bombing, attacking Nigerian oil and naval installations - tipping bombs out of the door. It crashed in Mar69 at Uli. The former 5N-AAK was taken over from Nigerian control in Apr67, and 9G-AAD was seized in Jun67.

BOLIVIA

As Bolivia was on the Allied side during WWII, it was supplied with Lend-Lease equipment, and the first four C-47s came from this source to the **Fuerza Aérea Boliviana** in Jan45. These and all later C-47s were used by Transporte Aéreo Militar (TAM) on military and domestic services. The latter were aimed at opening up areas of the country which could not be served economically by commercial airlines. Many of these operations were flown alongside C-46s of Corporacion Boliviano de Fomento. Further C-47s were supplied under Lend-Lease and then MAP, as well as by direct purchase from the US and four donated by Argentina. Technically, aircraft are operated by the Transportation Squadron of the Fuerza Aérea Boliviana, based at El Alto, La Paz, and although some thirty C-47s have been owned, attrition has been heavy and there have rarely been more than ten in service at one time. Military operations were few, but in the mid-sixties the air force was occupied with the hunt for Che Guevara in the area around Santa Cruz de la Sierra.

About seven C-47s remained in use with TAM until 1981, and since then most have been sold or scrapped. One BT-67 has been bought.

Where c/ns are quoted, histories are given in the Production History chapter.

TAM-01	c/n 1934	
'TAM-01'	26666	ex TAM-16
TAM-02		derelict La Paz, Jan81 - Jan97
TAM-03	13839	
TAM-04		cr 21Jan58
TAM-05		cr 08Nov58
TAM-06	20241 ?	
TAM-07		w/o
TAM-08		
TAM-09	9030	
TAM-10		
TAM-11		USAAF serial quoted as 42-9386, but probably 42-93786 c/n 13736. Cr 12Feb70 Laia, La Paz
TAM-12		
TAM-14	4569 ?	
TAM-15	26804	
TAM-16	26666	
TAM-17		i/s 1964; dbr 14Jul70; wreck noted at Trinidad Jan81 to Apr91
TAM-17	19173	to BT-67 for Mali AF
TAM-18		i/s 1964 to 1976
TAM-19	32989	
TAM-20	25673	
TAM-21		wfu prior to Jan81
TAM-22		i/s 1964; cr 04May71
TAM-23		cr 28Sep72; derelict Jan81
TAM-24	9207	
TAM-25	32626	i/s Nov73 to May82, wfu Apr91. Sold ex La Paz Dec94
TAM-26		i/s 1964/65, wfu Oct90 Trinidad
TAM-27		i/s 1976
TAM-28	33626	
TAM-30	11920	
TAM-31	19344	
TAM-32	19395	
TAM-33?	18968	
TAM-34		cr 11Nov74 nr Sorato Mt. Noted Feb79?
TAM-35		i/s 1964 to May82, wfu
TAM-36		wfu; std Trinidad Apr91
TAM-37		i/s 12Dec90. Std Trinidad Apr91
TAM-38	20507	BT-67 conversion
TAM-102		Dismantled Nov94. Ex FA Argentina T-102?

One unknown aircraft was w/o 04Jul66 at Rio Orton. Another cr. 24Feb49 on t/o Cuzco. Other deliveries:- c/n 6153 post-1946; c/n 9652 on 18Jan46; c/n 20080 on Jun48; c/n 25321 on 02Apr46.

BRAZIL

Brazil received its first C-47s in Sep44, when four were transferred by the USAAF at San Antonio, Texas under the Lend-Lease agreement. Seven more were handed over before the end of WWII. Two new transport units of the Brazilian Air Force/**Força Aérea Brasileira** were created on 05Oct44, 1° Grupo de Transporte and 2° Grupo, both based at Rio de Janeiro/Santos Dumont and Campo dos Afonsos. 10° Grupo already had Lodestars and only received one C-47, the remaining ten going to 2° Grupo de Transporte (2°GT). These retained USAAF serial numbers until Mar45, when serial numbers 01 to 11 were allotted. This series was short lived and in Aug45 they became C-47 2009 to C-47 2019 and further aircraft continued this series up to 2092, with the exception of 2054, 2057 and 2058. Twenty-two C-47s were delivered in 1946, 7 going to 1°GT and 15 to 2°GT. Twelve more arrived in 1947 for 1°GT, two being VC-47s, 2051 for the President and 2052 for the Air Minister. Between 1948 and 1950 a further six ex USAF C-47s were received and two were bought from Brazilian operators.

In Apr52 the Secao de Aviones de Comando was created, with equipment including four C-47s, its function being VIP and official transport. In Jan53 1°GT was reorganised into two Esquadroes of which the 1st Esquadrão retained C-47s. Similarly 2°GT was split and here 2/2°GT kept C-47s. Both Grupos were moved to Galeao Air Base in 1954. Early in 1957 the Grupo de Transporte Especial succeeded the Secao de Aviones de Comando, continuing to use some C-47s. In August of that year 2°/1°GT was formed and soon all C-47s from 2°GT were concentrated in the two Esquadroes making up 1°GT, with a complement of 39 aircraft.

During the years 1958 to 1974 further C-47s were acquired from a variety of sources. Three EC-47s were supplied to check radio aids in 1958, 1964 and 1965. 22 DC-3s were bought from various airlines as they were replaced by more modern equipment between 1958 and 1962 and two more in 1971 and 1974. Another was donated by the Acre Territory government. From 1958 onwards the strength of 1°GT was reduced to 16 C-47s in each Esquadrão and some aircraft were assigned to other units, bases etc. C-130s re-equipped 1°/1°GT in 1965 and the C-47s were passed to other units including 2°/1° Grupo de Aviação, 2°/6°GAV at Recife and the HQ of the 4th Air Zone.

In May69 6 Esquadroes de Transporte Aéreo (ETA) were formed, 1°ETA at Belem, 2°ETA at Recife, 3°ETA at Rio, 4°ETA at Sao Paulo, 5°ETA at Porto Alegre and 6°ETA at Brasilia. Each had 6 to 8 C-47s, except 3°ETA with about 15. By 1969 C-47s were no longer used by the Grupo de Transporte Especial and from 1974 onwards the EMB-110 began to replace the C-47 in the ETAs. Disposal of C-47s to civil operators started in 1976 and by 1979 the only unit using them was 1°ETA at Belem which was also using Catalinas. The last two (2018 and 2090) were retired on 24Jan83.

The C-47 in Brazilian Air Force service performed a great variety of essential roles in a country with very poor surface communications. They operated the extensive Correio Aereo Nacional (Military Mail service) and also carried civilians in areas where other air transport could not operate economically.

Serial numbers started, as explained earlier, with 01 to 11, re- numbered C-47 2009 to 2019. All later serials were prefixed C-47 except EC-47s 2065, 2088 and 2089. 2041, 2053 and 2064 were VIP style, but not prefixed VC-47. Several aircraft have had dubious c/ns quoted, and these are remarked upon in notes at the end:-

01/2009	c/n 25679	2051	13109
02/2010	25680	2052	18993
03/2011	25681	2053	19305
04/2012	25682	2055	4473
05/2013	25683	2056	19055
06/2014	25684	2059	20055
07/2015	25685	2060	20074
08/2016	25686	2061	20210
11/2017	26921	2062	20216
09/2018	26922	2063	20410
10/2019	26923	2064	20428
2020	34266	2065	19217
2021	34267	2066	13636
2022	34303	2067	27069 ?
2023	34365	2068	'45117' ?
2024	20555	2069	20244
2025	25397	2070	13822
2026	20459	2071	27069?
2027	20466	2072	20136
2028	11843	2073	4756
2029	9246	2074	33573 ?
2030	9985	2075	20519
2031	20206	2076	12356
2032	20414	2077	12147
2033	25416	2078	4755
2034	13823	2079	4704
2035	13821	2080	34299
2036	25418	2081	34296
2037	25426	2082	4621
2038	11837	2083	34366
2039	19775	2084	19008
2040	20048	2085	13156
2041	20451	2086	20586
2042	13844	2087	4703
2043	13538	2088	34268
2044	9932	2089	34249
2045	10177	2090	27198 ?
2046	10172	2091	2134
2047	13841	2092	42980
2048	9777	EDL	4910
2049	13862	BUQ	12616
2050	11811	FBR	6015

Notes: C-47s 2016 and 2019 crashed before taking up these serial nos. C-47 2067 is quoted as c/n 27069 as is 2071. The former was PP-ANW and the latter PP-AKC but it is probable that neither was c/n 27069 as this was relegated to the role of instructional airframe by the USAF in 1950. It is just possible that parts of 27069 were used to rebuild two aircraft. See the Production History chapter for further data. C-47 2068 has 45117 quoted as the c/n, but this is more likely to be a corrupted USAF serial number. However, it has not proved possible to trace which.

BULGARIA

A number of Li-2s were supplied to the **Bulgarian Air Force** by Russia after the war. Nothing is known of these aircraft.

BURKINA FASO - see also Upper Volta

Following the change of country name from Upper Volta (qv), C-47s 34334/XTMAA c/n 34334 (derelict by 1980) and 100865/XTMAB c/n 19328, continued for a time, and the latter may have survived into the nineties.

BURMA

About 17 C-47s were acquired by the **Union of Burma Air Force** during the early fifties, some from Burmese airlines and others through commercial sources, including the UK. They were used for general transport duties, but by 1978 they had been replaced by Fokker F.27s and the survivors were sold mainly to Nevada Airlines. Initially the C-47s were numbered in the block UBT-701 to UBT-717 and later renumbered in the series 5701 to 5717. Ex civil aircraft seem to run consecutively with their previous civil markings. 'UB-736' remained preserved in the Defence Services Museum, Yangon, late in 2005, ex RI-007 (Indonesia). The following are known in detail:-

UBT-702/5702	c/n 19920	UBT-713	26570
UBT-703/5703	13491	UBT-714/5714	25309
UBT-708/5708	13387	UBT-715/5715	10239
UBT-711/5711	19831	UBT-717/5717	19252
UBT-712/5712	33174		

It is also known that c/ns 12085, 12851, 12915, 13512 and 13888 were passed to the Air Force, possibly as UBT-707, UBT-710, UBT-709, UBT-705 and UBT-704 respectively.

BURUNDI

This small central African republic operated 23507 c/n 9369 ex French AF from 1969; the a/c was stored at Bujumbura as 9U-BRZ in 2001 (with 9U-BRY c/n 13460).

CAMBODIA / KHMER REPUBLIC / KAMPUCHEA

When Cambodia became independent from France in Nov53 a single C-47 was transferred for VIP use. The **Royal Khmer Aviation/Khmer Liberation Army** received a number of C-47s from 1956 onwards via US aid and other sources. When US military assistance resumed in 1970 after a six-year break, the (Cambodian) **Khmer Air Force** had 11 C-47s and several Il-14s and An-2s, nearly all of which were in need of major overhaul. The 11 C-47s transferred from PACAF bases between 12Aug70 and 24Sep70 are listed below, but most were destroyed in a shelling and sapper attack at Pochentong in Jan71. The Australians (two) and the US then provided more C-47s and some Cambodian crews received training in Australia.

Following the Communist take-over in Apr75 nine C-47s escaped to Thailand. They were 2100937, 348492, 349010*, 349210, 349254*, 349516*, 477152*, 51079* and 51116*, those marked * arriving in AC-47 configuration, suggesting that some would have been local Cambodian conversions. 349701 was passed to the Royal Thai Navy, date unknown. The remainder were either destroyed or taken over by the **Khmer Liberation Army**. Fourteen are believed to have been taken into Kampuchean service. A photograph taken at Phnom Penh in Feb80 showed six C-47s parked and apparently in use, but since then little has been heard of operations. Serial numbers used were a mix of the full or partial USAF serial number and the following have been reported:-

42-24055	c/n 9917	349701	26962
42-24139	10001	349703	26964
42-100937	19400	349426	26687
42-108865	12498	349516	26777
43-16105	20571	476337	32669
43-254	25629	76388	32720
	or 26515	O-76510	32842
348492	25753	76734	33066
348640	25901	477152	33484
349010	26271	45918	34179
349210	26471	51079	34349
349254	26515	51116	34386

1970 MAP deliveries were believed to have been:-

316254	20720	348946	26207
348492	25753	348960	26221
348562	25823	349085	26346

CHAPTER 3: MILITARY OPERATORS OF THE DC-3, C-47, R4D, DAKOTA AND LI-2

349236	26497	349701	26962
349373	26634	476282	32614
349433	26694		

The 1971 Australian supplies were c/n 9594 and 12076.

CAMEROUN

Six C-47s were supplied to the **Armée de l'Air du Cameroun** from French stocks from 1960 onwards, for use by the transport arm. Three were still in use in 1992. Call signs and serial numbers are employed.

TJXAA	93487	c/n 13404	TJXAK	76500	32832
TJXAC*	11705	11705	TJXAL	49608	26869
TJXAI	49536	26797			
TJXAJ	15504	19970	* later possibly TJXAB		

CANADA

The **Royal Canadian Air Force** (RCAF)/**Canadian Armed Forces** (CAF) received about 570 Dakotas during the war and many of these operated alongside the RAF in various theatres. 435 and 436 Squadrons were formed in India and served in Burma, while 437 Sq was formed at Blakehill Farm in England and served in Europe. These squadrons were disbanded in England in 1946 and their aircraft were flown back to Canada shortly afterwards. 435 Sq reformed at Edmonton on 01Aug46 and continued to use Dakotas until they were replaced by C-119s. 436 Sq was not reformed until 01Apr53 and joined 435 Sq on photo-survey work until it too was supplied with C-119Gs in 1952. Four of 436's Dakotas were used on UN work with 115 Air Transport Unit in Lebanon in 1958. During the war, several squadrons based in Canada used the Dakota for general transport duties; 164 Sq was formed in Jan43 and reformed as 435 Sq as mentioned above. 165 Sq only operated from Ju43 until it was disbanded in Oct45, while 168 Sq used some Dakotas in support of Transatlantic mail flights between Oct43 and Apr46. Other users of the Dakota post-war were 408 Photo, 413, 414 and 426 Sq for general duties and photographic survey work.

412 VIP Sq used the Dakota from 1952 onwards and 429 Sq continued to use the type until they were replaced by C-130Hs in 1974. Training in navigation was carried out by Dakotas of 1 Air Navigation School from its formation at Summerside in 1948 until they were replaced by C-130Hs. By 1979 nine Dakotas remained in CAF service, of which six were in use with 429 Comm Sq. Two remained with the Cold Lake Base Flight (12938 and 12959). Dakotas were finally retired from service on 31Mar89. In the final ceremony two aircraft were painted in wartime colours. Six of the final aircraft were sold to Erik Fleming who kept one in RCAF markings and passed the remainder to Basler. Three (12944, 12959 and 12963) have been placed on permanent display.

Many Dakotas operated with the RCAF in their original RAF serial numbers, and are only listed briefly, as they can be identified from the main production list. Others, supplied direct to Canada, were given serial numbers in the blocks 650 to 664 and 960 to 994. No. 1000 was supplied later for VIP work, and a further nine bought after overhaul during the fifties (10910 to 10918). With the formation of the Canadian Armed Forces in 1968 by the combination of the three arms, all aircraft were given new serial numbers in separate blocks. The Dakotas 12901 to 12971, now redesignated CC-129, were renumbered in 1970. There were also several aircraft in use for ground instruction. Some RCAF Dakotas used during the war were passed back to the RAF or sold to civil operators, including a batch for Trans Canada. Of the 111 carrying RAF serials post-war, 43 survived to be renumbered, the balance being made up from those with RCAF serial numbers. The last 70 odd were sold off steadily, both to Canadian and US operators, apart from a batch transferred to the Indian Air Force in 1962/63.

Unlike the RAF, the RCAF used a wide range of suffix letters to denote the aircraft function, in some cases just one aircraft being so designated. The letters were sometimes combined, eg IIINRO or IVMFP. The following are known to have been used:-

C	Converted to R1830-90C
D	Converted to R1830-92
M	Converted to R1830-92C
F	Freighter
FP	Freighter/Passenger
GS	unknown
N	Navigation Trainer
P	Photographic
R	Radio Trainer
RO	Radar-Observer Trainer
S	Special Duties, eg Snatch gear or camouflage trials
SC	Special Communications
SR	Search & Rescue
ST	Special Transport
T&R	Transport & Rescue
T/TT	Target Towing
U	Instructional
VIP	VIP Transport

Various abbreviations are used exclusively by the RCAF/CAF and these are decoded here:-

ADC	Air Defence Command
AETE	Aerospace Engineering Test Establishment, RCAF Uplands
AFF	Acceptance and Ferry Flight
AFHQ	PT Flt Air Force HQ
AMB	Air Material Base
AMC	Air Material Command
ANS	Air Navigation School
AMDU	Aircraft Maintenance & Development Unit
AOS	Air Observer School
ATC	Air Transport Command
ATU	Air Transport Unit?
CAC	Central Air Command
CEPE	Central Experimental & Proving Establishment
CFS	Central Flying School
CFTSD	Canadian Forces Technical Services Detachment
CJATC	Canadian Joint Air Training Centre
Comm Flt	Communications Flight
C&R Flt	Communications & Rescue Flight
EAC	Eastern Air Command
HQPtFt	HQ Piston Flight
KU	Composite Flight (as opposed to Comm Flt)
MAC	Maritime Air Command
MOTU	Maritime Operational Training Unit
NWAC	Northwest Air Command
OTU	Operational Training Unit
PT Flt	Piston Training Flight
RD	Repair Depot
S&R	Search & Rescue
TAC	
TC	Training Command
TFF	Transport & Ferry Flight
(T)OTU	(Transport) OTU
TSD	Technical Services Dept
TTFt	Target Towing Flight
WAC	Western Air Command

Bases used by RCAF/CAF Dakotas 1943 to 1989 are given below:-

Abu Sueir, Egypt	115 ATU, 115 CF
Calgary (Lincoln Park), Alta	129 AFF
Camp Borden, Ont	TTS
Centralia, Ont	AROS, RCS
Clinton, Ont	R&CS
Cold Lake, Alta	CEPE, AETE, 3 OTU, 448 Test Sq
Comox, BC	442 C&R Flt, 121 Comm Flt, 6 OTU
Dartmouth, NS	101 Comm Flt RCN
Downsview, Ont	ATC
Edmonton, Alta	435 Sq, C&R Flt
El Arish, Egypt	115 ATU
Fort Nelson, BC	NWAC
Gimli, Man.	TC, AFS = CFS
Goose Bay, Labrador	ATC
Greenwood, NS	103 RU, MAC, 2 MOTU
Grostenquin, France	2Wg
Lahr, Germany	109 KU
Lincoln Park, Alta (ex Calgary)	129 AFF
Marville, France	1 F Wg, 109 KU
Namao, BC	C&R Flt, 105 CR Flt, 435 Sq, CEPE
Naples, Italy	1 Air Div
North Bay, Ont	131 KU
Northolt, UK	4 ST
Rivers, Man	CJATC, 112 T Flt, 408 Sq
Rockcliffe, Qu	9 TGp, 408 Photo Sq, 412 Sq, 413 Photo Sq, 414 Photo Sq, HQPtFlt
St Hubert, Qu	104 Comm Flt
Saskatoon, Sask	402 CFTSD, 1005 TSD, AMDU, CFS
Sea Island, Vancouver, BC	121 C&R Flt
Shearwater, NS	VU32 RCN
Suffield, Alta	CEPE
Summerside, NS	ANS, CNS, TC, RCS

Trenton, Ont	129 AFF, 102 Comm Flt, 1 KTS, 4 (T) OTU, AMDU, CFS, TTFt, 424 C&RS
Uplands, Ont	AETE, CEPE, HQ FTU, 412 Sq
Vancouver, BC	121 KU, 32 OTU, 123 S&R
Weyburn, Sask	10 RD
Whitehorse, Yukon	NWAC, TAC, Comm Flt
Winnipeg, Man	ANS, AOS, 2 AOS, CFS, 111 Comm Flt, 429 Comp Sq, TC, 440 T&R Sq

RCAF and CAF serial numbers:-

650	9015		977	26005
651	9290		978	26004
652	9108		979	26641
653	9415		'KN979'	26641
654	9595		980	26644
655	9831		981	26643
656	9832		982	26642
657	9834		983	27133 *
658	9830		984	27135
659	9833		985	32683
660	10199		986	32681
661	10200		987	33115
662	10201		988	33116
663	10202		989	33466 *
664	10203		990	33467
960	12267		991	34219
961	12289		992	12217
962	12544		993	12483
963	12543		994	13476
964	12411		1000	33352
965	12876		10291	32540
966	12877		10910	9862
967	13086		10911	9186
968	13087		10912	4441
969	13343		10913	18986
970	13342		10914	32871
971	25370		10915	33540
972	25371		10916	32843
973	25368		10917	27074
974	25369		10918	12238
975	26003			
976	26002		* To Indian AF	

CAF series:-

			12936	9290
12901	26441		12937	9415
12902	27004		12938	9832
12903	27005		12939	9834
12904	33437		12940	9833
12905	33441		12941	10199
12906	33445		12942	13485
12907	27187		12943	12254
12908	27190		12944	12256
12909	27203		12945	12295
12910	27218		12946	13580
12911	32540		12947	25485
12912	12307		12948	25612
12913	12327		12949	26248
12914	12344		12950	12543
12915	12357		12951	12411
12916	12363		12952	13087
12917	32813		12953	13343
12918	12424		12954	13342
12919	12425		12955	25371
12920	12438		12956	25368
12921	32855		12957	26002
12922	32865		12958	26005
12923	32873		12959	26641
12924	12490		12960	26643
12925	32963		12961	33116
12926	33046		12962	33467
12927	13028		12963	12217
12928	13149		12964	12483
12929	13300		12965	33352
12930	13303		12966	9186
12931	13310		12967	4441
12932	13333		12968	18986
12933	13383		12969	33540
12934	13392		12970	27074
12935	13453		12971	12238

Instructional:-

			A.601B	13331
			A.628B	12267
A.508	9015		655B	32922
A.509	9108		A.754	27187
A.597	27135		A.7931	33430

RAF Serials:- FL595, 598, 615, 616, 618, 621, 636, 650; FZ557, 558, 571, 575, 576, 581, 583, 584, 586, 596, 634, 635, 665, 669, 671, 678, 692, 694, 695; KG312, 317, 320, 330, 337, 345, 350, 354, 368, 382, 389, 394, 395, 400, 403, 414*, 416, 423, 430, 441, 455, 479, 485, 486, 526, 545, 557, 559*, 562, 563, 568*, 577, 580, 587, 600, 602, 623, 632, 634, 635, 641, 665, 668, 692, 693, 713, 769, 808, 827, 828, 926; KJ936, 956; KK101, 102, 143, 160; KN200, 201, 256, 258, 261, 269, 270, 277, 278, 281, 291, 392, 427, 428, 436, 443, 448, 451, 485, 511, 666*, 676*; KP221, 224, 227; TS422, 425. *To Indian AF.

(See United Kingdom for index to c/ns)

CENTRAL AFRICAN REPUBLIC

The **Force Aérienne Centrafricaine** came into being in 1960 and in the following year a C-47 was supplied from French stocks. Several more followed. Two are believed to have survived until 1994. Call signs and serials are used.

TLJBA		c/n 9124 ?	TLKAB	348665	25926
TLJBB	141406	9172	TLKAC	93548	13472
TLKAA	232898	9124	TLKAD	48286	25547
TLKAA	49937	27198			

TLCAK has been reported, possibly in error for TLKAC.

CEYLON - see Sri Lanka

CHAD - see Tchad

CHILE

The first C-47 was delivered to the **Fuerza Aérea de Chile** in Oct46 from US surplus stocks. Four more were delivered in 1947, including one fitted out for Presidential use. These were assigned to Grupo Transporte 10 at Santiago. A further six ex-civil aircraft were bought in the USA in 1953 and joined the earlier C-47s in supply missions. By 1963 there were 15 C-47s in service, based at Los Cerillos. Some were used for passenger transport, including the weekly diplomatic exchange to Arica. One C-47 was operated for the Dirección de Aeronautica Civil during 1973/74 (A1/971), but reverted to military use in 1975. Reports suggest that about 6 C-47s remained with Escuadrilla de Enlace until retired in 1980 and replaced by CASA C.212s, the remainder having been replaced by Buffalo and Twin Otter aircraft.

FAC serial numbers are 901 and 950 to 972:-

901	c/n 20628		961	12937	(Note 2)
950	20628		962	12967 ?	(Note 3)
951(1)	13175 ?		963	12937	
951(2)	34260		964	33415	
952	12976		965	12676	
953	19465		966	9163	
954	25263		967	9701	
955	11702		968	26104	
956	4470		969	12557	
957	11864		970	19730	
958	3268		971	4148	(Note 4)
959	6151		972	20847	
960	20750	(Note 1)			

Deliveries from USAF stocks:- c/n 25265 Oct47; 13175 03Sep46 (951?).

Note 1: Another '960' has been a gate-guard for GA10 at Santiago-Benitez since at least 1988.
Note 2: Also reported as 963 i/s Jan74 to May79.
Note 3: 962 is unlikely to be c/n 12967 as this a/c cr with USAAF 14May44.
Note 4: Wore A1-971 1972-80.

Aviación Naval, the air wing of the Armada de República de Chile operated five C-47s on general transport duties to bases and harbour installations. They were replaced partly by CASA 212s in 1978. Serial numbers were 121 to 125, the first of these being noted in Feb69. Details for three are known: 121 c/n 13009, 122 c/n 26588 and 124 c/n 26958. 125 was w/o at Ritoque, 17Sep75.

CHINA

Originally 77 C-47s and 10 C-53s were supplied direct to China mostly for operation by **China National Aviation Corp**, under the Lend-Lease agreement during the war. These were used to move supplies forward to the war fronts with Japan, from bases supplied over the "hump" by the USAAF and RAF from India. Further aircraft were transferred from USAAF stocks in India. Some of these aircraft remained in use with the **Chinese Peoples Armed Forces Air Force** after the Communist take-over in 1950 and were supplemented by Li-2s though nothing definite is known. What is certain is that others escaped to Taiwan and have been identified in use as late as 1979. By the mid-eighties it is believed that about 100 Li-2s remained in use and by 1992 some fifty remained with the air force and twenty with the navy.

The following DC-3s are known to have been delivered from Mar42 onwards:- c/ns 4681, 4729/30, 4852/53, 4879/81/83, 4902/04/27/29/52/53, 6025/34/35/37/38, 6150, 6221/22, 6245, 7406/07, 9013/14, 9109/10, 9291/92, 9416/17, 9596/97, 9760/61, 9955/56, 10158/59, 13250/64/67/74/ 82/89/92, 13406, 13410, 13693/94/95, 13704/10/11/18, 18901/02/09/12, 19061/62, 19313/14, 19452/53, 19620/21, 19803/04/33/38/39, 19928/29, 20090/91, 20161/62, 20250/52/53/56/57/60/88/92/94, 20306/09/10/14/20/21/23-25/28/32/34/35/37/42/44/45/56/60/69/73/75/76/84/89/90-92/94, 20635/37/38/43/45/52/53/55/56/59/63/99; 20700-02/28; , 20803-20806/10/12/15/67-70/82/95, 25859//78/91, 25900, 25993, 26305/07, 26490/96, 26500, 26711, 26835/39/42/98, 26909/11/12/48/53, 27054/124, 32527/30/31/67/71/73/82/95, 32766, 32803/17/47/86, 32915/47/68/80/87/93/94.

A fleet list for CNAC dated 27Feb43 gives most of the earlier deliveries above, as no distinction was made in USAAF records as to whether the aircraft went to CNAC or the air force, as the former operated many of the aircraft with CNAC Plane Nos. See also the Commercial Operators chapter. In 1945 the CNAF used an ex-Japanese Showa 'Tabby' serial 405.

Prior to 1949 USAF serial numbers were used, but another series, of which 1022 to 1026 incl have been identified, was adopted. Only three other air force serials are known - 101 'National Day', 102 'China Youth' and 117.

Known Li-2s are 3018, 3019/'4766', 3028, 3029, 3049, 5011, 5021, 5070, 7103, 15/8205, 38043, 38046.

COLOMBIA

Colombia was amongst the major users of the C-47 in South America. The first of about three dozen was supplied to the **Fuerza Aérea Colombiana** in Sep44 and was still in service in 1978. Three more were delivered in 1946 and others were taken over from defunct airlines. A further nine were delivered under the ARP in May49 and thereafter more were acquired from various civil sources, including aircraft impounded for drug-running.

The C-47s were used on normal transport duties between FAC bases, though the majority were assigned to the 1st Transportation Squadron at Bogota and others at Madrid. Some were operated in camouflage in the mid-seventies, indicating a tactical support function. Others were used in public services to remote areas. These (marked *) were taken over by SATENA in 1962, (Servicio de Aeronavegación a Territorios Nacionales) which was formed in September as a unit of the FAC and supported by the government. They carried FAC serial numbers until Oct76, when a new series was instituted. As the C-47 was taken out of USAF service, so further aircraft were supplied to Colombia, three in 1964 and six more in 1976, followed by four more early in 1978. Deliveries continued into the nineties when four Basler BT-67 conversions were bought. These were fitted with FLIR, no doubt for the detection of drug barons' bases in the jungle. One of these was lost in an operational accident in 2001. Three more were delivered by the end of 2002, all known locally as the Fantasma AC-47T.

The FAC allotted the 600 series to transport aircraft, and C-47 numbers ran from 650 to 689, but some had 'A' suffixes, denoting either a rebuild or the second use of the serial. Later the 1600 series was used, but it does not appear that this came about by adding 1000 to the 600 series in every case. The SATENA series adopted in 1976 ran from 1120 to 1132 and six were still in use with SATENA in 1982, as well as about 16 with the FAC. Four were believed to be in service in 2000, one a C-117D, in addition to the four BT-67s. Known details are as follows:-

650	c/n 25501	
651		Jan47 to 1978
652		Jan47 to 1978
653		cr 06Apr62
653A	26189	
654		w/o 26Jul75 - O Disco
654A	26292	
655		Mar71 to Nov87; on dump 1989 to 1996 Bogota/El Dorado
656		Mar71 to 1978; nose on dump Madrid-Barroblanca, Feb95
657		Mar71 to Jan77
657A		C-53A
658*		w/o 28Jan64
658A*	4240	
659	32984	
660		1946 w/o 20Oct69
660A	26351	
661*		cr 21Jan72
662		cr 25May48 Apt, Bogota
662A		Mar71 to Jan77
663*		1948 to 01May75; cr Sardinata Norte de Santander
664		Feb50, wfu
664A		i/s 1982; w/o or wfu, at Madrid Jun90
665		Feb50
666		May68 to Jan77 (wreck May82 at Bogota/Eldorado). Reported at FAC Museum, El Dorado Feb95
667*		1964 to 1978, pres. Eldorado, FAC Museum, El Dorado Feb97
668		i/s Mar72, cr 21Feb78
669		Jul67 to Nov69, w/o
669A	34258	
670*	4824	
671		Aug50
672		Aug50
674		Oct50
675		
676*		1971, w/o 02Apr76 Puerto Liquizamo
676A	9108	
677	33550 ?	
677A		AC-47 i/s Aug86
679		Jan77
680		Sep66 to 1978
680A	4489	
681		Jan77 to 1978
682		Apr67 to Jan77
683		Mar72, derelict at Madrid Jun90
684*		Mar71, w/o 30Jul79
685		cr 08Sep69 nr Aspiany AB
685A		
686	25443	
687*	12446	
688*		Mar71, w/o 8Jan75 cr nr Docello
689*	20022	to 1121
689A	20032	
1120	12446	
1121	20022	
1122	19606	
1123	26044	
1124	26775	
1125	25976	
1126	33608	
1127	33038	
1128	4824	
1129		dam 25Jun81; wfu Madrid-Barroblanca Feb90, on dump Sep97
1130		in SATENA c/s Bogota Apr84; wfu Madrid-Barroblanca Jun90
1131		cr 13Nov80 80m NE Bogota
1132		i/s Aug85
1632		C-117D; i/s Sep97
1635		i/s Jun87; on dump May89 to Feb97+ Bogota/El Dorado
1639	19737	
1650		AC-47; w/o 29Aug88 nr Aname, on dump at Madrid Feb97
1651		at Madrid Tech School (TEDH) Feb97

1652		AC-47; On dump Feb95 to Sep97+ Madrid-Barroblanca
1654	26292	BT-67
1656		BT-67, serial in doubt
1658	32541	BT-67
1659	32984	BT-67, cr 02Sep00
1660		i/s Nov87; on dump Feb95 to Sep97 Madrid-Barroblanca
1667	19052	BT-67
1670	19125	BT-67
1674		i/s Jun87, on dump at Madrid-Barroblanca Jun93
1676	9108	
1677		i/s Nov87, on dump at Madrid-Barroblanca Feb93
1680		i/s Feb95
1681	33248	BT-67
1685	43382	C-117D
1686	25443	BT-67

Apart from the Basler BT-67 gunships other AC-47s were in use, but did not come from USAF stocks after conversion so it must be assumed that these were converted under separate contracts for the FAC.

Casualties:- one w/o Jul63; SATENA cr 3May75 NW Colombia.

Supplied ex USAF Stocks:- c/n 4824 (Sep52); 4840 (1952); 9809 (SATENA); 9893 (11May49); 9923, 9934, 18987, 19011, 19047 and 19118 (all 11May49); 20138 (15Apr65); 20346 (1954), 20534 (15Apr65), 33590 (Jan46), 34294 (Mar47) and 34302 (Jan46).

The **Policia Nacional de Colombia/PNC/Colombian National Police** needed extra capacity to move police around in the anti-drug cartel operations, and BT-67s have been acquired since 1991:-

PNC-211	25667		PNC-214*	
PNC-212	13110		PNC-0256	19685
PNC-213	20875 wfu 02Feb01			

* does not appear on Basler BT-67 conversion list, so may have been acquired later. PNC-0212 and 0214 have also been reported. One DC-3 was derelict in the PNC compound at Bogota/El Dorado in Feb95.

COMORES

In 1978/80 the **Comores Air Arm** included a C-47 in its inventory, supplied to the government in civil markings (D6-ECB c/n 20175).

CONGO BRAZZAVILLE / REPUBLIC OF THE CONGO

This ex-French colony received its first C-47 in Jun61 and by 1972 three had been supplied to the **Force Aérienne Congolaise**, but one crashed on 07Dec71. Two may still have been in use in 1994, though reports differ. TN210, listed below, is likely to be c/n 32835 or 33065.

TN210	c/n	(see above)
TN211		26984
TNKAM	76733	33065
	76503	32835

CUBA

Three C-47s were received by the **Fuerza Aérea Ejercito de Cuba** (FAEC) in Dec46 under ARP and a fourth a year later. These were all assigned to the Transport Squadron and were used for personnel transport. Five more C-47s were supplied under MAP in the early fifties. These were followed by a "Hi-per" C-53 for Presidential use (209).

Shortly before the revolution in 1959, nine C-47s and the C-53 remained in service with the Escuadron de Transporte. Two are known to have served with the **Fuerza Aérea Revolucionaria** (FAR) and one was shot down in 1964, but all were probably out of use by the early 1970s because of spares shortage.

Serial numbers were 200 to 211, of which 203 and 209 were later with FAR. 209 was named "Caballo de Batalla" first, then "G" and finally "Siem Maestro". It was delivered in Dec54. C/n 32724 was delivered in Dec46 (probably with 201 and 202).

200	c/n 9208		206	26223 ?	
201	32723		207		
202	33425		208		
203		to FAR	209	11643	to FAR
204	4528		210		
205	4397		211		

CZECHOSLOVAKIA

Some 25 surplus USAAF C-47s were diverted to the **Czech Air Force** from European stocks in 1945/46 and were given serials in the range D-01 to D-27, though from Jun57 they used the 'last four' of the USAAF serial instead. They were allotted to 1 and 2 Flights of the 1st LDP Air Transport Regiment, based at Kbely, Prague. The last were sold to France in 1960.

Li-2s were acquired in 1951/52. No 3 Flight was equipped with the Li-2 from 1951 onwards. As part of the DVLP (Paratroop Air Transport Regiment) these were transferred to Presov in Dec54. In July 1956 No 7 LO (Special Air Transport Section) was formed at Kbely as a VIP service. A further seven Li-2s were added in 1956/57 from CSA. Some Li-2s were redesignated Li-2F for use by FLS (Air Photo Group) at Hradcany. The Li-2s were replaced by Il-14s and withdrawn between 1963 and 1967.

C-47s:-			Li-2Ps:-		
D-01	c/n 26180		'D-24'	c/n 234 430 02	
D-02			D-29	234 421 05	
D-03	12948		D-30	234 421 06	
D-04	9199		D-31	234 427 03	
D-05	9371		D-32	234 427 08	
D-06			D-33	234 421 07	
D-07			D-34	234 421 09	(Li-2T)
D-08			D-35	234 428 01 ?	(Li-2D)
D-09			D-36	234 429 01	(Li-2D)
D-10			D-37	234 421 08	(Li-2T)
D-11			D-38	234 423 04	
D-12			D-37	234 427 10 ?	(Li-2D)
D-13	26447		1801	234 418 01	
D-14			2105	234 421 05	
D-15			2106	234 421 06	
D-16	26180		2107	234 421 07	
D-17	12948		2108	234 421 08	(Li-2T)
D-18	25667		2109	234 421 09	(Li2T)
D-19	12617		2209	234 422 09	(Li-2F)
D-20	25644		2210	234 422 10	
D-21	19474		2304	234 423 04	
D-22	26447		2305	234 423 05	
D-23	19580		2407	234 424 07 ?	
D-24	25653		2501	234 425 01	
D-25	26452		2703	234 427 03	
D-26	20740		2708	234 427 08	
D-27	19525		2710	234 427 10	(Li-2D)
D-36	19525		2801	234 428 01	(Li-2D)
0543	19006		2804	234 428 04	(Li-2F)
0866	19329		2891	234 428 01	(Li-2D)
3654	13654			(mis-paint of 2801)	
4053	9915				
5059	19525		2901	234 429 01	(Li-2D)
6274	20740		3002	234 430 02	
8392	25653				
8406	25667				

The missing C-47 c/ns are 9275, 9338, 11813, 12611, 12870, 19493, 19718

DAHOMEY - see Benin

DENMARK

The **Royal Danish Air Force** began operating C-47s in Sep53 when Eskadrille 721 formed a flight of two former SAS aircraft. In 1956 a further six were acquired from the Norwegian AF and they joined Esk-721 at Vaerlose. This unit continued to use them until 1982 when they were replaced by C-130Hs. All were retired and sold.

Initially the C-47s used a type prefix '68' to the serial placed above the individual number in small script. Thus 68 681 was the first aircraft received and 68 688 the last. By the early 'sixties this prefix had been replaced by the C-47 type letter 'K'.

CHAPTER 3: MILITARY OPERATORS OF THE DC-3, C-47, R4D, DAKOTA AND LI-2

K-681	c/n 9664	K-685	19291
K-682	20019	K-686	19475
K-683	19677	K-687	19200
K-684	19054	K-688	20118

DOMINICAN REPUBLIC

The first C-47 was delivered to the **Cuerpo de Aviación Militar** under MAP for ambulance duties, probably in the early fifties. Reorganisation as the **Fuerza Aérea Dominicana** followed, and about a dozen C-47s were used, of which 3401 to 3407 and 3412 are known. 3110 has been reported, probably in error. The only known c/ns are 3404 c/n 25530, 3407 c/n 20845. Many were noted in the mid-seventies, apart from 3110 not noted after May65; and 33425. By 1982 seven remained in use, falling to five in 1985. By 1991 three were reported derelict and only 3407 was reported airworthy in May98. 3406 crashed at Santiago-Cibao in Aug90 and the wreck remained there in Sep99, being scrapped by Apr00.

ECUADOR

The ARP provided the first **Fuerza Aérea Ecuatoriana** C-47s in Nov46 and six were in use by 1949 for general transport duties and social service routes throughout the country. Two commercial DC-3s were brought in 1952/53, but three aircraft had been lost by mid-1954, replaced by three ex USAF C-47s in 1957. By the end of 1963 all C-47s were grouped with the 1111th Transport Squadron at Quito, and one was in use as the Presidential transport in 1965. A further three DC-3s came from Brazil in 1967/68 but by May69 only nine C-47s remained in use.

In 1962 the Transportes Aéreos Militares Ecuatorianas (TAME) was formed to take over the social routes and the C-47 remained in use until 1971 when HS.748s were delivered. Four or five C-47s were withdrawn by May82, and another is preserved.

Initially the FAE used a numerical sequence of serial numbers, FAE 503 being supplied in Mar48 and FAE 506 following. Later the serial numbers were based on either the c/n or the USAF serial, and many also flew with civilian marks in the same sequence as other civil aircraft.

FAE 1969	HC-AUV	c/n 1969	also wore 31969
FAE 4341	HC-AUZ	4341	also CA4341
FAE 11747	HC-AUY	11747	also CA747
FAE 11775	HC-AVD	11775	
FAE 15677	HC-AUR	20143	also CA677
FAE 20120		20120	
FAE 20179	HC-AUX ?	20179	
FAE 23926		9788	
FAE 32016		2016 ?	
FAE 49785	HC-AUP	27046	
FAE 49789	HC-AUS	27050	
FAE 76448	HC-AUQ	32780	also CA448
FAE 77164	HC-AUT	33496	also CA164
FAE 92066	HC-AVC	11825	
'CA47'			pres. at Fort Patria with another DC-3

Also supplied were c/n 9252 on 30Sep47 (ARP); 12762 on 20Oct47 (del 1949) (ARP) and 19020 on 25Mar48 (ARP). These were probably all given serial numbers in the FAE 500 range. Ex-USAF 43-2028 was reported with the FAE in Jul53, c/n 2028 was quoted in error, and the true 43-2028 (c/n 4972) cr in N Africa in Feb43.

EGYPT

The **Royal Egyptian Air Force** was supplied with about six ex RAF Dakotas and USAAF C-47s between 1945 and 1947. The first of these, F3, then 113 c/n 32642 was given by the USAAF to King Farouk in Feb45. Others were rebuilt from abandoned USAAF C-47s at Payne Field, Cairo, but the only serial numbers known are 805, 807, 815, 816 and 817. Of these the first and last also operated with civil marks SU-AJG and SU-AJH respectively, while 807 was shot down by Israeli aircraft on 04Nov48 over the coast of Sinai. Two had been shot down earlier by a single Avia S-199 (Czech-built Me109) during a bombing raid on Tel Aviv in Israel on 03Jun48. Further aircraft were bought in Italy in 1948 (c/ns 4233, 25755, 26671, 26919, 26920 and 27048). At this time 10 C-47s had bomb racks and there were 20 transports, including C-46s and C-47s. The c/ns of the original ex RAF/USAAF aircraft were 9866, 10148, 25286, 25873, 25876 and 32642. Some were probably destroyed or damaged in various Israeli raids or during the 1956 Suez campaign when 22 C-47s were believed in use, 8 transports, 9 liaison and 5 in reserve. A squadron of 8 was reported in use by the **Arab Republic of Egypt Air Force** in the 1967 Six-Day War.

EL SALVADOR

One C-47 was supplied to the **Fuerza Aérea Salvadorena** by Jul49 and another by Jun54. They were used for routine transport duties with the 1st Transport Squadron, based at Ilopango. A further four were added in the mid-sixties, but one was in civil marks in 1968, possibly to allow it to overfly Honduras. A C-47 was lost in 1969 when it was shot down over Tegucigalpa during the 'soccer war'. A replacement was soon bought and in May74 a further eight came from USAF stocks. There has been no recent news of these C-47s but some saw action against 'guerillas' during 1982/83. Two BT-67s were supplied by Basler in 1990 and a further two in 1993, converted from newly-purchased aircraft.

101	c/n	i/s Jul49; on dump at San Salvador Feb02
102		shot down 1969?
103		i/s 1966 to Oct77; serial possibly used twice
104		i/s 1966 to Oct77
105	26759	
106		i/s 1966 to Aug99; std Feb02
107		i/s May74 to Oct77
108		i/s May74 to Jul78
109		i/s Jun74 to Jan79; wfu Feb02
110		i/s 1974 to Jul78; instr airframe Feb02, S Salvador
111		i/s Jun74 to Jul78
112		i/s Jul74, pres Aug99
113		i/s Jul74 to Oct77
114		i/s Jul74 to Oct77, pres. Aug99 San Salvador
115		on dump at San Salvador Feb02
116	33282	BT-67
117	25409	BT-67
118	33238	BT-67
119	6204	BT-67
123		
124		AC-47, i/s Aug99; std Feb02

C/ns 9256, 26766, 32710, 33536 and 33546 reportedly came from USAF stocks, the last four in May74. Three were destroyed at Ilopango on 27Jan82. C/n 13364 and 25418 were AC-47s out of six supplied.

ETHIOPIA

The **Imperial Ethiopian Air Force** used up to thirteen C-47s for general transport duties. The first of these was IEAF-1 c/n 13576, later 701. Further aircraft were 702 c/n 26586 or 33570; 703 c/n 12526; 705, 706, 707, 708, 709, 710, 711 c/n 19283, 712, 713, 715 c/n 32982 and 716. By 1993 ten C-47s were reported to be in store, and only one in service. The last five (706, 710, 713, 716 and one other), were stored at Debre Zeit where they were salvaged in 1998.

FINLAND

Douglas twins have long been used by the **Finnish Air Force/ Ilmavoimat**. The first of three DC-2s was donated by the Red Cross in 1940 for use in the war against Russia, and is now preserved. This was DC-1 (later DO-1) c/n 1354 and was armed with nose and dorsal guns, as well as bomb racks. In 1949 a further pair came from Aero O/y (DO-2 c/n 1582 and DO-3 c/n 1562). Nine DC-3s were taken over from Aero O/y (or later Finnair) between 1960 and 1970 and four of these remained in service with the transport flight at Utti until 18Dec84. These were put up for sale in 1986 and two F.27s were leased to carry out some of their work.

DO-4	c/n 25515	DO-9	11750
DO-5	19795	DO-10	12050
DO-6	19560	DO-11	6346
DO-7	19109	DO-12	12970
DO-8	19309		

FORMOSA - see Taiwan.

FRANCE

The **Armée de l'Air** received its first batch of C-47s in Sep44, when 22 were transferred from the USAAF at Mediouna, Morocco and allotted to Groupe de Transport 1/15 "Touraine" (GT 1/15). Soon after that another 36 were handed over to GT 2/15 "Anjou", completing WWII allocation. Post-war many more were acquired from a variety of sources, and a total of 264 have been traced.

In 1947 GT 1/15 became GT 1/61 and was based at Orleans along with GT 3/61 "Poitou" which joined them in 1953. The latter re-equipped with C-47s from USAF surplus stocks at Naples and Prestwick in 1949. Meanwhile GT 2/15 was sent to Saigon and became GT 2/64 after a brief period as Groupe de Marche en Extrême-Orient. The increasing need for transport in Indo-China resulted in MAP allotments and in 1951 new groups were formed or gave up their AAC.1s (Ju52/3ms) for C-47s. These were GT 2/62 "Franche Comté" at Haiphong and Hanoi, GT 1/64 "Bearn" at Nhatrang and later GT 2/63 "Senegal" also at Nhatrang. GT 1/25 "Tunisia" also used the C-47, but only after leaving its Halifaxes in Europe.

At first units usually had 25 to 30 aircraft and at the peak of operations in 1953/54 more than 100 C-47s were used in Indo-China. 75 of these came via MAP-Far East contracts and when the war ended many were returned to USAF stocks. The remainder were transferred to the new air forces of South Vietnam, Cambodia and Laos, with 12 remaining with Escadrille de Liaisons Aériennes 52 (ELA 52) at Saigon until 1958. Two were then with Escadrille Transport 1/65 and the rest returned to France or various colonies. In France, meanwhile, GT 1/64 "Bearn" moved to Bordeaux and later to Le Bourget joining GT 2/61 "Maine" which, in 1956, became GT 2/64 to form the 64e Escadre. At Orleans GT 2/62 became GT 4/61, and the 61e Escadre including GT 1/61 and GT 3/61 was re-equipping with the Noratlas.

In France the normal unit allotment was 16 aircraft but in North Africa local groups had 20. GT 1/62 "Algeria" received its C-47s at Algiers in 1955, to be replaced a year later by the N.2501. The C-47s were then transferred to a new unit, GT 3/62 "Sahara", also at Algiers. Nearby Boufarik housed Groupe de Liaisons Aériennes 45 (GLA 45), which included 10 C-47s on its strength and operated communications flights within Algeria. Similar but smaller units were ELA 46 in Morocco and ELA 47 in Tunisia. Desert units such as Groupe Saharien de Reconnaissance et d'Appui 76 (GSRA 76) at Ouargla and GSRA 78 at Colomb-Béchar used 10 to 12 C-47s each between 1958 and 1963.

Further afield local African liaison units were GLA 48 with six C-47s at Dakar, GLA 49 with up to 16 C-47s at Brazzaville and Bangui, Groupe Aérien Mixte 50 (GAM 50) at Tananarive, Madagascar (with 10), ESRA 77 at Fort Lamy with three C-47s and Groupe d'Outre Mer 88 (GOM 88) at Djibouti with four C-47s. Such aircraft were mostly used on regular routes to remote areas which could not be operated at a profit commercially, but also did SAR and paratroop training duties. After 1960 they were transferred progressively to the air forces of the newly independent territories.

In the West Indies Escadrille de Transport 58 (ET 58) had a few C-47s at Pointe à Pitre in Guadeloupe from 1961 to 1970, linking that island with Martinique and French Guyana. Two fuselages were still to be seen at Pointe à Pitre in Jan84.

During the sixties the Dakota was still active in metropolitan France with smaller units. Groupe de Liaison Aériennes Ministerielles 1/60 (GLAM 1/60) and Groupe Aérien d'Entrainement et de Liaison 2/60 at Villacoublay (GAEL 2/60) used varying numbers between 1952 and 1971, mainly for special detachments world-wide. ELA 56 at Persan-Beaumont, and later at Evreux, was charged with "special" missions. The remaining ELAs had the odd C-47 along with other types. ELA 55 at Lahr flew for the French forces in Germany, while ELA 41 at Dijon, ELA 43 at Bordeaux and ELA 44 at Aix-en-Provence covered their respective 'Regions Aeriennes'. Escadrille Electronique 54 at Lahr, and later at Metz, was an ECM unit, while Escadrille de Calibration 57 at Villacoublay checked radio navigation aids. Bomber Escadres 92e and 93e had a few 'hack' C-47s between 1965 and 1968 at Bordeaux and Istres, and at least one was used by Centre d'Experimentations Aériennes Militaires (CEAM) at Mont de Marsan.

Centre d'Instructions des Equipages de Transports 340 (CIET 340) at Toulouse used C-47s for pilot training between 1950 and 1969, while Escadrille d'Instructions des Troupes Aeroportées 341 (EITA 341) at Pau provided six C-47s for paratroop training from 1954 to 1957. Ecole de l'Air, alias Groupement Instruction 1/312 at Salon de Provence, also had up to six C-47s for transport. Base Aerienne 709 (BA 709) used 3 C-47s to train apprentices from African countries. Groupement Ecole 319 was the multi-engined flying school, transferring its 15 C-47s to GE 316 at Toulouse in 1965 for navigation training.

While most African based C-47s went to newly independent ex-colonies a few were retained and GLA 48's small fleet was shared with GT 1/63 at Thies, with Groupe Aérien Mixte d'Outre Mer 81 at Dakar and DATEF 168 at Bouake until 1965. Two remained with BA 172 at Fort Lamy until 1968 and Centre Inter-Armes d'Essais d'Engins Speciaux 343 (CIEES 343) at Colomb-Béchar, CSEM 330 and CEMO 325 at Reggan, provided air support to the French Nuclear Test Centre in the Sahara until 1967. Subsequently the C-47 was withdrawn and most survivors were stored at Chateaudun where many were scrapped. Some were sold to Israel in 1967, and 15 were transferred to the French Navy in 1969. Twelve went to Canada and the USA and 13 to Yugoslavia in 1972. These were allotted temporary French civil markings, but some were used only for ferrying and then broken up for spares, so several marks were used more than once.

The Air Force used a variety of unit codes on their aircraft. Each unit was allotted a block of 26 call signs starting, for example "FRASA". Sometimes the unit number and the last two letters were painted on, but often only the final letter was to be seen on the fin. They are not reliable means of identifying individual aircraft.

The French Navy or **Aéronavale** was the last user of the C-47 in France. They started with one which left Indo-China for Diego Suarez in 1956. Ten more were acquired around 1961 and were based at Dakar, Noumea etc. Finally 15 were taken over from the Air Force in 1969. Of these 26, twenty remained active with Escadrille 56S at Nimes-Garons where they were used for transport and training duties, until their replacement by Nord 262s or EMB-121 Xingus from 1984 onwards.

There were two other government operators of the C-47; **Centre d'Essais en Vol** (CEV) at Bretigny using C-47s for test and liaison work and the **Télécommunications Office** at Lannion, who used two for flights to Paris.

The list of serial numbers which follows was extracted from that published in 'Trait d'Union', the Journal of the French Branch of Air-Britain (Nos 28 to 33, 35, 37 to 39). Most French Air Force C-47s bore serial numbers directly related to the previous USAAF number, though some omitted one or both the year digits, usually the '4', depending on the total number involved. Records refer to some C-47s solely by their last three digits, and four of these have proved impossible to identify as all possible candidates have either been eliminated or have no obvious connections with France. A small group of aircraft bought in the fifties had the c/n applied to the fin in place of the USAAF serial, and another group, bought in the US, started at 701B, though later had USAAF serials substituted. In the index that follows, the last two groups are listed first, followed by the USAAF numbers. *These are not given in order of year, but in numerical order of the last five digits with the year omitted, though the year digit is given where it is known to have been used.* Two further anomalies are a captured Japanese L2D-2 4265, and 141406 believed to be c/n 9172. The latter is assumed to be a Scottish Aviation drawing number.

701B	c/n 9740	706B	10028
702B	4583	707B	26349
703B	20877		

c/n group:		15276	26721
13438	c/n 13438	15883	32631
13487	13487	'16140'	32888
13654	13654	34334	34334
14654	26099	141406	9172 ?
14655	26100	5141406	9172
14904	26349		

L2D-2:	
4265	?

USAAF serials:		315770	20236
15033	c/n 19499	835	20301
315072	19538	315984	20450
15073	19539	316014	20480
315135	19601	316156	20622
315400	19866	316164	20630
315504	19970	316286	20752
315511	19977	316328	20794
315545	20011	316390	20856
315587	20053	316409	20875
315666	20132	316410	20876
315693	20159	316411	20877

CHAPTER 3: MILITARY OPERATORS OF THE DC-3, C-47, R4D, DAKOTA AND LI-2

417836	4335	348729	25990	476420	32752	476977	33309
118338	4376	348759	26020 ?	476421	32753	980	33312
118401	4463	348772	26033	476423	32755	77011	33343
118474	4566	48789	26050	476450	32782	77049	33381
118491	4583	348800	26061	476498	32830	477069	33401
118516	4608	348823	26084	476499	32831	477071	33403
223386	9248	348859	26120	76500	32832	477101	33433
23402	9264	348874	26135	476502	32834	77116	33448
23474	9336	348876	26137	476503	32835	77232	33564
23480	9342	348931	26192	476505	32837	92060	11819
23507	9369	348962	26223	476556	32888	92449	12251
23509	9371	48978	26239	476557	32889	292457	12260
223602	9464	48990	26251	476559	32891	292499	12306
23639	9501	348994 (1)	26255	476560	32892	92857	12704
223710	9572	48994 (2)	9644	476561	32893	92872	12721
223782	9644	349035	26296	76562	32894	92880	12730
23878	9740	349047	26308	476669	33031	292972	12832
23940	9802	349048	26309	476717	33049	293087	12960
23941	9803	349049	26310	476721	33053	93510	13430
224055	9917	349050	26311	76725	33057	93519	13440
224062	9924	349051	26312	76726	33058	93537	13460
24069	9931	349089	26350	476733	33065	93715	13657
224125	9987	349113	26374	76746	33078	100509	18972
24166	10028	349115	26376	76786	33118	100543	19006
224336	10198	349129	26390	476787	33119	100580	19043
32898	9124	349145	26406	476791	33123	100666	19129
32931	9157	49194	26455	476792	33124	100823	19286
38592	4541	349216	26477	476795	33127	100865	19328
38672	6055	349296	26557	76835	33167	100880	19343
38693	6152	349345	26606	76921	33253	100895	19358
45918	34179	349356	26617	76974	33306	100956	19419
45991	34256	349364	26625	76975	33307	100962	19425
45993	34258	349384	26645	76976	33308	108993	13778
47985	25246	349418	26679				
348008	25269	349434	26695				
48018	25279	349454	26715				
48032	25293	49462	26723				
348058	25319	49468	26729				
348061	25322	49482	26743				
348071	25332	349524	26785				
348149	25410	49536	26797				
348151	25412	349545	26806				
48199	25460	349566	26827				
348267	25528	349593	26854				
48278	25539	349594	26855				
348279	25540	49604	26865				
48280	25541	49608	26869				
348281	25542	349664	26925				
348282	25543	349665	26926				
348283	25544	349666	26927				
348284	25545	349667	26928				
348285	25546	349685	26946				
348286	25547	349723	26984				
348287	25548	349781	27042				
348288	25549	349816	27077				
348289	25550	49821	27082				
348290	25551	49824	27085				
348291	25552	49853	27114				
348292	25553	349875	27136				
348306	25567	349876	27137				
348309	25570	349878	27139				
348336	25597	349879	27140				
48383	25644	349881	27142				
48392	25653	349882	27143				
48396	25657	349919	27180				
348399	25660	49927	27188				
348413	25674	349931	27192				
348415	25676	349937	27198				
348465	25726	49949	27210				
348470	25731	68819	11746				
348484	25745	76209	32541				
348504	25765	76216	32548				
48539	25800	476221	32553				
48555	25816	76229	32561				
348566	25827	476259	32591				
48585	25846	476307	32639				
348608	25869	476352	32684				
48619	25880	476353	32685				
348640	25901	476355	32687				
348665	25926	476356	32688				
348704	25965	476357	32689				
348714	25975	476404	32736				

351 quoted as c/n 32683 which went to the RCAF. Del to GT 2/15 in Dec45 on Lend-Lease. No other data.
748 Del 1945 to GT 2/15 Aug45 to Dec45. Possibly 41-38748 div to France Nov45.
793 Del 1945. DBF 29Jan46 Hanoi (Viet Cong action).

Note: The second 48994 was a rebuild of 42-23782 to replace 348994.

Unit rosters are as follows, listed in alphanumeric sequence:-

CIEES 343 41-18491, 18516, 42-23507, 92857, 93519, 93712, 108959, 43-48018, 48278, 48279, 48306, 48789, 49462, 44-76209, 76221, 76500, 76726, 76835, 76975, 77049, 77069

CIET 340 41-18338, 18474, 18516, 42-92872, 100509, 100543, 43-15504, 15545, 16409, 16410, 48018, 48199, 48279, 48285, 48585, 48608, 48619, 48789, 48823, 48838, 48839, 48931, 49049, 49454, 49462, 49468, 49482, 49604, 49608, 49723, 49824, 49853, 49876, 49879, 49927, 49937, 44-76221, 76229, 76307, 76420, 76423, 76450, 76500, 76505, 76562, 76717, 76721, 76725, 76733, 76786, 76795, 76835, 76974, 77011, 77049, 77071, 77116, 77232

ELA 56 41-18474, 38672, 42-23507, 24166, 92060, 92449, 93519, 93712, 43-16411, 47985, 48199, 48284, 48838, 49049, 49482

GAM 50 41-38592, 42-23507, 23878, 23940, 24069, 24166, 93562, 100823, 43-47985, 48199, 48838, 49816, 49821, 49824, 44-76216, 76562

GE 316 42-23878, 43-48278, 48306, 48555, 44-76229, 76503

GLA 45 41-18491, 18516, 38672, 42-23480, 23509, 23940, 68819, 93510, 100823, 100865, 100965, 43-15033, 16410, 48018, 48285, 48291, 48306, 48383, 48608, 48931, 48990, 49051, 49876, 49879, 49927, 44-76221, 76450, 76499, 76505, 76726, 76974, 76975, 77011, 77071, 77101, 45-1064

GLA 48 41-38592, 38693, 42-93715, 43-15072, 48278, 48336, 48484, 48990, 49593, 49608, 49937, 44-76307, 76356, 76699, 76746, 76974

GLA 49 41-7836, 18474, 18491, 32898, 42-23507, 92499, 43-48018, 48278, 48282, 48285, 48291, 48292, 49049, 49468, 49816, 49876, 49881, 44-76299, 76420, 76499, 76503, 76562, 76717, 76795, 77069, 77232

GLA 57 41-38592, 42-23602, 24069, 43-49608

GLAM 1/60 42-23940, 43-15072, 48280

GOM 50 42-23402, 23509, 93537, 43-16411

GOM 88 42-23782, 93537, 100823, 100865, 100962, 108959, 43-16410, 47985, 48292, 48392, 44-76216

GSRA 76 41-18516, 42-23602, 23782, 93510, 43-15504, 15546, 16410, 48018, 48285, 48396, 48539, 48990, 49876, 44-76420, 76450, 77071, 77101

GSRA 78 41-18474, 18491, 42-23509, 100823, 43-48018, 48279, 48396, 48608, 48931, 49824, 49853, 49876, 49879, 44-76423, 76450, 76500, 76726, 76791

GT 1/15 41-7836, 43-15835, 48278 to 48289, 48291/92, 48759, 49047 to 49051

GT 1/61 41-7836, 18474, 42-92499, 100509, 43-48018, 48278 to 48285, 48291, 48336, 48396, 48484, 48555, 48585, 48608, 48665, 48759, 48789, 48823, 48990, 48994, 49048, 49049, 49050, 49454, 49462, 49608, 49665, 49723, 49878, 49879, 49881, 49931, 49937, 44-76221, 76229, 76307, 76352, 76423, 76500, 76505, 76556, 76561, 76717, 76746, 76786, 76791, 76795, 76835, 76980, 77049, 77069, 77101, 77116

GT 1/62 41-7836, 18474, 42-23782, 43-16410, 48278, 48282, 48284, 48291, 48336, 48484, 48291, 48336, 48484, 48539, 48555, 48665, 48839, 48990, 49051, 49545, 49594, 49723, 49816, 44-76229, 76356, 76421, 76450, 76560, 76699, 76717, 76791, 76974, 76975, 76976, 76977, 77101

GT 1/63 43-48990, 44-76746.**GT 2/63** 42-23386, 24125, 43-15511, 16156, 16164, 48008, 48071, 48149, 48279, 48306, 48413, 48415, 48470, 48504, 48640, 48704, 48800, 48839, 49049, 49113, 49216, 49364, 49566, 49685, 49919

GT 1/64 42-23386, 23782, 24055, 24125, 24336, 92499, 100509, 100666, 100895, 108993, 43-15135, 15400, 15504, 15511, 15587, 15666, 15693, 15984, 16014, 16156, 16164, 16328, 48008, 48071, 48149, 48280, 48282, 48306, 48309, 48396, 48413, 48415, 48465, 48484, 48504, 48555, 48566, 48608, 48619, 48640, 48704, 48729, 48800, 48823, 48859, 48874, 48876, 48978, 49035, 49113, 49115, 49129, 49216, 49345, 49356, 49364, 49418, 49434, 49454, 49462, 49468, 49545, 49566, 49593, 49604, 49608, 49685, 49781, 49816, 49824, 49875, 49881, 49919, 49931, 44-76209, 76229, 76259, 76307, 76420, 76421, 76423, 76502, 76503, 76717, 76721, 76726, 76733, 76746, 76786, 76835, 77011, 77069, 77071, 77101

GT 1/65 43-48008

GT 2/15 42-92972, 43-49664 to 49667, 49875/76/79/81/82, 44-76352/53/55/56, 76357/59/60/61/62, 76786/87/91/95, 76974/75/76/77/80

GT 2/61 42-92499, 43-16410, 48282, 48306, 48484, 48539, 48555, 48608, 48839, 48990, 49051, 49593, 49594, 49666, 49816, 49876, 49937, 44-76209, 76221, 76307, 76356, 76500, 76560, 76699, 76717, 76721, 76726, 76746, 76791, 76835, 76976, 77011, 77069, 77071, 77101, 77116

GT 2/62 42-23386, 24055, 24125, 24336, 92457, 93087, 93519, 100580, 100895, 43-15135, 15400, 15511, 15545, 15984, 16014, 16328, 16390, 48061, 48151, 48306, 48396, 48399, 48413, 48585, 48714, 48823, 48994, 49089, 49115, 49356, 49418, 49594, 49685, 49723, 49931, 49949, 44-76209, 76356, 76357, 76404, 76502, 76503, 76560, 76562, 76699, 76725, 76726, 76786, 76835, 77011

GT 2/64 42-92499, 100509, 108993, 43-15135, 15504, 15587, 16286, 48278, 48279, 48280, 48283, 48285, 48291, 48306, 48336, 48396, 48539, 48555, 48585, 48608, 48619, 48704, 48772, 48876, 48931, 48962, 48990, 49049, 49051, 49145, 49345, 49384, 49545, 49594, 49604, 49608, 49665, 49667, 49723, 49781, 49876, 49881, 49931, 49937, 44-76229, 76352, 76356, 76357, 76500, 76503, 76505, 76556, 76560, 76562, 76699, 76786, 76791, 76795, 76974, 76975, 76976, 76980, 77011, 77049, 77069, 77116

GT 3/61 41-18338, 18474, 42-92499, 43-15504, 48539, 48555, 48619, 48931, 48990, 49816, 44-76221, 76229, 76307, 76423, 76717, 77069, 77116

GT 3/62 41-7836, 38672, 42-100865, 43-15545, 16410, 48018, 48284, 48291, 48336, 48665, 48823, 48823, 49051, 49816, 49824, 49853, 49879, 49881, 44-76356, 76450, 76499, 76560, 76699, 76786, 76791, 76795, 76835, 76974, 76975, 76976, 76977, 45-1064

GT 4/61 43-15504, 15545, 48018, 48285, 48306, 48396, 48585, 48789, 48931, 48978, 49468, 49604, 49723, 49824, 49879, 49937, 44-76209, 76420, 76423, 76503, 76717, 76721, 76725, 76726, 76733, 76746, 76786, 76835, 77011

GTLA 2/60 41-18401, 42-23480, 23509, 23602, 23639, 23782, 23941, 24069, 68819, 92060, 92499, 92872, 92880, 93150, 93537, 100543, 100823, 100865, 100956, 43-15072, 48279, 48280, 48292, 48383, 48396, 48484, 48539, 48585, 48931, 48978, 49049, 49051, 49194, 49296, 49460, 49462, 49608, 49821, 49937, 44-76499, 76505, 76721, 76725, 76726, 76733, 76791, 76835, 76921, 76974, 77011, 77069, 77232

Initially, most C-47s in Aéronavale service bore numbers similar to the Air Force, as many came from that source. However, the numbers were later contracted to 1, 2 or 3 digit serials, using part of the original serial. All C-47s used by Aéronavale were finally withdrawn in Aug84, after a final tour in formation by three aircraft. Many were sold after a period of storage, but some were broken up.

6/48406	c/n 25667	701/77101	33433
10/32810	9036	709/76209	32541
11/23411	9273	711/77011	33343
23/17223	13321	716/77116	33448
25/100825	19288	720/76420	32752
35/13835	13835	721/76721	33053
36/23936	9798	725/76725	33057
59/15059	19525	726/76726	33058
71/12471	12471	729/76229	32561
84/18984	18984	735/76835	33167
87/18487	4579	771/77071	33403
424/49824	27085	919/93519	13440
485/48585	25846		

GABON

The **Force Aérienne Gabonaise** was formed on independence in 1960 and a C-47 was transferred from French stocks. Two more were added later but by 1995 only one was believed to survive, probably TRKBB. TRKCK, reported earlier, is known to be TRKLK but no c/n is known.

TRKBA	17836	c/n 4335	TRKBD?	348292	25553
TRKBB	348284	25545	TRKLK		
TRKBC?	348789	26050			

GERMANY

Various DC-2s and DC-3s were captured by German forces in Czechoslovakia, Poland and finally in Holland between 1938 and 1940. Some of them were used for transport work with the **Luftwaffe** but Lufthansa also received a number. At least one is believed to have been used for operations behind Allied lines with KG.200. Aircraft of this era included:-

DC-2s:-			PC+EB	1364
NA+LD	c/n 1355		NA+LF	1365
PC+EC	1356		NA+LC	1366
SG+KV	1363		VG+FJ	1565
DC-3s:-			NA+LB	2036
PC+EA	1935		VE+RR	2110
NA+LC	1943		NA+LE	2142

When the West German Air Force (Luftwaffe) was reformed in 1956, 20 C-47s were supplied from USAF stocks for use by Transportgeschwader 61 (most of them came as surplus from RAF MUs). 1/LTG61, initially at Erding and then at Neubiberg, actually received 18 aircraft in Aug57 (coded GA-101 to GA-118) although two were passed immediately to the Special Air Mission of the Ministry of Defence (FlBerBMVg, also known as the Flugbereitschaftstaffel or FBS). Thus the FBS initially used four aircraft (CA-011 to CA-014) and eventually this code range was extended to CA-017 with up to seven in use. The FBS operated its C-47s from Wahn (Koln) until 1965.

Use with LTG61 was relatively brief and, after re-equipping with the Noratlas, eleven C-47s were transferred from 1/LTG61 to Flugzeugfuhrerschule (FFS-S) for use as multi-engine trainers (codes were AS-581 to AS-591). Section 'S' (FFS-S) were based at Wunsdorf by the time the C-47s arrived but their stay was to be extremely brief as, once more, they were replaced by the Noratlas in 1959. In late 1959, nine of these C-47s returned to Neubiberg where they rejoined the five aircraft that had remained with LTG61 and two of the FBS machines (CA-013 and CA-014) to form a temporary reserve squadron within LTG61. After some minor juggling these aircraft were re-coded GR-101 to GR-116. At that time the four other Luftwaffe aircraft were coded AS-588, AS-590, CA-011 and CA-012.

In early 1961 the LTG61 aircraft were dispersed to several units. An April 1961 fleet snapshot reveals six FBS aircraft (CA-011, CA-012 and CA-014 to CA-017), four with the FFS (AA-589 of FFS-A Landsberg and AB-588, AB-590 and AB-591 of FFS-B Diepholz), two pairs with each of the two command groups Luftwaffengruppe Sud (ND-105 and ND-106) and Luftwaffengruppe Nord (ND-201 and ND-202) and six with the Luftwaffe calibration squadron Luftvermessungsstaffel 61 (LVSt612) at Lechfeld (XA-111 to XA-116). LVSt612 was later renamed the 4 Fernmelde-und Versuchsregiment (Communications Instrument and Evaluation Regiment) and used C-47s, some with NASARR nose modifications, until 1970. Additional later-used codes included XA-117 (a unique additional C-53 acquired in 1962) and XA-118 to XA-124 (although the identity of XA-122 – if correct – remains untraced). Only one other 'new' user received C-47s in the 'sixties and that was Waffenschule 50 at Furstenfeldbruck that inherited AB-590 and AB-591 as BD-590/591 when FFS-B became WS-50. Other units to which no codes were allocated included the Materialubernahmekommando (Metukdo – the Equipment Acceptance Command) that accepted the aircraft in 1956 and Erprobungsstelle 61 at Manching, the WGAF's test and evaluation unit.

Although the Luftwaffe alpha-numeric codes precisely identified the users of all aircraft (and in the case of the C-47s were usually changed only to reflect a change of unit), all aircraft were identified administratively by construction numbers or MDAP/USAF serials. C-47 'serials' were the original USAAF identities and they were worn on the tail in 25mm characters beneath the national flag. The alpha-numeric codes were abandoned formally on 01Jan68 when the Luftwaffe allocated every aircraft a permanent new serial number. The surviving C-47s were given the range 1401 to 1411 as permanent identities. In the listing below aircraft are tabulated showing the codes used progressively through their careers. Reference to the individual histories should clarify understanding.

c/n			
4911	42-6459	XA-117	
26716	43-49555	GA-115, GR-115, CA-015	
26977	43-49716	GA-118, GR-118, GR-108, CA-016	
26989	43-49728	GA-117, GR-117, GR-107, XA-111	1401
32725	44-76393	GA-105, GR-105, XA-112	1402
32728	44-76396	GA-116, AS-581, GR-101, AS-589?, AA-589, XA-118	
32739	44-76407	GA-113, AS-582, GR-102, AB-591, BD-591	
32814	44-76482	GA-114, GR-114, CA-017	
33021	44-76689	GA-103, AS-583, GR-103, XA-113	
33024	44-76692	GA-112, AS-584, GR-104, ND-201, XA-120	1403
33052	44-76720	GA-108, AS-588, AB-588, AA-588, XA-119	1404
33064	44-76732	GA-101, CA-013, GR-113, CA-014, ND-106, XA-123	1405
33143	44-76811	GA-107, CA-014, GR-116, ND-202	
33153	44-76821	GA-110, AS-590, AB-590, BD-590	1406
33194	44-76862	CA-012, XA-124	1407
33203	44-76871	GA-109, AS-589, GR-112, ND-105	1408
33238	44-76906	GA-102, AS-587, GR-111, ND-106, CA-014	
33273	44-76941	GA-106, AS-591, GR-106, XA-114	1409
33353	44-77021	CA-011	
33429	44-77097	GA-104, AS-585, GR-109, XA-115	1410
33552	44-77220	GA-111, AS-586, GR-110, XA-116	1411

GREAT BRITAIN - see United Kingdom of Great Britain & Northern Ireland

GREECE

The **Royal Hellenic Air Force/Hellenic Air Force/Elliniki Polemiki Aeroporía** operated C-47s continuously from 1947 onwards, three remaining in use in 2001. They saw some action, starting with the civil war in 1947 and later with the United Nations in Korea between 1950 and 1955. They were used primarily for transport duties, but bomb racks were fitted during the civil war between 1944 and 1949, and attacks were made on communist-held buildings in Athens and elsewhere. Greece joined NATO in 1952 and further C-47s were supplied. Friction with Turkey over Cyprus and the key position of the Greek Islands for watching Russian Fleet movements kept Greek forces alert in later years.

The first of 78 C-47s came from Royal Air Force and USAF surplus stocks between 1947 and 1949. Then further C-47s were supplied by the USAF under MDAP after overhaul in the USA. The final group of aircraft was taken over from Olympic Airways in 1963. The great majority of the fleet served with 355 and 356 Moira (squadrons) at Elefsis although their controlling Wing occasionally changed. From 1969 C-47s were replaced gradually, first by the Noratlas and then by the C-130 and other sundries. In 1974, Greece formally became a republic and the **Hellenic Air Force** was created. By 1999 at least 18 aircraft remained in storage with a few more still in active use. In 2002 at least five aircraft still survived within 355 Moira although detached from the main station of Elefsis to Sedes. This unit was known as 355 MTM-Stm1.

Ex Royal Air Force Dakotas. These carried the RAF serial numbers.

KJ950	c/n 26242	KN384	32758
KJ960	26252	KN398	32821
KJ989	26428	KN475	32952
KJ991	26430	KN527	33075
KK105	26555	KN542	33146
KK156	26740	KN575	33199
KK169	26860	KN616	33263
KK171	26862	KN672	33378
KK181	26872	KN691	33404
KK219	27001	KP253	33555
KN272	27206	KP255	33557

Supplied ex USAF from 1947 onwards. Some were ex RAF Dakotas returned to the Field Liquidation Commissioner, but retaining their RAF serials. Where a USAF serial number is given this is an assumption in most cases, as these aircraft were supplied ex USAF storage.

316264	c/n 20730	348865	26126
316272	20738	348900	26161
316348	20814	349086	26347
316406	20872	349111	26372
348379	25640	349188	26449
KJ841	25705	349246	26507
KJ844	25783	349249	26510
348604	25865	349424	26685
348782	26043	349532	26793
348804	26065	KN339	32653

348656 c/n 25917 has also been reported.

A batch of 30 C-47s was supplied under MDAP in the 1949 fiscal year. Few details have come to light, but all were bought used and were overhauled for the USAF by Aviation Maintenance Corp, Van Nuys, CA, some seeing service in Korea.

49-2612	c/n	del 06Sep49, w/o 26May51
49-2613		del 06Sep49, pres Mikra Apt. Nov00
49-2614		del 28Oct49
49-2615	12843	
49-2616		del 28Sep49, w/o in collision with USAF F-80C on runway at K-13, Korea, 22Dec52 (13 Flt)
49-2617		del 28Sep49, i/s Oct72
49-2618		del 03Oct49, i/s 1973
49-2619	4749	
49-2620	4481	
49-2621		del 05Dec49, i/s 1992 114 Apt, wfu Athens 1996 to Nov00
49-2622	20474	
49-2623		del 28Nov49, i/s 1973 std Sedes, derelict Nov96
49-2624	9658	
49-2625	4409 ?	or 4609
49-2626		del 24Oct49, std Thessaloniki, pres Elefsis Nov00-2005
49-2627	4658	
49-2628		del 24Oct49, std Elefsis
49-2629		del 16Dec49, i/s 1977, std Sedes. On dump 2000
49-2630		del 24Oct49, I/s 1973, std Athens 1992 to 1996, on dump 1999 - 2001
49-2631		del 15Nov49, i/s 1973, pres Thessaloniki Nov93
49-2632		del 28Dec49, pres Tripolis AFB 1999-Nov00
49-2633	10246	
49-2634	13836	

49-2635		del 13Dec49, std Sedes 1996-Nov00
49-2636		del 09Nov49
49-2637	19983	
49-2638	9720	
49-2639		del 05Dec49
49-2640		del 15Nov49, inst a/fr Tatoi Apr67
49-2641		del 28Nov49, became restaurant 'Kate DC-10' on Mt Tassos 1996
?		crashed into a mountain after take-off from Taegu, Korea, 27May51 (13 Flt)

Unattributed c/ns among the MDAP supply are 4268, 4762, 6134, 10128, 10240, 13634, 19712, 20004 and 20489.

The last C-47s acquired came from Olympic Airways in 1963. The c/ns were used as tail numbers, except 23325.

9187	c/n 23325	ex SX-BAN
12304	12304	ex SX-BBC
12351	12351	ex SX-BAE
12373	12373	ex SX-BBA
12677	12677	ex SX-BAA
13012	13012	ex SX-BBD
19274	19274	ex SX-BAC

GUATEMALA

C-47 operations by the **Fuerza Aerea Guatemalteca** began on 26Dec45 with two aircraft which were with AVIATECA. These were T-1 and T-2 that flew officially by day as LG-AGA and LG-AHA and by night with the FAG. They were used in May49 in an abortive attempt to invade the Dominican Republic, but both survived in AVIATECA service for a number of years thereafter. Photos of both aircraft in FAG colours show no signs of any civil connections.

In 1946 two ex USAAF C-47s were delivered, c/n 20469 on 26Nov46 and c/n 34406 on 10Dec46 (delivered direct to XH-TAF). These were followed by c/n 20046 on 24Oct50. The former two came under an ARP project and the last under MAP. By 1962 further C-47s had been supplied and seven were in use, based at La Aurora. In the late sixties and seventies further deliveries came from USAF stocks and of the total of 19 supplied, only those converted to BT-67s now remain.

Apart from the original aircraft, T-1 and T-2 (possibly c/ns 6142 and 6052), two distinct series of numbers have been used. In the fifties 0515, 0653 and 0749 were observed, probably the initial post-war trio. Parts of 0961 which crashed on 27Oct51 are preserved at Flores.

There followed a sequence from 500 to 590 (in multiples of '5') which was in use from 1966. Final deliveries were BT-67s from Basler Turbo Conversions. Reports conflict on how many as serial numbers duplicate known FAG numbers and some new aircraft are known to be ex-civil aircraft, while others were FAG C-47s rebuilt.

500	c/n	i/s May67 to Oct80
505		i/s 1967 to Dec78
510	12196	
515		i/s Apr82
520	20046	
525		i/s Dec76 to 1992
530	20031	BT-67 (TG-FAG-6)
535	20732	
540	25425	
550	26286	
555	33499	BT-67 (TG-FAG-5)
560(1)	34398	BT-67 (TG-FAG-4)
560(2)	33542	mispainted
565		i/s Feb79. poss. w/o
570		i/s Dec78 to Oct80
575	19674	BT-67 (TG-FAG-3)
580(1)		i/s Dec 78 to Apr82
580(2)	9100	BT-67 (TG-FAG-1)
585		
590	33542	BT-67 (TG-FAG-2)

Five accidents have been reported, one in Oct51, one in 1963, another on 01Mar80 N of Guatemala City. Another was dbr in mid-1963, and BT-67 580 was dbr in Mar04.

GUINÉ-BISSAU

Known as Portuguese Guinea until independence was gained in 1974 after a prolonged civil war was ended by a change of power in Portugal, the **Force Aérienne da Guiné-Bissau** took over four C-47s left behind by the Portuguese AF, but these were little used.

6151	c/n 11765		6156	33093
6155	32675		6163	26144

HAITI

C-47s have been in use since the early fifties when three were operated by Cie Haitienne de Transports Aériens, an airline operated as a branch of the **Corps d'Aviation de l'Armée d'Haiti**. These aircraft were also used on Air Force duties. A further C-47 was in use by Jul60, at which time serial numbers were applied which formed part of the USAF serial or c/n. From 1969 a sequential system was adopted. Three were reported in use in 1994.

3681	c/n 13681	
4262	4262	
5878	34137	
9175	9175	
1233		i/s 1969 to May91 (derelict)
1235		i/s 1979 to May91 (derelict)
1238		
1275		
1281		
1282		

HOLLAND - see Netherlands

HONDURAS

The first C-47 was acquired by the **Fuerza Aérea Hondurena** in Dec47 to supplement smaller liaison types. Further aircraft were delivered from time to time, mainly from USAF surplus stocks, until about 1976 by which time some 15 had been supplied. They were mainly used on routine transport duties, but in Jul69 306 attempted to bomb Toncontin International Airport, San Salvador and the C-47s were all involved in the "Soccer War", moving troops around the border areas. By 1982 about eleven C-47s remained in service, based at Tegucigalpa. Three years later 14 C-47s were in use and the first C-130s had begun to arrive, and only seven C-47s remained by 1992. TV shots taken during the 1998 hurricane disaster showed a C-47 still active.

The serial number system is straightforward, apart from one re-numbering, possibly for VIP use.

300	c/n 12786	
301	6096	
302	11696	
303	25746	
304	12962	
305	19426	
306	13642	
307	26765	
308	34300	
309	25978	
310		i/s Apr81, cr San Pedro Sula, date unknown
311		i/s Apr82 (damaged in accident 17Oct87). On dump at Tegucigalpa Mar02
312		i/s Apr82, preserved. Tegucigalpa Mar02
313	20839	
314	20631	
315	26178?	
319	26541?	
321	11696	

Four C-47s were delivered in Oct74 ex USAF stocks:- 43-16373, 43-48717 (both 16th Oct, the former becoming 313, the latter 309), 44-76395 and 45-1009 (both 23rd Oct).

HUNGARY

No mention has been found of any C-47s being used by the **Magyar Légierö** or Hungarian Air Force, which is controlled by the Army. A number of Li-2s were supplied by Russia for transport work in 1949-51

CHAPTER 3: MILITARY OPERATORS OF THE DC-3, C-47, R4D, DAKOTA AND LI-2

and others were taken over from MALEV, and in 1951 returned in many cases. All were replaced by Il-14s and later An-26s.

(007)	c/n 234 410 07	(Li-2P)	307	184 393 07	(Li-2T)
008	234 410 08	(Li-2P)	310	184 393 10	(Li-2T)
109	184 331 09	(Li-2T)	503	184 395 03	(Li-2P)
201	184 332 01	(Li-2T)	504	184 395 04	(Li-2P)
203	184 332 03	(Li-2T)	505	184 395 05	(Li-2P)
206	234 412 06	(Li-2T)	803	234 428 03	(Li-2P)
209(1)	184 332 09	(Li-2T)	901	184 359 01	(Li-2T)
209(2)	234 412 09	(Li-2T)	902	184 359 02	(Li-2T)
210	234 412 10	(Li-2T)	(S101)	184 331 09	(Li-2T)
301	234 413 01	(Li-2T)	(S102)	184 332 01	(Li-2T)
303	234 413 03	(Li-2T)	(S103)	184 332 03	(Li-2T)
306(1)	184 363 06	(Li-2P)	(S104)	184 332 09	(Li-2T)
306(2)	184 393 06	(Li-2T)			

INDIA

The **Royal Indian Air Force** was formed in 1946 and 12 Sq, equipped with Dakotas, provided the transport support. Unfortunately a cyclone destroyed most of the initial 10 aircraft at Panagarh late in 1946. In 1947 6 Sq was in the process of changing from Spitfires to Dakotas, when partition transferred this unit to Pakistan. The initial Dakotas came from RAF stocks, comprising VP901 to VP926, a block of numbers not otherwise used by the RAF.

The new arm was blooded early as trouble developed in Jammu and Kashmir in Oct47, ceasing in Dec49, and Dakotas were no doubt used for supply work. Further trouble in May48 necessitated the use of 12 Squadron's Dakotas to supply isolated areas in Kashmir, landings being made at Leh at a height of 11,554 ft. Most Dakotas were overhauled by Hindustan Aviation, who handled over 100 aircraft from RAF and USAAF stocks left in India, between 1947 and 1951.

India became a republic in Jan50 and the **Indian Air Force** was created. At this time 12 Sq used Dakotas and Devons. 11 Sq was formed with Dakotas in Sep51. By 1954 C-119s began to replace Dakotas with 12 Sq, and these were passed to 43 Sq. By 1959 49 Sq was also equipped with Dakotas. The Dakotas saw more action in Oct62 when China took over Tibet and attacked border posts at Ladakh in the following month. More recent active service was in 1971 when war broke out with Pakistan and E Pakistan was invaded.

Dakotas were used regularly to supply outposts on the long frontiers with Pakistan and China and also to drop supplies during the many flood disasters. They were also used by the Multi-engined Training Unit, the Parachute Training School, the Transport Training Wing and the Navigation & Signals School. The last's seven Dakotas were replaced by HS.748s from 1971 on. This type also replaced 11 Sq's Dakotas. Apart from surplus Dakotas, aircraft came from other sources. At least 70 were in use in 1954, and in Nov62 (6) and Mar63 (2) eight came from Canada as emergency aid (BJ762-BJ767 and BJ912-BJ913). Between Dec61 and Mar68 another 20 were taken over from Indian Air Lines. From 1962 onwards 109 Dakotas saw service with the IAF, but records of sources are incomplete.

As of Jun80 there were 73 Dakotas on charge, but by 1983 fatigue problems, brought on no doubt by the extreme environment of the Himalayas, caused the type to be grounded pending checks, never to fly again. They were then sold as scrap, being replaced by Fairchild C-119s and they in turn by Antonov An-32s. Units using Dakotas in the early 80s were 11, 43 and 49 Squadrons.

Official information on Dakota serial numbers is confined to a list kindly supplied by the Air Attaché in London. This has allowed us to identify the more recently acquired aircraft, but not the surplus aircraft supplied earlier.

The following Dakotas were overhauled by Hindustan Aircraft Corp prior to independence:-

VP901	c/n 12258		VP910	13039
VP902	9326		VP911	13163
VP903	25300		VP912/V	12144
VP904	12817		VP913	12157
VP905	12581		VP914	12183
VP906	12498		VP915	13549
VP907	12499		VP916	13566
VP908	12813		VP917	13567
VP909	13024		VP918	13568
VP919	25305		VP923	9309
VP920	25308		VP924	9495
VP921	9181		VP925	9537
VP922	9237		VP926	9763

Apart from the above there were five other early aircraft ex RAF stocks which must have been transferred to the RIAF at its inception, namely:- MA963 c/n 9324; MA964 c/n 9681; MA965 c/n 12819; MA966 c/n 13588 and MA968 c/n 13551. These serial numbers do not fall into the RAF system (all being DH.89As). MI965, possibly an error for MA965, crashed on 31Oct47 in South Kashmir, but was not found until Aug80. The Indian Air Force adopted a serial number system based on that used by the RAF, and all aircraft were re-numbered into it. The Dakotas fell into the HJ, IJ, BJ and J series, but one exception is L1397 which may be an observation error. On the assumption that the various blocks listed shortly were all Dakotas, some 150 aircraft can be accounted for; while more than this are known to have been acquired, some may have been used only for spares. The following additional aircraft are known to have been transferred to the Indian Government in 1946/early 1947:-

C/ns 4779, 4796, 4856, 4920, 6145, 6174, 6240, 6244, 9069/70, 9184, 9239/40, 9312/15/19/25, 9493/96, 9535/47, 9679/84/85/87/90/93, 9764/65/70, 9824/76, 9952/54, 10026/27, 10115, 10219/24/26, 11912/31/76/97/99, 12002/22/23/29/40, 12043/44, 12167/71, 12201/81, 12316, 12480/95, 12978, 13034, 13185/89/90, 13247/49/72/77/81, 13386, 13547/63/85/86/87/89, 13631, 13714, 13792/93/95, 19155/61, 19518, 19855/56/57/59/63/72/75, 20263, 20726, 20878, 25303/07, 25462, 25849/92/93, 26125/29, 26709, 26895, 26904/45/47, 32575/85.

Observed Indian AF Dakotas are as follows:-

BJ449	c/n 19431		BJ762	13476
BJ478			BJ763	13160
BJ496	12494		BJ764	12449
BJ497	20259		BJ765	33369
BJ498	19519		BJ766	33384
BJ499	19151		BJ767	13151
BJ616			BJ910	
BJ617	13290		BJ912	27133
BJ618	13295		BJ913	33466
BJ619	12382		BJ920	13696
BJ620	18906		BJ921	26710
BJ621	12193		BJ922	6078
BJ622	25842		BJ923	13278
BJ623	12928		BJ1045	20276
BJ691			BJ1046	20170

HJ205	c/n	i/s 30Jun80
HJ206		i/s 30Jun80
HJ207		to spares 1976
HJ209/F		i/s 30Jun80
HJ211		i/s 30Jun80
HJ212		i/s 30Jun80
HJ213		i/s 30Jun80
HJ214		to spares 1976
HJ215		i/s 30Jun80
HJ217		Cat E Sep65
HJ218		cr 15Apr65
HJ219		Cat E
HJ220		i/s 30Jun80
HJ223		i/s 30Jun80
HJ224/C		i/s 30Jun80
HJ226		
HJ227		i/s 30Jun80
HJ228		i/s 30Jun80
HJ230		i/s 30Jun80
HJ231		cr 1965
HJ232		i/s 1958
HJ233		i/s Feb79
HJ234		Cat E
HJ235		cr 23Aug80
HJ236		i/s 30Jun80
HJ238		i/s 30Jun80
HJ239		i/s 30Jun80
HJ240/F		i/s 30Jun80
HJ241		i/s 30Jun80
HJ242		i/s 1958
HJ243		i/s 1958
HJ244		cr 06May67
HJ245		
HJ246		
HJ247		i/s 30Jun80

HJ248		i/s 30Jun80
HJ249		i/s 30Jun80
HJ251		i/s 1958
HJ252/Y		i/s Aug53
HJ253		i/s 30Jun80
HJ254		cr 26Apr74
HJ274		
HJ822		
HJ850		i/s 30Jun80
HJ851		i/s 30Jun80
HJ857		
HJ879		i/s 30Jun80
HJ881		
HJ882		i/s 30Jun80
HJ883		i/s Oct57
HJ885		i/s 30Jun80
HJ905		i/s 30Jun80
HJ907/U		i/s 30Jun80
HJ908	11912	
HJ910/J		i/s 30Jun80
HJ911/S		spares 1976
HJ912		i/s 30Jun80
HJ915		i/s 30Jun80
HJ916		cr 07Aug73
HJ917		i/s 1958
HJ918		
HJ919		i/s 30Jun80
HJ920		
HJ921		i/s 30Jun80
HJ922		i/s 30Jun80
IJ205		
IJ236		i/s 1958
IJ239/N		spares 1976
IJ240		i/s 30Jun80
IJ242/W		spares 1976
IJ244		cr Sep65
IJ245		i/s 30Jun80
IJ246		i/s 30Jun80
IJ247		i/s 30Jun80
IJ249		i/s 1969
IJ292		cr Sep65
IJ293		i/s 30Jun80
IJ294		i/s 30Jun80
IJ295		Cat E pre-1984
IJ296		i/s 30Jun80
IJ297		cr 25May77
IJ298		i/s 30Jun80
IJ302		i/s 30Jun80
IJ304		cr 04Apr68
IJ305		i/s 30Jun80
IJ341		cr 03Feb73
IJ386		cr Sep65
IJ387		spares 1976
IJ389		i/s 1958
IJ391		i/s 30Jun80
IJ392/B		i/s 30Jun80
IJ393/R		spares 1976
IJ394		i/s 30Jun80
IJ395		i/s 30Jun80
IJ397		i/s 30Jun80
IJ398		i/s 30Jun80
IJ817		i/s 30Jun80
IJ818		cr 04Feb75
IJ819		i/s 30Jun80
IJ820		cr 21Feb69
IJ822		i/s 30Jun80
J-973	20792	
J-975	20289	
J-978	13380	

BJ496 and BJ764 both preserved at Bangalore Jan94. HJ905 preserved at Agra Jan94, IJ817 stored at IAF Museum, Palam, Dec98, and IJ302 with the IAF Vintage Flt, Palam Oct97. HJ879 fitted with a long nose by Marshall, Cambridge.

INDONESIA

The **Indonesian Air Force/Angkatan Udara Republik Indonesia (AURI)** was formed in 1947 when the Netherlands gave independence to the islands making up the Netherlands East Indies. C-47s had been used by the RNEIAF 19 Sq when it was attached to the RAAF in 1945/46, the aircraft being allotted DT serial numbers and carrying Australian call signs on the tail. With independence many of the Australian call signs were used with VH changed to PK and the serial numbers NI-470 onwards were adopted, probably indicating Netherlands Indies pre-independence. They all went to Garuda Indonesian Airways. With independence a new series starting around T-429 came into use for C-47s with SkU 2 Sq. Assuming the series was continuous for C-47s, about 55 were used by the AURI, and in 1982 2 Sq was reported to be using a dozen C-47s. These were replaced by F.27-400Ms and IPTN CN235M-100s by 1993. The Air Force is now known as **Tentara Nasional Indonesia - Angkatan Udara (TNI-AU)**.

Apart from the air force, there were about six C-47s with the **Indonesian Navy/Angkatan Laut Republik Indonesia (ALRI)**, later **TNI-Angkatan Laut (TNI-AL)**, starting at U-601. The Army, **TNI-Angkatan Darat (TNI-AD)**, also had two C-47s in 1980. Apart from the post-independence forces, mention should also be made of the clandestine forces in 1946/47, when at least four C-47s were bought to support operations against the Dutch forces (serials RI-001 on).

The NI- series C-47s were:-

NI-470	c/n 42954		NI-476	13535
NI-471	19005		NI-477	19658
NI-472	13619		NI-478	13766
NI-473	19279		NI-479	13052
NI-474	12719		NI-480	12514
NI-475	13463			

Ten of these went to Garuda as PK-DBA to PK-DBJ.

Clandestine C-47s were:-

RI-001	c/n 26903	
RI-002	20578	
RI-007		bought in USA Jan49
RI-009	4823	chartered from Philippines
RI-1	12664	(ALRI)

'RI-001' also worn by c/n c/n 34228, and by c/n 13503 which may be included among preserved examples at Banda Aceh, N Sumatra (since 1984), Taman Mini Indonesia theme park, S Jakarta and at the Abri Satria Mandala Museum, central Jakarta.

AURI post-independence C-47s:-

T-429	c/n	i/s Jul59
T-430		i/s Aug59
T-431		i/s Oct59
T-433		i/s Mar57/Nov58
T-437	12036	
T-438	11972	
T-439	12279	
T-440	12097	
T-442	12878	
T-443	13344	
T-444	13345	
T-445	32691	to AT-4745
T-446	32692	
T-447		poss. cr 10Feb48
T-449	33475	
T-450	33477	
T-451	9281	
T-452	13207	to AT-4752
T-453	6032	
T-454	6199	
T-455		
T-457		i/s Jul50
T-458		i/s Jul78
T-459	9551	
T-462	13497	
T-463	12636	
T-464	25496	
T-467	13607	
T-468	13123	
T-469	12664	
T-470	9518	to ALRI Jun59
T-471	19902	
T-472	9753	to ALRI
T-473	9727	
T-474	12719	
T-475	13503	to AT-4775

CHAPTER 3: MILITARY OPERATORS OF THE DC-3, C-47, R4D, DAKOTA AND LI-2

T-476	9399	
T-477	13766	
T-478	13493	
T-479	13616	
T-480	11804	
T-481	9808	
T-482	25489	
T-483	9583	
T-484	19566	
T-485		noted 1970
T-486		
T-487		noted 1970
T-488		
T-489		
T-490		to AT-4790
T-491	12514	
T-492		wfu Apr88 Bandung
T-493		
T-494		
T-495		
T-496		
T-497		
T-498		
T-499		
T-500	27093	to A-4700
T-501		
T-502	33605	
T-503	33007	
T-504	27128	
T-505	33452	to A-4705
T-506		i/s Nov58
T-507		to A-507, stored Juanda NAS Apr00
T-508		to A-508, stored Juanda NAS Apr00
T-510		i/s May58
T-512		i/s Jul58
T-513		i/s Apr59
T-515		i/s Apr58
T-516		i/s Nov58
T-517		i/s Jul58
T-521		
T-526		i/s May59
T-527		
T-528		i/s Sep59
T-529		
T-530		i/s Jun59
T-531		i/s Oct59
T-532		i/s Jan60
T-540		
T-563		

It has been suggested that the NI- series were renumbered in the T- series, but this seems unlikely. It is known that T-444 and T-462, at least, remained until 1973. Apart from these the USAAF diverted c/ns 9518 and 9808 to the AURI. Previously they were with the Netherlands Navy. In 1970 it was reported that 14 Sq was using P.504 c/n 27128, and in 1973 A-9036 and A-9038 were noted, with the TNI-AD, both stored at Pondak Cabe Apr00. By Oct82 T-462, A-4700 c/n 27093 and A-4705 c/n 33452 were observed in Jakarta. They were being replaced by Buffalos in 1997.

Meanwhile, the Navy had up to seven C-47s (U-601 c/n 19510, U-602 c/n 12017?, to U-607 incl U-603 c/n 4500). They were operated from 1965 by SkwU and remained in service until about 1993. These included c/n 9753 which is known to have gone to the Navy. One Navy C-47 crashed at Bekasi in Feb48. U-603/04/05 & 07 were stored at Juanda NAS, Surabaya in Feb91, and U-601/03/04/05 & 07 were stored in Nov97, with U-603 remaining in Apr00. They were replaced by DHC-5 Buffalos.

FASI - **Satuan Udara Federasi Aerosport Indonesia** have five C-47s: AF-4752 c/n 13207 i/s 1994; AF-4775 c/n 34228 (as RI-001 Apr99); AF-4776 c/n 13334 ex PK-VTO i/s 2001; AF-4777 c/n 9281 ex PK-VTM i/s 1994; and AF-4790 i/s 1993-1999.

IRAN

The **Imperial Iranian Air Force** bought a number of surplus C-47s in 1948/49 and by 1958 there were ten of the type in use. By 1974 they had been replaced by C-130Hs and F.27s. No C-47s survived until the fall of the Shah. Serial numbers were in the series 5-01 to 5-23, but the only known c/ns are:-

5-01	c/n 10237		5-11	25331
5-10	19283			

Apart from these it is known that the following were supplied to the IIAF by the USAF in 1949:- c/ns 19442, 19669, 19682, 20130, 20168; c/n 20490 was added in 1957. Nine were reported passed on by the Turkish AF in Aug49:- c/ns 9498, 9800, 10055, 11856, 12764, 12903, 13444, 13674 and 19602.

ISRAEL

The C-47 served the **Israel Defence Force/Air Force (IDF/AF)** from its formation. Two were acquired in early 1948 from South Africa via Boris Senior (a serving SAAF officer) and three more were 'loaned' by Dutch millionaire Mr. van Lir. Added to these were an abandoned ex-Air France DC-3 F-BAXN and possibly one example from Belgium. One was lost when it crash-landed at its base, returning from a bombing mission against Syrian positions in Oct48. Initially numbered as 'S' (Transport) aircraft with numbers 81-86, the C-47 became operational on 25May48 at Sde Dov, moving to Ramat-David in Jun48 (and later Hatzor, Ekron and, finally, Lod). C-47s were used in a variety of roles during the 1948/49 war of independence, including transport, bombing and aerial photography. Further C-47s were added in 1950/51, at which time the call sign block from 4X-FAA was allotted. These call signs were used on overseas flights to pick up supplies etc in various parts of Europe. By 1956 there were 16 C-47s in service and these saw combat during the Israeli operations against Egypt (Operation Kadesh) in support of the Anglo-French attack on Suez on 29Oct56. The entire 16-strong C-47 fleet was used to drop 395 parachutists and equipment on the Mitla Pass in southern Sinai in the opening phases of the campaign, escorted by Meteor F.8s and Ouragans.

Following the 1956 war some of the aircraft were sold to Arkia for airline use, but between 1959 and 1963 further C-47s were acquired from various commercial sources in Australia and America. Others were bought as scrap and reconditioned in Israel. Just before the 1967 'Six-Day War' a further 15 C-47s were bought from French stocks, to make a fleet of 30. These were allotted call signs in the 4X-FNx series as the 4X-FAx series was by then used by the Noratlas. They took part in a variety of transport duties in the 1967 operations, supplying troops in the Negev and Sinai areas.

The 1967 operations marked the end of the C-47 as a major part of the IDF/AF transport fleet. Five were scrapped and three sold to Uganda. During the early seventies they were used mainly as instrument trainers and for second-line transport duties. By the outbreak of the Yom Kippur War on 06Oct73 only about ten remained in service. They were used for general duties including casualty evacuation, some reaching as far as Fayid, near Cairo. In 1976 the number was again increased, as three were taken over from civil operators (Arkia?) and the Ugandan fleet was returned to Israel. The C-47 saw further service in the 1982 war in the Lebanon when 18 remained in use.

IDFAF records, prior to 1973, have been destroyed and information is sparse, but during more than 34 years' service only two C-47s were lost to accidents. One C-47 was destroyed when a bomb fell off while landing at Ramat-David on 13Jul48 as it returned from an operation. The other was lost from engine failure on 24Oct48 over Ekron air base in the Negev, causing the only fatalities in Israeli C-47 operations. A survey in 1994 suggested that at least twenty C-47s remained on charge. 4X-FMJ was the last to be withdrawn, on 05Feb01 at Lod.

Serial number detail is limited. In the first series the Hebrew letter 'U' corresponds more or less to 'S' meaning "Si-yuah" or support, and was used prior to Nov48:-

S-81/81U	c/n 6223	coded 4X-FAG/04, to 1401(2)
S-82/82U	6224	coded 4X-FAH, to 1402
S-83/83U	10142	to 1401(1) ntu
S-84/84U	10146	to 1403
S-85/85U	12486	to 1404
S-86/86U	19420	to 1405

In Nov48, new designations were created with '7' (for Transport) and '14' (for C-47/DC-3) and an individual number, eg '71401', but '7' was not always worn, nor was '14', so markings appeared as '1401' or '01'. Confusingly, aircraft marked '00x' are not always the same as those marked '140x' or '0x'. The following post-Nov48 markings are known:

1401(2)	c/n 6223	4X-FAG/04
1402	6224	4X-FAH
?	19400	4X-F /06

?	26972	4X-FAA?/07
?	6227	4X-FAI/009
?	9050	4X-FAJ/010
1403	10146	4X-FNF/03
1404	12486	4X-FNL/04, then /004, then /04
1405	19420	4X-FNB/005
1406	33049	4X-FNK/006
1407	26792	4X-FNA/007
1408	26054	4X-FAH, then 4X-FNI/008
	11923	4X/FNF?/10, then 003
1416	25869	4X-FNN/016
1417	19446	4X-FNH/017
1418	32553	4X-FNO/018
1422	27137	4X-FNQ/022
1426	32837	4X-FNG/026
	33307	4X-FNT/029(1)
1429	12060	4X-FNT/029(2)
1430	25795	4X-FAK/030, then 4X-FNW/030
1432	4463	4X-FNE/032
1434	33123	4X-FND/034
1435	32755	4X-FNV(2)/035
1436	26310	4X-FNV(1)/036
1437	33031	4X-FNW/037
1438	33307	4X-FNZ/038
	6223	4X-FMF/040
1442	33031	4X-FMJ/042
1444	32755	4X-FMP/044

4X-FAA, a maritime radar conversion, was noted in use in 1956, and 4X-FNR, 4X-FNS, 4X-FNU and 4X-FNX remain to be identified. Serial numbers 002, 025, and 028 have also been noted. Apart from the above, various other aircraft are known, usually passing through the UK on delivery:- 4X-FZB (in Oct 1956); 4X-AF27; 4X-407, 4X-528 and 1708 (in 1954). As yet unidentified aircraft destined for Israel were c/ns 12306, 25687 4X-AOJ, 25800, 32669, 32675, 33093 and 33306. C-47 '59' was stored for the IDF/AF Museum at Hatzerim AB in Jul86, before moving to Kibbutz Revivim.

ITALY

The first DC-3 used by the **Aeronautica Militare Italiano (AMI)** was a SABENA example captured in North Africa in 1940 while in RAF service. It became MM60520 c/n 2093 and was used alongside DC-2 MM60436 c/n 1319 taken over from Aviolinee Italiane in 1940. Both reverted to civil use late in 1940. Post-war, USAAF surplus C-47s and C-53s were bought from stocks at Naples and most of Alitalia's surplus DC-3s were added later.

Units which have used C-47s and C-53s since 1948 are described below in chronological order, courtesy of MCP's Italian Military Aviation:

4 Gruppo (part of SAT) used C-53s from 1948 to Dec54 when it became Scuola Instruzione Equipaggi, coded SF-. It then became Scuola Addestramento Plurimotori on 03May55, using code SP-. In Dec61 it was further re-named Scuola Volo e Avanzato ad Elica. The C-47s were retired in 1969.

Reparto Volo Stato Maggiore operated C-47s from Dec48 until 1970, with codes SM-1 to SM-34. A particular aircraft might use several different codes.

Comando Aeronautica della Somalia used C-47s from Mar50 until 01Jun60 when it became the Mogadisciou Base Flight, using codes AS-1 to AS-5. They then passed to the Somali AF on independence.

Centro Radiomisure used C-47s from 1952 until 01Oct64 when it became Reparto Radiomisure, using code CR-. The latter continued 01Jun76 when it was disbanded and the aircraft transferred to 14. The code was then changed to 14-40 to 14-50.

306 Gruppo was formed on 01Sep52 and operated C-47s and C-53s, based at Roma Centocelle, being used for training and specialised duties. Initially they used code ZR- but RR- later. It was incorporated into the re-formed RVSM in Oct63 but transferred to 31 on 06Oct76 when the RVSM was disbanded. C-47s were then withdrawn.

307 Gruppo, part of RVSM, received some C-47s in 1959, but RVSM was disbanded later in the year.

315 Gruppo comprised 550 Squadriglia with C-47s and 551 Sq. It was formed on 01Oct64 at Pratica di Mare to check navaids and radar. The C-47s were passed to 316 Gruppo on 30Sep75 and this, in turn, went to 14 Stormo on 01Jul76.

2 Reparto Volo Reggionale was a liaison unit formed on 01Nov65, with C-47s based at Guidonia, and coded RR.

71 Gruppo Guerre Eletronica was formed in 1972 and operated some EC-47s. It was absorbed by the newly formed 14 Stormo on 01Jun76. The code was CR-. Fiat G.222RMs replaced the EC-47s from 1983 on.

8 Gruppo Sorveglianza Eletronica was re-formed on 01Jun76 with seven C-47s, as well as other types. The C-47s were replaced from 1981.

The *Scuola Caccia Ogni Tempo* had one C-47 between Mar55 and 30Sep57, coded SO-1. It had a radar nose and was used to train night fighter radar operators.

The last C-47, probably MM61893, was retired in the late eighties.

The following are known C-47s and C-53s used by Italy. C/ns for a few are still lacking and for these known unit details are given; for the remainder these details are incorporated in the Production History chapter:-

MM61764	(C-53)	c/n	Fiat Dec49 to Jan50; SqTrCA Somalia '1' Mar50 to Jun51; RVSM; SP-21; RR-05 May77 to Jul79; 14-48 Apr80; std Pratica di Mare Jan83. Scrapped at Pratica di Mare
MM61765	(C-53)	11681	
MM61766	(C-53)		SqTrCA Somalia '3' Mar50 to Jun51; RVSM (SP-2) Jun64; RR-04 Nov73 to Jul75; std Guidonia Jul77 and derelict to Oct80. Scrap 1988
MM61767	(C-53)		SqTrCA Somalia '4' Mar50; AS-4 1957 to Jun60; Somali AF 01Jul60
MM61768	(C-53)	11760	
MM61769	(C-53)		SM-9, SqTrCA Somalia AS-6, w/o 15Mar55 Nairobi, Kenya
MM61770	(C-47)		SqTrCA '5' Mar50; cr in sea off Brindisi 20Jan60
MM61775	(C-47)	19016	
MM61776	(C-47)	19194	
MM61777	(C-47)	9910	
MM61778	(C-47)	18964	
MM61784	(C-47)		RVSM Jun50; SM-29 pre-1968
MM61799	(C-47)		
MM61800	(C-47)	4260	
MM61815	(C-47)	26800	
MM61816	(C-47)	26646	
MM61817	(C-53)	7325	
MM61818	(C-53)	7397	
MM61823	(C-47)	4389	
MM61824	(C-47)	4506	
MM61825	(C-47)	4221	
MM61826	(C-47)	4380	
MM61832	(C-47)		RVSM/Ufficio Informazione; SM-16 Feb72; Cr 23Nov73 Venice
MM61893	(C-47)	4236	
MM61894	(C-47)	4261	
MM61895	(C-47)	6011	
MM61896	(C-47)	4316	
MM61897	(C-47)	4291	

It should be noted that most of the dates given are from observation rather than official records. Of the missing c/ns, it is known that the following were also delivered to the Italian Air Force:- c/ns 7322 (C-53), 11740 (C-53), 11753 (C-53), 11756 (C-53 possibly MM61764). This accounts for all but four C-47s. Seven wrecks still exist at Rome-Guidonia and Pratica di Mare.

IVORY COAST

The first C-47s were transferred to the **Force Aérienne de Côte d'Ivoire**, as was customary, from French Air Force stocks, but two others were delivered in 1965. The last was sold in 1977, following replacement by F.27s and F.28s. Call signs and serial numbers were used.

TUVAA	76795	c/n 33127	TUVAB(2)	11705	11705
TUVAB(1)	4164	20777	TUVAC	76786	33118

JAPAN

Japanese-built aircraft form a sub-section of Chapter 1 to which reference should be made for the little that is known of pre-war and wartime use.

COLOUR GALLERY

NC13717 DC-2-118B c/n 1368 - One of the few DC-2s to survive, this aircraft entered service with Pan American in 1935 and progressed through several PAA subsidiaries in Central America before returning to the USA in 1952. The DC-2 was acquired by the Donald Douglas museum in 1975 and was restored to fly in an early TWA colour scheme, as seen here at Santa Monica, CA on 17Jan79. [Dave Musikoff via P J Marson]

PH-AJU DC-2-112 c/n 1286 - Preserved in false (and somewhat fading) marks at Albury, NSW and photographed in Feb02, this was RAAF A30-11 ex-NC13736. It was modified with cargo doors in 1944 and was used later by S D Marshall for spares in 1946. [Rob Tracz]

NC16004 DST-144 c/n 1498 - American Airlines 'Flagship California', the name applied until taken over by the USAAC in May42. This aircraft eventually became N67000 and finished its career in South Africa on 28Dec73 when it crashed near Durban. [American Airlines via A Pearcy]

HH-GP1 DC-3-208 c/n 1964 - Haiti Overseas Airways operated this DC-3 briefly in 1973, the photo being taken in Florida in May74.
[P Evans - Stephen Piercey collection via P J Marson]

OH-VKB DC-3A-214 c/n 1975 - Kar-Air fitted this aircraft with magnetometer survey gear in 1969, seen at Joensuu, Finland in Aug74. Originally delivered to ABA, Sweden in 1937, it was withdrawn from use in Apr87 and donated to the Finnish Air Museum.   *[Paul Zogg via P J Marson]*

C9-ATG DC-3A-197 c/n 1984 - Interocean, registered in 1987 after repair following an accident, and photographed at Lanseria, South Africa on 09May92. Originally United's NC18112, delivered in 1937, this aircraft remains at Johannesburg-Rand, South Africa with Phoebus Apollo.   *[Andy Heape]*

COLOUR GALLERY

III

N18121 DC-3-210 c/n 1997 in the livery of The Great Silver Fleet of Eastern Air Lines, preserved at the Pearson Air Museum, Pearson, Vancouver, WA, where it was seen on 03Jul01. [Dave Peel]

NC21729 DC-3-201B c/n 2141 - An early example of an ever-increasing trend to paint aircraft in pseudo-military colours is seen in this photo taken at Oshkosh, WI on 31Jul77. The DC-3 here never saw military service, but spent the first thirteen years of its life with Eastern Air Lines before progressing through a succession of corporate or private owners in the USA. The aircraft is currently registered to a group in Canada. [P A Kirkup via P J Marson]

N32B DC-3A-253A c/n 2145 - After use with the Army Air Corps as a C-41A, this aircraft passed through a succession of private owners in the USA and received this registration in 1971. It was in use with a turkey farmer entitled 'Tinsley's Boss Bird' when this photo was taken in Mar81. This DC-3 has been re-registered several times since and is believed to be still flying. [Stephen Piercey collection via P J Marson]

N132BP DC-3A-253A c/n 2145 - This aircraft was delivered originally to the USAAC as C-41A 40-70 and is shown here in the colours of Bob Pond on 05Oct90 at Chino, CA. Named 'Miss Angela', it has 'maximiser' doors. [R A Scholefield]

N139D delivered as a DST-217A c/n 2165 - Shown in Pacific National colours at Las Vegas, NV in Jul82, this aircraft served with American, USAAF, Chicago & Southern and Colonial as well as sundry corporate owners. [Eric Wagner]

N26MA DC-3-313 c/n 2169 photographed at Lake Elsinore Parachute Center, CA on 19Oct97, this aircraft was still resident in Oct01, operated by Paralift Inc. [Roger Syratt]

COLOUR GALLERY

V

N1000A DC-3A-269B c/n 2184 - Formerly NC25609 of Northwest Airlines, photographed on 25Oct82 at Fort Lauderdale International, FL where it was later scrapped in Jan02. [Roger Syratt]

YV-440C DC-3-277B c/n 2201 - Aeroejecutivos, Venezuela. Ex N31PB, this DC-3 operates tourist flights from Caracas, Venezuela where it was seen landing on 30Mar03. Originally NC21797, its intended sale to American Airlines for possible restoration did not apparently proceed. [Paul Seymour]

N34PB DC-3-277B c/n 2204 of Provincetown-Boston Airline at Naples, FL on 11Nov82, this aircraft served originally with American Airlines as NC25658, before USAAF service and twenty years based post-war in Texas. [Roger Syratt]

N922CA DC-3-277B c/n 2204 in a later manifestation (see previous picture), appeared at the EAA Convention, Oshkosh, WI in 2004. [Dave Partington]

N139PB DC-3-314A c/n 2239 of Eastern Express, the last surviving part of Provincetown- Boston. Originally delivered to Braniff in 1940, this aircraft remained in airline use until shortly after this photo was taken at Naples, FL in Dec87. [via P J Marson]

N28AA DC-3A-314A c/n 2239 - Alexander Aeroplane supplies materials for kitplane builders, and this aircraft was very much at home at the EAA Convention, Oshkosh, WI on 05Aug92. [Jennifer Gradidge]

Colour Gallery   VII

LV-HOJ DC-3A-343 c/n 2265 - After use by Western Air Express and United, this aircraft was sold in Argentina in 1962 and was in use with the Provincial Civil Aviation Authority of Santiago del Estero when this photo was taken in Sep78. The DC-3 returned to the USA the same year, but as nothing has been heard of it since the mid-1980s, this probably means that it ended its days on a smuggling flight. [Stephen Piercey collection via P J Marson]

XA-FUJ DC-3A-197D c/n 3262 - Another United DC-3 sold in Mexico, to LAMSA in 1946 and thence to Aeronaves de Mexico in Jul52, with whom it remained until 1970. This photograph was taken at Nogales, Mexico in Mar63. [Clay Jansson]

NC28344 DC-3-357 c/n 3281 - Almost certainly this 65-year-old air-to-air photograph was taken when the aircraft was new in Dec40, although the aircraft lasted another 23 years before sale in 1963. Delta has restored another DC-3 of the same vintage to airworthy condition. [Delta Air Lines]

N600NA DC-3A-228D c/n 3291 - This aircraft began its career with Pan American in 1941, and after a post-war spell in Venezuela, was operated by several owners in Texas and Florida before reaching Smilin' Jack's Air Service, with whom it was photographed at Opa-Locka, FL on 20Nov96.
[Roger Syratt]

N74B DC-3A c/n 3299 - After use by TWA, this aircraft served for many years with Flight Safety Inc as an 'advanced aircraft trainer' according to the inscription on the roof. It was photographed at Oakland, CA in the early 1970s. It was used subsequently for spares after storm damage in Honolulu, HI.
[Stephen Piercey collection via P J Marson]

N33644 DC-3A-197E c/n 4123 seen in Western Airlines colours, is owned by Mike Kimbrell and kept at his ranch strip at Oakville, WA. The photo shows it at an EAA Chapter Fly-In at nearby Hoquiam on 07Jul01.
[Dave Peel]

COLOUR GALLERY

TI-SAA C-47-DL c/n 4231 - After service as 41-7744 with the 8th AF in North Africa, this aircraft was sold in Colombia in 1947 before progressing to Costa Rica in 1970. Passing through several Costa Rican registrations, the aircraft had been bought by SANSA by Feb80 when this photo was taken. It survived another thirteen years with the airline before being sold in Venezuela. [B G Lundkvist via P J Marson]

N728G C-47-DL c/n 4359 - Serving as 41-7860 during WW2, a lengthy life in mainly corporate ownership followed, this aircraft appearing at the EAA Convention, Oshkosh, WI in 2004. [Dave Partington]

HZ-TA3 R4D-1 c/n 4363 - This ex-Navy DC-3 has so far operated in four continents, starting in Colombia. The photo shows it after conversion for Prince Talal Bin Abdul Aziz with the name 'Sara' on the nose. Note the 'maximiser' undercarriage doors, close-cowled engine and panoramic windows. After use in Saudi Arabia for about ten years the aircraft was sold in South Africa as ZS-MRU in 1990 and at the time of writing had been flown to the UK to be prepared for a new owner in Iceland. [Stephen Piercey collection via P J Marson]

VR-HDB C-47-DL c/n 4423 - Martin Willing rescued this C-47 from New Guinea and flew it home to Hong Kong, where it now lives in a museum. It was the first aircraft operated by Cathay Pacific in 1946 and was sold by them in 1955 to New Guinea Airways. This air-to-air was taken on delivery over Hong Kong on 23Sep83. [Cathay Pacific via Martin Willing]

Colour Gallery

XI

41-18392 C-117C c/n 4430 - This aircraft was unusual in being returned to the United States Air Force after lease to Pioneer Airlines for four years in the post-war period. It was in use with the Air University when this photo was taken at Andrews AFB, MD on 31Jan70. Note the abbreviated presentation of the serial on the fin.
[Stephen H Miller via P J Marson]

C-FYED R4D-1 c/n 4433 - After a military and civil career spanning three decades, this aircraft started a new life as an aerial survey platform in the early 1970s. This photo was taken in Canada in Jul82 when operated by Questor International Surveys and shows a number of survey modifications.
[Stephen Piercey collection via P J Marson]

N220GB R4D-1 c/n 4438 - A spray-equipped aircraft of Monroe County Mosquito Control District, photographed at its Marathon, FL base on 13Nov96.
[Roger Syratt]

N330 C-47-DL c/n 4479 wearing Argas titles, photographed after rework at the MIACO facility, Malta in May84. It was later sold to the Spanish operator Aeromarket Express as EC-EJB before storage at San Bonet, Majorca. [Roger Syratt]

N57626 C-47-DL c/n 4564 of Nord Aviation, photographed at its Santa Teresa, NM base on 08Oct97. [Roger Syratt]

N34952 C-53 c/n 4944 - After time with Pan American, Mid-Continent and Braniff, this aircraft spent five years with Trans-Texas. This photograph was taken in Feb64 at Albuquerque, NM. [Chalmers Johnson]

COLOUR GALLERY

XIII

HB-ISB C-47-DL c/n 4667 - Bought by Classic Air AG in Jan86, this beautiful air-to-air was taken shortly thereafter. It started life with the USAAF in Africa in 1942, returning to the USA for disposal and eleven years with Canadian Pacific Airlines. [Classic Air via A Pearcy]

HB-IRN C-53 c/n 4828 - Although painted in Swissair colours this was never the real HB-IRN, which is c/n 33393 and resides at the Verkehrshaus der Schweiz in Luzern, but came to Germany in 1976 from Finland. Displayed as '65371' on the terminal building roof at Frankfurt for many years, it was moved to Munich's Franz-Josef Strauss airport in 1993 where this photo was taken on 19Jan97. [Frank van Vliet]

NC49551 DC-3 c/n 4940 operated by TWA between 1945 and 1952. [via Airline History Museum]

HR-SAH C-47-DL c/n 6102 - Acquired in 1954 by SAHSA, then registered XH-SAH, this aircraft saw service for nearly forty years with the same owner, becoming HR-SAH in 1961. This photo was taken at La Ceiba, Honduras on 02Mar78, shortly after being repainted in the airline's new colours. [Karl Krämer]

COLOUR GALLERY

XV

TG-AGA C-47-DL c/n 6142 - After serving with the 5th AF in the SW Pacific theatre, this aircraft returned to the USA for disposal to be bought by AVIATECA in 1945. It was at first LG-AGA before re-registration as TG-AGA in 1948, flying as such until it crashed on 18Nov75. This photo was taken on 27Sep59 at San Francisco, CA.
[Doug Olson]

C-FTDJ C-49J c/n 6261 - Still registered in the registration series of its first civil owner Trans-Canada Air Lines, this aircraft flew for the same basic company, Goodyear Tire & Rubber, from 1948 until its withdrawal and presentation to the National Aviation Museum at Rockcliffe in Feb84. The photo was taken during an air-to-air sortie from Toronto, Ont in Oct82. *[Stephen Piercey via P J Marson]*

OH-LCH DC-3A-453 c/n 6346 - Having flown in Finland for Aero O/Y since 1948, a cargo door was installed in 1963 and service with the Finnish AF followed from 1970 until the aircraft was bought by Airveteran in 1986, with whom it was restored to Finnish Airlines colours, and was photographed at Tampere, Finland on 01Jun96. *[Bas Stubert]*

XVI   THE DOUGLAS DC-1, DC-2, DC-3 – THE FIRST SEVENTY YEARS

XA-CUC C-47-DL c/n 7377 - As 42-5683 this aircraft spent its wartime in the USA and found its way to Mexico in 1951 for further government service as XC-ABF. It became XA-CUC in 1973 and was bought eventually by Baja Air with whom it was photographed at Brown Field, TX on 18Oct87.
[Paul Howard]

N81B C-47-DL c/n 7382 was being operated anonymously by Sky Charter Inc with an unusual window configuration when photographed at Opa-Locka, FL on 22 Oct98 - only the fuselage remained there at the end of 2001.
[Andrew Griffiths]

N75142 C-47A-1-DL c/n 9173 - This aircraft has spent most of its civilian life in Alaska, including a period of ten years flying scheduled services and charters with Reeve Aleutian Airways. This photo was taken in Aug73 at Anchorage, AK towards the end of its life with the airline.
[Bruce Drum via P J Marson]

Four R4D-6s were supplied by the US Navy to the **Japan Marine Self Defence Force** from 1958 on, remaining in service until 1974. One of these was an R4D-6Q fitted with electronic countermeasures equipment. They were used by units 205 Atu, 205 Ats and 61FS. All but one were sold. The last (9023) is preserved.

| 9021 | c/n 26088 | 9023 | 33095 |
| 9022 | 26118 | 9024 | 33227 |

JORDAN

The **Royal Jordanian Air Force** used four C-47s between 1967 and 1977 when they were replaced by C-130s and CASA 212s, and then returned to the USAF. The only known details are:-

| 111 | c/n 19460 |
| 112 | |

JUGOSLAVIA - see Yugoslavia

KAMPUCHEA - see Cambodia

KATANGA

During the civil war in the former Belgian Congo in 1961, Katanga seceded and set up an independent air force with at least four C-47s. These included:-

| KAT-02 | c/n 32558 | KAT-4 | 26259 |
| KAT-03 | 32557 | KAT-40 | 20455 |

KOREA, NORTH

During the fifties it has been reported that a small transport formation of the **Korean People's Armed Forces Air Force (KPAFAF)** had about a dozen Li-2s in service. Two (501 and 504) were noted at Pyongyang in 1983.

KOREA, SOUTH

The **Republic of Korea Air Force (ROKAF)** was supplied with a small number of C-47s from USAF stocks in 1954/55. A few of these survived until about 1974, but C-46s and C-123s made up the bulk of transport aircraft. One VC-47D is known, 43-48301 c/n 25562, plus one C-47D 049570/D-7 c/n 26831 and one EC-47Q c/n 20495, stored at Taegu.

LAOS

The **Laotian Army Aviation Service** was supplied initially with six former French C-47s in 1956. During the next ten years or so a dozen more were obtained from sundry sources with most arriving as MAP aid from the United States and by late 1968 there were 16 on strength. In 1969 it was planned to convert four to AC-47 configuration but this plan was abandoned for a more complex solution. Eight former SVNAF C-47s were received in 1969 (five in July, the last in October) and by late Sep69 five had been modified into gunships. The first AC-47 action took place on 07Oct69. The inactivation of the USAF's 3rd SOS at Phan Rang, Vietnam, in 1969 then allowed the direct transfer of eight former 3rd SOS AC-47Ds in Dec69 and by Jan70 a total of 13 were in use.

By late 1970 the total **Royal Laotian Air Force** (as it had become) C-47 strength is said to have been 34 including nine AC-47s (although at least 13 gunships had been received or modified). At least one aircraft was supplied as Australian aid in 1971. Relatively little is known of the movements and fates of these aircraft in subsequent years, although it seems possible that additional USAF AC-47Ds may have been received in 1970 and 1972 (see Vietnam notes). By 1977 the new **Lao People's Army Air Force** was in the process of replacing the C-47s with An-24s, although reports suggest that at least seven survived into the early 'nineties.

The following were known up to 1974 (listed in c/n order):-

998	c/n 9998	30678	13829
24178	10040	100937	19400
976	13608	666	20132

315666	20132	501	26762
O-48159	25420	349685	26946
O-43263	25524 (AC-47D)	322	32654
43-263	25524 (AC-47D)	76510	32842
565	25826 or 26826	632	32964
348704	25965	76644	32976
348909	26170	991	34256
349129	26390	117	34387 (AC-47D)
49356	26617	51127	34397
49468	26729		

348263 (43-263) and 51117 (117) were two of a batch of eight ex-USAF AC-47Ds received in late 1969. The other six are from 349211, 349423, 349516, 476370, 50927, 51047, 51057 and 51121.

Also known is '563' which cannot be identified positively, but is probably the 'last three' of a USAF serial for an unidentified aircraft.

LIBERIA

Two C-47s were reported to be in use with the **Liberian Army/Air Reconnaissance Unit** according to Flight's 1982 survey, probably ex Air Liberia. However they have not been reported for many years.

LIBYA

A number of C-47s were supplied to the **Royal Libyan Air Force** by the USAF when the country was still a kingdom, and despite upheavals since then, it is reported that nine continued in use for navigational training with the **Libyan Republic Air Force** for some years. Two were sold to the Turkish Air Force but none now remain. Those that have been identified are:-

15537	c/n 20003	O-49015	26276
16163	20629	349199	26460
16395	20861	49217	26478
348468	25729	49691	26952

MADAGASCAR

The **Armée de l'Air Madagascar** was equipped initially with one former French aircraft supplied in 1961. Two more followed in 1964 and 1965. In 1969 the first aircraft was returned to France and was replaced by two more former Armée de l'Air aircraft. Five surplus Air Madagascar C-47s were received additionally in the early 1970s. By 1982 at least five remained in service. 5RMMG was supplied from Basler stocks in 1989.

A report during 1995 indicated that most surviving C-47s were stored off the end of the runway at Tamatave. One unknown C-47 crashed, grossly overloaded. Four were sold to Aero Air of South Africa for overhaul in 1998 leaving two of those listed below, one of which crashed.

Call signs and serials have been used, and details are:-

5RMMA	693	c/n 6152	5RMMC	333/MC	12333
5RMMB	216	32548	5RMMD	761/MD	12761
5RMMC	593	26854	5RMME	927/ME	27188
5RMMD	454	26715	5RMMF	726/MF	11726
5RMMA	368/MA	13368	5RMMG	525/MG	19525
5RMMB	104/MB	19104			

MALAWI

The **Malawi Air Wing** has a transport arm which has been reported to possess four C-47s. Two were bought in 1990 from Basler and were placed for sale in 2002.

| 76-20 | c/n 13850 |
| 76-21 | 27005 |

MALI

Two C-47s were supplied by France in 1969 to form part of the Escadrille de Transport of the **Force Aérienne de la République du Mali**. They were TZ341 c/n 9644 and TZ343 c/n 25540, which were withdrawn by

1981 when they were replaced by An-24s. Two Basler BT-67s were ordered in 1996 but the first conversion crashed before delivery, TZ-389 c/n 26002. TZ-389 was re-used on c/n 26744 which was lent to Mali until TZ-390 c/n 19173 was delivered in Sep97. TZ-391 c/n 13383 was the second BT-67, supplied in Jul98.

MAURITANIA

The first **Mauritanian Islamic Air Force/Force Aérienne Islamique de Mauritanie** C-47 was supplied by France in 1962, followed by three others at intervals over the next ten years. Four probably remained in use until about 1978 but Buffalos were delivered during 1979 replacing them. Two Basler BT-67s had been delivered by the end of 2005. Details of call signs and serials were:-

5TMAA	48198	c/n 25459	5TMAE	48990	26251
5TMAB	92871	12720	5TMAF	93715	13657
5TMAC	48032	25293	5TMAH		12543
5TMAD	48383	25644	5TM..		27137

MEXICO

C-47s were delivered to the **Fuerza Aérea Mexicana** in Dec45 where they joined three Lodestars with the Transportation Squadron in Mexico City. One of these is believed to have crashed in 1946 and another in 1947, though it may have returned to the USAAF earlier. The third went back to the USAF in 1948. Six more C-47s were added under ARP in 1947 and another in 1948, to be used on general supply and personnel transport. By 1954 the number in use had grown to 10, two being assigned to the Presidential flight, being replaced by Fairchild F.27s in 1958 and reverting to general government work.

Recently between 7 and 10 C-47s are believed to remain in use, based at Mexico City, some having been added during the seventies to replace older aircraft. Units using C-47s were 8 Grupo Aéreo, Esc Aéreo de Transporte Ejecutivo and 9 Groupo Aéreo Esc Aéreo 311 & 312. In 1979 the executive flights were all merged as UTAPEF - Unidad de Transporte Aéreo del Poder Ejecutivo Federal, but only one C-47 has been identified. The remainder are probably with the Medium Transport Group. Little is known of many early C-47s, and the serial system with prefixes indicating function is somewhat confusing. In recent years C-47s have been taken over from various sources including impounded drug runners. The list below accounts for eight C-47s in service or under overhaul during 1993. The missing numbers in the series below are mostly Curtiss C-46s. By 2000 only one C-47 was believed to survive.

AP-0201	c/n 19409 ?	
AP/TP-0202	43083	
TP-0203		i/s Aug74
TP-304/XC-UPD		was with UTAPEF in Aug79
TED/ETM-6006		i/s Sep50 to 1993 Esc 311 "Plan de Ayala"(Oct76)
TED-6007		i/s Oct71 to Oct79 "Galiana" (Oct76)
TTD-610/6010		i/s Jun48
TTD/ETM-6011	9252	
FAM-6012		
FAM-6013		
TTD-6016		i/s Feb48
TP-6017		
TTD-6020		
TTD-6021		i/s Feb71
TED/FAM-6023		i/s Feb71 to Apr82 "Antonio Cordemas R" (Oct76)
TED-6024		i/s Oct71 to Apr82
TTD/ETM-6025	4383	
TP-6026		
TTD-6028		i/s Jul76 to Apr82
TTD-6032		i/s Jun72
TED-6035		i/s Jul76 to Apr82
TED-6036		i/s Jul76 to Apr82
TED-6037		i/s Jul76 to Apr82
TED/ETM-6040	43076	
ETM-6042	9276	
ETM-6043	4588	
ETM-6044	'198958'	Esc 312, broken up 1993
ETM-6045	3283	
ETM-6046	12647	
ETM-6047		i/s 1993
ETM-6048	25534	
ETM-6049		i/s 1993
ETM-6053	33346	
ETM-6054	25957	
ETM-6055	19238 ?	
ETM-6056	20698	
ETM-2118		very doubtful

ETM = Escuadrón de Transporte Miedano
TED = Transporte Ejecutivo Douglas
TTD = Transporte de Tropas Douglas
AP = Avión Presidencial
TP = Transporte Presidencial

Armada de Mexico, or the Mexican Navy, is known to have had their first C-47 in Oct68, when one was based at Mexico City for general transport duties. By the mid-seventies four were in use, but an F.27 and later a Buffalo had replaced all but one by 1980.

MT-101	c/n	i/s Oct63 to Oct71, possibly then MT-201
MT-201		
MT-202	11815	
MT-203		i/s Sep76
MT-204		i/s Sep76 to Oct79.
MT-330		noted Jan95

C-47s supplied by the USAF were:- c/n 10154 (05Oct47); 12715 (05Oct47); 13770 (30Sep47); 18989 (05Oct47); 19015 (03Aug48); 19097 (19Sep47) and 19376 (14Sep47). The early deliveries were 44-77255 and 45-1017 on 13Dec45, salvaged 22Dec50, plus 45-968 crashed 26Oct47. Two accidents have been reported, one a w/o in Oct53 and another w/o on 02Oct46 at Hermosillo.

MONGOLIA

A number of Li-2s are known to have been supplied to **Air Force of the Mongolian People's Republic** by Russia in the years immediately after the end of WWII. Noted were 501 and 504.

MOROCCO

The **Forces Armées Royales Marocaines** acquired its first C-47 from Royal Air Maroc in 1959 followed by a second from commercial sources in 1961. Six surplus USAF aircraft were then received in 1962. Between 1963 and 1971 at least another five were acquired from commercial and MAP sources. The survivors (ten in number) were sold in Jul78 to Euroworld for delivery to the USA, though some did not get that far. Known aircraft, with call signs and serials are:-

CNALA	42-5682	c/n 7376	CNALH	05936	34198
CNALB	76607	32939	CNALI	292136	11903
CNALC	316141	20607	CNALJ	49819	27080
CNALD	49206	26467	CNALK	13139	13139
CNALE	05928	34189	CNALM	20669	10073
CNALF	49436	26697	CNALN	348310	25571
CNALG	49493	26754			

Note that CN-ALL was a Potez 841.

MOZAMBIQUE

About five ex-Portuguese Air Force C-47s were taken over by the **Mozambique Air Arm** when independence was gained, but not all of these are known. All have been derelict for some years now.

CR-AHB	c/n 9948	FP-501	
75-15	10076	FP-502	20111
6170	11698		

MUSCAT & OMAN

The **Sultan of Oman's Air Force** used two C-47s briefly from 1968 to 1970 when they were traded in to buy Caribous. They were:-

501	c/n 26977
502	10201

CHAPTER 3: MILITARY OPERATORS OF THE DC-3, C-47, R4D, DAKOTA AND LI-2

NEPAL

Two DC-3s were used by the **Royal Nepal Air Force/Royal Army of Nepal**, based at Kathmandu. They were 9N-RF2 c/n 25471 and 9N-RF10 c/n 9950. The latter crashed on 13Sep72 near Panchkhall, Nepal.

NETHERLANDS

The **Koninklijke Luchtmacht/Marine Luchtvaartdienst** used C-47s fairly widely, both in Europe and in the East Indies. The first were used for communications during the latter part of the war by the Dutch Transport Flight, and most of these were handed over to KLM in 1946 to resume services (see NL- series). Within Europe two early aircraft (X-1 and X-2) were obtained commercially in the late 'forties followed by sixteen MDAP aircraft in 1952 from Belgium (the re-used X-2 to X-5) and the RAF (X-6 to X-17). These aircraft entered service with 334 Sq at Valkenburg wearing the large side codes 'ZU-1' etc (the use of these codes was abandoned in Sep59). The squadron moved to Ypenburg in late 1957 where the C-47s were replaced eventually by F.27 Troopships in 1960. In Indonesia 321 Sq of the MLD (Navy) used 15 C-47s at Biak until Feb50 when its Dakota flight became 8 Sq (at Biak). These aircraft were passed originally to the Dutch in 1945 wearing the 'Q' serials (listed below) that later became the 'W' series. In Feb46 this KLU sequence was abandoned and replaced by the MLD sequence 23-2 to 23-16. Their use was brief and most passed into Indonesian ownership in 1950.

When 334 Sq released its C-47s in 1960 two were passed to the MLD's 321 Sq at Biak as 018 and 019 in February followed by two more in May as 078 and 079 (these were previously vacant serials in the new 1959-vintage MLD system). The rest were withdrawn from use and disposed of in 1961-62. In Oct61 the KLU formed 336 Sq at Biak and received the three surviving MLD aircraft from 321 Sq (now returned to 'X' serials) as well as two new aircraft from Australia in late 1962 (X-18 and X-19). However, 336 Sq disbanded almost immediately in Oct62 when the Dutch transferred their last local territories to Indonesia and the C-47s were withdrawn and disposed of.

The serial lists below also include the range DT-937 to DT-992. These aircraft were used by the **Netherlands East Indies Army** between 1944 and 1950 (surviving aircraft were re-numbered with 'T' prefixes in May48 and DT-982 to DT-992 became NI-471 to NI-480 and NI-470). They were used by 19 and 20 Squadrons until May48 when 19 Sq disbanded. 20 Sq survived until 1950. The Indonesian Air Force (AURI) accepted the survivors, some 23 or so having earlier passed to Interinsulair Bedrijf (a KLM subsidiary, later Garuda) in Aug47.

Details are:-

Dutch Transport Flight (1316 Flight, RAF):-
NL201	c/n 2022		NL206	12767
NL202	1980		NL207	19785
NL203	1584		NL208	12953
NL204	12173		NL209	19510
NL205	20597		NL210	12734

All DC-3 except NL 203 (DC-2).

Netherlands Air Force (Europe):-
X-1	c/n		X-10/ZU-10	26714
X-2/(1)	19795		X-11/ZU-11	32613
X-2/ZU-2(2)	20879		X-12/ZU-12	33248
X-3/ZU-3	32632		X-13/ZU-13	33285
X-4/ZU-4	26996		X-14/ZU-14	33289
X-5/ZU-5	33323		X-15/ZU-15	25608
X-6/ZU-6	32657		X-16/ZU-16	26104
X-7/ZU-7	33252		X-17/ZU-17	33411
X-8/ZU-8	33415		X-18	25367
X-9/ZU-9	33362		X-19	9815

X-1 was bt 29Feb52; cr 06Feb53 at Valkenburg

Netherlands Navy (MLD):-
Q-1	VHPAA	c/n 19705
Q-2/W-2	VHPAB	13123
Q-3/W-3	VHPAC	9518
Q-4/W-4	VHPAD	19902
Q-5/W-5	VHPAE	9753
Q-6/W-6	VHPAF	9727
Q-7/W-7	VHPAG	25489
Q-8/W-8	VHPAH	13503
Q-9/W-9	VHPAI	9399
Q-10/W-10	VHPAJ	13493
Q-11/W-11	VHPAK	13616
Q-12/W-12	VHPAL	13210
Q-13/W-13	VHPAM	12664
Q-14/W-14	VHPAN	11804
Q-15/W-15	VHPAO	9808
Q-16/W-16	VHPAP	9583
018		26996
23-019		33323
078		32613
079		33285

Q-2/W-2 to Q-16/W-16 became 23-2 to 23-16 in Feb46. Q-1 crashed on delivery.

Netherlands East Indies AF:-
DT-937	VHRDG	c/n 12036	
DT-938	VHRDH	11972	
DT-939	VHRDI	12279	
DT-940	VHRDJ	12097	
DT-941	VHRDK	12880	
DT-942	VHRDL	12878	
DT-943	VHRDM	13344	
DT-944	VHRDN	13345	
DT-945	VHRDY	32691	
DT-946	VHRDZ	32692	
DT-947	VHREA	33128	
DT-948	VHREB	33130	
DT-949	VHREC	33475	
DT-950	VHRED	33477	
DT-951	VHREE	9281	
DT-952	VHREF	13207	
DT-953	VHREG	6032	
DT-954	VHREH	6199	
DT-955	VHREI		
DT-956	VHREJ		b/u 1946
DT-957	VHREK	20669 ?	
DT-958	VHREL	27132	
DT-959	VHREM	9550	
DT-960	VHREN		
DT-961	VHREO		b/u 1946
DT-962	VHREP	13497	
DT-963	VHREQ	12636	
DT-964	VHRER	25496	
DT-965	VHRES		cr 26Feb47, Southport, Australia
DT-966	VHRET		b/u 1946
DT-967	VHREU	13607	
DT-968	VHREV		b/u 1946
DT-969	VHREW		b/u 1946
DT-970	VHREX	20407	
DT-971	VHREY	20041	
DT-972	VHREZ		cr 12Mar47, Boerangpang, NEI
DT-973	VHRCO	19690	
DT-974	VHRCP	19719	
DT-975	VHRCQ	19623	
DT-976	VHRCR	19611	
DT-977	VHRCT	13639	
DT-978	VHRCU	19672	
DT-979	VHRCV	19844	
DT-980	VHRCW	12933	
DT-981	VHRCY	13731	
DT-982	VHRCZ	19005	
DT-983	VHRCA	13619	
DT-984	VHRCB	19279	
DT-985	VHRCC	12719	
DT-986	VHRCD	13463	
DT-987	VHRCE	13535	
DT-988	VHRCF	19658	
DT-989	VHRCG	13766	
DT-990	VHRCH	13052	
DT-991	VHRCI	12514	
DT-992	VHRCJ	42954	

Note: Douglas give c/n 42954 as DT-993, but all other sources give DT-992. C/n 4706 was used as a spares source, and c/n 18938 also went to the NEIAF.

NEW ZEALAND

The **Royal New Zealand Air Force** received its first Dakotas under the Lend-Lease programme in Feb43 and by the end of 1945, 49 had been taken on charge. These were operated by 40 and 41 Transport Squadrons and detached flights served in forward areas in the Pacific war zones. Five were lost in accidents before the end of 1945. Thereafter the type was run down steadily by sale or scrapping, and many went to National Airways. Bristol Freighters and Handley Page Hastings replaced the Dakotas of 41 Sq in the early fifties, but 42 Sq kept six in service until they were replaced finally by Andovers in 1977. Some of the last were, in fact, those returned to the RNZAF by National when this operator retired the type. A summary of Dakota serial numbers follows:-

NZ3501	c/n 9111	NZ3535	32695
NZ3502	9418	NZ3536	32696
NZ3503	9420	NZ3537	32895
NZ3504	9419	NZ3538	32897
NZ3505	9422	NZ3539	32899
NZ3506	9421	NZ3540	32896
NZ3516	12545	NZ3541	33131
NZ3517	12546	NZ3542	33134
NZ3518	13099	NZ3543	33135
NZ3519	13088	NZ3544	33315
NZ3520	25373	NZ3545	33316
NZ3521	25374	NZ3546	33313
NZ3522	25375	NZ3547	33478
NZ3523	25376	NZ3548	33480
NZ3524	25377	NZ3549	33482
NZ3525	26006	NZ3550	33481
NZ3526	26007	NZ3551	34223
NZ3527	26008	NZ3552	34222
NZ3528	26649	NZ3553	34225
NZ3529	26650	NZ3554	34226
NZ3530	26651	NZ3555	34224
NZ3531	27144	NZ3556	34227
NZ3532	27146	NZ3557	34228
NZ3533	27145	NZ3558	34229
NZ3534	32693		

Instructional airframes:

INST 114	9111	INST 117	13099

NICARAGUA

The DC-3 has served with the **Fuerza Aérea de Nicaragua** since 1948, but throughout that period there has been no clear distinction between their aircraft and those of the National Guard and the airline LANICA, all of which were controlled by the Somoza family. The first C-47s were seized by the government from the Costa Rican airline LACSA in Jun48 and passed on to the National Guard. They were returned to LACSA in 1951 and little is known of their use in Nicaragua. They were all sold after return. During the 1950s four C-47s were supplied to the FAN under MAP, further aircraft being acquired regularly until May76, when six were reported. A few may have been destroyed in the civil war, and in 1980 the name was changed to **Fuerza Aérea Sandinista**, and recently only two remained in service. Apart from aircraft with FAN serial numbers, at least two with civil marks have been used:

208	c/n	
410		i/s Nov66 to Feb79
411		i/s Dec68
412		i/s Feb67 to Mar75
414		i/s Feb72 to Feb79
416		i/s Nov71 to Feb79
417	12780	
418		del 19May76, i/s Feb79
203		i/s 1994
AN-ASP	4519	
AN-AWT	4174	

A C-47 was reported to have crashed near Quilali, 65km south of Honduras on 28Aug84.

NIGER

The **Force Aérienne du Niger** received one C-47 in Dec61, followed by three more by 1969. By 1980 it was reported that three were in store and the fourth had been sold. Call signs and serials were:-

5UMAA	18474	c/n 4566	5UMAC	48280	25541
5UMAB	48990	26251	5UMAD	77069	33401

NIGERIA

The **Federal Nigerian Air Force** took over the remaining Nigerian Airways C-47s in 1967 at the start of the civil war with Eastern Nigeria.

Five more were bought from Sabena in 1969. They were replaced by C-130Hs in 1971 and the survivors were all dumped at Lagos in 1972, to be broken up in 1978.

'AAL'	c/n 25364	NAF303	25292
'AAM'	6071	NAF304	20776
'AAN'	13606	NAF305	12318
'AAP'	13304	NAF306	9865
'AAQ'	9874	NAF307	12767

Note: 5N-AAK was impounded at Enugu on 05Apr67 after a scheduled flight from Lagos and was never 'AAK' with the Nigerian Air Force.

NORTH KOREA - see Korea (North)

NORTH YEMEN - see Yemen (North)

NORWAY

The **Royal Norwegian Air Force** received ten C-47s in Apr-Sep45. These were passed to DNL in 1946. A further aircraft, c/n 12447, was acquired in 1947 in a damaged state, for fire practice as an instructional airframe, marked 10412. Ten more were supplied under the MDAP in 1950 for use by 335 Sq at Gardermoen, replacing Lodestars. Of these, six were passed to the Royal Danish Air Force in 1956, three were sold in the USA in 1975, and one has been preserved for the Air Force Museum. Call signs were allotted to the later aircraft. In full, these were, for example 'JWBWC', but only the last three letters were painted on.

215558	c/n 7353	'O'
23802	9664	'S'
223923	9785	'V'
268711	11638	'P'
268770	11697	'R'
93797	13749	'T-AO', 'BW-D/L'
30673	13824	'Z'
2100591	19054	'T-AI', 'BW-I/K'
2100737	19200	'T-AP', BW-P'
2100838	19291	'T-AU', 'BW-C'
100995	19458	'U'
2101012	19475	'T-AR', BW-D/R'
315208	19674	'T-AM', 'BW-M'
315211	19677	'T-AL', BW-B/S'
315545	20011	'T'
315553	20019	'X'
315613	20079	'T-AK', 'BW-K'
315652	20118	'T-AN', 'BW-N/T'
316096	20562	'Y'
48247	25508	'T-AS', 'BW-E/N'

PAKISTAN

The **Pakistan Air Force** used in excess of 20 former RAF Dakotas from 1947. They were transferred from Indian stocks at the time of partition and initially equipped 6 Sq at Drigh Road and later Mauripur. They were used until 1950 when they were withdrawn into storage at 102 MU Drigh Road to be replaced by (unsuitable) Bristol Freighters. In part consequence some were later taken from storage and were then used by 12 (Composite) Sq, Mauripur, until final retirement from the PAF in 1955. Many of the survivors were sold to Field Aircraft Services for overhaul and re-sale. In service use one aircraft had been equipped for VIP work.

H-701	c/n 26089	H-712	32761
H-702		H-713	25802
H-703		H-714	33517 ?
H-704	33517 ?	H-715	
H-705		H-716	33564
H-706	12498	H-717	32945
H-707		H-718	27108
H-708		H-719	25793
H-709	33277	C-400	12813
H-710	27114	C-406	25309
H-711		C-407	33246

C/ns 27189 and 32867 were also supplied to Pakistan, in Feb48 and Nov47 respectively. Only one of the above can be identified positively as coming from the VP series (see India). Three others were VP902 c/n 9326, VP907 c/n 12499 and VP918 probably c/n 13568. An unknown C-47 was preserved at Islamabad in 1991. H-702 was sold in France 03Apr56.

CHAPTER 3: MILITARY OPERATORS OF THE DC-3, C-47, R4D, DAKOTA AND LI-2

PANAMA

Until Jan69, when the **Fuerza Aérea Panamena** was established, Panama relied on the USAF to provide defence needs. The first two DC-3s were supplied in 1969 for presidential transport, followed in Jan70 by a further two to operate a countrywide support network. One of the latter C-47s flew in the colours of Transporte Aereo Militar. Early in 1975 two C-47s were replaced by Twin Otters and transferred to a government agency, but the others survived until about 1980, when one crashed.

201		del Jan69. This and 202 are believed to have been HP-291 and HP-11, possibly in that order. i/s Feb 78
202		del Jan69
203	20436	
204	10267	

One C-47, reported as 210, but probably 201, crashed on 27Aug80.

PAPUA NEW GUINEA

Four Dakotas were supplied from RAAF stocks in 1975/76, when the **Papua New Guinea Defence Force** was founded. A further aircraft (A65-122 c/n 33455) was delivered for ground instruction in 1980 and two more (A65-63 and A65-65) were due in 1981, but only the first was used. Initially the Dakotas were numbered P65-001 etc, but changed to P-001 etc., and finally P2-001 on. P2-005 was sold in Australia and the remainder stored pending sale, which took place in 1994, some again in Australia.

P2-001	c/n 33109		P2-004	27130
P2-002	32877		P2-005	26001
P2-003	26638			

PARAGUAY

The Paraguayan government started operating social services within the country in the late forties, using Beech C-45s and Bonanzas. In Mar54 they were coordinated under Transporte Aéreo Militar, when the first C-47 was delivered. Three more were supplied in Jun55 and there were five in use by mid-1957. In the early sixties two more followed under MAP and another came from the USAF mission. Four more were supplied in 1964 and five in 1967, again under MAP. These were supplemented by a DC-6 and a Convair T-29. Initially the C-47s were numbered from T-21 to T-85 (odd numbers only), but in 1980 the **Fuerza Aérea del Paraguay** adopted a new system from 2001 to 2023. 32 aircraft were known in the T- series and 15 in the new sequence, of which 12 were in use in 1982, and four in 1993. In April 2000 one was airworthy and three others in store.

T-21	c/n	i/s 1953 to Nov76	T-57	20857	to 2024
T-23		i/s Apr55. To 2003. C/n quoted 15378 i.e. 28623	T-59	34347	
			T-61	34263	to 2012
			T-63	12850	to 2015
			T-65	13621	to 2017
			T-67	12190	
T-25	2183		T-69	27148	to 2016
T-27	19246	to 2005	T-71	25757	to 2014
T-31		i/s Jan79	T-73	32774	to 2022
T-35	4362	to 2007	T-75	26610	to 2019
T-37	34346	to 2009	T-77	25961	to 2021
T-39	19438		T-79	26068	to 2026
T-41	19002	to 2004	T-81	32630	to 2010
T-43	9517	to 2011	T-83	34320	to 2020
T-45	25936	to 2006	T-85	34376	to 2023
T-47	32926	2013 ntu	2028	33415	
T-49	26900		2030	12557	
T-51	34380	to 2008	2032	27098	
T-53	34208	2018 ntu	2034	26922	
T-55	26825	to 2025			

The **Paraguayan Navy** used T-26 c/n 13469.

PERU

The first three C-47s were delivered to the **Fuerza Aérea del Perú** in 1946, a further three in 1948 and three more in the early fifties. These were used mainly by the 41st Transport Squadron at Limatambo to operate the Transportes Aéreos Militares mountain and jungle social services, replacing the Faucett F.19, DH.89A and Grumman Goose. They were also used for military supply work between coastal cities. In 1960 TAM was re-formed as Servicio Aéreo de Transportes Comerciales (SATCO), with 7 C-47s and 3 C-46s. These were placed on the civil register where they are indexed in this volume. SATCO itself remained the 41st Squadron, forming part of the larger Grupo 8.

Two more C-47s were transferred to SATCO in 1961 and another two in 1963. At the same time a further 16 C-47s were supplied under MAP, 4 in 1962, 2 in 1963 and 10 in 1964, all assigned to Grupo 8, now based at Jorge Chavez in Cillao. Some operated away from base for long periods, particularly at Iquitos and Talara. They also provided the weekly Tacna-Lima diplomatic link with Chile. As routes were developed by TAM many passed to Faucett and in 1973 SATCO was reorganised as Aero Perú and the C-47s returned to the FAP with the introduction of F.27s and F.28s. Many of the C-47s had high hours and were withdrawn from use at this time. In 1977/78 16 An-26s were delivered and almost all the remaining C-47s were withdrawn from use, although a few continued in service into 1983.

Serial numbers were initially a complex Squadron/type/serial number, but no C-47s are known in this sequence. In the late forties a three-digit sequence was adopted, in order of acquisition. Finally in 1960 a new sequence, starting at 300 for transports, and prefixed by the year of delivery, was started. In a final change, late in the life of the Peruvian C-47s, the delivery-year prefix was dropped for all aircraft types.

Series one:-

403	c/n		488	4800
424			489	2192
483	34270		552	
484			677	34369
485	11718		696	4830
486	20057		697	11771
487	4177			

403 crashed on 16Nov54 at Jirishanga, Cerro de Pasco and 484 crashed on 09Jan58 nr Rioja. The gaps in the above series were probably filled by c/n 10155 and 19174 (del 18Feb48), 34269 (del 22Mar47) and 34271 (del 27Mar47). Two other crashes occurred on 24Feb49 at Cuzco and 20Jan51 at Pulco, Sacsara. One more supplied to FAP flew in civil marks only (c/n 20546).

Series two:-

47-301	c/n 34270		62-357	25273
55-302	11718		62-358	25342
48-303	20057		63-359	19269
55-304	4177		63-360	19679
49-305	4800		64-364	20530
50-306	2192		64-365	13843
53-307	25986		64-366	9994
58-311	34369		64-367	19749
60-314	4830		64-368	13743
60-315	11771		64-369	20177
47-319			64-370	13049
61-320	26683		64-371	20566
62-355	19532		64-372	13774
62-356	20009		64-373	18994

The Peruvian Navy or **Armada Peruana** operated a few aircraft for liaison work and coastal patrol in the early sixties and acquired their first DC-3 in 1965 plus one from Faucett in 1966. About eleven have seen service, mostly acquired from the Peruvian AF. These were used to supply naval ports along the Pacific coast, and also for patrol work until F.27s were delivered. Five were believed to remain in service in 1983, and one probably by 1988.

502	c/n 9980
503	
AT-510	
AT-511	
AT-512	i/s Apr72
AT-513	i/s Apr72
AT-520	i/s Aug73 to Mar79
AT-521	i/s Feb65 to Jul88. To ET-521.
AT-522	i/s Feb65 to Oct73
AT-523	i/s Dec73
AT-524	i/s Mar79
AT-528	i/s May85

Other known c/ns are 32737 and 34328.

PHILIPPINE REPUBLIC

The **Philippine Air Force (Hukbong Himpapawid NG Pilipinas)** was formed in Jul46 with about 30 C-47s supplied from local USAAF stocks. Small numbers of additional aircraft were received in the 'fifties but the next significant delivery took place in 1962-63 when at least 14 aircraft were received from the US. There were then few additions until the early 'seventies when further surplus USAF and Australian (two) aircraft were received between 1973 and 1976. One batch of about 20 surplus SVNAF C-47s ferried to Clark AFB in Jan73 has proved difficult to rationalise with approximately six aircraft reported to have entered PAF service, four going to an unidentified country (perhaps the Philippines) as MAP aid, seven having been broken-up at Clark and at least two definitely going to Thailand. Further deliveries included at least five from surplus USAF stocks in Thailand in 1974, two ex-SVNAF aircraft in 1975 and probably the last two ex-USAF aircraft in 1976.

At least 67 aircraft can be identified definitely from the records as having been used by the Philippine AF but clearly the in-service number at any given time was far lower. The 206th and 207th Air Transport Squadrons at Nichols AFB typically used about 18 during the 'sixties. Other units included the 303rd Air Reconnaissance Squadron within the 204th Composite Wing and some aircraft are reported to have been used by the 901st Weather Squadron. The 303rd ARS is reported to have used 'AC-47s' at some stage, but it should be noted that no former USAF/SVNAF AC-47Ds have been identified by serial number as delivered to or serving with the PAF and it is assumed that locally-modified aircraft were used in the attack/gunship role. By 1982 only five aircraft remained airworthy and these were stored and subsequently sold.

223417	c/n 9279	316113	20579
223493	9355	316140	20606
223643	9505	316163	20629
223663	9525	316310	20776
223789	9651	316324	20790
223907	9769	347964	25225
224260	10122	348064	25325
292257	12037	348076	25337
293246	13136	348154	25415
293565	13491	348229	25490
293673	13611	348301	25562
330717	13868	348476	25737
330737	13888	348599	25860
2100494	18957	349029	26290
2100791	19254	349387	26648
2100925	19388	349497	26758
315068	19534	349753	27014
315237	19703	349756	27017
315268	19734	349900	27161
315272	19738	349902	27163
315325	19791	349908	27169
315429	19895	349909	27170
315450	19916	349910	27171
315480	19946	349911	27172
315584	20050	476432	32764
315586	20052	476558	32890
315601	20067	476632	32964
315604	20070	476962	33294
315686	20152	477138	33470
315743	20209	477141	33473
315777	20243	477155	33487
315891	20357	477201	33533
316091	20557		

POLAND

Two C-47s were supplied to Poland in 1947 (c/ns 9106 and 9165) possibly as spares for LOT and others were operated initially by the **Polish Air Force/Polski Wojska Litnicze**, prior to transfer to LOT (qv). Apart from these the following aircraft are known to have gone to the Polish AF:- c/ns 9257, 9898, 12531, 12704*, 12774, 13144, 13146, 13217, 13348*, 13349*, 13552*, 19525 and 19580. Those marked * came from aircraft initially supplied to Russia and may have been used before the end of WWII by a Polish unit. Others came from USAAF surplus stocks in Europe. Apart from these Russia supplied a quantity of Li-2s which were used by the Air Force and some then transferred to LOT, as with the C-47s. Li-2s remained in service as late as 1965, being returned to the air force by LOT. Code numbers were used by the air force, but were subject to change.

01	c/n 184 362 03	(Li-2)	
02(1)	184 362 04	(Li2F)	later 39
03(1)	184 162 08	(Li-2T)	later 3
03(2)	184 362 05	(Li-2F)	
03(3)	234 427 04	(Li-2P)	later 40
04(1)	184 362 06	(Li-2)	later 1 and 44
04(2)	184 391 01	(Li-2T)	later 41 (Li-2F)
05	184 391 02	(Li-2)	later 027
06(1)	184 391 03	(Li-2T)	
07	234 426 09	(Li-2P)	later 42
08	234 426 10	(Li-2P)	later 028
09	234 427 01	(Li-2P)	later 029 and 02(2)
012	234 427 07	(Li-2P)	later 43
014	234 449 05	(Li-2P)	later 06(2)
	184 162 01	(Li-2T)	
10	234 427 02	(Li-2P)	later 026
11	184 161 10	(Li-2T)	later 4
12?	184 162 04	(Li-2T)	
15	184 162 07	(Li-2T)	
	184 197 04	(Li-2T)	
	184 198 02	(Li-2T)	
27	184 381 02	(Li-2)	
63	184 226 10	(Li-2P)	
64	184 232 06	(Li-2P)	

PORTUGAL

Portugal acquired their first C-47 during the war (250, a C-47A), but in all 29 were used by the **Força Aérea Portuguesa**. Ten came from USAF stocks in 1961. Prior to that four were taken over from TAP in 1958 for use by Esquadra 81, and two were supplied from Israel. Then a further twelve came from several African sources, mainly Portuguese colonial territories. A few remained in use with GIPN (Grupo de Instrução de Pilotagem e Navegação) in 1975. By 1978 most had been replaced by CASA 212s and a few remained in Angola and Mozambique, transferring to their respective air forces.

250/6150	c/n 19773	6165	26667
6151	11765	6166	25522
6152	11668	6167	13018
6153	11675	6168	20173
6154	10049	6169	42968
6155	32675	6170	11698
6156	33093	6171	33532
6157	19755	6172	13140
6158	19818	6173	11763
6159	20111	6174	12760
6160	20587	6175	19393
6161	10076	6176	9948
6162	25579	6177	18977
6163	26144	6178	12066
6164	26468		

RHODESIA - See Zimbabwe

ROMANIA

Russia supplied a number of Li-2s to the **Romanian Air Force** in 1951 and these served alongside a few Ju52/3ms and He111Hs. They were replaced by Il-14Ps.

008	c/n 234 410 08	(Li-2P)
102		
502	184 275 02	(Li-2P)
505	184 275 05	(Li-2P)
607		
702	234 447 02	(Li-2T)
802	234 418 02	(Li-2P)
804	184 238 04	(Li-2)
805	184 398 05	(Li-2)
807	184 398 07	(Li-2)
905	234 419 05	(Li-2P)
1001	234 410 01 ?	(Li-2P)
1002	234 410 02 ?	(Li-2P)
1003	234 410 03 ?	(Li-2P)
1004*	234 410 04	(Li-2P)
4506	234 445 06	(Li-2P)
8002	184 280 02	(Li-2P)
8004	184 280 04	(Li-2P)
	234 448 03	(Li-2)

* later 004

CHAPTER 3: MILITARY OPERATORS OF THE DC-3, C-47, R4D, DAKOTA AND LI-2

RUSSIA

Under Lend-Lease the Soviet Union was supplied with about 700 C-47s between Jan43 and the end of the war. These were delivered via the short route from Alaska to Siberia. American crews ferried them to Fairbanks, where the **Soviet Air Force** took delivery. So far as is known, two aircraft crashed on delivery before hand-over, but virtually nothing is known of subsequent use in the Soviet AF. A few were passed to Aeroflot for use on the internal sectors, and others went to Poland and some were also used on airline operations into Iran in the late forties. So far as military use is concerned, the C-47s (sometimes referred to as Si-47s) were used alongside the Li-2s, although probably not in the same units, due to lack of spares commonality. Because of a shortage of spares post-war, the C-47 probably faded out of service long before the Li-2.

USAAF records indicate those C-47s which were diverted to Russia and the following is a list of their c/ns:- 4765/68/70/71/99,6000/01/02/04/05, 6228 to 6237 incl; 7367, 9016 to 9025 incl; 9112 to 9121 incl; 9293 to 9302 incl; 9423 to 9441 incl; 9598 to 9615 incl; 9837 to 9854 incl; 10002 to 10016 incl; 11879/81/84 to 11887/89 to 11897/99 to 11902/29/30/34 to 37/39 to 11947/49 to 11957/59 to 11966/69; 12030 to 12034/46; 12117 to 12136 incl; 12224 to 12227 incl; 12229 to 12237 incl; 12239 to 12245 incl; 12390 to 12392 incl; 12394 to 12410 incl; 12599 to 12608 incl; 12698 to 12707 incl; 12796/97/99 to 12806; 12881 to 12890 incl; 12993 to 13002 incl; 13089 to 13098 incl; 13211 to 13220 incl; 13346 to 13355 incl; 13548/50/52/53/54/75; 25378 to 25391 incl; 25687 to 25704 incl; 25903 to 25912 incl; 26009 to 26018 incl; 26225 to 26234 incl; 26314 to 26323 incl; 26327 to 26336 incl; 26543 to 26552 incl; 26652 to 26657 incl; 26659 to 26662 incl; 26844 to 26853 incl; 26929 to 26938 incl; 27055 to 27062 incl; 27064/65; 27147/49 to 27153 incl; 27155 to 27158 incl; 32599/600; 32602 to 32604/06 to 08/10/11; 32697/99 to 32701/03 to 05/07 to 09; 32797 to 32801/04 to 32808; 32900 to 32905; 32907 to 09/11; 33004/08/11/15/17/22/26/29/33/36/40/44/47/51/55/59/63/67/70/ 74/77/81/84/88/91/94/98; 33101/04/08/11/14/17/20/22/25/29/32/36/39/ 42/45/48/51/54/58/62/66/69/73/77/81/84/93/95/98; 33202/05/08/12/14/ 18/22/29/31/34/37/40/54/58/64/68/71/74/80/84/88/93/96/98; 33311/18/ 24/30/33/34/39/42/47/50/54/56/61/66/70/74/77/80/83/87/91/95/98; 33402/05/09/13/17/20/24/27/32/35/39/42/46/50/54/58/62/ 65/69/72/76/ 79/83/86/90/93/97; 33500 to 33516 incl; 33522 to 33531 incl; 34156 to 34167 incl; 34169 to 34176 incl; 34232/33/35/37-42/44-48/51/52; 34304/07/08/10/19/21/22/24.

Known Soviet AF serials, where worn, followed the USAAF form; e.g., 349894 for c/n 27155 that visited Croydon, UK on 08Nov45.

Apart from C-47s, the Soviet AF must have used the majority of the Li-2s built before batch 161, but few c/ns have come to light. The constructor's number was usually applied externally, on the fin.

Li-2s known to have been operated by the Soviet AF have been summarised below courtesy of the authors of the excellent 'More than Half a Century of Soviet Transports', 4th edition, July 2004, to which readers are recommended.

c/n 1841314 (PS-84); 1843603 (PS-84); 1846310; 1846602 (Li-2VP); 18411906 (Li-2NK); 18412004; 18414808; 18416602 (Li-2VP); 18421001 (Li-2T); 18424702; 18426105; 18430005.

External numerical/colour markings have been identified as follows:

001	234 440 07	
01	184 386 06	
01 yellow	184 334 10	(Li-2T)
01 yellow	184 381 01	later 17 yellow
02	184 379 03	
02 yellow	234 441 01	
03	234 438 04	
03 yellow	234 416 05	(Li-2T)
05 red	184 332 05	(Li-2T)
05 yellow	234 412 01	(Li-2T)
06	184 392 01	
6 red	184 87 03	
07	234 442 09	
08 yellow	234 406 03	(Li-2REO)
08 yellow	234 434 08	(Li-2T)
09 red	234 442 05	(Li-2T)
011 white	234 423 03	(Li-2P)
17 white	184 96 06	
021 blue	234 425 05	(Li-2T)
39	184 188 09	(Li-2T) later 08 yellow
55 yellow	234 407 06	(Li-2T)
1052	184 110 52	
4026	184 40 26	
4027	184 40 27	
5408	184 54 08	(PS-84VP)

Unidentified Li-2s have been recorded as follows:

I-897; 4117; L4171; N-455 white; 03 red, 04 red, 22, 25, 40, 50 white, 490 white, 1004 black, 4054 white (PS-84).

RWANDA

Two C-47s were reported in use by the **Force Aérienne Rwandaise** during 1982. Their origin is uncertain but they may have come from the United Nations which used a number in that area after the civil war.

SAUDI ARABIA

C-47s were supplied to the **Royal Saudi Air Force** by the USAF under MDAP in 1952. Re-use of registrations and (probably) serials has made positive identification difficult. 402 and 403 are thought to have previously been HZ-AAN(1) and HZ-AAQ(1), and to have become HZ-AAB/C c/n 25276 and 32978, respectively. HZ-AAL(1) is believed to have become 401 and may be the a/c reported on the dump at Jeddah in Sep80. HZ-AAL(2) has also been reported as 451 c/n 11861. The RAF supplied c/n 25287 in Mar47.

SENEGAL/SENEGAMBIA

Eight C-47s have been used by **Armée de l'Air du Sénégal/Sénégambia**. All came from French sources between 1961 and 1973, some from Air France. They were sold to France or the USA in 1986.

6WSAA	348336	c/n 25597	6WSAE	293510	13430
6WSAB	476356	32688	6WSAF	2100611	19074
6WSAC	38748	6207	6WSAG	48555	25816
6WSAD	76746	33078	6VAAE	13836	25281

SOMALIA

Four C-47s were in use between 1960 and 1982, mostly transferred to the **Somalian Aeronautical Corps** from the Italian Air Force units based there before independence. These retained their earlier serial numbers.

MM61767	c/n	coded AS-4
MM61816	26646	coded AS-4
MM61824	4506	coded AS-5
	13111	coded AS-6?

SOUTH AFRICA

The first Dakotas arrived in South Africa in Jun43 and between then and Jul45, 58 were delivered direct from the USA from RAF orders and allotted **South African Air Force (SAAF)** serial numbers 6801 to 6858. They were operated by 5 (Transport) Wing, mainly on the shuttle service between South and North Africa and later into Italy. 28 Sq was formed at Almaza, Egypt in Jul43 and received five Dakotas from RAF stocks from 29Jul (along with Ansons and Wellingtons). This was followed on 27Apr44 by 44 Sq which was formed a month earlier from 43 Sq. Both units operated under RAF command on services within the Mediterranean area, as far as Karachi in the east and Takoradi in the west. Four of the Dakotas used were detached to help 267 Sq RAF carry supplies behind enemy lines in the Balkans and bring out wounded. All the Dakotas used retained their RAF serial numbers. 44 Sq was disbanded at Bari, Italy on 05Dec45, but 28 Sq returned to South Africa with its 26 Dakotas in Oct45, joining 5 Wing in carrying home troops. These aircraft were transferred to the SAAF, becoming 6859 to 6884.

A list of Dakotas issued to 28 Sq and 44 Sq while attached to the RAF is provided towards the end of this section.

With the end of the war 5 Wing was disbanded and most of the Dakotas put into store at 15 AD (Air Depot), just 15 being retained by 28 Sq. A few were used by 60 Sq between 1948 and 1950 for aerial survey work and also by the Photographic Flight. 44 Sq was re-formed from 25 Sq in Nov53 with Dakotas, as an Active Citizen Force (ACF) unit. In Jan63 28 Sq was re-equipped with C-130 Hercules and the Dakotas passed to 44 Sq. The Air Navigation School also operated Dakotas at this time.

In Feb68 the VIP flight of 28 Sq was renumbered 21 Sq with three VIP Dakotas but these were replaced by HS.125s in 1970. Also in 1968, 25 Sq was formed from the Ysterplaat Station Flight as an inshore reconnaissance unit, using Dakotas. The most recent unit to use Dakotas was the Multi Engine Training Unit (METU), now known as 86 AFS. There were 47 Dakotas left in 1994, serving with 25 Sq at Ysterplaat, 44 Sq at Swartkop (also with DC-4s) and 86 AFS at Bloemspruit. These include five bought from South African Airways in 1971 (6885 to 6889) and several others bought clandestinely to avoid sanctions. These included five from the RNZAF via the Comores in 1977 (incl 6890, 6891, 6871 and 6880). The last two had re-used serial numbers. Most Dakotas were camouflaged and saw active service in the war against Angola and in the Namibian border campaign. When the Shackletons were retired, 35 Sq was re-equipped with Dakotas modified with radar in the nose.

Some SAAF Dakotas were sold but 34 were rebuilt with extended fuselages and PT-6A-65 engines (indicated below by TP). However, by 1998 many of those converted had been sold in the USA to Dodson Aviation Inc of Ottawa, KS - some in a dismantled state. 19 C-47TPs remained in service at the end of 2000 (marked * below), with two more R-1830 Dakotas (6832 and 6859) in museums. A few remained active in 2003, but most had been placed in store by 2001, with seven fuselages stored at Wonderboom by Nov03, encoded by F-1 to F-7 and other markings:

F-1	c/n 12166	(Unit 581)	F-5	33552	(DC-3-1)
F-2	27199	(DC-3-2)	F-6	32825	
F-3	33134		F-7	12582	(Unit 848)
F-4	33478				

Index of SAAF Dakotas:-

6801	c/n 9492		6847	26115
6802	9628		6848	26438
6803	9629		6849	26439
6804	9630		6850(1)	26746
6805	9877		6850(2)	27099
6806	9878		6851	26745
6807	9879		6852* TP	27002
6808	10106		6853 TP	27199
6809	10104		6854* TP	32635
6810	10105		6855(1)	32937
6811* TP	11986		6855(2) TP	32961
6812	11987		6856	33373
6813	11989		6857 TP	33375
6814* TP	11990		6858(1)	33376
6815	12016		6858(2) TP	32897
6816 TP	12112		6859*	12586
6817	12159		6860	12000
6818	11979		6861	25939
6819	12166		6862	10110
6820 TP	12115		6863(1)	32946
6821	12107		6863(2) TP	33313
6822	12049		6864* TP	12580
6823	12073		6865(1)	27000
6824	12055		6865(2)	33478
6825* TP	12160		6866	12090
6826	12161		6867	9836
6827	12158		6868 TP	32948
6828* TP/AEW	12415		6869	11911
6829	12413		6870(1)	26743
6830	12414		6870(2) TP	33211
6831	12595		6871(1)	11991
6832	12478		6871(2)	34225
6833	12579		6872	9539
6834* TP/MR	12590		6873	11926
6835(1)	12596		6874(1)	32651
6835(2) TP	20175		6874(2)	32825
6836	13018		6875(1)	12065
6837* TP	13539		6875(2)* TP	11746
6838	13541		6876	12582
6839* TP	13540		6877* TP	11925
6840* TP	25311		6878	32951
6841	25312		6879 TP	9766
6842	25310		6880(1)	9948
6843	25609		6880(2) TP	25546
6844 TP	25610		6881	32961
6845(1)	26114		6882* TP/MR	32644
6845(2)* TP	26087		6883	25940
6846(1)	26116		6884* TP	12064
6846(2) TP	33134		6885* TP	12596
6886	12166		6889	9492
6887(1)	12049		6890	33552
6887(2)* TP	12704		6891 TP	33024
6888	12107		6892 TP	26439

Serial numbers have been re-used, almost certainly to cause confusion as the second-use aircraft were sometimes bought secretly.

RAF allocations to 28 Sq and 44 Sq prior to the end of 1945 were:

28 Sq: FD768, 884/86/87/91, 925/27/31/33/38/62, FJ711, FL527/50/51/ 53/55/64/65/83/90/92, 617/37/38, FZ553/55/70/74, KG456/70/71/74/76/ 97/98, 525, 711, KJ841/51, KK158, 218, KN332/34/37, 470/71/72/74/ 76/83.

44 Sq: FD792, 804/07/41/43/91, 925/31/35, FZ559, KG471/87/99, 503/09/11, KG626/88/89/90, 703/04/05/09/10/11/14/27, KJ829/30/41/ 43/51, KK157/58, 219, KN474/78/79.

In the early nineties, Dakotas continued in service with 25, 35 and 44Sq. 25 Sq is known to have had 6814, 6816, 6820, 6832, 6840, 6846, 6857, 6863, 6877 and 6885. No 35 Sq used 6811, 6814, 6825, 6828, 6829, 6832, 6834, 6835, 6837, 6839, 6840, 6845, 6846, 6848, 6852, 6854, 6858, 6862, 6863, 6864, 6867, 6870, 6873, 6875, 6876, 6877, 6880, 6884, 6885, 6887 and 6891. Finally 44 Sq had 6811, 6820, 6825, 6828, 6837, 6846, 6850, 6852, 6853, 6857, 6864, 6868, 6870, 6874, 6875, 6879, 6880, 6882, 6885, 6886, 6887, 6888, 6890, 6891 and 6892.

SOUTH ARABIA/SOUTH YEMEN

Four C-47s were bought by the **South Arabian Air Force** following independence in 1963, but only 202 and 203 are known to have served with the **Air Force of the South Yemen People's Republic** from 1967 onwards. A survey dated 1989 indicated that four C-47s remained in use, suggesting acquisition of at least one more, 201 having been sold to Indonesia in 1974.

201	c/n 25427		203	32867
202	27108		204	32943

SOUTH KOREA - see Korea (South)

SOUTH VIETNAM - see Vietnam (South)

SPAIN

Douglas twins were used by both sides in the Spanish Civil war between 1936 and 1939. The **Spanish Republican AF** took over three DC-2s and the sole DC-1 from LAPE in the summer of 1936 and two more were bought subsequently. They operated with their original civil markings until the end of the war, EC-XAX, EC-EBB, EC-BFF, EC-AGA and DC-1 EC-AGN surviving to be taken over by the **Spanish Nationalist AF**. EC-AAY was destroyed, as was c/n 1527 for which no registration mark is known.

One DC-2 was captured by the Nationalists in Jul36 and became 42-1 c/n 1521 and was used by General Franco throughout the war. At the end of the war the surviving Republican DC-2s were taken into the Nationalist AF, becoming 42-3 (c/n 1330), 42-4 (c/n 1417) and 42-5 (c/n 1320). It can only be guessed that 42-2 would have been the DC-1 (c/n 1137) which also survived to fly with Iberia, which took over all DC-2s (to become EC-AAA to EC-AAE).

Some C-47s were acquired by accident during the war after they force-landed in Spain, most notably in 1943 while en route from the UK to North Africa. These interned aircraft were subsequently returned to the USAAF and did not form any part of the post-war **Ejercito del Aire**.

In post-war military use the C-47 was known in Spain as T.3 and between 1947 and 1966 a total of 69 aircraft was acquired including two navigation-aid calibration aircraft that were operated in civilian markings. Following the initial receipt of two ex-RAF aircraft, briefly on Iberia's books in 1947, T.3s were acquired in four tranches. Twenty-two were received as US-aid in 1956-1957, 30 were commercially purchased in 1962-1963, two more came as aid in 1963 and finally 11 former Iberia aircraft were received in 1965-1966. The two calibration aircraft, EC-ANV and EC-ARV, were acquired in 1958 and 1963 respectively for use by the Servicio de Comprobacion de Ayudas at Madrid-Barajas where they were operated by Escuadron 401.

In Spanish use the aircraft were used broadly as transports in the 'fifties and 'sixties and in more specialised training roles in the 'seventies. This was a period of constant re-structuring for the Ejercito del Aire and the T.3s changed hands regularly, so that a listing of the operating units is somewhat complex.

The Grupo de Estado Mayor (the General Staff communications unit at Getafe) used the T.3 continuously from 1947 until 1978, initially with only one aircraft. Within the GEM the operating unit was Grupo 90 and the early code prefix '90-' reflected this on the T.3s and other types. In 1967 Escuadron 901 was created within Grupo 90 and the codes changed to reflect this. In 1971 Grupo 91 replaced Grupo 90 and Escuadron 911 replaced Escuadron 901. When withdrawn from use Escuadron 911 had eight T.3s on strength.

The major early user (1956-1963) was Ala 35 at Getafe. Initially the aircraft served with Escuadron 353 (code prefix '35-') but when C-54s were acquired in 1959 the T.3s were re-distributed to Escuadrones 351 ('351-') and 352 ('352-') to replace the C-352 (Ju-52). When more C-54s arrived in the early 'sixties they replaced the T.3s in Escuadron 352 and the Ala 35 aircraft were consolidated into Escuadron 351 until finally replaced by the Azor in 1963. Ala 37 at Albacete was re-equipped with T.3s in 1963 and they were used by Escuadrones 371 until 1973 and 372 until 1967. (In 1967, Ala 37 became Grupo 37 but reverted to Ala status in 1971.) When used at Albacete the T.3s were coded initially '37-') and then '371-' and '372-'. A third transport unit was Escuadron 98 (later Escuadron 981) at Torrejon that was briefly a T.3 user from late 1962 until mid-1964. Codes used were (presumably) '98-' and (certainly) '981-'. In June 1970 Escuadron 461 (within Ala 46 Mixte at Gando, Canaries) re-equipped and remained a major user until March 1976 when the T.3 was withdrawn. At that time eight had been in use with code prefixes '461-', although previously greater numbers had been used.

Training units to use the C-47 included the variously titled multi-engined training school at Jerez from 1961 until 1963 and then at Matacán from 1963 until 1978. Latterly known as the Escuela Militar de Transporte y Transito Aereos, its T.3s were coded initially '77-' and then '744-' and '745-' for Escuadrones 744 and 745. When withdrawn in 1978 each squadron held eight aircraft with a few in use with Escuadron 741. The Escuela Militar de Paracaidismo (the parachutists' school) used T.3s at Alcantarilla from 1973 until 1976. When withdrawn from use, eight T.3s had been in service with the school's Escuadron 721 (code prefix '721-'). The third major school user was the Academia General de Aire (AGA) at San Javier. The T.3 served with the AGA's Escuadron 792 ('792-') from 1973 until 1977. Six were withdrawn in 1977.

Other users of small numbers of T.3s included the Escuela Superior de Vuelo at Matacán (the first user of a C-47 in 1947), Escuadrilla 902 del Cuartel General de la Aviacion Tactica (one at Tablada from 1970), Escuadrilla 905 del Mando Aereo de Defensa at Torrejon (circa 1972), Escuadrilla de Base 534 at Reus (brief use) and Escuadrilla 604 at Gando (from 1973).

The T.3 fleet was withdrawn progressively from use from 1976 until 03Feb78 when it departed officially in favour of the equally ubiquitous CASA212. Approximately 48 aircraft survived to retirement although nearly half were scrapped at Cuatro Vientos as surplus to US needs. Most of the rest, free of MDAP re-sale restrictions, were sold to the commercial market in the UK, Germany and the USA.

Virtually all Ejercito del Aire T.3s wore unit codes. The prefix digits indicated the Ala or Grupo allocation (two digits, early use) or Escuadron or Escuadrilla (three digits, later use). Various suffix systems were used, sometimes matching the serial but often not. The allocation of the early codes has not been well recorded by enthusiasts (certainly not by those outside Spain), and there were many changes as aircraft moved units. In the following list, known codes are listed sequentially reading left to right. The asterix (*) indicates the code worn at withdrawal.

Serial	c/n	Codes
T.3-1	c/n 12164	wfu 10Sep64
T.3-2	13378	91-30(?), 90-30, 90-2, 901-2, 911-2, 911-05*
T.3-3	27154	wfu 29May68
T.3-4	11781	461-1, 461-04*
T.3-5	19270	744-05, 905-1, 901-5, 461-05*
T.3-6	19604	wfu 06Dec62
T.3-7	20497	902-1*
T.3-8	13068	35-122, 90-8, 901-8, 911-8, 792-3(?), 745-08*
T.3-9	26053	371-9, 721-2*
T.3-10	34139	721-1*
T.3-11	26611	90-4, 745-11*
T.3-12	13650	37-12, 461-09, 792-6*
T.3-13	19624	77-13, Feb72
T.3-14	12943	371-14, 744-14, 461-14(?), 721-5*
T.3-15	25241	90-5, 35-123, 37-15, 461-15(?), 461-14, 721-8*
T.3-16	25349	90-6, 901-6, 911-6, 911-06*
T.3-17	27035	371-17, 461-17, 911-11*
T.3-18	26607	77-18, 371-18, 744-18, 721-6*
T.3-19	33328	744-19
T.3-20	25764	77-20, 744-20, 461-32(?), 745-20* (last used by Esc.741)
T.3-21	26773	wfu 09Jul66
T.3-22	26986	371-22, wfu 16Oct68
T.3-23	26621	745-23
T.3-24	33554	745-24, 792-10*
T.3-25	9037	wfu 02Oct73
T.3-26	20471	wfu 10Apr62
T.3-27	20002	901-7, 911-7, 745-27, 792-5*
T.3-28	9914	901-4, 744-28*
T.3-29	19975	90-9, 901-9, 911-9, 911-09*
T.3-30	25531	461-10, 461-30*
T.3-31	12692	37-31, 461-27, 461-07, 461-31*
T.3-32	26899	461-03, 461-32*
T.3-33	20596	461-11, 721-3(?), 744-33, 745-23* (out-of-sequence code)
T.3-34	20721	461-15, 461-34, 721-7*
T.3-35	25836	37-35, 371-35, 461-26, 461-35*
T.3-36	20600	35-???, 77-??, 37-??, 77-??, 37-??, 461-16, 721-9*
T.3-37	26179	371-37, wfu 11Apr73
T.3-38	32779	wfu 07Sep64
T.3-39	20525	37-39, wfu 12Nov65
T.3-40	33604	461-08, 792-2*
T.3-41	26457	371-41, 461-05, 792-?*
T.3-42	4225	745-42, 911-07*
T.3-43	13772	wfu 06Jul70
T.3-44	19750	Ala 37, cr 21Apr63
T.3-45	34357	37-45, 371-45, 744-45*
T.3-46	32776	744-46, 461-13, 461-46*
T.3-47	32734	461-25, 721-4*
T.3-48	25399	371-48, 461-21, 745-48*
T.3-49	26692	745-49, 461-28, 792-1*
T.3-50	34361	461-50, 745-50*
T.3-51	25505	371-51, 461-51, 744-51*
T.3-52	33037	461-24, 744-52* (last used by Esc.741)
T.3-53	33243	wfu by 26Jan78 (corrosion)
T.3-54	34214	372-54, 744-54*
T.3-55	9634	372-55, 792-2, 744-55 (last used by Esc.741)
T.3-56	12690	981-15, 461-23, 745-56, wfu 14Jul75
T.3-57	4885	534-57, 744-57*
T.3-58	4890	745-58, 911-09*
T.3-59	4263	534-59, 744-59, 911-10*
T.3-60	4293	604-60, 744-60, 911-11*
T.3-61	10100	901-12(?), 745-61*
T.3-62	25450	901-12, 911-12, 744-62
T.3-63	33032	792-7
T.3-64	26342	744-64*
T.3-65	19268	745-65*
T.3-66	12758	745-66, 911-12*
T.3-67	13375	745-67, (604)-67*

SRI LANKA (Ceylon)

Two ex Air Ceylon DC-3s were taken over by the **Sri Lanka Air Force** in 1978 and were used for social services as well as military duties. They were withdrawn but one was overhauled in Oct88 as the civil war was stretching air force capacity. They were replaced by Chinese Y-8s and later CASA C-212s. At least one was then preserved.

CR-821	c/n 25464
CR-822	33556

SUDAN

Three DC-3s, possibly up to five, were known to have been acquired by the **Sudanese Air Force** from Sudan Airways in 1962. They were replaced by An-24s some years ago.

421	c/n 26732		425	26990
424	27099			

SWEDEN

The **Royal Swedish Air Force (Flygvapnet)** operated a small fleet of C-47s for over thirty years in a variety of roles. Initially two aircraft, from SAS, known as Tp79 in military use, were acquired in 1948-49 for SIGINT use. 79001 and 79002 were modified extensively before their respective acceptance by the Air Force in January and Jun51. They entered service with F8 Wing at Barkaby together with the more 'standard' aircraft 79003, accepted in Mar51 (codes are thought to have been '71', '72' and '73'). 79001, up from Bromma, was unfortunately lost to Russian fighters over the Baltic 13Jun52. F8 continued to use Tp79s until the early 'seventies, 79007 '77' having been added in March 1961. The F8 aircraft were passed to other units before the wing's closure in 1974.

F7 at Satenas was the recipient of the fourth aircraft, 79004 '74', in Jan53. It subsequently received 79005 '75' in 1955, 79006 '76' in 1960 and 79003 '73' (from F8) in the 'sixties. The Satenas aircraft were used as light transports and paratroopers and were regular visitors to European cities. They were eventually replaced at F7 by the C-130 with 79005 going first (to F3), followed by 79006 and then 79003 and 79004 (all to F13M) in 1981.

F3 at Malmslatt was a short-lived user before its closure in 1974. It used 79002, recoded '78' from its previous '72', 79005 '79' (ex '75') and 79007 '77'. When F3 disbanded in 1974 the Tp79s were transferred to a flight of F13 now operational at Malmslatt as F13M. F13M continued to operate the aircraft until the Tp79's operational retirement in 1981. Those used were 79002 '78' (later '72' and '792'), 79003 '793', 79004 '794', 79005 '79' (this was damaged beyond repair in a cross-wind landing at Nykoping 9Oct74), 79006 '76' ('796'), 79007 '77' ('797') and 79008 '78' ('798') – the 1975 replacement for 79005.

The long-used double-digit codes were replaced by new three-digit codes in 1980 and this affected the six surviving aircraft of F7 and F13M. These six were withdrawn progressively from use from late 1981, all six being officially stricken from the record in 1984.

79001	c/n 9001	F8/71(?), shot down 13Jun52
79002	9103	F8/72, F3/78, F13M/78, F13M/72, F13M/792
79003	9010	F8/73, F7/73, F7/793, F13M/793
79004	19771	F7/74, F7/794, F13M/794
79005	33246	F7/75, F3/79, dbr 9Oct74
79006	13883	F7/76, F13M/76, F13M/796
79007	13647	F8/77, F3/77, F13M/77, F13M/797
79008	33153	F13M/78, F13M/798

SYRIA

C-47s were acquired by the **Syrian Arab Air Force** during 1949-51, possibly from Syrian Airways. Six were reported to be in use during the six-day war in 1967 and "Flight" magazine continued to quote four in 1982. One Israeli source suggests that 20 to 30 might have been at Damascus during 1967, but it is thought that these were not airworthy at the time, and none was used then, nor have they been reported since. No serial numbers are known.

TAIWAN (Formosa)

The **Chinese Nationalist Air Force** left mainland China ahead of the Communist forces in 1950, taking with them some of the Lend-Lease C-47s supplied by the USAAF during WWII. Further aircraft were transferred from USAF stocks and about 20 were thought to remain in use in 1982 with the Air Transport Wing.

"Flight" magazine's 1994 survey suggested nine remained, mostly stored, but another report suggests nineteen were in service. All had been retired by 1995. Those originally supplied to China are listed under that entry. The following have been reported in Taiwan by observation:- 7022, 7026, 7031, 7209, 7214, 7244, 7285, 7288, 7294, 7295, 7307 (i/s 1978) and possibly 7624, but this series seems to have been replaced by a five digit series, eg C-51303, C-51310, the last three digits being used as a code no.

15055	c/n 19521	7311	16169	20635	7320
15481	19947		16197	20663	
15794	20260	7273	16262	20728	
15848	20314	7252	16349	20815	
15857	20323	7243	16404	20870	
15924	20390	7231	17251	25626	
16087	20553		24062	9924	7346
25657	6245		49331	26592	7344
48732	25993		49648	26909	
48806	26067	7219	49687	26948	
49046	26307		49793	27054	7270
49106	26367		76241	32573	
49235	26496		45933	34195	
49239	26500		451055	34325	7347

C/n 20717 arrived via MAP in Mar72 and c/n 12041 was donated for spares Dec 81.

TCHAD

The **Escadrille Tchadienne** was formed in 1961 and its equipment included one former Armée de l'Air C-47. Between 1964 and 1969 five more were added including three surplus to French needs. A second batch of five surplus Armée de l'Air aircraft followed circa 1971. At the height of operations between 1975 and 1982, nine were reported to be in use. Of these, one crashed on 28Jan78 at Tibesti. C-47s have now been replaced by the C-130 and none remained in service after 1985.

TTLAA	49594	c/n 26855	TTLAF	15883	32631
TTLAB	348291	25552	TTLAG	100509	18972
TTLAC	348861	26122	TTLAH	118516	4608
TTLAD	48978	26239	TTLAI	49462	26723
TTLAE	477049	33381	TTLAJ	23940	9802

THAILAND

Thailand's armed forces and police services have operated the C-47 in various guises from 1946 until the present day albeit that the current Royal Thai Air Force fleet entirely comprises Basler BT-67 conversions. The last of the piston-engined aircraft, latterly operated by the Royal Artificial Rainmaking Unit at Don Muang, were withdrawn in 1995 and the final flight by any conventional military C-47 was made in 1997.

The indigenous serial numbering system employed by the **Royal Thai Air Force** identifies with certainty 55 aircraft received between 1946 and 1976. Six of these aircraft later became Basler conversions and these were augmented with three 'new' BT-67 conversions to give a total of 57, all of which are listed below. Another six aircraft, unofficially reported to have been with the RTAF, are discussed in the penultimate paragraph.

Deliveries commenced in Aug46 when five former RAF aircraft were transferred from surplus stocks in India. These were followed in Nov46 by three from USAAF stocks including one previously used by the Air Attache in Bangkok. In Oct53 three more ex-USAF aircraft were acquired via MDAP and four were purchased from Qantas. Between 1957 and 1959 another 14 MDAP aircraft were received, all of which were former French aircraft previously used in the Indo-China theatre. In early 1964 three more ex-USAF aircraft, one of which was a navigational aids-checking EC-47D, were received as MAP aid. In Sep67 two of the RTAF aircraft (L2-2/00 and L2-25/01) were modified by the SVNAF from their 'regular' C-47 standard to that of AC-47 gunship. One of these was lost in Dec67 and appears to have been replaced in Mar68 by a former USAF AC-47D (the first to be so transferred out of the USAF inventory). In Sep70 two aircraft were transferred from the Thai Police to the RTAF and they were followed in early 1971 by three former Cambodian aircraft, the latter presumably as US-orchestrated MAP transfers. Both of the Police transfers and all three of the Cambodian aircraft were then locally converted to AC-47 standard. In Mar71 a former Air America HC-47D was received via MAP followed in late 1972 by another two ex-USAF C-47As.

In the second half of 1975 nine aircraft were taken on strength as MAP aid. However, their provenance is complicated as all had seen previous MAP use with at least one other US-friendly nation. Evidence is that most, possibly all, came from Cambodia although some of them had certainly seen earlier use with the SVNAF. That said it looks unlikely that any of them were transferred (or escaped) from South Vietnam directly to Thailand but it is conceivable that the MAP references that appear on the Thai records could reflect retrospective legitimisation of one or two SVNAF 'escapees'. To further complicate the picture, Thai records indicate that six of them were received configured as AC-47 gunships although only two of them were original USAF conversions that were later transferred to the SVNAF. The assumption is that these two had been transferred to Cambodia post-1972 and that the other four were field conversions in Cambodia. The picture is complex and we tread carefully.

The final acquisitions took place in 1976 when three former Air America and two one-time SVNAF aircraft were taken on strength as MAP aid. Again the

Chapter 3: Military Operators of the DC-3, C-47, R4D, Dakota and Li-2

process of transfer is unclear although two of the Air America aircraft ('559' and '147') are recorded as escapees from Saigon in 1975. One the former SVNAF aircraft has previously been used in 'RC-47' configuration.

Initially the eight or so aircraft equipped 1 Sq at Don Muang, Bangkok from where they were used for general purposes. One aircraft, L2-8/90, was allocated permanently to the Thai Royal Flight. In Jun51 three aircraft, L2-2/90 '102', L2-3/90 '103' and L2-5/90 '105', were allocated permanently to the Thai UNO contingent in Korea. 2/90 was lost in a crash in Japan in 1957 but the commitment remained until the late 'sixties (the two survivors were replaced in 1964 by two aircraft that later became L2-30/07 and L2-31/07).

The acquisition of more aircraft in 1953 facilitated a restructuring of the transport fleet at Don Muang with 61 and 62 Sq becoming active within 6 Wing, the latter unit surviving with C-47s until about 1978 when it was re-numbered 602 Sq. Shortly afterwards the 602 Sq aircraft were re-mustered in a new 603 Sq at Don Muang. With an active strength of up to 25 aircraft between 1957 and 1972, several other units were able to operate small numbers of support aircraft and they are known to have included the Flying Training School with two or three in use 1961-1965. Tactical units using one or two each in the 1964-1967 period included 20, 21, 22, 23, 41 and 42 Sqns. The influx of aircraft during the later stages of the war in South-East Asia increased strength to a maximum of about 40 in 1976. By then the JL2/AC-47 gunships had been operational for several years having been established initially as a flight of two in 1967/1968. By about 1972 there were five in use (one had been lost in 1967) and post-1975 this number had increased to 14 (one had been lost in 1967). Between 1967 and 1977 they were used by 61 and 62 Sqns (mainly the latter) but in May 1977, 12 aircraft were consolidated into 42 Sq within 4 Wing at Takhli (42 Sq was re-numbered 402 Sq circa 1978). They were joined by the two remaining JL2s in Oct77 and Mar78. Attrition was surprisingly low and between 1983 and 1985 the 13 survivors, by now reconverted to standard (L2) configuration, were transferred to 603 Sq within 6 Wing. There were six TL2/RC-47 conversions that included three of the Air America acquisitions and they were in use in the 1977-1981 period. Squadron allocation is unclear but may have been with 41/402 Sqns. All were later reconfigured to basic L2 standard or wfu.

After 1980 the in-service numbers began to dwindle as aircraft were progressively withdrawn from use. In 1986 a budget restriction led to a directive that numbers should be reduced to ten operational aircraft in the period 1987-1991. Many of the surplus airworthy aircraft were taken into storage at Lopburi during this period. Several others were retired for display duties. The final operational piston-engined C-47 unit was the Royal Artificial Rainmaking Unit that was active with six aircraft at Don Muang from 1991 until 1995. It was these six that were intended to become the Basler conversions. Five of them were successfully converted and delivered between Feb98 and Mar99 but one, L2-38/14 (45-0883), was found to be too badly corroded for conversion and was replaced by a new airframe (c/n 9290) that was delivered in May98. A second new airframe (c/n 20082) became the seventh Basler conversion in 2002 and eighth and ninth conversions were delivered in 2004. All the BT-67 conversions are operated currently by 461 Sq at Phitsanulok.

RTAF C-47s, in common with all RTAF aircraft since 1949, were identified administratively by a local serial system as well as by their former USAAF serials (frequently truncated to a large 'last three') and, when appropriate, unit codes. [The full USAF serials would have been necessary for MAP/USAF administrative purposes; the 'last three', once adopted, were more used operationally.] The Thai serials did not always appear on the exterior of the aircraft and, when worn, were usually in small Thai characters on the fuselage. However, the system appears to have been used consistently throughout the life of the C-47 and very few, if any, genuinely operated Thai aircraft have not been allocated such a serial. The more visible USAF/MAP serials (including at least two quasi-USAF serials based on the c/n) have always been worn and since the Vietnam-era the large 'last threes' were displayed very prominently.

The basic type number for the C-47 roughly translates as 'BL2', abbreviated to 'L2'. Sub-variant prefixes have also been used although it is unclear whether such designations have appeared as external paintwork. Thus JL2 was the attack/transport variant (the AC-47) and TL2 was the observation/transport variant (the so-called 'RC-47'). The one former USAF EC-47D confirmed in RTAF service (43-49250) received the unique prefix L2Or as well as a unique serial range. The BT-67 conversions received a 'new' designation, BL2k, and serial range in which the 'k' suffix indicated the first major sub-type of the basic C-47. The serial system itself therefore identifies the aircraft type, the sequence in type and the Thai year of acquisition. Thus the former USAF VIP and Thai Royal Flight aircraft 44-76517 in the RTAF museum at Don Muang,

acquired in 1946, was allocated the serial L2-08/90 in 1947 (1947 was the Buddhist year 2490). The camouflaged and derelict 42-100547 '547' that stands nearby was a late MAP aircraft taken on strength in Sep72 (the year 2515) and has the serial L2-39/15. The present fleet of nine BT-67s have the serials BL2k-01/41 to 09/47 and also now wear the 461 Sq codes '46151' to '46159'.

In the following list all aircraft were received as 'standard' C-47A/D unless noted otherwise and full previous histories can be found in the Production History chapter. Dates quoted below are the 'toc' date and should be understood to mean the actual date of entry into RTAF service, although occasionally they indicate the date of the documentation recording the entry into service. Where there are significant gaps between the RTAF toc date and any MAP date in the Production History, this may indicate previous use by an unidentified MAP-aid recipient. Bracketed entries show the source (or likely source) of each aircraft. JL2 and TL2 conversions are also indicated.

Serial	c/n	USAF	Date (Source)
L2-1/90	(Note 1)		
L2-2/90	12913	293045	19Aug46 (RAF)
L2-3/90	13562	293629	19Aug46 (RAF)
L2-4/90	9542	223680	19Aug46 (RAF)
L2-5/90	10216	224354	19Aug46 (RAF)
L2-6/90	18999	2100536	06Nov46 (USAAF). VIP conversion
L2-7/90	19572	315106	06Nov46 (USAAF). TL2 conversion. To BT-67
L2-8/90	32849	476517	06Nov46 (USAAF)
L2-9/96	20764	316298	14Oct53 (MDAP)
L2-10/96	32590	476258	Oct53 (MDAP)
L2-11/96	34203	50941	23Oct53 (MDAP)
L2-12/96	12248	'212248' (2108840)	22Oct53 (Qantas)
L2-13/96	12872	'212872' (293008)	26Oct53 (Qantas). VIP conversion
L2-14/96	12667	'212667' (292824)	Oct53 (Qantas)
L2-15/96	25491	'125491' (348230)	10Nov53 (Qantas)
L2-16/00	25674	348413	16Apr57 (France). TL2 conversion To BT-67
L2-17/00	9987	224125	16Apr57 (France)
L2-18/00	20053	315587	14Sep57 (France)
L2-19/00	26137	348876	15Sep57 (France). JL2 conversion
L2-20/00	26679	349418	15Sep57 (France). JL2 conversion
L2-21/00	25410	348149	04Nov57 (France)
L2-22/01	19866	315400	20Jul58 (France)
L2-23/01	25269	348008	Aug58 (France). TL2 conversion. To BT-67
L2-24/01	26806	349545	05Oct58 (France)
L2-25/01	27180	349919	05Nov58 (France). JL2 conversion
L2-26/02	13778	2108993	19Nov58 (France)
L2-27/02	19977	315511	27Jan59 (France)
L2-28/02	20794	316328	12Mar59 (France)
L2-29/02	27042	349781	20Apr59 (France)
L2-30/07	26902	349641	13Mar64 (USAF). JL2 conversion
L2-31/07	34288	51021	13 Mar64 (USAF). To BT-67
L2-32/11	25762	348501	30May68 (USAF)
L2-33/13	12487	292662	Sep70 (Thai Police)
L2-34/13	13740	293789	Sep70 (Thai Police). JL2 conversion
L2-35/14	12498	2108865	16Feb71 (Cambodia?). JL2 conversion
L2-36/14	13112	293224	08Feb71 (Cambodia?). JL2 conversion
L2-37/14	33066	476734	27Jan71 (Cambodia). JL2 conversion
L2-38/14	34142	50883	24Mar71 (Air America). TL2 conversion
L2-39/15	19010	2100547	12Sep72 (USAF)
L2-40/15	20421	315955	29Aug72 (USAF)
L2-41/18	26471	349210	28Aug75 (SVNAF at U-Tapao)
L2-42/18	26515	349254	09Sep75 (Cambodia at Udorn). To BT-67
L2-43/18	26777	349516	09Sep75 (Cambodia? at Udorn)
L2-44/18	33484	477152	Sep75 (? at Udorn)
L2-45/18	34386	51116	12Sep75 (Cambodia? at Udorn)
L2-46/18	26271	349010	11Nov75 (? at Udorn)
L2-47/18	34349	51079	14Nov75 (? at Udorn)
L2-48/18	19400	2100937	28Nov75 (Cambodia at Udorn)
L2-49/18	25753	348492	14Nov75 (? at Udorn). To BT-67
L2-50/19	34363	51093	30Mar76 (SVNAF? at U-Tapao)
L2-51/19	34141	50882	19Mar76 (SVNAF? at U-Tapao)
L2-52/19	20025	315559	20Jan76 (Air America at Takhli)

L2-53/19	20613	316147	20Jan76 (Air America at Takhli). TL2 conversion
L2-54/19	34259	50994	29Jan76 (Air America at Takhli). TL2 conversion
L2Or-1/07	26511	349250	26Jan64 (USAF). Recvd as EC-47D

Note 1: L2-1/90 is c/n 9871 (42-24009) or 13546 (42-93615), both toc 19Aug46.
Note 2: All (France), (USAF), (Cambodia?), (SVNAF?) and (Air America) were received under MAP, (?) indicates source unknown

BT-67 conversions are summarized below:

L2k-01/41	19572	'106'	(ex L2-7/90)	coded '46151'
L2k-02/41	34288	'021'	(ex L2-31/07)	coded '46152'
L2k-03/41	9290	'883'	(ex N46949)	coded '46153'
L2k-04/41	25674	'413'	(ex L2-16/00)	coded '46154'
L2k-05/42	25269	'008'	(ex L2-23/01)	coded '46155'
L2k-06/42	26515	'254'	(ex L2-42/18)	coded '46156'
L2k-07/43	20082	'882'	(ex N6898D)	coded '46157'
L2k-08/47	25753	'492'	(ex L2-49/18)	coded '46158'
L2k-09/47	33010		(ex N2685W)	coded '46159'

L2-38/14 c/n 34142 and L2-51/19 c/n 34141 were shipped to Basler but not converted to BT-67.

Reportedly, the **Royal Thai Navy** has used at least 13 C-47s of which nine are listed below. All of these aircraft appear to have been post-1972 MAP deliveries direct from USAF stocks and from previous MAP recipients in the region (the former SVNAF aircraft may have passed through other hands before reaching Thailand and some had been returned formally to the USAF before reaching Thailand). In the 1970s and 1980s, the naval C-47s were operated initially from U-Tapao by 2 Sq and then by 201 Sq and 202 Sq (the re-numbered 2 Sq). The Navy continued to operate the C-47 until the mid 1990s (the USAAF serials are as worn in Thai use):

25362	48101	(SVNAF?)
26038	48777	
26356	49095	(USAF)
26474	349213	
26962	349701	(see tailpiece notes)
27186	49925	(USAF)
32750	76418	(USAF)
34313	51044	(SVNAF?) (EC-47P in previous USAF/SVNAF use)
34397	51127	(Laos?)

A number of C-47s were purchased by the Thai government and were supplied as MAP-aid for use by other agencies, most notably the **Royal Thai Army** and the Police Air Wing. Identification of the Army aircraft remains difficult and only four of those listed below appear to have been verified positively as seeing Army service.

9414	'9414'	(223552)	Confirmed as Army
11669		(268742)	Assumed Army but never reported in use
13560	'213560'		Active at least 1985, latterly as '13560'
20764	316298		(ex-RTAF L2-9/96)
25420	48159		(MAP, probably ex-Laos)
25768	'125768'		Reported as Army but unconfirmed in use
26729	49468		Confirmed as Army
32970	76638		Confirmed as Army; previously a SVNAF VC-47D

The C-47 destroyed in a take-off crash at Don Muang on 21Jun77, when it struck the wing of a C-123, was from the Royal Thai Army.

At least four aircraft have been identified as operated by the **Royal Thai Police Air Wing** at various times but perhaps until no later than 1970. Their histories are not well understood although two aircraft are known to have been transferred to the RTAF in 1970. The list below includes one former RTAF airframe displayed since 1993 at the RTP Museum, Bangkok.

12487	'212487'	(292662)	To RTAF in 1970 as L2-33/13
13740	293789		To RTAF in 1970 as L2-34/13
19895	'319895'	(315249)	Acquired for Police 09Apr54 but only used temporarily
20349	315883		
26777	349516		(ex-RTAF L2-43/18)

[Unconfirmed aircraft 26908 (349647) left US charge as FLC 20Aug47, reportedly for the Thai Police. Much later unconfirmed sightings of '647' should not necessarily be linked to 26908].

The above lists are thought to have captured all the RTAF aircraft and most of those used by the other armed services. However other aircraft have been reported as in use with the Thai military and a few of them still cannot be explained as definite errors. Of those that have not been derived from documentation (such as mis-interpretation of MAP data), almost all involve sightings - particularly in the 'seventies and 'eighties at Don Muang and usually involve aircraft officially disposed of by the USAF as MAP aid to unidentified recipients. 'Possibilities' therefore include '103' (probably EC-47D 349103 to MAP 09Jan64) seen at Don Muang in 1984/85, '647' (C-47D 349647? to FLC 20Aug47 and vaguely reported as Thai Police) and '236' (presumably C-47D 349236 to MAP 13Aug70 from overhaul at Don Muang) reported in 1989. Several other sightings involve Cambodian and Laotian aircraft seen at Don Muang in the 'seventies and USAF aircraft in maintenance in Thailand prior to release as MAP aid elsewhere. There is also a suggestion that three former USAF/432nd TRW 'RC-47s' (348492, 348946 and 349701) based at Udorn were perhaps loaned to the RTAF in the 1968-69 period, presumably for special tasks. This is conceivable but their transfer to MAP did not occur until Aug70 and the evidence is that they did not then initially go to Thailand (it may have been Cambodia). In any event 348946 has never been reported in Thai use post Aug70.

A surprisingly large number of Thai C-47s (certainly in excess of 35) survives in various states of dilapidation both on military premises and elsewhere in Thailand. The individual histories contain such details as well as some accident data. An additional unidentified accident was at Nong Hard reservoir, Sakon Nakhon town on 28Feb84.

TOGO

The **Togolese Air Force/Force Aérienne Togolaise Escadrille de Transport** used two C-47s originally acquired from France. One crashed in 1974 and the other was withdrawn in 1980.

5VMAC	13438	c/n 13438
5VMAG	23941	9803

TURKEY

The **Turkish Air Force/Türk Hava Kuvvetieri** was supplied with 99 C-47s or Dakotas between 1946 and 1949. The first 18 were acquired in 1946, and were flown from Cairo in Egypt to the Kayseri Maintenance Centre in Nov/Dec. Eight had been delivered to the Hava Nakliye Bolugu (Air Transport Company) by the end of the year. A further 81 were supplied under MAP from stocks in Germany between 17Nov48 and 24Apr49. Two Air Transport Regiments were formed on 10May50 (11nci at Eskisehir and 12nci at Kayseri) each with four eight-aircraft groups. By 1953, the C-47s were spread across five squadrons (221-225 Filo), with the 12th Air Communications Base at Etimesgut.

Nine aircraft had been exported in 1949 (probably to Iran), but six more were purchased from THY in 1966 to serve in the VIP role. Four more were added in 1978 including two from the Libyan AF. Seventy aircraft remained on charge in 1960, but the number had fallen to 46 by 1983, operated by seven different units.

Most of the C-47s were employed on general transport duties and probably saw no active service until the invasion of Cyprus by Turkey in Jul74, when alongside Transalls and C-130s they were used to drop parachutists. As of late 1994 223 Hava Ulastirma Filo (Air Tpt Sq) had given up C-47s and 7 Electronic Flight had four EC-47s which saw service in the Gulf War on the Turkish-Iraqi border. 224 Filo received CN-235Ms in 1994. All C-47s have now been retired, with the final C-47 flight taking place on 08Jan98.

Units using the C-47 were:-

Irtibat Nakliye TB/2.Bl 1946/47
1 Nakliye TB 1/2.Bl 1947/Mar48, 11 Nakliye TB 3/4 Bl 1947/01Mar48
Hava Nakliye Alayi 1/2/3/4. Bl 01Mar48/09May50
11 Nakliye Alayi 1/2/3/4. Bl. Eskisehir 10May50/20Apr51
12 Nakliye Alayi 1/2/3/4. Bl. Kayseri 10May50/20Apr51
Irtibat Nakliye Ucus Grubo/I.Bl 10May50/20Apr51
221 Filo 20Apr51/1971 - became 223 Filo 1971/94. Etimesgut
222 Filo 20Apr51/1960 - became Ozel Filo 1960/71 - became 224 Filo 1971/94. Etimesgut
223 Filo 20Apr51/1957 - became Harita Mans Kitaati 1957/70 - became Hava Harp Okulo - Egitim Irtibat Mns. Kit'asi 1970/98. Etimesgut
Eskisehir Hava Ulastirma Filo 20Apr51/Oct53 - became 224 Filo 1953/71 - became 222 Filo 1971/95. Etimesgut

Kayseri Hava Ulastirma Filo 20Apr51/Oct53 - became 225 Filo 1953/71
Hava Okulo/4.Alet Filo Oct51/1956 - became Hv.Egt.K.Egt.Irt.Kt. 1956/95.
1 Taktik Hava Kuvveti Egitim Irtibat Kit'asi to 1994
3 Taktik Hava Kuvveti Egitim Irtibat Kit'asi to 1972, became 2 Taktik Hava Kuvveti Egitim Irtibat Kit'asi to 1972/1994

The serial number system comprises a block from 6001 to 6099 prefixed by the last two digits of the year of manufacture. For many years a serial number, comprising a base code and the last two of the serial number, was used on the fuselage side. More recently a unit code was used in place of the base code.

43-6001	20881 ?	
43-6002	20880	ETI-02
43-6003	25970	12-003
43-6004	26145	CBK-04
43-6005	20746	
43-6006	4971	
43-6007	25843	
43-6008	26456	H-008
43-6009	26168	ETI-09
43-6010	25715	CBK-10, ETI-10, 12-010, 1-010
43-6011	26956	TAKA-11, TK-11, H-011
6012	26506	
43-6013	26454 ?	
43-6014	26295	
43-6015	20883	CBK-15, OK-15, ETI-15, HEK-15
43-6016	25971	CBK-016
43-6017	26047	
43-6018	26160 ?	
42-6019	19017	ETI-19
43-6020	19608	CBK-20
42-6021	19494	METE-21, TK-21, H-021
43-6022	25598	
43-6023	19595	KR-23, ETI-23, 12-023
42-6024	10064	OK-24, YSL-24
43-6025	19531	YSL-25, H-025
42-6026	12965	YSL-26
43-6027	13878	ETI-27
43-6028	19668	CBK-28, ETI-28
42-6029	9905	
42-6030	19300	
42-6031	13622	ETI-31, 12-031
42-6032	18973	CBK-32, ETI-32, 12-032, '052'
42-6033	12950	ETI-033, E-033
42-6034	19322	CBK-34, ETI-34
42-6035	10132	ETI-35, 2-035, 12-035
42-6036	19330	CBK-36, METE-36, TK-36, 12-036
42-6037	12910	CBK-37, ETI-37, 1-037, 12-037
43-6038	19565	ETI-38, OKUL-38, 1-038, H-038
42-6039	13436	ETI-39, H-039
43-6040	25812	
43-6041	25513	ETI-41, 12-041, 1-041
42-6042	12949	ETI-42, 12-042
44-6043	32711	
43-6044	19973	CBK-44, OKL-44, ETI-44, YSL-44, H-044
43-6045	19729	CBK-45
42-6046	20117	ETI-46, 12-046
42-6047	12752	ETI-47, YSL-47, 12-047
43-6048	19516	CBK-48, TK-48, YSL-48, 12-048
42-6049	9363	H-049
43-6050	19600	
43-6051	13867	CBK-51, OKUL-51, ETI-51
43-6052	13877	YSL-52
42-6053	13653	H-053
42-6054	12713	TAKA-54, TK-54, 1-054
43-6055	25621	CBK-55, YSL-55
42-6056	19341	TAKA-56, TK-56, 1-056, H-056
43-6057	25711	YSL-57
42-6058	9922	
42-6059	12757	CBK-59, ETI-59, 12-059
43-6060	19724	CBK-60, ETI-60, H-060
42-6061	9379	TK-61
43-6062	20112	TK-62, E-062
42-6063(1)	13737	CBK-63, ETI-63
42-6063(2)		E-063 (EC-47) wfu 19Jun96
42-6064	12956	
42-6065	19294	
42-6066	9925	YSL-66, H-066
44-6067	32619	12-067
43-6068	13880	12-068, H-068
42-6069	19308	ETI-69, 12-069
42-6070	12563	TAKA-70, TK-70, 12-070, H-070
42-6071	19228	
42-6072	12564	12-072, H-072
43-6073	19529	OKUL-73, 12-073
42-6074	9908	YSL-74, H-074, 12-074, 2-074
42-6075	19357	OK-75, 1-075, 12-075
42-6076	12771	CBK-76, ETI-76, 2-076, E-076
43-6077	20512	CBK-77, ETI-77
42-6078	12900	CBK-78, ETI-78
43-6079	19644	CBK-79, ETI-79, YSL-79, H-079
42-6080	12966	
43-6081	26731	CBK-081
42-6082	19114	ETI-82
42-6083	19199	
43-6084	19557	
42-6085	13428	
42-6086	12615	
42-6087	12764	
42-6088	12903	
42-6089(1)	11856	
43-6089(2)	4971	ETI-089, 12-089
42-6090(1)	9498	
43-6090(2)		12-090 (EC-47D) wfu 13Sep88
43-6091(1)	19602	
42-6091(2)	9261	TK-91, 12-091
42-6092(1)	9800	
42-6092(2)	12577	ETI-92
42-6093(1)	13674	
42-6093(2)	12825	
42-6094(1)	10055	
42-6094(2)	7354	
	or 12769	ETI-094 cr Antalya 17Jan77
42-6095(1)	13444	
43-6095(2)	20115	2-095
42-6096	12955	ETI-96, E-096, ETI-96
42-6097	19250	
43-6098	26034	OKUL-98
43-6099	19825	
43-16395	20861	
43-49691	26952	ETI-691, 12-691
43-26258	26258	12-258, H-258
70-1478	9340	12-478

The base and unit abbreviations, also employed in the Production History chapter, are:- CBK Cubuk, ETI Etimesgut, YSL Yesilkoy, METE Diyarbakir, TAKA (later TK) Eskisehir, OKUL Izmir, H HHO, 12 12ciAHU. An unidentified C-47 of 12ciAHU cr nr Etimesgut 16Apr59.

UGANDA

Six C-47s were supplied to the **Ugandan Air Force** by Israel between 1963 and 1968. Of these U-401 c/n 6223 returned to Israel in 1973, and U-402 to U-406 remained derelict at Entebbe in 1993 after storage in Cyprus in 1976. In 1997 c/n 9410 was leased as 5X-TAL, later becoming 3D-ATH.

UKRAINE

Former Soviet AF Li-2 54 red was noted on 20May04 at the Kiev Park War Memorial, but no further information is available from this recently-established democracy.

UNITED KINGDOM OF GREAT BRITAIN & NORTHERN IRELAND

The **Royal Air Force** Dakotas were used by a very wide range of units. At least 46 Squadrons are known to have had the type on charge as the major equipment or jointly with other transport types. Apart from the operational units there were another 30 or so equipped with the type for training, either operational or conversion, or for various other purposes such as communications, research and development. Many of these units applied code letters to their aircraft, but these changed at intervals as aircraft moved to Maintenance Units for repair and back again, and the code was often limited to a single letter applied to the aircraft. Hence they are not mentioned in the production list. However, the unit part of the code letters are listed in the following summary of the unit histories, though some are incomplete, and in other cases several code groups were used at different times.

Detailed RAF squadron and unit allocations for overseas units have not survived and much information was not recorded on individual aircraft movement cards once an aircraft had gone overseas. During the Berlin Airlift, the Air Ministry only recorded all allocations as being either to the Oakington Transport Wing or the Waterbeach Wing. In practice, the Dakotas generally had individual squadron codes, 10, 18 (for a time), 27 and 30 Squadron in the case of Oakington, and 18, 53, 62 and 77 in the case of Waterbeach, details of which are given below, rather than in the Production History chapter. For each unit a list of the individual aircraft known to have been on charge at one time or another is given. These may well not be complete.

10 Squadron India Sep45-Dec47 and Oakington Oct48-Feb50 (Initially code ZA in India plus individual letter, then only individual underlined fuselage letters, call sign ODV plus individual letter, the last two letters being carried on the nose; at Oakington call sign OFA plus an individual letter, the last two letters being carried on the nose).

10 Sq was transferred to Transport Command in May45 and Dakotas replaced Halifaxes at Broadwell in August. It transferred to India in Oct45 and continued general transport duties from Bilaspur and later Poona until disbandment there on 20Dec47. On 05Nov48 238 Sq at Oakington was renumbered 10 Sq and operated on the Berlin Airlift. At that time Dakotas were held in pool but the personnel still operated as a Squadron. During this period, the aircraft are listed on their record cards by their maintenance base, i.e. Oakington, rather than the unit. 10 Sq was disbanded on 20Feb50.

FZ624/81, KG349/51, 447/54, 561, 650, KJ854/61/65/66/70/93, 900/07/52/89, KK101/20/27/29/31/36/51/53, 204, KN217/30/35/53/60/96, KN318/30/49/39/79/83/90/93/97, 402/06/15/28/33/42/48/50/52/60/93/97/98/99, 508/14/16/18/20/25/27/54/55/66/70/73/77/81/82/ 86/89, 601/03/08/23/31/43/44/51/52/56/59/73/78/91/94, 700/01, KP214/17/36/38/40/44/45/52/53/70/73, TS426.

18 Squadron Waterbeach Dec47-Feb50 (Individual letters only? Call sign MOFA plus individual letter).

This unit was reformed at Waterbeach on 08Dec47, using Dakotas, and taking part in the Berlin Airlift. It was disbanded on 20Feb50.

KJ865/66/86, 907/52/61/70/98, KK128/31/33/41/48/93, 212, KN217/23/30/55/60/67/69/81/85/93, 402/10/19/33/34/46/50/76/88/91/92/93/95/97/99, 506/08/14/18/23/28/50/53/66/73/81/86, 607/08/23/25/29/31/32/38/40/49/52/60/80/96, 701, KP213/14/17.

21 Squadron Aug65-Sep67.

While based at Khormaksar, Aden, Dakota KN452 was on charge along with Twin Pioneers and Andover C.2s in support of Army operations in the Radfan.

24 Squadron Hendon; Waterbeach; Oakington Apr43-Nov50 (In 1943 code ZK plus individual letter. In 1944/46 code NQ plus individual letter. From 1946, call sign ODA (later MODA) plus individual letter, the last two letters being carried on the nose - excess aircraft had an additional W suffix).

24 Sq was a communications unit between 1920 and the outbreak of war and used a wide variety of transport types as well as smaller types. The Dominie was in use when 24 Sq was transferred to Ferry Command in Apr42. A year later a flight of Dakotas was added to the mixed fleet which also included DC-3 OO-AUI. These were used on regular flights to Gibraltar returning with senior German and Italian prisoners. On D-Day supplies were carried over to France and casualties brought back. By Oct44 19 Dakotas and eight Ansons were on charge, increasing to 30 Dakotas by May45. Many VIP passengers were carried at this time, including Winston Churchill who was flown to France in Nov44. Regular services between Blackbushe and Prestwick were started in Sep45 to connect with transatlantic flights. In Feb46 the unit moved to Bassingbourn and was joined by the Yorks and Lancasters of 1359 VIP Flt. By 1947 the Dakotas gave way entirely to Yorks.

OO-AUH/AUI, FD772/82/89/92/94/95/97/98, 826/28/64/69/70/73/79/92, 904, FL518/59/84/88, 613/26/34, FZ549,629/31/33/34/36/37/46, KG518/28/83, 621/24/37/46/51/56/57/68/84, 729/70/82, KJ837/76, 926/30/32/52/73/74/79/80/83/94/97, KK153/91, 200/09, KN282/84/92, 386, 433/88/89/95, 508/12/13/14/15/19/20/21/22/70/71/74, 628/47/48/49/51, KP208/20/33/48/49/51/58, TJ167.

27 Squadron Oakington Nov47-Feb50 (Individual letters, call sign MODC plus individual letter).

This unit took Dakota IVs on charge when it was reformed as a transport squadron at Oakington on 24Nov47. Its main operation was the Berlin Airlift as part of 46 Group, at Wunstorf, Fassberg and Oakington. The unit was disbanded on 10Nov50 at Netheravon.

KJ878, 907/72/75/95, KK141/51, 213/19, KN238/41/74, 335/56/61/67/83/85/88/93/95, 410/15/33/42/46/62/91/92/97, 507/09/14/18/20/70/73, 605/10/23/29/31/38/41/56/57/94, 701, KP133, 214/23/79.

30 Squadron Oakington; Abingdon Nov47-Jan51 (Code JN plus individual letter, also just individual letters with Oakington Transport Wing; call sign MODF plus individual letter).

Dakotas equipped 30 Sq when it was reformed at Oakington on 24Nov47. Subsequently they were operated on the Berlin Airlift and in Nov50 Valettas began to replace them.

KJ930/75/94, KK127/29/51, KN214/31/38/92, 330/35/55/60/67/69/71/79/80/83/88/93/97, 402/06/10/15/19/28/33/42/52/87/92/95/97/98/99, 507/09/12/14/18/20/27/41/50/66/67/70/73/77/81/90, 607/08/23/28/31/38/40/47/52/56/57, 700, KP214/17/23/65/73.

31 Squadron India and Burma Jun42-Sep46 and India Nov46-Dec47 (Individual letters wartime 1942-46. Individual letter with call sign ODU plus individual letter, the last two letters being carried on the nose 1946-47).

31 Sq had a long association with aerial support and supply dropping, having served in India before the war. At the outbreak of WWII Vickers Valentias were in use and when Rashid Ali seized power in Iraq in Apr41 these were still with 'A' Flight, but 'B' Flight had some DC-2Ks (as the ex US airline DC-2s were designated). Four of the latter flew to Shaibah from Karachi with troops to help suppress the rebellion. These (DG468 to DG471) remained at Shaibah where they were joined by a further four US-registered DC-2s which were taken over from their American crews there. They were used to evacuate British civilians and to bring in more troops during May. The NC registered DC-2s returned to Pan American.

Unfortunately, the Germans had supplied fighter aircraft to Iraq, and six Me110s attacked Habbaniya destroying DC-2K NC14290. With the defeat of Rashid Ali, 31 Sq remained in Iraq until Aug41, when the DC-2Ks moved back to Karachi. In October seven flew to the Suez Canal Zone where they joined 117 Squadron's DC-2Ks at Bilbeis to carry supplies to forward areas in the Western Desert. Another DC-2K (DG475) was shot down by Bf109s, but without loss of life (one pilot was Flt Lt DSA Lord who later won a posthumous VC at Arnhem).

Upon Japan's entry into the war only two DC-2Ks remained airworthy at Lahore, where they had moved in September (the rest being in Egypt), and in the following January one of these was destroyed at Mingaladon in an air raid. Further aircraft were obtained and carried stores south, evacuating casualties on return. The DC-2s were wearing out and the first DC-3 (LR230) arrived in Apr42 from America. While the remaining DC-2s were overhauled, the DC-3 and one DC-2K continued operating in Burma. Six DC-3s had arrived by May, but two of these were destroyed by Japanese bombing on the following day at Myitkyina (LR230 and LR231). A third, piloted by Flt Lt Howell (who was pilot of DG475 when shot down in N Africa) managed to evacuate the crews and 65 refugees and wounded. Over 4000 persons were evacuated by 31 Squadron's Douglas transports.

The offensive began in 1943 with the first Wingate expedition. 31 Sq had 5 DC-3s to support the Chindits, who relied on them for all their needs from their base at Agartala. By Apr43 the first Dakotas had arrived and these were used throughout the next two years to supply troops in Burma when under Japanese attack and later when the 14th Army started to advance towards Rangoon, which was reached in Apr45. With the end of the war the Squadron moved on to Singapore and from there, in "Operation Mastiff", carried in supplies and returned with prisoners to India, operating 90 sorties over 3 weeks. One Dakota flew to Sarawak and took over from the Japanese. The unit flew into Java until replaced by Dutch units and 31 Sq was disbanded on 30Sep46. Only a month later, on 01Nov, 77 Sq was renumbered 31 Sq at Mauripur in India and Dakotas were again used on general duties until this too was disbanded at Mauripur on the last day of 1947.

DC-2:- AX755/67/69, DG468/69/70/71/74/76/77/79, HK820/21/37/47.
DC-3:- LR230/31/32/33/34/35, MA925/28/29/43.
Dakota:- FD775/76/80/81/83/87/88/91/92/93/99, 800/01/02/07/09/10/11/13/20/23/34/37/38/44/75/85/97/99, 909/16/18/19/24/32/34/36/48/49/51/53/62/64, FL507/12/13/27/35/36/37/40/41/43/55-59/66/71/73-79/94, 611/42, FZ579/85/97, 612/16/17/27/48/84, KG481, 520/41/42/

Chapter 3: Military Operators of the DC-3, C-47, R4D, Dakota and Li-2

51/54/60, 680/85/98/99, 720/25/58, KJ817/44/46/49/51/59/60/83/95, 915/16/18/19/34/51/54/56/57/60/67, KK117/18/19/64/66/67/73/74/78/79/84/85, 214/15, KN205/06/11/12/21/23/26/31/37/39, 301/04/06/09/26/84/88/89/99, 419/21/26/98, 501/03/35/36/45/46/60/69/75/76/86/96, 606/11/18/19/23/37/39/56/68/72/77/79/88/90/93, KP225/28/29/32/34/39/42/45/50/63/72/75.

46 Squadron Stoney Cross; Manston; Abingdon; Oakington Feb46-Feb50 (Code XK plus individual letter, also call sign code OFG plus individual letter carried on the nose).

Stirlings were received in Jan45 when 46 Sq became a transport unit, but Dakotas took over in Feb46 and were used on the Berlin Airlift from Wunstorf, Fassberg and Lubeck. They continued until the squadron disbanded on 20Feb50 at Oakington.

KJ801/10/37, 968/75, KK141/51/56/97, 213, KN238/41/76, 382/97, 402/08/10/16/32/33/37/42/46/47/49/87/91/92/98, 507/09/18, 641/81/90, KP214/41/79.

48 Squadron Down Ampney and Far East Mar44-Jan46 and Far East Feb46-Jul51 (Individual letters, also A or U plus individual letter, then code I2 plus individual letter, also I2-A and I2-U plus individual letters changing May45 to I2-M and I2-W plus individual letters; also call sign ODR plus individual letter, the last two letters being carried on the nose).

Hudsons based on Gibraltar were used until early 1944, when 48 Sq returned to the UK to join 46 Group and to re-equip with Dakotas at Down Ampney on 23Feb44, as part of Transport Command. In June, following intensive training, the unit took part in the Normandy landings, losing one Dakota. This was followed by Arnhem, where losses were more severe (eight Dakotas). The Rhine crossing in 1945 was the last wartime action, but during the whole period general transport operations and casualty evacuation had made up the bulk of the Squadron's work.

In Jul45 preparations were made to move to India and South East Asia Command (SEAC) and general transport duties continued there from Patenga, into Bengal and Burma and later down to Singapore, Java and Thailand. These operations continued until the unit was disbanded on 16Jan46. This was not the end of 48 Sq as on 15Feb46 215 Sq at Seletar was renumbered and its Dakotas took part in the anti-terrorist operations in Malaya. A detachment in Hong Kong later formed the Far East Communications Flight in Oct47. 48 Sq continued to use Dakotas until they were replaced by Valettas in May51.

FD898, 960/66, FL510/56/90/93, FZ551/92, 617/20/24/31/58/60/71/84/93, KG317/21/26/31/37/38/46/56/64/70/86/91/93/94/95/97, 401/04/06-09/11/14/16/17/19/21/23/26/28/36/39/48/52/56/86, 524/25/32/46/63/79/80/87/92/99, 610/24/32/45/59/78, 790, KJ822/24/43/44/49/58/87/95/96/97, 916/18/57/87/96/97, KK104/06/09/14/20/22/23/25/46/48/49/76, 207/10/13, KN209/22/27/31/38/40/44/48/53/61/70, 301/02/08/09/10/22/23/40/41/82/87, 402/04/12/13/33/36/54/58/59/61/62/65/69/85/87/97/98, 501/04/07/09/12/24/25/27/32/37/46/47/54/55/61/64/65/76/83/92/96/98/99, 606/11/14/16/19/20/22/26/33/92/99, KP211.

52 Squadron Far East Jul44-Jun55 (Individual letter, also nose code ODW plus individual letter; also nose codes TAW, TBW, TCW, etc.).

The Squadron was reformed at Dum Dum, Calcutta on 01Jul44 from C and D flights of 353 Sq, using Dakotas. These it flew over the "hump" into China and into forward airstrips in Burma, without any accidents. At the end of the war they moved down to Mingaladon at Rangoon in Oct46 and on to Changi, Singapore in 1947. In the following year aircraft were detached to Butterworth for anti-communist terrorist activities until Valettas replaced the Dakotas in 1951. The Squadron again took on some Dakotas in 1959 when the Voice Flight detachment of 209 Sq from Penang joined them. Their aircraft were fitted with loud-hailing equipment for anti-terrorist psychological operations and were used until the end of the emergency in Jul60. These aircraft were also used to drop smoke markers to aid RAAF Lincolns bombing the jungle, and in their own right to drop leaflets and calibrate navigational aids in the Far East theatre.

FD788/99, 803/09/13/19/22/44/82/96, 916/17/54, FL507/12/35/37/55/56/73/75, FL612/23/40/43, FZ595, 608/73/84, KG463, 521/55/56/73, 679/89, 702/18/19/22/24/64/85/86, KJ810/13-17/19/20/22/24/42/43/47/50/53/56/94, 904/13/14/16/17/23/26/32/45/47/52/55/62/63/72, KK106/10/17/22/83/90, 202, KN203/04/10/11/12/19/31/36/37/39/40/62/64/92/97/99, 301/03/07/08/10/16/19/22/41/50/52/58/59/83, 467/69, 501/ 06/34/36/47/72, 600/04/20/30/33/81/83, KP211/77.

53 Squadron Netheravon; Waterbeach Nov46-Jul49 (Code PU plus individual letter, also nose code ODT plus individual letter; call sign MODB plus individual letter by Nov47, the last two letters being carried on the nose).

Following the disbandment of the Liberator equipped 53 Sq in Transport Command on 15Jun46, the unit was reformed with Dakotas at Netheravon on 01Nov46. It took part in the Berlin Airlift from Waterbeach and Schleswigland but was again disbanded in July 1949 and the Dakotas gave way to the Hastings.

FL512, KK129/93, KN238, 381/85, 423/25/34/35/39/46/90/99, 508/77/90, 608, KN632/57, 700/01, KP215/17/23.

62 Squadron Far East Jul43-Mar46 and Sep46-Jun49 (Believed individual letter, also nose code ODE plus individual letter; later call signs MODC and MOFC plus individual letter).

62 Sq was withdrawn for training in supply dropping in May43 at Chaklala, India and its Hudsons were replaced by Dakota IIIs two months later. They started dropping supplies to the 14th Army in Burma in Jan44 and helped in every action in that theatre until the end of the war. Trooping and courier flights continued in South East Asia until disbandment at Mingaladon, Burma, on 15Mar46. The squadron was reformed from 76 Sq at Mingaladon on 01Sep46, with Dakota IVs and moved back to Palam, India in Mar47. By June the Squadron was up to full strength, but on 10Aug47 it was again disbanded. The Squadron was re-formed yet again, but at Waterbeach in Dec47 and again with Dakotas. These it used on the Berlin Airlift until final disbandment on 01Jun49.

FD840/46/82/89, 910/13-16/24/28/46/49/50/52, FL503/05/29/56/58/69, 600/02/32/44/46, FZ548/84/98, 627, KG457, 517/21/36/38/51/52, 676/79/95, 715/18/20/56/85, KJ824/42/43/56/66/74/94, 901/03/04/05/15/25/47/48/59/60/98, KK105/13/19/22/24/25/28/31/33/68/69/71/81/83/85/86/96, 211/13/14/73, KN204/07/09/37/38/45/72/76/79, 300/07/11/23/25/30/55/60/81/85/93, 434/46/55/57/90/92/98/99, 506/08/09/23/33/51/52/59/66/73/77/90, 607/08/23/25/32/40/42/57/60/81/96, 701, KP217/23/33/57.

70 Squadron Egypt May48-May50 (Codes, if any, unknown).

70 Sq became a Dakota C.4 unit on 01May48 when 215 Sq was renumbered at Kabrit in Egypt. These only remained until Valettas replaced them in Jan50.

KJ864/82, 906/10, KK147/58, 204, KN266/73, 554/55/60/75, 658/88/94/97/99, KP226/63.

76 Squadron Holme-on-Spalding Moor; Broadwell; India May45-Sep46 (Coded MP plus an individual letter initially, later just individual letters in India).

Having passed the war as a bomber unit, 76 Sq re-equipped with Dakotas on 08May45 at Broadwell and took them to India for general transport duties from Tilda in the following September. It disbanded at Palam on 01Sep46 when it was renumbered 62 Sq.

FZ686/88, KG321/86, 410, KJ863/64/72, 934/69, KK177, 204, KN237/93, 317/98, 402/25/32/46/52/56, 526/49/50/59, 664/67, KP225/37/43/46/56/57/59/60/61/62/63/66/67/68/69/71.

77 Squadron Broadwell; Full Sutton; India Jul45-Nov46 and Manston; Waterbeach Dec46-Jun49 (Code KN plus individual letter initially, with nose code U plus individual letter, call sign ODU, then in India just individual letter plus nose code U and individual letter. On reforming, code YS plus an individual letter, with nose code U plus individual letter, call sign MOFB).

77 Sq relinquished its Halifax bombers in Europe in Aug45. Dakotas were taken on charge at Broadwell in July/August and the unit moved to Mauripur, India in Sep45. It was renumbered 31 Sq on 01Nov46 but after a short interval, 271 Sq at Broadwell assumed 77 Sq's identity (01Dec46) as a Dakota unit in 46 Group. It was disbanded on 01Jun49, after spells at Manston and Waterbeach.

KG358/98, 407/52, KJ863/64/66/73/74/75/77/81, 906/07/34/67/88, KK128/31/50, KN252/74/76, 330/93, 434, 523/51/52/53/66/77/90, 605/07/25/37/39/56/60/62/65/68/72/77, KN690/93/96/97/99, KP219/23/24/25/28/29/32/33/34/39/42/50/64/72/75.

78 Squadron Egypt Jul45-Jul50 (Code EY plus individual letter, later possibly just individual letters, nose code J plus individual letter, call sign ODJ plus individual letter).

78 Sq transferred from Bomber Command and re-equipped with Dakotas before going to Almaza, Egypt on 20Sep45, moving to Kabrit a year later. It remained there until the Dakotas were replaced by Valettas in Jul50, operating in the Mediterranean and Middle East.

FD817/45, 927, FL524, 624, KG398, 402/07, 524/85, 629, 706, 808, KJ801/08/70/72/82, 908/14/98, KK127/56/57/58, KN243/65/66/85, 354/77/78/92/98, 435/53/77/78/81/86, 515/22, 638/50/52/53/54/58/74/75/80/92/94/95/98/99, KP210/18/33/35/43/47/55/56/65/74/77/78.

82 Squadron Benson Nov46-Dec52 (Individual letter codes).

While the squadron was engaged in photographic survey of West Africa, a few Dakotas were attached, presumably for transport support of the Lancasters. Three out of six were written off while with the squadron.

KK163, KN300, 431/38/58/93, 515, 650, KP215.

96 Squadron Far East Mar45-Sep46 (Code 6H, possibly not carried, plus individual letter, call sign unknown).

Halifaxes gave way to Dakotas when 96 Sq collected their aircraft at Cairo West at the end of Mar45. It then moved out to Bilaspur in India in May45 and was engaged in training paratroops and glider crews until it moved to Hmawbi, Burma in September for general duties in SEAC. At the end of the war the unit moved to Hong Kong in Apr46 where it was disbanded on 15Jun46 and all Dakotas passed to 110 Sq.

FD847/91, 936, FL509/32, 610/17/24, FZ553, 689, KJ497, 887/89, 913/20/52/63, KK107/15/19/88, KN213/14/21/47/63/64, 304/39/49/53/73/97, 400/04/05/11/12/14/19/21/22/30/67/68/69/70/79, KN543/70/72/79/88, 612/15/16/18/87, KP254.

110 Squadron Kai Tak (Hong Kong) Jun46-Jun47 and Changi (Singapore) Sep47-Jun52 (Individual letters only throughout, nose code Q plus individual letter Jun46-Jun47).

110 Sq took over Dakotas when 96 Sq was renumbered on 15Jun46 at Kai Tak and operated general duties in the Far East. It moved to Singapore in Sep47 and re-equipped there with Valettas by Apr52.

KJ843/87, 945/50/52/62/89, KK106/07/14/46/49/52/55/82/88, 202, KN212/13/21/31/40/47/97, 301/09/39/40/49/53/65/73/97/99, 400/04/05/14/30/56/67, 534/45/47/69/70/72/76/79/86/92/98/99, 611/16/20/22/33/58/81/87, KP254.

113 Squadron Aqir (Palestine) Sep46-Apr47 and Fairford May47-Sep48 (Possibly individual letter codes).

This unit was reformed when 620 Sq was renumbered on 01Sep46 as a transport unit with Halifaxes. Dakota IVs were added a few weeks later and both types remained in service until disbandment at Aqir, Palestine, on 01Apr47. Re-formation followed on 01May47 at Fairford, where Dakotas were again used. However final disbandment took place on 01Sep48.

FD793, KG344, KJ939, KN485, 675.

114 Squadron Egypt Aug47-Nov49 (Possibly individual letter codes, with call sign MOFM plus an individual letter).

Having operated Mosquitoes until 1946, 114 Sq was reformed at Kabrit on 01Aug47 with Dakotas for general transport duties. These continued until Valettas took over in Sep49.

KJ876/82, 906/55/81/88/98, KK127/47/57/58, 204, KN328/31, 473/75/85/86, 522/55, 639/53/56/58/75/77/79/81, KN689/92/94, KP209/10/18/33/63/77.

117 Squadron Egypt; Far East Jun43-Dec45 (Individual letter codes; possibly call sign ODF or OFF, plus an individual letter, the last two letters being carried on the nose).

In Oct41 117 Sq began to convert to DC-2Ks and moved to Bilbeis, near Cairo. It helped to evacuate Malta and flew General Alexander to take command in Burma. In May42 Lodestars and Hudsons replaced the DC-2Ks which went to 31 Sq. The Hudsons began to give way to Dakotas in Jun43 and these took part in the invasion of Sicily, moving on to Italy in September, where Bari became the base for supply dropping.

117 Sq was ordered to India on 25Oct, to help in the Burma campaign. By this time Wingate's second penetration into northern Burma was in contact with the Japanese, and 117 joined 62 and 194 Squadrons as part of 177 Wing to drop supplies and men. By Feb44 preparations had begun for the battle of Imphal which was to be the start of the move back to Rangoon, but before this took place the Chindits had completed their mission and had to be evacuated by 117 Sq.

The long haul to Rangoon followed and 117 helped with supply drops all the way. After VJ-Day it began helping to evacuate prisoners of war from Indo-China and Siam and this work as well as general supply duties continued until the Squadron disbanded at Hmawbi on 17Dec45.

DC-2:- AX767/68/69, HK820/21/37/47.
DC-3 LR231, MA925.
Dakota:- FD768, 820/33/34/36/39/47/75/84/85/90/94/95/96/98, 922/26/28/29/30/33/36/37/63/64/67, FJ709/10/11, FL512/24/25/36/52/56/73, 601/20/46, FZ590, 602/12/45, KG319, 413/35/58/61/82, 504/05/73/75, 626/84/96/98, 701/20/22/55, KJ892/97, 903/15/17/93, KK103/11/18/19/20/23/63/64/66/68/88, 211, KN209/11/18/21/45/48/57, KN303/313/15/16/17/20/26, 400/21/61, 502/62/67/69/87/93/97/98, 602/13/23/82/93, KP252/72.

147 Squadron Croydon Sep44-Sep46 (Code 5F allocated but no evidence of use. Carried call signs ODF and individual letter as fuselage code, the last two letters being carried on the nose. Post-war, some aircraft on the Croydon-Munich-Vienna run carried CMV markings with 110 Wing plus an individual number with different prefix letters for other routes).

This Squadron was re-formed with Dakotas at Croydon on 05Sep44 as part of 110 Wing which operated between the UK, France and Belgium, and later Italy. These services continued until 13Sep46 when the civil airlines had become re-established.

KG569, 730/34/45/48/49/50/68/71/75/76/80/83/96, 800/02/03/06, KJ801/03/08/10/38/39/62/65/78/80, 972, KK136/53/56, 212, KN268, 438/44/47/94.

167 Squadron Blackbushe Jul45-Feb46 (Markings unknown).

167 Sq used Dakotas from Blackbushe for a short while when their Warwicks were grounded for technical reasons between July and Sep45.

FZ696, KG361, 569, 730/49/50/76/80, 803, KJ801/10/38/39/62/65/73/80, KK136/53, 212, KN444/47/94.

187 Squadron Merryfield; Membury; Netheravon Mar45-Nov46 (Code PU plus an individual letter; code 5L also allocated later, but no evidence of use. Call sign OFT, later ODB, both with an individual letter, the last two letters being used as nose codes).

Although 187 Sq had a brief life in 1918 it did not reappear until Feb45 when it took on Halifaxes. However it was decided to equip with Dakotas and these began to arrive at Merryfield on 01May45. From then until 16Mar46 regular troop flights to India were flown. They operated to N Germany and Belgium from Oct45. A detachment flew to Italy and Austria in Jul46 and in October the main base became Netheravon, where the squadron was renumbered 53 Sq on 01Nov46.

FZ628/68, KG363/91, 598, KJ906/66/70/71/88, KK193, KN286/88/92, 371/79/80/81/82/83/88/93/94/95, 401/06/15/18/23/24/25/29/34/35/39/46/90/99, 506/08/10/17/18/90, 608/32/55/57/61, 700/01, KP215.

194 Squadron Far East May43-Feb46 (Individual letter codes only. Probably four letter call signs later).

The Squadron was formed at Lahore in India on 13Oct42, using Hudsons for communications duties between India and Ceylon. Preparatory to taking on Dakotas, two DC-3s were borrowed from 31 Sq (MA943 and LR235). The first Dakota (FD812) was allotted on 29May43 and the Hudsons were steadily replaced. Mail flights were taken over from Indian National Airlines in July, but this duty was handed on to 353 Sq in September and 194 Sq moved to Basel where it formed part of 177 Wing with 62 and 267 Squadrons.

194 Sq then became an Airborne Forces Squadron or "The Friendly Firm". They assisted 31 Sq in supplying the Chindits during their first expedition into Burma. Parachute supply training followed and on 01Jan44. They became operational with the Allied Troop Carrier Command under the USAAF, taking part in the Arakan campaign. They helped to land two brigades 200 miles behind Japanese lines near Imphal - dropping on "Broadway" and "Piccadilly" strips and eventually landing there alongside their USAAF counterparts. Other strips, with names such as "White City", "Blackpool" and "Clydeside" were opened later.

On 04Jun Troop Carrier Command ceased and 194 Sq came under the HQ 3rd Air Force. They helped to relieve Kohima and Imphal. Accidents were not infrequent because of the terrible weather and the restricted nature of many of the strips used. By mid-December the Squadron moved to Agartala and to Imphal. Supply dropping to the 14th Army continued through New Year 1945, as the Squadron moved down towards Rangoon and in August the unit moved there from Akyab. With the end of the war the emphasis was on supply work and prisoner evacuation from Bangkok. Disbandment came on 15Feb46 by which time the unit had played a crucial part in supporting all the important campaigns in Burma.

DC-3:- LR234/35, MA943.
Dakota:- FD801/12/19/21/22/31/35/43/54/56/77/78/80/81/82/94, 911/23/48/52, FL504/06/11/12/13/33/34/35/38/39/40/41/42/56/78, 619/43/44, FZ550/82/89/ 94/95/99, 600/12/16/44/64/73, KG413/45/59/62/65/81/93, 519/20/23/39/52/53/60/72/74/75/76, 678/79/94, 702/14/15/16/56/59/60/62/64/85/91, KJ854/59/85/86/88/94/95/97/98, 905/16/44/46/50/96/97, KK104/05/12/14/15/20/21/24/44/65/68/70/71/72/73/74/75/76/77/78/79/83/84, 207, KN202/16/29/43/46, 300/06/07/18/24/25, 466, 542/56/58/70/74/ 79/80/87/89/97, KN600/01/08/11/16/18/27/74.

204 Squadron Kabrit (Egypt) Aug47-Aug49 (Believed uncoded; call sign either ODN or OFN plus an individual letter, the last two letters being carried on the nose in some instances).

After operating flying boats throughout the war, 204 Sq was re-formed at Kabrit on 01Aug47 as a transport squadron with Dakotas. These were replaced by Valettas in 1949.

KJ876, 903/06/14/34/38/55/88, KK127/56/57/58/85, KN273, 378, 441/73/75/78/85/86, 522/55/74, 650/54/56/58/75/77/81, KP218/33/55/63/65/73/74/78.

206 Squadron Waterbeach Jan50-Feb50 (Believed uncoded).

Dakotas were used briefly during 1945/46, based on the Azores, supplementing Liberators.

KN367/69, 573, 608, 701.

209 Squadron Kuala Lumpur 1959.

This unit was formed from 267 Sq on 01Nov58 and initially operated Pioneers and Twin Pioneers from Kuala Lumpur in Malaya. Two Dakotas fitted with "Skyshouting" loudspeakers were taken over from 267 Sq shortly afterwards (KJ955 and KP277 named "Hope" and "Faith" when they passed on to 52 Sq in November of the same year). All three units used them for the same purpose, conducting psychological warfare against the communist guerillas in the Malayan jungle.

KJ955, KP277.

215 Squadron Far East Apr45-Feb46 and Kabrit (Egypt) Aug47-May48 (Individual letter codes only; call sign unknown).

215 Sq re-equipped with Dakotas for supply dropping in Apr45 and worked with the 14th Army over Burma. It moved on to Singapore in October where it was renumbered 48 Sq on 15Feb46. The squadron did not lapse for long as it was re-formed at Kabrit on 01Aug47, again with Dakotas, carrying out transport duties in the Middle East. This only lasted until 10May48, however, when a further renumbering took place, and the unit became 70 Sq.

FD780/99, 814/37/94, 930/54, FL510/32/37, 619, FZ589, 612, KG319, 795, KJ824/44/49/64/87/91/95-97, 906/18/34/38/49/78/82/91/93/98, KK104/08/10/19/20/25/27/30/40/48/76, 207/10/11/15/22, KN209/23/42/43/49/53/54/62/80/83/94, 302/09/10/23/24/31/83/90/91/99, 418/21/40/59/62/85/86, 522/47/79/80/83/86/88/89/92/96, 614/16/17/19/22/50/52/54/56/57/58/74/75/77/81/84/97/99, KP209/28/33/65/73/74/78.

216 Squadron Egypt Mar43-Jul50 (Individual letter codes, except around 1945/46 when used GH plus an individual letter. Call sign ODH (later MODH) plus an individual letter, the last two letters being sometimes carried on the nose).

This Squadron had the distinction of using the Dakota for longer than most units, receiving its first at Cairo West in Mar43 to replace the Bristol Bombays and Hudsons used on the run from Egypt to West Africa and for casualty evacuation from the Western Desert. Confusingly it was part of 216 Group. In Apr44 a detachment was sent to Agartala for two months, but otherwise the remainder of the war was spent maintaining communications in the Mediterranean and the Middle East based on Fayid and Kabrit, where Valettas were delivered from late 1949 onwards.

FD768/78/79/83/84/85/90/92, 804/05-08/14/16/17/18/28/29/30/31/33/39/40/42/45/47/49/52/53/57/59/66/75/76/86/88/92/93/96/98, 921/23/27/60/61/63, FJ711, FL510/22/24/30/33/34/35/49/52/52/54/73/75/89/99, 605/24/33, FZ551, 689, HK867, KG510/22/24/30-34/40/49, 689, 705/06/07/11/12/53, 808/31/70/73/76, 906/18/38/39/55/64/81/88, KK122/27/56-58, 217, KN218/64/65/66/73, 307/28/29/31/33/34/36/78, 471/73/75/77/79/80/81/82/85/86, 631/54/75/81/89/92/99, KP210/18/78.

231 Squadron Dorval (Canada) Sep44-Sep45 (Believed uncoded).

231 Sq was reformed at Dorval, Canada on 08Sep44 to carry out long-range transport services to Iceland and the UK. Consolidated Coronados were among the types on charge, but some Dakotas were also used from 45 Group, operating an airline type schedule for a few months between factories in the US and 45 Group HQ at Dorval.

FL528, KG740/77, KJ930/32, KK191/98, 204, KN673, KP210/17/76.

233 Squadron Blakehill Farm; Odiham; India Mar44-Dec45 (Code 5T plus individual letter, also 5T-A and 5T-U plus individual letters; also call sign OFU plus an individual letter, the last two letters being often carried on the nose; possibly individual letters only in the Far East).

233 Sq was re-equipped with Dakota IIIs at Blakehall Farm on 05Mar44 and on D-Day thirty aircraft towed gliders or took paratroops to Normandy. Twenty-one supply flights followed later the same day, four aircraft being lost. Casevac flights from the beachhead followed. Then, in September, there were 37 sorties to Arnhem during the first two days and 35 re-supply missions, when three aircraft were lost. General transport duties followed until the Rhine crossing when 24 Dakotas took part. 233 Sq moved to Odiham on 08Jun45 and on 15Aug to Tuliha, India, too late to take an active part and on 15Dec45 the squadron was merged with 215 Sq.

FD878, 931, FL526, FZ591, 665/66/69/72/78/79/80/81/85/86/88/92, KG313/14/15/29/41/51/56/98/99, 400/03/10/12/15/20/24/27/28/29/30/33/37/40/41/47/48/51/55, 529/55/59/61/66/85/86/89, 635, 700, KJ818/23/44/56/88/93/98, 902/03/55/64, KK106/23/41/69, 215, KN242/45/58, 313/14/21, 443, 550/86, 681/83/85/88/93/95, KP233.

238 Squadron Merryfield; India; Parafield (Australia) Jan45-Dec45 and Abingdon; Oakington Dec46-Oct48 (Australian call signs VMYxx plus two letters initially, then code WF plus individual letter. Call signs ODC and OFR plus individual letter, later MODD plus individual letter).

Having spent the bulk of the war as a Spitfire unit, 238 Sq was re-formed at Merryfield on 01Dec44 as a transport squadron. The intended Albemarles gave way to Dakotas which started arriving in Jan45. In the following month they flew to India to support operations in Burma but then went on to Parafield, Australia in support of the British Pacific Fleet, as part of 300 Wg. This proved unnecessary and disbandment came on 27Dec45. In the following year, on 01Dec46, 52 Sq became 238 Sq at Abingdon and Dakotas again flew in the latter's colours. They served on the Berlin Airlift, but on 05Nov48 the unit was again renumbered, to become 10 Sq.

KJ829, 982/87/89/91/93, KK127/30/32/40/41/48/49/51/54/89/90/95/96, 203, 315, KN203/07/08/10/14/15/32/33/34/36/37/39/43/44-48/50/51/55/57/59/60/62/63/64/72/87/92/98, KN356/60/67/79/82/85/88/93/96, 416/17/24/53/65/86/93/97, 507/12/14/18/20/28/40/43/44/46/47/65/66/72/73/81/83/90/96/99, 603/04/05/06/07/08/24/25/29/30/31/32/34, KP214.

While part of 300 Wg, some of these aircraft were allocated call signs in the VMYxx series, but most, while serving in India did not bear them. Those used were: VMYAD KK148, VMYAL KK149, VMYAP KK151, VMYAQ KN250, VMYBB KN528, VMYBG KN367, VMYBQ KN356, VMYBS KN360, VMYCN KN607, VMYCO KN605, VMYCP KN603, VMYCQ KN624, VMYCR KN634, VMYCS KN596, VMYCT KN604, VMYCU KN599, VMYCV KN631, VMYCW KN606, VMYCX KN608, VMYCY KN625, VMYCZ KN629, VMYDA KN543, VMYDB KN632, VMYDC KN465, VMYDD KN247, VMYDE KN544, VMYDF KN590, VMYDG KN572, VMYDH KN565, VMYDJ KN566, VMYDK KN581, VMYDL KN573, VMYDM KN260, VMYDO KN583, VMYDP KN540, VMYDQ KN396, VMYDR KN547, VMYDS KP211, VMYDT KP212, VMYDU KP213, VMYDV KP214, VMYDW KP215. These call signs remained with the aircraft while with 300 Wg, even when transferred to another unit within the Wing.

243 Squadron Camden (Australia) Feb45-Apr46 (Australian call signs VMY plus two letters).

243 was a Spitfire Squadron until 30Sep44 but when re-formed on 15Dec, it sailed to Canada and Dakotas were taken over at Dorval. On completion of training in Jan45, 15 Dakotas were flown across the Pacific to Australia, followed by a further echelon a month later. They provided scheduled services in support of Allied forces from Camden, NSW, as part of 300 Wg, to Manus Island, HQ of the British Pacific Fleet, to Leyte and later on to Singapore and Hong Kong. The Squadron disbanded on 15Apr46.

KJ995, KK115/29/34/44/46/47/48/49/51/52/55/87/88/92/99, KN240/47/50, 324/38/39/40/41/42/43/46-53/56-59/63-67/72/73/75, 528/29/30/31/65/81/99, 604/05, KP211-13.

Call signs used were: VMYAA KK155, VMYAB KK146, VMYAC KK129, VMYAD KK148, VMYAE KK147, VMYAF, KK152, VMYAG KJ995, VMYAH KN359, VMYAJ KK199, VMYAK KK144, VMYAL KK149, VMYAM KK134, VMYAN KK192, VMYAO KK188, VMYAP KK151, VMYAQ KN250, VMYAR KN346, VMYAS KK187, VMYAT KN530, VMYAU KN348, VMYAV KN341, VMYAW KN342, VMYAX KN339, VMYAY KN240, VMYAZ KN347, VMYBA KN363, VMYBB KN528, VMYBC KN338, VMYBD KN350, VMYBE KN364, VMYBF KN349, VMYBG KN367, VMYBH KN353, VMYBJ KN357, VMYBK KN351, VMYBL KN352, VMYBM KN340, VMYBN KN366, VMYBO KN375, VMYBQ KN356, VMYBR KN358, VMYBV KN341, VMYCD KN365, VMYCH KN529, VMYCJ KN531, VMYCL KN372, VMYCM KN373, VMYCO KN605, VMYCP KN603, VMYCT KN604, VMYCU KN599, VMYDK KN581, VMYDT KP212, VMYDU KP213, VMYDV KP211. See also 238 Sq.

267 Squadron Middle East; Far East Aug42-Jul46 and Kuala Lumpur (Malaya) Feb54-Oct58 (Individual letters, also A1, B1, etc., later also AW, BW, etc. Around 1945/46 used O or R plus individual letters, possibly the last two letters of the individual call sign. Names only with Voice Flight 1954/58).

267 Sq started the war as a communications squadron based at Heliopolis in Egypt. It was among the earliest to take Dakota Is in Aug41 and, with interruptions, used them until Nov58. They operated throughout the Mediterranean theatre, including support for the partisans in Yugoslavia, casualty evacuation and general duties. They moved to Bari, Italy in Nov43 and remained there until Feb45 when they were ordered to India to support the 14th Army in Burma. Disbandment took place there on 30Jun46. The Squadron was re-formed at Kuala Lumpur in Feb54 and again there were a few Dakotas on strength. These were fitted with loudspeakers and were used for four years before 267 Sq was renumbered 209 Sq on 01Nov58.

DC-3:- AX755, FJ711, HK867, HK993, 33642.
Dakota:- FD768/74/75/80, 815/18/30/34/40/41/43/45/48/49/50/51/52/53/55/57/58/63/65/75/76/78/79/83/86/89/91/92, 919/20/26/27/55/65/66/67, FJ711, FL529/30/32/44/67/89/93, FZ551, HK867, KG453/66/69/72/73/75/77/96, 511/23/46, 752/54, KJ810/42/43/47, 925/37/55/59/97/98, KK169/78/85/89, 208, KN205/07/08/11/25/30/60, 302/05/09/15/23/25/40/51/96, 400/20/58, 501/04/14/40/64/68/82/85/89/91/95, KN603/06/10/19/21/22/24/26/83/85/86, KP277.

271 Squadron Doncaster; Down Ampney; Odiham; Broadwell Aug43-Dec46 (DV plus individual letters initially, soon changed to YS plus individual letters with nose code OFV plus individual letter [call signs OFV, ODN and OFB]; later YS plus two-letter combinations).

This Squadron transferred from Bomber Command to Transport Command in 1943 and Dakota IIIs arrived at the end of that year. They moved from Doncaster to Down Ampney in Feb44 with 30 Dakotas on strength, to share the field with 48 Sq and 233 Sq, and for the next few months concentrated on preparations for D-Day, carrying out some night-time leaflet dropping raids. On 5-6 June the Squadron was responsible for the early paratroop drops over Normandy, and later for towing Horsa gliders. There followed regular shuttle flights taking over supplies and bringing back the casualties. On 17Sep 24 Dakotas took part in operation Market Garden to try to take the bridges at Arnhem. Two days later Flt Lt DSA Lord, DFC, gave his life and won a posthumous Victoria Cross while on a re-supply mission, flying Dakota KG374. On the 21st another member of the Squadron, Flt Lt Jimmy Edwards was shot down while flying his regular Dakota KG444 "The Pie Eyed Piper of Barnes". Fortunately he managed to force land behind Allied lines, and in saving his crew, gained the DFC.

In Mar45 12 Dakotas towed Horsa gliders from Britain in the Rhine crossing operations and a month later repatriation of British prisoners-of-war started and flying returned to routine transport duties. A move to Odiham was made in August and in October they went to Broadwell whence they carried troops to India for several months. There then followed passenger and freight services to the Mediterranean, until on 01Dec46 the squadron was re-numbered 77 Sq.

FD904, FL604/07/08/13/26/29/34/35/41/49/52/92, 601/07/13/14/15/22/25/26/28/33/38/39/41/55/60/67/68/90, KG314/18/27/40/45/50/53/57/58/62/65/67/72/74/75/76/78/87/89/90/91, 406/07/08/11/19/30/44/88/89, 500/12/14/15/16/45/50/57/58, KG561/62/64/84/89, 620/21/22/29/51/72/77, KJ866/72/73/74/77/81/82, 907/10/75/77, KK128/31/47/53/97, KN252/76/91, 330, 403/41, 523/51/52/53/57/77, 607/25/35/42/60/62/66, KN696, KP241.

353 Squadron India Apr44-Oct46 (Individual letter codes only; later carried nose code Y plus an individual letter, being the last two letters of the call signs which were possibly OFY plus an individual letter).

353 Sq transferred from patrol duties using Hudsons for transport work in Aug43, when it was moved to Palam, near Delhi, India. Dakotas supplemented the Hudsons in Apr44 and the remaining Hudsons were replaced by Warwicks from Nov44, only to be replaced by Dakotas in Apr45 and by Beech Expeditors. The unit was disbanded on 01Oct46.

FD780/87/88/99, 801/04/09/10/19/44/50/52/54/65/85/86/97, 912/17/18/50/53/54/59/64, FL503/07/08/09/13/35/41/55/57/66/70/71/73/75/77/78/79, 600/03/11/23/40/42/43, FZ554/79/87/97, 603/08/16/27/43/73/84, KG463/64/65/92, 521/37/39/41/42/56/57, 676/79/82/94, 702/16/17/19/95, KJ885, 905/23/46/47/55/56/58/63, KK112/17, KN231, 301/16/22/90/91, 454, 534/37, 600/33.

357 Squadron India; Burma Jan45-Nov45 (Single letter codes; probably with four-letter call signs later, the last two letters being carried on the nose).

Dakota IVs replaced Hudsons in Jan45 for operations into enemy-occupied Burma from Jessore, landing agents and supplies. The unit was disbanded on 15Nov45.

KG490, KJ889, 913/14/19/20/21/22/24/25/26/27, KK104/05/07/66/80/83, 263, KN304/57, 584.

435 Squadron India; Burma; Down Ampney Sep44-Mar46 (Individual letters only in Burma 1944/45; unit code 8J allocated in UK 1945/46 but not used, instead used call sign OFM plus an individual letter, call signs ODM and OFC also allocated).

This unit was formed with Canadian crews on 20Aug44, but the first Dakotas did not arrive until September when they were based at Chaklala, India. In December 435 Sq moved to Tulihal, Assam on the Burma front and became engaged in supply dropping to the 14th Army until Aug45. They were often under fighter attack during these operations. Once the Japanese troops had been driven out of Burma, 435 Sq returned to Down Ampney in England, and in Sep45 began flying from Croydon to various parts of Europe. These operations continued until Mar46 when, on the last day of the month, they disbanded and the aircraft started leaving for Edmonton, Canada.

FD821/31/34, 915/46/55, FL526/37, FZ658/71/78, KG313/17/20/37/41/97, 400/03/14/15/16/20/23/33/37/39/41/48/55/63/86/90/97, 557/59/63/80/87, 632/35/41/59/68/97, 713/57/59/62/88/92/93/94, KJ818/21/23/46/48/49/52/56/57/83/84/88/91/93/97/98/99, 902/12/15/48/49/50/53/57, KK105/06/08/16/43/69, KN208/27/41/58/61/70/77, 314/21, 413/27/36/40/43/48/51, 511/14/63/86, 665/66/76/83/85, KP220/21/24/26/ 27/41/75, KP241/75, TS422/25.

436 Squadron India; Burma; Down Ampney Sep44-Jun46 (Individual letters only in Burma 1944/45; unit code U6 allocated in UK 1945/46 but not used, instead used call sign ODC plus an individual letter, call signs ODM and ODN also allocated).

436 Sq was formed on the same day as 435 Sq and the Dakotas were taken on charge at Gujrat during October. They moved to Burma in mid-January, joining 435 Sq in supplying the 14th Army in the Burmese jungle. They followed a similar path back to Down Ampney and flew to Europe in October, continuing these operations until the following May, when the Dakotas started leaving for Canada. The unit disbanded in the UK on 22Jun46, but re-formed as part of the RCAF in Canada.

FD844/56/78, 934/64, FL532/37/52/78, FZ607/58/65/71/78, KG313/17/20/37/41/50, 400/03/14/15/16/20/23/30/33/37/39/41/48/55/86, 505/59/62/63/75/80/87, 632/35/59/68/78/97, 713/24/55/63/90/94, KJ820/21/44/45/51/52/53/55/56/58/85/87/93/96, 904/12/64/65/96, KK107/09/

CHAPTER 3: MILITARY OPERATORS OF THE DC-3, C-47, R4D, DAKOTA AND LI-2

10/13/26/43/81, KN208/10/13/15/16/20/22/25/41/58/61/77, 305, 413/27/43/48/51/56/58/61/62, 501/04/05/11/32/37/63/69/78/80/88, 620/55/65/66/76/78, KP221/24/26/75, TJ170, TS423.

437 Squadron Blakehill Farm; Europe; Odiham Sep44-Jun46 (Unit code Z2 plus DA onwards on NA onwards; from Aug45 Z2 plus an individual letter, also call sign ODO plus an individual letter, of which the last two letters carried on the nose; call sign changed to OFA May46; additional call signs suffixed by a letter W).

437 Sq was formed in England, at Blakehill Farm on 04Sep44. It took on Dakotas and within two weeks took part in Operation Market Garden to Arnhem. Subsequently it engaged in general transport duties and casualty evacuation flights between the UK and the Continent. In Mar45 gliders were towed over during the Rhine crossing and two months later the squadron moved to Belgium. Detachments operated in Norway from July to Nov45 and from Odiham between August and November, when the rest of the squadron moved back to the UK. Operations ceased at the end of May46 and by mid-June its aircraft had flown to Canada. Disbandment took place on 16Jun46.

FD870, FZ639/55/56/69/71/79/92/94/95, KG310/12/15/25/30/38/39/45/54/68/76/87/89/94/95, 409/12/22/25/27/37/52/89, 501/29/45/57/65/68/77/89, 600/02/10/23/34/39/50, 808, KN256/69/77/78/81/91, 436/43, 676, KP221/27/28.

510 Squadron 1943 to 1944.

Among a mixed collection of smaller communications aircraft a few Dakotas were used by 510 Sq within the UK. In Apr44 it was replaced by the Metropolitan Communications Squadron. No Dakota has been identified.

511 Squadron Lyneham Oct43-Jul44 (No evidence that individual letters or squadron codes ever carried).

Based at Lyneham in Wiltshire, 511 Sq operated Liberators and Albemarles to Gibraltar and Malta. The latter were replaced by Dakotas from Oct43 onwards. By Jul44 only long-range flights to India were being flown using Liberators and Yorks, and the Dakotas were dispensed with.

FD869, 900/02/05/39/40/44/45, FL515/17/46/47/59/61/62/63/85/86/88/96/97, FL649, KG432, KN653/63.

512 Squadron Hendon; Broadwell; Belgium; Holme-on-Spalding Moor; Palestine; Italy; Lyneham Jun43-Mar46 (Initially HC plus an individual letter which was sometimes suffixed by a figure 1; from Jul44 HC plus AA onwards or UA onwards; from Jul45 no unit code letters carried, instead used call sign ODK plus an individual letter, of which the last two letters carried on the nose; call signs sometimes suffixed by a letter W).

This unit was formed at Hendon with Dakotas on 18Jun43 to operate between the UK and North Africa. It moved to Broadwell in Feb44 to become an airborne forces unit and on D-Day towed gliders to Normandy, later bringing back casualties. 46 gliders were towed to Arnhem in September and 24 to the Rhine crossings in Mar45. In that month part of the Squadron was based at B.56 Evere, Belgium, returning in July to Holme-on-Spalding Moor when flights to the Middle East started in October. It moved on to Egypt in Oct45 and then back to Southern Italy to cover Italy and the Balkans. It returned to England in February and disbanded on 14Mar46.

FD772/82/89/94/95/97/98, 826/28/64/69/70/72/73/99, 900/02/03/04/05/39/40/44/45, FL515/17/18/19/44/45/46/59/66/68/84/96/97, 603/04/05/08/09/10/11/12/19/23/27/32/33, FZ548/50/56/60/63/68/69, 609/10/13/16/27/29/36/37/40/47/49/51/56/58/90/94/96, KG314/22/23/24/30/33/44/47/48/49/54/59/61/63/65/66/68/69/71/73/77/79/90/92, 407/18/22/31/32/80/86, 522/44/58/60/65/70/82, KG590/91/93/98, KN330/35/46/54/55/56/60/61/64/68/69/70/75, 441/76/99, 523/31, 641/55/57/61, 700, KP214.

525 Squadron Weston Zoyland; Lyneham; Membury; Abingdon Apr44-Dec46 (Code WF plus individual letter. Later allocated 8P but no evidence of use. Allocated call signs ODD and ODP).

Initially formed in Sep43 with Warwicks, these were grounded in Apr44 and 525 Sq took Dakotas on charge in Jun44. In September services to Allied bases in France and Belgium began and with the end of the war extended to the Mediterranean. Trooping ceased in Mar46 and instead mail and newspapers were carried to the Continent. On 01Dec46 the Squadron was renumbered 238.

FL562/88, 649, FZ628/68, KG345/90/91, 550/69/82, 637, 731/33/35/37/41/44/51/73/74, 808, KJ829/61, 966/68/70/71/72, KK147/51/56/93, 213, KN234/38/41/50/76/85/92, 367/78/79/80/82/88/93/94, 401/02/06/08/10/15/16/17/18/23/24/25/32/41/42/46/49/53/76/87/91/92/93/97/98/99, 500/07/09/12/14/20/38/73/90, 657/61, 700.

575 Squadron Hendon; Broadwell; Melbourne; Blakehill Farm; Italy; Egypt Feb44-Aug46 (Coded I9 plus an individual letter or pair of letters; from 1945 call signs ODS, OFD, OFN and ODK [or OFK] plus an individual letter, the last two letters being carried on the nose).

575 Sq was formed on 01Feb44 at Hendon from part of 512 Sq and two weeks later moved to Broadwell with Dakotas. It engaged in training exercises with the airborne forces until the invasion in June, when it helped to carry the 6th Airborne Division to Normandy. It also took part in the Arnhem landings, meanwhile carrying out general supply and casualty evacuation duties. Its final operation was the Rhine crossing, when 24 gliders were towed. In Jan46 it moved to Bari in Southern Italy to cover Italy, Austria, the Balkans and the Central Mediterranean area until it disbanded on 15Aug46.

FD873, 900/02/45, FL518/66, 605/10/11/12/23/33, FZ593, 613/16/23/36/40/46/62/65/68/74/83/95/96/98, KG310/11/12/20/23/25/26/27/28/32/34/39/43/48/49/55/59/61/63/80/86/88, 402/25/31/32/34/38/42/49, 501/11/22/29/44/50/67/93, 602/08/15/20/30/34/46/47/54, 774, 864, 906/66/88, KK154, KN258/73/75/90, 431, KN513/22/48, 636/40/63.

620 Squadron Aqir (Palestine) Jun46-Sep46 (Possibly uncoded).

This unit operated Dakotas briefly from Jan46 when it moved to Aqir, Palestine, until it was renumbered 113 Sq on 01Sep46.

KG344, KJ939, KN476, 675.

1314 (Transport) Flight Accra was formed in Jul44 and used Dakotas until disbanded on 30Sep45.

FD782/94/98, 828/64/70/71/72, KG495, 528, 675, 713/32/39/42/43/47, KJ747, 839/37/40, KN445/86/96, 646.

1315 (Transport) Flight was formed at Merryfield on 01Jan45 with an establishment of 15 Dakota IVs, for service in the South-West Pacific. It arrived at RCAF Station, Lachine on 20Mar and on 04Apr its aircraft began to leave for Australia. The flight was based at Archerfield from 01May and provided transport support for the British Pacific Fleet, as part of 300 Wg. Detachments operated as far afield as Hong Kong, Manus Island and, after Aug45, Japan. On 02Mar46, aircraft began leaving for the UK and the Australian headquarters was disbanded on 29Mar46. The Hong Kong detachment continued and moved to Iwakuni in Japan as part of the Commonwealth Occupation Force until the flight was disbanded on 21Aug46.

KJ980, KN344/54-58/60/61/62/65/66/68-76, 529/31, 649, KP213/14/15. These had VMYxx call signs applied in full. VMYBJ KN357, VMYBN KN366, VMYBO KN375, VMYBP KN376, VMYBR KN358, VMYBS KN360, VMYBT KN361, VMYBU KN368, VMYBV KN369, VMYBW KN370, VMYBX KN371, VMYBY KN374, VMYBZ KN354, VMYCC KN362, VMYCD KN365, VMYCE KN355, VMYCF KN344, VMYCG KN362, VMYCH KN529, VMYCJ KN531, VMYCL KN372, VMYCM KN373, VMYDU KP213, VMYDV KP214, VMYDW KP215.

1316 (Dutch) Flight operated six Dakotas alongside various light transports from formation at Hendon on 21Jun45 until disbanded on 04Mar46.

NL201/02/08/09.

1325 Flight Dishforth; Christmas Island; Changi Aug56-Apr60.

KJ945, KK129/93, 210, KN434, 598, 649.

1577 (Special Duties) Flight was formed at Lyneham on 09Aug43 to carry out trials of the Lancaster III and Halifax V in India. In May44 Dakota KG490 was allocated for glider-towing trials at Mauripur. It was replaced by KG463 on 24Dec44. The trials ended in Apr45 and KG463 went to 3 PTS.

1680 (Transport) Flight (code MJ plus an individual letter) maintained air services to bases in the Hebrides and flew some Dakotas from Prestwick from Jun44 until disbanded on 07Feb46.

FD772, FZ670, KG647/99, KJ977.

13 Operational Training Unit (OTU) had one Dakota on charge, KG489.

32 OTU

FL595/98, 615/16/18/21, FZ557, KG485.

105 OTU (code 8F plus an individual letter) at Bramcote replaced its Wellingtons with Dakotas in Jun45, becoming 1381 TCU on 10Aug45.

FD789, 904, FL547/86, KG353, 568/77/80/84/99, 600.

107 OTU (codes ZR & CM with individual letters) was formed on 03May44 at Leicester East with Dakotas for the conversion of transport and glider-tug crews and became 1333 TSCU on 01Mar45.

FD782, FL519/84, 604/08/09/13/26/29/31/34/35, FZ578/91, 626/29/36/37/64/72/91/93/95/97, KG360, 405/38/50, 513/27/43/47/78/95/97, 601/04/06/08/09/12/14/17/18/29/40/43/48/52/57/65/70/71, 728, KJ906, TP181, TS424/33/34/35/36.

108 OTU (individual letters, also A1, B1, C1, etc) was formed on 10Oct44 at Wymeswold with an establishment of 40 Dakotas and became 1382 TCU on 10Aug45.

FD789, 904, FL586/96, KG393, 567/81/88/94/96, 603/05/07/11/13/28/31/36/63/67, 778/82, KJ806/35/61/63/64/66/70/72/73/74/75/77/81/82, 907/10/11/12, KJ931/34.

109 OTU (individual letters then individual numbers 1-25, except 13) was formed at Crosby-in-Eden on 11Aug44 with 20 Dakotas and became 1383 TCU on 10Aug45.

FL626/52, FZ609, KG502, 619/33/38/39/42/44/49/51/55/57/58/60/61/62/64/66/69, 726.

240 Operational Conversion Unit (code NU plus an individual letter) was formed from 1382 TCU at North Luffenham on 05Jan48 and its Dakotas were replaced by Valettas by the middle of 1951.

KJ810/38/61/65/78, 972/83/95, KK129/31/33/34/41/97/98, KN252/68, 312/47/55/61/75/80, 408/31/37/38/49/62/88/94, 521/28/31/44/64, 629/31/34/73/80, KP231/33/51/76/79.

1330 Conversion Unit (Two digit numbers then call sign ODS plus an individual letter, the latter two numbers being sometimes displayed on the nose) was formed from No 1 Middle East Check & Conversion Unit at Bilbeis, Egypt on 01Aug44 and flew Dakotas until disbanded on 01Mar46.

FD779/92, 803/04/05/07/08/14/16/18/30/41/61, FJ711, HK867.

1331 Conversion Unit was formed at Risalpur, India on 01Sep44 and was disbanded on 15Jan46.

FD882/83, 964, FL611/42, KG349, 573, 883/89.

1333 (Transport Support) Conversion Unit (TSCU) (Codes DA, DB onwards initially, then individual numbers 21 to 54, then finally code ZR from about Jan46 plus an individual letter, sometimes with a bar over it; call sign ODY plus an individual letter, the last two letters being displayed on the nose) was formed from 107 OTU at Leicester East on 01Mar45, moving to Syerston on 25Oct45, passing its aircraft to 240 OCU on 05Jan48.

FD864, FL509, 613/26/31, FZ578/91/93, 613/64/66/72/91/93/97, KG360/71, 405/38/42/50/54, 513/43/78/95/97, 601/06/08/09/12/14/17/18/40/43/44/48/51/52/62/65/70, 728, KJ808/38/65/78/80, 972, KK133, KN252/85, 347/61, 531/44/66, 629/31/34/41, KP231/79.

1334 TSCU (individual letters only) was formed in Mar45 from the Transport Support Training Unit at Chaklala and disbanded on 31Mar46.

FD877/95/97, 950, FL556, FZ559/87, KG453/60, 571/76, 676/77/80/96, 717/63/85/86/87/91, KJ926/62, KK119, KN225/87/94/96, 321/89, 457, 535, KP237/74.

1336 (Transport) Conversion Unit (TCU) (code ZS plus an individual letter) was formed at Welford on 30Jun45 and disbanded on 01Mar46.

FD939, FZ549/92, 622/24/25/81/86/88, KG321/49/51/64/98, 402/07/10/36/40/47/52/54, 514/61/78/85, 629/45/50/71, TS426.

1380 TSCU (codes EZ and KG) was formed at Tilstock on 10Aug45 and was disbanded on 21Jan46.

FL631.

1381 TCU (individual letters only, then code 7Z plus an individual letter, then 8F) was formed from 105 OTU at Bramcote on 10Aug45, moving to Desborough on 19Nov45 and later to Dishforth. On 18Feb48 the unit was disbanded.

FD828/69, 902/40/44, FL517/18/47/59/62/84/85, 634, FZ549/92, 623/29, KG321/49/51/59/64/91/98, 402/07/10/36/51/65, 583, 645/46/56/57/58, 731/33/35/37/41/44/45/51/73, 875, 970/83/95, KK129/34/91/98, 212, KN268, 342/46/69, 401/18/31/76/95, 541/66/81, 640, KP248, TS426.

1382 TCU (initially individual letters, or individual letters plus 1, later code NU plus an individual letter) was formed from 108 OTU at Wymeswold on 10Aug45, moving to North Luffenham on 10Dec47 where it became 240 OCU on 05Jan48.

FD864, 904/39, FL567/84/86/96/97, 614/33/35, FZ628/33/46, KG314/80/92, 408/40/47/73, 561/64/67/81/88/89/94/96, 603/05/07/11/13/17/21/28/31/36/50/55, 778, KJ838/39/65/78, 912/72/73/83/95, KK133/41/47/97, KN252, 347/54/55/75/80, 408/15/31/38/49/88/94, 521/28/31/44/73/77/90, 602/07/25/29/31/34/41/73, KP231/51/76/79, TP187, TS424/27/32/33/34/35.

1383 TCU (code GY plus individual numbers to Sep45, then GY plus individual letter) was formed from 109 OTU at Crosby on 10Aug45 and disbanded on 26Jun46.

FD872, FL626/52, FZ609/23/51/98, KG314/33/73/92, 454, 502/43, 619/33/38/42/44/49/51/55/57/58/60/62/63/64/66/67/69/71, 726, KJ911/83, KN361.

1384 (Heavy Tr Conversion Unit) (HTCU) (code Q6 allocated but usage unknown) converted from Wellingtons in Dec45 at Ossington and disbanded on 30Jun46.

FD798, TS432.

TRAINING SCHOOLS

1 Parachute Training School (1 PTS) (See 1 Parachute and Glider Training School below). Received Dakotas at Ringway in Jan44. A move to Upper Heyford took place in Mar46 staying until Dec47.

FL531, 638/39, FZ560/64/66, KG357/60/65/72/78, 419, KJ882, 910/61/71/75/77, KK104/27/28/29/31/33/35/38/97, 212, KN215/50/86, 371/95, 403/18/23, 513/17, 605/42, 700.

1 Parachute and Glider Training School (1 PGTS) (call sign MODA plus an individual letter) Upper Heyford, seems to have overlapped 1 PTS as they operated concurrently. The first aircraft to operate with 1 PGTS arrived at the begining of 1948, moving to Abingdon in Jun50, when Hastings and Valettas were delivered.

KG393, KJ919/77, KK104/27/29/35/38/97, 212, KN250/95, 342/71/94/95, 403/18/23, 517/28/38, 605/41, 700.

3 Parachute Training School (3 PTS) was formed from the Air Landing School at Chaklala, India on 26Feb44, becoming the Transport Support Training School (later Unit) on 03Jun44 and 1334 TCU in Mar45.

FD801, FL623, FZ559/69, KG556, 601, KN222/36, 502.

Glider Pick-Up Training Flt, Ramsbury Jan45-Nov45.

TS424/25/33/34/35/36, TP181/87.

6 Lancaster Finishing School, Ossington, received some Dakotas before becoming part of 1384 HTCU on 01Nov45. Only one serial number is known.

FL635.

UNITS

Air Transport Tactical Development Unit (ATTDU) at Netheravon used Dakotas between Jun44 and Sep45.

FD826, FL639/51, FZ560, 650/87, KG360, 450/51/52, KN285/97, TP187, TS424.

CHAPTER 3: MILITARY OPERATORS OF THE DC-3, C-47, R4D, DAKOTA AND LI-2

Heavy Glider Servicing Unit (1 HGSU), mainly operated Dakotas equipped with towing gear for moving Hamilcar gliders around, based at Netheravon Mar44-Dec46.

KK143, KN641/62, TS422/24/25/26/27/32/34.

1 Middle East Check & Conversion Unit (MECCU), Bilbeis, Egypt Jun43-Jul44.

HK867(DC-3), FD805/08/14/18/30/41, FJ711

Transport Command Development Unit (TCDU), Brize Norton used Dakotas between Jan46 and Jul48, then Abingdon until Oct51.

FZ650/87, KG915, KJ861, KN274/85/95/96/97, 356/80, 641/42/61, KP208.

Transport Support Training Unit (TSTU) was formed from 3 PTS at Chaklala, India on 03Jun44. In Mar45 it became 1334 TCU.

FD879/85/86/97, 912/47/50, FL531/33/38, 556/57, KG460/92, 538/56/71/76, 676, 790/01, KJ865, KN361/93.

COMMUNICATIONS FLIGHTS AND SQUADRONS

Aden Communications Flight, Khormaksar Jan48-Mar51: FD943, KJ876, 964, KN215, 307/23/36, 453, KP210.
AHQ Italy Communications Flight, Marcianese and Udine Nov45-Oct47: FD892.
Allied Expeditionary Air Forces, Communications Flight, Heston Dec43-Oct44: TJ167.
Allied Forces Northern Europe, Norway Feb62-Sep67: KN645, KP208.
AOC Air Command S E Asia, Ratmalana; Changi Jan45-Nov46: HK983, FD800/03/79, 967, FL510, FZ631, KG507/17/18, KG682, 761/95, KK203/05, KN300.
Austria Communications Flight, Vienna Dec45-Jan47: KG528.
Bengal/Burma Comm Sq, Baigachi Dec44-Apr45: KG453, KJ961, KK103/11/21/25.
Bomber Command Communications Squadron (BCCS), Halton Aug44-Sep46 (code HZ): KG782
British Air Forces of Occupation Communications Flight/Squadron/Wing, ex 1315 Flt: KJ930, 980, KN340/57, 422, 612/17/49, KP213. Buckeburg, Germany Jul45-Jan47: KG770, KJ994, KK200/09, KN386, 628,45/47, KP222. Miho, Japan: see CommAF Japan below.
British Air Forces S E Asia Comm Sqn, Willingdon (Delhi) Oct44-Apr46: FD879, 920/67, FL542, KG507/18, 682, 723/61/65/95, KN300.
Burma Communications Flight, Mingaladon Apr45-Dec47: FD779, 803/22/83, FL510, KJ887, 932/62, KK202/05, KN467, 534/58/98.
Central Flying School (CFS): KJ994, KN647.
Coastal Command Communications Flight (CCCF), Bovingdon Feb53-Nov56: KN452, KP208.
Commonwealth Air Forces, Japan, Miho, Japan; KJ887, 980/94, KN340/72, 422, 547, 611/12/17/49, KP213.
East Africa Communications Flight, Eastleigh, Kenya Jul44-Dec50: KJ840, 979, KP238.
Empire Central Flying School: KP248.
Empire Flying School: KN282.
Far East Air Force Examining Squadron, Changi, Singapore: KN341
Far East Communications Squadron (FECS), Changi and Tengah, Singapore Oct47-Feb52: KG624, KJ887, 930/32/52/62, KK114/210, KN303/72/73, 561/72/76/98, 620/49.
Fighter Command Communications Squadron (FICCS), Bovingdon: KJ930
Flying Training Command Communications Flight (FTCCF): KK209.
AHQ India Communications Squadron, Palam Oct44-Apr46: FD879, FL510/42, KG507/18, 723/65, KK163, KN287, 325, 543, 682.
2 (India) Group Communications Flight: KG765, KN300, KP263.
3 (India) Group Communications Flight: KJ819.
Iraq (and Persia) Communications Flight, Habbaniya May45-May50: FD863, KG495, 509/73, KJ880, 956, KN290, 435, 519/43, 622/33.
Malaya Communications Squadron, Kuala Lumpur Oct45-Nov46: KG458, 505, KJ822, KK114, KN598.
AHQ Malta Communications Flight/Squadron, Luqa Jun48-Aug56, call sign MBRB plus a single letter: KK129, KN279, 452, 598, 645/47.
Mediterranean Middle East Communications Squadron, Heliopolis, Cairo Feb44-Apr46, call sign MODL: FZ553/73, KG706, KJ981, KK200, KN377, 478/81/82, 659.
Metropolitan Communications Squadron (MCS), Hendon Apr44-Apr46: KG738, KN645, TJ167.
Middle East Communications Squadron (MECS), Akrotiri, Cyprus Apr44-Jul79: HK983, KJ876, 955/81, KK200, KN377, 452/78/82.
Netherlands East Indies Communications Squadron, Kemajoran Nov45-Aug46: KK106/14, 205, KN618.
Second Tactical Air Force Communications Squadron (dispersed) Aug44-Jul45: FD799, KG736, KJ803, KK200/09, KN628/45/47
SHAEF Communications Squadron, Gatwick and Detmold Oct44-Jul45: KJ994, TJ170.
Signals Flying School: KK202.
Southern Communications Squadron (SCS): KJ882, KN328/77, 478.
Special Transport Flight, Kabrit, Egypt Jan50-Jul50: KJ876/82, 981, KK200, KN328/77, 478.
Technical Training Command (13 MU), Henlow Feb45-Jan48: KG311.
Third Tactical Air Force Communications Squadron, Comilla, India Oct44-Dec44: FD783/99, 803/19/22, KK111/21/25, 205.
Training Command Examining Unit, Manston and Brize Norton: KJ810, 984, KN290, KN394, 449/52, 564.
West Africa Transport & Communications Squadron, (Also Dakota Flight, WA), Takoradi, Gold Coast Oct46-Nov47: FD794, KG528, KJ836/37/40, KG528,675, KN496.

RESEARCH ESTABLISHMENTS

Aeroplane & Armament Experimental Establishment, Boscombe Down: FZ564, KN407, TS423, 41-18608.
Airborne Forces Experimental Establishment, Sherburn-in-Elmet Nov45-Jan52: FD943, KK127, TS431/32.
Central Fighter Establishment, W Raynham: KN700.
Electronic Countermeasures Establishment,: FD791.
Parachute Test Unit, Henlow: KJ836/52/74.
Royal Aircraft Establishment, Farnborough and West Freugh: FL519, FZ564, KJ836, KJ993, ZA947.
Telecommunications Research Establishment, Defford Apr44-Jul44: FZ564, 646.

Group and Wing COMMUNICATIONS FLIGHTS and SQUADRONS

18 Group Communications Flight: KN649.
42 Group: KN515.
45 Group was formed to handle aircraft deliveries across the Atlantic. The Communications Sq Dakotas were used to return ferry pilots to the plants, but others, unfortunately, were lost during the delivery flight, so remained on charge: FD864/78, 900, FL528/30, FZ676/97, KG396, 411/468, KG509, 740/46/79/84, 801, KJ984/86, KK129/87/88/91/98, KN271/74, 345, 409, 673, KP231.
46 Group Communications Flight: KP220.
110 Wing: KG776.
112 Wing: KN289.
113 (Transport) Wing Comm Flt, Nassau Apr43-Jul45: FD900, FL528, KG508.
117 Wing Communications Flight, Calcutta Sep44-Mar46: FD803.
144 Wing (1314 Flight): KG713/39.
216 Group, MMEAF: HK867(DC-2), FD782/94/98, 864/70/73, KG615, 774, KJ966/80, KK156, KN273/90, 640,61.
221 Group Communications Sq: KJ961.
224 Group Communications Sq, Ratmalana, Ceylon: KN585.
228 Group Communications Flight: KJ819.
282 Wing: KG705.
300 Group: KN581, 608.
300 Wing was the parent body for RAF units in Australia providing support for the British Pacific Fleet. It comprised 243 Sq, 238 Sq and 1315 Flt and moved to Hong Kong at the end of the war. Dakotas were allotted initially to the Wing and then to individual units: KN342/46/47/71/73/96, 528.
500 Wing: KJ993.

STATION FLIGHTS

Individual Dakotas were allotted to many airfields as station flights.

Blakehill Farm	KN369
Changi	KN240, 309, 598
Delhi (Air Attache)	KP208
Dishforth	KN538
Gatow	KG783, TS423
Gibraltar - North Front	KN446/52
Hendon	KG621, KJ994, KN645
Henlow	KG311, KJ852/74
Iwakuni	KN547, 649
Kabrit Wing	KJ840
Kasfareet	KN245
Lajes, Azores	FD864, KN274, 385
Little Rissington	KN506

Lübeck	KN370
Malta C & TTF	KN452, 598
Mauripur SF/CF	KG507, 723/65, KK163, KN260, 543, 603/24/82
Netheravon	KN361
Northolt	KJ994, KN508, KP208, TJ167
Oslo (Air Force N Europe)	KN645, KP208. SHAPE KJ994
Pretoria (Brit. Mil. Mission):	KN290
St Eval	KN274, 385
Seletar	KN572, 611/79
Sofia, Bulgaria (Brit. Mil. Attache)	KN513
Tempsford	KG544
Vistre Flight	KN356, KP279
Wymeswold	KG604

MAINTENANCE AND OTHER UNITS

Maintenance Units were No 5, Kemble; No 8, Little Rissington; No 12, Kirkbride; No 13, Henlow; No 22, Silloth; No 33, Lyneham; No 44, Edzell; No 107, Kasfareet; No 390, Seletar. No doubt some of the aircraft allotted to the station flights may have been with the MU for storage, and MUs are given in the Production History chapter of the book if storage was long-term.

A few units are not listed here as although they appear in the Production History entries the aircraft with these units were just 'passing through' in most cases:

An Aircraft Delivery Unit (ADU) probably kept an aircraft for the period of a delivery, unless it was damaged during that time.

A Ferry Unit (FU) had a few Dakotas for returning pilots to the pool.

R & SU Repair and Servicing Units were responsible for repairs on site and needed the occasional Dakota to carry spares.

No 85 R & SU ex Airborne Salvage Section performed a massive role in India recovering damaged aircraft, and used a number of Dakotas: KG536, 758, KJ819/54, 961.

SP or Staging Posts looked after aircraft while on delivery, and if an aircraft was damaged or written off while on their charge an SP may be listed.

Miscellaneous units:
Airwork Ltd:	TS423
C in C Med:	KJ981
Ferranti:	TS423
Queen's Flight:	KN452, 645
ACM Tedder:	TJ170

BERLIN AIRLIFT

During the Berlin Airlift, Dakotas were allotted to Bassingbourn, North Luffenham, Oakington, Waterbeach, Honington, Upper Heyford and Abingdon:

Abingdon	KK395
Bassingbourn	FL510, KG631, 738, KN352, 647
Honington	KN250, 368, 517
North Luffenham	KJ810, KN312
Oakington	KJ865/66/74/94, 907/52/61/70/77/97/98, KK127/28/29/31/36/51/53, 212/13, KN235/38/76/92, 330/55/60/67/69/79/80/81/85/88/93/97, 402/06/10/15/19/24/28/33/34/42/46/50/76/87/91/92/95/97/98/99, 506/07/08/09, KN514/18/20/41/50/51/52/66/72/73/77/81/86/90, 607/08/23/25/31/32/38/40/41/52/56/57/60/94/96, 700/01, KP204/17/65/73
Upper Heyford	KN394/95, 517/38, KP265
Waterbeach	KJ866/74, 907/61/70/75/77, KK131, KN292, 330/60/67/69/81/85/93, 446/99, 520/23/51/66/67/73/90, 607/08/32/40/57/60/96, KP214/17/23

BRITISH OVERSEAS AIRWAYS CORPORATION

The RAF serial, Transport Command call signs and UK civil registrations are given below. The call signs were ODZ and OFZ plus single or double letters painted on the fuselage sides:

FD769	ODZBK/G-AGFX	FD773	ODZAK/G-AGGB
FD770	ODZCK/G-AGFY	FD777	ODZDK/G-AGGA
FD771	ODZEK/G-AGFZ	FD796	ODZFK/G-AGGI

FD824	ODZZ/G-AGHF	FZ638	ODZF/G-AGJV
FD825	ODZY/G-AGHH	FZ641	ODZD/G-AGJW
FD860	ODZHK/G-AGHK	KJ802	OFZY/G-AGKA
FD861	ODZHL/G-AGHL	KJ804	OFZK/G-AGKB
FD862	ODZT/G-AGHP	KJ807	OFZW/G-AGKC
FD867	ODZX/G-AGHJ	KJ811	OFZV/G-AGKD
FD868	ODZV/G-AGHN	KJ867	OFZU/G-AGKE
FD901	ODZW/G-AGHM	KJ868	OFZT/G-AGKF
FD941	ODZU/G-AGHO	KJ871	OFZR/G-AGKH
FD942	ODZP/G-AGHU	KJ879	OFZS/G-AGKG
FL514	ODZS/G-AGHR	KJ928	OFZQ/G-AGKI
FL516	ODZR/G-AGHS	KJ929	OFZO/G-AGKK
FL520	ODZQ/G-AGHT	KJ933	OFZP/G-AGKJ
FL544	ODZO/G-AGIP	KJ935	OFZN/G-AGKL
FL548	ODZLK/G-AGIO	KJ976	OFZJ/G-AGNA
FL560	ODZN/G-AGIT	KJ985	OFZK/G-AGMZ
FL604	ODZC/G-AGJX	KJ990	OFZL/G-AGKN
FL607	ODZM/G-AGIS	KJ992	OFZM/G-AGKM
FL608	ODZB/G-AGJY	KK137	OFZH/G-AKNB
FL628	ODZH/G-AGIX	KK139	OFZD/G-AGNE
FL629	ODZA/G-AGJZ	KK142	OFZF/G-AGND
FL647	ODZMK/G-AGIZ	KK145	OFZG/G-AGNC
FZ561	ODZK/G-AGIA	KK201	OFZC/G-AGNF
FZ567	ODZL/G-AGIY	KK206	OFZA/G-AGNK
FZ614	ODZG/G-AGJU	KK216	OFZB/G-AGNG
FZ630	OFZJ/G-AGIW		

RAF Serial/Constructor's number Index:-

Although it has proved possible to identify almost all the c/ns for RAF aircraft, one or two remain outstanding. RAF record cards do not carry any means of identifying an aircraft beyond the serial number, though in a few cases, the USAAF identity is given. In such cases this has proved a mixed blessing, as some do not agree with data which were thought to be correct. It must be pointed out here that it has been assumed that RAF Dakota serial numbers were allotted in the same order as the USAAF numbers and in the vast majority of cases nothing has come to light to disprove this theory. A few very early aircraft probably did not follow this hypothesis and this is commented upon in the Production History chapter. Aircraft diverted from USAAF stocks do not follow any order, but the RAF cards record the USAAF serial number. One temporary diversion was 41-18608 which was used by the Aircraft & Armament Experimental Establishment at Boscombe Down to test the type in late 1942 before Lend-Lease aircraft arrived. It went back to the USAAF in January 1943. Also unidentifiable are one or two aircraft which are known or thought to have been built up from spares. HK893 is well known, being named appropriately! It now seems possible that HK993 might be the same as HK893.

Other missing aircraft were diverted from the USAAF but not documented as such, as they were almost certainly transfers in India where records were sketchy. Indeed, it will be noted that unit allocations are incomplete for some aircraft sent to ACSEA during war-time, though matters improve post-war.

It has only proved possible to identify many allocations by searching the Operational Record Books at the PRO, Kew, and for many of the smaller units entries were confined to staff postings.

In the following tabulations, space is saved by not listing every serial and its respective c/n; instead the ranges of consecutive serials and c/ns, where they occur, are shown separated by an oblique (/).

Douglas DC-2
AX755	c/n 1309	DG475	1410
AX767	1239	DG476	1251
AX768	1249	DG477	1237
AX769	1367	DG478	1403
DG468	1314	DG479	1240
DG469	1315	HK820	1350
DG470	1316	HK821	1406
DG471	1244	HK837	1371
DG472	1402	HK847	1313
DG473	1308	HK867(1)	1311
DG474	1401		

(*Note:* HK867 crashed on delivery and was used again on a DC-3.)

Dakota I
FD768	4445	FD789/98	9043/52
FD769/73	6223/27	FD799/808	9077/86
FD774/88	6238/52	FD809/18	9126/35

Chapter 3: Military Operators of the DC-3, C-47, R4D, Dakota and Li-2

Dakota III
FD819/28	9181/90
FD829/38	9235/44
FD839/58	9307/26
FD859/68	9405/14
FD869/78	9487/96
FD879/98	9531/50
FD899/908	9621/30

FD909/28	9676/95
FD929/35	9762/68
FD936	9770
FD937/38	9835/36
FD939/58	9860/79
FD959/67	9945/53

Dakota II
FJ709	4931
FJ710	4933

FJ711	4954
FJ712	7313

Dakota III
FL503	9954
FL504/13	10022/31
FL514/33	10097/116
FL534/43	10209/18
FL544/48	11903/07
FL549/57	11909/17
FL558/66	11919/27
FL567/69	11931/33
FL570/71	11975/76
FL572/80	11979/87
FL581/89	11989/97
FL590/98	11999/12007
FL599/607	12009/17
FL608/16	12019/27
FL617	12029
FL618/23	12039/44
FL624	12047
FL625/26	12049/50
FL627/30	12052/55
FL631	12057
FL632/40	12059/67

FL641/49	12069/77
FL650/52	12079/81
FZ548/53	12082/87
FZ554/81	12089/116
FZ582/622	12137/77
FZ623/31	12179/87
FZ632/40	12189/97
FZ641/49	12199/207
FZ650/58	12209/17
FZ659/63	12219/23
FZ664	12208
FZ665	12238
FZ666/67	12246/47
FZ668/73	12253/58
FZ674/75	12266/67
FZ676/78	12271/73
FZ679/85	12276/82
FZ686	12284
FZ687	12286
FZ688/92	12291/95
FZ693/98	12299/304

Dakota II
HK867(2)	4909

HK893	ex spares

Dakota I
HK983	4653

Dakota III
KG310/15	12305/10
KG317/32	12314/29
KG333/34	12332/33
KG337/52	12344/59
KG353/80	12362/89
KG381/96	12411/26
KG397/466	12432/501
KG467/86	12579/98
KG487	12807
KG488/96	12809/17
KG497/505	12819/27
KG506	12829
KG507/26	12911/30
KG527/56	13010/39
KG557/76	13149/68
KG577/94	13300/17
KG595/606	13326/37
KG607/19	13366/78
KG620/36	13380/96
KG637/50	13449/62
KG651/71	13468/88
KG672/723	13539/90
KG724/28	13725/29
KG729	13733
KG730/69	25274/313
KG770/809	25447/86
KJ801/39	25585/623
KJ840	25625
KJ841/42	25705/06
KJ843/79	25782/818
KJ880/82	25825/27
KJ883/93	25913/23
KJ894/912	25925/43
KJ913/15	26080/82
KJ916/19	26084/87
KJ920/23	26089/92

KJ924/27	26094/97
KJ928/31	26099/102
KJ932/35	26104/07
KJ936/39	26109/12
KJ940/42	26114/16
KJ943/65	26235/57
KJ966/69	26259/62
KJ970/72	26264/66
KJ973/76	26409/12
KJ977/80	26414/17
KJ981/85	26419/23
KJ986/99	26425/38
KK100/02	26439/41
KK103/07	26553/57
KK108/11	26559/62
KK112/15	26564/67
KK116/19	26569/72
KK120/23	26574/77
KK124/27	26579/82
KK128/31	26584/87
KK132	26589
KK133/36	26714/17
KK137/41	26719/23
KK142/49	26725/32
KK150/62	26734/46
KK163/81	26854/72
KK182/85	26879/82
KK186/92	26884/90
KK193/96	26969/72
KK197/200	26974/77
KK201/04	26979/82
KK205/08	26984/87
KK209/12	26989/92
KK213/16	26994/97
KK217/20	26999/27002

Dakota IV
KN200/01	27004/05

KN202/04	27066/68

KN205/09	27070/74
KN210/20	27076/86
KN221/25	27088/92
KN226/37	27094/105
KN238/43	27107/12
KN244/49	27114/19
KN250/51	27121/22
KN252/53	27178/79
KN254	27181
KN255/57	27183/85
KN258/61	27187/90
KN262/64	27192/94
KN265	27196
KN266/67	27198/99
KN268/70	27201/03
KN271/73	27205/07
KN274/77	27209/12
KN278/80	27214/16
KN281	27218
KN282/83	27220/21
KN284	27223
KN285/87	32532/34
KN288/89	32536/37
KN290/92	32539/41
KN293/95	32543/45
KN296/99	32547/50
KN300/02	32552/54
KN303/05	32556/58
KN306/07	32560/61
KN308	32587
KN309	32592
KN310	32594
KN311/12	32612/13
KN313/15	32615/17
KN316/18	32619/21
KN319	32623
KN320	32625
KN321/23	32627/29
KN324/26	32631/33
KN327/29	32635/37
KN330/32	32639/41
KN333/35	32643/45
KN336	32649
KN337/39	32651/53
KN340/42	32655/57
KN343/45	32659/61
KN346/48	32663/65
KN349/51	32711/13
KN352/54	32715/17
KN355/57	32719/21
KN358/60	32723/25
KN361/62	32728/29
KN363/65	32731/33
KN366/68	32735/37
KN369/71	32739/41
KN372/74	32743/45
KN375/77	32747/49
KN378/80	32751/53
KN381/87	32755/61
KN388	32763
KN389	32809
KN390/95	32811/16
KN396/402	32819/25
KN403/09	32827/33
KN410/16	32835/41
KN417/20	32843/46
KN421/22	32848/49
KN423/27	32851/55
KN428/36	32857/65
KN437/43	32867/73
KN444/45	32912/13
KN446/49	32916/19
KN450/53	32921/24
KN454/57	32926/29
KN458/64	32931/37
KN465/69	32939/43
KN470/71	32945/46
KN472/73	32948/49
KN474/79	32951/56
KN480/85	32958/63
KN486/88	32965/67
KN489/90	33005/06

KN491/92	33009/10
KN493/94	33013/14
KN495	33016
KN496/98	33019/21
KN499/500	33024/25
KN501	33027
KN502/03	33030/31
KN504/05	33034/35
KN506/07	33038/39
KN508/09	33041/42
KN510/11	33045/46
KN512/13	33049/50
KN514/15	33052/53
KN516/18	33056/58
KN519	33060
KN520	33062
KN521/22	33064/65
KN523/24	33068/69
KN525/26	33072/73
KN527	33075
KN528/29	33078/79
KN530/31	33082/83
KN532/33	33086/87
KN534	33089
KN535	33092
KN536	33107
KN537/38	33137/38
KN539/40	33140/41
KN541	33143
KN542/43	33146/47
KN544/45	33149/50
KN546/47	33152/53
KN548/49	33156/57
KN550	33159
KN551	33161
KN552/54	33163/65
KN555/56	33167/68
KN557/58	33171/72
KN559/61	33174/76
KN562/63	33178/79
KN564/65	33182/83
KN566	33185
KN567/71	33187/91
KN572	33194
KN573/74	33196/97
KN575/76	33199/200
KN577/78	33203/04
KN579	33207
KN580/81	33210/11
KN582	33213
KN583	33215
KN584	33217
KN585/87	33219/21
KN588/91	33223/26
KN592	33228
KN593	33230
KN594	33233
KN595/96	33235/36
KN597/98	33238/39
KN599/607	33242/50
KN608/09	33252/53
KN610	33255
KN611	33257
KN612/16	33259/63
KN617/18	33265/66
KN619/20	33269/70
KN621/22	33272/73
KN623/26	33276/79
KN627/28	33281/82
KN629/31	33285/87
KN632	33289
KN633	33317
KN634/36	33319/21
KN637	33323
KN638/41	33325/28
KN642/43	33331/32
KN644/46	33334/36
KN647	33338
KN648/49	33340/41
KN650/51	33343/44
KN652	33346
KN653/54	33348/49

KN655/56	33352/53	KN692/94	33406/08
KN657	33355	KN695/97	33410/12
KN658/59	33357/58	KN698/700	33414/16
KN660	33360	KN701	33418
KN661/64	33362/65	KP208	33419
KN665/66	33368/69	KP209/11	33421/23
KN667/69	33371/73	KP212/13	33425/26
KN670/71	33375/76	KP214/17	33428/31
KN672/73	33378/79	KP218/19	33433/34
KN674/75	33381/82	KP220/22	33436/38
KN676/78	33384/86	KP223/24	33440/41
KN679/81	33388/90	KP225/27	33443/45
KN682/84	33392/94	KP228/30	33447/49
KN685/86	33396/97	KP231	33451
KN687/89	33399/401	KP232/36	33517/21
KN690/91	33403/04	KP237/79	33539/81

DC-3

LR230	4173	LR235	1949
LR231	1915	MA925	4116
LR232	4130	MA928	4931
LR233	1923	MA929	4933
LR234	4851	MA943	4118

Dakota II

TJ167	4930	TJ170	unknown

Dakota III

TP187	12609/19536?	TS431	19613
TS422	19345	TS432	19361
TS423	19347	TS433	19579
TS424	19350	TS434	19574
TS425	19353	TS435	19566
TS426	19569	TS436	19349
TS427	19551		

DC-3C Troop Contract

WZ984(1)	6208	XF648	33331
WZ984(2)	9172	XF667	33331
WZ985	9803	XF746	33408
XB246	25275	XF747	32716
XE280	26735	XF748	33416
XF619	33042	XF749	27078
XF623	32943	XF756	26717
XF645	33390	XF757	25925
XF646	25825	XG331	26411
XF647	26082		

Dakota III

'KG661'	10200	ZD215	27127
ZA947	10200		

Ground Instructional Airframes

3493M	ex 8 AF - PTS Ringway 08Jan43	6253M	11922
		6291M	12220
3494M	ex 8AF - PTS Ringway 08Jan43	6292M	13369
		6297M	12197
4838M	9984	6298M	12277
4844M	9930	6299M	12156
4926M	12423	6300M	13733
4957M	13316	6301M	13382
4981M	13451	6302M	12388
4989M	13010	6345M	33005
5097M	25590	6346M	12376
5201M	13471	6348M	33069
5245M	25473	6357M	12388
5351M	9188	6358M	13382
5566M	12220	6359M	13733
5567M	12453	6360M	12156
5742M	12918	6410M	11992
5749M	11905	6507M	25473
5949M	6226	6596M	25289
6053M	25814	6729M	33287
6229M	32917	6731M	33451
6230M	13461	6763M	27121
6252M	4930		

'4987M' was noted 03Feb57 at Field Aviation, Tollerton, painted in error for 4981M.

(Total 1929 DC-3 & Dakota)

UNITED STATES OF AMERICA

US Army Air Corps interest in the DC-2 began with the purchase in 1935 of an 'off the shelf' example for evaluation as the XC-32. The value of such a transport was quickly appreciated and two C-34s were ordered with special interiors for delivery in Apr36. These were assigned to the First Staff Sq at Bolling Field, DC and one was used by the Secretary of State for War. At this time 18 C-33s were also ordered. These had a cargo loading door and were distributed in ones and twos to units associated with the Air Depots and Air Corps bases.

Between January and September 1939 the much modified C-39 was delivered and the 35 aircraft were assigned to transport squadrons and Air Depots, some with as many as five aircraft. In 1939 the units were the 1st Transport Sq at Patterson Field, OH; 2nd at Langley Field, VA (and to Olmstead, PA early in 1940); the 3rd at Duncan Field, TX; the 4th at McClellan Field, CA; the 5th at Olmstead and then Patterson; the 6th at Olmstead and the 7th at McClellan. They were absorbed into the Transport Groups by 1941 and carried the brunt of domestic army transport work following the attack on Pearl Harbor.

Even before the outbreak of war in 1941 the **US Army Air Forces** (so named after 20Jun41) had ordered further transports. Amongst these were 545 C-47s in Sep40 and 92 C-53s in mid-1941 as well as a further 200 C-47s. The first C-54s were also ordered at this time, to meet long range needs. In Sep41 a further 70 C-47s and 50 C-53s were ordered, using production capacity initially planned for airline orders. Early in 1942 the massive wartime orders began to be placed, with 1270 C-47s and 65 C-53s, followed in July by 134 more C-47s and in September by 2000 C-47As to be built at the new plant at Oklahoma City. In Dec42 a further 2000 C-47As and C-47Bs were ordered from the Long Beach plant. The next orders were placed in Feb44 for 2000 C-47As and C-47Bs from Oklahoma City and in Jun44 for 1100 C-47Bs, again from Oklahoma City. The last order was for 1469 C-47Bs and 131 C-117As in Jul44 from Oklahoma City, but some were cancelled at V-J Day.

Although the first C-53s were delivered in late 1941 and the first C-47s in early 1942, these were inadequate for current needs, and only in early 1944 did supply begin to match demand. The use to which the various models were put is discussed under Air Transport Command and the various theatre Troop Carrier Commands.

Air Transport Command

Air Transport Command was formed as Air Corps Ferry Command on 29May41 to undertake the task of ferrying British lend-lease aircraft from their factories to the Atlantic coast for transfer to British crews at Montreal and the Atlantic crossing. South Atlantic ferry services also had their origins in the delivery of British orders and in Mar41, even before legislation authorising Lend-Lease, a request was made for 50 transport aircraft to operate across Africa from Takoradi to Cairo. Twenty Lodestars were the first aircraft bought through the USAAF from US owners and in the absence of any available Air Corps pilots the British government entered into an agreement with Atlantic Airways Ltd, a subsidiary of Pan American Airways, and they delivered the first ten aircraft from Miami on 21Jun41, via Belem in Brazil (where they were interned for three days by neutral Brazil). Later deliveries were made under US ownership until Africa was reached.

On 26Jun41, Pan American Airways agreed to establish a ferrying service and an air transport service from Miami to the west coast of Africa and on to Khartoum. Pan American Air Ferries handled delivery of many aircraft supplied direct to Britain. Following extensive training, the first DC-3 service from Bathurst in the Gambia to Khartoum did not leave until 21Oct41 and only ten transports had left by the time of Pearl Harbor. Ferry Command itself flew two survey flights to Cairo via the South Atlantic route in late 1941, using converted B-24s. While four-engined types were the only practicable means of servicing the long over-water segments, DC-3s were pressed into service on many other routes.

Initially the vast experience of the airlines with the DC-3 was used, and contracts were placed for the operation of new USAAF C-53s (and later C-47s) on some routes. Pan American began with five C-53s between Miami and Natal, Brazil in Feb42, later expanding to 14 aircraft. Eastern began a service from Miami to South America, Trinidad, Puerto Rico and Nassau under contract to Air Service Command on 01May42 and on to Natal in June to connect with services across the South Atlantic.

Other contracts were placed with Northeast to fly Goose Bay, Greenland, Iceland and finally to Prestwick by Jul42 using two C-53s. Northwest flew to Fairbanks, AK; American to Iceland; Western to Edmonton, Canada and United from Dayton to Alaska. The DC-3s remained on the Alaska run throughout the war, and continued to Brazil for some time.

Early in 1942 Ferry Command was split into a Domestic Wing with six US sectors, and a Foreign Wing with four sectors. The latter were the North Atlantic Sector at Presque Isle, ME, the Transatlantic Sector at Bolling Field, DC, the South Atlantic sector at Morrison Field, W Palm Beach, FL and the Pacific Sector at Hamilton, CA. These sectors became Wings a few months later and the South Atlantic Wing moved to Georgetown. Two new Wings were added, the Caribbean Wing at Morrison and the Africa-Middle East Wing at Cairo and later at Accra in the Gold Coast. Ferry Command was renamed Air Transport Command on 20Jun42 but on 30Apr42 the 50th Transport Wing which combined the domestic transport squadrons, became the nucleus of Troop Carrier Command with the responsibility for most intra-theatre transport. During this period, on 06May42, the War Department took over many of the civil airlines' DC-3s leaving only 200 to continue domestic services.

The oldest route to come under the ATC was the Pan American-Africa service from Bathurst, Gambia which eventually reached as far as Cairo. They had seven DC-3s in Oct41, but later eleven were used, still in civil markings, though their exact status is not clear. All were ex-airline DC-3s, several acquired within a few weeks of manufacture. Some were sold to the USAAF and others to the British and on 18Feb42 an order was given that the trans-Africa service was to become a military operation as soon as practicable. The eleven DC-3s were allotted USAAF serial numbers (42-38250 to 38260) on 14Mar42, but all had been transferred to the RAF ten days earlier. USAAF C-53s were then assigned to the route and by June 38 were in use, but Pan American's involvement did not end until December, and they continued their South Atlantic operations.

As the situation in China deteriorated, 25 airline DC-3s were transferred to open a supply line across the Himalayas into China. This was the AMMISCA project or American Military Mission to China. In the event the civil aircraft were considered under-powered, and all but seven C-47s with R-1830s were reassigned within the US and replaced by 15 C-53s and at least eight new C-47s. Crewed by reserve officers they formed the 1st Ferrying Group of the 10th Air Force, India, and 26 aircraft left Morrison for Karachi between 19Apr and 13May42. In India the Trans-India Ferry Command and the Assam-Burma-China Ferry Command were formed with four DC-3s and ten borrowed from PAA - Africa and began carrying fuel for the Doolittle Tokyo raid. They were then diverted to assist General Stilwell in northern Burma, as a crisis in the Middle East led to the diversion of twelve 10th Air Force transports.

Late in 1942 the first Ferrying Group moved from Karachi to Assam. By mid-December, 15 of the 62 DC-3s sent to India had been destroyed and four were still in the Middle East. Many others were unserviceable, and the Assam airfields were in poor condition. ATC took over the "Hump" operation on 01Dec42 and began plans to replace the C-47s with C-46s. Despite this, 85 C-47s were in use before the first C-46s arrived, and 160 C-47s remained in the China-Burma-India theatre even in 1945. The ATC allotted its aircraft to the various base units attached to airfields from which the aircraft operated.

Other ATC services using C-47s mainly did so late in the war, operating a regular long-haul intra-theatre supply service mentioned later.

EUROPE AND NORTH AFRICA

Northern Europe 1942

Project 'Bolero', the USAAF build-up in the UK started in May42. The 8th Air Force was formed in Jan42 as the air element of a proposed North African invasion task force. However, demands in the Pacific caused this plan to be abandoned a month later, and the 8th became the organisation for 'Bolero'. Three Troop Carrier Groups (TCG 60th, 62nd and 64th), each with four squadrons with a nominal strength of 13 C-47s (and a few C-53s in the 62nd) were assigned to the 8th AF on 12Jun, 06Sep and 18Aug respectively. The air echelons of each group were ferried to the UK. Plans called for a build up to 15 TCGs in the 8th AF by the end of 1943. In Aug42, however, the North African landings were reinstated and the first three groups became part of the 51st Troop Carrier Wing (TCW) on 01Sep42 and were transferred to the 12th AF in the Middle East. The 315th TCG, with only two squadrons of C-47s and C-53s, was assigned to the 8th AF on 01Dec42, but in May43 16 of its 22 aircraft were detached to serve with the 12th AF. On 16Oct43 the group was assigned to the 9th AF and with two new squadrons added it reverted to troop carrying duties.

North Africa and the Western Desert

When Rommel launched his offensive in Jan42, forcing the British forces back into Egypt, help was sought from the United States. In Jun42 all available bombers were moved from India to the US Army Middle East Air Force. Initially the transport element comprised 12 borrowed C-47s (or C-53s). In the following November the 316th TCG was sent from Texas to Deversoir, Egypt, with 52 C-47s, eventually being based at El Adem as the transport element of the newly formed 9th AF, a function which it fulfilled for seven months.

As plans for the invasion of North Africa progressed, the 60th TCG was teamed with the 2nd Battalion, 503rd Parachute Infantry Regiment. On 07Nov this force left St Eval and Predannack in Cornwall, SW England to make a drop near Oran at La Senia and Tafaraoui on the following day. This was Operation 'Torch'. The C-47s straggled along North Africa to Gibraltar and three were interned in Spanish Morocco (later becoming part of Iberia's fleet), but most reached their destination by late afternoon. The 64th TCG with 39 C-47s followed on 09Nov from St Eval to Gibraltar and took the 3rd British Parachute Battalion to Algiers. 34 C-47s reached their destination on 11Nov and 26 dropped 312 paratroops at Duzerville, 6 miles SE of Bone on the 12th. They then ferried in supplies and on the 16th followed up with a further drop of 384 British paratroops at Souk-el-Arba, 90 miles west of Tunis. Meanwhile the 60th TCG at Maison Blanche Airport, Algiers, dropped 350 more paratroops at Youks-les-Bains on 12Nov. The C-47s then air-supplied the 14th Fighter Group (P-38s) and the 15th Bomb Squadron (A-20s) for operations from Youks. The 62nd and 64th TCGs dropped 530 paratroops at Depienne, 10 miles northeast of Pont du Faks to attack Tunis from the southwest in the last major paratroop drop in North Africa.

In Dec42 the 51st TCW was assigned to the Central Algerian Composite Wing at Algiers, but this was stillborn and on 05Jan43, it went to the 12th AF, operating as the Northwest African Air Service Command, carrying out routine transport duties. At this time 135 of the original 154 C-47s were still operational. When plans for the invasion of Sicily were approved, the 51st TCW was transferred to the Northwest African Air Force Troop Carrier Command. The 52nd TCW was later earmarked, comprising the 61st, 313th, 314th and 316th TCGs, all with C-47s. Meanwhile, control of North Africa was completed on 13May43.

Sicily and Southern Italy

The first airdrop in the invasion of Sicily was 'Ladbroke' and took place on 09Jul43. In this a total of 147 planes, including 112 C-47s from the 51st TCW, towed 137 Waco CG-4s and 8 Horsas all with British pilots and carrying 1600 troops of the British 1st Airborne Division from the El Djem area of Tunisia. The gliders were released near Syracuse and Floridia in southeast Sicily. There were no losses among the tugs and the operation was the most successful of the invasion. Later in the night the second mission 'Huskey No 1' involved 226 C-47s of the 52nd TCW (amongst which were 35 from the 316th TCG) and 3405 paratroops of the US 82nd Airborne Division were dropped over North Gela. Eight aircraft were lost to enemy action and the troops were badly scattered in the dark. Because of this and the unexpectedly weak opposition met by the first drop, the next drop was delayed and 'Huskey No 2' on the 11Jul was nearly a disaster. 144 C-47s of the 52nd TCW tried to drop 2000 troops of the 504th Regimental Combat Team to reinforce the 82nd Airborne Division, but lack of coordination resulted in 23 aircraft being shot down by both sides, and 60 damaged. Some casualties were caused by allied naval units, but many crews were saved. The next operation was 'Fustian' on 13Jul, when 132 C-47s of the 51st TCW carried British troops. 14 planes were lost, 50 damaged and 27 returned without completing their drops.

Operations by the 9th AF in the Mediterranean ceased in Aug43 and its only troop carrier unit, the 316th TCG, was transferred to the 12th AF's XII TCC on 23Aug.

Training for the invasion of Italy was carried out in Tunisia during August with units of XII TCC (51st and 52nd TCW) and they moved to southern Sicily with the 82nd Airborne Division between 02 and 06Sep. The troops were landed by sea at Reggio and Salerno, and the C-47 units were used to drop supplies until airfields were ready. Casualties were evacuated by the 29 TCS (313 TCG, 52nd TCW) as well as two US and one RAF squadron from the Northwest African Air Service Command.

On 13Sep 82 C-47s and C-53s of the 61st, 313th and 314th TCG dropped 1300 men of the 504th Regiment of the 82nd Airborne Division south of the Sele River, with no losses. On the following day two more drops were made. 125 aircraft dropped 1900 men of the 505th regiment in the same area and 40 aircraft of the 64th TCG attempted a drop at Avellino, but the men were scattered. After the later Anzio landings, the need for troop carrier units diminished and the 52nd TCW returned to the UK and the 9th AF on 14Feb44, while the 51st TCW came directly under the 12th AF from 05Mar, when XII TCC was disbanded. It remained under the Mediterranean Allied Tactical Air Force. In Feb44 the 7th and 15th TCS of the 62nd TCG were sent to Brindisi to support partisans in Yugoslavia, Albania and Greece. Such operations averaged 35 C-47 sorties a night and the squadrons were attached temporarily to 334 Wing, RAF. These squadrons were replaced by all four squadrons of the 60th TCG from 16Mar on, and continued supply drops as well as 194 landings during Jul44. Ten C-47s were lost (one for every 458 sorties). The 7th TCS returned to this activity in October, followed by the 51st TCS and in the following March by the 16th TCS (64th TCG) which took over for the rest of the war.

Meanwhile, back in Italy, the 62nd and 64th TCGs were assigned to supply dropping operations in support of the 15th Army Group as it moved through Italy. The 62nd ceased these operations on 09Jan and the 64th took over two days later and continued until 07May45. Other duties in Italy included the 10th and 28th TCS (60th TCG) which evacuated wounded partisans from the Balkans.

ATC's intra-theatre operations in North Africa began in Jan43 from Accra to Marrakech, later under the Mediterranean Theatre's Mediterranean Air Transport Service, largely a British operation until early 1944. Eventually services flew to Tunis, Cairo, Naples, Rome and Marseille, but the latter was taken over by the European Wing in Oct44.

The only C-47s of the 15th AF were four used for the Aircrew Rescue Unit 1 which evacuated aircrews from the Balkan area, especially Yugoslavia.

Northern Europe

In preparation for the invasion of France, troop carrier strength had to be built up and from one half group in Jun43, there were 14 TCGs in the UK by Jul44. As part of this, the 9th AF units were absorbed by the 12th AF in the Mediterranean once operations in the Middle East ended, and the 9th AF took over all the 8th AF tactical aircraft so that the 8th could concentrate on strategic bombing. Both Air Forces came under USAAF UK, established in Oct43.

The 9th AF took over, on 16Oct43, the 315th TCG (two squadrons at first, and two more later) and the 434th TCG recently arrived from the US. These made up the nucleus of IX Troop Carrier Command based at Cottesmore and later Grantham and came under 50th TCW. The 435th TCG arrived at Langar on 03Nov43, followed by the 436th TCG at Bottesford on 03Mar44. With the arrival of the 53rd TCW from the US and the 52nd TCW (with the 61st, 313th, 314th and 316th TCGs) from Sicily in Feb44 there was much reorganisation and the 53rd TCW took over most of the 50th's groups and the newly arrived 437th, 438th and 439th TCGs. The 52nd TCW acquired the 315th TCG, while the 50th eventually took on the 439th TCG and three more groups fresh from the US, the 440th, 441st and 442nd TCGs.

On 25Feb44 XII TCC took over IX TCC and training for the Normandy landing began. By then the TCGs were at six bases in East Anglia, five in Berkshire and Wiltshire and three in the West Country. Two thousand gliders were assembled at Greenham Common in Berkshire during April and May. Training for the TCGs included troop flying and supply and medical evacuation missions in the UK, relying heavily on the experience of the four groups with experience in the Mediterranean.

The Invasion of France

On D-day, 06Jun44, the combined USAAF/RAF transport strength was 2316 aircraft. The attack started with 19 pathfinder aircraft in six 'serials' dropping teams to mark the six drop zones near St Mére Eglise in north east Normandy 30 minutes prior to the main drop. From each of the 14 IX TCC airfields, two batches of 15 aircraft each carried troops of the 82nd and 101st Airborne Divisions to the drop zones. The 82nd used 432 aircraft (and 50 gliders later) and the 101st used 369 aircraft and 52 gliders. A further 20 aircraft were used by specialised units. This drop lasted from 00:16 to 04:04 (am) and of the 821 C-47s and C-53s dispatched, 805 reached their targets and only 21 aircraft were lost. These were followed by 104 C-47s of the 434th and 437th TCGs, each towing a Waco CG-4A or Horsa glider. Only one C-47 failed to reach the landing zone, and one other failed to get home. The first resupply was in the early evening of 06Jun and early the next morning when nine groups, comprising 408 tow aircraft and a similar number of gliders was sent off. Eight failed to reach their targets but many gliders landed in the middle of the battle at St Mére Eglise. Further supply drops on the morning of 07Jun by 320 C-47s and C-53s were scattered, some landing in enemy held areas.

In total it would appear that 1672 C-47s etc and 512 gliders were despatched, of which 1606 aircraft and all the gliders set out across the Channel. Nine gliders did not reach their landing zones and 25 aircraft failed to complete their drops. In all 41 aircraft were lost and 449 damaged, the gliders being considered expendable.

On 16Jul IX TCC was redesignated Provisional Troop Carrier Air Division and from 31Aug was controlled directly by the US Strategic Air Forces in Europe. The Division also controlled the 51st TCW in the Mediterranean which was to take part in the invasion of Southern France (Operation "Dragoon"). For this 416 tow planes and 226 glider pilots were moved from England to Italy to join the 51st TCW and early in the morning of 15Aug, 396 aircraft with 5100 paratroops, both US and British, took off from the west coast of Italy and dropped at Le Muy, between Nice and Marseille. This was followed by 40 C-47s towing gliders and later the same day by drops from 41 more aircraft and two further glider attacks. One of these, known as Operation 'Dove' involved 332 gliders. Losses were very light and drops continued to prevent the troops outrunning their supplies.

'Market Garden' - Arnhem

The next major air assault was the drop in the Arnhem and Nijmegen areas to attempt the crossings of the Waal and the Rhine - Operation 'Market Garden' which started on 17Sep. This was the biggest airborne assault so far. The 101st Airborne Division dropped over and to the north of Eindhoven, the 82nd Division over Nijmegen and to the south, while the British 1st Airborne Division and the Polish 1st Independent Parachute Brigade dropped over Arnhem. A total of 1546 aircraft (C-47s, C-53s and Dakotas) were drawn from IX TCC and RAF 38 and 46 Groups. There were also 478 gliders and all took off from 24 bases in England:- Spanhoe, Cottesmore, Saltby, Langar, Folkingham, Balderton, Barkston Heath, Fulbeck, Broadwell, Brize Norton, Fairford, Down Ampney, Blakehill Farm, Chalgrove, Membury, Welford, Ramsbury, Keevil, Greenham Common, Aldermaston, Tarrant Rushton, Chilbolton, Chipping Ongar and Boreham. Of the combined fleet 1481 aircraft and 425 gliders reached their targets with the loss of 35 aircraft and 13 gliders. On the following day 1306 aircraft and 1152 gliders were dispatched and losses were 22 aircraft and 21 gliders. By 26Sep a total of 4242 aircraft sorties and 1899 glider sorties had been made with the loss of 98 aircraft and 137 gliders as well as rather more that had to turn back for various reasons.

Following the failure at Arnhem came the Battle of the Bulge in which IX TCC took part. On 23Dec44 allied troops were surrounded at Bastogne and 260 C-47s were used to drop supplies, followed by a further 160 sorties the following day. Bad weather prevented a further drop on the 25th, but on the 26th and 27th further large drops were made, eventually relieving the situation.

The last airborne assault in Europe was Operation 'Varsity' in which two British Airborne Divisions of the First Allied Airborne Army were dropped across the Rhine between Wesel and Rees on 24Mar45. A 2.5 hour long train of aircraft comprising 2046 aircraft and gliders of IX TCC and 890 aircraft and gliders from RAF 38 and 46 groups were used to drop 14,365 troops and their equipment.

As the ground forces moved through France the tactical forces followed them, but the transports of TCC remained in England pending the later operations described above. Aircraft were taken off supply operations well in advance of drops, etc, to allow for adequate training and to avoid the disaster in the Sicily invasion. By Oct44 the four groups of the 52nd TCW began moving into France, first to the Le Mans area and then to Chartres. The 50th and 53rd did not move until Feb45 and by April the 50th was at Amiens and the 53rd in the Orleans area.

Other European Transport Use

The VIII Air Force Service Command acquired three C-47s as early as Jul42 for intra-theatre use. These were incorporated into the 8th AF Ferry and Transport Service in Oct42, joining some B-17s. In Apr43 it was based at Hendon as the 27th Air Transport Group, borrowing aircraft from IX TCC and ATC as well as British Oxfords. The 315th TCG also served as an 8th AF Transport Group until it was detached to Algeria in May43. It returned to troop carrying with the 9th AF in Oct43.

The 9th AF's transport unit was the 31st ATG (IX Air Force Service Command) with C-47s. The 31st began operating to France a few days after D-day and moved to landing field A-21C at St Laurent-sur-Mer by 30Jun44. The 27th ATG moved to Heston on 07Jan44 and came under the Air Service Command, USSTAF in Mar44. When the 31st ATG was placed under the same control in Sep44 the two groups formed the 302nd ATW and received 100 new C-47s from ATC's allotment, bringing its strength up to 184 aircraft.

Air Transport Command, while primarily responsible for providing transport from the US to the war theatres, began to operate scheduled services within these theatres late in 1943 as more C-47s became available. In Europe this comprised a daily Prestwick - Hendon flight from

Oct43 and later that year twice daily from St Mawgan to Hendon. With the liberation of Paris a UK-Paris service was started. ATC also helped supply Patton with petrol in Sep44 and moved SHAEF from London to Versailles with 75 flights. By Jun45 regular services were operated to Frankfurt, Naples, Stockholm, Budapest and Lisbon, with many stops in between.

The South-West Pacific

The Pacific war was divided into two theatres, the Southwest Pacific Area (Australia, New Guinea, Borneo, Philippines, Java and part of the Solomons) under MacArthur in Australia, and the Pacific Ocean Area (North, Central and South Pacific) under Nimitz. The US Army Forces HQ in the S Pacific at Suva, Fiji moved to Noumea, New Caledonia at the end of Jul42 and on 03Sep42 the Air Force element in SWPA was constituted as the 5th AF with headquarters at Brisbane. The AAF elements in the SPA became the 13th AF on 13Jan43 with their HQ at Espiritu Santo, New Hebrides.

New Guinea

The original transport element in Australia, the 21st and 22nd TCS had 32 Lockheed and Douglas aircraft, mainly KLM escapees from the East Indies as well as a few old B-17s and two LB-30s. These were assigned to the Directorate of Air Transport under Capt Harold Gatty. Forty-one US aircraft out of 78 assigned were on hand by Sep42, but 15 were only fit for spares. Two Troop Carrier Squadrons of 13 C-47s each were assigned, the first arriving in mid-October. The second was retained temporarily by the Pacific Ocean area and seven C-47s shuttled from Noumea to Guadalcanal for a month.

The 374th TCG was activated by the 5th AF to contain four squadrons and their first action was supply dropping in the Buna area of New Guinea during Operation "Hatrack" in Oct42. They also flew Australian troops to Wanigela strip in October/November continuing landing or dropping supplies in the area until 23Jan43 as well as evacuating casualties. Late in January they also flew troops into Wau airstrip with a 12% slope. Losses were comparatively light, and of 11 aircraft involved, five were eventually salvaged or rebuilt.

During Jan43, the 317th TCG flew 52 new C-47s from California to Australia. These were transferred to the 374th TCG and the 317th inherited the latter's tired mixture of C-47s, C-49s, C-60s, LB-30s and B-17s. By 30Jun43, three and a half TCGs were scheduled to be on hand, with a further group due in the third quarter. At this stage, the strategy was to hold the enemy, while concentrating on the European theatre. Aircraft sent to the 5th AF still had winter equipment, and this was removed in Australia until May43, when it was deleted before delivery. Control of the growing troop carrier element in Australia was carried out by the 54th TCW constituted in Feb43. It functioned from Port Moresby in May43 and by the first week in July only the 374th TCG was assigned. At this time four new TCSs arrived, followed by two more soon after and another TCG in September, to give 14 squadrons.

During the Spring and early summer of 1943 the campaign in New Guinea steadily developed and a major base was developed at Dobodura, supplied solely by air. In June a further airfield was built at Tsili Tsili requiring 150 C-47 trips per day. This operation was largely unmolested by the Japanese, but on 15Jul fighters shot down two C-47s moving the first fighter squadron ground crews into the field. Following a seaborne landing at Lae on 04Sep 1943, 79 C-47s of the 54th TCW took 1700 troops (US and Australian) across the 9000 ft Owen Stanley Mountains to a drop at Nadzab, 15 miles northwest of Lae to capture a site for an airfield and to cut off the Japanese at Salamaua. The airfield at Nadzab was in use on the following day and within ten days dispersals for 36 transports has been completed. Although Salamaua fell on 11Sep, and Lae on the 16th, Nadzab was supplied by air for several months, continuing until the Lae-Nadzab road was completed in Dec43, with about 200 C-47 flights a day.

Progress in New Guinea was relatively slow but following a landing in the Hollandia vicinity, the 65th TCS moved to the Tadji airstrip near Aitape and C-47s also began using Cyclops airfield at Hollandia on 29Apr. The 41st TCS moved in on 04May. After this it was a matter of keeping the ground forces supplied from the air, building more strips and clearing the Japanese troops from the rest of New Guinea. The 54th TCW with help from ADAT played a major part in this. The 65th, 66th and 68th TCSs operated out of Aitape, and then the various islands were attacked by air and invaded by sea or air, though air drops resulted in a high injury rate and were used mostly to capture airstrips.

The first C-47 equipped unit with the 13th AF was the 13th TCS. Aircraft were assigned as needed to SCAT. A second TCS was added in Mar43, but B-17s were used by the 39th and 69th TCSs of the 375th TCG for much supply dropping until early 1944. They moved up into New Guinea in Aug43.

Philippines and Beyond

The activities of the 5th and 13th AFs increasingly overlapped and on 15Jun44 the transport work was combined in the Far East Air Forces (Provisional). The Navy and Marines did most of the island hopping in 1944, taking Kwajalein, Eniwetok, Guam etc, culminating in the seaborne landing in the Philippines in Leyte on 20Oct44. Lack of airfields limited the 317th TCG C-47s to supply dropping. The third Air Commando Group (with P-51s and C-47s) arrived at Leyte on 01Dec44, assigned to the 54th TCW. This wing took over units of ADAT when it was disbanded on 03Oct44 and became the 322nd TCW on 30Dec44, being assigned to the Far East Service Command. The 54th TCW remained with the 5th AF.

Plans had been laid for an airborne invasion of Mindanao, for which 650 C-47s were to be used to tow 735 gliders. However, in the event, the island was bypassed and few of the gliders were used. After the invasion of Mindoro on 15Dec44, the 8th Fighter Group flew in. A fuel shortage threatened and C-46s and C-47s were used to bring in 600 drums of petrol a day. The C-47s came from the 317th TCG based on Leyte. The next island invasion was Luzon on 09Jan45, by sea. By the 16th Lingayen airfield was in use for transports and C-47s of the 54th TCW from Mindoro dropped over 2000 paratroops on Tagaytay Ridge on 03Feb without loss. Following this the 317th TCG C-47s dropped over 2000 men on the island fortress of Corregidor. It fell much more rapidly than expected without loss of aircraft and just over 200 casualties. There followed two more paratroop drops in the Pacific war. On 23Feb ten C-47s of the 65th TCS from Nichols Field, Manila, dropped 125 men on Los Banos Agricultural College to free over 2000 Allied internees. The last major drop involved the 317th TCG C-47s and some C-46s from the 433rd TCG towing gliders. They dropped nearly 1000 men on 23Jun to help in the assault on Acala, Calalaniugan.

Subsequent operations to take the Netherlands East Indies, Borneo, Mindanao etc were seaborne and C-47s were only used for landing some troops and evacuating casualties. The 54th TCW finally took overall command of 'Mission 75', in which 100 C-47s and 272 C-46s together with 180 C-54s of ATC occupied Japan on 28Aug45.

ATC in the Pacific

The Pacific was, of course, largely an area for long range transports, and C-54s in particular, but as the war progressed lines of communication grew longer and in Jul43 the first ATC intra-theatre service from Port Moresby via Townsville and Amberley to Sydney was started, using five C-47s. In May44, 15 C-47s from ATC Southwest Pacific Wing based at Guadalcanal started a daily service from Tontouta (Noumea) via Espiritu to Guadalcanal. One hundred C-47s from ATC's allotment were sent to Australia at 25 per month from May to Aug44 to operate the Brisbane-Nadzab service, augmenting the ADAT flights. It started on 26Jun44 and by August there were 17 daily flights. It extended to Hollandia in September and a route between Nadzab and Milne Bay started at this time.

China-Burma-India

Probably the most important and well-known transport operation in the China-Burma-India theatre was the ATC "Hump" operation already discussed under the ATC section earlier. However, when in Dec42 the only significant transport operation in the 10th AF was transferred to the ATC, it became necessary to provide further troop carrier units for intra-theatre duties. Of the 12 C-47s or C-53s lent to the Middle East in Jun42 only eight returned and these were only kept airworthy by fitting R-1830-47s intended for Chinese P-43s. By the spring of 1943, the 10th AF had two C-47 squadrons, the 1st and 2nd TCS, although the latter was nominally a 14th AF unit operating in India. Additionally another TCS, probably the 27th, was provided for use by Stilwell in Burma. By Dec43, when the joint British-US Eastern Air Command (EAC) was established, TCC in the 10th AF comprised four C-47 squadrons, the 1st, 2nd, 27th and 315th TCS.

The first major tactical use of the troop carrier element was in Wingate's counter attack west of Imphal, Burma, on 05Mar44. A task force comprising 13 C-47s from the 27th TCS, 12 UC-64s and 150 CG-4As was assembled. 67 gliders were dispatched on what turned out to be a most unsatisfactory mission. Only 32 reached the landing zone at "Broadway" where three landed safely, nine in hostile territory, two were lost and the remaining 18 returned to base. The next day 12 gliders were sent to Chowringhee and between 13 and 19Mar C-47s of the 27th TCS flew 156 sorties and dropped over 800,000 lb of supplies. Aerial supply for Wingate's force continued and the 27th was joined by the 315th TCS and 117 Sq RAF. While the Wingate expedition was in progress the Japanese were attacking at Imphal and TCC was swamped with requests for help. The 64th TCG (4th, 16th, 17th and 35th TCS) arrived on 08Apr along with 216 Sq RAF, both on emergency detachment from the Middle East to help relieve Imphal. They remained into early July, when the 3rd Combat Cargo Group arrived.

Also in Apr44, Stilwell launched an attack from Ledo towards Myitkyina using troops of the 50th Chinese Division flown in by the India-China Wing ATC and onwards by the 1st TCS to Burma. Another attack was made across the Salween River from Yunnan and from May to November the 27th TCS was attached to the 69th Composite Wing, 14th AF to support the Salween crossing. The airfield at Myitkyina was taken on 17May44, allowing C-47s of the TCC to make over 500 sorties a day into the strip, but the city itself was not taken until 03Aug, while the Chinese were forced to withdraw southwards. The 322nd TCS was added to the Chinese American Composite Wing (later the 68th CW) in April and by October 50 C-47s were based in China for intra-theatre use, to be replaced by C-46s shortly after.

Burma

With the advance into Burma came the formation of two new types of group, the Air Commando Group and the Combat Cargo Group. The Air Commando Group was formed with two squadrons of 25 P-51 Mustangs, one TCC squadron of C-47s and 32 CG-4As, plus three liaison squadrons with L-5s and UC-64s. The Combat Cargo Group had four C-47 squadrons, each with 25 aircraft (later C-46s). The 10th AF TCC was abolished on 04Jun44, with the 3rd CCG passing to the 3rd Tactical Air Force (10th AF) to join the 2nd ACG. The EAC was formed with the 1st ACG, the 1st CCG and with RAF Wing 177 became Combat Cargo Task Force (CCTF) on 14Sep. This had 163 aircraft in October and had expanded to 354 by Spring 1945, with two more RAF Wings, an extra CCG (probably 4th CCG) and another ACG. The 10th AF retained the 443rd TCG and the 11th CCS.

In Sep44, CCTF carried supplies from Assam to northern Burma in preparation for the advance south from Myitkyina. The various units of CCTF were based at Dinjan in Assam, Ledo and Warazup in Burma, Shinbwiyang, Luliang in China, Tulikal in India and Myitkyina. The Burma campaign got off to a successful start and the 14th and 22nd Chinese Divisions were returned to China between 05Dec44 and 05Jan45. Aircraft used were 10th AF C-47s from a TCG, C-47s from the 317th and 319th TCS (of the ACGs) and China based CCG C-47s, all used to carry the 14th, with the loss of three C-47s. C-46s carried the 22nd Division. With the flank protected, the forces driving south through Burma crossed the Irrawaddy River and took Meiktila airfield in Feb45 and C-47s of the 1st and 2nd ACGs flew in troops for the attack on Mandalay, which fell on 11Mar45.

C-47s of the 317th and 319th TCSs and ten from the 2nd and 4th CCS moved to Kalaikunda for paratroop training in Apr45 and on 02May45, flying from Akyab, 83 aircraft dropped paratroops 20 miles south of Rangoon without casualties and Rangoon fell without opposition with the amphibious landing (Operation Dracula). Although this operation was completed very quickly, CCTF involvement was considerable, carrying in 330,000 tons of supplies, 340,000 men and evacuating 94,000 casualties. In the later stages of the war, there were about 500 operational C-47s in the China-Burma-India theatre, comprising about 130 in India-Burma service, about 160 with ATC, about 140 with the 10th AF and 40 with the 14th AF. It was only in May45 that the number of C-46s exceeded 500, and the C-47 bore the brunt of operational flying in this theatre.

Hawaii

The 7th AF in Hawaii had no troop carrier unit for most of the war, but the 17th TCS was assigned to it and its advanced HQ moved to Tarawa and then Kwajalein in Mar44. The 7th AF was transferred to FEAF on 14Jul45 for the projected invasion of Japan, but the war came to an end before it could be used.

Alaska

The possibility of a Japanese attack on Alaska was very real because of its proximity to Japan via the Aleutian chain. Northwest Airlines flew a survey flight to Alaska as early as 27Feb42 under contract, and was later joined by Western and United Airlines. The threat was proved to be real when the Japanese attacked Dutch Harbor on 03 to 05Jun42. By Sep42 Northwest was using 15 DC-3s on the run from Great Falls, MT to Fairbanks, AK, while Western had four on the Ogden, UT to Anchorage run. The importance of Alaska was further increased when Lend-Lease deliveries to Siberia started in Aug42 and the Alaskan Wing of ATC was formed on 17Oct42.

The 11th AF had one squadron of C-47s, the 42nd TCS, by Jun42. The 54th TCS joined it by Aug43 and between them they carried 7500 tons of cargo and 15,000 men per month on intra-theatre flights, mainly to Attu, Adak and Shemya in the Aleutians. United operated the Anchorage - Adak shuttle for ATC (at the request of the 11th AF) in Sep and Oct43. When there was a possibility that the 11th AF would lose its Troop Carrier Squadrons in Jan44, Northwest began an Anchorage-Adak service, extended to Attu in Jul44. Four C-54s and a few C-46s were also used, but C-47s and DC-3s bore the brunt of the work.

Mainland United States

Many C-47s were retained for use in the USA by various training units of ATC, TCC and the paratroop division. As they became more numerous they began to be used as hacks, test aircraft etc, throughout the USA. ATC began ferry training at 1 OTU, Rosecrans Field, St Joseph, MO, in Jul42 and established a school for transport pilots (2 OTU) at Homestead AFB, FL in Nov42. 1 OTU became a specialised OTU for C-47 pilots about Aug42. Most Troop Carrier Squadrons were formed in the USA learning formation flying, parachute dropping, glider towing etc using older C-47s before taking on new aircraft and departing the USA at Hamilton, CA, for the 5th AF or Morrison, FL for onward flight to N Africa or India.

Post-War Use

With the end of the war in Europe and the Far East USAAF operations changed considerably and with the occupation of Western Europe and Japan there was, initially, an increased need for transport and communications aircraft. C-47s served both as personnel and cargo transports throughout the newly occupied areas, ferrying in urgent supplies and repatriating prisoners. Other C-47s returned to the USA for storage, helping to take personnel home and within six months of VJ-day the number of operational aircraft was halved. Aircraft returning home were operated by Air Transport Command and usually saw landfall at Hamilton from the 5th AF or Bradley, CN or Hunter, GA from Europe.

Storage depots were set up overseas at Oberpfaffenhofen in Germany, Naples in Italy, Cairo in Egypt, Karachi in India, and Tacloban and Manila in the Philippines. Aircraft were sold from these depots by the ANLC (Army Navy Liquidation Commission) and later by the FLC or Field Liquidation Commission. Those C-47s that were ferried home to the US were put in store with the Reconstruction Finance Corp (RFC) during 1945/46 and this body was responsible for surplus sales to airlines during this period. This work was taken over by the War Assets Administration (WAA) in 1947. Many C-47s were simply sold for salvage overseas or reclaimed for usable parts. Some of these ended up as scrap but a large number were rebuilt and some of the latter are still flying 60 years later. It has not proved possible to trace all the sales and many were sold only as a source of spares to concerns specialising in overhaul. The main home storage base was Davis-Monthan which had several units looking after the stored aircraft in the dry desert conditions.

With the formation of the **US Air Force** on 18Sep47 a new command structure was set up, with Strategic Air Command (SAC) taking over the 8th and 15th AFs which included some C-47s for freight and VIP transport. Tactical Air Command (TAC) also included C-46s, C-47s and C-54s of the 3rd AF in its inventory, for tactical air transport. These were passed on to Continental Air Command on 01Dec48.

The Air National Guard programme was initiated in Apr46 under the control of Air Defense Command and C-47s were assigned to most state units. The Air Transport Command continued from 1946 with three global divisions (Pacific, Atlantic and European), in place of the nine wartime divisions. This was integrated with the Naval Air Transport Service on 01Jun48 as MATS (Military Air Transport Service) and 239 C-47s were taken over.

Berlin Airlift

Soon after the formation of MATS the Russians stopped trains bound for Berlin and on 21Jun48 a massive airlift was started by the USAFE and the RAF to keep the city supplied with all necessities including food and coal. On 26Jun 32 C-47 flights from Wiesbaden had carried 80 tons of supplies into Tempelhof. Less than 100 C-47s, mostly from European Air Transport Service were available. Six RAF Dakotas joined them initially, but as momentum built up more RAF aircraft from 38 and 46 Groups joined. Further details of the units involved in the latter operation are given under the British military section.

Within three weeks 60 TCG, USAF, had 105 C-47s in use, but the C-54 was found more suitable and bore the brunt of the operation. By 01Oct the USAF C-47s were withdrawn, although the RAF continued until 'Operation Plainfare' ceased in the following year.

On 01Sep49 Air Defense Command gave way to Eastern and Western Air Defense Forces under Continental Air Command.

Korean War

The Korean War, which started in Jun50, involved TAC's C-54s as well as some C-47s but the latter played a comparatively minor role due to the distances involved in ferrying supplies from the USA. They mainly plied from Japan to Korea on local supply work but on 20Oct50 40 C-47s and 71 C-119s were used in the UN drive into North Korea when Combat Cargo Command dropped 2860 paratroops and 300 tons of supplies north of Pyongyang.

Following Chinese intervention early in 1951 the FEAF Combat Cargo Command was replaced by the 315th Air Division. RC-47Ds were used as flare droppers to allow B-26s to attack the Chinese by night as they drove south. During these operations C-47s were used to evacuate the wounded of the 1st Marine Division trapped in the Chosin Reservoir area and 4689 troops were flown out from an airstrip at Hagaru. The Korean war eventually reached a stalemate in May53 and on 27Jun an armistice was agreed.

One result of this war was the expansion of Tactical Air Command and on 01Dec50 it separated from Continental Air Command, together with 520 aircraft, amongst which were C-47s, C-46s and C-119s for troop transport. The C-46s gave way to C-119s by 1963, but the C-47 soldiered on for a little longer, and many were used as unit transports, carrying spares etc.

C-47 Variations

Most C-47Bs were modified to C-47D standard when the high altitude blowers were removed from 1946 on. Some did revert back to the C-47B when they were needed to operate in the Andes of South America, Colombia, Peru etc. VIP transport was provided in all theatres by the soundproofed VC-47A and VC-47D variants, fitted with airline seats etc., though judged by the way some aircraft switched back and forth the changes were, at most, cosmetic. These remained in service for many years with various Command Headquarters and also with air attaches around the World. The VC-47s were replaced by VC-131s or the C-12 Super King Air.

Most C-47s operated by the Air Rescue Service (the MATS Air Rescue Service after 1948) in the early post-war years were modified to SC-47 configuration. They were equipped with search and rescue equipment including a small lifeboat for dropping to survivors in the sea. Large circular windows were fitted fore and aft to some aircraft to aid searches. However, some of these modified MATS aircraft were used without formal record of their change (i.e., on their individual record cards) and were thus still C-47As and C-47Ds until a rationalisation of the MATS rescue fleet and SAC's Aircrew Recovery Program fleet in 1954. This exercise transferred control of SAC's recovery C-47s to MATS and simultaneously caused a clerical 'catch-up' of all these C-47s to SC-47A and SC-47D regardless of history and, one suspects, their precise modification state (SAC's C-47s were JATO-equipped). However, by 1954 many of the ARS S/C-47s had been replaced with more modern aircraft including helicopters and for the next few years most aircraft were dedicated to the Aircrew Recovery Program. The handful of SC-47s that survived until the 1962 adoption of tri-service designations were re-named HC-47s.

In 1953, 26 C-47s, already in service with the Airways and Air Communications Service of MATS (AACS), were further modified by Hayes, gaining more sophisticated navigational-aid checking equipment. The aircraft were progressively re-designated AC-47D (and there was one AC-47A) after the first pair were designated briefly RC-47D. AC-47s were easily recognisable at distance by their distinctive nose radomes and copious amounts of day-glo paint! In the 1962 rationalisation of designations, the AC-47Ds became EC-47Ds but by then the type was being withdrawn in favour of more modern jet aircraft. The AACS became the Air Force Communications Service in Jul61 (and was detached from MATS) and a few aircraft soldiered on until going to storage in the mid 'sixties. In good condition, the AFCS EC-47Ds were virtually all disposed of via MAP programs to several nations. However, with the exception of the disposals to Brazil and South Vietnam, future use would not be as navaid-checkers and the paper title 'EC-47D' became an irrelevance.

One further variant, mentioned already, was the RC-47A or D, fitted with cameras for aerial reconnaissance. These were also used in Korea for flare dropping.

The C-47E designation was yet another modification for high altitude work, having the Wright R-1820-80. Only about nine of these were modified, some of them finding their way to the US Army later.

Between Korea and Vietnam

MATS continued to use the C-47, but only for local work. The AC-47s served on in their intended role, based on Bovingdon, Herts and also in Japan and elsewhere, while the SC-47s continued to serve from Prestwick, covering the Eastern Atlantic and similar units were to be found elsewhere. A few C-47s remained with MATS until it became Military Airlift Command (MAC) on 01Jan66, continuing until at least 1969.

In 1954 the Air National Guard was reorganised and in addition to fighter-bomber units becoming interceptor units, there were 13 troop carrier wings and 6 Air Supply and Transport Squadrons, equipped with C-46s, C-47s and C-119s. Also most units had their own C-47 for communications, some surviving into the early seventies.

Air Commandos and Vietnam

By 1961 the USAF was generally only operating the C-47 in the light transport and communications role. While most first-line and reserve combat units still possessed them as hacks, large numbers were being released as surplus to friendly nations and sold on the commercial market. Others were being scrapped. There were no C-47 tactical squadrons of any significant size with any command although several communications units still possessed double-digit quantities. This steady downward spiral would be slowed to some extent by the forthcoming war in south-east Asia, but aircraft continued to be disposed of throughout the decade. Certainly there was no suggestion then that C-47s would once again become important combat aircraft. However, in 1961 the concept of unconventional commando forces, involved in 'counter-insurgency' activity, was gaining interest within the USAF.

The 4400th Combat Crew Training Squadron ('Jungle Jim') was formed in Apr61 at Hurlburt Field, FL (Eglin Auxiliary Field 09) to develop appropriate 'commando' tactics and to deploy operational detachments wherever necessary. Several aircraft types were used including the C-47. With an authorised strength of 16 C-47s, the unit initially received about 24 C-47s gathered from many sources, the great majority of which were SC-47s. Unfortunately, many of these old warriors were simply too tired for the new task and they were quickly given up to storage and scrapping. Of course, they were replaced rapidly, but the unit settled down as a C-47 outfit with only about eight SC-47s remaining on strength. The subsequent lineage of this unit is to say the least complicated. In Apr62, the 1st Air Commando Group was activated at Hurlburt and then, in Jun63, it became the 1st Air Commando Wing. The 4400th CCTS was replaced by the 1st Material Squadron in Apr62 and then by the 4410th CCTS (date uncertain), but remained a component of the 1st ACW until Dec65 when the 4410th CCTW was formed at Hurlburt. This was preparatory to a re-shuffle of accountabilities and the 1st ACW moved to England AFB in Jan66.

During its time at Hurlburt several other units had formed within the 1st ACW. One of them, the 317th ACS, formed in Jul64 with C-47s in the air commando role and, post-transfer, the squadron was eventually operational again with the 1st ACW at England in Jul66. A handful of the new AC-47D 'Spooky' gunships remained on strength with the 317th ACS and then the 4410th SOTG (qv) until 1972. The 4412th CCTS formed at England in Aug66 to meet the growing training need and was integrated into the 1st ACW in Oct67. Having been re-designated the 1st Special Operations Wing in Jul68, the 1st SOW returned to Hurlburt Field in Jul69 and, in the process, exchanged its squadrons with the 4410th CCTW that transferred from Hurlburt to England the following month. As a result of this move, virtually all TAC C-47 operations were concentrated at England within the 4410th CCTW. In Dec69 more than 50 aircraft were on strength including three AC-47D and three TC-47D. The unit continued to meet all C-47 training needs (becoming the 4410th Special Operations Training Group in Sep70) until its inactivation in Jul73 when the few surviving aircraft were passed to the 1st SOW at Hurlburt (the 1st SOW had only used staff transport C-47s after 1970). These aircraft were used subsequently by the 603rd SOTS at Hurlburt to train foreign crews until Jul74 after when the 1st SOW phased out the C-47.

To return to 1961, the 4410th CCTS sent a detachment to Bien Hoa, South Vietnam, in Nov61. Det 2A was a composite unit that included four SC-47s and the deployment, intended to be a six-month instructional

TDY, was code-named 'Farm Gate'. Of course, 'Farm Gate' developed into more activity than had been foreseen and even within the scope of the USAF's C-47 operations it is a complicated story to tell. Perforce we concentrate here on very basic details.

With the creation of the 1st ACG in Apr62, the detachment became det 2A 1st ACG and remained so until Jul63 when it became the 1st ACS, assigned to the 34th Tactical Group at Bien Hoa. With no organisational links to the 1st ACG/ACW the 1st ACS remained at Bien Hoa until Jan66 when it moved to Pleiku. During this period it was reassigned to the 6251st TFW in Jul65 (at which time it passed the [now] HC-47s to the 5th ACS) and then the 2nd AD in Feb66. In Mar66 it was again reassigned to the 14th ACW (Nha Trang) and at that time was equipped with six standard 'ash and trash' aircraft used in support of its A-1 and U-10 fleet. In Dec67, the 1st ACS was reassigned to the 56th SOW at Nakhon Phanom. After becoming the 1st SOS in Aug68, it was finally reassigned to the 18th TFW (Kadena) in 1972 although by now no longer a C-47 operation (after 1965 the 1st ACS was primarily an A-1 operation). The original 'Puff' was a 1964-vintage 1st ACS C-47D . . .

In Aug65, det 8 of the 1st ACW was activated at Forbes AFB to organise the final training and work-up of two new units, the 4th and 5th ACS. The 4th ACS was to be the first C-47 unit (although the aircraft were at that time still known as FC-47), while the 5th ACS was to be a psychological warfare unit. The 4th ACS was the first to deploy to Vietnam in Nov65 when it arrived at Tan Son Nhut (qv).

Theoretically the 5th ACS was activated at Nha Trang in Aug65 although it was not until Mar66 that it was assigned to the newly-formed 14th ACW. The 5th ACS was a mixed-asset unit (it also used U-10s) that initially took on charge six of the C-47s previously used by the 1st ACS at Bien Hoa including the five (but soon to be four) surviving HC-47s. Known as the 'Quick Speak' 'psywar' squadron, it provided detachments from Nha Trang to Bien Hoa, Binh Thuy, Da Nang and Pleiku and in Mar67 it provided the nucleus of the new 9th ACS (the second 'psywar' squadron, also equipped with six C-47s and U-10s). Having become the 5th SOS in Aug68, the unit was eventually inactivated at Nha Trang in Oct69 and its assets, including the four HC-47s, were dispersed.

The 606th ACS was a composite squadron activated at Nakhon Phanom, Thailand, under the 634th CSG in Mar66. It was reassigned to the 56th SOW when that wing was activated at Nakhon Phanom in Apr67 and, having become the 606th SOS in Aug68, it was finally activated in Jun71. The 606th ACS was a mixed-asset unit that included B-26s and C-123s and its C-47s were only briefly on strength. On activation the squadron also received three specially-modified C-47Ds, officially known as RC-47s although the designation does not appear on record cards, for use as communications-relay aircraft over Laos in a programme known as 'Halfmoon'. In the absence of sufficient ABCCC C-130s, the 7th Air Force used these three aircraft to relay information from ground forces via the Savannakhet operations centre to the tactical air control centre. The three aircraft were received by the 606th ACS in May66 and were based at Udorn within its det 1 alongside three standard aircraft operated by the local 630th CSG. They became operational in early Dec66 and in Jan67 all six aircraft became part of the Udorn-based 432nd TRW, the 'Halfmoon' trio leaving the 606th ACS det that was then discontinued in the third quarter of 1967. Eventually, in Nov69, the three RC-47s joined the 56th SOW at Nakhon Phanom where they remained until withdrawal in Jun70. All three were transferred subsequently to the RTAF in Aug70. The 606th ACS was also, very briefly in Oct66, the operator of eight newly-modified AC-47Ds at Nakhon Phanom. However, these aircraft were transferred quickly to the 14th ACW at Nha Trang where they facilitated the conversion of the 9th ACS into a 'Spooky' unit.

The Vietnam War saw the development of two major new activities for the old Gooney Bird. One, the electronic listening role, proved to be its definitive Vietnam activity and, indeed, its final USAF flourish. However, another task was certainly its most spectacular. The unlikely role of the AC-47D 'Spooky' gunship was developed in 1964 and resulted in 53 production aircraft, almost all of which served in the theatre. First deliveries were to the 1st ACW at Hurlburt in Sep65 while the 4th ACS worked up at Forbes and the first 20 aircraft were ferried rapidly to Tan Son Nhut where they were accepted formally in mid-November. The 4th ACS was assigned initially to the local 6250th CSG, 2nd AD, but was transferred to the new 14th ACW at Nha Trang in Mar66. The squadron made its physical move to Nha Trang that July but maintained detachments throughout the region for all its life. In Aug68 it became the 4th SOS before moving to Phan Rang in Oct69. The 4th SOS flew its final mission on 01Dec69 before inactivating on 15Dec.

The second operational AC-47D unit was the 9th ACS that became active in Mar67 within the 14th ACW at Pleiku although it, too, was highly mobile and maintained detachments at many bases in Vietnam and Thailand. The unit moved to Nha Trang in Sep67, became the 9th SOS in Aug68 but had lost its gunships by the time it moved to Tuy Hoa in Sep69. The third and final unit was the short-lived 14th ACS operational only from Jan-Apr68 at Nha Trang within the 14th ACW. It was replaced numerically by the 3rd ACS, activated in May68 at Nha Trang, renamed 3rd SOS in Aug68 and inactivated in Sep69. From Mar69 three aircraft were retained, initially as a det 4th SOS, as a flight within the 432nd TRW at Udorn, Thailand (until May70), and three more were retained by the 4410th SOTG at England until passed on as MAP aid in 1972. In truth, flying Spooky was dangerous and, with 17 lost in less than four years, early withdrawal was probably inevitable. After mid-1969, virtually all the Spooky gunships were transferred rapidly to the South Vietnamese and Laotian air forces.

In contrast, the EC-47 fleet, the plain-Jane EC-47N/P and the up-rated EC-47Q, saw many years of reliable service with relatively few losses. The 460th TRW, activated at Tan Son Nhut in Feb66, was the first and principal user of all these aircraft. The first EC-47N/P electronic reconnaissance aircraft (originally known as RC-47s) were delivered to Tan Son Nhut in 1966 and the 360th and 361st TRS, based at Tan Son Nhut and Nha Trang respectively, were activated in April of that year (both became TEWS in Mar67). The 362nd TEWS was activated in Feb67 within the 460th TRW, but was based at Pleiku where it replaced det 1 of the 361st TRS. All three squadrons maintained permanent detachments away from their home bases and some shuffling of the home stations also occurred with the 361st TEWS moving to Phu Cat in Sep69. The EC-47Q was received in 1968 and was eventually used exclusively by the 362nd TEWS. All three squadrons were reassigned organisationally to the 483rd TAW at Cam Ranh Bay in Aug71 and then physically in a second round of reorganisations in Feb72 to the 377th ABW at Tan Son Nhut (360th TEWS) and the 366th TFW at Da Nang (362nd TEWS). The 361st TEWS was reassigned to the 56th SOW, Nakhon Phanom, in Sep72. The first squadron to be inactivated was the 362nd TEWS at Da Nang in Jun72 with its equivalent strength of EC-47N/Ps passing to the South Vietnamese Air Force. The 360th TFS then inactivated at Tan Son Nhut in Nov72 leaving only the 361st TEWS operational within the 56th SOW. The 361st TEWS was now a large squadron flying all three versions of the EC-47 from its bases in Thailand (there was a detachment at Ubon) and the EC-47 soldiered on until old age and 'peace' finally caught up with it. The 361st TEWS was eventually inactivated in Jun74. By then most of its aircraft were beyond use to anyone and more than 20 were scrapped at Clark and Udorn in 1974-75.

Although most of the USAF's 'sixties tactical operations involving C-47s took place in south-east Asia, the Air Commando/Special Operations philosophy had global implications although beyond TAC and PACAF few units were made operational. The largest, by a distance, was the 605th ACS established at Howard, CZ (Canal Zone), in Nov63 within the 5700th ABW, headquartered at nearby Albrook AFB. Within USAF's Southern Command the 605th ACS undertook a wide variety of regional tasks in support of the US military and civilian authorities before its eventual inactivation in Sep72. The parent unit became the 24th Composite Wing (at Howard) in Jan68, the 24th Air Commando Wing in March and the 24th Special Operations Wing in Jul68. The 605th ACS consequently became the 605th SOS. In 1966-67, C-46s operated alongside the C-47s (presumably meeting numerical shortfall), but by late 1968 the Commandos had gone and the 24th SOW C-47 numbers ballooned to more than 30, including the embassy and other special mission aircraft. The C-47 era ended abruptly in 1970 when at least 24 aircraft were disposed of as MAP-aid.

Elsewhere the only 'tactical' C-47s were those in Alaska and Germany. Between Nov66 and Oct68, six C-47s temporarily replaced C-123s within the 21st Composite Wing's 21st Operations Squadron at Elmendorf. In Europe, the 7th ACS was formed at Sembach in Jul64 within the 38th ABG and its mixed fleet initially included six C-47s. Organisational changes saw it reassigned to the 603rd ABW in Sep66, re-named the 7th SOS in Jul68 and transferred to Ramstein the following month. On transfer, four of the C-47s were returned to Otis AFB where they became det 1 of the 1st SOW (re-named the 7th Special Operations Flight in Jul69). This arrangement lasted until Apr70 when the four 7th SOF aircraft were withdrawn to desert storage. Meanwhile, as part of a mixed-fleet, the two surviving C-47s at Ramstein continued in use until final withdrawal from the 7th SOS in May73.

Camouflage and Coding

The war in south-east Asia brought about the widespread and belated camouflaging of all USAF tactical aircraft. This affected all the C-47s used in that theatre as well as many of the TAC aircraft in the USA. By the late 'sixties, some of the special operations aircraft had begun to appear in nondescript grey colours but, by and large, the non-tactical C-47s remained in their white-top schemes until the end. The two-letter tactical codes that appeared initially on PACAF aircraft and then on other tactical aircraft were also applied to C-47s at squadron level but only to those in south-east Asia, at Hurlburt Field and at England. Codes known to have been applied to C-47s are as follows: 'AA' - 7th SOF, 'AH' - 603rd SOTS, 'AJ' - 360th TEWS, 'AL' - 361st TEWS, 'AN' – 362nd TEWS, EL' - 3rd ACS, 'EN' - 4th ACS, 'EO' - 5th ACS, 'ER' - 9th ACS, 'IA' - det 1 1st ACW (Otis), 'ID' - 317th ACS, 'IG' - 4412th CCTS, 'IJ' - probably the 4410th SOTG, 'OS' - 432nd TRW (AC-47D det).

The Final Years

While the tactical C-47s slugged it out over the jungles of south-east Asia, the once-huge fleet elsewhere was run-down gradually in favour of less-old and even a few brand-new communications aircraft. Many were passed to friendly nations under sundry aid programmes and for those not quite up to making the trip home safely, the local scrap-man was waiting. When the last was retired in 1975 the bulk of those still on the inventory were to be found in storage at Davis-Monthan AFB awaiting sale and/or scrapping. Aircraft went for scrap or as a source of spares, others to overhaul and further flying. By the time that Basler visited in 1994, only four were found to be suitable for purchase. Known storage codes are given at the end of the US section of this chapter.

USAAF/USAF Unit Identification Codes

The system used by the USAAF, which started in 1942 and evolved from that used by the US Army Air Corps, was fairly simple. Any units attached to a particular field or base was part of the Base Unit, coded variously as AAFBU or BAS, but here given as BU. Units which were on active duty and liable to move base had their own system, for example TS or Transport Squadron under the USAAC became Troop Carrier Squadron in the USAAF.

Not all bases had a BU number, those in Europe had a prefix indicating the country (F for France, G for Germany etc), as did those in Japan. Those in Britain had no prefix, but Australian bases had no number. Those in India and China had BU numbers. There is no record of any in Africa or Italy.

With the formation of the USAF in 1948 everything changed and codes were generally adopted which indicated the function of the unit. The system was infinitely more complex than that used previously and slowly evolved to that in use today, using fewer letters as time went by. Often five or six letter codes were used, but in this volume every attempt has been made to reduce this to three, though this has not always proved possible if confusion is to be avoided. In the list which follows the codes as used in this volume are given first, followed by the full unit designation and then the codes used in the USAAF/USAF records. The codes used here are given in alphabetical order - but where it has proved impossible to decode the original longer codes these remain.

In the production list the system used should be self explanatory. For each entry a two or three letter code indicates the command or organisation, eg TC for Training Command, ATC for Air Transport Command. Then follows the base, the unit and the date acquired. The overall command is only given when this changes and the base is only given when there is a move to another. Transfer within a base only warrants repeat of the base if the command changes. Where the unit is redesignated while remaining at the same base, the base is omitted. If the unit moved base only the new base is given.

In wartime, few changes were reported back to the USA, and no units were given on the aircraft card, but these have often been identified from MACRs (Missing Aircrew/Aircraft Reports) which were completed by the unit losing an aircraft, giving comprehensive details. Some accident reports have been identified and these give unit, serial number, command, date and place, often replacing the 'Cond.' date given on the cards. Unit rosters or census lists and lists of aircraft available for an operation have also proved useful. Often there are several units known for any one aircraft, but not the order. Dates are given in day/month/year order where a definite transfer date is known. If the date is in brackets, this indicates that the aircraft was with that unit at that time, possibly from a roster, transfer order or operation list. A colon (:) between the unit and loss details indicates that that unit sent in the report.

Unfortunately it is clear that much information has been lost prior to 1948 when an aircraft served outside the USA. When an aircraft left the inventory prior to about 1952, units were not given in documents available, just the base, so although Base Units could be hazarded at, they have not been added. Beyond that time, complete records have been extracted from the microfilm copies of the aircraft cards, up to the final retirement of the C-47 in 1975. Some records were probably pilfered, lost or destroyed before transfer to microfilm, and a complete history may never be recorded.

USAAF Transport Units

Initially units were designated as Transport Squadrons which formed parts of Transport Groups. The TSs were redesignated Troop Carrier Squadrons in Jul42 when the AAF was reorganised. Later, as the need arose other squadrons were formed, as Air Commando Squadrons, Combat Cargo Squadrons and Pathfinder Squadrons, all of which used C-47s and C-53s and some the C-33 or C-39. Later C-46s replaced some C-47s and then in 1945 the C-54 began to take over.

The states in which US bases were located are shown in the Bases Used section that follows this section.

10th Troop Carrier Group was activated on 20May37 as the 10th Transport Group, and trained with Bellanca C-27s and Douglas C-33s. It was assigned initially to the logistics organization of the Office of the Chief of the Air Corps and in 1941 to the Air Service Command (ASC), providing transport for supplies, material and personnel within the USA. It was assigned to Air Transport Command in Apr42 (later I Troop Carrier Command) and redesignated 10th T C Group in Jul42. In 1943 it converted to C-47s and trained cadres for Troop Carrier Groups and training replacement crews. It disbanded on 14Apr44.

Stations used were:- Patterson 20May37, Wright 20Jun38, Patterson 17Jan41, Mitchell 25May42, Pope 04Oct42, Dunnellon 13Feb43, Lawson 30Nov43, Grenada 21Jan44, Alliance 08Mar44 to 14Apr44.

The 10th TCG comprised the following TCSs which are described below. Most transferred to other Groups: 1, 2, 3, 4, 5, 27, 38, 307 and 308th. The 38th was inactivated as early as 14Apr44.

Several Troop Carrier Squadrons operated only within mainland USA, primarily as transport units or for training. These are described first.

3rd TCS This was activated as the 3rd Transport Squadron on 05Jul35, becoming the 3 TCS on 04Jul42. It was formed at San Antonio AD with C-27s, but C-33s joined in 1936. It became part of 10th TG on 20May37, moving to Duncan Fld on 05Jul37. C-39s were taken on in 1938, serving until 1942, when C-47s and C-53s were added. The 3 TS joined the 63rd TG on 10May41. It disbanded on 14Apr44.

Wartime base moves were:- Camp Williams 29May42; Dodd 18Sep42; Victorville 16Nov42; Lawson 07May43; Grenada 03Jun43 and Sedalia 19Jan44.

From 1943 on the 3 TCS was responsible for training replacement aircrews.

5th TCS This was activated on 14Oct39 as the 5th Transport Squadron, becoming a TCS on 04Jul42. It was part of the 10th TG until that time, when the group became the 10th TCG but was attached to the 314th TCG between 22Feb43 and 08Apr43.

Stations were Patterson Fld, until May42, when it moved to Billy Mitchell Fld,. On 04Oct42 it went to Pope, and to Lawson on 02Dec42. On 26Jan44 it transferred to Grenada and on to Alliance on 12Mar44. It disbanded on 14Apr44.

C-33s and C-39s were used until 1942, C-47s and C-53s thereafter. This was an operational training unit until the end of 1942, when it started training replacement glider crews. The only C-47 known to have served with 5 TCS was 42-93223.

9th TCS Initially activated as the 9th Transport Squadron, this became the 9th TCS on 04Jul42. 9 TS joined the 63rd TG (later TCG) on 01Dec40 when it was activated. From May42 until Feb44 it was responsible for crew training and replacement pilot training, being based at Patterson initially, then moving progressively to Brookley on 18Sep41, Camp Williams on 24May42, Dodd on 18Sep42, Stuttgart on 11Nov42, Victorville on 18Dec42, Ft Sumner on 04Mar43, Lawson on 07May43 and Grenada on 03Jun43. It joined the 7th AF on 03Feb44 moving to Hickam on 21Feb44 and to Abermama Island on 27Mar44 and Saipan on 04Aug44. During this period it was assigned to VI Air Service Area Command from 25Jul45, to AAF Middle Pacific from 15Dec45, to Pacific Air Command on 01Jan46 and to the 54th TCW on 15Jan46. It moved to Guam in Jul46, and was responsible for aerial transportation in the Central, Western and Southwestern Pacific from 21Feb44 until Jul46.

Equipment included most DC-3 derivatives, C-33s, C-34s and C-39s up to 1941, C-47s, C-50s and C-53s from 1942, but C-46s arrived in 1945 and C-54s in 1946. C-47s remained until 1946.

C-47s used: 41-38598, 42-15533.

24th and **25th TCS** These two units followed identical histories. They were constituted on 19Jan42 and activated on 01Feb42, when they were assigned to the 89th TG (later TCG). Initially both were Transport Squadrons, becoming TCSs on 04Jul42. Responsible for transition pilot training, they moved from Daniel to Harding on 08Mar42, to Camp Williams on 22Jun42, to Sedalia on 10Sep42 and finally to Del Valle on 19Dec42, where they disbanded on 14Apr44.

26th TCS was formed on 19Jan42 and assigned to the 89th TG, later TCG. Initially it was based at Daniel, GA, moving to Harding, LA on 08Mar42 and to Camp Williams, WI on 22June of that year. A further move to Sedalia, MO took place on 10Sep and the final move was to Del Valle, TX on 19Dec42. It was disbanded on 14Apr44. The 26th had responsibility for operational and replacement training and did not see action.

30th and **31st TCS** These units were formed on 28Jan42, being assigned to the 314th TG on 02Mar42 and on 15Jun to the 89th TG (later TCG). The bases were Drew Fld, FL from 02Mar, Camp Williams from 10Jun42, Sedalia on 10Sep42 and Del Valle from 16Dec42 until disbandment on 14Apr44. They were responsible for transition and pilot replacement training.

60th TCS This was formed on 13Oct42 and activated on 26Oct as part of the 63rd TCG. Stations were Dodd Fld, moving to Victorville on 19Nov, then to Lawson Fld on 10May43. Next was Grenada AAF on 03Jun43 and finally Sedalia on 19Jan44. It was concerned with training replacement pilots and was disbanded on 14Apr44.

C-47s used: 41-18387, 18467, 18470, 18578, 18590, 38598, 42-6496, 15533, 15537, 23339, 23345, 23360, 23387, 23777, 23806, 24071, 24097, 24123, 24307, 24320, 47379, 68770, 68790, 68795, 68797, 68844, 43-30666, 30676, 30688, 30690

307th TCS This unit was constituted and activated on 15Mar43 and disbanded just over a year later on 04Apr44. It was assigned to the 10th TCG, and was based at Baer Fld initially, moving to Grenada AAF on 06May, Lawson Fld on 05Jun, back to Grenada on 28Jan44 and finally to Alliance AAF on 12Mar44. The 307th was responsible for operational training until Jul43, when it took on replacement training for glider crews.

C-47s used: 41-18396, 18416, 42-23360, 68735

308th TCS Activated on 15Mar43, the 308th formed part of the 10th TCG and was stationed initially at Baer Field, moving to Grenada on 6th May and to Lawson on 05Jun43. The next move was back to Grenada on 28Jan44, and then to Alliance on 12Mar44, where the squadron was disbanded on 14Apr44. Initially it was an operational training unit, but from Jul43 it undertook replacement training for glider crews.

C-47s used:- 42-68781, 92042

316th TCS This was constituted on 07Dec43 and activated a week later, when it was assigned to 1 Troop Carrier Command and attached to 61st TCW passing to 1st Provisional TCG on 30Feb44. On 04Nov44 it passed to VI Air Service Area Command and to the 7th AF on 22Jul45. On 01Sep45 it went to the 8th AF, joining the 54th TCW on 15Feb46. It was disbanded on 25Mar46. Bases were Sedalia from 15Dec43, Alliance from 25Jan44, Camp Marshall from 10Mar44 to 30Sep44, Kahuku on 04Nov44, Bellows Fld on 16Feb45, and Okinawa from 22Aug45 until disbandment on 25Mar46. C-47s were used only until 1945, when they were replaced by C-46s. After initial training the unit was responsible for transport in the Hawaiian Islands and to forward bases in the Pacific.

C-47s used:- 42-24405, 42-93101, 93180, 43-15774, 15777, 15780, 16057, 16093

320th TCS This TCS was constituted on 09Dec44 and activated on the 17Dec, being assigned to the 509th Composite Group. It was based initially at Wendover until 26Apr45, moving to North Field, Tinian on 30May45 in support of the 509th's atomic warfare activities. It moved back to Roswell AAF on 06Nov45, by which time C-54s had replaced the C-47s. 42-93163 and 43-48401 were used from Jun46.

Europe and North Africa

The TCSs used by the 8th, 9th and 12th Air Forces were transferred from one to another, so are listed here as a whole. The 8th AF passed the transports to the 9th AF or 12th AF, although at an early stage they were still part of the 8th. Reference is sometimes made to the 8th when an aircraft was lost. This seems to have been a paper transfer to expedite write-off, or because the 8th carried out repair work and salvaged a damaged aircraft.

60th TG comprising 10, 11, 12 and 28 TCS, was activated on 01Dec40 at Olmstead, transferring to Westover in May41. It became part of the 8th AF on 12Jun42 and ferried to the UK between 07Aug42 and 11Oct42 to Chelveston and Aldermaston. It became part of the 51st TCW, 8th AF on 01Sep42 and transferred to the 12th AF on 12Sep42, being assigned to the XII Air Force Service Command on 05Jan43 and then transferred to the Northwest African AF TCC (Prov) for the invasion of Sicily. 12th AF took direct control when XII TCC was disbanded. Finally to PTCAD on 16Aug44.

10 TCS 41-7750, 7765, 7766, 7799, 7800, 7805, 7807, 7816, 7818, 7820, 7825, 7830, 7836, 7838, 7846, 18342, 18344, 18348, 18388, 18409, 18536, 18685, 19473, 19486, 38700, 38707, 42-23468, 23471, 23473, 23481, 23515, 23525, 23526, 68714, 68740, 68748, 68749, 68750, 68754, 68762, 68851, 100959, 43-15378, 30649
11 TCS 41-7741, 7749, 7771, 7801, 7813, 7828, 7830, 7845, 7850, 18367, 18388, 18409, 18636, 18698, 19473, 38685, 38701, 42-23411, 23472, 23516, 23528, 100944, 100958
12 TCS 41-7725, 7749, 7764, 7765, 7767, 7769, 7774, 7812, 7814, 7815, 7816, 7819, 7821, 7828, 18351, 18386, 18418, 18685, 19463, 19485, 42-23465, 23469, 23471, 23478, 23519, 23522, 100958, 101033, 43-15348, 15362
28 TCS 41-7800, 7805, 7806, 7820, 7836, 7846, 7855, 18342, 18344, 18346, 18348, 18384, 18471, 18650, 19483, 41-38594, 38705, 42-23410, 23475, 23508, 23515

C-47s and C-53s also used by 60 TCG: 41-7748, 7773, 7776, 7779, 7824, 7826, 18337, 18347, 18361, 18365, 18386, 18471, 18515, 38695, 42-6482, 23405, 23411, 23465, 23471, 23472, 23643, 23934, 23967, 24062, 24072, 24214, 68748, 68750, 68754, 68762, 68806, 68811, 68812, 68814, 68851, 92097, 92292, 92686, 92886, 93090, 93091, 93526, 93734, 93753, 93820, 100502, 100593, 100746, 100768, 100807, 100817, 100820, 100847, 100858, 100883, 100950, 100961, 100963, 43-2027, 15045, 15066, 15075, 15107, 15133, 15135, 15138, 15158, 15213, 15295, 15344, 15363, 15521, 15668, 15672, 15700, 15992, 16026, 16039, 47979, 47981, 47987, 47988, 48241, 48244, 48248, 48251, 48261, 48267, 48314, 48318, 48591, 48686, 48790, 48899, 49384, 49386, 49405, 49413, 49420, 49421, 49865

61st TCG comprising 14, 15, 53 and 59 TCS (activated 04Jul42) was assigned to the 52nd TCW, 12th AF, and to XII AFSC on 05Jan43. It moved to Northwest African AF TCC (Prov) in 1943 but on 17Feb44 returned to Barkston Heath in England to join the 9th AF. From 26Aug44 it became part of 52nd TCW, PTCAD. The group was disbanded on 31Jul45. The Codes listed form part of the same system as used by the RAF, use being confined to Western Europe.

14 TCS code 3I 42-5684, 5691, 15531, 23335, 23638, 23642, 24172, 24204, 24379, 24381, 32807, 32872, 32917, 42-92067, 93072, 93798, 100975, 43-15340, 15609, 47979, 47980, 48261, 48913, 49024
15 TCS code Y9 41-7816, 42-5693, 5694, 5704, 23300, 23307, 23330, 23332, 23336, 23340, 23637, 23933, 24208, 24322, 24332, 32925, 32930, 32933, 32934, 92776, 92836, 92875, 92897, 100894, 43-15047, 15074, 15183, 15210, 15309, 16024, 30647, 47975
53 TCS code 3A 41-38699, 42-23407, 23408, 24173, 24181, 24201, 24206, 24379, 32806, 32829, 32832, 32837, 32870, 32877, 32919, 92066, 92773, 92778, 92842, 92882, 93781, 100896, 100983, 100984, 108888, 108909, 43-15047, 15096, 15324, 15335, 30732, 48723, 48939, 49679
59 TCS code X5 41-19486, 42-5701, 23304, 23306, 23329, 23333, 23334, 23335, 23338, 23406, 23932, 32927, 32931, 32932, 32935, 43-15097

C-47s also known to have served with 61TCG are: 41-7811, 42-32917, 42-23356, 23398, 23929, 23967, 24035, 24067, 24177, 24267, 24375, 24390, 42-92457, 92467, 92835, 92841, 92877, 92889, 92898, 92907, 93067, 93072, 93074, 93075, 93511, 93699, 93708, 93720, 93722, 93729, 93731, 93780, 93794, 93817, 93818, 42-108889, 108902, 108981, 100678, 100804, 100872, 100883, 100912, 100950, 100986, 101028, 101033, 43-15079, 15107, 15115, 15130, 15133, 15145, 15170, 15171, 15172, 15191, 15194, 15221, 15226, 15292, 15310, 15312, 15327, 15334, 15346, 15348, 15505, 15514, 15521, 15622, 15639, 15661, 15671, 15700, 16364, 43-47979, 47980, 47988, 48245, 48251, 48257, 48261, 48316, 48594, 48686, 48816, 48913, 48915, 49024, 49098, 49185, 49207, 49208, 49865, 49893, 44-76294

CHAPTER 3: MILITARY OPERATORS OF THE DC-3, C-47, R4D, DAKOTA AND LI-2

62nd TCG comprising 4, 7, 8 and 51 TCS was activated at McClellan on 11Dec40. It joined the 51st TCW, going to the 8th AF on 09Sep42 at Keevil in the UK. Shortly after, on the 14Sep42, the Wing joined the 12th AF and thereafter followed 60th TG. The 62nd Group was inactivated on 13Dec45.

4 TCS 41-18419, 18421, 18424, 18425, 18428, 18442, 18444, 18452, 18455, 18456, 38580, 38585. 38591, 42-23510, 24187, 24202, 24207, 24333, 24336, 24373, 24378, 92680, 92683, 92702, 92992, 93251, 92354, 93784, 93785, 93787, 93818, 100949, 43-15361, 15375, 47972, 49530
7 TCS 41-7818, 18423, 18426, 18433, 18445, 18446, 18447, 18457, 18460, 38580, 42-23527, 24209, 24390, 92680, 93253, 93820, 100950, 100955, 43-15115, 15116, 15118, 48312, 48317, 49414, 49539, 49779, 49947, 44-76450
8 TCS 41-7853, 18358, 18360, 18412, 18438, 18439, 18443, 18469, 18520, 18616, 18681, 38589, 38712, 42-23511, 23517, 24207, 24214, 24375, 24391, 92696, 92701, 92704, 93254, 93276, 93784, 93785, 93818, 100593, 100953, 43-15117, 15375, 15376
51 TCS 41-18344, 38591, 42-24178, 24179, 24186, 24191, 24193, 24203, 24327, 24330, 24383, 92990, 93255, 100951, 43-15532, 30653

Also used by 62 TCG were:- 41-18375, 18382, 18422, 18453, 18461, 38591, 38695, 42-6469, 6497, 15531, 15540, 23476, 23521, 24318, 24388, 47372, 47382, 92054, 100963, 43-15278, 15287, 15606,30714, 49410, 49419, 49424, 49409

64th TCG comprising 16, 17, 18 and 35 TCS was activated at Duncan Field on 04Dec40. It joined the 51st TCW, 8th AF on 18Aug42 at Ramsbury, England, transferring to the 12th AF on 14Sep42 and then followed 60th TG's movements. The 64th TCG plus 4 TCS were loaned to the CBI, leaving Sicily on 02Apr44 and arriving in India five days later. They were required to help stem the Japanese advance in the Kohima-Imphal sector of the Burma front. They returned to Sicily on 09Jun44, having lost eleven C-47s, but Myitkyina was secured.

16 TCS 41-7807, 7824, 7837, 7845, 18341, 18345, 18348, 18349, 18360, 18365, 18376, 18380, 42-23503, 23639, 100954, 43-48268
17 TCS 41-7809, 7817, 7856, 18344, 18352, 18354, 18355, 18368, 18370, 18375, 18382, 18448, 19469, 42-68758, 68759, 68766, 92700, 92929, 43-15245, 15246, 15247, 15248, 15249, 15250
18 TCS 41-7812, 7844, 7847, 7852, 7853, 7858, 7866, 18356, 18357, 18358, 18374, 18515, 18520, 42-23927, 45-1032
35 TCS 41-7818, 7825, 7828, 7846, 7850, 18338, 18354, 18358, 18367, 18369, 18378, 18458, 18502, 18603, 42-23383, 23520, 23648, 68759, 68766, 92676, 92998

C-47s also used by 64 TCG: 41-7803, 7811, 7841, 18340, 18351, 18353, 18361, 18366, 18389, 18419, 18450, 18502, 18685, 18698, 19473, 42-6482, 6497, 23468, 23932, 23936, 24182, 24192, 24196, 24199, 24205, 24213, 24382, 24385, 68805, 68807, 68808, 92684, 93823, 100947, 100954, 108901, 43-15361, 15363, 47983

313th TCG comprising 29, 47, 48 and 49 TCS was formed in the USA on 04Jul42 and moved to the 52nd TCW, 12th AF in 1943. It then followed the 61st TG and returned to Folkingham in the UK in Feb44, as part of the 9th AF. It converted to C-46s in 1945, and all but the 48th were inactivated on 22Sep45. The 48th survived until 15Nov45.

29 TCS Code 5X 41-7812, 7813, 7814, 7815, 7816, 7817, 18542, 18629, 18632, 38602, 38698, 38704, 38749, 42-23306, 23646, 23649, 24184, 24198, 24270, 24373, 38602, 38749, 32808, 32810, 32880, 32921, 92060, 92718, 92916, 93005, 93518, 93703? 93715, 93792, 93793, 100525, 100878, 100966, 43-15107, 15110, 15160? 15166, 15202, 15294, 15297, 15323, 15330, 15345, 15616, 15650, 15768, 16031, 16098, 48074, 48953, 49038, 49040, 49083
47 TCS code N3 41-18633, 20129, 42-5700, 5702, 5703, 42-23509, 23529, 23644, 24386, 32827, 32865, 32867, 32875, 32877, 32920, 32923, 68849, 92726, 92870, 92970, 93027, 93519? 93814, 43-30723, 43-15066?, 15075, 15176, 15619, 15649, 16265?
48 TCS code Z7 41-18350, 18367, 18487, 18519, 18563, 18593, 18633, 42-5676, 5703, 23383, 23474, 23636, 23647, 23648, 24211, 32863, 32873, 32911, 32916, 68766, 93511, 100514, 43-15079, 15101, 15145, 15156, 15198, 15260, 15267, 16122, 15632, 48727
49 TCS code H2 41-18633, 42-5690, 5699, 42-23636, 24177, 42-68694, 68695, 68696, 68697, 68698, 68699, 68700, 68701, 68702, 68705, 68758, 42-92064, 92868, 92880, 93062, 93076? 93091, 93099, 93507, 93521? 108991, 100639, 100640, 100849, 100852, 100854, 100859, 100860, 100893, 43-15048, 15082, 15110, 15166, 15191, 15506, 15637, 15662? 16049, 43-30648, 48856, 49564, 49698

C-47s TCS unknown: 42-93706, 93712, 100547, 100848, 100891, 43-15163, 30652, 43-48403, 48415, 49784

314th TCG comprising 32, 50, 61 and 62 TCS was formed in the USA on 04Jul42 (32nd and 50th). The 61st was activated on 26Oct42 and the 62nd on 05Dec42. They joined the 52nd TCW, 12th AF in 1943. Thereafter it followed the 61st TG's movements, returning to Saltby in the UK in Feb44, and joining the 9th AF. It had some C-109s late in the war. Inactivation was between Sep45 and 26Aug46.

32 TCS code S2 41-38679, 42-23303, 23361, 23362, 23366, 23368, 23647, 32873, 92903, 93077, 93794, 100892, 100982, 100976, 108982, 43-15146, 15508, 30715
50 TCS code 2R 42-23331, 23344, 23356, 23363, 23393, 23394, 23395, 23399, 23401, 23402, 23429, 24069, 24239, 24335, 24384, 32924, 42-68708, 68720, 68761, 42-92862, 92876, 93065, 93088, 93288, 93710, 100894, 43-15150, 15180, 15214, 15347, 15505, 15631, 15645, 30651
61 TCS code Q9 41-18487, 18632, 42-5689, 5690, 5700, 5702, 5703, 42-23303, 23344, 23403, 23643, 24268, 24325, 24331, 68759, 68771, 68809, 42-92055, 92719, 92839, 92841, 92893, 93001, 93026, 93807, 43-15149, 15198, 15643, 15647, 15664, 15678, 16051, 30716, 47970
62 TCS code E5 42-23337, 23929, 24334, 32810, 32910, 32924, 42-68706, 68707, 68708, 68713, 68716, 68720, 68763, 68766, 68849, 42-92725, 93002, 42-100846, 100896, 108990, 43-15093, 15151, 15221, 15305, 15623, 16026, 43-47980

Other C-47s used by the 314th TCG are:- 42-23396, 23397, 23871, 24328, 24335, 32931, 42-93100, 93521, 42-100841, 43-15287, 15606, 48935

315th TCG comprising 34, 43, 309 and 310 TCS was activated at Olmstead on 14Feb42. 34 and 43 TCS moved to Aldermaston in the UK as part of VII ASC, 8th AF on 01Dec42. 16 aircraft were detached to Blida, Algeria to the 12th AF in May43. The Group joined 50th TCW, IX TCC, 9th AF on 16Oct43 on return to the UK (Welford on 06Nov43 and Spanhoe on 07Feb44), when 309 and 310 TCS were added. They transferred to 52nd TCW, IX TCC, 9th AF in Feb44 and to PTCAD on 16Aug44. The 309th and 310th inactivated on 31Jul45.

34 TCS code NM 41-20063, 20064, 20072, 20125, 20127, 42-6461, 15565, 15567, 23509, 23609, 24172, 24174, 24269, 24389, 92056, 92682, 92733, 92734, 92736, 92737, 93031, 93035, 93063, 93067, 93697, 93719, 100970, 43-15058, 15091, 15106, 15173, 15175, 15188, 15199, 15206, 15224, 15259, 15293, 15308, 15321, 15359, 15878, 15881, 15885, 15887, 15893, 16022, 16023, 30650
43 TCS code UA 41-18427, 18441, 18458, 18468, 18502, 18506, 18514, 18515, 18516, 18520, 18589, 38600, 42-23479, 24175, 24176, 68811, 92734, 92738, 92849, 93704, 100875, 108871, 108905, 43-15071, 15157, 15199, 15227, 15251, 15254, 15255, 15256, 15266, 15300, 15342, 16032
309 TCS code M6 42-92833, 92864, 92873, 93029, 93032, 93061, 108873, 108883, 43-15187, 15208, 15341, 15346
310 TCS code 4A 42-92888, 108969, 43-15339, 15612, 43-48395, 48399, 48404

C-47s known to have been with the 315th are:- 42-23412, 24189, 42-68812, 42-92727, 92742, 92779, 92780, 92877, 92890, 92895, 92902, 93037, 93064, 93085, 93512, 93515, 93520, 93698, 93701, 93702, 93706, 93707, 93719, 93799, 93811, 93815, 42-100514, 100516, 100872, 100881, 108906, 108912, 108960, 108977, 108980, 43-15096, 15164, 15193, 15204, 15212, 15225, 15253, 15257, 15314, 15317, 15324, 15325, 15333, 15495, 15509, 15513, 15614, 15617, 15634, 15648, 16122, 16263, 16281, 30652, 43-48402, 48724, 48923, 48931, 49694

316th TCG comprising 36, 37, 44 and 45 TCS was activated in Texas on 04Jul42. It went to the 9th AF on 23Nov42 and ferried to Deversoir (Egypt), El Adem on 10Dec42. It became part of Northwest African AFF TCC (Prov) (XII TCC) on 23Aug43. The Group returned to Cottesmore, UK in Feb44 to IX TCC, 9th AF and to PTCAD on 26Aug44. Inactivation for the 36th and 37th did not occur until 23Jun48 and 44th on 25Mar46, the 45th on 26Dec45, when the latter two were using C-46s.

36 TCS code 4C 41-18420, 18422, 18511, 18519, 18522, 18525, 18527, 18529, 18531, 18533, 18534, 18535, 18536, 18606, 20129, 38608, 38620, 38704, 42-5704, 15533, 15546, 23383, 23503, 23505, 23513, 23623, 23931, 24389, 68700, 68760, 68765, 68766, 68769, 68785, 92679, 93754, 93780, 100517, 100872, 100973, 108902, 108909, 43-15179, 15185, 15205, 15227, 15258, 15265, 15634, 15638, 15643
37 TCS code W7 41-18503, 18528, 18532, 18595, 18599, 18600, 18633, 18696, 38607, 38608, 38611, 38616, 38617, 38625, 42-23428, 23601, 23602, 23918, 24328, 24392, 68772, 92725, 92774, 92846, 92884, 93100, 93734, 93775, 93755, 100502, 100875, 43-15093, 15171, 15212, 15277, 15281, 15288, 15292, 15295, 15498, 15509, 15510, 15610, 15617, 16263, 16265, 16266, 16269, 16270, 16273, 16281, 30652,

30721, 48263, 48293, 48394, 48399, 48402, 48403, 48414, 48415, 48721, 48722, 48948, 48949, 49682, 49685, 49688, 49705
44 TCS code 6E 41-20055, 20068, 20122, 20126, 20128, 20129, 20136, 42-5682, 15533, 15546, 15548, 15549, 15553, 15884, 23492, 23505, 23507, 24189, 24269, 42-68772, 68782, 92056, 92727, 92777, 92886, 93071, 93753, 93815, 100516, 100714, 100970, 100971, 108877, 43-2020, 15095, 15189, 15203, 15317, 15324, 15496, 15513, 15516, 15614, 15615, 15648, 15671, 48293, 48390, 49682
45 TCS code T3 41-18505, 18512, 18513, 18541, 18542, 18596, 18627, 38601, 38603, 38605, 38613, 38622, 38624, 38739, 42-23404, 23506, 23507, 23523, 23639, 23935, 24181, 92832, 92846, 92861, 93075, 93511, 93512, 93754, 100499, 100883, 43-15106, 15184, 15194, 15207, 15225, 15305, 15334, 15495, 15497, 15633, 15641, 15648, 15659, 16122, 47972

C-47s also used by the 316th TCG were:- 41-18482, 18653, 38610 [HQ], 38622 [HQ], 42-15546 [HQFlt], 23308, 23387, 23772, 23788, 23793, 24096, 32915 [HQ], 42-92738, 93167, 93187, 93543, 93607, 93754, 42-100487, 100488, 100489, 100494, 100560, 100597, 100603, 100632, 100635, 100673, 100710, 100782, 100861, 100931, 100997, 108886, 108922, 43-15106, 15161, 15227, 15256, 15270, 15272, 15273, 15276, 15277, 15278, 15280, 15281, 15283, 15292, 15300, 15497, 15501, 15554, 15561, 15563, 15566, 15573, 15576, 15586, 15593, 15594, 15602, 15603, 15604, 15634, 15678, 15683, 15685, 15689, 15691, 15765, 15778, 15950, 16040, 16059, 16061, 16067, 16069, 16074, 16091, 16093, 16100, 16123, 16279, 47905, 47972, 48010, 48012, 48056, 48058, 48059, 48065, 48069, 48071, 48073, 48081, 48085, 48092, 48096, 48131, 48135, 48145, 48446, 48447, 48458, 48470, 48480, 48481, 48492, 48504, 48505

349th TCG comprising 23, 312, 313 and 314 TCS was formed in the USA and allotted to the 52nd TCW. The 23rd was activated only on 21Nov44, the remaining units on 01Nov43. It joined PTCAD in Mar45 as a C-46 unit. The 314th was inactivated on 31Jul46 and the other three on 07Sep46.

23 TCS code Q8
312 TCS code 9E 42-15554, 23797, 23866, 42-92115, 42-100493, 100494, 43-15283, 30664, 48066
313 TCS code 3F 41-18627, 42-23308, 23782, 23793, 92115, 100663, 100712, 43-15082, 30664
314 TCS code LY 42-23777, 23866, 23925, 68741, 100783, 43-15684

C-47s used by the 349th TCG:- 42-93185, 93187, 93222, 93223, 100487, 100488, 100489, 100568, 100597, 100714, 43-15268, 15276, 15278, 15281, 15284, 15287, 15550, 15554, 15559, 15561, 15573, 15594, 15606, 15683, 15685, 15689, 15691, 16137, 16200, 47970, 48069, 48071, 48072, 48073, 48081, 48100, 48135

434th TCG comprising 71, 72, 73 and 74 TCS activated on 09Feb43, and was to have gone to the 8th AF, but was reassigned to the 50th TCW, IX TCC, 9th AF on 22Feb44. Bases in England were Greenham Common, Fulbeck and Welford Park on 10Dec43, then Aldermaston. It had joined the 53rd TCW, IX TCC by May44 and the PTCAD on 31Aug44. All were inactivated on 31Jul46. The 74th had some C-46s by 1946.

71 TCS code CJ 42-24022, 24024, 24028, 24030, 24038, 42-93795, 42-100507, 43-15101, 15349, 15611, 16028
72 TCS code CU 42-100500, 100505, 100506, 100671, 108992, 43-15220, 15628, 15663, 16031, 16033, 16034
73 TCS code CN 42-24040, 24044, 24047, 24048, 24050, 42-92887, 93040, 93803, 43-15666, 16037
74 TCS code ID 42-6488, 24053, 24060, 24062, 24192, 24199, 92080, 43-15196, 15350, 15502, 15627, 30717

C-47s also used by the 434th TCG were: 42-23918, 24051, 42-92087, 92919, 93187, 93607, 42-100504, 100520, 100531, 100560, 100568, 100635, 100670, 100673, 100805, 100806, 100890, 101000, 101024, 108991, 43-15035, 15068, 15103, 15268, 15277, 15278, 15491, 15504, 15565, 15574, 15586, 15610, 15629, 15675, 16027, 16050, 16086, 16137, 16200, 43-47970, 48064, 48100, 48134, 48145, 48255, 48924.

435th TCG comprising 75, 76, 77 and 78 TCS activated on 25Feb43 and went to the 50th TCW, IX TCC, 9th AF on 03Nov43, based at Langar and Welford Park in the UK on 25Jan44. Transferred to 53rd TCW in Feb44 and to PTCAD on 31Aug44. The 75th gained C-46s in 1945 and the 77th in 1946. The 76th and 78th inactivated on 15Nov45, the 77th on 10Jun46 and the 75th survived until 22Nov49.

75 TCS code SH [CK after D-Day] 42-68720, 68734, 92052, 92099, 93543, 100879, 43-15272, 16059, 16074, 16099, 30717?, 30718, 30735, 43-48065, 48092, 48472, 48716, 48718, 48720, 48734

76 TCS code CW 42-24111, 24122, 24127, 42-68731, 68737, 68738, 100508, 100897, 43-48389, 48407, 48499, 48711, 48725, 48803, 48870, 48926, 48938, 48944, 48946, 48960, 48961
77 TCS code IB 42-23928, 24042, 24077, 24095, 24121, 24132, 24192, 42-68752, 68792, 42-92094, 92716, 92844, 42-100510, 43-15192, 15297, 43-30720, 30734
78 TCS code CM 42-24026, 24072, 24074, 24099, 24134, 42-68736, 42-92086, 92099, 92866, 93812, 42-100668, 100669, 100897, 43-15169, 15209, 15222, 15261, 15618, 43-30731, 48355, 48391

C-47s & C-53s known to be with 435th, TCS unknown:- 42-68734, 42-100549, 100636, 100769, 100888, 43-15108, 15113, 15162, 15306, 15315, 15493, 15516, 43-48332, 48914.

436th TCG comprising 79, 80, 81 and 82 TCS activated on 01Apr43 and went from the US to 50th TCW, IX TCC, 9th AF on 04Feb44 and to Bottesford and Membury in the UK on 03Mar44. Transferred to 53rd TCW, IX TCC, 9th AF in Feb44 and to PTCAD on 31Aug44. They inactivated on 15Nov45.

79 TCS code S6 42-5690, 23529, 24015, 24041, 24045, 24114, 68707, 68782, 92707, 93067, 93607, 100519 to 100531 inc, 100670, 108991, 43-15068, 15091, 15096, 15153, 15327, 15332, 15358, 15640, 43-30652, 48188, 48468, 48714, 49035, 49043, 49089, 49526, 49653
80 TCS code 7D 42-24066, 32872, 32917, 68743, 68830, 42-100532 to 100542 inc. 100544, 100898, 43-15091, 15109, 15215, 15262, 15610, 15670, 43-48332
81 TCS code U5 42-23329, 24034, 24039, 24063, 24064, 92704, 100501, 100504, 100522, 100547 to 100558 inc., 100667, 100674, 43-15224, 15265, 15318, 15501, 15504, 15661, 30723, 47980, 48931
82 TCS code 3D 42-24032, 24069, 42-92092, 93072, 93279, 42-100559 to 100571 inc., 100672, 100673, 43-15080, 15291, 43-30728, 30729, 48263, 48948

C-47s and C-53s with the 436th TCG were:- 42-5693, 24119, 32873, 32919, 42-24054, 68716?, 68811, 68835?, 42-100506, 100545, 100665, 100884, 100887, 100898, 100936, 43-15085, 15147, 15188, 15195, 16369, 30719, 48489, 44-76230

437th TCG comprising 83, 84, 85 and 86 TCS was formed in the USA on 01May43 and allotted to the 53rd TCW, IX TCC, 9th AF in Mar44 at Ramsbury, England. It went to PTCAD on 31Aug44. Inactivation was on 15Nov45.

83 TCS code T2 42-92863, 92867, 100572 to 100579, 100581, 100582, 100801, 100877, 100895, 100972, 100974, 43-15315, 15344, 15678, 48225, 48244, 48246, 48255, 48387, 48456
84 TCS code Z8 41-18364, 42-24385, 68765, 93007, 42-100565, 100583, 100584, 100586, 100589 to 100593, 100631, 100638, 100651 to 100655, 100658, 100659, 100660, 100661, 100676, 100803, 100804, 100881, 100888, 100889, 100978, 100982, 108884, 43-15167, 15302, 15311, 15313, 15315, 15493, 15630, 15657, 15676, 48357, 48405
85 TCS code 9O 42-23351, 23385, 23783, 23918, 23921, 24055, 24126, 24133, 68797, 92077, 92078, 42-100632, 100634 to 100638, 100647, 100648, 100649, 100650, 100805, 100806, 108889, 43-15252, 15356, 15511, 15651, 15655, 15659, 16035, 16389, 48253
86 TCS code 5K 42-68774, 42-92098, 92881, 42-100657, 100660, 100884, 100982, 43-15313, 48473

C-47s known to be with 437th TCG:- 42-93508, 42-108870, 100547, 100575, 100633, 100656, 100886, 43-15100, 15102

438th TCG comprising 87, 88, 89 and 90 TCS was formed in the USA on 01Jun43 and allotted to the 53rd TCW, IX TCC, 9th AF on 09Feb44 at Langar, UK and then Greenham Common on 16Mar44. It passed to PTCAD on 31Aug44. Closure came on 22Sep45.

87 TCS code 3X 42-24182, 24387, 24182, 68815, 92847, 92871, 93003, 93025, 93034, 93605, 100738 to 100745, 100747, 100748, 100749, 100750, 108979, 43-15296, 15320, 15326, 15620, 15673, 48384, 49218
88 TCS code M2 42-24102, 68807, 68808, 92087, 42-100751 to 100763, 100887, 43-15174
89 TCS code 4U 42-24196, 42-92097, 93073, 42-100764, 100765, 100768, 100770, 100772, 100776, 100887, 43-15298, 15336, 15512, 15620
90 TCS code Q7 42-23932, 92899, 93709, 100781, 100810, 100811, 100813, 108983

C-47s TCS unknown:- 42-23839, 92705, 92716, 92894, 42-100567, 100570, 100766, 100774, 100856, 100882, 43-15500, 30731, 48213, 48332, 49249

439th TCG comprising 91, 92, 93 and 94 TCS was formed in the USA on 01Jun43 and allotted to the 53rd TCW, IX TCC, 9th AF in Feb44. It was based at Balderton and Upottery in England on 26Apr44 and transferred to the 50th TCW, PTCAD on 26Aug44. Some C-46s were allotted in 1945 and all but the 94th closed on 10Jun46, the latter on 31Jul46.

91 TCS code L4 42-92912, 93095, 42-100642, 100644, 100818, 100819, 100823, 100832, 100833, 100847, 100885, 100889, 43-15049, 15660
92 TCS code J8 42-92735, 93797, 93801, 100822, 100824, 100825, 100826, 100827, 100828, 100830, 100831, 43-15045, 15046, 15629, 15652, 16050
93 TCS code 3B 42-23601, 68733, 92717, 92774, 92775, 92900, 92908, 92917, 92920, 93069, 93705, 93726, 93730, 93797, 100509, 100642, 100731, 100734, 100736, 100737, 100821, 100835 to 100840, 100842, 100844, 100845, 100846, 100872, 100876, 100880, 100932 to 100935, 100937 to 100942, 108910, 43-15044, 15067, 15083, 15088, 15092, 15168, 15182, 15191, 15217, 15649, 15669, 16043, 16053, 47978, 47993, 48408, 48410, 48805, 48856
94 TCS code D8 42-93003, 93098, 42-100848, 100852, 100853, 100856, 100858, 100860, 100862, 100893, 43-15159, 15635

C-47s used by 439th TCG:- 42-23306, 23918, 24124, 24304, 24308, 24313, 42-92099, 92919, 93004, 93094, 93717, 42-100817, 100820, 100821, 100829, 100859, 100883, 43-15050, 15272, 15294, 15323, 15351, 15509, 15650, 15651, 15678, 16052, 48397, 48927

440th TCG comprising 95, 96, 97 and 98 TCS was formed in the USA on 01Jul43 and allotted to the 50th TCW, IX TCC, 9th AF in April 1944 and based in England at Bottesford and Exeter on 18Apr44. It transferred to PTCAD on 26Aug44. Inactivation was on 18Oct45.

95 TCS code 9X 41-7802, 18409, 18503, 38695, 42-5674, 32931, 32932, 68738, 68814, 68832, 92740, 92780, 92872, 92884, 92914, 93006, 93097, 93705, 93753, 100509, 100730, 100731, 100899 to 100909 inc, 100911, 100965, 43-15073, 15084, 15087, 15121, 15295, 15658, 30717, 48388, 48453, 48474, 48861, 49084
96 TCS code 6Z 41-18428, 18461, 18505, 18600, 42-24210, 92295, 92706, 92728, 92870, 92872, 92884, 93081, 93542, 93730, 100642, 100731, 100732, 100733, 100821, 100880, 100901, 100908, 100910 to 100920 inc, 100965, 100977, 108886, 43-15067, 15087, 15137, 15140, 15295, 16270, 47966, 47969, 47974, 48400, 48858, 48937, 49014, 49188
97 TCS code W6 41-7802, 7851, 42-5673, 32803, 32863, 68701, 68702, 92066, 92259, 92295, 92717, 92726, 92729, 92771, 92880, 93084, 93278, 93519, 93735, 100734, 100809, 100894, 100921 to 100931 inc, 100936, 108891, 43-15069, 15070, 15076, 15078, 15099, 15626, 15636, 15654, 15658, 15672, 48390, 48392, 48402, 48464, 48801, 48807
98 TCS code 8Y 41-18441, 18599, 42-23503, 68748, 68840, 92717, 92718, 92775, 92900, 92920, 93033, 93096, 100736, 100737, 100932 to 100942 inc, 108910, 43-15083, 15168, 15182, 15669, 16043, 43-47966, 47992, 48413, 48477, 49099, 49698

C-47s & C-53s, TCS unknown, were:- 41-18696, 42-68695, 68700, 42-92774, 93034, 42-100527, 100550, 100961, 100997, 43-15217, 15503, 15656, 48408, 48410, 48468

441st TCG comprising 99, 100, 301 and 302 TCS was formed in the USA on 01Aug43 and allotted to the 50th TCW, IX TCC, 9th AF in Apr44 and based at Langar and Merryfield in the UK on 25Apr44. It went to PTCAD on 26Aug44. The 99th and 100th inactivated on 27Mar46 and the 301st and 302nd on 27May46.

99 TCS code 3J 42-92719, 92731, 92905, 93028, 93036, 100863, 100864, 101003 to 101013, 43-15094, 15200, 15218, 15348, 15355
100 TCS code 8C 42-92459, 92467, 92470, 92677, 92732, 92741, 92843, 92918, 93041, 93078, 93079, 93454, 93681, 42-100865, 100866, 101004, 101014 to 101024, 101034, 43-15042, 15086, 15098, 15102, 15186, 15197, 15357, 15646, 16042, 30725, 43-47968, 48875, 48956
301 TCS code Z4 42-5693, 23394, 92681, 92911, 92921, 93036, 93038, 93082, 93708, 93720, 100867, 100868, 100870, 101025 to 101035, 108910, 43-15216, 15219, 15353, 15644, 16042, 16045
302 TCS code 2L 42-92730, 92771, 92872, 92904, 92914, 92921, 93068, 93082, 93084, 42-100867, 100869, 100870, 101027, 108886, 100891, 43-15033 to 15043, 15066, 15067, 15073, 15078, 15135, 15152, 15189, 15348, 15353, 15621, 16379, 48260, 48880, 48951

C-47s and C-53s, TCS unknown:- 42-32870, 42-23331, 24056, 42-68843, 42-92845, 43-16348, 43-47976, 48256,

442nd TCG comprising 303, 304, 305 and 306 TCS was formed in the USA on 01Sep43 and allotted to the 50th TCW, IX TCC, 9th AF on 29Mar44, based at Fulbeck and Weston Zoyland in England in Jun44. To PTCAD on 26Aug44. The TCG inactivated on 30Sep46.

303 TCS code J7 42-92415, 92739, 92879, 42-100895, 108837, 108842, 43-15081, 48924
304 TCS code V4 42-92380, 92422, 92456, 92459, 92462, 92915, 43-15111, 15119
305 TCS code 4J 42-93042, 93087, 93093, 93732, 43-15064, 15120 to 15126, 15128 to 15131, 15158, 15263, 15354
306 TCS code 7H 42-92740, 92743, 92865, 92918, 93681, 93717, 100874, 43-15065, 15090, 15132, 15133, 15134, 15136 to 15143, 15149, 16048

C-47s, TCS unknown:- 42-92418, 92424, 92452, 93071, 93700, 42-100643, 100842, 43-15098, 15199

IX Troop Carrier Pathfinder Group. Four Pathfinder Squadrons were formed to lead Troop Carrier Squadrons to drop zones and they were operational in time for the Market Garden operations to Eindhoven. Some aircraft, at least, were fitted with radar, though these do not appear to have had new designations.

1 Pathfinder Sq 42-92717, 93097, 93540, 93542, 93543, 93681, 43-15161, 15163, 15678, 30725, 47968, 47969
2 Pathfinder Sq 42-92740, 93604, 93685?, 93752, 93799, 100964, 108977, 43-15200, 15322, 15328, 15329, 47967, 47974, 49008
3 Pathfinder Sq 42-92706, 92837, 93086, 93605, 93606, 93680, 93682, 93821, 108969, 108993, 43-48056
4 Pathfinder Sq 42-92707, 92885, 93079, 93096, 93099, 93544, 93755, 43-15325, 15668, 48266

Also used were 42-100981, 108837

5th Air Force - Southwest Pacific Area, Australia

54th Troop Carrier Wing was constituted on 26Feb43, activated in Australia on 13Mar43 to form part of the 5th Air Force. It comprised the following Groups:- 2nd Combat Cargo Group, 317th Troop Carrier Group, 374th TCG, 375th TCG and 433rd TCG. Codes under ADAT comprised civil registration marks for use within mainland Australia, but Field or nose numbers were also used in blocks allotted to each unit.

317 TCG comprising 39, 40, 41 and 46 TCS. This was activated at Duncan Fld on 22Feb42, subsequently operating from Bowman Fld on 19Jun42, Lawson Fld on 11Oct42, Maxton from 03Dec42, then to Townsville on 23Jan43, to Pt Moresby in Sep43, Finschhafen in Apr44 and finally to Hollandia, NEI in Jun44. 39 TCS joined 317 TCG on 22Feb43 and was inactivated on 14Sep49.

39 TCS [Field Nos 6 to 25]:- 38-519, 38-530, 38-532, 41-18498, 18564, 18568, 18588, 18646, 18648, 18649, 18651, 18653, 18658, 18660, 18665, 18666, 18667, 18668, 19470, 19472, 19475, 38659, 38662, 38664, 38668, 38676, 38750, 42-23421, 23488, 23498, 23581, 23584, 23585, 23586, 23587, 23588, 23590, 23592, 23653, 23655, 23661, 23664, 23685, 23946, 23947, 23952, 23953, 23954, 23955, 23956, 23958, 23959, 24256, 24394, 24411, 32831, 92032, 92038, 92804, 93242, 93494, 100466, 100476, 100477, 100481, 100622, 100627, 43-15240, 15426, 15437, 15440, 15441, 15442, 15459, 15460, 15471, 15472, 15475, 15483, 16012, 16014, 16015, 16016, 16018, 16019, 16021, 16111, 16115, 16230, 16238, 16304, 16320, 16344, 30761, 49914
40 TCS [Field Nos 26 to 50]:- 41-7732, 7733, 41-18498, 18538, 18539, 18564, 18577, 18584, 18586, 18588, 18601, 18646, 18647, 18648, 18653, 18682, 38630, 38634, 38747, 42-23418, 23465, 23485, 23586, 23587, 23588, 23589, 23598, 23651, 23661, 23662, 23664, 24222, 24223, 24225, 24226, 24256, 24257, 24403, 24407, 92788, 92822, 92823, 93235, 93236, 93240, 93496, 100460, 100464, 100474, 100480, 100486, 100618, 100624, 100717, 100725, 108928, 108957, 108976, 43-15412, 15426, 15444, 15446, 15448, 15456, 15467, 15478, 16011, 16012, 16014, 16015, 16019, 16021, 16026, 16114, 16116, 16241, 16288, 16298, 16334, 30747, 49913, 49914
41 TCS [Field Nos 51 to 75]:- 38-511, 515, 41-7690, 7708, 7712, 7732, 7842, 7843, 18413, 18459, 18478, 18480, 18487, 18498, 18507, 18523, 18526, 18568, 18570, 18577, 18588, 18591, 18595, 18597, 18601, 18602, 18612, 18646, 18648, 18652, 18656, 18662, 18663, 18665, 18671, 18673, 18680, 18682, 19465, 19472, 38602, 38629, 38630, 38634, 38661, 38675, 38678, 38680, 38682, 38737, 42-15566, 23418, 23486, 23582, 23583, 23598, 23599, 23654, 23657, 23844, 23856, 23858, 24215, 24260, 24261, 24395, 24411, 24412, 24413, 56107, 93497, 93500, 100624, 100719, 100721, 43-15230, 15413, 15414, 15428, 15435, 15438, 15447, 15449, 15455, 15458, 15465, 15480, 15481, 15488, 16014, 16015, 16019, 16021, 16304, 47996

46 TCS [Field Nos 76 to 100]:- 41-7686, 7687, 7690, 7691, 7693, 7694, 18586, 18595, 18597, 18649, 18660, 18661, 18671, 18683, 19467, 19487, 38658, 38659, 38660, 38665, 38666, 38674, 38675, 38736, 42-23489, 23490, 23491, 23582, 23587, 23650, 23651, 23653, 23654, 23656, 23658, 23659, 23660, 23662, 23665, 23698, 23708, 23712, 23831, 23959, 24224, 24261, 32830, 32831, 92074, 92817, 93233, 93238, 93493, 93499, 100475, 100717, 100725, 108927, 108957, 108976, 43-15240, 15451, 15452, 15467, 15474, 15476, 16014, 16019, 16104, 16208, 16221, 16225, 16241, 16298, 16329, 30761, 47996

374 TCG, **54 TCW** comprising 6, 21, 22, and 33 TCS. The 6th and 33rd were activated in the USA on 04Jul42, the 21st and 22nd on the following day. The group was activated in Australia on 12Nov42 at Brisbane, moving to Pt Moresby in Dec42, Townsville on 07Oct43, Nadzab in Sep44 and finally Biak, NEI in Oct44. All had gained C-46s in 1945-46. All but the 6th inactivated in 1946 (21 and 22 on 31Jan and 33 on 15Feb). The 6th redesignated on 21May48.

6 TCS [Field Nos 501 to 525]:- 41-18498, 18538, 18539, 18560, 18564, 18568, 18571, 18577, 18583, 18584, 18585, 18586, 18588, 18595, 18597, 18601, 18602, 18615, 18667, 18697, 19466, 38601, 38602, 38615, 38631, 38676, 42-23418, 23422, 23590, 23650, 23653, 23654, 23722, 23856, 23874, 23956, 24260, 24261, 24395, 24406, 24409, 24415, 32874, 92035, 92783, 92784, 92785, 92793, 92794, 92797, 92799, 92802, 92805, 92806, 92829, 92830, 92856, 100464, 100465, 100466, 100467, 100471, 100475, 100485, 100486, 100623, 43-15436, 15464, 16103, 16199, 16228, 16230, 16312, 16314, 16316, 16317, 16320, 16324, 16332, 16333, 30749, 30750, 30754, 49761, 49762, 49765, 49905 plus C-46s
21 TCS [Field Nos 526 to 550]:- C-39s 38-505, 508, 519, 527, 530, 532, 41-1941, 1944, 41-7685, 7686, 7687, 7688, 7690, 7691, 7693, 7694, 7695, 7697, 7698, 7702, 7733, 41-18567, 18571, 18585, 18587, 18615, 18628, 18648, 18649, 18651, 18653, 18656, 18660, 18662, 18667, 18668, 19472, 20051, 20053, 20054, 20066, 20070, 38647, 38676, 42-23418, 23420, 23587, 23610, 23707, 23721, 23947, 92785, 92789, 92790, 92791, 92796, 92797, 92799, 92802, 92805, 92806, 92808, 92820, 92821, 100465, 100471, 100483, 100484, 108878, 108957, 43-15325, 15400, 15432, 15483, 15932, 16014, 16103, 16217, 16226, 16227, 16228, 16229, 16230, 16236, 16237, 16246, 16293, 16295, 16315, 16318, 16320, 16330, 16346, 30745, 30752, 30755, 30757, 30758, 48006, 48302, 49023, 49129, 49144, 49219, 49161, 49405, 49653, 49680, 49751, 49755, 49762, 49764, 49903, 49905, 49906, 44-76639, 76933, 77094, 77261, 83226, 83227, 83228, 83229, 45-941, 950, 1007, 1021, 1029, 1089
22 TCS [Field Nos 551 to 575]:- 41-7732, 7733, 18539, 18602, 18612, 18642, 18645, 18662, 18663, 18670, 18673, 19466, 19467, 19479, 20051, 38623, 38628, 38631, 38662, 38663, 38664, 38665, 38666, 38668, 38673, 38678, 38680, 38761, 41-1941, 1944, 42-23487, 23489, 23491, 23502, 23533, 23534, 23535, 23651, 23656, 23659, 23662, 23664, 23698, 23700, 23721, 23949, 23953, 24044, 24220, 24224, 24229, 24255, 24400, 32805, 32830, 32840, 92701, 92781, 92786, 92811, 92814, 92820, 92821, 92827, 100465, 100466, 100472, 100473, 100718, 43-15436, 15477, 16103, 16105, 16199, 16226, 16228, 16229, 16293, 30742, 30747, 30751, 30752, 30757, 30759, 49910
33 TCS [Field Nos 576 to 600]:- 41-18538, 18564, 18583, 18584, 18587, 18588, 18595, 18597, 18598, 18601, 18602, 18628, 18651, 18652, 18653, 18658, 18660, 18662, 18663, 19472, 38601, 38602, 38628, 38629, 38630, 38631, 38634, 38658, 38660, 38669, 38675, 38682, 38666, 42-23487, 24255, 24403, 24414, 32830, 92789, 92792, 92800*, 92801, 92803, 92807, 92808, 92814, 92818, 92819, 92820, 92956, 100467, 100480, 108878, 43-15429, 15434, 15436, 15464, 15470, 16018, 16207, 16217, 16229, 16231, 16292, 16318, 16324, 30741, 30744, 30748, 30760, 49906, 49910

375 TCG comprising 55, 56, 57 and 58 TCS, was activated on 18Nov42 at Bowman, then moving to Sedalia on 23Jan43, to Laurinburg-Maxton on 05May43, to Baer on 02Jun43, whence it departed for Brisbane, forming there on 13Jul43. Further moves were to Pt Moresby on 31Jul43, to Dobodura on 19Aug43, to Pt Moresby on 19Dec43, to Nadzab on 22Apr44 and Biak, NEI on 27Sep44. The final base was San Jose, Mindoro on 17Feb45. Curtiss C-46s supplemented C-47s in June 1945.

55 TCS [Field Nos 101 to 125]:- 41-38673, 38681, 38732, 42-23388, 23532, 23610, 23651, 23876, 23947, 24223, 24257, 32800, 32805, 32840, 32876, 92027, 92029, 92031, 92033, 92035, 92036, 92812, 92825, 92828, 93236, 93243, 93663, 93686, 100622, 100625, 100729, 108957, 43-15419, 15437, 15443, 15444, 15473, 15482, 15487, 16016, 16113, 16210, 16242, 16317, 16323, 16327, 49769, plus C-46s
56 TCS [Field Nos 126 to 150]: - 41-18628, 38733, 38742, 42-23500, 23502, 23532, 23533, 23534, 23537, 23610, 23618, 23946, 23956, 24220, 24396, 32876, 92035, 92037, 93229, 93237, 93241, 100478, 100626, 100628, 108882, 43-15413, 15482, plus C-46s

57 TCS [Field Nos 151 to 175]:- 41-38623, 42-23589, 23611, 23612, 23613, 23614, 23616, 23617, 23697, 23701, 23703, 23705, 23709, 23720, 23922, 24221, 92030, 92032, 92033, 93232, 93233, 93235, 93240, 100437, 100468, 100479, 100627, 100628, 100629, 100729, 108882, 43-15424, 16020, 16296, 16312, 16327, 30749, plus C-46s
58 TCS [Field Nos 176 to 200]:- 41-18408, 18431, 18647, 38623, 38647, 38731, 38733, 42-23419, 23590, 23690, 23702, 23703, 23720, 23950, 23960, 23961, 24221, 24410, 92030, 92782, 92783, 92824, 93233, 100466, 100485, 100621, 43-15416, 15418, 15422, 15424, 15437, 15442, 15482, 15489, 16288, 16302, plus C-46s

11th AF Alaska comprised the 42nd and 54th TCS. The 42nd was activated on 02May42 as a Transport Squadron which was redesignated a TCS on 05Jul42. The unit was based at Elmendorf from its formation until 18Feb44. It moved to Lawson Fld on 06Mar44, and was disbanded on 14Apr44. The 54th was formed as a Transport Sq on 01Jun42, and redesignated a TCS on 04Jul42, forming part of the 64th Transport Group. It moved to the 315th TCG on 11Jun42 and to the 4th AF on 23Oct42. On 15Nov42 it transferred to XI Service Command which formed part of the 11th AF. Formation was at Hamilton Fld and it moved that year to Bowman and was at Florence between 03Aug42 and 17Oct42. Transfer to Elmendorf was on 15Nov42 and disbandment on 05Mar44.

42 TCS 41-18415, 18473, 18474, 18486, 18499, 18507, 18510, 18530, 38632, 38633, 38635, 38636, 38637, 38641, 38642, 38643, 38644, 38645, 38648, 38649, 42-24276
54 TCS 41-38602, 38604, 38606, 38609, 38623, 38635, 38640, 38641, 38642, 38643, 38644, 38645, 42-23608, 23837, 23838, 23842, 23845, 23846, 23848, 23849, 23850, 23853, 23854, 23861, 23867, 23870, 23963, 24274, 24275, 92831, 93000, 93280, 93602, 108868, 43-15723, 15733, 15737, 15742, 15761, 48496, 48497, 48620, 48893, 49123, 45-892, 893, 894, 895, 972, 979, 985, 988, 1037, 1040, 1042, 1043, 1045, 1046, 1047, 1048, 1050, 1053

13th AF SW Pacific

13th Transport Squadron was activated as such on 01Dec40 and assigned to the 61st Transport Group. On 04Jul42 it became the 13th Troop Carrier Squadron, reporting to the 61st Troop Carrier Group when Troop Carrier Command was formed. 13 TCS was assigned overseas to the South Pacific on 10Oct42 and left the 61st TCG. It was assigned to the 13th AF on 13Jan43, joining the 13th AF Service Command on 01Jul43. On 22Aug43 it was assigned to the 403rd TCG which arrived in the S Pacific in Jul43, and remained with this Group until 15Oct46 when the 13 TCS was inactvated. The 13th TCS was based as follows:-

Patterson 01Dec40; Drew 13Jul41; Pope 25May42; Lockbourne 08Aug42; To S Pacific 23Sep42 to 09Oct42; Tontouta, New Caledonia 10Oct42; Espiritu Santo 02Nov42; Biak 21Sep44; Dulag 17Jun45 and Clark 07Jan46 to 15Oct46.

The 13th TCS was unusual in being a lone unit, operating in the Central Pacific, and was not involved with the 5th AF.

13 TCS 41-18559, 18572, 18574, 18575, 18576, 18578, 18579, 18580, 18581, 18582, 18590, 18592, 18675, 42-23605, 23711, 23722, 24418, 43-16325

403 TCG, part of the 13th AF at Noumea, comprised 63, 64, 65 and 66 TCS. This was activated on 12Dec42 and moved from Baer Fld in Jun/Jul43. 64 TCS was ordered to proceed from Hamilton Fld to Nandi, Fiji on 17Jul43 and there report to the Commanding General, 13 AF. All aircraft listed below for this unit were reported on the aircraft card as shipment code OTARU. It was at Espiritu Santo from 15Sep43, finally moving to Biak, NEI on 04Oct44. The 65 and 66 TCS were assigned to the 5th AF on 26 and 21Jul and to the 54th TCW on 13Aug43, going to 433 TCG on 09Nov43 and returning to 403 TCG on 20Feb45, being inactivated on 27Jan and 15Jan46 respectively.

63 TCS [Field Nos probably 251 to 275]:- 41-18573, 38742, 43-16219, 30739
64 TCS [Field Nos 276 to 300]:- 41-18675, 38737, 38751, 42-23689, 23690, 23696, 23707, 23711, 23712, 23714, 23718, 23722, 23724, 23725, 23844, 43-49754
65 TCS [Field Nos 201 to 225]:- 41-38661, 38750, 38761, 42-23353, 23498, 23499, 23536, 23615, 23712, 23717, 23851, 23857, 24228, 24397, 24398, 24413, 92025, 92034, 92038, 92074, 92798, 92826, 100469, 100715, 100724, 100728, 108880, 108881, 43-15411, 15421, 15450, 15456, 16111, 49902, An unknown but named C-47 was "Freight Train from Hell"
66 TCS [Field Nos 226 to 250]:- 41-38609, 38750, 42-23493, 23498,

CHAPTER 3: MILITARY OPERATORS OF THE DC-3, C-47, R4D, DAKOTA AND LI-2

23651, 23658, 23691, 23692, 23694, 23695, 23700, 23703, 23704, 23708, 23709, 23713, 23714, 23720, 23723, 23948, 23958, 24229, 92038, 92039, 92063, 92805, 92813, 93234, 93493, 93495, 93498, 100461, 100466, 100468, 100482, 100619, 100620, 100623, 100719, 100720, 108927, 43-15410, 15422, 15425, 15428, 15450, 15461, 16010, 16017, 16111, 16112, 16216, 16219, 16225, 16291, 16294, 16304, 30746, 30750, 47996, Also "Oklahoma Limited" and "Sandy"

433 TCG comprising 65, 66, 67, 68, 69 and 70 TCS, [65 & 66 to 403TCG]. This group was activated on 09Feb43 at Florence Fld, moving via Baer Fld in early Aug43, to Pt Moresby by 25Aug43. It finished at Biak, NEI on 17Oct44.

67 TCS [Field Nos 301 to 325]:- 41-18588, 38750, 42-23493, 23498, 23653, 23654, 23658, 23660, 23691, 23703, 23708, 23709, 23713, 23720, 23723, 23835, 23840, 23843, 23844, 23847, 23878, 23882, 23886, 23924, 24402, 92046, 92048, 92049, 92051, 100486, 43-15441, 15453, 15483, 16344, and named C-47s with no known serial: The Green Banana II, Heradnaw II, Dixie, Cock O' The Walk, Hustlin' Hoosier III, Yingle Yangle, Ginnie V, Ginnie VI
68 TCS [Field Nos 326 to 350]:- 41-38740, 38750, 42-23651, 23791, 23858, 23860, 23862, 23863, 23865, 23868, 23879, 23880, 23881, 23883, 23885, 23914, 23917, 23959, 24044, 24218, 24258, 24404, 92041, 92045, 92048, 92050, 92803, 93234, 100473, 100481, 100486, 108868, 108927, 43-15417, 15428, 15448, 15459, 15461, 16020
69 TCS [Field Nos 351 to 375]:- 41-18601, 18668, 38623, 42-23651, 23791, 23841, 23856, 23871, 23872, 23876, 23881, 23883, 23884, 23887, 23889, 23922, 23959, 24217, 24218, 24219, 24353, 92028, 92035, 92804, 92816, 93227, 100460, 100625, 100722, 100728, 108880, 108927, 108951, 108957, 43-15427, 15459, 16294, 16323, 16335, 16344, 43-30746, 30756
70 TCS [Field Nos 376 to 399]:- 42-23583, 23662, 23857, 23868, 23869, 23874, 23875, 23919, 23920, 23945, 24259, 24401, 92047, 92059, 92062, 93227, 100480, 100715, 100716, 100717, 100719, 100722, 100723, 100729, 108927, 43-15427, 15457, 16343, 30756

2 CCG was activated on 01May44 at Syracuse, and assigned to the 5th AF in Nov44, operating between New Guinea, Australia and the Philippines, and then moving to Leyte in Mar45. Then on to Okinawa and Yokota, Japan. It was deactivated on 15Jan46. It comprised 5th, 6th, 7th and 8th CCSs. Although C-47s were reported in use, the Curtiss C-46 was the prime equipment. 6 CCS had C-47A 43-15443 in May45 and 8 CCS 43-15445 in Jun45.

C-47s allotted to 2 CCG incl:- 42-93188, 93190, 93223, 93224, 43-15686, 15689, 15690, 48062, 48064, 48065

3 Air Commando Group (ACG) was formed in Florida in 1944, comprising two P-51 squadrons and an L-5 Liaison Squadron, plus the 318th TCS. The latter was activated at Sedalia on 01Oct43 as the 310th TCS, as part of the 443 TCG. The 310th was split into the 318th TCS and the 343rd Airdrome Sq in May44 when the 443 TCG was deactivated. The unit had moved to Alliance in Jan44, and to Camp Mackall on 04Mar44. Glider tow training with CG-14s and Horsas was carried out in May44. They moved to Dunnellon for Air Commando operations in Jul44 and then back to Camp Mackall on 13Sep44. The full complement of 16 C-47s were ready at Baer Fld on 30 Sep44, and on 11Oct44 318 TCS left for the west coast, via Amarillo to Fairfield, departing on 15Oct44 for Hawaii, then Christmas Is, Canton Is, and Nadzab, New Guinea on 26Oct44. Further moves were to San Rogue, Leyte in Jan45, to San Jose, Mindoro in the same month, to Mingaladon, Luzon in March and on to Laoag, Luzon by 19Apr45. The next move to Ie Shima was completed on 25Aug45 and finally to Atsugi, Tokyo in September. The 318th TCS was deactivated in 1946.

C-47s used were:- 42-108955, 43-15813 to 15818, 42-93450 to 452, 42-93481 to 93486, three unknown and 42-23835 (nose numbers A001 to A020 resp.). Used prior to overseas duty were:- 42-24125, 24130, 92079, 101001, 43-15268, 15280, 15288, 15566, 16068, 16073, 16084

6th AF Panama

The **20th TCS** was activated on 05Jul42 as part of the 6th AF in the Canal Zone. C-46s were added in 1945. The unit was inactivated on 17Jun48.

20 TCS 38-510, 524, 534, 41-7689, 7692, 7715 to 7721, 7761, 7762, 7770, 7782 to 7785, 42-23596, 23597, 43-48000, 48006, 48301, 49141, 45-1032, 1101

7th AF - Hawaii

The **19th TCS** was activated as the 19th Transport Squadron on 01Jan41 and was redesignated on 05Jul42. It was assigned to the Hawaiian Air Force (later the 7th) when it was activated, forming part of the VI Air Service Air Command from 15Aug44, and AAF, Middle Pacific from 15Dec45. It joined Pacific Air Command on 01Jan46. It was stationed at Hickam Field from the start, returning there in 1946 after moving to John Rogers Airport on 29May42. The 19th was mainly responsible for transport within the Hawaiian Islands and to forward bases in the Pacific. C-33s were used in 1941 - 1942, C-53s until 1945 and C-47s from 1943 to 1946, when C-46s and C-54s took over. Lodestars were also used.

C-47s used were:- 41-20045, 20046, 20069, 20071, 20073, 42-23965, 24265, 92930, 92932, 92933, 92934, 92935, 100988, 100993, 100994, 43-15056, 15248, 30736, 48621, 49528, 49553, 49554, 49556, 49558, 49560, 49569, 49570, 49572, 44-77164, 77204

The **311th TCS** was activated on 01Nov43 at Sedalia as part of the 349th TCG, moving to Alliance on 19Jan44 and Pope on 08Mar44. It became part of 1 TCC on 01Dec44, and was briefly based at Baer from 8 to 20Jan45, moving to Kahuku on 09Feb45 when it joined VI Air Service Area Command. The 311th moved to Bellows Field on 15Feb45 and became part of the 7th AF on 22Jul45. It moved to Okinawa on 22Aug45 and became part of AAF, Middle Pacific on 31Jul45. C-46s replaced C-47s in 1945, and it inactivated on 15May46.

C-47s used were:- 42-68744, 93223, 100487, 100488, 100489, 100493, 100712, 43-15281, 15691, 30692

10th Air Force - India - Burma

The first transport units in the CBI belonged to the ATC and the first TCS to become operational on 02Feb43 was the 1st TCS (activated 04Jul42) which was attached to the India-China Wing of the ATC until 07Mar43, when it joined the 10th AF. The 2nd TCS (also activated 04Jul42) joined the 1st TCS on 17Feb43, being attached to the ATC between 09Mar and 01Jul43 for operations over the 'Hump'. Further units were added, the 315th TCS on 01Jan44, the 27th TCS (activated 04Jul42) on 12Jan44 and on 15Feb44 the 443rd TC Group was transferred from the USA to become the command force for the four TCSs listed earlier. At the end of the war the 443rd TCG moved to China and helped move the Nationalist army from inland China to the Eastern region to secure Nanking in Sep45. All but the 27th had C-46s by 1945, and were inactivated as follows:- 1st on 18Dec45, 2nd on 24Dec45, 27th on 27Dec45 and 315th on 28Dec45.

Known C-39s and C-47s used by these units were:-
1 TCS 38-513, 515, 533, 41-19468, 42-24272, 24419, 92975, 100444, 100595, 100693, 100694, 108984, 43-15052, 48628, 42-93372?
2 TCS 38-516, 518, 41-19471, 19476, 19480, 19497, 38684, 38687, 38696, 38702, 38706, 38708, 38709, 38721, 38726, 38734, 42-23520, 32868, 92971, 92972, 92973, 93275, 93488, 93490, 93740, 93741, 93743, 100458, 100463, 100607, 100614, 100615, 100642, 100696, 100969, 43-15369, 15370, 15395, 15403, 30640, 30641, 30642, 30645, 48626, 48637, 44-76245
27 TCS 42-92974, 92976, 92980, 93276, 93759, 93768, 93771, 93775, 100680, 100681, 100682, 100684 to 100692, 100702, 108930, 43-15368, 16169, 16182, 16185, 16350, 16403, 16425, 48732, 48733, 48761, '860'(100680?)
315 TCS 41-38585, 42-93749, 100587, 100683, 100695, 100697, 100700, 100704, 43-15051, 15366, 15371, 15785, 16188, 48634

On 01May44, the **317th TCS** was activated and assigned to the 2nd ACG to provide transport support to this air strike force in Burma, dropping paratroopers in the assault on Rangoon. It was deactivated on 28Feb46 when it rejoined the 10th AF.

Known C-47s are:- 317 TCS 43-15694 to 15699, 15819 to 15829, 16170, 16180. Used during training in the US were:- 42-23789, 24125, 24130, 24295, 92075, 93176, 93181, 93183, 93184, 93188, 93190, 93193, 93195, 93224, 43-15268, 15270, 15275, 15280, 15289, 16055

On 01Sep44 the **319th TCS (Commando)** was activated in India to provide transport support to the 1st Air Commando Group. It continued to support the 1 ACG until 27Sep45 when it was reassigned to the 10th AF and deactivated on 27Dec45.

Known C-47s were:- 43-16195, 16422, 43-48230, 49645

1 CCG was activated 15Apr44 at Bowman Fld with C-47s and left for CBI theatre in Aug/Sep44. It was used to support the British XIV Army in the Arakan campaign as part of the Combat Cargo Task Force until May45, when it was assigned to the 69th Composite Wing in China, returning home in Nov45. 1, 2, 3 and 4 CCS were attached. One squadron (1 CCS) was detached for service in China on 29Jan45 with the 14th AF. The 1st and 4th CCS re-equipped with C-46s in Jun45. The 1 CCG was re-designated the 512th TCG in Sep45, and 1 CCS became 326 TCS on 29Sep45 and 2 CCS became 327 TCS on 31Oct45, 3 CCS to 328 TCS and 4 CCS 329 TCS, both on 29Sep45. They were inactivated in Dec45 at Morrison Fld.

Known C-47s were:-
1 CCS 43-15841, 15844, 15847, 15850, 15878, 15879, 15901, 15904, 15905, 15906, 15908, 15909, 15910, 15912, 15914, 15916, 15917, 15919 to 15925, 16173, 16179, 16181, 16182, 16191, 16363, 16404, 43-48625, 48627, 48633, 49120, 49636, 49793,
2 CCS 41-19471, 43-15819, 15834, 15876 to 15900, 15919, 15927, 16182, 16357, 16363, 49642, 49645, 49647, 44-76233,
3 CCS 42-93356, 93748, 43-15836, 15839, 15851, 15853, 15860, 15861, 15862, 15863, 15864, 15865, 15870, 15875, 15913, 15917, 16176, 16186, 48627, 48731, 49121, 49578, 44-76669
4 CCS 42-92976, 93276, 93356, 93384, 100688, 43-15830, 15831, 15832, 15835, 15837, 15838, 15840, 15842, 15843, 15845, 15846, 15849, 15852, 15867, 15911, 15928, 16179, 16181, 48625, 49578, 49636, 49646, 49650, 49793
329 TCS 43-15874, 49646

C-47s attached to 1 CCG were:- 42-93161, 43-16068

3 CCG was activated at Sylhet, India on 05Jun45, and supported the British XIV Army in Burma and relieved the 64th TCG. It re-equipped with the Curtiss C-46 in 1945. It comprised 9, 10,11 and 12 CCS which were redesignated 330, 331, 332 and 333 TCS by 01Oct45. These were inactivated between 1946 and 1948.

The following C-47s are known:-
9 CCS 42-93329, 93330, 93333, 93334, 93335, 93336, 93337, 93338, 93341, 93348, 93349, 93353, 93357, 93359, 93365, 93742, 93746, 100445, 108941, 43-15789, 15792, 16084, 16192, 48638, 44-76649
10 CCS 42-92981, 93343, 93359, 93361, 93366, 93369, 93371, 93377, 93378, 93389, 93390, 93391, 93747, 93773, 100613, 108944, 43-15781, 15788, 15794, 15800, 15804, 15812, 16234, 44-76234
11 CCS 41-18554, 42-93333, 93360, 93372, 93385, 93387, 93744, 93745, 93751, 93761, 43-15372, 15782, 15783, 15784, 15795, 15802, 15805, 15811, 15873, 16352, 16356
12 CCS 42-93350, 93354, 93367, 93758, 93767, 93772, 108943, 108945, 43-15796, 15801, 15806, 15809, 16177
330 TCS 42-93276, 43-15916, 16169, 16427, 44-76436, 76657, 76665, 76670
332 TCS 42-93386, 43-15369, 16424, 49792, 44-76640, 76656

4 CCG was activated at Syracuse in Jun44 with C-47s and C-46s, but only the latter were used once India was reached in Nov44.

C-47s known to have been with 4 CCG were :- 42-100714, 43-15765, 15768, 15770, 15772, 15773, 15774, 15777, 15778, 15780, 16054, 16055, 16057, 16058, 16059, 16065, 16067, 16069, 16072, 16073, 16074, 16082, 16084, 16085, 16086, 16091, 16093, 16100, 48075

14th Air Force - Burma - 322 TCS (68th Composite Wing). This was part of the 443rd TCG, and was activated on 09Sep44, gained C-46s later and was inactivated on 06Jan46.

Known C-47s: 41-19478, 38677, 38696, 38708, 42-93288, 93760, 93763, 100441, 108986, 43-15366, 15380, 15381, 15384, 15925, 49577, 44-76238

Bases used by USAAF, USAF, US Navy and US Marine Corps DC-3 variants

The following list of airfields covers all those which have been mentioned in records of the type's service between 1940 and 1975. So far as possible units based at these fields are listed, but in some cases only a single aircraft may have been involved, or the use was transitory. Units sometimes remain unknown. USAAF and USAF fields are designated as Air Force Station, Air Base, Army Air Field, Air Force Base, Field, Air National Guard Base, Royal Air Force (RAF), and many were up- or downgraded over their period of use. Others were also used by the Navy, as Naval Air Station, Naval Air Field or Marine Corps Air Station and are known to have had R4Ds based. For many no designation is known, and there may have been none, so such designations have been omitted. Bases in Korea, Japan, France and Germany were allotted codes such as K-1, J-1, F-1 or G-1. Fields in Great Britain had a number but no prefix. Many bases were renamed during the period and the old or new names are given (in brackets). Where no unit is given against a place name, this is because none has been identified.

Aberdeen, PA	6570 COTG/TEG
Abermama Isl.	9 TCS
Abidjan, Ivory Coast	1127 FAG, 513 TAW
Abilene, TX	261 BU, 341 ABG, 819 ABG [to Dyess Dec56]
Accra, Gold Coast, W Africa	ATC Africa-M East
Adair, Corvallis, OR	
Adak, AK, Aleutian Is.	19 ADR
Adams, AR	154 FS/RTS/TRS, 8154 ABS, SAS HQ
Adana, Turkey	7216 ABG/ABS
Addis Ababa, Ethiopia	1130 SAG, 1171 FAG/FMS, 1172 FMS
Agana, Guam Is	Fasron-118, VR-6, VR-7, VR-8 Det, VR-21 Det, VR-23 Det, 1503 SS
Agra, India	ATC - 1303 BU
Aitape, New Guinea	5 AF: 65, 66, 68 TCS
Akron, OH	112 FIS, BAR, NART, Goodyear
Akyab, New Guinea	5 AF: 2 CCS, 4 CCS, 317 TCS, 319 TCS
Alamagordo, NM	231 BU, 4145 BU [to Holloman Jan48]
Alameda, CA	Fasron-8, Fasron-116, Fasron-885, VR-2, VR-4, VR-5 Det, VR-23, 12 ND, NARTU, 61 FW, 111 RDCD, 194 FS
Albany, GA	RVAH-3
Albrook, CZ	1 RS, 3 BCS, 6 WS, 16 ABS, 18 TCS, 20 TCS, 153 ACS, 783 BU, 1806 AACG, 1937 AACS, 5506 HQF, 5700 ABG/W, 5701 MS/MSG, 5702 MS/ABG, IAA SC
Albuquerque, NM	AECm
Alconbury RAF, Hunts, England	10 TRW, 7560 ABG
Aldermaston, RAF Berks, England	[467] 9 AF: 60, 62, 63, 315 & 434 TCG
Alexandria, LA	107 RDCD, 132 BW/FBW, 137 FBW, 329 BU, 366 FBW, 4416 BCS [to England May55]
Algiers, Algeria	12 AF: 51 TCW, ATC base
Alliance, NB	5 TCS, 10 TCS, 308 TCS, 311 TCS, 316 TCS, 318 TCS 434 TCG, 805 BU, 816 BU
Altus, OK	11 ABG/ABW/BW/CSG/STAW, 63 TCW, 96 ABG/BW, 443 MITW
Alvin Callender, New Orleans, LA	122 FIS, 159 CAMS
Amarillo, TX	1739 FYS, 3320 MSG/TTW, 3701 BU, AOTC
Amberley, Brisbane, Australia	5 AF
Amchitka, AK	5022 ABS
Amiens-Glisy, France	50 TCW [B-48]
Anacostia, Washington, DC	AvDivHQ, HQMCFltSect, MCAD, NARTU [See Bolling]
Anchorage, AK (Kulis)	144 ATS, 517 ABG, 1455 BU, 1701 ABG/ATD
Andersen, Guam Is (ex Harmon)	3 AD, 2 RG, 11 RG/RS, 19 BW, 79 ARS, 327 ADHQ, 3960 ABG/ABW, 6319 ABW
Andrews, Camp Springs, MD	1 BU, 2 ADRG/ARR, 4 ABG, 4 ADRG, 4 FG, 4 MSG, 4 WG, 26 AD, 60 BU, 64 BU, 65 BU, 85 AD, 95 FIS, 113 FW/TFW, 121 FS, 122 BU, 131 FS, 188 ACSS, 401 ABS, 709 NGHQ, 1001 ABW/CW, 1050 ABG/W/MSG, 1101 ABW, 1298 ATS, 1401 ABW, 2259 RFC, 2523 INSD, ACR Sr, MATS HQ, MTCS, SASH, HQMCFltSect
Ankara, Turkey	37 BU, 1172 FMS, 7217 ABS, 7250 SG/SS, TRK AM, NavMiss
Ann Arbor, MI	Univ. of Michigan
Arcata, CA	BAL, TOAIC, Landing Aids Exptl Stn.
Ardmore, OK	309 TCG
Argentia, Ft McAndrew, Newfoundland	Fasron 106
Arnold EDC, Tullahoma, TN	6560 ABS, AEDC
Ashiya, Kyushu, Japan	3 RS/G, 21 TCS, 39 ARS, 374 TCW, 403 TCW, 483 TCW, 6122 ABW, 6461 ATS
Asuncion, Paraguay	24 ACW/CW/SOW, 1134 SAD, 5500 FMS, 5700 ABW, Par Dt/Ft
Athens-Hellenikon, Greece	1127 FAG, 1130 SAG, 1141 SAS, 1172 FMS, 1602 ATD/ATS, 7168 ATS, 7206 ABG/ABS/ATS/CSG/ SG, 7907 BU, GREAM, JUSMAG, DAO, NavAtt
Atkinson, NB	5918 ABS
Atlanta, GA	35 BU, 4115 BU, 4204 BU, NART
Atlantic City, Bader Fld, NJ	119 FIS, VX-3
Atsugi, Honshu, Japan [J-2]	VR-23, Fasron-11, FAWPra, H&MS-11, H&MS 13, 318 TCS
Atterbury, IN	434 TCG, 2466 ARTC
Augusta, ME	8132 ABS, RFC, SASH
Austin, TX	
Aviano, Italy	12 AF: 40 TACG, 7207 ASBS, 7227 CSG/SG
Avon Park, FL	325 BU
Bad Kissingen, Germany	316 STCS

CHAPTER 3: MILITARY OPERATORS OF THE DC-3, C-47, R4D, DAKOTA AND LI-2

Location	Units
Baer, Ft Wayne, IN	1 CCG, 1 TC, 122 FIW, 163 FS/FBS/FIS/TFS, 307 TCG, 308 TCG, 311 TCS, 317 CMOS, 318 TCS, 375 TCG, 403 TCG, 433 TCG, 439 BU, 715 NGHQ, 806 BU, SASH
Baghdad, Iraq	1127 FAG, 1130 SAG
Bainbridge, GA	3306 TNS
Bakalar, IN	5 AFRD, 434 TCW, 930 TCG, 2466 ABS/RFC [ex Atterbury]
Balboa, CZ	
Balderton RAF, Notts England	439 TCG [482]
Baltimore, MD (Glenn L Martin)	104 FS/FBS, MAR BM, BAR
Banana River, Cocoa Beach, FL	NAL, NATTC/GCA [to Patrick]
Bangalore, India	ATC 1309 BU
Bangkok, Don Muang, Thailand	2 ADH, 3 TFW, 405 FW, 631 CSG, 1020 SAW, 1130 SAG, 1131 SAS, 1134 SAS, 6200 ABW/MATW, MDAP, JusMag
Bangor, ME	134 FD
Barbados, BWI	316 TCD
Barber's Point, Oahu, HI	Fasron 117, 14ND, VR-21, VMR-12
Bari, Italy	12 AF
Barksdale, Bossier City, LA	2 AF/ABG, 19 TAC, 26 SMW/SRW, 31 FW/SFW, 47 ABG, 91 ABG/SRW, 97 ABG/SRW, 174 BU, 301 BW/ABG/ABW, 307 BW, 312 BU, 331 BU, 376 BW, 805 ABG, 2000 BU, 2621 BU, 3500 AFY, 3908 SEVG/SSTG, 4238 ABG/CSG/SRW, ATC HQ, TRCC
Barkston Heath RAF, Lincs, England [483]	61 TCG
Barnes, MA (Westfield)	104 CAMS/TFG, 131 FIS/FS/TFS
Barrackpore, India	10 AF, ATC 1304 BU
Bartow, FL	340 BU, 3303 TNS,
Battle Creek, MI	[See Kellogg]
Beale, Marysville, CA	456 STW, 4126 CSG/SRW
Beane Fld, St Lucia, BWI	26 ADRS, 5916 ABS
Beaufort, SC	H&MS-31, H&MS-32
Bedford, MA	1 EES, 4146 BU, 4147 BU, 4148 BU, 4161 BU, ProjCAST [to Hanscomb Jun48]
Beirut, Lebanon	60 TCG/TCW, 61 TCW, 85 ADW, 1127 FAG, 1130 SAG, NavAtt
Belgrade, Yugoslavia	1127 FAG, 1130 SAG, 1134 SAS, 1172 FM Sq, MDAP
Bellows, Waimanalo, Oahu, HI	311 TCS, 316 TCS
Benghazi, Libya	Wg ATC, 1141 SAS, 1171 FMS, MAAG
Benguerir, Fr Morocco	3926 ABG/ABS/CSG
Bentwaters RAF, Suffolk, England	81 FBW/FIW/TFW, 3 AF
Beograd, Yugoslavia	[see Belgrade]
Bergstrom, Austin, TX	12 ABG/FEW/SFW, 27 ABG/FG/FEW/FW/MSG/SFW, 29 TCS, [ex Del Valle] 62 TCG, 75 CSG/RCW/TRW, 131 FW/FBW, 311 BU, 313 ABG/MSG/TCG, 340 BW, 349 TCG, 434 TCG, 807 BU, 808 ABG, 2413 ABG, 4016 ABS, 4130 ABG/CSG/SRW, 4414 ABS
Berlin-Tempelhof, W Germany	[see Tempelhof]
Bermuda, Kindley	55 ARS, 1389 BU [see Kindley]
Bern, Switzerland	1130 SAG
Berry, Nashville, TN	74 ABS, 105 ATS/FS/RTS/TRS, 118 ATG/CW/MALG, 8105 ABS, CAP Rg, SASH
Bethpage, Long Island, NY	BAR
Biak, New Guinea	5 AF: 374, 375 & 433 TCG, 13 TCS
Bien Hoa, S Vietnam	1 ACG/ACW, 2 ADH, 3 SOS, 3 TFW, 4 SOS, 9 SOW, 14 ACW/SOW, 6251 CSG
Biggs, El Paso, TX	1 TOWS, 5 RS, 9 RU, 19 TAC, 20 FG, 47 ABG/BG/MSG, 62 BU, 95 BW, 97 ABG/ABW/ADRG/BW, 204 BU, 305 BU, 309 BU/ADR, 362 FG, 810 ABG, 1900 AACS, 2151 RD/RU
Big Spring, TX	3560 PTW [to Webb]
Binghamton, NY	BAL
Binh Thuy, S Vietnam	5 SOS, 9 SOS, 14 ACW/SOW, 22 TASS, 632 CAMS
Birmingham, AL (Smith ANGB)	35 BU, 81 RS, 106 BS/TRS, 117 TRG, 118 TRW, 160 FS/RTS, 2587 ARTC, 4139 BU, 8160 ABS, SASHQ, NART
Bitburg, Germany	1 PBS, 12 AF: 10 TRW, 36 FB/FDW/FIW/MS/TFW, 49 TFW, 86 FIS, 1807 AACW, EAAAR
Blackbushe RAF, Hants, England	Fasron-76, Fasron-Spec 200
Blackland, Waco, TX	
Blakehill Farm, Wilts England [459]	9 AF
Blida, Algeria	12 AF: 315 TCG, 34 & 43 TCS
Bluethenthal, Wilmington, NC	130 BU, 812 BU
Blytheville, AR	97 BW/CSG, 461 BTW, 809 BU
Boca Raton, FL	3501 BU, 4150 BU
Bogota, Colombia	COL Ft/Dt, 1134 SAS, 5500 FMS, 7409 MMS, NavMiss
Boise, ID	124 CAMS/FG, 190 FIS/TRS, 8190 ABS, SASH [ex Gowen]
Bolleville, France	[A-25C] 302 ATW
Bolling, DC	1 ABU/BU/STS, 6 AG, 16 MSG/SAMG, 35 BU, 91 ABG, 311 PMCW, 1100 ABW, OG/MSG/OG/SAMG, 1110 SAMG, 1147 SAG, 1299 ATS, ACH SR, CAP, HQ Command Base,
Bonn, Germany	1127 FAG, 1130 SAG, 1141 SAS, 1147 SAG, 1171 FMS, ATTAT, MAAG
Bordeaux, Merignac, France	12 AF, 81 RS, 82 RS, 126 BS/BW, 7413 ABG/ABS/SG, [Y-37] SFERMA
Borinquen, PR	1 RS, 24 CW, 48 SR ADG, 82 RS, 334 TCS, 785 BU, 4017 EMP
Boston, MA	1 AFPO, 67 FW, DCA SR, INSMAT
Bottesford RAF, Leics, England [481]	436 TCG, 440 TCG
Bovingdon RAF, Herts England	3 AF: 16 SAM, 1171 FMS, 1858 AACF/FCF, 7500 ABG, [112] 7531 ABS, 7900 ABG, JAAGp, MDAP
Bowman, Louisville, KY	1 CCG, 4 CCG, 35 BU, 41 TCS, 54 TCS, 317 TCG, 375 TCG, 808 BU, 1077 BU
Bradley, CN	[Windsor Locks] 103 FG/FIW/FW/CAMS, 118 FBS/FIS/FS/TFG, 121 BU, 8118 ABS
Brady, Fukuoka, Kyushu, Japan	21 TCS
Brainard-Hartford, CN	103 FIW, 118 FBS/FIS, 8118 ABS
Brazzaville, Congo	1127 FAG
Bremen, Germany	[R-40] 764 BU, 2040 LSC, Attache
Brienne, Beaune, France	48 TFW
Brindisi, Italy	60 TCG, 62 TCG
Brisbane, Qld, Australia	5 AF: 374 TCG, 375 TCG, VR-3, COM AIR 7th Flt
Brize Norton RAF, Oxford, England	30 ADW, 3909 ABG, 3920 ABG/CSG, 7503 BCS/ABG, 7508 ABG, 7530 ADFG
Brookley, Mobile, AL	9 TCS, 13 ATS, 146 AACS, 521 ATG/ATS, 776 BU, 925 DFS, 1100 BU, 1103 BU, 1601 ATG, 702 ATD, 1703 ATG, 1735 ATS, 1919 AACS, 2850 ABW, 3191 AACG, 4007 BU, 4119 BU, MOB AMA
Brooks, San Antonio, TX	12 AF, 16 SAMG, 35 BU, 170 BU, 182 FBS/FIS, 306 BU, 363 RCG, 1100 SAMG, 1103 BU, 1116 SAMS, 1734 ATS, 1736 ATS, 2316 ATS, 2423 IND, 2577 RFC, 2595 ABG, 6960 HQG, ASM CN, USSS
Brown, CA	VU-7
Brownsville, TX	568 BU, PAW/PWA BT, BWR FR, NB PRO,
Brownwood, TX	375 TCW
Bruning, NB	264 BU
Brunswick, ME	Fasron-108, 1 ND
Bruntingthorpe RAF, Leics, England	3912 ABS/CSG
Brussels, Belgium	1171 FMS, 7485 ADW, ADEFA, OARHQ
Bryan, TX	3530 PTW, ATC
Bucharest, Romania	Attache
Buchschwabach, Germany	
Buckingham, Ft Myers, FL	2117 BU
Buckley, Denver, CO	3 GCS, 7 GCS, 16 PHS, 86 FW/NGW, 91 PCS/PMS, 109 RDCD, 120 FS/FBS/FIS/TFS, 140 CAMS/FW/FBW/TFG/TFW, 3415 MSG, 3702 BU, 3718 BU, SASH
Budapest, Hungary	1130 SAG
Buenos Aires, Argentina	24 CW/SOW, 5500 FMSq, 7405 MMS, 7413 MMD, ArgDt, Nav.AdvGp
Buffalo, NY	Bell RRD, Curtiss RRD
Bunker Hill, Peru, IN	305 BW/CSG, 323 FBW, 4041 ABG [to Grissom May68]
Burbank, CA (Lockheed AT)	6 AFPO, 7 AFPO, 1350 PHG, Lockheed RD, NSF

103

Burlington, VT	14 CAMS, 75 ABS, 134 FS/FIS, 158 CAMS/FG, 517 ADFG, 8134 ABS, SAS HQ	Cherry Point, Havelock, NC	AES-46, Hedron-2, H&MS-14, H&MS-24, H&MS-27, H&MS-32, MAG-11, MAG-15, MAG-24, MAMRON-24, MAMRON-14, MARS-27, MWSG-27, MAG-7, MAG-14, MAG-62, MAW-2, MAW-3, VMR-252, VMGR-252, AFMFLANT, SO&ES, SAES-2
Burtonwood RAF, Lancs, England	3 AF, 3 AD, 59 ABG/ADW/HBS, 68 ARS, 1602 SS/TSW, 1625 SS, 1807 AACW, 1858 AACF, 1965 AACS, 1979 AACS/W, 3110 MG, 3113 FMS, 7520 ABDG, 7540 MDG, 7550 ABDG, 7552 MAG, 7559 MDG/MG, ENTF		
		Cheyenne, WY	140 FBW/FW, 153 CAMS, 187 FBS/FS/FIS/AMTS/TAS, 8187 ABS, SASH, Lockheed/LAI CW
Bush, Augusta, GA	RFC	Chicago, O'Hare, IL	106 RDCD, 4032 BU, CNATT [see O'Hare]
Bushy Park RAF, Middx, England	3 AD, 813 AACG [see Teddington]	Chicago Mun, IL (Midway)	35 BU, 108 BS, 4200 BU, CECCI
Richard E Byrd, Richmond, VA	149 BS/FIS/TFS/TS, 192 TFG, 4638 SS, ADFS, SASH	Chico, Sacramento, CA	433 BU, 488 BU
Cable, CA	MRIAC	Chievres, Mons, Belgium [A-84]	
Cairo, Egypt	1130 SAG, 1134 SAS, A-ME/ATC, NavAtt	Chilbolton, Hants, England [404]	IX TCC
Calcutta, India	1345 BU, ATC HQ [Western Wg]		
Camden, NJ	RCA	China Lake, Inyokern, CA	11 ND, RDT&E, R&T
Campbell, Hopkinsville, KY	68 BW, 340 BW, 4002 ABS/BSS	Chincoteague, MD	Fasron-121, NAOTS, NOTS, VX-2
Camp Blanding, FL	1134 SAS	Chinhae, S Korea [K-10]	75 AD, 18 FBW
Camp Carson, CO	3904 ABW/CW		
Camp Davis, Wilmington, NC	1079 BU	Chino, CA	PAM CP
Camp Douglas, WI	[To Camp Williams]	Chitose, Hokkaido, Japan	4 FW/FIW/FBW, 6029 SG, 8092 HAAD
Camp Kearney, San Diego, CA	MAG-25	Christchurch, New Zealand	VX-6
Camp Lejeune		Chu Lai, S Vietnam	H&MS-12, H&MS-13, H&MS-36
Camp Mackall, Hoffman, NC	316 TCG/TCS, 317 CMOS, 318 TCS/CMOS, 800 BU	Chunchon, S Korea [K-47]	6147 TCLG
Camp Springs, MD	122 BU, 161 BU [to Andrews]	Chungking, China	
Camp Williams, WI	3, 9, 24, 25, 30 & 31 TCS [see Camp Douglas]	Cigli, Izmir, Turkey	41 TATCG, 116 BFD, 7231 CSG/SG/TTG
Cam Ranh Bay, S Vietnam	12 TFW, 483 TAW	Cimarron, OK	RFC
		Cincinnati, Lunken, OH	[see Lunken]
Canberra, Australia	Nav. Attache	Clark, Luzon, Philippines	2 RS, 5 RVP, 6 SVG, 13 TCS, 18 ABG/ABS/FBW, 21 TCS, 22 TC, 24 MDG/MG/MNG, 35 BSS, 338 RVM, 405 FW/FMS, 432 TRW, 1503 ABS/ATD/ATG, 1506 SS/ATS, 1867 FCS, 6424 ADW, 6200 ABW/MSG/MATW/TCS, MDAP, SMPAR, SOMAR, VR-21
Cannon, NM	27 TFW, 832 ABG [ex Clovis Jun57]		
Cape, AK	5023 ABS, CAB DT [ex Ft Glenn]		
Capetown, S Africa	Naval Attache		
Capital, Springfield, IL	170 FBS/FIS/TFS, 183 TFG		
Caracas, Venezuela	24 CW/SW, 1127 FAG, 1130 SAG, 1134 SAS, 5500 FMS, 5700 ABW, 7423 MMS, Ven Dt/Ft, NavMiss.		
		Cleveland, OH	112 BS, 2240 ARTC, 4163 BU, ADEFA, NACA, NACL, Lewis Flt. Prop.
Carswell, TX	7 ABG/BW/MSG/CSG, 8 AF, 11 BW, 33 BU, 105 ACSS, 735 BU, 824 ABG/CSG, 1803 ACSG, 1921 ACSS, 3908 SEVS, 3941 SEVS, 6592 TES, FLS [ex Ft Worth]	Clinton County, Wilmington, OH	35 BU, 2252 ABS/RFC, 2223 IND, 2523 IND, 2760 ABG, 4090 CSG, 4143 BU, 4152 BU, NANS, TTF
		Clinton-Sherman, OK	7 BW, 70 BW, 4123 ABG/CSG/STW
Casablanca, Fr Morocco	ATC [see Cazes]	Clovis, NM	50 FBW, 140 FBW, 312 FBW, 388 FBW, 4445 ABS [to Cannon Jun57]
Caserta, Italy			
Casper, WY		Cocoa Beach, FL	6 WS, LRPD [to Patrick]
Castle Merced, CA	40 BW, 55 SRCW/RCNS, 93 ABG/ADG/BW/CSG/MSG, 200 BU, 482 BU	Coco Solo, CZ	FASRON 108, 15 ND, StaOper
		Coffeyville, KS	379 BU
Cazes, Casablanca, Fr Morocco	80 ADW, ATC	Colombo, Ceylon	ATC 1310 BU
		Colorado Springs, CO	ComNavConad [to Peterson]
Cecil, FL	CQTU, 6 ND, Fasron-9, VUU	Columbia, SC	[see Congaree] 129 BU
Celle, Germany [B-118]	317 ABG	Columbus, MS	166 FS/FT, 434 TCG, 454 BW, 2113 BU, 3301 PTS/TNS, 4228 CSG/SRW, BAR NART
Chabua, Assam, India	ATC E Sect HQ, 1333 BU	Comiso, Sicily	12 AF: 64 TCG
Chambley, France	10 TRW, 21 FBW, 25 TRW, 163 TFS, 366 TFW	Concord, CA	111 RDCD, 194 FS
Chanute, Rantoul, IL	134 BU, 733 BU, 1114 SAMS, 1853 AACF/FCHF, 2314 ATS, 3345 MSG/TTNW, 3499 MTG/TAW, 3502 BU, 3505 RCG, 3718 BU, 4430 ATG, 4440 ADG, CTTC	Congaree, SC	157 FBS/FIS/FS, 169 CAMS, 8157 ABS, SAS HQ, MFG-52 [see Columbia & McEntire]
		James Connally, Waco, TX	3501 SS, 3565 AOTW/BPTW/NTW/OTW/MSG, 4501 SS, FTN AF
Chanyi, China	ATC	Cooke, Lompoc, CA	392 ABG, 1 MSLDV [to Vandenburg]
Charleston, SC	113 BU, 167 FS, 193 BU, 437 MAW, 444 FIS, 593 BU, 1608 ATW/FMS, 8167 ABS, SAS HQ, Electronics Proj.	Coolidge, Antigua, BWI	25 ADRS, 5914 ABS
		Copenhagen, Denmark	1130 SAG, 1141 SAS, 1171 FMS, MAAG, MDAP, NavAtt
Chartres, France [A-40]	52 TCW	Corpus Christi, TX	ATTU, ATU-12VP, CNABT, NAATC, NAAWFS, VMU, VT-28, VT-29
Chase, TX	NAATC		
Chateauroux, France	17 AF, 73 ADFW, 322 AD, 1602 ATW, 1616 SS, 3130 ABG, 3131 ARS/MG/MU, 7029 BCS, 7322 ABG/ABW, 7373 ABG/ADW/MG	Corry, Pensacola, FL	NABTC, NAIT, Trans Pool, VUU
		Corvallis, OR	MAG-35
		Cottesmore RAF, Rutland, England [489]	316 TCG
Chatham, Savannah, GA	2 ABG/ABW/BG/BW, 114 BU, 158 FS, 165 TAG		
		Courtland, AL	
Chaumont, France	48 FBW/TFW, 137 FBW, 141 TFS, 366 TFW	Craig, Selma, AL	44 BU, 501 AUW, 3615 FTW/PTW, 3840 AUW
Cheli, Maywood, CA		Cuba	[see Guantanamo Bay]
Chelveston RAF, Northants, England [105]	3 AF, 60 TCG, 62 TCG, 63 TCG, 3914 ABG	Cubi Point, Luzon, Philippines	Fasron-113, H&MS-11
		Culver City, CA	Hughes Acft
Chengkung, China	ATC 1339 BU	Custer, Battle Creek, MI	4627 ABS/SS
Chennault, LA	68 BW/CSG/ABW, 806 ABG/CSG [ex Lake Charles]		

Location	Units
Daggett, CA	420 BU, 444 BU, Douglas Mod Center
Dakar-Yoff, Senegal	DMI, NavAtt
Dale Mabry, Tallahassee, FL	335 BU
Dalhart, TX	232 BU
Dallas, TX	69 TCS, 136 FG, 181 FS/FIS/TAS, 555 BU, 2223 IND, 2423 IND, 2596 ABS/ARTC/FTRC/RFC, Lockheed Mod Ctr, BAR, BWRFr, NART [ex Hensley Field]
Damascus, Syria	1130 SAG, 1134 SPA
Da Nang, S Vietnam	2 ADH, 4 SOS, 9 SOS, 35 TFW, 56 SOW, 362 TEWS, 366 TFW, 483 TAW, 6498 ABW, FASU, H&MS-11, H&MS-17, HMM-163, HMM-365, HedSupAct.
Daniel, Augusta, GA	24 TCS, 25 TCS
Dannelly, Montgomery, AL	106 RTS, 117 TRW, 160 RTS/TRS, 187 TRG, 701 NGA Hq, 11 SAS HQ
Davis, Adak, AK	19 ADRS, 321 ABG/DW, 5020 ABS/G/HQW
Davis-Monthan, Tucson, AZ	15 FIS, 43 ABG/BW/MSG, 100 SRW, 233 BU, 248 BU, 303 BW/CSG, 803 ABG/CSG, 2704 ASDG [01Aug 59 to 01Feb65], 3040 ASD/ASS [24Aug48 to Jan50], 4080 SRW, 4105 BU [Nov45 to 24Aug48], MASCE [01Feb65 to Feb74], [Dates indicate storage unit]
Davis, Muskogee, OK	1929 ACSS
Dayton, Vandalia, OH	162 FBS/FIS/FS, BAGR CentDist
Del Valle, Austin, TX	24 TCS/CS, 25 TCS, 26 TCS, 30 TCS, 31 TCS [To Bergstrom 1943]
Denver, CO	140 CAMS, NART [see Buckley]
Dergaon, India	ATC Stn no 22
De Ridder, LA	314 BU
Des Moines, IA	124 FBS/FIS/FS/TFS, 132 CAMS/FEW/FG/FW, 4209 BU, 8124 ABS
Detroit, MI	4 AFPO, CEPDI, EAPDI [probably not at airfield]
Detroit-Wayne, MI	107 BS/FS, 127 FW/FBW/TRG, 171 FS/FBS/TRS, 191 TRG, CAPR [to Selfridge]
Deversoir, Egypt	12 AF: 316 TCG
Dhahran, Saudi Arabia	1172 FMS, 1414 ABG/ABS, 7244 ABG/S, ARS, HQ CMEF
Dinjan, Assam, India	10 AF: 1 ACG, 1 CCG, 2 TCS, 4 TCS, 64 TCG
Dobbins, Marietta, GA	3 ARR, 32 AD, 35 AD, 54 FW, 104 RDCD, 116 ATG/CAMS/FBW/FIW/MALG/TFG, 128 ATS/FBS/FIS/FS, 445 TCW/DT 918 ATG/MALW/MALG/TCG, 1115 SAMS, 2223 IND, 2315 ATS, 2523 IND, 2589 ABG, 4430 ATG, 4433 ATS, 4440 ADG, 4632 SS, 8128 ABS, SAS HQ
Dobodura, New Guinea	375 TCG
Dodd, Ft Sam Houston, TX	3 TCS, 9 TCS, 60 TCS
Dohazari, India	1 CCG
Donaldson, Greenville, SC	18 AF, 61 TCW, 63 TCG/TCW, 64 TCG, 77 TCS, 375 TCG, 443 TCG, 465 TCG, 4501 HQS/SS [ex Greenville AFB]
Don Muang, Thailand	[see Bangkok]
Douglas, Charlotte, NC	156 FSS, 145 AMTG/AMTS/CAMS/MALG, SASH
Dover, DE	80 ABS, 125 BU, 148 FIS, 436 MAW, 1607 FMS/MSG/MSS/TSW, 1619 BFS, 1737 FYS
Dow, ME	7 ABS, 14 ABG/ADRG/FG/MSG, 101 CAMS/FG/FW, 132 ABG/FS/FBW/FEW/FIS, 506 SFIW/ABG, 765 BU, 1379 BU, 4038 CSG/SRW, 4060 ABG/CSG [ex Bangor]
Down Ampney RAF, Glos., England [458]	9 AF
Downey, CA	Consolidated Vultee
Dress, Evansville, IN	
Dreux, France	60 TCW, 106 TRS, 7117 TRW, 7305 ABS
Drew, Tampa, FL	13 TCS, 30 TCS, 31 TCS, 301 BU, 327 BU
Dublin, Eire	1130 SAG, 1134 SAS
Dulag, Leyte, Philippines	13 TCS, FEAF
Dulles, Chantilly, VA	MPI FV
Duluth, MN	73 ABS, 148 FG, 179 FS/FI, 343 CAMS/FG, 515 ADFG, 4787 ABG
Dum Dum, Calcutta, India	ATC 1305 BU
Duncan, San Antonio, TX	3 TS, 64 TCG, 317 TCG [Part of Kelly from 1943]
Dunnellon, FL	1 TC, 10 TCG, 317 CMOS, 318 TCS/CMOS
Dyersburg, TN	330 BU
Dyess, Abilene, TX	64 TCW, 96 BW/CSG/STW, 516 TCW, 819 ABG/CSG [ex Abilene AFB]
Eagle, Dos Palos, CA	
East Base, Gt Falls, MT	1455 BU
East Kirkby RAF, Lincs, England	3 AF, 61 ARS, 63 ARS/RS, 64 ARS/RS, 3917 ABG/ABS
Echterdingen, Stuttgart, Germany	7005 ABS [R-50]
Edenton, NC	H&MS-14, Hamron-11, MAG-15
Edmonton, Alta, Canada	122 AACU, 752 BU, 1455 BU, 1705 ATD, 1851 AACS, 3904 CW
Edwards, CA	2759 EXW, 4485 TEW, 6510 ABW/ADW, 6515 MAG, AFFTC, NLO [ex Muroc]
Eglin Aux Fld 09, Ft Walton Beach, FL	1 SOW, 1 ACW, 1 MAS, 834 TCW, 4400 CCTS/MATS, 4410 CCTW, 4412 CCTS, 4751 ADW [Hurlburt Fld]
Eglin, Valparaiso, FL	1 EGMG, 10 CW, 17 BW/BTW, 14 AF, 48 ARS, 550 GMW, 609 BU, 610 BU, 611 BU, 616 BU, 3200 PTG/TW, 3201 ABG/ABW, 3203 MSG, 3205 DRG, 4485 TEW, AATC, ADTC, AFAC, APGC, ATG, ATSD, OTC, ATKG, PGP
Eielson, Fairbanks, AK	58 SMS/SRWS/WES, 90 SMW, 375 RVWS, 517 ABG, 5010 ABS/ABW/CW [ex Mile 26 Fld]
El Adem, Libya	316 TCG
El Centro, CA	Para Exp Unit, NPF, NPU, NavAerORecFac, MAG-35
El Djem, Tunisia	51 TCW
El Geneina, Sudan	ATC 1207 BU
Ellington, Houston, TX	47 RS, 63 FW, 108 RDCD, 111 FS/FBS/FIS, 147 CAMS/FG, 446 TCW, 1602 ATD, 2223 IND, 2423 IND, 2517 BU, 2578 ABG/ABS/RFC, 3605 BTW/NAW/OTW, CAP HQ
Ellsworth, Rapid City, SD	28 ABG/BW/CSG/SRW, 821 STAD [ex Rapid City]
Elmendorf, Anchorage, AK	2 RDCS, 6 RDC, 7 AWG/WG, 10 RS, 11 WS, 21 CW, 32 ENG, 39 ADW, 42 TCS, 54 TCS, 57 ABG/ABW/ADRG/MS/MSG/FW/FIW, 59 AACS, 64 TCS, 65 FS, 66 FS, 71 ARS, 110 RDCF, 114 ABS/POS, 709 BU/BFS, 1455 BU, 1727 SS, 1804 AACG, 1855 AACF, 2107 WG, 5006 ATS, 5039 ATG/ATS/ABW/ADG/ADW/BFLS, 5040 OF/CAMG, AACM, Alaska AD, CAPW
El Paso, TX	ATC, 578 BU [became Biggs AFB]
El Segundo, CA	VR-1, BWGR West Dist, Douglas RRD
El Toro, Santa Ana, CA	HAMRON-15, MAMRON-15, SAES-1, MARS-37, AIRFMFPAC, MAG-12, MAG-15, MAG-25, MAG-33, H&MS-15, H&MS-33, H&MS-37, MAM-15, MAMS-37, MTG-10, NPTR, SO&ES, SOS-1, VMAT-10, VMR-152, VMR-352, SOS-1, SERVRON 25, HHS AfmfPac.
Elyria, OH	
England, Alexandria, LA	1 SOW, 1 ACW, 17 SOS, 317 ACS/ACW, 366 FBW, 548 SOTS, 4403 TFW, 4410 CCTW/SOW/SOTG, 4412 CCTS [ex Alexandria]
Enid, OK	2518 BU, 3575 AFG/PTW [to Vance Jul49]
Eniwetok Atoll, Stickell Fld, Marshall Is	4930 TEG/SG/SS, 4931 TES, 4951 SS, SWC
Ent, Colorado Springs, CO	2101 AWG
Ephrata, WA	430 BU, 464 BU
Erbenheim, Germany	60 TCG, 7160 ABG, 7165 CG
Erding, Germany [R-91]	3 RBS, 12 AF, 43 TCS/HBS, 85 ABG/ADFW/MG, 7030 ABW/SG, 7210 MG/MS, 7230 ABG, 7280 ABG, 7485 ADW/SW, 8085 MG
Ernest H Harmon, Stephenville, Newfoundland	6 RS, 52 RS, 136 AACS, 537 ABG, 766 BU, 1226 ABG, 1856 AACF, 1933 AACS, 4081 ABG/ARW/CSG/SRW, 6602 ABG, 6605 ABW
Esenboga, Turkey	
Esler, Alexandria, LA	313 BU, 353 BU
Espiritu Santo, New Hebrides	403 TCG, 13 TCS
Etain, France	49 FBW/FTW/TFW, 166 TFS, 366 TFW, 388 FBW, 7005 ABS, 7121 TFW
Evansville, IN	RA RRD - Republic
Evreux-Fauville, France	317 ABG/CAMS/TCW, 322 ADW, 465 TCW, 513 TCW, 7333 ABG/CSG
Ewa, Oahu, HI	Air Pac, MAG-15, MAW-3, Servron-15, SMS-15, VMR-352

Location	Units
Exeter, Devon, England [463]	50 TCW, 440 TCG
Fairbanks, AK	ATC
Fairchild, Spokane, WA	92 ABG/ABW/BW/SRW/STAW, 98 BW, 99 SRW, 111 SRW, 814 ABG, 2834 ADFG, Spokane AD/AMC [ex Spokane AFB]
Fairfax, Kansas City, KS	555 BU, 569 BU, 4101 BU, 4610 ABS/SW, 2472 ARTC, 4676 ADG
Fairfield-Suisun, CA	1 WS, 5 ABG/SRW, 9 ABG/BW/SRW, 10 STU, 55 RVWS, 59 BU, 92 BW, 98 BW, 99 SRW, 308 WRG, 374 RVWS, 375 RVWS, 530 MSG, 814 ABG, 1501 MSG/ATG, 1503 BU, 1504 BU, 1702 ATG, 1704 ATG, 1733 ATS, 2078 WEA/RCNS [to Travis]
Fairford RAF, Glos, England	3919 ABG/CSG, 7504 ASW, 7507 ABGFallon, NV 12 ND
Fargo, Hector, ND	178 FIS/FS, 8178 ABS, SAS HQ
Farmingdale, NY	FAC FN, Republic RRD
Fassberg, Germany [B-152]	513 ABG, 1966 AACS
Felts, Spokane, WA	116 FS
Fenny, Bengal, India	10 AF: 18 TCS
Finschhafen, New Guinea	5 AF: 317 TCG
Florence, Italy	7167 SAMS, 7233 HQS, 7235 HQS
Florence, SC	42 TCS, 54 TCS, 127 BU
Floyd Bennett, Brooklyn, NY	[see New York NAS]
Folkingham RAF, Lincs, England [484]	9 AF: 313 TCG [29, 47, 48, 49 TCS]
Fontainebleau, France	7495 HQG
Forbes, KS	2 AF, 7 GCS, 21 AD, 55 ABG/SMW/SRW, 90 ABG/BW/SMW/SRW, 190 TRG, 311 AD, 313 TCW/TALW, 814 ABG, 815 ABG/CSG, 8127 ABS, SASH [ex Topeka]
Ft Benjamin Harrison, IN	2463 ABG
Ft Benning, GA	[see Lawson Fld]
Ft Bragg, NC	[see Pope Fld]
Ft Dix, Trenton, NJ	2 EES, 449 BU, 592 BU, 4149 BU [to McGuire Jan48]
Ft Douglas, Salt Lake City, UT	SASH
Ft George Wright, Spokane, WA	60 FW/NGW, 142 FW
Ft Glenn, Umnak Is, AK	56 AYSD [to Cape AFB]
Ft Hayes, Columbus, OH	736 NGHQ, SAS HQ
Ft Lamy, Chad, Africa	Attaché
Ft Lauderdale, FL	VTB 1
Ft Lee, Petersburg, VA	4638 ABS/SS
Ft Lewis, Tacoma, WA	SAS HQ
Ft McAndrew, Argentia, Newfoundland	8 WA, 66 ACG, 716 BU, 1230 ABS, 1805 AACG
Ft Monmouth, Red Bank, NJ	DOA SC, Pro DV
Ft Nelson, BC, Canada	517 ABG, 1701 ABG
Ft Randall, Cold Bay, AK	55 AYD
Ft Richardson, Anchorage, AK	57 ADRG
Ft Smith, AR	184 TNPS/TRS, 188 TRG
Ft Snelling, Minneapolis, MN	31 AD
Ft Sumner, NM	9 TCS, 267 BU
Ft Totten, NY	90 BU
Ft Wayne, IN	163 TFS [ex Baer]
Ft Worth, TX	3 AF, 6 AF, 7 MSG, 33 BU, 39 BU, 58 BW, 62 BU, 204 BU, 233 BU, 735 BU, 2000 BU, 2003 BU, 2519 BU, Convair, SAPDI [to Carswell Jan48]
Joe Foss, Sioux Falls, SD	114 CAMS/FG, 175 FS/FIS/TFS, 211 BU, 8175 ABS, SAS HQ
Foster, Victoria, TX	450 FBW/FDW/TFW, 2539 BU, 3580 PTW
France, CZ	4 BCS/TRS, 5620 ABS, 5621 MSG, 5625 ABG
Frankfurt, Germany	763 BU, 6900 SCW [see Rhein-Main]
Freeman, Seymour, IN	4120 BU
Freising, Germany	4 IMS, 156 AACS, 1854 AACS
Fresno, CA	144 CAMS/FG, 194 FIS
Friendship, Baltimore, MD	4 WG, 104 FBS, 6590 HQG/SG, HQ ARDC
Fuchu, Honshu, Japan	1 WG, 10 WG
Fulbeck RAF, Lincs, England [488]	9 AF: 434 TCG, 442 TCG
Furstenfeldbruck, Germany [R-72]	2 WW, 5 TOWS, 12 AF, 36 ABG/FBG/FBW, 45 TNPS, 47 STCS, 83 ARS, 84 RS, 1807 AACW, 1857 AACF, 1944 AACS, 7301 ABG, 7330 FTW/TNW, 7365 ABS/MSG
Futema, Okinawa	H&MS-16, MWHS-1
Gainesville, GA	NATTC, PnAvRadSc
Galveston, TX	
Garden City, KS	4132 BU
Gary, TX	530 ADFG, 3585 PTW [ex San Marcos]
Gaya, India	ATC 1311 BU
Geiger, Spokane, WA	84 CAMS/FG, 87 ABS, 116 FIS/FS, 141 FIG, 142 CAMS/FW, 463 BU/CAMS, 530 ADFG, 4702 DEW, 4751 ABS, 8116 ABS
Gen. Spaatz, Reading, PA	103 RDCD, 109 RDCD, 112 ABG, 140 AMTS, 148 FS/FBS/FIS, 2237 ARTC
Geneva, Switzerland	Attaché
George, Lawrenceville, IL	805 BU
Georgetown, Br Guiana	7408 SU, SAW/ATC [see Atkinson]
George, Victorville, CA	1 FIW, 4 TS, 21 FBW, 131 FBW, 146 FBW, 338 BU, 434 TCG, 479 FBW/FDW/TFW, 805 BU, 831 ABG [ex Victorville AFB]
Giebelstadt, Germany	36 FBW, 7030 ABW/SG, 7312 SS
Gilbert, Marshall Isl.	Commarshalls
Gioia del Colle, Italy	305 MUMS, 3505 MUMS, 7230 SS/TTG
Glasgow, MT	13 FIS, 91 BW, 476 FG, 4141 CSG/SRW
Glendale (Grand Central), CA	GCA CP
Glenview, IL	NART, NRT TRS PI
Glynco, Brunswick, GA	NAR
Godman, Ft Knox, KY	108 FBW, 118 BU, 123 FBW, 165 FBS, 315 BU, 351 BU, 405 FBW, 2236 ARTC, 4444 ABS
Goodfellow, San Angelo, TX	6 WW, 9 WRG, 31 AWD, 1110 BAG/BAS, 1212 BU/BAS, 2533 BU, 3545 BFY/BPTW/PTW, CRCCE
Goose, Goose Bay, Labrador, Canada	3 TF, 6 RS, 22 HELS, 54 ARS, 59 FIS, 108 FBW, 538 ABG, 1227 ABG, 1383 BU, 4082 ABG/CSG/SRW, 6603 ABW/ABG, 6606 ABW, 6615 ATS
Gore, Great Falls, MT	5 STU, 120 CAMS, 186 FS, 557 BAS, 1455 BAS, 8186 ABS, SAS HQ [to Great Falls]
Gotha North, Germany [R-4]	
Gowen, Boise, ID	190 FS/FES, 424 BU, 425 BU
Graham, Marianna, FL	
Grand Forks, ND	319 BW, 478 FG
Grand Island, NB	242 BU
Grand Rapids, Kent County, MI	BAL, LER GR
Grandview, Kansas City, MO	328 FG, 2472 RFC, 4676 ADFG [to Richard Gebaur]
Grantham RAF, Lincs, England	9 TCC
Gravelly Pt, VA (Washington Nat Apt)	501 ATG, 503 BU, 520 BU, 1100 BU, 1254 ATS, 1298 ATS, DOI SC, FLS HQ
Gray, Ft Lewis, WA	
Great Bend, KS	
Greater Pittsburgh, PA	54 FG, 71 FIS, 81 ABS, 112 ABG/CAMS/FG/FIW, 146 FIS/FBS, 147 FBS/FIS/FS, 459 TCW, 500 ADFG, 575 BU, 758 TCS, 911 MATS/MG/TCG, 2253 ABG
Great Falls, MT	7 FYG, 29 AD, 120 CAMS/FG, 186 FES/FIS, 407 ABG/SFW, 517 ATG/MSG, 1271 ATS, 1300 ABW, 1455 BU, 1701 ABG/ATG/ATS/ATW/MSG, 8186 ABS, SAS HQ [to Malmstrom Oct 55)
Theodore F Green, Hillsgrove, RI	143 ACG/ASLS/SOG/TAS/TCS/TCG, 152 FBS/FIS
Greenham Common RAF, Berks, England [486]	61 ARS, 62 ARS, 434 TCG, 438 TCG, 3909 ABG/CSG
Greensboro ORD, NC	106 BU, 1060 BU
Greenville, MS	3300 PTS, 3505 PTW, 4197 BU
Greenville, SC	29 TCS, 37 TCS, 47 BG Dt, 63 TCW, 64 TCW, 105 RDC DT, 303 BU, 309 BU, 313 BU, 316

CHAPTER 3: MILITARY OPERATORS OF THE DC-3, C-47, R4D, DAKOTA AND LI-2

Location	Units
Greenwood, MS	ABG/MSU/TCG, 330 BU, 375 TCW, 433 TCW, 434 TCG, 804 BU, 2603 SBS, 4418 BCS, HQSq 568 BU
Grenada, MS	3 TCS, 5 TCS, 9 TCS, 10 TCG, 60 TCS, 307 TCG, 317 TCG
Grenier, Manchester, NH	82 ABG/ADRG/FG/MSG, 90 BU, 101 CAMS/FIW, 102 RDCD, 106 RDCD, 112 BU, 126 RDCD, 133 ATS/FIS/FS, 732 TCS, 1377 BU, 2235 ABS, 2263 SBS, 3247 SAS/SS, 4234 SAS, 4681 ABS, 8133 ABS, SAI NH, SASH
Griffiss, Rome, NY	1 FIG, 7 RS, 12 RS, 27 FIS, 63 TCW, 102 RDCD, 109 RDCS, 138 FD, 925 DPF, 1100 BU, 2751 ABG/EXW, 2845 ABG/DEW, 2856 ABW, 2905 SDG, 3087 ABG, 3135 ELS, 3171 ERS/ERG, 4149 BU, 4713 REVS, 6530 ABW, 6531 FTS, Rome AMA, RAD, RDP, RODC [ex Rome AAF]
Grissom, Peru, IN	305 ARW/BW [ex Bunker Hill AFB]
Grosse Isle, MI	NART
Guadalcanal, Solomon Is.	SWPac/ATC
Guam Is (Anderson), Orote	9 TCS, VR-21, HDN MAG-24 [see Agana]
Guantanamo Bay, Cuba	VU-10, 10 ND
Guatemala City, Guatemala	24 ACW/COW/SOW, 1134 SAG, 5500 FMS, 5713 ABS, 7414 MMS, GMLD
Gulfport, MS	328 BU
Gunter, Montgomery, AL	476 BU, 2586 ARTC
Guntersville, AL	JLR PG, LRPD
Hagerstown, MD	Fairchild AC
Hague, The, Ypenburg, Netherlands	17 DAP, 1130 SAG, HQ MDAP
Hahn, Germany	12 AF, 36 FDAW/TFW, 50 FBW/TFW, 367 TFW, 7425 ABG/FMS/SG
Haifa, Israel	1137 SAS
Half Moon Bay, CA	61 NGW
Hamilton, San Rafael, CA	1 FW, 4 AF, 6 ARR, 8 RU, 11 RDCS/STU, 16 SAMG, 21 TCS, 28 AD, 33 BU, 35 BU, 41 ARS/RS, 51 AACG, 54 TCS, 78 ABG/FG/FIW/FW/MSG, 108 RDCD, 112 RDCD/RDCS, 174 TFW, 325 ABG, 400 BU, 401 BU, 460 BU, 566 ABG/ADFG, 701 BU, 1100 SAMG, 1117 SAMS, 1503 BU, 1801 AACG, 1850 AACF/FCF, 1856 AACF/AACS, 2223 INS, 2317 ATS, 2323 INS, 2346 RFC, 2347 MATD, 4430 ATG, 4435 ATS, 4440 ADG, 4661 MATS, 4702 DW, 4754 REVF, CAP, FLS, WADF
Hammer, Fresno, CA	403 BU
Hanau, Germany	45 ADG
Hancock, Syracuse, NY	32 AD, 138 TFS, 174 TFG, 4624 SG/ABS [ex Syracuse AAB]
Haneda, Tokyo, Japan [J-9]	540 MSG, 1503 ABG/MAS/MSG/ATW, 1539 BU, 1808 AACW, ATC, 2143 AWW, 8083 MAAD, FEAF, MAG-33, MAW-1, ComNavJap, VR-21
L G Hanscom, Bedford, MA	9 TCW, 94 TCW, 2223 IND, 2234 RFC, 3245 ABW, 2523 IND, 6520 ABW/TEW, AFDDV, CARCE, ELD, MITCM [ex Bedford AAF]
Hanshiu	Hamron-16
Harbor, Baltimore, MD	104 FBS/FIS/FS
Harding, Baton Rouge, LA	24 TCS, 25 TCS, 26 TCS
Harlingen, TX	2123 BW, 3610 OTW/TNW
Harmon, Guam, Marianas Islands	6 RS, 7 AF, 19 ABG, 20 RD, 21 TCS, 24 HBS, 30 WS, 46 FS, 541 ABG, 1504 ABG, ATC, VR-8 Det.
Harris, Cape Girardeau, MO	
Harrisburg, PA	[ex 196 TEWS Olmstead AFB]
Hartford, CT	246 BU, Pan American, Pratt & Whitney
Hassani, Athens, Greece	14 TCS, 60 ABG/TCG, 85 ADW, 1632 ABS, 7156 MD/MS, [to Ellinikon] 7166 CS, 7167 SAMS, 7907 BU, MDAP, UNBCt, GREAM
Hathazari, India	10 AF: 1 CCG
Hattiesburg, MS	
Havana, Cuba	1127 FAG, 1130 SAG, 1134 SAS, CUBFt/Dt
Hawkins, Jackson, MS	183 ATS/AMTS/RTS
Hawthorne, CA	Northrop RRD
Hayward, CA	111 RDCD, 129 ACG/TCG/TCS, 144 FBW/FW/FIW, 194 FBS/FIG/FS, 2349 ABW
Hector, ND	119 CAMS/FG, 178 FIS [see Fargo]
Hellinikon, Athens, Greece	[see Athens]
Helsinki, Finland	1130 SAG
Hendon RAF, Middx, England	27 ATG, 1127 FAG, 1130 SAG, 1134 SPA, VR-24, VR-25 [575] VRU-4, Fasron-76
Hensley, Dallas, TX	35 BU, 181 FBS/FIS/FS, 735 BU, 2596 ARTC/FTRC, 4122 BU
Heston RAF, Middx, England [510]	27 ATG
Hialeah, FL	
Hickam, Honolulu, Oahu, HI	7 AF: 9TCS, 11 RS, 15 ABW, 19 TCS, 71 ACS, 76 ARS, 154 FG, 199 FS/FBS/FIS, 531 ATG/MSG, 775 BU, 1500 ABG/ATW/FMS/MSG/OS/OW, 1521 BU, 1801 AACG, 6486 ABW, VR-8
Hill, Ogden, UT	62 BU, 140 FBW, 461 BTW/BW, 467 BU, 925 DFS, 1100 BU, 1729 ATS, 2344 RTC, 2489, ABW, 4013 BU, 4135 BU, 4677 REVF, OGAMA
Hillsgrove, Providence, RI	152 FS
Hobbs, NM	59 ADG/HBS, 4160 BU
Hollandia, New Guinea	5 AF: 41 TCS, 317 TCG
Holloman, Alamogordo, NM	2754 ABG/EXW, 3205 DG, 4802 GMS, 6540 MTW, HLDC, MDC CE
Holman, St Paul, MN	109 FS/FIS, 133 FW/FIW, 8109 ABS, SAS HQ
Homestead, FL	2 OTU/ATC, 19 BW, 31 TFW, 125 FIG, 379 ABG, 435 TCW, 563 BU, 823 ABG/CSG, 1127 FAG, 2223 INS, 4531 FTW
Hondo, TX	2523 BU, 3304 TNS, 3706 BU, HACHT
Honduras	7416 MMS/SU [see Tegucigalpa]
Hong Kong	SPAMA
Honolulu, HI	VR-8, VR-11 [see Hickam]
Houston, TX	111 FBS/FIS, NARF
Howard, Balboa, CZ	1 ACW/RS, 4 TRS, 6 FW, 23 ABG, 24 ACW/SOW, 36 FG, 582 SVG, 605 ACS, 5601 ABS, 5602 MSG, 5605 ABG, 5700 ABW, 6 AF
Hubbard, NV	192 FBS [See Reno]
Hulman, Terre Haute, IN	113 FIS/TFS, 181 TFG [see Terre Haute]
Hunter, Savannah, GA	2 ABG/BG/BW, 158 FS, 302 BU, 308 BW, 487 BU, 804 ABG
Hurlburt, FL	1 SOW, 834 TCW [to Eglin 09]
Hutchinson, KS	117 TRS, 190 TRG, ATU-600VP, ATU-601 VP, NAATC
Ie Shima Island, Okinawa	318 TCS
Ilion	
Imeson, Jacksonville, FL	125 CAMS/FIG/FG, 159 FBS/FIS
Imphal, Assam, India	
Incirlik, Turkey	7216 ABG/ABS/CSG
Independence, KS	4185 BU
Indian Springs, NV	4935 ABS, SWCC
Indio, CA	
Industriehafen, Germany	10 ARS
Inglewood, CA	6 AF, 6592 SG, AF Ballistic Missile Div, ARD CM, North American, BAR
Inyokern, CA	NOTS [ex Harvey]
Isla Grande, San Juan, PR	198 FBS/FIS
Itami, Osaka, Japan	60 ARS, 67 RTW/TRW
Itazuke, Fukuoka, Kyushu, Japan [J-13]	5 ADHQ, 8 ABG/FBW/TFW, 21 TCS, 27 FEW, 51 FIW, 58 FBW, 136 FBW, 452 BW, 6143 ABG/OS, 6160 ABW
Iwakuni, Honshu, Japan [J-14]	MARS-17, MAMS-17, MWHS-1 Adv.Base, Fasron-120, NAMD, 3 BW, 75 ADFW, 6133 ATW
Iwo Jima, Bonin Is.	6361 ABS
Izmir, Turkey	1130 SAG, 1141 FMS/SAS, 7231 CSG/TTG, 7266 SS, 7470 HQSS/SS
Jackson, MS	183 TAS, 2588 ARTC, 4103 BU
Jacksonville, FL	159 FIS/FS, 4203 BU, 8159 ABS, AT Dept, ATU VP- MS-10, Fasron-109, C&R, ADAU, HDN FAW-8, NATTU, NARTU, 6 ND, CNAAT, CANOT
Jakarta, Indonesia	405 FW, NavAtt, DAO
Jefferson Barracks, MO	71 FW
Jerusalem, Israel	1137 SAS
Jiwani, India	ATC 1349 BU
Johnson, Irumagawa, Honshu, Japan	3 BW, 3 RG/RS, 3 BTAW, 4 FIW, 35 FIW, 36 ARS, 1505 ABG, 6041 ABG, 6162 ABW, 6314 ABW, 6517 ABG

Location	Units
Johnston Island, C Pacific	1010 ABG, 1505 ABG, 1509 ABS/SS, 1521 BU, 1525 ABG/ABS, 6486 ABW, ATC
Johnsville, Warminster, PA	NADC, NADS Flt Dept, 4 ND [to Warminster]
Jorhat, Assam, India	ATC 1330 BU
Kabul, Afghanistan	1127 FAG, 1130 SAG, 1134 SAS
Kadena, Okinawa	2 RG/RS, 15 WS, 18 FBW/TFW, 33 ARS, 313 ADD, 1811 AACG, 6313 ABW, 6332 ABW, ComFltAct
Kahuku, Oahu, HI	311 TCS, 316 TCS
Kanawha City, Charleston, WV	130 ACG, 167 FBS/FIS
Kaneohe Bay, Oahu, HI	Fasron 117, H&MS-13, H&MS-24, HQSFMFP, 14 ND
Kansas City, MO	VR-3
Karachi, India	10 AF, 1127 FAG, 1130 SAG, 1141 SAS, ATC 1306 BU, ICHD
Karamursel, Turkey	6900 SECW
Kaufbeuren, Germany	12 TCS, 60 ABG/TCW/TCG, 116 AACS, 156 AACS, 746 BU, 1944 AACS, 7280 ABG, 7320 AFW, 7323 MSG, 7331 TTW
Kearney, NB	27 FG/MSG, 200 BU, 485 BU,
Kearns Tr Ct, UT	467 BU, 1050 BU
Keesler, Biloxi, MS	3380 MSG/TTW, 3704 BU, 4425 SCHS, Keesler TTC,
Keevil RAF, Wilts, England [471]	62 TCG
Keflavik, Iceland	53 ARS, 1400 ABG/CAMS/FMS/MATS/MSG, NavSta
Kellogg, Battle Creek, MI	110 TRS, 172 FS/FIS/TRS, 435 TCG, 817 BU, 4180 BU
Kelly, San Antonio, TX	6 WD, 24 WS, 33 BU, 53 AACS, 59 ADG, 62 TCG, 70 BU, 103 WG, 149 CAMS/FG, 182 FIS, 518 ATG, 703 BU, 708 BU, 1003 INGG, 1100 BU, 1275 TSS, 1700 FMS/MAS/ATG/ATS, 1708 FYG, 1738 FYS, 1803 AACG, 2103 AWG, 2851 ABW, 4121 BU, 6960 HQG/SG, CONDV, SAAMA
Kenitra, Morocco	NavTraCom
Key, Meridian, MS	153 FS/RTS/TRS, 186 TRG, 301 BU, 347 BU
Key West, FL	VF-101, VX-1, 6 ND, FallWeaTraLant
Kiangwan, China	1369 BU
Kimpo, S Korea [K-14]	3 RG, 4 FIW, 8 FBW, 40 TCS, 46 TCS, 51 FIW, 67 RTW, 136 FB, 679 RTW, 2157 ARS, 6130 ABG/ABU, 6131 TSW, 6147 ABG/TCG, 6151 ABU, 6167 ABG/SS, 6314 ABW/SW, 6401 FMU, 6461 ATS/TCS
Kincheloe, Kinross, MI	507 CAMS/FIW/FW, 4609 ABG [see Kinross]
Kindley, Bermuda	55 ARS, 522 ABG, 1389 BU, 1604 ABG/ABW/FMS/MSS/MATS
Kingman, AZ	4184 BU
Kingsley, Klamath Falls, OR	408 FG
Kingsville, TX	NAATC
Kinloss RAF, Morayshire, Scotland	
Kinross, MI	507 CMS/FG [to Kincheloe Sep59]
Kinston, NC	3308 TNS
Kirtland, Albuquerque, NM	2 CMOD, 34 ADHQ, 81 ABG/FIW, 93 FIS, 150 CAMS/FG/TFG, 188 FBS/FIS/FS, 237 BU, 428 BU, 2758 ABG, 3078 ABG, 4900 ABG, 4901 ABW/SW, 4910 ABG, 4925 SWG/TEG, 8188 ABS, AEC KM, NASWF, NWEF, SWC
Kisarazu, Honshu, Japan	10 WG, 86 FIW, 2723 ABS/ADG, 6408 ADG
Knollwood, Southern Pines, NC	
Knoxville, TN	BAL
Kodiak, AK	17 ND, Fasron-114
Komaki, Nagoya, Honshu, Japan [J-21]	3 RS, 5 AFH, 30 WS, 37 ARS, 49 FBW, 67 TRW, 347 FW, 1861 AACF, 6101 ABW, 6106 ABS/ABU/ABW
Korat, Thailand	388 TFW, 631 CSG
Kotzebue, AK	503 ABS
Kulis, AK	[see Anchorage]
Kunming, China	14 AF, ATC 1340 BU
Kunsan, S Korea [K-8]	3 BW, 6170 ABG/ABS, 6175 ABG, 6314 ABW/SW
Kurmitola, India	ATC 1345 BU
Kwajalein Atoll, Marshall Is	17 TCS, 532 ABS, 1502 ABG/ATS/SS, 1535 BU, NAB, NAS, VR-23 Det
Kweilin, China	ATC 1365 BU
Lackland, San Antonio, TX	352 BU, 3543 BU, 3700 BTRW/INW/MIW, LMCC
Ladd, Fairbanks, AK	4 FD, 10 RS, 72 RVPS, 74 ARS, 82 FG, 91 SRW, 321 ASG/SVG, 449 FWS, 517 ABG, 1701 ABG/ATD, 5001 ABG/ABS/ABW/ADRG/CW/MSG/MS/OS, 5060 CAMG/OS, PGC 5064 CMTS/CMTU/COS, Transfer base for Russian C-47s
La Guardia, New York, NY	502 BU
Lajes, Azores (Lagens)	57 ARS, 523 ABG, 1605 ABG/ABW/FMS/MSG/MSS/MS
La Junta, CO	249 BU
Lake Charles, LA	44 ABG/BW, 47 BG, 68 BW, 307 BU, 340 BW, 806 ABG [to Chennault Nov58]
Lake City, FL	OTU, ATU VB2-2
Lakehurst, NJ	NARTU, NATTU, Para Unit, 4 ND, ZW-1
Lakeland, FL	352 BU
Lakenheath RAF, Suffolk, England	48 TFW, 301 BW, 3904 CW, 3909 ABG, 3910 ABG/CSG, 3913 ABS, 7504 ABG/ASG
Lalmai, Bengal, India	16 TCS, 17 TCS
Lalmanirhat, Assam, India	ATC 1326 BU
Lambert, St Louis, MO	71 NG, 107 RDCD, 110 BS/BTS/FG/FIS/FS/TFS, 131 BW/CW/TFG, 726 NGAHQ/SASHQ, 798 NGAS, 4210 BU, 8110 BS, ACHC
Landsberg, Germany	31 WS, 7030 HQG, 7351 MG,
Landstuhl, Germany	86 FBW/FIW, 7030 HQG
Langar RAF, Notts, England [490]	435 TCG, 438 TCG, 441 TCG
Langley, Hampton, VA	1 AACW, 2 ATS, 2 WSG, 3 BU, 4 ABG/FIG/FIW/MSG, 8 BU, 9 AF, 20 FBW, 47 BW, 65 BU, 76 BU, 84 BS, 85 BU/BS, 111 FBS, 117 BS, 122 BS, 126 FBW, 136 FBW, 161 RCS, 300 BU, 304 BU, 315 TCG, 345 BTG/TBMG, 363 ABG/MSG/RCG/RCW, 405 FBW, 423 BS, 424 BS, 441 BU, 734 BU, 836 ABG, 1001 INGU, 1800 AACW, 2102 WG, 3539 BU, 4405 OS, 4430 ABW, 4440 ADG, 4500 ABW/SS, HQS, NACA, TACCM
Laoag, Luzon, Philippines	318 TCS
Laon-Couvron, France	38 BTW/BW/TACW, 66 TRW, 126 BW
La Paz, Bolivia	1130 SAG, Bol Dt/Ft, 7406 MMS
Laredo, TX	3640 PTW
Larson, Moses Lake, WA	61 TCG, 62 ABG/TCG/TCW, 71 SRFW, 81 FIW, 82 FIS, 101 FIW, 462 STAW, 4170 CSG/CSS/SRW, 4703 DEW, MATS [ex Moses Lake AFB]
Las Cruces, NM	WHS
Lashio, Burma	
Las Vegas, NV	3021 BU, 3595 PTW [to Nellis Apr50]
Laughlin, Del Rio, TX	3645 CCTW/FTW
Laurinburg/Maxton, NC	317 TCG, 375 TCG, 810 BU
Lawson, Ft Benning, Columbus, GA	3 TCS, 5 TCS, 9 TCS, 41 TCS, 42 TCS, 60 TCS, 10 TCG, 60 TCG, 75 TCS, 117 RTG, 119 RTW, 307 TCG, 316 TCG, 317 TCG, 319 BU, 434 TCG, 464 TCG, 811 BU, 4408 ABS
Ledo, India	CCTF
Leesville, LA	138 BU
Le Mans, France [A-35]	52 TCW
Lemoore, CA	12 ND
Leopoldville, Congo	1127 FAG, MSN HQ
Leyte Island, Philippines	2 CCG, 317 TCG, 318 TCS, ComPhilSeaFron
Liberal, KS	
Lima, Peru	24 ACW/SOW, 1127 FAG, 1130 SAG, 5500 FMS, 7421 MMS, PER Dt/Ft, NavMis
Limestone, ME	42 ABG/BW, 4215 BSS [to Loring Oct54]
Lincoln, NB	35 BU, 98 ABG/ABW/BW, 132 ABG, 155 CAMS/FG/FIG/TRG, 173 FBS/FES/FIS/FS, 307 BW, 818 ABG/CSG, 2004 BU, 3541 BU, 8173 ABS, SASH, NART
Lindsey, Wiesbaden, Germany	
Lingayen, Luzon, Philippines	
Linliang, China	CCTF
Lisbon, Alverca, Portugal	1127 FAG, 1171 FMS, MDA, MAAG, OGMA
Litchfield Pk, Goodyear, AZ	11 ND, Storage [when closed, aircraft in store were flown or roaded to Davis-Monthan, or scrapped]

CHAPTER 3: MILITARY OPERATORS OF THE DC-3, C-47, R4D, DAKOTA AND LI-2

Location	Units
Little Rock, AR	43 BW, 123 TRW, 189 TRG/TRS, 384 BW, 825 ABG/CSG, 3947 SEVS
Liuchow, China	1 CCG, ATC 1363 BU
Lockbourne, OH	13 TCS, 26 SMW, 31 TCS, 91 ABG/SMW/SRW, 105 RDCD, 112 BS, 121 ABG/FBW/FW, 166 FS, 301 ARW/BW, 317 TCW/TAW, 318 BU, 332 ABG/MSG, 801 ABG, 2114 BU, 4152 BU, 4220 BSRS
Lockheed Air Terminal, Burbank, CA	62 FW, 112 RDCD, 115 BS, 126 BW, 146 CW, 6 AFPO, 7 AFPO, 1350 PHG, NSF, Lockheed RRD, PAM CP
Logan, Boston, MA	101 FG/FIW/FS/RDCD/TFS, 102 CAMS/FG/FIW/TFG, 722 SASH/NGAH
London, Lincoln, ND	20 FBG?
Long Beach, CA	115 FBS, 188 FIS, 416 BU, 556 BU, 1728 FYS, 1737 FYS, 1738 FYS, 2223 IND, 2323 IND, 2347 ABG/RFC, 4860 PHG, ARTC, Douglas
Loring, Limestone, ME	42 BW [ex Limestone]
Los Alamitos, CA	NART
Los Angeles AFS, CA	6592 SG/SW, AFD Fr, LA SX, BagrWestDist
Los Negros, New Hebrides	13 TCS
Louisville, Standiford, KY	165 FS/FB, CV-MOD
Love Fld, Dallas, TX	555 BU, CAPRg, LO MOD CN
Lowry, Denver, CO	9 RU, 19 AWS, 33 BU, 44 ARS, 62 BU, 106 AACS, 110 ABG, 736 BU, 930 EVS, 1100 BU, 1110 ASG/BAG, 1733 ATS, 1910 AACS, 2151 RU, 3415 MSG/TTW, 3705 BU, 7625 OS, ACDC, CAPR, FLS, LTC
Lubbock, TX	2527 BU, 3500 PTW [to Reese Nov49]
Luigi Bologna, Taranto, Italy	7230 TNG/TTG
Luke, Glendale, AZ	58 TFW, 127 FW/PTW, 197 FS, 3028 BU, 3600 CCTW/FTW, 4510 CCTW, SASH
Luliang, China	329 TCS
Lunken, Cincinnati, OH	446 BU, 586 BU
MacArthur, Islip, NY	CAPR
MacDill, Tampa, FL	1 TFW/RS, 5 RS, 7 GCS, 15 TFW, 62 BU, 300 BU, 305 BW, 306 ABG/BG/BW, 307 ABG/MSG/SMW, 311 RCW, 326 BU, 330 SVG, 338 BU, 465 BU, 737 BU, 809 ABG, 2582 ARTC, 3908 SEVS, 4750 ADFW
Madison, WI	176 FIS
Madrid, Spain	1127 FAG, 1130 SAG, 1134 SAG, 1148 SAS, 1171 FMS, 1859 AACF, 3090 ADFL, 7600 ABG/CSS/SS, CASA, SPAMA NavAct
Maison Blanche, Algeria	60 TCG
Malden, MO	815 BU, 3305 TNS
Mallory, Memphis, TN	
Malmstrom, Great Falls, MT	29 AD, 341 CSG/SMW, 407 ABG, 4061 ABG/CSG, 4642 SS [ex Great Falls]
Malta, Mediterranean	Fasron-201 Spec.
Mamadan, Iran	MDAP
Managua, Nicaragua	5500 FMS, NicDt
Manchester, NH	NOLD BAS [to Grenier]
Manila, Luzon, Philippines	405 FW, 1020 SAW, 1130 SAG, 1173 FMS, 1175 FMS, 1134 SAG, 6200 MATW, JMPGp
Mansfield-Lahm, OH	164 FS/FIS/TFS/FBS, 179 TFG
Manston RAF, Kent, England	31 FEW, 66 ARS/RS, 123 FBW, 405 FBW/FW, 406 FIW, 3917 ABG, 7512 ASG, 7582 ABS,
Manus Island, Admiralty Is	
Maracay, Venezuela	Ven Ft
Marana, AZ	3307 PTS/TNS
Marble Mt, S Vietnam	H&MS-16
March, Riverside, CA	1 ABG/FG/FW/MSG, 4 RS, 8 RS, 9 WS, 12 RS, 12 AF, 22 ABG/BW/CSG, 33 BU, 42 RS, 44 FBW, 58 BW, 62 BU, 67 ABG/MSG, 101 AACS, 106 BW, 312 BU, 320 BW, 321 BU, 412 FG, 420 BU, 731 BU, 807 ABG/CSG, 1801 AACG, 1907 AACS, 2101 AWG, 2150 RU, 2223 IND, FLS
Marfa, TX	818 BU, 3025 BU
Marham RAF, Norfolk, England	7503 BCS
Marietta, GA	16 SAMG, 35 BU, 54 FW/NGW, 58 BW, 128 FS, 1100 SAMG, 1115 SAMS, 2589 ARTC, 4115 BU, 4204 BU, WRAMA [to Dobbins Feb50]
Marks, Nome, AK	5030 ABS
Marrakech, Fr Morocco	ATC N Africa Wg
Marshall, Ft Riley, KS	356 BU, 4406 ABS
Glenn L Martin, Baltimore, MD	104 FIS/TFS, 135 ACG, 175 TFG
Martinsburg, WV	167 AMTS/FIS/TFS
Mather, Sacramento, CA	1505 BU, 2622 BU, 3535 BTW/OTW/NTW
Matsushima, Japan	46 TCS, 6141 ABS
Maxwell, Montgomery, AL	33 BU, 42 BU, 48 RS, 160 RTS, 502 AUW, 738 BU, 1100 SAMG, 1118 SAMS, 1922 AACS, 2100 BU, 3800 ABW/Air University, FLS
Mayport, FL	
McAndrew, Newfoundland (Argentia)	8 WS, 66 AACG, 716 BU, 1805 AACG
McChord, Tacoma, WA	8 RS, 33 BU, 43 ARS, 61 TCG, 62 TCG/TCW/ABG/ADRG/MALW/MSG, 102 AACS, 314 BU, 318 FIW, 325 FG/FIW/FW/MSG, 406 BU, 464 BU, 517 ABG, 567 ADG, 1455 BU, 1501 ATG, 1726 SS, 2150 RS, 4704 DEW, 4740 DEW, FLS, MATS
McClellan, Sacramento, CA	4 TS/WG, 6 WD, 7 TS, 8 ADFD, 10 AWS, 55 SRWS, 62 TCG, 68 BU, 101 WG, 552 AEWCW, 594 BU, 701 BU, 925 DFS, 1100 BU, 1730 ATS, 2101 AWG/WG, 2852 ABW, 4127 BU, 4701 AEWCS, SMAMA
McConnell, Wichita, KS	7 TS, 23 TFW, 127 FIS/TFS, 184 TFG, 381 SMW, 388 TFW, 3520 CCTW/FTW, 4347 CCTW
McCook, NB	
McCoy, Orlando, FL	306 BW, 321 ABG/BW/CSG, 1360 MATS, 4047 CSG/STW (ex Pinecastle)
McEntire, Congaree, SC	157 FS, 169 FG, 741 NGHQ
McGhee-Tyson, Knoxville, TN	74 ABS, 134 ATG/CAMS/FG, 151 ARS/FIS, 355 FG, 516 ADG, BAL
McGuire, Ft Dix, NJ	2 FIS, 5 FIS, 52 ABG/FW/FIW, 91 ABG, 119 FIS, 141 FBS/FIS/TFS, 332 FIS, 438 MAW, 539 FIS, 568 ADG, 601 CAMS, 1161 ATW/FMS/MAS/MS/OS, 1611 ATW/FMS/OS, 2223 IND/INS, 4709 DEW [ex Ft Dix]
McMurdo Sound, Antarctica	VX-6
Meiktila, Burma	
Melbourne, Australia	1130 SAG, 1134 SAS, NavAtt
Membury RAF, Wilts, England [466]	9 AF: 436 TCG
Memphis, Millington, TN	VR-791, NATTC
Memphis Apt, TN	3 AFRD, 35 BU, 62 BU, 118 TRW, 155 ATS/FS/TNPS/TRS, 445 TCAD, 550 BU, 554 BU, 920 TCG, 2584 ABS, 2854 RFC
Merced, CA	444 BG, 482 BU [to Castle Jan46]
Meridian, MS	NABTC
Merryfield RAF, Somerset, England [464]	441 TCG
Mexico City, Mexico	1127 FAG, 1130 SAG, 1134 SAS, LIAF, MexDt, NavAtt
Miami, (36th St Apt,) FL	8 AACW, 9 STU, 20 FYG, 92 BU, 154 BU, 473 BU, 1105 BU, 2223 IND, 2252 RFC, 2523 INT, 2585 ABS/ARTC/RFC, 4006 BU
Miami Apt., FL	AACMF, AAIMF, ADXMF, AIIMF, AINMF, H&MS-31, MWSG- 37, NARTU, SO&ES, SOS-3
Midland, TX	555 BU, 2528 BU
Middletown AD, PA	[see Olmsted]
Midway, Pacific Ocean	NavSta
Miho, Honshu, Japan	17 BW, 452 BW, 6135 ABS
Mildenhall RAF, Suffolk, England	2 BW, 3 AD, 93 BW, 322 AD, 509 BW, 513 TAW/TCW, 1602 ATW, 3904 CW, 3910 ABG, 3913 ABS/CSG, 7350 CSG, 7511 ABS/ASW, 7513 ABG/ABS/TACG, 7543 ABS, US Navy
Miller, Staten Island, NY	
Mills, San Francisco, CA	[to San Francisco Apt]
Millville, NJ	
Mindoro, Philippines	54 TCW, 318 TCS, 375 TCG
Mineola AMC, NY	AILMY
Mines, Los Angeles, CA	4208 BU [to Los Angeles Apt]
Mingaladon, Burma	318 TCS
Mingan, Quebec, Canada	1225 ABG, 1235 ABS

Location	Units
Minneapolis Apt, MN	5 AFRD, 31 AD, 56 FIW, 72 ABS, 96 TCS, 109 ATS/FIS, 133 CAMS, 137 BU, 440 TCW, 47 FG/CAMS, 514 [to Minneapolis St Paul] ADFG, 934 MATG/MATS/TAG/TCG, 1334 ABG, 2223 IND, Apt] 2423 IND, 2465 ABG/RFC, 2473 RFD, CAP Rg, MHRCM
Minneapolis NAS, MN	VR-812, NART
Minot, ND	5 BW, 32 CAMS/FG, 450 BW, 4136 SRW
Minter, Bakersfield, CA	3000 BU, 3008 BU
Miramar, San Diego, CA	11 ND
Misamari, Assam, India	ATC 1328 BU
Misawa, Honshu, Japan [J-27]	3 RG/RS, 21 FMS, 38 ARS, 39 AD, 49 FBW, 116 FBW, 475 TFW, 512 RVWS, 6016 ABW, 6139 ABG, 6163 ABW
Mitchel, Hempstead, NY	1 AF, 2 AFPO, 2 TOWS, 8 WG, 10 TCG, 12 RDCD, 12 AWS, 16 SAMG, 26 AD, 35 BU, 52 ABG/AACG/AACS/FWG/MSG, 63 BU, 74 BU, 100 BU, 102 BS/WG, 104 BU, 110 BU, 114 BS, 702 BU, 1100 BU, 1102 BU, 1112 SAMS, 1802 AACF/AACG, 1851 AACF, 1856 AACG/AACS/AACW, 2102 WG, 2230 ARTC, 2233 RFC, 2313 ATS, 2500 ABG/ABW, 2523 IND, 3501 RCG, 4400 ABG, 4431 ATS, ARD FA, CNCCM, EAP DI
Gen Mitchell, Milwaukee, WI	5 TCS, 126 FIS/FS, 128 ATRG/CAMS/FIS/FIW/FW, 2423 IND, 2473 RFC, 8176 ABS, SASH
Mobile AD, Brookley, AL	4119 BU, MAD [see Brookley]
Moffett, Sunnyvale, CA	VR-3, VR-4, VR-5, VR-14, VR-44
Mohanbari, Assam, India	ATC 1352 BU
Mojave, CA	MASG-51
Molesworth RAF, Northants, England	582 ASLG, 7560 ABG, 7582 ABS/MATS/SS
Momote, Los Negros Is, Admiralty Is.	13 TCS, 338 RVM, 338 RVP
Momauk, Burma	
Monrovia, Liberia	DAO, NavAtt
Montevideo, Uruguay	24 SOW, 1130 SAS/G, 5500 FMS, URU Dt
Moody, Valdosta, GA	146 FBW/FEW, 321 FID, 2225 BU, 3550 CCTW/FTW/MSG/TNW, 4756 ADFG
Moore, Mission, TX	Training
Moriyama, Honshu, Japan	10 WG, 20 WS
Moron, Seville, Spain	3973 ABG/CSG, 7473 ABG/CSG
Morris, Charlotte, NC	156 FS/FBS/FIS, 333 BU, 8156 ABS
Morrison, W Palm Beach, FL	1 CCG, 5 ERS, 11 STU, 41 TCS, 53 RCS/RCG, 54 RCS, 55 RCS, 62 BU, 65 BU, 103 BU, 308 WRG, 325 ABG/FW, 723 BU, 785 BU, 806 BU, 900 BU, 1100 BU, 1103 BU CARDBAS
Morton, PA	BAR
Moscow, Russia	1130 SAG
Moses Lake, WA	81 FIW, 325 ABG/FW [to Larson]
Mountain Home, ID	5 ABG, 7 GCS, 9 ABG/BW/CSG, 67 TRW, 426 BU, 706 ABG, 1300 ABW, 1706 ABG, 4205 ABG
Mt Carmel, IL	2471 ARTC
Munich, Germany [R-82]	60 TCG, 1812 AACG
Muroc, CA	421 BU, 608 BU, 620 BU, 2759 ABG/EXW, 3208 COTG/SBTS, 4144 BU [to Edwards Dec49]
Muskogee, OK	349 BU
Mustin, Philadelphia, PA	Adm
Myitkyina, Burma	9 TCS, 11 CCS, 12 CCS, 315 TCS, ATC 1348 BU, CCTF
Myrtle Beach, SC	317 BU, 354 TFW, 4554 TFW
NACA, Ames	
Nadzab, New Guinea	318 TCS, 374 TCG, 375 TCG,
Nagoya, Honshu, Japan	20 WS, 1809 AACG [see Komaki]
Naha, Okinawa, Japan	33 ARS, 51 ABG/FIW, 64 ARS, 1503 ATD, 1507 SS, 6313 ABW, 6351 ABG/ABW, 6431 ABG
Nakhon Phanom, Thailand	4 SOS, 56 SOW, 360 TEWS, 361 TEWS, 362 TEWS, 366 TFW, 460 TRW, 483 TALW, 606 ACS, 1507 SS, 6498 ABW
Nanking, China	14 AF, 1130 SAG, AAG, CTGG, Nav. Att.
Nanning, China	ATC 1364 BU
Naples, Capodichino, Italy	1141 FMS/SAS, 7470 HQSS/SS, MAAG, Fasron-77, VR-24, VR-25
Narsarssuak, Greenland	6 RS, 51 ARS/RS, 1003 ABS, 1231 ABG/ABS, 1385 BU, 6611 ABG/ABS
Nashua, NH	SAINH [Saunders Ind]
Nashville, TN	20 FYG, 105 FS, 118 MALG, 558 BU, ANG
Nassau, Windsor Fld, Bahamas	Delivery point for RAF
Needles, CA	
Nellis, Las Vegas, NV	474 TFW, 3595 CCTW/FTW/PTW, 4520 CCTW, 4525 SCS
Neubiberg, Germany [R-85]	5 TOWS, 10 RTW, 86 ABG/CG/FG/FBW/FT, 317 TCW, 7101 SG
Newark, NJ	108 FW, 114 BU, 119 FS/FT/FBS, 150 AMLS, 170 ATG, 1100 BU, 4108 BU
New Castle, Wilmington, DE	2 TS, 4 FIW, 47 ARS, 82 CAMS/FG, 113 FIW, 142 ATG/FBS/FIS/FS/TFS, 166 ATG/CAMS, 525 ADFG, 552 BU, 2237 RFC, 4652 ABS, 4710 DEW, 8142 ABS, Bellanca, SAS HQ
New Cumberland, PA	53 FW, 103 RDCD, 112 FW
New Delhi, India	1127 FAG, 1130 SAG, 1134 SAS, HQ-ATC ICW, NavAtt
New Haven, CT	3510 BU
New Orleans, LA	122 FIS, 159 CAMS, 159 FG, 4159 BU, NART
Newport, AR	MAG-34
New River, Jacksonville, NC	H&MS-26
New York, NY (Floyd Bennett)	2 AFPO, 102 AMTS/BS/FIS, 106 ABG/BG/CG, 114 BS/BTS/FIS, 510 BU, 2230 ARC/RFC, 2310 ATF, EAP DI, ONR-SDC, VRF-1, VRS-1, NART
Nha Trang, S Vietnam	2 ADH, 3 TFW, 4 SOS, 5 ACS/SOS, 6 SOS, 9 SOS, 14 ACW/SOW, 361 TEWS, 460 TRW
Niagara Falls, NY	15 CAMS/FG, 76 ABS, 107 FW/FIW/TFG, 136 FS/FIS/TFS, 328 TCS, 518 ADFG, 2237 RFD, 2242 RFD, 2256 RFC, 2523 IND, 4621 SG, NART
Nichols, Manila, Luzon, Philippines	13 TCS, 65 TCS
Nome, AK	53 AYS
Norfolk, VA	Fasron-3, Fasron-102, FAW-5, VR-1 Det, VRF-1, VRF-31, VRJ-2, VR-22, VRU-22, VR-31, 5 ND Fairbetulant, Faetulant
Norman, OK (Westheimer)	185 FS
North Field, Guam, Marianas Is	19 ABG, 320 TCS, 514 RVWS [to Anderson Oct49]
North Island, Coronado, CA	Faetupac, Fasron-4, VR-32, VRF-32, VU-3, 11 ND (ex San Diego NAS) [usually known as NORIS]
North Luffenham RAF, Rutland, England [477]	9 AF
Northolt RAF, Middx, England [387]	66 TRW, 302 ATW, 513 TCW, 3918 ABS/CSG, 7500 ABG, 7513 TAG, 7560 ABG
Norton, San Bernardino, CA	1 FIW, 27 AD, 61 RS, 63 ARS/RS, 64 ARS/RS, 88 RS, 1002 ING, 1738 FYS, 2848 ABG/ABW, 4705 DW, LASX, SB AMA (ex San Bernardino)
Nouasseur, Casablanca, Morocco	7 BW, 11 BW, 17 AF, 80 ADW, 357 FIS, 1603 SS,1815 AACG, 3150 MG, 3153 FMS, 3922 ABG/CSG/MATS, 7280 ABG/ADW/MG
Noumea/Tontouta, New Caledonia	13 TCS, 403 TCG
Oahu Is, HI	7 AF
Oakland, CA	4114 BU, 61 FW, 111 RCDC, VR-4, NART
Oak Ridge, TN	AEC OT, FAC OT
Oberpfaffenhofen, Germany	10 HBS, 7290 ABG
Oberwiesenfeld, Germany	60 TCG
Oceana, VA	Fasron-5, 5 ND, VX-3
Offutt, Omaha, NB	1 ABW, 3 WW, 35 BU, 130 BU, 131 BU, 189 AACS, 759 BU, 1802 AACG, 1911 AACS, 2101 AWG, 2473 ARTC, 3902 ABG/W, 4131 BU
Ogden, UT	[see Hill]
O'Hare, Chicago, IL	56 CAMS/FG, 64 TCS, 66 FW, 106 RDCD, 108 ATRS/BS/FBS/FIS, 126 ARG/ATG/BW/CW, 142 FIW/FIS, 168 BS, 403 TCW, 501 ADG, 928 TAG/TCG, 1114 SAMS, 2223 IND, 2242 RFD, 2310 ATF, 2314 ATS, 2423 IND, 2471 RFC, 2473 RFC, 4032 BU, 4432 ATS, 4706 DEW, 8108 ABS, CECCI
Okinawa Is, Ryukyu Is, Japan	2 CCG, 311 TCS, 316 TCS, 1503 ATD, CNABS

Location	Units
Oklahoma City, OK	[see Will Rogers]
Okmulgee, OK	137 FBW
Olathe, KS	2472 ARTC/RFC, NART, NATTC
Olmsted, Middletown, PA	2 TS, 5 TS, 6 TS, 10 TCS, 11 TCS, 12 TCS, 28 TCS, 33 BU, 34 TCS, 43 TCS, 56 CLMS, 60 TCG, 105 BU, 140 AMTS, 168 ATG/MALG, 193 SOG, 309 TCS, 310 TCS, 315 TCS, 430 BU, 734 BU, 2855 ABW, 3180 WEFS, 3502 RCW, 4112 BU, 4149 BU, FLS, MAMA,
Ondal, India	ATC 1312 BU
Onote, Guam	MAG-24
Ontario Int, CA	87 RS, 163 CAMS/FG/FIG, 196 FIS/TASS, 420 BU, 443 BU, BWR,
Oppama, Honshu, Japan	Fasron-120, Japan AdvBase
Oran, Algeria	36 TCS
Orchard Place, IL	16 SAMG, 35 BU, 66 FW/NGW, 108 BS, 141 BU, 168 BS, 1100 SAMG, 1114 SAMS, 2471 ARTC [To O'Hare Sep49] [see Park Ridge]
Orlando, FL	11 PBS/TMS, 17 TMS, 438 TCG, 455 BU, 466 BU, 588 TMG, 902 BU, 1360 ABG/MATS, 2583 ABG/SBS, 4504 SS, BSS, HQSS
Orleans-Bricy, France [A-50]	98 TCS
Orly, Paris, France	117 RTW, 1127 FAG, 1130 SAG, 1171 FMS, 1602 ATD, 1606 MSS, 1630 ABG/ABS, 7415 ABG/SG, 7495 HQG, HQ OECA,
Orote, Guam	[See Agana]
Osan, S Korea [K-55]	5 AF, 18 FBW, 30 WS, 51 ABW, 58 FBW, 67 TRW, 117 RTW, 1863 AACF, 6100 SW, 6171 ABW, 6314 ABG/ABW/SW
Oscoda, MI	63 FIS, 84 ABS, 527 ADG
Oslo, Norway	3 AF, 1130 SAG, 1141 SAS, 1171 FMS, 7167 SMS, 7240 HQS/SS, MAAG, MDAP, NavAtt.
Otis, Falmouth, MA	1 ACW/SOW, 33 FG/FIW/ABG/MSG, 101 RDCD, 102 FIW, 551 AES/AEWCW, 564 ADFG, 4707 DEW, 4784 ABG
Ottawa, Ontario, Canada	1130 SAG, 1132 SAS, CCS OC, FM SF
Oxnard, Camarillo, CA	414 FG/CAMS, 533 ADFG
Page, Ft Myers, FL	338 BU
Paine, Everett, WA	57 FG, 86 ABS, 110 RDCD, 116 FSS, 326 CAMS/FG, 529 ADFG, 2343 RFD, 2346 RFD
Palau Island, Pacific	ComPalau
Palestine, IL	7280 MG
Palm Beach, FL	12 RS, 81 RS, 83 RS, 84 RS, 87 RS, 1371 MCS, 1372 MCS, 1707 ABW/ATW/FMS/MAS [ex Morrison]
Palm Springs, CA	560 BU
Panama City, CZ	PAN AD, Com-15
Paoshan, China	
Park Ridge, Chicago, IL	106 RDCD, 4803 BU [see Orchard Place]
Parks, CA	3275 INW/MTW, 3506 RCG
Patrick, Cocoa Beach, FL	6 WS, 6550 ABS/ABW, 6555 GMW/TS, AFMCE, LRPD, (ex Banana River) Nth American
Patterson, Fairfield, OH	1 TS, 5 TCS, 9 TCS, 10 TCG, 29 TCS, 550 BU, 733 BU, 901 TS, 1100 BU, 4000 BU, 4100 BU, 4140 BU [To Wright-Patterson Jan48]
Patuxent River, MD	NART, VX-6, VR-1, VR-3, VR-21, VW-2, FASRON-106 [Pax.R.] AirR&D Adm. Sup. Div., Elect Test, Radio Test, Tact.Test
Pearl Harbor, Ford Is, HI	A&T, Fasron 11
Pease, Portsmouth, NH	100 BW, 157 ARG/MAG, 509 BW, 817 ABG/CSG [ex Portsmouth AFB]
Peiping, China	ATC
Pendleton, OR	4115 BU
Pensacola, FL (Corry)	ADAU, NABTC, CNAT
Peoria, IL	169 FBS/FIS/FS/TFS/TASS, 182 TASG/TFG
Pepperrell, St Johns, Newfoundland	6 RS, 64 AD, 535 ABG, 1225 ABG, 1380 BU, 1805 AACG/AACW, 1856 AACF, 4737 ABW/ABG, 6100 ABG, 6600 ABG/ADG/ADW, 6604 ABW
Perrin, Sherman, TX	2537 BU/BW, 3555 BFTW/BPTW/CCTW/FTW/MSG, 4780 ADW
Perry, FL	342 BU
Peterson, Colorado Springs, CO	3 AWG, 15 AF, 200 BU, 201 BU, 204 BU, 209 BU, 264 BU, 268 BU, 3904 CW, 4600 ABG/ABW, 4614 CAMS
Phalsbourg, France	66 TRW, 86 FIW, 102 TFW, 366 TFW
Phan Rang, S Vietnam	3 ACW, 9 SOS, 14 SOW
Philadelphia, PA	103 BS/FBS/FIS, 111 BG/CAMS/CW, 117 BG/BS/FBS/FIS, NAMC
Phillips, Aberdeen, MD	608 BU, 613 BU, 2800 COTG, 3208 COTG, 3210 COTG, 6570 COTG/TEG
Phoenix, AZ	161 CAMS, 197 FBS/FIS, 8197 ABS, SASH, Goodyear
Phu Bai, S Vietnam	360 TEWS, H&MS-36
Phu Cat, S Vietnam	9 SOS, 12 TFW, 14 ACW/SOW, 37 TFW, 337 TFW, 361 TEWS, 460 TRW, 483 TAW
Pievre	
Pinecastle, FL	321 ABG/BW, 621 BU, 813 ABG, 903 BU [to McCoy May58]
Pinellas, St Petersburg, FL	341 BU
Pittsburgh, PA	444 BU, 500 ADG, 575 BU, 2239 ARTC
Plattsburg, NY	380 BW/CSG/STW, 820 ABG/CSG
Pleasantville, NY	GPLPY
Pleiku, S Vietnam	2 ADH, 3 SOS, 4 SOS, 9 SOS, 12 TFW, 14 ACW/SOW, 360 TEWS, 362 TEWS, 460 TRW, 633 CAMS/CSG/SOW
Pocatello, ID	
Pohang, S Korea [K-3]	MAW-1, Hedron-1
Point Mugu, CA	NAMTC, PAU, PMR, RD&DE
Pollacksville	MTG-51, MFG-51
Ponce, PR	
Ponte Olivo, Sicily, Italy	64 TCG
Pope, Fayetteville, NC	5 RS, 5 TCS, 10 ABG/TCS/TCG/MSG, 13 TCS, 16 SAMG, 35 BU, 45 TCS, 50 TCW, 62 MSG/BU, 310 BU, 311 TCS, 313 TCS, 316 TCG, 349 TCG, 437 TCG, 464 TAW/TCW, 812 BU, 815 BU, 1100 SAMG, 1113 SAMS, 2313 ATS, 2600 ABG/ABS, 4415 ABG
Port-au-Prince, Haiti	HAI FT, HAT DT, 5500 FMS
Porterfield	3 AF
Porterville, CA	473 BU,
Portland, OR	89 ABS, 123 FIS/FS, 142 CAMS/FG, 337 FG/CAMS, 357 FIS, 432 BU, 503 ADFG, 2343 ARTC/RFC, 2346 RFD, 4735 ABS, 8123 ABS, CAP, ADC, SAS HQ
Port Lyautey, Morocco	7019 BSC, VR-24, Fasron-104
Port Moresby, New Guinea	317 TCG, 374 TCG, 375 TCG, 433 TCG
Portsmouth, NH	100 ABG, 817 ABG [to Pease Sep57]
Port Washington, WI	SDC
Prague, Czechoslovakia	1130 SAG, 1134 SAS, Div Mil Int.
Pratt, KS	246 BU
Presque Isle, ME	2 STU, 23 CAMS/FG/FIW/MATS, 28 TA, 26 AD, 528 ADO, 1102 BU, 1380 BU, 4654 BCS, 4711 DEFW, NAS
Prestwick, Ayrshire, Scotland [500]	3 AF, 21 ATG, 32 ADHD, 67 ARS/RS, 1602 ATW, 1631 ABS/ABG/MATS
Pretoria, S Africa	1127 FAG, 1130 SAG, 1134 SAS, Attaché
Princeton	HMM-362
Pusan, S Korea [K-1 & K-9]	17 BW, 18 FBW, 35 FIW, 75 ADW, 452 BW, 2710 ADFW, 6002 ATW, NavAtt
Pyongtaek, S Korea [K-6]	1863 AACF, 6147 ATG/ATS, Hamron-12
Pyongyang, N Korea [K-24]	
Pyote, TX	2753 ASD/ASS
Quantico, VA	AES-12, SO&ES
Quito, Ecuador	EcuFt/AM/Dt, 5500 FMS, 7411 SS/MMS, NavAirMis
Quonset Point, RI	VX-6, A&R, A&T, CNAOT, 1 ND,
Rabat-Sale, Morocco	5 AD, 17 AF/HQS, 1127 FAG, 1859 AACF, 7221 ABG/ABS/HQS/SS, MUSOF
Ramey, Aguadilla, PR	1 RS, 24 CG/CW, 48 SVG, 55 ABG/SRW, 63 ARS, 72 ABG/BW/CSG/SRW, 73 AACG, 305 BW, 334 TCS, 521 ATG, 1370 PMD, 1601 ATG, 1806 AACG, 4017 EMP, 5900 ABS/ABW/CW, 5904 ABG [ex Borinquen]
Ramsbury RAF, Wilts, England [469]	64 TCG, 437 TCG
Ramstein, Germany	7 SOS/SOW, 26 TRW, 31 WS, 81 FIW/OS, 1857 AACF, 7030 ABW/CSW/HSS/OS/SG/SOG/SOW
Randolph, San Antonio, TX	6 ARR, 8 WG, 27 AF, 1116 SAMS, 1700 ATD, 1736 ATS, 1854 AACF/FCF, 2316 ATS, 2500 BU,

Location	Units
	2532 BU, 3300 SS, 3510 BPTW/CCTW/FTW/MSG, 3515 SS, 4430 ATG, 4434 ATS, Avn Med. Sch.
Rangoon, Burma	405 FW, 1130 SAG, 6200 ABW/MATW,
Rapid City, SD	28 ABG/BG/BW/MSG/SRW, 54 FIS, 175 FIS, 354 BU [to Weaver Jan48, then Rapid City Jun48 and Ellsworth Jun53]
Reading, PA	103 RDCD, 109 RDCD, 112 ABG, 148 FS/FBS/FIS, 438 BU, 2237 ARTC, HRS SP [to Gen. Spaatz Fld]
Ream, Imperial Beach, CA	FaetuPac
Red Bank, NJ	3151 ELG
Redmond, OR	401 BU
Reese, Lubbock, TX	3500 PTW
Reilly, Ft McClellan, AL	
Reno, NV	3 OTU, 192 FBS/FIS/FS, 8192 ABS [to Stead Jan51]
Reno Apt, NV	152 CAMS/TRG
Reykjavik, Iceland	
Rhein-Main, Frankfurt, Germany [Y-73]	2 WG, 12 AF, 60 TCG/TCW, 61 ABG/TCS/TCG/TCW, 84 ARS/RS, 86 ATS, 133 AACS, 322 TAW, 763 BU, 1000 ABG, 1408 BU, 1614 SS, 1629 ABS/SS, 1857 AACS/AACF/FCF, 1945 AACS, 7167 ATS/SAMS, 7310 ABG/ABW/MATS/SG, 7499 SG
Ribatejo, Portugal	OGMA
Rice, CA	
Richards-Gebaur, Kansas City, MO	328 CAMS/FW, 2423 IND, 2472 RFC, 4676 ABG [ex Grandview]
Richmond-R E Byrd, VA	61 BU, 120 BU, 149 FS/TFS/BS/FIS/TS, 4638 SS, ADFS, SASHQ
Rio de Janeiro, Brazil	1127 FAG, 1130 SAG, 1134 SAS, 5500 FMS, BMCD, BRAM, JBMC, NavMis.
Rio Hato, Panama	4 RCT, 5 BCS
Roanoke, VA	Penn. Central R4D school
Roberts, Birmingham, AL	
Robins, Warner-Robins, GA	3 ARR, 4 WG, 6 WD, 14 AF HQ, 25 AWS, 65 BU, 67 BU, 71 BU, 104 WG, 737 BU, 925 DPF, 930 EVS, 1100 BU, 1702 ATG, 1727 ATG/ATS, 1803 AACG, 1814 AACG, 1852 AACF, 1856 AACS, 2077 WF, 2104 AWG, 2853 ABG/ABW, 4005 BU, 4117 BU, 4197 BU, WRAMA
Rochester, MN	137 FS, 553 BU
Rockwell, Coronado, CA	
John Rogers, Honolulu, HI	19 TCS
Rome, Italy	1127 FAG, 1130 SAG, 1141 SAS, 1171 FMS, MAAG, NavAtt
Rome, NY	111 BU, 4002 BU, 4104 BU [to Griffis Jan48]
Romulus, MI	136 BU, 553 BU [see Detroit-Wayne]
Roosevelt Roads, PR	HAMRON-14, HAMRON-24, MAMRON-14, MAW-2, 10 ND Fasron-109
Rosecrans, St Joseph, MO	1 OTU/ATC, 126 BW, 139 ATG, 180 ATS/BS/BTS/FIS/TRS, 561 BU
Roslyn, Hempstead, NY	26 AD
Ross, Arcadia, CA	
Roswell, NM	320 TCS, 427 BU, 509 MSG [to Walker]
Rota, Cadiz, Spain	Fasron-104,
Rye Lake RRD	
Sacramento, CA	[see McClellan]
Saigon, S Vietnam	[see Tan Son Nhut]
St Eval RAF, Cornwall, England	
St Joseph, MO	180 TAS [to Rosecrans]
St Louis, MO	3500 BU, NART
St Paul, MN	109 FS, MAT-NW, NW MOD
St Thomas, VI	
Saipan Island, Marianas Is	9 TCS
Sale-Rabat, Morocco	[see Rabat]
Salinas, CA	451 BU, 483 BU
Saltby RAF, Lincs, England	314 TCG [32, 50, 61, 62 TCS]
Salt Lake City, UT	35 BU, 140 FW, 151 ATG/CAMS, 191 ATS/FBS/FIS/FS, 8191 ABS
Salzburg, Austria [R-80]	1142 SAS
Sampson, Geneva, NY	3650 MIW/INW
San Angelo, TX	108 FBW
San Antonio AD, Duncan Fld, TX	3 TCS, 1045 BU, 3543 BU, 3700 BTW, IDV [see Duncan] [to Kelly]
San Bernardino AD, CA	126 BU, 196 FS, 4126 BU, SBAMA [to Norton Mar50]
San Diego, CA	Fasron-7, Fasron-11, Fasron-110, Fasron-691, FAW-14, VR-5, VR-23, VR-32, VRF-2, VRU-3, VRU-32, VU-7, 11ND, Buweps, Faetupac, MABG-2, VMJ-152, MAW-2, ComFairWC, HDN MAR AIR WC, MAG-35, Convair [to North Island]
Sanford, FL	HATU, RVAH-3, VAH-3, 6ND
San Francisco, CA	68 BU, FOR SV
Sangley Point, Luzon, Philippines	VR-21, VR-23, VRU-23, Fasron 119, NavSta
San Jose, Costa Rica	58 AYD, 1134 SAS, 5713 ABS
San Juan, PR (Isla Grande)	156 CAMS/FG, 198 FS/FBS/FIS, ARS, VR-22 Det, 10 ND
San Marcos, TX	2532 BU, 2536 BU, 3585 LHTG/PTW [to Gary]
San Roque, Basilan Is, Philippines	318 TCS
San Salvador, El Salvador	24 ACW/CW/SOW, 5500 FMS, 5700 ABW, ES Dt/Ft
Santa Ana, CA	Hamron-16, Mamron-16, MAW-1, 1040 BU, 3000 BU
Santa Cruz, Bombay, India	ATC 1308 BU
Santa Maria, CA	321 BU, 440 BU, 449 BU
Santa Monica, CA	6 AF, Douglas RRD, PRO DV, M&S
Santa Rosa, CA	434 BU
Santiago, Chile	1127 FAG, 1130 SAG, 1134 SAS, 5500 FMS, 5700 ABW, 7408 MMS, Chile Dt/Ft
Santo Domingo, Dominican Rep.	24 ACW/COW/SOW, 5500 FMS
Sarasota, FL	
Savannah, GA	165 MALG
K I Sawyer, Marquette, MI	56 CAMS/FW, 410 BW, 473 FG
Schenectady, NY	109 CAMS, 139 ATS/FS/FIS/TFS
Schilling Salina, KS	310 BW/STAW [ex Smoky Hill]
Scott, Belleville, IL	8 WG, 9 WG, 16 AWS, 62 BU, 113 FIS, 139 BU, 169 FIS, 1405 ABW, 1731 ATS, 1918 AACS, 2469 RFC, 3300 HQS, 3310 TTW, 3500 BU, 3505 BU, ACC CN, ACSS, AWCS, TEC, TRCCM
Sculthorpe RAF, Norfolk, England	3 AD, 47 BW/BTW/SG, 67 RS, 97 BW, 3911 ABG, 7375 CSG, 7502 ABG/ASW/BCS
Seattle, WA	110 RDCD, NARTU, VR-5, VR-23, VRU-3, 13 ND [see Boeing Fld]
Sedalia, Knob Noster, MO (Whiteman)	1 TC, 3 TCS, 24 TCS, 25 TCS, 26 TCS, 30 TCS, 31 TCS, 60 TCS, 311 TCS, 316 TCS, 318 TCS, 322 BU, 340 ABG/BW, 375 TCG, 439 TCG, 802 BU, 813 BU [to Whiteman Oct55]
Selfridge, Mt Clemens, MI	1 FG/FW, 1 MSG/OMS, 5 ARR, 9 RS/RU, 10 AF, 30 AD, 49 ARS, 56 ABG/FG/FIW/MSG, 62 BU, 63 TCG, 106 RDCD, 136 BU, 146 BU, 575 ADG, 2151 RD, 2242 RFC, 2423 INS, 2465 MATD, 4708 ADW
Selman, Monroe, LA	2530 BU
Sembach, Germany	3 TMW, 7 ACS, 36 TFW, 38 ABG/TMW, 66 RTW/TW/TRW, 81 ARS, 603 ABW, 7127 SG, 7227 SG
Seoul, S Korea [K-16]	30 WS, 58 FBW, 374 TCW, 403 TCW, 483 TCW, 1130 SAG, 1818 AACG, 1863 AACF, 6146 ADG/FTG, 6147 ABG, 6167 ABG, 6461 TCS, AttUsna
Seville, Spain	3977 ABG, 7602 SW,
Sewart, Smyrna, TN	3 TOWS, 64 TACW, 104 RDCD/RDCF, 313 TCG, 314 TCG, 314 TCW, 316 TCG, 4413 TCW
Seymour Johnson, Goldsboro, NC	4 TFW, 83 FDW, 123 BU, 191 FIG
Shamshernagar, India	ATC 1347 BU
Shanghai, Kiangwan	ATC 1369 BU, VRU-3 Det2, VRU-23
Shaw, Sumter, SC	18 TRS, 20 ABG/FBW/FG/MSG, 35 BU, 66 RTW, 118 TRW, 139 BU, 316 BU, 363 RCW/TRW/TW, 376 BU, 837 ABG, 4411 CCTG, 4502 SS, CAPR
Shawnee, OK	StaOps
Shemya, AK	19 ADS, 5021 ABS
Shepherd's Grove RAF, Suffolk, England	81 FBW/FIW/TFW

Location	Units
Sheppard, Wichita Falls, TX	3706 BU, 3750 BTG/BTW/MSG/TTW, FTN AF, SHTTC
Sherman, Ft Leavenworth, KS	355 BU, 2223 ABS, 4405 ABS
Shingbwiyang, Burma	1 TCS, 2 TCS
Shiroi, Japan	
Sidi Slimane, Morocco	45 FS, 56 RS, 1159 AACF, 1859 AACF, 3906 ABG/CSG, ARS
Sigonella, Catania, Sicily	
Sikeston, MO	813 BU
Singapore	1127 FAG, 1130 SAG/SAW
Sioux City, Sergeant Bluff, IA	53 CAMS/FG/MATS, 79 ABS, 106 RDCS, 140 BU, 174 FS/FES/TFS, 185 TFG, 211 BU, 224 BU, 521 ADFG, 4616 ABS, 4644 ABS/SS
Sioux Falls, SD	211BU, 3507 BU [see Joe Foss]
Sitapur, India	
Sky Harbor, Phoenix, AZ	161 ATF, 197 ATS
Smoky Hill, Salina, KS	2 ABG, 40 BW, 204 BU, 247 BU, 301 ABG/MSG, 310 BW, 802 ABG [to Schilling]
Smyrna, TN	314 ABG/ATS/TCG/TCW, 316 TCG, 342 BU, 2140 BU, 2601 LTLS [to Sewart Mar50]
Sofia, Bulgaria	1130 SAG, 1134 SAS
Sondrestromfjord, Greenland	1385 BU, 4684 ABG, 6621 ABG/ABS, 7167 ARS, 8408 ABG, HIRAICT Gp
Sookerating, Assam, India	18 TCS, 64 TCG [TDY], ATC 1337 BU
South Plains, Lubbock, TX	2527 BU, 4168 BU [see Lubbock]
South Weymouth, MA	VR-3, Storage, NADU
Spangdahlem, Germany	10 RTW/TRW, 36 TFW, 49 TFW, 82 ARS, 83 ARS/RS
Spanhoe RAF, Northants, England [493]	315 TCG
Spence, Moultrie, GA	3302 TNS
Spokane, WA	84 FG, 92 ABG/BG/BW/MSG, 98 BW, 116 FIS, 141 FIG, 203 BU, 376 SRG, 4134 BU [to Fairchild Nov 50]
Springfield, OH	162 TFS/FIS, 170 FS, 178 TFG, SASHQ
Squantum, Boston, MA	NART, ProjCAST
Srinagar, Kashmir, India	MOK Gp
Stallings, Kinston, NC	Training
Standiford, Louisville, KY	123 TRG, 165 FS/FBS/FIS/TRS, 2236 ARTC
Stead, Reno, NV	8 RG, 61 ARS/RS, 62 ARS/RS, 63 ARS, 3635 CCTW/FTW, 3904 CW [ex Reno]
Stephenville, Newfoundland	1388 BU [see Ernest Harmon]
Stewart, Newburgh, NY	32 AD, 105 MAG, 115 BU, 329 CAMS/FG/MSS, 2002 BU, 2232 ARTC, 4400 ABG, 4603 ABG/CAMS, 4700 ABG/ADFG, EADF
Stockholm, Sweden	1127 FAG, 1130 SAG,
Stockton, CA	591 BU
Stout, Indianapolis, IN	113 FS, 122 FW/FIW, 315 TCG, 331 BU, 800 BU, 814 BU, 2466 ARTC, 8113 ABS, SAS HQ
Strother, Winfield, KS	269 BU
Sturgate RAF, Lincs, England	63 ARS/RS, 3928 ABG
Sturgis, KY	
Stuttgart, AR	9 TCS
Stuttgart, Echterdingen, Germany [R-50]	7005 ABS
Suffolk County, Westhampton, NY	45 FIS, 52 CAMS/FG, 77 ABS, 103 FIW, 118 FIS, 519 ADFG, 106 ARRG
Suwon, S Korea [K-13]	8 FBW, 18 FBW, 51 FIW
Sweetwater, TX	261 BU
Sylhet, Assam, India	1 CCG
Syracuse, NY	2 CCG, 4 CCG, 138 TFS/FS/FIS, 3650 INW, 4202 BU [to Hancock]
Tachikawa, Honshu, Japan [J-6]	1 TCG/ING, 13 ARS, 36 ARS, 347 TCW, 374 TCW, 1020 SAW, 1127 FAG, 1170 FMS, 1173 FMA, 1861 AACF/FCF, 2710 ABW, 6000 SG/SW, 6100 ABW/SW, 6200 MATW, 6400 ADW, 6485 OS, AMPAR, FEAMCOM, FELFR, JAMA, NMPAR, TAD
Tacloban, Leyte, Philippines	Storage
Taegu, S Korea [K-2]	5 AD HQ, 30 WS, 45 TRS, 49 FBW, 58 FBW, 67 RTW, 374 TCW, 474 FBW, 1818 AACG, 6147 ABG/TCS/ATW, 6167 ABG, 6153 ABS
Taejon, S Korea [K-5]	6146 ABU
Taichung, Taiwan	NCLTT
Tainan, Taiwan	58 FBW, 432 TFW, 868 TMS, 6214 SS/TACG, AAITT
Taipei, Taiwan	1 Det, 13 AFH, 327 ADHD, 405 FW, 1127 FAG, 1129 SAW, 1130 SAG, 1170 FMS, 6200 ABW/MATW, 6213 SS, MAAG, MAG AS, MDAP, ChNavSec, MAAG, H&MS-11, JOC
Takhli, Thailand	355 TFW, 6200 MATW
Takoradi, Gold Coast (Ghana)	Staging post
Tananarive, Madagascar	1127 FAG
Tangier, Morocco	1130 SAG, 1134 SAS
Tan Son Nhut, Saigon, S Vietnam	2 ADH, 4 ACS, 9 SOS, 360 TEWS, 366 TFW, 375 CG, 377 ABW/CSG, 405 FW, 460 TRW, 483 TAW, 1020 SAW, 1127 FAG, 1173 FMS, 6200 MATW, 6255 CSS, 6498 ABW, MAAG, MDAP, HedSupAct NSA
Taranto, Italy	[see Luigi Bologna]
Tarawa Atoll, Gilbert Is	17 TCS
Teddington, Middx, England	83 RS [not an airfield] [see Bushy Park]
Tegucigalpa, Honduras	24 CW/ACW/SOW, 7416 MMS/SU, Hon Dt
Teheran, Iran	1127 FAG, 1130 SAG, 1172 FMS, 1176 FMS, MDAP, ATC N Afr Wg, IAM
Tel Aviv, Israel	1130 SAG
Tempelhof, Berlin, Germany	158 AACS, 788 BU, 1946 AACS, 2025 LSC, 7350 ABG/ABS/BCS/SG/SS/SW, 7908 BU, HQCnfGer
Terminal Isle, San Pedro, CA	
Tezgaon, India	ATC 1346 BU
Tezpur, Assam, India	
Thermal, CA	
Thomasville, AL	
Thornbrough, Cold Bay, AK	5024 ABS
Thule, Greenland	3 TF, 55 RS, 332 FIS, 4083 ABG/ABW, 4683 ABG/ADFW, 6607 ABW, 6612 ABG
Thunderbird, Glendale, AZ	
Tingkawk Sakan, Burma	
Tinker, Oklahoma City, OK	3 MCG/MCS, 6 WDt, 33 AD, 59 WG/WW, 67 BU, 506 TFW, 513 RCS/RVWS, 925 DFS, 1100 BU, 1702 ATG, 1728 ATS, 1800 AACW, 1856 AACS, 1865 AACF/FCF, 1869 FCS, 2059 WW, 2078 AWS, 2854 ABW, 4136 BU, COAAR, OKAMA
Tobyhana, PA	
Tokyo, Japan	10 WG, 30 WS, 1173 FMS, 1503 FMS, 1808 AACW, 6000 SW, 6048 ABW, FEAF
Toledo Exp, Swanton, OH	112 TFS, 180 TFG
Tonopah, NV	422 BU
Tontouta, New Caledonia	13 AF: 13 TCS, 403 TCG
Topeka, KS	7 GCS, 55 ABG/MSG, 190 ARG, 594 BU, 736 BU, 853 TDPD, 1100 BU, 2832 SPD, 4136 BU [to Forbes Jun49]
Topsham, N Brunswick, ME	4626 ABS/SS, ADFS Maine
Torrejon, Spain	497 FIS, 1864 AACF/FCF, 3970 CSG/ABG/SRW
Toul-Rosieres, France [A-98]	10 RTW/TRW, 26 TRW, 50 FBW/TFW, 110 TFS, 117 RTW, 465 TCW, 497 FIS, 7131 TFW, 7352 ABS, 7430 ABS, 7514 SG, 7544 CSG/SG
Townsville, Qld, Aust.	317 TCG, 374 TCG
Traverse City, MI	StaOps, SwTTEU, TTF
Travis, Fairfield, CA	5 ABG/SRW, 60 ATS/MAW, 75 ATS, 1501 FMS/MS/TSW, 1733 ATS, 1800 AACW, LERGR (ex Fairfield-Suisun)
Travis, Savannah, GA	158 FBS/FIS/ATS, 165 CAMS/ATG
Trenton, NJ	141 FS
Trinidad, BWI	
Tripoli, Libya	ATC N Africa Wg

Truax, Madison, WI	115 CAMS/FG, 128 FIW/TFW, 176 FIS/FIW/FS, 327 FG/CAMS/FMS, 520 ADG, 3508 BU, 4631 ABS
Truman	
Tso Ying, Formosa	MAAG
Tsuiki, Kyushu, Japan	4 FIW, 49 FBW, 51 FIW, 67 RTW, 6131 TSW, 6150 TSW,
Tsuyung, China	1 CCG
Tucson, AZ	152 FIS/TFS, 162 CAMS/FG, GCA CP [see Davis-Monthan]
Tulihal, India	1 CCG, CCTF
Tulln, Vienna, Austria	2043 LSC, 7100 SW, 7351 ABS, 7360 ABG/BCS
Tulsa, OK	125 ATS/FBS/FIS/FS/TFS, 138 CAMS, 555 BU
Tunis, Tunisia	31 FEW, ATC
Turner, Albany, GA	31 ABG/FBW/FEW/MSG/SFIW, 108 FBW, 357 BU, 508 FEW/SFIW, 1370 CAMS/PMS/PMW, 1803 AACG, 1814 AACG, 1926 AACS, 2109 BU, 4138 CSG
Tuskegee, AL	2143 BU
Tutuila Is, Samoa Islands	VRU-1, VRU-3
Tuy Hoa, S Vietnam	9 SOS, 31 TFW, 6257 ABS
Tyndall, Panama City, FL	308 BU, 500 AUW, 3625 CCTG/CCTW/FTW/TNW/TTG, 3820 AUW, 4756 ADFG/ADFW/MSG, ADFWC
Ubon, Thailand	4 ACS, 8 TFW, 9 SOS
Udorn, Thailand	2 ADH, 3 TFW, 14 SOW, 56 SOW, 405 FW, 432 TRW, 606 ACS, 630 CSG, 6200 MATW
Upottery RAF, Devon, England [462]	439 TCG
Upper Heyford RAF, Oxford, England	20 TFW, 66 TRW, 3904 CW, 3912 ABS, 3918 ABG/CSG, 7509 ABG
U Tapao, Thailand	635 CSG, 636 CSG
Valawa	
Valley RAF, Anglesey, Wales	1407 BU
Valparaiso, Chile	NavMis.
Vance, Enid, OK	3560 PTW, 3575 PTW [ex Enid AFB]
Vandalia, OH	See Dayton
Vandenburg, Lompoc, CA	392 ABG/CSG, 4392 CSG/AEG [ex Cooke]
Van Nuys Metro, CA	62 NGW, 112 RDCD, 115 ATS/BS/FBS/FIS/TFS/TAS, 146 CG/FBW, 195 ATS/FBS/FS/TFS/TRS, 441 BU, AMV, AVM BA,
Venice, FL	337 BU
Vergiate, Italy	Macchi
Vernam, Jamaica	24 ADRS, 5912 ABS,
Vicenza, Italy	1141 SAS, MAAG
Victoria Rd, Middx, England	7500 ABG, HQ 3rd AF & 7th AD [not an airfield]
Victorville, CA	1 FIW, 3 TCS, 9 TCS, 60 TCS, 116 FBW, 452 BW, 4196 BU [to George Jun50]
Vienna, Schwechat, Austria	160 AACS, 746 BU, 1130 SAG, 1948 AACS
Vientiane, Laos	405 FW, 1020 SAW, 6200 MATW, Att.
Vincent, Yuma, AZ	34 AD HQ [ex Yuma AFB]
Waco, TX	3545 BFY, 3565 BPTW, FTN AF [to James Connally]
Walker, NM	6 STAW/BW, 9 BW, 33 FG, 509 ABG/BW/MSG, 812 ABG [ex Roswell]
Walla Walla, WA	200 BU, 423 BU
Waller, Trinidad	1 RS, 27 ADRS, 5920 ABG, 5922 MSG, 5925 ABG
Walnut Ridge, AR	RFC [storage]
Walterboro, SC	126 BU
Warazup, Burma	CCTF
Warminster, PA	NADC (ex Johnsville)
Francis E Warren, Cheyenne, WY	389 ABG/CSG/SMW, 706 SMW, 809 CSG, 3450 TTW
Warrensburg, MO	
Washington, Camp Springs, MD	DOI DC [see Andrews]
Watertown, NY	619 BU, CWT
Waycross, GA	345 BU
Wayne County, Detroit, MI	[see Detroit-Wayne]
Weaver, Rapid City, SD	28 ABG/ADR [to Rapid City Jun48]
Webb, Big Spring, TX	3560 PTW (ex Big Spring AFB)
Weeksville Storage	[USN]
Welford Park RAF, Berks, England [474]	315 TCG, 434 TCG, 435 TCG
Wellington, N Zealand	1130 SAG, 1134 SAS, ATC 1307 BU,
Wendover, UT	216 BU, 320 TCS, 4100 MB, 4432 ABS
Westchester County, NY (White Plains)	52 FW, 102 ARRS, 102 RDCD, 105 CAMS, 106 FIW, 137 AMTS/FIS/FS/TFS, 160 FIW, GPLPY
Westheimer, Norman, OK	185 FS [see Norman]
West Malling RAF, Kent, England	VR-24, Fasron-200
Weston Zoyland RAF, Somerset, England [447]	442 TCG
Westover, Chicopee Falls, MA	5 RS/WG, 6 RS, 8 WG, 46 ARS/RS, 60 TCG, 62 BU, 108 BU, 112 BU, 520 ABG/ATG, 716 BU, 814 ABG/CG, 1100 MAS, 1377 BU, 1388 ABG, 1600 ABG/ATG/ATW/MS/MSG, 1702 ATG, 1732 ATS, 1802 AACG, 1856 AACF/FCF, 1917 AACS, 2108 AWG/WG, 4050 ABG, 6600 ABG, 8405 ABG, VR-6
West Palm Beach, FL	41 TCS, CARDBAS [see Morrison]
Wethersfield RAF, Essex, England	20 FBW/TFW, 7522 ABS
Wetzlar, Germany	6608 ADFW
Wheeler, Wahiawa, Oahu, HI	
Wheelus, Tagiura, Libya	5 TOWS, 17 AF, 41 ATS, 58 ARS/RS, 60 TCW, 61 TCW, 62 ARS, 526 ABG, 580 ARCW, 1602 ATW, 1603 ABG/ATS/ATW, MS, 1615 SS, 1859 AACF, 3904 CW, 7272 ABW/FTW, 7910 AFS/BU
Whidbey Island, WA	Faetupac Det.2, Fasron-112, 13 ND
Whiteman, MO	340 BW, 351 SMW [ex Sedalia]
White Plains, NY	[see Westchester Co]
White Sands, NM	DOA OR
Whiting, Milton, FL	BTU-6, ATU VB4.4
Wichita, KS	51 AFPO, 127 FBS/FS, 3520 FTW/CCTW/TNW, 4034 BU, SASH, Boeing [To McConnell Apr54]
Wiesbaden, Germany [Y-80]	5 AACW/AACG/WG, 18 AWS/WS, 31 WS, 60 ABG/TCG/TCW, 89 BU, 117 RTW, 501 SVG, 1130 SAG, 1807 AACG/AACW, 2058 AWG, 2105 AWG, 7100 HQSW/MSG/SW, 7101 ABS/ABW, 7150 ABG, 7167 ATS/SAMS, 7405 SG/SS, 7499 CS/ SG, EATS
William Northern, Tullahoma, TN	AED CN
Williams, Chandler, AZ	13 TCS, 3010 BU, 3021 BU, 3525 AFG/CCTW/FTW/PTW, 4530 CCTW
Willow Grove, PA	2223 IND, 2237 RFC, 2523 IND, ElecTTU, HQSq APS, VR-3, NART
Willow Run, Ypsilanti, MI	30 AD HQ
Will Rogers, Oklahoma City, OK	118 TRW, 137 CAMS/FBW, 185 ATS/FBS/FIS/FS/TRS, 8117 ABS,CAA, SAS HQ
Wilmington, DE	[see New Castle Co Apt]
Winslow, Flagstaff, AZ	
Winston Salem, NC	8 BU
Wold-Chamberlain, Minneapolis, MN	[see Minneapolis Apt]
Woodbridge RAF, Suffolk, England	81 TFW
Wright-Patterson, Dayton, OH (ex Wright Fld & Patterson Fld)	1 WS, 4 WG, 6 WG, 10 TCG, 51 ARD, 72 BU, 103 AACS, 901 ATS, 1726 ATS, 1914 AACS, 2750 ABG/ABW, 3500 RCW, 4000 BU, AED DV, ADEF, ASD, Inst of Tech, URS SR, WADC, BAGRCentDist, BWFltRepCen
Wurtsmith, Oscoda, MI	379 BW/CSG, 412 CAMS/FG, 527 ADFG [ex Oscoda AFB]
Wyton RAF, Hunts, England	2 BW
Yalova, Turkey	6933 SG
Yangkai, China	ATC
Yokosuka, Japan	ComNavForJapan
Yokota, Fussamachi, Honshu, Japan [J-38]	2 CCG, 3 BTAW/BW, 3 OMS, 35 FIW, 67 TRW, 421 ATR/RFBS, 6007 RCG, 6023 REVF, 6033 OMS, 6091 RFBS, 6102 ABW, 6106 ABS, 6161 ABW
Yongdungpo, S Korea [K-27]	3 RG/RS, 5 AD HQ, 502 TCTG, 6153 ABS, 6167 ABG/ABW, 6933 SG
Yongil-wan, Pohang, S Korea	6033 OMS, 6150 TSW

CHAPTER 3: MILITARY OPERATORS OF THE DC-3, C-47, R4D, DAKOTA AND LI-2

Location	Units
Yontan, Okinawa	6351 ABW
Youngstown, OH	459 TCS, 502 ADFG, 757 TCS, 910 MATS/TAG/TCG
Ypsilanti, MI	[see Willow-Run]
Yuma, AZ	3036 BU, 4750 ABG/ADFG/ADW/TNG [to Vincent]
Yunnanyi, China	ATC
Zaragoza, Spain	3974 ABS/CSG, 7603 ABS

Unit Codes used for C-47 Units in USAAF & USAF in official records

In the course of transcribing the USAF C-47 records from microfilms and cards, codes have been identified for the various units listed. These codes have evolved over the years from a system with simple abbreviations, for example Air Transport Squadron became AT Sq or TSP Sq. Under the USAAF, units operating C-47s were either active service, such as TCS, CCS, etc., or Base Units, usually abbreviated as BAS and covering Air Transport Command as well as all the training units. However, when the USAF was formed in 1948, a plethora of units emerged with titles indicating their function and abbreviated accordingly. With time these codes tended to change, becoming shorter, as they are today. Some, particularly contractors, had an indication of the place and state where the base was situated. Over time the same code was used for different units, a cause for confusion if the date of use was unknown. Fortunately, here, dates are known.

At one stage there was an indicator letter for the type of unit, eg L, M or H for Light, Medium or Heavy, usually applied to Bomb or Transport squadrons, but these have been omitted here. There is a range of suffix letters, indicating command level, etc., S for Squadron, W for Wing, G for Group, as well as D for Detachment, C for Center, F for Flight and U for Unit. However, other meanings sometimes apply, for example D for Depot, but these are given in full in the following list. However, some codes have resisted decoding.

Codes Used Here	Unit	Codes on Official Data Sources
AACM	Alaska Air Command	AA CM
AACS/F/G/W/U	Army Airways Communications System (1943-1946) ACS Sr, Airways & Air Communication Service (1946-1961) Air Force Communications Service (1961 on)	ACSFt/Sq.Gp/Wg/Ut
AAG	Army Advisory Group	AAG
AAG	Air Advisory Gp	AAD Gp
AATC	Air Force Armament Test Center	AATCN
ABDG	Air Base Depot Group	ABDGp
ABG/S/W	Air Base Gp/Sq/Wg	ABGp/Sq/Wg, ABSWg, ABH Gp
ACC	Air Communications Center	ACC CN
ACDC	Air Force Academy Command	ACD CM
ACE	Army Corps of Engineers, Omaha, NB	ACEON
ACG/S/W	Air Commando Gp/Sq/Wg	AC Gp/Sq, ACOWg, ACRWg
ACHC	Aeronautical Chart & Information Center	ACH CN
ACH Sr	AACS Checking Service	
ADC SC	Air Defense Command San Diego, CA	ADC SC
ADCYH	Avio Diepen Corp, Ypenburg, Netherlands	ADCYH
ADEF	Air Development Force	ADE FR
ADEFA	Air Research & Development Facility	ADEFA
ADFW/G/Sx/C	Air Defense Wing/Group/Sector/Center	AD Wg, ADF Gp, ADF Wg, ADF Sx
ADG/F	Aircraft Delivery Group/Facility	ADG, ADF, ADEGp, ADYGp AD HQ Air Div Headquarters (ADH HQ, ADH Dv, Air Div ADLG)
ADGp	Air Depot Group	ADGp
ADRG/S	Airdrome Group/Squadron	ADR Gp/Sq
ADTC	Armament Development & Test Center	ADTC
ADV HQ	Advance HQ	ADV HQ
ADWC	Air Defense Weapons Center	ADWCE
ADXMF	Aerodex Inc, Miami, FL	ADXMF
AEC	Atomic Energy Commission, Kirtland, NM	AEC KM
AEDC	Arnold Engineering Development Center	AED CN
AEDD	Air Engineering Development Div	AED DV
AEWCW	Airborne Early Warning & Control Wg	AEW Wg
AFAC	AF Armament Center	AFA CN
AFATT	Air Force Attache	AFATT, ATTAT
AFDDV	AF Command & Control Development Div	AFDDV
AFDFR	AF Ballistic Missile Div. Frontier	AFD FR
AFFTC	Air Force Flight Test Center	AFTCE
AFH	Air Force Headquarters	AFH Dt, AFH HQ
AFG	Advanced Flying Group	AFY
AFMC	Air Force Missile Test Center	AFM CE
AFOPD	Air Force Operations Plans Div.	AFOPD
AF PO	Air Force Procurement Office	AF PO
AFRD	Air Force Reserve Detachment	AFR Dt
AFS/W	Air Force Squadron/Wing	AFSq/Wg
AIIMF	[Air International, Miami, FL] [American Airmotive Corp]	AINMF, AAIMF, AACMF
AILMY	Mineola Air Material Center, Aircraft Instruments Lab, Mineola, NY	AILMY
Air America	Air America, Tainan, Taiwan	AAITT
AMCPac	Air Material Command, Pacific Area	AMPAR
AMS	Aviation Medicine School	AVM Sc
AMTS	Aeromedical Transport Squadron	AML Sq
AMV	Aviation Maintenance Corp, Van Nuys, CA	AVM Cp
ANTAD	Antilles Air Depot	ANTAD
AOTC/W	Air Observers Training Center/Wing	AOT CN/Wg
APGC	Air Proving Ground Center	APG Ce
APS	Air Pictorial Service	APS
ARCW	Air Resupply & Communications Wing	ARC Wg
ARDC/F	Air Research & Development Command/Fac	ARD CM/F ARGAD
ARG Dt/Ft	Argentine Det/Flight	ARG Dt/Ft
ARP	American Republics Program	ARP
ARR	Air Force Reserve Region	ARG RG
ARS	Air Rescue Sq	ARS (see RS?)
ARS	Aircraft Repair Sq	ARE Sq, ARP Sq
ARTC/S	Air Reserve Training Center/Squadron	ART CN/Sq
ARW	Air Refuelling Wing (Heavy)	ARH Wg
ASD	Aeronautical Systems Division	AOD Dv
ASDG	Aircraft Storage & Disposition Group	ASD Gp
ASG	Aerospace Support Group/Air Service Gp	AES Gp, ASG
ASLG/S	Air Resupply Group/Squadron	ASL Gp, Sq
ASMC	Aerospace Medical Center	ASM CN
ASS	Aircraft Storage Sq/Depot	AST D/Sq??
ASW/G	Aircraft Service Wing/Group	AS Wg/Gp
ATD	Armament Test Division	ATS Dv
ATH	Armament Test Group	ATS Gp
ATKG	Air Task Group	ATK Gp
ATRS	Air Refuelling (Tactical) Sq	ATR Sq
ATS/G/W	Air Transport Sq/Gp/Wg	AT Sq/Gp/Wg, TSP Sq etc.
AUW	Air University Wing	AUW
AWCS	Airways & Air Communications Service	AWC Sr
AWS/G/W/D	Air Weather Squadron/Group/Wing/Det	AEW Sq/Gp/Wg/Dt
AYSD	Airways Det.	AYS
BADE	Canal Zone	BADE
BAL	AF Bailment	AF BALLI
BAS	Balloon Activities Squadron/Group	BA Sq, Gp, BLA Sq
BCS	Base Complement Squadron	BC Sq
BFS/D	Base Flight Squadron/Det.	BFL Sq/Dt
BFTG/W	Basic Flying Training Group/Wing	BFY Gp/Wg
BMCD	Brazil Military Com. Det.	BMC Dt
BOL Dt/Ft	Bolivian Det./Flight	BOL Dt/Ft
BPTW	Basic Pilot Training Wing	BPT Wg
BRAM	Brazil Air Mission	BRA AM
BRVM	[Far East]	
BSS	Base Service Squadron	BSR Sq
BTrW/Gp	Basic Training Wing/Group	BTN Wg/Gp
BTW/S	Bombardier Training Wing/Squadron	BMT Wg/BTA Wg/Sq

BU	Base Unit	BAS
BUD	Base Unit District	BUD
BW, BS, BS	[Bomb Wing (Heavy or Medium)]	BHWg, BMWg, BG, BS
	[Bomber Light (Jet) Wing]	BJL Wg, BL Sq
CAMS/G	Consolidated Aircraft Maintenance Sq/Gp	CAM Sq, CLM Sq/Gp
CAP/W	Civil Air Patrol/Wing	CIV AP, CAP Rg/Wg
CARCE	Cambridge Research Center	CARCE
CASA	Construcciones Aeronauticas SA, Madrid	CASAM, CAFMS
CASAM	Casco Air Service, Albuquerque, NM	CASAM
CCG/S	Combat Cargo Group/Squadron	CCGp, CCSq, CBC Gp
CCG/S	Combat Cargo Group/Squadron	CCG/S
CCM Gp	Combat Commando Gp	CCM Gp, CCS Gp
CCTG/S/W	Combat Crew Training Gp/Sq/Wg	CCT Gp/Sq/Wg
CDB	Caribbean Delivery Base	CARDBAS
CDM	Continental Division Mil. Tpt. Cmd.	CON Dv
CECCI	Cook Electric Co, Chicago, IL	CECCI
CEPDI	Central Air Procurement District	CEPDI, CHD
Chile Ft	Chile Flight	CHL Ft
CMO D/S	Troop Carrier (Commando) Dt/Sq	CMO Dt, CMO Sq
CMTS/U	Cold Weather Material Test Sq/Unit	CMT Sq/Ut
CNCC	Continental Air Command	CNC CM
COAA	Continental AACS Area	COOAR
Col Ft/Dt	Colombia Flight/Det	COL Ft/COL Dt
COTG	Calibration & Ordnance Test Group	COT Gp
CRC	Cambridge Research Center	CARCE
CRYC	Cryptological Center	CRC CE
CSG/W	Combat Support Group/Wing	COS Gp, CS Gp, Cos Wg
CSV	Communications Service	CSV
CTG	Composite Test Group	COT
CTTC	Chanute Technical Training Center	CTC CN
CUD	Cuba Detachment	CUBA Dt
CVS	Consolidated Vultee, San Diego, CA	CVC SD
CW	Composite Wg	CT Wg
CW/G/S	Composite Wing/Group/Squadron	CMP Wg, CMP Gp, CMP Sq
CWTD	Cold Weather Test Detachment	CWT Dt
DET Dt	Detachment	DET Dt
DEW	Defense Wing	DEF Wg
DFS	Depot Feeder Squadron	DPF Sq
DFt	Air Depot Flight	DEP Ft
DG	Drone Group	DRO Gp
DMI	Division of Military Intelligence	Div Mil Int
DM Sq/Wg	Air Defense Missile Squadron/Wing	DM Sq, DM Wg
DOA OR	Dept of the Army, Ops Range, White Sands, NM	DOA OR
DOI DC	Dept of Interior, DC	DOI DC
Douglas	Douglas, Chicago, IL	DC RRD
Douglas	Douglas, Santa Monica, CA	DUG SM
DW	Depot Wing	Dep Wg
EAA AR	European African Middle East AACS Area	EAA AR
EADF	Eastern Air Defense Frontier	EAD Fr
EAPD	Eastern Air Procurement District	EAP DI
ECA	Economic Cooperation Administration	ECA
ECD/F	Ecuador Det./Flight	ECU Dt/Ft
EDC	Engineering Development Center	EDC
EES	Electronics Experimental Squadron	EEL Sq
EGMG	Experimental Guided Missile Group	EGMGp
ELDDV	Electronics Development Div., Hanscom	ELDDV
ELS	Electronics Squadron	ELE Sq
ENG	Air Engineering Squadron	ENG
ENTF	European Northern Disposition Task Force [see ERG below?]	ENTF
ERDG	Electronics Research & Development Gp	ERD Gp
ERG/S	Electronic Research Group/Squadron	ER Gp/Sq, ERE Sq
ESD	Electronics Systems Division	ELD, EMP
ESF	El Salvador Flight	ES Ft
EVS	Evacuation Squadron	EVSq
EXW	Experimental Wing	EXW
FAC BM	Fairchild Aircraft Co, Baltimore, MD	FAC BM
FAC FN	Fairchild Aircraft Co, Farmingdale, NY	FAC FN
FAC HM	Fairchild Aircraft Co, Hagerstown, MD	FAC HM
FAC OT	Fairchild Aircraft Co, Oak Ridge, TN	FAC OT
FAG	Field Activities Group	FA Gp
FAMC	Far East Air Material Command	FAM CM
FBW	Fighter Bomber Wing	FB Wg
FCF/S	AACS Field Checking Flight/Sqn	FCH Ft/Sq
FDT	Fighter Det.	FDt
FEA AF	Far East Air Force	FEA AF
FEAMCOM	Far East Air Material Command	FEAMCOM
FEF	Far East Air Logistics Frontier	FELFR
FERBF	SFERMA, Bordeaux, France	FERBF
FEW	Fighter Escort Wing	FE Wg
FG/FW/FS	[Fighter Group/Wing/Sq]	FTR Gp/Wg, Fs Sq
FIS/W	Fighter Interceptor Sq/Wg	FI Sq/Wg
FLS	Flight Service	Flt Sr
FLTS	Flight Test Squadron	FLT Sq
FMSt	Foreign Mission Staff	FMSt, FM SF
FMS/U	Field Maintenance Squadron/Unit	FDMSq/Ut, FM Sq, FLMSq
FOG	Flight Operations Group	FLO Gp
For Sv	Forestry Service	FOR SV
FSH	Flight Service HQ	FLS HQ
FS/W	[Fighter Day Sq/Wg]	FDA Sq/Wg
FTN AF	Flying Training Air Force	FTN AF
FTRC	Flying Training Center	FTR CN
FTS	Flight Test Squadron	FLT Sq
FTW/G	Flying Training Wing/Group	FTA Wg, FTN Wg, FTN Gp
FWS/W	[Fighter All Weather Sq/Wg]	FWSq/Wg
FYG/S	Ferry Group/Squadron	FRY Gp, FER Sq, FRY Sq
GCA	Grand Central Aircraft Co	GCA CP
GCS	Geodetic Control Sq	GEC Sq
GLRRD	General Electric RRD	GLRRD
GMW/S	Guided Missile Wing/Squadron	GMW/Sq
Goodyear	Goodyear, Akron, OH	GDYAO
GPLPY	General Precision, Pleasantville, NY	GPLPY
GREAM	Greek Air Mission	GRE AM
GSA	General Services Admin.	GSA-AID
GUF/D	Guatemala Ft/Det	GML Ft/Dt
HAA	Heavy Administrative Airplane Det.	HAA Dt
HACHT	Hughes Acft Co, Hondo, TX	HAC HT
HADC	Holloman Air Development Center	HLD CE
HATD/F	Haiti Det/Ft	HAT Dt/Ft
HBS/S	HQ & Base Services Air Depot/Sqn	HBS AD, HBS Sq
HIRAICTGP	Hiran Air Composite Gp	HIRAICTGp
HOND/F	Honduras Detachment/Flight	HON Dt/Ft
HQG/W	Headquarters Group/Wing	HQS Gp/Wg
HQSS	Headquarters Support Gp/Sq	HQS Gp/Sq? HRS Sp
HS	Helicopter Squadron	HEL Sq
Hughes	Hughes Aircraft Co, Culver City, CA	HAC CU
IAASC	Inter American Air Forces Academy School	IAASC
ICHD	India-China Div, ATC	ICHD
IDT	Indoctrination Detachment	IND Dt
IDV/Wg	Indoctrination Division, Wing	IND Dv, Wg
IMS	Installation & Maintenance Sq	IM Sq
INGG/S	Inspector General Group/Sq	ING Gp/Sq, ING
INSD	Instructor Det/Sq	INS Dt/Sq
IRAM	Iran Air Mission	IRNAM
ITHQ	Institute of Technology HQ	ITHQ
JAAGp	Joint American Advisory Group	JAAGP
JAMA	Japan Air Material Area	JAMA
JBMC	Joint Brazil/US Mil. Comm.	JBUSMC
JLRPG	Joint Long Range Proving Ground	JLR PG
JMAG	Joint US Military Advisory Group	JUGJM
JMP Gp	Joint US Military Advisory Gp to Philippines	JMP GP
JMS	Joint US Military Group (Spain)	JMS
JUSJM	Joint US Military Aid to Greece	JUSJM

Chapter 3: Military Operators of the DC-3, C-47, R4D, Dakota and Li-2

KTTC	Keesler Technical Training Center	KTCCN
LA SX	Los Angeles Sector	LA SX
Lear	Lear Inc, Grand Rapids, MI	LERGR
LHT Gp	Liaison Helicopter Training Group	LHT Gp
LIAFT	Liaison Flight, Mexico	LIAFT
LMC	Lackland AMC	LMC CM
Lockheed	Lockheed Act Ind., Cheyenne, WY	LAICW
LOGC	Logistics Command	LOG CM
LOMC	Lockheed Modification Center	LO MOD CN
LRPD	Long Range Proving Ground Division	LRP Dv
LSC	Labour Supervision Company	LS Co
LTC	Lowry Technical Training Center	LTCCE
LTL Sq	Assault Sq (Light)	LTL Sq
MAAD	Medium Administration Aircraft Det.	MAA
MAAG	Military Assistance Advisory Group	MAG MG
MAAG	Military Assistance Advisory Group	MAG AS
Macchi	Macchi, Vergiate, Italy	MACVI
MALG/W	Military Airlift Group/Wing	MAL Gp/Wg
MAMA	Middletown AMA, Olmsted, PA	MID AR, MAAAR
MATS/W	Material Squadron/Wing	MAT Sq/Wg
MATSS	Military Air Transport Service Sq	MATS Sq
MBS	Maneuver Base Sq	MB Sq
MCG	Mobile Communications Group	MOCGp
MCS	Mapping & Charting Squadron	MCH Sq
MD	Missile Division	MSL Dv
MDAP	Mutual Defence Aid Program	MDAPr
MDC CE	Military Development Test Center	MDC CE
MDG	Maintenance Depot Group	MND Gp
MDP DP	Manila Air Depot	MDP Dp
MHRCM	Minneapolis Honeywell Reg, Minneapolis, MN	MHRCM
MID	Military Intelligence Div	MID
MIT	Massachusetts Institute of Technology Cambridge, MA	MITCM
MMS	Military Mission Service	MMS
MOAMA	Mobile Air Material Area	MOB AR, MOAAR
MOKG	Military Observer Group in Kashmir	MOK Gp
MS/G	Maintenance Sq/Gp Fairfax Co, VA [Contractor]	MAI Sq/Gp/Ut MPI FV MRI AC
MSG/S	Maintenance & Supply Gp/Sq	MSU Gp/Sq
MSLD	Missile Division	MSL Dv
MSN Hq	Congo Mission HQ	MSN HQ
MSTW	Missile Test Wing	MST Wg
MTCS	Military Transport Command Service	MTC Sr
MTG	Mobile Training Group	MBT Gp
MTGW	Military Airlift Training Wing	MTG Wg
MTW	Military Training Wing	MIT Wg
MUMS	Munitions Maintenance Sq	MUMSq
MUSOF	Morocco US Logistics Office, Rabat	MUSOF
NACA	Natl Adv Cttee for Aeronautics Lab.	NACL
NAFCE	National Avn. Facilities Exptl Center	NAFCE
NAMIC	North American Avn, Inglewood, CA	NAMIC
NASWF	Naval Air Special Weapons Facility	NASWF
NCCTT	Nationalist China? Taichung, Taiwan	NCCTT
NGA HQ/W/S	National Guard HQ/Wing/Squadron	NGA HQ, NG Wg, NGA Sq
NICD	Nicaragua Detachment	NIC Dt
NOLDBAS	North Atlantic Delivery Base	NOLDBAS
NPAMA	Northern AMA, Pacific	NMP AR
NSF	Nuclear Support Force	NSF
Northrop	Northrop Aircraft, Hawthorne, CA	NTHHC
NW MOD	Northwest Airlines Modification Ctr	NW MOD
OAR HQ	European Office of Aerospace Research, Brussels	OAR HQ
OASC	Ogden Air Service Command	OASC
OF/OG/OS	Operations Flight/Group/Squadron	Op Ft/GP, OPR Sq, OPS
OGAMA	Ogden Air Material Area	OGDAR
OGMA	Of. Ger. de Mat. Aeron., Ribatejo, Portugal	OGM RP
OKAMA	Oklahoma City Air Material Area	OKL AR, OCAAR?
OMS	Organizational Maintenance Sq	OM Sq
OTC	Operational Test Center	OTC CE
OTW	Observer Training Wing	OBT Wg
PAL	Philippine Air Lines, Manila	PALMI
PAM Cp	Pacific Airmotive Corp	PAM Cp
PAN AD	Panama Air Depot	PAN AD
PAO	Port Air Officer	PAO
PARF/AM	Paraguay Flight/Air Mission	PAR Ft/AM
PAWA	Pan American World Airways, Brownsville, TX	PAW BT, PWA BT
PBS	Pilotless Bomber Squadron	PBL Sq
PCS	Photo Charting Squadron	PCS
PDP DP	Philippine Air Depot	PDP DP
PERD	Peru Detachment	PER Dt
PGC	Air Proving Ground Command Center	PGC CE
PGP	Proving Ground (Provisional)	PGP
PHG/S	Photo Group/Squadron	PHOGp/Sq
PMS	Periodic Maintenance Sq	PEM Sq
PMW/D/S	Photo Mapping & Charting Wing/Det/Sq	PMC Wg/Dt/Sq
PRO Dv	Procurement Division	PRO DV
PTCS	Provisional Troop Carrier Squadron	PTCS
PTG/W	Proof Test Group/Wing	PTS Gp/Wg
PTW	Pilot Training Wing	PTN Wg
RAD	Rome AF Depot	RDP DP
RA RRD	Republic Aircraft, Evansville, IN	RA RRD
RCG/W	Recruiting Group/Wing	REC Gp, REC Wg
RCS/G	Reconnaissance Sq/Group	(RCM Sq, RCN Sq, RCW Gp, RC Gp, RC Sq)
RDCD/F/S/U	Radar Calibration Det/Ft/Sq/Unit	RDC Dt/Ft/Sq/U
REVS/F	Radar Evaluation Squadron/Flight	REV Sq, RDE Ft
RFC/D	Air Force Reserve Flying Center/Det	RFC CN/DT
RFBS	Air Refuelling (Fighter Bomber) Sq	RFB Sq
RG/RS/RD/RU	Rescue Group/Squadron/Det/Unit	(RES Gp, Sq, Dt, RCU Sq, Res UT)
RODC	Rome Air Development Center	RODCE, ROM AR
RRD	Resident Representative Delivery	RRD
RTW/S/G	Reconnaissance Wing/Sq (Tactical)	RCT Wg, RCT Sq, RCT Gp
RVM	Reconnaissance V Long Range Mapping Sq	RVM
RVPS/G	Reconnaissance V Long Range Photo Gp	RVPSG, RVP Gp
RVWS	Reconnaissance Very Long Range Weather	RVLRWSq, RVW Gp, RVWSq
SAAMA	San Antonio Air Mat Area	SAAAR
SAD/G/S/W	Special Activities Det/Gp/Sq/Wg	SPA Dt, Gp, Sq, Wg, SPESq
SAINH	Saunders Assocs Inc, Nashua, NH	SAINH
SAMA	Sacramento Air Material Area	SMAAR, SAR AR
SAMG/S	Special Air Missions Group/Squadron	SAM Gp, Sq
SAPDI	Southern Air Processing District	SAPDI
SBAMA	San Bernardino Air Material Area	SB AR, SBAD
SBTS	Stratospheric Bomb Test Sq	SBT Sq
SBS	Standby Base Sq	STBSq
SCS	School Sqn	SCH Sq
SCU	Statistical Control Unit, TSP	SCU TSP
SDG	Specialized Depot Group	SPD Gp
SECW	Security Wing	SCWg
SEVG/S	Strategic Evaluation Group/Squadron	SEVG/S, SST Gp
SFW	Strategic Fighter Wing	SFI Wg
SG/SS/SW	Support Group/Wing	SUP/SUT/SUSGp/Sq/Wg
SHTC	Sheppard Test Center	SHT CE
SLA Sc	USAF School for Latin America	SLA Sc
SMW	Strategic Missile Wing	SM/STM Wg
SMWg	Strategic Recon. Medium Wing	SM Wg?
SOG/W	Special Operations Group/Wing	SOP Gp, Wg
SOMAR	Southern Air Material Area Pacific	SOMAR
SOS	Special Operations Sq	
SOTG	Special Operations Training Group	SOT Gp
SPAMA	Southern Pacific AMA	SMPAR/SMPA
SPP	Special Project	SPEPRJ
SR ADG	[unknown]	

SRFW	Strategic Reconn. Flight Wing	SRFWg
SRG/W	Strategic Reconnaissance Gp/Wg	SRG, SRC/SRH/ STR Wg
SRWS	Strategic Recon. Weather Sqn	SMWS
SS	Search Squadron	SSq
SSTG	Strategic Standardisation Group	SSTGp
STAW	Strategic Aerospace Wing	STA Wg
STC	Staging Command	StC
STCS	Station Complement Squadron	STC Sq
STSq	Staff Squadron	STSQ
STU/G	Station Unit/Group	STA Unit/Gp
SVG	Servicing Group	Sr Gp
SWC/Gp	Special Weapons Center/Group	SPW CE/GP
SWCC	AF Special Weapons Command Center	SWC CE
SWRS	Strategic Weather Reconnaissance Squadron	SMW Sq
TAC	Tactical Center	TAC Cn
TACd	Tactical Air Command	TAC AC
TACC	Tactical Command	TAC CM
TACG/W	Tactical Air Command Group/Wing	TAC Gp, TAC Wg
TACTG	Tactical Group	TAT Gp
TAD	Tachikawa Air Depot	TAD DP
TAM	Turkish Air Mission	TRK AM
TASS/G	Tactical Air Support Sq/Gp	TAS Sq/Gp
TAW/G	Tactical Airlift Wing/Group	TAL Wg/Gp
TBG	Tactical Bomb Group	TBM Gp
TC	Training Command	TRC
TCAW/D	Troop Carrier Assault Wg/Det	TCAW, TCADt
TCG/S/W	Troop Carrier Group/Sq/Wg	TC/TCM/ TCH Gp, Sq, Wg
TCTG	Tactical Control Group	TCL/TCT Gp
TD	Topeka AF Depot	TDP Depot
TEG/S/W	Test Gp/Sq/Wg	TES Gp, Sq, Wg
TEWS	Tactical Electronic Warfare Sq	TEWS
TF	Task Force	TSK Fr
TFG/S/W	Tactical Fighter Gp/Sq/Wg	TFG Gp, Sq, Wg, TFT Wg
TMW	Tactical Missile Sq/Wg	TM Sq, Wg
TNG/S/W	Training Gp/Sq/Wg	TNG Gp, Sq, Wg
TNPS	Tactical Night Photo Sq	TNP Sq
TOAIC	Transocean Airlines Inc	
TRAW	Training Aids Wing	TA Wg
TRC	Training Command	TRC CM
TRG/S	Tactical Photo Jet Gp/Sq	TPJ Gp, Sq,
	Tactical Night Jet Sq	TNJ Sq
TRW/S/G	Tactical Reconnaissance Wing/ Sq/Gp	TR Wg, TR Sq, TRN Wg, TR Gp
TS/G	Tow Squadron	TOW Sq
TSW/S	Tactical Support Wing/Sqn	TST Wg, TS Sq
TTW/G	Technical Training Wing/Group	TTA/TTN Wg, TTA Gp
UNB CT	UN Committee to the Balkans, Hassani	UNB CT
UOMAM	University of Michigan	UOMAM
URD	Uruguay Detachment	URGDt
URS	USAF Recruiting Service	URS Sr
USSS	USAF Security Service	USSR
VEND/F	Venezuela Det/Ft	VEN Dt, VEN Ft
WADC	Wright Air Development Center	WRD CN
WADF	Western Air Defense Force	WAD Fr
WCW	[unknown]	WCW
WEFTS	Weather Equipment Flight Test Sq	WEF Sq
WF/G/S/W/ D/U	Weather Flight/Gp/Sq/Wg/Det/Ut	WEA Gp, Fl, Sq, Wg, Dt, Ut
WHS	White Sands, NM	WHS
WRAMA	Warner Robins Air Material Area	WRAAR, WRAD
WRS/G	Weather Reconnaissance Squadron/ Group	WER Sq/Gp

Air Force Commands

The abbreviations used for Air Force Commands are given below:

AAC	Alaska Air Command [Oct46]
ACD	AF Academy Command
ADC	Air Defense Command
AFC	Air Ferry Command
AFE	Air Force Europe
AFR	Air Force Reserve?
AMC	Air Material Command – AMO = AM Overseas
ANG	Air National Guard
ARD	AF Research & Development Command
ARO	AF Research & Development Command Overseas
ASC	Air Service Command
ATC	Air Transport Command – ATO = AT Overseas – ATS?
ATSC	Air Technical Service Command [Aug44]
BFC	Bolling Field Command
CAC	Caribbean Air Command (or Central America Cmd?)
CAF	Continental Air Forces
CEN	AAF Center
CG	Commanding General
CNC	Continental Air Command
CNR	Continental Air Command Reserves
CO1	Commanding Officer 1st AF etc
CSO	Facility Checking Service Overseas
CSV	Facility Checking Service
CTC	Continental AF Troop Carrier Cmd
C21	Commander 21st Bomb Wing
FEA	Far East Air Force [Dec45]
FFC	Ferry Flight Command
HQC	Headquarters Command – HQO = HQ Overseas
LOG	Logistics Command [Apr61]
LRP	Long Range Proving Ground Command
MATC	Material Command
MTC	Military Transport Command – MTO = MT Overseas
NEA	North East Air Command
PAC	Pacific Air Command
PAF	Pacific Air Forces [Jul57]
PDC	Personnel Distribution Command
SAC	Strategic Air Command [Mar46] – SAO = SA Overseas
SOU	Southern Command
SYS	Systems Command [Apr61]
TAC	Tactical Air Command [Mar46] – TAO = TA Overseas
TCC	Troop Carrier Command
1TC	1st Troop Carrier Command
3 AD	3rd Air Division

USAAF Serial/Constructor's Number Index

Apart from a few serial numbers that were allotted but never used, and some others that are not absolutely confirmed, the USAAF presents no problems. The vast majority of DC-3 derivatives were ordered in huge blocks of numbers issued in order with the c/ns. Errors in applying the c/ns were outlined in Chapter 1 and are now fully understood. Some confusion arises with those aircraft which remained in use for over ten years. These received a prefix "O" for Over Ten Years old, to avoid confusion with aircraft issued with later fiscal year prefixes.

Thus, 42-100710 was reduced to "O-2710" but the more usual form might be 0-48098 for 43-48098. Indeed, serials were applied to aircraft almost exclusively with the digit 0, not the capital letter, as photographs in this book illustrate. Some C-47s had two or even three variants in their serial number, causing much confusion during the years from 1955 to 1957 when the system was standardised on a "O" plus either the last five digits or the last four and the fiscal year digit. In this edition the letter "O" has been omitted except for a few non-standard uses.

The main problem in trying to include such numbers is that reports often have no date given, so the order of use is unknown. What is known is that every aircraft carried such numbers, in whatever form.

By 1969 when tactical aircraft were camouflaged, some C-47s used in Vietnam acquired a further variant on the serial numbers, using the last five digits, at first as the last three in white plus two further digits in black and much smaller. These two could be the fiscal year or the last of these plus one from the aircraft number. A further complication involves some

Chapter 3: Military Operators of the DC-3, C-47, R4D, Dakota and Li-2

supplied under aid programmes in Africa, where only the last three were applied. Some of these went to the Congo. Others were supplied to Vietnam, Laos or Cambodia, some of which have not been identified with certainty.

In the following tabulation, as with the United Kingdom, space is saved by not listing every serial and its respective c/n; instead the ranges of consecutive serials and c/ns, where they occur, are shown separated by an oblique (/).

DC-2 derivatives:-

Serial	Type	c/n
36-1	C-32	c/n 1414
36-70/87	C-33	1503/20
[36-70 to C-38]		
36-345/46	C-34	1415/16
38-499/501	C-39	2057/59
38-503	C-42	2060
38-504/35	C-39	2061/92
41-1374	C-32A	1374
41-1375	C-32A	1375
41-1376	C-32A	1376
(42-53527)	C-32A	1239
42-53528	C-32A	1249
42-53529/31	C-32A	1310/12
(42-53532)	C-32A	1367
42-57154	C-32A	1252
42-57155	C-32A	1298
42-57156	C-32A	1300
42-57227	C-32A	1250
42-57228	C-32A	1254
42-58071	C-32A	1238
42-58072	C-32A	1313
42-58073	C-32A	1406
42-61095	C-32A	1242
42-61096	C-32A	1245
42-65577	C-32A	1243
42-65578/9	C-32A	1293/4
42-68857	C-32A	1297
42-68858	C-32A	1246
42-70863	C-32A	1241
(44-83226)	C-32A	1375
44-83227	C-32A	1376

DC-3 derivatives:-

Serial	Type	c/n
38-502	C-41	c/n 2053
40-70	C-41A	2145
41-7681	C-48	3256
41-7682/84	C-48A	4146/48
41-7685/89	C-49	3270/74
41-7690	C-49A	3282
41-7691/93	C-49B	4094/96
41-7694	C-49	3297
41-7695	C-50C	4083
41-7696	C-50D	4084
41-7697/700	C-50	4119/22
41-7701	C-52C	4136
41-7702	C-51	3289
41-7703/05	C-50B	4109/11
41-7706/07	C-52B	4127/28
41-7708	C-52	4112
41-7709	C-50D	4131
41-7110/11	C-50A	4804/05
41-7712/13	C-50D	4134/35
41-7714	C-52A	4813
41-7715	C-49C	4814
41-7716/20	C-49D	4141/45
41-7721	C-49C	4815
41-7722/25	C-47-DL	4200/03
41-7726/42	C-47-DL	4205/21
41-7743/92	C-47-DL	4230/79
41-7793/807	C-47-DL	4285/99
41-7808/60	C-47-DL	4307/59
41-7861/66	C-47-DL	4369/74
41-18337/94	C-47-DL	4375/432
41-18395/97	C-47-DL	4442/44
41-18398/465	C-47-DL	4460/527
41-18466/536	C-47-DL	4558/628
41-18537/603	C-47-DL	4662/728
41-18604/38	C-47-DL	4765/99
41-18639/72	C-47-DL	6000/33
41-18673/99	C-47-DL	6079/105
41-19463/99	C-47-DL	6106/42
41-20045	C-53-DO	4810
41-20046	C-53-DO	4816
41-20047/50	C-53B-DO	4817/20
41-20051	C-53-DO	4821
41-20052	C-53B-DO	4822
41-20053/56	C-53-DO	4823/26
41-20057/59	C-53B-DO	4827/29
41-20060/136	C-53-DO	4830/4906
41-38564/78	C-47-DL	4445/59
41-38579/600	C-47-DL	4528/49
41-38601/25	C-47-DL	4629/53
41-38626/50	C-47-DL	4729/53
41-38651/75	C-47-DL	6034/58
41-38676/83	C-47-DL	6071/78
41-38684/763	C-47-DL	6143/222
42-5635/70	C-47-DL	6223/59
42-5671	XC-47C-DL	7365
42-5672/92	C-47-DL	7366/86
42-5693/704	C-47-DL	9000/11
42-6455/504	C-53-DO	4907/56
42-6505	C-52D	3275
42-14297/98	C-68-DO	4173/74
42-15530/69	C-53-DO	7325/64
42-15870/94	C-53-DO	7387/411
42-23300/4407	C-47A-1-DL	9162/208
42-23347/55	C-47A-5-DL	9209/17
42-23356/79	C-47A-10-DL	9218/41
42-23380/412	C-47A-15-DL	9242/74
42-23413/537	C-47A-20-DL	9275/399
42-23538/80	C-47A-25-DL	9400/42
42-23581/787	C-47A-30-DL	9443/649
42-23788/961	C-47A-35-DL	9650/823
42-23962/4088	C-47A-40-DL	9824/950
42-24089/138	C-47A-45-DL	9951/10000
42-24139/321	C-47A-50-DL	10001/183
42-24322/37	C-47A-55-DL	10184/99
42-24338/407	C-47A-60-DL	10200/69
42-24408/19	C-47-DL	13779/90
42-32786/935	C-47-DL	9012/161
42-38250	C-49H-DO	4116
42-38251	C-49H-DO	4118
42-38252	C-49G-DO	1915
42-38253	C-49H-DO	4130
42-38254	C-49H-DO	1993
42-38255	C-49G-DO	1949
42-38256	C-49D-DO	1923
42-38257	C-49H-DO	2126
42-38258	C-48C-DO	3276
42-38259	C-48C-DO	4114
42-38260	C-48C-DO	3275
42-38324	C-48B-DO	2223
42-38325	C-48B-DO	3263
42-38326	C-48B-DO	3264
42-38327	C-48C-DO	2147
42-38328	C-49H-DO	4133
42-38329	C-49H-DO	4099
42-38330	C-49H-DO	2272
42-38331	C-49H-DO	4107
42-38332/34	C-48C-DO	4170/72
42-38335/36	C-48C-DO	4175/76
42-38337	C-48C-DO	4178
42-38338	C-48C-DO	4182
42-43619	C-49E-DO	1494
42-43620	C-49E-DO	2165
42-43621	C-49E-DO	2149
42-43622/23	C-49E-DO	2263/64
42-43624	C-49D-DO	1916
42-47371/82	C-53-DO	7313/24
42-56089	C-48B-DO	4113
42-56090	C-48B-DO	1957
42-56091	C-48B-DO	1955
42-56092	C-49E-DO	1499
42-56093	C-49E-DO	1976
42-56094	C-49E-DO	1549
42-56095	C-49E-DO	1500
42-56096	C-49E-DO	1498
42-56097	C-49E-DO	1495
42-56098	C-48B-DO	1960
42-56099	C-48B-DO	1958
42-56100	C-48B-DO	1953
42-56101	C-48B-DO	1977
42-56102	C-48B-DO	2222

42-56103	C-49E-DO	1496
42-56104	C-49E-DO	2216
42-56105	C-49E-DO	1497
42-56106	C-49E-DO	2217
42-56107	C-49E-DO	2127
42-56609	C-48B-DO	1959
42-56610	C-48B-DO	3265
42-56611	C-48B-DO	1952
42-56612	C-48B-DO	1951
42-56613	C-49F-DO	2224
42-56614	C-49G-DO	1948
42-56615	C-49G-DO	1971
42-56616	C-49F-DO	2225
42-56617/18	C-49E-DO	4081/82
42-56619	ntu	
42-56620/21	C-49F-DO	1931/32
42-56622	ntu	
42-56623	C-49F-DO	2028
42-56624	ntu	
42-56625	C-49E-DO	1933
42-56626	C-49E-DO	4132
42-56627	C-49E-DO	2267
42-56628	C-49F-DO	2255
42-56629	C-48B-DO	2185
42-56630/31	C-49G-DO	1997/98
42-56632	C-49G-DO	1999 or 2246
42-56633	C-49F-DO	2226
42-56634	C-49E-DO	2271
42-56635	C-49G-DO	1996
42-56636	C-49F-DO	4129
42-56637	C-49F-DO	3251
42-57157	C-84-DO	1922
42-57506	C-49H-DO	2198
42-57511	C-84-DO	1924
42-57512	C-84-DO	1934
42-57513	C-84-DO	2027
42-65580	C-49H-DO	2167
42-65581	C-49H-DO	2203
42-65582	C-49H-DO	2205
42-65583	C-49-DO	4091
42-65584	C-49D-DO	3280
42-68687/89	C-49H-DO	2179/81
42-68693/851	C-53D-DO	11620/778
42-68860	C-49D-D0	3285
42-78026	C-48C	1954
42-78027	C-48C	4125
42-78028	C-48C	1905
42-92024/091	C-47A-DK	11779/853+
42-92092/415	C-47A-1-DK	11854/12213+
42-92416/572	C-47A-5-DK	12214/387+
42-92573/743	C-47A-10-DK	12389/577+
42-92744/923	C-47A-15-DK	12579/777+
42-92924/3283	C-47A-20-DK	12779/13177+ except
42-93159	C-47B-5-DK	13040
42-93284/823	C-47A-25-DK	13179/777+
42-100436/635	C-47A-65-DL	18899/9098
42-100636/835	C-47A-70-DL	19099/298
42-100836/1035	C-47A-75-DL	19299/498
42-107422	C-49H-DO	2189
42-108794/993	C-47A-xx-DL	11788-13778*
43-1961	C-49J-DO	4996
43-1962/67	C-49J-DO	4987/92
43-1968	C-49J-DO	4997
43-1969/71	C-49J-DO	4993/95
43-1972/73	C-49J-DO	6313/14
43-1974	C-49J-DO	4998
43-1975/78	C-49J-DO	6315/18
43-1979	C-49J-DO	4999
43-1980/81	C-49J-DO	6263/64
43-1982	C-49J-DO	5000
43-1983/85	C-49J-DO	6259/61
43-1986	C-49J-DO	6342
43-1987	C-49J-DO	6262
43-1988/89	C-49J-DO	6343/44
43-1990/94	C-49J-DO	6319/23
43-1995/99	C-49K-DO	4982/86
43-2000/11	C-49K-DO	6325/36
43-2012	C-49K-DO	6324
43-2013/17	C-49K-DO	6337/41
43-2018/21	C-53C-DO	4964/67
43-2022/24	C-53C-DO	4978/80
43-2025/32	C-53C-DO	4969/76

43-2033/34	C-53C-DO	6346/47
43-14404/05	C-53-DO	4960/61
43-15033/453	C-47A-80-DL	19499/919
43-15454/632	C-47A-85-DL	19920/20098
43-15633/16132	C-47A-90-DL	20099/598
43-16133/46432	C-47B-1-DL	20599-20898
43-30628/39	ntu	6059/70
43-30640/761	C-47A-DL	13791/912
43-36600	C-53-DO	4809
43-47963/48262	C-47A-30-DK	25224/523
43-48263/562	C-47B-1/2-DK	25524/823
43-48563/912	C-47B-5/6/7/8/9-DK	25824/26173
43-48913/49262	C-47B-10/11/13-DK	26174/523
43-49263/612	C-47B-15/16/18-DK	26524/873
43-49613/962	C-47B-20/23-DK	26874/27223
44-52990/91	C-48C	3286/87
44-76195/538	C-47B-25/27/28-DK	32527/870
44-76539/854	C-47B-30-DK	32871/33186
44-76855/7184	C-47B-35-DK	33187/516
44-77185/294	C-47B-40-DK	33517/626
44-83228	C-49H-DO	1941 ntu
44-83229	C-49H-DO	1944 ntu
45-876/10584	C-47B-45-DK	34134/34324 (except C-117As between 34129/318 see below)
45-1055/139	C-47B-50-DK	34325/34409
[Various C-47Bs were built as TC-47B]		
45-2545/48	C-117A-1-DK	34129/32
45-2549	C-117A-5-DK	34133
45-2550	C-117A-1-DK	34136
45-2551	C-117A-1-DK	34145
45-2552	C-117A-1-DK	34168
45-2553	C-117A-1-DK	34191
45-2554	C-117A-1-DK	34212
45-2555	C-117A-1-DK	34234
45-2556	C-117A-1-DK	34250
45-2557	C-117A-1-DK	34264
45-2558	C-117A-1-DK	34278
45-2559	C-117A-1-DK	34291
45-2560	C-117A-1-DK	34305
45-2561	C-117A-1-DK	34318
49-2612/41	C-47-DL	R Hellenic AF (few c/ns known)
51-3817	YC-129	43158

+ c/ns ending in "8" excluded
* c/ns ending in "8" only; every tenth aircraft with a c/n ending in digit '8' fitted into the serial range 42-108794 to 42-108993 between c/n 11788 to 13778, inclusive
C-47Cs fitted with amphibian floats are believed to comprise:- 41-18582, 42-5671, 42-92577/92699, 108868

Known instructional airframes are as follows:
G-4   33023   ex 44-76691
G-18   11840   ex 42-92079
G-19   34230   ex 45-967

Derivative C-47 Models

As described in Chapter 2, there were many derivative models of the C-47, some of which were production-line embodiments. Others were the result of modification programmes that continued almost until the aircraft was withdrawn from USAF use in the seventies. An overview of every known military variant is provided in Chapter 2, but here serials are listed by mission letter and operational purpose. Reference to individual serials will provide greater clarity. It should be remembered that the numbers of aircraft involved in any given programmes have not been well documented and many totals quoted in standard reference works do not stand up to close scrutiny when cross-referenced with USAF record cards. The record cards themselves can be unreliable (for a number of reasons) and even the most microscopic analysis does not provide absolute certainty about the numbers involved in any given programme. Obvious card errors have been 'corrected' here. All that said, all known derivative details with the exception of the ubiquitous VC-47 aircraft are listed below.
AC-47A/D (later EC-47D) – Used by the AACS/AFCS for nav-aid checking purposes, there were 26 conversions: 43-48139/599/708/ 783/892/902/904/905, 49029/095/103/190/250/331/387/705/776/930, 44-76598/643, 77290, 45-946/979/985, 1002/077.

AC-47D (previously FC-47D) – Gunship conversion extensively used in south-east Asia. Total of 53 excludes proof-of-concept aircraft 43-48462 and early field conversions such as 43-48491 and 43-48579 (the original

Chapter 3: Military Operators of the DC-3, C-47, R4D, Dakota and Li-2

'Puff"): 43-16065/133/159/368, 48263/356/466/501/591/686/701/801/ 916/921/925/929, 49010/021/124/211/268/274/330/339/421/423/492/ 499/503/516/517/546/770/859, 44-76207/290/354/370/394/534/542/593/ 606/625/722, 77263, 45-919/927, 1047/057/117/120/121.

EC-47A/B/D (some later to JC-47A/D, NC-47A and RC-47D as well as C-47A/D and VC-47A) – Exempt status aircraft. Use of this prefix was discontinued after 1955. A highly unreliable total of 26 identified from record cards: 42-23918, 24313, 292033, 293177/543, 100606*/662, 43-15264/550/956, 16065/133/158, 48150/263/273/726/870/881, 49009/ 076/085/214, 44-77152, 45-1097/127
(*42-100606 was previously EVC-47A).

EC-47D for MATS/AFCS – See AC-47D.

EC-47D for PACAF – One EC-47Q aircraft, 45-1131, briefly listed as EC-47D 1967-68 before becoming EC-47Q.

EC-47N – See RC-47N.

EC-47P – See RC-47P.

EC-47Q for TAC/PACAF – Electronic reconnaissance C-47A/D with up-rated engines. 16 aircraft in total: 42-24304, 93704, 43-15204/ 681, 16029, 30730, 48009/087/636/959, 49208/570/771, 44-76304, 45-1131*/133 (*45-1131 previously designated EC-47D until 'Q' suffix allotted).

FC-47D for TAC/PACAF – See AC-47D.

GC-47D – At least three ground instructional airframes at Howard AFB and Albrook AFB, Panama: ('D' models according to 1973-vintage records): G-4 ex 44-76691, G-18 ex 42-92079, G-19 45-967.

HC-47A/D (previously SC-47A/D) – At least 27 aircraft recorded as being re-designated HC-47 post-1962 but the exact total is likely to be in excess of this as other former SC-47s survived beyond 1962. Known serials are: 42-23775, 92111/916, 93181/794/812, 43-15270/297/ 311/537/540/541/548/558/561/574/773/933, 16087*/157, 30717, 48074, 49008/220/353/368/430, 45-883.
(*43-16087 was briefly a JHC-47A).

JC-47A/D (most were previously EC-47A/D) – At least 24 identified from record cards: 42-23918, 92033, 93177/780, 100606/662, 43-15264/ 550/956/983*, 16065/133, 48150/263/273/953, 49009/076/085/096/214, 44-77152, 45-1097/127 *43-15983 became NC-47A).

NC-47A/B – Two aircraft: 43-15983 and 43-16277.

RC-47A/B/D – At least six conversions for photo-mapping purposes and used by MATS/APCS for much of their careers although card records suggest early use with ATC: 42-92990, 43-48726, 49522/554/783, 45-1134.

RC-47A – At least one aircraft officially designated in 1944 (42-23643). Purpose unconfirmed.

RC-47D – One aircraft, 44-77222, was used from 1949 for reconnaissance work out of Furstenfeldbruck and Wiesbaden, West Germany. Two Hayes-modified C-47Ds that were designated as RC-47D 1952-53 before re-designation as AC-47D for MATS/AACS (44-76643 and 45-979).

'RC-47' (C-47D) – Three aircraft modified in 1966 by PACAF for use as communications relay aircraft over Laos. System went live in Dec66 and was reportedly discontinued in 1969 ('radios removed') with aircraft returned to standard configuration and disposed of to MAP in 1970: 43-48492/946 and 49701.

RC-47N – At least 25 C-47A converted to electronic reconnaissance capability in 1966 for use in the Vietnam theatre. All aircraft survived until May67 when they became EC-47N. Serials were: 42-23520/ 882, 24300/313, 93161/166/735/814, 100513/665/950/984, 108980, 43-15112/133/603/668/979/980, 16055/095/123, 48072/153/158.

RC-47P – At least 30 C-47D converted to electronic reconnaissance capability in 1966 for use in the Vietnam theatre. 28 survivors became EC-47P in May67. Serials were: 43-48402/480/702/767/871/886/933/ 947, 49009/013/100/126/201/260/491/547/679/703/865, 44-76524/668, 77016/254, 45-925/937, 1044/046/102.

SC-47A/D – Search and rescue/recovery. The history of this designation is complex. Original conversions from the 1950-52 period are said to number 26 but few of these aircraft can be found obviously from aircraft record cards. It was not until mid-1954 when SAC's large fleet of C-47A/Ds, dedicated to its 'Aircrew Recovery Program', was assimilated by MATS that we see evidence of updating the cards to show SC-47A and SC-47D designations. The great majority of SC-47s thus appear in the records in mid-1954 and as more records were updated 'new' SC-47s continued to appear until mid-1957. By the time of the 1962 tri-service designation change to HC-47A/D many aircraft had been returned to C-47 status (at least in name), were in storage or had been sold. Only 27 aircraft received the new designation on their paper record. At least 90 SC-47A/D are known from their record cards: 42-23771/775, 24057, 92111/916, 93086/181/183/513/794/812, 100670, 101000/028, 108944, 43-15194/209/270/277/284/297/311/345/537/540/541/542/544/548/558/ 561/574/616/689/732/773/808/933, 16087/134/145/157/160/161/250/ 277/367/376/400/411, 30717, 48074/ 307/393/398/446/575/765/951/957, 49099/207/220/341/353/368/370/ 430/431/508/523/565/567/638/656, 44-76214/306/330/444/447, 77272/ 280/286, 45-883/933, 1013/087/090/ 091/123.

TC-47A – At least 11 C-47A modified (?) for training use, most for ATC in 1947. All survivors eventually returned to C-47A standard. From record cards: 42-23490/655, 92073, 93101, 43-15586/684/930/943, 16040/ 118/119.

TC-47B/D – Officially 133 TC-47B conversions were undertaken on the production line. Of these, at least 39 were delivered directly to the USN and thus never became TC-47Ds. The conversion of the TC-47B to TC-47D was automatic once the superchargers were removed. Aircraft built as TC-47Bs for the USAAF included the following: 43-48641, 49033/268/348/351/703/751/760/790/808/814/832/852/880/903/921/939/ 956, 44-76206/214/223/240/248/257/265/273/282/290/298/306/314/ 322/330/338/346/354/362/370/378/386/394/402/410/418/430/438/446/ 454/494/502/510/518/524/534/550/553/558/566/574/578/582/588/593/ 598/606/612/618/625/632/638/645/652/658/663/668/675/680/686/691/ 696/700/705/711/716/722/729/734/794.

Virtually all of the TC-47B conversions subsequently became TC-47D, regardless of use or status. At least 17 standard C-47D also became TC-47Ds. These re-designations reflected role rather than modification state and fell into two categories. At least eight were used by AMC at their Warner-Robins and Wright depots between 1948 and 1951. The others were used (as TC-47Ds) by ATC in 1947-48 alongside the TC-47As. These aircraft included: 43-48397/503/705/807/946, 49261/274/278/331/ 343/349/360/ 361/370/375/685 and 45-1135. The TC-47A and TC-47D identities were lost as roles changed and the last designations (but not necessarily the aircraft!) disappeared in the late 'fifties.

VC-47A/B/D – A considerable number of C-47s were modified for VIP and executive duties. Among the most fluid of all USAF identities, no attempt is made to list them here and the reader is referred to the individual aircraft histories.

C-47E – The nine C-47D aircraft modified by Pan American for airways use were: 43-15306/563/688/764, 30658, 48133/875/906, 45-1109.

VC-117A/B – The C-117A was by definition a VIP aircraft and continued to be so after deletion of the superchargers and re-designation to C-117B. Aircraft were re-designated VC-117A and VC-117B before stabilising as either VC-117A or C-117B.

C-117C – The 10 aircraft known to have been acquired from Pioneer Airlines for VIP use at the time of the Korean war were the former C-47s: 41-18348/384/392, 42-92873, 93040/518/601, 100769, 108866, 43-15265.

US Navy and Marine Corps

The first DC-2s or R2D-1s, as they were designated, were delivered to the Navy and Marine Corps in 1935 to replace the Ford Trimotors then used by utility squadrons. The Navy R2Ds were based at Anacostia and San Diego and the Marine Corps unit was VJ-6M with two based at Quantico. These five R2Ds carried on into the early forties, by which time two had been destroyed and two dismantled. The last survived the war and is preserved today in the colours of KLM as PH-AJU/N39165.
Initial R4D deliveries were to Navy orders but all later aircraft came from USAAF orders though they never carried the latter's colours apart from some later transfers.

The Naval Air Transport Service was authorised on 12Dec41, with three wings, the Pacific, West Coast and Atlantic Wings. The first Navy R4D squadron was VR-1 formed at Norfolk, VA, then VR-2 at Alameda, CA and

VR-3 at Kansas City, KS, in Feb, Apr and Jul42, respectively. VR-1 operated between Boston and Corpus Christi, TX, Argentia, Newfoundland and Trinidad, BWI and later to Iceland and Rio de Janeiro. VR-2 flew between California and Alaska in the North and to Corpus Christi. VR-3 operated in the Pacific and as far as Australia. These units made up the NATS in the early months of the war.

As footholds in the Pacific islands were gained so transport services were started and SCAT or South Pacific Combat Air Transport Service was formed, functioning from Aug42. This carried fuel into Guadalcanal and evacuated casualties out of the various combat zones. In the Central Pacific, the Central Pacific Combat Air Transport Group or TAG came into being and both SCAT and TAG were used for jungle supply drops and transport to the battle fronts. They were rarely used to drop paratroops because the jungle conditions resulted in heavy loss of men and equipment.

NATS continued to operate over the longer strategic supply routes, and flew over the Hump into China and from Karachi via Africa, S Atlantic, S America to the USA, carrying important raw materials such as drugs, tin, rubber, tungsten etc. Eventually the R4Ds used by VR-1, VR-2 and VR-3 were replaced by the larger and longer range R5Ds, though some R4Ds remained on strength as late as 1948. Many other VR units were formed subsequently and R4Ds are known to have served with VR-4 (Mar43), VR-5 (Aug44), VR-6 (Aug45), VR-7 (Mar43), VR-8 (Sep44), VR-9 (Dec44), VR-10 (Nov44), VR-11 (Aug44), VR-13 (Aug44), VR-22 (Aug47), VR-23 (Jun48), VR-24 (Jan48), VR-32 (Jun48) and VR-44 (Jul48). Most of these units continued to use R4Ds until well after the end of the war, and eventually, on 01Jul48, the NATS was merged with MATS.

A variety of other Navy units are recorded as having used R4Ds at various times during the war and others. These include VE-1, VE-2 and VE-3 (probably special electronics): VH-2, VH-3, VH-5 and VH-14 (probably ambulances); VJ-4, VJ-7, VJB-1 and XVJ-25 (weather reconnaissance), VRJ-2; VRF-1 to 4 (fighter supply units); VRS-1 (anti-submarine training?), VRU-2, VRU-3, VRU-4, VRU-22 and VRU-23 (transport utility); VX-2 and VX-6 (experimental work in the Antarctic etc.).

One spectacular post-war operation was the flight of six R4D-5Ls with skis off the deck of the carrier "Philippine Sea" using JATO to assist take-off, for operation by VX-2 in the Antarctic on 29Jan47. Unfortunately there was no way these aircraft could be flown back to the carrier so they were abandoned at "Little America" at the end of the season on 21Feb47. Later, in 1956, VX-6 was equipped with R4Ds and one of their aircraft "Que Sera Sera", was the first aircraft to land at the South Pole on 31Oct56. This aircraft is now preserved for the Smithsonian at Pensacola NAS. The operation levelled the Navy with the USAF which had landed a C-47 at the North Pole. Operation Deep Freeze used 7 R4D-5Ls, 4 R4D-6Ls and 6 R4D-8Ls. Apart from units equipped with R4Ds for specific duties, most US Navy stations had the odd R4D on their roster, and although these could not be identified to a particular base during wartime, with peace they soon acquired the name of their home base or a code on the tail to indicate this - though the codes changed from time to time. The Navy did not operate R4Ds in Korea or Vietnam in large numbers, but they still played their part in these two theatres, and by the end of the last conflict the R4D, or C-47H & C-47J as it had been redesignated in 1962, had reached the end of the road and almost all were retired by the late seventies. A few C-117Ds remained in service until the early eighties and some remain at Davis Monthan in the 'yards'.

The US Marines used their R4Ds for transport and utility work in the various Pacific war theatres and at home. Five units were so equipped during 1942/43, namely VMJ-152, 153, 252, 253 and 353. These continued (except for 252) to use the type until the end of 1946 when they were redesignated VMR-152 etc, the last giving up the type in Mar48. These units were VMR-152, 153, 252, 253, 313, 352 and 353. In the production list which follows, other Marine Corps units, groups or wings are referred to. These are Marine Air Wings 1, 2 and 3 (MAW-1, MAW-2, MAW-3), plus the reserve wing MAW-4. Various Marine Air Groups (MAG) are listed, numbered from 7 to 94 as well as various Marine Corps Air Stations.

As will be obvious from the production list, aircraft moved back and forth between the Navy and the Marine Corps, and there is confusion in the official records as to aircraft assignments. Some units listed are clearly errors. Some units will be noted that have not been explained. These include HDN or Headquarters Squadron, Fasron or Fleet Aircraft Service Squadron, Servron or Servicing Squadron (the USN equivalent of an MU). Generally, the latter have been omitted, as most aircraft were attached temporarily during overhauls. A few others are listed, but it has not proved possible to decode the abbreviated unit numbers.

US Navy abbreviations for units mentioned are:-

ADAU	Administration Aviation Unit
Adv Base	Advance Base
Adv Gp	Advisory Group
AES	Aircraft Engineering Squadron
AFMF LNT/PAC	Air Fleet Marine Force Atlantic/Pacific
ALUSNA	Allied US Naval Advisor
ANRS	Air Navigational Radio School
A&R	Assembly & Repair
A&T	Acceptance & Transfer
ATD	Aviation Training Dept
ATU	Advanced Training Unit
BAGR Dist	Bu Aer General Representative District (Central or Western)
BAR	Bureau of Aeronautics Representative
BTU	Basic Training Unit
BWFLTRREP CEN	Bureau of Naval Weapons Fleet Readiness Representative Central
BWR FR	Bureau of Naval Weapons Representative, Fleet Readiness
CASU	Carrier Air Service Unit
ChNavSec MAAG	Chief Navy Section MAAG
CMEF	Com. Middle East Forces
CNABT	Chief Naval Air Basic Training
CNAVGR JUSMMA	Chief Naval Advisory Gp, Joint US Military Mutual Aid Turkey
CNFGER/JAP	Com. Naval Forces Germany/Japan
CNME	Com. Naval Mid East
ComAirPacSCF	Com. Air Pacific Submarines Command Forward
Com Air Phil SF	Commander Air Philippine Sea Frontier
ComFair	Commander Fleet Air
ComFltAct	Commander Fleet Activities
COMNAB-10	Commander Naval Air Bases. 10 Naval District
ComNavConAd	Commander Naval Continental Air Defense
ComNavForJapan	Commander Naval Forces Japan
COMPHIB	Commander Amphibious Force
COM USTDC	Commander US Taiwan Defense Command
COM-17	Commander ND 17
CQTU	Carrier Qualification Training Unit
DAO	Defense Advisory Officer
DCASR	Defense Contract Admin. Service Region
FaetuLant	Fleet Airborne Electronics Training Unit - Atlantic
FaetuPac	Fleet Airborne Electronics Training Unit - Pacific
FairBetulant	Fleet Airborne Electronics Training Unit - Atlantic
FALLWEATRA LANT	Fleet All Weather Training Unit - Atlantic
FASRON	Fleet Air Service Squadron
FAWPra	Fleet Air West Pacific Repair Activity
Fleet Dept NADS	Fleet Dept. Naval Air Development Station
F&M	Ferry & Maintenance
FMF	Fleet Marine Force
ForAvaHQGru	Marine Forces Aviation HQ Group
GCA	Ground Control Approach
HAMS	HQ & Maintenance Squadron
HATU	Heavy Attack Training Unit.
HEDRON	Marine HQ Squadron
HEDSUPACT	HQ Support Activity
HML	Marine Light Helicopter Squadron
H&MS/HAMRON	HQ & Maintenance Squadron
HQ	Headquarters
HQ MC Flt Sect	HQ Marine Corps Flight Section
INSMAT	Inspector of Naval Material
JOC	Joint Operations Centre
LANT	Atlantic
MAAG	Military Assistance Advisory Group
MAG	Marine Air Group
MAMS	Marine Aircraft Maintenance Squadron
MARS	Marine Aircraft Repair Squadron
MARTD	Marine Air Reserve Training Det.
MAW	Marine Air Wing [Pac/Lant]
MBDW	Marine Base Defense Wing
MBG	Marine Bombing Group
MCAD	Marine Corps Aviation Division
MCAS	Marine Corps Air Station
MFG	Marine Fighter Group
MNFG	Marine Night Fighter Group
MOTE	
M&S	Maintenance & Support
MTG	Marine Training Group
MWHS	Marine Wing HQ Squadron
MWSG	Marine Wing Service Group

CHAPTER 3: MILITARY OPERATORS OF THE DC-3, C-47, R4D, DAKOTA AND LI-2

MWSS	Marine Wing Service Squadron
NAAS	Naval Auxiliary Air Station
NAATC	Naval Air Advanced Training Command
NAAWFS	Naval Air All Weather Flight School
NABTC	Naval Air Basic Training Command
NactuLant	Night Attack Combat Training Unit Atlantic
NADC	Naval Air Development Center
NADS	Naval Air Development Station
NADU	Naval Air Development Unit
NAF	Naval Air Facility
NAG	Naval Advisory Group
NAIT	Naval Air Intermediate Training
NAMC	Naval Air Material Center
NAMD	Naval Aviation Maintenance Dept
NAMT	Naval Air Missile Test Center
NANS	Naval Air Navigation School
NAOTS	Naval Aviation Ordnance Test Station
NARF	Naval Air Rework Facility
NART	Naval Air Reserve Training
NARTU	Naval Air Reserve Training Unit
NAS	Naval Air Station
NASWF	Naval Air Special Weapons Facility
NATC	Naval Air Test Center
NAT&E	Naval Airship Training & Experimental
NaTechTrau	Naval Air Technical Training Unit
NATF	Naval Air Test Facility
NatParaTest Range	National Parachute Test Range
NATTC	Naval Air Technical Training Center/Command
NATTU	Naval Air Technical Training Unit
NavAct	Naval Activity
NavAeroRecovFac	Naval Aeronautical Recovery Facility
NavSecJusmag	Navy Section Joint US Military Advisory Group
NavSta	Naval Station
NavTraCom	Naval Air Advance Training Command
NBPRO	Naval Base Plant Rep. Officer
ND	Naval District
NightDevronLant	Night Development Squadron Atlantic
NLO	Naval Liaison Officer
NOTS	Naval Ordnance Test Station
NPF	National Parachute Facility
NPRO	Naval Plant Rep. Officer
NPU	Naval Parachute Unit
NRTRS PL	Naval Reserve Training Transportation Pool
NSA	Naval Support Activity
NSAWF	Naval School All Weather Flight
NWC	Naval Weapons Center
NWEF	Naval Weapons Evaluation Facility
ONR	Office of Naval Research
O&R	Overhaul & Repair
PAC	Pacific
PAU	Pilotless Aircraft Unit
PEU	Parachute Experimental Unit
PMR	Pacific Missile Range
RD&DE	Research & Development Design & Engineering Groups
RDT&E	Research, Development Test & Evaluation
R&T	Research & Test
SAES	Station Aircraft Engineering Squadron
SDC	Special Devices Centre
Servron	Service Squadron
SO&ES	Station Operation & Engineering Squadron
SOS	Station Operation Squadron
SWTTEU	Special Weapons Test & Tactical Evaluation Unit
TTF	Training Task Force
USCG	US Coast Guard
USMC	US Marine Corps
USN	US Navy
VAH	Heavy Attack Squadron
VE	Evacuation Squadron
VH	Rescue Squadron
VMAT	Marine Attack Training Squadron
VMF	Marine Fighter Squadron
VMR	Marine Transport Squadron
VR	Air Transport Squadron, then Fleet Tactical Support Squadron and lastly Fleet Logistics Support Squadron
VRF	Air Ferry Squadron (1943 - 1948); Aircraft Ferry Sq (1957 - 1986)
VRJ	Utility Transport Squadron (1945 - 1946)
VRU	Transport Utility Squadron (1946 - 1948)
VT	Training Squadron
VX	Air Development Sq (1946 - 1968); Air Test & Evaluation Sq (1969 -VXE Antarctic Development Squadron
ZW	Airship Early Warning Squadron

US Navy and Marine Station and Unit codes

These codes are usually painted on the fin and rudder. During wartime no codes were used, for security reasons. In the early fifties a single letter indicated the station, but few of these are known, as follows:

A	Anacostia
B	Atlanta
R	New York
V	Glenview
Z	Squantum and S Weymouth

In the later fifties and up to the end of C-47 service two letters or one digit and one letter were used. When tail codes are prefixed '3' they are advanced training, '4' refers to Naval Technical Training Command, '5' to Marine Air Reserve Squadrons, '6' to Naval Reserve Training Unit, '7' to Naval Reserve Squadrons and '8' to Naval Reserve Training Detachments.

Codes known to have been used on R4Ds, C-47s and C-117Ds are:-

AZ	USMC		3B	VT-28
BH	VMGR-252		3C	VT-29
BL	HML-268		4B	Glynco
BZ	HS FMF LANT (USMC)		4F	Philadelphia
CE	VMA-225		4L	Lakehurst
CN	H&MS-14		4M	Memphis
CZ	H&MS-27		4P	Pensacola
DA	H&MS-32		5A	Andrews/Washington
EL	H&MS-26		5B	Atlanta
EW	H&MS-24		5D	Dallas
EX	H&MS-31		5F	Jacksonville
FK			5G	Alameda
FT	FASRON-200 from Jun57		5L	Los Alamitos/El Toro
GJ	RVAH-3		5M	Memphis
HH	H&MS-40		5N	Lakehurst
JA	VX-1		5S	Norfolk
JD	VXE-6		5T	Whidbey Island
JK	VR-1		5V	Glenview
JM	VR-24		5X	New Orleans
JP	VRF-32		5Z	South Weymouth
JX	VX-6		6A	Anacostia/Washington
LZ	VP-94		6F	Jacksonville
MV	(USMC)		6G	Alameda
QF	H&MS-37/MARS-37		6M	Memphis
RE			6N	Lakehurst
SC	VMAT-102		6S	Norfolk
SZ	H&MS-17		7E	Minneapolis
TM	H&MS-11		7R	New York
TN	VMCJ-3		7W	Willow Grove
TX			7X	New Orleans
UH	VU-7		7Y	Detroit
WA	H&MS-12		7?	Seattle
WZ	HS FMF PAC		8H	North Island (NORIS)
XV				
YU	Hamron-13			

US Navy serial number index

9620/22	R2D-1	c/n 1325/27	05073/74	R4D-3	4863/64
9993/94	R2D-1	1404/05	05075/76	R4D-3	4877/78
3131	R4D-1	4204	05077/78	R4D-3	4893/94
3132/39	R4D-1	4222/29	05079/80	R4D-3	4917/18
3140/43	R4D-1	4280/83	05081/82	R4D-3	4942/43
4692	R4D-1	4284	05083/84	R4D-3	4955/56
4693/99	R4D-1	4300/06	06992/93	R4D-3	7408/09
4700/06	R4D-1	4360/66	06994	R4D-3	7411
4707	R4D-2	4097	06995	R4D-3	7339
4708	R4D-2	4098	06996/97	R4D-3	7350/51
01648/9	R4D-1	4367/8	06998/99	R4D-3	4969/70
01977/85	R4D 1	4433/41	07000	R4D-4	4962
01986/90	R4D-1	4550/54	07001	R4D-4	6345
05051/53	R4D-1	4555/57	07002/03	R4D-4	6348/49
05054/61	R4D-1	4654/61	12393/404	R4D-1	6059/70
05062/72	R4D-1	4754/64			

12405/08	R4D-5	9177/80	17127/28	R4D-5	12263/64	50761	R4D-6	26273	50799	R4D-6	26613
12409/12	R4D-5	9231/34	17129/30	R4D-5	12269/70	50762	R4D-6	26278	50800	R4D-6	26618
12413/16	R4D-5	9303/06	17131	R4D-5	12275	50763	R4D-6	26283	50801	R4D-6	26624
12417/19	R4D-5	9357/59	17132	R4D-5	12290	50764	R4D-6	26288	50802	R4D-6	26658
12420	R4D-5	9442	17133	R4D-5	12330	50765	R4D-6	26293	50803	R4D-6	26663
12421/24	R4D-5	9401/04	17134	R4D-5	12283	50766	R4D-6	26298	50804	R4D-6	26668
12425/29	R4D-5	9482/86	17135	R4D-5	12331	50767	R4D-6	26303	50805	R4D-6	26673
12430/32	R4D-5	9527/29	17136/37	R4D-5	12287/88	50768	R4D-6	26313	50806	R4D-6	26678
12433/37	R4D-5	9616/20	17138/40	R4D-5	12296/98	50769/71	R4D-6	26324/26	50807	R4D-6	26683
12438/42	R4D-5	9671/75	17141/43	R4D-5	12311/13	50772	R4D-6	26353	50808	R4D-6	26688
12443/46	R4D-5	9756/59	17144/53	R4D-5	12334/43	50773	R4D-6	26358	50809	R4D-6	26693
17092	R4D-5	11788	17154/58	R4D-5	12427/31	50774	R4D-6	26363	50810	R4D-6	26698
17093	R4D-5	11798	17159/68	R4D-5	12515/24	50775	R4D-6	26368	50811	R4D-6	26703
17094	R4D-5	11808	17169/73	R4D-5	12552/56	50776	R4D-6	26373	50812	R4D-6	26708
17095	R4D-5	11818	17174	R4D-5	12679	50777	R4D-6	26378	50813	R4D-6	26713
17096	R4D-5	11828	17175	R4D-5	12779	50778	R4D-6	26383	50814	R4D-6	26718
17097	R4D-5	11838	17176	R4D-5	12733	50779	R4D-6	26388	50815	R4D-6	26724
17098	R4D-5	11848	17177	R4D-5	12743	50780	R4D-6	26393	50816	R4D-6	26733
17099	R4D-5	11858	17178	R4D-5	12753	50781	R4D-6	26398	50817	R4D-6	26824
17100	R4D-5	11868	17179	R4D-5	12768	50782	R4D-6	26403	50818/23	R4D-6	26873/78
17101	R4D-5	11878	17180	R4D-5	12778	50783	R4D-6	26408	50824	R4D-6	26883
17102	R4D-5	11888	17181	R4D-5	12780	50784	R4D-6	26413	50825	R4D-6	26893
17103	R4D-5	11898	17182	R4D-5	12879	50785	R4D-6	26418	50826	R4D-6	26924
17104	R4D-5	11908	17183	R4D-5	12798	50786	R4D-6	26424	50827	R4D-6	26958
17105	R4D-5	11918	17184	R4D-5	12808	50787	R4D-6	26524	50828	R4D-6	26963
17106	R4D-5	11928	17185	R4D-5	12818	50788	R4D-6	26558	50829	R4D-6	26968
17107	R4D-5	11938	17186	R4D-5	12828	50789	R4D-6	26563	50830	R4D-6	26973
17108	R4D-5	11948	17187	R4D-5	12838	50790	R4D-6	26568	50831	R4D-6	26978
17109	R4D-5	11958	17188	R4D-5	12847	50791	R4D-6	26573	50832	R4D-6	26983
17110	R4D-5	11968	17189	R4D-5	12788	50792	R4D-6	26578	50833	R4D-6	26988
17111	R4D-5	11978	17190/91	R4D-5	12979/80	50793	R4D-6	26583	50834	R4D-6	26993
17112	R4D-5	11988	17192/98	R4D-5	13003/09	50794	R4D-6	26588	50835	R4D-6	26998
17113	R4D-5	11998	17199	R4D-5	13079	50795	R4D-6	26593	50836	R4D-6	27003
17114	R4D-5	12008	17200/07	R4D-5	13100/07	50796	R4D-6	26598	50837	R4D-6	27008
17115	R4D-5	12018	17208	R4D-5	13179	50797	R4D-6	26603	50838	R4D-6	27024
17116	R4D-5	12028	17209	R4D-5	13108	50798	R4D-6	26608	50839	R4D-6	32790
17117	R4D-5	12038	17210	R4D-5	13180						
17118	R4D-5	12048	17211/18	R4D-5	13221/28						
17119	R4D-5	12058	17219	R4D-5	13279	91104	R4D-1	9051	99843	R4D-7	33256
17120	R4D-5	12068	17220/27	R4D-5	13318/25	99099	R4D-7		99844	R4D-7	33267
17121	R4D-5	12078	17228	R4D-5	13379	99824	R4D-7	33095	99845	R4D-7	33275
17122	R4D-5	12088	17229/34	R4D-5	13591/96	99825	R4D-7	33100	99846	R4D-7	33283
17123	R4D-5	12178	17235/37	R4D-5	25314/16	99826	R4D-7	33105	99847	R4D-7	33291
17124	R4D-5	12188	17238	R4D-5	25324	99827	R4D-7	33110	99848	R4D-7	33299
17125	R4D-5	12198	17239	R4D-5	25424	99828	R4D-7	33144	99849	R4D-7	33305
17126	R4D-5	12261	17240/48	R4D-5	25438/46	99829	R4D-7	33155	99850	R4D-7	33314
						99830	R4D-7	33160	99851	R4D-7	33322
						99831	R4D-7	33170	99852	R4D-7	33329
17249	R4D-6	25525	39072/76	R4D-5	10092/96	99832	R4D-7	33180	99853	R4D-7	33337
17250	R4D-6	25624	39077/81	R4D-5	10204/08	99833	R4D-7	33186	99854	R4D-7	33345
17251/63	R4D-6	25626/38	39082/85	R4D-5	13811/14	99834	R4D-7	33192	99855	R4D-7	33351
17264	R4D-6	25724	39086/91	R4D-5	13855/60	99835	R4D-7	33201	99856	R4D-7	33359
17265/77	R4D-6	25768/80	39092/95	R4D-5	19063/66	99836	R4D-7	33206	99857	R4D-7	33367
17278	R4D-6	25824	39096	R4D-6	32791	99837	R4D-7	33133	(138659)	R4D-8X	43158
17279	R4D-6	25924	39097	R4D-6	32793	99838	R4D-7	33216	138820	R4D-8X	43158
17280/82	R4D-6	25944/46	39098	R4D-6	32794	99839	R4D-7	33227	150187	R4D-6	20842
17283/91	R4D-6	25948/56	39099	R4D-6	32795	99840	R4D-7	33232	150188	R4D-6	25654
30147?	R4D-1	4401	39100	R4D-7	32796	99841	R4D-7	33241	150189	R4D-6	26212
33615/21	R4D-4R		39101	R4D-7	32802	99842	R4D-7	33251	150190	R4D-6	26218
33815/20	R4D-4	6350/55	39102	R4D-7	32810						
37660	R4D-1	6036	39103	R4D-7	32818						
37661	R4D-1	6152	39104	R4D-7	33121	12410	R4D-8	43348	17108	R4D-8	43369
37662	R4D-1	6153	39105	R4D-7	33076	12412	R4D-8Z	43399	17111	R4D-8	43304
37663/68	R4D-1	6253/58	39106	R4D-7	33080	12419	R4D-8	43316	17116	R4D-8	43307
37669/72	R4D-1	9039/42	39107	R4D-7	33085	12420	R4D-8	43312	17119	R4D-8	43378
37673/6	R4D-1	9073/76	39108	R4D-7	33090	12422	R4D-8	43305	17122	R4D-8	43335
37677/80	R4D-1	9122/25	39109	R4D-6	27197	12425	R4D-8	43396	17123	R4D-8	43333
39057/61	R4D-5	9855/59	39110	R4D-5	20588	12428	R4D-8	43370	17124	R4D-8	43310
39062/66	R4D-5	9940/44	39111	R4D-5	20133	12431	R4D-8	43395	17127	R4D-8	43336
39067/71	R4D-5	10017/21				12435	R4D-8	43353	17140	R4D-8	43385
						12437	R4D-8	43393	17149	R4D-8	43383
						12438	R4D-8	43319	17150	R4D-8	43311
50740/41	R4D-6	25957/58	50751	R4D-6	26118	12439	R4D-8	43328	17152	R4D-8	43364
50742	R4D-6	26024	50752	R4D-6	26124	12440	R4D-8	43351	17153	R4D-8	43345
50743	R4D-6	26079	50753	R4D-6	26128	12441	R4D-8	43389	17154	R4D-8	43373
50744	R4D-6	26083	50754	R4D-6	26133	12443	R4D-8	43327	17156	R4D-8	43342
50745	R4D-6	26088	50755	R4D-6	26138	12445	R4D-8	43314	17158	R4D-8	43368
50746	R4D-6	26093	50756	R4D-6	26143	17092	R4D-8	43381	17160	R4D-8	43331
50747	R4D-6	26098	50757	R4D-6	26224	17097	R4D-8	43371	17165	R4D-8	43341
50748	R4D-6	26103	50758	R4D-6	26258	17098	R4D-8	43340	17166	R4D-8	43347
50749	R4D-6	26108	50759	R4D-6	26263	17102	R4D-8	43330	17169	R4D-8	43350
50750	R4D-6	26113	50760	R4D-6	26268	17103	R4D-8Z	43400	17171	R4D-8	43309

CHAPTER 3: MILITARY OPERATORS OF THE DC-3, C-47, R4D, DAKOTA AND LI-2

17175	R4D-8	43301	39081	R4D-8	43397	2446	c/n 9759	17243	25441
17177	R4D-8	43306	39084	R4D-8	43355	17183	12798	17247	25445
17179	R4D-8	43346	39087	R4D-8	43315	17235	25314		
17182	R4D-8	43375	39096	R4D-8	43338				
17188	R4D-8	43384	39097	R4D-8Z	43302				
17190	R4D-8	43365	39104	R4D-8	43325				
17191	R4D-8	43379	39109	R4D-8	43313				
17194	R4D-8	43352	50762	R4D-8	43308				
17196	R4D-8	43357	50772	R4D-8	43337				
17211	R4D-8	43391	50780	R4D-8	43398				
17216	R4D-8	43334	50782	R4D-8	43366				
17219	R4D-8	43323	50784	R4D-8	43380				
17241	R4D-8	43343	50786	R4D-8	43386				
17242	R4D-8	43392	50796	R4D-8	43361				
17248	R4D-8	43374	50801	R4D-8	43356				
17253	R4D-8	43377	50804	R4D-8	43320				
17255	R4D-8	43318	50808	R4D-8	43394				
17258	R4D-8	43390	50812	R4D-8	43358				
17270	R4D-8	43387	50821	R4D-8	43322				
17273	R4D-8	43303	50823	R4D-8	43317				
17281	R4D-8	43359	50826	R4D-8	43363				
17284	R4D-8	43367	50833	R4D-8	43349				
17287	R4D-8	43372	50834	R4D-8	43324				
39061	R4D-8	43344	50835	R4D-8	43321				
39064	R4D-8	43376	50836	R4D-8	43388				
39070	R4D-8	43360	50838	R4D-8	43329				
39071	R4D-8	43326	99845	R4D-8	43362				
39072	R4D-8	43382	99853	R4D-8	43339				
39080	R4D-8	43354	99857	R4D-8	43332				

Note 1: 99099 is an ex-PAA DC-3A.
Note 2: c/ns for 150187 - 150189 may be interchanged.

United States Army

The US Army used 39 C-47s between the early sixties and the mid-seventies. The majority were used for general support duties but some operated in connection with missile trials at the Army's Missile Command and Kwajalein test site in the Pacific. In addition two were used at various times by the "Golden Knights" Parachute Team. One was a higher powered C-47E originally converted for high altitude operations. Others were fitted with wing racks for carrying test equipment, flares, etc. The majority of the Army's C-47s (about 25) came from the Navy, the remainder being ex-USAF. Their serial numbers were often corrupted from those used originally and have caused some confusion as a result. Ex-Navy aircraft had the "O" prefix, e.g. O-50781, and another Navy serial had the fiscal year added, e.g. 43-9095 for Bu 39095. The following are known:-

ex US Navy
12436	C-47H	c/n 9619	O-39103*	NC-47K	32818
12444	SC-47H	9757	43-39106**	NC-47H	33080
17096	C-47H	11828	O-39107	TC-47K	33085
7168	TC-47H	12524	50740	C-47J	25957
17181	VC-47H	12780	O-50761	C-47J	26273
17203	C-47H	13103	O-50781	C-47J	26398
7220	C-47H	13318	O-50787	C-47J	26524
17256	C-47J	25631	50790	TC-47J	26568
41-7276	C-47J	25779	50806	C-47J	26678
39058	TC-47H	9856	99827	TC-47J	33110
43-39074	VC-47A	10094	O-99831	C-47J	33170
43-9095	C-47H	19066	99848	C-47J	33299

* also wore 9103.   ** also wore 39106.

ex USAF
42-93101	C-47D	12975	O-15982	C-47A	20448
42-93173	VC-47A	13055	6277	NC-47B	20743
42-93780	JC-47A	13730	O-30665	C-47A	13816
42-100847	C-47A	19310	43-48950*	C-47D	26211
15688	C-47E	20154	43-49281	VC-47D	26542
43-15700	VC-47A	20166	45-0972	C-47B	34236
43-15701	VC-47A	20167	66-8836	C-47H	13105
O-15760	C-47A	20226			

* also wore 43-8950.

United States Coast Guard

About eight R4D-5s are believed to have been used by the USCG for general support duties. Some of these were based at the Headquarters in Washington, DC. Known aircraft are:-

NASA - National Aeronautics and Space Adminstration

c/n 12287	NASA 017 then NASA 817, to N817NA
25771	NASA 268 then NASA 10, to N10NA, N423NA
26367	NASA 106
26787	NASA 501, to N501NA, N636NA, N817NA, N827NA
33110	NASA 18 then NASA 701, to US Army

See the Production History chapter for further details.

MASDC C-47 and C-117 Storage Codes

The Military Aircraft Storage and Disposition Center, located at Davis-Monthan AFB, south-east of Tucson, AZ, had 255 C-47s in storage by 31Jul46. Each was coded in the CB sequence, and known identities are given below, together with those known for C-117s. Type descriptions are those current at the time of entering MASDC.

CB001-			CB407	45-0999	VC-47D
CB095		unknown	CB408	42-93173	VC-47A
CB096	43-49008	C-47D	CB409	44-76269	VC-47D
CB113	43-49518	C-47D	CB410	43-48411	C-47D
CB226	42-100662	C-47D	CB411	43-48458	C-47D
CB243	43-49786	C-47D	CB412	43-48928	C-47D
CB251	43-15577	C-47A	CB413	42-93184	VC-47A
CB268	42-93807	C-47D	CB414	42-100743	C-47A
CB269	43-48859	C-47D	CB415	44-76203	VC-47D
CB276	43-16156	C-47D	CB416	45-0948	VC-47D
CB278	43-16164	C-47D	CB417	43-16004	C-47A
CB279	43-48151	C-47D	CB418	43-49272	VC-47D
CB286	43-15718	C-47D	CB419	45-0997	VC-47D
CB287	43-49113	C-47D	CB420	45-0876	C-47D
CB292	43-15611	C-47A	CB421	43-48160	VC-47A
CB293	43-48415	C-47D	CB422	43-49420	VC-47D
CB294	43-49216	C-47D	CB423	43-15951	C-47A
CB295	45-0993	C-47D	CB424	43-48913	VC-47D
CB296	44-76410	C-47B	CB426	43-16155	VC-47D
CB298	44-76502	C-47D	CB427	43-49514	C-47D
CB300	43-48058	C-47D	CB428	43-48343	C-47D
CB307	43-49688	C-47D	CB430	42-24302	VC-47A
CB309	43-49301	C-47D	CB431	45-0920	VC-47D
CB310	44-77276	C-47D	CB433	44-77214	VC-47D
CB317	43-49295	C-47D	CB434	43-48783	EC-47D
CB318	43-48488	C-47D	CB435	39074	VC-47A
CB320	43-49333	C-47D	CB436	43-49366	C-47D
CB321	43-48715	C-47D	CB437	43-49358	C-47D
CB322	42-23774	C-47D	CB438	43-48490	C-47D
CB325	44-76600	C-47D	CB439	39058	C-47H
CB328	43-15619	C-47D	CB440	43-48705	C-47D
CB332	43-16387	C-47D	CB441	43-15140	C-47A
CB334	44-76642	C-47D	CB442	43-49090	C-47D
CB336	43-49556	C-47D	CB443	45-1009	C-47D
CB338	44-76933	C-47D	CB445	44-76378	TC-47D
CB339	44-76706	C-47D	CB447	44-76395	C-47D
CB374	42-24311	VC-47A	CB448	44-77204	VC-47D
CB393	45-1074	C-47D	CB449	43-49485	C-47D
CB394	44-77253	C-47D	CB450	43-16373	C-47D
CB397	45-0942	VC-47D	CB451	45-1101	C-47D
CB398	45-0894	C-47D	CB452	43-48717	C-47D
CB399	42-93727	VC-47A	CB453	43-49505	C-47D
CB400	43-48092	C-47A	CB454	43-49349	C-47D
CB402	12444	NC-47H	CB455	50806	C-47D
CB403	43-15274	C-47A	CB456	39106	NC-47H
CB404	43-16061	VC-47A			(ex ZB014)
CB405	43-49845	VC-47D	CB457	45-0972	C-47D
CB406	44-76449	VC-47D			(ex ZB013)
CE001	17108	C-117D	CE003	138820	C-117D
CE002	12422	C-117D			
CE012	45-2548	C-117B	CE013	45-2547	C-117A

By the mid-1980s, many had gone through surrounding local 're-processing' companies, being returned to flying status or scrapped. The following list gives the known codes/aircraft in the 1970s/1980s for aircraft at the yards of Allied

Aircraft Sales (AA), Desert Air Parts (DA - formerly Petroski's) and Dross Metals (DM). Again, type descriptions are those current at the time of entry to the 'scrapyard' areas.

2C035	17269	C-47L	AA	6C035	50796	C-117D	DM
2C039	17112	C-47H	AA	6C036	12428	C-117D	DM
2C041	50817	C-47J	AA	6C037	17156	C-117D	
2C049	50789	C-47J	AA	6C038	12431	C-117D	
2C052	12416	C-47H	AA	6C039	17119	C-117D	
	17192	C-47H	DA	6C040	39061	C-117D	
6C005	17160	TC-117D	AA	6C041	39097	C-117D	
6C006	17127	C-117D	AA	6C042	17190	C-117D	
6C007	12425	C-117D	AA	6C043			
6C008	17111	C-117D	AA	6C044	99857	C-117D	
6C009	50826	C-117D		6C045	12422	C-117D	
6C010	99845	C-117D	AA	6C046			
6C011	17149	C-117D	AA	6C047	50834	C-117D	
6C012	17287	C-117D	AA	6C048	17248	C-117D	DA
6C013	17258	C-117D	DA	6C049	17122	C-117D	
6C014	50808	C-117D		6C050	50786	C-117D	
6C015	17194	C-117D	AA	6C051	39080	C-117D	
6C016	12443	C-117D		6C052	17165	C-117D	
6C017	17216	C-117D	AA	6C053	138820	C-117D	
6C018	12441	C-117D	AA	6C054	39081	C-117D	
6C019	50784	C-117D		6C055	12420	C-117D	
6C020	17150	C-117D	DM	6C056	17108	C-117D	
6C021	17092	C-117D	AA	6C057	17116	C-117D	
6C022	39071	C-117D	AA	6C058	12419	C-117D	AA
6C023	50812	C-117D	AA	6C059	50782	C-117D	
6C024	39104	TC-117D		6C060	39064	C-117D	DA
6C025	17177	C-117D	AA	6C061	12437	C-117D	
6C027	39070	C-117D	DM	6C062	17166	C-117D	
6C028	17102	C-117D	DM	6C063	17140	C-117D	
6C029	17097	C-117D			12441	C-117D	
6C030	12412	VC-117D	DM		17153	C-117D	DM
6C031	17182	C-117D	DM		17175	C-117D	
6C032	17153	C-117D	DM		17177	C-117D	
6C033	39072	C-117D			17248	C-117D	DA
6C034	39109	TC-117D					

UPPER VOLTA: see also Burkina Faso

C-47s were supplied by France to the **Force Aérienne de Haute Volta** in Dec64 (34334/XTMAA c/n 34334) and in 1971 (100865/XTMAB c/n 19328). XTMAA is known to have been derelict in 1980. There may have been another as a survey indicated that two remained in use ("*Flight*" Magazine 1983), but neither now survives.

URUGUAY

The first C-47s supplied to the **Fuerza Aérea Uruguaya** were delivered in 1947 for use by the general transportation squadron based at Montevideo. A further two were bought in 1950 and another soon after. In 1955 the first four of ten ex-USAF C-47s were delivered under treaty obligations. The 14 C-47s used during the mid-sixties were all operated by Transporte Aéreo Militar Uruguayo (TAMU) which flew social services as well as military supply missions. In 1969 the Uruguayan government reorganised the whole air transport system with the merger of the bankrupt PLUNA and TAMU, so that PLUNA came under government control. From that point all aircraft used on domestic services carried FAU serials as well as civil registration marks. At first four C-47s were taken over, followed by two more in the mid-seventies. With the delivery of F.27s, FH-227s and Bandeirantes, the C-47 was withdrawn slowly from service and by late 1979 there were only about ten in use with the Brigada Aerea No.1. Only one survived in 1994. The aircraft used are mostly well-documented and serial numbers were:-

G4-507	c/n 25268	517	33411
G4-508	13744	518	25983
G4-509	32551	519	33431
T-510	19021	520	26623
T-511(1)	19301	521	19231
511(2)	34381	522	25733
G4-512	25392	T-523	9226
513	19617	524	4471
514	20604	525	13306
515	32770	527	
T-516	25608		

The prefix G4 was used for some years, but was dropped after G4-512. It is probable that 511 was used twice as 45-1111 has been quoted also, possibly in error. A further C-47 was delivered on 31Oct47 (c/n 19545) and may have been G4-506.

VENEZUELA

The first **Fuerza Aérea Venezolana** C-47 was one intended for Brazil that was diverted in 1946. This, together with seven others delivered in 1947-48 under ARP, formed the initial equipment of the Transport Wing at Caracas Maiquetia (when a second squadron was later equipped with C-123s, this unit then became the 1st Transport Squadron – see serial notes below). Aircraft were allocated to two flights, 'A' and 'B', as early as 1947. More C-47s were received during the 'fifties and 'sixties with the in-use total perhaps peaking at as many as 20 aircraft. In Jun61 the transport squadrons (with C-47s and C-123s) were reorganised into the new Grupo Aéreo de Transporte 6. In the early 'seventies, four aircraft were sold to the civil market and others withdrawn.

The FAV have used two serial number systems since 1946 and both have been complex. Initially, C-47s were marked to show the higher unit, flight allocation and the individual number in the flight. Thus, 'serial' 4-B-T, circa 1947, indicated the fourth aircraft of 'B' flight of the Transport Squadron ('T'). When a second squadron formed, this same aircraft would have become 4-BT-1 to indicate that it now belonged to the 1st Sq. In the list below note that other types 'fill gaps', an example being the C-54 7-AT-1. An example of a 2 Sq aircraft is C-123 4-BT-2.

A completely new serial system was introduced after 1965 using apparently random four-digit numbers.

4AT-1		3BT-1	i/s 1965
5AT-1		4BT	
6AT-1	i/s 1960	6BT-1	
8AT-1		7BT-1	i/s Sep60
1BT-1	i/s 1958	8BT-1	i/s 1960
2BT-1	i/s Jan64		

1023	i/s Oct78
1127	i/s Aug66
1162	i/s May68
1250	i/s Feb67 to 1972 then to LAV
1311	i/s 1972 then to LAV
1330	i/s Jan74
1544	i/s Oct73 to Oct78 and derelict at Caracas
1547	
1570	i/s Jul68
1593	i/s May67
1633	i/s 1972 then to LAV
1660	i/s Mar68 to Mar77, poss re-serialled 1840 by Nov00
1923	i/s May68
2111	
2315	
4984	Preserved in the Museo Aeronautica FAV, Maracay

Two unidentified fatal FAV C-47 accidents occurred when an aircraft hit a mountain in Los Teqes (3k) on 12Jul52 and in Dec66 when an aircraft hit Mt Estado Tachira (4k).

The **Armada Republica Venezolana** established a small fixed-wing transport force in the early seventies, with two C-47s, probably ex FAV. One remained in 1977, with an ex-Aeropostal HS.748. Serial numbers originally noted were ARV-12 and ARV-14 (i/s 1972 to Mar77). Later TR-0102 c/n 25278, was noted in Oct78, and TR-0202 was also seen.

Amongst C-47s supplied to Venezuela by the USAF during 1945-47 were the following:

c/n 9459	13046
9902	20595
10045	25264
11852	26267
11869	34399

VIETNAM (SOUTH)

Thirty years later it is perhaps possible to forget that, for a brief period, the **South Vietnam Air Force/SVNAF** was the world's fourth largest air force and probably the second largest military operator of the C-47. More than that, the history of the SVNAF was one of constant conflict and its battle-proven fleet included some of the most sophisticated and heavily modified of all the military C-47s.

When created in the closing years of the French presence in Indo-China, the SVNAF comprised a single C-47 unit at Tan Son Nhut, Saigon – the

CHAPTER 3: MILITARY OPERATORS OF THE DC-3, C-47, R4D, DAKOTA AND LI-2

312th Special Missions Squadron. A single aircraft was also based at Nha Trang within a liaison flight. By July 1955 the US had sanctioned the transfer of a squadron of French MDAP aircraft (the former aircraft of GT 2/63) to form the 1st Air Transport Sq with 16 aircraft, and in Jun56 a second squadron, the 2nd ATS, had formed with further MDAP-supplied C-47s. These aircraft had also been used formerly by the French Air Force. The 312th SMS was discontinued and replaced by the 314th SMS for VIP work, its mixed fleet including three C-47s. All aircraft were based at Tan Son Nhut, the 1st Air Transport Group having been created in Jun56 to control the 1st and 2nd ATS. By that time, at least 36 C-47s had been received.

Between 1956 and 1966 only a handful of MAP aircraft was added including two VIP-configured C-47Ds but, as the guerilla war began to escalate and US involvement increased, organisational changes were made and new units appeared. The 33rd Tactical Wing was established at Tan Son Nhut in Jan64 comprising three C-47 units, the 413rd Transportation Sq (the former 1st ATS), the 415th TS (formerly the 2nd ATS) and the 314th SMS (with C-47s and T-28s) together with a helicopter squadron. A handful of C-47s equipped the 83rd Special Operations Sq, also at Tan Son Nhut (in Jan66 the 83rd SOS, now part of the 33rd TW, was renamed the 83rd Tactical Group). In early 1965 the two transport squadrons possessed 35 aircraft. The first identified 'non-standard' aircraft to join the SVNAF appear to have been an EC-47D in 1964 and a C-47D described by the SVNAF as an 'RC-47' in 1965.

There was an influx of at least 22 aircraft, including two C-47Ds locally described as 'RC-47', in early 1967 and this resulted in more unit changes. The 417th TS formed at Tan Son Nhut in Jan67 and when the 413rd TS re-equipped with C-119s, the latter's C-47s were passed to another new Tan Son Nhut unit, the 419th TS. However, the return of 12 of the older MDAP aircraft to USAF storage in 1968 together with attrition was not offset by about four new arrivals that year, and the 419th TS was soon deactivated, its aircraft passing to an enlarged 415th TS that continued to operate the C-47 until its deactivation in 1973. Another new unit to appear in 1966/67 was the 716th Reconnaissance Sq at Tan Son Nhut, initially equipped with the three 'RC-47s' (C-47Ds 43-48937, 44-77264 and 45-882) and the EC-47D (43-48905).

At least another eight standard C-47s were acquired in 1969/70, presumably to replace attrition (seven C-47s were lost in accidents between 1965 and 1971). By now aircraft were coming as MAP aid from in-theatre USAF units as they upgraded their own forces and from USAF storage. Major changes occurred in mid-1969 following the USAF's decision progressively to transfer in-theatre AC-47D gunships to the SVNAF as units deactivated. The transfer of 14th SOW AC-47Ds began in Jun69 when five aircraft were handed-over to the 817th Attack Sq, initially within the 33rd TW but later the 62nd TW, at Nha Trang (the 417th TS had been re-numbered and moved in anticipation of this acquisition). Sixteen AC-47Ds were transferred to the SVNAF from the inactivating 3rd SOS in mid-1969 and, following the inactivation of the 4th SOS later in the year, a further three followed by Jan70. [The USAF released three more theatre AC-47Ds to MAP in Jun70, followed by the last three on USAF strength in Jul72, but it is unclear who was the recipient – but see serial notes.] The receipt of the 3rd SOS AC-47Ds by the SVNAF enabled it to release eight C-47s for permanent transfer to the Royal Laotian Air Force between May and Oct69. By late 1970, the 33rd TW fleet at Tan Son Nhut and Nha Trang comprised the 314th SMS ('VC-47'), the 415th TS (C-47), the 716th RS ('RC-47' and U-6A) and the 817th AS (AC-47D).

At least 16 more conventional C-47s were received in 1971/72 mainly from local USAF sources as well as additional 'specials'. Three special operations HC-47s were received from local USAF units in early 1971 and in early 1972 another EC-47D (43-49029) and a C-47D (43-48620 but described by the SVNAF as 'SC-47') arrived. The two latter aircraft joined the 716th RS but it is unclear to which unit(s) the HC-47s were attached.

In 1972 there was another major influx of specialised aircraft as part of the US-inspired 'Project Enhance'. US sources have described the C-47 element of 'Enhance' as comprising the transfer of 12 'RC-47' and 33 'EC-47' from in-theatre USAF units. However, examination of other evidence suggests a slightly different story. We can identify at least 41 transfers in calendar 1972 comprising 11 C-47s, the 'SC-47' and EC-47D mentioned earlier, three (assumed) AC-47Ds, 11 EC-47Ns and 14 EC-47Ps. The final known transfers took place in Feb73 and they comprised six more EC-47Ns and two EC-47Ps (and it should be remembered that the EC-47N/P were identical mission aircraft and that until mid-1967 they had been designated RC-47N/P). We can therefore identify the 33 'EC-47s' but have to assume that the 12 'RC-47s' were actually a combination of other versions. 'Enhance' necessitated the activation of a new radio intelligence gathering squadron, the 718th RS at Tan Son Nhut, attached to the 33rd TW and equipped exclusively with the EC-47N/P.

The huge increase in C-47 numbers coupled with a general and very rapid expansion of the SVNAF led to an unmanageable situation with many aircraft placed in storage. Moreover, in Nov72 the USAF exerted pressure on the SVNAF to return all C-47s, C-119s and C-123s in order to release crews to fly the more capable C-130. Although the Vietnamese resisted this to a degree and retained some C-47s, in Jan73 at least 20 aircraft, including some that had been received only recently, were returned to the USAF and were re-distributed to other nations or scrapped. A US figure (date uncertain) suggests that 34 C-47s went into storage at some time in the early 'seventies. Prior to the return of these aircraft, a snapshot of the SVNAF C-47 units in late 1972 counts 22 active C-47s with the 415th TS and another six in storage, 22 EC-47N/Ps active with the 718th RS, an unknown total (but all) AC-47Ds with the 817th TS, six 'VC-47Ds' with the 314th TS and a mix of two EC-47Ds, three 'RC-47s' and the 'SC-47' with the 716th TS. Presumably, the three HC-47s and probably other C-47s were distributed among the operational bases.

Following the cease-fire of 27Jan73, the SVNAF gradually disintegrated although its structure remained superficially intact until close to the end. The 415th TS was deactivated in 1973 as more advanced types undertook the more basic transport work. The other major units survived until at least late 1974 with the 718th RS establishing a detachment at Da Nang within the 41st TW. It is unclear to what extent the US may have orchestrated any further transfers of C-47s from the SVNAF directly to other air arms or agencies, but after early 1973 we do not see any 'forced gain' entries on USAF record cards to indicate the return of MAP aircraft from South Vietnam. After the fall of Saigon on 30Apr75 an estimated 38 intact C-47s of all marks were taken by North Vietnamese forces and at least 16 others are thought to have escaped to Thailand. What we see, therefore, are some aircraft recorded properly as returned to the USAF and redistributed, others such as the AC-47Ds that probably operated with other nations in the region but whose transfers are not recorded on cards and several, including some of the 1975 'escapees', that were taken subsequently into use by other nations. Few of those that remained in Vietnam after May75 saw very much use.

By 1978, Russia had supplied 20 Li-2s to the new combined Vietnamese Air Force and they were used alongside some of the surviving C-47s. However, a shortage of spare parts and a history of hard work made their lives relatively short and none survived for long.

Throughout its life, the SVNAF maintained the individual aircraft radio call/code system that it had inherited from the French. The 'last two' of the call-sign were worn on a yellow disc on the tail, the first (smaller) letter indicating the squadron and the second (larger) identifying the individual aircraft. Code prefixes were as follows: 314th TS 'C', 1st ATS/413rd TS 'N', 2nd ATS/415th TS 'E', 417th TS 'H', 716th RS 'M', 718th RS 'W' and 817th TS 'K'.

The following lists identify in excess of 150 aircraft of all marks that we are fairly confident served with the SVNAF. However, this is a particularly complex air force to research and omissions and errors are likely, although we have striven to minimise the latter. For ease of reference they are presented by the SVNAF type identification which, in a few instances, is at variance with the USAF record at the time of transfer. The aircraft source has been short-handed to 'MAP' (all ex-USAF aircraft whether theatre transfers or from US storage depots), 'France' (former French aircraft redirected on US authority either directly or via storage), and 'Local' (covering all other acquisitions). Greater clarity will come by referring to individual histories:

C-47A/C-47D:-

Serial	c/n	Date/Source	Notes
224062	c/n 9924	23Jul56 (France) 'E', 'EC' (64)	to Taiwan by Apr72
224336	10198	16Mar56 (France)	
292295	12080	21Sep71 (MAP)	
292836	12681	30Apr68 (MAP) 'EA' (72)	
293087	12960	03Aug56 (France) 'EH' (63), 'EC' (63)	to USAF 05Aug68
293354	13256	Nov53 (Local)	
2100666	19129	30Aug56 (France) 'CM' (64), 'EC' (66)	to Laos?
315648	20114	post Apr56 (Local)	
315718	20184	post Apr56 (Local)	
315984	20450	20Feb56 (France) 'ED'	
316140	20606	17Jul69 (MAP)	to Philippines by Apr72
316156	20622	20Oct55 (France)	to USAF 27Aug68
316164	20630	22Oct55 (France) 'B'	to USAF 02Sep68
348014	25275	10Apr56 (Local) 'F' (58)	crashed 1960

348058	25319	24Oct55 (France) 'K' (64), 'C'	to USAF 31Oct68
348071	25332	24Oct55 (France)	
348101	25362	28Feb61 (MAP)	to Thailand by 78
348151	25412	21Aug56 (France)	to USAF 01Sep68
348387	25648	15Apr67 (MAP) 'EN' (72)	to USAF 10Jan73
348394	25655	31Mar67 (MAP)	
348415	25676	24Oct55 (France) 'NI'	to USAF 27Sep68
348465	25726	post 13Feb56 (France) 'EF' (64)	
348476	25737	06May67 (MAP) 'EQ' (72)	to USAF 09Jan73
348491	25752	08Sep69 (MAP) 'EY'	to USAF 19Jan73
348504	25765	22Oct55 (France) 'B' (64)	
348599	25860	16Nov67 (MAP) 'ED' (72)	to USAF 04Jan73
348704	25965	24Oct55 (France) 'D', 'I' (64), 'NB'	to Laos by Dec70
348729	25990	post 13Feb56 (France) 'EC'	current 1964
348772	26033	21Oct54 (France)	
348777*	26038	09Sep72 (MAP) 'EY' (72)	to Thailand
348800	26061	24Oct55 (France)	
348816	26077	10Feb67 (MAP) 'ES' (72)	to USAF 06Jan73
348859	26120	24Oct55 (France) 'EA' (64)	to USAF 12Aug68
348874	26135	post 13Feb56 (France) 'A' (63)	
348879	26140	25Feb67 (MAP)	
348909	26170	04Jan66 (MAP)	to Laos by Sep69(?)
349035	26296	16Mar56 (France) 'EP'	
349095	26356	15Nov67 (MAP) 'EK' (72)	to USAF 07Jan73
349113	26374	24Oct55 (France) 'N' (65)	to USAF 13Sep68
349114	26375	07May61 (MAP) 'EB' (64)	
349210	26471	04May68 (MAP) 'EC' (72)	to Thailand by 75
349215	26476	08May67 (MAP)	
349216	26477	24Oct55 (France) 'J' (64), 'D'	to USAF 27Sep68
349344	26605	01Apr67 (MAP) 'EL' (72)	to USAF 09Jan73
349345	26606	post 13Feb56 (France) 'EB' (64)	
349361	26622	14Nov69 (MAP) 'EU' (72)	to USAF 04Jan73
349364	26625	24Oct55 (France) 'E'	
349425	26686	22Apr67 (MAP)	
349495	26756	17Nov69 (MAP) 'EZ' (72)	to USAF 05Jan73
349497	26758	13Mar67 (MAP) 'EJ' (72)	to USAF 08Jan73
349500	26761	10May62 (MAP) 'EW'	
349519	26780	21Jun62 (MAP) 'EP' (?)	
349524	26785	24Oct55 (France)	extant Tan Son Nhut 95
349545*	26806	post 15Apr58 (MAP)	to Thailand by 68
349566	26827	24Oct55 (France) 'K', 'A'	
349680	26941	23Aug72 (MAP)	later to Thailand
349783	27044	14Nov69 (MAP) 'ET' (72)	
349814	27075	07Oct71 (MAP) 'EI' (72)	to USAF 12Jan73
349907	27168	04May68 (MAP)	
349925	27186	01Apr67 (MAP) 'EF' (72)	to USAF 06Jan73
476259	32591	20Feb56 (France) 'EA' (64)	
476418	32750	04May68 (MAP) 'EB' (72)	to USAF 21Jan73
476454	32786	27Nov67 (MAP)	
476460	32792	24Jul72 (MAP)	in storage Nov72
476502	32834	24Oct55 (France) 'H' (64)	to USAF 18Oct68
476558	32890	14Nov69 (MAP) 'EV' (72)	to USAF 08Jan73
476578	32910	09Sep71 (MAP)	to USAF 06Mar73
476632	32964	10Aug72 (MAP) 'EE' (72)	to USAF 07Jan73
476643	32975	03Nov67 (MAP) 'EC'	destroyed by mortar fire at Tan Son Nhut 18Feb68
477012	33344	03May67 (MAP) 'ER' (72)	
477162	33494	14Aug72 (MAP)	in storage Nov72
477218	33550	16Aug72 (MAP)	in storage Nov72
477283	33615	08Sep72 (MAP) 'EO' (72)	to USAF 05Jan73
477284	33616	29Jul72 (MAP) 'EG' (72)	to USAF 22Jan73
50887	34147	25Jul72 (MAP)	in storage Nov72
50939	34201	17Jun62 (MAP) 'R'	
50945	34207	26Jan67 (MAP) 'MC'	
50950	34213	07Sep71 (MAP)	
50993	34258	20Feb56 (France)	to USAF 28Sep68
51062	34332	31Mar70 (MAP)	
51080	34350	07Aug72 (MAP) 'EH' (72)	to USAF 20Jan73
51093	34363	26Jul72 (MAP)	in storage Nov72, to Thailand

*348777 and 349545 were VC-47Ds when they left USAF service.

'VC-47D' (SVNAF designation):-

348586	25847	04Jan66 (MAP) 'EF', 'CG' (72)	
349257*	26518	25Feb67 (MAP) 'CH' (72)	to USAF 26Feb73 escapee to Thailand 75
476302*	32634	31Jan67 (MAP) 'CL' (72)	
476417*	32749	09Mar67 (MAP) 'CI' (72)	
476638	32970	21Jul62 (MAP) 'CF' (72)	to Thailand by 77
476686	33018	26Apr62 (MAP) 'CE' (72)	

*349257 was a 'genuine' VC-47D when withdrawn from USAF service. 476302 and 476417 had been VC-47Ds earlier in their USAF careers.

EC-47D:-

348905	26166	17Jan64 (MAP) 'MA' (72)	
349029	26290	07Feb72 (MAP) 'MF' (72)	later to Philippines

'RC-47' (C-47D):-

348937	26198	02Jun65 (MAP) 'EO' (68), 'MG' (72)	
477264	33596	26Jan67 (MAP) 'MB' (72)	
50882	34141	26Jan67 (MAP) 'MC' (72)	to Thailand by 76

'SC-47' (C-47D):-

348620	25881	13Jan72 (MAP) 'ME' (72)	

HC-47A/HC-47D:-

293812	13765	29Jan71 (MAP)	
315773	20240	09May71 (MAP)	
50883	34142	22Mar71 (MAP)	to Thailand by Nov72

AC-47D:-

316065	20531	15Jul69 (MAP)	
316133	20599	07Jun70 (MAP)	
316368	20834	31Dec69 (MAP) 'KT'	
348466*	25727	20Jul72 (MAP)	
348501*		11Apr68 (MAP)	to Thailand
348686	25947	30Jul69 (MAP)	
348701	25962	06Apr69 (MAP)	
348801	26062	30Jun69 (MAP)	
348916	26177	31Jul72 (MAP)	
348929	26190	30Jul69 (MAP) 'KL'	
349010*	26271	07Jun70 (MAP)	
349211*	26472	31Dec69 (MAP)	
349339	26600	30Jul69 (MAP) 'KI'	
349421	26682	20Aug69 (MAP)	later to VN-C508
349423*	26684	28Dec69 (MAP)	
349503	26764	15Jul69 (MAP) 'KF'	
349516*	26777	28Dec69 (MAP)	
349517	26778	30Jul69 (MAP)	
349572	26833	29Jan71 (MAP)	
349770	27031	30Jun69 (MAP) 'KD'	
476354	32686	15Aug69 (MAP)	
476370*	32702	24Dec69 (MAP)	
476394	32726	15Aug69 (MAP)	
476593	32925	15Aug69 (MAP)	
476606	32938	15Jul69 (MAP)	
476625*	32957	07Jun70 (MAP)	
476722	33054	30Jun69 (MAP)	
477263*	33595	23Jul72 (MAP)	
50919	34180	30Jun69 (MAP) 'KC'	
50927*	34188	01Jan70 (MAP)	
51047*	34316	01Jan70 (MAP)	
51057*	34327	26Dec69 (MAP)	
51121*	34391	05Jan70 (MAP)	

*348501 was transferred to MAP in 4.68, a year before other transfers began and it is uncertain whether this aircraft ever did serve with the SVNAF. When the USAF's 4th SOS inactivated at Phan Rang in Dec69, it possessed 14 aircraft. Only three of them (316368 and two unidentified) initially went to the SVNAF. Eight others went to the RLAF and three were retained in Thailand by the USAF's 432nd TRW for another six months. Thus, the SVNAF will have received two from 349211, 349423, 349516, 476370, 50927, 51047, 51057 and 51121. It may also have received the three 432nd TRW aircraft (316133, 349010 and 476625) in Jun70 and perhaps the three that went to MAP in Jul72 (348466, 348916 and 477263). It did not receive 348263 and 51117 as they are known to have gone from the 4th SOS to the RLAF as part of the batch of eight in 1969.

EC-47N:-
223520	9382	15Nov72 (MAP) 'WX' (72)	
293161	13042	17Feb73 (MAP)	
293166	13047	03Nov72 (MAP) 'WN' (72)	
293735	13680	08Nov72 (MAP) 'WS' (72)	
2100513	18976	01Nov72 (MAP)	
2100950	19413	13Nov72 (MAP) 'WV' (72)	
2100984	19447	03Nov72 (MAP) 'WM' (72)	to USAF. Extant Pima County
2108980	13468	17Feb73 (MAP)	
315112	19578	10Nov72 (MAP) 'WT' (72)	
315603	20069	06Nov72 (MAP) 'WP' (72)	
315668	20134	17Feb73 (MAP)	
315979	20445	17Feb73 (MAP)	
315980	20446	17Feb73 (MAP)	
316055	20521	06Nov72 (MAP) 'WO' (72)	
316095	20561	24Aug72 (MAP) 'WI' (72)	
316123	20589	17Feb73 (MAP)	
348158	25419	21Nov72 (MAP) 'WE' (72)	

EC-47P:-
348480	25741	19Aug72 (MAP) 'WD' (72)	
348767	26028	23Aug72 (MAP) 'WG' (72)	
348871	26132	22Aug72 (MAP) 'WF' (72)	
348886	26147	01Aug72 (MAP) 'WB' (72)	
348933	26194	22Aug72 (MAP) 'WH' (72)	
348947	26208	25Aug72 (MAP) 'WK' (72)	
349009	26270	08Nov72 (MAP) 'WQ' (72)	
349013	26274	08Nov72 (MAP) 'WR' (72)	
349126	26387	10Nov72 (MAP) 'WU' (72)	
349703	26964	17Feb73 (MAP)	in Thailand by 95
349865	27126	09Nov72 (MAP)	
476524	32856	09Nov72 (MAP)	
476668	33000	08Nov72 (MAP) 'WL' (72)	
50925	34186	16Feb73 (MAP)	
51044	34313	01Aug72 (MAP) 'WA' (72)	to Thailand
51046	34315	19Aug72 (MAP) 'WC' (72)	

YEMEN (NORTH)

Three C-47s were acquired by the **Yemen Arab Republic Air Force** prior to 1957. Nothing is known of individual aircraft, but they probably came from Yemen Airlines.

YEMEN (SOUTH) - see South Arabia.

YUGOSLAVIA

At first Li-2s supplied by Russia were used by the **Yugoslav Air Force/Jugoslovensko Ratno Vazduhplovstvo** in 1946/47. Later these were supplemented or replaced by C-47s from various sources including France and the USAF. The latter supplied a batch in 1953/54 after overhaul at Bordeaux and by Avio Diepen in Holland. In 1980 it is reported that about 15 remained in use, destined to be replaced by An-26s. Several were sold in the USA during 1980. Little is known of the detail of the Yugoslavian C-47s but it is thought that two serial systems were used. The first post-war sequence commenced with 7301 and 7329 seems to be the highest-noted example. That sequence appears to have been replaced in the 1960s by one starting at 71201 and may reflect a simple re-numbering exercise. The later sequence reached at least 71258 (with an aberrant '71273' reported). Other reported sequences now appear to be in error.

Known Li-2s are 7103 (preserved nr Bosanski Petrovac), and 7011 (ex 71103) c/n 18422308, locally known as an Li-3, combining an Li-2 fuselage with Pratt & Whitney engines.

C-47s detected so far are mainly relics:
7304	c/n	noted 1948
7311	26720	later 71202
7313		
7314		
7315		
7317	33355	
7318		noted 1958
7321		
7323	33220	later 71214
7329		
71202	26720	
71203		preserved at Zadar (Apr 96)
71204		
71206		
71209		
71210		noted 1960s
71212		noted at Nis, near Bihach AB 1991 to 1996
71214	33220	
71216		wfu post-11Jan77. At Mostar 1992
71218		noted at Zagreb. Present Jul95 - Jun01
71219		
71229		noted Oct74
71237	11746	
71241	12704	
71245		wfu Batajnica AFB near Belgrade 1970s
71248		wfu Rajlovac, nr Sarajevo, present Sep91
71253		donated 10Dec80 to a Slovene museum for display at partisan field, Otok near Metlika - in place 18Aug84. In RAF c/s in 1986, present Jan97
71254	25546	
71255	26557	
71258		
71273		noted 1974

Amongst candidate ex-French C-47s was c/n 4608. Those supplied from USAF stocks included c/ns 25791, 26096, 26256?, 26720, 26742, 27081, 32545?, 32827?, 33041, 33060, 33062?, 33165, 33220, 33250, 33319, 33327?, 33355. Those marked '?' left USAF stocks at a time when others went to Yugoslavia.

ZAIRE/DEMOCRATIC REPUBLIC OF CONGO

The **Force Aérienne Congolaise/Force Aérienne Zairoise** acquired a fleet of C-47s following the civil war in 1961. Most of these originated in the United Nations fleet, though some probably came from Air Zaire. About ten C-47s were in use between 1974 and 1979 with 191 and 192 Squadrons, though their serviceability was doubtful. None now remain, though a survey in 1993 suggested that six might be in service. Ten C-47s were supplied from USAF stocks in 1964 via MAP (9T-PKA to 9T-PKJ?), four more ex MAP in the autumn of 1965 and a further ten from various sources in the late 60s. Some details have come to light from pilot log books and observations, but no official data is known.

9T-PDX	c/n	possibly ex UN
9T-PIF	7367	also 9T-P23
9T-PKA		ex USAF, cr Jul68
9T-PKB	25344 ?	
9T-PKC		ex USAF, seized by rebel mercenaries at Kisangani in Jul67; cr Jul67 at Bukavu
9T-PKD	25242	
9T-PKE	25357 ?	
9T-PKF	25502	
9T-PKG		ex USAF, cr 08Apr69 at Mushie
9T-PKH		ex USAF
9T-PKI	20149	
9T-PKJ	25516	
9T-PKK	19541	
9T-PKL	13348	
9T-PKM	25357 ?	
9T-PKR	6339	
9T-PKS	4144	
9T-PKT	13486	
9T-PKU	10129	
9T-PKV	12734	
9T-PKW		quoted as 13486, alternate for 9T-PKT
9T-PKY		
9T-PKZ	19551	
9T-JDM	34409	
9T-MSS	34409	ex 9T-JDM
9T-TAB		
9T-TAC		
9T-TAU		
9T-TAZ		
9T-TCA		
9T-TCB	25518	to Congo Jun64

Other possible FA Congolaise/Zaire AF candidates are c/n 9938 (9T-P24), 13842, 19815 and 32742.

ZAMBIA

Eleven C-47s have been reported as serving with the **Zambian Air Force**, but none now survives. Those acquired in 1964 came from the Rhodesian Air Force and two others may have come from Zambian Airways whose C-47s are not all accounted for.

Serial numbers are:

AF-101	c/n 32715		AF-107	1973
AF-102	33547		AF-108	1973
AF-103	33072		AF-109	1973
AF-104	33182		AF-110	
AF-105		i/s Oct69	AF-111	25339
AF-106		i/s Oct69		

ZIMBABWE / RHODESIA / SOUTHERN RHODESIA

The first Dakota was supplied to the **Southern Rhodesian Air Force** by the SAAF in 1947 and was given the serial number SR-25. In 1954/55 seven ex RAF Dakotas were overhauled by Scottish Aviation for the **Royal Rhodesian Air Force** as it had become on 31Dec53, for use by 3 Transport Sq (SR/RRAF 152 to 158). Four more followed in 1964, this time from South Africa (703, 706, 707, and 709), and further aircraft were later bought through various channels. During the Unilateral Declaration of Independence (UDI), the RRAF became the **Rhodesian Air Force**, and clandestine sources were used to support the ground forces in suppressing the "rebellion". Later C-47s arrived in ones and twos to replace losses.

The serial numbering system was changed several times during the period, using different prefixes to suit the regime in power. SR denoted Southern Rhodesia, RRAF the Royal Rhodesian Air Force, and R for the post-UDI Rhodesian Air Force on 11Nov65. With the formation of Zimbabwe on 18Apr80, the "R" was dropped by the **Zimbabwe Air Force**. A series starting at 700 was used by Rhodesia, but to this was added the squadron number 3, amongst the digits, probably to confuse. It is fairly clear that the "3" has not always remained in any particular position, to add to confusion. It is believed that the following have been used at various times:

Apart from those listed in the accompanying table (see below), it is known that c/n 33552 was delivered to Rhodesia in 1975, possibly for spares use, as it has not appeared subsequently. Ten Dakotas were in store at Harare-Manyame (marked *) in Feb98 but 7039 and 7310 were moved to Wonderboom in S Africa in 2001.

Sthn Rhod AF 28Nov47-31Dec53	Call sign	Royal Rhod AF 31Dec53-01Mar70	Rn RRAF	Rhod AF 01Mar70-18Apr80	Zimbabwe AF 18Apr80 to date	c/n
SR-25	VPYZA	25 then 151	702	R3702	-	25310
SR-152	VPYZB	152	703(1)	-	-	32715
SR-153	VPYZC	153	704	R7034	-	33410
SR-154	VPYZD	154	705(1)	-	-	33547
SR-155?	VPYZE	155	706(1) then 705(2)?	R7053	7053*	32759
SR-156	VPYZF	156	707(1)	-	-	33072
SR-157	VPYZG	157	708(1)	-	-	33182
-	-	-	-	R3700	3700*	13164
-	-	-	-	R3701 later R7301	7301*	33083
-	VPYZB	-	703(2)	R7303	7303*	25312
-	VPYZE	-	706(2)	R3706 later R7036	7036*	25939
-	VPYZF	-	707(2)	R3707 later R7307	-	32946
-	-	158	708(2)?	R7038 later R3708	3708*	33138
-	VPYZH	-	709	R3709 later R7039	7039*	32651
-	-	-	-	R7310	7310*	42978
-	-	-	-	R7311 later R3711	3711	12049
-	-	-	-	R7312	7312	9492
-	-	-	-	R7313	7313*	32741
-	-	-	-	R7314 later R7134	7134*	26437

Royal Rhodesian Air Force C-47B '158' c/n 33138 awaits the results of a discussion taking place around the door on this unidentified mountain-backed airstrip during the sixties. As shown in the table above, this aircraft went on to serve in the Rhodesian and the Zimbabwe Air Forces.
[Cliff Minney]

CHAPTER 3: MILITARY OPERATORS OF THE DC-3, C-47, R4D, DAKOTA AND LI-2

FA Argentina *C-47A T-20 c/n unknown* - This pre-delivery photograph taken at Idlewild, NY shows a C-47A equipped with skis for Antarctic use. It was attached to Grupo de Transportes Aereas Antarticas and crashed on 19Mar56. A second C-47 numbered T-20 was c/n 2012. [William Steeneck]

Argentine Navy *C-47A 0281 3-Gt-12 c/n 12732* - This early C-47 (it has small hinges on the cargo doors) was awaiting delivery, probably in the New York area in 1948. 3-Gt indicates the 3rd Naval Air Force General Transport Unit. Such unit codes changed regularly. This C-47 is believed to have crashed on 03Apr63. [Warren D Shipp]

Biafran AF *C-47B-25-DK '803' c/n 32725* - Seen at Abidjan, Ivory Coast in Apr69, this aircraft had been built as 44-76393, delivered to the RAF as KN360 and eventually passed to the WGAF, its final marks being XA+112 when operated by LVSt 612 at Lechfeld, Germany. When sold as surplus it became N10803 and was sold for supply to the Biafran AF. On arriving at Faro the 'N10' portion of the registration was blanked out.[Roger Caratini via Bill Fisher]

FA Brasileira C-47B C-47 2009 c/n 25679 - This was the first C-47B supplied to Brazil as FAB no. 01, and is unusual in having twin DF loops behind the cockpit. It is now preserved at the Museo Aeroespacial at Rio de Janeiro, Brazil. [via David Lucabaugh]

Burmese AF C-47A-30-DK UB714 c/n 25309 - This Dakota was supplied to Burma ex G-ANZE and this photograph was taken at Bovingdon, UK, probably in Jul55. It was sold as N2271C in Jul78 and stored at Bangkok until 1993 when it was delivered to Archerfield, QLD where it has remained ever since with all movable parts stripped out. [A Pearcy]

Cambodian AF C-47B 43-254 c/n 26515 - This photograph, taken at Paya Lebar, Singapore on 25Mar72 suggests that this aircraft is perhaps more likely to be c/n 25629, previously US Navy R4D-6 17254 than ex-USAF C-47 43-49254. It has a 'knob' under the nose on which was originally mounted a DF loop of the type fitted to R4Ds and not to USAF C-47s. Its profusion of aerials suggests that it was an ELINT aircraft. [R F Killick]

CHAPTER 3: MILITARY OPERATORS OF THE DC-3, C-47, R4D, DAKOTA AND LI-2

Royal Canadian AF *C-47B 'KG828' c/n 25612* - Belonging to 1 Air Command, this aircraft was based in Europe and the photograph was taken at Odiham, UK on 17Sep68 whilst visiting for the SBAC show at nearby Farnborough. The aircraft is actually KJ828 and was so in Oct59, and became 828 in 1961 before becoming KG828 post-1965 and then 12948. [Jennifer Gradidge]

Chinese Nationalist AF *C-47D 293* - Nothing more is known of this aircraft as this rare photograph is undated, and the serial system has changed several times over the years. [MAP]

Chinese Nationalist AF *C-47B-7-DK 48806, later 7219 c/n 26067*, is now preserved at the Academy Museum at Kangshan AB in Taiwan where it was photographed on 27Jul95. [Bas Stubert]

FA Colombiana C-47D 1124 c/n 26775 of SATENA, the government-owned local-service operator is shown in this photograph taken at Villavicencio, Colombia in Feb82. Radar equipment is advertised on the nose - a most useful asset in the mountainous terrain. [Karl Krämer]

FAE de Cuba C-47A-DL 204 c/n unknown - taken possibly in Miami, FL before 1959. [H G Martin]

Czech AF C-47A-DL D-19 c/n 12617 - Delivered ex-USAAF in May46, this was not one of the Czech AF examples that was later sold to the French AF. [Unknown]

CHAPTER 3: MILITARY OPERATORS OF THE DC-3, C-47, R4D, DAKOTA AND LI-2

FA Ecuatoriana *C-47D FAE 76448/HC-AUQ c/n 32780* - Delivered via MAP from USAF stocks in Panama, this aircraft was used by Transportes Aereos Militar Ecuador on commercially uneconomic domestic services, and survived until about 1985. *[via A Pearcy]*

Imperial Ethiopian AF *C-47 707 c/n unknown* - The IEAF had as many as thirteen C-47s in use at any one time, and this photograph was probably taken before delivery from the UK. *[APN]*

Finnish AF *C-53D-DO DO-9 c/n 11750* - This aircraft was delivered from USAF stocks in Jul48 and registered OH-LCG for Finnair. After twenty-one years, it was transferred to the National Board of Survey with the Finnish AF and various extra aerials, as well as an observation window behind the cockpit, can be seen. It was sold eventually to Warbirds of Norway in 1986. *[Peter Bish]*

Armée de l'Air VC-47D 349545 c/n 26806 - This photograph was taken in Apr58 at Clark Field in the Philippines, when the aircraft was returned to the USAF. It later went to the S Vietnam AF and then to Thailand (see later photograph). Interestingly, it has a DF loop mounted under the nose, as usually fitted to US Navy R4Ds. [Merle Olmsted]

Luftwaffe Dakota 1408 c/n 33203 - This aircraft served with the Luftwaffe for twenty years until it took up US marks and eventually went to Colombia, where it was stored at Eldorado in 1993. [unknown]

R Hellenic AF C-47B-DK 349111 c/n 26732 - This aircraft was delivered to the Greek AF from USAF stocks in Jun48, and has been preserved at Tatoi, Greece since 1996. [MAP]

CHAPTER 3: MILITARY OPERATORS OF THE DC-3, C-47, R4D, DAKOTA AND LI-2   137

CA de l'Armée de Haiti *C-47D 4262 c/n 4262* - COHATA or Compagnie Haitienne de Transports Aeriens operated as a branch of the Corps d'Aviation de l'Armee de Haiti, and used 4262 in the early 1950s, ex NC54327.   [H G Martin via P J Marson]

Royal Indian AF *C-47B/Dakota HJ922 c/n unknown* - Little is known of Indian AF Dakotas, except that most came from RAF stocks in India in 1946. HJ922 was still in service in Jun80, but by 1983 fatigue problems were beginning to show and few survived much longer.   [A J Jackson collection]

Imperial Iranian AF *C-47A-DL 5-07 c/n unknown* - This aircraft is probably an ex-USAF C-47 on delivery through Croydon, Surrey, UK to the IIAF in about 1949.   [via Merle Olmsted]

Israel Defence Force/Air Force *C-47B 4X-FNN/1416 c/n 25869 - This aircraft was supplied from French AF stocks to the IDF/AF in Jan67, just in time for the 'Six-Day War'. It was sold recently in the US as N47SJ.*
[MAP]

Aeronautica Militare Italiano *C-47A-40-DL MM61777/CR-43 c/n 9910 - After leaving USAAF service this aircraft passed to KLM and then to the Italian AF in 1950. CR- indicates Centro Radiomisure and there are many tell-tale aerials and sensors mounted on top of and below the fuselage. It was re-coded 14-43 in May76, when this photograph was taken at Milan-Malpensa, Italy and was one of the last Italian AF C-47s in service. Its remains were still at Rome-Guidonia in 2001.*
[Carlo Gallo]

Ivory Coast AF *C-47B 76795/TUVAA c/n 33127 - Supplied to the Ivory Coast from French AF stocks in 1961, and photographed at Dakar, Senegal in Nov64, this aircraft eventually passed to Air Transivoire in 1977 as TU-TJM.*
[Roger Caratini]

CHAPTER 3: MILITARY OPERATORS OF THE DC-3, C-47, R4D, DAKOTA AND LI-2

Japan *DC-3 or L2D-3 c/n unknown* - This pre-war aircraft was waiting at Fukuoka, Japan in Oct45 in case General MacArthur allowed Japan Airways to resume commercial operations. The aircraft is nominally all-white with a green cross, then a requirement for any airworthy Japanese aircraft. Another example, sitting behind on its belly, is engineless. When flying did re-start in Japan in 1954, DC-3s were imported, so this pair seems not to have survived.
[US Marine Corps]

Laotian Army Aviation Service *C-47A-DL 666 c/n 20132* - This aircraft was acquired via the French AF in Aug56, its full serial being 43-15666. When and where this photograph was taken are unknown, but the pristine condition of the aircraft suggests that it was newly overhauled/acquired.
[via A Pearcy]

Royal Libyan AF *C-47B-DK O-49015 c/n 26276* - This C-47 was photographed prior to delivery following overhaul at Miami, FL in Aug65.
[via A Pearcy]

FA Mexicana C-47A-DL AP-0201 c/n 19409 unconfirmed - There is some doubt as to the identity of this Presidential C-47, named 'Revolucionario'. It was photographed at Dallas-Love Field, TX on 02Oct64 when AP-0201 was also registered XC-PAZ. [Erwin J Bulban]

FA Royales Marocaines C-47B-DK 49436 c/n 26697 - After overhaul by Fairchild, this was delivered to the Moroccan AF in 1962, but by 19Mar64, when this photograph was taken at Dakar, Senegal, the roundels had been painted out and nothing further is known of it. Most other Moroccan AF C-47s were sold in the US in 1970. [Roger Caratini]

Koninklijke Luchtmacht Dakota 4 X-8/ZU-8 c/n 33415 - A visitor to Blackbushe, UK on 03Sep57 for the SBAC show at nearby Farnborough, this aircraft was delivered to the Royal Netherlands AF from RAF stocks in 1952. It returned to the USAF in Mar61, being passed to Chile in 1962 and Paraguay in 1993. [Jennifer Gradidge]

CHAPTER 3: MILITARY OPERATORS OF THE DC-3, C-47, R4D, DAKOTA AND LI-2
141

Royal New Zealand AF *Dakota 3 NZ3517 c/n 12546* - On taking-off from Piva strip, Bougainville in the Solomon islands in Jan45, the main gear is just retracting and flaps are not needed. The roundels are modified USAAF but retain the central red circle, reduced in size. The aircraft was broken up in 1948. [RNZAF]

Royal Norwegian AF *c/n 19674 C-47A-DL 315208* - Before joining 335 Squadron of the Royal Norwegian AF, this was the original 'Fassberg Flyer' on the Berlin Airlift in Jun50. It was photographed at Bodo, Norway in Mar69 and was sold eventually in the USA as N62102 in Aug74. Later it was converted to a Basler BT-67, going to Guatemala in 1993. [C P Russell-Smith via P J Marson]

Philippine AF *C-47B-DK 377155 c/n 33487* - This aircraft was delivered to the Philippine AF in 1945 and survived until 1980. The serial is wrongly painted and should read 477155. This photograph was taken at Nichols Field, Philippines in Apr57. [Merle Olmsted]

Forca Aérea Portuguesa *C-47A-80-DL 250 c/n 19773* - As 43-15307 this 8th AF C-47 was interned in Portugal on 12Apr44 on its way to North Africa. Any damage was repaired and it was taken into the Portuguese AF as D-1, later becoming 250, CS-EDA and 6150. This photograph was taken in Portugal in 1946.
[Portuguese AF]

Sudanese AF *Dakota 425 c/n 26990* - Scottish Aviation overhauled numerous Dakotas and this example went through their works in Aug62 after it had been transferred from Sudan Airways (ST-AAL) to the air force. It reverted later to ST-AAL and in 1971 went to Ethiopian Airlines. [J A Watts]

Escadrille Tchadienne *C-47B-DK 49594 c/n 26855* - Coded TTLAA, this was the Presidential aircraft in its day, being photographed on 06Nov70 at Abidjan, Ivory Coast. Originally an RAF Dakota, it transferred to the French AF in May49 after overhaul by Scottish Aviation, going to Tchad in Jun61.
[Roger Caratini]

CHAPTER 3: MILITARY OPERATORS OF THE DC-3, C-47, R4D, DAKOTA AND LI-2

Royal Thai AF *C-47D-DK O-39545 c/n 26806* - An earlier photograph shows this aircraft whilst in French AF service. It passed through USAF ownership in Apr58, and then as a VC-47D went via the S Vietnam AF to Thailand. In the absence of any further dating, it is just possible that this aircraft did not serve in Vietnam. The photograph was probably taken at Don Muang, Thailand, where the 603rd Squadron was based. [Norm Taylor]

United Kingdom *Dakota III KG496 c/n 12817* - The Royal Air Force had the largest fleet of C-47s apart from the USAAF and many can be seen in this photograph taken at Bari in southern Italy in 1944. The unit code for 267 Sq is A-1. KG496 went on to India in 1945 and passed to the R Indian AF as VP904. [G S Leslie/R C Sturtivant]

United States Army Air Corps *C-49 (ex DC-3-362) 41-7694 c/n 3297* at Felts Field, WA in Mar41. This C-49 was delivered on 22Mar41, and is therefore brand new. The only identification is the number '94' on the fin, the last two of the USAAC serial. This aircraft was ordered originally by TWA and has R-1820s; it went to the 5th AF in Australia in Sep42 and went missing the following April. [Boardman Reed]

United States Army Air Force C-53-DO 41-20062 c/n 4832 at Wright Field, OH, taken on 24Nov41. This aircraft belonged to the 10th Transport Group, being delivered on 17Nov41. '62' is the last two of the full serial. It was used only within the USA and survived the war to be sold to Iberia as EC-CAZ, with whom it crashed at Madrid in Dec46.
[via David Lucabaugh]

United States Army Air Force C-47-DO VHCFQ c/n 4722 was photographed at Port Moresby, New Guinea, about to embark men going on leave in Dec43. The USAAF serial was 41-18597, but aircraft serving with the Australian Directorate of Air Transport (ADAT) carried a 'registration' for security reasons, as they operated into Australian civil airports.
[via David Lucabaugh]

United States Army Air Force C-53-DO 42-15887 c/n 7404 over the Californian coastline in Aug42. This aircraft went to the 8th AF, served in Europe with the 9th AF and was sold post-war to Brazil as PP-CCZ.
[Harry Gann/Douglas]

CHAPTER 3: MILITARY OPERATORS OF THE DC-3, C-47, R4D, DAKOTA AND LI-2   145

United States Army Air Force *C-47A-DL 42-24275 c/n 10137* at Alexai Point, Attu in the Aleutian Islands. Mail is being unloaded from an 11th AF C-47 in 1943. This aircraft went to Elmendorf, AK in Sep43 and was salvaged in Mar45.   *[via David Lucabaugh]*

United States Army Air Corps *C-39 VHCCH/38-532 c/n 2089* at Sydney, NSW in Nov43. This aircraft was operated by Australian National for the USAAF 21 TCS. There is a cargo door, but it is in one piece - a field modification. Here the marking has a hyphen, but in this book, the hyphen is generally omitted to indicate military use.   *[via David Lucabaugh]*

United States Army Air Force C-53-DO 42-6467 c/n 4919 at Accra, Gold Coast (now Ghana) in May43. Accra was the main staging post for delivery from Brazil and on to East Africa. This aircraft was based with the Central African Air Wing ATC, and retains the old 'meat ball' roundel, having been delivered in Dec42. Post-war it went to United Airlines as NC19925. Eleven other C-47s and two B-24s are also visible. [via David Lucabaugh]

United States Army Air Force C-47-DL 41-38665 c/n 6048 'Jayhawk' somewhere in N Australia. This C-47 was an airborne workshop and is carrying a wing, type unknown, under its belly. This is the second 'Jayhawk', 41-18598 having been lost in Dec43. [Harry Gann/Douglas]

Unites States Army Air Force C-47A-DL 43-15271 c/n 19737 probably taken close to delivery in Mar44. This aircraft stayed in the USA and was used for training in glider snatching, the equipment being fitted under the rear fuselage. It was sold post-war as NC73508, going to Colombia in 1992.
[Harry Gann/Douglas]

CHAPTER 3: MILITARY OPERATORS OF THE DC-3, C-47, R4D, DAKOTA AND LI-2

United States Army Air Force *C-47A-DL 42-100444 c/n 18907 at Hailakandi, India with 1 Air Commando Sq, 10th AF. Glider snatch-gear is fitted.*
[USAF via David Lucabaugh]

United States Army Air Corps *C-53D-DO 42-68716 c/n 11643 at A.64 Strip, St. Dizier, France on 19Sep44. With unit code E5-L, this aircraft was operated by 62 TCS of 314 TCG 9th AF. D-Day stripes are still prominent, but reduced, and not under the wings.* [William L Swisher via David Lucabaugh]

United States Army Air Force *C-47A-DL coded L4-W about to snatch a Waco CG-4A glider from a field in France, probably evacuating casualties back to England. The code L4 indicates 91 TCS or 439 TCG. A hook trailed below the aircraft catches the nylon tow-rope between the two poles. The rope stretches to absorb the shock.*
[USAAF]

United States Army Air Force *C-47A-DL 42-100898 c/n 19361 at Membury, England in Sep44. 7D-Q indicates 80 TCS. Two missions were flown by this aircraft on D-Day, piloted by Peter Boisseau, the second towing a Horsa glider. Subsequently, this aircraft was transferred to the RAF as TS432 to help satisfy their need for snatch-gear-equipped C-47s. It later became G-AJVZ with Scottish Aviation.* [Peter Boisseau]

United States Army Air Force *C-47A-70-DL 42-100798 c/n 19261 serving with the 7th AF in the Pacific theatre, receiving attention alongside three Curtiss C-46s at Falalop Island on 04Apr45.* [via David Lucabaugh]

United States Army Air Force *C-47A-DL 43-15109 c/n 19575 at Membury, England on 10Feb45. Operated by 80 TCS (code 7D-R) the D-Day stripes are vestigial and very dirty. This aircraft survived to see post-war service in the USA.* [Peter Boisseau]

CHAPTER 3: MILITARY OPERATORS OF THE DC-3, C-47, R4D, DAKOTA AND LI-2

United States Army Air Force C-47A-DK 42-93607 c/n 13537 at Melun-Villaroche, France on 23Feb45. S6-X indicates 79 TCS, and this photograph shows radar fitted for pathfinder duties. The aircraft survived until 1968, ending its life with Air America. [Peter Boisseau]

United States Army Air Force C-47B-DK 43-48884 c/n 26145 at an airfield somewhere in England (judged by the architecture), loading drop tanks. It appears to have suffered some battle damage as a new port wing has been fitted. Behind is 223941 and another. Two of the three aircraft have decorated engine nacelles and B-24 Liberator 44-50772 can also be seen in the background. [via Dave Benfield]

United States Air Force C-47D 45-951 c/n 34214 was modified to VC-47D standard in Jul48 and posted to 6 Weather Sq with MATS in Apr50, based at Cocoa Beach (later Patrick), FL. It is now preserved at the Berlin Airlift Memorial, Germany having served with the Spanish AF. [via A Pearcy]

United States Air Force C-47D 45-1012 c/n 34279 of the USAF Air Rescue Service in Jun48. ARS Det 6 was part of 8 Rescue Sq, based at Hamilton, CA and although this aircraft was not re-designated SC-47D as the designation was not introduced until some years later, the last window ahead of the roundel is bulged for downwards observation. [William T Larkins?]

United States Air Force HC-47A-DK 42-92111 c/n 11875 at Phu Cat, S Vietnam with 12 TFW on 20Sep70. By this time, the aircraft had been modified as an HC-47A but it was a unit hack and lacks the bulged window usual for this modification. [Norm Taylor via George Pennick]

United States Air Force C-47D 43-49361 c/n 26622 flying over Vietnam dropping leaflets from a hatch in the rear cargo door, attempting to persuade the Vietcong to surrender. Its operating unit was the 5th Air Commando Sq of 14 ACW that worked out of Bien Hoa in 1967. [Harry Gann/Douglas]

CHAPTER 3: MILITARY OPERATORS OF THE DC-3, C-47, R4D, DAKOTA AND LI-2

United States Air Force C-47D O-3403 [43-49403] c/n 26664 was operated by the 117th FBS, with Pennsylvania Air National Guard in 1955. The serial shows the 'O-' prefix for over ten years' service, but before the system had been standardised. This aircraft was a unit hack based at Philadelphia, PA, seen here flying with the port engine stopped. It crashed in Alaska in Nov57. [USAF]

United States Air Force C-47B-40-DK 44-77200 c/n 33532 - One of the few C-47s to last long enough in USAF service to carry Military Airlift Command markings, this aircraft was operated by the Base Flight at Lajes, in the Azores, where this photograph was taken on 25Oct69. The aircraft flew subsequently with the Portuguese AF and ended up on relief flights in Ethiopia in 1981, being last reported derelict at Addis Ababa, Ethiopia in 2003.
[C P Russell-Smith via P J Marson]

United States Navy R4D-4/DC-3A-447 07003 c/n 6349, taken on charge by the US Navy in Dec42, this aircraft remained in service until 1956, operating with the Naval Air Transport Service (badge on nose). The photograph was taken before 1948, when NATS merged with MATS. The aircraft was sold as N2087A and then went to Japan. [via A Pearcy]

United States Navy *R4D-2/DC-3-388 4707 c/n 4097* was delivered to the US Navy at Anacostia, MD on 12Mar41, but this photograph was taken at San Francisco, CA on 04Oct41. The aircraft is a standard DC-3 with left-hand door. Sold in May46 as NC28389, it ended its life with Air Madagascar in 1969.
[William T Larkins]

United States Navy *R4D-1 3131 c/n 4204* - This aircraft was the first cargo R4D delivered to the US Navy in 1942 to NAS Anacostia. Most of its later life was spent with the US Marine Corps.
[US Navy via David Lucabaugh]

United States Navy *R4D-5-1-DK 17100 c/n 11868* - The nose code indicates that this aircraft was with VR-5, part of NATS. The photograph was taken at Massacre Bay, Attu in the Aleutian Islands, less than a month after delivery, and was the first landing of an aircraft on this airstrip on 07Sep43.
[via David Lucabaugh]

CHAPTER 3: MILITARY OPERATORS OF THE DC-3, C-47, R4D, DAKOTA AND LI-2

United States Marine Corps *R4D-5 17184 c/n 12808 ran off the end of the runway at Falalop Island, Ulithi Atoll, Espiritu Santo in the SW Pacific on 03Nov44 whilst operating with the USMC VMR-253. Salt water corrosion caused it to be stricken on 30Nov44.* [via David Lucabaugh]

United States Navy *LC-117D 12441 c/n 43389 sitting on the snow at Williams Field, McMurdo Sound, Antarctica on 10Jan67. Named 'City of Invercargill' with VX-6, this aircraft operated out of New Zealand in the winter season, and in the 'summer' season supported land parties. It returned to C-117D (no skis) in 1971 and then spent almost thirty years in the Davis-Monthan, AZ area, some in the ownership of Basler Turbo Conversions.* [US Navy via A Pearcy]

United States Navy *R4D-5 17238 c/n 25324 taking off with JATO assistance from the carrier 'USS Philippine Sea' on 29Jan47 for 'Little America' in the Antarctic for 'Operation Hi Jump'. The canisters under the outer wing are believed to be for flotation. It was abandoned in Antarctica in 1948 and had sunk through the ice by 1955.* [Navy Dept, US National Archives]

United States Navy *R4D-5 12415 c/n 9305 was another of the six R4D-5s flown to 'Little America' in 1947, and was the first aircraft to fly over the South Pole. Here the wheels have been removed and skis only are used. JATO bottles are fitted, and the wide red bands painted on the fuselage and wings are to aid location in the event of a forced landing on the snow. Note the MATS titling overpainted on the roof.* [US Navy via David Lucabaugh]

United States Navy *R4D-5 17237 c/n 25316 has acquired the name 'Honolulu Snowboat', but the snow is so hard-packed by 22Feb47 when this photograph was taken that wheels have replaced skis and JATO bottles were no longer needed. All six of the R4D-5s used in Antarctica were stricken on 30Apr47 when they were abandoned at the end of the operation, there being no way of recovering them at the time.*

[US Navy via David Lucabaugh]

Fuerza Aérea Uruguaya *TC-47B-25-DK 515 c/n 32770 - One of a large number of C-47s operated by the Uruguayan AF, 515 was received from USAF stocks in 1961. The aircraft heads a line-up of similar machines at Carrasco, Uruguay in May79.* [A Fabius via P J Marson]

Chapter 4

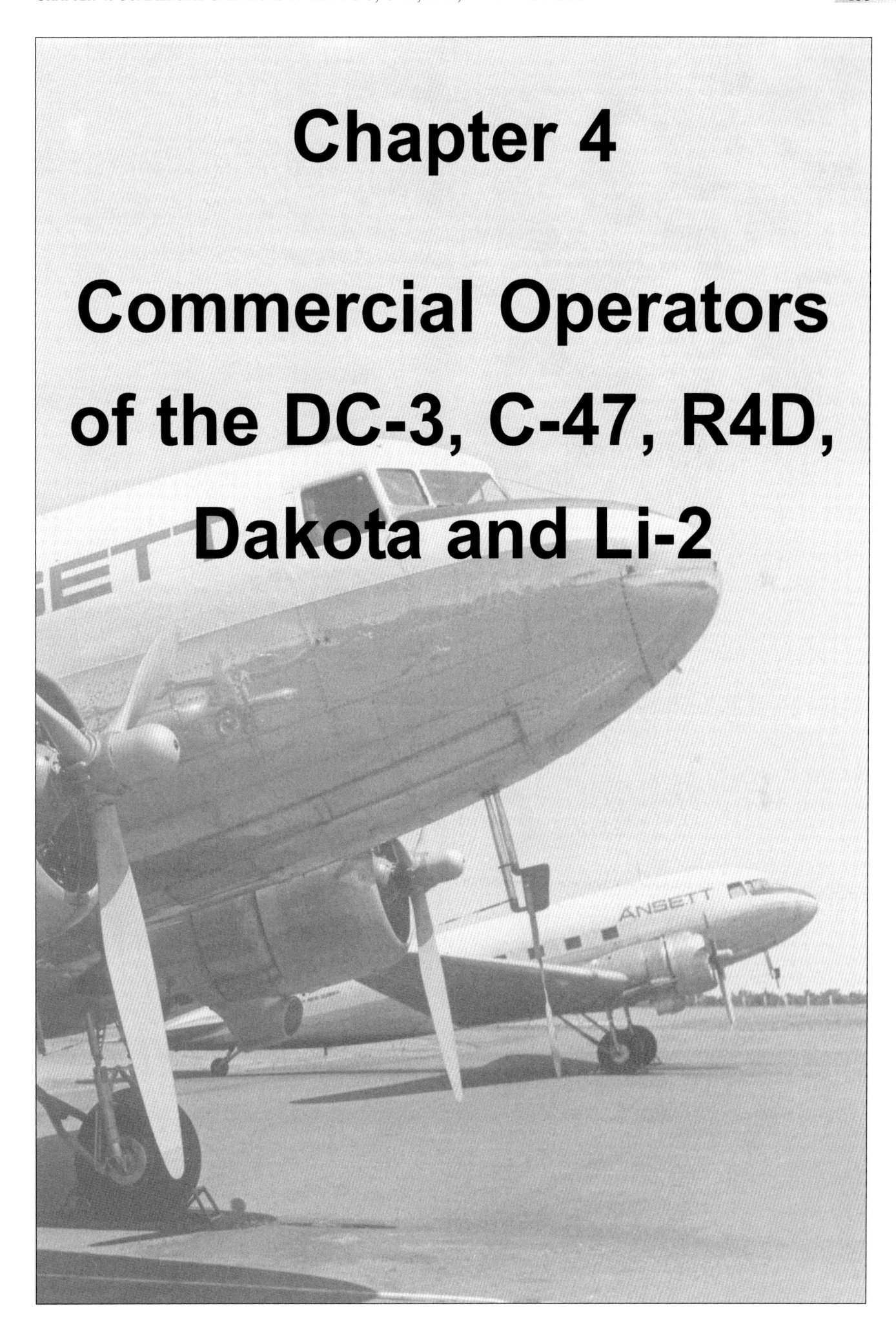

Commercial Operators of the DC-3, C-47, R4D, Dakota and Li-2

So many DC-3s and their derivatives have seen service with scheduled airlines and charter operators that the following section has been broken down by country to make it more manageable. As the DC-3's career has already spanned 70 years, many of the countries listed have suffered political changes involving new names, boundaries, mergers or partitions, and operators have come and gone even more frequently. The countries have been referred to by the name current at the time the last DC-3 was in use or the present name if they are still in use, but cross-referenced to later or earlier titles. Operator name changes due to merger or takeover are indicated and are emboldened when the DC-3s remained in use.

So far as is possible each operator is listed with a brief history of its use of the DC-2 or DC-3 and a list of the registration marks for each aircraft used. At the end of each country's operators will be found an index of the markings used and the constructor's numbers wherever possible to allow cross-reference to the production list. Occasionally, the c/ns given may not be correct in the index, but discrepancies are explained so far as is possible. In some cases details are incomplete but the data that has come to light is given at this point with comments. Changes of nationality marking with political status or independence are noted for any aircraft which are known to have operated with more than one marking within a country, e.g. VR-A to 7O- when Aden became South Yemen.

DC-2s and C-39s are indicated in the indices, and where markings have been used more than once, even if not taken up, (1), (2) or (3) are used to indicate the order of use. An oblique stroke indicates re-registration while with the airline. Registrations indicated as not taken up in individual histories are shown in brackets in this index wherever possible.

ADEN - VR-A and 7O See Yemen.

AFGHANISTAN - YA

Ariana Afghan Airlines, Kabul, was formed in 1955 with help from Indamer Co Ltd, but Pan American took over their 49% share. Domestic services using DC-3s started in 1956 and the last was sold in 1972 after storage. Four were owned, one re-registered following government ownership.

Index:-

YA-AAA	c/n 4242	YA-AAD	18910
YA-AAB	4275	YA-AAE	4242
YA-AAC	6135		

ALGERIA - F and 7T

Until late 1963 Algeria was a Département of France and several DC-3 operators were based there though all except Air Algérie moved out prior to independence. French-registered aircraft are indexed under France.

Aérotechnique SA, Duclos, Algiers, used DC-3s on scheduled and charter services from 1948 until Apr62 when they were taken over by Airnautic.

F-BEFI; F-BEIK; F-BEIS; F-OAID; F-OAQR; F-OAYM; F-OBDS.

Africair - Sté. Algérienne de Constructions Aéronautiques, Algiers. Two DC-3s were used on charter flights in North Africa from 1964 until about 1969 when they (7T-VBB and 7T-VBC) became derelict at Toulouse.

Air Algérie - Sté. Algérienne de Constructions Aéronautique, Algiers. Air Algérie was formed in 1946 and in the following year DC-3s replaced the French-built Ju52/3ms (AAC.1). The airline merged with Cie Air Transport in 1953 to form **CGTA-Air Algérie**.

F-BCYF to F-BCYO incl; F-BEFP; F-OAFQ; F-OAFR.

Air Algérie - Cie Générale de Transports Aériens, Air Algérie, Algiers. Formed in April 1953 by the merger of Air Algérie and Air Transport, this airline became Air Algérie following Algerian independence in 1963. At that time three DC-3s were still in use (7T registered), and one remained in store as late as 1978.

F-BCYM/7T-VAM; F-BCYN/7T-VAN; F-OAVR; 7T-VAV.

CATA - Cie Algérienne de Transports Aériens, Philippeville. Operations started with two DC-3s in 1947 and two more were added by the time Aigle Azur had taken over in Jan50.

F-BEFA; F-BEFB; F-BESS; F-BEST.

Cie Chérifienne du Pont Aérien. Although initially based in Algeria the two DC-3s were used briefly in Morocco in the summer of 1954 and in Indo-China in the following winter, as a subsidiary of Air Outremer.

F-OANI; F-OAPD; F-OAQE; F-OAQJ.

Cie Générale Transaharienne. Two DC-3s (F-BEIX and F-BEIY) were operated in North Africa from 1948 until they were sold to Air France early in 1950.

SATT - Sté. Africaine de Transports Tropicaux t/a Aéro Africaine. Two DC-3s were used briefly in 1947/48 but were exchanged for nine Lodestars.

F-BCYP; F-BCYQ.

Sté Transafricaine d'Aviation, Orly. Operated to French West Africa. Three DC-3s saw brief service in 1952/53.

F-BFGE; F-BFGG; F-BFGI.

Index:-

7T-VAM	c/n 33207	7T-VBB	4387
7T-VAN	25916	7T-VBC	11706
7T-VAV	12380		

ANGOLA - CR-L and D2

Until 1973 Angola, on the west coast of Southern Africa, was a Portuguese colony, but civil war lead to independence and the nationality mark CR-L gave way to D2- used on the last two DC-3s.

DTA - Direcção de Exploração dos Transportes Aéreos, Luanda. Surplus C-47s were bought in 1945/46 to replace the pre-war Rapides, and some continued in service for another 28 years, when the airline was nationalised following Angola's independence in Oct73 becoming TAAG about two years later.

CR-LBK; CR-LBL; CR-LBM; CR-LCA; CR-LCB; CR-LCC; CR-LCY; CR-LCZ; CR-LDK

TAAG - Transportes Aéreos de Angola SARL, Luanda. This company was formed about 1975 following independence in Oct73 although it had existed earlier as DTA. The remaining DC-3s were finally replaced by F.27s in 1976, two being sold in Cuba.

CR-LBL; CR-LBM; CR-LCA; CR-LCB; CR-LCY; CR-LCZ; CR-LDK.

Index:-

CR-LBK	c/n 13769	CR-LCZ	12711
CR-LBL	12904	CR-LDK	12445
CR-LBM	18979	CR-LOH	
CR-LCA	20456	CR-LOI	
CR-LCB	10195	D2-EPL	32664
CR-LCC	20173	D2-FDK	12445
CR-LCY	20592		

CR-LOH and CR-LOI were owned by C.T.A., probably an abbreviation for Companhia de Transportes Aéreos, thought to be a government agency.

ANGUILLA - VP-L - See Leeward Islands.

ANTIGUA - VP-L - See Leeward Islands.

ARGENTINA - LV and LQ

Post-war the DC-3 was the mainstay of many Argentinian airlines. Nationalisation into Aerolineas Argentinas reduced the number of operators in 1950, but the DC-3s remained until replaced by HS.748s in the early sixties. Apart from the airlines, DC-3s were used by a number of government and state agencies, registered for a time in the LQ- series.

Aerolineas Argentinas - Empresa del Estado, Buenos Aires. Aerolineas was formed in May49 to take over FAMA, ALFA, Aeroposta and ZONDA with effect from 01Jan50. DC-3s were taken over

CHAPTER 4: COMMERCIAL OPERATORS OF THE DC-3, C-47, R4D, DAKOTA AND LI-2

from all these companies and remained in use for a further 12 or more years. The last few were passed on to LADE for use on social service routes.

LV-ABE; LV-ABH; LV-ABT; LV-ABU; LV-ABX; LV-ABY; LV-ABZ; LV-ACD; LV-ACE; LV-ACF; LV-ACG; LV-ACH; LV-ACI; LV-ACJ; LV-ACL to LV-ACQ incl; LV-ACW; LV-ACX; LV-ACY; LV-ACZ; LV-ADF; LV-ADG; LV-ADJ; LV-AET; LV-AFE; LV-AFS; LV-AFW; LV-AGD; LV-AGE; LV-AGF.

Aeroposta Argentina SA, Buenos Aires. Aeroposta's origins go back to 1928. Pre-war equipment was replaced by DC-3s when the airline was renamed Aeroposta Argentina Soc. Mixta on 15Apr47. In 1950 ALFA and Aeroposta Argentina were taken over and nationalised with FAMA and ZONDA. As will be appreciated from individual aircraft histories, the situation was somewhat more complex than the above statement suggests, but the following appear to have been owned by Aeroposta:-

LV-ABX; LV-ABY; LV-ABZ; LV-ACD; LV-ACE; LV-ACH; LV-ACJ; LV-ACM; LV-ACN; LV-ACW; LV-ACX; LV-ACY; LV-ACX; LV-ADF; LV-ADG; LV-AET.

A.L.A. - Aerotransportes Litoral Argentina SA, Rosario. Six DC-3s were bought to operate services from Apr58 onwards, when the monopoly of Aerolíneas was broken following Peron's downfall. A 30% share in the airline was taken by Cia Argentina de Transportes Aéreas (founded 1957) in 1965. The two companies merged 06Sep71 as **Austral Líneas Aéreas** by which time only two DC-3s remained.

LV-FYH; LV-FYI; LV-FYJ; LV-FYL; LV-GHZ; LV-GIB.

A.L.F.A. - Aviación del Litoral Fluvial Argentina, Buenos Aires. ALFA was formed to take over Dodero's operations in part. It was absorbed into Aerolineas in 1949.

LV-ABE; LV-ABF; LV-ABH.

Cia. Argentina de Cargas Aéreas Internas. Two C-47s (LV-AHD and LV-AHE) were used on internal cargo services between 1951 and 1954.

Cia. Argentina de Aeronavegación - t/a Aeronaves Dodero, Buenos Aires. Sr Dodero bought up the pre-war Italian-sponsored airline 'Corporación' in 1945 and operated about five DC-3s, some DC-4s and Cessna T-50s until bought out by ALFA and FAMA in May46.

LV-ABE; LV-ABF; LV-ABG(?); LV-ABH; LV-ABT; LV-ABU.

FAMA - Flota Aérea Mercante Argentina, Buenos Aires. FAMA was formed in Feb46 with state and private funds (including Sr Dodero's). International services were flown with various types, including DC-3s. In May49 nationalisation took FAMA into Aerolineas Argentinas. Earlier some of Dodero's fleet had come under FAMA control because the law forbade him holding a share in more than one airline.

LV-ABT; LV-ABU; LV-ACG; LV-AFE; LV-AFW; LN-AGF.

LACAS - Líneas Aéreas Commerciales Al Sur. DC-3s LV-AFX, LV-AHD and LV-AHE were used between 1948 and 1951.

LADE - Líneas Aéreas del Estado, Buenos Aires. The Argentine Air Force operated DC-3s (some ex Aerolineas) on routes which were not commercially viable, from 1946 until they were replaced by F.27s in 1969. It is not certain which C-47s were so used, but all serial numbers are listed in the military section.

Servicios Aéreos Rio Negro, San Justo, used DC-3 LV-JIG between 1968 and the early seventies when the company ceased trading.

Servicios Aéreos Santa Isabel, Buenos Aires, operated two DC-3s from about 1961 onwards. LV-GYP and LV-HOJ arrived in Miami for sale in 1978, and LV-GYP eventually came to Eire in 1984.

TRANSAER - Transportes Aéreos Terrestres y Maritimos bought three C-39s from the Navy during 1959/60 for use on domestic cargo charters.

LV-GGT to GGV incl.

ZONDA - Zonas Oeste y Norte de Aerolineas Argentinas Soc Mixta, Buenos Aires, was formed in Feb46 to operate a large fleet of C-47s bought from Canadair as well as some DH.89As. Services started in the following January, continuing until nationalisation in May49.

LV-ABX; LV-ABY; LV-ABZ; LV-ACD; LV-ACE; LV-ACF; LV-ACH; LV-ACI; LV-ACJ; LV-ACL to LV-ACQ incl; LV-ADD; LV-ADJ.

Index:-

LV-ABE	c/n 6015	LV-FYI	19524
LV-ABF	19965	LV-FYJ	26158
LV-ABG		LV-FYL	34283
LV-ABH	13621	LV-GGT (C-39)	2060
LV-ABT	18992	LV-GGU (C-39)	2074
LV-ABU	19278	LV-GGV (C-39)	2083
LV-ABX	13435	LV-GHZ	25354
LV-ABY	12850	LV-GIB	20472
LV-ABZ	13473	LV-GIX	4556
LV-ACD	13328	LV-GJT	12678
LV-ACE	13373	LV-GYP	2108
LV-ACF	25455	LV-HOJ	2265
LV-ACG	33538	LV-JIG	20817
LV-ACH	13027	LV-JNB	4754
LV-ACI	13156	LV-JTC(1)	2122
LV-ACJ	13336	LV-JTC(2)	19026
LV-ACL	12020	LV-NQU	20093
LV-ACM	9490	LV-PCV	2108
LV-ACN	12246	LV-PDJ	25775
LV-ACO	25277	LV-PKP	26114
LV-ACP	11920	LV-PTY	2265
LV-ACQ	13159	LV-ROT	12845
LV-ACW	12057	LV-RRY	4731
LV-ACX	12387	LV-XEO	19659
LV-ACY	12291	LV-XEP	20093
LV-ACZ		LV-XFR	9936
LV-ADD	19545	LV-XFS	19479
LV-ADF	20158	LV-XFT	19997
LV-ADG	33430	LV-XFU	19542 ?
LV-ADJ	13150	see	19642
LV-AET	19961	LV-XFV	19026
LV-AFE	6176	LV-XFW	19344
LV-AFS	12025	LV-XFX	19395
LV-AFW	19790	LV-XFY	18968
LV-AFX	20473	LQ-ACF	25455
LV-AGD	9162	LQ-ACW	12057
LV-AGE	20083	LQ-ADG	33430
LV-AGF	20405	(LQ-CAA)	2012
LV-AHD	12845	LQ-GIX	4556
LV-AHE	4731	LQ-GJT	12678
LV-AHI (DC-2)	1351	LQ-INL	25775
LV-AVJ (C-39)	2057	LQ-IOS	2012
LV-FDF	20473	LQ-IPC	4280
LV-FIF(DC-2)	1252	LQ-JNB	4754
LV-FYH	26052	LQ-MSP	26114

Notes:- LV-ABG is believed to have been operated by ALFA, but no other details are known. The LV-P. series are provisional marks used on delivery. Likewise, the LV-X. group was used for delivery, but all these went to the Air Force.

AUSTRALIA - VH

The DC-2 was introduced to Australian airlines in Apr36 and the DC-3 in Dec37, joining Lockheed 10s and replacing older British types on many routes. These aircraft were used briefly by the RAAF, but returned to airline use when cargo C-47s became available to the Air Force. With the end of the war the Government purchased surplus C-47s and leased these to established operators and, at the same time, formed Trans Australia Airlines. The DC-3 was replaced on the longer routes by more modern equipment in the early fifties and relegated to intrastate services and also to cargo work and other mundane duties.

DC-3 use in Australia has been complicated by the ramifications of the Ansett group, but once this group gave up the DC-3 its use steadily declined, and many aircraft were sold or given to S E Asia for civil and military use. The relatively small number remaining were used in ones and twos by small operators. There had been somewhat of a resurgence in the nineties with Dakota National Air using a respectable-sized fleet.

Adastra Aerial Surveys Pty Ltd, Mascot, NSW, operated regular services in New South Wales pre-war, but then concentrated on survey work, using Hudsons and DC-3 VH-AGU. This was taken over with Adastra's assets by East-West in May73.

Aircrafts Pty Ltd, Brisbane, Qld, was controlled by Butler Air Transport and ordered its first DC-3, VH-BBV, in 1947. The name was changed to **Queensland Airlines** in 1948.

Airlines of Australia, Sydney, NSW, was formed in Oct35 to take over New England Airways. Control passed to Australian National in 1937 via Bungana Investments, but it operated separately until Jul42 with DC-2s VH-UYB, VH-UYC and DC-3 VH-UZJ.

Airlines of New South Wales Pty Ltd, Sydney, NSW, was formerly **Butler Air Transport** until renamed in Dec59. It operated services in NSW and by 1968 had been renamed Ansett Airlines of NSW Pty Ltd.

VH-ANH; VH-ANJ; VH-ANM; VH-ANQ; VH-ANR; VH-ANS; VH-ANZ; VH-AOH; VH-AOI; VH-AVL; VH-BDU; VH-BUR; VH-INB; VH-INC; VH-ING; VH-INI.

Airlines of South Australia Pty Ltd, Adelaide, SA, was formerly **Guinea Airways**, but was purchased by Ansett in 1959. In 1968 it was styled **Ansett Airlines of SA**.

VH-ABR; VH-ANH; VH-ANN; VH-ANP; VH-ANS; VH-ANW; VH-ANX; VH-ANZ; VH-INB. VH-EWF was leased in 1965.

Air North, Darwin, NT, bought DC-3 VH-MMA in Jul83, followed later by VH-CAN which was sold in 1989. It became Air North International by 1993. VH-MMA was then operated under lease from Vintage Aircraft Co.

Air Queensland, Cairns, Qld, previously **Bush Pilots Airways**, operated DC-3s VH-BPL; VH-BPN; VH-EDC; VH-PNM; VH-PWN and VH-SBL. The last named went to General Cargo in 1981 and the four remaining active aircraft went directly to Air Rambler/DC-3 Queensland PL in Feb88. N5590K was acquired during the 1980s.

Air Rambler (Australia) Pty Ltd, Freshwater, Qld, a division of Rambler Tours obtained VH-BPL, VH-BPN, VH-EDC and VH-PWN from Air Queensland in 1988 for operation as **DC-3 Queensland**, see below.

Air Tasmania Pty Ltd, Hobart, Tas., was formed in Jul73 using DC-3 VH-MMF on internal routes, ceasing operations in Sep77.

Ansett Airways Pty Ltd, Melbourne, Vic., was formed in 1936 and bought three DC-3s from the US FLC in 1946. Its parent company, Ansett Transport Industries bought Australian National in Oct57 and the two were then merged to form **Ansett-ANA**.

VH-RMA/VH-BZA; VH-AMJ/VH-RMJ/VH-BZJ; VH-AMK/VR-RMK/VH-BZK; VH-AML/VH-RML/VH-BZL; VH-BZB; VH-BZC; VH-TAG.

Ansett-ANA, Melbourne, Vic., was formed on 04Oct57 by the merger of Ansett and ANA. Much interchange of aircraft with other members of the Ansett Transport Industries fleet took place. The trading name was changed to **Ansett Airlines of Australia** in Nov68.

VH-AAU; VH-ABR; VH-ANH; VH-ANJ; VH-ANM; VH-ANN; VH-ANO; VH-ANP; VH-ANR to VH-ANT incl; VH-ANV to VH-ANX incl; VH-ANZ; VH-AOH; VH-AOI; VH-BZB; VH-BZC; VH-BZK; VH-INB; VH-INC; VH-IND; VH-ING; VH-INI.

Ansett Airlines of Australia Pty Ltd, Melbourne, Vic. By the time this trading name was adopted in Nov68 only DC-3s VH-ABR and VH-ANH remained.

Ansett-Mandated Airlines Ltd, Lae, PNG, often called Ansett-MAL, was the trading name for Mandated Airlines following its take-over by Ansett in 1961. It was renamed **Ansett Airlines of Papua New Guinea** in Jun68.

VH-AAU; VH-AOI; VH-BDU; VH-MAB; VH-MAC; VH-MAE; VH-MAL; VH-MAN; VH-MAR; VH-MAS; VH-MAT; VH-MAV.

Ansett Airlines of Papua New Guinea Pty Ltd., Lae, PNG, was the trading name adopted in Jun68 by **Ansett-MAL** and used until the formation of Air Niugini in Nov73.

VH-AOI; VH-MAB; VH-MAE; VH-MAL; VH-MAN; VH-MAR; VH-MAT; VH-MMA; VH-MMD; VH-MMF; VH-MML; VH-PNA; VH-PNB; VH-PNM.

Ansett (P&NG) Pty Ltd, Boroko Lae, PNG, was formerly **Papuan Airlines Pty Ltd**. It used the following DC-3s:-

VH-MAB; VH-MAL; VH-MAN; VH-MAT; VH-MMA; VH-MMD; VH-MMF; VH-MML; VH-PNA; VH-PNB; VH-PNM.

Australian National Airways Pty Ltd, Melbourne, Vic. was formed in Jul36 by the merger of West Australian Airways, Adelaide Airways, Holymans Airways and shipping interests. By this time Holymans already used one DC-2, and more were ordered from the makers in 1936. DC-3s followed in 1937 and others taken over from surplus stocks in 1945/46. In addition some were used on lease during the latter part of the war, operating in military call-signs. All DC-3s were fitted with Wright R-1820 Cyclones. Control of the airline passed to Ansett in Oct57 but the identity was not lost as the new company operated as **Ansett-ANA** until 1968.

DC-2s:- VH-ADQ/AEN; VH-ADZ; VH-ARA; VH-ARB; VH-ARC; VH-CRH; VH-USY; VH-UXJ; VH-UYB; VH-UYC.
DC-3s:- VH-ABR; VH-ACB; VH-AEO to VH-AETincl; VH-AEV; VH-AFK; VH-AKG; VH-ANH to VH-ANZ incl; VH-INA to VH-ING incl; VH-INM; VH-INN; VH-UZJ; VH-UZK.

The following were operated by ANA using their military call-signs: VHCCF; VH-CCG; VH-CCH; VHCDA; VHCDB (x2); VHCDC (x2); VHCDD; VHCDE (x2); VHCDG (x2); VHCDH; VHCDJ; VHCDK (x2); VHCXD; VHCXL (x2).

BBA Air Cargo - See Brain & Brown.

Brain & Brown Airfreighters Pty Ltd, Moorabbin and Essendon, Vic, used three DC-3s, VH-BAA; VH-BAB; and VH-BAM for cargo work from 1960, replacing Ansons. When control passed to Air Express Holdings in Nov76, the name was changed to **BBA Air Cargo Pty Ltd**. It ceased trading in 1979.

Bush Pilots Airways Ltd, Cairns, Qld, used DC-3s on their scheduled services from 1970. They bought Queensland Pacific Airways in 1972 thus adding to their DC-3 fleet, of which five remained in 1979. Bush Pilots became **Air Queensland** in 1982.

VH-AEQ; VH-BPN; VH-EDC; VH-EDD; VH-MAL; VH-PNM; VH-PWM; VH-PWN; N5590K; "VH-BPA".

Butler Air Transport Pty Ltd, Sydney, NSW, acquired its first DC-3 in 1948 to replace DH.84s and DH.89As. It gained control of Aircrafts Pty Ltd in 1948, renaming it Queensland Airlines. Control passed to Ansett in Feb58 and it became **Airlines of New South Wales** in Dec59, via Bungana Investments.

VH-AKR/VH-INF; VH-ANR; VH-AOG; VH-AOH (twice); VH-AOI; VH-BDU; VH-BNH; VH-INI.

Connair Pty Ltd, Alice Springs, NT, added DC-3s to the fleet in 1973 to supplement Herons on scheduled services. The airline was bought out by East-West Airlines in Dec79 and renamed **Northern Airlines**.

VH-EDC; VH-EWE; VH-MIN; VH-MMA; VH-PWM; VH-UPQ.

Cranways Pty Ltd, Launceston, Tas, was formed in 1980 to operate charters with DC-3s VH-EWE, VH-SBL and VH-TAK and traded as **General Cargo Australia**. The company no longer exists.

Dakota Downunder operated DC-3 VH-JGL.

Dakota National Air, Bankstown, NSW, operated a fleet of DC-3s mainly for charter work, both passenger and freight, starting in 1995. It was renamed **Discovery Airways** and went into administration in Feb04 re-emerging as **Discovery Air Tours**. Only VH-DNA, VH-MIN and VH-SBL were still active in 2005.

VH-ATO; VH-BPN; VH-DNA; VH-MIN; VH-PTE; VH-PWN; VH-SBL and VH-UPQ.

DC-3 Queensland Pty Ltd, Freshwater, Qld, bought four DC-3s from Air Queensland in Feb88. This was a division of Rambler Tours which was associated with Australian Roadway Tours. VH-BPL; VH-BPN; VH-EDC; and VH-PWN were all sold by auction in Jun92.

Dick Lang's Desert Air Safaris, Adelaide, SA, bought DC-3s VH-BPN and VH-PWN (2) for pleasure flying. These were sold to Dakota National Air in 1995.

East-West Airlines Ltd, Tamworth, NSW, replaced its Ansons with DC-3s in 1953 and used them on scheduled services in NSW. They were replaced by F.27s. The last was used for research into microwave landing systems for CSIRO. Pacific & Western was a subsidiary. Both Adastra and Connair were bought out, in 1973 and 1979 respectively. DC-3s were subject to much re-registration during their life.

CHAPTER 4: COMMERCIAL OPERATORS OF THE DC-3, C-47, R4D, DAKOTA AND LI-2

VH-AEQ; VH-AER/VH-EWF/VH-EWE; VH-AEZ/VH-EWD; VH-AGU; VH-DAS; VH-EWA/VH-EWF/VH-PWN; VH-EWB/VH-PWM; VH-EWF. *(An oblique stroke indicates a change of mark, but the same mark may have been used on several aircraft at different times).* VH-SBN was leased in 1968.

Fleet Air Services (Tasmania) Pty Ltd, Melbourne, Vic, operated charter flights from Essendon from 1976 until bought by the IPEC group in 1977 and sold in 1979. DC-3 VH-EWE was used.

Flight Australia, Bankstown, NSW, had VH-CAN in joint partnership with Winrye Aviation. It was delivered on 17Feb89, but repossessed in Jul91.

Forrestair Pty Ltd, Essendon, Vic (Forrester Stephen Pty), used DC-3s on charter cargo work to Tasmania and Bass Strait Islands from 1974 until Oct78 when high costs forced a cessation of operations.

VH-EDD; VH-MMF; VH-SBL; VH-TAK.

General Cargo Australia - see Cranways.

Golden West Airways, Chinchilla, Qld, operated DC-3 VH-AGU briefly. It was sold in Jun89 to Peachbrand PL, but still operated for Golden West in 1993.

Golden Wings Australia, Hobart, Tas, used DC-3 VH-SBL, but this was sold to Travair in 1986. VH-CAN was leased to Air North in May84.

Guinea Air Traders Ltd, Lae, PNG, was formed in New Guinea in 1946, using two C-39s (VH-ARB and VH-ARC). DC-3s were also used until 1951.

VH-BFW; VH-BZB; VH-GAT; plus G-AGHN and G-AKNB on lease.

Guinea Airways Pty Ltd, Adelaide, SA., was originally formed to operate in New Guinea in 1927 with services extended to Australia in 1937, but by 1946 only flew in South Australia in pool with ANA. A few DC-3s were operated in wartime call-signs, later others came from ANA and in 1959 the airline became part of the Ansett group, forming **Airlines of South Australia**.

DC-2 VH-UYB was leased 1939. *DC-3s:-* VH-AER; VH-AEU; VH-AEX; VH-ANH; VH-ANI; VH-ANN/VH-GAH; VH-ANP/VH-GAI; VH-ANS/VH-GAJ; VH-ANW/VH-GAK; VH-AVK; VH-AVL; VH-AVM; VH-INB/VH-GAL. Call-signs: VHCCB; VHCDJ; VHCDK; VHCGM.

Holymans Airways Pty Ltd, Melbourne, Vic., bought two early DC-2s in 1936 before becoming part of ANA.

VH-USY; VH-UXJ.

IPEC (Interstate Parcel Express), Essendon, Vic., took over DC-3 VH-EWE with Fleet Air on 11Mar77. IPEC colours were applied in Apr79 but it was sold in Dec79.

Jetair Australia Ltd, Sydney, NSW, operated as Jetairlines of Australia on commuter and charter services, using DC-3s from Nov69 until Nov70.

VH-BUR; VH-EQB; VH-EQN; VH-EQO; VH-SBN; VH-TAI.

Koomeela Australia DC-3 VH-UPQ carried this title in Feb89, but having bought **Rebel Air** changed to that title by Jun89. Similarly VH-MIN used Rebel Air titles. The company also traded as **Colbinra Transport**, Maitland, NSW. VH-TMQ was bought ex RAAF in 1988, but it never entered service.

Macair Air Charter Service, Sydney, NSW, was formed by Charles M MacDonald in 1948 to operate migrant charters between Europe and Australia. DC-2s were owned, but only one flight in Mar48 was known.

VH-ARB; VH-ARC; VH-CDZ.

MacRobertson Miller Aviation Co Pty Ltd, Perth, WA, was owned until 1955 by Commercial Aviation Co, trading as MMA. In that year it merged with Airlines (WA) Ltd, and became MacRobertson Miller Aviation Pty Ltd on 01Oct55. DC-3s began to replace Ansons in 1947 and remained in use until 1971 when F.28s replaced them. MMA became a subsidiary of Ansett in 1963 and was styled MacRobertson Miller Airline Services Pty, Ltd.

VH-AEU; VH-ANX; VH-ANZ; VH-MMA; VH-MMD; VH-AXM/VH-BXM/VH-MME; VH-MMF; VH-MMK; VH-MML; VH-MMM; VH-MMO/VH-MMB; VH-MMT. VH-EWD was leased 1965/6.

Mandated Airlines Ltd, Lae, PNG, started post-war operations with DH 84s, but in 1947 the first DC-3 was bought. Many more followed, until in Jan61 Ansett gained control and operations continued as **Ansett-MAL**.

C-39:- VH-ARB.
DC-3s:- VH-AOI; VH-BFV/VH-MAE; VH-BFW/VH-MAC; VH-MAH/VH-MAV; VH-MAL; VH-MAM/VH-MAB; VH-MAN; VH-MAR; VH-MAS; VH-MAT.

Marshall Airways Pty Ltd, Sydney and Bankstown, NSW. DC-2 VH-CDZ was used on charter flights and joy-rides until 1955.

Masling Commuter Services Pty Ltd, Cootamundra, NSW, used DC-3 VH-MWQ on charter work and newspaper deliveries until it was sold in 1979 at which time VH-EWE was also regd. C/n 11973 was used for spares from 1977.

New Holland Airways Pty Ltd, Sydney, NSW, was formed in 1948 to fly migrants to Australia, using DC-2 VH-AEN, DC-3 VH-BNH (used as I-TROS also) and the last DC-5 VH-ARD. Few flights were recorded.

North East Airlines, Cairns, Qld, Started operations using DC-3 VH-SBL on 18Dec87, but this was sold early in the following year.

Northern Airlines Ltd, Alice Springs and Darwin, NT, was formed in Jun80 by East-West from Connair. DC-3s VH-MIN and VH-UPQ were used until replaced by Metros.

Papuan Air Transport Ltd, Port Moresby, PNG, used DC-3s on charter flights from 1958 and on scheduled flights from 1963 onwards. The title **Papuan Airlines** ("Patair") was adopted prior to its take-over by Ansett in Jul70. The name was changed to **Ansett (P&NG) Ltd** in 1972.

VH-PAT; VH-PNA; VH-PNB; VH-PNM. VH-SBD was lsd from Sep67.

Paradak Pty Ltd, Essendon, Vic, was formed in 1978 with DC-3 VH-CAN to operate charters, mainly for parachute dropping. This was sold in May84. VH-PTS was added in 1981. It went to Splitters Creek Airlines of Albury.

Peachbrand Pty Ltd, Archerfield, Qld, t/a Dakota Airways, had VH-AGU which was leased by G Twycross in 1987 and then owned by him.

Qantas Empire Airways Ltd, Sydney, NSW, operated C-47s in the latter part of WWII on loan from the USAAF and subsequently converted a fleet of DC-3s for passenger work in Australia and New Guinea. The latter services were bought from W R Carpenter, but the assets were passed to TAA in Dec60, along with most DC-3s. The remaining pair were sold in 1961.

VH-AEO; VH-AES; VH-AEU; VH-AEY; VH-AEZ; VH-AFA; VH-AIH/VH-EBH; VH-AII/VH-EBI; VH-AIJ/VH-EBJ; (VH-BAJ)/VH-EAK; (VH-BAK)/VH-EAL/VH-EBH/VH-EBW; (VH-BAL)/VH-EAM; (VH-BAM)/VH-EAO/VH-EBX; VH-BHB; VH-BHD; VH-BHE; VH-EAN/VH-EBF/VH-EBU; VH-EAP/VH-EBY; VH-EAQ; VH-EAR; VH-EBE/VH-EBT; VH-EBF; VH-EBG/VH-EBV; VH-EDC; VH-EDD.

Military call-signs used included: VHCCB; VHCCC (x2); VHCDC; VHCDE; VHCDL; VHCDM; VHCGM; VHCWA.

Queensland Airlines Pty Ltd, Brisbane, Qld, was formed as Aircrafts Pty Ltd and was renamed in 1948 after control had passed to Butler Air Transport. In Feb58 Ansett took over and operations ceased in Dec66.

VH-AAU; VH-ANM; VH-AOH; VH-AOI; VH-AVL; VH-BBV; VH-IND.

Queensland Pacific Airways Ltd, Brisbane, Qld, was formed in 1971 to use DC-3s VH-EDC; VH-EDD; VH-PWM and VH-PWN. These were sold to Bush Pilots Airways in Jun72.

Rebel Air Pty Ltd, Sydney, NSW, started charter operations with DC-3 VH-PWM in Dec79. VH-MIN and VH-UPQ were added later and then VH-TMQ ex RAAF. Rebel Air was bought by Koomeela in 1989 and its name was then adopted by the joint company. VH-RRA was used for spares.

Setair, Melbourne, Vic (Scientific and Educational Tours), operated charter flights and night newspaper flights from Melbourne from 1979, using a total of five DC-3s. All had been sold by Jul83.

VH-EWE; VH-MIN; VH-MWQ; VH-SBL; VH-UPQ.

South Pacific Airmotive, operated VH-EDC in Feb93, but this force-landed in Botany Bay. They also owned VH-MIN; VH-MMF and VH-SPY/N65388, but these were sold in 1998.

Trans Australia Airlines, Melbourne, Vic, is the operating name for the Australian National Airlines Commission which started services with DC-3s in Sep46. These remained in use, latterly in New Guinea from Sep60, until the Sunbird Services were taken over by Air Niugini in 1973. VH-EWE was leased briefly in 1972/3.

VH-AEO to VH-AES incl; VH-AEU; VH-AEV; VH-AEX to VH-AFA incl; VH-AII; VH-AIJ; VH-DAS; VH-SBA to VH-SBO incl; VH-SBW; VH-TAE to VH-TAN incl; VH-TAT to VH-TAW incl; (VH-TAY); VH-PNB.

Travair DC-3 VH-SBL was sold in 1987.

Travmar Holdings Pty Ltd, Rutherford, NSW, started operations in 1977 with charter work, but commuter services did not get started. Three DC-3s were owned, VH-DAS being used for spares. It is no longer trading.

VH-DAS; VH-MMD; VH-SBO.

Up Over Down Under (UODU Air) were due to start 'Back-packers' flights on 27Mar94 and had imported one DC-3, N2271C, of three due from Thailand. This arrived at Archerfield, Qld, in Nov93 but operations never began due to the poor condition of the aircraft and further purchases were abandoned.

Victorian Air Coach Services, Essendon, Vic, started operations in Dec61 over the routes of Southern Airlines in Victoria, Tasmania and S Australia. DC-3s were used until the last operations on 29Aug66.

VH-ANH; VH-ANJ; VH-ANO; VH-ANP; VH-ANQ; VH-ING.

Index:-
This index attempts to list only those aircraft which carried civil type markings for airline or other use. However, due to a shortage of US personel, in WWII airlines such as ANA, Guinea and Qantas operated DC-3s of various models on loan from the ADAT fleet of the USAAF on military transport duties, commencing 1944. They carried military call-signs as registration marks and were issued with Certificates of Airworthiness. Where it is confirmed that an aircraft was airline-operated the mark is included here, shown without a hyphen, but many other marks are known in the same series, that were issued for military use only. The RAAF used series VHDAA to DAC; VHCTA to VHCUZ and VHRFA to VHRGZ. Most of the 'civil' DC-3s used call signs in the VHCCx and VHCDx blocks. See RAAF section in which all ADAT C-47s are listed using the call signs which lack the hyphen. Many VHCxx series were used and re-used by the USAAF and the VHRCA to VHREZ block was used by the Netherlands East Indies AF Nos. 19 and 20 Squadrons.

VH-AAU	c/n 19904	VH-AID	33097
VH-ABC	12285	VH-AIG	9594
VH-ABR	2029	VH-AIH	25491
VH-ACB	2030	VH-AII	13622
VH-ADQ(DC-2)	1259	VH-AIJ	12667
VH-ADZ(DC-2)	1376	VH-AIQ	32672
VH-AEN(DC-2)	1259	VH-AIX	32880
VH-AEO	6051	VH-AKG	4969
VH-AEP	6023	VH-AKR	12647
VH-AEQ	6024	"VH-ALT"	1941
VH-AER	6007	VH-AMJ	9740
VH-AES	6021	VH-AMK	13362
VH-AET	6013	VH-AML	13606
VH-AEU	6108	"VH-ANA"	33113
VH-AEV	6122	VH-ANH	4120
VH-AEX	6071	VH-ANI	4119
VH-AEY	9815	VH-ANJ	9105
VH-AEZ	9811	VH-ANK(1)	13906
VH-AFA	9813	VH-ANK(2)	9999
(VH-AFE)	10001	VH-ANL	20571
(VH-AFF)	9998	VH-ANM(1)	9347
(VH-AFG)	13085	VH-ANM(2)	18923
VH-AFK	9592	VH-ANN	3272
"VH-AFK"(DC-2)	1375	VH-ANO	4094
"VH-AFL"(DC-2)	1376	VH-ANP	4096
VH-AGU	32668	VH-ANQ	3271
VH-AIC	12076	VH-ANR	1944

VH-ANS	6010	VHCDK(2)	20763
VH-ANT	10078	VHCDL	19920
VH-ANU	13521	VHCDM	19902
VH-ANV	10082	VH-CDZ(DC-2)	1376
VH-ANW	13624	VHCGM	9811
VH-ANX	18949	VH-CRH(DC-2)	1288
VH-ANY(1)	13612	VHCWA	4840
VH-ANY(2)	6172	VHCXD	1941
VH-ANZ	9559	VHCXL(1)	1944
VH-AOG	10083	VHCXL(2)	19950
VH-AOH(1)	13603	VH-DAS	6051
VH-AOH(2)	12790	VH-DMV	25495
VH-AOI	19694	VH-DNA	27130
VH-ARA (C-39)	2087	(VH-DNF)	33109
VH-ARB (C-39)	2076	VH-EAE	33096
VH-ARC (C-39)	2089	VH-EAF	33106
VH-ASD	13506	VH-EAK	12872
VH-ASJ	32991	VH-EAL	13084
VH-ATO	33109	VH-EAM	9286
VH-AVK	13612	VH-EAN	12187
VH-AVL	13906	VH-EAO	25367
VH-AVM	9590	VH-EAP	12873
VH-AXM	9350	VH-EAQ	11971
VH-AXT	9749	VH-EAR	12035
VH-BAA	13084	VH-EBE	10000
VH-BAB	25495	VH-EBF(1)	12248
(VH-BAJ)	12872	VH-EBF(2)	12187
(VH-BAK)	13084	VH-EBG	12541
(VH-BAL)	9286	VH-EBH(1)	25491
(VH-BAM)(1)	25367	VH-EBH(2)	13084
VH-BAM(2)	9811	VH-EBI	13622
(VH-BAT)	12790	VH-EBJ	12667
VH-BBV	12360	VH-EBT	10000
(VH-BDR)	12790	VH-EBU	12187
VH-BDU	12041	VH-EBV	12541
VH-BFV	11917	VH-EBW	13084
VH-BFW	13587	VH-EBX	25367
VH-BHB	19950	VH-EBY	12873
VH-BHC	20401	VH-EDC	12874
VH-BHD	25427	VH-EDD	25367
VH-BHE	19934	VH-EQB	25826
"VH-BLM"	33099	VH-EQN	25998
VH-BNH	26675	VH-EQO	33463
"VH-BPA"	12187	VH-EWA	9286
VH-BPL	12873	VH-EWB	11970
VH-BPN	32945	VH-EWD	9811
VH-BUR	19934	VH-EWE	6007
VH-BXM	9350	"VH-EWE"	13084
VH-BZA	4651	VH-EWF(1)	6007
VH-BZB	9414	VH-EWF(2)	9286
VH-BZC	33242	VH-EYB	12037
VH-BZJ	9740	VH-EYC	33294
VH-BZK	13362	VH-GAH	3272
VH-BZL	13606	VH-GAI	4096
VH-CAN	13506	VH-GAJ	6010
VH-CAO	25495	VH-GAK	13624
VH-CAQ	12285	VH-GAL	9285
VH-CAR	12874	VH-GAT	4651
VH-CBA	9749	VH-INA	12252
VHCCB	4823	VH-INB	9285
VHCCC(1)	4824	VH-INC	12045
VHCCC(2)	9906?	VH-IND	13529
VHCCF (C-39)	2087	VH-INE	9452
VHCCG (C-39)	2076	VH-INF	12647
VHCCH (C-39)	2089	VH-ING	19951
VHCDA	3270	VH-INI	12252
VH-CDA	32675	VH-INM	25427
VHCDB(1)	3272	VH-INN	4969
VHCDB(2)	20665	VH-JGL	26640
VH-CDB	32669	VH-JVF	12874
VHCDC(1)	9906?	VH-JXD(1)	33102
VHCDC(2)	3282	VH-JXD(2)	33297
VH-CDC	33093	VH-MAB	9749
VHCDD	4094	VH-MAC	13587
VHCDE(1)	4096	VH-MAE	11917
VHCDE(2)	27016	VH-MAH	12875
VHCDG(1)	3271	VH-MAL	4423
VHCDG(2)	20705	VH-MAM	9749
VHCDH	6010	VH-MAN	12647
VHCDJ	9397	VH-MAR	12035
VHCDJ	4120	VH-MAS	9592
VHCDK(1)	4119	VH-MAT	13340

CHAPTER 4: COMMERCIAL OPERATORS OF THE DC-3, C-47, R4D, DAKOTA AND LI-2

VH-MAV	12875	VH-SBF	12541
VH-MIN	13459	VH-SBG	12873
VH-MJR	6353	VH-SBH	25367
VH-MMA	9593	VH-SBI	6122
VH-MMB	34228	VH-SBJ	13622
VH-MMD	33301	VH-SBK	6023
VH-MME	9350	VH-SBL	12056
VH-MMF	12540	VH-SBM	11967
"VH-MMF"	13624	VH-SBN	10001
VH-MMK	19950	VH-SBO	6108
VH-MML	32945	VH-SBT	26480
VH-MMM	13612	VH-SBW	27110
VH-MMO	34228	VH-SMH	13157
VH-MMT	6353	VH-SMI	13459
VH-MWQ	9593	VH-SPY	33113
VH-NVD	32879	VH-TAE	12056
VH-NVZ	32883	VH-TAF	11967
VH-OVM	33102	VH-TAG	12875
VH-PAT	33242	VH-TAH	10001
VH-PNA	33103	VH-TAI	9998
VH-PNB	26789	VH-TAJ	13085
VH-PNM	26480	VH-TAK	13338
VH-PTE	26638	VH-TAL	25366
VH-PTM	25826	VH-TAM	25364
VH-PTS	33113	VH-TAN	9592
VH-PWM	11970	VH-TAT	13083
VH-PWN(1)	9286	VH-TAU	13340
VH-PWN(2)	26001	VH-TAV	13622
"VH-QLD"	6024	VH-TAW	12539
VH-RMA	4651	(VH-TAY)	12037
VH-RMJ	9740	VH-TMQ	32884
VH-RMK	13362	VH-UPQ	33300
VH-RML	13606	VH-USY(DC-2)	1580
VH-RPA	33099	VH-UXJ(DC-2)	1561
VH-RRA	33099	VH-UYB(DC-2)	1563
VH-SBA	6021	VH-UYC(DC-2)	1566
VH-SBB	10000	VH-UZJ	2002
VH-SBC	11971	VH-UZK	2003
VH-SBD	12187	"VN-BME"	20041
VH-SBE	12539		

A road vehicle marked "VHDAK" used parts of c/n 13210.

AUSTRIA - A and OE

Apart from DC-2 A-500 bought for government use before WWII, DC-3s were used only briefly in Austria.

Austria-Flugdienst, Vienna, used DC-3s OE-FDA and OE-FDB (later OE-GDB) between 1958 and 1964 on charter work.

Austrian Airlines (Osterreichische Luftverkehr AG), Vienna, used three DC-3s on local services between 1963 and 1966, when they were replaced by HS.748s.

OE-LBC; OE-LBD; OE-LBN.

Index:-

A-500(DC-2)	c/n 1320	OE-LBC	12324
OE-FDA	13332	'OE-LBC'	13073
OE-FDB	1972	OE-LBD	42976
OE-GDB	1972	OE-LBN	42963

AZORES - See Portugal

BAHAMAS - VP-B

The first DC-3 came on to the Bahamas register in 1949 with Bahamas Airways. This was followed by Flamingo and then by Bahamasair, but no DC-3s remained by 1980.

Bahamas Airways Ltd, Nassau. DC-3s were introduced on inter-island services when BOAC took over the airline from BSAAC in 1949. In 1959 the holding company was sold to Skyways who supplied further DC-3s. However BOAC regained control in 1960 and sold most of the DC-3s. One more was leased in 1965 but all were sold by 1968.

VP-BAA; VP-BAB; VP-BAH; VP-BAP; VP-BAQ; VP-BAU; VP-BBL; VP-BBM; VP-BBN; VP-BBR; VP-BBT; VP-BBU; VP-BCC; N142HD (Lsd); N203ZZ (Lsd).

Bahamasair, Nassau. This was formed by the merger of **Flamingo** with **Out Island** and DC-3s were operated on lease between 1975 and 1979.

N8563, N14931, N25651, N23WT.

Flamingo Airlines, Nassau. Services started as a subsidiary of Bahamas World in March 1971 with DC-3s (N407D and N338G) amongst other types. Following the merger with Out Island, **Bahamasair** was formed in 1975.

Helda Air operated DC-3s N21783 and N123BA.

Kwin Air, see Kwin Aircraft Corp in US section.

Lucaya Air, LBAS, Freeport, used N12954 on lease in the early nineties.

Taino Air, Freeport, operated DC-3s N165LG and N166LG on lease.

Index:-

VP-BAA	c/n 19999	VP-BBM	25623
VP-BAB	25623	VP-BBN	33159
VP-BAH	33159	VP-BBR	12299
VP-BAP	13114	VP-BBT	26725
VP-BAQ	9885	VP-BBU	9885
VP-BAU	33518	VP-BCC	12450
VP-BBL	19999		

BAHRAIN

Gulf Aviation Co Ltd, Bahrain was a subsidiary of BOAC and operated DC-3s on local scheduled services between 1958 and 1972 when the last was retired. The first three were leased from Kalinga (VT-AXF, VT-AZU and VT-DGS), but by 1966 six British examples had been bought. These remained until the F.27 replaced them. They were G-AGKE; G-ALVZ; G-AMVA; G-AMZZ; G-ANEG; G-AOFZ.

BANGLADESH - S2

Biman Bangladesh, Dacca, started scheduled services in Feb72 using a DC-3. This crashed on the 10th of that month, at Dacca, but its identity is unknown. It was probably leased, never appearing on the Bangladesh civil register.

BARBADOS - 8P

Carib-West Airways Ltd, Christchurch. Charter services were started in Mar71, using three DC-3s. These were retired by 1976 when a US-registered example was leased.

8P-AAA; 8P-AAB; 8P-AAC; N63440.

Tropic Air (Tropical Air Services), Christchurch, used four DC-3s on charter services between Feb73 and 1980. In 1979 the operator was taken over by the Canadian company, Air Dale Ltd, who supplied two of the DC-3s for winter use.

8P-CAW; 8P-DON; 8P-OOW; 8P-WGO.

Index:-

8P-AAA	c/n 9978	8P-DON	4812
8P-AAB	12892	8P-OOW	13342
8P-AAC	26363	8P-WGO	4932
8P-CAW	27078		

BECHUANALAND - See Botswana

BELGIUM - OO

The DC-3 was used briefly in Belgium by Sabena before the war, but post-war it featured prominently in both the European and Congo operations of Sabena, Sobelair etc. Several smaller operators used the type and Delta had the distinction of flying the last DC-3 service in Belgium. A few DC-3s were used by the state, on lease from the Air Force.

Air Congo/CFL operated in the Congo using DC-3s OO-AWN, OO-SBD and OO-SBE.

BIAS - Belgian International Air Services, Antwerp, was founded in 1959 but only started using DC-3s in 1965 when it bought up Sabena's Libyan operation on behalf of **Linair**, in whose colours the aircraft continued to operate until 1972.

OO-AUW; OO-AWJ; OO-CBX; OO-CBY; OO-SBC; OO-SBH; OO-UBT.

COBETA - Cie Belge de Transports Aériens, Brussels, was formed in 1947 and used DC-3s on charters from 1948 until 1950 within Europe. They also operated scheduled services between Brussels and Manchester from Apr48 until Sep49.

OO-APB (x2); OO-APC; LX-LAA (Lsd).

Delta Air Transport, Antwerp, began DC-3 operations in 1968, operating local services for KLM and later for Sabena. The last DC-3 flight was in Oct72, by which time the Convair 440 had replaced the type.

OO-AUV; OO-AUX; OO-AVG; OO-CBU; OO-DVG; OO-GVG; OO-KVG; OO-VDF; PH-MAG (Lsd).

John Mahieu Aviation, Brussels. DC-3s were used in 1948 for some European services (see COBETA). These were the first OO-APB, OO-APC (Lsd to SABENA 1949) and LX-LAA on lease.

SABENA - Sté. Anonyme Belge d'Exploitation de la Navigation Aérienne, Brussels. The first two DC-3s were delivered in 1939 and taken over by the RAF in 1940 but lost during that year, one to bombing and the other in North Africa. When operations were restarted in 1946, C-47s were bought from RAF and USAAF surplus stocks, and further aircraft direct from Douglas after rebuild. They were used extensively on European and Congo services until replaced by more modern aircraft. Those in the Congo went to Air Congo in 1960, but others were used on charter to Linair in Libya from 1959 until the operation was bought by BIAS in 1965. The last DC-3s were sold to Nigeria and to Delta by 1970.

OO-AUH; OO-AUI; OO-AUL to OO-AUS incl; OO-AUV to OO-AUZ incl; OO-AWF to OO-AWH incl; OO-AWJ to OO-AWN incl; OO-AWZ; OO-CBA; OO-CBB; OO-CBC; OO-CBJ; OO-CBK; OO-CBL; OO-CBN; OO-CBO; OO-CBT; OO-CBU; OO-CBW; OO-CBX; OO-CBY; OO-SBC; OO-SBD; OO-SBE; OO-SBH; OO-SBI; OO-SBK; OO-UBJ; OO-UBT; plus on lease:- OO-APC (from COBETA) OO-SBF; OO-SBG (from Sobelair) and OO-SMA to OO-SMD incl (Lsd from the AF). OO-CBH was written-off on delivery.

SOBELAIR - Sté Belge de Transports Aériens, Brussels. Formed originally in 1946 as **Sté d'Etude du Transport Aérien** to operate charters to the Belgian Congo and East Africa. SABENA acquired a 75% interest in 1949. The last DC-3 was sold in Jan56.

OO-SBA to OO-SBG incl; OO-TBA.

Index:-

OO-APB(1)	c/n 11923	OO-AWK	9865	
OO-APB(2)	25292	(OO-AWL)(1)	12420	
OO-APC	4930	OO-AWL(2)	19551	
OO-AUH	2093	OO-AWM	12318	
OO-AUI	2094	OO-AWN(1)	19574	
OO-AUL	42968	OO-AWN(2)	12767	
OO-AUM	42973	(OO-AWO)	13153	
OO-AUN	42977	OO-AWZ	25292	
OO-AUO	10129	OO-CBA	6327	
OO-AUP	10063	OO-CBB	6339	
OO-AUQ	10241	OO-CBC	4144	
OO-AUR	4549	OO-CBH	10070	
OO-AUS	9093	OO-CBJ	43092	
(OO-AUV)(1)	26045	OO-CBK	26045	
OO-AUV(2)	43087	OO-CBL	12420	
OO-AUW	26297	OO-CBN	13450	
OO-AUX	43088	OO-CBO	12454	
OO-AUY	43089	OO-CBT	19536	
OO-AUZ	43090	(OO-CBU)(1)	25880	
OO-AVG	19458	OO-CBU(2)	25799	
OO-AWF	13486	OO-CBW	20776	
OO-AWG	43091	OO-CBX	33224	
OO-AWH	43154	OO-CBY	11982	
OO-AWJ	9626	OO-DVG	43089	
OO-GVG	43090	OO-SBK	26980	
OO-KVG	4346	OO-SMA	26501	
"OO-PTG"	13331	OO-SMB	32557	
(OO-SBA)(1)	12185	OO-SMC	26046	
OO-SBA(2)	13332	OO-SMD	26048	
OO-SBB	13033	OO-SNC	32664	
OO-SBC	13457	OO-TBA	12172	
OO-SBD	25457	OO-UBJ	43092	
OO-SBE	12734	OO-UBT	19536	
OO-SBF	12050	OO-VDF	9410	
OO-SBG	13472	(OO-VDH)	25799	
OO-SBH	11979	(OO-VGK)	4346	
OO-SBI	13474			

Note: A DC-3 fuselage was painted "OO-DAC" for use as a clubhouse at Diest Aero Club, Schaffen/Diest, Belgium, between about 1958 and 1964 but its identity remains unknown.

BELIZE - See British Honduras

BENIN - See Dahomey

BOLIVIA - CB and CP

Despite Bolivia's mountainous terrain, the DC-3/C-47 found an important niche there, although C-46s and B-17s were more suited to the high altitude cargo work. Few C-47s remain today. The nationality mark CB was used until Oct53, when it was changed to CP and 500 added to the number. LAB was the only DC-3 user prior to 1953. By the new century only about four remained on the register.

Aerolíneas Abaroa, La Paz, used DC-3s for charter work between 1961 and 1969 when the company went out of business.

CP-565; CP-639; CP-691; CP-695; CP-710; CP-720; CP-729; CP-755.

Aerolíneas Condor, La Paz, used DC-3s for freight work between 1958 and 1963.

CP-639; CP-645.

Aerolíneas La Paz, La Paz. The type was flown briefly during 1977/1978 before operations ceased. The last two were still at La Paz in Mar81.

CP-755; CP-820; CP-1243; CP-1416; CP-1417; CP-1418; CP-1419.

Air Beni, La Paz, was using DC-3 CP-2290 from 1997 to 2001.

Bolivian Air Flying (BAFIN), La Paz, used one DC-3 CP-735, which went missing in Oct90.

Bolivian Air Tourmen, La Paz. A single DC-3 (CP-820) was operated between 1971 and 1977.

Cía Aerovías Bolivia, Cochabamba. DC-3 CP-720 was in use on domestic cargo services.

Cía Boliviana de Aviación, Cochabamba, a further DC-3 operator, not to be confused with the one below, used CP-639, CP-1419 and CP-1990. Operations ran from about 1987 to 1989 or later.

Cía Boliviano de Aviación, La Paz. Domestic cargo services were operated with two DC-3s (CP-720 and CP-755) between 1969 and 1977.

CADET - Cooperativa Aérea de Transportes, Cochabamba. Three DC-3s saw service between 1971 and 1977.

CP-572; CP-607; CP-820.

Corporación Boliviano de Fomento, La Paz. This government-owned corporation included two DC-3s in its fleet, providing air cargo services to undeveloped areas.

CP-734; CP-735.

Frigorifico Santa Rita, La Paz. DC-3 CP-529 was used for bulk meat transport from 1977, it was destroyed by fire in 1993. CP-607 was used in 1992 to 1994.

CHAPTER 4: COMMERCIAL OPERATORS OF THE DC-3, C-47, R4D, DAKOTA AND LI-2

Frigorifico Cooperativo "Los Andes" SA, La Paz. Freight and bulk meat work started in 1950, an unidentified DC-3 being included in the fleet.

Frigorifico Reyes, La Paz, used DC-3s CP-1622 and CP-2178 for meat transport but these were replaced by Convairs and larger aircraft.

Horizontes. A single DC-3 (CP-728) was in use from 1973 to 1976.

Líneas Aéreas Canedo, Cochabamba, started charter services in about 1980 using DC-3s. These mostly gave way to Convairs by 1992 but CP-2255 remained in 2000 and CP-1960 was acquired, followed by P-2421 in 2002.

CP-583; CP-733; CP-1059; CP-1128; CP-1960; CP-2255; CP-2421.

Lloyd Aéreo Boliviano - LAB, Cochabamba. LAB was the major Bolivian DC-3 operator, starting in Aug45 and using them until the last was replaced by F.27s in 1978.

CB-29/CP-529; CB-30/CP-530; CB-31; CB-32; CB-33; CB-34/CP-607; CB-35/CP-535; CB-36/CP-536; CB-68/CP-568; CB-72/CP-572; CB-73/CP-573; CB-83/CP-583; CB-84/CP-584; CB-91/CP-591; CB-100/CP-600; CB-101/CP-601; CP605; CP-733; CP-734; CP-735.

NOLI, Santa Cruz, operated DC-3 CP-1074 on freight services from at least 1978 to 1982.

Servicios Aéreos Cochabamba, La Paz. A single DC-3, CP-680, was used on domestic cargo services from 1960 to 1964.

Servicios Aéreos Virgen de Copacabana, Cochabamba. DC-3 CP-733 was in use in 1979, CP-1668 remained until 1991 and CP-1952 was sold earlier. CP-1128 was in store by 2000.

Cia Sudamericana C & S. DC-3 CP-529 was operated between 1973-7.

Transalfa operated DC-3s CP-583 and CP-733 in 1986. Both were sold.

Trans Oriental Ltda, Santa Cruz. DC-3 CP-1074 was in use between 1974 and 1986, and CP-1742 was in use in 1986, but operations ceased in the late eighties.

Transportes Aéreos Acre operated DC-3 CP-645 between 1960 and 1965.

Transportes Aéreos Itanez. During 1976/77 three DC-3s were owned; CP-728; CP-1059 and CP-1128.

Transportes Aéreos Luwior had DC-3s CP-1940 and CP-1941, but the latter was sold. The company ceased operations in 1991.

Transportes Aéreos Militares, La Paz. See Bolivian Air Force for further details.

Transportes Aéreos San Antonio, Cochabamba, bought CP-1940 and CP-1941 by October 1987. CP-1940 remained in 2000.

Transportes Aéreos San Jorge, owned CP-1960 from about 1986 on.

Transportes Aéreos San Miguel used DC-3s CP-583, CP-1059, CP-1622 and CP-1952 but all had been sold or otherwise disposed of by 1991.

Transportes Aéreos Tadeo, La Paz. A single DC-3, CP-607 was in use in the late eighties, but was sold in 1988.

Transportes Aéreos Tauro used DC-3s CP-1419 and CP-1465but ceased operations by 1989.

Transportes Aéreos Virgen de Carmen, Cochabamba, used DC-3 CP-607 in 1999. CP-1419 was acquired for spares.

VEBAS Ltda, La Paz. Three DC-3s were operated from 1974 to 1978:- CP-583; CP-735; CP-1243.

Index:-

CB-29	c/n 4980	CB-35	4867
CB-30	34351	CB-36	20619
CB-31	13837	CB-65	19236
CB-32	19445	CB-68	19024
CB-33		CB-72	1549
CB-34	12570	CB-73	4682
CB-77		CP-735	33553
CB-83	9668	CP-755	4294
CB-84	19226	CP-820	19176
CB-91	20200	CP-897	19721
CB-100	2181	CP-1020	9028
CB-101	2182	CP-1059	2173
CP-529	4980	CP-1074	1967
CP-530	34351	CP-1128	1998
(CP-534)	12570	CP-1226	
CP-535	4867	CP-1243	32609
CP-536	20619	CP-1416	
CP-565	19236	CP-1417	26804
CP-568	19024	CP-1418	19344
CP-572	1549	CP-1419	32988
CP-573	4682	CP-1465	32682
CP-583	9668	CP-1470	19395
CP-584	19226	CP-1607	
CP-591	20200	CP-1622	13336
(CP-600)	2181	CP-1660	
CP-601	2182	(CP-1668)	7386
CP-605	32542	CP-1668	25764
CP-607	12570	CP-1742	2134
CP-639	7375	CP-1940	2120
CP-645	20199		or 12798 ?
(CP-666)		CP-1941	4084
CP-680	13371	CP-1952	9074
CP-691	32724	CP-1957	34268
CP-695	19389	CP-1960	18993
CP-710	20230	CP-1990	27069/a
CP-720	34351	CP-2178	20472
CP-728	19689	CP-2255	25951
CP-729	32546	CP-2290	32626
CP-733	2182	CP-2421	43365
CP-734	34311	(CP-2486)	9276

Notes:-
CB-33 was owned by LAB and was destroyed in the civil war on 29Aug49.
CP-1226 was allotted to Coop. Aerea de Transportes, but ntu.
CP-1416 owner J L Suarez, ex TAM.

BORNEO - See Malaysia.

BOSNIA-HERZEGOVINA - T9

C/n 32935 was noted at Malta as T9-ABC from 1995 but was not delivered to Bosnia and is now (Mar06) in the Malta Aviation Museum.

BOTSWANA - A2 (Previously Bechuanaland - VQ-Z.)

Air Botswana (Pty) Ltd, Gaborone. This was known at first as **Botswana Airways** which was formed from Botswana National in 1969 and reorganised in Aug72, when DC-3 A2-ZHR was in use. XS-EJK was leased.

Bechuanaland National Airways (Pty) Ltd, Francistown, was formed with DC-3s VQ-ZEA and VQ-ZEB in 1965. It was liquidated in 1968 when Botswana National Airways took over operations and one DC-3 was returned to S Africa.

Botswana National Airways (Pty) Ltd, Gaborone, succeeded Bechuanaland National in 1968, taking over A2-ZEB from the latter and adding A2-ZHR. The latter passed to Botswana Airways in 1969.

Wenela Air Service, Francistown, used DC-3s and DC-4s between 1968 and 1978 on the Witwatersrand Native Labour Association operations. The DC-3s were A2-ZEM to A2-ZEP inclusive, of which the first three came to be operated by **Air Travel**. Wenela also used South African registered DC-3s such as ZS-DJK - see also under Rhodesia and Africair, South Africa.

Index:-

VQ-ZEA	c/n 33581	A2-ZEA	33581
VQ-ZEB	33083	A2-ZEB	33083
A2-AAA	26439	A2-ZEM	33257
A2-ACF	6154	A2-ZEN	32961
A2-ACG	13331	A2-ZEO	26087
A2-ACH	9581	A2-ZEP	26439
A2-ADB	11989	A2-ZFD	32656
A2-ADL	33581	A2-ZHR	13164

BRAZIL - PP and PT

Brazil is second only to the United States in the number of DC-3s that have been registered, though at least 10% have carried more than one Brazilian marking during their life in Brazil. The first DC-2 arrived in 1939 and the first DC-3 was diverted from the USAAF in 1943 via Pan American. Thereafter every major operator used the type. To-day only one remains active, although a few remain on the register, PP-VBN being used for tourist flights at Belem Novo, Porto Alegre in 2003. Several companies used PP-X.. marks for delivery flights of their aircraft.

Aero Geral Ltda, Rio de Janeiro. Two DC-3s (PP-AGF, PP-AGG) together with some Catalinas and C-46s were used on scheduled operations between 1948 and 1951, when the airline was absorbed by VARIG.

Aeronorte - Empresa de Transportes Aéreos Norte do Brasil Ltda, Sao Luiz. Feeder services began in 1950 and control passed to Aerovias Brasil in 1953 who supplied three DC-3s. These were taken over by REAL in 1959 but Aeronorte continued to operate as a separate division and a further two DC-3s added. Varig's take-over two years later ended this arrangement.

PP-ANV; PP-NBJ; PP-NBK; PP-NBL; PP-YPC; PP-YPI; PP-YPK; PP-YQN; PP-YQS; PP-YPY.

Aerovias SA, Belo Horizonte, Minas Gerais. One DC-2 and two C-39s were used between 1946 until 1949 when only one remained and bankruptcy stopped operations. PP-AVH was also intended but ntu.

PP-AVG; PP-MGA; PP-MGB.

Aerovias Brasil, SA, Empresa de Transportes, Rio de Janeiro, started life as a subsidiary of TACA in August 1942 (Empresa de Transportes Aéreos Carga Aerovias Brasil). It became independent of TACA in January 1947 prior to which two DC-2s were bought. Subsequently about 30 DC-3s were acquired. VASP gained control in 1949 but lost it in 1950 and then in September 1954 REAL took over and **REAL-Aerovias** titles were used on the aircraft until VARIG gained control in 1961.

DC-2s:- PP-AVG; PP-AVH. DC-3s:- PP-AVI to PP-AVW incl; PP-AVY; PP-AVZ; PP-AXD to PP-AXG incl; PP-AXI to PP-AXL incl; PP-AXT; PP-AXV; PP-AXW; PP-AXY; PP-AXZ; YS-22 and YS-24 (leased from TACA de Salvador).

Central Aérea Ltda, Rio de Janeiro. This was formed in 1948 with three DC-3s PP-IBA to PP-IBC and in 1950 merged with Consórcio Nacional de Transportes Aéreos, retaining its identity until 1953. PP-XEZ/PP-ANH was acquired in 1950. PP-ANB was used from 1954 until 1959.

CONAGRA - Colonizadora e Consutoria Agrária, Rio de Janeirohas operated four ex Brazilian AF C-47s. These were all sold by 1988.

PT-KVJ to PT-KVM incl.

Consórcio Nacional de Transportes Aéreos, Rio de Janeiro. This airline was formed in 1951 as a consortium of Central Aérea Ltda, Transportes Aéreos Nacional Ltda, OMTA (not a DC-3 user) and VIABRAS. Some aircraft were leased from individuals, but operated in Nacional colours. Operations were taken over by **REAL** in 1956 together with many of the DC-3s previously flown in the colours of the constituent companies (see REAL for details of DC-3s used).

Cruzeiro - Serviços Aéreos Cruzeiro do Sul SA, Rio de Janeiro. DC-3s were bought in 1943 to supplement the remains of the pre-war fleet of German types. In 1950 an interest was acquired in Viação Aérea Gaúcha and in Catarinense. By 1969 the DC-3s had all been replaced by YS-11s. A single C-39 was used for aerial survey work for many years.

C-39:- PP-CEC; DC-3s:- PP-AJC; PP-AJD; PP-CBS to PP-CBV incl; PP-CBX to PP-CCE incl; PP-CCK to PP-CCP incl; PP-CCR; PP-CCT; PP-CCV to PP-CCZ incl; PP-CDB; PP-CDC; PP-CDD; PP-CDG to PP-CDP incl; PP-CDR to PP-CDV incl; PP-CEB; PP-CED; PP-CES; PP-PED; PP-SAD; PP-SAE; PT-AOB; PT-BHP.

Empresa de Transporte Aéreo Brasileiro Ltda, Rio de Janeiro. Four DC-3s were in use between October 1946 and May 1947 when they were leased to Aerovias Brasil. In January 1949 the airline became part of Aerovias.

PP-ACA to PP-ACD incl.

JARI Florestal, Belém, used DC-3 PP-AJD from 1975 to 1983 and PP-CDT in the eighties.

Linha Aérea Transcontinental Brasileira SA, Rio de Janeiro. Five DC-3s were used on scheduled services from 1945. Operations were partly amalgamated with Viação Aérea Santos Dumont in 1949 and finally the airline was bought by REAL in August 1951.

PP-ATF; PP-ATG; PP-ATH; PP-ATJ; PP-NAL.

Linhas Aéreas Brasileiras, Rio de Janeiro. Scheduled services were flown between 1946 and 1949, when bankruptcy intervened. Three of the DC-3s were bought by Nacional.

PP-AJA; PP-AJB; PP-BRA to PP-BRF incl.

Linhas Aéreas Natal, Natal. This airline was formed in July 1946 with four DC-3s. They were taken over by REAL in May 1950.

PP-JAA to PP-JAD incl.

Linhas Aéreas Paulistas SA, Rio de Janeiro. DC-3s were bought soon after the war ended and scheduled services started. The airline was bought out by Loide in 1949.

PP-LPB to PP-LPG incl.

Loide Aéreo Nacional SA, Rio de Janeiro. Founded as **Transportes Carga Aérea** in 1947 and re-named LAN in 1949 when Paulistas and TAB were bought. VASP took control in 1962. Apart from DC-3 PP-ASC inherited from TCA, PP-LPC; PP-LPE; PP-LPF and PP-LPG from Paulistas were used.

Nacional - See Transportes Aéreos Nacional Ltda.

Navegação Aérea Brasileira, SA, Rio de Janeiro. Four DC-3s were bought in 1946 to supplement the Lockheeds and Beechcraft used since 1939, but operations were suspended between 1948 and 1951. The airline was reformed as NAB Nova Organização in 1951 and took over Panair do Brasil's DC-3 fleet. VASP gained control in 1962.

PP-NAK to PP-NAN incl; PP-NAR to PP-NAZ incl; PP-NMA; PP-NMB.

PAB - Panair do Brasil SA, Rio de Janeiro. PAB operated two DC-2s from just before the war until 1942 and DC-3s from 1945. By 1958 most of the large fleet had been transferred to NAB, but two were taken back in 1962. The airline was declared bankrupt in 1965.

DC-2s:- PP-PAY; PP-PAZ; DC-3s:- PP-PBS to PP-PBU incl; PP-PBW; PP-PBY to PP-PCA incl, PP-PCC; PP-PCD; PP-PCE; PP-PCH to PP-PCP incl; PP-PCS to PP-PCV incl; PP-PED; PP-PEE.

Projeto Rondon was a regional development agency operating flights for students. A fleet of DC-3s was used for this work up to the late seventies.

PP-FNE/PT-KTW; PP-FOI/PT-KUA; PP-FOZ/PT-KTZ; PP-NAM; PP-NAT/PT-KTY; PP-SPO/PT-KUB; PP-SQA; PP-SQJ/PP-FOP/PT-KTX; PP-SQK/PT-KUC; PP-SQO/PT-KUD.

Paraense Transportes Aéreos SA.` Two DC-3s, PP-BTU and PP-BTX, were used from 1962 until 1969.

REAL - SA Transportes Aéreos, Sao Paulo. This airline was formed in 1946 as **Redes Estaduais Aéreas Ltda** and two DC-3s were used to start operations early that year. Other DC-3 operators were taken over:- LA Transcontinental Brasileira in August 1951, Aerovias Brasil in 1954, Nacional in 1956 and T A Salvador in 1957. In turn, REAL was taken over by Varig, in August 1961. This listing includes takeovers:

PP-AKA to PP-AKD incl; PP-ANE; PP-ANI; PP-ANO; PP-ANS; PP-ANT; PP-ANW; PP-ANX; PP-ANZ; PP-AVF; PP-AVJ; PP-AVK; PP-AVL; PP-AVN; PP-AVP; PP-AVQ; PP-AVS; PP-AVT; PP-AVU; PP-AVY; PP-AXD to PP-AXF incl; PP-AXI to PP-AXL; PP-NBJ; PP-YPA to PP-YPC incl; PP-YPG to PP-YQB incl; PP-YQF to PP-YQH incl; PP-YQJ to PP-YQS incl.

RICO - Rondonia Importação, Exportação, Industria e Comércio, Manaus, has used over 30 DC-3s on charter and contract freight work, but only two remained by 1988.

PP-AJC; PP-AJD; PP-CCM; PP-CED; PP-CES; PP-SAE; PP-VBW; PT-BHP; PT-KTV; PT-KTX to PT-KUA incl; PT-KUC; PT-KUD; PT-KUR; PT-KUW; PT-KUY; PT-KVK; PT-KVN; PT-KVR; PT-KVS; PT-KVT; PT-KVU; PT-KVX; PT-KXR; PT-KYX; PT-KYZ; PT-KZH; PT-KZJ; PT-KZM; PT-KZV; PT-KZW?; PT-LBK; PT-LBL; PT-LBM.

CHAPTER 4: COMMERCIAL OPERATORS OF THE DC-3, C-47, R4D, DAKOTA AND LI-2

Royal Taxi Aéreo, Belem operated PT-KZE and PT-KZG in 1988, but operations ceased.

SA Viacao Aérea Gaúcha - SAVAG, Rio Grande do Sul. Operations started in 1948 with Lodestars. Control passed to Cruzeiro in September 1950 and two DC-3s were supplied, PP-SAD and PP-SAE. The operation was absorbed by Cruzeiro in 1966.

SADIA SA Transportes Aéreos, Sao Paulo. Operations with DC-3s and C-46s started in April 1956. Sadia operated in association with REAL from 1957 until 1961 and took over T A Salvador in 1962.

PP-AND; PP-ASJ; PP-ASK; PP-ASN to PP-AST incl.; PP-AVY; PP-SLL.

SAVA - Serviçios do Aerotaxis e Abastecimento do Vale Amazônica, Manaus, used DC-3 PT-KVJ but by 1988 it was out of use.

Scala Taxi Aéreo, Cuiabá, used PT-KVM for a while in the 1980s but sold it.

Taxi Aéreo Fortaleza, Fortaleza, operated DC-3 PT-AOB during 1980-1983, later adding PT-KYW and PT-KZF. All were withdrawn from use.

Taxi Aéreo Lider Ltda, Belo Horizonte, used DC-3 PT-CEV on taxi operations from 1964 until 1967.

Taxi Aéreo Uirapuru, Fortaleza, operated DC-3 PP-VBW during 1980-2.

Transportes Aéreos Bandeirantes Ltda, Rio de Janeiro. This was formed as T.A. Bacia Amazônica in 1947 and the name changed in 1948. From January 1950 it operated under contract from Loide and Paulistas from whom aircraft were chartered. PP-BLC and PP-XDW are the only DC-3s known.

Transportes Aéreos Ltda, Rio de Janeiro, operated scheduled services from 1948 until merged into Catarinense in 1950, using DC-3s PP-AJA and PP-AJB.

Transportes Aéreos Catarinense SA, Florianópolis. This was formed in 1949 when Cia Catarinense de Transportes Aéreos and Transportes Aéreos Ltda were merged. In September 1950 the airline was taken over by Cruzeiro but continued to operate under its former name until 1966 when it was absorbed in Cruzeiro's network.

PP-AJA; PP-AJC; PP-AJD; PP-AJE.

Transportes Aéreos Nacional Ltda - TAN, Rio de Janeiro. Scheduled services started in 1947 and in 1951 VIABRAS, Central Aérea and OMTA were taken over. REAL took 85% control in 1957 but operation as Nacional continued until it was integrated into Varig in January 1962 (see also **Consórcio Nacional**).

PP-AKA to PP-AKD incl; PP-AKI; PP-ANA to PP-ANZ incl; PP-AOA; PP-AOD; PP-BRC; PP-XNN

Transportes Aéreos Salvador Ltda, Salvador, Bahia. DC-3s were supplied to TAS by REAL from 1958 until 1961. TAS was connected with Sadia in 1962 and integrated with it in 1963. DC-3s used were PP-AND; PP-ANE; PP-YPS/PP-SLL.

Transportes Aéreos Sul Americanos SA, DC-3 PP-SVA was used between May 1948 and January 1949, when the company was declared bankrupt.

Transporte Carga Aérea SA. Three DC-3s were used for cargo work in 1948/49 but two were lost in accidents and the third passed to Loide when the company was reformed. They were PP-ASA to PP-ASC incl.

VARIG - SA Empresa de Viação Aérea Rio Grandense, Porto Alegre. Varig was formed originally with German assistance, but this ceased after the war and DC-3s were then bought. Aero Geral was absorbed in 1951, followed in August 1961 by the REAL-Aerovias Brasil network and finally by Nacional in January 1962. This resulted in a very large fleet of DC-3s, but by 1971 sales, accidents and retirements had removed the type from service.

PP-AKA; PP-AKI; PP-ANG; PP-ANL; PP-ANN; PP-ANP; PP-ANT; PP-ANU; PP-ANV; PP-AVJ; PP-AVN; PP-AVT; PP-AXL; PP-CDS; PP-VAW to PP-VBC incl; PP-VBF; PP-VBG; PP-VBH; PP-VBK; PP-VBL; PP-VBN; PP-VBO; PP-VBP; PP-VBR; PP-VBT; PP-VBV; PP-VBW; PP-VCD; PP-VCH; PP-VCS; PP-VDL; PP-VDM; PP-YPC; PP-YPI; PP-YPJ; PP-YPK; PP-YPO; PP-YPT; PP-YPU; PP-YPY; PP-YQN; PP-YQQ.

VASP - Viação Aérea São Paulo SA, São Paulo. VASP was formed by German interests, but came under Brazilian control in 1945. DC-3s were bought in the following year and more were added with the purchase of Loide and NAB in 1961. Aerovias Brasil came under VASP's control in 1949, but this passed to REAL a year later. The DC-3s gave way to YS-11s by 1972. VASP Aerofoto used C-39 PP-CEC for some time.

PP-NAM; PP-NAT; PP-SPK to PP-SQA incl; PP-SQG to PP-SQM incl; PP-SQO; PP-SQP.

VIABRAS - Viação Aérea Brasil SA, Sao Paulo. DC-3s were in use from July 1947 until 1956 when Nacional gained control after joint operation from 1950.

PP-ANJ; PP-IBA; PP-KAA to PP-KAD incl.

Viação Aérea Bahiana, Salvador. Three DC-3s were bought in December 1947 and sold in 1952, following bankruptcy in 1951.

PP-BHD to PP-BHF incl.

Viação Aérea Santos Dumont SA, Rio de Janeiro. Cargo services were operated with a Catalina, a Budd Conestoga and later DC-3s from 1944 until 1956 when Nacional gained control. DC-3s used were PP-ANL; PP-SDD; PP-SDE.

VOTEC - Serviçios Aéreos Regionales SA, Belem-Val de Cans. DC-3s were bought in 1978 from the Air Force for cargo services. None remained by the late eighties.

PT-KYW; PT-KYX; PT-KZE; PT-KZF; PT-KZG.

Index:-

PP-AAA	c/n 26683	PP-AOA	20193
PP-ABE	4419	PP-AOB	"33573"
PP-ACA	13326	(PP-AOC)	27069/b
PP-ACB	12356	PP-AOD	20136
PP-ACC	12147	PP-ASA	19843
PP-ACD	25295	PP-ASB	20467
PP-AGF	4115	PP-ASC	20200
PP-AGG	19972	PP-ASJ	4103
PP-AJA	11844	PP-ASK	20182
PP-AJB	9971	PP-ASN	27098
PP-AJC	20402	PP-ASO	32785
PP-AJD	6193	PP-ASP	4306
PP-AJE	3288	PP-ASQ	9203
PP-AKA	20193	PP-ASR	19176
PP-AKB	"33573"	PP-ASS	12985
PP-AKC	27069/b	PP-AST	9659
PP-AKD	20136	PP-ATF	34292
PP-AKI	11747	PP-ATG	34272
PP-ANA	9203	PP-ATH	34293
PP-ANB	19238	PP-ATJ	26683
PP-ANC	4306	PP-ATT	20519
PP-AND	9004	PP-AVG (DC-2)	1245
PP-ANE	34299	PP-AVH (DC-2)	1252
PP-ANF	19438	PP-AVI	4825
PP-ANG	4307	PP-AVJ	7333
PP-ANH	20187	"PP-AVJ"	20555
PP-ANI	34293	PP-AVK	4910
PP-ANJ	20182	PP-AVL	9886
PP-ANK	13773	PP-AVM	32746
PP-ANL	19871	PP-AVN	27222
PP-ANM	4365	PP-AVO	19113
PP-ANN	1992	PP-AVP	19214
PP-ANO	19830	PP-AVQ	11653
PP-ANP	4341	PP-AVR	19779
PP-ANQ	20519	PP-AVS	19792
PP-ANR	4704	PP-AVT	25227
PP-ANS	4280	PP-AVU	19389
PP-ANT	9714	PP-AVV	32785
PP-ANU	1545	PP-AVW	4754
PP-ANV	26172	PP-AVY	13632
	and/or "5994"	PP-AVZ	9156
PP-ANW	27069/a	(PP-AXB)	13372
PP-ANX	13048	PP-AXD	13326
PP-ANY	4756	PP-AXE	12356
PP-ANZ	13822	PP-AXF	12147

PP-AXG	25295	PP-FBK	6015	PP-SDF	26683	PP-XEC	19972
PP-AXI	25235	PP-FBO	12616	PP-SLL	1500	PP-XEE	20463
PP-AXJ	6177	PP-FBR	6015	PP-SPK	32706	PP-XEM	25588
PP-AXK	13636	PP-FNE	32682	PP-SPL	34274	PP-XEP	12025
PP-AXL	20463	(PP-FNF)	26601	PP-SPM	34151	PP-XEQ	19278
(PP-AXT)	13048	PP-FOI	32785	PP-SPN	34296	PP-XER	18992
PP-AXV	4419	PP-FOP	11863	PP-SPO	34285	PP-XES	13621
PP-AXW	4957	PP-FOR	19230	PP-SPP	27063	PP-XET	6015
PP-AXY		PP-FOZ	26343	PP-SPQ	27036	PP-XEU	13156
PP-AXZ	20244	PP-FVA	4473	PP-SPR	20544	PP-XEZ	20187
PP-AZA	9154	PP-FVI	4703	PP-SPS	26343	PP-XNN	19830
PP-BAD	19238	PP-FVN	10042	PP-SPT	20543	PP-YPA	19446
(PP-BAG)	4419	PP-IBA	4704	PP-SPU	20729	PP-YPB	13658
PP-BHD	2012	PP-IBB	4341	PP-SPV	25985	PP-YPC	20719
PP-BHE	1992	PP-IBC	4360	PP-SPW	34364	PP-YPG	13776
PP-BHF	1989	PP-JAA	13488	PP-SPX	12257	PP-YPH	4692
PP-BLC	9154	PP-JAB	12303	PP-SPY	10102	PP-YPI	4361
PP-BRA	9004	PP-JAC	12190	PP-SPZ	4649	PP-YPJ	20179
PP-BRB	13764	PP-JAD	13371	PP-SQA	4742	PP-YPK	20181
PP-BRC	13773	PP-KAA	4280	PP-SQG	1919	PP-YPL	4569
PP-BRD	34299	PP-KAB	4365	PP-SQH	1545	PP-YPM	4241
PP-BRE	34366	PP-KAC	4704	PP-SQI	13048	PP-YPN	4755
PP-BRF(1)	9714	PP-KAD	9714	PP-SQJ	11863	PP-YPO	20529
PP-BRF(2)	4704	PP-LDA	20200	PP-SQK	4347	PP-YPP	19176
PP-BTU	25235	PP-LPB	12723	(PP-SQL)	2248	PP-YPQ	12985
PP-BTX	9203	PP-LPC	19120	PP-SQM	4621	PP-YPR	9659
PP-CBS	4963	PP-LPD	19226	PP-SQO	19778	PP-YPS	1500
PP-CBT	4968	PP-LPE	9668	PP-SQP	1952	PP-YPT	13488
PP-CBU	4981	PP-LPF	19226	PP-SSE (DC-2)	1252	PP-YPU	12303
PP-CBV	4977	PP-LPG	26267	PP-SVA	19438	PP-YPV	12190
PP-CBX	11658	PP-MGA (C-39)	2058	PP-VAW	32690	PP-YPW	13371
PP-CBY	11692	PP-MGB (C-39)	2079	PP-VAX	32754	PP-YPX	9154
PP-CBZ	11767	PP-NAK	26601	PP-VAY	34276	PP-YPY	11670
PP-CCA	27177	PP-NAL	42979	PP-VAZ	34287	PP-YPZ	11699
PP-CCB	32682	PP-NAM	42980	PP-VBA	26183	PP-YQA	13621
PP-CCC	32593	PP-NAN	4521	PP-VBB	32652	PP-YQB	12025
PP-CCD	32559	PP-NAR	26019	PP-VBC	32732	PP-YQF	34292
PP-CCE	19829	PP-NAS	11743	PP-VBF	10156	PP-YQG	34272
PP-CCK	4750	PP-NAT	11683	PP-VBG	9209	PP-YQH	26682
PP-CCL	25247	PP-NAU	4884	PP-VBH	34301	PP-YQJ	25228
PP-CCM	19613	PP-NAV	4544	PP-VBK	26823	PP-YQK	4731
PP-CCN	10042	PP-NAW	9137	PP-VBL	6014	PP-YQL	2012
PP-CCO	12616	PP-NAX	11775	PP-VBN(1)	25360	PP-YQM	25871
PP-CCP	4226	PP-NAY	2134	PP-VBN(2)	26921	PP-YQN	1919
PP-CCR	32609	PP-NAZ	7387	PP-VBO	27138	PP-YQO	2248
PP-CCT	4703	PP-NBJ	4957	PP-VBP	9666	PP-YQP	34373
PP-CCV	20402	PP-NBK	4419	PP-VBR	4947	PP-YQQ	4615
PP-CCW	34366	PP-NBL	20244	PP-VBT	25588	PP-YQR	9719
PP-CCX	7341	PP-NMA	7396	PP-VBV	26889	PP-YQS	4914
PP-CCY	"20126"	PP-NMB	26272	PP-VBW	25989	PP-ZNU	"20126"
PP-CCZ	7404	PP-PAY (DC-2)	1351	PP-VCD	9031	PR-MGF	33581
PP-CDB	19008	PP-PAZ (DC-2)	1324	PP-VCH	19972	PT-ACV	3288
PP-CDC	13764	PP-PBS	11747	PP-VCS	19757	PT-AEC	4615
PP-CDD	26818	PP-PBT	11743	PP-VDL	4115	PT-ANX	19830
PP-CDG	19245	PP-PBU	11683	PP-VDM	7333	PT-AOB	9068
PP-CDH	11730	PP-PBW	4884	"PP-VRG"	1545	PT-AOS	1919
PP-CDI	4684	PP-PBY	26183	PP-XAS	19446	PT-APC	34373
PP-CDJ	19278	PP-PBZ	32609	PP-XAT	13658	PT-ASJ	4103
PP-CDK	18992	PP-PCA	34283	PP-XAU	13773	PT-ATP	2197
PP-CDL	6015	PP-PCC	4703	PP-XAV	19226	PT-AYC	27098
PP-CDM	6193	PP-PCD	4544	PP-XAX	12723	PT-BEJ	19176
PP-CDN	13156	PP-PCE	9137	PP-XAZ	9668	PT-BEK	12985
PP-CDO	11790	PP-PCH	4087	PP-XBA	19290	PT-BEL	9659
PP-CDP	3288	PP-PCI	2197	PP-XBB	19120	PT-BFU	2248
PP-CDR	4891	PP-PCJ	4103	PP-XBI	9203	PT-BHP	19245
PP-CDS	4823	PP-PCK	26158	PP-XBM	13048	PT-BIG	25235
PP-CDT	4442	PP-PCL	26052	PP-XBP	4241	PT-BJC	19214
PP-CDU	13452	PP-PCM	19524	PP-XCC	4360	PT-BQX	32732
PP-CDV	26601	PP-PCN	3284	PP-XCD	12985	PT-BUQ	12616
PP-CEB	20586	PP-PCO	11775	PP-XCF	26818	PT-BUR	6015
PP-CEC (C-39)	2079	PP-PCP	2134	PP-XCJ	26683	PT-CEV	20182
PP-CED	7386	PP-PCS	7387	PP-XCL	9666	PT-CGL	7333
PP-CES	11689	PP-PCT	7396	PP-XCM	4947	PT-FAG	"20126"
PP-DLM	20586	PP-PCU	26272	PP-XDE	11670	"PT-JAS"	32540
PP-DOK	4649	PP-PCV	25871	PP-XDF	3288	PT-KTV	6015
PP-DQA	4307	PP-PED	2134	PP-XDG	4615	PT-KTW	32682
PP-DSC	19230	PP-PEE	7396	PP-XDH	6177	PT-KTX	11863
PP-DSU	26818	PP-RSX	25235	PP-XDI	11699	PT-KTY	11683
PP-EDL	4910	PP-SAD	13764	PP-XDN	26267	PT-KTZ	26343
PP-ENB	27098	PP-SAE	18992	PP-XDP	11730	PT-KUA	32785
PP-ETE	19055	PP-SDD	20435	PP-XDU	13636	PT-KUB	34285
PP-FBJ	12616	PP-SDE	20519	PP-XDW	4115	PT-KUC	4347

CHAPTER 4: COMMERCIAL OPERATORS OF THE DC-3, C-47, R4D, DAKOTA AND LI-2

PT-KUD	19778	PT-KVX	20210
PT-KUR	9932	PT-KXR	19055
PT-KUW	34303	PT-KYW	34267
PT-KUY	19008	PT-KYX	13821
PT-KVA	4756	PT-KYZ	11837
PT-KVB	20136	(PT-KZB)	2134
PT-KVC	42980	PT-KZE	34266
PT-KVH	20451	PT-KZF	20244
PT-KVI	25397	PT-KZG	26921
PT-KVJ	27069/a	PT-KZH	10172
PT-KVK	34296	PT-KZJ	13538
PT-KVL	19305	PT-KZM	4621
PT-KVM	25684	PT-KZV	19775
PT-KVN	18993	PT-KZW	34268
PT-KVP	4910	PT-LBK	13156
PT-KVR	9985	PT-LBL	20055
PT-KVS	20428	PT-LBM	20586
PT-KVT	12147	PT-LGO	4433
PT-KVU	12356	PT-WXE	33581

Notes:- PP-AXY has been quoted with the c/n 45117. This may be a garbled USAAF serial, but apart from its transfer to the Air Force as 2068, no more is known.
PP-ANW and PP-AKC are both quoted as c/n 27069.
PP-ANV c/n 26172 is also quoted as "5994".

BRITISH GUIANA - See Guyana.

BRITISH HONDURAS - VP-H (also Belize)

Maya Airways Ltd, Belize. A DC-3, VP-HAI c/n 4814 was leased from Mexico from September 1963 until March 1964.

BRITISH VIRGIN ISLANDS - See Leeward Islands.

BULGARIA - LZ

No DC-3s are known to have been used in Bulgaria, although Russian built Li-2s were.

TABSO - Bulgarian Civil Air Transport. A number of Li-2s operated by Bulgarske Vazdusne Sobstenie, were taken over by TABSO in 1949. Only LZ-TUA to LZ-TUH incl; LZ-TUM; LZ-TUO; LZ-TUQ and LZ-40 have been identified, with around half of the c/ns known. One crashed on 06Dec52 en route Sofia-Varna.

Index:-

LZ-LIA	c/n	LZ-TUF	184 318 03
LZ-LIO	234 435 01	LZ-TUG	
LZ-TUA	234 435 07	LZ-TUH	
LZ-TUB	184 323 02	LZ-TUM	
LZ-TUC	184 318 08	LZ-TUO	
LZ-TUD		LZ-TUQ	
LZ-TUE	184 323 03	LZ-40	234 435 01

BURMA - XY

Airways Burma Ltd, Rangoon, used DC-3s on charter operations from 1949 onwards, but all are believed to have been taken over by the Burmese Air Force.

XY-ABZ; XY-ACA; XY-ACB: XY-ACC; XY-ACG to XY-ACK incl.

Burma Airways Corp. - See Union of Burma Airways. When the new title was adopted in 1972 the following probably remained in use:-

XY-ABF; XY-ACF; XY-ACM; XY-ACO; XY-ACT; XY-ADD.

Burma National Airways, Calcutta, which had a monopoly of internal air services until Aug47, operated DC-3 VT-CHT between 1946 and 1950.

Peacock Airlines, Rangoon, was a Burmese-American company and a subsidiary of Pan American had a Government mail contract 1945-48 and is believed to have owned one DC-3. It later became Sky Freighters.

Union of Burma Airways, Rangoon. UBA was formed in 1948, using DC-3s to operate many domestic services. The name was changed to Burma Airways in December 1972, following corporate changes. By this time many DC-3s had been transferred to the Air Force. The remainder were sold to Ethiopia in 1977.

XY-ABF; XY-ACC; XY-ACF; XY-ACH; XY-ACL; XY-ACM; XY-ACN(x2); XY-ACO to XY-ACU incl; XY-ADB to XY-ADD incl. VR-HEN was leased.

Index:-

XY-ABF	c/n 25288	XY-ACN(1)	9043
XY-ABZ	19920	XY-ACN(2)	12073
XY-ACA	13491	XY-ACO	13026
XY-ACB	13888	XY-ACP	9131
XY-ACC	13512	XY-ACQ	12579
XY-ACF	18914	XY-ACR	9629
XY-ACG	12085	XY-ACS	9877
XY-ACH	13387	XY-ACT	12981
XY-ACI	12915	XY-ACU	9334
XY-ACJ	12851	XY-ADB	33517
XY-ACK	19831	XY-ADC	25793
XY-ACL	25818	XY-ADD	26089
XY-ACM	26979		

BURUNDI - 9U

Air Burundi or STAB - Sté. de Transports Aériens du Burundi, Bujumbura, started scheduled local services in April 1971 under the name STAB. Air Burundi was adopted in June 1975. The DC-3s have been out of use since about 1986, but were still in storage in June 1993. In 2000 9U-BHL was briefly registered to Kivu Air.

Index:-

9U-BAB	c/n 9369	9U-BAE	25541
9U-BAC	13460	9U-BHL	25546

CAMBODIA - XU

As a French Protectorate the area used F- until becoming part of Indo-China in Nov49 using F-O. When independent from 09Nov53 Cambodia used F-KH but adopted XU- in 1960, first with numbers, then with letters. This war-torn country had a number of DC-3 operators but there are more mystery aircraft than in any other area of a similar size. As civilisation ceased to exist in the area for a while, it seems almost impossible that these problems will ever be unravelled. Even the airline titles are somewhat difficult to interpret, as some appear to be translations of others. Many aircraft went on flying until they could no longer get off the ground and they were then cannibalized for spares.

Cambodair - See Cambodia Air Commercial.

Cambodia Air Commercial is known to have used two DC-3s between 1972 and 1974, both on lease from Laos. These were XW-TDA, destroyed on 02Oct72, and XW-TFL which crashed on 20Apr74 at Suay Rieng. If this operator is related to **Cambodair**, they used F.E.A.T. DC-3 B-261 still bearing Taiwanese registration. The company may be linked to Air Union which operated some of the following, all of which have been photographed with C.A.C.: XW-TDM; XW-TFN; XW-PHV and XW-PHW all of which were written off between Jul72 and May74.

Cambodian Air Service operated DC-3 N88750 registered since Dec72 to C E Wroten of Phnom Penh.

Golden Eagle Airlines (Also known as Tri-9 which operated Khmer Airlines CV.440s) used DC-3 N64422 in the early 70s until corrosion caught up with it. XW-TFB, operated in Vietnam by Lane Xang, was also used.

Hang Meas Airlines used DC-3 XW-TDF, see Xiengkhouang Air Transport, Laos.

Kampuch Airways used DC-3 N90715 at least.

Khmer Airlines, Phnom Penh/Pochetong. This was formed in June 1973 to succeed Khmer Akas and may have also adopted its sub-title. It also used **Air Cambodge** titles for international routes. At least six Cambodian and two Laotian DC-3s are known to have been used. XU-AAE; XU-CAF; XU-GAJ; XU-HAK; XU-KAL; XU-LAN; XW-PKX and XW-PKY.

Khmer Akas (Réseau Aérien Intérieur Cambodgien), Phnom Penh, was formed in 1970 and used DC-3s to start operations. In 1973 Convair 340s were introduced, but in June that year it became **Khmer Airlines**. At least ten DC-3s are known:

XU-AAE; XU-CAF; XU-DAG; XU-EAH; XU-FAI; XU-GAJ; XU-HAK; XU-IAL; XU-KAL; XU-LAN.

Khmer Hansa (also known as **United Khmer Airlines**) apparently taken over by Khmer Akas. The following are believed to have been used between 1959 and 1971:-

XU-DAG; XU-EAH; XU-FAI; XU-HAK; XU-IAL.

Lane Xang Airlines, Vientiane - see Laos.

Royal Air Cambodge (later **Air Cambodge**), Phnom Penh, started operations in Nov56 with help from Air France and Aigle Azur, the latter providing two chartered DC-3s to commence services. The later name was adopted in mid-1970. Two DC-3s were owned and several leased:-

XU-FAG; XU-IAJ; XV-NIA; XW-PDE; XW-PFT; XW-TFB/N48230; N82AC; N83AC; B-245/N85AC; B-257/N86AC and B-1553.

Senaki Peanich Airlines, based in Thailand, operated DC-3s XW-TDA and XW-TFJ, the former having been with Cambodia Air Commercial.

Sté Khmer Aviation (Sté Khmère des Agences de Voyage et de Tourisme), Phnom Penh, had XU-CAF and XU-LAN by mid-1972 both of which found their way to Khmer A/l, whose address the company shared.

Sorya Airlines of Laos had DC-3s XW-PNB and XW-PKT in Cambodia.

United Khmer Airlines included DC-3s XU-EAH and XU-FAI between 1971 and 1975, both also appearing in Khmer Hansa colours at this time. C/n 33097 was acquired in 1977, XU- regn unknown.

Index:-

XU-AAD	c/n 12039	XU-IAJ	"45-109"
XU-AAE	19256	XU-IAL	19569
XU-CAF	32569	XU-KAL	4811
XU-DAG	13366	XU-LAN	18934
XU-EAH	10082	XU-PFE	
XU-FAG	11717	XU-PFX	
XU-FAI	4094	XU-PFY	
XU-GAJ	13384	XU- ?	33097
XU-HAK	26237		

Notes:- The XU-P.. series were provisional marks, possibly for cargo only, or as conversions from XW-P . . regns.
Several casualties to unknown aircraft are known:- DC-3 XW-PNC of Samaki A/L damaged at Phnom Penh on 10Mar75; DC-3 of Khmer Hansa destroyed by rocket attack at Pochetong on 11Mar75; DC-3 of Air Cambodge destroyed at Kampot on 04May73.
C/n 9559 is quoted as XU-GAJ and also as XU-IAL.
The Cambodian Government used F-OAQE/F-KHAA c/n 12498 and F-OAPD/(F-KHAB) c/n 20571.
For XW- registrations, see Laos.
For XV- registrations, see Vietnam.
For B- registrations, see Taiwan.

CAMEROUN - TJ

Air Cameroun S/A des Avions Meyer et Cie, Douala. DC-3 TJ-ABJ was bought in February 1965, after lease as F-BAIE in 1963. F-OAID and F-OAIU were used in the 1950s and F-BGXN was leased in 1963.

Cameroons Air Transport Ltd, Victoria, used DC-3 TJ-ACF from February 1969 until January 1970, supplementing its Doves.

Sté. de Transports Aériens Camerounais, Douala, was formed as a subsidiary by Sté Alpes Provence in October 1950 with three DC-3s (F-BEIV; F-BEFH; F-BEIL), ceasing work a year later.

Index:-

TJ-AAA	c/n 11705	TJ-ABJ	26925
TJ-AAC	13404	TJ-ACF	26414

CANADA - CF, C-F and C-G

Canada has always been a stronghold of the DC-3 but by 1999 less than thirty remained with operators, mainly in the northern parts of the country, supplying isolated communities. Next to the United States, Canada and the United Kingdom have had the largest number of DC-3 operators, mostly cargo in Canada's case.

In January 1974 the Canadian nationality mark was changed from CF- to C-F and C-G and all aircraft were expected to be repainted in the new mark within the next year. All C-G series were registered as such, but CF- series aircraft have retained the old marks for much longer, often until the aircraft needed to be repainted, so the index only gives the marks used when the aircraft was first registered. Only when the date of applying the new mark is known is this fact referred to in the production list.

Aero Trades Western, Winnipeg, Man. Three DC-3s were used on passenger and cargo charter work in northern Manitoba. Operations ceased after bankruptcy in 1984.

C-FAAD; C-FBKQ; CF-KBU; C-GCXD; C-GCXE; C-GWIR.

Air BC, Vancouver, BC. Formed by the merger of Air West and Trans Provincial in 1980, used DC-3s C-GSCB and C-GWUG, but these were sold.

Air Brazeau, Rouyn, PQ. Starting in 1974 DC-3s were used on scheduled services, but the name was changed to Quebec Aviation in 1978. Two DC-3s remained in 1980, but are no longer owned.

CF-CSC; C-FIRW; C-GABG; C-GABH; C-GABI; C-GAXT.

Air Caravane Inc, Dorval, PQ, used DC-3s on charter operations from 1973 until these ceased in 1980.

CF-EEX; CF-TAS; C-FWIC.

Air Creebec, Val d'Or, PQ, acquired DC-3 C-FBJE in 1984 and sold it to Air Ontario in 1988.

Air-Dale Ltd, Sault Ste Marie, Ont. Charter operations were carried out with DC-3s from 1973. In 1979 the Barbados airline Tropic Air was acquired. The DC-3 fleet was sold by 1989/90.

CF-ADB; CF-IAR; C-FLED; CF-OOW; CF-WGO; C-GRMH; C-GWYX.

Air Gaspé Inc, Havre de Gaspé, PQ., was the name adopted by **Trans-Gaspésian** in 1962. DC-3s were used for a time on scheduled services. One was sold in 1969, the other crashed in 1973.

CF-QBB; CF-SAW.

Air Gava Ltd, Schefferville, PQ., used two DC-3s on charter work from 1975 onwards, one remaining in 1980.

C-FEEX; CF-POY; C-GADY.

Air Inuit, Fort Chimo, PQ, used DC-3s C-FIRW, C-FPIK and C-FTAS to serve various Eskimo communities between 1977 and 1985.

Air North Charter, Whitehorse, Yukon, used DC-3s on passenger services and charter work for the oil exploration industry from 1979. Only C-GZOF remained in 1999.

C-FCUG; C-FGHL; C-FIMA; CF-OVW; and C-GZOF.

Air Ontario, Sarnia, Ont, was taken over by Austin on 01Jul87, adopting the old name. DC-3s C-FAAM; C-FBJE; C-FQBC; C-GNNA and C-GWYX were in the old Austin fleet but these had been sold by 1990.

Alberta Northern Airlines Ltd, Calgary, Alta., used DC-3s from 1973, but the last was sold in 1983.

CF-TKX; C-GWIR; C-GWUG; C-GWUH; C-GCTE/C-GXAV; C-GXAU(2).

Arctic Air, Fort Simpson, NWT, used three DC-3s between 1971 and 1977 for charters.

CF-DXU; CF-HBX; CF-PIK.

CHAPTER 4: COMMERCIAL OPERATORS OF THE DC-3, C-47, R4D, DAKOTA AND LI-2

Arctic Outpost Camps, Edmonton, Alta, was using DC-3 CF-VQV 1978-81 to serve outlying communities.

Associated Airways Ltd, Edmonton, Alta, operated charter services in Alberta and NW Territory with a variety of aircraft. DC-3 CF-INE was used for a year commencing 12.55

Astro Airlines, St Jean, PQ. DC-3s CF-ECY; CF-FAY and CF-IAX were used briefly in 1973/74.

Atlantic Central Airlines, Saint John, NB, used DC-3s CF-BFV; CF-BKV (briefly) and CF-HPM on scheduled operations between 1974 and 1976.

Austin Airways Ltd, Timmins, Ont. DC-3s were used extensively on services in the northern parts of Canada from 1956. The assets were acquired by White River Air Services in 1975 and operations continued with the remaining two DC-3s, but have now ceased.

CF-AAB; CF-AAC; CF-AAH; CF-AAL (two uses); CF-AAM; CF-BJE; C-FIAX; CF-ILQ; CF-JMX; CF-NAO; C-FQBC; C-GNNA; C-GWYX.

Aviation Boréal, Val d'Or, PQ, a newcomer to DC-3 operations, bought its first in 1989 and two remained in service in 2000.

C-FQBC; C-GCKE; C-GCXD; C-GCZG.

Bayview Air Services Ltd, Slave Lake, Alta. DC-3s C-GKFC and C-GWMY were used on regular services within Alberta until 1976.

Bearskin Lake Airways, Sioux Lookout, Ont., added DC-3s C-FKAZ, C-FKBU in 1983. The last DC-3 was sold in Jan87.

Bradley Air Services Ltd, Carp, Ont. Scheduled services with DC-3s were operated from 1975 under the trading name 'First Air'. The operator was taken over by Air Inuit on 26Sep90, and the last DC-3s were sold by 1993.

CF-FAX; C-FFST; CF-GKZ; C-FIQR; CF-ITH; CF-LFR; CF-MOC; CF-QNF; CF-TVK; CF-TVL; C-GUBT; C-GWMY; C-GWUG; C-GWUH.

Buffalo Airways, Fort Smith, NWT, uses DC-3s on cargo charters. Six were owned in 1983. In receivership 18Jul85, but operations continued until 1987 when the airline was renamed **Northwestern Air Lease**. It now operates again as **Buffalo Airways Ltd**, owning ten DC-3s, some of which are stored.

C-FBZI; C-FCUE; C-FDTB; C-FDTH; C-FFAY, C-FGHL; C-FLFR; C-FMOC; C-FNWU; C-FROD; C-GCZG, C-GJKM; C-GPNR; C-GPNW; C-GPOA; C-GRTM; C-GWIR; C-GWZS.

Calm Air, Thompson, Man, used DC-3 C-GCKE but this was sold.

Canadian Colonial Airways, Montreal, PQ. This pre-war subsidiary of American Colonial Airways used DC-2 CF-BPP on their route to New York from August 1939 until September 1942.

Canadian Pacific Airlines, Vancouver, BC. DC-3s were used for scheduled services on the Canadian west coast from 1945 until 1969. The last was sold in 1974 after use for crew training.

CF-BZN; CF-CPV to CF-CPY incl; CF-CRW to CF-CRZ incl; CF-CUA to CF-CUG incl; CF-DIG.

Central Mountain Air, Smithers, BC bought two DC-3s from Air Ontario, C-FAAM and C-GWYX, and C-FQNF ex First Air. All were lost in accidents by 1993. C-FBXY was also used during 1991.

Central Northern Airways Ltd, St James, Man. CNA used DC-3 CF-TET from December 1955 until the following September when Transair was formed. CF-ICU was leased in 1956.

Chaparal Air (Chaparal Charters Inc), Dorval, PQ operated C-FPIK and C-FTAS between 1981 and 1984.

Contact Airways, Fort McMurray, Alta. DC-3s were operated from August 1975. The last was sold in 1987.

CF-QHY; CF-RTB; CF-TFV; C-GABG; C-GWZS; C-GZOF.

Cotenair, Québec, PQ, owned DC-3 C-FBVF, previously leased to Trans Côte.

Crown Charter Services, Brantford, Ont, trades as Crown Mail and Delivery Services, and operates four C-117Ds with Gateway Airlines titles. Two were stored in 2000.

C-GDIK, C-GDOG, C-GGKE, C-GJGQ.

Eastern Provincial Airways Ltd, St Johns, Nfld. DC-3s were used on scheduled routes from July 1961 until the airline was taken over by Nordair in 1969. Some were acquired with Maritime Central in September 1963. During 1965/66 CF-HGL was leased to Air St Pierre, operating from French St Pierre et Miquelon.

CF-CRW; CF-FAJ; CF-GHX; CF-GOC; CF-HBX; CF-HGL; CF-HTH; CF-ILW; CF-JNR; CF-RTB; CF-RTY.

Eldorado Aviation, Edmonton, Alta, used DC-3s and DC-4s for the carriage of passengers and freight for Eldorado Nuclear Ltd and Northern Transportation Co in the late seventies.

CF-CUG; CF-DGJ; CF-OVW.

Enterprise Air, Oshawa, Ont, used DC-3 C-FOOW from 1996 and DC-3TP C-GEAI from 2001 until they were registered to Triumph Air in mid-2005.

A. Fecteau Transport Aérien Ltée, Senneterre, PQ. This subsidiary of Quebecair used DC-3s on scheduled services between 1970 and 1975.

CF-FSJ; CF-IAR; CF-ILZ; CF-POY; CF-QBI.

First Air - see Bradley Air Services.

Frontier Air Service, Kapuskasing, Ont, leased DC-3 C-GCTE in Jul85. This was leased to Rog-Air and the two operators merged, continuing as Frontier. The DC-3 was sold in Jun90.

Gander Aviation Ltd, Gander, Nfld. DC-3s CF-BKX and C-FWIC were used between 1974 to 1977 on charter work. CF-GHX was acquired in 1971 for instructional use only.

Gateway Airlines Ltd, Brantford, Ont took over three C-117Ds from Crown Mail in 2001. C-GDIK, C-GDOG, C-GGKE.

Gateway Aviation Ltd, Edmonton, Alta. DC-3s were used on scheduled and charter services in the Arctic but operations were taken over by Northward Avn in 1979 and the latter company went into liquidation in 1980.

CF-CUC; CF-JWP; CF-PIK; CF-PWG; CF-QJZ; CF-RTB; C-GWZS.

Golfe Air Quebec Ltd, Baie Comeau, PQ. DC-3s were used on third level services since 1976, linking Baie Comeau with Rimouski, Mont Joli and Forestville. All were sold by early 1982.

CF-EEX; CF-FAX; CF-WGM.

Great Lakes Air Services Ltd, Sarnia, Ont. DC-3s CF-GLA; CF-GLB and CF-YED were used to start scheduled services in 1967. The company name changed to **Great Lakes Air Lines** Jan68 and the DC-3s were replaced by Convair 440s in 1974.

Great Northern Airways Ltd, Calgary, Alta. DC-3s were used on charter work from 1960 until bankruptcy closed the airline in 1971.

CF-CPY; CF-CUC; CF-JWP; CF-PWH.

Great Northern Freight, Sault Ste Marie, Ont, acquired DC-3s CF-OOW and C-FWGO in 1988. The former was sold to Enterprise Air in 1996, the latter to Collingwood Air in 1994.

Gulf Aviation Inc, Rimouski, PQ. Gulf used DC-3s from 1948 onwards, in association with Rimouski Airlines. They were merged as Quebecair in 1953.

CF-GVZ; CF-TDK; CF-TDL.

Harrison Airways Ltd, Vancouver, BC. Ex-CP Air DC-3s were used to open charter services in 1969. They were taken over by **Futura Airways** in January 1979 but sold off.

CF-CPX; CF-CRX; CF-CRZ.

Hollinger Ungava Transport Ltd, Montreal, PQ. Operations began in 1948 to serve various mining companies in Labrador, and others requiring cargo transport. The last DC-3s were sold by 1959.

CF-DME; CF-DXO; CF-DXR; CF-FBS; CF-FKZ; CF-FST; CF-GHX; CF-GKV; CF-HGD.

Hooker Air Services Ltd, Sioux Lookout, Ont. DC-3 C-FGHL, bought in April 1971, was used in association with Transair on scheduled services. It became part of White River Air Services in 1978.

Hudson Bay Air Transport Ltd, Flin Flon, Man, used DC-3s CF-ETE and CF-IOC from 1963 until 1985.

Ilford-Riverton Airways Ltd, Winnipeg, Man. Passenger and cargo services were operated in the Arctic with DC-3s, the first of which was bought in 1970. Four were in use in 1980. It was re-named **Northland Air Manitoba** in 1986. CF-POY was leased during 1975.

CF-ABA; CF-ADD; CF-AII; CF-AOH; C-FBKQ; CF-CQT; CF-ETE; CF-IAX; CF-IAZ; CF-IKD; C-FKAZ; CF-XPK; C-GSCC; C-GWYX.

International Jet Air Ltd, Calgary, Alta. Used DC-3s CF-CPY and CF-CUC from mid-1971 until they were sold. CF-JWP may have been leased.

Kelowna Flightcraft Charter, Kelowna, BC, used DC-3 C-FGXW in 1985/86 for a promotional Round the World tour. C-GWUG was bought in 1989, but was later sold.

Kenn Borek Air Ltd, Dawson Creek, BC, took over DC-3s with Kenting's fleet in 1975 and one was still used on Arctic charter flights in 2000.

CF-CRW; CF-DXU; C-FIQR; CF-OOY; CF-PIK; CF-QHF; C-GGKG; C-GOZA; C-GWMX.

Kenting Aviation Ltd, Toronto, Ont. DC-3s were bought in 1972/73 for charter work in the Arctic. In 1973 the name became **Kenting Atlas Aviation** and operations were taken over by **Kenn Borek Air** in 1975 although operations continued as Kenting until at least 1978.

CF-DXO; CF-DXU; CF-ILW; CF-IQR; CF-ITH; CF-OOV; CF-OOX; CF-OOY; CF-QHF; C-GOZA.

Knight Air Ltd, Fort St John, BC. DC-3s CF-BXY and CF-JUV were used in support of the Mackenzie Valley Oil exploration industry in the 1970s.

Knox Air Service, Pickle Lake, Ont bought C-FFAY in 1990. It went to Buffalo in 1993. C-GRSA was leased in 1991.

Labrador Airways, Goose Bay, Lab, became **Air Nova**, but continued to use the old name, operating DC-3 C-FQBI.

Lambair Ltd, The Pas, Man. Cargo, charter and scheduled services were operated with a variety of types, including DC-3s. Bankruptcy led to a cessation of operations on 18Feb81.

CF-BFV; CF-BKX; CF-DBJ; CF-DXO; CF-FAY; CF-QHF; CF-TAT; CF-TAU; CF-TES; C-GWIR.

Laurentian Air Services Ltd, Dorval, PQ, used DC-3s on charter work within Quebec, the last one being disposed of in 1983.

CF-ADB; CF-ECY; CF-GKZ; CF-IAR; CF-ITH; CF-KAZ; CF-PAG; CF-POX; CF-POY; CF-PWI; C-FTAT.

Maritime Central Airways Ltd, Charlottetown, PEI, used DC-3s on scheduled work from 1946 until taken over by Eastern Provincial in Oct63.

CF-BXZ; CF-BZH; CF-BZI; CF-DJT; CF-FAJ; CF-FBY; CF-FCQ; CF-FKQ; CF-GHQ (1 & 2); CF-GKZ; CF-GOC; CF-HGD; CF-HGL; CF-HTH; CF-HTP; CF-IQR; CF-MCC.

Matane Air Services Ltd, Matane, PQ, bought DC-3s for scheduled services in 1954 and used some until 1969.

CF-TDO; CF-TDR; CF-TDT.

Midwest Airlines Ltd, Winnipeg, Man. DC-3s CF-IHH and CF-WCM were used on scheduled routes from 1966 until 1972.

Millardair Ltd, Toronto, Ont. DC-3s were used from 1963 on third level services, but later only charter work was done, primarily in support of the automotive industry. C-117Ds were added in 1983. Operations ceased, due to bankruptcy, on 31May90.

CF-DTV; CF-ITQ; CF-WBN; CF-WCM; CF-WCN; CF-WCO; CF-WGM (two); CF-WGN; CF-WGO; CF-WIC; CF-WTU; CF-WTV; (CF-ZKR); C-GDIK; C-GDOG; C-GGCS; C-GGKE; N2071X/C-GGKG; C-GGVU; C-GJGN; N116DT/C-GJGQ; C-GNOA.

Mont Laurier Aviation Co Ltd, Roberval, PQ, introduced DC-3s on schedules in 1955, but was taken over by Nordair in 1957.

CF-IHH; CF-IQK.

Montreal Air Services Ltd, Montreal, PQ. DC-3s CF-DME; CF-IQR and CF-JIZ were used for charter work between 1953 and 1963.

Nahanni Air Service, Norman Wells, NWT, operated DC-3s C-GCTE and C-GWUG, these being sold by 1985.

Norcanair - North Canada Air Ltd, Prince Albert, Sask, was formed when the services operated by **Saskatchewan Govt. Air Services** were taken over in March 1965. Two DC-3s were used initially, and more were acquired later. The last remaining example was sold to Time Air in Mar87.

CF-CTA; CF-CTB; CF-CTD; CF-IHH; CF-KBU; CF-YDH.

Nordair Ltd, Montreal, PQ, was formed in Nov56 by the merger of Mont Laurier Aviation (from which two DC-3s came) and Boreal Airways. A fleet of the type was built up between 1956 and 1976, some being leased to subsidiary **Sudair Ltd** in the early sixties.

CF-AOH; C-FCSC; CF-GKZ; CF-HGD; CF-HTH; CF-IHH; CF-IQD; CF-IQF; CF-IQK; CF-IQR; CF-MCC; CF-NAG; CF-NAH; CF-NAO; CF-NAR.

North Cariboo Air, Fort St. John, BC, acquired DC-3 C-FJUV in May 1980, and C-FBXY in Jan82. The latter was sold to Central Mountain Air in 1991.

North Coast Air Services, Prince Rupert, BC, used DC-3 CF-CQT on some schedules between 1970 and 1975.

Northern Thunderbird Air, Prince George, BC, operated DC-3 CF-JUV on their routes between 1976 and 1978.

Northern Wings Ltd (Les Ailes du Nord Ltée), Sept Iles, PQ, used DC-3s on schedules from 1955, became a division of Quebecair and ceased flying by 1983.

CF-BZN; CF-FSJ; CF-GHQ; CF-GKV; CF-ILY; CF-ILZ; CF-NAG; CF-ORD; CF-QBC; CF-QBI.

Northland Airlines Ltd, Winnipeg, Man, used three DC-3s on charter work between 1961 and 1969.

CF-IHH; CF-PIK; CF-SAW.

Northland Air Manitoba, Winnipeg, Man, was renamed as such from Ilford Riverton early in 1986. All DC-3s had been disposed of by 1993, and the airline was renamed **Air Manitoba** in Jul91.

C-FADD; C-FAOH; C-FCQT; C-FGHL; C-FIKD; C-GCZG; C-GSCC; C-GWYX.

Northward Aviation, Edmonton, Alta., acquired three DC-3s for local operations in 1971/72. It took over **Gateway Avn** in 1979 and operated schedules until financial problems forced closure in March 1980.

CF-BKX; CF-CUC; CF-JWP

Northwest Territorial Airways Ltd, Yellowknife, NWT, bought DC-3s for cargo charter work in 1965 and four remained in 1980. All have now been sold.

CF-BZI; CF-NTF; CF-NWS; CF-NWU; CF-QHF; CF-QHY; CF-XXT; C-GWIR; C-GWMX; C-GWMY; C-GWZS.

Northwestern Air Lease, Fort Smith, NWT, alias **Buffalo**, was operating DC-3s in 1993, some leased out. Buffalo is now the operating name.(qv)

C-FCUE; C-FDTB; C-FFAY; C-FLFR; C-FNWS; C-FROD; C-GJKM; C-GPNR; C-GWIR; C-GWZS.

Nunasi Central Airlines, Red Lake, Ont, ex Ontario Central, was re-named **Nunasi-Northland Airlines** in 1987. DC-3s were used until the airline ceased operations by 1993, when only two survived.

C-FGHL; C-FIAR; C-FYQG; C-GCKE; C-GCZG

Ontario Central Airlines Ltd, Kenora, Ont., used the DC-3 from 1969, primarily for charter work in northwestern Ontario. It was taken over by White River Air Services in 1978 and owned by Austin, though five DC-3s continued in use under the original name. None now remains.

CF-ABA; C-FBFV; CF-BJE; CF-BKS; CF-BKV; C-FBKW; C-FBKX; CF-BKZ; CF-DXO; CF-GHL; C-FIAR; C-FIAZ; CF-KAZ; CF-TTZ; CF-XPK; CF-XUS; CF-YQG; C-GCKE; C-GCZG; C-GSTA.

Pacific Coastal Airlines, Nanaimo, BC. Local services were flown with DC-3s from 1977 until 1980 when it was taken over by Airwest.

C-FKAZ; C-FPWI.

Pacific Western Airlines Ltd, Vancouver, BC, was founded in May 1953 by the merger of Queen Charlotte and Associated Airways with Central BC Airways. Some of QCA's DC-3s continued to be used on scheduled services until 1968.

CF-EPI; CF-HCF; CF-ONH; CF-PWC; CF-PWF; CF-PWG; CF-PWH; CF-PWI.

Patricia Air Transport Ltd, Sioux Lookout, Ont., used two DC-3s, C-FHBX and C-FBKV on charter work during 1977/78.

Pem-Air Ltd, Pembroke, Ont. Regular services were operated with DC-3s from 1971, but operations ceased in 1981.

CF-GKZ; CF-GLA; CF-GLB; CF-NAO; CF-TKX; C-GWUH.

Perimeter Airlines, Winnipeg, Man., bought DC-3s C-FDBJ, C-FBFV in 1982. C-FFAY was added in 1984, originally as a ground test-rig, but a year later it was restored. C-GCKE was leased from Nunasi Central. All were sold by 1990.

Points North Air Services, Points North Landing, Saskatoon, leased a DC-3 in 1990. C-FNTF was bought in 1988, and C-FCQT and C-FNWS later. The last two remain in use in 2001.

Quebecair Ltd, Dorval, PQ, was formed in 1947 as Rimouski Airlines which operated in association with Gulf Aviation and merged with it in 1953 to form Quebecair. Matane Air Services was bought in 1965 and Northern Wings became a subsidiary. A disastrous hangar fire in July 1958 destroyed five DC-3s. The remainder had been sold by 1971.

CF-CRW; CF-GEH; CF-GVZ; CF-HVM; CF-QBB to CF-QBI incl; CF-QBM; CF-TDK; CF-TDL.

Queen Charlotte Airlines Ltd, Vancouver, BC, used two DC-3s, CF-EPI and CF-HCF, on charter work between 1953 and 1955, when the airline merged into Pacific Western, whose CF-PWI was regd to QCA later.

Reindeer Air Services, Inuvik, NWT. DC-3s were used between 1971 and 1976 on what must have been the most northerly based services by the type. They were taken over by Kenn Borek Air.

CF-ABA; CF-AOH; CF-CRW; CF-TFV; CF-TKX; CF-TQW.

Rimouski Airlines Ltd, Rimouski, PQ, operated DC-3s in its own name and with those owned by **Gulf Aviation** from 1947 until they merged in 1953.

CF-FKY; CF-FSP; CF-GEH; CF-TDK; CF-TDL.

Rog-Air, Port Loring, Ont, leased DC-3 C-GCTE until 1990.

Royalair Ltd, Montreal, PQ, operated DC-3s CF-HVH and CF-QBB on lease from September 1968 until insolvency in January 1969.

Sabourin Lake Airways, Sabourin Lake, Man, bought C-GRSA and leased C-FBXY in 1992. C-GCKE was later added, and continued into 1999.

St Felicien Air Services Ltd, St Felicien, PQ. Scheduled and cargo flights with DC-3s were operated from 1969 until 1978, when the last was in store.

CF-FKZ; CF-FST; CF-IRW; CF-LFR; C-GLUC.

Saskatchewan Government Airways (Saskair), Prince Albert, Sask. Two DC-3s, CF-KBU and CF-SAW, were used on scheduled services between 1957 and 1965 when Norcanair took over operations.

Sioux Narrows Airways, Winnipeg, Man., have used DC-3 C-FQHY on charter work since 1979.

Skycraft Air Transport Inc, Oshawa, Ont., used four DC-3s from 1976 to 1982 in support of the Ontario automobile industry.

C-FRTB; C-GSCA to C-GSCC incl; C-GUBT; C-GYBA.

Skyfreighters, Terrace, BC, acquired four C-117Ds from Millardair in August 1995. They were sold to Crown Charter.

C-GDIK; C-GDOG; C-GGKE; C-GJGQ.

Slate Falls Airways, Sioux Lookout, Ont., used DC-3s C-FIAR, CF-KBU and C-GWUH on bush charter services from 1977, the last being sold by 1983.

Soundair, Toronto, Ont., and Vancouver, BC, had DC-3s for charter work, but by 27Apr90 a receiver was appointed and operations ceased.

C-FFBS; C-FIAR; C-FIMA; C-FQBI; C-FTVL; C-GCXD; C-GSCA; C-GUBT.

Southern Frontier Air Transport, Calgary, Alta., was using DC-3 CF-CUC in 1979, this was sold in 1985. C-GWMX was used in 1980/81.

Sterling Air Services, Red Deer, Alta., used DC-3s between 1971 and 1975.

CF-FAX; CF-FAY; CF-QNF.

Sudair. This subsidiary of Nordair used four DC-3s on charter work between 1964 and 1967.

CF-HGD; CF-HTH; CF-IQR; CF-MCC.

Superior Airways Ltd, Thunder Bay, Ont. DC-3s were used on charter work from 1970 until operations with DC-3s ceased by 1982.

CF-ABA; CF-AOH; CF-AUQ; C-FBKZ; CF-BYK; CF-DXO; C-FKAZ; CF-POY; C-FPWI; CF-TKX; CF-TTZ; CF-XXT.

Survair Ltd, Ottawa, Ont., operated scheduled services between 1976 and 1977 with DC-3s, on ex-Nordair routes. All had been sold by about 1978.

CF-FBS; CF-FKZ; CF-FST; CF-IMA; CF-IQR; C-FIRW; CF-LFR; CF-NAR.

Transair Ltd, Winnipeg, Man. was formed by the merger in 1956 of Central Northern and Arctic Wings, both of which contributed DC-3s. Further aircraft were added until 1963 but all had been sold by 1972.

CF-CPV/CF-TAR; CF-CPW/CF-TAS; CF-DIG/CF-TAT; CF-ICU; CF-LJS/CF-TAU; CF-TEA; CF-TES; CF-TET.

Trans-Canada Air Lines, Montreal, PQ. Thirty DC-3s were acquired surplus between 1945 and 1947 and formed the mainstay of operations within Canada. Some remained in service until 1963 when the last was sold to Transair. None was lost in any accident, a proud record.

CF-TDJ to CF-TEJ incl; CF-TER to CF-TET incl.

Transfair, Sept Iles, PQ, was known earlier as **Transport Aérien Sept Iles**, the name being changed about 1985. DC-3s C-FDTT and C-FPOY were used from 1993, the last being retired by 2000.

Trans Gaspésian - See Air Gaspé.

Trans-Labrador Airlines Ltd, Mont Joli, PQ. DC-3s were used on charter operations from 1956 until 1963.

CF-BZN; CF-ILZ; CF-JNR.

Trans North Air, Whitehorse, NWT, also known as **Trans North Turbo Air**, used DC-3s C-GABI and C-GWUH from 1980 until 1985.

Transport Aérien Sept-Iles, Sept Iles, PQ. owned a number of DC-3s probably mostly leased out to other operators for some of the time, from 1973 until the name was changed to **Transfair**, in about 1985.

C-FBZN; C-FDTT; C-FIRW; C-FPOY; C-FQBC; C-GABG.

Trans Provincial Airlines Ltd, Terrace, BC, used DC-3s CF-KAZ, CF-PWI and C-GWUG on scheduled services between 1970 and 1980, when they were sold.

Triumph Airways Ltd, Oshawa, Ont, registered C-FOOW and C-GEAI, ex Enterprise Air, in 2005.

Waglisla Air (t/a Wagair), Vancouver, BC, used C-FTFV between 1983 and 1988 and from time to time others were leased (CF-CUG, C-FIMA, C-GZOF and N707BA).

Wheeler Airlines Ltd, Montreal, PQ. DC-3s were used on scheduled services from 1955 until the airline was taken over by Nordair in 1964.

CF-HGD; CF-HTH; CF-IHG; CF-IQF; CF-IQR; CF-JIH; CF-MCC.

Williston Lake Air Service, Mackenzie, BC, bought DC-3s C-FGKZ and C-FTVL in May 1990, but only PA-31s are now used.

World Wide Airways Inc, Montreal, PQ, used DC-3 CF-JNN on charter work from 1957 to 1959. Others such as CF-DME and CF-ILS were sales stock.

Yellowbird Air, Vancouver, BC. DC-3 C-GYBA was used on general charter work between 1976 and May 1984 when it was sold to Skycraft.

Index:-

CF-AAB	c/n 12289
CF-AAC	25369
CF-AAH	12528
CF-AAL(1)	26828
CF-AAL(2)	10202
CF-AAM	9862
CF-ABA	20562
CF-ADB	33540
CF-ADD	26324
CF-AII	19353
C-FALL	43385
CF-AOH	13860
CF-AUQ	26726
CF-BFV	7340
CF-BJE	13453
CF-BKP	12438
CF-BKQ	26441
CF-BKR	33437
CF-BKS	32865
CF-BKT	25371
CF-BKU	33116
CF-BKV	4441
CF-BKW	32540
CF-BKX	32813
CF-BKY	25485
CF-BKZ	27074
(CF-BLL)(DC-2)	1411
CF-BPP (DC-2)	1411
CF-BVF	12317
CF-BXY	25980
CF-BXZ	4695
CF-BYK	25611
CF-BZH	6079
CF-BZI	13448
CF-BZN	25290
CF-CAR	9452
CF-CBL	6319
CF-CPV	4594
CF-CPW	4666
CF-CPX	6085
CF-CPY	4666
CF-CQT	9813
CF-CRW	18958
CF-CRX	19276
CF-CRY	20592
CF-CRZ	20180
CF-CSC	6183
CF-CTA	32843
CF-CTB	12435
CF-CTD	9633
CF-CUA	4518
CF-CUB	12711
CF-CUC	19366
CF-CUD	6187
CF-CUE	12983
CF-CUF	12855
CF-CUG	9891
CF-DBJ	6135
CF-DGJ	25454
CF-DIG	11850
CF-DJT	19039
CF-DME(1)	13177
CF-DME(2)	20432
CF-DOT	4733
CF-DSW	12850
CF-DTB	12597
CF-DTD	12253
CF-DTH	12591
CF-DTT	25615
CF-DTV	12192
CF-DXO	12437
CF-DXR	13376
(CF-DXT)	33430
CF-DXU	12930
CF-DYK	13435
CF-ECN	4702
CF-ECY	9264
CF-EEX	9700
CF-EPI	7408
CF-ESO	12369
CF-ETE	12005
CF-FAJ	12099
CF-FAX	33518
CF-FAY	4785
CF-FBS	6070
CF-FBY	26888
CF-FCQ	6208
CF-FKQ	4301
CF-FKY	6246
CF-FKZ	9052
CF-FOL	25483
CF-FSJ	25880
CF-FSP	20219
CF-FST	9041
CF-FTR	32843
CF-FVX	6176
CF-FYN	34326
CF-GBG	32963
CF-GBH	32843
CF-GBI	33540
CF-GBJ	27074
CF-GEH	6179
CF-GEI	12377
CF-GHL	12475
(CF-GHQ)(1)	12416
CF-GHQ(2)	19122
CF-GHX	11780
CF-GJZ	12196
CF-GKV	25282
CF-GKZ	9395
CF-GLA	2140
CF-GLB	1547
CF-GOC	7362
CF-GON	25799
CF-GOR	12055
CF-GVZ	26997
CF-GXE	12159
CF-GXW	25313
CF-HBX	13854
CF-HCF	2198
CF-HFT	11636
CF-HGD	13041
CF-HGL	12712
(CF-HHR)	12332
CF-HPM	4989
CF-HTH	27000
CF-HTP	19140
CF-HVH	43074
CF-HVM	26184
CF-HXS	4854
CF-IAE	4563
CF-IAR	20877
CF-IAS	11657
CF-IAX	19499
CF-IAZ	33564
CF-ICF	6319
CF-ICU	19721
CF-IHG	13368
CF-IHH(1)	12939
CF-IHH(2)	26058
CF-IHO	4880
CF-IKD	"33569" see 9531
CF-ILQ	12377
CF-ILS	26216
CF-ILW	4352
CF-ILY	4410
CF-ILZ	13033
CF-IMA	13070
CF-INB	9089
CF-INE	9397
CF-IOC	13456
CF-IQD	20427
CF-IQF	6101
CF-IQK	25944
CF-IQR	11876
CF-IQV	20439
CF-IRW	9834
CF-ITH	20228
CF-ITQ	9108
CF-JIH	10052
CF-JIP	9452
CF-JIZ	26700
CF-JMX	25615
CF-JNN	20058
CF-JNR	4595
CF-JRY	4585
CF-JUV	19394
CF-JWP	9089
CF-KAB	20199
CF-KAH	27184
CF-KAZ	19345
CF-KBU	4683
CF-KCI	19433
CF-KZO	12055
C-FLED	43375
CF-LFR	13155
CF-LJS	11877
CF-MCC	13399
C-FMKB	19560
CF-MOC	12741
CF-NAG	12458
CF-NAH	10052
CF-NAO	12332
CF-NAR	13154
CF-NTF	12344
CF-NWS	12419
CF-NWU	6095
CF-ONH	12857
CF-OOV	13300
CF-OOW	13342
CF-OOX	12238
CF-OOY	12411
CF-ORD(1)	6319
CF-ORD(2)	9210
CF-OVW	12267
CF-PAG	20444
CF-PIK	27202
CF-POX	20875
CF-POY	10028
CF-PQE	6319
CF-PQG	12055
CF-PWC	9397
CF-PWF	9089
CF-PWG	20439
CF-PWH	2198
CF-PWI	4880
CF-QBB	10081
CF-QBC	27026
CF-QBD	3256
CF-QBE	9649
CF-QBF	12092
CF-QBG	13337
CF-QBH	20219
CF-QBI	6179
CF-QBM	6187
CF-QCM	4854
CF-QHF	13392
CF-QHY	26005
CF-QJZ	9831
CF-QKU	12528
CF-QNF	26643
CF-QZU	20444
CF-RBC	6319
C-FROD	13028
CF-RTB	13803
CF-RTY	27078
CF-SAW	12332
C-FSAW	4644
CF-TAR	4594
CF-TAS	4667
CF-TAT	11850
CF-TAU	11877
CF-TDJ	6261
CF-TDK	6319
CF-TDL	6343
CF-TDM	12004
CF-TDN	12007
CF-TDO	12026
CF-TDP	12027
CF-TDQ	12039
CF-TDR	12042
CF-TDS	12092
CF-TDT	12093
CF-TDU	12106
CF-TDV	12110
CF-TDW	12139
CF-TDX	12141
CF-TDY	12191
CF-TDZ	12192
CF-TEA	12412
CF-TEB	12591
CF-TEC	12597
CF-TED(1)	12930
CF-TED(2)	12487
CF-TEE	13559
CF-TEF	13560
CF-TEG	25313
CF-TEH	12440
CF-TEI	12442
CF-TEJ	13337
CF-TER	12253
CF-TES	11906
CF-TET	13393
CF-TFV	34295
CF-TKX	10202
CF-TQW	12598
(CF-TQZ)	9830
CF-TTZ	33116
CF-TVK	27004
CF-TVL	32855
CF-UZA	19028

CHAPTER 4: COMMERCIAL OPERATORS OF THE DC-3, C-47, R4D, DAKOTA AND LI-2

CF-VQV	3264	C-GGVU	25449
CF-WBN	25888	C-GJDM	20721
CF-WCM	9053	C-GJGN	43312
CF-WCN	43082	C-GJGQ	43307
CF-WCO	19737	C-GJKM	13580
CF-WGM(1)	13394	C-GKFC	4200
CF-WGM(2)	10168	C-GLUC	4760
CF-WGN	33368	C-GNNA	12483
CF-WGO	4932	C-GNOA	19627
CF-WIC	11625	C-GOZA	26111
CF-WOR	3296	C-GPNR	13333
CF-WTU	25802	C-GPNW	13028
CF-WTV	12300	C-GPOA	12307
CF-XPK	19433	C-GQHK	4545
CF-XUS	12352	C-GRMH	20196
CF-XXT	27212	C-GRSA	13485
CF-YDH	12301	C-GRSB	12295
CF-YED	4433	C-GRTM	13310
CF-YQG	4654	C-GSCA	27190
(CF-ZKR)	10168	C-GSCB	33441
C-GABE	12363	C-GSCC	33352
C-GABG	19661	C-GSTA	10201
C-GABH	25659	C-GUBT	12424
C-GABI	26815	(C-GUKU)	13948
C-GADY	11982	C-GWIR	9371
C-GAXT	12255	C-GWMX	12357
C-GCKE	27203	C-GWMY	25368
C-GCTE	13087	C-GWUG	32963
C-GCUW	27078	C-GWUH	33046
C-GCXD	25612	C-GWXP	10199
C-GCXE	12254	C-GWYX	13343
C-GCZG	34385	C-GWYY	18986
C-GDAK	2141	C-GWZS	12327
C-GEAI	33053	C-GXAU(1)	12295
C-GDIK	43369	C-GXAU(2)	13310
C-GDOG	43374	C-GXAV	13087
C-GERD	43330	C-GYBA	20215
(C-GFGZ)	27218	C-GYJG	33467
C-GFHP	26792	C-GYJH	9186
C-GGCA	4998	C-GYJJ	33445
C-GGCS	32529	C-GYJK	"194377"
(C-GGJF)	33441		see 9290
(C-GGJG)	27190	C-GYJL	32873
(C-GGJH)	33352	C-GZCR	12425
C-GGKE	43366	C-GZOF	20833
C-GGKG	43354	C-GZYF	2206

CAYMAN ISLANDS - VR-C, VP-C

For Cayman Airways Ltd see under Costa Rica

CENTRAL AFRICAN REPUBLIC - TL

Air Bangui, Cie Centre Africaine, Bangui. Formed in 1966 with DC 3 TL-AAD, the former Presidential TL-JBB.

Air Centrafrique was formed in 1964 and TL-AAD was bought from Air Bangui in 1971.

Ste Nationale Inter RCA, Bangui was formed from Air Centrafrique in July 1980, with DC-3s TL-AAD and TL-AAX.

Index:-

TL-AAD	c/n 6212	TL-JBB	9172
TL-AAX	9172		

CEYLON - VP-C, CY and 4R See Sri Lanka

CHILE - CC

Chilean aircraft histories are complicated by the way in which many of the older aircraft have been registered in four separate series. Fortunately the only operator to survive the whole period was LAN, and they used the majority of DC-3s registered in Chile. The first series started with CC-CBG and may not have been used. The second began at CC-CLA, the third CC-CLDG and the final one from CC-CAA onwards in 1963. No DC-3s remain in use.

Aerocargo Regional Ltda, Los Cerillos, Santiago, bought DC-3s CC-CBO, CC-CJL, CC-CLK and CC-CLL for cargo work in 1991/92.

Aeroservicios Parrague Ltda, Los Cerillos, Santiago, used DC-3 CC-CLL for forest fire fighting from 1993.

Aerosur - Soc de Transportes Aéreos Gidemi Ltda. Aerosur operated two DC-3s, CC-CBT and CC-CLB between 1961 and 1970, both being lost in accidents. In 1962 the name was changed to **Soc. Aerosur Ltda**, to **Eduardo Rubio Guardera** on 13Sep66 and finally to **Emp. Aero Aysen** on 26Feb67.

Aerocor - Aerolíneas Cordillera Ltda, Santiago. Four DC-3s were used between 1971 and 1979, but none are now in use.

CC-CBN; CC-CBO; CC-CBP; CC-CBW.

CINTA - Cía Nacional de Turismo Aéreo, Santiago. Two DC-3s operated domestic services from May 1956 until merged into ALA in 1957. The routes were taken over by LADECO in Nov58.

CC-CBK; CC-CBM.

LADECO - Línea Aérea del Cobre SA, Santiago, was founded in Sep58 to take over CINTA's domestic operations. The DC-3s were replaced by Boeing 727s.

CC-CAO; CC-CBK; CC-CBM; CC-CBZ.

LAN-Chile - Línea Aérea Nacional de Chile SA, Los Cerillos, Santiago. DC-3s were bought from 1946 onwards to replace various earlier types such as the Lockheed 10 and 18. The DC-3s were replaced by HS.748s by 1969.

Series 1:- CC-CAL; CC-CBG to CC-CBJ [Possibly not used]

Series 2:- CC-CLD; CC-CLH; CC-CLI; CC-CLK; CC-CLL; CC-CLM; CC-CLO to CC-CLQ incl.

Series 3:- CC-CLDG to CC-CLDX incl.

Series 4:- CC-CBN to CC-CBZ incl.

Línea Aérea TAXPA Ltda, Santiago, had three DC-3s, CC-CBO, CC-CBW and CC-CJL. In 1993 all were for sale. They were operated by Carlos Griffin.

Soc Aerovias Bochetti Ltda acquired DC-3 CC-CBZ from Ladeco in Jan 1966 and operations ceased in August 1972.

Index:-

CC-CAL	c/n 6190	CC-CLL(2)	26794
CC-CAO	4219	CC-CLM	34260
CC-CBB		CC-CLO	13872
CC-CBG	9716	CC-CLP	9742
CC-CBH	26906	CC-CLQ	19383
CC-CBI	26704	CC-CLR?	13727
CC-CBJ	13296	CC-CPF	6190
CC-CBK	11664	CC-CLDG	26277
CC-CBM	6330	CC-CLDH	34255
CC-CBN	34255	CC-CLDI	34260
CC-CBO(1)	34260	CC-CLDJ	19218
CC-CBO(2)	6190	CC-CLDK	13872
CC-CBP	19218	CC-CLDL	9742
CC-CBQ	13872	CC-CLDM	19383
CC-CBR	9742	CC-CLDN	13727
CC-CBS	13727	(CC-CLDO)	11883
CC-CBT	26172	CC-CLDO	26172
CC-CBU	7395	CC-CLDP	9716
CC-CBV	26906	CC-CLDQ	7395
CC-CBW	26704	CC-CLDR	26906
CC-CBX	13296	CC-CLDS	26704
CC-CBY	9783	CC-CLDT	13296
CC-CBZ	9927	CC-CLDU	9783
CC-CJL	26958	CC-CLDV	9927
CC-CLB	26277	CC-CLDW	26277
CC-CLD	19218	CC-CLDX	6190
CC-CLH	11883	CC-PJN	26958
CC-CLI	7395	CC-PLU	26794
CC-CLK(1)	26277	CC-PQF	6190
CC-CLK(2)	20158	CC-PQG	26704
CC-CLL(1)	34255	CC-PQI	26958

CHINA - XT and B

Douglas twins were used in China pre-war by Pan American's subsidiary CNAC and both DC-2s and DC-3s were supplied. The aircraft were numbered in sequence from #1 upwards but international prefix marks were rarely used. Politics and war then intervened. CNAC's operations suffered at the hands of Japanese fighters and bombers. Post-war the Communist advance steadily took over China and eventually the pro-American side was confined to Formosa, or Taiwan as it became known (see later). A large proportion of CNAC's aircraft and those of CATC found their way to Hong Kong where, after much legal wrangling, they ceased to be Chinese property.

Immediately after the war many USAAF surplus C-47s were acquired and operated by the re-formed airlines and by relief organisations. With the Communist victory in 1949 some were taken over and used, though in recent years only Li-2s are known, flying with a few captured C-46s.

The nationality mark XT was used by China and Formosa for a number of years until about 1951 but this was reallocated to Upper Volta. The mark B was issued, although only Formosa used this for many years. Mainland China flew without a nationality letter as such but around 1950 numbers were assigned that were prefixed with "Civil Aviation" in Chinese characters. DC-3 types appear to have been allocated numbers in the range 101 through 113; 109 was named "China Youth" and 110 was "National Day" originally. As happened in Russia, these were re-engined with the M62IR in 1954. In China they were known as the TS-62 Gexin (translated as 'innovation'). The last, #102, was retired in January 1967.

As far as is known, Chinese Li-2s (which only flew within the country) used plain numbers.

Central Air Transport Corp (CATC), Beijing. (Formerly Eurasian Avn Corp) Twelve C-47s were acquired from ex-USAAF stocks in India in 1945, and further aircraft were bought in 1946, many for spares. In the early post-war period these were given a simple number prefixed by CA as follows.

CA1	c/n 4483	CA34	
CA2	4781	CA35	
CA3	20388	CA36	
CA4	7313	CA38	32769
CA5	13410	CA39	13296
CA6	13236	CA41	20894
CA7	10229	CA43	32578
CA8	13186	CA47	20387
CA9	6133	CA48	32986
CA10	4246	CA50	20160
CA11	4214	CA54	26906
CA29	32588	CA56	20891
CA31	32574	CA57	20817
CA32		CA59	25888
CA33		CA62	4859

In January 1947 the 'Plane Numbers' were changed to XT- marks in the XT-Txx series (see index below). Known are XT-T10, XT-T21 to XT-T24, XT-T31 to XT-T34, XT-T36, XT-T37, XT-T67, XT-T68, XT-T70 and XT-T74. In early 1948 this was changed to a series between XT-501 and XT-541, odd numbers only. XT-543 was also used but this was flown by the World Lutheran Mission as a replacement for XT-T72.

By 1948 there were about 22 C-47s in use and these survivors were bought by Civil Air Transport in 1949, being registered N8324C to N8342C in the process. XT numbers known for CATC aircraft were from XT-503 to XT-543, odd numbers only. The following CATC aircraft were flown by defecting pilots to the Communist side: XT-501 on 25Aug49, XT-507 on 27Oct49 and XT-525 on 09Nov49..

China National Aviation Corp, (CNAC), Shanghai. CNAC started operations in October 1929 and was 45% owned by Pan American from 1933 onwards, reducing to 20% in 1946. Both DC-2s and DC-3s were supplied before the war. Further C-47s were supplied under the Lend-Lease program during and additional examples from surplus USAAF stocks were obtained after the end of the war. As with CATC, the capital was taken over by Civil Air Transport in Dec49 and with this several DC-3s. Initially, aircraft were identified using a simple number assigned by the airline on or near delivery.

DC-2s known to have been supplied were c/ns 1302, 1369, 1567/8, and 1600. These cannot with *complete* certainty be proved to tie up with the aircraft numbers quoted below. Additionally #32 was rebuilt and then became #39; while #36 and #40 were also DC-2s but their origins have yet to be determined.

DC-3s bought pre-war were c/ns 2135, 2148, and 2261, while surplus C-47s known are c/ns 4573, 20309, 20310 and 32968.

#24 (DC-2)	c/n 1369	#67	6151
#26 (DC-2)	1302	#68	6221
#28 (DC-2)	1600	#69	6222
#31 (DC-2)	1567	#70	9014
#32 (DC-2)	1568	#71	9013
#36 (DC-2)		#72	9110
#39 (DC-2)	1568	#73	9109
#40 (DC-2)	1560	#74	9291
	or 1598 ?	#75	9416
#41	2135	#76	9417
#46	2148	#77	9596
#47	2261	#78	9597
#48	4852	#79	9760
#49	4853	#80	9761
#50	4871	#81	9955
#51	4879	#82	9956
#52	4902	#83	10159
#53	4904	#84	10158
#54	4927	#85	18902
	later 9069	#86	18901
#55	4929	#87	19062
#56	4881	#88	19061
#57	4883	#89	19313
#58	7407	#90	19314
#59	7406	#91	19452
#60	4681	#92	19620
#61	4729	#93	19621
#62	4730	#94	19803
#63	6034	#95	19804
#64	6035	#96	20091
#65	6037	#97	20253
#66	6150	#98	20252

C/n 19453 did not reach China but crashed on delivery 07Mar44 ex Miami.

See production list for casualty details of the above.

The remaining aircraft have yet to be identified with any certainty. However, they are probably from 20803 to 20806, 20867, 20868, 26305, 26306, 32527, 32530, 32531, 32803, 32817 and 32847, not necessarily in order. *The following entries must therefore be considered speculative:*

#99	20804?	No further details
#100	20806?	Re-registered XT-T20 in 1947
#101	20803 or 20805?	Lost wing in turbulence between Sadiya and Ft Hertz, over Hump 07Oct44, cr nr Kobo
#102	20803 or 20805?	Lost over Hump, Talifu, N Yunnan 07Jan45.
#103	20867?	Re-registered XT-T83 in 1947
#104	20868?	Cr 20Oct45 about 20 mls NE of Suichang, Zhejiang on Shanghai to Hong Kong flight
#105	26305 or 26306?	Cr. Hukawng Valley 16Feb45 - crew baled out after pilot lit cigarette and set plane on fire!.
#106	26305 or 26306?	Cr. over Hump 25Nov44 - crew baled out.
#107	32527?	Re-registered XT-84 in 1947
#108	32530?	Re-registered XT-T58 in 1947
#109	32531?	Still active in early 1947
#110	32803?	No further details
#111	32817?	Re-registered XT-T81 in 1947
#112	32847?	Re-registered XT-T52 in 1947

In late 1945 additional aircraft were acquired from surplus USAAF stocks. They remain unidentified. Known examples are #136, #138, #140, #141 and #145, with #139 likely.
#117 was in use from 12.49 to 1966 and is reported to Changping as PLAAF 97042.
#136 re-registered XT-56 in 1947 may be c/n 4573.

In January 1947 the 'Plane Numbers' were changed to XT- marks initially and briefly into the XT-xx or XT-Txx series. Known are XT-T20, XT-T45, XT-T48, XT-T51, XT-T52, XT-T54 to XT-T56, XT-T58, XT-T60 and XT-T81 to XT-T92. Note that it is not certain if the second T was always used.

Then , in early 1948, this was changed to a series of numbers between XT-111 and XT-141 for C-47s (odd numbers only).

CHAPTER 4: COMMERCIAL OPERATORS OF THE DC-3, C-47, R4D, DAKOTA AND LI-2

Other unidentified casualties recorded between 1946 and 1949 include:-
19Mar46 #139 (C-47 not confirmed but likely) Missing on flight from Chonqing to Shanghai, near Enshi, Hubei.
25Dec46 #140 Crashed due to fog, Lungwha Airport, Shanghai.
25Jan47 #138 Hit high ground en route Guangzhou to Chonqing in Sichuan.
28Jan47 #145 Crashed due to engine fire Zhou Jia Wan, Tian Men County, SE of Wuhan, Hubei.
25Apr47 #141 Engine failed on take-off, overshot when attempting to abort, Lungwha Airport, Shanghai.
27Oct47 XT-T89 Shot down by PLA on approach to Yulin. (Reported simply as #89 but this does not fit original #89)
12Dec48 XT-113 Hit mountain on approach to Taipei, 32 mls NE of Dan Bei.

In 1949 survivors were bought by CAT and registered between N8348C and N8362C.

The followingCNAC aircraft were flown from Hong Kong to the Communist side by defecting pilots on 09 November 1949: XT-115, XT-121, XT-123, XT-125, XT-129, XT-131 and XT-139.

China National Relief & Rehabilitation Administration (CNRRA) Air Transport was formed on 25Oct46. Five C-47s were acquired in the Philippines. These are likely to be c/ns 20681, 20705, 25833, 26832, and 26167. CNRRA Air Transport formally became **Civil Air Transport (CAT)** on 28May48. The five C-47s likely became XT-801 to 809 (odd numbers only) in early 1948 although only XT-801 has been identified with certainty. XT-805 crashed in Southern Yunnan on a flight from Mengtzu to Haiphong on 08Nov49. XT-811 was also allocated although this was XT-543 of the World Lutheran Federation re-registered on 10Nov49. See Taiwan/Formosa for additional information on CAT.

China People's Airline Company was formed on 15Jul52. Prior to that the service had been operated under the direction of the Central People's Government Civil Aviation Bureau, commencing on 01Aug50. Initial equipment consisted of aircraft that had been flown out of Hong Kong and elsewhere by defecting pilots. In 1952 ten DC-3 variants were in use, most or all of which would be the former CATC and CNAC aircraft listed above. Lisunov Li-2s were added gradually. China People's Airline was discontinued on 01Mar54, when the Civil Aviation Bureau resumed control. The name was formally changed to the Civil Aviation Administration of China on 10Nov54.

Civil Aviation Administration of China (CAAC) - Minhaiduy, later known as the **General Administration of Civil Aviation of China**, Beijing. CAAC was formed in 1954 to succeed SKOGA and the China People's Airline. At least 29 Li-2s were used, some remaining in service as late as 1980.

301	c/n 184 336 01	315	184 331 01
302	184 338 06	316	184 363 04
303	184 336 02	317	
304	184 338 04	318	184 338 09
305	184 402 06	319	
306	183 338 03	320	184 339 04
307	184 396 02	321	
308	184 338 08	322	184 396 08
309	184 336 06	323	184 396 03
310	184 397 04	324	
311(1)	184 337 07	325	184 405 08
311(2)	184 397 03	326	
312	184 335 10	327	184 405 09
313	184 336 08	328	
314	184 363 05	329	184 402 05

Of the above B-301 is the only example noted using the B-nationality prefix - on 06Oct88, wfu. 323 was noted in service as recently as August 1987.

Two CAAC DC-3s are known to have used only names initially:

"National Day" became 101 (Dec49 to 1964) and then went to the China Aviation Museum as CNAC XT-115.
"China Youth" became 102 (Dec49 to 1964) and is displayed as such at Beijing Aeronautical Institute.

Great China Aviation Corp. This company was formed around Oct45. A small number of C-47s was acquired, however, they were unable to begin full operations die to political pressures. Their aircraft were flown with CATC markings as CA32 to CA36, see above.

Hamiata was founded on 15Nov39 as a joint Soviet-Chinese company that came about as a result of an agreement between the Russian and Chinese Governments. Services were operated between Alma Ata in Russia and points in NW China.The operation was largely run by Russia, which supplied two DC-3s and later two C-47s for the services. All were registered in Russia - see that section for details. The agreement was renewed in May49 and it is likely that this formed the framework for the similar agreement that led to the vreation of SKOGA.

SKOGA (or SKOAGA) - People's Aviation Corp of China was formed on 27Mar50 with Soviet help as Sovietsko-Kitaysko Aktsioneren Obschestvo Grazhdanskoi Aviatsii (Sino-Soviet Civil Aviation Joiny Stock Company). First services were flown on 01Jul50 from Beijing to destinations in the Russian Far East. Initially Lisunov Li-2s were used. The service continued until 01Jan55, when responsibility was turned over to China and operated by CAAC.

Index:-
It is not certain that the second T in the registrations below was always carried.

XT-T10	c/n 13186	XT-125	
XT-T20	20806 ?	XT-127	
XT-T21	7313	XT-129	
XT-T22	32588	XT-131	
XT-T23	4483	XT-133	32530
XT-T24	20388	XT-135	
XT-T31	13296	XT-137	
XT-T32	26704	XT-139	
XT-T33	32578	XT-141	
XT-T34	20387	XT-501	
XT-T36	20160	XT-503	
XT-T37	26906	XT-505	
XT-T45	4927	XT-507	
XT-T48	19313	XT-509	
XT-T51	19062	XT-511	
XT-T52	32847 ?	XT-513	
XT-T54	19452	XT-515	
XT-T55	4929	XT-517	
XT-T56	4573 ?	XT-519	
XT-T58	32530 ?	XT-521	
XT-T60		XT-523	
XT-T67	20891	XT-525	
XT-T68	20817	XT-527	
XT-T70	25888	XT-529	
XT-T72	(see note)	XT-531	
XT-T74	44859	XT-533	
XT-T81	32817 ?	XT-535	
XT-T82	4730	XT-537	
XT-T83	20867 ?	XT-539	
XT-T84	32527 ?	XT-541	
XT-T85	19620	XT-543	19932
XT-T86	18901	XT-801	20681
XT-T87	6151	XT-803	20705
XT-T88	6221		or 32987 ?
XT-T89		XT-805	27167
XT-T90	4871	XT-807	
XT-T91	2135	XT-809	
XT-T92	2261	XT-811(1)?	19932
XT-111		XT-811(2)?	18947
XT-113		XT-813	
XT-115		XT-815	19258
XT-117		XT-817	19256
XT-119		XT-819	
XT-121		XT-821	
XT-123		XT-823	13399

Note: XT-T72 World Lutheran Mission; acquired 13May46, "St Paul"; Cr 10Feb49, Payang Kweiyang, Kweichow Province. A second C-47 was acquired for spares only as "St Peter". XT-T72 was replaced by XT-543.

XT-BTA and XT-BTB were two surviving pre-war DC-3s reported in 1943. XT-DBF (or -OBF?) was DC-2 ex #40, c/n either 1560 or 1598.

COLOMBIA - C and HK

Many DC-3s as well as a few C-39s have been used on Colombian airline routes. Although the major Colombian airlines have given up the DC-3, smaller operators continue to use them on flights to places that cannot take a jet. In fact in the past ten years the number in use has increased by about 50%, but lack of spares was taking its toll by 2000. Registration marks are somewhat complicated by the change in nationality mark from C- to HK- in 1948. At that time most aircraft with numbers below C-100 were given new numbers, but higher-numbered aircraft retained their original marks. Unfortunately it has not proved possible to clarify some of the earlier aircraft histories as the files have been destroyed.

Aerocondor - Aerovías Condor de Colombia Ltda, Barranquilla, was formed in February 1955 as **Línea de Aviación "Condor" Ltda** to operate scheduled domestic and cargo services. It was soon renamed Aerocondor. The last DC-3 was sold in 1967.

HK-500; HK-503; HK-873.

ADES - Aerolíneas del Este, Villavicencio, operated DC-3s HK-3177 which crashed in May 1991 and HK-3220, sold to Trans Oriente in 1990. They had HK-1149 and HK-2663 still registered in 2005.

Aerolíneas TAO Ltda, Neiva/Bucaramanga. TAO was formed as **Transportes Aéreos Opita** in 1957, but renamed **Taxi Aéreo Opita** in the early sixties, taking its final name in 1970, a year before the DC-3s were replaced by Viscounts.

HK-556; HK-595; HK-1078; HK-1202.

Aero Norte - Aerovías del Norte Ltda, Cucuta/Barranquilla, bought two DC-3s in 1977. These were HK-122 and HK-329, neither remaining after 1980.

Aerosucre Ltda, Barranquilla, used DC-3 HK-1078 between 1974 and 1979.

AEROTAL - Aerovías Territoriales de Colombia, Villavicencio/Bogota. Operations started in 1953 as **Taxi Aéreo "El Llanero" Ltda** using single engined types. The final name was adopted in 1973. Four DC-3s have been used. Operations ceased in the autumn of 1983.

HK-1333; HK-1338; HK-1393; HK-2214.

Aerotaxi de Calamar used DC-3 HK-3462, withdrawn in 1992, and sold.

Aerovanguardia, Villavicencio, had DC-3 HK-1503 in 1997 and by 1999 had added HK-2663, followed by HK-3199.

Aerovilla, Villavicencio, started operating DC-3s in late 1993, and has used HK-3199, 3292 and 3349. HK-3292 was the last in service and returned to Air Colombia in 2001.

AFRYPESCA - Empresa de Aviación Refrigeración y Pesca used DC-3s to carry refrigerated fish and other cargo, in the early fifties.

HK-127; HK-708; HK-709; HK-1003

AIDA - Agencia Interamericana de Aviación Ltda used DC-3s on domestic charters from May47.

C-1002; C-1003.

Air Colombia, Bogota, was using DC-3 HK-3292 by Nov87, and HK-3293 in 1988. Two DC-3 BT-67s were bought from Basler, to be HK-3575 and HK-3576 but were impounded by the DEA for drug offences and never delivered. The company moved to Villavicencio in 1996, and HK-3293 was operational in 2005, along with HK-3292 returned from Aerovilla and HK-3359.

ALCOM, Villavicencio, was operating DC-3 HK-3349 and HK-4045 in Sep97, the latter remaining in 1999, withdrawn from use.

ALIANSA - Aerolíneas Andinas SA, Villavicencio, used DC-3 HK-140, wfu by 1992, HK-337, HK-2581 and HK-2820, all of which were in service in 1997. HK-337 was lost in 1999, HK-122, HK-3037 and HK3462 being added.

ALICOL of Villavicencio, operated DC-3 HK-3176 from 1993, adding HK-140 in 1996.

APEL Express SA, Bogota, bought three DC-3s from Ecuador in 1987. They were sold to SAEP by 1992.

HK-3348; HK-3349; HK-3350.

ARCA - Aerovías Colombianas Ltda, Bogota, used DC-3s on scheduled services between 1954 and 1982.

HK-166; HK-337; HK-339; HK-766.

AVIANCA - Aerovías Nacionales de Colombia SA, Bogota. As well as a few C-39s, a large fleet of DC-3s was used from 1942 until about 1972, when HS.748s replaced the last few. In 1952 the fleet was increased by the purchase of LANSA and SAETA. Because of the high altitude of some Colombian airports, many DC-3s were modified as Hiper DC-3s to give improved performance.

C-39s:- C-102; C-103; C-106; *DC-3s:-* C/HK-100; 101; 102(2); 104; 105; 107 to 111; 116 to 127; 140; 142; 143; 149; 150; 153 to 155; 159 to 161; 166; 167; 303; 308; 312; 314; 316 to 319; 324 to 329; 500; 502; 508; 1201; 1202; 1203; 1204; 1315; 1316; 1340 and 1341. See index for those which were only C- registered.

AVISPA - Aerovías Pilotos Asociados, Medellin, flew DC-3s and Cessna 180s on taxi and charter operations until about 1962.

HK-524; HK-525.

Cessnyca Ltda, Medellin, operated DC-3s on commuter services between 1971 and 1974.

HK-1212; HK-1216; HK-1351.

Cia. Trasandina de Aviación SA, Cartagena, used DC-3 C/HK-805 until 1948 to supplement a fleet of Lodestars.

CORAL - Coronado Aerolíneas, Bogota, operated DC-3 HK-3527X

COSTA - Cia Sinuana de Transporte Aéreo Costa, Cerete, had a single DC-3 HK-3199. It was sold to Aerovilla.

El Venado - See Taxi Aereo El Venado.

Empresa Aerovías del Pacifico Ltda (ARPA). DC-3 HK-385 was used until November 1956 when it was destroyed.

Expreso Aéreo Ltda, Cia, Bogota, was formed in May 1947 to operate two DC-3s on cargo services.

C/HK-900; C-901.

Interandes - Cia Interandina de Aviación, Bogota, operated cargo DC-3s HK-1149 and HK-3177. The former remained in service until 1997, but was sold to ADES Colombia by 1998.

LAC Colombia - Líneas Aéreas del Caribe, Barranquilla. DC-3 HK-805 was used to support C-46 cargo services.

LACOL - Líneas Aéreas Colombianas, Villavicencio, had four DC-3s, HK-124, HK-1340, HK-3213 and HK-3215, but operations ceased around 1995.

LAICA - Líneas Aéreas Interiores de Catalina, Villavicencio. Two DC-3s were used on domestic freight services.

HK-166, HK-329.

LANC - Líneas Aéreas del Norte de Colombia, Villavicencio. The only DC-3 HK-2497 was dismantled by 1999.

LANSA - Líneas Aéreas Nacionales SA, Barranquilla. Scheduled services were started in October 1945 as **Limitada Nacional de Servicio Aéreo**. This name was changed in June 1947 and the airline was taken over by Avianca in October 1951.

C-67; C-68; C-69; C-74; C-76; C-78; HK-140; HK-149; HK-160; HK-161; C/HK-303 to 319; HK-324 to 329; HK-1201. It is uncertain where the 300 series changed from C- to HK-.

LAOS Ltda - Líneas Aéreas Orientales Ltda, Villavicencio, used DC-3s on third level services until 1977.

HK-101; HK-102; HK-122; HK-124; HK-166; HK-772.

LATINA, Villavicencio, DC-3 HK-1212 was active in 2000 and HK-2006 has been acquired since.

Líneas Aéreas Darien Uraba, Medellin, bought C-117D HK-3586 in 1990, but it is believed no longer in use.

Líneas Aéreas del Mar, Cali, had DC-3s HK-3630 and HK-4045 in service in 1996, but the latter was sold to ALCOM, and operations ceased.

Líneas Aéreas El Dorado, Bogota, bought six DC-3s. Operations ceased in 1987.

HK-122; HK-2663; HK-2664; HK-2665; HK-2666; HK-3361.

Líneas Aéreas La Urraca, Bogota, was formed in January 1963 to operate scheduled domestic services with DC-3s, one of which remained in 1980.

HK-500; HK-772; HK-1175; HK-1270; HK-1315.

Líneas Aéreas Petroleras, Bogota, operated a single DC-3 HK-1514 from at least 1982 until 1999, but it is no longer in use.

Líneas Aéreas TACA de Colombia, Bogota, started joint services with TACA de Venezuela to Caracas in January 1945, but gave up in May 1947 when bankruptcy intervened. One C-39 and 13 DC-3s were used:-

C-39:- C-157; DC-3s:- C-168; C-169; C-170; C-203 to 205; C-209 to 215 incl. YS-26 was also used.

[Note: Further TACA group entries will be found under Costa Rica, El Salvador, Honduras and Venezuela]

Rutas Aéreas de Colombia Ltda, Medellin, took over scheduled services operated by Soc. Aeronautica Medellin SA in July 1955. DC-3s HK-523, HK-524 and HK-525 were used.

Rutas Aéreas SAM Ltda was formed in January 1955 and became **Rutas Aéreas de Colombia** in 1957 with help from KLM. Services returned to SAM in 1961.

HK-523, HK-524; HK-525.

SADELCA - Servicio Aérea del Caqueta, Neiva, used DC-3s on charter work from 1975, and about five remained in 2000.

HK-124; HK-1212; HK-1338; HK-1340; HK-1351; HK-1514; HK-2494; HK-2663; HK-2664; HK-2665; HK-2666; HK-3199; HK-3263; HK-3286; HK-3349; HK-3993; HK-3994; HK-4189.

SAEP - Servicios Aéreos Especializados en Transportes Petroleros, Bogota, had DC-3s but all were stored by 1999.

HK-2006; HK-2494; HK-2663; HK-3031; HK-3176; HK-3213; HK-3348; HK-3349 and HK-3350.

SAETA - Sociedad Aérea de Tolima SA, Bogota. SAETA was formed in February 1947 with aid from AVIANCA, but operations were absorbed by the latter by 1952. DC-3s were C/HK-1200 to 1204 incl.

SAM - Sociedad Aeronáutica Medellin SA, Medellin. DC-3s started operations in September 1946 but the name was changed in 1955 to **Rutas Aéreas SAM** (see earlier). Reorganisation followed and the name became **SA Medellin Consolidada**. In 1962 it became a subsidiary of AVIANCA and its owned associate Aerotaxi. Some DC-3s were registered in the early C- series and C-75 is known to have become HK-505. Others were C/HK-500 to 510; HK-521 to HK-526 and HK-338. C-521 also reported.

SARPA - Servicios Aéreos del Putumayo, Puerto Asis, used DC-3 HK-3199, since sold.

SATENA - Servicio de Aeronavegación a Teritorios Nacionales, Bogota. See military section. All DC-3s were disposed of by 1987.

SCOLTA - Sociedad Colombiana de Transportes Aéreos Ltda, Bogota, was formed in August 1947 to operate cargo services. Three DC-3s were used but only C-34 and C-71 (1) have come to light. The latter crashed in October 1948 and was rebuilt by AVIANCA as HK-140.

SELVA, Villavicencio, began charter operations in 1980, using DC-3s HK-122 and HK-2213 - these remaining until the mid-nineties.

Sociedad Transportes Aéreos Boyacenses, Tunja, Boyaca State. Domestic charter services were operated using DC-3s during the sixties.

HK-500; HK-503 and HK-766.

TACA - See Líneas Aéreas TACA de Colombia

TACATA - Taxi Aéreo Caqueta, Barrancabermeja/Bogota, used two DC-3s HK-166 and HK-766 from 1959, until it went out of business around 1970.

TAERCO - Taxi Aereo Colombiano, Villavicencio, used DC-3 HK-1315 in 1997, but it was withdrawn in 1999.

TALA Ltda - Transportes Aéreos Latinamericanos, Bogota, operated DC-3s HK-2580; HK-2581 briefly until in November 1982 the fleet was impounded by the Ministry of Justice. HK-3037 was in use in 1990 after overhaul, so it would seem that the impounding was temporary. This was later sold to Aliansa.

TANA - Transportes Aéreos Nacional, Bogota, started operations in April 1972 using DC-3s and Beech 18s for charter work. It earlier operated as Taxi Aereo Nacional, merging with TAVINA in 1978.

HK-140; HK-149; HK-1511; HK-1512; HK-1514; HK-1517; HK-2006.

TAO - Taxi Aéreo Opita - See Aerolineas TAO.

TAXADER - Líneas Aéreas Taxader, Bucaramanga, was formed in August 1947 as **Taxi Aereo de Santander** (hence the later name). DC-3s were in use from 1955 until 1965.

HK-410; HK437; HK-793; HK-794; HK-862; HK-864; HK-873.

Taxi Aéreo "El Llanero" - See Aerotal.

Taxi Aéreo El Venado, Villavicencio. Third level services were started in 1973 with DC-3s. The name **Aéreos El Venado Ltda** was later adopted. Operations ceased in September 1981.

HK-122; HK-124; HK-140; HK-149; HK-329; HK-556; HK-1078; HK-1315; HK-1340.

Transamazonica, Villavicencio, began operations in 1980 with five DC-3s, adding further aircraft. Three remained in 1999, but operations were later suspended.

HK-124; HK-140; HK-500; HK-772; HK-1175; HK-1315; HK-1340; HK-2497; HK-3348; HK-3359; HK-3360; HK-3361.

VIARCO - Vías Aéreas Colombianas, Medellin. Operations started in June 1945 using a fleet of DC-3s. Many were sold to SAM in 1948 when operations ceased following bankruptcy.

C-400 to C-403 incl; C-407 to C-412 incl.

An airline of the same name bought DC-3 HK-2820X in 1983. It was sold in 1992. HK-1212, HK-1315 and HK-3349 were reported subsequently.

Index:-
Because of the dual nationality marks and doubts about the changing over from C- to HK-, aircraft are listed numerically regardless.

Suffixes have the following significances: X - delivery/ferry, E - Especiales or special purpose, G - Government agencies, P - private, W - Executive use. They are sometimes changed during aircraft use, and X may be retained for some time on the aircraft following delivery. Only those definitely known to have been carried are included in this index.

C-34X	c/n 12513	C-110	4181
C-60	6158	C/HK-111	4105
C-67	10194	C/HK-116	4786
C-68	9388	C/HK-117	9139
C-69	19758	C/HK-118	6182
C-71(1)	6354	C-119	6217
C-71X(2)	9993	C/HK-120	4314
C-74	10032	C/HK-121	4370
C-75	9380	C-122(1)	4688
C-76	12977	C/HK-122(2)	4414
C-78(1)	19101	C/HK-123	6160
C-78(2)	13830	C/HK-124	4349
C-90?	12977	C/HK-125	4410
C-100	2012	C/HK-126	4290
C/HK-101	4688	C/HK-127	4332
C/HK-102	4231	C/HK-140	6354
C-103 (C-39)	2058	C/HK-142	1957
C-104	1992	C/HK-143	10088
C-105	1989	C/HK-149	4593
C-106 (C-39)	2079	C/HK-150	4697
C/HK-107	11723	C/HK-153	4711
C-108	4829	C/HK-154	6215
C/HK-109	4753	HK-155	4338

Reg	c/n	Reg	c/n	Reg	c/n	Reg	c/n
C-156 (C-39)	2070 ?	C/HK-708	9041	HK-3462X	11759	HK-3630X	25449
C-157 (C-39)	2086	C/HK-709	4433	HK-3527X	(see notes)	HK-3993	26343
HK-159	6068	HK-711	9124	HK-3575	33053	HK-3994	4319
HK-160	19540	HK-766	26272	HK-3576	20875	HK-4045	25808
HK-161	19630	HK-772	11743	HK-3586X	43325	HK-4189	4319
HK-166	12560	HK-793	4240				
HK-167	4272	HK-794	4551				
C-168	19141	C/HK-805	12853				
C-169	19725	HK-862	12374				
C-170	19242	HK-864	4466				
C-203	19141	HK-873	2199				
C-204	19725	C-900	4363				
C-205	19242	C-901(1)?	10251				
C-209	12062	C-901(2)?	4727				
C-211	25481	HK-961X	(see notes)				
C-212	4410	HK-962X	(see notes)				
C-213	4290	C-1002	6252				
C-214	4332	C/HK-1003	19757				
C-215	4338	HK-1078	9884				
C-301		HK-1109G	9809				
C-302		HK-1110G	11789				
C/HK-303	10032	HK-1149G	26593				
C/HK-304	19101	HK-1175	20432				
C/HK-305		C/HK-1200	(see notes)				
C/HK-306	12977	HK-1201	4479				
C/HK-307	10194	HK-1202	4402				
C/HK-308	19758	C/HK-1203	9970				
C/HK-309	(see notes)	C/HK-1204	13746				
C/HK-310	13807	HK-1212	4987				
C/HK-311	20183	HK-1216	1905				
HK-312	4757	HK-1221G	9703				
"HK-313"	10177	HK-1270	4544				
HK-314	4436	HK-1315	4307				
C/HK-315	9073	HK-1316G	9714				
C/HK-316	6253	HK-1333	27051				
HK-317	9091	HK-1338	11687				
C/HK-318	6173	HK-1340X	11704				
C/HK-319	19680	HK-1341	11716				
C/HK-324	4351	HK-1351	42958				
C/HK-325	19654	HK-1393	19053				
C/HK-326	4631	C/HK-1503W	34331				
C/HK-327	19513	HK-1504E	19998				
HK-328	20224	HK-1505W	20473				
HK-329	4404	HK-1511W	6138				
HK-337	11831	HK-1512E	19039				
HK-338	(see notes)	HK-1514E	11741				
HK-339G	11994	HK-1515E	4484				
HK-385	1971	HK-1517E	4997				
C-400	4792	HK-2006X	43086				
C-401	4527	HK-2213	11752				
C-402	4725	HK-2214X	11627				
C-403	13643	HK-2494	33105				
C-407	6158	HK-2497	27079				
C-408	11865	HK-2540P	13816				
C-409	6061	HK-2580	19127				
	see also 4732	HK-2581	27006				
C-410(1)	6152	HK-2663X	10201				
HK-410(2)	4955	HK-2664X	12352				
C-411	4763	HK-2665X	19433				
C-412	4659	HK-2666X	32540				
HK-437E	4697	HK-2819X	2242?				
C/HK-500	19637	HK-2820X	20171				
C/HK-501	18986	HK-3031	10202				
C/HK-502	19653	HK-3037	20548				
C/HK-503	10171	HK-3176	19606				
C/HK-504	10062	HK-3177	26775				
C/HK-505	9380	HK-3199	26044				
C/HK-506	6061	HK-3213	25659				
	see also 4732	HK-3215X	26111				
C/HK-507	4725	HK-3220	11808				
C/HK-508	4527	HK-3234X					
C/HK-509	4763	HK-3241X	1970				
C/HK-510	6152	HK-3263					
(HK-521)	12953	HK-3286	6144				
(HK-522)	11994	HK-3292	19661				
(HK-523)	12017	HK-3293X	9186				
HK-523	42965	HK-3348X	11775				
HK-524	12075	HK-3349	11825				
HK-525	9904	HK-3350	1969				
(HK-526)	11831	HK-3359	34295				
HK-556	4958	HK-3360	33052				
HK-595	19238	HK-3361X	33203				

Notes:-
HK-309 crashed on 15Apr50 at Santa Ana.
HK-338 was reported as c/n 11831 but this is now believed to be HK-337.
HK-961X and 962X were probably never delivered although photos taken in the USA are in the Editor's collection.
HK-1200 of S A Tolima SA, crashed on 13Aug49 at El Dorado, Bogota.
HK-2663 to HK-2666 were mispainted during overhaul - see histories.
HK-3527X was cancelled on 26Jun90.

COMORES - F-O and D6.

Air Comores SARL, Moroni, Comores, was formed in 1963 and used two DC-3s from 1971 until 1976. F-OCEN and F-OCRR were sold before the new marking was adopted. The D6-CAx series were imported clandestinely for export to the SAAF.

Index:-
D6-CAD	c/n 33478	D6-CAG	33313
D6-CAE	34225	D6-CAH	33134
D6-CAF	32897	D6-ECB	20175

CONGO, REPUBLIC of - TN

Air Congo, Cie Congolaise de Transports Aériens, Pointe Noire. Two DC-3s, TN-AAB and TN-AAF were in use between 1962 and 1965, when Lina Congo took over.

Lina Congo, Brazzaville, was formed in March 1964 to take over Air Congo. The new name was adopted in August 1965 and the DC-3s TN-AAB, TN-AAF plus TN-ABI were replaced by F.27s in 1976.

Index:-
TN-AAB	c/n 10101	"TN-ADS"	12704
TN-AAF	13388	TN-ADT	25546
TN-ABI	9511		

CONGO, DEMOCRATIC REPUBLIC - See Zaire.

COSTA RICA - TI

Costa Rica, situated in Central America between Nicaragua and Panama, had nine DC-3 operators, though none now survives. The major users were LACSA and TACA, though many of the latter's were short-lived, being passed on to other TACA subsidiaries in Venezuela and Brazil. Nearly 50 DC-3s were in use at some time.

Aerolíneas Nacionales SA (ANSA), San Jose, operated internal services between 1958 and 1960 using two DC-3s and a C-46. One of the former was written off in 1960 and may have brought about the airline's demise.

TI-1021; TI-1023.

Aeroservicios Puntarenas SA, (APSA), San Jose. Three DC-3s were used on domestic passenger charter work until replaced by a Convair 440 in 1976. A further DC-3 was bought in May 1978, but all services were suspended in 1979. One unknown DC-3 crashed at Managua, Nicaragua on 15Feb74.

TI-1051C; TI-1082C/TI-AHA; TI-AMS.

Aerovías Cariari SA, (ACASA), San José, started scheduled services in 1970 using four DC-3s before operations ceased in 1979.

TI-1075C/TI-ACB; TI-1078C/TI-ACC; TI-ALX; TI-AMS. In addition, HP-729 was leased.

Caribbean Airlines used two DC-3s and a C-46 on internal services from 1966 until 1967.

TI-1051C; TI-1052C.

CHAPTER 4: COMMERCIAL OPERATORS OF THE DC-3, C-47, R4D, DAKOTA AND LI-2

Cayman Airways Ltd, Grand Cayman, BWI. This company was operated by LACSA, the main shareholder, and later became **Cayman Brac Airways**. LACSA provided DC-3s until 1977.

TI-1051C; TI-1052C; TI-1067C/TI-LRE.

LACSA - Líneas Aéreas Costarricenses SA, San José acquired its first DC-3s in June 1946 with Pan American assistance. TACA de Costa Rica's surviving DC-3s were taken over in 1952. At one time the DC-3 made up the bulk of the fleet, but the last was in use with Cayman Brac in 1977 and was sold in May 1978.

TI-16; TI-17; TI-18; TI-1000; TI-1002; TI-1003/1003C; TI-1004C; TI-1005/1005C; TI-1006/1006C; TI-1051C; TI-1052C; TI-1067C/ TI-LRE; TI-AHA.

RANSA - Ruta Aérea Nacional SA, San José, was formed in 1979 acquiring two DC-3s from Aerovias Cariari. SANSA took over domestic services in 1980.

TI-ACB; TI-ACC.

SANSA - Servicios Aéreos Nacionales SA, San José, began operations in 1980 taking over LACSA's and RANSA's domestic services, using DC-3s.

TI-AMS; TI-SAA; TI-SAG. HR-SAH was leased.

TACA de Costa Rica SA, San José was part of the Waterman Airlines complex formed by Lowell Yerex and controlled by him until 1947 as Transportes Aereos Centro-Americanos. It then passed to Waterman Steamship Co and the various constituents were sold gradually, TACA de Costa Rica going to LACSA in 1952. DC-3s made up a large part of the fleet, replacing the pre-war Fords, Lockheed 14s and 18s, and Twin Beeches post-war. [*Note*: Further TACA group entries will be found under Colombia, El Salvador, Honduras and Venezuela]

TI-62; TI-71; TI-73; TI-75; TI-101 to 106; TI-115; TI-119; TI-120; TI-156; TI-157; TI-159; TI-160; TI-1000 to 1004 incl.

TAN - Transportes Aéreos Nacionales SA, San José, used several DC-3s on low cost charter and schedules in the fifties, under C N Shelton's management.

TI-107 to TI-109 incl; TI-161; TI-1023.

Index:-
Costa Rica has used four distinct systems for registering its civil aircraft. Initially the series started at TI-1, reaching about TI-161. In late 1949 commercial aircraft were put in a series starting at TI-1000. In the mid-fifties a suffix was added denoting the function (C for commercial). Some aircraft simply had the C added, but vacant numbers in the 1000 block were re-used. Lastly, at the beginning of 1975, a letter system was adopted, all then current aircraft being re-registered.

TI-16	c/n 4957	TI-1002	26078
TI-17	9061	TI-1003(1)	12312
TI-18	4419	TI-1003/C(2)	19046
TI-62	19046	TI-1004	4889
TI-71	4910	TI-1004C	9884
TI-73	25481	TI-1005/C	4959
TI-75	7333	TI-1006/C	4960
TI-101	19214	TI-1021	4541
TI-102	19779	TI-1023	
TI-103	25227	TI-1042C	33612
TI-104	19242	TI-1051C	26700
TI-105	9884	TI-1052C	20191
TI-106	19389	TI-1067C	7345
TI-107	4444	TI-1075C	4231
TI-108	6158	TI-1078C	6215
TI-109	6218	TI-1082C	10127
TI-115		TI-ACB	4231
TI-119	25278	TI-ACC	6215
TI-120	25452	TI-AHA	10127
TI-156	43078	TI-ALX	26725
TI-157	43077	TI-AMS	7345
TI-159	6350	TI-AON	34394
TI-160	12062	(TI-AQL)	25526
TI-161		TI-LRE	7345
TI-1000	6138	TI-SAA	4231
TI-1001		TI-SAG	9137

Notes:-
TI-161 was destroyed by fire on 24Apr48.
TI-1001 may have crashed in Nicaragua.
TI-1023 crashed on 25May60.
C/n 19593 was a TI- candidate around 1947/8.

CUBA - NM and CU

Between 1945 and 1959, when the Communist revolution took place, there were six DC-3 operators in Cuba. Thereafter only Cubana retained any DC-3s until spares shortage forced their retirement, however there was a slight resurgence when Aero Caribbean imported a few.

Aero Caribbean, Havana bought its first DC-3 in 1983 and later three were in use. These moved on to Aerotaxi in 1997.

CU-T113/CU-T127; CU-T123; CU-T124.

Aerotaxi added Aero Caribbean's DC-3 fleet to its own in 1997.

CU-T123; CU-T124; CU-T127, CU-T1058, CU-T1059, CU-T1192.

Aerovías Cubanas Internacionales, Havana, started charter operations in 1945 as **Cuban International Airways**. One DC-3 is known to have crashed on 27Aug48.

Aerovias "Q" SA, Havana, used DC-3s on scheduled operations from April 1946 until 1959 when most aircraft were sold.

NM-42; CU-T2; CU-T3; CU-T4; CU-T5; CU-T88; CU-T100; CU-T101; CU-T104; CU-T115; CU-T144; CU-C312; CU-C313; CU-C314. C/n 19035 was delivered in 1946, but its fate is unknown.

Cía Cubana de Aviación SA, Havana, was a subsidiary of Pan American until 1953. In 1946 most schedules were flown by DC-3s, but few of these survived the revolution in 1959, when Cubana was renamed Empresa Consolidada Cubana de Aviacion.

NM-39/CU-T7; NM-40/CU-T8; NM-43/CU-T9; CU-T38; CU-T102; CU-T128; CU-T138; CU-T172; CU-T266; CU-T586; CU-T808; CU-T810; CU-T826; CU-T836.

Cuba Aeropostal SA, Havana. Scheduled and charter mail and freight operations were started in 1949 with DC-3s and C-46s. DC-3s were CU-T265 and CU-T333.

Expreso Aéreo Inter-Americano SA, Havana, used several DC-3s along with C-46s on scheduled internal services until operations ceased in 1958 following financial difficulties. Several aircraft went to Aerovias "Q". In 1946-49 it had links with **Transair Inc**, of New York (qv).

CU-T100; CU-T101; CU-T104; CU-T115. C/n 19449 is unidentified.

Index:-

NM-39	c/n 11646	CU-T127	11645
NM-40	11744	CU-T128	4104
NM-42	19770 ?	CU-T138	2229
NM-43	32722	CU-T144	4466
CU-T2	34289	CU-T172	11671
CU-T3	9667	CU-T265	20558
CU-T4	19770	CU-T266	11684
CU-T5	19236	CU-C312	
CU-T7	11646	CU-C313	
CU-T8	11744	CU-T314	
CU-T9	32722	CU-T333	19122
CU-T38	4100	CU-T586	
CU-T88		CU-N702	13331
CU-T100	13681	CU-T808	4397
CU-T101	12717	CU-T810	32723
CU-T102	6321	CU-T826	20186
CU-T104	20463	CU-T836	
CU-T113	11645	CU-T1058	32664
CU-T115	25360		or 12445 ?
CU-T123	12445	CU-T1059	11645
CU-T124	32664	CU-T1192	10028

Note:- CU-N702 was an executive aircraft.
C and T prefixes were used for Transport aircraft, many of which were delivered with a P (Provisional) prefix.

CURAÇAO - See Netherlands West Indies.

CYPRUS - 5B

Cyprus Airways, Nicosia, started operations in April 1948, with help from British European Airways, using British registered DC-3s. Further aircraft were added in 1951. All were replaced by Viscounts in 1958, but two DC-3s were used briefly in the seventies.

G-AKII to G-AKIK incl; G-AGND; G-AKGX; G-AMHJ; 5B-CBC; 5B-CBD.

Index:-

5B-CAV	c/n 4381	5B-CBB	33235
5B-CAW	10106	5B-CBC	11924
5B-CAY	33444	5B-CBD	9623
(5B-CAZ)	25806	5B-CBE	10106
5B-CBA	10099		

CZECHOSLOVAKIA - OK

CLS - Ceskoslovenská letecká spolecnost, Prague. DC-2s and DC-3s were bought via Fokker before the war. These were used on scheduled services in Europe until 1938, when the airline was taken over by Germany and the aircraft registered there and used by Lufthansa.

DC-2s:- OK-AIA to OK-AID incl; OK-AIZ.
DC-3s:- OK-AIE to OK-AIH incl.

CSA - Ceskoslovenske státní aerolinie, Prague. When this airline was reformed post-war aircraft were bought from various sources and included numerous USAAF surplus C-47s. Following the Communist take-over in 1949 a few Li-2s were added from Russian stocks. Later Il-12s and Il-14s were used and the remaining DC-3s sold to France for Air Force use from 1958 onwards. Apart from the pre-war aircraft given above, all those indexed below seem likely to have seen service with CSA.

Index:-

DC-2:		OK-AIC	1562
OK-AIA	c/n 1581	OK-AID	1565
OK-AIB	1582	OK-AIZ	1564
DC-3:		OK-WDI	9501
OK-AIE	2023	OK-WDJ	9931
OK-AIF	2024	OK-WDK	12549
OK-AIG	2095	OK-WDL	12730
OK-AIH	1973	OK-WDN	12894
OK-VAJ	9915	OK-WDO	19006
OK-VAV	9371	OK-WDP	19286
OK-VDA	26180	OK-WDQ	19329
OK-VDS	9199	OK-WDR	9157
OK-VDZ	13654	OK-WDS	11854
OK-WAA	19343	OK-WDT	13438
OK-WAB	9367	OK-WDU	9798
OK-WAK	9996	OK-WDV	9962
OK-WAP	12721	OK-WDW	9264
OK-WAR	13430	OK-WDY	12725
OK-WAT	19439	OK-WDZ	9385
OK-WAX	9802	OK-WHA	9798
OK-WBA	4608	OK-WZA	25667
OK-WBC	9369	OK-WZB	9798
OK-WCN	9802	OK-WZC	
OK-WCO	9996	OK-WZD	
OK-WCP	12721	OK-WZE	
OK-WCR	13430	OK-WZF	
OK-WCS	9367	OK-WZG	
OK-WCT	12974	OK-XAA	26452
OK-WDA	9464	OK-XAB	25644
OK-WDB	9503	OK-XBC	19538
OK-WDC	12176	OK-XDG	19535
OK-WDD	19102	OK-XDH	19587
OK-WDE	19419	OK-XDM	19539
OK-WDF	19474	"OK-XDM"	1995
OK-WDG	9342	OK-XDU	13802
OK-WDH	9373	OK-XDY	12974 ?
Li-2:		OK-BYO	234 421 05
OK-BYA	234 423 01	OK-BYP	234 421 08
OK-BYQ	234 423 09	OK-GAG	234 428 04
OK-GAA	234 421 05	OK-GAH	234 430 02
OK-GAB	234 418 01	OK-PYP	234 427 10
OK-GAC	234 423 05	"OK-WDI"	234 427 10
OK-GAD	234 422 09	OK-XDN	234 418 01
OK-GAE	234 422 10	"OK-1962"	234 418 01
OK-GAF	234 425 01		

DAHOMEY - TY (Now Benin)

The only C-47s registered in Dahomey were used by the Air Force, but they carried call signs in civil style and two of them were leased to Air Afrique in 1965, using these marks.

Transports Aériens du Benin acquired two ex Aéronavale C-47s TY-BBO and TY-BBQ in late 1983. Neither now survives. They were probably used by the Benin AF.

Index:-

TY-AAB	c/n 32639	TY-BBO	33433
TY-AAC(1)	27142	TY-BBQ	25846
TY-AAC(2)	4775		

DENMARK - OY

Apart from many DC-3s used by DDL and a few by Farøe Airways, Denmark was the brief resting place for some Polish DC-3s which had been supplied to Russia and eventually found their way to Iran.

DDL - Det Danske Luftfartsselskab A/S, Copenhagen. DC-3s were bought surplus from the USAAF in Europe for conversion by Canadair and others direct from Douglas who rebuilt them as DC-3Cs. Services were combined into Scandinavian Airlines System in 1948, but ownership always remained with DDL. The last was sold in 1957.

OY-AAB; OY-AEB; OY-AIB; OY-AOB; OY-AUB; OY-AYB; OY-DCA; OY-DCE; OY-DCI; OY-DCO; OY-DCU; OY-DCY; OY-DDA; OY-DDE; OY-DDI; OY-DDO; OY-DDU; OY-DDY; OY-KLA; OY-KLE; OY-KLI.

Farøe Airways A/S, Copenhagen, bought three DC-3s in 1965/66 and operated them under the name "Fairline". Services ceased on 28Sep67.

OY-DMN; OY-DNC; OY-DNP.

Index:-

OY-AAB	c/n 12422	OY-DDA	19288
OY-AEB	12473	"OY-DDA"	9664
OY-AIA	19499	OY-DDE	19218
OY-AIB	13312	OY-DDI	13727
OY-AIC	12704	OY-DDO	20453
OY-AOB	13761	OY-DDU	19865
OY-AUB	19632	OY-DDY	19771
OY-AYB	19634	OY-DMN	13637
OY-BPB	20019	OY-DNC	42962
OY-DCA	4828	OY-DNP	11638
OY-DCE	4865	OY-ITC	10043
OY-DCI	7330	OY-KLA	12422
OY-DCO	42962	OY-KLE	4828
OY-DCU	42963	OY-KLI	19218
OY-DCY	42976		

DJIBOUTI - See Somaliland (French)

DOMINICAN REPUBLIC - HI

This state in the West Indies has never had many based DC-3s but eight operators used the type.

Aerovías Nacionales Quisqueyanas, Santo Domingo, operated DC-3s on scheduled cargo and passenger services from 1962 until 1978 when the fleet was sold to Aerolineas Dominicanos.

HI-64; HI-78; HI-115; HI-117; HI-159; HI-221; HI-252; N18101 and N44993 leased.

Chapter 4: Commercial Operators of the DC-3, C-47, R4D, Dakota and Li-2

Alas del Caribe, Santo Domingo, used DC-3 HI-237 for cargo work from June 1974 until it crashed in April 2000.

Carga Aerolíneas Dominicanas, Santo Domingo, took over Quisqueyanas' last DC-3, HI-252 in 1978, continuing its operation into the early eighties.

Compañia de Carga, Santo Domingo, had DC-3 HI-465. This was withdrawn in 1987.

CONFISA, Santo Domingo, used DC-3 HI-463 until it was grounded.

Dominicana - Cía Dominicana de Aviación C por A., Santo Domingo, started scheduled services in July 1944 and DC-3s were added to the fleet in 1947, the last being retired in the early sixties.

HI-6; HI-7; HI-12; HI-40.

LANSA - Líneas Aéreas Nacionales SA, Santo Domingo, owned DC-3 HI-222 from mid-1973 unti it was destroyed at the end of Jan75.

Taino Airlines, Santo Domingo, leased C-117D HI-477. It was seized by the US Customs in 1989.

Index:-

HI-6	c/n 4735	HI-252	4498
HI-7	4539	HI-374	33224
HI-12	11766	HI-445	7392
HI-40	20455	HI-463	9635
HI-64	3279	HI-465	4621
HI-78	3281	HI-477	43378
HI-115	6324	HI-477CA	43378
HI-117	2172	HI-502	12254
HI-159		HI-521SP	43335
HI-221	6322	HI-525	32624
HI-222	2189	HI-545CT	43365
HI-237	2107		

Notes:- HI-159 was w/o on 18May69.

ECUADOR - HC

Thirteen DC-3 operators are known for this republic in the north-western part of South America, between Colombia and Peru, but none has been in use for some years now.

AECA - Aeroservicios Ecuatorianos, Guayaquil, bought DC-3 HC-BQZ in July 1991.

Aero Transportes Ecuatorianas SA, owned DC-3s HC-SGF and HC-SGG between Sep48 and Feb49, when it was taken over by AREA.

ANDES - Aerolíneas Nacionales del Ecuador SA, Guayaquil, used a single DC-3 HC-ATG for a time, but nothing is known of it.

AREA - Aerovias Ecuatorianas, Quito, started operations in Feb49 using a variety of types, including four DC-3s.

HC-ACL; HC-SJB; HC-SJE; HC-SJI.

ATESA - Aero Taxis Ecuatorianas SA, Quito, used four DC-3s between 1966 and 1975 on oil rig charter work.

HC-ALD; HC-ATJ; HC-AUC; HC-SJE.

Cia de Aviación Aero Amazonas operated DC-3 HC-ANJ between Nov67 and Nov71, when it crashed.

Líneas Aérea Condor bought DC-3 HC-ALD in 1979.

SAETA - Sociedad Ecuatoriana de Transportes Aéreos, Quito, was formed in 1967 with three DC-3s, operating domestic services. Viscounts supplemented them in 1970.

HC-APT; HC-AVQ; HC-AXP.

SAN - Servicios Aéreos Nacionales, Guayaquil, used two DC-3s to start services in 1964. These remained in use until 1977/78.

HC-ALD; HC-SJI.

SANTA - Servicio Aéreos Nacionales de Territoriales Andes, operated DC-3s HC-SMB and HC-SMC on domestic services in 1949 and 1950. HC-SMA may also have been another SANTA example.

Taxi Aéreo Opita used DC-3 HC-ALC between October 1965 and 1971.

TAME - Transportes Aéreos Militar Ecuador, Quito. TAME was set up as a branch of the Air Force to operate commercially uneconomic domestic services. DC-3s were used at first, but all were replaced by Electras and HS.748s. All the aircraft were flown with civil registration marks and their c/ns on the fin.

HC-AUP to HC-AUT incl; HC-AUV; HC-AUX; HC-AUY; HC-AUZ; HC-AVC; HC-AVD.

Transportes Aéreos Orientales, Quito, started operations in May 1948, using UC-64s and Ju52/3ms, but these gave way to DC-3s in 1965 and the last of these was sold in November 1973.

HC-AFQ; HC-ALC; HC-ALK; HC-AMT.

Index:-

HC-ACL	c/n 19779	HC-AUY	11747
HC-AFQ	34272	HC-AUZ	4341
HC-ALC	19871	HC-AVC	11825
HC-ALD	19046	HC-AVD	11775
HC-ALK	27222	HC-AVQ	12299
HC-AMT	26183	HC-AXP	26725
HC-ANJ	20719	HC-AYB	
HC-AOP	4082	HC-BOT	9831
HC-APT	26882	HC-BQZ	2216
HC-ATG		HC-SBR	12374
HC-ATJ		HC-SBS	25272
HC-AUC		HC-SGF	4425
HC-AUP	27046	HC-SGG	9980
HC-AUQ	32780	HC-SJB	12374
HC-AUR	20143	HC-SJE	4425
HC-AUS	27050	HC-SJI	34394
HC-AUT	33496	HC-SMA	4202 ?
HC-AUV	1969	HC-SMB	1549
HC-AUX	20179	HC-SMC	4682

Notes:-
HC-AUC of ATESA was written off on 02May74.
HC-AYB was owned by SARCO, an otherwise unknown operator. Noted Apr75, Canx.

EGYPT - SU

Little is known about DC-3s used in Egypt during the fifties, but Misrair appears to have operated a number, probably jointly with the Air Force as some carried dual markings in the same manner as more recent An-12s and C-130s.

International Air Cargo, Cairo, leased DC-3 SU-AZI from Intra Airways during 1976/77.

Misrair SAE, Cairo. Misrair was formed from Misr Airwork in May 1949 and the first DC-3s were used from 1957 onwards. In the following year the airline became **United Arab Airlines** and was merged with Syrian Airways in 1960, taking over their DC-3s. So far as is known, most other DC-3s were used jointly with the Air Force.

SU-AJG; SU-AJM; SU-AJW; SU-AJX; SU-AKZ; SU-ALP; SU-ALR to SU-ALT incl.

Nile Delta Air Services, Cairo, leased several DC-3s in 1976 pending delivery of two from Belgium. One unknown example crashed in the sea off Alexandria on 05Nov78. Operations ceased about 1987.

SU-AZE; SU-AZF; SU-AZM to SU-AZP incl.

Pyramid Airlines, Heliopolis, Cairo, used chartered DC-3s from June 1977 on non-scheduled services. Many of these had been leased in Malta from a US registered company. Operations ceased in the mid-eighties.

N330; N565; N893; N894; N920/SU-BFY; N925; N169AP; N219F; N480F; N486F; N535M; N3455/SU-BFZ; N3161Q; N3176Q; N3177Q; N3178Q; SU-AZP.

Index:-

SU-AHN	c/n	SU-ALP	26107
SU-AHO	26882	SU-ALR	
SU-AHP		SU-ALS	33559
SU-AHR		SU-ALT	25669
SU-AHS		SU-AMM	34216
SU-AHT		SU-AZE	
SU-AHU		SU-AZF	32716
SU-AHV		SU-AZI	13468
SU-AJG		SU-AZM	25851
SU-AJJ		SU-AZN	32664
SU-AJM		SU-AZO	25756
SU-AJW		SU-AZP	
SU-AJX		SU-BFY	19754
SU-AKZ		SU-BFZ	33379

Notes:-
SU-AHN/HO/HR/HS to USA 1951. SU-AHP/HT/HU/HV to Egyptian AF.
SU-AJG, regd in Aug 1957, crashed on 15Jan68 at Zifta, Nile Delta, Egypt. It also operated as Egyptian AF 805.
SU-AJM, regd in Aug 1957, crashed on 15May62 nr Cairo. Ex EAF 817.
SU-AJW, regd 1957, was destroyed in June 1965 at Cairo.
SU-AJX, regd 1957, crashed on 12May63 at Ayayda, Cairo.
SU-ALR has been quoted with c/n 10101, ex Syrian Airways. See production list for further comment.

EIRE - See Ireland.

EL SALVADOR - YS

El Salvador forms a small, but important, part of the Central American region and was the last country to give a home to TACA, once widespread throughout the area. No DC-3s are now registered.

Aerolineas El Salvador, San Salvador, used DC-3 YS-34C in 1971, but no longer trades.

Aerovias Latino Americanas SA, San Salvador, had a single DC-3, YS-30, in 1947 but it crashed and operations were taken over by TACA.

TACA de El Salvador, San Salvador, or Transporte Aereos Centro Americanos, operated in various countries, but this branch still survives. It changed its name to TACA International Airlines in March 1960, by which time all DC-3s had long disappeared.

YS-21 to YS-24 incl; YS-31 to YS-39; YS-41; YS-47; YS-58; YS-70.

World Aviation Enterprises Inc, used YS-43C.

Index:

YS-21	c/n 7333	YS-35	13372
YS-22	11724	YS-36	25278
YS-23	11653	YS-37	13449
YS-24	4825	YS-38	12204
YS-26	2210	YS-39	12061
YS-26C	9256	YS-41	43079
YS-30	4461	YS-43C	25449
YS-31	9090	YS-47	4773
YS-32	25481	YS-53C	6061
YS-33	20235	YS-58	13819
YS-34	12062	YS-70	6350
YS-34C	9456		

EQUATORIAL GUINEA - 3C

A single DC-3, believed ex-Medavia and owned by NCA International, made unsuccessful test flights at Malta in March/April 1995 before being re-registered T9-ABC and ending its career in Malta Aviation Museum.

3C-JJN   c/n 32935

ESTONIA - ES

A single DC-3 ES-AKE was registered in Estonia in 2000, an escapee from Zaire (9Q-CUK), whose owner lives in Sweden.

ES-AKE   c/n 33445

ETHIOPIA - ET

Ethiopian Airlines Inc, Addis Ababa, inaugurated services with TWA assistance in April 1946, using DC-3s from surplus stocks. Although all the original fleet was written off, further aircraft have been added from time to time, but by 1992 none remained in use. The markings were changed to a lettered system in 1962.

ET-T-1; ET-T-2/ET-AAP; ET-T-3/ET-AAQ; ET-T-4/ET-AAR; ET-T-5; ET-T-10; ET-T-12; ET-T-14/ET-AAS; ET-T-15/ET-AAT; ET-T-16; ET-T-18; ET-AAO(2); ET-ABE; ET-ABF; ET-ABI; ET-ABQ; ET-ABR; ET-ABX; ET-ABY; ET-ADC; ET-AEJ; ET-AFW; ET-AGG to ET-AGI incl; ET-AGK; ET-AGM; ET-AGO; ET-AGP; ET-AGQ; ET-AGR; ET-AGT to ET-AGX incl.; ET-AHG; ET-AHP; ET-AHQ; ET-AHR; ET-AIA; ET-AIB; ET-AIJ.

RRC - Refugee Relief Commission used DC-3s for the carriage of relief supplies, but this operation has now ceased.

ET-AGV; ET-AGX; ET-AHS; ET-AIJ; ET-AJG; ET-AJH.

Index:-

ET-T-1	c/n 10053	ET-ABR	4297
"ET-T-1"	9628	ET-ABX	4292
ET-T-2	13181	ET-ABY	12205
ET-T-3	20174	ET-ACZ	25606
ET-T-4	9465	ET-ADC	26162
ET-T-5	19416	ET-AEJ	26990
	or 19418 ?	ET-AFW	33429
ET-T-6	26503 ?	ET-AGG	11652
ET-T-8	26498 ?	ET-AGH	9501
ET-T-10	13576	ET-AGI	19006
ET-T-12	20874	ET-AGK	26465
ET-T-14	13454	ET-AGM	20874
ET-T-15	13483	ET-AGO	26732
ET-T-16	13305	ET-AGP	26475
ET-T-17		ET-AGQ	12278
ET-T-18	12926	ET-AGR	11711
ET-T-20	9321	ET-AGT	25288
ET-T-21	9469	ET-AGU	13026
ET-T-22	13556	ET-AGV	12073
ET-T-32	33570 ?		see also 26979
(ET-AAO)(1)	10053	ET-AGW	12981
ET-AAO(2)	12526	ET-AGX	26089
ET-AAP	13181	ET-AHG	25471
ET-AAQ	20174	ET-AHP	12210
ET-AAR	9465	ET-AHQ	4607
ET-AAS	13454	ET-AHR	13311
ET-AAT	13483	ET-AHS	33532
(ET-AAU)	13305	ET-AIA	9628
ET-ABE	32846	ET-AIB	42969
ET-ABF	6069	ET-AIJ	32982
ET-ABI	12000	ET-AJG	13576
ET-ABQ	4325	ET-AJH	19283

FIJI - VQ-F (later DQ)

Fiji Airways, Suva, Fiji, leased DC-3s including VH-EDC from Qantas in March 1965 and also from New Zealand National to replace Herons in 1966. The company name changed to **Air Pacific** 31July71 and the nationality prefix to DQ in Oct71. HS.748s replaced the DC-3s in 1972.

Index:-

VQ-FAH	c/n 34227	VQ/DQ-FBF	27144
VQ-FAI	18923	VQ/DQ-FBJ	32899

FINLAND - OH

Aero Oy - Finnish Airlines / Finnair, Helsinki. Two DC-2s were acquired in March 1941 from Germany, who had taken them over from Czechoslovakia in 1938. They were passed to the Air Force in 1949, when DC-3s, acquired in 1946 by the Finnish Government, had replaced them. Ownership passed to Aero Oy on 14Sep49. The DC-3s, in their turn, were passed on to the Air Force, when replaced by Convairs from 1962 onwards.

DC-2s:- OH-DLA/OH-LDA; OH-DLB/OH-LDB;
DC-3s:- OH-LCA to OH-LCI incl; OH-LCK.

CHAPTER 4: COMMERCIAL OPERATORS OF THE DC-3, C-47, R4D, DAKOTA AND LI-2

KAR-AIR Oy - Karhumaki Airways, Helsinki; formerly **Veljekset Karhumaki Oy**, Halli; operated scheduled services with DC-3s from 1954 onwards. One was used for survey work, but the rest were replaced by Convair 440s in 1957/58, and OH-VKB is now with the Finnish Aviation Museum.

OH-VKA to OH-VKD incl.

Index:-

OH-DLA(DC-2)	c/n 1582	OH-LCI	19560
OH-DLB(DC-2)	1562	(OH-LCJ)	12050
OH-LCA	9799	OH-LCK	12050
OH-LCB	19109	OH-LDA(DC-2)	1582
OH-LCC	25511	OH-LDB(DC-2)	1562
OH-LCD	19309	OH-VKA	4828
OH-LCE	12970	OH-VKB	1975
OH-LCF	25515	OH-VKC	42970
OH-LCG	11750	OH-VKD	4346
OH-LCH	6346		

FORMOSA - See Taiwan

FRANCE - F

French-registered DC-3s have been operated in France and in all French colonial territories throughout the world. Colonial operators are described under the present name for these countries, but the aircraft are indexed under France to avoid confusion. Those aircraft in the F-A... , F-B... and F-G... series were normally home-based or owned by home-based companies. The F-O... series were owned and based overseas with a few exceptions, while the F-OG.. series are based in the West Indies. F-D... covered pre-independence Morocco; F-KH.. Cambodia. Those used in Vietnam (F-VN.. series) are indexed there. When the French Air Force sold its remaining C-47s, many were bought by dealers and received temporary civil marks for delivery - possibly their only civilian flight as they were sold for spares. Some marks were re-issued to other types (see series F-BRGA to F-BRGQ; F-BSGN to F-BSGZ and F-BTDA to F-BTDK). Apart from the occasional DC-3 preserved in airworthy condition, none is now used.

Ste Aéro Cargo, Lyon. Four DC-3s were used on cargo services from Nov47 until Aigle Azur took over in 1955.

F-BEFG; F-BEIV; F-BFGL; F-BFGN.

Aigle Azur, Paris, Nice, Marseille; commenced operations Sep46 as a charter service, then operated scheduled routes in France, the Mediterranean and Africa. It was taken over by UAT 01May55. Aigle Azur Indochine was a subsidiary which merged with Aéro Cargo to become Aigle Azur Extrême Orient - *see entry under Indo-China*.

F-BCYZ; F-BEFA to F-BEFG incl; F-BEFJ; F-BEIA; F-BESS; F-BEST; F-BFGA to F-BFGC incl; F-BFGL; F-BFGN; F-BGXD; F-OABJ; F-OABK; F-OAPB; F-OAPC; F-OAQA.

Air Antilles, Pointe-à-Pitre, Guadeloupe, was formed as Antilles Air Services in 1954 and re-named in 1961. Two DC-3s, registered to J-P Le Cozannet, were used on schedules from 1969 until Mar78.

F-OGDZ; F-OGFJ; plus F-OGFI for spares.

Air Atlantique, Bordeaux, used DC-3 F-BJUT briefly in 1963.

Air Dakota, Dinard, operated F-GIAZ/F-GIDK from 1991 until 1997.

Air Dauphine, Grenoble/Nice, used DC-3 F-BEIY in 1969 and the name was changed to **TAR - Transports Aériens Réunis** in Dec70.

Air France, Orly & Le Bourget, Paris, plus overseas bases. A single DC-2 F-AKHD was leased by Air France from the Government for trials in 1939. Nearly 70 DC-3s were used on services within Europe and in various overseas colonies. Many of the latter aircraft were transferred to the new airlines on independence. In later years DC-3s were used mainly by the CEPM (Centre d'Exploitation Postale Métropolitaln) or "Postale de Nuit" as it was commonly known. This started with Ju52/3ms, but DC-3s took over in 1948 to be replaced by DC-4s and F.27s from 1968. The training section or SFP, Section de Formation des Pilotes, also used DC-3s. A single DC-3 was actually bought before the war for use in South America, where it was sold.

DC-2:- F-AKHD. *DC-3s:-* F-ARQJ; F-BAIE to F-BAIJ incl; F-BAOA to F-BAOE incl; F-BAXA to F-BAXT incl; F-BBBA; F-BBBE; F-BCYA; F-BCYC; F-BCYD; F-BCYE; F-BCYK; F-BCYP to F-BCYV; F-BCYX; F-BEFH; F-BEFI; F-BEFL to F-BEFO; F-BEHC; F-BEHF; F-BEIE; F-BEII; F-BEIK; F-BEIX; F-BEIY; F-BFGE; F-BFGT; F-BFGU; F-BGOU; F-BHKU; F-BHKV; F-BHKX; F-BJRY; F-OART; F-OCOA.

Air Guadeloupe, Pointe-à-Pitre, operated DC-3s F-OGDZ and F-OGFJ of **SATA - Sté Antillaise de Transports Aériens** between 1978 and the early 1980s.

Air Inter, Orly, Paris, leased DC-3s from TAI in 1961 to start internal services. They were soon replaced by other types. Only F-BFGX, F-BGXN and F-BJUT are known.

Air Martinique, Fort de France, was the trading name of **SATAIR - Sté Antillaise de Traitements Aériens**, operating F-OGFJ from 1978 to 1983.

Airnautic GECA, Nice. The last remaining DC-2 in Europe was bought in 1959 and used until 1962 when it was allowed to rot away. Six DC-3s were bought with Aerotec, but leased out and then sold soon after.

DC-2:- F-BJHR; *DC-3s:-* F-BBOS/F-OBDS; F-BEFI; F-BFGM; F-BIID/F-OAID; F-BHQR/F-OAQR; F-OAYM.

S A Air Nolis. This short lived DC-3 operator used the type for charter work between about Apr48 and Mar50, two having been written-off.

F-BEFO; F-BEFQ; F-BEIH; F-BEII.

Air Normandie, Caen. DC-3 F-BEFS was used in Algeria between Jul49 and 1951.

Cie Air Transport, Paris, used four DC-3s for various periods between 1948 and 1962, transferring them to or from Air France, a major shareholder.

F-BEFO; F-BEIK; F-BEIX; F-BEIY.

Bretagne Air Services, Dinard, was formed in Feb76 to operate charter and taxi services. Scheduled flights were started to Guernsey in May of that year, and DC-3s F-BEIG and F-BYCU were used for charter work until about Jul80.

Fretair, Paris, had a fleet of seven DC-3s for cargo charters from Feb70 until most had been sold to Uni-Air between 1973 and 1975. Operations never started.

F-BAIF; F-BCYD; F-BCYT; F-BCYV; F-BCYX; F-BEHF; F-BHKX.

Hemet Exploration used ten DC-3s on aerial survey work in southern Africa and elsewhere, but by 1993 all had been sold.

F-BFGX; F-BJBY; F-BJHC; F-BVJH; F-GEOA; F-GEOB; F-OCKH; F-OCUY; F-ODHB; F-ODQL.

Normandie Air Services, Caen, leased DC-3s F-BCYX and F-BEIG until operations ceased, about 1981.

Rousseau Aviation, Dinard, operated DC-3s from 1963 until about 1975 on scheduled and charter flights. Many others were bought from the Air Force for spares or re-sale with temporary marks F-WSGN to F-WSGZ.

F-BAXH; F-BAXI; F-BAXP; F-BAXR; F-BFGM; F-BHKX; F-BNPT; F-BRGN; F-BTDB; F-BTDF; F-BTDG; F-BTDK.

Sté Aérienne de Transports Alpes Provence, Marseille. DC-3s were operated to North Africa from Apr48 to 1952. **Sté des Transports Aériens Camerounais** was a subsidiary using two DC-3s in 1951/52.

F-BEFH; F-BEFK; F-BEII; F-BEIL; F-BEIM; F-BEIV; F-BEIZ; F-BFGO; F-BFGU.

Sté Les Avions Bleus, Perpignan, was owned by François Moreau and DC-3s were used between about 1949 and May52 on routes to Algiers.

F-BEFF; F-BEIJ; F-BEIL; F-OADR.

Sté Transatlantique Aérienne. DC-3s were used on charters to Africa and Madagascar from Mar48 until Nov52 when the name was changed to **Sté Transafricaine d'Aviation**.

F-BEFL; F-BEIB; F-BEIC; F-BFGD to F-BFGI incl.

Stellair, Toulouse-Blagnac, operated DC-3s F-BEIG; F-BYCU; F-GEOM; F-GESB(ntu). Operations ceased about 1991.

TAI - Cie de Transports Aériens Intercontinentaux, Orly, Paris. Four DC-3s were used in Noumea from 1956 onwards, but later one of these was leased to Air Inter. The remainder were then used by Air Madagascar and sold to them in 1963.

F-BGSE; F-BGSF; F-BGXN; F-BJUT and F-OBCT.

Trans Europe Air, owned DC-3 F-BCYX in 1978, but ceased trading in 1981, and the DC-3 became derelict. It had been intended to use F-BSGV but this was ntu.

Transports Aériens Réunis, Nice, was formed in Dec70 from **Air Dauphine** and the sole DC-3, F-BEIY, remained in use until May71.

Transvalair, Air Charter Express, Caen, started operating two DC-3s, F-GDPP and F-GDXP, in 1984 for overnight cargo work parcels service. They were withdrawn from service by 1989.

Uni-Air, Toulouse-Blagnac, started DC-3 operations in Apr73, when aircraft were bought from Fretair for passenger and charter work. The last was sold in 1979, as F.27s were bought as replacements.

F-BAIF; F-BAXR; F-BCYD; F-BCYT; F-BCYV; F-BCYX; F-BEHF.

UAT - Union Aéromaritime de Transport, Le Bourget, Paris, bought DC-3s initially in 1952 but sold them to Autrex in 1954, when Herons replaced them. Aigle Azur was taken over on 01May55. A final aircraft was bought from Airnautic in 1964 but sold soon after, by which time UAT had merged with TAI.

F-BEFF; F-BEFI; F-BEFS; F-BEIL. F-BFGA was leased.

Vargas Aviation, St Brieuc. Three DC-3s were bought for charter work from November 1970 onwards, one surviving until May 1973.

F-BCYT; F-BCYV; F-BHKX.

Index:-

F-AKHD(DC-2)	c/n 1333
F-ARQJ	2122
F-AZTE	9172
F-BAIE	26925
F-BAIF	33119
F-BAIG	25549
F-BAIH	25548
F-BAII	25550
F-BAIJ	25547
F-BAOA	11708
F-BAOB	11714
F-BAOC	11717
F-BAOD	11720
F-BAOE	11769
F-BAXA	42970
F-BAXB	42971
F-BAXC	42972
F-BAXD	42975
F-BAXE	25250
F-BAXF	13139
F-BAXG	13142
F-BAXH	25243
F-BAXI	13677
F-BAXJ	13173
F-BAXK	20012
F-BAXL	20047
F-BAXM	20245
F-BAXN	19420
F-BAXO	20488
F-BAXP	19799
F-BAXQ	25251
F-BAXR	20100
F-BAXS	13138
F-BAXT	9274
F-BAXV	12380
F-BAXX	12255
F-BAXY	32848
F-BAXZ	33226
F-BBBA	6207
F-BBBE	6212
"F-BBBE"	9172
F-BBOS	25875
F-BCBB	4463
F-BCCL	4464
F-BCYA	13256
F-BCYB	12832
F-BCYC	19071
F-BCYD	19075
F-BCYE	20301
F-BCYF	25252
F-BCYG	12526
F-BCYH	4376
F-BCYI	4502?
F-BCYJ	4572
F-BCYK	4509
F-BCYL	6112
F-BCYM	33207
F-BCYN	25916
F-BCYO	12101
F-BCYP	9158
F-BCYQ	19328
F-BCYR	4495
F-BCYS	9894
F-BCYT	4398
F-BCYU	10151
F-BCYV	10141
F-BCYX	10144
F-BCYY	13460
F-BCYZ	7362
F-BEFA	10073
F-BEFB	12251
F-BEFC	9339
F-BEFD	13657
"F-BEFD"	9172
F-BEFE	12685
F-BEFF	6055
F-BEFG	19105
F-BEFH	4635
F-BEFI	9463
F-BEFJ	13368
F-BEFK	19471
F-BEFL	19104
F-BEFM	13467
F-BEFN	12892
F-BEFO	26042
F-BEFP	26058
F-BEFQ	25807
F-BEFS	12416
F-BEFT	32831
F-BEHC	13472
F-BEHF	12489
F-BEIA	19211
F-BEIB	26561
F-BEIC	27210
F-BEID	19405
F-BEIE	25848
F-BEIF	20865
F-BEIG	10253
F-BEIH	26857
F-BEII	12761
F-BEIJ	32554
F-BEIK	25856
F-BEIL	19362
F-BEIM	32822
F-BEIN	32831
F-BEIO	26260
F-BEIP	4517
F-BEIQ	12099
F-BEIR	26888
F-BEIS	11746
F-BEIT	26355
F-BEIU	25875
F-BEIV	19870
F-BEIX	4505
F-BEIY	4775
F-BEIZ	32733
F-BESS	19498
F-BEST	19100
F-BFGA	9336
F-BFGB	11819
F-BFGC	33253
F-BFGD	10046
F-BFGE	12939
F-BFGF	13440
F-BFGG	19387
F-BFGH	19561
F-BFGI	13652
(F-BFGJ)	25874
(F-BFGK)	19592
F-BFGL	13824
F-BFGM	19865
F-BFGN	9785
F-BFGO	26107
F-BFGT	9978
F-BFGU	12333
F-BFGV	11700
F-BFGX	11722
F-BGOU	25606
F-BGSE	4097
F-BGSF	13368
F-BGSM	27108
F-BGXD	13312
F-BGXN	11706
F-BHKU	25457
F-BHKV	20001
F-BHKX	11995
F-BHQR	9511
F-BIEE	26042
F-BIID	12422
F-BJBY	7390
F-BJHC	25756
F-BJHR(DC-2)	1332
F-BJRY	12255
F-BJUT	4387
(F-BLOZ)	13142
(F-BNFB)	19074
F-BNPT	25459
F-BRAM	9644
F-BRAN	33401
(F-BRGA)	9931
(F-BRGB)	9172
(F-BRGC)	9336
(F-BRGD)	32831
(F-BRGE)	19006
(F-BRGF)	4541
(F-BRGG)	9501
(F-BRGH)	"9516" ?
(F-BRGI)	11746
(F-BRGJ)	27140
(F-BRGK)	12730
(F-BRGL)	19343
(F-BRGM)	12704
(F-BRGN)	9172
F-BRGO	9336
(F-BRGP)	19006
F-BRGQ	9501
F-BRQG	26743
F-BSGV	32820
F-BTDA	26743
F-BTDB	10028
F-BTDC(1)	
F-BTDC(2)	19006
F-BTDD	25460
F-BTDE	25546
F-BTDF(1)	19539
F-BTDF(2)	9501
F-BTDG	20875
F-BTDH	26984
F-BTDI	26721
F-BTDJ	19006
F-BTDK	4608
F-BVJH	9366
F-BYCU	12720
F-DAAZ	7376
F-GBOL	13590
F-GDPP	9172
F-GDXP	32561
F-GEFU	19074
F-GEFY	25281
F-GEFX	6207
F-GEOA	32752
F-GEOB	33058
F-GEOM	9798
(F-GEOV)	33433
F-GESB	13835
F-GIAZ	33352
F-GIDK	33352
F-GILV	32935
F-GNFD	32561
F-KHAA	12498
(F-KHAB)	20571
F-OABJ	25874
F-OABK	19592
F-OABV	7376
F-OABX	19634
F-OACA	6241
(F-OADA)	26107
F-OADR	20562
F-OAEL	19795
F-OAFP	20000
F-OAFQ	26100
F-OAFR	26728
F-OAFS	25281
F-OAGZ	12358
F-OAHY	12793
F-OAIC	11705
F-OAID	12422
F-OAIE	11726
F-OAIF	11711
F-OAIG	12489
F-OAIU	19785
F-OAMU	19252
F-OANH	6172
F-OANI	25427
F-OAOE	12017
F-OAOR	11979
F-OAPA	13472
F-OAPB	32761
F-OAPC	4969
F-OAPD	20571
F-OAPH	12090
F-OAPP	33564
F-OAQA	33174
F-OAQC	32631
F-OAQD	27114
F-OAQE	12498
F-OAQJ	12075
F-OAQR	9511

CHAPTER 4: COMMERCIAL OPERATORS OF THE DC-3, C-47, R4D, DAKOTA AND LI-2

F-OART	4479	(F-ODQE)	9172
F-OASQ	20001	F-ODQL	32935
F-OASR	11995	F-OGDI	
F-OAVR	25965 ?	F-OGDZ	33282
F-OAYM	20777	(F-OGFI)	26455
F-OAYR	12813	F-OGFJ	6055
F-OBCT	20874	F-WSGN	19499
F-OBDS	25875	F-WSGO	19538
F-OBZI	12720	F-WSGP	33564
F-OBZR	26828	F-WSGQ	9264
F-OCEN	20175	F-WSGR	20877
F-OCKH	9336	F-WSGS	4583
F-OCKT	4495	F-WSGT	9464
F-OCKU	25810	F-WSGU	26865
F-OCKV	26719	F-WSGV	19286
F-OCKX	27215	F-WSGX	25567
F-OCOA	11717	F-WSGY	9371
F-OCRR	25606	F-WSGZ	25880
F-OCUY	7390	F-WZIG	25347
(F-ODEL)	26729	F-WZII	25571
F-ODHB	25756	F-WZIR	25368

See also Operators under Indo-China.

GABON - TR

SOACO - Sté Anon. de Constructions, Libreville. Two DC-3s, TR-LKN and TR-LVZ, were used on charter work. Neither survived beyond the mid-eighties.

Transgabon - Transports Aériens du Gabon, Libreville. DC-3s were operated on scheduled services between 1965 and 1975, by which time the name Air Gabon had been adopted, and newer aircraft purchased.

TR-LKL to TR-LKN incl; TR-LML. TN-AAB was leased

Index:-

		TR-LKN	25549
TR-LKL	c/n 26042	TR-LML	12422
TR-LKM	4505	TR-LVZ	9511

GERMANY - D

Germany's first Douglas twin was a DC-2 bought by Lufthansa from Fokker in 1936. This was followed by DC-2s and DC-3s taken over from Czech airlines in 1938 and from KLM in 1940, when much of the KLM fleet was captured at Schiphol. At least one of the latter DC-3s was recovered post-war and one of the DC-2s that was sold to Finland is believed to be stored there. Post-war several DC-3s were acquired by more conventional means but none of the type now remains in use in Germany, though several are on display in various locations.

Bavaria Fluggesellschaft, Munich, bought three DC-3s from Lufthansa in 1960, to operate the latter's cargo services. They were traded in for BAC One-Elevens in March 1967.

D-CADE; D-CADO; D-CORA.

Deutsche Lufthansa AG, Berlin/Cologne. DC-2 D-ABEQ was bought in 1936 and used on trial flights for a year, when it was sold to Poland. Three DC-2s were taken from CLS in 1938 and used until 1941, when the surviving pair went to Finland. A further six captured DC-2s were flown during the war, but none survived. Four ex CLS DC-3s were also taken in 1938 and six more came from KLM in 1940, and all were used during the war years by Lufthansa and the Luftwaffe at various times. At least one was used by the Luftwaffe for special duties with KG.200. When flying restarted in 1956 a further three DC-3s were bought for cargo work, but two were sold to Bavaria Flug in 1960. PH-MAA was leased in 1963 for two months.

DC-2s:- D-AAIB; D-AAID; D-AAIO; D-ABEQ; D-ABOW; D-ADBK; D-AEAN; D-AIAS; D-AIAV; D-AJAW.
DC-3s:- D-ABBF; D-AAIE; D-AAIF; D-AAIG; D-AAIH; D-ABUG; D-AOFS; D-ARPF; D-ATJG; D-ATZP; D-CADE; D-CADI; D-CADO.

Deutsche Lufttransport Gesellschaft mbH, bought DC-3 D-CABA in Aug55 with backing from Haniel & Co and Skyways. Operations ceased in 1956.

Nordseeflug Sylter Lufttransport, Hamburg, started operations using DC-3 D-CNSF in Aug66, but it was sold to Airwork Services in May68.

Index:-

D-AAIB(DC-2)	c/n 1582	D-ATZP	2093
D-AAID(DC-2)	1565	D-CABA	13173
D-AAIE	2023	D-CABE	25667
D-AAIF	2024	D-CABI	1972
D-AAIG	2095	D-CABU	ntu
D-AAIH	1973	D-CADE	27108
D-AAIO(DC-2)	1562	"D-CADE"	25450
D-ABBF	2110	D-CADI	19795
D-ABEQ(DC-2)	1318	D-CADO	25427
D-ABOW(DC-2)	1365	D-CAFA	6043
D-ABUG	1935	(D-CAFE)	43087
D-ADBK(DC-2)	1355	D-CCCC	7353
D-AEAN(DC-2)	1363	(D-CDRY)	12679
D-AIAS(DC-2)	1364	D-CDST	32935
D-AIAV(DC-2)	1366	D-CNSF	26977
D-AJAW(DC-2)	1356	D-COLA	ntu
D-AOFS	2036	D-CORA	32867
D-ARPF	1943	"D-CORA"	25450
D-ATJG	2142	D-CXXX	32872

Note: Hamburger Luftreederei (Hr.Ermer) applied for registrations D-CABU and D-COLA for DC-3s to be acquired from the USA. Marks were reserved 29Mar57 with no identities quoted and cancelled 10Mar58 as not imported. See also D-CABI, D-CAFA histories.

GHANA - 9G

Ghana Airways Ltd, Accra, was formed in Jul58 to take over the Ghana portion of WAAC, with help from BOAC. Four DC-3s were bought in Feb59 and used until replaced by HS.748s in about 1970.

Index:-

9G-AAC	c/n 33609	9G-AAE	12054
9G-AAD	12199	9G-AAF	9407

GREECE - SX

Hellenic Air Transport Co Ltd, Athens (Aeroporike Metaphore Hellados). This company was formed in 1948 with DC-3 SX-BAM, to operate charter flights. It survived a gale in Dec50 which destroyed their only other aircraft, and in Jul51 they merged with Hellenic Airlines and TAE to form National Greek Airlines.

Hellenic Airlines SA, Athens, was formed in association with Scottish Airlines, but was merged with National Greek in Jul51.

SX-BBA to SX-BBF incl.

National Greek Airlines, Athens, resulted from the amalgamation of Hellenic Air Transport, Hellenic Airlines and TAE in July 1951. It was taken over by the government on 11Jul55, following financial trouble, and became **Olympic Airways** on 05Apr57.

SX-BAA to SX-BAH incl; SX-BAK to SX-BAN incl; SX-BBA to SX-BBF incl.

Olympic Airways SA, Athens, took over the assets of National Greek on 06 Apr57. The remaining DC-3s were operated until replaced by DC-6Bs on 01May70, when they were sold, transferred to the Air Force or scrapped.

SX-BAA to SX-BAH; SX-BAK; SX-BAL; SX-BAN; SX-BBA; SX-BBC to SX-BBF incl.

Technical & Aeronautical Exploitation Co Ltd, Athens, known as **TAE**, was reformed in 1946 with help from TWA. It merged with Hellenic in July 1951 to form National Greek Airlines.

SX-BAA to SX-BAI incl; SX-BAK to SX-BAN incl.

Index:-

SX-BAA	c/n 12677	SX-BAH	26565
SX-BAB	18981	SX-BAI	12162
SX-BAC	19274	SX-BAK	26095
SX-BAD	9491	SX-BAL	25923
SX-BAE	12351	SX-BAM	20184
SX-BAF	12322	SX-BAN	9187
SX-BAG	26880	SX-BBA	12373

SX-BBB	12332	SX-BBF	4860
SX-BBC	12304	SX-ECD	"92632"
SX-BBD	13012		see 26242
SX-BBE	26459	SX-ECF	33206

Notes:-
SX-ECD and SX-ECF were Government-owned. 'ECD is quoted as 92632, being delivered on 15Dec58. It is derelict at Athens-Hellenikon.

GUATEMALA - LG and TG

Three DC-2 and DC-3 operators in Guatemala are known, but none now includes the DC-3 in their fleet. LG- was used as the nationality mark until Oct48, when TG- was adopted and aircraft current at the time repainted.

Aero Express, Guatemala City, used four DC-3s for charter work from Jun74 onwards. Operations probably ceased around 1990.

TG-BAC; TG-CAH; TG-GER; TG-PAW.

AVIATECA - Aerolíneas de Guatemala Aviateca, Guatemala City, was formed in 1945 by the government as Cia Guatemalteca de Aviacion to take over Aerovias de Guatemala who owned two DC-2s. The airline traded as Empresa Guatemalteca de Aviacion SA until mid-1974 when the present name was adopted. The first DC-3s were bought in Jan46 being shared with the Air Force, but the DC-2s were only sold in 1952. In all, twelve DC-3s have been used, the last three being bought as recently as 1979. DC-3s have not been used since 1987.

DC-2s: LG-ABA; LG/TG-ACA. *DC-3s:* LG/TG-AGA, LG/TG-AHA; LG/TG-AJA; LG/TG-AKA; LG/TG-AMA; LG/TG-ANA; LG/TG-APA; TG-AFA, TG-AMA, TG-ASA; TG-ATA; TG-AXA.

TAPSA - Transportes Aéreos Profesionales SA, Guatemala City, used DC-3 TG-SAB briefly on scheduled services to Puerto Barrios. It was registered in Feb79 and crashed on 07May79. Reported repaired at Guatemala City and w/o in forced landing at Bay City, TX 16Jan83 in an attempted drug drop.

Index:-

LG-ABA(DC-2)	c/n 1599	TG-BAC	25775
LG/TG-ACA(DC-2)	1368	TG-CAH	4477
TG-AFA	12255	"TG-CHP"	11741 ?
LG/TG-AGA	6142	TG-O-CNA	19495
LG/TG-AHA	6052	TG-GAC	
LG/TG-AJA	11874	TG-GER	4258
LG/TG-AKA	13327	TG-LAM	26063
LG/TG-AMA	13484	TG-PAW	10127
TG-AMA(2)	12435	TG-SAA	13854
LG/TG-ANA	12371	TG-SAB	
LG/TG-APA	19454	TG-SAL	
TG-ASA	4369	TG-TAG	2250
TG-ATA		TG-WIZ	26590
TG-AXA	6053		

Notes:-
TG-ATA lay derelict at La Aurora Apt, Guatemala, following a crash on 26Jul78 in a swamp near Flores.
TG-GAC and TG-SAL have no owner or c/n details quoted. Neither is in use.
TG-TAG was used by Transportes Aéreos Gautemalticos.
"TG-CHP" was an intercepted drug runner 14Sep03.

GUINÉ - BISSAU (Portuguese Guinea) CR-G and J5

Linhas Aéreas da Guiné Bissau, Bissau, originated in Transportes Aéreos da Guiné Portuguesa which bought a DC-3 shortly before the airline was reformed on independence. Seven DC-3s are believed to have been owned, but some may have been used only for spares. Several came from the Portuguese Air Force, but their origins are obscure. The last three were delivered in Aug78, with ex-French c/n 4398 following in 1979. All were withdrawn from service by about 1991, by which time the airline had become **Transportes Aereos da Guinee-Bissau**.

Index:-

CR-GBL	c/n 25606	CR-GBQ	
CR-GBM		CR-GBR	
CR-GBN		CR-GBS	25475
CR-GBO		J5-GAR	
CR-GBP		J5-GAX	

Note:- The aircraft which came from the Portuguese Air Force are believed to include c/ns 11765, 20587, 25522, 26144, 32675 and 33093.

GUINEA - 3X

Formerly French Guinea until independence in 1958. **Air Guinée** owned DC-3 3X-GAD, derelict at Conakry in 1977.

3X-GAD   c/n   ?

GUYANA (British Guiana) - VP-G and 8R

Guyana Airways, Georgetown, was formed before WW2 by American interests, and bought DC-3s in late 1946. They operated in US markings until Dec50 when Guyanan VP-G marks were applied. All the original aircraft survived to pass into Guyana Airways' fleet in 1963, when the country gained independence. The last two were sold in 1979.

Index:-

VP/8R-GAF	c/n 19759	VP/8R-GAS	19691
VP/8R-GAG	19603		(rebuild of VP-GAH)
(VP-GAH)	19691	VP/8R-GCF	33196

HAITI - HH

Airlines operating originally in Haiti were part of the Air Force, with serial numbers that formed part of the c/n or USAF serial number. None of these passed into civil use, presumably remaining with the Air Force.

COHATA - Cie Haitienne de Transports Aériens, Port au Prince, used three DC-3s on domestic services between 1945 and 1974 when the Air Force operations were taken over by Haiti Air Inter.

"3681" c/n 13681; "4262" c/n 4262; "5878" c/n 34137.

Haiti Air Inter, Port au Prince, was formed in 1974 to take over COHATA's operations, but not its aircraft. It used two DC-3s, HH-CND and HH-CNE from the late 70s to the early 80s, but these were bought from Haiti Air Transport, if known dates are accepted.

Haiti Air Transport, Port au Prince, had two DC-3s, HH-CN2 and HH-CN3, which some reports suggest went to Air Inter, and others that they came from that airline.

Haiti Overseas Airways, Port au Prince, used DC-3 HH-GP1 during 1973/74.

Perle Air operated HH-PRD, but ceased operations in Feb86. HH-PRD appears to have been re-registered HH-EBA

Pipirite Air, Port au Prince, operated DC-3 HH-ABA in 1981 and this was stored at Port au Prince by Feb96.

Index:-

HH-ABA	c/n 25888	HH-EBA	26441 ?
HH-CMG	12254	HH-GP1	1964
HH-CND/		HH-PRD	26441 ?
HH-CN2	20865	HH-1233	
HH-CNE/		HH-1294	
HH-CN3	11700		

Notes: HH-1233 and 1294 were noted at Middleton Apt, DE, ex Haiti AF.

HONDURAS - XH and HR

Honduras, in the middle of the Central American chain, formed one of the many bases for the pre-war TACA empire that survived until 1948. Three other airlines, all DC-3 operators, followed, and one still used the type in 2001. The nationality mark changed from XH- to HR- in Feb61.

ANHSA - Aerovías Nacionales de Honduras SA, Tegucigalpa, was formed in 1950, with three DC-3s, to operate scheduled services. Stock was bought out by SAHSA in Nov57 but separate operations continued until about 1999.

XH/HR-ANA; XH/HR-ANB; XH-ANC; HR-AND; HR-SAH.

LANSA - Líneas Aéreas Nacionales SA, La Ceiba, started scheduled services in 1967 with four DC-3s. Others were bought later and three were believed still to be in use in 1982.

HR-LAD to HR-LAH; HR-LAK; HR-LAL; HR-LAQ.

SAHSA - Servicio Aéreo de Honduras SA, Tegucigalpa, started operations in Oct45 with help from Pan American. DC-3s were used from 1950 onwards, some remaining in service in 1982. In 1953 the stock of TACA de Honduras was bought out and in 1957 a share was obtained in ANHSA.

XH-ANB; XH-SAA; XH/HR-SAB; XH/HR-SAC; XH/HR-SAD; XH/HR-SAE; XH-SAF; XH-SAG; XH/HR-SAH/HR-ATH; XH/HR-SAI; HR-SAZ; HR-SHC.

SETCO, Tegucigalpa, operated a semi-scheduled passenger service with DC-3s HR-AJY and HR-ALU, reported withdrawn by 1999.

TACA de Honduras, Tegucigalpa, used DC-3s to replace the Lockheed 14 which started services in 1944. About 10 DC-3s were probably used, but only six have come to light. [*Note*: Further TACA group entries will be found under Colombia, Costa Rica, El Salvador and Venezuela]

XH-TAB; XH-TAE; XH-TAF; XH-TAG; XH-TAR; XH-TAZ.

Index:-

XH-ANA	c/n 13301	HR-ALU	
XH-ANB	9146	HR-AMJ	32761
XH-ANC	"33567"	HR-ANA	13301
XH-AND		HR-ANB	9146
XH-SAA	19667	HR-AQI	2216
XH-SAB	4299	HR-ATH	6102
XH-SAC	4232	HR-CNA	19495
XH-SAD(1)	7317	HR-LAD	19999
XH-SAD(2)	4477	HR-LAE	9885
XH-SAE	9090	HR-LAF	
XH-SAF	34406	HR-LAG	12450
XH-SAG	25245	HR-LAH	12412
XH-SAH	6102	HR-LAK	9140
XH-SAI	"33567"	HR-LAL	32761
XH-TAB	43078	HR-LAQ	12450
XH-TAE	9090	HR-SAB	4299
XH-TAF	34406	HR-SAC	4232
XH-TAG	25245	HR-SAD	4477
XH-TAR		HR-SAE	9090
XH-TAZ	19046	HR-SAH	6102
XH-T001	13301	HR-SAI	"33567"
XH-T002	9146	HR-SAZ	19495
HR-AIF	11696	HR-SHC	19513
HR-AJY	6068	HR-291	4258

Notes:-
XH-ANC - the c/n is as given officially, but see production list.
XH-TAR is believed to have crashed on 08Sep53.
HR-AIJ noted at Opa Locka on 04Oct80.
HR-ALU - first noted Sep92.
HR-AMJ noted wfu at Tamiami Jul94.
HR-AQI was operated by Caribbean Air.
HR-LAF is believed to have been allotted to a DC-3, but nothing further is known.

HONG KONG - VR-H

Two airlines operated DC-3s from Hong Kong in the fifties. Others were used by various dealers for resale in the area.

Cathay Pacific Airways Ltd, Hong Kong, was founded in 1946 to operate to Manila. DC-3s were replaced by DC-4s in the mid-fifties. VR-HDB returned to Hong Kong in 1983, for preservation.

VR-HDA; VR-HDB; VR-HDG; VR-HDI; VR-HDJ; VR-HDW; VR-HEN.

Hong Kong Airways Ltd, Hong Kong, started operations in December 1947 as a subsidiary of BOAC. DC-3s were replaced by Viscounts in 1957.

VR-HDN to VR-HDQ incl.

Index:-

VR-HDA	c/n 32991	VR-HDQ	9863
"VR-HDA"	9525	VR-HDW	25430
VR-HDB	4423	VR-HEC	26903
VR-HDG	20576	VR-HEN	12793
VR-HDI	19904	VR-HEP	32530
VR-HDJ	20763	VR-HES	11780
VR-HDN	12019	VR-HET	19895
(VR-HDO)(1)	9408	VR-HEX	19932
VR-HDO(2)	11907	VR-HFE	33200
VR-HDP	11921	VR-HFR	20794

HUNGARY - HA

While, with the exception of HA-TSA, no DC-3s are known to have been used in Hungary, Russia supplied a number of Li-2s for use by Maszovlet when the war ended. Further aircraft were sold to MALEV when that was formed from the former airline in 1955. HA-LIX was restored to airworthiness in 2002.

MALÉV - Magyar Légiköziekedési Válialat, Budapest, was formed on 25 November 1954 and inherited nine Li-2s from Maszovlet when Soviet participation came to an end. Many were withdrawn in 1964, by which time the Il-14 had replaced them on international routes.

HA-LIA to HA-LII; HA-LIK to HA-LIZ incl; HA-TSA.

MASZOVLET - Magyar-Szovjet Polgári Légiformgalmi Társaság, Budapest, was formed in October 1946 with technical and financial help from Russia. Operations started in December 1947 with 11 Li-2s. The airline became MALEV in 1954 when Russian assistance ceased.

HA-LIA to HA-LII incl; HA-LIK; HA-LIL.

Index:-

Complete details of Li-2s are given in Volume 2.

HA-LIA	c/n 184 235 03	HA-LIO	184 395 05
HA-LIB	184 235 06	HA-LIP	184 395 04
HA-LIC	184 235 07	HA-LIQ	234 412 06
HA-LID	184 235 08	HA-LIR	234 413 03
HA-LIE	184 235 10	HA-LIS	234 413 01
HA-LIF	184 256 04	HA-LIT	184 359 01
HA-LIG	184 266 01	HA-LIU	184 393 06
HA-LIH	184 270 05	HA-LIV	184 393 10
HA-LII	184 270 06	HA-LIW	184 393 07
HA-LIK	184 275 01	HA-LIX	184 332 09
HA-LIL	184 280 03	HA-LIY	184 332 03
HA-LIM	234 410 07	HA-LIZ	234 412 07
HA-LIN	234 428 03	HA-TSA	20492

ICELAND - TF

Although four airlines have used DC-3s within Iceland, only Icelandair used any number. Only one remains to-day, occasionally used for top dressing and appropriately registered TF-NPK. Another is stored for preservation.

Flugfélag Islands hf - Icelandair, Reykjavík, bought six DC-3s to operate internal scheduled services between August 1946 and June 1954. A further two were leased from Britain in 1963/64. The last was sold in 1975.

TF-FIO; TF-FIS; TF-ISA; TF-ISB; TF-ISD; TF-ISG to TF-ISI incl.

Flugfélag Norðurlands sf, Akureyri, leased DC-3 TF-ISB from Flugfélag Islands in 1975.

Flugsyn, Akureyri, used DC-3s TF-AIO, TF-AIV and TF-VON to operate scheduled services from the summer of 1966, but operations ceased in September 1969.

Loftleiðir hf, Reykjavík, used a DC-3, along with other types, to operate internal services from June 1948 until November 1951, when a second was added. They were sold to Iberia in 1952/53 when Flugfélag Islands took over the services.

TF-RVM; TF-RVP.

Index:-

TF-AIO	c/n 33416	TF-ISG	12482
TF-AIV	32872	TF-ISH	13861
TF-AVN	4363	TF-ISI	13389
TF-FIO	26569	TF-NPK	13861
TF-FIS	12000	TF-RVM	13057
TF-ISA	12184	TF-RVP	34280
TF-ISB	9860	"TF-SUO" /"TF-SUN" /	
TF-ISD	4327	TF-VON	26101

INDIA - VT

The DC-3 played a considerable part in post-war Indian aviation, forming the backbone of all the newly formed airlines in 1945/46. Even before this a number of DC-2s were registered, but after a few months in dual markings and Indian National's colours, they passed to 31 Sq RAF. The considerable stocks of surplus DC-3s, both RAF and USAAF, provided a ready supply of aircraft and spares. Various dealers bought up batches and registered them as such, overhauling whenever a customer appeared. It seems likely that some of these had their identities mixed up and others were built up from parts of several aircraft, being given constructors numbers by the overhauling company, so that their origins are impossible to sort out. So far as possible these problem aircraft are discussed at the end of the index. By December 2001, no DC-3s remained airworthy in India, though there are plans to restore VT-AUI to airworthiness in the near future.

Air-India Ltd, Bombay, originated in **Tata Air Lines**, who bought C-47s in some numbers for overhaul and scheduled operation. The new name was adopted on 1 August 1946, and disappeared on nationalisation in August 1953.

VT-ARI; VT-ATI; VT-ATK; VT-ATV; VT-ATY to VT-AUG incl; VT-AUQ; VT-AUR; VT-CCA; VT-CCC; VT-CCD; VT-CFG; VT-CFK; VT-CFL; VT-CFY; VT-CHH; VT-DAT.

Air-India International Ltd, Bombay, used DC-3 VT-CGP for charter work and engine transport.

Air Services of India Ltd, Bombay, resumed scheduled services in May 1946, using the DC-3. These continued until nationalisation in 1953.

VT-AUQ; VT-AUS to VT-AUV incl; VT-AXA to VT-AXD incl; VT-AXF; VT-AYH; VT-COJ; VT-CPQ.

Airways (India) Ltd, Calcutta, was formed in September 1945 and started scheduled services in April 1947 with numerous DC-3s. Non-scheduled services continued after the schedules were taken over in 1953 at nationalisation, until about 1973, but the bulk of the DC-3s went to Indian Air Lines.

VT-AUH to VT-AUJ incl; VT-AVR to VT-AVT incl; VT-AZW; VT-CGG; VT-CGI; VT-CGZ; VT-CHB; VT-CJH; VT-CKU; VT-CMD; VT-CSB; VT-CUZ; VT-CZO; VT-DBA; VT-DDW.

Airworks India Ltd, Bombay, bought DC-3s VT-AUR, VT-AUU, VT-CGA, VT-DFM and VT-DTS for charter work at various times between 1964 and 1981.

Ambica Air Lines Ltd, Bombay, operated DC-3s on scheduled services from January 1947 until February 1949.

VT-AYG; VT-AYH; VT-CGA; VT-CGB; VT-CLE; VT-CXN; VT-CXP.

Bharatair, Delhi, were using DC-3 VT-AUM in 1983.

Bharat Airways Ltd, Calcutta, used DC-3s to start charter operations in January 1947, and scheduled services in the following June. It was nationalised in August 1953.

VT-CGA; VT-CGG; VT-CGL to VT-CGR incl; VT-CLE; VT-CML; VT-CRE; VT-CTZ; VT-DBD; VT-DDK

Dalmia-Jain Airways Ltd, New Delhi, was formed in 1946 for charter and survey work. It bought out Indian National in July 1946 but this continued separate operations until nationalisation, and Dalmia-Jain was liquidated in June 1952.

VT-ARH; VT-ATT; VT-CDY to VT-CEB incl; VT-CEI; VT-CEN; VT-CEO; VT-CYG; VT-CYH.

Darbhanga Aviation, Calcutta, was started by the Maharaja of Darbhanga in March 1950, using DC-3s, probably for charter work. Operations ceased in March 1954 when VT-DEM was lost.

VT-AYG; VT-AZX; VT-CME; VT-DEM.

Deccan Airways Ltd, Begumpet, Hyderabad, used DC-3s to begin non-scheduled operations in April 1946 and schedules in July. It was nationalised in August 1953.

VT-AUM to VT-AUP incl; VT-AUS; VT-AXE; VT-CEN; VT-CEO; VT-CGC; VT-CHF; VT-CJC; VT-CJD; VT-CLR; VT-CNC; VT-CQL; VT-CYH; VT-CYX; VT-DDD.

Himalayan Aviation Ltd, Calcutta, was formed in 1947 for charter and survey work with DC-3s. Night mail flights began in October 1949, but Deccan took these over in June 1951. Most of the aircraft passed to Indian Air Lines in 1953.

VT-AXB; VT-CHE; VT-COZ; VT-CYM; VT-CYN; VT-DAZ; VT-DDR.

Indamer Co (Pvt) Ltd, Bombay, used DC-3s to start charter work in 1947. By 1960/61 the aircraft were leased to Kalinga Airlines.

VT-ARH; VT-AXF; VT-AZU; VT-CGB; VT-CHT; VT-COI; VT-CRA; VT-CXR; VT-CYW; VT-DDR; VT-DDT; VT-DFZ; VT-DGP; VT-DGR; VT-DGS; VT-DGV ; VT-DGX. NC65350 was intended but dbf on delivery.

Indian Airlines Corp, New Delhi, was formed by the nationalisation of all the major Indian airlines in August 1953. By that time airline operation had become highly competitive and non-profitable. Initially operations were run on a 'line' basis, each line being formed from one of the constituent companies, but later the operation was rationalised. The fleet was dominated, at first, by the DC-3, of which about 80 joined the fleet. These were sold off fairly steadily, many going to the Indian Air Force, but some were retained for at least fifteen years, and one remained in 1977 for cargo work. They were replaced mainly by F.27s and HS.748s, but outlasted the Vikings by many years.

VT-ATR; VT-ATT to VT-ATV incl; VT-ATZ to VT-AUB incl; VT-AUE; VT-AUH; VT-AUL; VT-AUM; VT-AUP to VT-AUV incl; VT-AVR to VT-AVT incl; VT-AXA to VT-AXC incl; VT-AYH; VT-AZW to VT-AZY incl; VT-CCC; VT-CCD; VT-CDY; VT-CEA; VT-CEB; VT-CEI; VT-CEN; VT-CEO; VT-CFB; VT-CFG; VT-CGA; VT-CGC; VT-CGG; VT-CGI; VT-CGL; VT-CGN to VT-CGR incl; VT-CGZ; VT-CHE; VT-CHF; VT-CHH; VT-CJC; VT-CJH; VT-CMD; VT-CML; VT-CNC; VT-COJ; VT-COZ; VT-CQL; VT-CSB; VT-CTZ; VT-CUA; VT-CVB; VT-CVC; VT-CYF to VT-CYH incl; VT-CYM; VT-CYN; VT-CYX; VT-DBA; VT-DDD; VT-DDR; VT-DDW; VT-DEV; VT-DFM; VT-DGK; VT-DGN; VT-DGO; VT-DGQ.

Indian National Airlines Ltd, New Delhi, started operating before the war and used a pair of ex-RAF DC-2s between 1942 and 1945. DC-3s were bought at the end of the war and ownership passed to Dalmia Jain, although INA's operating name was retained until nationalisation in August 1953.

DC-2s:- VT-ARA; VT-ARB; *DC-3s:-* VT-ARH; VT-ARI; VT-ATB; VT-ATR to VT-ATU incl; VT-AUL; VT-AUM; VT-AUR; VT-CFB; VT-COH; VT-COK; VT-CVB; VT-CVC; VT-CYG; VT-DGN.

Indian Overseas Airlines Ltd, Bombay, started life as Mistri Airways in September 1946 and the new name was adopted in 1947. DC-3s were used until services ceased in September 1950 and they were sold.

VT-AUH to VT-AUJ incl; VT-AZC; VT-AZU to VT-AZZ incl; VT-CCG; VT-CCH; VT-CTV; VT-CTZ; VT-CUA; VT-CXP; VT-CYW.

Jamair Co (Pvt) Ltd, Calcutta, was formed by private interests in 1948 to run passenger and cargo charters using DC-3s and DC-4s. Two of the former were believed in use until 1981.

VT-ATT; VT-ATZ; VT-AZV; VT-COU; VT-CQL; VT-CTR; VT-CZC; VT-DGO; VT-DTQ.

Jupiter Airways Ltd, Vepery, Madras, operated a route to New Delhi, using DC-3s, from 1948 to March 1949, when operations ceased.

VT-CHA to VT-CHI incl, but VT-CHD and VT-CHE were ntu.

Chapter 4: Commercial Operators of the DC-3, C-47, R4D, Dakota and Li-2

Kalinga Air Lines (Pvt) Ltd, Calcutta, started DC-3 operations in 1947 and continued these until nationalised in 1953. Charter work resumed in 1958, continuing until February 1972 in cooperation with Darbhanga and Jamair who provided some aircraft.

VT-AUQ; VT-AXF; VT-AZU; VT-AZV; VT-AZX; VT-CEI; VT-CGB; VT-CGP; VT-CMD; VT-CNZ; VT-COA; VT-COU; VT-CQL; VT-CRA; VT-CTR; VT-CXR; VT-CYF; VT-CYW; VT-DAY; VT-DAZ; VT-DDR; VT-DDT; VT-DFM; VT-DFN; VT-DFZ; VT-DGK; VT-DGP; VT-DGR; VT-DGS; VT-DGX.

Mistri Airways, Bombay, operated DC-3s VT-AUH to VT-AUJ incl; VT-AZC; before becoming Indian Overseas. See earlier.

Nalanda Airways Ltd, Patna, Bihar, started government-controlled operations in 1948. Four DC-3s are known to have been used, possibly leased.

VT-AUH to VT-AUJ incl; VT-AZY.

Orient Airways Ltd - Calcutta, then Karachi.- See also Pakistan. Formed in 1946, services began in April 1947 with equipment originally registered in India. On partition later that year the fleet was re-registered in Pakistan. Indian registrations, used or intended, were:

VT-CIC; (VT-CIE); VT-CIF to VT-CIH incl; VT-CIJ; (VT-CPA to VT-CPK, VT-CPN).

Safari Airways, Bombay, was formed in 1971 using two ex IAL DC-3s. Scheduled services gave way to charter work, but that ceased by 1981.

VT-CYG; VT-DDD.

Tata Air Lines, Bombay, was another pre-war airline to survive and restart operations. Two DC-2s were operated on loan from the RAF in 1942-44. In October 1945 a fleet of surplus DC-3s was bought. The name was changed to **Air-India Ltd** in August 1946.

DC-2s:- VT-AOQ; VT-AOU. DC-3s:- VT-ATI; VT-ATK; VT-ATV; VT-ATY to VT-AUG incl; VT-CCA to VT-CCD incl; VT-CFG; VT-CFK; VT-CFL.

Index:-

DC-2:
Reg	c/n
VT-AOQ	c/n 1315
VT-AOR	1316
VT-AOS	1244
(VT-AOT)	1402
VT-AOU	1314
VT-AOV	1308
(VT-AOW)	1401
(VT-AOX)	1410
VT-AOY	1251
VT-AOZ	1237
(VT-APA)	1403
VT-APB	1240
VT-ARA	1239
VT-ARB	1313

DC-3:
Reg	c/n	Reg	c/n	Reg	c/n	Reg	c/n
VT-ARH	4851	VT-AUS	20289	VT-CCH	12851	(VT-CPE)	19032
VT-ARI	4118	VT-AUT	13720	VT-CDY	26505	(VT-CPF)	4562
VT-ATB	4116	VT-AUU	13687	VT-CDZ	25867	(VT-CPG)	4356
VT-ATI	4922	VT-AUV	20318		(see note)	(VT-CPH)	12089
VT-ATK	4946	VT-AVR	20311	VT-CEA	32973	(VT-CPI)	12501
VT-ATR	20259	VT-AVS	13696	VT-CEB	26491	(VT-CPJ)	9546
VT-ATS	20359	VT-AVT	13295	VT-CEI	20355	(VT-CPK)	11982
VT-ATT	20363	VT-AXA	19874	VT-CEN	26710	(VT-CPN)	12222
VT-ATU	20358	VT-AXB	20172	VT-CEO	26485	VT-CPQ	13558
VT-ATV	4182	VT-AXC	20303	VT-CFB	13626	VT-CQL	20792
VT-ATY	13714	VT-AXD	13294	VT-CFG	4888	VT-CRA	12505
VT-ATZ	13689	VT-AXE	19160?	VT-CFK	26049	VT-CRE	13081
VT-AUA	13245		(see note)	VT-CFL	20248	VT-CRP	19117
VT-AUB	13278	VT-AXF	13259	VT-CGN	12989	VT-CSB	13290
VT-AUC	18914	VT-AXX	19831	VT-CFY	9767	VT-CTR	9003
VT-AUD	13716	VT-AYG	12848	VT-CGA	25467	VT-CTV	10178
VT-AUE	19519	VT-AYH	19072	VT-CGB	9945	VT-CTZ	13061
VT-AUF	13712	VT-AYK	13298	VT-CGC	12500	VT-CUA	6078
VT-AUG	4175	VT-AZC	4331	VT-CGE	11982	VT-CUZ	13029
VT-AUH	18906	VT-AZU	13232	VT-CGG	12821	VT-CVB	13037
VT-AUI	13231	VT-AZV	13253	VT-CGI	20176	VT-CVC	25471
VT-AUJ	19149	VT-AZW	13684	VT-CGL	10031	VT-CXN	2209
VT-AUL	20265	VT-AZX	13285	VT-CGM	9320	VT-CXP	19275
VT-AUM	18905	VT-AZY	19154	VT-CGO	13542	VT-CXR	11846
VT-AUN	13405	VT-AZZ	4267	VT-CGP	12928	VT-CYF	25842
VT-AUO	13265	VT-CCA	25298	VT-CGQ	13573	VT-CYG	13019
VT-AUP	19151	VT-CCB	25475	VT-CGR	13579	VT-CYH	12493
VT-AUQ	19431	VT-CCC	25299	VT-CGZ	13581	VT-CYM	19317
VT-AUR	13686	VT-CCD	25468	VT-CHA	12915	VT-CYN	19988
		VT-CCG	19851	VT-CHB	13023	VT-CYT	32992
				(VT-CHC)	12320	VT-CYW	4242
				(VT-CHD)	12346	VT-CYX	13543
				VT-CHE	12193	VT-CZC	12103
				VT-CHF	"11810"	VT-CZO	20725
				VT-CHG	25297	VT-DAT	13168
				VT-CHH	13380	VT-DAY	12085
				VT-CHI	13555	VT-DAZ	11916
				VT-CHJ	25274	VT-DBA	13165
					(see note)	VT-DBD	"43-14038"
				VT-CHT	20662		(see note)
				VT-CIC	9543	VT-DBY	33559
				(VT-CIE)	9143	VT-DCM	10230
				VT-CIF	19032	VT-DDD	13584
				VT-CIG	4562	VT-DDK	25483
				VT-CIH	4356	VT-DDR	12070
				VT-CIJ	12089	VT-DDT	20170
				VT-CJC	13025	VT-DDW	9949
				VT-CJD	12826	VT-DEM	13792
				VT-CJH	12477	VT-DET	9689
				VT-CJT	12501	VT-DEU	9952
				VT-CJU	9546	VT-DEV	9950
				VT-CKU	25302	VT-DFM	20269
				VT-CLA	26916	VT-DFN	13628
				VT-CLE	4653	VT-DFZ	4647
				VT-CLR	25475	VT-DGK	"KAL-2"
				VT-CMD	12491	VT-DGN	"INA/D-499"
				VT-CME	20276	VT-DGO	32934
				VT-CML	19868	VT-DGP	9549
				VT-CMZ	25463	VT-DGQ	9072
				VT-CNC	12382	VT-DGR	4457
				VT-CNZ	12163	VT-DGS	4273
				VT-COA	25304	VT-DGT	4275
				VT-COH	13387	VT-DGU	6135
				VT-COI	13137	VT-DGV	18910
					(see note)	VT-DGW	33140
				VT-COJ	10051	VT-DGX	12142
				VT-COK	12095	VT-DLZ	"HAL/5001"
				VT-COU	13570	VT-DTH	10139
				VT-COZ	13569	VT-DTQ	20681
				(VT-CPA)	26423	VT-DTS	20012
				(VT-CPB)	6241	(VT-DTT)?	26056
				(VT-CPC)	9543	VT-DUP	26057
				(VT-CPD)	9143	VT-EEL	13290

Notes:-
VT-AXE - c/n 19160 is quoted, but USAAF records state that this c/n suffered a structural failure on 20Aug44 and was written off.
VT-CDZ - Indian DCA records give KJ8606 which was a corruption of 43-48606 c/n 25867.
VT-CHJ - c/n 19566 has been quoted for this, but known details do not tie up so it would seem that c/n 13829/25274, as given in the Air-Britain SE Asia register, is more likely.

VT-COI - c/n 25482 has been quoted but this was N64794 from 1946 until 1977 with the same owner and is now preserved. C/n 25482 is the corrected c/n for 14037 given in Indian records. C/n 14027 is recorded as going to the Indian government, so is a possible candidate, but 13137 is now preferred.

VT-DBD - Official records give 43-14038 which it had been assumed was an error for 43-15038. However this was salvaged in December 1944, and 43-16038 was salvaged in Europe in 1946, so both seem unlikely candidates. C/n 14038/25483 is possible, being also with Bharat as VT-DDK which may have been a re-registration.

VT-DGK - c/n KAL-2 was registered to Kalinga Airlines in January 1953, having been rebuilt from parts. It was w/o on 19Oct56 at Agartala, but it is not certain if it was with Indian Air Lines at this time.

VT-DGN - c/n INA/D-499 is presumably a rebuild by Indian Airlines, possibly from two damaged aircraft. It was last reported on the April 1978 register.

VT-DGO - c/n is quoted officially as 16166 which would make it 32914. This was in USAF service until it became N710Z and is current, whereas VT-DGO crashed in 1954. One possible candidate is c/n 16186/32934 which is known to have been disposed of by the RAF to FLC on 27Nov47.

VT-DLZ - c/n quoted as HAL/5001, a rebuild by Hindustan Aviation Ltd. It was registered in October 1959 and cancelled on 23Jan60 on transfer to the Indian AF.

INDO-CHINA - F-O ...

Before France gave independence to the various countries which made up Indo-China (Cambodia, Laos and Vietnam), several DC-3 operators were based there. Aircraft were used increasingly on supply missions to areas under attack by the Vietcong based in the north and a number of DC-3s were lost as a result of enemy action. Some owners used aircraft that had been 'home' based, and moved out to help in the emergency. This accounts for the F-B series DC-3s, some of which may never have been to Indo-China, but as their owners operated there they are listed here.

AFRIC - Air France régie indo-chine. The French High Commission in Indo-China used DC-3s F-BCYA, F-BCYB, F-BCYC and F-BCYE which, except for F-BCYB which went to Air Vietnam, were operated in Indo-China from 1947 by Air France. F-BCYP, F-BCYQ and F-BAXB were added later and some were transferred to Air Vietnam 15 October 1951.

Aigle Azur d'Extrême Orient, Hanoi (previously Nice, Marseilles, Le Bourget, Casablanca and Saigon). **Aigle Azur** was formed in September 1946 principally as a charter service with Ju52/3ms but these were replaced by DC-3s in 1947/48. CATI was taken over in January 1950, with four DC-3s, and more were added until 1954. **Aigle Azur Indochine** was formed in October 1949 to continue operations in Indo-China and by 1952 had 12 DC-3s. On 01 May 1955 the scheduled operations in France, the Mediterranean and Africa were taken over by UAT. In November 1955 Aigle Azur Indochine merged with Aéro Cargo to form **Aigle Azur d'Extrême Orient**. Some DC-3s were lost to enemy action. The last was sold to the French Air Force in 1960, when only Stratoliners remained.

F-BCYY; F-BGSM; F-OAPA; F-OAPP; F-OAQC; F-OAQD. In addition F-OAOE was leased from Autrex.

For details of remainder of Aigle Azur fleet operated in Europe and North Africa, see entry under France.

Air Outre-Mer, Hanoi, operated DC-3s between July 1949 and January 1958 under the ownership of Roger Colin (better known as Roger Caratini). He started as Ets Roger Colin in 1948 and then formed **Cie Aérienne de Transports Indochinois (CATI)** in July 1950. Air Outre-Mer was the operating name adopted in 1953 and this was retained when CATI became **CTAC (Cie de Transports Aériens et de Commerce)** in July 1953.

F-BCYG; F-BCYL; F-BEIO; F-OABX; F-OACA; F-OAEL; F-OAFR; F-OAHY; F-OAIF; F-OANH; F-OANI; F-OAOR; F-OAPD; F-OAPH; F-OAQE; F-OAQJ; F-OBDS; F-VNAG; F-VNAH.

CATI - Cie de Transports Indochinois, Hanoi - See Air Outre-Mer.

Cie Autrex, Hanoi, founded January 1948 by Jean Le Breton with an Auster (Auster Extrême-Orient), trading as Autrex; Le Breton, Lopez Loretta et Cie, operated supply flights in Indo-China from January 1952 until 1956. By the end of 1955 nine DC-3s had been sold.

F-BCYI; F-BCYJ; F-BEFF; F-BEFP; F-BEFS; F-BEFT; F-BEIL; F-BEIP; F-BFGE; F-BFGI; F-OAMU; F-OAOE.

CTAC - Cie de Transports Aériens et de Commerce - See Air Outre-Mer.

STAEO - Sté de Transports Aériens en Extrême Orient, Saigon, took over **COSARA** (Comptoir Saïgonnais de Ravitaillement) in 1949. The remaining four DC-3s eventually passed to Air Vietnam in May 1956.

F-BCCL; F-BEIB; F-BEIM; F-BEIT; F-BEIU; F-BFGG.

For cross reference to F-Oxxx and F-VNxx registrations, see under FRANCE and VIETNAM respectively, also Cambodia and Laos.

INDONESIA - (Netherlands East Indies) - PK

Douglas twin-engined transports played a considerable part in opening up airline operations in the Indonesian archipelago. KLM transferred three DC-2s to the Eastern division as early as 1935. These were followed by DC-3s in 1940, but the Japanese invasion in early 1942 resulted in the destruction of some and the remaining DC-2s, DC-3s and DC-5s escaped to Australia, where they were used by the USAAF. One of the DC-3s is preserved there today. With post-war independence, Garuda was formed and used a large number of DC-3s inherited from KLM. In later years, when the left-wing dictatorship fell, greater freedom was given for the formation of independent airlines, and DC-3s were used widely by these. In addition to the companies listed below, a number of oil companies operated DC-3s in Indonesia, including Pertamina, Caltex-Pacific, Shell and Stanvac. Only one DC-3 is believed to remain airworthy.

PT Airfast Indonesia, Djakarta, took over oil support operations in September 1974, having four DC-3s on strength at one time, amongst a wide range of aircraft types. Most of these were taken over by Pelita Air Services. PK-OAZ was the last DC-3 used commercially in Indonesia.

PK-AKR; PK-AKT; PK-OAZ; PK-OBK; PK-SVD/OBJ; N11AF.

PT Air Indonesia, Mendan, intended to use DC-3s PK-IDA, PK-IDB and PK-IDH for air freight and cargo operations in Sumatra but only the last of these went into service, in 1968.

PT Bouraq Indonesia Airlines, Djakarta, used three DC-3s to start scheduled services in 1970. One remained airworthy until 1985.

PK-IBA; PK-IBI; PK-IBS.

PT Dirgantara Air Services, Djakarta, had up to five DC-3s for scheduled services but the last was withdrawn in 1987.

PK-NDG; PK-NDH; PK-NDK; PK-VTM; PK-VTN; PK-VTO.

PN Garuda Indonesia Airways, Djakarta, jointly owned by KLM and the Indonesian Government at first, took over the fleet of 22 DC-3s used by KLM in December 1949, when independence was granted. They were used on routes to the many islands forming the new country, with Convairs operating the longer routes. Following the annexation of Netherlands New Guinea (or Irian Jaya) in 1961, De Kroonduif's fleet of DC-3s was added. Subsequently the DC-3 was replaced steadily by the F.27 and the last was sold in September 1970. Various re-registrations occurred over the years, complicating identification of individual aircraft. Such changes are not listed here.

PK-DPA to PK-DPK incl; PK-GDA to PK-GDI incl; PK-GDK to PK-GDZ incl; PK-RCO to PK-RCR incl; PK-RCT to PK-RCW incl; PK-RCY; PK-REE; PK-REU; PK-REX; PK-RFY.

Indonesian Airways was set up by pre-independence forces to run the Dutch blockade as a semi-civil operation 1945-49, mainly from bases in Burma. Aircraft used an RI- prefix (Republic Indonesia). Four DC-3s are known, RI-001, -002, -007 and -009. Others operated were VH-HDJ (using call-sign IR-1) and VT-CLA.

KNILM (Koninklijke Nederland-Indische Luchtvaart Maatschappij), Djakarta, operated in the East Indies in the late twenties and by 1935 the East Indies division of KLM had received three DC-2s. These all escaped to Australia in 1942, together with four of the seven DC-3s sent out in 1940. Surplus DC-3s were bought post-war and one came direct from Douglas. All the early aircraft served initially with No 19 Squadron RAAF, with Dutch aircrews. Exactly which aircraft served post-war is difficult to unravel as all those registered in the PK-RCx/RDx and REx series may have been used, coming direct from similar VH- series. KLM continued to operate in the

Chapter 4: Commercial Operators of the DC-3, C-47, R4D, Dakota and Li-2

East Indies as KNILM but on 1 August 1947 the services were absorbed by KLM. On independence in December 1949 Garuda Indonesia was formed, being owned jointly by the government and KLM. The latter's share was finally bought out in September 1956.

DC-2s: PK-AFJ to PK-AFL incl; *DC-3s:* PK-AFV; PK-AFW; PK-AFZ; PK-ALN; PK-ALO; PK-ALT; PK-ALW; PK-DBA; PK-DBC; PK-DBG; PK-DBH; PK-DBK incl; PK-DPA to PK-DPK incl., and some of PK-RCO to PK-REY incl.

Mandala Airlines, Djakarta, operated four DC-3s during 1979 to 1981, but none remains in use. Three were operated for PENAS Cargo.

PK-OSA; PK-VDM; PK-VDN; PK-VDO.

PENAS Cargo (Perusahaan Negara Areal Survey), Djakarta, used three Mandala DC-3 freighters in the eighties.

PK-VDM; PK-VDN; PK-VDO.

PN Merpati Nusantara Airlines, Djakarta, was formed in 1963 to take over responsibility for De Kroonduif's operations from Garuda. Two DC-3s were leased initially from the Air Force and then more from Garuda, making up a fleet of 13 DC-3s, as well as many smaller types. Most DC-3s had been sold by 1980, some to Dirgantara.

PK-NDA to PK-NDM incl; PK-GDK; PK-GDN; PK-GDO; PK-GDP; PK-GDS; PK-GDW; PK-GDX.

PT National Air Charter, Djakarta, operated DC-3s on charter work. None now remains in service.

PK-WWH to PK-WWL incl.

PT Safari Air, Balikpapan, used DC-3 PK-OAZ on charter work in 1978, and PK-JDE earlier, from 1969.

Sempati Air Transport, Djakarta, started operations in March 1969 with two DC-3s, later rising to four. The last was withdrawn in 1982.

PK-JDA; PK-JDB/PK-JDG; (PK-JDC); PK-JDD; PK-JDE.

PT Seulawah Air Service, Djakarta, was formed in June 1968 and started using DC-3s on scheduled services in September of that year. All had been sold by 1980.

PK-RDA to PK-RDC incl; PK-RDE to PK-RDH incl.

Transna Indonesia (Trans National Airways / Trans Nusantara Airways PT), Djakarta, used four DC-3s on charter services beginning about November 1970. The last was retired in 1985.

PK-EHA; PK-EHC; PK-EHD; PK-GDC.

PT AOA Zamrud Aviation Corp, Denpasar, Bali, was formed in 1968 and eleven DC-3s were bought from Lake Central soon afterwards. Only six of these were delivered, and some may have been used for spares. These were used on scheduled (until 1971) and charter services but none remain.

PK-GDF; PK-JDG; PK-WWL; PK-ZDA to PK-ZDI incl; N65134 cr on delivery.

Index:-

PK-AFJ (DC-2)	c/n 1374	PK-CAB	9051		
PK-AFK (DC-2)	1375	PK-DBA	19005		
PK-AFL (DC-2)	1376	PK-DBC	19279		
PK-AFV	1965	PK-DBG	19658		
PK-AFW	1982	PK-DBH	13766		
PK-AFZ	1981	PK-DBK	42954		
PK-AKF	19566	PK-DPA	42954		
PK-AKG	12333	PK-DPB	19005		
PK-AKJ	26867	PK-DPC	13619		
PK-AKP	25427 ?	PK-DPD	19279		
PK-AKR	12209	PK-DPE	12719		
PK-AKT	12485	PK-DPF	13463		
PK-ALN	1936	PK-DPG	13535		
PK-ALO	1937	PK-DPH	19658		
PK-ALT	1941	PK-DPI	13766		
PK-ALW	1944	PK-DPJ	13052		
PK-CAA	12500	PK-DPK	12514		
PK-EHA	2238	PK-RCP	19719		
PK-EHC	27129	PK-RCQ	19623		
PK-EHD	33456	PK-RCR	19611		
PK-GDA	9281	PK-RCT	13639		
PK-GDB	20407	PK-RCU	19672		
PK-GDC	20041	PK-RCV	19844		
PK-GDD	19690	PK-RCW	12933		
PK-GDE	19719	PK-RCY	13731		
PK-GDF	19623	PK-RDA	19510		
PK-GDG	19611	PK-RDB	32895		
PK-GDH	13639	PK-RDC	6023		
PK-GDI	19672	PK-RDD	12017		
PK-GDK	19844	PK-RDE	11967		
PK-GDL	12933	PK-RDF	12035		
PK-GDM	13731	PK-RDG(1)	12036		
PK-GDN	19549	PK-RDG(2)	6353		
PK-GDO	13377	PK-RDH(1)	11972		
PK-GDP	13334	PK-RDH(2)	13085		
PK-GDQ	12500	PK-RDI	12279		
PK-GDR	19154	PK-RDJ	12097		
PK-GDS	13619	PK-RDK	12035		
PK-GDT	12719	PK-RDL	12878		
PK-GDU	13463	PK-RDM	13444		
PK-GDV	13535	PK-RDN	13345		
PK-GDW	19658	PK-RDY	32691		
PK-GDX	13766	PK-RDZ	32692		
PK-GDY	13052	PK-REA			
PK-GDZ	12514	PK-REB			
PK-IBA	12652	PK-REC	33475		
PK-IBI	13514	PK-RED	33477		
PK-IBS	33579	PK-REE	9281		
(PK-IDA)	32725	PK-REF	13207		
(PK-IDB)	13366	PK-REG	6032		
PK-IDH	12433	PK-REH	6199		
PK-JDA	33456	PK-REI			
PK-JDB	32878	PK-REK			
(PK-JDC)	27129	PK-REM	9550		
PK-JDD	33112	PK-REN			
PK-JDE	27129	PK-REP	13497		
PK-JDG	32878	PK-REQ	12636		
PK-JJM	9858	PK-RER	25496		
PK-JJS	20715	PK-REU	13607		
PK-MVD	9281	PK-REX	20407		
PK-NDA	12664	PK-REY	20041		
PK-NDB	19566	PK-SVD	19249		
PK-NDC	13123	PK-SVE	19032		
PK-NDD	19549	PK-VDM	9551 ?		
PK-NDE	13377	PK-VDN	13607		
PK-NDF	13334	PK-VDO	13207		
PK-NDG	34228	PK-VJS	12433		
PK-NDH	19694	PK-VTM	9281		
PK-NDI	19154	PK-VTN			
PK-NDJ	13766	PK-VTO	13334		
PK-NDK	9281	PK-WWH	19690		
PK-NDL	19658	PK-WWI	25427		
PK-NDM	13619	PK-WWJ	19032		
PK-NZA	13123	PK-WWK	20407		
PK-OAZ	19623	PK-WWL	3275		
PK-OBC	12485	PK-ZDA	2212		
PK-OBJ	19249	PK-ZDB	3275		
PK-OBK	12209	PK-ZDC	2146		
PK-OSA	6353	PK-ZDD	2123		
PK-PAA	20832	PK-ZDE	4390		
PK-PAB	9051	PK-ZDF	19648		
PK-PIA	10082	PK-ZDG	13365		
PK-PIB	4094	PK-ZDH	9746		
PK-RCA	13619	PK-ZDI	19844		
PK-RCC	12719	RI-001	26903		
PK-RCD	13463		(see note)		
PK-RCG	13766	RI-002	20578		
PK-RCH	13052	RI-007			
PK-RCI	12514	RI-009	4823		
PK-RCO	19690				

Notes:- There has been some confusion over a number of Indonesian DC-3s. PK-AKF now seems more likely to have been c/n 19566 than 25427, which is more likely to be PK-AKP, but further information may come to light. PK-REA, PK-REB may relate to DT947 and DT948.

At least 4 DC-3s exist painted as Indonesian Airways RI-001 "Seulawah", one is said to be 26903, the others include 13503 and 34228. RI-007 is said to be ex-Burma, returned Oct50 to be preserved in Myanmar as UB-736.

IRAN - EP

DC-3s have been used in Iran since the end of WW2. Immediately after the war it has been reported that Russia was operating Lend-Lease C-47s on services into Iran, but as this infringed the terms under which they were supplied, it is believed they were sold in Iran. A report in Aviation Week (12 Nov 1958) suggested that the president of Iranian Airways, Reza Afshar, out-manoeuvred the Russian government who were supporting the Tudeh Party in northern Iran. With American agreement, 19 C-47s were purchased which the Russians were operating, and possession of the aircraft was to have been taken "as is" and "where is", not only in Iran, but in other parts of the Middle East. Unfortunately, we have not been able to confirm this report, as all Iranian DC-3s are of known origin, and none came from amongst those supplied to Russia under Lend-Lease. They may, of course, have been used only for spares. Iranian Airways overhauled a number of surplus C-47s stored in the Middle East, but none of these seems to have had any Russian connections.

Air Service Co, Abadan, used DC-3s and FH-227Bs on charter flights in support of the oil industry. The DC-3s all came from the sister company, Air Taxi Co, from about 1968 onwards.

EP-ADL; EP-AEH; EP-AEO; EP-AIQ; EP-AML.

Air Taxi Co, Teheran, was formed in 1958 for charter and survey work, using ex-Iranian Airways DC-3s. The last of these was transferred to Air Service Co in 1976/77.

EP-AAK; EP-ABG; EP-ADG; EP-ADL; EP-AEH; EP-AEO; EP-AGZ; EP-AIQ; EP-AML.

Iranian Airways Co, Teheran, was formed in December 1944 with help from TWA. DC-3s were used to start services in May 1946 and later Transocean supplied some aircraft. Persian Air Services was merged with Iranian in 1961 forming Iran National Airlines Corp (Iranair).

EP-AAF to EP-AAH incl; EP-AAJ; EP-AAK; EP-AAL; EP-AAP; EP-ABB to EP-ABE incl; EP-ACI to EP-ACL incl; EP-ACU; EP-ACV; EP-ADG; EP-ADI/N3980C; EP-ADL; EP-AED to EP-AEI incl.

Iranair - Iran National Airlines Corp, Teheran, was formed in 1961 by the merger of Iranian Airways and Persian Air Services. A number of DC-3s were taken over and continued in use until about 1967. Several went to Air Taxi Co.

EP-AAK; EP-ABB; EP-ABC; EP-ACU; EP-ADG; EP-ADI; EP-ADL; EP-AED to EP-AEI incl.

Index:-

EP-AAF	c/n 20618	EP-ACU	4113
EP-AAG	9453	EP-ACV	12919
EP-AAH (1)	9321	EP-ADG	10237
EP-AAH (2)	26498	EP-ADI	6350
EP-AAJ	13572	EP-ADL	19275
EP-AAK	13016	EP-AED	7367
EP-AAL	9469	EP-AEE	13348
EP-AAM?	"9331"	EP-AEF	19289
EP-AAP	13556	EP-AEG	9938
EP-ABB	6043	EP-AEH	12774
EP-ABC	13652	EP-AEI	13552
EP-ABD	33340	EP-AEO	20813
EP-ABE	33163	EP-AGZ	26868
EP-ABG	13568	EP-AIQ	32840
EP-ACI	27115	EP-AML	33163
EP-ACJ	9692	EP-HIQ	32730 ?
EP-ACK	25615	EP-IWB	12680
EP-ACL	9308		

Notes:-
Some of the above did come from Russia, but via Poland.
EP-HIQ is reported but unidentified, presumably with Imperial connections but the quoted c/n 32730 was in use with the USAF until after EP-HIQ was registered.

IRAQ - YI

Iraqi Airways, Baghdad, leased DC-3s from BOAC during 1946/47 pending delivery of their Vikings to operate routes on which the Rapides could no longer cope with traffic demands.

Index:-

YI-GHJ	c/n 9413	YI-GNB	26719
YI-GKH	25810	YI-HCZ	11924

IRISH REPUBLIC/ IRELAND/ EIRE - EI

DC-3s were in use in Eire since before WW2, and continued until 1982.

Aer Lingus Teoranta, Dublin, bought its first DC-3 just before WWII, but expansion of the fleet had to wait until 1946 when further aircraft were bought direct from Douglas, and others from surplus stocks in Europe. The type remained in use until F.27s were delivered, having outlasted the Vikings intended to replace them. The last few were used for cargo work until sold in 1963/64.

EI-ACA; EI-ACD to EI-ACI incl; EI-ACK to EI-ACM incl; EI-ACT; EI-ADW to EI-ADY incl; EI-AFA to EI-AFC incl; EI-AFL; EI-AHG.

Aer Turas Teoranta, Dublin, operated DC-3 EI-ANK on charter services between April 1964 and January 1965, when it was sold.

Apple Air Services Ltd bought EI-BSI and EI-BSJ in Jun86, but operations never started.

Clyden Airways, Dublin, a subsidiary of Mercantile Aviation and Trading, was registered to operate DC-3s in 1978 on mail services to Manchester. Operations ceased on 22Jan81 and the aircraft were sold in Jan 1982.

EI-BDT; EI-BDU.

Hibernian Airlines Ltd, Dublin, was founded as Air Charters of Ireland in 1966, but traded as Hibernian and operated charters. All of the fleet were leased to Emerald (in Northern Ireland - see United Kingdom entry) at one time or another.

EI-APB; EI-APJ; EI-ARP; EI-ARR.

Index:-

EI-ACA	c/n 2178	EI-AFL	33447
(EI-ACB)	2261	EI-AHG	32761
EI-ACD	9140	EI-ALR	4579
EI-ACE	42956	EI-ALS	9036
EI-ACF	42957	EI-ALT	12471
EI-ACG	4579	EI-ANK	9813
EI-ACH	12893	EI-APB	25600
EI-ACI	9036	EI-APJ	33042
EI-ACK	19503	EI-ARP	33010
EI-ACL	11861	EI-ARR	13164
EI-ACM	12899	EI-AYO	1911
EI-ACT	12471	(EI-BDT)(1)	10144
EI-ADW	26107	EI-BDT(2)	32872
EI-ADX	26728	(EI-BDU)(1)	4398
EI-ADY	26997	EI-BDU(2)	9043
EI-AFA	19632	(EI-BKJ)	26569
EI-AFB	20453	EI-BSI	33379
EI-AFC	20135	EI-BSJ	19754

ISRAEL - 4X

ARKIA - Israel Inland Airlines Ltd, Tel Aviv, obtained DC-3s from the Israeli Air Force in October 1955, adding further aircraft until 1961. The last was retired from scheduled services and charter work in September 1968.

4X-ACW; 4X-ADA; 4X-AEO; 4X-AES; 4X-AEZ; 4X-ASR.

El Al Israel Airlines, Tel Aviv, used DC-3 4X-ATA in February 1951 for a short time. It was then returned to the Air Force, but later went to Arkia.

Israelair, Haifa, operated six DC-3s in association with **Pan African Air Charter** from Haifa to Rome and Paris, mostly ex-Westair Transport, in South African markings. All found their way to Arkia or the IDF/AF later.

ZS-AVM; ZS-BCJ; ZS-DAH; ZS-DCY; ZS-DCZ; ZS-DDJ.

Colour Gallery

XVII

C-GWIR C-47A-DL c/n 9371 - As 42-23509 this C-47 served with the 8th AF in Europe, then the Czech AF and finally spent twelve years with the Armée de l'Air in France. After overhaul in France the aircraft has been in Canada for the past thirty years. It visited the 50th anniversary gathering at Abbotsford, BC on 08Jun86, whilst with Northwest Territorial. [Eric Wagner]

12937 Dakota IIIF c/n 9415 - This was delivered to the RCAF in 1943 and was in its final year in 1990, with the by-then-renamed Canadian Armed Forces, when this air-to-air photograph was taken. [CAF via A Pearcy]

CP-583 C-47A-DL c/n 9668 - This aircraft spent its wartime years in the USA and was sold surplus to Brazil in 1946. It passed to Bolivia in 1951, to be withdrawn there in 1990. This photograph shows it at Santa Cruz, Bolivia on 07Nov84. [M Magnusson]

F-GEOM C-47A-DL c/n 9798 - For this C-47A the war started in North Africa with the 8th AF, passing to the 9th in 1944, and then to CSA-Czech Airlines in 1947. The French Navy used it for the next 25 years until it was sold to Stellair as F-GEOM in 1985. It operated from Bournemouth, UK until 2002, earning its keep day-tripping to France and to British airshows as G-DAKK. [via A Pearcy]

OD-AAN C-47A-40-DL c/n 9894 - Beginning life with the 8th AF in Europe in 1943, this aircraft served with Air France until 1947. Seen with the short-lived dual titles 'Middle East Airlines-Air Liban', this photo was taken at Beirut, Lebanon in Oct65. The aircraft spent the next 40 years in the Middle Eastern area prior to its sale in Venezuela, where it flew with SERVIVENSA. [Stephen Piercey collection via P J Marson]

YV-505C C-47A-DL c/n 9894 - After service with Air Liban, this aircraft became US-owned, but remained in Europe and North Africa until its purchase by MIDAS in 1988. It later became YV-610C with AVENSA, but this photo was taken on 20Sep89 at Caracas, Venezuela while still owned by MIDAS. [M Magnusson]

Colour Gallery

G-AGHS C-47A-50-DL c/n 10099 - This Dakota was one of the examples to see service with BOAC during the later war years, after which it served with BEA, who converted it to a 'Pionair'. In Mar61 it was acquired by Cambrian Airways and was one of the few in the fleet to be painted in the later colour-scheme, as seen here at Southampton, UK on 20Apr68. After sale the following year, the aircraft was soon withdrawn from use in Beirut, Lebanon and later scrapped. [P J Marson]

PP-VBF C-47A-DL c/n 10156 - VARIG bought this aircraft via the Hughes Tool Company in 1947 and it operated in Brazil until about 1971, when it was set up in the Parque do Flamengo, Rio de Janeiro. This photo was taken in May75 before it suffered from vandalism and was removed for post-restoration display at Rio-Galeao, Brazil. [Stephen Piercey collection via P J Marson]

39078 R4D-5S c/n 10205 - Operated by the US Navy, this photo was taken at NAF Litchfield Park, AZ, around 1960, prior to service with the Arctic Research Laboratory at Barrow, AK fitted with skis and radome. [Doug Olson]

N136FS C-47A-DL c/n 10267 - Four Star Air Cargo operates a fleet of DC-3s from the US Virgin Islands, having bought this aircraft in 1987. The photograph was taken at its former San Juan, PR base on 15Jun00. [Michael Prophet]

N700RC C-53-DO c/n 11628 formerly with Red Carpet Airlines, was being operated by Key West Airlines at Fort Lauderdale International, FL when photographed on 25Oct82. [Roger Syratt]

N7500A C-53D c/n 11693 - This DC-3 was owned by Britt Aarvik (Odin Air) and was used for parachute jumping, operating from Zephyr Hills, FL. Note the stylised SAS-style cheat-line and Norwegian flag, plus the inscription 'Norge' reflecting the original nationality of the owner. The photo was taken on an unknown date, some time after 1984. The aircraft is fitted with Wright R-1820s. [via Franc v.Vliet]

Colour Gallery

XXI

7T-VBC C-53D c/n 11706 - Afric Air bought this C-53 in 1964 from UTA for charter work, but it was withdrawn by the following May. Probably taken at Toulouse-Montaudran, France.
[Roger Caratini via David Lucabaugh]

N130Q C-53D c/n 11761 - This aircraft was fitted with amphibious floats by Folsome Air Service, Bangor, ME for HBF Inc. Photo taken at Manchester, NH on 20Sep90.
[Ken Marshall]

268835 C-53D c/n 11762 - After service with the 8th AF in Europe, this aircraft was operated post-war by American Airlines and then passed through several owners. It was found disused at Gainesville, FL and then flown to McClellan AFB, CA to become part of the base museum, where this photo was taken on 25Sep95.
[Michael Prophet]

PT-KYZ C-47A-DK c/n 11837 of the Brazilian operator RICO was at Opa-Locka, FL on 01Nov82 where it was photographed before restoration at Madrid AFB, Colombia in mid-1995. [Roger Syratt]

ZK-AMR/UN281 C-47A-DK c/n 11970 - Delivered to the RAAF in Dec43, this aircraft spent its life in Australia until sold in New Zealand in 1986. It was then leased to the UNO in Oct93, serving in Cambodia and Somalia. It was last noted stored at Harare, Zimbabwe in 1996. [D A Noble]

HS-TDD C-47A-DK c/n 11977 - This aircraft served with Thai Airways between 1951 and 1977, passing to Sky of Siam in 1980. This photo was taken at Bangkok, Thailand on 13Feb73. [J G Prozesky via P J Marson]

Colour Gallery   XXIII

N123DZ C-47A-1-DK c/n 12004 once served with the RCAF as FL595 and eventually joined Florida Air Cargo, with whom it was operating when photographed at Opa-Locka, FL on 20 Nov96. [Roger Syratt]

N4995E C-47A-DK c/n 12039 - After service with the RCAF as FL618 and Trans-Canada as CF-TDQ, this aircraft was purchased by Frontier in Oct58 and named 'Sunliner Lincoln'. The photo was taken by an anonymous photographer between 1958 and 1966.

ET-ABY C-47A-1-DK c/n 12205 - After service with the RAF, this Dakota was civilianised for airline use in Turkey, where it spent 20 years before being passed on to Ethiopia. The airline's colour-scheme is probably one of the most attractive of its era. The photo was taken in Sep68, possibly in Nairobi, Kenya. [Stephen Piercey collection via P J Marson]

42-92577 C-47C-DK c/n 12393 - One of five amphibian conversions, this aircraft served with the 5th AF in New Guinea and then the 7th AF at Elmendorf, AK. The conversions were not a great success. The fate of 42-92577 is uncertain as it has been confused with US Navy Bu 12393 c/n 6061. This rare wartime air-to-air photo was probably taken in Oct44. [Harry Gann/Douglas]

ZS-BXJ C-47A-DK c/n 12413 - This Dakota was supplied via the RAF to the SAAF in 1944 as 6829 and continued in that service until it passed to South African Airways around 1977, still showing signs of its use for maritime reconnaissance. Photo taken at Johannesburg, South Africa on 29Jan97. [S Morrison]

N700CA C-47A-10-DK c/n 12438, named 'Mary Lou' with Champlain Air, was photographed at Pompano Beach, FL on 17Nov96, having operated in Canada for the first 27 years of its life. [Roger Syratt]

Colour Gallery

N54AA C-47A-DK c/n 12475 - As Dakota KG440 this aircraft served with various units in the UK, before going to Canadair for overhaul in 1946 and service in Canada for the next 50 years or so. This photograph was taken at Opa-Locka, FL in Sep99, while with Allied Air Transport. [Michael Prophet]

F-BEHF C-47A-DK c/n 12489 - After service as a Dakota with the RAF, this aircraft was sold to Ciro's Aviation as G-AKJN and then to Air Atlas, eventually spending 14 years with Air France on the night postal service. [via A Pearcy]

N100SD C-47A-DK c/n 12853 - After eighteen months with the ATC and ten civil markings, N100SD was flown by Aero Virgin Islands for nearly ten years, but had only recently joined this airline when this photo was taken at San Juan in Apr80. It was stored at San Juan, PR in a dismantled state in April 1989, only to be destroyed by Hurricane Hugo on 17Sep89. [Stephen Piercey via P J Marson]

VH-EDC C-47A-DK c/n 12874 - After wartime service with the RAAF, twelve years were spent with the Department of Civil Aviation before going to QANTAS for another eleven years. Bush Pilots bought it in 1972 and this photo was taken in Sep73 at Bankstown, NSW. Thereafter, it had several more owners until it ditched on take-off into Botany Bay, Sydney in Apr94, but was recovered. [Neville Parnell]

VT-CYG C-47A-DK c/n 13019 - One of many Dakotas acquired by Indian Airlines post-war from RAF stocks, VT-CYG survived much longer than most and came to Great Britain in Jun94 where it was photographed at Elstree, Herts on the 11th. Subsequently it became N47AZ and was stored at Nairobi-Wilson, Kenya after famine relief work in 1999. [Jennifer Gradidge]

N47FL C-47A-20-DK c/n 13087 photographed wearing the titles of its previous operator, Spanish company ARM, at Elstree, UK in Sep95. [Jennifer Gradidge]

COLOUR GALLERY

XXVII

C-FLFR C-47A-DK c/n 13155 - Initially flown with the RAF, this Dakota went to Canada with the RCAF, serving with the UNO in 1960. It was sold in 1969 and remains with Buffalo Airways, with whom it was photographed at Yellowknife, NWT on 27Jun98. [Michael Prophet]

CC-CBX C-47A-DK c/n 13296 - A complicated history started with the USAAF ATC in China and then with CATC and storage in Hong Kong, the subject of a legal dispute. As N4660V it returned to the USA and found its way to LAN Chile under various registrations before passing to the Direccion de Aeronautica by 1972. It is now preserved in the museum at Los Cerillos, Santiago back in LAN colours, where it was photographed in Aug00 in a very tired condition. [Eric Wagner]

23 R4D-5 c/n 13321 - As 17223 this aircraft spent about 20 years with the US Navy before being sold to the French Navy with 56S and eventually becoming No.23. It was used as a navigation trainer and has an astrodome further back than usual. When Aeronavale retired their fleet it passed to Basler, who converted it to a BT-67 turboprop N96BF in 1990. It was used as a demonstrator and crashed in Africa in Dec94. [Aéronavale]

XXVIII THE DOUGLAS DC-1, DC-2, DC-3 – THE FIRST SEVENTY YEARS

ZS-CRV C-47A-25-DK c/n 13331 - After a career that included service with the RAF and spells with Cuban, US and Botswanan operators, this aircraft is currently operating air safari flights with Rovos Air from Lanseria in South Africa, where it was photographed on 14Nov02. [Dave Becker]

AF-4776 C-47A-DK c/n 13334 - Satuan Udara FASI must have a strange sense of humour, demonstrated by this outrageously-painted female, named 'Den Bey', on display at Jakarta, Indonesia in 1997. It was earlier reported wfu in 1991 as PK-VTO. [Paul Jackson]

9V-BAL C-47A-DK c/n 13384 - Malaysia-Singapore Airlines took this aircraft over from Malaysian Airways on 01Jan67 and in 1969 it was sold to Khmer Airlines as XU-GAJ. Photographed at Singapore in 1967, it was destroyed by a rocket attack at Phnom Penh, Cambodia in Feb75.
[Stephen Piercey collection via P J Marson]

COLOUR GALLERY

VH-MIN C-47A-DK c/n 13459 - Since being registered to the Bureau of Mineral Resources in 1954, this C-47 has had many owners and was one of seven with Dakota National Airways in 1998. Photographed on 02May00 at Sydney (Bankstown), NSW. [Al Bovelt]

ZS-CAI C-47A-25-DK c/n 13541 spent over 40 years with the South African Dept of Transport as a calibration aircraft before it was sold in 2002. Here it is seen at Pretoria-Wonderboom, South Africa on 08Oct03. [Chris Chatfield]

CF-AOH C-47A-DL c/n 13860 - At the time this photo was taken at Abbotsford, BC on 10Jun86, this aircraft was registered to Northland Air Manitoba and the name Air Manitoba was not adopted until Jul91. [Eric Wagner]

N99131 C-47A-65-DL c/n 18949 was photographed at its Honolulu International, HI base when in daily use by Genavco Air Cargo as an inter-island freighter in Oct95. It had been overhauled after ten years' storage at Honolulu, following thirty years' operations in Australia since its original delivery from the factory. [Roger Syratt]

TAM-17 C-47A-DL c/n 19173 - Basler bought this C-47A from the Bolivian AF for conversion to BT-67 standard and it eventually went to Mali. It was photographed at Oshkosh, WI on 02Aug93, and the marking 46BF can just be discerned on the fuselage. [Jennifer Gradidge]

N96H C-47A-70-DL c/n 19224 had carried the same registration since 1954 and had been stored in a damaged condition at Albuquerque, NM by the time it was photographed on 12Oct97. [Roger Syratt]

COLOUR GALLERY

XXXI

PK-SVD C-47A-70-DL c/n 19249 - After brief post-war use in the USA, this aircraft was exported to Indonesia in 1950, where it flew with several owners before being bought by Airfast in 1974. This photo was taken shortly after entering service with the airline before the registration letters of its original Indonesian operator, <u>S</u>tandard <u>V</u>acuum Oil, were replaced by the marks PK-OBJ. The C-47A was written-off in Indonesia in 1982.
[Stephen Piercey collection via P J Marson]

K-685/N3240A C-47A-DL c/n 19291 - Valiant Air Command bought this C-47 from the Danish Air Force in 1982 after it had been used in the film 'A Bridge Too Far'. It has long been used for parachute jumps but remains in Danish AF colours. Photo taken 29Jul89 at Oshkosh, WI.
[Jennifer Gradidge]

N147DC C-47A-DL c/n 19347 - This Dakota served first with the 8th AF before transfer to the RAF in 1944, being fitted by the USAAF with glider snatch gear. Subsequently it was used for various radar trials and at RAE Farnborough, UK before its sale to Aces High who used it in several films in a range of civil and military colours. Here it is in a USAAC scheme, 10 TG indicating the 10th Transport Group and 07 supposedly indicating the last two digits of the USAAC serial (erroneously in this case, as the original serial was 42-100884). Because it has rarely earned its keep this aircraft is one of the lowest-hours DC-3s, with little over 3000 hours on the airframe. This photo was taken at its North Weald, Essex base in England on 23Sep00. [Jennifer Gradidge]

PK-GDN C-47A-DL c/n 19549 - This aircraft was acquired when Garuda took over de Kroonduif in 1963 and this photo was taken during a visit to Bankstown, NSW on 04Feb67, probably for overhaul.
[Neville Parnell]

CF-WCO C-47A-80-DL c/n 19737 - After wartime use, this aircraft was civilianised by Remmert-Werner in 1946 and flew for numerous owners in the USA before it was sold to Millardair in Canada in 1967. It served that airline for nearly fourteen years before moving from the Florida area to Venezuela in the 1980s. This photo was taken on 04Jan74 in Canada.
[Larry Milberry via Stephen Piercey collection]

PH-DDZ C-47A-80-DL c/n 19754 taken at the DC-3 Fly-In at Texel in the Netherlands on 05May87, shortly after acquisition by the Dutch Dakota Association and still wearing the colours of its previous owner Pyramid Airlines.
[Roger Syratt]

CHAPTER 4: COMMERCIAL OPERATORS OF THE DC-3, C-47, R4D, DAKOTA AND LI-2

Index:-

4X-ACW	c/n 26054	4X-AOE	6224
4X-ADA	26792	4X-AOJ	25687
4X-AED	26972	4X-AON	19400
4X-AEO	6227	4X-ASR	10146
4X-AES	11923	4X-ATA	6227
"4X-AES"	6223	4X-DCA	25625
4X-AEZ	6224	4X-DCB	33031
4X-AOA	25667	4X-DCE	32755
4X-AOB	33093	4X-DCF	6223
4X-AOC	19503	4X-DNA	25625

Note:- Most IDF/AF C-47s carry civil type call signs in the 4X-F.. series on their fins. These are listed in the military section.

ITALY - I

Italy was among the first countries in Europe to use the DC-2, a single example of which was delivered in 1935. A captured ex-Belgian DC-3 was used during WW2 by Ala Littoria following a short spell with the Italian Air Force, but the main influx came from USAAF surplus stocks at Naples, in 1945/46. A number of operators sprang up, but disappeared almost as quickly.

Aereo Teseo SA (Orario Linee Aereo Teseo) acquired a fleet of nine DC-3s from April 1947 and used them until December of that year, when operations ceased temporarily. They were restarted by Salpanavi Soc. di Navigazione Aerea in January 1948, but were finally ended in July, and most aircraft sold to Egypt.

I-BARI; I-BOLO; I-GENO; I-NAPI; I-PALU; I-REGI; I-TORI; I-VENE; I-ZOLI - all using the first four letters of cities they served ! However, no identity is known for I-NAPI while I-ZOLI was apparently not taken up.

ALITALIA - Linee Aeree Italiane, Rome, acquired DC-3s when it took over LAI in November 1957. The last of these was sold in Ethiopia in 1965.

I-LALO; I-LENE; I-LEON; I-LICE; I-LIDA; I-LINA; I-LONA; I-LORD; I-LORO; I-LUCE; I-LULA; I-LUNA.

Aviolinee Italiane SA, Rome, bought DC-2 I-EROS in 1935 and used it until 1940, when it was taken over by the Italian Air Force.

Avio Linee Italiane - Flotte Riunite, Rome, was formed in January 1949 by the merging of Airone, A.L.I., SISA, Transadriateca and SNA. DC-3s acquired with some of these companies were used until January 1952, when the assets were sold to LAI.

I-COSU; I-EBRO; I-ELFO; I-ENOS; I-ETNA, I-LUNA; I-SOLE; I-TRAS; I-TRES; I-TRIS; I-TROS; I-TRUS; I-VARO; I-VELE.

ITAVIA - Società di Navigazione Aerea SpA, Rome, bought DC-3s in 1962 to replace DH Herons on scheduled services. These, in turn, were sold to pay for Heralds two years later.

I-TAVA; I-TAVE; I-TAVI; I-TAVO.

Linee Aeree Italiane SpA - LAI, Rome, started operations in Apr47, using DC-3s with help from TWA. Those that survived were taken over by Alitalia on 01Nov57.

I-EBRO; I-ENOS; I-LAIL; I-LALO; I-LAMA; I-LEDA; I-LENE; I-LENT; I-LEON; I-LETR; I-LICE; I-LIDA; I-LILI; I-LINA; I-LINC; I-LIRA; I-LODO; I-LONA; I-LORD; I-LORO; I-LOTT; I-LUCE; I-LULA; I-LUNA; I-TRAS; I-TRUS.

Nucleo Ala Littoria, Rome, operated airline services during the war, from September 1940 until June 1943, when the Luftwaffe took over the equipment, which included DC-2 I-EROS and DC-3 I-EMOS.

Salpanavi, Società di Navigazione Aerea, Milan, started operations on 19 July 1947, using DC-3s leased from SISA. They merged with Aereo Teseo in January 1948.

I-NAVE; I-PADO.

SAM - Società Aerea Mediterranea, Rome, operated as a charter subsidiary of Alitalia, with four of the latter's DC-3s. These were replaced by DC-6Bs in 1962.

I-LALO; I-LENE; I-LORD and I-LORO.

SISA - Società Italiane Servizi Aerei, Trieste, started scheduled services on 8 June 1947, using DC-3s, but merged with Avio Linee Italiane in October 1948.

I-COSU; I-LUNA; I-NAVE; I-SOLE; I-VARO; I-VELE.

Transadriateca, Società di Navigazione Aerea SpA, Venice, began DC-3 operations in April 1947, but merged with Avio Linee Italiane in January 1949.

I-PADO; I-TRAS; I-TRES; I-TRIS; I-TROS; I-TRUS.

Index:-

I-BARI	c/n 26671	I-LORO	4297
I-BOLO	27048	I-LOTT	4506
I-COFR	12679	I-LUCE	4387
I-COSU	4291	I-LULA	4291
I-EBRO	7325	I-LUNA	4346
I-ELFO	4260	I-NAPI	see note
I-EMOS	2093	I-NAVE	4345
I-ENOS	7397	I-NEBB	18964
I-EROS (DC-2)	1319	I-PADO	4329
I-ETNA	4396	I-PALU	4233
I-GENO	26920	I-REGI	4312
I-LAIL	4308	I-RIBE	4380
I-LALO	19484	I-SOLE	4506
I-LAMA	4389	I-TAVA	13652
I-LEDA	4411	I-TAVE	12083
I-LENE	4325	I-TAVI	33225
I-LENT	4548	I-TAVO	33392
I-LEON	4316	I-TORI	25755
I-LETR	4686	I-TRAS	26800
I-LICE	6011	I-TRES	25573
I-LIDA	4261	I-TRIS	26707
I-LILI	25573	I-TROS	26675
I-LINA	4236	I-TRUS	26646
I-LINC	9101	I-VARO	6011
I-LIRA	4380	I-VELE	4548
I-LODO	4221	I-VENE	26919
I-LONA	4500	(I-ZOLI)	see note
I-LORD	4496		

Notes:- I-NAPI was registered to Aereo Teseo on 29Nov48 and cancelled as sold abroad on 09Mar49, probably to the Egyptian AF with others from the same company. Its c/n is unknown. I-ZOLI appears to have been reserved for Aereo Teseo but not to have been officially registered, possibly due to the company closure.

IVORY COAST - TU

Air Afrique, Abidjan, was formed by Air France and representatives of 11 African countries on 28Mar61 to operate scheduled services throughout the ex-French colonial territories in W Africa. A few DC-3s were used on local services for a time. Two were leased from the Dahomey Air Force, and two from Air Ivoire.

TU-TIA; TU-TIB; TU-TCL; TY-AAB; TY-AAC; 6V-AAP.

Air Ivoire, Cie Nationale, Abidjan, began scheduled services in mid-1964 using two DC-3s. These were replaced by YS-11s in 1973.

TU-TIA; TU-TIB; 5U-AAJ; 6V-AAP.

Sté. Airtransivoire, Abidjan, used DC-3 TU-TJM on air taxi and charter work in 1978/79. It was wfu by 1986.

Index:-

TU-TCL	c/n 25875	TU-TIB	42959
TU-TIA	42955	TU-TJM	33127

Note:- The TU-V.. series is covered in the military section.

JAMAICA - VP-J and 6Y

British Caribbean Airways Ltd, Kingston, used two DC-3s to start scheduled services in July 1948, but in October of the following year they were taken over by BWIA.

VP-JAP; VP-JAQ.

Jamaica Air Services, Kingston, leased a US registered DC-3 to start services in 1963, but nothing further is known of this.

Trans-Jamaican Airlines, Montego Bay, bought DC-3 Viewmaster 6Y-JJQ in 1980. It was probably sold in 1986.

Index:-

VP-JAP	c/n 13114	6Y-JJQ	9108
VP-JAQ	9885		

JAPAN - J and JA

Japan made early use of the Douglas DC-2 and DC-3. Nakajima bought a single DC-2 (NC14284 which became J-BBOI) in October 1934 and followed this with five unassembled aircraft. With the experience gained they designed their own twin, the Nakajima AT-2, bearing a superficial resemblance to the DC-2. The DC-3 followed with 20 delivered as parts, and two DC-3As. These served as patterns for licence production by Showa as the L2D. Dai Nippon used nine L2Ds from 1941. Japanese production is described earlier. Post-war, when aviation was again permitted in 1954, DC-3s were used to open internal routes and 18 examples were bought in the USA. Some were also leased by Northwest Airlines for use in Japan.

All Nippon Airways Co Ltd, Tokyo, was established in March 1958 by the merger of Far East Airlines with Japan Helicopter and Aeroplane Transport Co. The latter already had two DC-3s and others were bought after the merger, the final DC-3 being retired in 1968.

JA5018; JA5019; JA5024; JA5025; JA5027; JA5039; JA5040; JA5043; JA5045; JA5050; JA5072; JA5077; JA5078; JA5080; N493/JA5128 (lsd).

Dai Nippon Airways (DNKKK), Tokyo, operated a DC-2 supplied by Nakajima in 1938 (J-BBOI "Niitaka" ex NKYKK and Army). One DC-3 J-BFOB "Tsubaki" is known to have been in use early in 1940. A batch of nine Nakajima built DC-3s, J-BHOR to J-BHOZ were delivered in 1941, named as follows:- J-BHOR name unknown; J-BHOS "Kusunoki"; J-BHOT "Hinoki"; J-BHOU "Kashi"; J-BHOV "Nara"; J-BHOW name unkn; J-BHOX "Kaba"; J-BHOY "Tsuga" and J-BHOZ "Momi". A further eight DC-3s followed during 1941:- J-BIOA "Sugi"; J-BIOB "Matsu"; J-BIOC "Ume"; J-BIOD "Momo"; J-BIOE "Kiri"; J-BIOF "Yanagi"; J-BIOG "Sakaki"; J-BIOJ "Azusa". Eleven further aircraft have been identified as J-BKOA "Mutsu"; J-BKOF "Higo"; J-BKOJ "Take"; J-BKOL "Kunugi"; J-BKOV "Kawachi"; J-BKOY "Tushima"; J-BOOA "Satsuma"; J-BOOB "Ohsumi" J-BOOJ "Kamo"; J-BOOQ "Shima"; J-BOOU "Izumo".

The following fates are known:- J-BIOA, shot down Aug43 near Sulawesi (Celebes); J-BIOC, crashed into mountain near Taipei (Formosa) Dec43; J-BIOF, crashed near Malay Peninsula Aug 44; J-BIOG, crashed Cebu Island Oct 42; J-BKOA, lost between Denpasar and Surabaya 24Jan45; J-BKOJ, ditched north of Formosa Mar42; J-BKOL, lost Formosa Jan44; J-BKOV, shot down en route Taipei (Formosa) 05Mar45; J-BOOJ, crashed into mountain in Formosa Dec44; J-BOOQ, forced landing after take-off from Matsuyama (Formosa) Apr45.

Greater Japan Air Lines, Tokyo, was formed in August 1939 by the reorganisation of Japan Air Lines, ceasing operations on 24 August 1945. Showa-built L2Ds were used.

Japan Air Lines, are known to have started operations using DC-3s in 1951. Their origin remains somewhat of a mystery, with a photo of a DC-3 in JAL c/s showing a Philippine Airlines flag on the tail, but no registration mark visible.

Japan Helicopter and Aeroplane Transport Co (JHAT), Tokyo, bought two DC-3s to start operations in March 1954, using them until JHAT merged with Far East Airlines in March 1958, forming All Nippon.

JA5018; JA5019; JA5024; JA5025; JA5027; JA5039; JA5043; JA5045.

Nihon Koku Yuso KK - NKYKK, (Japan Air Transport Co),Tokyo, imported six DC-2s in 1934/35. These were evaluated by Nakajima and purchased by the Army. Evidence exists of nine registrations: J-BBOH, J-BBOI "Niitaka", J-BBOO "Kirishima", J-BBOQ "Tsukuba", J-BBOR "Atago", J-BBOT, J-BBOU "Kongo"; J-BBOV "Ibuki"; J-BDOH. One was named "Fuji". J-BBOT crashed on 05Feb40 at Uotsuri Isle, 115m N of Formosa.

North Japan Airlines, Sapporo, Hokkaido, bought two DC-3s in the USA between 1955 and 1959. They were taken over by **Japan Domestic Airlines** when NJA merged with Nitto and Fuji.

JA5015; JA5058.

Index:

DC-2:

J-BBOH	c/n	J-BBOT	
J-BBOI	1323	J-BBOU	
J-BBOO		J-BBOV	
J-BBOQ		J-BDOH	
J-BBOR			

DC-3:

J-BDOI	2009 ?	J-BKOL (L2D)	
J-BDOJ		J-BKOV (L2D)	
J-BDOK		J-BKOY (L2D)	
J-BDOL		J-BOOA (L2D)	
J-BDOM		J-BOOB (L2D)	
J-BFOB		J-BOOJ (L2D)	
J-BHOR (L2D)		J-BOOQ (L2D)	
J-BHOS (L2D)		J-BOOU (L2D)	
J-BHOT (L2D)		JA5015	2217
J-BHOU (L2D)		JA5018	6006
J-BHOV (L2D)		JA5019	4247
J-BHOW (L2D)		JA5024	13194
J-BHOX (L2D)		JA5025	13510
J-BHOY (L2D)		JA5027	1996
J-BHOZ (L2D)		JA5039	3253
J-BIOA (L2D)		JA5040	6349
J-BIOB (L2D)		JA5043	3258
J-BIOC (L2D)		JA5045	7336
J-BIOD (L2D)		JA5050	11729
J-BIOE (L2D)		JA5058	4806
J-BIOF (L2D)		JA5072	4811
J-BIOG (L2D)		JA5077	2185
J-BIOJ (L2D)		JA5078	6173
J-BKOA (L2D)		JA5080	4436
J-BKOF (L2D)		JA5100	1553
J-BKOJ (L2D)		JA5128	3251

Notes:-
DC-2s known to have been supplied are c/ns 1323, 1418 to 1422 incl. Of these c/n 1323 was a pattern aircraft and the other 5 were assembled by Nakajima. Some re-registration may have occurred.

Sixteen DC-3s were supplied, via Great Northern Airways (Canada) as agents for Mitsui and Nakajima, on the following dates: Nov37: 2009, 2025; Dec37: 1979, 2026; Apr38: 2037, 2038; May38: 2039, 2040, 2041; Aug38: 2048, 2049, 2050, 2051; Sep38: 2052; Oct 39: 2055; Apr40:2056. With the possible exception of 2009 no regn tie-ups are known. Some aircraft listed as L2Ds above may have been Douglas-built.

JORDAN - JY; TRANSJORDAN - TJ

Four airlines, all to some extent related to each other, have used DC-3s in Jordan, or Transjordan as it was previously known until April 1949. The nationality mark was changed from TJ- to JY- in 1954.

Air Jordan Co, Amman, was formed in July 1950 and operated five DC-3s until 1958, when it merged into Air Jordan of the Holyland.

JY-AAB; JY-ABE; TJ/JY-ABH; TJ/JY-ABI; JY-ABW.

Air Jordan of the Holyland, Amman, resulted from the merger of Air Jordan Co and Arab Airways in December 1958, with help from Transocean. Two DC-3s were inherited, one from each operator, but both were disposed of by the late fifties.

JY-ABR; JY-ABW.

CHAPTER 4: COMMERCIAL OPERATORS OF THE DC-3, C-47, R4D, DAKOTA AND LI-2

Index:-

4X-ACW	c/n 26054	4X-AOE	6224
4X-ADA	26792	4X-AOJ	25687
4X-AED	26972	4X-AON	19400
4X-AEO	6227	4X-ASR	10146
4X-AES	11923	4X-ATA	6227
"4X-AES"	6223	4X-DCA	25625
4X-AEZ	6224	4X-DCB	33031
4X-AOA	25667	4X-DCE	32755
4X-AOB	33093	4X-DCF	6223
4X-AOC	19503	4X-DNA	25625

Note:- Most IDF/AF C-47s carry civil type call signs in the 4X-F.. series on their fins. These are listed in the military section.

ITALY - I

Italy was among the first countries in Europe to use the DC-2, a single example of which was delivered in 1935. A captured ex-Belgian DC-3 was used during WW2 by Ala Littoria following a short spell with the Italian Air Force, but the main influx came from USAAF surplus stocks at Naples, in 1945/46. A number of operators sprang up, but disappeared almost as quickly.

Aereo Teseo SA (Orario Linee Aereo Teseo) acquired a fleet of nine DC-3s from April 1947 and used them until December of that year, when operations ceased temporarily. They were restarted by Salpanavi Soc. di Navigazione Aerea in January 1948, but were finally ended in July, and most aircraft sold to Egypt.

I-BARI; I-BOLO; I-GENO; I-NAPI; I-PALU; I-REGI; I-TORI; I-VENE; I-ZOLI - all using the first four letters of cities they served ! However, no identity is known for I-NAPI while I-ZOLI was apparently not taken up.

ALITALIA - Linee Aeree Italiane, Rome, acquired DC-3s when it took over LAI in November 1957. The last of these was sold in Ethiopia in 1965.

I-LALO; I-LENE; I-LEON; I-LICE; I-LIDA; I-LINA; I-LONA; I-LORD; I-LORO; I-LUCE; I-LULA; I-LUNA.

Aviolinee Italiane SA, Rome, bought DC-2 I-EROS in 1935 and used it until 1940, when it was taken over by the Italian Air Force.

Avio Linee Italiane - Flotte Riunite, Rome, was formed in January 1949 by the merging of Airone, A.L.I., SISA, Transadriateca and SNA. DC-3s acquired with some of these companies were used until January 1952, when the assets were sold to LAI.

I-COSU; I-EBRO; I-ELFO; I-ENOS; I-ETNA; I-LUNA; I-SOLE; I-TRAS; I-TRES; I-TRIS; I-TROS; I-TRUS; I-VARO; I-VELE.

ITAVIA - Società di Navigazione Aerea SpA, Rome, bought DC-3s in 1962 to replace DH Herons on scheduled services. These, in turn, were sold to pay for Heralds two years later.

I-TAVA; I-TAVE; I-TAVI; I-TAVO.

Linee Aeree Italiane SpA - LAI, Rome, started operations in Apr47, using DC-3s with help from TWA. Those that survived were taken over by Alitalia on 01Nov57.

I-EBRO; I-ENOS; I-LAIL; I-LALO; I-LAMA; I-LEDA; I-LENE; I-LENT; I-LEON; I-LETR; I-LICE; I-LIDA; I-LILI; I-LINA; I-LINC; I-LIRA; I-LODO; I-LONA; I-LORD; I-LORO; I-LOTT; I-LUCE; I-LULA; I-LUNA; I-TRAS; I-TRUS.

Nucleo Ala Littoria, Rome, operated airline services during the war, from September 1940 until June 1943, when the Luftwaffe took over the equipment, which included DC-2 I-EROS and DC-3 I-EMOS.

Salpanavi, Società di Navigazione Aerea, Milan, started operations on 19 July 1947, using DC-3s leased from SISA. They merged with Aereo Teseo in January 1948.

I-NAVE; I-PADO.

SAM - Società Aerea Mediterranea, Rome, operated as a charter subsidiary of Alitalia, with four of the latter's DC-3s. These were replaced by DC-6Bs in 1962.

I-LALO; I-LENE; I-LORD and I-LORO.

SISA - Società Italiane Servizi Aerei, Trieste, started scheduled services on 8 June 1947, using DC-3s, but merged with Avio Linee Italiane in October 1948.

I-COSU; I-LUNA; I-NAVE; I-SOLE; I-VARO; I-VELE.

Transadriateca, Società di Navigazione Aerea SpA, Venice, began DC-3 operations in April 1947, but merged with Avio Linee Italiane in January 1949.

I-PADO; I-TRAS; I-TRES; I-TRIS; I-TROS; I-TRUS.

Index:-

I-BARI	c/n 26671	I-LORO	4297
I-BOLO	27048	I-LOTT	4506
I-COFR	12679	I-LUCE	4387
I-COSU	4291	I-LULA	4291
I-EBRO	7325	I-LUNA	4346
I-ELFO	4260	I-NAPI	see note
I-EMOS	2093	I-NAVE	4345
I-ENOS	7397	I-NEBB	18964
I-EROS (DC-2)	1319	I-PADO	4329
I-ETNA	4396	I-PALU	4233
I-GENO	26920	I-REGI	4312
I-LAIL	4308	I-RIBE	4380
I-LALO	19484	I-SOLE	4506
I-LAMA	4389	I-TAVA	13652
I-LEDA	4411	I-TAVE	12083
I-LENE	4325	I-TAVI	33225
I-LENT	4548	I-TAVO	33392
I-LEON	4316	I-TORI	25755
I-LETR	4686	I-TRAS	26800
I-LICE	6011	I-TRES	25573
I-LIDA	4261	I-TRIS	26707
I-LILI	25573	I-TROS	26675
I-LINA	4236	I-TRUS	26646
I-LINC	9101	I-VARO	6011
I-LIRA	4380	I-VELE	4548
I-LODO	4221	I-VENE	26919
I-LONA	4500	(I-ZOLI)	see note
I-LORD	4496		

Notes:- I-NAPI was registered to Aereo Teseo on 29Nov48 and cancelled as sold abroad on 09Mar49, probably to the Egyptian AF with others from the same company. Its c/n is unknown. I-ZOLI appears to have been reserved for Aereo Teseo but not to have been officially registered, possibly due to the company closure.

IVORY COAST - TU

Air Afrique, Abidjan, was formed by Air France and representatives of 11 African countries on 28Mar61 to operate scheduled services throughout the ex-French colonial territories in W Africa. A few DC-3s were used on local services for a time. Two were leased from the Dahomey Air Force, and two from Air Ivoire.

TU-TIA; TU-TIB; TU-TCL; TY-AAB; TY-AAC; 6V-AAP.

Air Ivoire, Cie Nationale, Abidjan, began scheduled services in mid-1964 using two DC-3s. These were replaced by YS-11s in 1973.

TU-TIA; TU-TIB; 5U-AAJ; 6V-AAP.

Sté. Airtransivoire, Abidjan, used DC-3 TU-TJM on air taxi and charter work in 1978/79. It was wfu by 1986.

Index:-

TU-TCL	c/n 25875	TU-TIB	42959
TU-TIA	42955	TU-TJM	33127

Note:- The TU-V.. series is covered in the military section.

JAMAICA - VP-J and 6Y

British Caribbean Airways Ltd, Kingston, used two DC-3s to start scheduled services in July 1948, but in October of the following year they were taken over by BWIA.

VP-JAP; VP-JAQ.

Jamaica Air Services, Kingston, leased a US registered DC-3 to start services in 1963, but nothing further is known of this.

Trans-Jamaican Airlines, Montego Bay, bought DC-3 Viewmaster 6Y-JJQ in 1980. It was probably sold in 1986.

Index:-

VP-JAP	c/n 13114	6Y-JJQ	9108
VP-JAQ	9885		

JAPAN - J and JA

Japan made early use of the Douglas DC-2 and DC-3. Nakajima bought a single DC-2 (NC14284 which became J-BBOI) in October 1934 and followed this with five unassembled aircraft. With the experience gained they designed their own twin, the Nakajima AT-2, bearing a superficial resemblance to the DC-2. The DC-3 followed with 20 delivered as parts, and two DC-3As. These served as patterns for licence production by Showa as the L2D. Dai Nippon used nine L2Ds from 1941. Japanese production is described earlier. Post-war, when aviation was again permitted in 1954, DC-3s were used to open internal routes and 18 examples were bought in the USA. Some were also leased by Northwest Airlines for use in Japan.

All Nippon Airways Co Ltd, Tokyo, was established in March 1958 by the merger of Far East Airlines with Japan Helicopter and Aeroplane Transport Co. The latter already had two DC-3s and others were bought after the merger, the final DC-3 being retired in 1968.

JA5018; JA5019; JA5024; JA5025; JA5027; JA5039; JA5040; JA5043; JA5045; JA5050; JA5072; JA5077; JA5078; JA5080; N493/JA5128 (lsd).

Dai Nippon Airways (DNKKK), Tokyo, operated a DC-2 supplied by Nakajima in 1938 (J-BBOI "Niitaka" ex NKYKK and Army). One DC-3 J-BFOB "Tsubaki" is known to have been in use early in 1940. A batch of nine Nakajima built DC-3s, J-BHOR to J-BHOZ were delivered in 1941, named as follows:- J-BHOR name unknown; J-BHOS "Kusunoki"; J-BHOT "Hinoki"; J-BHOU "Kashi"; J-BHOV "Nara"; J-BHOW name unkn; J-BHOX "Kaba"; J-BHOY "Tsuga" and J-BHOZ "Momi". A further eight DC-3s followed during 1941:- J-BIOA "Sugi"; J-BIOB "Matsu"; J-BIOC "Ume"; J-BIOD "Momo"; J-BIOE "Kiri"; J-BIOF "Yanagi"; J-BIOG "Sakaki"; J-BIOJ "Azusa". Eleven further aircraft have been identified as J-BKOA "Mutsu"; J-BKOF "Higo"; J-BKOJ "Take"; J-BKOL "Kunugi"; J-BKOV "Kawachi"; J-BKOY "Tushima"; J-BOOA "Satsuma"; J-BOOB "Ohsumi" J-BOOJ "Kamo"; J-BOOQ "Shima"; J-BOOU "Izumo".

The following fates are known:- J-BIOA, shot down Aug43 near Sulawesi (Celebes); J-BIOC, crashed into mountain near Taipei (Formosa) Dec43; J-BIOF, crashed near Malay Peninsula Aug 44; J-BIOG, crashed Cebu Island Oct 42; J-BKOA, lost between Denpasar and Surabaya 24Jan45; J-BKOJ, ditched north of Formosa Mar42; J-BKOL, lost Formosa Jan45; J-BKOV, shot down en route Taipei (Formosa) 05Mar45; J-BOOJ, crashed into mountain in Formosa Dec44; J-BOOQ, forced landing after take-off from Matsuyama (Formosa) Apr45.

Greater Japan Air Lines, Tokyo, was formed in August 1939 by the reorganisation of Japan Air Lines, ceasing operations on 24 August 1945. Showa-built L2Ds were used.

Japan Air Lines, are known to have started operations using DC-3s in 1951. Their origin remains somewhat of a mystery, with a photo of a DC-3 in JAL c/s showing a Philippine Airlines flag on the tail, but no registration mark visible.

Japan Helicopter and Aeroplane Transport Co (JHAT), Tokyo, bought two DC-3s to start operations in March 1954, using them until JHAT merged with Far East Airlines in March 1958, forming All Nippon.

JA5018; JA5019; JA5024; JA5025; JA5027; JA5039; JA5043; JA5045.

Nihon Koku Yuso KK - NKYKK, (Japan Air Transport Co),Tokyo, imported six DC-2s in 1934/35. These were evaluated by Nakajima and purchased by the Army. Evidence exists of nine registrations: J-BBOH, J-BBOI "Niitaka", J-BBOO "Kirishima"; J-BBOQ "Tsukuba", J-BBOR "Atago", J-BBOT, J-BBOU "Kongo"; J-BBOV "Ibuki"; J-BDOH. One was named "Fuji". J-BBOT crashed on 05Feb40 at Uotsuri Isle, 115m N of Formosa.

North Japan Airlines, Sapporo, Hokkaido, bought two DC-3s in the USA between 1955 and 1959. They were taken over by **Japan Domestic Airlines** when NJA merged with Nitto and Fuji.

JA5015; JA5058.

Index:

DC-2:

J-BBOH	c/n	J-BBOT
J-BBOI	1323	J-BBOU
J-BBOO		J-BBOV
J-BBOQ		J-BDOH
J-BBOR		

DC-3:

J-BDOI	2009 ?	J-BKOL (L2D)	
J-BDOJ		J-BKOV (L2D)	
J-BDOK		J-BKOY (L2D)	
J-BDOL		J-BOOA (L2D)	
J-BDOM		J-BOOB (L2D)	
J-BFOB		J-BOOJ (L2D)	
J-BHOR (L2D)		J-BOOQ (L2D)	
J-BHOS (L2D)		J-BOOU (L2D)	
J-BHOT (L2D)		JA5015	2217
J-BHOU (L2D)		JA5018	6006
J-BHOV (L2D)		JA5019	4247
J-BHOW (L2D)		JA5024	13194
J-BHOX (L2D)		JA5025	13510
J-BHOY (L2D)		JA5027	1996
J-BHOZ (L2D)		JA5039	3253
J-BIOA (L2D)		JA5040	6349
J-BIOB (L2D)		JA5043	3258
J-BIOC (L2D)		JA5045	7336
J-BIOD (L2D)		JA5050	11729
J-BIOE (L2D)		JA5058	4806
J-BIOF (L2D)		JA5072	4811
J-BIOG (L2D)		JA5077	2185
J-BIOJ (L2D)		JA5078	6173
J-BKOA (L2D)		JA5080	4436
J-BKOF (L2D)		JA5100	1553
J-BKOJ (L2D)		JA5128	3251

Notes:-

DC-2s known to have been supplied are c/ns 1323, 1418 to 1422 incl. Of these c/n 1323 was a pattern aircraft and the other 5 were assembled by Nakajima. Some re-registration may have occurred.

Sixteen DC-3s were supplied, via Great Northern Airways (Canada) as agents for Mitsui and Nakajima, on the following dates: Nov37: 2009, 2025; Dec37: 1979, 2026; Apr38: 2037, 2038; May38: 2039, 2040, 2041; Aug38: 2048, 2049, 2050, 2051; Sep38: 2052; Oct 39: 2055; Apr40:2056. With the possible exception of 2009 no regn tie-ups are known. Some aircraft listed as L2Ds above may have been Douglas-built.

JORDAN - JY; TRANSJORDAN - TJ

Four airlines, all to some extent related to each other, have used DC-3s in Jordan, or Transjordan as it was previously known until April 1949. The nationality mark was changed from TJ- to JY- in 1954.

Air Jordan Co, Amman, was formed in July 1950 and operated five DC-3s until 1958, when it merged into Air Jordan of the Holyland.

JY-AAB; JY-ABE; TJ/JY-ABH; TJ/JY-ABI; JY-ABW.

Air Jordan of the Holyland, Amman, resulted from the merger of Air Jordan Co and Arab Airways in December 1958, with help from Transocean. Two DC-3s were inherited, one from each operator, but both were disposed of by the late fifties.

JY-ABR; JY-ABW.

CHAPTER 4: COMMERCIAL OPERATORS OF THE DC-3, C-47, R4D, DAKOTA AND LI-2

Arab Airways (Jerusalem) Ltd, Amman, bought DC-3s to operate scheduled services in October 1953 and a further aircraft was leased for a while in 1956. One of these went to Air Jordan on its merger with Arab Airways.

JY-AAA; TJ/JY-ABN; TJ-ABO; TJ/JY-ABR; JY-ABS. TJ-ABQ possibly.

ALIA - Royal Jordanian Airlines, Amman, replaced Jordan Airways, alias Jordanian, in December 1963 and in July 1967 a DC-3 (JY-ADE) was bought. However, this was sold to UTA for spares a month later.

Jordan Airways, Amman, was formed to take over Air Jordan in Sep61 and leased DC-3 JY-ACJ from MEA between 1961 and 1963.

Index:-

JY-AAA	c/n 26057	TJ-ABQ	25810
JY-AAB	4113	TJ/JY-ABR	26105
"JY-AAE"	26569	JY-ABS	4273
JY-ABE	26569	JY-ABW	26423
TJ/JY-ABH	4223	JY-ACJ	26057
TJ-ABI		JY-ACN	26105
TJ/JY-ABN	25806	JY-ADE	9004
TJ-ABO	25586		

Note:- TJ-ABI was sold in the USA in August 1958.

JUGOSLAVIA - See Yugoslavia

KATANGA - KA

Air Katanga, was formed in early 1961 in part of the ex Belgian Congo which had seceded from the Democratic Republic of Congo. A few DC-3s were leased from Sabena and one was bought in South Africa but operated by Air Couriers, whose relationship with Air Katanga is unknown. It was destroyed by bombing before any registration had taken place.

KA-DFN; KA-TCA ; OO-AUL; OO-AUX; OO-AWF; OO-AWL; OO-AWN; OO-AWZ; OO-CBX.

Index:-

KA-DFN	c/n 12161	KA-TCA	26244

KENYA - VP-K and 5Y

The first DC-3s were used in Kenya before the three territories making up East Africa gained their independence from British Colonial rule. At that time they were registered in the VP-K.. series, as were all aircraft owned by EAA. Subsequent to independence some of the aircraft were registered in Tanzania and Uganda, though for convenience they are listed here to avoid repetition in the entries for EAA under these countries.

Air Kenya have used three DC-3s on scheduled services. The airline was formed in 1986 as a joint venture with Sunbird. Two were on lease from Sunbird Air Charter and a third was bought in 1990. They were replaced by Dash 8s in 1997.

5Y-AAE; 5Y-BBN; 5Y-BGU; 5Y-DAK.

East African Airways Corp - EAAC, Nairobi, used DC-3s on scheduled services from October 1949 until January 1977, when financial difficulties forced their sale to Caspair. Independence in 1965 resulted in some being re-registered in Tanzania (5H-) and Uganda (5X-).(qv)

VP-KHK; VP-KHN; VP-KIF; VP-KJP/5Y-AAD; VP-KJQ/5Y-AAE; VP-KJR/5X-AAQ; VP-KJS/5X-AAR; VP-KJT; VP-KJU/5Y-AAF; VP-KLA/5H-AAJ; VP-KLC/5H-AAK; VP-KKH; VP-KKI/5H-AAL; VP-KNU; VP-KTS/5X-AAS.

Caspair Ltd, Nairobi, took over the Kenya based DC-3s from EAA in 1977 to operate domestic services. These included some non-Kenyan registered aircraft stranded in Kenya when operations by EAA ceased. Some were sold to the Sudan or to Sunbird Air Charter in 1979, but two remained in use in 1982.

5Y-AAE; 5Y-BAX; 5Y-BBL to 5Y-BBN incl.

Skyways, Nairobi, also trades as Sincereways, and operates a single DC-3 5Y-BMB, the last in Kenya.

Skyways (E Africa) Ltd, Nairobi, a subsidiary of the UK company Skyways Lyd, operated VP-KGI, VP-KGL commencing 1948 as non-African charter companies were banned from the colonial territories. The service was suspended in 1949.

Sunbird Air Charter, Wilson, Nairobi, took over some DC-3s from Caspair in 1979, two of which were sold and two written-off in accidents.

5Y-AAE; 5Y-BAX; 5Y-BBN; 5Y-DAK(1).

Index:-

VP-KGI	c/n 9623	5Y-AAE	32844
VP-KGL	13182	5Y-AAF	33325
VP-KHK	26099	5Y-ACF	25372
VP-KHN	26721	5Y-ADI	13447
VP-KIF	25606	5Y-AKB	32923
VP-KJP	32825	5Y-BAX	26095
VP-KJQ	32844	5Y-BBL	32955
VP-KJR	32845	5Y-BBM	32628
VP-KJS	33211	5Y-BBN	32845
VP-KJT	33278	5Y-BFO	12073
VP-KJU	33325	5Y-BGU	4890
VP-KKH	33568	5Y-BIL	42963
VP-KKI	32955	5Y-BLL	4082
VP-KLA	32628	5Y-BMB	34375
VP-KLC	25815	5Y-BNK	27047
VP-KLJ	20228	5Y-DAK(1)	32954
VP-KNU	12166	5Y-DAK(2)	12073
VP-KTS	32656	5Y-DCA	26733
5Y-AAD	32825	5Y-RDS	27085

KOREA, NORTH

UKAMPS, Pyong-Yang, started operations with Li-2s supplied by Russia, but these were replaced by Il-14s. No details of individual aircraft are known.

KOREA, SOUTH - HL

Relatively little is known about the DC-3s used in Korea by the two airlines that have used the type. It is possible that some of the early aircraft came from Hong Kong Airways, as these have never come to light.

Korean National Airlines, Seoul, started using DC-3s in 1950 and continued, with disturbance due to the war of 1950-53, until June 1962 when Korean Air Lines was formed. The DC-3s were registered and operated in the HL0x series and were almost certainly re-registered when KAL was formed, but there is some confusion over dates. HL06 was hijacked to N Korea on 16Feb58 and may never have been returned.

HL03; HL05; HL06; HL07; HL08.

Korean Air Lines, Seoul, succeeded KNA in June 1962. One DC-3 was leased from Japan in that year and others probably taken over from KNA and re-registered. Further DC-3s were registered from about 1965 in the HL200x series.

HL2001; HL2002; HL2003; HL2005; HL2010; HL4005; HL4007; HL4008; HL4009.

Index:-

HL03	c/n	HL2003	25969
HL05		HL2005	
HL06		HL2010	32810
HL07	33200	HL4005	2185
HL08		HL4007	
HL2001	12017	HL4008	
HL2002	20203	HL4009	33200

Notes:- Photos of HL05 and HL06 taken in Aug 1953 and June 1954 respectively, show KNA markings, though of a different style. HL2010 has been reported as owned by Far East Airlines, so its listing under Korean may be an error.

KUWAIT - G and 9K

Kuwait Airways, Kuwait, acquired DC-3s as Kuwait National in 1953, adopting the present name in 1955. Some were only on lease. One

DC-3 survived until 1959. C/n 25806 is preserved as "G-AMZZ" painted in KNA colours.

G-AMPO; G-AMSL; G-AMSM; G-AMVA; G-AMZZ; G-ANTC.

LAOS - XW

As a French Protectorate the area used F- until becoming independent within the French Union 1949 using F-O, then F-L from 1955. The XW-prefix was allocated in 1959 and came into use in 1960. Because of the disturbed state of this country since independence, many mysteries exist about the DC-3s used by numerous operators, though the type was the mainstay of operations. It is most unlikely that the problems evident later will ever be solved. Two series of markings were used from 1960, XW-Pxx and XW-Txx, but apart from the fact that Bird & Sons' aircraft are all in the first series, there seems no obvious distinction between the two. Laos now uses the nationality mark RDPL, but there is no evidence that any DC-3s survived to adopt the new marks in 1977.

Air Laos SA, Vientiane, was formed as a partnership between the Laotian Government, Air France and Aigle Azur in October 1952. Operations began in November 1952 with two DC-3s leased from Aigle Azur. Activities ceased in 1961 when its operating certificate was withdrawn.

F-BEIA; F-BFGA; F-BFGC; F-BFGN; F-OAQD; XW-PAD; XW-PXK.

Air Vientiane Laos, Vientiane is believed to have used XW-TAH from 1964 to 1967 and also c/n 20434 in XW-Txx marks in the late sixties.

Lane Xang Airlines, Vientiane, has been reported as using four DC-3s for a time, at least until the end of 1974, the last two DC-3s below operated in Cambodia with Khemara Air Transport in 1974. Lane Xang also operated other types in Cambodia as Cambodia International Airlines.

XW-PKD; XW-PKT; XW-TFB; XW-TFI.

Lao Airlines - Sté. Anon. de Transports Aériens, Vientiane, was formed in September 1967 to operate scheduled services and was bought by Royal Air Lao in Dec73. Some five DC-3s are known to have been used between March 1968 and 1975.

XW-TDD; XW-TDH; XW-TDI; XW-TDO; XW-TFC.

Laos Air Charter, Vientiane, is known to have used about eight DC-3s between March 1967 and 1973. One is believed to have remained in use until about 1975. This company also operated in Cambodia.

XW-PFA; XW-PFN; XW-PFY; XW-TDA; XW-TDJ; XW-TDK; XW-TDL; XW-TDM; and possibly XW-TFJ.

Royal Air Lao, Vientiane, succeeded **Air Laos** Transports Aériens in 1962, maybe only by the addition of "Royal" to the title. Six DC-3s have been reported, two remaining until 1975.

XW-PAD; XW-PAR; XW-TAD; XW-TAE; XW-TAF; XW-TDR.

Sorya Airlines, Vientiane, used DC-3 XW-PKT and also operated XW-PNB in Cambodia.

Xiengkhouang Air Transport, Vientiane, is known to have used three DC-3s, one of which was used from December 1967 until 1975.

XW-PFA; XW-TDC; XW-TDF.

Index:-

	c/n		
XW-PAA		XW-PFT	12539
XW-PAD	26696	XW-PFV	11971
XW-PAR		XW-PFW	13524 ?
XW-PCM	27211	XW-PFX	13529
XW-PDE	10160	XW-PFY	20049 ?
XW-PDF		XW-PGJ	
XW-PDG	13184	XW-PGK	
XW-PDL		XW-PGW	
XW-PEE	13623	XW-PHV	
XW-PFA	13906	XW-PHW	
XW-PFC		XW-PKD	
XW-PFM		XW-PKT	
XW-PFN	20763	XW-PKX	
XW-PKY		XW-TDI	27145
XW-PNB		XW-TDJ	13529
XW-PNC		XW-TDK	20763
XW-TAD		"XW-TDK"	10078 ?
XW-TAE	32991	XW-TDL	27082
XW-TAF	20328	XW-TDM	10078
XW-TAH	20213	XW-TDO	26006
XW-TDA	13729	XW-TDR	33481
XW-TDB		XW-TFB	34298
XW-TDC	33612	XW-TFC	
XW-TDD	4119	XW-TFI	4119
XW-TDF	27105 ?	XW-TFJ	26651
	or 13906 ?	XW-TFL	9559
XW-TDH	26008	XW-TFN	

Notes:-
XW-PAR has been reported as ex B-1523, but this was w/o on 21Aug67.
XW-PFC has been reported as a Porter and as a DC-3, the latter w/o on 21Dec71. This may have been confused with XW-TFC w/o on the same date.
XW-PFM reported with Lao Cathay, lost 07Dec67.
XW-PGJ Bird & Sons Inc, lsd to CASI, was w/o 2Jan70 at Long Cheng.
XW-PGK Bird & Sons Inc, fate unknown.
XW-PHV Air Union Co., w/o 03Dec73 Phnom Penh.
XW-PHW lsd to Cambodia Air Commercial, w/o 07Jul72 at Kompong Som, Cambodia.
XW-PKD Lane Xang Airlines, dbr 12Sep73 at Kampot, Cambodia.
XW-PKT Lane Xang Airlines, Sorya (?), w/o 03Jul74 at Kompong Som.
XW-PKX Khmer Airlines. w/o 08Oct74 Krakor, Cambodia.
XW-PKY op by Khmer Akas, w/o 04May73, Kampot.
XW-PNB Sorya, w/o Phnom Penh 11Apr75.
XW-PNC Angkor Intl, to Sakami Khmer A/l, w/o Phnom Penh 10Mar75.
XW-TAD Royal Air Lao, w/o 24Feb68 between Luang Prabang and Vientiane.
XW-TDB reported with Lane Xang.
XW-TFL Air Union Co./CAC w/o 20Apr74 at Suay Rieng.
XW-TFN Air Union Co. w/o 28May74 at Kompong Som.

LEBANON - LR and OD

Lebanon was still under French control to some extent when the first DC-3s were supplied to Air Liban in April 1945. At the same time Pan American was supporting a rival which is now the survivor. The nationality mark LR- was used until May 1951 when it was changed to OD-.

Air Liban - Cie Générale de Transports (CGT), Beirut, started operations in April 1945 with help from Air France. At this time it was known as CGT, but the name Air Liban was adopted in 1951. It merged with Middle East Airlines in 1965. DC-3s replaced Ju52/3ms in August 1947, using them until the merger.

LR/OD-AAM; LR/OD-AAN; LR/OD-AAV; LR-AAX; LR-ABC; LR-ABI; OD-ABK; OD-ABN; OD-ABQ.

Lebanese Air Transport (Charter) Co, Beirut, leased two DC-3s for some months from April 1956, for oil support work.

OD-AEP; OD-AEQ.

Middle East Airlines Co, SA, Beirut, bought DC-3s, with Pan American help, in 1945 and used them on scheduled services until the airline merged with Air Liban in November 1965, when the last was sold.

LR-AAA; LR/OD-AAB; LR/OD-AAG; OD-AAN; LR/OD-AAO; LR/OD-ABB; LR/OD-ABD; LR/OD-ABE; OD-ABO.

Index:-

LR-AAA	c/n 13192	LR/OD-ABD	26056
LR/OD-AAB	20175	LR/OD-ABE	25709
LR/OD-AAG	10139	LR-ABI	26042
LR/OD-AAM	4495	OD-ABK	25243
LR/OD-AAN	9894	OD-ABN	26107
LR/OD-AAO	10239	OD-ABO	4284
LR/OD-AAV	42970	OD-ABQ	20012
LR-AAX	13138	(OD-ADN)	42968
LR/OD-ABB	26057	OD-AEP	33444
LR-ABC	13138	OD-AEQ	32872

CHAPTER 4: COMMERCIAL OPERATORS OF THE DC-3, C-47, R4D, DAKOTA AND LI-2

LEEWARD ISLANDS - VP-L

The Leeward Islands form the northern end of a chain of islands stretching from Trinidad in the south, to Puerto Rico in the north. To the south are the Windward Islands. The Leeward Islands comprise Antigua & Barbuda (VP-LAA to -LJZ), Anguilla & St Kitts, Nevis (VP-LKA to -LLZ), Montserrat (VP-LMA to -LUZ) and British Virgin Islands (VP-LVA to -LZZ).

Air Anguilla operated DC-3 N90830 on lease during the summer of 1976.

Air BVI Ltd, Tortola, British Virgin Islands, used DC-3s on scheduled internal services. They operated initially in US markings on lease in November 1975 but were registered locally a few months later. Five were in use in 1982, but all were sold to **Aero Virgin Islands** in 1984/85.

VP-LVH to VP-LVK incl; VP-LVM.

Leeward Islands Air Transport Services Ltd, St John's, Antigua, used DC-3 VP-LIL on scheduled services during 1965/66, on lease from BWIA.

Seagreen Air Transport, St John's, Antigua, used DC-3s VP-LAO and VP-LIX on cargo charter work from 1968. The former was sold in 1982, and the latter became V2-LIX, then N4797H, continuing to be used on lease until 1986.

Index:-

VP-LAO	c/n 33196	VP-LVJ /	
VP-LIL	13114	N62548 /	
VP-LIX /		N4577Z	9795
V2-LIX /		VP-LVK /	
N4797H	25623	N5117X	6054
VP-LVH /		VP-LVM	12195
N4425N	1963		
VP-LVI/			
N4471J	6187		

LESOTHO - 7P

Formerly Basutoland, Lesotho became independent in 1966.

Lesotho Airways leased DC-3s ZS-DRJ and ZS-EJK from Commercial Air Services of South Africa and a First-Day Cover of the innaugural flight from Johannesburg to Maseru on 02Oct67 shows a DC-3.

LIBERIA - EL

Air Liberia Inc, Robertsfield, was formed by the merger of Liberian National and Ducor Air Transport in January 1974. Two DC-3s were inherited from the former (EL-AAB and EL-AAZ).

Liberian International Airways, Robertsfield, formed June 1948, was the predecessor to Liberian National. Two DC-3s (NC33372 and NC33373) passed through Prestwick on delivery on 8 August 1948, the latter becoming EL-ADH. LIA apparently became LNA in 1951, after the assets were taken over by the government in 1949.

Liberian National Airways, Robertsfield, started operations in 1951, probably taking over Liberian International's operation and aircraft - though this cannot be confirmed apart from the use of one DC-3 in common. Four DC-3s appear to have been used, starting in 1951, and two remained when Air Liberia was formed (see note).

EL-AAB; EL-AAZ; EL-ADH.

Index:-

EL-AAB(1)	c/n 4284	EL-ADH	4368
EL-AAB(2)	12054	EL-AWB	9410
EL-AAZ	11652		

Note:- Confusion exists over the use of registration EL-AAB. It has been assumed that the first EL-AAB had connections with NC33372 c/n 4284 and it is reported as going to MEA in 1953. Photographic evidence shows the existence of an EL-AAB (2?) in August 1960 and of 9G-AAE in September 1960. 9G-AAE (12054) was canx 09Nov70 becoming EL-AAB (3?) and crashed as such on 19Apr75. Another accident to an EL-AAB is recorded on 25Jun70 at Tchien involving starboard wing and undercarriage damage. This could be the demise of the unidentified EL-AAB(2?) or a repairable accident to EL-AAB(3) if the actual transfer pre-dated the Ghanaian cancellation paperwork by a few months. Clarification is still sought.

LIBYA - 5A

Various DC-3s have been used in Libya over the years since oil was first discovered there, but all have been leased or operated by foreign companies, and none has been registered there.

Air Libya, Benghazi, was formed by American interests to operate DC-3s in support of desert oil companies. **All World Aviation** owned the aircraft in 1977, but ceased trading in 1 January 1980 when its operating certificate was withdrawn.

N98392; N718A; N166J; N172K; N292L.

Libyan Aviation, Benghazi, began using DC-3s on oil support work about 1965 in association with **International Aviation Development Corp**, and later **Diamond Leasing Co**. The survivors were taken over by the Libyan government and used for target practice.

N330; N219F; N480F to N489F incl (also used in earlier marks).

Linair - Libyan National Airways, Tripoli, was formed jointly by Sabena and various oil companies. The operations were taken over by BIAS in 1966 and continued until 1973 when the aircraft were sold.

OO-AUV; OO-AUW; OO-AWJ; OO-AWM; OO-CBC; OO-CBU; OO-CBW; OO-CBX; OO-CBY; OO-SBH; OO-UBT.

United Libyan Airlines, Benghazi, operated three British registered DC-3s in the early 196Os, all owned by Autair. By 1964 G-AGHJ, G-AGYX and G-AJIC were in **Libyan Aviation** colours, and were sold by Autair in August 1965.

LUXEMBOURG - LX

European Air Transport, SA, Luxembourg, was reported to have started operations with three DC-3s in 1962. The aircraft were probably leased and operations did not last long.

Luxembourg Airlines (later Luxair) - SA Luxembourgeoise de Navigation Aériens, Luxembourg, began services with help from Scottish Aviation, on 2 February 1948. These ceased temporarily, in 1958, by which time all the DC-3s had been sold.

LX-LAA; LX-LAB; LX-LAC.

Index:-

LX-DKT	c/n 10253	LX-LAB	25292
LX-LAA	10101	LX-LAC	12373

MADAGASCAR - F and 5R

Air Madagascar, Tananarive, was formed in 1947 and DC-3s were first supplied by TAI in 1956/57 together with financial and technical assistance. In 1961, when Madagascar became independent, a new airline was formed with the same operating name and aircraft, as **Sté. Nationale Malgache de Transports Aériens**. From 1 January 1962 it operated as **Madair**, reverting to the present name exactly a year later. At that time new nationality marks were adopted. Several more DC-3s had been added since those supplied by TAI and in 1963 seven were in use. By 1971 they had been replaced by a Nord 262 and Twin Otters and six were transferred to the Air Force.

F-BEII; F-BEFL; F-BFGU; F-BGSE; F-BGSF; F-OAYR; F-OBCT. These were later registered 5R-MAF to 5R-MAK incl and 5R-MAV.

Index:-

5R-MAA	c/n 11726	F-BEII/5R-MAI	12761
F-BGSF/5R-MAF	13368	F-OAYR/5R-MAJ	12813
F-BFGU/5R-MAG	12333	F-OBCT/5R-MAK	20874
F-BGSE/5R-MAH	4097	F-BEFL/5R-MAV	19104

MALAWI - VP-Y and 7Q

Air Malawi, Blantyre, was formed as a subsidiary of Central African Airways in March 1964, but became independent of Rhodesia in 1967 with UDI. Three DC-3s were used, but all had been sold by 1970 when Viscounts and HS.748s replaced them.

Index:-

VP/7Q-YKM	c/n 32935	7Q-YKN	33211
VP-YKN	32741		

MALAYA/MALAYSIA/SINGAPORE - VR-R; VR-S; 9M; 9V; and BORNEO - VR-O

As the political situation in the Malaysian peninsular and adjacent island states was so complex at the time DC-3s were used in the area, all such aircraft and operators, including those in Borneo, are best covered under one heading. Pre-war the Federated Malay States used VR-R registrations; post-war the Federation of Malaya used VR-R until independence and on 01Jan59 9M- was adopted. Singapore had taken over VR-S from Straits Settlements after the war and initially all Malayan Airways aircraft used this series. When Singapore became self-governing in 1959, some DC-3s were put in the VR-R series briefly, but soon took up the 9M- series. British North Borneo (later Sabah) used VR-O, Sarawak VR-W and Singapore VR-S, but all joined Malaya to form Malaysia in September 1963 using 9M-. Singapore withdrew in August 1965 and the 9V- register thus came into use in February 1966.

Kris Air, Singapore used DC-3 N64422 in the late seventies, with C-46s.

Malayan Airways Ltd, Singapore, acquired DC-3s in 1947 to replace Airspeed Consuls. For a time after Malayan independence the airline continued to operate under the old name, but **Malaysian Airways** was adopted on 16Sep63.

VR-SCB; VR-SCC; VR-SCG/9M-AMU; VR-SCM/VR-RCM/9M-ALM, VR-SCN/VR-RCN/9M-ALN; VR-SCO/VR-RCO/9M-ALO; VR-SCP/VR-RCP/9M-ALP; VR-SCQ/VR-RCQ/9M-ALQ; VR-SCR; VR-SCW; VR-SDD; VR-SDH; VR-SEI.

Malaysian Airways Ltd, Singapore, was formed on 16 September 1963 from Malayan Airways, inheriting six DC-3s. The name **Malaysia-Singapore Airlines** was adopted on 01Jan67. Borneo Airways' operations were taken over on 20May64.

9M-ALM; 9M-ALP; 9M-ALQ; 9M-AND/9V-BAL; 9M-ANE; 9M-ANF/9V-BAM; 9V-BAN; 9V-BAO.

Malaysia-Singapore Airways, Singapore, resulted when Malaysian was renamed on 01Jan67. Although sources differ somewhat, it seems that seven DC-3s remained in use at this time, though all were sold by the time Malaysian separated from MSA in 1972.

9M-ALM; 9M-ALP; 9M-AMU; 9M-ANE; 9V-BAL; 9V-BAM; 9V-BAN; 9V-BAO.

Pan Malaysia Air, Kuala Lumpur registered DC-3 9M-AUJ in January 1975, but the marking was never taken up although still listed in 1978. N722A was owned about 1976.

Saber Air Pte Ltd, Singapore, bought DC-3 9V-BAN from MSA in 1970, but sold it in the following February.

Borneo Airways Ltd, Labuan, was supplied with DC-3s by Malayan Airways between August 1962 and June 1963. A further aircraft was added in 1964 when Borneo had become part of Malaysia. Separate operations ceased on 1 April 1965.

VR-OAH/9M-AND; VR-OAI/9M-ANE; VR-OAJ/9M-ANF; 9M-AMU.

Index:-

VR-OAH	c/n 13384	VR-SCB	20792
VR-OAI	26237	VR-SCC	20763
VR-OAJ	20763	VR-SCG	12006
VR-RCM	19569	VR-SCM	19569
VR-RCN	12209	VR-SCN	12209
VR-RCO	13366	VR-SCO	13366
VR-RCP	12433	VR-SCP	12433
VR-RCQ	13729	VR-SCQ	13729
VR-SCR	9189	9M-AMU	12006
VR-SCW	13384	9M-AND	13384
VR-SDD	33423	9M-ANE	26237
VR-SDH	26867	9M-ANF	20763
VR-SEI	26237	(9M-AUJ)	33444
9M-ALM	19569	9V-BAL	13384
9M-ALN	12209	9V-BAM	20763
9M-ALO	13366	9V-BAN	13366
9M-ALP	12433	9V-BAO	13729
9M-ALQ	13729		

MALI - CT and TZ

Air Mali, Bamako, was given three DC-3s by the British Government in 1961. These were registered provisionally CT-ABA etc, but later TZ-ABA etc prior to delivery. They survived most Russian supplied aircraft, but were out of service by 1974.

Transport Aérien du Mali, Bamako, is believed to have bought DC-3 TZ-AJW in June 1991, when it was cancelled from the US Register. It returned to Europe in 1995.

Index:-

CT-AAA/TZ-ABA	c/n 12222	CT-AAC/TZ-ABC	12208
CT-AAB/TZ-ABB	12096	TZ-AJW	11737

MARTINIQUE - F-OG..

Air Martinique (Satair), Fort de France, was formed in 1964 to operate scheduled services. Various DC-3s are known to have been leased as N63440 (1974), N755VM (1974), N211M (1978/9) and F-OGFJ was registered 1978-83 until replaced by Twin Otters, and other twins. See also under France.

MAURITANIA - 5T

Air Mauritanie - Soc Nationale Air Mauritania, Nouakchott, used DC-3s to start scheduled services in 1963. Several were leased from time to time, from Spantax which provided financial help, and from Air Senegal. None now remain.

5T-CAA to 5T-CAC incl; 5T-CAE; 5T-CJQ; EC-ARZ; 6V-AAA; 6V-AAK.

Index:-

5T-CAA	c/n 12939	5T-CAE	9463
5T-CAB	12720	5T-CAH	9511
5T-CAC	1984	5T-CJQ	25293

MEXICO - XA, XB and XC

Mexico has been a major DC-3 user ever since the end of WW2, but DC-2s and DC-3s were supplied to Mexicana before the war by Pan American. Of the many post-war operators only about two still use the DC-3. Tracing the history of Mexican aircraft is complicated by the way in which markings are changed according to the use the owner makes of the aircraft. The XA series is reserved for airlines, XB for private and executive use and at first by government agencies. The last moved to the XC series. Some individual DC-3s have had marks in all three series. It has not proved possible to identify all the earlier DC-3s on the Mexican register, as the early published register quoted no constructor's number - and in some cases did not indicate the model, so a few Douglas B-18s and C-39s may have been included. Where doubt is known to exist this is mentioned in the notes.

Aéreo Panini - See Servicio Aéreo Panini.

Aero California, La Paz, used DC-3s XA-HOI, XA-IOR, XA-JAE, XA-JIE, XA-RAM and a DC-9 on passenger services starting about 1982/83. DC-9s took over completely by 1989.

Aero Libertad SA, a subsidiary of Mexicana, bought three ex PBA DC-3s, operating the first service in Sep89. They were out of service by 1991.

XA-RPE; XA-RPN; XA-RPO. XA-REP was noted with a company of the same name in 1998.

CHAPTER 4: COMMERCIAL OPERATORS OF THE DC-3, C-47, R4D, DAKOTA AND LI-2

Aerolíneas California Pacifico, Guerrero Negro, was using one DC-3 from 1979 onwards. Later a Convair 440 was added and two more DC-3s by 1995, of which one remained in 1999, possibly the last year of DC-3 operations.

XA-CUC; XA-RPI; XA-VIZ.

Aerolíneas del Pacifico SA, La Paz, Baja California, started scheduled and charter services in prior to 1976 and continued to use DC-3s until about 1984.

XA-HOI; XA-POK; XA-SUY; XA-TEH; XB-FOO.

Aerolíneas Mexicanas SA, Mexico City, was formed by Aeronaves de Mexico to operate unprofitable domestic services. It was absorbed into Aeronaves in 1960.

XA-FUW; XA-GUX; XA-HUF.

Aerolíneas Moxi had DC-3 XA-FUW in use in the sixties. It crashed in 1967.

Aerolíneas Vega SA, Mexico City, was formed as **LAGOSA** in 1950 and the name changed in 1963. Operations ceased in about 1969.

C-39s: XA-DOH; XA-DOJ; XA-KIC. DC-3s:- XA-JAN; XA-JER; XA-NAA.

Aeromaya SA, Merida, Yucatan, was formed in November 1966 by the merger of Aero Safari and Aereo Gomez Mendez SA. The latter operated several DC-3s. The airline was taken over by SAESA in September 1969.

XA-CAG; XA-FEG; XA-GEU; XA-NIJ.

Aero-Mitla, Oaxaca, operated a single DC-3 XA-KIK, acquired in 1980.

Aeronaves Alimentadoras, Mexico City, was formed as a subsidiary of Aeronaves de Mexico to operate feeder services. DC-3s were used from December 1968 until September 1970.

XA-FUA; XA-FUV; XA-GUF; XA-JUT.

Aeronaves de Mexico SA, Mexico City, used DC-3s on scheduled services from 1946 onwards. LAMSA was taken over in 1952, followed by Aerovias Reforma in 1954, Aerolineas Mexicanas in 1960 and Trans Mar de Cortes in 1962. It traded as **Aero Mexico** from 1972.

C-39s:- XA-DOI; XA-DUF. DC-3s:- XA-FIX; XA-FIY; XA-FUA; XA-FUJ; XA-FUM; XA-FUV; XA-FUW; XA-GAU to XA-GAX incl; XA-GEW; XA-GII; XA-GUF, XA-GUN; XA-GUQ; XA-GUS; XA-GUX; XA-HEP; XA-HIP to XA-HIR incl; XA-HIY; XA-HUE to XA-HUI incl; XA-JUT; XA-KAD; XA-XYZ(1).

Aero Pacifico, La Paz, had three DC-3s, some used for cargo work.

XA-JAE; XA-JIE; XA-RAM.

Aeroservicios de Sonora, Nogales, used DC-3 XA-CEG between 1971 and about 1976, and XA-CIL from 1972.

Aero Transportes SA (also Aerovías Transportes), Mexico City, started operations in 1944 using Boeing 247Ds. These were replaced by DC-3s, but in 1952 financial difficulties forced a merger with Mexicana.

XA-GAF to XA-GAI incl; XA-GIA; XA-GIE; XA-GIR; XA-GOH; XA-GOR; XA-GUQ; XA-HEZ; XA-HIA.

Aero Transportes del Sureste SA, Mexico City, started operations soon after the end of WW2, using four DC-3s. It probably ceased operating about 1951.

XA-GAA; XA-GAE; XA-GEM; XA-GEX.

Aerovías Braniff SA, Mexico City, started scheduled services in April 1945 as a subsidiary of Braniff. DC-3s were used, but after October 1946 only charter and local services were flown, ceasing about 1949.

XA-DUI; XA-DUJ; XA-GEF; XA-GEG.

Aerovías Coahuila lost a DC-3 XA-HOU on 10Oct49 when it crashed near Saltillo, en route Mexico City - Piedras Negras.

Aerovías Contreras, Mexico City, operated DC-3s on scheduled services in the late forties. The proprietor was Manuel Contreras Farfas.

DC-2:- XA-GEP. DC-3: XA-GEO; XA-GIZ; XA-HIE to XA-HIG incl; XA-HIK.

Aerovías Internaciónales, Mexico City, used three DC-3s between about 1946 and 1951 when it was taken over by **Aero Transportes**. Operations ceased in 1953. It appears to have inherited aircraft from Aerovías Latino Americanas

XA-GEQ; XA-GOH; XA-GUQ.

Aerovías Latino Americanas - ALASA formed in 1946 from amalgamation of Com.Aéreas de Veracruz SA and Cia Aeronáutica del Sur SA, taken over itself by Aero Transporte SA in 1951. It operated XA-GEQ, XA-GOH and XA-GUQ.

Aerovías Oaxaquenas SA, Oaxaca, was formed in 1979 with three DC-3s. Two remained by 1995, both out of use.

XA-IOH; XA-JIH; XA-JII.

Aerovías Reforma SA, Mexico City, was formed as **Aerovías Internacionales de Mexico** in November 1946, initially with Boeing 247Ds. DC-3s were widely used on scheduled services until the airline was taken over by **Aeronaves de Mexico** in 1954.

XA-CAY; XA-FIX; XA-FIY; XA-GAV to XA-GAX incl; XA-HIP; XA-HIQ?; XA-HIR; XA-HIY; XA-HUE to XA-HUI incl.

Aerovías Rojas SA, Oaxaca, operated scheduled passenger and cargo services to Ixtepec, between about 1965 and 1977.

XA-JAN/XB-KOQ; XA-GEV; XA-JER/XB-KOM.

Aerovías del Sur SA, Iguala de Guerrero, used DC-3s on scheduled cargo and passenger services between about 1966 and 1969, when operations ceased.

XA-FIL; XA-GIB; XA-SUR.

Aerovías Transcontinentales, Guadalajara, Jalisco, used four DC-3s in the early fifties until they were sold.

XA-GUM; XA-GIR; XA-HEZ; XA-HIA.

Communicaciónes Aéreas de Veracruz SA, Japala, Vera Cruz, operated three DC-3s until 1947 when the name was changed to **Aerovias Latino Americanas**. Only two are identified, XA-FOZ which crashed in 1946, and XA-GEQ.

Cia Mexicana de Aviación SA, Mexico City, started using DC-2s supplied by PAA (which owned 45% of the company) in 1937. They were sold in 1942. C-39s were bought in 1944 to supplement the DC-3s delivered in 1939. A large fleet of the type was used until the last was retired in 1969.

DC-2s:- XA-BJG; XA-BJI; XA-BJL(1); XA-BJL(2); XA-BJM; XA-BKO; XA-BKQ; XA-BKV; XA-BKY.
C-39s:- XA-DOB; XA-DOH; XA-DOJ; XA-DOQ; XA-DOS; XA-DOT.
DC-3s:- XA-BLN; XA-BLO; XA-BLW; XA-CAB; XA-CAG; XA-CAM; XA-CAO; XA-CAY; XA-DEE; XA-DIH; XA-DIK; XA-DIN; XA-DUG; XA-DUH; XA-DUK; XA-DUM; XA-FEG; XA-FIL; XA-GAM; XA-GEC; XA-GEU to XA-GEW incl; XA-GIB; XA-GIN; XA-GOC; XA-GUJ; XA-HAO; XA-HIY; XA-HUS; XA-JAE; XA-JAG; XA-JAM to XA-JAO incl; XA-JAT; XA-JAX; XA-JER; XA-JID; XA-JIP; XA-LEX.

Cia Tabasquena de Aviación SA, Mexico City, started scheduled local services in 1948, using smaller types. DC-3 XA-JAE was used between 1965 and 1968.

Líneas Aéreas del Centro, Guadalajara, was using DC-3 XA-JAL during 1979. Other reports suggest it was bought in 1984.

Líneas Aéreas del Pacifico SA - LAPSA, Baja California, used DC-3 XA-JUI on charter work from 1947 until the early fifties, when it was taken over by Trans Mar de Cortes.

Líneas Aéreas Guerrero-Oaxaca - LAGOSA, Mexico City, had two C-39s, XA-DUF(?) and XA-KIC, in its cargo fleet from 1950.

Líneas Aéreas Mexicanas SA - LAMSA, Mexico City, operated as a subsidiary of United Airlines who supplied Boeing 247Ds and DC-3s. The latter were in use between 1946 and 1952, when Aeronaves de Mexico took over operations.

XA-FIY; XA-FUA; XA-FUJ; XA-FUM; XA-FUV; XA-FUW; XA-GAJ; XA-GUX; XA-JUT.

Líneas Aéreas Unidas SA - LAUSA, Mexico City, was formed as Aeronaves de Oaxaca, but was renamed in 1951 after Transportes Aereos Tampico was taken over in 1950. It became **Líneas Aéreas Unidas Mexicanas** (LAUMSA) in 1962. Four C-39s were used at first, but two DC-3s also appeared, and may have been used until the early sixties.

C-39s:- XA-DOB; XA-DOH?; XA-DOI; XA-DOQ;
DC-3s:- XA-FIK; XA-HUH.

Maya Airways had DC-3 XA-MAI in 1970, at Mexico City. See Servicio Aereo Gomez Mendez for Aero Maya.

Omega Aero Transportes, Ensenada, were using DC-3 XA-ROM in 1999, but operations were suspended by 2000.

Rutas Aérea Mexicana SA - RAMSA, Mexico City, operated two DC-3s, amongst other types, on scheduled services about 1950.

XA-FUC; XA-HOS.

Servicio Aéreo Gomez Mendez, Huajuapam de Leon, used five DC-3s on scheduled services. Some were registered initially to Manuel Gomez Mendez. The airline was taken over by Aero Safari in November 1966, to form **Aero Maya**.

XA-CAG; XA-FEG; XA-GAQ; XA-JEW; XA-NIJ.

Servicio Aéreo Panini, Mexico City, founded 1936, operated scheduled services using Boeing 247Ds and DC-3s. Two DC-2s, bought from CMA, were also used, one unknown example crashing on 28Dec47. Operations were taken over by Aerovias Reforma in 1949.

DC-2s:- XA-BKY and XA-BKO or BKQ; XA-GEE?;
DC-3s:- XA-FUX; XA-FUZ; XA-GEE?; XA-HIQ; XA-HIR.

Servicios Aéreos, La Paz, was using DC-3 XA-JAE in 1979/80.

Servicios Aéreos Especiales SA - SAESA, Mexico City, was formed in 1960 using a DC-3 to start charter and scheduled operations. This was lost in 1968 but later replaced. Aero Maya was taken over in September 1969 but operations ceased shortly afterwards, when Aeronaves de Mexico took over some routes.

XA-GEU; XA-JAE; XA-SAE.

Taxis Aéreos Nacionales SA, Mexico City, started charter and air-taxi operations with two DC-3s in 1947 until at least 1952. XA-HOT is known.

Trans Mar de Cortes SA, La Paz, Baja California, used DC-3s to start cargo charters in 1947. Líneas Aéreas del Pacifico was taken over in 1952. In 1962 the airline was itself taken over by Aeronaves de Mexico.

XA-FIR; XA-HUE; XA-HIY; XA-JEL.

Transportes Aéreos de Nayarit SA, Tepic, Nayarit, used a DC-3 to start scheduled passenger services in 1954. One DC-3 remained in use until the late seventies. An operator under the same name appeared in 2000 with two DC-3s, XA-IUI and XA-RZF.

XA-BIK/XA-TAN; XA-COM; XA-CUD; XA-HAQ.

Transportes Aereos Jalisco, Guadalajara, Jalisco, used C-39s and DC-3s between 1945 and 1955, when CMA took over the routes.

C-39s:- Unknown; DC-3s:- XA-GAU; XA-GIW; XA-GUM.

Transportes Aereos Mexicanos SA - TAMSA, Yucatan, used DC-3s until the airline was taken over by Mexicana in 1960.

XA-GAF to XA-GAI incl, XA-GEL; XA-GIO; XA-HEY.

Transportes Aereos Tampico S de RL de CV, Tampico, used various types including two DC-3s until 1950 when LAUSA took the airline over.

XA-FIK; XA-GER.

Index:-

XA-BIK	c/n 9088	XA-GEM	
XA-BJG(DC-2)	1367	XA-GEO	
XA-BJI (DC-2)	1304	XA-GEP (DC-2)	
XA-BJL(1)(DC-2)	1255	XA-GEQ	4563
XA-BJL(2)(DC-2)	1368	XA-GER	
XA-BJM(DC-2)	1249	XA-GEU	4281
XA-BKO(DC-2)		XA-GEV	7339
XA-BKQ(DC-2)	1408	XA-GEW	4088
XA-BKV(DC-2)	1599	XA-GEX	
XA-BKY(DC-2)	1371	XA-GIA	19766
XA-BLN	1989	XA-GIB	9000
XA-NLO		XA-GIE	19649
XA-BLW		XA-GII	3293
XA-CAB	2128	XA-GIN	
XA-CAG	2228	XA-GIO	13113
XA-CAM	2330 ?	XA-GIR	
XA-CAO	2231	XA-GIW	19683
XA-CAY		XA-GIZ	11790
XA-CDV	4419	XA-GOC	4101
XA-CEG	19593	XA-GOH	
XA-CIL	4218	XA-GOR	25452
"XA-CMA"	9276	XA-GUE	
XA-COI	25961	XA-GUF	1931
XA-COM	19409	XA-GUJ	25354
XA-CUC	7377	XA-GUM	4756
XA-CUD	25356	XA-GUN	7358
XA-DEE	2196	XA-GUQ	2149
XA-DIH		XA-GUS	4491
XA-DIK	3292	XA-GUX	4383
XA-DIN	7359	XA-HAO	2193
XA-DOB(C-39)	2088	XA-HAQ	34342
XA-DOH(C-39)	2064	XA-HEP	7361
XA-DOI C-39)	2069	XA-HEX	
XA-DOJ(C-39)	2080	XA-HEY	13432
XA-DOQ(C-39)	2077	XA-HEZ	
XA-DOS(C-39)	2091	XA-HIA	
XA-DOT (C-39)	2075	XA-HIE	
XA-DUF (C-39)	2072	XA-HIF	
XA-DUG	11713	XA-HIG	
XA-DUH	11725	XA-HIK	
XA-DUI	4926	XA-HIN	13822
XA-DUJ	4891	XA-HIP	4926
XA-DUK	11721	XA-HIQ	4891
XA-DUM		XA-HIR	3290
XA-DUS(C-39)	2069 ?	XA-HIY	20472
XA-FEG	4180	XA-HOE	19662
XA-FIK	4328	XA-HOF	
XA-FIL	11748	XA-HOI	
XA-FIR	13702	XA-HOS	1497
XA-FIX	19217	XA-HOT	1551
XA-FIY	6102	XA-HOU	2208
XA-FOZ		XA-HUE	12891
XA-FUA	3259	XA-HUF	19802
XA-FUC	19770	XA-HUG	19242
XA-FUH	4392	XA-HUH	20554
XA-FUJ	3262	XA-HUI	18978
XA-FUM	3255	XA-HUS	7388
XA-FUV	3261	XA-IOH	4225
XA-FUW	3260	XA-ION	13378 ?
XA-FUX		XA-IOR	1547
XA-FUZ		XA-IUI	11719
XA-GAA		XA-JAE	4961
XA-GAE		XA-JAG	4814
XA-GAF		XA-JAL	4258
XA-GAG		XA-JAM	6043
XA-GAH		XA-JAN	9088
XA-GAI		XA-JAO	13818
XA-GAJ	3258	XA-JAT	4905
XA-GAM	4350	XA-JAX	
XA-GAO		XA-JEL	12990
XA-GAQ		XA-JER	4889
XA-GAU	4085	XA-JEW	
XA-GAV	9927	XA-JID	4588
XA-GAW	9783	XA-JIE	9049
XA-GAX	10160	XA-JIH	9904
XA-GEC		XA-JII	20416
XA-GEE		XA-JIP	4301
XA-GEF	4442	XA-JOI	4992
XA-GEG	34364	XA-JOK	
XA-GEL	20427	XA-JOV (DC-2?)	

Chapter 4: Commercial Operators of the DC-3, C-47, R4D, Dakota and Li-2

Reg	c/n	Reg	c/n
XA-JOY		XB-JIP	
XA-JUI		XB-JIX	26281
XA-JUT	3257	XB-JOX	4218
XA-KAD	4240	XB-JUO	
XA-KAF	25526	XB-JUX	19409
XA-KEQ	4918	XB-KEK	19015
XA-KIC (C-39)	2069	XB-KEM	2193
XA-KIK	4369	XB-KOH	
XA-KTB	2118	XB-KOI	
XA-LEX	19201	XB-KOM	4889
XA-MAI		XB-KOQ	9088
XA-MIR		XB-KTB	2118
XA-MOC		XB-KUB (C-39)	2069
XA-NAA	4419	XB-KUR	
XA-NAD	34373	XB-LAH	
XA-NIJ	11713	XB-LAX	
XA-NIW		XB-LIY	
XA-POK	4100	XB-LOR	
XA-PUR	9715	XB-LUB	
XA-RAM	2130	XB-LUZ	
XA-REP	9049	XB-MEQ	
XA-ROM	12287	XB-MEX	4918
XA-RPE	2137	XB-MIL	2193
XA-RPI	19662	XB-MIQ	4936
XA-RPN	2167	XB-MOP	
XA-RPO	1953 ?	XB-NAE	20454
XA-RTC	2219	XB-NEF	
XA-RZF	12192	XB-NIW	"43159"
XA-SAE	20554	XB-NOB	25356
XA-SCF	6343	XB-POA	7355
XA-SUR	11682	XB-POH	19822
XA-SUY	2219	XB-QUC	"156621"
XA-SYN	13485	XB-SIO (C-39)	2064
XA-TAN	9088	XB-TEY	13432
XA-TEH	19057	XB-UNO	9276
XA-TMR	43301	XB-VUT	12726 ?
XA-VIZ	9726	XB-WIP	4301
XY-XYZ-1(1)	4419	XB-YAV (C-39)	2072
XA-XYZ-1(2)	4756	XB-ZAT	43076
XB-AEA	11713	XC-ABF	7377
XB-BIS	13445	XC-ABW	19217
XB-CIW	34364	XC-BCE(1)	7377
XB-COC	19201	XC-BCE(2)	12192
XB-DIY	26297	XC-BEX	4218
XB-DPN	34292	XC-BII	26281
XB-DYD		XC-BIN	13050
XB-DYO		XC-BIY	4936
XB-DYP(1)	19239	XC-BNH	4104
XB-DYP(2)	4491	XC-BNO	4104
XB-DYU	33213	XC-BUQ	10189
XB-ECG		XC-BUR	9276
XB-FAA	9142	XC-CAM	4905
XB-FAB	43083	XC-CFE	1551
XB-FAQ	12740	XC-CIC	34292
XB-FAW		XC-CIJ	4383
XB-FEP	11790	XC-CIY	3293
XB-FIR	13702	XC-CNI	12736 ?
XB-FIS		XC-CTM	4282
XB-FOO	4491	XC-DAK	19201
XB-FOZ	43073	XC-DAP	10096
XB-FUA	11790	XC-DOE	43076
XB-FUJ	4100	XC-DOJ	4383
XB-FUX	12785	XC-DOS	11815
XB-GED	19029	XC-FAB	6315
XB-GEL	4174	XC-HDA	
XB-GEN	"2438"	XC-INI	9279 ?
XB-GUB	12740	XC-JBC	4763
XB-GUI	2130	XC-OPS	4588
XB-HAH	11713	XC-PAA	19409
XB-HED	1920	XC-PAB	43083
XB-HIZ	4491	XC-PAT	4905
XB-HUZ	4795	XC-PAZ	19409
XB-JAD	1920	XC-PMX	9795
XB-JBR	3261	XC-REX	13818
XB-JEE	6200	XC-SAG	9276
XR-JEX	19449	XC-SRH	
XB-JIN	13050	XC-UPD	

Notes:-
XA-BKO was quoted as C-39 c/n 2092.
XA-CAM was owned by Mexicana and may have been c/n 2230 (by interpolation).

XA-FOZ was owned by Comm. Aereas de Veracruz and crashed on 13Nov46.
XA-GAA and XA-GAE were owned by Aerotransportes del Sureste.
XA-GAF to XA-GAI incl were all owned by Aerovias Transportes Mexicanos SA.
XA-GAO was owned by C Davalos, Guadalajara.
XA-GAQ was owned by M Gomez, Huajuapam de Leon.
XA-GEE of Servicio Aereo Panini may be either a DC-2 or DC-3.
XA-GER was owned by Felipe Gutierrez de Lara, Tampico.
XA-GEX owned by Aero Transportes del Sureste SA, is listed as a 2-seater so may have been a cargo aircraft.
XA-GIN was owned by Carlos Cervantes Perez, Ensenada.
XA-GOC is doubtful as c/n 4101 as this was involved in two accidents while with Pan American, and may not have been repaired after the second.
XA-GUE and XA-HEX were owned by Carlos Cervantes Perez.
XA-ION of Aerovias Oaxaquenas, derelict at Oaxaca in Feb03 is thought to be c/n13378.
XA-JEL was owned by Lineas Aereas Portuarias.
XA-JEW was owned by Manuel Gomez Mendez of Pueblo (another 2-seater - cargo?).
XA-JOV was owned by Servicio Aereos de Chiapas SA of Tuxtla Gutierres, and is listed as an 18-seater. This may be a DC-2 variant or a B-18.
XA-MIR cr 29Jan86.
XA-UDY noted with California Pacifico early in 2006.
XB-DPN "Usila", noted on a freight charter.
XB-DYD at Laredo, TX Oct87.
XB-DYP cr on t/o Laredo, TX 23Jan89.
XB-DYU noted Tucson, AZ Aug89.
XB-ECG noted 1989.
XB-FAW was owned by Manuel Villegas.
XB-FIS was owned by Finaciera Industrial.
XB-GEN is quoted with c/n 2438. This may be part of a complete serial or a fuselage number. It was owned by Alfonso Fernandez Aponte of Tijuana. It was a 2-seater.
XB-JEX was registered to the "President" and may have been transferred to the XC-series.
XB-JIP was owned by Joaquin Maza Sotier.
XB-JUO was owned by Antonio Rodriguez Otegui y Soc.
XB-KOH was owned by Maderera del Tropico SA, Mexico City. It was an 18-seater, so may have been a DC-2 or B-18.
XB-KOI was owned by Hotel Club de Pesca, Acapulco, and was listed as a 50-seater, but later amended to a 23-seater, so may have been a DC-4.
XB-KUR was owned by Carlos Panini Binosi.
XB-LAH was owned by Atlantic Northern Airlines, Mexico City.
XB-LAX was registered to "Presidencia" as a 7-seater (executive interior?) and may have been transferred to the XC- series.
XB-LIY was a 32-seater owned by Naviera y Comercial of Ensada.
XB-LOR was owned by Felix Cabanos Hdoa, another 2-seater.
XB-LUB was another 2-seater, owned by Francisco Munoz Ceballos.
XB-LUZ was registered to Secretaria de Hacienda, a candidate for the XC- series.
XB-MEQ was owned by Mario Moreno of Mexico City.
XB-MEX was owned by Lic. Miguel Alaman V. of Mexico City.
XB-MOP was owned by Abastecedora de Sotavento SRL, Mexico City - a 2-seater.
XB-NEF was owned by Abelardo L Rodriguez, Mexico City. It was named "Pitic" and was active in 1954.
XB-NIW quoted as c/n 43159 but possibly 43-159 . .?
XC-HDA was registered to the Secretaria de Hacienda and named "Lalmbarcacion".
XC-SRH was registered to Secretaria de Recursos Hirualicos.
XC-UPD of unknown ownership, was noted at Mexico City on 6Oct79.

Many of the above details were drawn from a Mexican register published in 1951. The XC- series was adopted a year or two later. The register just quotes Douglas as the type, and while 24-seaters are assumed to be DC-3s, and 2-seaters could be A-24s, it is more likely that they were C-47 cargo models. It is known, for example, that XA-GIO which is listed as a 3-seater, is a DC-3. The 16- and 18-seaters are possibly DC-2s, or C-39s, and one or more may have been B-18s.

MONGOLIA - MT

Formerly Outer Mongolia, in 1939 known as the Mongolian People's Republic.

Far East Fur Trading Co Ltd was used merely as an agency through which six DC-3As were exported to the Soviet Union in January and

February 1939, being shipped via Japan. They were allocated marks MT-16 to MT-21 incl.

Mongolian Air Transport Co was another Soviet 'customer', 3 DC-3s c/ns 1974, 1987 and 1988, were shipped to Cherbourg in 1937 for Fokker and after assembly flown on to Russia all marked as "F-2", subsequently being used by the Soviet Air Force.

Index:-

MT-16	c/n 2096	MT-19	2099
MT-17	2097	MT-20	2100
MT-18	2098	MT-21	2101

Note: See under Russia for subsequent histories.

MOROCCO - F and CN

Morocco gained independence from France in 1957 and prior to that all aircraft were flown in French marks. Such aircraft are indexed under France and only four of them survived to join the CN- series. The CNALx series are military aircraft and listed in that section.

Aigle Azur Maroc, Casablanca, an operating subsidiary of Aigle Azur, was using up to five of the parent company's DC-3s in 1951. See main entry under France.

Air Atlas - Soc. Chérifienne de l'Air, Casablanca, was formed in September 1946 using Ju52/3ms. These were replaced by DC-3s supplied by Air France in 1949. The airline merged with Air Maroc in July 1953 to form Cie Chérifienne de Transports Aériens - Air Atlas - Air Maroc, the progenitor of Royal Air Maroc.

F-BAXE; F-BAXF; F-BAXG; F-BAXJ; F-BAXM; F-BAXY; F-BEFA; F-DAAZ; F-OABV; F-OAIG.

Air Maroc - Soc. Marocaine de Construction Aéronautique, Casablanca, was a private company, formed in 1947 and operations with DC-3s began in July 1948. Air Atlas was taken over in July 1953 and the airline became Royal Air Maroc in 1957, when four DC-3s remained.

F-BEFS; F-BEFT; F-BEIN to F-BEIR incl.

Royal Air Maroc - Cie Nationale de Transports Aériens, Casablanca, was formed when Air Maroc was renamed in February 1957 and four DC-3s taken over. Some of these were passed to the Air Force from 1959 onwards.

CN-CCI to CN-CCL incl.

SCANA - Sté Commerciale d'Aviation Nord Africaine, Casablanca, operated F-OASQ in 1955/6.

Index:-

| CN-CCI | c/n 13139 | CN-CCK | 7376 |
| CN-CCJ | 25250 | CN-CCL | 10073 |

MOZAMBIQUE - CR-A and C9

Mozambique was a Portuguese colony until 25 June 1975, but only one colonial DC-3 survived that long, eventually adopting the C9- nationality mark.

African Air Carriers used DC-3s C9-ATG and N6907/C9-ATH from 1988. Taken over by Interocean, Lanseria and used for famine relief work, from 1993.

DETA - Direcção de Exploração dos Transportes Aéreos, Lourenco Marques, bought DC-3s in 1945 to replace the Ju52/3ms in use since before WW2. The DC-3s were all replaced by F.27s prior to independence. One was taken over by the Servicio da Aeronautica Civil.

CR-ABJ; CR-ABK; CR-ABQ; CR-AGC; CR-AGD; CR-AGU; CR-AHB.

SCAN Air Charter, Maputo, operate a single DC-3 C9-STF on charters.

Index:-

CR-ABJ	c/n 11699	CR/C9-AHB	9948
CR-ABK	11763	C9-ASQ	33257
CR-ABQ	12760	C9-ATG	1984
CR-AFR	13018	C9-ATH	9410
CR-AGC	13140	C9-STE	19006
CR-AGD	19393	C9-STF	12205
CR-AGU	33325		

NAMIBIA - ZS

Namib Air, Windhoek, was the name adopted by Suidwes Lugdiens in 1978 when South West Africa was declared independent of South Africa.

ZS-DIW: ZS-DJZ.

NEPAL - 9N

Royal Nepal Airline Corp, Ltd, Kathmandu, was formed in July 1958 to take over Indian Airlines' DC-3 operations in Nepal. Some aircraft were transferred from Indian Airlines, and others bought, the last in 1971. No DC-3s remained in use after about 1978.

9N-AAB to 9N-AAE incl; 9N-AAH; 9N-AAI; 9N-AAL; 9N-AAM; 9N-AAO to 9N-AAQ incl; 9N-AAX; 9N-AAY.

Index:-

9N-AAB	c/n 20311	9N-AAO	20135
9N-AAC	20681	9N-AAP	42956
9N-AAD	19792	9N-AAQ	9950
9N-AAE	26475	9N-AAX	25998
9N-AAH	6216	9N-AAY	19934
9N-AAI	7338	9N-RF-2	25471
9N-AAL	19632	9N-RF-10	9950
9N-AAM	12893		

NETHERLANDS - PH

The influence of KLM and Fokker on the DC-2 and DC-3 gave the Netherlands an important role in the development of the types. Although they were never built by Fokker, most of those supplied pre-war to European airlines were assembled at Schiphol and KLM was one of the major users of both types until 1940. Another claim to fame was the performance of their DC-2 PH-AJU in coming first in the transport section of the England-Australia race of 1934 and second overall. To-day, only the Dutch Dakota Association keeps DC-3s and a DC-2 in the air and under preservation.

Aero-Holland NV, Ypenburg, started charter operations in April 1948 continuing to use the DC-3 and smaller types until 1950.

PH-TBG; PH-TFA to PH-TFC incl.

Fairways, Rotterdam, began life as **Transaero Rotterdam**, starting operations in 1961 with two DC-3s on charter work. A scheduled service to Southampton was flown in 1963 until the airline was taken over by Martins in 1964.

PH-SCC; PH-SSM.

KLM - Koninklijke Luchtvaart Maatschappij NV, Amsterdam, ordered DC-2s very early in the life of the type, and was still using them at the time of the German invasion in May 1940. One escaped to Britain and re-entered service in 1945. DC-3s were added to the fleet in 1936. Many were destroyed by bombing in 1940 but some were taken over by Lufthansa. A few escaped to Britain to resume operations in 1946, along with many more bought from surplus stocks. They remained in use until the last was passed to **KLM Aerocarto** for survey work in 1970. Various DC-2s and DC-3s were transferred to the East Indies and DC-3s to the West Indies to support KLM subsidiaries in these areas.

DC-2s PH-AJU; PH-AKG to PH-AKT incl; PH-ALD to PH-ALF incl; PH-TAZ; PH-TBF. *DC-3s* PH-ALH; PH-ALI; PH-ALN to PH-ALW incl; PH-ARA; PH-ARB; PH-ARE; PH-ARG; PH-ARW to PH-ARZ incl; PH-ASK; PH-ASM; PH-ASP; PH-ASR; PH-AST; PH-AXH; PH-AZR to PH-AZT incl; PH-TAY; PH-TAZ; PH-TBA; PH-TBD to PH-TBI incl; PH-TBK to PH-TBP incl; PH-TBR; PH-TBV to PH-TCC incl; PH-TCG to

PH-TCI incl; PH-TCK to PH-TCM incl; PH-TCR to PH-TCW incl; PH-TCY; PH-TCZ; PH-TDR to PH-TDW incl; PH-TDY; PH-TDZ; PH-TEU to PH-TEW incl; PH-DAA to PH-DAD incl; PH-DAI; PH-DAL; PH-DAM; PH-DAR; PH-DAT to PH-DAX incl; PH-DAZ. (The last group were earlier aircraft re-registered).

KLM Aerocarto, an aerial survey and mapping subsidiary of KLM, has operated three DC-3s, two in Surinam marks.

PH-DAA; PH-DAW/PZ-TLA; PZ-TLC.

Martins Air Charter, Amsterdam, used DC-3s on charter flights from 1960 until they were replaced by Convair 340s in 1967. Fairways' operations including scheduled service were taken over in 1964.

PH-MAA; PH-MAB; PH-MAG; PH-DAA; PH-DAB; PH-SCC; PH-SSM. LN-RTA was leased.

Moormanair - Moorman Vliegtuigonderhoudsbedrijf, NV, Amsterdam, used DC-3s on charters carrying cargo between 1968 and about 1971.

PH-MAB; PH-MAG; PH-MOA.

Schreiner Aerocontractors NV, The Hague, operated charter services with two DC-3s between 1963 and 1967. The airline was renamed Schreiner Airways in 1966.

PH-DAC; PH-ERZ.

Index:-

DC-2s:
PH-AJU(1)	c/n 1317	PH-AKL	1358
PH-AJU(2)	1288	PH-AKM	1359
"PH-AJU"	1286	PH-AKN	1360
"PH-AJU"	1404	PH-AKO	1361
PH-AKF(1)	1318	PH-AKP	1362
PH-AKF(2)	1319	PH-AKQ	1363
PH-AKF(3)	1320	PH-AKR	1364
PH-AKF(4)	1330	PH-AKS	1365
PH-AKF(5)	1331	PH-AKT	1366
PH-AKF(6)	1332	PH-ALD	1583
PH-AKG	1335	PH-ALE	1584
PH-AKH	1354	PH-ALF	1585
PH-AKI	1355	PH-ALZ	1564
PH-AKJ	1356	(PH-FOK)	1319
PH-AKK	1357	PH-TBB	1584

DC-3s:
PH-ALH	1935	PH-DAA	11855
PH-ALI	1590	PH-DAB	19510
PH-ALN	1936	PH-DAC	9410
PH-ALO	1937	PH-DAD	7338
PH-ALP(1)	1938	PH-DAI	12720
PH-ALP(2)	1965	PH-DAL	9511
PH-ALR	1939	PH-DAM	19549
"PH-ALR"	32966	PH-DAR	12017
PH-ALS	1940	PH-DAT	13334
PH-ALT	1941	PH-DAU	12485
PH-ALU	1942	PH-DAV	12083
PH-ALV	1943	PH-DAW	13458
PH-ALW	1944	PH-DAX	12075
(PH-ARA)	1979	PH-DAZ	13377
PH-ARB	1980	PH-DDA	19109
PH-ARE	1981	(PH-DDZ)(1)	19560
PH-ARG	1982	PH-DDZ(2)	19754
PH-ARW	2019	PH-ERZ	20518
PH-ARX	2020	PH-MAA	33213
PH-ARY	2021	PH-MAB	4500
PH-ARZ	2022	PH-MAG	12472
PH-ASK	2036	PH-MOA	33353
PH-ASM	2142	(PH-NCR)(1)	12184
PH-ASP	2109	PH-NCR(2)	13462
PH-ASR	2110	PH-NDV	4860
PH-AST	2111	PH-PBA	19434
PH-AXH	2147	(PH-RIC)	32872
PH-AZR/G-AGJR		PH-SCC	19458
	11995	PH-SSM	13182
PH-AZS/G-AGJS		PH-TAY	11995
	12173	PH-TAZ	12173
PH-AZT/G-AGJT		PH-TBA	12172
	12172	(PH-TBC)	7338

PH-TBD	1980	PH-TCL	9511
PH-TBE	2022	PH-TCM	11831
PH-TBF	1943	PH-TCR	25479
PH-TBG	9510	PH-TCS	12919
PH-TBH	19194	PH-TCT	13334
PH-TBI	11855	PH-TCU	13472
PH-TBK	9910	PH-TCV	12309
PH-TBL	18964	PH-TCW	13460
PH-TBM	19549	PH-TCY	9410
PH-TBN	12775	PH-TCZ	13368
PH-TBO	13638	PH-TDR	12382
PH-TBP	9904	PH-TDS	13480
PH-TBR	19211	PH-TDT	25281
PH-TBV	19795	PH-TDU	12485
PH-TBW	20122	PH-TDV	12083
PH-TBX	9978	PH-TDW	13458
PH-TBY	12767	PH-TDY	12181
PH-TBZ	19785	PH-TDZ	13377
PH-TCA	12953	PH-TEU	13396
PH-TCB	19510	PH-TEV	13301
"PH-TCB"	9836/19434	PH-TEW	13026
PH-TCC	12734	PH-TFA	13462
PH-TCG	9158	PH-TFB	12172
PH-TCH	19328	PH-TFC	27079
PH-TCI	12720	PH-UEV	12083
PH-TCK	19016	(PH-WWW)	33353

NETHERLANDS NEW GUINEA - JZ

De Kroonduif - Nederlands New Guinea Luchtvaartmaatschappij "De Kroonduif" began operations in West New Guinea (Irian Barat) on 01 January 1947 using DC-3s leased from KLM. Six were re-registered in JZ- marks from Jan56. These were taken over by Garuda in Feb63, following transfer of the territory to Indonesia as West Irian.

Index:-

JZ-PDA	c/n 11855	JZ-PDD	19549
JZ-PDB	19510	JZ-PDE	13377
JZ-PDC	9410	JZ-PDF	13334

NETHERLANDS WEST INDIES - PJ

KLM (West Indies Divn.), Curaçao, bought a number of war surplus C-47s in 1945 to replace the Lockheed 14s and Lodestars then in use. These DC-3s were, in turn, displaced by Convair 340s in 1962.

Index:-

PJ-ALA	c/n 7392	PJ-ALG	12953
PJ-ALB	7345	PJ-ALH	11994
PJ-ALC	7338	PJ-ALI	13301
PJ-ALD(1)	42965	PJ-ALP	11831
(PJ-ALD)(2)	12017	PJ-ALT	9904
PJ-ALE	19247	(PJ-ALZ)	11831

NEW GUINEA - P2

For many years New Guinea was administered by Australia and all airlines operating there were Australian-owned and registered. DC-3s were used by various airlines, including Qantas, Papuan Air Transport, Guinea Air Traders, Mandated, Ansett-MAL and Trans Australian's Sunbird Service. The last two operations combined to assist in the formation of a new airline when New Guinea became independent in 1973.

Air Niugini, Port Moresby, commenced operations on 1 November 1973 with finance provided by the government, Qantas, Ansett and TAA. DC-3s were provided by the latter two and continued to operate alongside F.27s until these and F.28s had replaced them by 1977.

Index:-

P2-MAB/P2-ANX	c/n 9749	P2-SBB/P2-ANN	10000
P2-MAN/P2-ANY	12647	P2-SBD/P2-ANO	12187
P2-MAT/P2-ANZ	13340	P2-SBG/P2-ANP	12873
P2-MMA/P2-ANS	9583	P2-SBL/P2-ANR	12056
P2-MMD/P2-ANU	33301	P2-SBO/P2-ANT	6108
P2-MML/P2-ANV	32945	P2-SBW/P2-ANQ	27110

NEW ZEALAND - ZK

Of the four users of the DC-3 in New Zealand, only New Zealand National operated scheduled services for any great length of time, or used DC-3s in any numbers. Apart from the airline operators, one of the most interesting aspects of the DC-3's use has been its modification as an aerial topdresser to improve sheep pastures. The main operator in this field was James Aviation, but Fieldair and Airland also took part in the work. Another DC-3 was used for the carriage of live deer from hunting areas. Despite their agricultural uses, these DC-3s were kept immaculately.

Classic Air, Palmerston North, operated DC-3s for topdressing work, but they were later leased to Fieldair and operated as **Air Freight**, which also owned ZK-BBJ.

ZK-AMR; ZK-AWP.

Mount Cook & Southern Lakes Tourist Co, Christchurch, started scheduled services in 1961, using the first of three DC-3s. Two more were added later and by January 1967 the airline was operating as **Mount Cook Airlines**. HS.748s were bought from 1968 onwards and they had replaced all the DC-3s by 1980.

ZK-AOD; ZK-AOF (lsd 1972-74); ZK-BEU; ZK-BKD; ZK-CAW (lsd 1969-71).

New Zealand National Airways Corp, Wellington, was formed by the merger of Union Airways, Air Travel and Cook Strait Airways. DC-3s were used from 1947 onwards, replacing the smaller Lodestars entirely. Several were operated as pure freighters and fourteen of the passenger aircraft were *Skyliner* conversions with large windows. In turn the DC-3s were displaced by F.27s and none remained in 1970. Some of them were leased to Fiji Airways for a while, and the remainder were returned to the RNZAF who only retired them in 1979.

ZK-AOD to ZK-AOF incl; ZK-AOH to ZK-AOJ incl; ZK-AOZ to ZK-APB incl; ZK-APK; ZK-AQP; ZK-AQS to ZK-AQU incl; ZK-AWO to ZK-AWQ incl; ZK-AYK; ZK-AYL; ZK-AYZ; ZK-AZA; ZK-AZL to ZK-AZN incl; ZK-BBJ; ZK-BEU; ZK-BKD; ZK-BKE; ZK-BQK; ZK-CAW. VH-TAE was leased in 1960.

South Pacific Airlines of NZ, Auckland, started scheduled services in 1960, using DC-3s leased from Ansett which was a substantial shareholder. The three DC-3s were *Viewmaster* conversions. These remained until 1965 by which time the airline was in the hands of receivers.

ZK-BYD; ZK-BYE; ZK-CAW. G-AMKE was leased Dec61-Feb62 and ZK-AQU in 1965.

Index:-

ZK-AMR	c/n 11869	ZK-AXS	32743
ZK-AMS	9286	ZK-AYK*	26006
ZK-AMY	13506	ZK-AYL*	26008
ZK-AOD*	27146	ZK-AYZ*	26649
ZK-AOE	33131	ZK-AZA*	27144
ZK-AOF*	32899	ZK-AZL	33316
(ZK-AOG)	32897	ZK-AZM	33478
ZK-AOH	34228	ZK-AZN*	33481
ZK-AOI	34226	ZK-BBJ*	34222
ZK-AOJ*	27145	ZK-BEU*	13099
(ZK-AOK)	34227	ZK-BKD	13521
ZK-AOZ	32895	ZK-BKE	4119
ZK-APA*	34224	ZK-BQK*	33315
ZK-APB	32693	ZK-BYD	13906
ZK-APK*	34227	ZK-BYE	13529
ZK-AQP	32897	ZK-BYF	20051
ZK-AQS	32695	ZK-CAW	18923
ZK-AQT	32696	ZK-CHV	34360
ZK-AQU	33134	ZK-CQA	26030
ZK-AUJ	26651	ZK-DAK	26480
ZK-AWO	33480	ZK-ERI	34225
ZK-AWP*	33135	"ZK-RFS"	26030
ZK-AWQ	33313	"ZK-SAL"	33316

Note: * indicates Skyliner conversion.

NICARAGUA - AN and YN

Various airlines have operated DC-3s in Nicaragua since WW2, but only LANICA has been of any significance. Several small operators are known to have existed, but little is known of them. Recent political changes and the civil war may well have destroyed some survivors. The nationality mark YN- was adopted in 1979.

AERONICA, Managua, took over a few DC-3s from Lanica when that operator became bankrupt in 1981. Only YN-BVK is known.

Flota Aérea Nicaraguense. Nothing is known of this operator except that DC-3 AN-ADJ crashed on 15 July 1950 at Monte Carmelo, Nicaragua.

LANICA - Líneas Aéreas de Nicaragua SA, Managua, started operations in 1946 with help from Pan American. DC-3s replaced the Boeing 247Ds and eventually 17 of the type had been used, and one remained by 1981, when the airline was declared bankrupt.

AN-ACN; AN-ACR to AN-ACT incl; AN-ACX to AN-ACZ incl; AN-ADD; AN-ADJ; AN-ADK; AN-ADM; AN-ADQ; AN-AEC; AN-AOK; AN-ASP; AN-AWT; YN-BVK. N53192, N56800 were leased.

TACA de Nicaragua, Managua, operated services until 1946, when their contract was cancelled by the government. At this time Ford Trimotors had just been replaced by DC-3s.

AN-ACE to AN-ACG incl; AN-ADB; AN-ADD.

Index:-

AN-ACE	c/n 25245	AN-ADD	9884
AN-ACF	25246	AN-ADJ	9061
AN-ACG	13819	AN-ADK	6083
AN-ACN	6090	AN-ADM	32722
AN-ACR	20120	AN-ADP	6096
AN-ACS		AN-ADQ	9212
AN-ACT	12856	AN-AEC	12312
	(see note)	AN-AOK	19046
AN-ACX		AN-ASP	4519
AN-ACY		AN-AWT	4174
AN-ACZ	4662	YN-BVK	6215
AN-ADB			

Note: AN-ACT has also been quoted as c/n 3293 but this seems more likely to have become XA-GII.

NIGER - 5U

Air Niger, Niamey, was formed in 1966 with help from UTA. Two DC-3s were used at first to operate domestic services, but have now been retired:-

5U-AAC; 5U-AAJ.

Index:-

5U-AAC	c/n 12358	5U-AAL	4566
5U-AAJ	4505		

The 5U-MAA series are military markings.

NIGERIA - VR-N and 5N

DC-3s used in Nigeria by West African Airways were at first in the colonial VR-N series, but with independence this was changed to 5N- in 1960. On the outbreak of civil war in the Eastern region (or Biafra) in 1967, some Nigerian Airways DC-3s were taken over by the Air Force of Biafra, and subsequently dumped at Lagos until scrapped.

Arax Airlines, Lagos, uses DC-3s on local services and in support of oil drilling. The airline is assisted by International Development Corp, from whom some aircraft were leased, from 1967, and registered from 1974.

N3102Q/N485G/5N-ARA; N895/5N-ARB; N330/(5N-ARC); N3455.

Nigeria Trade Wings Airways, Ikeja, originally bought two DC-3s in Britain (5N-AJE and 5N-AJF), but these were never delivered because of financial problems. In 1974 two more were bought but they were out of use by 1981. The operator was taken over by Autair Malta Ltd.

5N-ATA; 5N-ATB.

CHAPTER 4: COMMERCIAL OPERATORS OF THE DC-3, C-47, R4D, DAKOTA AND LI-2

WAAC (Nigeria) Ltd, Lagos, traded as **Nigeria Airways**, taking over the operations of WAAC on 1st October 1958 and with them their DC-3 fleet. These were re-registered in the 5N- series in 1960/61, when the Nigerian government bought out BOAC's and Elder Dempster's shareholding. Most of the DC-3s went to the Nigerian Air Force in 1967, by which time F.27s had replaced them.

VR-NCK to VR-NCP incl/5N-AAK to 5N-AAP incl; VR-NCS/5N-AAQ.

West African Airways Corp, Lagos, added DC-3s to their fleet in 1957, mostly bought in Australia. Services were taken over by **Nigeria Airways** in October 1958.

VR-NCK to VR-NCP incl; VR-NCS.
G-AGHJ; G-AKJH; G-AMPZ and G-AOUD were leased.

Index:-

VR-NCK	c/n 25366	5N-AAO	9813
VR-NCL	25364	5N-AAP	13304
VR-NCM	6071	5N-AAQ	9874
VR-NCN	13606	5N-AJE	33346
VR-NCO	9813	5N-AJF	26582
VR-NCP	13304	5N-ARA	33042
VR-NCS	9874	5N-ARB	33273
5N-AAK	25366	(5N-ARC)	4479
5N-AAL	25364	5N-ATA	12472
5N-AAM	6071	5N-ATB	33609
5N-AAN	13606		

NORTH BORNEO - VR-O - See Malaya.

NORWAY - LN

Eleven Norwegian-based operators have used the DC-3 since the war, but apart from DNL, only in small numbers and generally for short periods.

Bergen Air Transport AS, Bergen, bought DC-3 LN-TVA in 1973 and used it for charter work until it was sold in August 1975.

BRAATHENS - South American and Far East Air Transport AS (SAFE), Oslo, bought one DC-3 for charter work in 1947 and added a second in 1957 for scheduled services.

LN-PAS; LN-SUK.

DNL - Det Norske Luftfartsselskap AS, Oslo, was reformed in 1946 using DC-3s previously operated by the Norwegian Air Force. Others were bought from USAAF surplus stocks. The aircraft remained registered to DNL but from August 1948 operated in **Scandinavian Airlines System** colours. All had been sold by 1957.

LN-IAF to LN-IAI incl (last three later LN-IKG to LN-IKI); LN-IAK to LN-IAT incl; LN-LMR. LN-NAB was leased to SAS.

Fred Olsen's Flyselskap AS, Oslo, bought three DC-3s for charter work in 1946. Two of them were lost in 1952 and replaced by one bought from DNL and another on short term lease. The last was sold in 1961 and replaced by Viscounts.

LN-IAS; LN-LMK(2); LN-LMR; LN-NAB; LN-NAD; LN-NAE.

Mey-Air AS, Oslo, leased DC-3 LN-RTW briefly during 1969.

Nor-Fly, Oslo, used DC-3 LN-KLV on oil charter work between 1972 and 1976.

Norwegian Overseas Airways AS, Oslo, owned DC-3 LN-TVA between August and October 1975, but it does not appear that any operations took place.

Polaris Air Transport AS, Oslo, was formed in 1964 to use DC-3s on charter flights. They were replaced by Convair 240s in 1969.

LN RTE; LN-RTO. SE-BSN was lsd briefly in 1965.

Riis Flyrederei AS, Oslo leased to other operators such as Wideroe's and Transair Sweden.

LN-PAS; LN-RTA; LN-RTE; (LN-LMI); LN-LMK(1); LN-LMR.

Stellar Air Freighter used DC-3 LN-LMK (2) on charter operations during 1972.

Wideroe's Flyveselskap AS, Oslo, operated scheduled services to northern Norway using DC-3s for a short time in 1964 on lease.

LN-LMR(2); LN-PAS; LN-RTA; LN-RTE.

Index:-

LN-IAF	c/n 13883	LN-LMK(1)	42969
LN-IAG	12712	LN-LMK(2)	43091
LN-IAH	13647	LN-LMR(1)	19771
LN-IAI	11638	LN-LMR(2)	13652
LN-IAK	7353	LN-KLV	4828
LN-IAL	11697	LN-NAB	12324
LN-IAM	9785	LN-NAD	12148
LN-IAN	20562	LN-NAE	12372
LN-IAO	13824	LN-PAS	12181
LN-IAP	9664	LN-RTA	4327
LN-IAR	20011	LN-RTE	11697
LN-IAS	19458	LN-RTO	33185
LN-IAT	20019	LN-RTW	4346
LN-IKG	12712	LN-SUK	4327
LN-IKH	13647	LN-TVA	10201
LN-IKI	11638	LN-WND	11750
(LN-LMI)	13652		

Note:-
Confusion has existed over LN-IAG and LN-IAH. Officially these were listed with c/ns 13647 and 12712 respectively. However, it seems likely that the airframes were mixed during conversion by Canadair Ltd or the paper work confused at purchase. The data plate for LN-IKH was checked while in service with Linjeflyg and later with the Swedish AF and found to bear c/n 13647. LN-IKG became CF-HGL and is reported in Canadian paper work as c/n 13647, so it seems that no-one has checked this aircraft's data plate since its arrival there.

PAKISTAN - AP

Crescent Air Transport Ltd, Karachi, used a single DC-3 (AP-AED) to start charter operations in August 1949. It crashed in July 1954.

Orient Airways Ltd, Karachi, began charteroperations in April 1947 and scheduled services in June 1947 using DC-3s which were at first Indian-registered, although it is unlikely that they ever operated in these marks, as the series concerned (VT-CPA onwards) was not used. The first two aircraft were leased from BOAC pending availability of their own aircraft. Orient's operations were merged into Pakistan International's in April 1955. (See under India for VT- registrations)

AP-AAA to AP-AAK incl; AP-AAN; AP-AAX to AP-ABD incl; AP-ACV; AP-ACW; AP-ACY to AP-ADA incl; AP-AEI; AP-AGD; AP-AGG.

Pak-Air Ltd, Karachi, was formed as **Pakistan Airways Ltd** in 1947 with help from Transocean. Services were suspended in 1949 and the aircraft sold.

AP-ABW; AP-ACD; AP-ACE; AP-ACF; AP-ADH to AP-ADJ incl.

Pakistan International Airlines Corp, Karachi, took over Orient's DC-3 fleet when the airlines merged in April 1955. All had been replaced by F.27s by 1965.

AP-AAC; AP-AAG to AP-AAI incl, AP-ABA to AP-ABD incl; AP-ACY; AP-ACZ; AP-AEI; AP-AGG; AP-AJH; AP-AJS; AP-AJT.

Index:-

AP-AAA	c/n 26423	AP-AAX	10123
AP-AAB	6241	AP-AAY	20776
AP-AAC	9543	AP-AAZ	12670
AP-AAD	9143	AP-ABA	6213
AP-AAE	19032	AP-ABB	6216
AP-AAF	4562	AP-ABC	6069
AP-AAG	4356	AP-ABD	6258
AP-AAH	12089	AP-ABW	12159
AP-AAI	12501	AP-ACD	27114
AP-AAJ	9546	AP-ACE	12775
AP-AAK	11982	AP-ACF	13480
AP-AAN	12222	AP-ACV	33224

AP-ACW	33559	AP-AFH	33246
AP-ACY	27082	AP-AFK	33277
AP-ACZ	33561	AP-AFL	33517
AP-ADA	33174	AP-AGD	32631
AP-ADH	9878	AP-AGG	32846
AP-ADI	4841	AP-AJH	13568
AP-ADJ	11636	AP-AJS	12501
AP-AED	20777	AP-AJT	26868
AP-AEI	26868	AP-AMC	20058

Note:- Surviving aircraft ending in the letter "I" resulting in call-sign "India" were re-registered AP-AJS/JT.

PANAMA - RX and HP

Panama, strategically placed on the Panama Canal, is better known as a "flag of convenience" country for shipping, but a number of airliners have been registered similarly while "in transit". However, the relatively few DC-3s used in the area have been somewhat more stable, and one (HP-86 of COPA) was with that airline for about 40 years - which must be some kind of record. RX- gave way to HP- in 1952.

Aerovías Urraca SA, Panama, used DC-3s between 1971 and early 1973.

HP-560; HP-629; HP-698.

Alas Chiricanas. DC-3s HP-86 and HP-446 were used. They were replaced by EMB-110s.

Cia Chitreana de Aviación SA, Chitre, Herrera, has been reported as using three DC-3s, but only two have identified and were sold between 1984 and 1988.

HP-490; HP-729.

COPA - Cia Panamena de Aviación SA, Panama City, started scheduled services in May 1947, using two DC-3s supplied by Pan American. Three others were added at various times, of which two survived in 1982. RX-76 may never have been used as it crashed in November 1946. The last was sold about 1986.

RX-76; RX/HP-86; RX/HP-87; HP-190; HP-446; HP-665.

Panama Cargo Three, Panama City, had two DC-3s, but one was sold.

HP-1176CTH; HP-1178CTH.

RAPSA - Rutas Aéreas Panamenas SA, Panama City, started operations in September 1958, using DC-3s. The last was sold in 1975.

HP-291; HP-309; HP-327; HP-496; HP-563.

Index:-

RX-76	c/n 20590	HP-490	13746
RX/HP-86	6144	HP-496	6068
RX/HP-87	4541	HP-560	19242
HP-182		HP-563	19513
HP-190	34374	HP-629	26700
HP-191	1996	HP-665	6068
HP-212	12374	HP-671	43073
HP-291	9091	HP-698	
HP-309	7392	HP-729	7392
HP-327	7345	HP-837	9920
HP-335	4484	HP-1126P	
HP-390	9137	HP-1176CTH	25808
HP-393	33612	HP-1178CTH	10131
HP-446	9137		

Notes:- HP-698 was current in 1977, though withdrawn.

PARAGUAY - ZP

Lineas Aereas Paraguayas SA, Asuncion, operated scheduled services, using DC-3 ZP-CCG under Air Force management between 1972 and 1978.

Transporte Aereo Militar, Asuncion, used DC-3s on domestic routes that were not economic commercially. At least seven are believed to have been used, and are listed in the military section.

Index:-

ZP-CCG   c/n 4362

PERU - OB

Apart from Faucett, no commercial operator in Perú was a major DC-3 user. However, at various times, three military operators used the type on domestic/social services, each passing on its DC-3s to the organisation which took them over, until Aero Perú gave up the type. The lettered registration marks gave way to a numbered series in 1964, in which a prefix letter indicated the function of the aircraft. The numbers were the registration certificate numbers which often appeared on the aircraft when the lettered series was used.

Aerolineas Peruanas SA, Lima, is reported to have used two DC-3s when operations first started in 1957. They have not been identified, but by 1958 only C-46s were in use.

Aeronorte SA bought C-117D OB-T-1325 in July 1988. Operations ceased in 1989/90.

Aero Perú, Lima, was formed in October 1973 to take over SATCO's operations and their remaining DC-3s. These were used on uneconomic domestic services, but were replaced by F.27s and F.28s.

OB-R-535; OB-R-539; OB-R-540.

Alpa Aerotaxis, Lima, bought DC-3 OB-T-1043 for charter work in late 1973. It ceased operations.

Cia Aérea Trans-America Peru SA (ATAPSA), Lima, bought DC-3 OB-R-774 in April 1965 for domestic freight charters, but it was out of use by 1972.

Faucett - Cia de Aviación Faucett SA, Lima, is one of the oldest airlines in South America, having started in 1928. DC-3s were introduced in 1946 and at least one remained until 1980.

OB-PAL; OB-PAM; OB-PAQ/R-167; OB-PAS/R-199; OB-PAT/R-200; OB-PAU; OB-PAV; OB-PAX; OB-PAY; OB-PBA/R-246; OB-PBD/456; OB-PBF/R-473; OB-PBG/R-500; OB-PBH; OB-PBI; OB-PBJ/R-544; OB-PBK/R-551; OB-PBN; OB-PBO/R-676; OB-PHI/R-516;

SATCO - Servicio Aéreo de Transporte Commerciales, Lima, took over TAM's domestic services in June 1960, including eleven DC-3s. It became Aero Perú in 1973.

OB-XAA/R-534; OB-XAB/R-535; OB-XAC/R-536; OB-XAD/R-537; OB-XAF/R-539; OB-XAG/R-540; OB-XAK/R-568; OB-XAP/R-581; OB-XAT/R-653; OB-XAU/R-654.

TAM - Transportes Aéreos Militares, Lima, took over Linea Aerea Nacional in May 1946 and soon afterwards bought DC-3s. These are detailed in the military section.

Taxi Aéreo Selva had DC-3 OB-1345 in 1989.

Trans-Peruana de Aviación SA registered two DC-3s in 1965, OB-R810 and OB-R811; the first operated for three years but the latter was unused.

Index of lettered series:-

OB-LHC-499	c/n 26405	OB-PBA-246	9980
(OB-LHZ-568)	26683	OB-PBD-456	34356
(OB-LIS-632)	34135	OB-PBF-473	7384
(OB-LIT-633)	26112	OB-PBG-500	20225
OB-PAL-145	34362 ?	OB-PBH-530	7331
OB-PAM-146	34206	OB-PBJ-544	13177
OB-PAQ-167	34328	OB-PBK-551	4801
OB-PAS-199	32729	OB-PBN-659	25839
OB-PAT-200	32737	OB-PBO-676	26360
OB-PAU-201	32740	OB-PHI-516	26184
OB-PAV-223	26819	OB-WAI-473	7384
OB-PAX-224	25882	OB-WBT-500	20225
OB-PAY-226	25819	OB-XAA-534	11718

OB-XAB-535	4177	OB-XAK-568	26683
OB-XAC-536	4800	OB-XAP-581	4830
OB-XAD-537	2192	OB-XAT-653	34369
OB-XAF-539	34270	OB-XAU-654	25986
OB-XAG-540	20057		

Index of numerical series:-

OB-R-167	34328	OB-R-551	4801
OB-R-199	32729	OB-R-568	26683
OB-R-200	32737	OB-R-581	4830
OB-R-224	25882	OB-M-632	34135
OB-R-246	9980	OB-R-653	34369
OB-R-473	7384	OB-R-654	25986
OB-M-499	26405	OB-R-676	26360
OB-R-500	20225	OB-R-774	10052
OB-R-516	26184	OB-R-810	12110
OB-R-534	11718	OB-R-811	13074
OB-R-535	4177	OB-I-818	20546
OB-R-536	4800	OB-I-900	9796
OB-R-537	2192	OB-T-1043	12876
OB-R-539	34270	OB-T-1325	43347
OB-R-540	20057	OB-1345	11771
OB-R-544	13177	OB-1756	13177

Notes:-
OB-PAL has c/n 34365 quoted officially, but this has an alternative history. As c/n 34362 was supplied to Peru, this is preferred.
Those in the OB-I series were government-owned.

PHILIPPINE REPUBLIC - PI and RP

Because of the large number of islands making up the Philippine Republic this was an ideal site for the development of air transport and as soon as WW2 was over the ready supply of surplus C-47s from USAAF storage depots there soon led to a considerable expansion in air services, with the DC-3 as mainstay. Much confusion has arisen over the identity of many of the Philippine-registered DC-3s, as the official records are less than adequate and because the 1973 change in nationality mark from PI- to RP- has caused further complications. In some cases the same aircraft changed from PI- to RP-, but in others, a second DC-3 took up the number earlier used by another of this type. The number of operators has fallen drastically and two users with four aircraft remained by 2001.

Air Link International Airways, Manila, use a single DC-3 amongst Beech twins.

RP-C1101.

Air Manila Inc, Manila, was formed in February 1964 to operate DC-3s bought from Frontier Airlines in the USA. One crashed on delivery, but the Philippine identities of many used have remained a mystery. Domestic services started in January 1965 and further aircraft were acquired when it merged with Fairways and was taken over by Philippine Air Lines in 1973. Seven DC-3s were destroyed in a hurricane in 1970.

PI-C368; PI-C854 to PI-C857 incl; PI-C859 to PI-C863 incl; PI-C941; PI-C943; PI-C946 and PI-C960; probably including c/ns 12139, 12191 (cr on delivery), 12440, 19003, 19542 ex-Frontier.

Asean Air Freight operated DC-3 N102DH on lease in 1994/95.

Astro Air Transport, Pasay City, started domestic non-scheduled services in May 1976, initially with DC-3s, but these were replaced by C-46s in 1979.

RP-C1O; RP-C649.

Commercial Air Lines Inc, Manila, started charter operations in February 1946 and scheduled services in July of the following year, using a large fleet of DC-3s from USAAF surplus stocks. The airline was taken over by PAL in August 1948.

PI-C2; PI-C4; PI-C7; PI-C9; PI-C15; PI-C17; PI-C19; PI-C23; PI-C40; PI-C42; PI-C125; PI-C126; PI-C140 to PI-C151 incl.

Commercial Air Transport Inc, Pasay City, was operating DC-3s from about November 1977, when one was written off, but by 1981 the last was derelict.

PI/RP-C141; PI/RP-C647; PI/RP-C649; RP-C653.

Commuter Air Philippines, Manila, founded in 1985, were operating DC-3 RP-C1101 in 1992.

Continental Airways used DC-3 RP-C132. They ceased operations by 1976.

Delta Airways, Pasay City, had used DC-3 RP-C14 on charter operations, along with smaller types, but it was lost in 1989.

FAIRWAYS - Filipinas Orient Airways, Manila, operated scheduled domestic services from January 1965 until its take-over by PAL in April 1973. DC-3s, bought mainly from Southern Airlines, were used.

PI-C368; PI-C490; PI-C941 to PI-C948 incl; PI-C960 and PI-C961.

Far Eastern Air Transport Inc, Santa Cruz, Manila, bought a small number of DC-3s in 1946 but services were suspended in the following January and the airline was bought out by PAL in May 1947.

PI-C1; PI-C5; PI-C6; PI-C40; PI-C96; PI-C97; PI-C99; PI-C103.

FAST - Fleming Airways System Transport, Pasay City, started DC-3 operations in 1956 with low-fare domestic services. They ceased early in 1966.

PI-C262; PI-C567 to PI-C570 incl.

Mabuhay Airways, Pasay City, began operations as **First United Air**, adopting its present name in November 1973. DC-3s ceased to form part of the fleet by 1986.

RP-C74; RP-C84; RP-C643; RP-C2122.

Manila Air Transport System operated DC-3 RP-C23; RP-C81, RP-C82 and RP-C83 from 1984-85 until as late as 1994.

OASIS Inc - Orient Air Systems and Integrated Services Inc, Pasay City, originated as Far East Aviation Services and operated charter flights using a few DC-3s in 1980/82 with C-46s and Convairs.

RP-C2, RP-C40, RP-C570.

Philair, Passay City, has operated DC-3s RP-C550 and RP-C631. Both were sold but a third, RP-C287 was w/o in 1983.

Philippine Airlines Inc (PAL), Manila, restarted operations after the war on 25 February 1946, using surplus DC-3s. A large fleet of the type was built up and further aircraft were acquired from various operators. In 1947 Far East Air Transport was taken over, and in the following year Commercial Air Lines joined them, followed in 1950 by Trans Asiatic. In January 1974 Air Manila and Filipinas Orient were taken over but by the end of the seventies the DC-3 had been phased out of service.

PI-C2 to 9 incl; 10 to 12 incl; 14 to 17 incl; 19; 22 to 25 incl; 36; 38; 40 to 43 incl; 47; 53 to 59 incl; 90 to 92 incl; 94 to 99 incl; 103; 125 to 133 incl; 138; 140 to 151 incl; 199; 270; 439; 481; 485 to 490 incl; 941; 943; 946; 960; 961. Some survived to use the RP-C prefix.

Philippine Express Co, Manila, lost a DC-3 in an accident at Carrio Rizal on 2 November 1947, but nothing further is known of operations.

Sky Tours Inc, Manila, used an unknown DC-3 on charter work.

A.Soriano Air Cargo, Manila, operated a single C-117D RP-C473 through the early nineties.

Swiftair Inc, Zamboanga City, started operating charter flights to the S Philippines in August 1972. Most DC-3s were withdrawn from use, but two remained in 1999.

RP-C147, RP-C368, RP-C488; RP-C860, RP-C862, RP-C868.

Trans Air Service, Manila, had three DC-3s but all their aircraft were sold.

RP-C141, RP-C142, RP-C649.

Trans Asiatic Airlines Inc, Manila, began operations in June 1946, using DC-3s. They were taken over by PAL in late 1950. There was also a Thai based subsidiary.

PI-C180 to PI-C184 incl.

Victoria Air Inc, Manila, which operated DC-3s RP-C138 and RP-C142 was taken over by Village Airways. Reports suggested that the airline continued to operate separately in the early 90s using RP-C95 which became RP-C535; RP-C14; RP-C550; RP-C631; RP-C646 and RP-C845. Of these, RP-C550 and RP-C550 were still current in 2005.

Village Airways, Pasay City, uses DC-3s to run cargo charter services. Five aircraft are thought to have been used, but see Victoria Air.

RP-C95; RP-C138; RP-C140; RP-C490; RP-C646.

Index:-

PI-C1	c/n 25436	PI/RP-C141	19251
PI/RP-C2	25428	PI-C142	13397
PI-C3		RP-C142	13848
RP-C3	26209	PI-C143	13780 ?
PI-C4	10123	PI-C144	13403
PI-C5	9754	PI-C145	10269 ?
PI-C6	9807	PI-C146	10269 ?
PI-C7	18934	PI/RP-C147	20767
PI-C8	19183	PI-C148	18925
PI-C9	12648	RP-C148	34280
PI-C10		PI-C149	4823
RP-C10	25572	RP-C149	19785
	or 13848 ?	PI-C150	4824
PI-C11	19181	PI-C151	4840
PI-C12	13508	PI-C180	20583
PI-C13	4736	PI-C181	18947
PI-C14	13193	PI-C182	26816 ?
RP-C14	26088	PI-C183	19258
PI-C15	25435	PI-C184	19252?
PI-C16	13908	PI-C199	12793
PI-C17	20573	PI-C262	
PI-C19	12652	PI-C270	13808
PI-C22	12628	RP-C287	26118
PI/RP-C23	25431	PI/RP-C368	2217
PI-C24	19904	PI-C439	13514
PI-C25	19920	RP-C472	
PI-C34	20669 ?	RP-C473(C-117D)	
PI-C36			43327
PI-C38		PI-C481	33579
PI/RP-C40	12529	PI-C485	
PI-C41	13194	PI-C486	26480
PI-C42	11780	PI-C487	32569
PI-C43		PI/RP-C488	33239
PI-C47	20777	PI-C489	32863
PI-C53		PI/RP-C490	20626
PI-C54	19932	RP-534	9525
PI-C55	13510	RP-C535	27016
PI-C56		RP-C538	
PI-C57	19895	RP-C549	
PI-C58	20776	RP-C550	25737
PI-C59	19254 ?	RP-C563	
PI-C72		PI-C567	26811
RP-C74	25572	PI-C568	25231
RP-C81	25325	PI-C569	20396
RP-C82	20209	PI/RP-C570	25452 ?
RP-C83	25562	RP-C631	12037
RP-C84		PI/RP-C643	26996
PI-C90	10081	PI-C646	27174
PI-C91	13364	RP-C646	13848
PI-C92	12672 ?	PI/RP-C647	9786
PI-C94	27026	PI-C648	
PI/RP-C95	27016	PI/RP-C649	13510
PI-C96	27174	RP-C653	
PI-C97	26389	RP-C716	2217
PI-C98	33491	PI-C718	4806
PI-C99	20811	RP-C758	19738
PI/RP-C103	20769	RP-C782	20209
RP-C124		RP-C845	25415
PI-C125	12670	PI-C854	13559
PI-C126	20593	PI-C855	
PI-C127	9397	PI-C856	
PI-C128	13365	PI-C857	
PI-C129	9746	PI-C859	
PI-C130	9719	PI-C860	19003 ?
PI-C131		RP-C860	33239
PI/RP-C132	19897	PI-C861	
PI-C133		PI/RP-C862	19996
PI/RP-C138	20811	PI-C863	
PI/RP-C140	19253	RP-C868	

PI/RP-C941	4107	PI/RP-C960	2179
PI-C942	1926	PI/RP-C961	11666
PI/RP-C943	2240	RP-C1101	9525
PI-C944	42967	RP-C1352	25347
PI-C945	4822	RP-C1353	25368
PI/RP-C946	4106	RP-C1354	25571
PI-C947	1909	(PI-C1937)	33457
PI-C948	4892	PI/RP-C2122	9310

Notes:-

PI-C3 was owned by PAL and w/o in 1948.
PI-C10 was owned by PAL and w/o in 1948. It is not thought to be related to RP-C10, for which two c/ns are reported from 1976.
PI-C38 was owned by PAL and crashed on 30Dec52 off Formosa.
PI-C43 was owned by PAL, fate unknown.
PI-C53 was owned by PAL and destroyed on the ground by a typhoon on 26Dec47.
PI-C56 was owned by PAL, fate unknown.
PI-C59 was owned by PAL and crashed on 13Sep47 at Zamboanga but it is thought to be c/n 19254 which was reported w/o 01Oct46.
PI-C131 was owned by PAL, fate unknown.
PI-C133 was owned by PAL and crashed on 23Nov60 on Mt Baco.
PI-C143 was owned by PAL and crashed on 17May48 at Cebu. Thought to be c/n 13780, either this, PI-C145 or PI-C146 was c/n 10269 and all three originated with Commercial.
PI-C145 was owned by PAL (see above) and crashed on 21Jan48 at Iloilo.
PI-C184 owned by Transasiatic, crashed on 18Jan50 at Rangoon, Burma.
PI-C262 owned by Fleming A/ws was w/o on 22Mar58.
PI-C485 was owned by PAL and crashed on 13Oct62 at Cagayan de Oro Airport.
PI-C648 owned by the Aguinaido Development Corp, was w/o on 14Oct67.
PI-C854 to PI-C863 probably comprise the original equipment of Air Manila. Little is known of them except that most came from Frontier Airlines and PI-C856 crashed on 16Dec65.
N490, a DST c/n 1954 was exported to the Philippines in Aug64.

POLAND - SP

Poland bought about ten C-47s from USAAF surplus stocks in 1946 while Russia supplied a large batch of Li-2s which were operated by the 7th Independent Civil Aviation Squadron from 01Apr45. Both groups of aircraft later became part of LOT.

Polskie Linie Lotnicze "LOT", Warsaw, bought DC-2s from Fokker in 1935 and used these on scheduled services until September 1939, when they were lost. Russia supplied about 30 Li-2s in 1945 for use by the Air Force, but later by LOT when they restarted operations. They were supplemented by a batch of USAAF surplus C-47s the last of which were sold via Denmark in about 1959, while the Li-2s probably remained in use a little longer, as one is known to have crashed in 1960.

DC-2s:-

SP-ASJ	c/n 1318	SP-ASL	1378
SP-ASK	1377		

DC-3s:-

SP-LCA	7367	SP-LCF	9938
SP-LCB(1)	10044	SP-LCG(1)	9165
SP-LCB(2)	12704	SP-LCG(2)	12774
SP-LCC(1)	9903	SP-LCH(1)	9106
SP-LCC(2)	13348	SP-LCH(2)	13552
SP-LCD	19499	SP-LCJ	9801
SP-LCE	19289		

Li-2s:-

SP-LAA	184 227 02	SP-LAP	184 232 04
SP-LAB	184 227 03	SP-LAR	184 240 03
SP-LAC	184 227 04	SP-LAS	184 232 03
SP-LAD	184 227 05	SP-LAT	184 232 05
SP-LAE	184 240 01	SP-LAU	184 232 06
SP-LAF	184 240 04	SP-LAW	184 240 09
SP-LAG	184 232 02	SP-LBA	184 220 09
SP-LAH	184 232 01	SP-LBB	184 198 02
SP-LAJ	184 240 05	SP-LBC	184 190 10
SP-LAK	184 240 02	SP-LBD	184 198 04
SP-LAL	184 240 08	SP-LBE	184 202 03
SP-LAM	184 226 10	SP-LBF	184 202 05
SP-LAN	184 240 06	SP-LBG	184 183 08
SP-LAO	184 240 07	SP-LBH	184 196 02

CHAPTER 4: COMMERCIAL OPERATORS OF THE DC-3, C-47, R4D, DAKOTA AND LI-2

SP-LBJ	184 197 04	SP-LKE	234 420 02
SP-LDA	184 391 02	SP-LKF	334 445 10
SP-LKA	184 385 05	SP-LKG	334 448 01
SP-LKB	184 385 04	SP-LKH	334 445 07
SP-LKC	234 410 10	SP-LKI	334 448 04
SP-LKD	234 415 01		

PORTUGAL and AZORES - CS

Aero Portuguesa Ltda, Lisbon, leased one DC-3 until it was taken over by TAP in 1953.

CS-ADB.

CTA - Companhia de Transportes Aéreos operated DC-3s CS-TDX and CS-TDZ in 1946. Its routes were taken over in July 1947 by TAP and the DC-3s went to Angola.

SATA - Soc. Açoriana de Transportes Aéreos Ltda, Azores, used DC-3s on inter-island scheduled services to replace Doves in 1964. They were replaced, in turn, by HS.748s in 1975. (CS-TAI was also used by Atlantico Interplano, a private company)

CS-TAD; CS-TAE; CS-TAI.

TAP - Transportes Aéreos Portugueses SARL, Lisbon, used DC-3s on scheduled services from 1946 until the aircraft were transferred to the Air Force or to Angola in 1958.

CS-TDA to CS-TDH incl.

Index:-

CS-ADB	20012	CS-TDB	10033
CS-AZL	26244	CS-TDC	11765
CS-DGA	19503	CS-TDD	11668
CS-EDA	19773	CS-TDE	11675
CS-EDB	19393	CS-TDF	18998
CS-TAD	9140	CS-TDG	13140
CS-TAE	32761	CS-TDH	10049
CS-TAI	12060	CS-TDX	20456
CS-TDA	19393	CS-TDZ	20173
"CS-TDA"	19503		

RHODESIA - See Zimbabwe

ROMANIA - YR

LARES - Liniile Aeriene Române Exploatate cu Statul, Bucharest, operated two Fokker-assembled DC-3s from 1937 until the outbreak of war, when one survived. Two DC-3 accidents are reported, both fatal. One crashed at Cluj, Romania on 23Aug40 and the other on take-off from Bucharest on 19Jun41. YR-PAF is known to have survived until 1964. DC-2 YR-GAD ex G-AGAD, which came from Poland and never got to BOAC, survived until July 1942 at least.

DC-2: YR-GAD;
DC-3s: YR-PAF; YR-PIF.

TARS - Transporturi Aeriene Româno-Sovietice, Bucharest, took over LARES' assets on 01Feb46 and, with Russian help, operated Li-2s from 1946 until the airline was taken over by TAROM in 1954, and the remaining aircraft passed to TAROM.

YR-DAB; YR-DAC; YR-MIG; YR-MIR; YR-TAA; YR-TAB; YR-TAC; YR-TAD; YR-TAE(2); YR-TAF; YR-TAG; YR-TAH; YR-TAI; YR-TAJ; YR-TAK; YR-TAL; YR-TAM; YR-TAN; YR-TAO(2); YR-TAP; YR-TAR; YR-TAS; YR-TAT; YR-TAV; YR-TAW; YR-TAX; YR-TAY; YR-TAZ.
DC-3s: YR-PAF; YR-PIF.

TAROM - Transporturi Aeriene Române, Bucharest, was formed in 1954 to take over TARS, and with it a number of Li-2s. The following have been reported.

YR-DAB; YR-DAC; YR-MIG; YR-MIR; YR-TAB; YR-TAD; YR-TAE; YR-TAF; YR-TAG; YR-TAK; YR-TAL; YR-TAM; YR-TAN; YR-TAO; YR-TAP; YR-TAR; YR-TAS; YR-TAT; YR-TAW; YR-TAX; YR-TAZ.

Index:-

YR-GAD(DC-2)	c/n 1378	YR-PIF (DC-3)	1985
YR-PAF(DC-3)	1986		

Li-2s:

YR-DAB	234 448 03	YR-TAJ	184 235 08
YR-DAC	234 415 07	YR-TAK	184 280 04
YR-MIG	234 448 02	YR-TAL	184 275 02
YR-MIR	234 445 05	YR-TAM	184 232 07
YR-PCB	184 398 07	YR-TAN	184 280 05
YR-PCD	184 398 05	YR-TAO(1)	184 235 10
YR-TAA	184 235 01	YR-TAO(2)	234 418 02
YR-TAB	184 232 08	YR-TAP	184 275 05
YR-TAC	184 235 03	YR-TAR	184 235 02
YR-TAD	184 235 04	YR-TAS	184 240 10
YR-TAE(1)	184 235 06	YR-TAT	184 328 02
YR-TAE(2)	234 419 05	YR-TAV	184 238 01
YR-TAF	184 235 05	YR-TAW	234 445 06
YR-TAG	184 280 02	YR-TAX	184 238 03
YR-TAH	184 235 07	YR-TAY	184 238 02
YR-TAI	184 235 09	YR-TAZ	184 238 04

RUSSIA/SOVIET UNION - URSS and CCCP

AEROFLOT - Grazhdanskogo vozdushnago flota, (Civil Air Fleet) Moscow, bought a number of Douglas twins before the war. The first was a DC-2 bought via Amtorg in August 1935. This may have been URSS-M25 c/n 1413 which crashed in August 1937. Some 27 DC-3s followed, supplied nominally to the Mongolian Air Transport Co., or via Ex-Cello and Northeast, both almost certainly acting as agents for Aeroflot. Those identified below are listed in the production section. Licence production as the PS-84 and later the Li-2 followed and Aeroflot used many of these following the war. They also used a number of the 707 C-47s supplied under Lend-Lease together with 3 from USAAF stocks in Alaska. None has survived but a single Li-2 restored to airworthy condition (RA-01300 c/n 23441605 - ex Soviet AF 03) unfortunately crashed.

While some of the imported DC-3s went to the Soviet Air Force, many were operated by Aeroflot and the GVF. The URSS- prefix was used for civil international flights already and some of the DC-3s were registered in a sequence commencing URSS-A in 1939. Some batches were delivered by sea to Cherbourg and following assembly were flown to Russia in ferry marks 'F-2' or 'F-6'. Another group, ostensibly sold to Far East Fur Trading, Mongolia, were registered MT-16 to MT-21 and were used by the Soviet Air Force for casualty evacuation in the Khalkhin - Gol conflict and the Winter War in Finland.

Post-war lack of spares meant that many C-47s in Russia were re-engined with Ash-621R engines being designated TS-62, or with ASh-82FN engines as TS-82. The type remained in service with Aeroflot until 1957. Two DC-3s, URSS-M136 and -M137, were used by the Chinese-Soviet airline **Hamiata** in 1939 (see also under China).

Delivered as 'F-2' from Cherbourg: C/ns 1589, 1974, 1987, 1988, 2031, 2032, 2033, 2042, 2043, 2044, 2045, 2046, 2047.

Delivered as 'F-6' from Cherbourg: C/ns 2112, 2113, 2114, 2115, 2116, 2117.

Delivered as MT-16 to MT-21 resp: C/ns 2096 to 2101 incl.

Index:-

DC-2:
URSS-M25   c/n 1413

DC-3:

URSS-M132	1589	URSS-D	2096
URSS-M135	2032	URSS-G	2097
URSS-M136	2031	URSS-H	2046
URSS-M137	2033	URSS-K	2098
URSS-M138	2034	URSS-M	2031
	(see note)	URSS-N	2033
URSS-A	1589	URSS-L3403	2096
URSS-B (1)	2032	URSS-L3402	2097
URSS-B (2)	2035	URSS-L3407	2117
URSS-C	2047		

Identified C-47s are:-

CCCP-X361	c/n 4771	CCCP-L1026	33370
CCCP-L803	6234	CCCP-L1053	34307
CCCP-L867	12119	CCCP-L1059	34310
CCCP-L894	13097	CCCP-L1060	34322
CCCP-L976	26332	CCCP-L1201	33439
CCCP-L997	?	CCCP-L1212	34324
CCCP-L1008	?	CCCP-N-425	33432
CCCP-L1015	?	"CCCP-7245"	26735

Notes:-
URSS-M138 was supplied as a pattern aircraft without engines. It may have been assembled as PS-84 "841".
URSS-A was a DC-3-196, in service 12Jun39 until at least Jul41.
URSS-D was in service in Jul41.
CCCP-L867, -L997, -L1026 wore only numbers without prefix and were in camouflage c/s.
CCCP-L1008 was used in a film in Aeroflot markings.
CCCP-L1015 was noted with Aeroflot Jun49.
CCCP-N-425 served with Aviaarktika, 1945-47.
"CCCP-7245" appeared as such in a film
One pre-war DC-3 crashed on 25Apr41 on take-off from Moscow, in bad weather.
Further aircraft which are believed to be C-47s are CCCP-H328; H465; L879; L1403.
C-47s known to have been used by the Soviet Air Force include c/ns 11960, 33169, 33333, 33387, 33417. See also Military Operators.

All known Russian-registered Li-2s will be found in the Li-2 Production section Chapter 7 and Preserved examples are listed in Chapter 9. Those with known c/ns are also listed in the cross-reference Index Chapter 11.

ST LUCIA - VQ-L and J6

St Lucia Airways, Castries, St Lucia, used DC-3 VQ-LAX on charter services in the Windward Islands for a few months during 1977, but replaced it with an Islander. It leased the same DC-3 back in 1978 as N28346.

Index:-

VQ-LAX	c/n 6259

SAUDI ARABIA - SA and HZ

The first DC-3 operated in Saudi Arabia in 1945 was one given to the King by the US Government and registered SA-R-1 for operation by the Royal Flight. This was transferred later to Saudi Arabian Airlines, and is now preserved in its original markings. It may well have been the aircraft which flew as SA-T-1 with the airline, but that series was discontinued when HZ was adopted as the nationality mark in 1951. Data on Saudi DC-3s is somewhat confused by the way in which some marks have been re-used following transfer of the earlier aircraft to the Air Force, and their return in new markings.

Saudi Arabian Airlines, Jeddah, was supplied with DC-3s with help from TWA in 1946. Operations began on 14 March 1947, using five aircraft rising to eight, at least two of which still survived on the scrap heap at Jeddah until recently, following their replacement by F.27s leased in the USA. The SA-T- series was used by the airline.

HZ-AAA to HZ-AAE incl; HZ-AAJ to HZ-AAS incl; HZ-AAX; amongst which some marks used twice. SA-T-1, T-2, T-6, T-8, T-10, T-15, T-20, T-201.

Index:-

SA-R-1	c/n 32650	HZ-AAB	25276
SA-R-2	4607	HZ-AAC	32978
SA-R-3	4501	HZ-AAD	4607
SA-T-1	22680 ?	HZ-AAE	4501
SA-T-2	32979 ?	HZ-AAJ	26680
SA-T-6		HZ-AAK	32979
SA-T-8		HZ-AAL(1)	
SA-T-10		HZ-AAL(2)	11861
SA-T-15		HZ-AAM	
SA-T-20		HZ-AAN(1)	25276 ?
SA-T-201		HZ-AAN(2)	12899
HZ-AAA		SA/HZ-AAO	
HZ-AAP	25283	HZ-AAS	
HZ-AAQ(1)	32978 ?	HZ-AAX	32650
HZ-AAQ(2)		HZ-TA3	4363
HZ-AAR	33427 ?		

Notes:-
The following were acquired through TWA in 1948 and presumably registered in the SA-T- series: c/ns 9321, 9381, 9469, 13556, 26503.
SA-R-1 - a link has been proposed between this and SA-T-1 but remains unproven.
HZ-AAA/B and C are believed to have been operated by the Saudi Air Force as 401, 402 and 403, but while sources tend to confirm two of these connections, HZ-AAA is unidentified and 401 was reported as such on the Jeddah dump in Sep80. These RSAF DC-3s were earlier used as HZ-AAL, HZ-AAN and HZ-AAQ, all of which marks were re-issued later. HZ-AAL(1) is believed to have become Saudi AF 401, HZ-AAN(1) is known to have been 402 and HZ-AAQ(1) became 403.
HZ-AAM noted 1960, crashed on 24Jun67 at Khatif Nseir.
HZ-AAO crashed on 16Feb56 at Nejran.
HZ-AAQ(2) has been quoted as 11861 which conflicts with HZ-AAL(2) listed as such Feb58 and seen Nov63.
HZ-AAS was reported sold as YE-AAS.
SA-T-6 was seen at Karachi Nov47.
SA-T-10 was overhauled by Scottish Avn and delivered on 22Apr49.
SA-T-201 was owned by Missouri Airways Inc and was bought in Cairo in Jan47 for operations in the Middle East which ceased in Jul48.

SENEGAL - 6V

Air Sénégal - Cie Sénégalaise de Transports Aériens, Dakar, was formed in November 1962 to take over domestic services flown by **Ardic**. It was nationalised as **SONATRA Air Sénégal** (Sté. National Transport Aérien) on 1 July 1971. DC-3s were used from early 1963 until replaced by F.27s in 1977/78.

6V-AAA; 6V-AAE; 6V-AAK; (6V-AAM); 6V-AAO; 6V-AAP; 6V-ABB; 6V-ACA; 6V-ACW; 6V-ACZ and F-OAQR leased.

Index:-

6V-AAA	c/n 4351	6V-AAP	20505
6V-AAE	25281	6V-ABB	9511
6V-AAK	4757	6V-ACA	25475
(6V-AAM)	33581	6V-ACW	42959
6V-AAO	33089	6V-ACZ	25606

SINGAPORE - See MALAYA

SOMALILAND (FRENCH) - F-O

A French Overseas Territory post-war, becoming the Territory of the Afars and the Issas in 1967 and independent as Djibouti in 1977.

Air Djibouti - Cie Territoriale de Transports Aériens de la Côte Française des Somalis, Djibouti, operated scheduled services with DC-3s between 1965 and 1976, when the last two were sold and used in the film "A Bridge Too Far".

F-BGOU; F-OCEN; F-OCKT; F-OCKU; F-OCKV; F-OCKX; F-OCRR.

SOMALI REPUBLIC - 6OS/6O

Somali Airlines, Mogadishu, started scheduled services to Aden in July 1964 using DC-3s. Of the four used over this period two remained in 1980 and were sold in the USA. The registration prefix changed from 6OS- to 6O- on 31Oct70.

Index:-

6OS-AAA/6O-SAA		6OS-AAC/6O-SAC	20424
	c/n 19754	6OS-AAH/6O-SAH	13111
6OS-AAB/6O-SAB	20016		

SOUTH AFRICA - ZS

Some 100 DC-3s and two DC-2s have been registered in South Africa for commercial operations since 1946 and even now a sprinkling remain in use. The DC-3s originated not only in SAAF surplus Dakotas, but also in numerous imports as a result of trade with nearby states in Southern Africa, both for legitimate and clandestine purposes.

Aero Air registered DC-3s ZS-NZA to ZS-NZE and ZS-NTD in their name in 1997. Some were bought from the Madagascan Air Force, and may not yet be in service.

Africair Ltd, Johannesburg, was formed as **A.V. Air Transport** in 1946 (Anglo Vaal), and operated scheduled services for a time. The name Africair was adopted in 1949 and in the years that followed operated on behalf of **WENELA** (Witwatersrand Native Labour Assoc.), carrying labour for the South African gold and diamond mines from nearby countries. Some of these aircraft were registered in Rhodesia from 1960 until 1968, then moved to Botswana, but these operations ceased in 1977.

ZS-CCG; ZS-DBP/VP-YSJ; ZS-DBV; ZS-DCA/VP-YSK; ZS-DDC; ZS-DDV; ZS-DEF; ZS-DFN; ZS-DHO; ZS-DHW/VP-YSL; ZS-DHX; ZS-DHY/VP-YSM; ZS-DIV/VP-YSN; ZS-DJZ/VP-YSO; ZS-DKP/VP-YSP; ZS-DKR/VP-YSR; .

African Air Carriers (Pty) Ltd, Lanseria, formed in 1981, operated charter and cargo services using five DC-3s ex-Caprivi on Avex Air's licence. Operations ceased in 1984.

ZS-KEX; ZS-KHN; ZS-KIV; N6907; N99210; N9985Q.

Africa Charter Airlines registered DC-3 ZS-DRJ in 1997 but ceased by 2001.

Air Cape (Pty) Ltd, Cape Town, started scheduled services in March 1969 when one of SAA's routes was taken over. The first DC-3 had been bought for charter work in 1965 and in the end three were used, being replaced by HS.748s. The last was sold in Mar87.

ZS-EDX; ZS-EYN; ZS-EYO.

Air Lowveld, Johannesburg, used three leased DC-3s on third level services and became part of Magnum Airlines.

Airworld, Pretoria, operated three DC-3s for Speed Service Couriers. One remained in 2001.

ZS-MFY; ZS-MRU; ZS-NKK.

Air Zambezi bought DC-3 ZS-NTD in 2000.

Anglo-Vaal Air Transport, Johannesburg, used DC-3s from 1946 to 1949 prior to becoming Africair.

ZS-BCA; ZS-BCJ; ZS-BVF.

Avex Air, Johannesburg-Rand leased DC-3 ZS-JMP to Airworks Botswana, for air survey work.

Avia Air Charter, Wonderboom - see **Wonderair**.

Bazaruto Air Charter, Lanseria, used one DC-3, ZS-LVR being active in 1993.

Caprivi Airways, Windhoek, was formed in mid-1978 and scheduled operations using DC-3s began in October. Some remained US registered and never entered service. Operations ceased in late 1979 and the aircraft were sold to African Air Carriers.

N8044/ZS-KEX; N6907; N94468; N99210; N9985Q.

Comair - Commercial Air Services (Pty) Ltd, Johannesburg, bought DC-3s to replace their Lodestars from 1963 on. Five were used on scheduled services until 1980 when F.27s were bought. The trading name was Commercial Airways from November 1967.

ZS-DRJ; ZS-DXW; ZS-EJK; ZS-FRM; ZS-IWL.

Eyethu Air Cargo, had three DC-3s registered in 1999, all sold by 2000.

ZS-NTD; ZS-NTE; ZS-NZA.

Inter-Air, Lanseria, used DC-3 ZS-JMP in 1992 but this was sold to Jet Air.

Jet Air Charters, Lanseria, owned DC-3 ZS-JMP in 1999.

Magnum Airlines, Johannesburg, formed from the merger of Air Lowveld and Avna Air in 1970, leased DC-3 ZS-DRJ and ZS-FRM from Comair in the early eighties.

Maluti Air Services, bought DC-2 ZS-DFX in Nov54. It was leased to Silver City in 1957.

Mercury Aviation Services (Pty) Ltd, Johannesburg, used DC-3s for charter work during 1946 but after four had been lost in accidents in the next 18 months, operations ceased and the airline was declared bankrupt in December 1948. It was taken over by Sky Taxis Ltd.

ZS-BCA; ZS-BNB; ZS-BTN; ZS-BTO; ZS-BWX; ZS-BWY; ZS-BWZ; ZS-BXZ.

Namib Air - see Suidwes Lugdiens.

National Airways Corp, (Pty) Ltd, Baragwanath, Transvaal, operated scheduled services between 1965 and 1970 using DC-3s. The last one was passed to Swazi Air, a subsidiary.

ZS-DKR; ZS-EKK; VQ-ZJB.

Pan African Air Charter Ltd, Johannesburg, was an affiliate of Wm Dempster Ltd and operated cargo charters with a fleet of DC-3s from 1946 until about 1952. They were regular visitors to Britain, but also helped the newly-formed Israel - possibly in a clandestine manner.

ZS-AVK to ZS-AVO incl; ZS-AYB; ZS-BRW; ZS-BRX; ZS-BYX.

Phoebus Apollo, Lanseria, began operating DC-3s in 1997, with ZS-PAA, ZS-DIW and ZS-NTE.

Phoenix Airlines bought two DC-2s from Swissair in 1952 and used them until 1954. One was lost in an accident and the other sold to Maluti Air Services in November of that year.

ZS-DFW; ZS-DFX.

Pretoria Air Services, registered DC-3 ZS-KIV in April 1997.

Professional Airways, Lanseria, operates a single DC-3-65TP ZS-LJI.

Protea Airways (Pty) Ltd, Johannesburg, had ties with National and Swazi Air. It bought its first DC-3s before 1968 and used them on scheduled services, but all were sold in June 1977.

ZS-EKK; ZS-FKI; ZS-FRJ; ZS-IPP; ZS-KAT.

Regional Airlines, Johannesburg, bought DC-3 ZS-DIW in 1992. It ceased operations in 1993.

Rennies Air (Transvaal), Johannesburg, used DC-3 ZS-IPP on charter work for a while in the late seventies.

Rossair Executive Air Charter, Lanseria, owns two DC-3-65TPs, ZS-OBU, ZS-OJJ and leases 5Y-RDS.

Rovos Air, Lanseria, a subsidiary of Rovos Rail Tours (Pty) Ltd, operate a single 21-seat executive configuration DC-3 ZS-CRV on air safari work throughout southern Africa.

South African Airways, Johannesburg, bought DC-3s to operate scheduled services from 1946 onwards, when they progressively replaced Lodestars. They were themselves replaced by Viscounts and HS.748s and most were returned to the SAAF in 1971. Two were restored to service for the SAA Museum.

ZS-AVI; ZS-AVJ; ZS-BXF; ZS-BXG; ZS-BXI; ZS-BXJ; ZS-DJB; ZS-DJC; ZS-DJX.

Suidair International Airways Ltd, Johannesburg, was a subsidiary of President Motors and operated DC-3s between November 1946 and January 1950 when it was declared bankrupt. The later aircraft may only have been owned while awaiting sale.

ZS-BCY; ZS-BJZ; ZS-BWZ; ZS-BXZ; ZS-BYH; (ZS-BYI).

Suidwes Lugdiens (Edms) Beperk, Windhoek, SW Africa (now Namibia), originated as **South West Air Transport (Pty) Ltd** until it merged with Oryx Aviation in March 1959. The first DC-3 was bought in November 1953 and two remained in 1978 when **Namib Air** was formed.

ZS-DBP; ZS-DIW; ZS-DJZ.

TAC Air Services, operated two DC-3s in 1999: ZS-OJD and ZS-OJE bought from Kenya.

Trek Airways (Pty) Ltd, Johannesburg, used a single DC-3 to start non-scheduled services in conjunction with Air Safari between December 1953 and January 1955. ZS-DIY was later replaced by a Viking.

Tropic Airways (Pty) Ltd, Johannesburg, started charter operations with DC-3s in 1951 and continued until 1954.

ZS-DEF; ZS-DFB; ZS-DHO.

United Air Services (Pty) Ltd, Pretoria, began scheduled services in June 1972, using DC-3s. These were used in 1980 during Rhodesian independence negotiations in Botswana and were still in use in 1983. The parent company was **Sandriver Safaris**, to which some of the aircraft were registered. UAS was taken over by **Wonderair** in 1988.

ZS-GPL; ZS-PTG; ZS-UAS.

WENELA - See Africair above.

Wonderair, Pretoria, took over United Air Services in 1988, trading as **Avia Air Charter**. They also engaged in converting DC-3s to the AMI turbo prop version DC-3-65TP.

ZS-DHX; ZS-GPL; ZS-KCV(65TP); ZS-LJI(65TP); ZS-LYW(65TP); ZS-MFY; ZS-MRR(65TP); ZS-MRS(65TP); ZS-MRU; ZS-NKK(65TP); ZS-PTG; ZS-XXX.

Index:-

Reg	c/n	Reg	c/n	Reg	c/n
ZS-ASN	c/n 33581	(ZS-DBL)	12090	ZS-EYO	32935
ZS-AVI	9630	ZS-DBP	12066	(ZS-FFM)	42976
ZS-AVJ	12016	ZS-DBV	13182	ZS-FKI	33581
ZS-AVK	10142	ZS-DBZ	12000	(ZS-FKK)	13164
ZS-AVL	12981	ZS-DCA	12090	ZS-FRJ	42978
ZS-AVM	10146	ZS-DCY	9050	ZS-FRM	42963
ZS-AVN	11829	ZS-DCZ	6223	ZS-GPL	9581
ZS-AVO	9334	ZS-DDC	12445	ZS-IPP	33083
ZS-AYB	19584	ZS-DDJ	6227	ZS-IPX	26439
ZS-BAA	1984	ZS-DDR	9877	ZS-IWL	9628
ZS-BCA	13182	ZS-DDV	9628	ZS-JMP	2119
ZS-BCJ	12486	ZS-DDZ	12158	ZS-KAT	13164
ZS-BCY	13014	ZS-DEF	10105	ZS-KCV	26713
ZS-BJZ	9131	ZS-DEO	12073	ZS-KEX	2008
ZS-BNB	4098	ZS-DER	9629	ZS-KHN	19536
ZS-BRW	13468	ZS-DES	12055	ZS-KIV	33257
ZS-BRX	19566	ZS-DFB	12414	ZS-LJI	34225
ZS-BTN	2199	ZS-DFN	12161	ZS-LVR	20475
ZS-BTO	2205	ZS-DFW(DC-2)	1322	ZS-LYW	25802
ZS-BVF	12066	ZS-DFX(DC-2)	1332	ZS-MAP	32644
ZS-BWX	4254	ZS-DHO	11979	ZS-MFY	12073
ZS-BWY	6341	ZS-DHW	26087	ZS-MRR	9766
ZS-BWZ	9145	ZS-DHX	32656	ZS-MRS	13540
ZS-BXF	12107	ZS-DHY	33257	ZS-MRU	4363
ZS-BXG	12049	ZS-DIV	32961	ZS-NJE	9836
ZS-BXI	12166	ZS-DIW	11991	ZS-NKK	13143
ZS-BXJ(1)	12000	ZS-DIY	27000	ZS-NPI	33581
ZS-BXJ(2)	12413	ZS-DIZ	26743	ZS-NTD	26438
(ZS-BXZ)	12595	ZS-DJB	9492	ZS-NTE	11926
ZS-BYH	12579	ZS-DJC	32937	ZS-NZA	10110
(ZS-BYI)	12414	ZS-DJK	11989	ZS-NZB	27188
ZS-BYX	12587	ZS-DJX	12596	ZS-NZC	11726
(ZS-BZO)	4764	ZS-DJZ	26244	ZS-NZD	19104
ZS-CAI	13541	ZS-DKP	26439	ZS-NZE	13368
ZS-CCG	9948	ZS-DKR	33408	(ZS-NZF)	12205
ZS-CRV	13331	ZS-DLX	20228	ZS-OBU	27047
ZS-DAG	9050	ZS-DPO	1994	ZS-OIR	32948
ZS-DAH	6224	ZS-DRJ	12026	ZS-OJD	4890
ZS-DAI	6223	ZS-DXW	42969	ZS-OJE	32844
ZS-DAJ	6227	ZS-EDX	9452	ZS-OJI	26439
ZS-DAK(1)	1498	ZS-EJK	19484	ZS-OJJ	32961
ZS-DAK(2)	12073	ZS-EKK	9628	ZS-OJK	25610
(ZS-DBB)	12445	ZS-EYN	33211	ZS-OJL(1)	25546
				ZS-OJL(2)	33313
				ZS-OJM	25546
				ZS-OSO	12590
				ZS-PAA	1984
				ZS-PTG	13331
				ZS-UAS	6154
				ZS-XXX(1)	9766
				ZS-XXX(2)	12073

SOUTH KOREA - See Korea, South

SOUTH YEMEN - See Yemen

SPAIN - EC

Spain has a unique interest in the Douglas twin, since the DC-1 prototype found its way there during the Civil War, and made its last resting place there, working out its life with various LAPE and later Iberia DC-2s. Post war many DC-3s followed (as well as every other DC- model bar the DC-5). A number of minor mysteries exist, as on many registers where any number of aircraft are involved - see notes at end. The DC-2s are now less of a mystery than they were, thanks to Gerald Howson's *Aircraft of the Spanish Civil War*. The DC-1 and six DC-2s served with LAPE and four DC-2s as well as the DC-1 survived the war to pass to the Nationalist AF (one was captured early in the war). These passed to Iberia who used the last until April 1946.

Aeroflete, Alicante, used two DC-3s on cargo charters from 1968 until 1974, when both had become derelict.

EC-AQB; EC-ASP.

Aeromarket Express SA, Palma, was formed in 1988 to operate general cargo charter work from Majorca. Three DC-3s were bought initially, but accidents took their toll and by 1993 when the airline was known as **ARM** three remained in service, and operations ceased in that year.

EC-EIS; EC-EJB; EC-EQH; EC-FAH; EC-FDH; EC-FIN; EC-FNS.

Aero Transportes de España, Alicante, operated DC-3s EC-BUG and EC-CPO.

AVIACO - Aviación y Comercio SA, Madrid, used a small number of DC-3s to supplement other types on scheduled services between April and December 1962. They were leased from Sabena.

EC-ASK to EC-ASM incl.

IBERIA - Líneas Aéreas de España, Madrid, was formed on 07Jul40 to take over LAPE and with it the sole DC-1 and four DC-2s. These were registered EC-AAE and EC-AAA to EC-AAD respectively. The first DC-3s were wartime internees, both RAF and USAAF, but many others of the type were added post-war from a variety of sources. In 1966 eleven were transferred to the Spanish Air Force, and the remaining few withdrawn for sale. Three series of registrations appear to have been used.

EC-ABC; EC-ABK to EC-ABQ incl; EC-ACG to EC-ACI incl; EC-ACX; EC-ADR; EC-AEJ; EC-AET; EC-AEU; EC-AGO; EC-AGS; EC-AHA; EC-ALC; EC-ASE to EC-ASH incl; EC-CAU; EC-CAV; EC-CAX to EC-CAZ incl; EC-DAK; EC-DAL; EC-DAR; EC-DAS; EC-DAU; EC-DAV; EC-DAY.

Chapter 4: Commercial Operators of the DC-3, C-47, R4D, Dakota and Li-2

LAPE - Líneas Aéreas Postales Españolas, Madrid, bought five DC-2s in 1935/36. Between 1936 and 1939 when the civil war ended these and the sole DC-1 (EC-AGN fleet no 39) were used by LAPE Zona Rojas. The four pre-war DC-2s were EC-AAY; EC-BFF; EC-EBB and EC-XAX with LAPE fleet nos 22, 25, 24, and 21 respectively. EC-BFF was captured by the Nationalists (right wing) in July 1936. Nos 22 and 26 (the latter's registration unknown but EC-BBE has been reported) were destroyed. EC-AGA fleet no 27 was bought in October 1936, becoming EC-AAA with Iberia. The Douglas twins were used by the Republicans (left wing) for bombing as well as general transport duties, including the carriage of gold to France to pay for weapons. On one occasion EC-EBB and the by then Nationalist EC-BFF, both armed with cabin window mounted machine guns, had a dogfight during a raid on Badajoz!

SPANTAX SA, Madrid, bought DC-3s to operate charter flights from 1960 onwards. The last was sold in 1977.

EC-ACX; EC-ANV; EC-ARZ; EC-AQB; EC-AQE; EC-AQF; EC-ASP; EC-ATT; EC-AXS; EC-BEC; EC-BED; EC-BEG.

TASSA - Trabajos Aéreos del Sahara SA, Madrid, operated charter flights using DC-3s alongside larger aircraft from 1960 until 1965, when operations ceased.

EC-AQG; EC-AQH; EC-ASQ; EC-ATM; EC-AUG; EC-AUH.

Index:-
Spain has had several related registration systems, so for clarification we list these separately:

Pre-1946, 2nd and 3rd Register sequences:

EC-AAA (DC-2) c/n 1320		EC-CAY	7346
EC-AAB (DC-2)	1417	EC-CAZ	4832
EC-AAC (DC-2)	1521	EC-DAK	4885
EC-AAD (DC-2)	1330	EC-DAL	4890
EC-AAE (DC-1)	1137	EC-DAR	19553
EC-AAY (DC-2)	1334	EC-DAS	19334
EC-AGA (DC-2)	1320	EC-DAU	12758
EC-AGN (DC-1)	1137	EC-DAV	19332
EC-BBE (DC-2)	1527 ?	EC-DAY	19410
EC-BFF (DC-2)	1521	EC-EAB	20405 ?
EC-CAU	4256	EC-EAC	12154 ?
EC-CAV	4263	EC-EBB (DC-2)	1417
EC-CAX	4293	EC-XAX (DC-2)	1330

Post-1945, 4th Register sequence:

EC-AAA (DC-2)	1320	EC-ARZ	13474
EC-AAB (DC-2)	1417	EC-ASE	19268
EC-AAC (DC-2)	1521	EC-ASF	26342
EC-AAD (DC-2)	1330	EC-ASG	27200
EC-ABC	19334	EC-ASH	33032
"EC-ABC"	34361	EC-ASK	12767
(EC-ABK)	4256	EC-ASL	42968
EC-ABL	4263	EC-ASM	25292
EC-ABM	4293	EC-ASP	26980
EC-ABN	7346	EC-ASQ	12421
EC-ABO	4832	EC-ATM	33581
EC-ABP	4885	EC-ATT	1908
EC-ABQ	4890	EC-AUG	2176
EC-ACG	19553	EC-AUH	2006
EC-ACH	19332	EC-AXS	1984
EC-ACI	12758	EC-BEC	43089
(EC-ACK)	20405 ?	EC-BED	43090
(EC-ACL)	12154 ?	EC-BEG	43091
EC-ACX	19410	EC-BUG	32734
EC-ADR	10100	EC-CAR	26743
EC-AEJ	9344	EC-CPO	34361
EC-AET	13375	EC-EIS	32814
EC-AEU	25450	EC-EJB	4479
EC-AGO	13057	EC-EQH	33058
EC-AGS	13479	EC-FAH	9336
EC-AHA	34361	EC-FDH	11982
EC-ALC	19785	EC-FIN	13087
EC-ANV	26216	EC-FNS	9700
EC-AQB	12844	EC-177	4479
EC-AQE	25641	EC-187	9700
EC-AQF	26465	EC-220	33058
EC-AQG	26763	EC-530	9336
EC-AQH	20072	EC-659	13087
EC-ARV	33610	EC-699	11982

Notes:-
EC-AAA to AAD carried their registrations into the 4th series in 1945-46, although already damaged or wfu, they were not officially cancelled until 25Sep47.
EC-ACK, previously EC-EAB has c/n 20405 quoted in official records. This is known to have been NC86548 and later LV-AGF. There is a possibility that EC-EAB, which would have been registered by 1947, could have been sold to the Argentine in 1949 (with 'new' marks EC-ACK remaining unused). This is very much conjecture.
EC-EAC/EC-ACL presents more of a problem as the quoted c/n, 12154, was FZ599 which crashed in Burma on 8 May 1944, and never went near Spain. It too would have been registered about 1947.
EC-BBE has been suggested as the possible identity of LAPE's No.26.
EC numerical registrations are delivery marks.

SRI LANKA - VP-C, CY and 4R (formerly Ceylon)

Air Ceylon Ltd, Colombo, was founded in 1947 by the government. Five DC-3s were used while the country changed its name in 1972 and two remained in service until 1978, when financial difficulties caused the cessation of operations. These DC-3s (4R-ACG and ACI) went to the Sri Lankan Air Force, where they were operated by Helitours, its commercial arm, in the early eighties.

Index:-

VP-CAR/CY-ACF/		VP-CAT	11927
4R-ACF	c/n 25475	VP-CBA/CY-ACE	
VP-CAS/CY-ACG/			13452
4R-ACG	25464	4R-ACI	33556

SUDAN - SN and ST

Air Taxi was reported to be using DC-3 ST-AHL in 1979.

SASCO Air Lines, Khartoum operated ST-AHL in 1993.

Sudan Airways, Khartoum, bought DC-3s in 1954 to expand services started with Doves. They were retired for sale in August 1971 after replacement by F.27s, but ST-AAJ remained on aerial survey work until 1975.

SN/ST-AAG; SN/ST-AAH; SN/ST-AAI; SN/ST-AAJ; SN/ST-AAK; ST-AAL; ST-AAM.

Index:-

SN/ST-AAG	c/n 26732	ST-AAM	26969
SN/ST-AAH	27099	ST-AHH(1)	32628
SN/ST-AAI	26582	(ST-AAH)(2)	32845
SN/ST-AAJ	33083	ST-AHK	4890
SN/ST-AAK	33346	ST-AHL	26095
ST-AAL	26990		

Note:- It has been reported that in 1982 there were about twenty DC-3s abandoned at Khartoum airport, apparently reasonably intact. Most are believed to have been registered elsewhere. Security was too tight to allow close inspection.

SURINAM - PZ

Gum Air NV, Paramaribo, used DC-3 PZ-TLC inn the late seventies.

KLM Aerocarto - see Netherlands - used PZ-TLA and PZ-TLC.

Surinam Airways - Surinaamse Luchtvaart Maatschappij NV, Paramaribo, was formed in 1955 with help from KLM and used several DC-3s from 1960 onwards. All were replaced by Twin Otters.

PZ-TAM; PZ-TAW to PZ-TAY incl.

Index:-

PZ-TAM	c/n 19247	PZ-TAY	13173
PZ-TAW	33189	PZ-TLA	13458
PZ-TAX	13114	PZ-TLC	6053

SWAZILAND - VQ-Z and 3D

Swazi Air Ltd, Manzini, Swaziland, operated as a subsidiary of National Airways Corp, South Africa, using DC-3s from 1965. These were replaced by Viscounts by 1977.

VQ-ZJB/3D-AAH; ZS-EKK/3D-AAV; 3D-ABI.

Index:-

VQ-ZJB	c/n 13164	3D-ABI	42978
3D-AAH	13164	3D-ATH	9410
3D-AAV	9628		

SWEDEN - SE

AB Aerotransport/(ABA)/Swedish Air Lines, Stockholm, bought DC-3s in 1937 from Fokker, and also acquired C G von Rosen's DC-2 SE-AKE in 1940. Operations continued through the war, though not without casualties. Further aircraft were bought in 1946/47 from USAAF surplus stocks in Europe. From 1948 they operated in the colours of Scandinavian Airlines System, but ownership remained with ABA. The DC-3s were steadily replaced by SAAB Scandias and Convair 440s and the last was sold to Linjeflyg in 1957.

SE-APG; SE-BAA to SE-BAC incl; SE-BAF; SE-BAG; SE-BAL; SE-BAS to SE-BAU incl; SE-BAW; SE-BAY; SE-BAZ; SE-BBH; SE-BBI; SE-BBK to SE-BBR incl; SE-BSI; SE-BSM; SE-BSN.

Linjeflyg AB, Bromma, Stockholm, was formed as **Airtaco AB** to deliver newspapers within Sweden and to operate local passenger services. DC-3s were added to the fleet in 1953 and continued in use until they were replaced by Convairs in 1965.

SE-BBO; SE-BSM; SE-BSN; SE-BWF; SE-CAZ; SE-CBX; SE-CBZ; SE-CFM; SE-CFP to SE-CFW incl. OH-LCC was leased in 1959.

Loadair, Gothenburg, operated three DC-3s on cargo services from 1963 until September 1964, when operations were taken over by Torair.

LN-RTA (Lsd); SE-BSN; SE-CFT.

Scandinavian Airlines System - SAS was a consortium formed in August 1948 to coordinate the operations of ABA, DDL and DNL. Ownership of the aircraft was retained by the constituent companies and they continued to be registered in the parent countries. Externally this was the only way to distinguish ownership. See constituent operators in Denmark, Norway and Sweden for DC-3s used.

Skandinaviska Aero AB, Stockholm, started charter operations using three DC-3s in 1946, and bought another from Norrlandsflyg in 1947. Operations ceased in 1948 - see SILA.

SE-APW; SE-APZ; SE-ARX; SE-AYL.

SILA - Svensk Interkontinental Lufttrafik AB, Bromma, Stockholm, bought DC-3s from Skandinaviska Aero AB in June 1948 but probably never used them, selling them in 1948 either to the Swedish Air Force or to SAS.

SE-APW; SE-APZ; SE-ARX; SE-AYL.

Sverigeflyg AB operated DC-3 SE-EGR on charter work in Europe during 1965-66.

Svensk Flygjanst AB, op as **Swedair AB**, Stockholm-Bromma, used DC-3 SE-BSM on charter and calibration work from about 1972 and until its sale in 1988. SE-EDI was used temporarily in early 1965.

Torair AB, Gothenburg, was formed in September 1964 to take over Loadair and to operate cargo and passenger charters. The two DC-3s were sold to Faroe Airways in 1965/66.

SE-BSN; SE-CFT.

Transair Sweden AB, Malmo, acquired DC-3s in 1953 to operate inclusive tour charters and night mail services. Two were sold to the United Nations in 1961 for use in the Congo but the remainder returned to their owners after lease during 1963/64.

LN-LMR; LN-RTA; SE-BBO; SE-BSM; SE-BSN; SE-BWD; SE-BWE; SE-BWF.

Index:-

SE-AKE (DC-2) c/n 1354		SE-BBO	13637
SE-APG	11746	SE-BBP	25874
SE-APW	9103	SE-BBR	19592
SE-APZ	9001	SE-BSI	13312
SE-ARX	9010	SE-BSM	7353
SE-AYL	7376	SE-BSN	11638
SE-BAA	1947	SE-BWD	2205
SE-BAB	1972	SE-BWE	1947
SE-BAC	1975	SE-BWF	13652
SE-BAF	2133	SE-CAZ	12526
SE-BAG	2132	SE-CBX	6043
SE-BAL	11726	SE-CBZ	13332
SE-BAS	11700	SE-CFM	12324
SE-BAT	11705	SE-CFP	13883
SE-BAU	11711	SE-CFR	13647
SE-BAW	11722	SE-CFS	11697
(SE-BAX)	11726	SE-CFT	42962
SE-BAY	19559	SE-CFU	42963
SE-BAZ	20135	SE-CFW	42976
SE-BBH	19975	SE-EDI	33581
SE-BBI	20000	SE-EGR	42970
SE-BBK	20001	SE-GUL	33532
SE-BBL	20114	SE-IKL	33153
SE-BBM	20128	SE-IOK	12970
SE-BBN	12896		

SWITZERLAND - HB

Switzerland was an early user of the DC-2 and the DC-3, six of the former and five of the latter being pre-war. The only DC-3s remaining are two with a pleasure flight company and the DC-3 preserved in the Swiss Transport Museum at Lucerne.

ALPAR - Schweizerische Luftverkehr AG, Bern, bought five DC-3s for charter work in 1947 but financial problems resulted in the airline being taken over by Swissair and with one exception the aircraft were sold before they were used.

HB-ATA; HB-ATB; HB-ATI; HB-ATO; HB-ATU.

Balair AG, Basle, bought DC-3 HB-ITD in October 1967 for use in United Nations colours until its sale in 1974.

Classic Air, Zurich, has operated DC-3s HB-ISB and HB-ISC on pleasure flights since 1986.

Swissair - Schweizerische Luftverkehr AG, Zurich, bought its first DC-2 in December 1934 and continued to operate the type until the last two were sold in South Africa in 1952, so becoming the longest user of the type. The DC-3 was added to the fleet in 1937 and more were bought post-war and remained in service until replaced by Convairs. The last few were transferred to an air survey subsidiary until finally sold in 1969.

DC-2s:- HB-ISA; HB-ISI; HB-ITA; HB-ITE; HB-ITI; HB-ITO.
DC-3s:- HB-IRA to HB-IRI incl; HB-IRK to HB-IRO incl; HB-IRU; HB-IRX.

Index:-

(CH-447)(DC-2) c/n 1320		HB-IRI	1946
HB-ATA	26355	HB-IRK	20737
HB-ATB	9510	HB-IRL	26259
HB-ATD	25591	HB-IRM	32939
HB-ATI	26162	HB-IRN	33393
HB-ATO	11923	"HB-IRN"	4828
(HB-ATU)	25875	HB-IRO	2054
HB-IRA	1945	HB-IRU	2132
HB-IRB	42969	HB-IRX	26162
HB-IRC	42978	HB-ISA (DC-2)	1320
HB-IRD	26054	HB-ISB	4667
HB-IRE	2121	HB-ISC	9995
HB-IRF	26465	(HB-ISE)	25482
HB-IRG	25641	(HB-ISF)	11722
HB-IRH	13483	HB-ISI (DC-2)	1331

CHAPTER 4: COMMERCIAL OPERATORS OF THE DC-3, C-47, R4D, DAKOTA AND LI-2

HB-ITA (DC-2)	1329	HB-ITI (DC-2)	1321	
HB-ITD	33213	HB-ITO (DC-2)	1332	
HB-ITE (DC-2)	1322			

SYRIA - SR and YK

Syrian Airways Co, Damascus, used DC-3s to start operations in 1947 but these were taken over by the Air Force in 1948, the airline resuming operations in 1949. In 1960, when the United Arab Republic was formed, the airline merged with Misrair to form United Arab Airlines, and the aircraft were re-registered in Egypt until the union broke up.

SR-AAC; SR/YK-AAD; SR/YK-AAE; SR/YK-AAF; YK-AAG; YK-AAH; YK-AAK; YK-AAO.

Syrian Arab Airlines Co, Damascus, was reformed following the break up of the union with Egypt in October 1961 and operations resumed from Damascus. Only three DC-3s then remained and by 1975 these were retired, possibly again going to the Air Force.

YK-ACA to YK-ACC incl.

Index:-

SR-AAC	c/n		YK-AAK	33559
SR/YK-AAD	26349		YK-AAO	25709
SR/YK-AAE	26362		YK-ACA	
SR/YK-AAF			YK-ACB	33559
YK-AAG	26107		YK-ACC	25709
YK-AAH	10101 ?			

Notes:-
YK-AAF crashed 21Dec53 on a mountain at Dah-el-Kadeeb, nr Damascus.
YK-AAH is quoted with c/n 10101, but this is most unlikely as FL518 with this c/n was converted as LX-LAA by Scottish Avn, and is well documented until its cancellation in February 1975.

TAIWAN/FORMOSA - XT and B

Taiwan is the name currently used for Formosa, but it is also the sole remaining non-Communist part of the old China (though occupied by Japan from 1895 until 1945). It uses the nationality marks allocated to China, XT- being used until the new prefix B- was allocated c.1947 although this was not used immediately. The Nationalist Government was established in Formosa in 1949 and XT- was replaced by B- which it has since shared B- with mainland China. XT- was later reallotted to Upper Volta. There are a number of mysteries over Taiwan-based DC-3s, but little help has been forthcoming from the authorities, and as most of the aircraft are now defunct, it is unlikely that these will be resolved.

Air Asia Co Ltd, Taipei, was a subsidiary of Air America and operated aircraft, including DC-3s, supplied by Civil Air Transport. Operations included clandestine flights for the CIA to mainland China and other communist areas in S E Asia, but have now ceased. Known DC-3s are:-

B-817; B-829; B-879; B-933.

China Air Lines Ltd, Taipei, started domestic services in 1960 using DC-3s between 1965 and 1969.

B-309 (Lsd); B-1523; B-1531; B-1533; B-1537; B-1539; B-1553; B-1555 and XW-TAH (Lsd).

Civil Air Transport, Taipei, in 1947 took over **CNRRA Air Transport** (formed in October 1946 for famine relief work in China) but was dissolved by order of the Communist Government in August 1949. Operations were transferred to Hong Kong in 1949, when all aircraft were temporarily US-registered. A complex legal battle ensued and further details may be found under **CATI** in the US section. It seems that between 35 and 38 DC-3s may have been owned at some time during the period. The airline was renamed **Air Asia** and had CIA connections, but is no longer operating. DC-3s were originally registered between XT-801 and 829 (odd numbers only), but in the B- series only the following are known:-

B-801; B-809; B-811; B-815; B-817; B-823; B-827 and B-829. B-808, B-819 and B-828 have also been reported in this series, but may not have been owned by CAT. VR-HDP was acquired in Jan51.

Far East Air Transport Corp, Taipei, started operations in August 1957 and DC-3s supplemented Beech C-45s on domestic services from 1965 onwards. By 1978 only one DC-3 remained and that was withdrawn.

B-241; B-243; B-245; B-247; B-249; B-251; B-253; B-255; B-257; B-259; B-261.

Foshing Airlines, Taipei, originated in Fu Shing Aviation Corp, in 1950. Two DC-3s, B-1407 and B-1409, were used for a time.

Winner Airways Co, Taipei, bought DC-3s in 1966 to operate domestic services. These ceased about 1975.

B-301; B-304; B-305; B-307; B-308; B-309; B-311; B-312; B-313.

Index:-

B-112	c/n		B-809	19932
"B-126"	13612		B-811	18947
B-241	34195		B-815	19258
B-243	11832		B-817	19256
B-245	20794		B-818	
B-247	19904		B-819	
B-249	9592		B-823	13399
B-251	13587		B-827	13784
B-253	12041		B-828	
B-255	32695		B-829	34298
B-257	19950		B-879	34325
B-259	13612		B-933	13817
B-261	12875		B-1407	26696
B-301	12790		B-1409	32991
B-304	4808		B-1503	
B-305	3251		B-1505	
B-307	20213		B-1523	
B-308			B-1531	11729
B-309	12541		B-1533	2010
B-311	4811		B-1537	
B-312	3258		B-1539	
B-313	2185		B-1553	20434
B-801	20681		B-1555	34325
B-808				

Notes:-
B-112 was owned by Taiwan Aviation, a front for Air America, and crashed on 25Jul67 on Mt Pha Boh, nr Luang Prabang, Laos
B-301 is quoted in most sources as c/n 12790, but this has also been given for B-308.
B-808, B-818, B-819 and B-828 were reported with Air America Inc, but see US section.
B-1523 crashed on 21Aug67 but may have been repaired as XW-PAR.
B-1537 and B-1539 were both owned by China Airlines.
Registrations B-147, B-559 and B-994 are sometimes assumed but these operated without national prefix - see Air America, USA.

TANGANYIKA VP-T and TANZANIA 5H

Tanganyika was served by East African Airways and its aircraft are listed there while they were registered in Kenya. On the merger with Zanzibar to form Tanzania and following independence, the nationality mark 5H- was adopted and used for the surviving EAA aircraft. DC-3s used in the territory were:-

Index:-

VR/5H-TBI	c/n 32592		5H-AAJ	32628
VR-TBJ	32656		5H-AAK	25815
VR-TBT	20453		5H-AAL	32955

TCHAD - TT

Air Tchad, N'djamena, was founded in June 1966 and took over scheduled services previously flown by Air Afrique in August 1966. Two DC-3s were bought at this time and were still in use in 1982. TT-EAA's C of A was suspended in Nov84.

Index:-

TT-EAA	c/n 25548		TT-EAB	9157

THAILAND - HS

Thailand, known until 1939 as Siam, operated DC-3s in some numbers for a country of its size, due to the poor surface transport. Most of the operators were ephemeral and either merged with Siamese Airways or ceased to operate. The numerical system of registration used on some of the earlier aircraft presents somewhat of a mystery, but related only to foreign-owned operators.

Pacific Overseas Airlines (Siam) Ltd, Bangkok, was formed in early 1947 with government aid and help from Pacific Overseas Airlines of the USA. It was merged with Siamese Airways to form **Thai Airways** in November 1951.

HS-PC101; HS-PC-102/HS-POC; HS-PC-103; HS-POB (ex either HS-PC-101 or -103).

PMC Associated Co.Ltd, Bangkok, operated three ex Burmese AF C-47s on rain-making operations from 1980 until 1984.

N2270M; N2271C; N2271D.

Sahakol Air, Bangkok, formed as a subsidiary of Bangkok United Mechanical Co, leased three ex Continental AS C-47s from Air Alliance Inc between 1973 and 1975 for operation in Thailand and Laos during 1973 to 1975.

N11AF; N650K; N64422.

Senaki Peanich Airlines, Bangkok, are reported to have had a DC-3 HS-TFJ parked at Bangkok for a time. No hard evidence has been found and it is believed to have been confused with their C-47 XW-TFJ which was parked at Bangkok in 1978 and subsequently broken up there.

Siamese Airways Co Ltd, Bangkok, was formed in March 1947 to resume services after the war using DC-3s. The airline was merged with Pacific Overseas to form **Thai Airways** on 1 November 1951.

HS-SAA to HS-SAF incl.

Sky of Siam Co Ltd, Udon Thani, operated two DC-3s on freight services between 1980 and 1984, when they ceased operations.

HS-TDA; HS-TDD.

Thai Airways Co Ltd, Bangkok, resulted from the merger of Siamese Airways and Pacific Overseas on 01Nov51. DC-3s formed the backbone of operations until they were replaced on domestic services by HS.748s from 1964, the last two being retired in 1975 and the survivors broken up.

HS-TDA to HS-TDI incl.

Trans-Asiatic Airlines (Siam) Ltd, Bangkok, was formed as a subsidiary of Trans Asiatic of Manila in March 1947. It operated DC-3s in Burma between July 1948 and July 1950 byt activities were reduced and the company wound up in November 1952.

HS-TA180; HS-TA190; HS-TA191.

Index:-

	c/n		
HS-AUJ		HS-TDC	12585
HS-AUM		HS-TDD	11977
HS-DOA	26511	HS-TDE	13794
HS-OOO	3266	HS-TDF	9414
HS-POB	11977	HS-TDG	13362
HS-POC	13794	HS-TDH	9189
HS-SAA	13726	HS-TDI	12248
HS-SAB	12829	HS-TFJ	
HS-SAC	12585	HS-PC101	
HS-SAD		HS-PC102	13794
HS-SAE		HS-PC103	
HS-SAF	12150	HS-TA180	20583 ?
HS-TDA	13726	HS-TA190	
HS-TDB	12829	HS-TA191	

Notes:-
HS-SAE of Siamese Airways crashed on 9Apr51 at Cap d'Aguilar, Hong Kong.
HS-PC103 is said to have crashed on the west coast of Sumatra 25Oct48, in which case HS-POB would probably be ex HS-PC101.
HS-TA-180 of Trans Asiatic, crashed in early 1949 at Mingaladon, Burma. It may have been ex PI-C180.

TONGA - A3

Peau Vav'u Air, Tongatapu, managed by Pionair Adventures Ltd of New Zealand, acquired two of their DC-3s in June 2004 but they were not initially re-registered locally. ZK-AMY returned to Pionair in October 2005 but ZK-AWP remained in Tonga becoming A3-AWP in Mar06.

Index:-

A3-AWP   c/n 33135

TRINIDAD & TOBAGO - VP-T and 9Y

Trinidad was a British Crown colony until 1965 when independence was granted and the nationality mark 9Y- adopted.

Beach Airways, Port of Spain, Trinidad, owned DC-3 9Y-TDY briefly in 1973.

BWIA - British West Indian Airways, Port of Spain, Trinidad, acquired DC-3s in the first place from British Caribbean in 1949, but they were passed on to Bahamas Airways until 1952, when they finally came on to the Trinidad register. Three more followed, but all had been sold by 1967.

VP-TBE; VP/9Y-TBF; VP/9Y-TBJ; VP/9Y-TBW; 9Y-TCR.

Index:-

VP-TBE	c/n 9885	VP/9Y-TBW	13173
VP/9Y-TBF	13114	9Y-TCR	13114
VP/9Y-TBJ	33189	9Y-TDY	19759

TUNISIA - F and TS

Tunis Air - Sté. Tunisienne de l'Air, Tunis, was founded in 1948 with help from Air France who supplied four DC-3s. Those that survived by November 1959 went on to the new Tunisian register on independence.

F-BAXV/TS-AXV; F-BAXX/TS-AXX; F-BAXY; F-BAXZ/TS-AXZ; F-OAIG.

Index:-

TS-AXV	c/n 12380	TS-AXZ	33236
TS-AXX	12255		

TURKEY - TC

DHY - Devlet Hava Yollari - See THY.

THY - Türk Hava Yollari, Ankara, was formed as **Devlet Hava Yollari** and operated under this name from 1946 until 1956 when the present name was adopted. Until 1956 the airline was a government operation, but it became a corporation in that year with strong government connections. DC-3s were bought from USAAF and RAF surplus stocks in the Middle East and remained in service until they were replaced by F.27s and the last sold in 1971, some after prolonged storage. The following list does not distinguish DHY from THY ownership.

TC-ABA; TC-ACA; TC-ADA; TC-AFA; TC-AKA; TC-ALA; TC-ALP; TC-ANA; TC-AND; TC-APA; TC-ARA; TC-ARK; TC-ART; TC-ARZ; TC-ASA; TC-ATA; TC-BAC; TC-BAG; TC-BAL; TC-BAZ; TC-BEN; TC-BEY; TC-BUK; TC-ECE; TC-EFE; TC-EGE; TC-EKE; TC-ESI; TC-ETI; TC-TUG; TC-YOL; TC-YUK.

Index:-

TC-ABA	c/n 4971	TC-AND	12689
TC-ACA	7352	TC-APA	4292
TC-ADA	7354	TC-ARA	20455
TC-AFA	9276	TC-ARK	19509
TC-AKA	6095	TC-ART	19468
TC-ALA	4319	TC-ARZ	10196
TC-ALI	12830	TC-ASA	20454
TC-ALP	9261	TC-ATA	13183
TC-ANA	9340	TC-BAC	19548

CHAPTER 4: COMMERCIAL OPERATORS OF THE DC-3, C-47, R4D, DAKOTA AND LI-2

TC-BAG	19616	TC-EGE	9694
TC-BAL	19423	TC-EKE	12205
TC-BAZ	12769	TC-ESI	12825
TC-BEN	12577	TC-ETI	12319
TC-BEY	13571	TC-KOL	26258
TC-BUK	10107	TC-TUG	20115
TC-ECE	9310	TC-YOL	12060
TC-EFE	9307	TC-YUK	10107

Notes:-
TC-KOL c/n 26258 was used 1968-78 by a government agency "Devlet Hava Meydanlari" or Turkish State Airports, probably for checking radio aids. C/ns 10189 and 19433 were bought for spares by DHY but eventually sold as N60U and N59U respectively without being registered in Turkey.

TURKS & CAICOS - VQ-T

Turks & Caicos National Airlines Ltd, Grand Turk, acquired DC-3 VQ-TAF in April 1983 but had sold it by May 1986.

Index:-

VQ-TAF   c/n 12550

UGANDA - 5X

Until East African became insolvent, Ugandan airline operations were covered by EAA, though political problems had already caused difficulties. Three DC-3s were registered to EAA in Uganda and are given below (5X-AAQ/R/S). Only two other DC-3s were registered. See under Kenya for East African Airways details.

Uganda Aviation Services Ltd, Kampala, bought a single DC-3, 5X-UWJ, in 1972 and used it on charter services until it was sold to Caspair in 1977.

Index:-

5X-AAQ	c/n 32845	5X-TAL	9410
5X-AAR	33211	5X-UWJ	26095
5X-AAS	32656		

UNITED KINGDOM - G

The DC-1 made a brief sortie onto the British scene when bought by Viscount Forbes in May38, only to be sold a few months later for use in Spain. KLM DC-2s and DC-3s followed when they escaped from Holland in 1940 and continued to operate from British bases until 1945. However, most DC-3s came from surplus RAF stocks of Dakotas or BOAC's fleet. Many Dakotas were sold overseas after overhaul, but they were also the mainstay of BOAC's and BEA's operations for many years after the war, and many other smaller passenger and cargo operators used the type, sometimes only briefly when work was hard to come by in the late forties and fifties. The Berlin Airlift helped several to keep their Dakotas earning, and others were used on trooping contracts through Egypt, when they acquired temporary RAF markings again. Since the sixties there has been a steady decline in numbers earning their keep apart from an influx of ex-Spanish AF C-47s in the late seventies. Seven DC-3s were given Class B markings for test flights with turboprop engines or on overhaul for resale. These are listed at the end of the index.

At the time of writing Air Atlantique operates their last DC-3, and Aces High have one US-registered Dakota available for filming etc. In 1996 South Coast Airways started up to undertake scenic flights and visit air shows, and the Dakota Club had a US-registered example but both ceased operations in 2002.

Air Anglia, Norwich, was formed in Aug70 by the merger of Norfolk Airways, Anglian Air Charter and Rig-Air to operate scheduled and charter services with DC-3s. The last were retired from charter work in 1975, giving way to F.27s.

G-AGJV; G-AMPZ; G-ANTD; G-AOBN.

Air Atlantique / Atlantic Airways, Jersey and Coventry, was formed in Mar77 as Air Atlantique for freight charter work from Jersey, but subsequently moved to Coventry, becoming the only major UK DC-3 operator, with a contract for Marine Pollution control. Seven aircraft were equipped with spray bars under the tailplane for applying oil dispersant. Two other aircraft were retained for passenger charters, and night mail. Gradually the sprayers have been withdrawn, one aircraft, G-ANAF, was being used for radar systems testing and one reportedly reserved for the Midland Air Museum. By the end of 2005 only G-AMRA remained in the active fleet.

G-AMCA; G-AMHJ; G-AMPO; G-AMPY; G-AMPZ; G-AMRA; G-AMSV; G-AMYJ; G-ANAF; G-ANTC; G-APML; G-BPMP; G-DAKK.

Air Contractors Ltd, Blackbushe and Bovingdon. DC-3s G-AIWC to G-AIWE incl were used on charter work, including the evacuation of civilians from India and Pakistan at partition. The first entered service in Jan47 but all were retired at the end of the Berlin Airlift and then sold.

Air Freight Ltd - See Skyways Cargo Airlines.

Air Gregory Ltd, Newcastle, used DC-3 G-AKJH for charters between Apr65 and Oct68. It was also leased out to other operators.

Air Kruise Ltd, Lympne. The first DC-3 was bought in 1953 for charter work, but more were added and scheduled services to the continent started. The airline was absorbed by Silver City in 1958.

G-AMYV; G-AMYX; G-AMZB; G-ANLF; G-AOBN. G-AMSS was leased from Dan-Air in 1956/57.

Air Links Ltd, Gatwick, owned three DC-3s between 1959 and 1962, all being used on charter flights.

G-AMGD; G-AMKE; G-APUC

Air Luton charter company took over Air Atlantique's night mail contract in Jan85 and used three of their DC-3s, operating from 19Feb85 to 09Jan86. The contract was lost to Topflight in early 1986 and the DC-3s were sold to the latter. G-AMPY was leased and some services were operated by G-AMCA, G-AMRA, G-AMSV and F-GDPP.

G-AMHJ; G-AMPO; G-ANAF.

Air Transport Charter (C.I.) Ltd, Jersey and Blackbushe. Five Dakotas were bought between Apr47 and Sep50 and used on charter work. One operated 205 sorties on the Berlin Airlift. Flying ceased in Oct52 and the aircraft were sold.

G-AJBG; G-AJBH; G-AJVZ; G-AKIL; G-AKOZ.

Air Ulster, Belfast, was the trading name for Ulster Air Transport, formed in Dec67 with one DC-3 to take over Emerald Airways services. Further aircraft were bought, but operations ceased in Jan70.

G-AGJV; G-AKNB; G-AMJU; G-AMWV; G-AMWW.

Airwork Ltd, Blackbushe and Gatwick, was formed well before WW2, being involved in many aspects of aviation. DC-3s were bought between 1949 and 1954 some for use and others for overhaul and resale. Only one remained when the airline merged with Hunting Clan to form British United in Jul60.

G-AGIS; G-AGKC; G-AGYZ; G-AKJN; G-AMBW; G-AMRA; G-AMZD; G-AMZW; G-AMZX.

Autair Ltd, Luton, bought its first DC-3 in Apr60, and added further aircraft until 1966. Vikings began to replace them in 1962 and the last DC-3 was sold in 1967.

G-AGHJ; G-AGYX; G-AJIC; G-AKNB; G-ALTT; G-AMGD; G-AMNV; G-APPO; G-APUC.

BKS Air Transport Ltd, Southend and Newcastle. DC-3s were bought in Apr52 for charter work, and the first were used on scheduled services in May55 from Leeds to Belfast. Ambassadors steadily replaced the DC-3s followed by HS.748s from May58 and all DC-3s had departed by 1967.

G-AIWD; G-AIWE; G-AMSF; G-AMSH; G-AMVB; G-AMVC; G-ANAF; G-APPO.

Blue-Line Airways Ltd, Tollerton, used DC-3 G-AGNG on cargo charter work from Jan49 until operations ceased in August of that year.

British European Airways Corpn - BEAC, Northolt and Heathrow, London. BEAC was officially formed on 01Aug46 with aircraft leased from BOAC. On 01Feb47 various other internal airlines were taken over, of which only Railway Air Services was a DC-3 operator. Thereafter about 70 DC-3s were owned or leased for various periods, continuing in service until May63 when the last service out of Heathrow, flown by Pionair G-AGZB, ended ignominiously in a field near Birmingham.

G-AGHH; G-AGHJ; G-AGHL; G-AGHM; G-AGHP; G-AGHS; G-AGHU; G-AGIO; G-AGIP; G-AGIS; G-AGIT; G-AGIU; G-AGIW; G-AGIX; G-AGIZ; G-AGJV; G-AGJW; G-AGJZ; G-AGNF; G-AGNG; G-AGNK; G-AGYX; G-AGYZ; G-AGZB to G-AGZE incl; G-AHCS to G-AHDC incl; G-AIWD; G-AJDE; G-AJHY to G-AJIC incl; G-AJXL; G-AKII to G-AKIK incl; G-AKJH; G-AKNB; G-ALCB; G-ALCC; G-ALLI; G-ALPN; G-ALTT; G-ALXK to G-ALXN incl; G-ALYF; G-AMDB; G-AMDZ; G-AMGD; G-AMFV; G-AMJX; G-AMJY; G-AMKE; G-AMNV; G-AMNW; G-AMYB.

British Island Airways, Gatwick, was formed from British United Island Airways (BUIA) on 20Jul70. By this time only four DC-3s remained in service, one used for radar calibration duties. The remainder were cargo aircraft, and the last was withdrawn on 30May74.

G-AMHJ; G-AMRA; G-AMSV; G-AOBN.

British Midland Airways Ltd (BMA), East Midlands Airport. BMA was formed when **Derby Airways Ltd** changed its name on 01Oct64. Seven DC-3s were then in use on cargo charters and inclusive tours. The last was sold in Jul69.

G-AGJV; G-AKJH; G-AMSX; G-ANTD; G-AOFZ; G-AOGZ; G-APBC.

British Nederland Air Services Ltd, Tollerton and Bovingdon. Two DC-3s (G-AJZD and G-AJZX) were bought early in 1948 for charter work. One was sold in Nov50 and operations ceased a month later.

BOAC - British Overseas Airways Corpn, Heathrow, London. One DC-2, G-AGBH, registered to KLM, was used by BOAC in 1940. DC-3s were acquired soon after BOAC was formed in Apr40, when KLM aircraft were taken over on lease. Subsequently, considerable numbers were supplied from RAF orders as they were delivered to Britain. These were used on the run to Africa and beyond throughout the remaining years of the war. In all 82 Dakotas and DC-3s were operated, at first from Whitchurch, Bristol. Later some flew to Scandinavia from Leuchars in Scotland. Most of the earlier aircraft had dual markings, flying at times in RAF marks with four or five letter codes and crews in RAF uniforms. All aircraft were camouflaged at this time. With the end of the war the paint was stripped and aircraft used to open up routes in Europe and elsewhere. Shortly afterwards BEA was formed and after a short period when DC-3s were leased in BOAC colours, many of BOAC's DC-3s were handed over. The remainder were gradually replaced on BOAC services by faster, longer range aircraft and the last DC-3 departed in Mar52. Many sales were to BOAC subsidiaries in Aden, Hong Kong, Malaya etc.

DC-2:- G-AGBH. *DC-3s:-* G-AGBB to G-AGBE incl; G-AGBI; G-AGEN; G-AGFX to G-AGGB incl; G-AGGI; G-AGHE; G-AGHF; G-AGHH; G-AGHJ to G-AGHU incl; G-AGIO to G-AGIU incl; G-AGIW to G-AGIZ incl; G-AGJR to G-AGKN incl; G-AGMZ to G-AGNG incl; G-AGNK; G-AGYX; G-AGYZ to G-AGZE incl; G-AHCS to G-AHDC incl; G-AIAZ; G-AIBA; G-AIWC; G-AMMJ; G-AOJI. The last two were bought for subsidiaries, so were not used by BOAC.

British United Airways Ltd, Gatwick. BUA was formed on 01Jul60 by the merger of Airwork and Hunting-Clan. Various DC-3s came into the combined fleet but were operated by subsidiaries Morton Air Services, BU(CI) etc, although some were painted in BUA colours. The aircraft listed here all had some connection with BUA after it was formed, though not all wore the full colours.

G-AKNB; G-ALPN; G-AMHJ; G-AMJU; G-AMNL; G-AMPZ; G-AMRA; G-AMSJ; G-AMSV; G-AMWV; G-AMYJ; G-AMYV; G-AMYX; G-AMZB; G-AMZF; G-AMZG; G-ANAE; G-ANEG; G-ANTB; G-ANTC; G-AOBN; G-AOUD.

British United Island Airways Ltd (BUIA), Gatwick. BUIA was formed from BU(CI)A, BUA(Manx) and Morton on 01Nov68. Eight DC-3s were in service at the time of formation. The name was changed to **British Island Airways** on 20Jul70 when BUA was about to merge with Caledonian. By this time only four DC-3s remained.

G-AKNB; G-ALPN; G-AMHJ; G-AMRA; G-AMSV; G-AMYJ; G-AOBN; G-AOUD.

British Westpoint Airlines Ltd, Exeter. This airline was created when **Westpoint** changed its name in Oct63. At this time three DC-3s were in use and more were leased during 1964 but financial problems forced a cessation of operations in May66.

G-AJHY; G-ALYF; G-AMDB; G-AMPO.

Cambrian Airways Ltd, Cardiff and Liverpool. This was founded as **Cambrian Air Services** in 1935 and by 1955 two DC-3s were in use. On 22May55 the name was changed to Cambrian Airways and on 07May56 a ten year agreement with BEA resulted in the eventual retirement of smaller types and the acquisition over the next five years of a further eight DC-3s. The last of these was sold in Jul69, by which time Viscounts had taken over all routes.

G-AGHM; G-AGHS; G-AGIP; G-AHCZ; G-ALCC; G-ALXL; G-AMFV; G-AMJX; G-AMSW; G-AMSX.

Channel Airways Ltd, Southend. This company was formed as **East Anglian Flying Services Ltd** in Jan46 and the first DC-3s were bought in 1960. By that time Channel Airways had been adopted as the operating name, but it was not the trading name until 25Oct62, when nine DC-3s had been acquired and one lost in an accident. They remained in scheduled service for a number of years, but all had been withdrawn by Mar70 and broken up.

G-AGNK; G-AGZB; G-AGZD; G-AHCU; G-AHCV; G-AJIB; G-ALXN; G-AMDZ; G-AMNW.

Ciro's Aviation Ltd, Gatwick. Two DC-3s were bought early in 1947 and used on charter flights to East Africa. Later they took part in the Berlin Airlift, but were back on passenger services in 1949, continuing until early 1951, when they were sold and operations ceased.

G-AIJD; G-AKJN; G-AKVX.

Classic Air leased DC-3 F-GEOM in 1993 for pleasure flights in the West country, but ceased operations almost immediately and proposed UK marks G-OFOM were ntu.

Continental Air Transport Ltd, Southend, leased DC-3 G-AMGD from Autair during 1960, but sub-leased it to Arkia until operations ceased in Oct60.

Crewsair Ltd, Southend, took delivery of the first of two DC-3s in Mar50, using the type on cargo charters and later passenger work. By 1952 Vikings had replaced the DC-3s, which were sold.

G-AIWE; G-ALVZ. In addition G-AMSF was used briefly in 1959.

Dan-Air Services Ltd, Southend, Blackbushe and Gatwick. Dan-Air was formed in Mar53 and the first of four DC-3s was bought in June, followed by three more by 1963. These remained on charter work until the last was withdrawn in Sep70.

G-ALXK; G-AMPP; G-AMSS; G-AMSU.

Derby Aviation Ltd, Wolverhampton, bought their first DC-3 in 1955 followed by Montgomery's old mount (KN628) as G-AOGZ in the following year. By 1958 the name was changed to **Derby Airways Ltd** and a third DC-3 added. In 1961 eight DC-3s were in use, having replaced Miles Marathons. The airline name was changed to **British Midland** in Oct64.

G-AGJV; G-AKJH; G-AMSW; G-AMSX; G-ANTD; G-AOFZ; G-AOGZ; G-APBC.

Don Everall (Aviation) Ltd, Wolverhampton, used two DC-3s on inclusive tours and scheduled flights from Apr57 until the airline merged with Air Safaris in Nov60, and the last DC-3 was sold.

G-AMSF; G-ANEG.

Eagle Aviation Ltd, Luton and Blackbushe, bought its first DC-3 in Aug49 and changed its name to **Eagle Airways Ltd** on 01Jul53, by which time eight had been bought. A further four were added over the next twelve months but some were quickly sold after conversion and never operated by Eagle. Charter and scheduled services were operated until May54 but by then all but one had been sold. One or two more were bought later, solely for overhaul and re-sale.

G-AGNG; G-AGYZ; G-AHCT; G-AJPF; G-AMPO; G-AMPS; G-AMPT; G-AMSO; G-AMST; G-AMVA; G-AMYB; G-AMZZ; G-AOJI; G-AOYE.

CHAPTER 4: COMMERCIAL OPERATORS OF THE DC-3, C-47, R4D, DAKOTA AND LI-2

Eastern Airways Ltd, Humberside, was formed in Jul78 as a subsidiary of Lease Air Ltd, to operate three DC-3s on scheduled and charter flights until the aircraft were sold late in 1981.

G-AMPO; G-AMRA; G-AMYJ.

Emerald Airways, Eglinton, NI, was formed in Northern Ireland in January 1965, but apart from leasing one British registered DC-3, the remainder came from Hibernian. They were used on scheduled services until December 1967.

EI-APB; EI-APJ; EI-ARP; EI-ARR; G-AOGZ.

Executive Air Transport Ltd, Coventry, bought a single DC-3, G-ANEG, in Apr61, for charter work and internal scheduled services. It was sold in Aug62.

Fairflight Charters Ltd, Biggin Hill, Kent, used DC-3 G-AMFV from June to Sep70, on charter work.

Gibraltar Airways Ltd, originally founded in Gibraltar in 1931, began operating DC-3s in 1962 on its service to Tangier. Trading as **Gibair**, it owned G-AMFV, and at various times leased G-AGHS, G-ALTT and G-ALXL, until superceded by Viscounts in 1970.

Gregory Air Services - See Air Gregory.

Gulf Aviation Co Ltd - See under Bahrain.

Hornton Airways, Gatwick, flew DC-3 G-AKLL on charter flights from Jan48, including 108 sorties on the Berlin Airlift. It closed down in May50.

Humber Airways Ltd, Hull and Grimsby, bought four DC-3s from Macedonian Airways in Dec74 for oil rig work. They were never used and the airline closed down in the following January.

G-AMHJ; G-AMPO; G-AMRA; G-AMSV.

Hunting Air Transport Ltd, Bovingdon and Heathrow, was formed in Aug51, at which time Hunting Air Travel owned one DC-3, bought in June of that year. In Oct53 Clan Lines acquired control and the name **Hunting Clan Air Transport Ltd** was adopted. Eight DC-3s were used on scheduled and charter operations, but only two remained when the airline merged with Airwork to form BUA.

G-AMHJ; G-AMNL; G-AMSH; G-AMSJ; G-AMSK; G-AMSL; G-AMVB; G-AMYW; G-AOFZ.

Hunting Clan - see Hunting Air Transport.

Intra Airways, Jersey, was formed on 01Jan69 to operate a DC-3 on charter work, based on Jersey. By 1977 seven DC-3s had been used, and they also leased F-BCYT, but Viscounts began to replace them and by Jan79 all DC-3s had been sold when the airline merged with Express Air Freight to form part of Air Bridge Carriers as Jersey European Airways.

G-AKNB; G-AMHJ; G-AMPO; G-AMPY; G-AMPZ; G-AMRA; G-AMYJ.

Irelfly Ltd, Shoreham and Gatwick, used three DC-3s on charter flights from February 1966 until the airline closed in Nov67.

G-ALYF; G-AMPY; G-AMSH.

Jersey Airlines, Jersey, bought DC-3s for scheduled services in Apr59 but in the following year it was reorganised and Alares Development took over ownership of many of the aircraft. BUA took over the airline on 20May62, but the old name remained until 01Aug63 when it was changed to British United (Channel Islands) Airways.

G-AGHJ; G-AJHZ; G-AMSF; G-AMYJ; G-AMZF; G-AMZG; G-ANEG; G-ANTB; G-ANTC; G-AOUD.

Jersey European Airways, Jersey, was founded on 01Nov79 by the merger of Intra and Express, using DC-3s G-AMHJ and G-AMPY, but these were sold early in 1980.

Kearsley Airways Ltd, Stansted. Three DC-3s, the first bought in Oct47, were used for charter work. 246 sorties were flown on the Berlin Airlift, and charter work continued into 1949. Lack of work and a good offer to buy the fleet led to closure in Mar50.

G-AKAR; G-AKDT; G-AKOZ.

Kestrel Airways Ltd, Lydd and East Midlands, used a single DC-3, G-AMFV, for charter work from Oct70. OO-CBU was bought for spares, but the DC-3 was replaced by a Viscount.

Lancashire Aircraft Corp. Ltd, Blackpool. Four DC-3s were bought from Nov52 to operate scheduled services and charters. In Sep55 they were used to start the Skyways Coach-Air service to France. Subsequently the operation was taken over by British Aviation Services and LAC ownership of the DC-3s ceased in Dec56.

G-AHCT; G-AMSV; G-AMWV; G-AMWW; G-AMWX; G-ANAE.

Macedonian Aviation Ltd, Luton and Southend, started DC-3 operations in Nov72. The last of four was bought in Apr74 but financial problems overtook its expansion plans and all were sold to Humber Airways in December.

G-AMHJ; G-AMPO; G-AMRA; G-AMSV.

Manx Airlines Ltd, Ronaldsway, IOM, was formed by the change of name from Manx Air Charter when two DC-3s were bought in Feb53 to operate scheduled services. The airline was taken over by British Aviation Services in May56, but the old name remained until one aircraft was lost in an accident. The remaining DC-3 was transferred to Silver City.

G-AMZB; G-AMZC.

Mercury Airlines Ltd, Manchester, added DC-3 G-AMSN to their fleet in Apr64 for charter work, including night newspaper deliveries as well as some scheduled services. Operations stopped on 31Oct64.

Meredith Air Transport Ltd, Southend, used DC-3 G-AMSU on trooping contracts for Tropic Airways from Oct52 to Jun53 when it was sold to Dan-Air to start their operations.

Morton Air Services Ltd, Croydon and Gatwick, was already part of BUA when the first DC-3s were transferred from Jersey Airlines for cargo charter work. In 1965 a further three were taken over, making six in all, including BUA's radio calibration aircraft G-AOBN. G-APBC was leased in Sep68. On 01Nov68 the airline became part of BUIA.

G-AMHJ; G-AMRA; G-AMSV; G-AMYJ; G-AOBN; G-AOUD.

North-South Airlines Ltd, Leeds, added two DC-3s to its fleet in the summer of 1961, one on lease while the other was overhauled (G-ALXK and G-ALYF). Scheduled services were flown until Jan62 and the airline was wound-up two months later.

North-West Airlines (IOM) Ltd, Ronaldsway, IOM, bought two DC-3s in Jun49 and used them on scheduled services as well as freight charters. They were sold in Mar51 when "government policy" made long-term planning impossible.

G-AGHF; G-AGHO.

Payloads (Charter) Co Ltd, Croydon, used DC-3 G-AJGX between April and Oct47.

Railway Air Services Ltd, Renfrew, bought three DC-3s in Mar46 to operate the London-Glasgow route. One landed on the roof of a house on approach to Northolt, but the other two were taken over by BEA on 01Feb47.

G-AGYZ to G-AGZB incl.

Rig-Air Ltd, Norwich, bought DC-3 G-AMPZ in Nov69 for oil support work, having used chartered aircraft until then. The airline became part of **Air Anglia** in Aug70, but the old colours were retained for some time thereafter.

Scottish Airlines Ltd, Prestwick, was formed by Scottish Aviation in Jan46 and some 13 DC-3s were converted for use on scheduled and charter services or by the subsidiary airlines Luxembourg Airlines and Hellenic Airlines. The last was sold in Mar61 to Dan-Air, who took over the operations. Scottish Aviation were, of course, major converters of Dakotas for air forces and airlines post-war.

G-AGWS; G-AGZF; G-AGZG; G-AIOD to G-AIOF; G-AJBC; G-AJLZ; G-AJVY; G-AKNM; G-AMJU; G-AMPP; G-AMSI.

Silver City Airways Ltd, Langley, Blackbushe and Ferryfield/Lydd. Over twenty DC-3s formed part of Silver City's fleet between Oct46 and Mar62.

The first was delivered in Nov46 and was one of a batch of five used on charter work until Jun50 when all were sold. The next DC-3s were bought in 1953 and more were added until 1962 when the airline became part of BUA on 23Jan62, and one was transferred from Transair. They finally went to BU(CI)A on 01Jan63. Apart from DC-3s, DC-2 ZS-DFX was leased for use in Libya, and four Irish DC-3s were used similarly.

G-AIRG; G-AIRH; G-AIWC; G-AJAU; G-AJAV; G-AJZD; G-AKNB; G-ALPN; G-AMJU; G-AMPZ; G-AMWV; G-AMYV; G-AMYW; G-AMYX; G-AMZB; G-ANAE; G-ANLF; G-AOBN; EI-ACG; EI-ACI; EI-ACK; EI-ACT; and *DC-2* ZS-DFX.

Site Aviation Ltd, Aberdeen, bought British Island's last three DC-3s in Jan74, but only one entered service before BIA repossessed them for non-payment.

G-AMHJ; G-AMRA; G-AMSV.

Sivewright Airways Ltd, Manchester/Barton & Ringway, bought three DC-3s between July 1947 and July 1949 for use on the Isle of Man to Jersey scheduled service as well as worldwide charter work. One was used briefly on the Berlin Airlift. They were sold in March 1951 when BEA took over the Isle of Man/Jersey route.

G-AGNK; G-AKAY; G-AKSM.

Skyways Ltd, Langley, Dunsfold and Stansted. DC-3s were used over two different periods. The first batch included two ex-KLM DC-3s and was bought between Aug46 and Dec48, with another leased in 1951. The nine aircraft were all sold by Jan52 after use in East Africa and on charter work. Then, in 1957/59 four more were bought, two being used briefly by Bahamas Airways, but all were sold by Dec60.

G-AGBD; G-AGBE; G-AGHM; G-AGND; G-AGYZ; G-AICV; G-AIWC; G-AIWD; G-AIWE; G-AJDE; G-AKII; G-AKJH; G-APBP; G-APNK.

Skyways Cargo Airline Ltd, Lympne and Lydd. Operations started as **Air Freight Ltd**, formed in Apr67 as sales agents for Skyways Coach-Air. In 1970 Skyways' three DC-3s were transferred to Air Freight and in January 1971 Skyways Coach-Air was liquidated. Cargo and charter operations continued and in Oct72 a fourth DC-3 was bought together with the assets of South West Aviation. 1975 saw the addition of three more DC-3s and the airline reorganised as Skyways Cargo Airline. The DC-3s remained in service until some were replaced by FH-227s in 1979 and by 1980 the remainder were sold, following financial difficulties.

G-AGJV; G-AGYZ; G-AMSM; G-AMSV; G-AMWW; G-AOBN; G-APBC. In addition G-AMFV was used for spares.

Skyways Coach-Air Ltd, Lympne, bridges the gap between Skyways and Skyways Cargo as both had ties with Mr Eric Rylands. The Coach-Air service to Paris was started in Sep55 and Skyways Coach-Air became a separate company in Oct58. Operations continued until Jan71, when three DC-3s remained. Shortage of finance necessitated closure on 20Jan71; the aircraft were transferred to Air Freight Ltd and the remaining operations taken over by Skyways International, formed by a group of employees.

G-AMGD; G-AMSH; G-AMSM; G-AMWW; G-AMWX; G-APUC.

Southampton Air Services Ltd, Southampton, used ex-KLM DC-2 G-AGBH for a brief period in 1946 before it was lost off Malta. DC-3 G-AJPF was registered for a few months in 1947.

South Coast Air Services Ltd, Shoreham, Sussex, bought DC-3s G-AJHZ and G-AMSN early in 1965 for charter work. The first was leased for a time to British Westpoint, but both were later used for nightly newspaper flights. Operations ceased on 05Aug65 when British Westpoint took over the work and the DC-3s were sold.

South Coast Airways, Bournemouth, operated DC-3 G-DAKK during the summer from 1996 onwards, for flights to airshows etc. A second DC-3 N47FK was operated for The Dakota Club. Operations ceased on 11Jul02.

Southern International Ltd, Gatwick, was formed in Jun76 by BST Holdings and DC-3 G-AMCA used for cargo charter work until it was sold to Air Atlantique in 1977.

South West Aviation Ltd, Exeter, bought a DC-3 in Jul68 and a second in May69. They were used for charter work until financial problems forced their sale in Oct72.

G-AMYJ; G-APBC.

Starways Ltd, Liverpool/Speke. The first of eleven DC-3s was bought in Oct50, the first two being pre-war DC-3s. They were used on charter, and later scheduled services to various parts of Britain and abroad. Control was gained by J A and F H Wilson in 1954 and they were sometimes the registered owners of aircraft. Operations were taken over by British Eagle from 01Jan64 and the aircraft sold.

G-AJDC; G-AJDG; G-ALXK; G-AMJU; G-AMPO; G-AMPY to G-AMRB incl; G-AMSM; G-AMSN.

Strathair, Strathallan, was the trading name for Strathallan Air Services Ltd, who used two DC-3s, one in 1966 and the other from Apr67 until Mar69 for charter work, including oil-support. Schedules were flown for BUA in 1967 but the aircraft were sold.

G-AOGZ; G-APPO.

Surrey Flying Services Ltd, Southend and Stansted. DC-3 G-AMSR was bought in May52 for freight runs to Berlin in the colours of **Air Charter**, who became the aircraft's owner in late 1952.

Topflight Ltd, Luton, Beds, took over Air Luton, its night mail work and fleet of DC-3s in 1986 but did not survive for long.

G-AMHJ; G-AMPO; G-ANAF. Additionally G-AMPY was leased.

Transair Ltd, Croydon and Gatwick. The first of 18 DC-3s was bought in Jan53 being used to replace Ansons on newspaper delivery runs and later for charter and scheduled services to the Channel Islands. Four remained when Transair joined BUA on 01Jul60. Several were only bought for overhaul and resale.

G-AGBD; G-AGIS; G-AMPZ; G-AMRA; G-AMVK; G-AMVL; G-AMYJ; G-AMZD; G-AMZF; G-AMZG; G-ANAD; G-ANEG; G-ANTB; G-ANTC; G-ANYF; G-AOUD; G-APBC; G-APML.

Trent Valley Aviation Ltd, Nottingham, bought DC-3 G-AJPF in Feb48 for freight and passenger charter work. Eagle Aviation took over on 01Sep50.

Tyne Tees Air Charter Ltd, Newcastle and Sunderland, bought the first of four DC-3s in Mar62 for inclusive tour charters and for leasing. The name **Tyne Tees Airways Ltd** was adopted in Oct62. DC-3 G-AOXI was used for spares, but two remained until liquidation in Jan65.

G-AJHZ; G-AMNV; G-AOXI; G-APUC.

Ulster Air Transport Ltd, Belfast. See Air Ulster.

Westminster Airways Ltd, Blackbushe, bought three DC-3s between Apr47 and Jul48, of which two were used on refugee relief work in India, followed by the Berlin Airlift. A fourth, G-AJVY, was operated for London Express Newspapers. All were sold by Jul50.

G-AJAY; G-AJAZ; G-AJVY; G-AKNM.

Westpoint Aviation Ltd - See British Westpoint Airlines.

William Dempster Ltd, Stansted. The only DC-3, G-AMSS, was bought in Aug52 for charter work, but it was sold to Dan-Air when operations ceased in 1953.

Note:- For further details of British DC-3/Dakota operations the reader is referred to "British Independent Airlines 1946 - 1976" by A C Merton Jones. Much of the information given here has been extracted in a necessarily condensed form from this excellent work.

Index:-

G-AFIF(DC-1)	c/n 1137	(G-AGCH)(DC-2)	1312
(G-AGAD)(DC-2)	1377	(G-AGCI)(DC-2)	1239
G-AGBB	1590	(G-AGCJ)(DC-2)	1249
G-AGBC	1939	(G-AGCK)(DC-2)	1367
G-AGBD	1980	G-AGEN	4118
G-AGBE	2022	G-AGFX	6223
G-AGBH (DC-2)	1584	G-AGFY	6224
G-AGBI	2019	G-AGFZ	6225
(G-AGCF)(DC-2)	1310	G-AGGA	6241
(G-AGCG)(DC-2)	1311	G-AGGB	6227

Chapter 4: Commercial Operators of the DC-3, C-47, R4D, Dakota and Li-2

G-AGGI	9050	G-AHLZ	25453	G-ALXL	33235	G-ANLF	11979
G-AGHE	9189	G-AIAZ	13459	G-ALXM	33213	G-ANLI	32761
G-AGHF	9186	G-AIBA	9860	G-ALXN	26106	G-ANLJ	12498
G-AGHH	9187	G-AIBG	25467	G-ALXO	33447	G-ANLK	25802
G-AGHJ	9413	G-AICV	1943	G-ALYF	19350	G-ANLL	33564
G-AGHK	9406	G-AIJD	9049	G-AMBW	25275	G-ANLM	27114
G-AGHL	9407	G-AIOD	25292	G-AMCA	32966	G-ANLY	26089
G-AGHM	9623	G-AIOE	12373	G-AMDB	26432	G-ANLZ	33517
G-AGHN	9414	G-AIOF	12332	G-AMDZ	12911	G-ANMA	32945
G-AGHO	9862	G-AIOG	12482	G-AMFV	10105	G-ANMB	27108
G-AGHP	9408	G-AIRG	25288	G-AMGD	9628	G-ANMC	25793
G-AGHR	10097	G-AIRH	12445	G-AMHJ	13468	G-ANNT	12090
G-AGHS	10099	"G-AISH"	33331	G-AMJU	25925	G-ANTB	27207
G-AGHT	10103	G-AIWC	13474	G-AMJX	27080	G-ANTC	26111
G-AGHU	9863	G-AIWD	13475	G-AMJY	33556	G-ANTD	26414
"G-AGHY"	19347	G-AIWE	13479	G-AMKE	25928	G-ANYF	27000
G-AGIO	11907	G-AIYT	12486	G-AMMJ	33518	G-ANZE	25309
G-AGIP	11903	G-AJAU	12433	G-AMNL	33392	G-ANZF	26570
G-AGIR	11932	G-AJAV	12386	G-AMNV	33581	G-ANZG	33246
G-AGIS	12017	G-AJAY	13375	G-AMNW	25622	G-AOAL	33174
G-AGIT	11921	G-AJAZ	10100	G-AMPO	33185	G-AOBN	11711
G-AGIU	12096	G-AJBB	12477	G-AMPP	26717	G-AOCT	12813
"G-AGIV"	11975	G-AJBC	12304	G-AMPS	32741	G-AODD	10239
G-AGIW	12186	G-AJBD	13012	G-AMPT	32935	G-AOFZ	9131
G-AGIX	12053	G-AJBG	25448	G-AMPY	26569	G-AOGX	20777
G-AGIY	12102	G-AJBH	25460	G-AMPZ	32872	G-AOGZ	33282
G-AGIZ	12075	G-AJDC	2205	G-AMRA	26735	G-AOJI	33159
G-AGJR	11995	G-AJDE	13182	G-AMRB	33418	G-AOUD	25573
G-AGJS	12173	G-AJDG	2199	G-AMSF	25825	(G-AOXI)	25613
G-AGJT	12172	G-AJGX	12162	G-AMSH	33331	G-AOYE	10028
G-AGJU	12169	G-AJHY	13388	G-AMSI	26087	G-AOZA	32548
G-AGJV	12195	G-AJHZ	12421	G-AMSJ	33225	G-AOZI	32867
G-AGJW	12199	G-AJIA	12208	G-AMSK	32954	G-APBC	27121
G-AGJX	12014	G-AJIB	9624	G-AMSL	26411	G-APBP	13173
G-AGJY	12019	G-AJIC	9487	G-AMSM	27209	G-APKO	4123
G-AGJZ	12054	G-AJLC	4930	G-AMSN	33379	G-APML	25620
G-AGKA	25586	G-AJLX	25483	G-AMSO	33568	(G-APNK)	25623
G-AGKB	25588	G-AJLY	13452	G-AMSR	26244	(G-APPJ)	33609
G-AGKC	25591	G-AJLZ	10101	G-AMSS	32840	G-APPO	20453
G-AGKD	25595	G-AJNR	12095	G-AMST	32955	G-APUC	12893
G-AGKE	25806	G-AJPF	13456	G-AMSU	33548	G-ASDX	13331
G-AGKF	25807	G-AJRW	19569	"G-AMSU"	26717	G-ATBE	9813
G-AGKG	25818	G-AJRX	12209	G-AMSV	32820	G-ATXS	4103
G-AGKH	25810	G-AJRY(1)	13366	G-AMSW	32919	G-ATXT	4306
G-AGKI	26099	G-AJRY(2)	13331	G-AMSX	33196	G-ATXU	19176
G-AGKJ	26105	G-AJTO	12647	G-AMVA	33163	G-ATZF	12324
G-AGKK	26100	G-AJVY	12358	G-AMVB	26082	G-AVNF	9004
G-AGKL	26107	G-AJVZ	19361	G-AMVC	33390	G-AVPW	12476
G-AGKM	26431	G-AJXL	9628	G-AMVK	26975	G-AXJU	32923
G-AGKN	26429	G-AJZD	12333	G-AMVL	33408	(G-AZDF)	33346
G-AGMZ	26423	G-AJZX	9051	G-AMWV	25600	G-BFHA	25399
G-AGNA	26412	G-AKAR	26889	G-AMWW	33010	G-BFHB	25505
G-AGNB	26719	G-AKAY	12006	G-AMWX	32594	G-BFHC	12758
G-AGNC	26728	G-AKDT	25606	G-AMYB	33346	G-BFPT	19268
G-AGND	26725	G-AKGX	9874	G-AMYJ	32716	G-BFPU	26692
G-AGNE	26721	G-AKII	12299	G-AMYS	26554	G-BFPV	34357
G-AGNF	26979	G-AKIJ	13304	G-AMYT	25805	G-BFPW	33604
G-AGNG	26997	G-AKIK	13487	G-AMYV	32943	G-BFXA	4890
G-AGNK	26985	G-AKIL	25282	G-AMYW	33020	G-BFXB	4225
G-AGWS	6208	G-AKJH	13164	G-AMYX	33042	G-BGCE	13378
G-AGYX	12472	G-AKJN	12489	G-AMYY	26437	G-BGCF	20596
G-AGYZ	12278	G-AKLL	25450	G-AMYZ	33571	G-BGCG	20002
G-AGZA	12455	G-AKNB	9043	G-AMZA	33569	G-BHUA	9914
G-AGZB	12180	G-AKNM	25799	G-AMZB	26980	G-BHUB	19975
G-AGZC	12222	G-AKOZ	27188	G-AMZC	33270	G-BHUC	25764
G-AGZD	12450	G-AKPW	13729	G-AMZD	32860	G-BHUD	32776
G-AGZE	12416	G-AKSM	9860	G-AMZE	25813	G-BLDI	19475
G-AGZF	9172	G-AKVX	12587	G-AMZF	27078	G-BLFK	20721
G-AGZG	9803	G-ALBG	25459	G-AMZG	33416	G-BLFL	34214
G-AHCS	12348	G-ALCA	12159	G-AMZH	27110	(G-BLXV)	12970
G-AHCT	12308	G-ALCB	9878	G-AMZR	33083	G-BLXW	19560
G-AHCU	13381	G-ALCC	10106	G-AMZS	26582	(G-BLYA)	11750
G-AHCV	12443	G-ALEZ	12066	G-AMZW	27099	G-BMCR	9995
G-AHCW	13308	G-ALFO	20401	G-AMZX	26732	G-BPMP	10073
G-AHCX	13335	G-ALLI	19351	G-AMZZ	33340	G-BVOL	9836
G-AHCY	12355	G-ALPM	19566	"G-AMZZ"	25806	G-DAKK	9798
G-AHCZ	11924	G-ALPN	12158	"G ΛMZZ"	12254	G-DAKS	19347
G-AHDA	12177	G-ALTT	12000	G-ANAD	27215	"G-DJKP"	12254
G-AHDB	12077	G-ALVZ	33423	G-ANAE	26101	(G-OFON)	9798
G-AHDC	13481	G-ALWC	13590	G-ANAF	33436	G37-1	26106
G-AHLX	25480	G-ALWD	12911	G-ANAS	33257	G37-2(1)	26432
G-AHLY	25294	G-ALXK	32828	G-ANEG	33444	G37-2(2)	25613

G41-1-67	25427	G41-3-66	32872
G41-2-67	27108	G41-3-67	32867

UNITED NATIONS - UN

The United Nations leased 20 DC-3s for operations in the Congo following withdrawal of Belgian forces and during the subsequent civil war from July 1960. Some came from the USAF and others from civil operators such as Transair-Sweden. Their subsequent fates varied, some returning to their owners and others, such as the USAF C-47s, being sold locally to other African operators or for spares to support Air Congo. The last was stored in 1964. One C-47 crashed 02Dec62 between Leopoldville to Albertville. It remains unidentified. Several RCAF Dakotas were leased for use in Lebanon in 1958 and others have been used in the Middle and Far East. More recently, two were leased from New Zealand for use in Cambodia in 1993. Some aircraft have retained their registrations or serials without taking up any UN identity.

Index:-

UN-201	c/n 9957	UN-217	13700
UN-202	32532	UN-218	19781
UN-203	20010	UN-219	20505
UN-204	33089	UN-220	9780
UN-205	18983	UN-281	11970
UN-206	20068	UN-280	34222
UN-207	25855	UNO 8680	25941
UN-208	26122	HB-ITD	33213
UN-209	25927	SE-CFM	12324
UN-210	26974	SE-CFT	42962
UN-211	4757	5Y-BIL	42963
UN-212	19654	KN511	33046
UN-213	4351	KN666	33369
UN-215	2205	656(RCAF)	9832
UN-216	1947	989(RCAF)	33466

UNITED STATES - NC and N

As is only to be expected, by far the largest operator of Douglas twins, and DC-3s in particular, was the United States. Almost every major airline used them to carry the bulk of their passengers in the years immediately prior to WW2 and for a number of years thereafter. Many of these DC-3s were sold to smaller operators who used them to build up their business, and in turn became major airlines such as Texas International, US Air, Republic etc. Many other DC-3s were used, and some still are, by charter operators. Immediately after the war many new companies sprang up, dreaming of the profits to be made from such operations. The majority were short-lived, but some, such as Flying Tiger, grew to become major cargo carriers. Many existed to operate cheap transcontinental services, but gained a bad name because of their high accident rate. Most of the current charter companies are relatively small, and operate over limited areas. DC-3s have been used widely to smuggle cocaine and marijuana, the profits to be gained apparently being adequate to risk writing off the aircraft after one flight.

Another major use for the DC-3 was as an executive transport. The first of these was purchased new from Douglas pre-war, but the big expansion came after the war, though the rise in the price of Avgas and the evolution of smaller, more economical twins and jets has reduced the DC-3 fleets. Government use has been considerable. The CAA, and later the FAA, used many for checking radio aids etc, and others are still used by the USDA Forestry Service and others for pesticide spraying. So long as the DC-3 remains economical, it will continue to be part of the scene at American airports.

Considerable confusion exists over the system of licence numbers used in the USA. At first this was a simple chronological system, the higher the number, in general, the later it was issued. With increasing numbers of aircraft, suffix letters were used, singly at first, and later (from 1956 on) in pairs. These double suffix letters were not recorded in the first published registers as the computer printouts did not identify the second letters. Some pairs were personalised, to suit the company's name. From 1978 to about 1982 the practice of applying minute numbers was allowed, and it is often impossible to identify aircraft by licence number on photographs, but in recent years the numbers are of a more reasonable size. Category letters were used pre-war, NC for commercial, NR for restricted etc. NX was used on a few DC-3s flown for cross-wind landing gear or radar trials, but the letters were deleted on 31 December 1948 and after that date only 'N' was used. The category is now painted near the cockpit. In the following operator section, registrations except the first used are listed without NC/NR/NX, and reference should be made to the production list for the appropriate prefix information. In the production list section it has been assumed that aircraft registered prior to 1949 were NC and those later just N numbered, though the 'C' was often not deleted immediately.

It has not proved possible to identify owners for all DC-3s for which NC/N numbers are known. The FAA card index records each aircraft by c/n and licence numbers used. The index often records foreign markings and usefully ex USAF and USN serials, but it does not give owners. It is quite impossible to check all individual files, so reliance has had to be placed on published registers. These were only available regularly from 1963 onwards. Prior to this a list was produced in 1947 and in 1953 but without c/ns. Many allotted NC/N numbers were used for delivery from RFC stores, and then exported. Others were registered but the sale fell through and a new number was allotted. Such allocations are given in the index, but not all owners have been traced. A group of allotted numbers were given to aircraft on order for airlines and then cancelled when they were diverted to the USAAF in 1942. Wherever possible we have now included known 'ntu' registrations in the index as well as in the production list.

The criteria for inclusion in the operator list which follows are somewhat arbitrary. All airlines known to have operated scheduled services are included, as are charter companies with an operating certificate. Not all aircraft registered to a company may have actually been operated by it but they are nevertheless included if such ownership was recorded. Executive owners and fixed base operators are omitted, even though some of the former ran airline-type operations. Many companies which appear, from their name, to be operators, may only have leased out aircraft. If it has not proved possible to identify the nature of some such operations, mention has been omitted.

The latest development in the publication of the US Civil register is through the internet, but unfortunately the information is often far from accurate. Basler BT-67s are still recorded with R-1830 engines. The register has not been culled for more than ten years and aircraft remain listed even though their sale is reported, probably to scrap.

AAT Airlines - See Air Sunshine.

AAXICO - See American Air Export & Import Co.

Academy Airlines (Airline Aviation Academy Inc), Griffin, GA, operates air taxi and charter flights as well as training. Two of their many DC-3s were in use in 1983, but the fleet increased to four ten years later, working for Emery Worldwide. In 1995 the Emery contract had ceased and three DC-3s remained in 2002.

N1690; N33639; N130D; N132D; N133D; N136D; N143D; N230D; N232GB; N15M; N744V; N3433Y.

Accelerated Charter Express, Broomfield, CO, operated N2298C in 1984, when it was sold to Salair.

Admiral Air Service, Oakland, CA, was formed in August 1948 as Quaker City Airways and operated between Jan49 and Sep51. Operations re-started in 1960-61 with DC-3s, but the airline closed down in 1962.

N16069; N19935; N33607; N45398.

AeroDyne Airlines, Renton, WA, used the DC-3 from 1969 for charter and leasing. Some aircraft were leased to Aero-Transit in 1979, and four DC-3s remained in 1983. A single Twin Otter remained in 1984.

N44585; N44587; N44896; N65351; N74589; N107AD; N2025A; N1051N; N1280N. Additionally N91287, N91289 were acquired for spares.

Aero Finance Corp, Hialeah, FL, was formed by **C N Shelton & Co**, changing its name in 1950 and continuing until at least 1953. It became part of the Peninsular Group in 1951 and also traded as **Aero Coach**. Freight charter services were operated.

N54406; N65764; N66118; N66147; N66176.

Aero Freight Inc, El Paso, TX, bought DC-3 N471AF in Nov94 for cargo work. It was later registered N472AF after a spell in Mexico.

Aeronautical Services, Friday Harbour, WA, had DC-3 N403JB registered to them but it was sold. It was used for freight work.

Aero Services Inc, Van Nuys, CA, owned DC-3 NC18641 in 1947.

CHAPTER 4: COMMERCIAL OPERATORS OF THE DC-3, C-47, R4D, DAKOTA AND LI-2

Aerosun International, Clearwater, FL, ex **Red Carpet Airlines**, used DC-3 N600RC briefly from 15Nov82. Convairs replaced it by 1983.

Aero-Transit Inc, Spokane, WA, operated scheduled freight services from 1979 onwards, supplementing with DC-3s leased from Aero-Dyne and others.

N19906; N75142; N91314; N600JD are identified.

Aero Union Corp, Chico, CA were operating R4D-8s N55988 and N5597T as freighters until 1982 when the aircraft were put up for sale.

Aero Virgin Islands Corp, St Thomas, VI, operated scheduled services between Puerto Rico and St Thomas from 1976, using DC-3s, four of which remained in 1983. In 1985 there were seven in use. The entire fleet was destroyed when hurricane Hugo hit St Thomas in Sep89. See also **Air BVI** (Leeward Islands).

N15598, N25651, N25695, N28346, N45338, N101AP; N102AP; N4471J; N4425N; N331P, N100SD; N5117X; N4577Z.

Air America, Inc (AAM) was formerly **Civil Air Transport Inc** (CATI). It was formed in 1959 as a wholly-owned subsidiary of the Pacific Corporation, a cover organisation for the CIA. Its operational headquarters were at Taipei, Taiwan. Some C-47s were transferred from CATI and others were bailed from the USAF for operation in SE Asia. Air America had ten C-47s in Vietnam in Jan67. The company officially ceased to exist on 30Jun76.

083 (43-16083); 084 (43-48084); 147 (43-16147); 559 (43-15559); 607 (42-93607); 949 (43-15949); 994 (45-0994); 0-50883; B-809; B-815; B-817; B-827; B-829; B-841; B-879; B-929; B-933; EM-3 (B-1531); XW-PFT.

Notes:-
Quoted registrations B-147, B-559 and B-994 did not exist; the registration prefix B- has been added incorrectly in other sources to the 'last three' of USAF serials carried on these aircraft.
Of other quoted marks, '999' was probably an error for 994; 'B-808' was probably an error for B-809; B-811crashed in Oct54 while with CAT; B-819 was a PBY-5A; 'B-828' was probably an error for B-829.
EM-3 was B-1531 leased from China Air Lines and XW-PFT was leased from CASI.

Air Americana - See Skyway Airlines.

Airborne Transport Inc, Jamaica, NY, used DC-3 NC16002 on charter services until it crashed in Dec48.

Air Cargo America, San Juan, PR, operated DC-3 N10801 in 1979, but sold it in 1984. N705GB and N3749Q were leased.

Air Cargo Express Inc, Upper Montclair, NJ used DC-3 NC57672 in 1949/50.

Air Cargo Express/ ACE Air Cargo Express, Cleveland, OH, leased DC-3 N139JR during 1982. By 1985 the fleet had increased to six but DC-3s were no longer in the fleet by 1986, and in Aug88 operations came to an end.

N88FA; N136D; N139JR; N140JR; N141JR; N1213M.

Air Cargo Transport Corp, Newark, NJ, operated cargo flights from 1946 until it was declared bankrupt on 28Jan48. Three DC-3s* were lost in a hangar fire at Newark in Mar46.

NC8884; NC13719; NC13726*; NC14271; NC14941; NC36349; NC39188*; NC41798*; NC50520; NC50525; NC54417; NC60940; NC60941; NC60942; NC60943; NC88874; NC88875; NC88876.

Air Caribbean, Isla Verde, PR, operated DC-3s on scheduled services within Puerto Rico from Dec75 until they ceased in 1979. For a time the aircraft were owned by **Old South Air Service**.

N4795; N8661; N16096; N86584; N42FN; N285SE; N286SE; N1159S; N999Z.

Air Charter, San Juan, PR, owned DC-3s N31MC and N37AP, for freight work, the latter surviving in 2000.

Air Charter West, Oakland, CA, started as **Zoom Zoom Air** when charter and taxi services were flown. The name was changed in 1975, but operations later ceased and some of the aircraft reverted to parent company **Transwest Air Express**.

N60705; N63250; N50CE/N200ZZ; N4007C; N100ZZ; N300ZZ.

Air Chicago Freight, Chicago, IL, operated DC-3s N50321 and N51617 on lease about 1976.

Air Commuter Express - Airgo Inc, Dallas Love Field, TX & Warrentown, NC, was owned by A A Hulsey and operated as **Airgo Air Freight** from 1977 until about 1982. Passenger and cargo work was undertaken.

N520; N18255; N67873; N88794; N91314; N94530; N162E; N4990E; N55LT; N222MA; N258M.

Air East Inc, Jacksonville, FL, operated DC-3 N13300 briefly during the early seventies.

Air Florida, Miami, FL, took over **Air Sunshine** in Jul78, with four DC-3s. Scheerer Air was also involved.

N74KW to N77KW incl.

Air Freight Inc, Newark, NJ, had DC-3s NC54477, NC56645 and NC60897 used on flights to San Juan. They were sold in July 1947 due to bankruptcy.

Air Freight Inc, Jackson, FL, operated DC-3s on cargo charters from late 1972 until Nov74, many on lease from Jim Hankins.

N50321; N51617; N57131; N61721 to N61726 incl; N67873; N130D; N625E.

Air Fresh Sea Foods Inc, Memphis, TN, were using DC-3s NC7401 and NC8820 in 1947.

Airgo Air Freight - See Air Commuter Express.

Air Indiana, Indianapolis, IN, began DC-3 operations in 1978, initially from Detroit. Three remained when operations ceased about 1981.

N18944; N25646; N25677; N51071; N88874; N36AP; N37AP; N502PA; N8QE; N222TS; N711TD.

Air Indies Corp, St Thomas, VI, was formed in 1968 to operate scenic trips from Miami to Nassau. Third level services to Puerto Rico followed but business ceased on 17Jan74.

N6187; N4795; N39544; N91314; N285SE; N286SE.

Airline of the Virgin Islands, St Thomas, VI, operated DC-3s N101AP and N102AP between 1984 and August 1987 when they were sold.

Airline Transport Carriers Inc, Burbank, CA, started DC-3 operations in 1946, when owned by C C Sherman, who also owned California Central. Some aircraft were leased. Charters continued until 1955, with suspensions in 1951/52.

N12989; N13437; N15581; N15957; N18666; N33635; N36480; N79055; N79056.

Air Miami, Miami, FL, acquired DC-3 N11BC, re-registered N3XW in Nov79, to supplement their Heron. N3XW was used on lease until early 1983 and N6102 briefly in 1980.

Air Mid-America, Chicago, IL, was a certificated cargo carrier which used two DC-3s between Sep70 and sometime in 1971.

N18105; N25666.

Air Molokai, Kahului, HI, also known as **Tropic Airlines** operated DC-3s N104RP and N162E on scheduled and inter-island charter operations in dual titles. The last was sold in 1989.

Air Nashua, Nashua, NH operated DC-3s N8009 and N96H in the late seventies.

Air Nevada, Burbank, CA, operated DC-3 N33639 on scheduled services from Long Beach to Hawthorne, NV, as successor to Hawthorne Nevada Airlines and Mineral County Airlines Inc in 1964.

Air New England Inc, Barnstaple, ME, started third level services in Apr71 and DC-3s were soon introduced. These were replaced by FH-227Bs in 1975.

N18141; N18105; N25666; N33654; N60705 (lsd); N88874.

Airnews Inc, San Antonio, TX, was a certificated cargo carrier in Aug49 and used two DC-2s as well as two DC-3s and four Norsemen. Nothing has been reported on the DC-2s, but the DC-3s were N64744 and N75430. The certificate was surrendered in Oct51.

Air North, Fairbanks-Metro, AK, trading as **Yukon Air Service**, was operating DC-3s N95460 and N3FY from 1977. It was taken over by Liberty Air, and ceased operations, becoming bankrupt on 04Sep84.

Air Oasis Airline, Long Beach, CA, used DC-3 N61350 on charter work from 1959 to 1963 and also had N15570.

Air O'Hare, Chicago, IL, operated four DC-3s out of O'Hare, Chicago between 1974 and 1977.

N44998; N8BC; N9BC; N7CA.

Air Pacific International Inc, Tamuning, Guam, started commuter services within the US Trust Territory in 1969, using a single DC-3 N46496, possibly until 1978.

Airplane Charter by Mercer Inc, Burbank, CA, see Mercer Airlines.

Air Puerto Rico, San Juan, PR, used DC-3 N28381 in 1975.

Air Rajneesh, Carlsbad, CA, had three DC-3s in 1985, but legal problems forced closure in that year.

N2647; N31MC; N101ZG.

Air Resorts Airlines, Carlsbad, CA, formed in 1975 operated DC-3s during 1983, but these were sold to Air Rajneesh.

N31MC; N101ZG.

Air San Jose, Mountain View, CA, used DC-3 N41447 during 1970.

Air Services Inc, Newark, NJ, operated irregular services between 1948 and 1955, using C-46s and two DC-3s, of which one was N16004.

Air Siesta, McAllen, TX, operated DC-3 N10004 in 1982/83 and N5831B in 1985/86. They were sold and Air Siesta remains an FBO.

Air South - see **Florida Air Lines**.

Air Sunshine (AAT Airlines Inc.), Key West, FL, operated DC-3s from Miami to Florida Keys. The airline originated as American Air Taxi Inc in 1951 and commuter services were introduced in Jul71. The operations were taken over by **Air Florida**/Scheerer Air in Jul78.

N137PB; N73KW/N770SU; N74KW/N21712; N75KW/N30087; N76KW/N345A; N77KW; N4731S. Some of the DC-3s were re-registered in the KW sequence during service with Air Sunshine.

Air Taos, Taos, NM used DC-3 N4996E in 1978.

Air Taxi International, Miami, FL, founded in 1985 was operating DC-3 N376JC in 1993.

Air Texana, Beaumont, TX, had DC-3s N76KW and N600JD until 03Aug81.

Alamo Airways Inc, Las Vegas, NV, operated one DC-3, N64424, on non-scheduled services from 1964 to 1966.

Alaska Aeronautical Industries Inc, Anchorage, AK, used DC-3 N49319 very briefly, until it was damaged beyond repair in Mar71.

Alaska Airlines Inc, Seattle, WA, had at least seven DC-3s for scheduled and charter routes between 1945 and 1958.

NC15473; NC15572; NC91005 to NC91008 incl; N1310M.

Alaska Coastal - Ellis Airlines, Juneau, AK, operated DC-3 N25669 between about 1962 and 1968, when it was taken over by Alaska Airlines.

Alaska Island Air, Kotzebue, AK, operated a fleet of singles and one DC-3, N32AL, until 2000.

Alaskan Southern Airlines, Seattle, WA, used two DC-3s in Alaska for domestic services. These were owned by Pan American, and were incorporated into the airline in 1940.

All-American Airways Inc, Miami, FL, used one DC-3 on charter services in 1948, from New York to San Juan, later replaced by C-46s.

All American Airways Inc, Washington, DC, started operations as All American Aviation (a company of this name having DC-2 NC13783 in Jul44), adopting the above name in Sep48. DC-3s were bought in 1949 and the name changed to **Allegheny Airlines** in 1953.

NC88801; N91221 to N91234 (also operated under earlier licence numbers).

Allegheny Air Cargo Inc, Pittsburgh, PA, operated DC-3 NC20754 in 1947. Another DC-3 crashed near Allentown, PA on 22Jan47.

Allegheny Airlines Inc, Washington, DC, was formed when **All American** changed its name in 1953. The DC-3s were retired in 1963/64, by which time most had been re-registered in the series N141A to N155A, though some had been withdrawn for sale with marks unchanged.

N18943/N155A; N21914; N30087; N65136; N91221/N141A; N91222/N142A; N91223/N143A; N91224/N144A; N91225/N145A; N91226/N146A; N91227/N147A; N91228/N148A; N91229/N149A; N91230/N150A; N91231/N151A; N91232; N91233/N153A; N91234/N154A;

Allied Air Freight, Opa-Locka, FL. Operated cargo flights from Miami to the Bahamas and to Canada until 2001. Three DC-3s were used.

N8040L, N54AA, N57NA

Aloha Airlines Inc, Honolulu, HI, was formed as **Trans Pacific**, and renamed Aloha in Nov58. DC-3s remained in use until Jan61, when replaced by F.27s.

N15565; N62083; N62086; N63376; N65393; N90627; N91028; N2804D; N5631V.

Alpena Flying Services Inc, Alpena, MI, operated scheduled third level services as Detroit Northern Airlines during 1971, using DC-3 N50CE.

Alpha Airlines, Kings Point, NY, was using DC-3s N5009 and N46938 during 1978-82.

American Air Cargo - see Atkins Aviation.

American Air Export & Import Co - AAXICO, Miami, FL, started cargo charter operations in 1945 and the name AAXICO Airlines was adopted in Dec56. DC-3s were only used between Oct45 and 1951, often briefly prior to onward sale.

N16815; N17079; N19454; N36412; N53192; N54368; N54412; N57481; N57673; N74620; N79033; N88790; N88794; N3933C; N3957C; N1844M.

American Air Freight, Laredo, TX, operated DC-3 N88FA/N773AF/XB-DYP(1) amongst other cargo types to 1995. N337AF was used in 1987/88.

American Airlines Inc, New York, NY, ordered the DC-2 in 1934 to replace their uneconomical Curtiss Condors. The type remained in use until sold to the British Purchasing Commission via the USAAF in 1940. The DST and later the DC-3 were launched directly as a result of American's interest and the first of a fleet of about 90 delivered in Apr36. Further DC-3s were acquired towards the end of the war to replace those taken over by the USAAF in 1942. Convair 240s replaced all the DC-3s by the early fifties.

DC-2s:- NC14274 to NC14283 incl; NC14921 to NC14925 incl; NC14966.
DST and DC-3s:- NC12910; NC12923; NC12989; NC13353; NC14959; NC14988; NC15201; NC15575; NC15577; NC15579; NC15580; NC15581; NC15589 to NC15592 inc.; NC15957; NC16001 to NC16009 incl; NC16011 to NC16019 incl; NC16030; NC16096; NC17331 to NC17340 incl; NC18141 to NC18144 incl; NC17888; NC18662; NC18663; NC18666; NC18667; NC18669; NC19921; NC19922; NC19924(2); NC19974; NC21745 to NC21749 incl;

NC21752; NC21767; NC21768; NC21769; NC21793; NC21794; NC21795; NC21797; NC21798; NC21799; NC21914; NC25629; NC25658; NC25660; NC25661; NC25663; NC25664; NC25665; NC25670 to NC25673 incl; NC25676; NC25684; NC25685; NC25686; NC28310; NC28321; NC28323; NC28324; NC28325; NC28350; NC33317; NC33651; NC33653 to NC33657 incl; NC39544; NC45374; NC45383; NC45391; NC50591; NC50592; NC88787; NC88826; NC88827; NC88828; NC91082; NC91084.

DC-3 regns not taken up were:- NC14283(2); NC14922(2); NC25663(2); NC28359; NC28388(2); NC30050; NC30052; NC33627; NC33628; NC33662 (1) & (2); NC34969(1); NC34978(1) and the unregistered c/ns 6315, 6317 and 6318.

American Air Transport Inc, Miami, FL, used three DC-3s for charter work during 1948-51 and for schedules to Florida from San Juan in 1950.

N57481; N59278; N88741(2).

American Airways Charters, Miami, FL, operated two DC-3s on charters from Miami in 1980, but operations ceased in 1990.

N6102; N840MB.

American Flyers Airline Corp, Fort Worth, TX, was owned by Reed Pigman and began airline operations in Dec49. It adopted the trading name in 1951 but some aircraft remained registered to the owner until his death in 1971, when the DC-3s were sold.

N18111; N19919; N19922; N33656; N62253.

American Flyers Inc, Fort Lauderdale, FL, operated DC-3s N872A and N1300M during 1976-78.

American International Airways used DC-3 N912E briefly during 1975.

American Overseas Airlines Inc, New York, NY, was the name adopted following American's purchase of American Export Lines in 1945. Pan American took over AOA in Sep50 following a ruling that AA could not operate overseas, and the DC-3s continued in use on European feeder routes.

N25686; N90907; N90908.

Anguilla Airways, St Thomas, VI, was granted a permit to operate cargo services in Mar72, using a leased DC-3.

Apollo Airlines, Orlando, FL, used DC-3 N833M in 1984, but it was sold in Sep86.

Appalachian Flying Service Inc, Johnson City, TN operated DC-3 NC48990 in 1947.

Arabian American Oil Co - ARAMCO, San Francisco, New York and Dhahran, Saudi Arabia, operated scheduled services for its employees engaged on company business in Saudi Arabia, using predominantly DC-3s from 1946 until F.27s took over in 1977. All had earlier markings which are listed in the Production section.

N717A to N723A incl.

Arctic Frontier Airways, Seattle, WA, used DC-3 NC33317/N733A on charter work in 1948.

Arctic Pacific Inc, Seattle, WA, was incorporated in 1947 for non-scheduled operations, using DC-3s and C-46s. Operations ceased in 1952 after a C-46 accident. A (different?) company named Arctic Pacific Airlines used N1789B and N1399N in 1959.

Argonaut Airways Inc, Miami, FL, was incorporated in May46 and started coach services in 1951 using DC-3s and C-46s. It was certificated to fly irregular services from Jan59 until 1962 with DC-3s, being owned by Southern Pipeliners at that time.

N18101; NC57638; N142A; N153A.

Argosy Air Lines Inc, Fort Lauderdale, FL, used DC-3s on passenger and cargo services from 1974 until about 1979.

N14931; N18196; N407D.

Arizona Airways Inc, Phoenix, AZ, started airline operations using DC-3s in Sep45. It merged with Monarch to form Frontier on 01Jun50.

NC57985; NC64910; NC75028.

Arnold Air Services Inc, Seattle, WA, started passenger and cargo charter operations in 1947, using a fleet that included two unidentified DC-2s.

NC79087/NC49363; N91052; N91054.

Arrow Airways Inc, Burbank, CA, operated DC-3s on passenger and cargo charters within California between 1949 and Feb51.

N54357; N60256; NC62024; NC62025; NC68179; NC68180.

Aspen Airways Inc, Denver, CO, bought DC-3s in 1963 to fly an air taxi service to the Aspen ski resort. Services were scheduled in 1968 and Convairs flew the service from 1971.

N345A; N222LW; N22Z.

Astro Airways, Pine Bluff, AR, used three DC-3s for charter work between 1981 and 1995.

N25646; N88874; N6666A.

Atkins Aviation, McAllen, TX, trading as **American Air Cargo**, used DC-3s on cargo work from 1986 until operations ceased about Mar91.

N512AC; N513AC; N514AC; N515AC; N518AC; N117RR; N61724.

Atlantic Air Cargo, Miami, FL, was operating DC-3s N437GB and N705GB in 2002-03.

Atlantic, Gulf & Midland Corp, Little Ferry, NJ, used a DC-3, NC54578, on charter services between 1947 and Dec48.

Atlantic Northern Airlines Inc, New York, NY, started operations as Ocean Air Tradeways in Jan46. A DC-3 was leased for flights to Miami.

Atorie Air, El Paso, TX, linked to Scoben Investments, started using DC-3s on cargo operations in 1984, adding to the fleet in 1985 and ceasing in mid-1986.

N2647; N37AP; N25CE; N403JB; N31MC; N1213M; N222PV; N101ZG.

Audi Air Inc, Fairbanks, AK, started DC-3 operations about 1986, but the certificate was revoked in the summer of 1988.

N9663N; N8042X.

Avalon Air Transport Inc, Long Beach, CA, started scheduled services within California in Jun60, using DC-3s. The name was changed to **Catalina Airlines** in Jul63.

N330; N1132; N33607; N55L.

Aviation Corp. of Seattle, Seattle, WA, operated two DC-3s on non-scheduled services as **Westair Transport** in 1947.

B Airways, Miami, FL, operated DC-3 N2685W between Miami, Freeport and Nassau from 1983 until its sale in Nov89.

Ball Bros Inc, Anchorage, AK, used DC-3 N68363, plus larger types, for the carriage of fish from 1979 on. All aircraft were sold to Northern Pacific Transport by 1983.

Bar Harbor Airlines, Bangor, ME, began as an FBO in 1946. After certification in Aug65 began operating scheduled passenger routes in New England. Following a cooperative agreement with EAL in 1981 it became a unit of Eastern Air Express in 1986 and acquired Provincetown-Boston Airlines and its DC-3s in 1987, operating them in Eastern Express or Florida Express colours but withdrew most of them from service in 1988.

N32PB; N34PB; N35PB; N38PB; N40PB; N43PB; N130PB; N136PB; N137PB; N139PB.

Baron Aviation Services Inc, Vichy, MO, used up to seven DC-3s as freight carriers from 1979 onwards. Five remained in 1999.

N19721; N51938; N1350A; N6CA; N486C; N47FJ; N977W.

Basler Flight Services Inc, Oshkosh, WI, have owned DC-3s since 1957, using them for passenger charters at first, but then mostly for cargo, including mail and parcels for UPS. Overhaul and conversion work was also carried out. **Basler Turbo Conversions** were formed to take on the rebuilding of DC-3s to DC-3-BT-67 standard (see conversions listing in Volume 2) which had started in 1983, a new facility being built specially at Oshkosh, WI, in which the conversions took place.

N5009; N6110; N7772; N8056; N8383; N18255; N18944; N22357/ XA-RPN; N24320; N25641; N25695; N40359; N40386; N46496; N46877; N46938; N46949; N46950; N51071; N54542; N59314; N59316; N90830; N91379; N99663; N99665; N721A; N8064A; N707BA; N21BF; N28BF; N29BF; N46BF; N70BF; N72BF; N91BF; N95BF; N96BF; N97BF; N98BF; N100BF; N102BF; N103BF; N104BF; N105BF; N106BF; N107BF; N110BF; N300BF; N400BF; N555CR; N2237C/XA-RPE; N471DK; N472DK; N2668D; N6898D; N8187E; N99FS; N486F; N232GB; N240GB; N512GL; N513GL; N792G; N96H; N138H; N734H; N932H; N56KS; N165LG; N147M; N795M; N845MB; N115NA; N510NR; N3753N; N331P; N8059P; N29R; N573R; N578R; N4039S; N9923S; N387T; N744V; N45WT; N66W; N145ZA; N808Z, N907Z.

Bird & Sons, Inc, a private airline run by William H Bird, operated a variety of aircraft types (including some C-47s) in SE Asia as the aviation division of A Bird & Sons a heavy construction company operating in Vietnam and Laos. Company HQ initially in Seattle, WA but later moved to San Francisco, CA. Continental A/L bought the aviation division in 1965 and commenced operations in Sept65 as **Continental Air Services Inc (CASI)**. William Bird later formed Bird Air. The following C-47s, reported with Bird & Sons, were transferred to CASI unless otherwise stated:

N560, N7780C; N7781C; XW-PAD was dbr in shellfire at Vientiane, Laos 15Dec60; XW-PGJ & XW-PGK, c/ns unknown, may have been operated by Bird & Sons (see Laos)

Bixby Airlines, Long Beach, CA, owned by Diana Bixby, used two DC-3s in 1948.

NC57372; NC79077.

Blatz Airlines Inc, Burbank, CA, bought DC-3s in Jan48 to operate charter work. This continued until 1962.

N33639; N56990; N58731; N62086; N63107; N67588; N1399N.

Bonanza Air Lines Inc, Las Vegas, NV, bought DC-3s in 1949 when inter-state scheduled services started. The DC-3s were replaced by F.27s from 1959 onwards, and all had been sold by 1962. All aircraft operated in the marks used at the time of purchase before re-registration as N485 and N490 to N498 inclusive. Two, N15559 and N56589, were never re-registered.

Borinquen Air, San Juan, PR, started operating DC-3s out of Puerto Rico in Mar82 using the trading name of **Diaz Aviation Corp**. By 2003 two remained, used on cargo flights.

N18916/N28PR; N28341; N45379/N27PR; N86553; N29R.

Bo-S-Aire Corp, Greenville, SC, trading as **Bowman Aviation** operated charter flights using DC-3s from 1973 until operations ceased in May88 and the fleet was sold.

N18255/N28BA; N88794; N91314 lsd; N3BA; N4BA; N12BA; N230D/N19BA; N222MA. N67873 was painted in Bo-S c/s 1980.

Braniff Airways Inc (Braniff International), Dallas, TX, bought second-hand DC-2s in 1936 and used these on its airline routes until 1942. DC-3s followed in 1939, bought new, some of which were diverted to the USAAF in 1941. More were added from surplus stocks post-war and another batch taken over with Mid-Continent on 16Aug52. The last DC-3 was sold in 1961.

DC-2s:- NC13713; NC13715; NC13716; NC13719; NC13724; NC13727; NC13728.
DC-3s:- N15201; N17338; N17888; N18661; N18667; N21773 to N21776 incl; N21914; N25666 to N25670 incl; N25672; N25685; N25693; N28362 to N28364 incl; N28508; N28679; N33312; N33326; N33327; N33346; N34950 to N34952 incl; N34971; N41831; N45335; N45340; N45367; N49556; N59748; N59749; N61350; N61351; N61451; N65350; N65351; N65378; N95453.

Brooks Fuel, Fairbanks, AK, used DC-3 N95460 for carrying fuel from Sep95, though it was stored from 1996 onwards.

Bruning Aviation Inc, Springfield, MA, operated three DC-3s in 1947, NC15587, NC36498 and NC36699 but lost the second of these on 25Feb48 when it crashed and was burnt landing at Columbus, OH. The company was declared bankrupt in Oct48.

Buckeye Air Freight, Cleveland, OH, used DC-3s for cargo charter work between 1973 and 1978.

N60705; N3433E; N3433U.

Buker Airways, Springfield, VT, operated DC-3 N94441 briefly during the late sixties.

Burke Air Transport, Miami, FL, used four DC-3s on charter work between 1946 and 1949, by which time two had crashed. **Seattle Air Charter** was the trading name in Jan49.

NC54550; NC79023; NC79024; N79025.

Business Air, Burlington, VT, had five DC-3s painted in WW2 colours, used for cargo work. Most were out of use by 1995.

N54NA; N57NA; N58NA; N59NA; N107AD; N2025A.

Cal Aero Airways, Van Nuys, CA, used DC-3 N41447 during 1969/70.

California Air Tours, Los Angeles, CA, trading as **Sentimental Journeys**, have used various DC-3s for pleasure flights. None now remains.

N54542; N92578; N97H; N7043N; N8042X.

California Central Airlines, Burbank, CA, started scheduled operations in Jan49, using DC-3s leased from Airline Transport Carriers and later from C C Sherman.

N12935; N15570; N17318; N17397; N33660; N45333; N79055; N79056.

California Growers Air Express Inc, Van Nuys, CA, used a DC-3 at one time to carry agricultural produce.

NC63186.

Cal-Neva Air Inc, owned by J Duby, used two DC-3s during the sixties.

N62086; N63250.

Canadian Colonial Airways Inc, New York, NY, bought DC-2s and DC-3s in 1939, and used these until Apr42 when the name **Colonial Airlines** was adopted.

DC-2s:- NC14276; NC14925;
DC-3s:- NC21750; NC21751; NC21758; NC21759; NC28360; NC28361.

Cape Smythe Air Service, Barrow, AK operated DC-3 N19454 amongst a large fleet of smaller types during the late 1990s.

Capital Airlines Inc, Washington, DC, was formed in Apr48 when the name was changed from **Pennsylvania Central Airlines** (see PCA). In Jun61 financial difficulties forced a merger with United, although by then all but three DC-3s had been sold.

N18620; N19915; N19917; N21747; N21781 to N21785 incl; N21788; N21790; N25689; N25691N25694 to N25696 incl; N28324; N28360; N33677; N33678; N44993; N45338; N45366; N45373; N45379; N49553; N60705; N86588; N88835; N1549V and *Super DC-3s* N16012; N16016; N16019.

Capitol Airways Inc, Nashville, TN, started operations in Jan46, using a few DC-3s from 1951 until 1955/56, when C-46s made up the fleet.

N15596; N19193; N25629; N31538; N86584.

Carco Air Services Inc, Albuquerque, NM, used DC-3s on scheduled services to the Los Alamos nuclear research centre between 1966 and 1971. They were then returned to government agencies or sold.

N6387A; N137D; N709Z; N710Z; N808Z; N810Z; N811Z.

CHAPTER 4: COMMERCIAL OPERATORS OF THE DC-3, C-47, R4D, DAKOTA AND LI-2

CARIBAIR, Caribbean-Atlantic Airlines Inc, San Juan, PR, operated DC-3s on scheduled services from June 1945 until the airline was taken over by Eastern in 1973.

N16068; N18940; NC21787; N25679; N28323; N34970; NC55985; N65389; NC79044; N8011E; N1549V.

Carib Air Cargo, t/a GMD Air used DC-3s for cargo work until they were sold to Tol Air in 1989.

N80617; N722A; N783V.

Caribbean Air Services - CASAIR, St Croix, VI, traded as such from 1979 on, but is now known as **Caribbean Aviation Services** and based at Miami Springs, FL, using three DC-3s. They were associated with Southern Air Transport and their fleet was sold by Nov85.

N1546A; N7753A; N666DG; N23WT.

Caribbean American Airlines Inc, Miami, FL registered DC-3 NC1050M in Dec46.

Caribbean Aviation Services, Miami, FL used DC-3s N7753A, N666DG and N23WT on passenger and freight services in the early 1980s.

Caribbean Express, Miami, FL, operated DC-3 N889P briefly until its sale in Apr84.

Caribbean International Airlines, Miami, FL, used two DC-3s on charter work between Jul68 and 1971.

N1948; N401D.

Caribbean Island Airlines, San Juan, PR, used an unknown DC-3 about 1969.

Caribe Air, Birmingham, AL used DC-3 N51D(2) in 1978.

Caribe Airways, Miami, FL, proprietor A Mendez, operated four DC-3s prior to 1949 on low fare passenger services between New York and San Juan.

NC46858; NC55985; NC65742; NC66112.

Carriba Air, San Juan, PR, was reported as using DC-3s from Miami in the early eighties.

N79B; N77KW.

Cascade Air, Seattle, WA, had DC-3 N91314 in 1999, along with a C-46, and have since added N60049, N60154, N791HH and N272R, based at Ephrata Municipal, WA..

Catalina Flying Boats, Long Beach, CA, continue to operate two freight DC-3s, N403JB and N2298C. The former was bought in Feb94.

Catalina Pacific Airlines, Beverley Hills, CA, used DC-3s on scheduled services to Catalina Island and charters to Nevada gambling cities from 1956 until 1960.

N18101; N33644; N55L.

Central Airlines Inc, Fort Worth, TX, introduced DC-3s on scheduled services in 1950, continuing until their merger with Frontier in Oct67.

N15563; N15584; N15837; N17397; N18939; N19454; N19937; N39544; N49541; N75276; N75277; N88790; N88794; N91003; N285SE; N286SE; N287SE; N7820B.

Central American Airways Flying Services Inc, Louisville, KY, was a contract carrier which started operations with a DC-3 in Jul65. N272R was in use until 1981. N47965 was reported in 1947.

Central Cargo Inc, San Juan, PR, used three DC-3s on cargo charters between 1969 and 1976.

N15773; N17312; N28392.

Central Iowa Airlines, Davenport, IA, started operations about 1972, when the first of four DC-3s was reported. Operations probably ceased in 1975.

N18143; N25646; N28364; N144D.

Century Airlines, Pontiac, MI, founded in 1963 as **Cryderman Air Service**, (qv), used several DC-3s on charter work, as well as C-46s and Convairs. The last three were retired in 1993.

N18105; N19454; N25666; N33654; N54604; N2669A; N12BA; N19BA; N81B; N2668D; N2668K; N14MA; N15MA; N2668N; N272R.

Century Airlines, Kansas City, MO, traded as **SS Airways** and used DC-3 N211Q.

Challenger Airlines Co, Denver, CO, was formed as **Summit Airways** in 1946 and the name changed to Challenger in Jan47. It was taken over by Monarch to form **Frontier** in Dec49. DC-3s were the only equipment.

NC53376; N65135; N65276; N65385.

Champlain Air, Plattsburgh, NY, operate four DC-3s: N59NA, N122CA, N700CA and N922CA. They were bought in 1992 and at one time operated for US Air Express.

Charter Airlines, Gainesville, FL, started operations as Charterair in Feb77 but was changed to Charter Air Center and then to the above name in Dec78. The only DC-3 used was N28391 and operations were taken over by Mackey at the end of 1978.

Chesapeake Airways Inc, Salisbury, MD, started scheduled services with two DC-3s in Apr46.

NC60713; NC60714.

Chicago and Southern Airlines Inc, Memphis, TN, bought DC-3s in 1940 and continued to use them until the airline was taken over by Delta in May53 to form Delta C & S.

N12926; N12927; N12958; N15849; N17882; N18618; N19930; N19977; N25625 to N25628 incl; N28378; N30083; N31538; N38938; N38939; N44881; N75411; N86599.

Christler Flying Service, Thermopolis, WY were using DC-3s and L749A Constellations in the late seventies.

N498(2); N19922; N51041; N62374; N86462; N2204S.

Civil Aeronautics Admin/Federal Aviation Agency have used over eighty DC-3s in their work checking airways and providing transport for their staff. They were registered between NC1 and NC300, many being re-registered more than once, and readers should consult the index later in this section.

Civil Air Transport Inc (CATI), was formed in 1949 and incorporated under Delaware laws to act as the nominee of CAT S.A. in the legal battles over the ownership of the CATC and CNAC aircraft and other assets acquired in Dec49 by Claire L Chennault and Witing Willauer. Some of these aircraft and spares, which either remained on mainland China or were flown there from Hong Kong, were never handed over. Surviving aircraft were shipped to the USA in Sept52 for refurbishment and/or sale. CATI was acquired by the Airdale Corpn, the CIA's holding company, in 1950 and became Air America Inc in 1959. Civil Air Transport Company Limited continued in operation as a separate company, based in Taiwan (qv).

N8324C to N8342C incl; N8348C to N8350C incl; N8352C to N8362C incl; N8399C; N8421C.

Note:- Many of these aircraft were re-registered in the USA. N8351C has been quoted as a DC-3 c/n 16099/32847 but is now known to have been C-54D c/n 10699.

Classic Express Airways, Orange County, CA, are listed as owning DC-3 N103NA.

C & M Airlines, Fort Worth, TX were using DC-3 N86584 in 1985 but sold it in 1986.

Coastal Air Lines, Newark, NJ, started operations using DC-3s in Feb47 but ceased after two accidents, probably as early as 1948.

N60331; N74620.

Coastal Airways Inc, Miami, FL used DC-3s N14931, N76KW and N800RC in the 1980s. Operations ceased on 29Jun90.

Coastal Cargo Co Inc, Teterboro, NJ commenced charter operations in Feb47, mainly between Miami and Boston. Two DC-3s are known, NC53210 being w/o Jan49 and N74647 probably leased as replacement, but by 1951 Coastal Cargo was using only C-46s.

Coker Air Freight Inc, Grand Prairie, TX, bought DC-3s N101CA, N103CA and N104CA in Sep79, adding N94CA in 1981. They were taken over by Skyfreighters in 1984.

Colonial Airlines Inc, New York, NY, was formed when Canadian Colonial changed its name in Apr42. One DC-2 was inherited as well as several DC-3s, some of the latter remained in use when Eastern took over operations in Jun56. Some were sold to the Argentine in 1946, and may simply have been overhauled.

DC-2:- NC14925; DC-3s:- NC16096; NC21745; NC21751; NC21752; NC21758; NC21759; NC21795; NC21798; NC28323; NC28324; NC28350; NC28360; NC34968; NC34971; NC34978; NC37468; NC34970; N86547; N86548; N86586; N86591; N86592.

Columbia Air Cargo Inc, Portland, OR, used a single DC-3, NC95486, on irregular cargo services to Alaska until it was destroyed in Nov47.

Columbia Airlines, Woodland Hills, CA, operated as Air Cargo Express from March to Oct62, using leased DC-3 N1789B.

Comut-Aire, Pontiac, MI, used DC-3s to operate third level services to Detroit. Four aircraft are known to have been used, probably leased.

Conner Airlines Inc, Miami, FL, began operations in 1948 using two leased DC-3s on passenger and freight charter services, buying them later in the year, but selling them in 1949. Two DC-3s and three C-46s were insured in Jan51; they have not been identified but F A Conner himself owned N1549V in the sixties and N8666 in the seventies.

Consolidated Airlines, Oakland, CA, is known to have used two DC-3s c.1962/3, one being N1789B. Another four were used by an airline of this name in Apr49, all going to Robinson Airlines almost immediately.

N15590; N16018; N21749 and N25671.

Consolidated Air Transit Inc, Teterboro, NJ, operated four DC-3s on charters until Sep48 but only two are known.

NC36699; NC79057.

Consumers Air Freight Corp, Champaign, IL, earlier known as **Allied Air Carrier Corp**, operated DC-3 NC18638 on charter services in 1946/47.

Continental Air Lines Inc, Denver, CO, introduced DC-3s on scheduled services in 1945 retaining them until **Continental Air Services Inc** was formed in Sep65 as a wholly owned subsidiary, see below and also under Bird & Sons.

N15564; N15565; N16061; N16065; N16067; N16068; N16069; N16070; N16089; N18112; N18940; N18945; N19932; N25679; N25682; N33315; N44883; N45367; N45370; N61350; N61351; N61442; N61450; N61451; N64422; N67674; NC73726; NC73727; N86587; N86588; N86598; N620Z.

Continental Air Services Inc (CASI), Reno, NV, was formed in April 1965 as a wholly-owned subsidiary of Continental Air Lines Inc to operate aircraft and ground facilities in support of oil exploration, construction and engineering projects, USAID and other US Government agencies. In Aug65 the company took over much of the aviation division of Bird & Sons (qv) which was operating in Laos from a base in Vientiane. In 1966/7 CASI had five DC-3s in Viet Nam. Some C-47s were acquired from Bird & Sons and others were transferred from Continental.

B-933; N560/XW-PDE; N7302/XW-PFV; N13622/XW-PEE; N64422; N64910; N65385; N79971/XW-PDG; N719A; N7780C; N7781C; N4995E; N650K; N55L; N8744R; N620Z; XW-PFT.

Continental Charters Inc, Miami, FL, started operations on an irregular basis in 1947, when three DC-3s were reported in use, but only NC16083 has been identified. They ceased flying in Feb55.

Continental Sky-Van Inc, Oakland, CA, used three DC-3s to operate coast-to-coast cargo and passenger services in Aug46.

NC56968; NC56969; NC56970.

Cordova Airlines Inc, Anchorage, AK, started operating as Cordova Air Services with T-50s and smaller types. Two DC-3s were used in Alaska from Aug52 until about 1965.

N25669; N91314.

Corporate Express, Pontiac, MI, founded in 1983, operated ten DC-3s on freight services. By 1999 all had been sold.

N15MA; N56KS; N105CA; N302SF; N303SF; N514AC; N683LS; N8021Z; N9382; N68363.

Cryderman Air Services Inc, Pontiac, MI, used DC-3s on certificated charter operations to support DC-4s, from 1970 until about 1980. Some were leased out in later years.

N18105; N19454; N25666; N33654; N88794; N88874; N81B; N140D; N310K; N3MJ.

Crystal Shamrock Airlines, Minneapolis, MN, has operated DC-3s on charter flights since 1974. These were sold by 1988.

N12954; N38941.

Currey Air Transport Ltd, Oakland, CA, traded as **Trans Continental** until 1961, using DC-3 N74663 in 1955.

Davis Airways Inc, Boston, MA, used DC-3s NC57654 and NC88713 (re-regd NC56800) in 1946/47, for charter passenger and cargo work between the eastern states and Cuba.

Delta Air Lines Inc, Atlanta, GA, bought second-hand DC-2s in 1940, but sold them within the year to the British Purchasing Commission and replaced them with DC-3s. Further aircraft were bought in 1945 and in May53 Chicago & Southern's fleet was added. The last DC-3s were sold in 1963.

DC-2s:- NC14275; NC14921; NC14923; NC14924.
DC-3s:- NC12926; NC12927; NC12958; NC15748; NC15849; NC16055; NC17882; NC20750; NC20751; NC20752; NC25625; NC25626; NC25628; NC25656; NC28340 to NC28346 incl (but the first allocations of NC28345 to NC28347 were not delivered); (NC30045 to NC30047 ntu); NC30083; NC31538; NC33347; NC38938; NC39393; NC44881; NC49657; NC51359; NC57539; NC86553; NC88854; N1200M.

DHL Island Airways, Honolulu, HI, used DC-3s as well as larger cargo types retaining one in 1983.

N46496; N102BL; N103BL; N104RP.

Dodson International Air, Covington Mun, GA, have operated seven DC-3s since 1998. Four remained in 2000.

N2805J; N303SF; N308SF; N683LS; N4550J; N9382; N74589.

Eagle Air Freight Inc, Goleta, CA, operated DC-3s on cargo services between Dallas and Burbank from 1946 to 1948.

NC15558; NC57372; NC64722; NC79035; NC79042.

East Coast Flying Services Inc, Jacksonville, FL, operated DC-3s between 1961 and 1971 on charter services.

N1294; N91221; N50CE; N90Q.

Eastern Air Lines Inc, New York, NY, acquired DC-2s soon after EAL was formed as a division of North American Aviation on 17Apr34. The first was delivered at the end of September in the colours of General Air Lines, but by 15Dec the title Eastern Air Lines had been adopted. DC-3s followed in 1936 and while the DC-2s that survived were sold to the RAAF in Australia in Dec40, some DC-3s served through the war, others were diverted to the USAAF and many more were added from surplus stocks, continuing in service until 1953 when they were sold. A few more were acquired with Colonial, but these went early in 1957.

DC-2s:- NC13731 to 13740 incl; 13781; 13782; 14969; 14970.
DC-3s:- NC12945; NC12954; NC12978; NC15567; NC15570; NC15595 to NC15599 incl; NC15773; NC16070 to NC16072 incl; NC16081 to NC16083 incl; NC16094 to NC16096 incl; NC18120 to NC18124 incl; NC18196; NC18916; NC19134; NC19193; NC19963;

Chapter 4: Commercial Operators of the DC-3, C-47, R4D, Dakota and Li-2

NC19968 to NC19970 incl; NC21727 to NC21729 incl; NC21743 to NC21745 incl; NC21751; NC21758; NC21759; NC21795; NC21798; NC25646 to NC25648 incl; NC25650; NC25651; NC25656; NC28323; NC28345; NC28381 to NC28385 incl; NC28391 to NC28394 incl; (NC30029 to NC30039 ntu); (NC33630 ntu); NC33631; NC33632; NC33633; NC33634; (NC33635 to NC33639 ntu); NC33643; NC44792; NC45331; NC45332; NC45369; NC45381; NC54406; NC86562; NC86569; NC86584; NC86597; NC88808; NC88809; NC88871; NC88872.

Eastern Express - see under Provincetown-Boston Airline.

Economy Airways Inc, Newark, NJ, used one DC-3 in association with Economy Air Coach Inc.

Edde Airlines, Salt Lake City, UT, was formed in 1960 to operate non-scheduled services with DC-3s between 1962 and 1965.

N485; N498.

Empire Air Lines Inc, Boise, ID, was formed as Zimmerly Air Lines in Apr44. Empire was incorporated in 1946 and DC-3s were acquired. Operations were taken over by West Coast Air Lines in Aug52.

N62373 to N62376 incl, plus one other.

Empire Airlines, Fort Lauderdale, FL, used two DC-3s during the early seventies on charter work.

N18196; N22Z.

ERA Helicopters/Jet Alaska, Anchorage, AK, added a DC-3 N394CA to the fleet in 1994, and N1944H in 1995. N394CA became N1944M. They are used for tourist flights in Alaska.

Evergreen International Airlines, Marana, AZ and Missoula, MT, acquired Johnson Flying Services' certificate on 28Nov75 and with it, four DC-3s. These were used in support of fire-fighting work, but all had been withdrawn for sale by 1979. DC-3 N16070 is with Evergreen Helicopters for their museum in UAL colours.

N24320; N91378; N91379; N74Z.

Executive Air Transport Inc, St Louis, MO, used DC-3s on intra-state services between 1945 and early 1947. There seems to be some connection between this and the next operator as the first nine aircraft listed here were registered to Executive Transport Corp.

NC75408; NC75411; NC75412; NC75413; NC88788; NC88789; NC88790; NC88791; NC88794. NC28346 has also been quoted, but was registered in 1959-61.

Executive Transport Corp, Grand Prairie & Dallas, TX. operated DC-3s in 1946/47. Some were only overhauled for resale.

NC47755; NC47762; NC47763; NC62567; NC65134; NC65135; NC65136; NC65276; NC65278; NC65282; NC65283; NC65284; NC65357; NC65358; NC65384; NC65385; NC65388; NC65389; NC65390; NC75404; NC75405; NC75406; NC75407; NC75408; NC75409; NC75410; NC75411; NC75412; NC75413; NC88783; NC88788 to NC88791; NC88794; NC4425N.

Express Airways, Sanford, FL, sold N889P and leased out N3749Q. N688EA has also been used for cargo work. HI-502 was stored at Sanford for spares in 1989-93. Operations ceased in 1998.

Fairbanks Air Services, Fairbanks, AK, used DC-3s N46496 and N345A in Alaska, circa 1972-74.

Fairways Corp., Washington, DC, operated two DC-3s on charter work between 1953 and 1966.

N7654; N66W.

Falcon Airways Inc, Addison, TX, operated all-cargo services in mid-western and southern states from 1976 until bankruptcy intervened in early 1980.

N83FA; N85FA; N86FA; N87FA; N88FA; N355MJ (some also operated in earlier marks).

Federal Express Corp, Memphis, TN, leased DC-3s during 1976 for carriage of items larger than the Falcons could hold. They were replaced by Boeing 727s.

N19721; N6CA; N130D; N30FE. N47FJ was used in 1987.

Federated Air Lines Inc, New York, NY, used DC-3 NC25612 at one time for passenger charters.

Fireball Air Express, Long Beach, CA, was formed on 17Dec45 with DC-3 NC55297. It was renamed **Standard** in 1946.

Flamenco Airways, Culebra, PR, started using DC-3s in 1990, but the last was sold in 1999.

N2647; N68363; N37AP; N31MC.

Flamingo Air Services Inc, Teterboro, NJ, started cargo operations in 1946 and DC-3s were used until Jan49, when activities ceased.

NC54331 to NC54336 incl.

Fleetwood Airlines, Brownsville, TX was using DC-3 N25612 in 1955. It is unknown if it was connected with the Fleetwood A/w below.

Fleetwood Airways Inc, Westaco, TX, used DC-3s NC48130, NC48131 and NC48132 between 1946 and 1948.

Flightways Corp, Philadelphia, PA, used DC-3s N87651 and N87652 briefly around 1975/76.

Flite Services Inc, Panama City Beach, FL, operated N99FS from Sep87 until its sale in Mar89.

Florida Air Cargo, Opa Locka, FL, have been reported as using DC-3s N15MA and N123DZ from 1996/97. N130D was acquired in 2001. The similarly named **Florida Air Cargo Transfer**, Miami Springs, used N666DG in 1984/85.

Florida Air Lines Inc, Sarasota, FL, started operations as Florida Air Taxi, but it later bought DC-3s to start third level services and the new name was adopted in 1968. **Air South** and **Shawnee** were taken over in 1975 and for a while joint titles were used. The schedules were suspended on 11Jan80.

N6102; N8701; N19919; N21768; N28364; N33656; N77B; N79B; N149D; N4996E; N86U; N341W.

Florida Air Transport, Ft Lauderdale, FL, included C-117D N9663N in their cargo fleet but it was stored in 1999.

Florida Airways International used a single DC-3, N21712, probably on lease, in 1974.

Florida Commuter Airlines, Palm Beach International, FL (formerly **Red Baron Air**) lost DC-3 N75KW near Freeport, Bahamas on 12Sep80, on a charter flight. They were operating N76KW in 1982.

Florida Express - see Provincetown-Boston Airline.

Florida Fresh Air Express, Lakeland, FL, used DC-3s in 1946-47 for cargo work.

NC34099; NC47056; NC47057; NC50486; NC54438.

Florida National Airways, Ft Lauderdale, FL, operated DC-3s on charter work from 1974 to 1977.

N40FN/N6510; N42FN/N520TT; N48FN/N950FA; N49FN/N88752; N8661.

Flying Tiger Lines, Los Angeles, CA, started work as **National Skyways Freight Corp**, using Budd RB-1s in Jun45. These gave way first to DC-3s in 1946, when the above name was adopted, and then to the larger DC-4. The DC-3s were all sold by 1948, some in India. It has not proved possible to separate NSF from FTL ownership in every case and some NSF DC-3s may have served briefly with FTL.

NC17193; NC18927; NC19949; NC36802; NC58122; NC59277; NC59278; NC59279; NC59699; NC63164; NC63363; NC63364; NC64737.

Four Star Air Cargo, St Thomas, VI, bought their first DC-3s for cargo work in 1986 and four were in use by 1987. Most were re-registered in 1988 and six continued flying into 2003 operating as **Four Star Aviation**.

N67PA/N131FS; N333EF/N132FS; N53NA/133FS; N833M/N134FS; N63107/N135FS; N58296/N136FS; N303SF/N138FS; N29958/N139FS; N101AP; N57NA;

Freight Air Inc, Miami, FL, started charter work, passenger and cargo, with DC-3 NC51879 in Jul49, ending in May50.

Fromhagen Aviation, St Petersburg/Clearwater, FL used DC-3 N95C between at least 1978 and 1992.

Frontier Airlines Inc, Denver, CO, was formed in Jun50 by the merger of **Monarch** and **Arizona Airways**, both DC-3 users. DC-3s remained in use until Convair 340s were bought in 1961, and were not retired finally until 1968. In Oct67 further DC-3s were bought with **Central Airlines**, but were sold off rapidly.

N15563; N15584; N15837; N17397; N18939; N19193; N19937; N39544; N49541; N53376; N57985; N61442; N64421 to N64424 incl; N64910; N65135; N65276; N65385; N66610; N75028; N75430; N86596; N4990E to N4998E incl; N285SE to N287SE incl; N4946V. In addition, N75276; N75277; N88790; N88794; N91003 and N7820B were registered only to Central.

Frontier Flying Service, Fairbanks, AK, used a single DC-3, N59314, on charter work in the late 1970s. It remained in use in 2000 but has since been retired. N8042X has also been reported. This ditched in June89 so is presumably only for spares use. Similarly N99663 was w/o in Oct79.

Frontier Pacific Airlines operated DC-3 N33644 in 1979.

Gallagher Brothers, Drexel Hill, PA, operated a DC-3 on charter work in association with Bar Harbour Airways Inc, just post-war.

Genavco Air Cargo, Honolulu, HI were using DC-3s N65388 and N99131 in the early 1990s.

General Air Cargo Inc, Portland, OR, started passenger and freight charters in 1947. The name was changed to **General Airways** and operated until 1962.

NC4112; NC17314; NC41455; NC41748; NC47573.

General Air Lines, New York, NY, was formed by Eastern Air Transport in 1934, but became **Eastern Air Lines** in December of that year. Meanwhile four DC-2s were painted in General's colours.

NC13731 to NC13734 incl.

Gilley Airways Corp, Glen Falls, NY, started operating scheduled cargo services in about 1973 but ceased after a year or so.

N894A; N91GA; N92GA.

Glade Air, Ft Lauderdale, bought DC-3 N86U in May85 but it was sold in 1988.

Global Airways Inc, Vineland, NJ, used DC-3 NC53196 in 1946/47.

Globe Freight Airlines Inc, Hartford, CT, used DC-3 NC60331 on cargo charters in 1947 but sold it to Coastal Airlines.

Golden Gate Airways, Vallejo, CA, used DC-3 N63250 on intra-state services until Nov61.

Golden Isles Air Inc, Ft Lauderdale, FL, bought DC-3 N47GW in Apr80 and later used N47WG/N47CR in 1982-87.

Golden North Airways, Fairbanks, AK, owned DC-3 NC79077 in 1946/47.

Golden State Airlines Inc, Burbank, CA, operated DC-3 N33644 from 1972 until about 1979.

Great Circle Airways Inc, New Orleans, LA, used three DC-3s for freight work in 1946.

Great Lakes Airlines Inc, Burbank, CA, began operations in Apr46 and by 1948 two DC-3s were in use on charter work in association with Currey Air Transport, but aircraft were held in the name of Nevada Aero Trades and have not been identified.

Great Southern Airways, Atlanta, GA utilized DC-3s N4550J and N308SF for freight work in the early 1990s, probably leased from Dodson International.

Greek Railway Express, New York, NY, operated two DC-3s in 1947, NC60882 and NC60883

Gulf Air Taxi, Yakutat, AK, owned DC-3 N8064A from Jun87 until Mar88, when it was sold.

Gulf & Western Airlines Inc, Houston, TX, used a DC-3 on irregular charters until Sep48.

Hammond Forner Air Service, Jackson, MI, used DC-3 NC61990, in 1946-47.

Hankins Air Service - see Jim Hankins.

Harolds Air Service, Galena, AK, bought DC-3 N300TX in 1984. It was the first Turbo Express DC-3 later taken over by Basler. N8059P was also reported but probably never in service. Harolds was renamed **Friendship Air Alaska** on 04Oct86 and the DC-3s were returned to Baslers in Aug88.

Harrington's Inc, Cleveland, OH, used two DC-3s on passenger charter until 1949.

NC29086 plus one.

Havenstrite Aircraft Inc, Los Angeles, CA, used a single DC-3 N63250 on non-scheduled interstate passenger services.

Hawaiian Airlines Ltd, Honolulu, HI, bought its first DC-3 new in Aug41, adding more aircraft from surplus stocks post-war. They remained in use until replaced by Convairs and sold in Nov68.

N13437; N15576; N17883(lsd); N33606 to N33608 incl; N33649; N62044 to N62046 incl; N67872; N67873; N86598; N95469.

Hawkeye Airlines, Ottumwa, IA, operated DC-3s on third level services to Sioux City from 1974 to 1976.

N51071; N101KC.

Hawkins and Powers Aviation, Greybull, WY, owned four C-117Ds between Jan83 and Jun86, when all had been sold.

N2121U; N2123Y; N21270; N4504W.

Hawthorne Nevada Airlines, Hawthorne, NV, operated DC-3s as **Mineral County Airlines**, a name that was later incorporated. It became **Air Nevada** in 1969.

N15570; N33639; N61350.

Hemisphere Air Transport, New York, NY, operated a DC-3 on irregular charters under the ownership of J F Adelman, forming part of the "North American" group.

Hiawatha Airways Inc, Winona, MN, used DC-3 NC63800 in 1946/47.

HoganAir, Hamilton, OH, started a fleet of DC-3s for cargo work in 1984. It was re-named **Miami Valley Aviation** in 1988, qv.

N69HA/N79HA; N81HA/N8187E; N88HA; N89HA; N90HA/N907Z; N92HA; N93HA/ N932H; N98HA/N982Z; N13AT/N99HA/N9923S; N36AP.

Hoosier Air Freight, New York, NY, operated DC-3s until 1946 when it became Airborne Cargo Lines Inc.

NC45393; NC46484; NC46496; NC54325; NC54337; NC54453; NC54454; NC54555; NC57539; NC57626.

Horizon Air used DC-3 N401JB in 1979. The airline was renamed **Kahila A/L**.

Inland Air Lines, Los Angeles, CA, was taken over by **Western Air Lines** in 1943, but continued to operate separately with DC-3 NC15569, bought in 1945. It later flew in Western colours.

CHAPTER 4: COMMERCIAL OPERATORS OF THE DC-3, C-47, R4D, DAKOTA AND LI-2

Inter-Coastal Airways, Detroit-Willow Run, MI, used two C-117Ds from Sep84 until their sale in 1989.

N873SN; N973SN.

Intercontinental Air Transport Co Inc, Miami, FL. Three DC-3s were used in 1946. Owner was W A Stonnell.

NC42022; NC54090; NC88873.

Interior Airways Inc, Fairbanks, AK, originally traded as Interior Enterprises, and used three DC-3s between 1958 and the early seventies.

N46496; N75391; N95460.

Intermountain Aviation Inc, Marana, AZ, flew two DC-3s on a contract basis between 1964 and 1968.

N404D; N404U.

International Air Freight Inc, W Palm Beach, FL, used DC-3s during the late forties on irregular cargo services.

NC52710; NC54450; NC54451; NC54455; NC54551.

International Airlines - See Trans-Luxury.

International Airports Inc, Burbank, CA, used both C-46s and DC-3s (incl unidentified N4909V) on charter work, probably as a leasing concern.

International Air Service, Rochester, NY, used DC-3 NC60256 in 1946/47.

Interstate Airmotive Inc, St Louis, MO, owned DC-3s for charter services between 1968 and 1972.

N25695; N28346; N33678; N561R.

Interstate Air Services Corp, Santurce, PR, operated six DC-3s on charter flights between 1968 and 1977. One remained in 1982.

N21787; N28323; N34970; N65389; N79044; N8011E.

Island Air Ferries, Bohemia, NY, used three DC-3s between 1947 and 1951, N15583; N15592 and NC52630.

Island Airlines, Nantucket, ME, operated one DC-3, N92578, in 1992.

Island Airlines Hawaii, Honolulu, HI, formerly Air Cargo Hawaii, operated DC-3s N8064A and N96H in the late 1970s and early 1980s, presumably leased from Kahila and/or Trans National.

Island Air Transfer, Honolulu, HI, used DC-3 N99131 on all-cargo services from 1972 until about 1977, when it had become derelict.

Island Traders, San Juan, PR, used DC-3s N692A, N86596 and N87629 during 1979/80.

Jefferson State Airlines Inc, Klamath Falls, OR, used two DC-3s on charter work from 1972 to 1974.

N44998; N1213M.

Jersey Shore Air Freight, Wayside, NJ, used DC-3 N56990 between 1973 and 1974.

Jim Hankins Air Services Inc, Jackson, MS, operated DC-3s on scheduled mail and cargo services from 1970, but only one remained in 1983, and that was sold by 1987. It also operated as **Hankins Airways**. A number of DC-3s were leased to Air Freight Inc.

N17779N18122; N45338; N45366; N50321; N57131; N61722 to N61725 incl; N88874; N91314; N8061A; N3BA; N143D; N625E; N4996E; N842MB; N845MB; N1213M; N447RS.

Jimsair Aviation Services, San Diego, CA, used DC-3 N403JB from May to Aug80.

JLR Air Transport Inc, Brownsville, TX, also known as **SCS Air Transport**, was using DC-3s N1346, N14636; N16625; N6903; N69033/N60705; N101CA and N103CA in the early 1980s for freight carrying.

Johnson Flying Services Inc, Missoula, MT, used several DC-3s and a DC-2 to drop parachutists for fire-fighting work and on supplemental services from 1946 until the operation was taken over by Evergreen Helicopters in 1975.

DC-2:- N4867V; *DC-3s:-* N24320; N49466; N91378; N91379.

Kahila Airlines, Honolulu, HI, began life as **Horizon Air** in 1978, changing its name late in 1979. It was also known as **Trans National Airlines**, qv and later as **Swift Delivery Air Freight** by 1981. Operations ceased in 1983.

N8064A; N102BL; N96H; N401JB.

Kansas City Southern Skyways Inc, Kansas City, MO, used DC-3s on non-scheduled cargo services until 1949.

NC17140; NC15836; NC34999; NC58022; NC58024.

Key West Airlines, Boca Raton, FL, acquired DC-3 N700RC in Jul80, selling it in Mar88.

K & K Aircraft, Bridgewater, VA, use several DC-3s for spraying and cargo work in the early 1990s.

N2401; N47E/N7043N; N177H/N17334; N56KS; N307SF/N321L.

Kwin Aircraft Corp, Fort Lauderdale, FL, used DC-3s on third level services between 1973 and 1980, to the Bahamas.

N44993; N94486; N22KN; N9012/N55KN; N33MW.

Lake Central Airlines Inc, Indianapolis, IN, used DC-3s to start operations in Nov49, when they took over **Turner Airlines** and some assets of Nationwide Air Transport Services. The airline was taken over, in turn, by Allegheny in Jul68 and the last DC-3s sold.

N14967; N15573; N16065; N18667; N21711; N21712; N21713; N21714; N21715; N21716; N21777; N21914; N25670; N25672; N30087; N33312; N33326; N34950; N41831; N44998; N45335; N57131; N61351; N65134; N65136; N86551.

Lake Wales Air Services, Lake Wales, FL, had DC-3s N1021G and N341W. By 1987 it was only an aircraft rental concern.

LAPSA Inc, San Juan, PR, DC-3 N102AP was operated by Victoria Air when it crashed in 1991.

Legend Airways, Nashua, NH started operating DC-3 N25641 in about 1992. By 2001 it operated as **Legend Airways of Colorado**, out of Denver, CO, still with N25641 and N341A.

Legion Express, Opa-Locka, FL have been reported operating DC-3s, N2025A and N4797H.

Lone Star Cargo Lines, operated DC-3s briefly in 1946/47.

NC50037; NC50322; NC54228; NC79022; NC79026; NC79029.

Los Angeles Air Services Inc - LAAS, Burbank, CA, used DC-3s on charter work from 1948 until about 1954. Original owners seem to have been James W Porter and Lee C Taylor. It was sold to Kirk Kerkorian and Rose Pechulis, but later Kerkorian was sole owner.

N15559; N15589; N17318; N17319; N17397; N19925; N19941; N28393; N30022; N39572; N41441; N49542; N53011; N4618V.

Lynbird International, Fort Lauderdale, FL bought two DC-3s by 1985 and sold them by Oct87.

N124SF; N37FL/(N125SF).

Mackey Airlines Inc, Fort Lauderdale, FL, operated DC-3s on scheduled services to the Bahamas from 1953 until 1964.

N25648; N25651; N28392; N37469; N86584.

Magic Carpet Transport Co, Kansas City & Blue Springs, MO. DC-3 NC50788/NC61067 was used in 1946/47.

Maine Air Cargo Express Inc, Owls Head, ME, used DC-3 NC54080 on charter work in the late forties.

Maine Air Transport Co Inc, Rockland, ME, used a single DC-3 on charter work until Sep48.

The Maine Sea Food Airlines, Bath, ME. Operated DC-3 NC18776 in 1946-47.

Majestic Airlines, Salt Lake City, UT, used DC-3s N19454; N305SF, and N67588 on cargo charters, from 1988 to 2001 on. N19906 was probably leased. By 2001 it had moved to Anchorage, AK, as **Majestic Air Cargo**, still operating N67588 and N305SF in 2002.

Mannion Air Charter, Detroit, MI, used four DC-3s for charter work from 1972 until their sale in Jun82 and earlier owned N88790.

N12MA to N15MA incl.

Marian Air Service Inc, Savannah, GA, used four DC-3s for anti-mosquito spray work from at least the late seventies. Their last DC-3 was sold in Aug87.

N31MS to N34MS incl.

Massachusetts Air Industries (E Anthony & Sons Inc), New Bedford, MA, used a single DC-3, N54099, to operate third level services prior to 1952.

May Air X-Press, Dallas, TX, includes DC-3s N116SA and N25646 in their cargo fleet.

McFerrin Air Express Inc, St Louis, MO, started freight work in March 1946 using DC-3 NC52709 and a Lodestar.

McNeely Charter Services Inc, Memphis, TN, had three DC-3 freighters, two of which remained in 2001. N24320, N5831B and N59316, regd since 1993.

Mercer Enterprises and **Mercer Airlines**, Long Beach and Burbank, CA, originated as Airplane Charter by Mercer Inc operating charter services; bought DC-2 N39165 in 1954. DC-3s were used during the 1960s and 70s, the company name changing to **Pacific American Airlines** c.1977.

N16096; N18620; N31538; N86584; N95453; N7500A.

Mercury Airlines Inc, Ft Worth, TX, had a fleet of four DC-3s in 1946/47.

NC62373; NC62374; NC62375; NC62376.

Meridian Air Cargo Inc, Memphis, TN / Meridian, MI, started freight services as **Key Brothers Flying Service** in Apr74, using DC-3s under contract to Emery Air Freight, amongst others. Operations are believed to have ceased in 1979.

N56990; N721A; N3433E; N3433H; N1213M; N3433U; N744V; N3433Y.

Meteor Air Transport Inc, Teterboro, NJ, was formed in 1946 to operate cargo services. The last DC-3s were sold in 1955, but C-46s remained in use.

N53593; N53594; N53596; N54337; N1433V; N1549V.

Methow Aviation, Wenatchee, WA, owned a single DC-3 N91314 from 1985 to about 2000, equipped as a freighter.

Miami Airlines Inc, Greensboro, NC, operated DC-3s on charter work between 1946 and 1961. Owner was R W Duff.

N16096; N21798; N21919; N57667; N65743/N3935C/N5592A.

Miami Valley Aviation, Hamilton, OH, formerly **HoganAir** continued to use DC-3s from renaming in 1988 to at least 2003.

N36AP; N707BA; N8187E; N932H; N79HA; N9923S; N907Z; N982Z.

Michigan Central Airlines Inc, Flint, MI, used a DC-3 on scheduled and charter work within Michigan.

Mid-America Airlines, Tulsa, OK, started charter services as **Texoma Airways** in Jun67, but the airline was declared bankrupt in 1971. A different company with a similar name, **Mid America Air Transport Inc** of Chicago, earlier operated a DC-3 N129D.

N151D; N560R; N42V.

Mid-Continent Airlines Inc, Kansas City, MO, operated DC-3s from 1944 until the airline merged with Braniff on 15Aug52.

N15201; N17338; N17888; N18667; NC19918; N19928; N21914; N25670; N25672; N25685; N28508; N28679; N33312; N33326; N33327; N34950 to N34952 incl; N34971; N41831; N45335; N61350; N61351; N61451; N95453.

Midline Air Freight Inc, Elizabethtown, KY was operating DC-3 N683LS in 2003.

Midstate Air Services, Stuart, FL, operated DC-3 N87654 from Dec81. It was sold in 1985.

Midwest Air Freighters, Des Moines, IA, used DC-3s for cargo work between 1973 and 1977.

N18258; N395R.

Midwest Airways Inc, Cincinnati, OH, operated local services from Cleveland between 1969 and 1971, using DC-3s.

N30087; N33MW/N21914.

Midwest Aviation Inc, Janesville, WI, operated DC-3s on air taxi and scheduled services from 1966 until about 1970.

N344; N1346; N1348; N60705.

Mineral County Airlines - see Hawthorne Nevada Airlines.

Missionair, Orlando-Kissimee, FL, acquired and re-registered three DC-3s during the nineties but only N79MA was still active by 2003.

N21783/N217MA; N123BA/N213MA; N169LG/N79MA.

Missouri Airways Inc, St Louis, MO, used DC-3 NC15845 in 1947.

Modern Air Transport Inc, Newark, NJ, used C-46s to start operations in 1947 but after the airline was acquired by Gulf American Land Corp in 1965, a few DC-3s were added.

N25685; N28508; N33327; N34951; N34952; N62386; N1085M; N1093M.

Mohawk Airlines Inc, Utica, NY, was formed in Dec46 as **Robinson Airlines** to operate scheduled services with DC-3s. The name was changed to Mohawk in Aug52 and further DC-3s were added. They had given way to Convair 240s by 1963.

N15590/N407D; N15596/N408D; N16018/N400D; N18117/N401D; N18118/N402D; N18119/N403D; N21749/N404D; N25671/N405D; N25676/N406D; N28340/N409D; N33370/N410D.

Monarch Air Lines Inc, Denver, CO, was formed in 1946 and started scheduled services using DC-3s in November of that year. These continued until the airline merged with Challenger in Dec48 and with Arizona Airways in Apr50 to form Frontier.

N64421 to N64424 incl; N66610.

Montauk-Caribbean Airways, E.Hampton, NY, together with **Ocean Reef Airways**, Miami, FL, bought DC-3 N96H in 1983, selling it in 1984.

Mor-Fresh Air Express Inc, Council Bluffs, IA, used DC-3s NC64104 and NC64105 in 1947.

Mountainwest Aviation, Aspen, CO were using DC-3 N101ZG on charter work in 1977-78.

Mt McKinley Air Freight Inc, Anchorage, AK, used DC-3s NC49538 and NC74678 in 1946/47. NC57191 was ntu but was then used as NC91002.

Naples Airlines - See Provincetown-Boston Airlines.

National Air Cargo Corp, Los Angeles, LA used DC-3s NC13719; NC15559; NC63451 and NC90626 in 1946/47, for charter work.

National Air Express Co, Marshall, MO. operated two DC-3s, NC58022 and NC58024 in 1946/47 for charter work.

National Air Transport Co, Detroit, MI used DC-3s NC61989 and NC9562H in 1946/47.

National Air Transportation Service (NATS), Oakland, CA, used at least four DC-3s on charter work. NC38942 crashed in Oct46, and others were NC50788 (two acft), NC61067 and NC74589.

National Skyways Freight Corp, Los Angeles, CA, replaced their Budd RB-1s with DC-3s in 1946 and their name was changed to **Flying Tiger** towards the end of that year.

NC18927; NC58122; NC59277 to NC59279 incl; NC59699; NC62035; NC62570; NC63164; NC63351; NC63363; NC63364; NC64722; NC64737; NC64744; NC64747; NC88774.

Nationwide Airlines Inc, Detroit, MI, started DC-3 operations in 1947, merging with Lake Central in 1950.

NC51881; NC57131; N1075M.

Nationwide Air Transport Service Inc, Miami Springs, FL, used DC-3s for charter work between 1946 and 1951, in association with Nationwide Airlines. The assets were taken over by Resort in 1951 and the DC-3s disposed of. Three DC-3s have been identified, but three others were involved in accidents on 01May46, 01Jan47 and 15Aug48 (at Carmel, NJ). Four were said to be in use in the late forties, so some casualties may have been repaired.

NC50046; NC57131; NC60941.

Nenana Air Services, Fairbanks, AK, are reported to have used DC-3 N3FY in 1984.

Nevada Airlines Inc, Las Vegas, NV, operated scheduled services to the Grand Canyon and charter flights on demand, using at least three DC-3s. A number of others were bought from the Burmese Air Force in 1978, but never left the Far East. The airline was out of business in 1980.

N17332; N138D; N139D/N110SU; N163E; N101SF; N711TD; N2270M; N2270N; N2270W; N2270Z; N2271B; N2271C; N2271D; N2271F; N139HH.

New England Air Express Inc, Teterboro, NJ, started charter operations primarily to and from Alaska, in 1947. DC-3 NC58121 was used to support C-46s.

New Mexico Flying Service, Albuquerque, NM, founded in 1983, operated DC-3s N25646 and N403JB(2) on freight services in 1989-92.

Nord Aviation, Pembina, ND, carried freight in three DC-3s operating for Federal Express between 1979 and 2003 when one remained.

N102DH; N3784Y; N57626.

Norseman Air Transport Inc, New York, NY, incorporated in Nov45, leased DC-3 NC60326/NC58181.

North American Airlines, Miami, FL, formerly **Air Miami** (qv) operated two DC-3s during 1981-82 and leased N6102 from American Airways Charters during this period..

N6102; N889P; N3XW.

North American Skyliners, Long Beach, CA, used DC-3 NC67234 in 1946/47.

North Cay Airways Inc, San Juan, PR, was formed in 1970 as **Air Indies Corp,** to operate third-level services. It became a subsidiary of Airways Enterprises Inc in 1973, but operations ceased in 1976.

N4795; N5925; N16060; N39544; N86596; N87628; N87629; N91314; N69B; N285SE; N286SE.

North Central Airlines Inc, Minneapolis, MN, was formed as **Wisconsin Central** in 1948, adopting the new name on 16Dec52, by which time the fleet was all DC-3. The last of these was sold at the end of 1968, though N21728, with 83,454 flying hours, was preserved.

N817; N1945; N2400; N2401; N5649; N12954; N12978; N14931; N15598; N15748; N15773; N17312; N17318; N17320; N18196; N18949; N21728; N21729; N25648; N25651; N26214; N28341; N28381; N28385; N33347; N33632; N33633; N38941; N38943; N44997; N86553; N88854; N88C; N408D.

Northeast Airlines Inc, Boston, MA, used DC-2s briefly in 1942 and bought DC-3s in the same year. The DC-2s were later fitted with DC-3 outer wing panels. The DC-3s and further aircraft bought or leased post-war continued in use until 1967, though partly replaced by Convair 240s.

DC-2s:- NC13717; NC13720; NC13783; NC13784; NC13787.
DC-3s:- N14967; N16060; N18941; N18953; N19428; N17891; N19942; N25612; N28323; N28324; N30087; N33621; N33622; N33623; N34417; N45362; N45388; N44992; N44997; N44998; N65134; N65136; N65282; N65384; N65390; N86558.

Northern Air Cargo, Anchorage, AK, used DC-3s N19906 and N75142 for cargo work in 1976, and N9382 in 1982. The last was sold in 1987.

Northern Airlines Inc, Seattle, WA, owned DC-3 NC16839 and NC54312 in May46.

Northern Airways, Burlington, VT, used seven DC-3s from 1984 taken over by Business Airways on 28Jul86.

N53NA; N54NA; N56NA; N57NA; N58NA; N59NA; N400RS.

Northern Consolidated Airlines, Anchorage, AK, flew DC-3s on some scheduled services from 1947 until the airline was taken over by Wien in Mar68.

N21748; N75142; N95460; N4766C.

Northern Pacific Transport, Anchorage, AK, acquired DC-3 N68363 in May83, selling it in Mar85.

Northland Air Cargo Inc, Anchorage, AK, owned NC91053 in 1946/47.

Northwest Airlines Inc, St Paul, MN, first bought DC-3s in Mar39 to replace their Lockheed 14s. Services continued throughout the war under contract to the USAAF. The DC-3s were supplemented by DC-4s, but the last was not sold until 1958.

N12935; N13437; N14236; N17397; N19925; N19928; N21711 to N21716 incl; N21777; N25608 to N25610 incl; N25621 to N25623 incl; N28679; N33324 to N33327 incl; N33329; N33331; N33332; N33334; NC39340; N39544; N45333; N59409; N70003; N79055; N79056.

Old South Air Services, Isla Verde, PR, traded as **Air Caribbean** from 1978 (qv).

Onyx Aviation Inc, Oklahoma City, OK, used DC-3 N86553 for charter work until 2000.

Ortner Air Service, Wakeman, OH, used DC-3 N144A for charter work between 1964 and 1974.

Overseas Airways, Ft Lauderdale, FL, operated DC-3 N401D on charters between Jul74 and 1976. Reports suggest that this company was originally named Haiti Overseas.

Ozark Air Lines Inc, St Louis, MO, used DC-3s to inaugurate scheduled services on 26Sep50. They remained in use until replaced by F.27s and FH-227Bs in 1968. The DC-3s were re-registered as below, sometimes well after acquisition.

N128D to N151D incl; N163J to N166J incl; N52V. Additionally, N1399N was briefly leased in 1960.

Pacific Air Cargo Inc, San Bruno, CA, used DC-3 N41447 for cargo charters between 1970 and 1972.

Pacific Airlines Inc, Los Angeles, CA, used DC-3 NC18775 in 1946-47. The company was originally entitled Pacific Coast Airlines Inc.

Pacific Air Lines Inc, San Francisco, CA, started operations as **Southwest Airways Co** in 1946, but changed name in Mar58. DC-3s were used until about 1964, when Martin 202s and 404s had replaced them.

N15570; NC50474; N54369; N54370; N63104 to N63107 incl; N63440; NC66634; N67588; N67589; N6678C.

Pacific Alaska Air Express Inc, Anchorage, AK, used DC-3 NC66637 on non-scheduled services during 1946. It crashed in May48, but was not listed in 1947 register.

Pacific Alaska Airlines, Fairbanks, AK, was started by Don Gilbertson as **Aero Retardant Inc**, for aerial fire fighting. The name Pacific Alaska was adopted in 1972 and the DC-3s had all been sold by 1976.

N19971; N21748/N666DG; N91314; N777DG; N364K.

Pacific American Airlines, Burbank, CA, started life as **Mercer** but only two DC-3s, N16096 and N7500A, remained in use when the new name was adopted. Operations ceased in 1978.

Pacific Coast Airlines, Los Angeles, CA, started cargo charters around 1972/73 but the DC-3s were later sold.

N50CE; N5647V.

Pacific National Air Express, Santa Monica, CA, used several DC-3s in 1946/47.

NC38944; NC53219; NC53225; NC54330; NC56990; NC79037; NC79989; NC90626.

Pacific National Airways, Burbank, CA, were reported to be operating DC-3s during 1980, but operations were suspended in 1981.

N138D; N139D; N163E; N74KW.

Pacific Northern Airlines, Seattle, WA, used DC-3s at various times between 1946 and 1967 when the airline was taken over by Western. They were used on scheduled services and charter work in Alaska.

NC33676; NC34970; NC37465; NC37469; NC37470; N49277; N49319.

Pacific Northern Airlines, Portland, OR, operated third-level services using two DC-3s in 1973/74.

N998Z; N999Z.

Pacific Southwest Airlines Inc, San Diego, CA, had various DC-3s, some on lease, when they started local scheduled services in May49 in California. They were replaced by DC-4s in 1955.

N14959; N17085; N17186; N17333; N25644; N49840; N60256; N95487.

Page Airways Inc, Rochester, NY, started DC-3 scheduled services soon after the war, but in 1946 only charter work was undertaken. This continued until about 1970. The early aircraft are unknown, but later DC-3s were N15773; N12978; N25641; N45363; N54334; N611CB and N711SE.

Pan American Airways Inc, New York, NY, was a major user of both the DC-2 and the DC-3 before WW2. The first DC-2s were bought in 1934 but none remained by 1941. Some had gone to subsidiaries such as China National, Panair do Brasil and Mexicana, while others were sold to the RAF. In all 18 were owned. DC-3s were ordered in 1937 and more were bought surplus post-war. Some of those used during the war saw service in Africa with PAA-Africa and others were operated for the USAAF in that area, on ferry operations. The final additions were two DC-3s taken over with American Overseas in 1950.

DC-2s:- NC13723; NC13729; NC14268 to NC14273 incl; NC14290 to NC14292 incl; NC14295 to NC14297 incl; NC14950; NC14978; NC16049; NC30076.
DC-3s:- NC14283(2); NC15568; NC15582; NC17316; NC18109; NC18113 to NC18117 incl; NC18646; NC18937; NC19118; NC19912; NC19914; NC19916; NC19948; NC19949; NC21717; NC21902; NC22429; NC22434; NC25641 to NC25645 incl; NC25653 to NC25657 incl; N25686; NC28301 to NC28308 incl; NC30010 to NC30012 incl; NC30089; NC30093 to NC30097 incl; NC33320 to NC33322 incl; NC33370 to NC33374 incl; NC33609 to NC33614 incl; NC34925; NC34947; NC34948; (NC34949 to NC34962, not del); NC36802; NC36803; NC44786; NC45375; NC45396; NC49549; NC49552; NC50616 to NC50618 incl; NC50625; NC51182; NC51183; NC51657; NC54227; NC54310; NC54705; NC54726; NC54727; NC54728; NC54731; NC59299; NC59410; NC60002; NC60003; NC67902; NC79001 to NC79011 incl; NC88731; NC88732; NC88773; NC88877; N90908; N9947F.

Notes:-

PAA also operated the following known C-47s on behalf of the USAAF or US Navy in military marks:

41-7757, -7810, -7827, -7829, -7831, -7834, -7835, -18362, -18371, -18398, -18399, -18677, -20088 to 20090, -20092, -38569, -38574, -38576, -38584; 43-2002, -15497, -15567; 44-77263, -77264, -77269, -77279, -77284, -77286, -77287; 45-887, -936, -938, -945, -946; USN 4692, 4704, 01649, 05058, 06955, 37660.

PAA-Africa - The following civil registrations are known, mostly used for delivery only by PAA crews to or via Africa, prior to application of military serials:

DC-2s:- NC13712; NC14280; NC14966; US.1 to US.3; US.8 to US.10.
DC-3s:- NC16082; NC16094; NC17313; NC18117 (used twice); NC21750; NC25623; NC33642; NC33653; NC33655; NC33675; NC34988; NC34989; NC34990.

The following C-47s are known to have been operated by PAA-Africa on delivery or on behalf of the USAAF:

41-7722, -7723, -7725 to 7730, -7738, -7739, -7754, -7756, - 7758 to 7760, -7796, -7798, -7831, -7864, -7865, -18400 to 18403, -20078 to 20081, -20084, -20085, -20099, -20101 to 20103, -20105, -20109 to 20111, -20113, -20115, -20117, -38564, -38566 to 38568, -38570, -38572, -38577, -38579, -38581 to 38583; 42-6455, -6457, -6458, -6462, -6467, -6470 to 6472, -6492, -6505, -14297, -14298, -47373, -47376, -47377.

Pan American-Grace Airways Inc ('Panagra'), New York, NY, used a large number of DC-2s and DC-3s on its routes in South America. Some of these came from Pan American, the first DC-2s being taken on in 1934 and the last scrapped in 1947. DC-3s followed in 1937 and some of these remained in use until 1960 when they were sold in Peru.

DC-2s:- NC13729; NC14268; NC14270; NC14272; NC14273; NC14292; NC14298.
DC-3s:- NC14967; NC14996; NC15583; NC18118; NC18119; NC18936; NC19364; NC19470; NC19912; NC19913; NC21718; NC25652; NC28334; NC28335; NC28380; NC30008; NC30014; NC30091; NC30092; NC33645; NC39334; NC49550; NC51657; NC54213; NC54311; NC86564; NC86565; NC88726; NC88754.

Parachute Air Cargo, Oakland, CA, owner John J Maggi, operated a DC-3 on cargo charters during 1946.

Paradise Airlines, Oakland, CA, was formed for charter work in 1963, but operations ceased in Mar64 when their Lockheed 049 crashed.

N63106; N63440.

Parks Air Lines bought a number of DC-3s in 1948 with the intention of starting scheduled services. This was not possible and all but one were sold soon after. One went to Ozark Airlines who in 1950 activated the routes that Parks had failed to start.

NC16009; NC25665; NC25670; NC25672; NC55115.

PBA - see Provincetown-Boston Airline.

Pearson-Alaska Inc, Anchorage, AK, used an unknown DC-3 for charter work.

Pegasus Air Freight Corp, Philadelphia, PA, had DC-3s NC51764 and NC58156.

Peninsular Air Transport, Miami Springs, FL, (H B Robinson) operated charter services on the East Coast in association with Associated Airlines Agency from 1946 until 1951, using three DC-3s.

NC18776; NC53416; NC53420.

CHAPTER 4: COMMERCIAL OPERATORS OF THE DC-3, C-47, R4D, DAKOTA AND LI-2 235

Pennsylvania-Central Airlines Corp, Washington, DC, bought its first DC-3s in 1939 and continued to fly scheduled services throughout the war. The name was changed to **Capital Airlines** in Apr48.

NC12919; NC18620; NC19915; NC19917; NC21781 to NC21790 incl; NC25689; NC25691; NC25692; NC25693; NC25694 (two aircraft); NC25695; NC25696 incl; (NC33675, NC33676, NC33679, NC33680, NC33682 ntu); NC33677; NC33678; NC44993; NC45338; NC45366; NC45373; NC45379; NC49553; NC53668; NC60705; NC65135; NC65276; NC65384; NC65385; NC86588; NC88834; NC88835.

Philips Flying Service Inc, Harbour Springs, MI, used a DC-3 to start commuter services in Sep64. This may have been leased, but has not been identified.

Piedmont Air Cargo, Gastonia, NC, started operating freight DC-3s in 1994, ex Bo-S-Aire.

N3BA; N19BA; N81B; N272R.

Piedmont Aviation Inc, Winston Salem, NC, started local airline services with DC-3s on 20Feb48, trading as **Piedmont Airlines**. The DC-3s were used until replaced by F.27s and Martin 404s in 1963. Those used before 1953 were flown in the markings used at purchase, but were placed in one block of numbers by 1953.

N40V to N58V incl (with N59V, N60V ntu), N3946A; N9519C; N8014E.

Pilgrim Airlines, New London, CT, had a Dart-powered Super DC-3 but it is uncertain if it was used on scheduled commuter services in Nov74 due to lack of certification. It became derelict after ground damage.

N156WC/N156PM.

Pinehurst Airlines Inc, Pinehurst, NC, was formed in 1973 for general charter work, using DC-3s. Commuter services were operated in N Carolina for a time. The DC-3s were finally replaced by YS-11s in Nov79.

N6896; N57131; N311A; N132D; N136D; N148D; N166E; N3433P; N52V.

Pioneer Air Lines Inc, Dallas, TX, bought DC-3s from the USAF to replace their Lockheed 10s on scheduled services. Operations started as **Essair**. The DC-3s were later replaced by Martin 202s and the DC-3s sold back to the Air Force, where they became C-117Cs. When the CAB forced Pioneer to sell its Martin 202s, ten DC-3s were leased mostly from Leeward Aero, all ex United/Continental.

N16061; N16065; N16067; N16068; N16070; N16089; N18112; N18940; N18945; N25679; NC47968; NC47995; NC47996; NC48132; NC53425; NC54357; NC54366; NC54729; NC55303; NC57902; NC62384; NC79021; NC95433.

Plains Airways operated Beech D18Ss on passenger flights out of Cheyenne, WY in 1946-48 but owned or dealt with DC-3s from 1949.

N17883; N25622; N25681; N33642.

Pompano Airways, Pompano Beach, FL, operated three DC-3s, two leased, from 1982 until bankruptcy intervened in Jun85.

N47WG; N165LG; N166LG.

Pro Airlines Inc, Rapid City, ND, operated scheduled mail and charter services with Beech 18s and DC-3s during 1975/76. Would appear to be linked to a Pro-Air in California which operated N17778 and N37AP.

N17778; N18196; N37AP; N403UB.

Pro-Air Services, Opa-Locka, FL, successor to the above, used DC-3s between Miami and Key West during 1979/81. Only N18196 remained in 1982 and operations ceased on 18Mar88.

N14931; N17778; N18196; N25670; N74KW; N76KW; N800RC; N403UB.

Pronto Air Services, El Paso, TX, bought N3433U in 1982 and is believed to have leased DC-3 N47FJ during 1984-87. The similarly-named **Pronto Aviation Services**, Las Cruces, NM had N102BL and N1213M in 1982.

Provincetown-Boston Airline/Naples Airlines, Provincetown, MA and Naples, FL, first bought DC-3s in Jan68 to replace their ageing Lockheed 10s on commuter services from Boston. Naples Airlines was the southern division using some of the aircraft when they were not required in Massachusetts during the winter months. All DC-3s were re-registered after purchase, two of them twice over. Twelve were in use in 1984. PBA filed for Chapter 11 in Mar85. Part of the operation was taken over by **People Express** in 1986. **Bar Harbor** took over this part of the latter's operation, but operations finally ceased on 06Sep88. For a while some DC-3s operated in **Eastern Express** and **Florida Express** colours, but the DC-3s were steadily sold.

N31PB/N21797; N32PB/N832PB/N34951; N33PB/N233PB/N233P/N34952; N34PB/N25658; N35PB/N25685; N38PB/N18141; N40PB/N21768; N43PB/N18105; N130PB/N30PB/N25673; N136PB/N18121; N137PB/N33327; N139PB/N25666.

Puerto Rico Air Transport, San Juan, PR DC-3 NC51894 was damaged in Jan47. NC51881; NC66001 and NC66016 were also used.

Purdue Aeronautics Corp, Lafayette, IN, used DC-3s primarily on pilot training, some were sold on quickly but from Dec61 some charter work was done. Name changed to **Purdue Airlines Inc** from 03Apr68 and the remaining aircraft were sold to Basler in 1971.

N3588; N12954; N12978; N18196; N28385; N33632; N33633; N44792/N792G; N45331/N331PA; N391N; N6899D/N386T; N387T.

Quaker City Airways Inc, Philadelphia, PA, used two DC-3s on charter services during the early fifties. See Admiral Airways.

N25612; N53460.

Rainbow Airlines Inc, New York, NY, owner B F Reinauer, had seven DC-3s in 1946. **Rainbow Airlines of Honolulu** operated NC95469 in 1947.

NC32624; NC32975; NC50264; NC50311; NC50312; NC50314; NC57672.

Rainier Air Freight Lines Inc, Seattle, WA, operated three DC-3s on charter work from Aug46 until 1948.

NC58775; NC58776; NC66637.

Rapid Air, Grand Rapids, MI, owned two DC-3s, N346AB and N707BA, but by 1999 they were stored.

RCR Air Transport Inc, Tavington, NY, used DC-3 NC50041 in 1946/47.

Reading Aviation Services, Reading, PA, operated DC-3s on scheduled services to Newark in 1958 and between 1968 and 1972.

N7772; N51D; N85K.

Red Baron Air, W Palm Beach, FL, operated local services with DC-3s in 1980. It was renamed **Florida Commuter Airlines** (qv).

Red Carpet Flying Services Inc, St Petersburg, FL, used DC-3s on charter work between 1973 and 1977. It was re-named **Aerosun International** on 15Nov81.

N600RC; N700RC; N800RC; N100SD; N72WL.

Reeve Aleutian Airways Inc, Anchorage, AK, owner Robt Reeve, operated charter services with DC-3s until 1948, when scheduled services were developed. The last DC-3 was sold in 1978.

N19906; N46567; N49319; N49363; N75142; N91016; N2768A.

Regina Cargo Airlines Inc, Miami, FL, started freight charters in Jun48 with DC-3s, but the operating certificate was revoked in 1950. It later reformed as **Regina Airlines/Imperial Airlines**.

NC15587; NC19941; N28392; NC36699.

Resort Airlines Inc, New York, NY, used several DC-3s probably leased from the RFC or WAA, to start charter services in 1945-46. The operations were based on New York, but moved to Oakland when C-46s were used to replace the DC-3s.

NC15573; NC18639; NC86551.

Rhoades Aviation, Columbus, IN, bought DC-3s to operate on behalf of Federal Express, starting on 10Apr89, from Houston to Dallas. One was a DC-3-65TP*. It later operated as **Rhoades International**. One remained in use in 2001, with two more stored.

N374AS; N376AS; N139JR; N140JR; N141JR; N142JR; N143JR; N145JR; N146JR*.

Rio Airways, Killeen, TX, used DC-3 N514X between 1977 and 1979 for third-level services.

Robinson Airlines Corp, Ithaca, NY, started life in Dec46 using a number of DC-3s on scheduled services. The name was changed to **Mohawk** in Aug52.

NC15590; NC15591; NC16018; NC17332; NC18118; NC18119; NC18936; NC21749; NC25671; NC25676; NC33370.

Roblex Aviation, San Juan, PR, operates cargo flights, using DC-3s N19BA and N50E.

Rockdale Flying Service, Rockdale, TX, used DC-3 N763A for charter work, from Jul68. It was sold in Jul84.

Royal Airlines Inc, Las Vegas, NV, had a single DC-3 in the early seventies for commuter services.

Royal Air Services, Salinas, CA, operated a DC-3 for charter work in 1948.

Royal West Airways, Las Vegas, NV, used two DC-3s during 1981/82.

N138D; N101KC.

Saber Cargo Airlines, Charlotte, NC, have operated DC-3s on cargo work since May84, initially as Saber Aviation. Four DC-3s remained operating as Saber Cargo Airlines until Dec03, when they were sold to First Flight Out.

N58NA; N115SA; N116SA; N12907; N74589; N79017.

Salair, Seattle, WA, used cargo DC-3s in the Washington area and Alaska from 1984 on. The fleet was to have been re-registered N350SA on, but this never took place. Services were operated for Emery Air Freight. All aircraft had been sold by 1996.

N19906; N44587; N75142; N2025A; N8061A; N707BA; N394CA; N2298C; N3FY; N3433Y; N145ZA.

Samoan Air Lines Inc, Hollywood, CA, began scheduled services between Apia and Pago Pago, Samoa, in Jul59 using DC-3 N33607. The aircraft was repossessed.

San Diego Sky Freight, San Diego, CA, used DC-3s NC67661 and NC90627 in 1946-48.

Santa Fe Skyway Inc, Wichita, KS, was formed by Santa Fe Railway on 04May46 to carry cargo. It used three DC-3s and some DC-4s, but operations ceased on 15Jan48.

NC57612; NC65278; NC66697.

Sea-Bear Air Transport, Togiak, AK, operated cargo flights using DC-3s. Both were sold in 1984.

N56KS; N3MJ.

Seaboard and Western Airlines Inc, New York, NY, used DC-3 N91221 on lease for European operations during 1959/60.

Seattle Air Charter Inc, Seattle, WA, began charter operations in 1947, using DC-3 NC79025. This crashed in Jan49. See also **Burke Air Transport** for which it was the trading name from 1949.

Sentimental Journey, Oakland, CA, later known as **Otis Spunkmeyer Air**, operated DC-3s N54595/N41HQ, N97H and N115NA during the 1990s.

Shamrock Airlines, Bethany, OK, used DC-3s on charter work between 1965 and 1969.

N14931; N18143; N18196.

Shawnee Airlines Inc, Orlando, FL, started scheduled commuter services in Jul68, introducing DC-3s in 1973. Control passed to **Air Florida** in 1975 and the DC-3s were replaced by Martin 404s in 1977. From Nov76 Shawnee operated "The Connection" using DC-3s, but most of these were withdrawn in 1978, association with Air Miami continuing until the following year.

N1301; N15584; N18111; N19919; N45338; N45366; N62101; N62102; N62103; N88854; N79B; N11BC/N3XW.

Shorter Airlines, Detroit, MI, started third-level services in 1968 and DC-3s were put into use in 1974/75 as required. They were leased, but all were withdrawn by 1976.

N14931; N15598; N18196; N25651.

Skyfreight Airlines Inc, Dallas, TX, used five DC-3s on transcontinental freight services in the late forties.

NC62384; NC62385; NC62386; NC62387; NC62388.

Skyfreight Airlines, Miami, FL, used DC-3s for cargo work from 1974, as trading name of Tropics International. Operations ceased around 1986.

N7868B; N4261P/N124SF; N341W.

Skyfreighters, Grand Prairie, TX, took over from **Coker Air Freight** their fleet of DC-3s, including two C-117Ds* in Aug84. All those remaining were re-registered in 1985. The DC-3s were gradually replaced by Convairs, and all had been sold by 1993.

N4BA/N305SF; N98BF/N308SF; N94CA/N302SF; N101CA/N301SF; N103CA/N303SF; N104CA; N58297/N307SF*; N8538R/N306SF*; N127SF* has also been reported, c/n unknown.

Skyline Inc, Coral Gables, FL, used DC-3s NC21935 and NC54206 in 1946/47.

Sky Train Air, McAllen, TX, bought DC-3s N498 and the short-lived N258M(2) in 1981. Another, N60705 was ntu.

Skyway Airlines, Ft Leonard Wood, MO, was the trading name for Skyway Aviation Inc, and used DC-3s N889P and N890P on commuter and charter flights between about 1974 and 1980. In later years Air Americana was the operating name.

SMB Stage Line, Des Moines, IA, was the operating name for Sedalia-Marshall-Boonville Stage Line, and operated an extensive network of mail services. DC-3s were introduced when commuter services started in 1974, but in 1979 Convair 600s were bought to replace all the DC-3s.

N9141; N41447; N62103; N100DW; N403D; N7CA; N200TA.

Sourdough Air Transport, Fairbanks, AK, used two DC-3s on charter work in the late forties. Only NC74663 is known.

South Central Air, Kenai, AK acquired DC-3 N12MA in 1981. It was cancelled in Oct84. N19454 was added later, and remained in use until 2000, when operations were suspended.

Southeast Airlines, Kingsport, TN, was operated by Southeastern Aviation Inc and used DC-3s to fly schedules in Tennessee from Nov56 until Aug60.

N25680/N285SE; N18938/N286SE; N18103/N287SE; N25682/N288SE; N289SE; N18941; N142A.

Southeast Airlines Inc, Miami, FL, operated DC-3s on scheduled services within Florida between 1968 and 1972.

N21712; N75028.

South East Airlines Inc, Charlotte, NC, operated DC-3 NC52818 in 1946/47.

Southern Air Express, Bartow, FL, used DC-3 NC36540 in 1946/47. Later another company of the same name at Boynton Beach, FL, used N625E from Dec77 to Jan79.

Southern Air Transport, Miami, FL, were using DC-3s N45860 and N59SC in 1982 on freight services.

Southern Airways Inc, Birmingham, AL, started scheduled services using DC-3s in Jun49. Many were re-registered. They were replaced by Martin 404s and DC-9s by late 1967.

N494 to N496 incl; N8820; N19193; N52818; N91232; N60SA to N71SA; N85SA to N96SA incl.

Southern Commercial Air Transport Inc, New Orleans, LA, used two DC-3s, NC54579 and NC79063 in 1946/47. They were leased to Skytrain Airways.

Southern Flyer, Hattiesburg, VA, operated DC-3s on charter work from 1979. They moved to Memphis, TN in Sep79, then to Lake Wales, FL and then operated freight out of San Juan, PR.

N37906; N45860; N134D; N310K; N59SC.

Southwest Airlines, Scottsdale, AZ, used DC-3 N88871 for charter work from Oct77 until 1979.

Southwest Airways Co, Beverly Hills, CA, began DC-3 operated scheduled services on 02Dec46. These continued until the name **Pacific Air Lines** was adopted on 06Mar58.

N15570; N54369; N54370; N63104 to N63107 incl; N63439; N63440; N67588 to N67590 incl.

Southwind Airlines, McAllen-Miller, TX, leased two DC-3s from Aviones Inc in 2000. They are N12BA and N514AC, still in operation 2005.

Southwind Aviation, Los Fresnos, TX, used four DC-3s at one time but all were sold by 1992.

N68363; N70003; N683LS; N890P.

SS Airways, Kansas City, MO, used DC-3 N211Q on mixed freight/passenger services in 1981-83.

S S W Inc, Oakland, CA, known also as "Supair" or "The Original Skycoach" used an unknown DC-3 to supplement C-46s on charter work.

Standard Air Cargo, San Diego, CA, started cargo operations in Apr46, using two DC-3s, NC17085 and NC38939.

Standard Air Lines Inc, Long Beach, CA, operated DC-3s on charter work between 1946 and Jun49 when its operating certificate was revoked. It was earlier Fireball Express.

N4245; N15584; N17186; N25644; N49840; N55297; N90627.

Standard Airways Inc, San Diego, CA, bought DC-3s for charter work in the early sixties, but replaced them with larger types by mid-1963.

N1132; N16069; N33607; N33644; N45398.

Starflite Inc, White Plains, NY, operated DC-3 N430SF on intrastate services in the late sixties.

State Airlines Inc, Charlotte, NC, owned three DC-3s between about 1964 and 1972.

N25686; N91006; N2077A.

Stewart Air Service, Los Angeles, CA, used DC-3s on charter services from Sep46 until about 1971.

N25626; N28679; N67578; N74678.

Strato Freight Inc, Windsor Locks, CT, flew DC-3 NC61190 between 1947 and Nov49 when the company's operating licence was revoked. NC53011 was used briefly in 1947 before being destroyed in May47. Another DC-3 crashed into a mountain near Sylvia, NC, on 16Oct47.

Suburban Airlines, originating as Readbank Air Taxi, later operated DC-3s on third-level services in the early 1970s as a subsidiary of **Reading Aviation Services Inc.** (qv)

N7772; N85K.

Summit Airways, Denver, CO, was formed in 1946 but the name was changed to **Challenger Airlines** in Jan47, (qv).

Summit Airlines, Philadelphia, PA, used DC-3s and other types on scheduled cargo services in the Eastern USA until 1979, when they were put up for sale.

N87652; N67PA; N502PA.

Sun Belt Airways, Huntsville, TX, used DC-3 N32B/N132BB from 1978 until Jun89 when the aircraft was sold.

Sun International Airways, San Juan, PR, leased three DC-3s in 1981.

N101AP; N102AP; N2VM.

Sunland Air Transport Co, Little Rock, AR, used DC-3 NC38944 on passenger charters in the late 1940s.

Swift Delivery Air Freight - see Kahila Airlines.

Tabors Luxury Airlines, San Juan, PR. had two DC-3s in 1946.

TBM Inc, Visalia, CA, operated C-117Ds N1334K, N8538C, N8538F, and N8538R on cargo work in the eighties.

Texas Airways, Brownsville, TX used DC-3s N132D, N136D and N148D on freight services in the early eighties.

Tol Air Services, San Juan, PR, operated DC-3s from 1989 onwards as freighters. Seven were in use in 2003.

N87T; N780T; N781T; N782T; N783T/N783V; N784T; N786T/N68363.

Trans Air, Ft Lauderdale, FL used DC-3 N600JD from about 1983 until its sale in Aug86, when the airline filed for Chapter 11.

Transair Inc, New York, NY, started irregular passenger and cargo operations on 01Feb46, initially with two DC-3s between New York, Miami and Havana, the Bahamas and Mexico. The company was disolved and all aircraft sold in 1949. In early 1947 it was connected with **Expreso Aereo Inter-Americano SA**, Havana, Cuba, holding a 17½% interest. The fleets were insured together and comprised seven DC-3s.

NC19136; NC44782; NC46858; NC55985; NC57673; NC59794; NC65742; NC62568/CU-T100; NC62565/CU-T101; NC66112; NC69329/CU-T104; NC69327/CU-P115; NC88801.

Trans-Air Hawaii Ltd, Honolulu, HI, began scheduled freight services in 1947, using four C-47s. Two more were bought a year or so later, but probably did not enter service. They were replaced by three C-46s by 1949.

NC62001; NC62039; NC62040; NC62072; N5602V, N5606V

Trans-Alaskan Airlines Inc, Burbank, CA, used DC-3s and DC-4s on supplemental services. The DC-3s were owned between about 1946 and 1955.

N4111; N16015; N21793; N1268N; N4946V; N4670V.

Trans American Airways, Burbank, CA, used a DC-3 and C-46 on charter services in the late 1940s.

Trans Caribbean Air Cargo Lines Inc, New York, NY, operated DC-3s in December 1945, along with C-46s and DC-4s, all used for cargo charters. It became **Trans Caribbean Airways** in 1948/49, when passenger charters began.

NC41748(1)/NC58090; NC41748(2); NC41757/NC58091; NC60818/NC50040; NC60819/NC50034; NC56012; NC56018.

Transcontinental Air Express Corp, Stockton, CA, operated non-scheduled cargo and passenger services in 1946, using DC-3s.

NC54369; NC54370.

Transcontinental and Western Air Inc - See Trans World Airlines.

Trans Eastern Airlines, New York City, NY, operated DC-3 NC54088 in 1947.

Trans Florida Airlines Inc, Daytona Beach, FL, used three DC-3s on charter services between 1972 and 1974, one remaining until 1978. N404D was painted in Holiday Hunters Air Travel Club titles.

N15598; N404D; N715F.

Trans Global Airlines, Long Beach, CA, owned a single DC-3 in the early sixties, N62086.

Trans Island Airways used DC-3 N222LW during the early seventies, probably on lease.

Trans-Luxury Airlines Inc, Teterboro, NJ/Chicago, IL, operated non-scheduled passenger services with DC-3s between 1946 and 1948. The parent company was International Airlines which probably owned some of the aircraft. Seven DC-3s were owned, two of which crashed in 1946.

NC13719; NC14937; NC17091; NC49952; NC51878NC54099; NC57850.

Trans Marine Airways, New York City, NY, leased two DC-3s from Colonial Airlines in 1945/46.

Trans National Airlines Inc, San Francisco, CA, operated air taxi and cargo flights using a DC-3 and two Doves during 1976/77. The DC-3 was N63250.

Trans National Airlines Inc, Honolulu, HI, were using DC-3s N8064A, N102BL, N96H and N401JB on charter work during 1980. Sold to **Swift Delivery Air Freight** May81. See also **Kahila Airlines**.

Trans New England Airlines, Nashua, NH, flew DC-3s on scheduled cargo commuter services from 1973 until 1976.

N1346; N14636; N60705; N333TS.

Transocean Air Lines, Oakland, CA, operated a number of DC-3s, mainly in support of other airlines, such as Iranian and Air Jordan. It seems unlikely that any were used on their own services except for charters.

N17314; N30022; N33641; N54595; N79907; N95433; N2703A; N3980C; N9820F; N9896F; N55L.

Trans-Pacific Airlines Ltd - See Aloha Airlines.

Trans Sierra Airlines operated DC-3 N407D from Oct60 for a brief period.

Trans South Airways, Lexington, TN, used DC-3 N140D/N222TS between 1973 and 1976.

Trans-Texas Airways, Houston, TX, started scheduled services using DC-3s in Oct47. They remained until 1969, a year after the name had been changed to **Texas International**, but the last few were, by then, awaiting sale.

N10608; N10616; N17112; N17331; N17336; N18105; N18121; N18141; N18143; N19968; N21768; N21797; N25646; N25658; N25661; N25666; N25668; N25673; N25685; N28364; N28391; N28508; N33327; N33654; N34951; N34952; N58V.

Trans Tropic Airlines, Miami Shores, FL, used four DC-3s in 1947.

NC54477(?); NC65745; NC65746; NC65747.

Trans West Air Express, Oakland, CA, traded in the seventies as **Zoom Zoom Air** and later as **Air Charter West**, operating N60705, N3433Y, N100ZZ and N300ZZ.

Trans World Airlines Inc, New York, NY, started life in 1927 as **Transcontinental and Western Air Inc**, and continued to trade under this name until 17May50. The operating name Trans World Airlines was painted on aircraft somewhat earlier than this, but the letters **TWA** were always carried, and DC-3s at one time flew just with "The Transcontinental Line" titling. Hence, in the production list, TWA is used regardless. TWA started the whole DC story by ordering the DC-1 NC223Y in 1933. Following successful trials the developed version, or DC-2 was ordered in May34, and they were used until the summer of 1942 when the last were bought by the British Purchasing Commision for the Royal Air Force in India. The first DC-3s were delivered in Apr37 and the type continued in use throughout the war, including a number operated in military marks for the USAAF. Post-war there were 76 of the type in the fleet in 1946, but these steadily gave way to DC-4s and later Martin 202s, and the last was sold in 1957, after cargo and training use. TWA also assisted in the acquisition of DC-3s post-war to airlines such as Ethiopian, Iranian and Saudi Arabian.

DC-2s:- NC13711 to NC13730 incl; NC13783 to NC13790 incl; NC14978; NC14979; NC16049. *DC-3s:-* NC1941 to NC1951 incl; NC12942; NC14931 to NC14933 incl; NC14988; NC15589; NC15591; NC16095; NC17312 to NC17324 incl; NC18040; NC18565; NC18573; NC18619; NC18949 to NC18954 incl; NC19939 to NC19941 incl; NC19974; NC21769; NC26214; NC28310; NC28321; NC28325; NC28350; NC28361; NC28383; NC28393; NC30079; NC30081; NC33621 to NC33623 incl; NC34417; NC34602; NC34985; NC38940; NC38941; NC38943; NC41750 to NC41752 incl; NC44881; NC44783; NC44897; NC44996 to NC44998 incl; NC45364; NC45365; NC45376; NC45397; NC45942; NC49551; NC51159; NX51165; NC51167; NC51171; NC51179; NC51194; NC51831; NC54548; NC86543; NC86544; NC86558; NC86567; NC86585; NC86589; NC88725; NC88822 to NC88825 incl.

Tricon International Airlines Inc, Dallas, TX, used DC-3s for cargo charter work, mainly mail, between about 1973 and 1976.

N403D; N101SF; N200TA.

Triple H Flying Service, Honolulu, HI, used DC-3 NC62034 in 1947.

Tropic Airlines, Honolulu, HI, used DC-3s N162E and N104RP in the mid-eighties. See also **Air Molokai**.

Tropics International Inc, Miami, FL, traded as **Skyfreight** and used three DC-3s on cargo flights to the Bahamas.

N7868B; N4261P/N124SF; N341W.

Turner Airlines, Indianapolis, IN, bought four DC-3s in Oct49 to operate scheduled services, but was taken over by Lake Central in Sep50.

N21711; N21713; N21716; N21777.

Twentieth Century Airlines operated three DC-3s for a brief period in 1946 when operations first started as part of the North American group.

NC52925; NC52935.

Union Flights bought N403JB in 1985, named 'Pegasus', it was sold in 1991.

Union Southern Airlines, New York, NY, operated DC-3s between Miami, Haiti, Venezuela etc in 1947, possibly on lease. NC53196 was lost on 04May47 at Newark, NJ.

NC53196; NC54099; NC79020.

United Air Lines Inc, Chicago, IL, ordered DC-3s and DSTs in 1936 to replace the smaller and uncompetitive Boeing 247Ds. They continued in service through the war years and well into the fifties. A few more were bought with the purchase of Capital Airlines in Jul61, but these were sold as soon as possible, and probably never operated in United colours. With 114 known DC-3s and DSTs, United's fleet was probably the largest of the type with the almost certain exception of Aeroflot Li-2s.

NC15586; NC16060 to NC16074 incl; NC16086 to NC16090 incl; NC17109; NC17397; NC17713; NC17883 to NC17885 incl; NC17890; NC18102 to NC18112 incl; NC18145; NC18146; NC18938 to NC18945 incl; NC19428; NC19453; NC19454; N19915; N19917; NC19919; NC19923; NC19925; NC19930; NC19932; NC19934; NC19935; NC19937; NC19946 to NC19948 incl; NC19964; N21781 to N21784 incl; N21790; NC25611 to NC25622 incl; NC25675; NC25677 to NC25683 incl; NC28360; NC28379; NC33640 to NC33642 incl; NC33644; NC33646; NC33647; (NC33648); (NC33649); NC38944; NC39572; NC41358; NC44991; NC44992; NC44995; N45338; N45373; N45379; NC45398; NC45399; NC49541; NC49543; NC49559; NC73417; NC75413; NC75430; NC86558; NC86593; NC86594; NC86596; NC88790; NC88794.

Universal Airlines Inc, New York, NY, operated non-scheduled passenger and cargo services to Puerto Rico, using DC-3s, until 1949. Two DC-3s crashed in 1946 and 1947.

NC18648; NC54374; NC57609.

US Air Express - see Champlain Air.

US Airlines Inc, Ft Lauderdale, FL, started regular operations in Feb46 using leased DC-3s and C-46s. These were used on scheduled cargo services, but the company was reorganised in Sept 1951 and thereafter used only C-46s. It also owned **Florida-Fresh Air Express Inc** (qv). Thirteen DC-3s are known, one of which crashed in Mar47.

NC21730; NC47057; NC54327; NC54328; NC54438; NC62566; NC65480; NC88802; NC88803; NC88804; NC88805; NC88806; NC88834.

US Forest Service, Boise, ID, were using Basler Turbo-67s N115Z (ex N146Z) and N142Z (ex N100Z) in 2003.

Vacation Airways, San Juan, PR, were using DC-3 N45379 during 1976.

Vance International Airways, Seattle, WA, initially as Consolidated Airlines, bought DC-3 N57131 in 1955 for charter work. It probably remained in use until about 1967.

Vero Monmouth Airlines, Vero Beach, FL, started commuter services in Jul74, but two DC-3s had been used since 1970 for charter work. They were initially owned by Wall Herald Co, which traded as **Monmouth Airlines**, and were sold in 1979.

N2VM; N5250V.

Veteran Airways Ltd, Westerly, RI, (possibly the above re-constituted) used two DC-3s in 1947 within Rhode Island and Connecticut and also for charter. One, still unidentified, remained in 1951.

Veteran's Air Express Co, Newark, NJ. used DC-3s NC58121 and NC86583. The airline was declared bankrupt on 09Dec46.

Viking Air Transport Co Inc, Burbank, CA, owned DC-3s briefly in 1946 operating from New York to the W. Coast.

NC53218; NC53219; NC53225; NC66688; NC79036.

Viking Express, t/a **Heritage Air Tours**, used DC-3 N21RB for transcontinental 'memory' flights. It was sold to Vintage Airways.

Viking Express, Chicago-Dupage, IL, which may not be related to the above, used DC-3s N12BA, N162E/N22RB; N12RB and N68363 on freight services from about 1993.

Viking International Airfreight Inc, Minneapolis, MN, started scheduled cargo services in 1969 and used DC-3s on this work from 1977. It was taken over by Corporate Air about 1984.

N56990; N721A; N6898D; N3433E; N1213M; N387T; N3433U; N744V.

Vintage Air Tours, Orlando, FL, was formed by Richard Branson as an offshoot of Virgin International, and began operating sightseeing flights from Orlando to Key West in Dec92. These were not a success and both DC-3s were wfu in 1997.

N12RB; N22RB.

Vintage Airways, Lafayette, LA, bought DC-3 N33VW in 1998. It was sold to the Cavanaugh Collection in 2001.

Virgin Air, St. Thomas, VI, bought DC-3s N46949 & N46950 from Marshall Air in 1982. They were out of use by 1984.

Virgin Island Air Service Inc, Miami, FL, started irregular services in 1947, using DC-3 NC1075M.

Virgin Islands International leased DC-3 N102AP in 1983.

Wallace Air Service Inc, Spokane, WA, operated three DC-3s in 1947.

NC49319; NC49322 are known.

Waterman Airlines Inc, Mobile, AL, owned NC75402.

West Coast Airlines Inc, Seattle, WA, operated DC-3s on scheduled services from Dec46. Four more aircraft were added when Empire was bought in Aug52 and they continued in use until all had been sold by 1968.

N44585; N44587; N44896; N56589; N62373 to N62376 incl; N65351; N74589; N91052; N2025A; N1051N; N1280N.

Western Air Lines Inc, Los Angeles, CA, bought their first DC-3s in 1937 when the airline was still known as **Western Air Express**. The present name was adopted on 11Mar41 and DC-3s remained in use until the last was retired in 1959.

NC15563; NC15569; NC16060; NC18101; NC18102; NC18600; NC18645; NC18646; NC19387; NC19964; NC28379; NC33621; NC33644; NC33647; NC33670; NC33671; (NC33672); NC45363; NC45395; NC49319; NC49554; NC56589; NC56592.

Westland Airlines Inc, San Angelo, TX used DC-3s NC65121 and NC75737 in 1947.

Wien Alaska Airlines Inc, Fairbanks, AK, started DC-3 scheduled services in 1945 and continued through several changes of name until their sale in 1968. **Wien Air Alaska** was adopted in 1966, and a merger with Northern Consolidated in Mar68 produced Wien Consolidated.

N19921; N21748; N21769; N57131; N91014; N2757A.

Willis Air Services Inc, Teterboro, NJ, was formed in Oct45 for charter cargo work. At least five DC-3s and two DC-4s were used. It was also known as "The Commander Line".

NC20969; NC53460; NC57190.

Winged Cargo Inc, Philadelphia, PA, used five DC-3s for cargo work, and also to tow Waco CG-4 cargo gliders.

NC25644; NC28802; NC48520; NC79054; NC88876(?).

Wisconsin Central Airlines Inc, Madison, WI, bought six DC-3s in 1950 to replace their Lockheed 10s, then in use. The name was changed to **North Central** in Dec52.

N1945; N14931; N15598; N17312; N17320; N18949; N21728; N26214; N38941; N38943.

Woods Air Fuel, Palmer, AK, continued to use DC-3s in Alaska into the nineties to fly diesel fuel to outlying parts.

N50CM; N777YA.

Yakima Sky Chief, Seattle, WA, was owned by R C Reed until Jun48, when G W Charters took over and an unknown DC-3 was used on charter work.

Yukon Air Service, Fairbanks, AK, owned N333EF in 1984 and has operated DC-3s N95460 and N3FY under the name of **Air North**, since 1979.

Yute Air Alaska, Dillingham, AK, operated a mixed fleet of aircraft, amongst which was DC-3 N777YA. This was sold in Feb91.

Zantop Air Transport Inc, Detroit, MI, used DC-3s on cargo services between 1953 and 1969.

N18101; N19193; N19923; N33639; N33644; N49363; N49551; N56990; N63107; N67588; N88825/N620Z.

Zoom-Zoom Air, Oakland, CA, the trading name for **Trans West Air Express**, used DC-3s on regular freight services from 1973/74 until the name was changed to **Air Charter West** in 1975 (qv).

N60705; N63250; N3433Y; N100ZZ; N200ZZ; N300ZZ.

Index:-

Note that the prefix N is used throughout this index, the categories NC (Commercial), NL (Limited), R (Restricted), NS (Special) and NX (Experimental) which may appear in individual histories are omitted here to simplify sorting. The order used in this listing differs from that of the master Index as it enables large batches and airline fleets to be identified more readily.

N1	c/n 4146	N8	4084
N2(1)	20426	N9	11859
N2(2)	4147	N10	4661
N3(1)	4147	N11	26283
N3(2)	20426	N12	2053
N5	4574	N13	26283
N6	4146	N14(1)	4080
N7(1)	20426	N14(2)	20443
N7(2)	25341	N14(3)	9526

Reg	MSN	Reg	MSN	Reg	MSN	Reg	MSN
N14(?)	20202	N74(2)	25954	N894	33203	N4002	33241
N15	25341	N76(1)	20560	N895	33273	N4003	11672
N16	4084	N76(2)	4279	N902	11701	N4111	4583
N17(1)	4279	N77	25627	(N916)	11928	N4112	26216
N17(2)	33206	N78	9486	N920	19754	N4245	20004
N17(3)	11859	N79(1)	6264	N925	20016	N4296	42962
N18	11859	N79(2)	26108	N950	20475	N4405	33232
N19	20403	N84	4148	N990	9247	N4585	4585
N20	4438	N86	4146	N993	7319	N4795	11772
N21(1)	9526	N99	4574	N1000(1) (DC-2)	1324	N4800(1)	4997
N21(2)	20202	N100(1)	20494	N1000(2)	3275	N4800(2)	4497
N21(3)	20443	N100(2)	20560	N1132	13138	N4848	25573
N22	20033	N107	4661	N1142	34326	N4849	33282
N23(1)	19320	N109	20403	N1187	4145	N5009	13850
N23(2)	12261	N112	20443	N1294	11653	N5050	32867
N24(1)	20443	N114	4661	N1301	4864	N5104	19851
N24(2)	4148	N118	20426	N1325	13658	N5106	9058
N24(3)	9526	N119	4438	N1346	25678	N5107	4837
N25(1)	26733	N160	20424	N1348	9395	N5108	12830
N25(2)	10243	N161	19754	N1621	6154	N5109	9100
N25(3)	25956	N162	20016	N1622	43080	N5117	6054
N26	26093	N181	9005	N1623	9053	N5144	9380
N27	33305	N182	20560	N1624	42981	N5170	6154
N28(1)	10243	N183	20419	N1690	2180	(N5410)	34370
N28(2)	26733	N199	33251	N1820	9053	N5414	34370
N29(1)	33206	N200	20400	N1822	43080	N5649	4090
N29(2)	33133	N202	20033	N1823	9053	N5658	34286
N30	33216	N203	25341	N1916	4545	N5867	9555
N31	26358	N206	4776	N1941	3266	N5925	4202
N32	33345	N214	34374	N1942	3267	N6062	34326
N33	26583	N226	6355	N1943	3268	N6102	11645
N34	33359	N300	33251	N1944	3269	N6110	9667
N35	32794	N330	4479	(N1945)	3270	N6187	6187
N36	33291	N342(1)	20202	N1945	3294	N6430	20698
N37	26713	N342(2)	9526	(N1946)	3271	N6510	4925
N38	33100	N344	19234	N1946	3295	N6574	4388
N39(1)	11808	N361	4470	(N1947)	3272	N6619	12458
N39(2)	26283	N400(1)	33241	N1947	3296	N6650	11631
N40	25824	N400(2)	13447	(N1948)	3273	N6677	32843
N41(1)	12261	N414	25248	N1948	3298	N6678	13154
N41(2)	19320	N415	10247	(N1949)	3274	N6680	12435
N42	26268	N416	13111	N1949	3299	N6811	43159
N43(1)	26258	N424	4147	(N1950)	3294	N6894	11982
N43(2)	2053	N473	26283	N1950	3286	N6896	33224
N44(1)	25775	N485	4848	(N1951)	3295	N6903	26297
N44(2)	33232	N490	1954	N1951	3287	N6907	9410
N45	33322	N491	2185	(N1952)	3296	N7007	43080
N46	33251	N492	1553	(N1953)	3297	N7119	4784
N47(1)	33155	N493	3251	N1953	3297	N7124	12679
N47(2)	26283	N494	2221	(N1954)	3298	N7222	6338
N48(1)	26268	N495	4819	(N1955)	3299	N7301	9042
N48(2)	33201	N496	2270	N1956	2014	N7302	11971
N49	26558	N497	4811	N2001	4903	N7401	26461
N50	4438	N498(1)	4595	N2005	19737	N7503	9028
N51	11928	N498(2)	1903	N2006	11741	N7654	11654
N52	20419	N500	13850	N2010	34130	N7709	12093
N53	26968	N502	3266	N2028	6164	N7756	26167
N54	25954	N503(1)	4939	N2400	26877	N7772	6338
N55	13004	N503(2)	11701	N2401	26263	N7775	2195 ?
N56	4279	N512	2108	N2503	4939	N8009	20806
N57	25627	N520	11851	N2568	26193	N8037	
N58	9486	N560	10160	N2614	12741	N8044	2008
N60	26874	N565	26400	N2615	19998	N8056	25735
N61	10096	N586	9555	N2627	4762	N8084	20624
N62(1)	34374	N590	20457	N2630	19593	N8097	34354
N62(2)	25951	N606	34326	N2636	13143	N8099	26520
N63(1)	11703	N645	26388	N2647	4862	N8383	26299
N63(2)	26108	N701	26388	N2700	20438	N8563	9830
N64	33232	N717	25356	N2979	6097	N8661	4951
N66	33144	N760	3269	(N2985)	9174	N8666	25957
N67(1)	25956	N812	20443	N2988	6315	N8701	11628
N67(2)	13004	N814	4661	N2989	6315	N8704	33048
N68	26874	N815	4438	N3000	42961	N8720	4807
N69(1)	26593	N816	4550	N3006	42961	N8783	26051
N69(2)	25951	N817	2121	N3262	12412	N8785	20494
N70(1)	19320	N818	20426	N3329	11651	N8820	13041
N70(2)	26133	N819	9040	N3339	12332	N8860	1970
N71(1)	9005	N837	9124	N3455	33379	N9012	4936
N71(2)	11928	N841	6253	"NC3519"	9381	N9141	20529
N73(1)	33206	N842	9526	N3588	20178	N9382	12331
N73(2)	26968	N843	4733	N3773	12042	N9434	19433
N74(1)	26733	N893	33052	N3898	19127	N9999	10101

CHAPTER 4: COMMERCIAL OPERATORS OF THE DC-3, C-47, R4D, DAKOTA AND LI-2

Registration	Serial	Registration	Serial	Registration	Serial	Registration	Serial
N28345(2)	2224	N30076 (DC-2)	1324	N33647	4126	N34967	42963
(N28346)(1)	4814	N30079	6264	(N33648)	4127	N34968	42964
N28346(2)	6259	N30081	4987	(N33649)(1)	4128	(N34969)(1)	6323
(N28347)	4815	N30083	6315	N33649(2)	4809	N34969(2)	42965
N28350	2264	N30084	4863	N33651	4115	(N34970)(1)	4993
(N28359)	6321	N30085	4658	N33653	4116	N34970	42966
N28360	2271	N30086	4660	N33654	4117	(N34971)(1)	4994
N28361	2272	N30087	4861	N33655	4118	N34971	42967
N28362	4106	N30088	6064	(N33656)(1)	4119	(N34972)(1)	4995
N28363	4107	N30089	7387	N33656(2)	4802	N34972(2)	42968
N28364	4108	N30091	11774	(N33657)(1)	4120	(N34973)(1)	4982
(N28370)	4109	N30092	11775	N33657(2)	4803	N34973	42969
(N28371)	4110	N30093	11620	(N33659)(1)	4121	(N34974)(1)	4983
(N28372)	4111	N30094	4960	N33659(2)	4981	N34974(2)	42970
N28378	3285	N30095	4961	N33660	25958	(N34975)(1)	4984
N28379	3283	N30096	7358	(N33662)	4122	N34975(2)	42971
N28380	3284	N30097	7359		and 6322	(N34976)(1)	4985
N28381	4089	N30743	11664	N33670	4811	N34976(2)	42972
N28382	4090	N31113	4992	N33671	4812	(N34977)(1)	4986
N28383	4091	N31179	33201	(N33672)	4813	N34977(2)	42973
N28384	4092	(N31214)	25604	N33675	4130	(N34978)(1)	6325
N28385	4093	N31310	43395	(N33676)(1)	4131	N34978(2)	42974
(N28386)	4094	N31538	6317	N33676(2)	43074	(N34979)(1)	6326
(N28387)	4815	N31654	4145	N33677	4132	N34979(2)	42975
(N28388)	4096	N32342	19662	N33678	4133	(N34980)(1)	6327
	and 6324	N32624	19843	(N33679)	4134	N34980(2)	42976
N28389	4097	N32975	19979		and 6263	(N34981)(1)	6328
(N28390)	4098	N33312	4842	(N33680)	4135	N34981(2)	42977
N28391	2268	N33315	4978		and 6264	(N34982)(1)	6329
N28392	2269	N33317	11636	N33684	4963	N34982(2)	42978
N28393	3251	N33320	7361	(N33685)	4964	(N34983)(1)	6330
N28394	3250	N33321	7391	(N33686)	4965	N34983(2)	42979
N28508	7349	N33322	7396	(N33687)	4966	N34984	42980
N28512	20467	N33324	1954	(N33688)(1)	4967	N34985(1)	42981
N28679	10035	N33325	4859	N33688(2)	43092	N34985(2)	12025
N28802	27138	N33326	4127	N33689	4968	N34988(1)	4827
N28889	20520	N33327	4128	(N33690)	4969	N34988(2)	10243
N29086	4304	N33329	11651	(N33691)	4970	N34989	4828
N29958	12357	N33331	7394	(N33692)(1)	4971	N34990	4829
N30000(1)	4809	N33332	7355	N33692(2)	43075	(N34999)(1)	4112
N30000(2)	43073	N33334	11674	(N33693)(1)	4972	N34999(2)	4565
N30000(3)	6017	N33346	7356	N33693(2)	43077	N36176	9632
N30000(4)	43158	N33347	6322	(N33694)(1)	4973	N36349	19845
N30000(5)	43159	N33370	4970	N33694(2)	43078	N36412	10239
N30000(6)	43301	N33371	7409	(N33695)(1)	4974	N36480	33598
N30001	4170	N33372	4284	N33695(2)	43079	N36498	12527
N30002	4171	N33373	4368	(N33696)	4975	N36516	7357
N30003	4172	N33374	4369	(N33697)	4976	N36540	4795
N30004	4173	N33606	4806	(N33868)	1964	N36699	19603
N30005	4174	N33607	4807	N34099	11816	N36802	4905
N30006	4175	N33608	4808	N34110	19039	N36803	7388
N30007	4176	N33609	4100	N34113	12550	N36815	4754
N30008	4177	N33610	4101	N34116	9247	N36898	4360
N30009	4178	N33611	4102	N34417	7337	(N36984)	4877
N30010	4179	N33612	4103	N34602	25452	N37465	42955
N30011	4180	N33613	4104	N34915	43076	(N37466)	42956
N30012	4181	N33614	4105	N34916	43082	(N37467)	42957
N30013	4182	N33621	3286	N34917	43080	N37468	42958
N30014	4183	N33622	3287	N34925	4957	N37469	42959
N30016	9774	N33623(1)	3288	N34947	4958	N37470	42960
N30021	4980	N33623(2)	20215	N34948	4959	N37497	43084
N30022	4841	(N33627)	4804	(N34949)	4960	N37499	43085
N30024	4977	(N33628)	4805	(N34950)(1)	4961	N37529	13378
(N30025)	4978	(N33630)	4136	N34950(2)	7399	N37737	33213
(N30026)	4979	N33631	4137	(N34951)(1)	4962	N37800	20806
N30027	4980	N33632	4138	N34951(2)	4827	"N37810"	33170
(N30029)	6331	N33633	4139	(N34952)(1)	6345	N37906	12712
(N30030)	6332	N33634	4140	N34952(2)	4944	N38114	33100
(N30031)	6333	(N33635)(1)	4141	(N34953)	6346	N38860	13649
(N30032)	6334	N33635(2)	12337	(N34954)	6347	N38938	4989
(N30033)	6335	(N33636)	4142	(N34955)	6348	N38939	4585
(N30034)	6336	(N33637)	4143	(N34956)	6349	N38940	6331
(N30035)	6337	(N33638)	4144	(N34957)	6350	N38941	6332
(N30036)	6338	(N33639)(1)	4145	(N34958)	6351	N38942	12971
(N30037)	6339	N33639(2)	4085	(N34959)	6352	N38943	3280
(N30038)	6340	N33640	3265	(N34960)(1)	6353	N38944(1)	3287
(N30039)	6341	N33641	4113	N34960(2)	20349	N38944(2)	19972
(N30045)	6342	N33642	4114	(N34961)	6354	N39165 (DC-2)	1404
(N30046)	6343	N33643	4129	(N34962)(1)	3289	N39188	19636
(N30047)	6344	N33644	4123	(N34962)(2)	6355	N39334	7331
(N30050)	6319	N33645	4124	N34963	34148	N39340(1)	4700
(N30052)	6320	N33646	4125	N34966	42962	N39340(2)	6062

N39354	19659	N45394	18978	N49558	11666	N52935	20017
N39393	4943	N45395	11642	N49559	11669	N52940	4551
(N39420)	26683	N45396	4814	N49657	9066	N53011	4276
N39544	11649	N45397	11625	N49686	11674	N53192	6178
N39572	20178	N45398	4892	(N49687)	11722	N53196	19435
N40160		N45399	11629	N49688	11650	N53210	13777
N40180	25824	N45727	13033	N49689	11654	N53216	12853
N40359	19125	N45860	12528	(N49690)	11723	N53218	19626
N40386	26120	N45864	9304	N49732	4557	N53219	19802
N41046	4282	N45873	12458	N49745	20179	N53225	20554
N41050	4241	N46484	9795	N49789	4227	N53315	43159
N41061	4341	N46496	9499	N49840	6006	N53376	19542
N41075	4302	N46567	9825	N49895	26167	N53416	4522
N41169	4704	N46858	9885	N49952	12680	N53420	4650
N41182	6061	N46877	9186	N49966	33144	N53425	12508
N41353	4327	N46938	27005	N50034	20080	N53426(1)	9380
N41358	9649	N46949	9290	N50037	4307	N53426(2)	19988
N41392	12855	N46950	32873	N50039	10240	N53457	20105
N41398	13050	N47027	9140	N50040	19980	N53460	11863
N41407	12983	N47028	32761	N50041	9030	N53471	19988
N41441	12985	N47056	6115	N50043	4759	N53474	20432
N41447	12987	N47057	10185	N50046	34373	N53480	33613
N41455	11876	N47060	19066	N50264	20235	N53593	20447
N41667	20594	N47071	25720	N50311	19691	N53594	20193
N41748(1)	19649	N47076	9971	N50312	19759	N53596	20433
N41748(2)	11827	N47218	4785	N50314	12868	N53668	13633
N41750	4857	N47259	13114	N50320	6173	N54075	6096
N41751	4856	N47573	9581	N50321	19239	N54080	4255
N41752	4870	N47574	26700	N50322	20002	N54088	13837
N41756	19024	N47656	13113	N50474	4563	N54090	20241
N41757(1)	19766	N47755	4381	N50486	10047	N54091	13730
N41757(2)	4240	N47762	4382	N50488	4219	N54099	19778
N41761	20406	N47763	4403	N50520	9555	N54206	4471
N41785	32785	N47764	4503	N50525	see 20323	N54213	4432
N41798	4208	N47780	20813		and 9986	N54215	13636
N41831	3275	N47965	9714	N50591	11731	N54227	19540
N42022	13432	N47968	4430	N50592	11703	N54228	4571
(N43861)	33265	N47995	4386	N50593	4895	N54229	6101
N44567		N47996	4422	N50616	11716	N54310	6090
N44585	9568	N48065	13816	N50617	11718	N54311	4830
N44587	12857	N48066	33110	N50618	11748	N54312	9723
N44782	4703	N48067	26524	N50619	4895	N54324	13656
N44783	4903	N48130	19995	N50620	4928	N54325	19176
N44786	7336	N48131	20427	N50621	7347	N54326	20185
N44792	6314	N48132	9147	N50622	11703	N54327	4262
N44881	4988	N48159	25779	N50623	11731	N54328	6134
N44883	11645	N48211	26718	N50624	11745	N54329	"32850"
N44884	4890	N48230	34298	N50625	11765	N54330	6164
N44896	9665	N48255	26568	N50786	19224	N54331	19992
N44897	4986	N48258	33085	N50788(1)	12891	N54332	20224
N44991	11706	N48284	25964	N50788(2)	4741	N54333	20186
N44992	11738	N48324	13105	N51041	19851	N54334	19998
N44993	6260	N48520	20184	N51071	4837	N54335	20217
N44995	11719	N48731	4226	N51080	12830	N54336	34331
N44996	4936	N48990	9247	N51091	9100	N54337	20136
N44997	11685	(N49249)	33536	N51159	26503	N54339	13836
N44998	11752	(N49250)	26766	N51165	7386	N54357	4595
N45331	7323	N49277	6098	N51167	7384	N54364	25235
N45332	11693	N49319	26676	N51171	9063	N54366	12907
N45333	6330	N49322	9210	N51179	20874	N54368	10051
N45335	4964	N49363	4556	N51182	4419	N54369	19240
N45338	11778	N49454	10177	N51183	4232	N54370	19220
N45339	11657	N49466	26705	N51194	4790	N54374	6177
N45340	4976	N49472	25416	(N51301)	4654	N54406	4095
N45362	4908	N49538	9700	N51359	13759	N54412	13137
N45363	4912	N49540	11651	N51362	10062	N54417	20440
N45364	11699	N49541	7340	N51617	9967	N54438	19871
N45365	11670	N49542	4947	N51657	19524	N54450	10128
N45366	11757	N49544	11644	N51764	19447	N54451(1)	25318
N45367	11751	N49543	11672	N51793	19276	N54451(2)	9174
N45369	11742	N49546	7394	N51831	4644	N54452	20037
N45370	11637	N49547	7349	N51878	4542	N54453	9993
N45373	6324	N49548	11682	N51879	4682	N54454	19249
N45374	4925	N49549	11702	N51881	4477	N54455	12957
N45375	11639	N49550	11771	N51894	4568	N54456	20529
N45376	11730	N49551	4940	N51938	25956	N54477	4749
N45379	11776	N49552	11652	N52200	19630	N54540	25989
N45381	11687	N49553	4820	N52630	12727	N54542	34378
N45383	4858	N49554	11729	N52709	4234	N54548	9274
N45388	7348	N49555	4965	N52710	19095	N54550(1)	4565
N45391	11633	N49556	7403	N52818	12513	N54550(2)	9965
N45393	12843	N49557	11653	N52925	7369	N54551	25318

Chapter 4: Commercial Operators of the DC-3, C-47, R4D, Dakota and Li-2

Registration	MSN	Registration	MSN	Registration	MSN	Registration	MSN
N54577	20439	N58099	13854	N62025	4200	N65134	19025
N54578	9068	N58121	34353	N62033	19716	N65135	13803
N54579	20123	N58122	4242	N62034	25882	N65136	19648
N54595	2053	N58139	20101	N62035	26819	N65162	12683
N54599	34189	N58156	10066	N62039	19712	N65266(1)	9995
N54602	27080	N58181	6216	N62040	26078	N65266(2)	19241
N54604	25571	N58216	12908	N62044	34345	N65276	19202
N54605	32939	N58296	10267	N62045	4810	N65278	19029
N54607	10073	N58297	43345	N62046	4816	N65282	9914
N54608	11903	N58492	4392	N62072	26590	N65283	19965
N54610	20607	N58731	13532	N62083	26789	N65284	9145
N54611	26467	N58775	13822	N62086	19713	N65331	11815
N54705	12844	N58776	13048	N62101	25508	N65350	4736
N54726	4786	N59277	9088	N62102	19674	N65351	19225
N54727	9061	N59278	6200	N62103	20079	N65357	9742
N54728	4299	N59279	6077	N62109	19468	N65358	6015
N54729	13439	N59299	4544	N62229	25631	N65371	4828
N54731	9139	N59314	12363	N62253	4621	N65378	19238
N55115	19800	N59316	18986	N62265	34280	N65384	18984
N55297	4683	N59345 (DC-2)	1297	N62266	19785	N65385	20542
N55303	12722	N59360	19999	N62303	32923	N65386	9742
N55330	11874	N59398	9965	N62373	19212	N65387	6015
N55414	34370	N59409	4700	N62374	12534	N65388(1)	19383
N55462	13746	N59410	11643	N62375	19028	N65388(2)	33113
N55892	12647	N59534	20145	N62376	19978	N65389	19382
N55894	9749	N59586	4649	N62384	13531	N65390	19402
N55985	12560	N59655	19236	N62385	20212	N65391	13872
N56001	4627	N59699	13061	N62386	19983	N65393	20051
N56012	20430	N59748	11877	N62387	20586	N65480	20235
N56018	19441	N59749	20196	N62388	9891	N65556	1911
N56589	4400	N59794	9137	(N62414)	19716	N65566	4481
"N56589"	19978	N60002	4372	N62427	26118	N65601	6148
N56592	6017	N60003	6083	N62428	26088	N65742	20439
N56645	4485	N60049	32553	N62443	19460	N65743	20432
N56743	4731	N60154	32755	N62472	19035	N65745	6014
N56780	4615	N60214	25795	N62548	9795	N65746	4742
N56800	4589	N60256	9201	N62565	12717	N65747	4388
N56801	9026	N60326	6216	N62566	13445	N65764	4525
N56968	4341	N60331	12968	N62567	13621	N65931	9124
N56969	4704	N60480	9530	N62568	13681	N66001	4270
N56970	4241	N60493	20518	N62570	13798	N66006	20120
N56990	20404	N60705	4638	N62574	19751	N66011	26134
N57123	33170	N60706	13732	N63104	20214	N66016	9031
N57131	19040	N60713	19122	N63105	20213	N66025	19637
N57132(1)	10244	N60714	13699	N63106	20434	N66054	19653
N57132(2)	25655	N60742	11851	N63107	20063	N66055	18986
N57135	4581	N60777	12741	N63122	34326	N66056	10062
N57136	9035	N60818	19980	N63164	11846	N66057	10171
N57190	11870	N60819	20080	N63186	26792	N66112	4272
(N57191)	20227	N60878	34364	N63250	34329	N66113	4528
N57278	19366	N60882	12677	N63255	11850	N66118	19593
N57372	10136	N60883	12740	N63288	33613	N66131	12856
N57481(1)	4202	N60897	4598	N63351	34328	N66147	6158
N57481(2)	4372	N60940	20188	N63363	13818	N66162	19790
N57539	9037	N60941	20219	N63364	10178	N66176	6218
N57540	4785	N60942	20158	N63376	13817	N66209	13851
N57609	4444	N60943	19543	N63400	12792	N66610	9786
N57612	34301	N60958	11850	N63439	20229	N66634	26281
N57626	4564	N60995	11832	N63440	20194	N66637	11800
N57638	19991	N61067	4741	N63451	19683	N66655	26400
N57650	4528	N61190	19400	N63689	12678	N66688	20438
N57654	19757	N61350	4535	N63800	9053	N66697	9990
N57667	6030	N61351	4390	N64104	19230	N66699(1)	4497
N57668	13851	N61442	9642	N64105	19317	N66699(2)	9040
N57669	4613	N61450	11631	N64181	12853	N66699(3)	2194
N57672	20035	N61451	4630	N64421	19003	N67000	1498
N57673	13736	N61518	6190	N64422	19476	N67082	33429
N57674	12732	N61677	4837	N64423	9251	N67125	20886 / 43086
N57700	1970	N61696		N64424	4424	N67136	6187
N57779	12830	N61721	20399	N64490	25360	N67178	
N57800(1)	19991	N61722	20077	N64605	13227	N67234	20181
N57800(2)	26058	N61723	26536	N64703	12505	N67422	
N57850	9214	N61724	13176	N64722	10052	N67562	20479
N57902	19232	N61725	19041	N64737	19275	N67578	19057
N57927	12255	N61726	20024	N64744	19234	N67588	20536
N57985	19996	N61849	20139	N64747	19117	N67589	19656
N58020	20187	N61938	33612	N64766	27218	N67590	20191
N58022	4609	N61981	2216	N64767	10199	N67651	4642
N58024	9378	N61989	9100	N64784	25482	N67661	11790
N58090	19649	N61990	4901	N64793	25471	N67674	33571
N58091	19766	N62001	4654	N64910	20062	N67776	20093
N58093	4423	N62024	6103	N65121	20061	N67796	12297

Registration	C/N	Registration	C/N	Registration	C/N	Registration	C/N
	or 34406	N75290	26184	N79971	13184	N87625	4858
N67797	26683	N75391	26366	N79987	9074	N87626	9988
N67809	6153	N75402	4523	N79989	19242	N87627	13660
N67825	4519	N75404	6154	N80617	20865	N87628	19747
N67826	4501	N75405	4559	N81235	4562	N87629	20749
N67827	4607	N75406	6204	(N81315)	9143	N87630	25449
N67828	4237	N75407	6097	N81384	6213	N87631	25678
N67872	4484	N75408	6183	N81388	20628	N86732	26783
N67873	9055	N75409	4309	N81394	19032	N87633	32546
N67902	4491	N75410	6054	N81397	4356	N87634	32678
N68000	13847	N75411	4498	N81907	33313	N87635	32762
(N68071)	25509	N75412	9058	N81949	12582	N87636	33612
N68179	4843	N75413	4383	N81952	32825	N87637	34295
N68180	4664	N75430	4490	N82103		N87638	7390
N68188	4348	N75431	4489	(N83017)	13105	N87639	9198
N68219	6181	N75483	9000	N86408	25707	N87640	9633
N68220	9154	N75489	6059	N86410	25707	N87641	10193
N68221	19055	N75583	10168	N86435	25531	N87642	11835
N68307	4211	N75737	25354	N86437	12692	N87643	13060
N68353	20402	N75885	19242	N86438	26899	N87644	19627
N68358	10156	N75959	13840	N86439	25836	N87645	19661
N68363	20238	N75984	4893	N86440	20721	N87646	19772
N68371	12789	N77112	25627	N86441	32734	N87647	20457
N68390	9175	N77777(1)	2238	N86442	34361	N87648	20563
N68392	20832	N77777(2)	10107	N86443	34357	N87649	20627
N68399	25819	N77777(3)	9342	N86444	20600	N87650	20833
N68459		N78125	9486	N86445	32779	N87651	25521
N68780	25888	N79001	26272	N86446	32776	N87652	25534
N68920	11844	N79002	26052	N86447	19750	N87653	25568
N69007	19454	N79003	26459	N86448	26179	N87654	25659
N69010	4756	N79004	26349	N86449	26692	N87655	26030
N69011	6062	N79005	25871	N86450	13772	N87656	26136
N69030	4588	N79006	25671	N86451	25399	N87657	26360
N69031	6193	N79007	26362	N86452	20525	N87658	26602
N69032	4932	N79008	25709	N86453	20596	N87659	26631
N69033	4638	N79009	26057	N86457	26687	N87660	26815
N69040	4519	N79010	26056	N86458	19173	N87661	26828
N69258	13057	N79011	26158	N86459	9919	N87662	26917
N69327	25360	N79014	9254	N86460	19397	N87663	27141
N69329	20463	N79015	9666	N86461	13758	N87664	32529
N69353	4425	N79017	19227	N86462	19581	N87665	32572
N69354	4397	N79018	12675	N86463	20230	N87666	32589
N69612	20054	N79020	26823	(N86464)	13809	N87667	32638
N70003	12938	N79021	19731	(N86465)	25394	N87668	33028
N72420	12871	N79022	20200	N86467	20716	N87669	33126
N72859	26457	N79023	9226	(N86468)	26803	N87670	33176
N73417	3258	N79024	9887	(N86474)	32977	N87671	34340
N73420	18925	N79025	10181	N86543	11737	N87672	34360
N73421	4824	N79026	20473	N86544	11689	N87673	34367
N73422	4840	N79028	20182	N86547	19961	N87674	34404
N73508	19737	N79029	20471	N86548	20405	N87682	20424
N73726	4894	N79032	11865	N86551	6179	N86783	19754
N73727	6352	N79033	9176	N86553	4715	N87684	20016
N73853	12446	N79034	19245	N86558	11665	N87696	13404
N73855	33604	N79035	19008	N86559	4975	N87745	6315
N73856	34214	N79036	20472	N86562	11761	N87788	12261
N73857	33244	N79037	20438	N86564	4415	N87805	33558
N73861	4884	N79038	20519	N86565	4516	N87814	33216
N74136	11923	N79040	13831	N86567	6044	N87815	26268
N74139(1)	4930	N79042	9394	N86569	4937	N87817	33251
N74139(2)	25485	N79043	13048	N86583	19411	(N87818)	4279
N74586	19711	N79044	9654	N86584	4935	N87819	26108
N74589	9926	N79045	13822	N86585	11741	N87880	26202
N74590	6213	N79054	19852	N86586	7395	N87907	33291
N74595	4562	N79055	20171	N86587	4951	N88706	6098
N74596	4356	N79056	20195	N86588	11628	N88713	4589
N74597	19032	N79057	10088	N86589	4939	N88725	19680
N74598	9143	N79062		N86591	20083	N88726	13056
N74611	12524	N79063	18922	N86592	9162	N88731	13820
N74620	4294	N79070	9775	N86593	11696	N88732	13835
N74647	9075	N79077	9715	N86594	11664	N88740(1)	6077
N74654	4211	N79087	4556	N86596	4975	N88740(2)	13070
N74663	6257	N79907	9470	N86597	11627	N88741(1)	6200
N74678	9726	N79960	33283	N86598	9392	N88741(2)	9146
N74827	10052	N79961(1)	13837	N86599	13759	N88743	9088
N74844	26458	N79961(2)	26893	N87604	19006	N88750	13114
N75028	6053	N79961(3)	26958	N87605	9501	N88752(1)	6069
N75029	6156	N79962	26098	(N87606)	26721	N88752(2)	4179
N75097	6151	N79963	26124	N87606	19742	N88753	9003
N75142	9173	N79966	12058	N87611	33105	N88754	34356
N75276	26568	N79968	20167	N87623	34195	N88756	13860
N75277	26288	N79970	25275	N87624	9147	N88757	20489

Chapter 4: Commercial Operators of the DC-3, C-47, R4D, Dakota and Li-2

Reg	c/n	Reg	c/n	Reg	c/n	Reg	c/n
N88758	13643	N91082	4631			N375AS	27008
N88771	4218	N91084	4351	N1AU	25771	N376AS	27047
N88772	4569	N91221	13860	N7AP	25341	N434A	4727
N88773(1)	6043	N91222	12789	N11AF	13817	N471AF	13485
N88773(2)	6258	N91223	10127	N13AT	25964	N472AF	13485
N88774	7366	N91224	9723	N23AJ	9247	(N511AA)	20444
N88775	19770	N91225	6098	N24AH	9526	(N512AA)	34358
N88776	19201	N91226	12528	N26AA	33444	N512AC	25534
N88783	12785	N91227	9175	N26AH	26093	N513AC	4346
N88787	19639	N91228	9254	(N27AA)	25806	(N514AA)	26568
N88788	13643	N91229	12792	N28AA	2239	N514AC	26558
N88789	4395	N91230	6178	N32A	33345	N515AC	1903
N88790	4628	N91231	9471	N32AL	33368	N517A	11627
N88791	4254	N91232	4595	N32AP		N518AC	43191
N88794	4357	N91233	9392	N34AH	43360	N534A(1)	4497
N88798	6255	N91234	20191	N36AP	13439	N534A(2)	4997
N88799	10127	N91244		N37AH	26713	N596AR	4877
N88801	19409	N91260	25372	N37AP	4430	N595AM	27203
N88802	4458	N91261	19495	N38AP	10217	N598AR	2145
N88803	9090	N91286	26324	N39AH	11808	N692A	7318
N88804	9921	N91287	26883	N43A	43086	N715A	6352
N88805	4461	N91288	12269	N44AF	6328	N717A	4498
N88806	4773	N91289	26138	N47AZ	13019	N718A	4503
N88807	20588	N91314	4538	N49AG	11737	N719A	4309
N88808	20137	N91315	33542	N51A(1)	4988	N720A	4381
N88809(1)	6253	N91374	26618	N51A(2)	2103	N721A	6204
N88809(2)	20058	N91375	33180	N51AD	2103	N722A	4382
N88822	13757	N91378	12296	N54AA	12475	N723A	4395
N88823	13073	N91379	13079	N61A	9667	N733A	11636
N88824	13678	N92578	9028	N68AH	26874	N751A	12060
N88825	25234	N93042	19685	N73AH	26968	N763A	4894
N88826	19776	N93043	25334	N76AB	20560	N773AF	19239
N88827	19654	N94218	4141	N82AC	10160	N872A	7403
N88828	19513	N94437	25453	N83AC	12539	N887AM	27085
N88829(1)	19415	N94441	26063	(N84AC)	12585	N894A	4978
N88829(2)	6253	N94442	26454	N85AC	20794	N906A	11751
N88834	12695	N94443	32885	N86AC	19950	N941AT	12907
N88835	19448	N94446	32977	N90A	4810	N999AT	20427
N88854	11677	N94447	20716	(N95AC)	9342	N1000A	2184
N88871	6313	N94448	26803	(N96AC)	19468	N1037A	43341
N88872	3274	N94449	13809	N97A	4813	N1350A	33032
N88873	13640	N94450	25394	N100A	4237	N1546A	20191
N88874	12693	N94451	19397	N101AP	12299	N1944A	19677
N88875	9212	N94468	19536	N102AP	2257	N2000A	11627
N88876(1)	4615	N94470	27006	N107AD	12438	N2001A	4497
N88876(2)	9249	(N94480)	25453	N129AG	11653	N2020A	9667
N88877	20225	N94486	19991	N130A	25483	N2025A	34375
N88882	32592	N94528	19851	N132AL	33368	N2027A	34289
N88916	32920	N94529	20401	N133AC	6260	N2077A	4479
(N88936)	32762	N94530	12172	N134A	4727	N2078A	20427
N88937	19524	N94531	27079	(N141A)	13860	N2082A	20439
N88967	12863	N94542	19122	N142A	12789	N2084A	12679
N90079	7392	N94590	9719	N143A	10127	N2087A	6349
N90545(1)	9920	N94597	9397	N144A	9723	N2669A	9700
N90545(2)	32785	N94598	27026	N145A	6098	N2700A	"33567"
N90600	43308	N94599	10081	N146A	12528	N2701A	"33569"
N90626	4327	(N94717)	33235	N147A	9175		see 9531
N90627	4642	(N94718)	25806	N148A	9254	N2702A	33542
N90628	43344	(N94719)	33444	N149A	12792	N2703A	26586
N90715	19548	N95433	4223	N150A	6178	N2719A	13177
N90795	9053	N95446	6070	N151A	9471	N2733A	11636
N90830	13050	N95453	7351	N153A	9392	(N2754A)	25956
N90856	19992	N95460	20190	N154A	20191	N2757A	25956
N90904	33552	N95466	9970	N155A	2010	N2768A	25980
N90905	33024	N95469	7350	N169AP	20457	N3240A	19291
N90907	4268	N95470	9209	N200A	4237	N3706A	26224
N90908	25228	(N95473)	10156	(N200AN)	33053	(N3910A)	25457
N91002	20227	N95475	6354	N241AG	19662	N3941A	4097
N91003	9708	N95481	4306	N242AG	12679	N3946A	12336
N91005	20203	N95486	6065	N300A(1)	20401	N3947A	9856
N91006	20208	N95487	4225	N300A(2)	4237	N3951A	33076
N91007	20199	N95488	13469	N300AL	4237	N4044A	27082
N91008	25422	N98392	26565	N301AK	19778	N4045A	27090
"N91008"	2245	N99131	18949	N311A	9968	N4046A	26864
"N91008"	6337	N99210	1984	N314A	12740	N4049A	9124
N91014	25768	N99346	26501	N337AF	12004	N4270A	20058
N91016	11853	N99435	32899	N341A	2145	N5211A	19677
N91026	4301	N99663	33467	N345A	9397	N5515A	9061
N91028	4362	N99665	33445	N345AB	13803	N5522A	6090
N91052	12863	N99857	43332	N346AB	33441	N5541A	13105
N91053	13174	N99873	26465	N347AB	20215	N5590A(1)	13560
N91054	9712	(N99886)	33444	N374AS	34154	N5590A(2)	12873

Registration	C/N	Registration	C/N	Registration	C/N	Registration	C/N
N5592A	20432	N107BK	4082	N78C	4994	N6516C	25954
N6387A	34358	N110BF	43381	N80C	2108	N6517C	13004
N6666A	12907	N111BC	25526	N81C	1971	N6634C	13399
N7500A	11693	N123BA	7320	N82C(1)	1996	N6678C	10096
N7502A	4985	N132BB	2145	N82C(2)	20438	N6679C	4228
N7753A	1977	N132BP	2145	N83C	20137	N6682C	20877
N7904A	"1240" ?	N190BB	4369	N84C	2268	N6696C	19766
N7998A	27008	N202B	4090	N86C	3253	N6697C	20072
N8041A	25450	N230BK	26882	N88C	4090	N6868C	34334
N8061A	6085	(N239BW)	11631	N89C	3252	N6870C	25537
N8064A	9831	N300BF	26744	N90C	2199	N6893C	4419
(N9416A)	2053	N300BG	4237	N92C	2008	N7069C	26358
N9838A	13139	N400B	11672	N93C	4979	N7071C	33206
N9839A	34198	N400BF	9415	N94C	6331	N7072C	26583
N9842A	10073	N477B	2252	N94CA	26705	N7073C	33216
(N9845A)	11903	N641B	12853	N95C(1)	3283	N7074C	33345
N9853A	34189	N707BA	33046	N95C(2)	20139	N7091C	33359
N9891A	9891	(N755BB)	2220	N96C	4550	N7092C	26583
		N915BD	43080	N97C	3258	N7147C	13177
N3BA(1)	20401	N999B	4255	N98C	1955	N7148C	26184
N3BA(2)	12172	N1788B	1954	N99C	11696	N7153C	4332
N4BA	6208	N1789B	2130	N101CA	20698	N7232C	11808
N8BC	4090	N1790B	2185	N103CA	9967	N7233C	33133
N9BC	9510	N1791B	2183	N104CA	25409	N7234C	26283
N11BC	34373	N1792B	2184	N105CA	25720	N7477C	33291
N12BA	10035	N1793B	4859	N122CA	4827	N7478C	32794
N19BA	4986	N1794B	7313	N213C	3291	N7488C	33100
N21BF	9832	N1795B	20388	N215CM	26792	N7489C	26713
N23BA	9342	N1796B	20346	N239CJ	20454	N7630C	33322
N28BA	4583	N1797B	20160	N322C	6090	N7631C	33201
N29BF	26002	N1798B	20817	N322CS	6090	N7632C	9486
N32B(1)	6061	N1799B	32578	N394CA	19394	N7633C	25775
N32B(2)	2145	N2271B	19362	N395CG	11651	N7634C	25824
N46BF(1)	4545	see also	19920	N486C	6325	N7674C	26258
N46BF(2)	19173	N2566B	25769	N505C	43335	N7675C	26268
N55B	2220	N2900B	26882	N545CT	43365	N7676C	26968
N62BA	6095	N2901B	4433	N555CR	4545	N7677C	33155
N66B	9667	N2902B	25655	N611CB	19992	N7678C	26558
N67B	11737	N2948B	4880	N700CA	12438	N7713C	
N68B	11741	N3937B	18978	N700CC	4903	N7714C	
N69B	1916	N5139B	4926	N770CC	43080	N7780C	25736
N70B(1)	3296	N5598B	43325	N814CL	34370	N7781C	26763
N70B(2)	4854	N5831B	19345	N821C	6336	N7874C	6156
N70BF	27085	N6201B	11657	N852C	9471	N7931C	25837
N71B	1967	N6387B	25406	N922CA	2204	N8014C	4200
N72B	2250	N7712B	34306	N951CA	34214	N8324C	20388
N72BF	33053	N7771B	10052	N952CA	20721	N8325C	13186
N73B	2252	N7820B	13006	N2237C	2137	N8326C	13296
N74B	3299	N7862B	26216	N2271C	25309	N8327C	20346
N75B	4992	N7868B	26669	N2298C	33201	N8328C	20160
N76B	4987	N8041B	10100	N2426C	13232 ?	N8329C	32588
N77B	20433			N3753C	20596	N8330C	26704
N78B	4140	N1C	27079	N3928C	2194	N8331C	32578
N79B	2257	N4C	4433	N3929C	2195	N8332C	26906
N80B(1)	2259	N4CP	4433	N3932C	18986	N8333C	20891
N80B(2)	11701	N6CA	33346	N3933C	4763	N8334C	20817
N80BA	2259	N7CA	26582	N3935C	20432	N8335C	25888
N81B	7382	N10CA	26603	N3937C	4732	N8336C	7313
N82B	4998	N10CR	4112	N3938C	9380	N8337C	4859
N83B	4862	N11CA	26613	N3943C	12853	N8338C	2183
N84B	11701	N12CA	12332	N3956C	4731	N8339C	2184
N85B	2233	N25CE	12476	N3957C	20473	N8340C	2130
N86B(1)	6328	N27C	20438	(N3958C)	12853	N8341C	2185
N86B(2)	13073	N28C(1)	7394	N3963C	9041	N8342C	1954
(N89BF)	12425	N28C(2)	4998	N3972C	11865	N8348C	19313
N89BJ	13228	N38CA	6343	N3975C	12717	N8349C	19620
N91BF	32541	N38CG	4760	N3980C	6350	N8350C	20806
N92BF	27187	N40CE	25409	N4007C	11719	N8352C	19452
N95BF	25667	N47CE	13456	N4700C	4903	N8353C	32817
N96BF	13321	N47CR	19770	N4766C	20475	N8354C	32530
N97BF	19525	N48CG	4932	N4776C	20715	N8355C	19062
N98BF	18984	N49CE	33186	N4788C	34325	N8356C	4573
N100BF	43361	N50CE	25409	N5000C(1)	32867	N8357C	6151
N102BF	43334	N50CM	13445	N5000C(2)	20475	N8358C	18901
N102BL	32654	N55C	26542	N5541C	12428	N8359C	2261
N103BF	13383	N55CE	26542	N5590C	12187	N8360C	2135
N103BL	20830	N62CC	13798	N6078C	11657	N8361C	4927
N104BF	12543	N67CR	4200	N6082C	26763	N8362C	4871
N105BF	43389	N68CW	25980	N6097C (C-39)	2072	(N8399C)	19932
N106BF	43396	N73CD	32529	N6200C	25445	N8421C	20681
N107B	4082	N75C	9028	N6494C	25352	N8538C	43347
N107BF	43352	N77C	4219	see also	26405	N9074C	32934

Chapter 4: Commercial Operators of the DC-3, C-47, R4D, Dakota and Li-2

Registration	c/n	Registration	c/n	Registration	c/n	Registration	c/n
N9075C	9549	N471DK	19446	N1FN	11685	N6666F	20454
N9076C	9072	N472DK	27137	N3FY	20562	N8538F	43369
N9077C	4457	N473DC	19345	N12F	6342	N9011F	9210
N9078C	4273	N473DK	6223	N12FL	6342	N9731F	19654
N9079C	4275	N517DC	6154	N30FE	34329	N9820F	26423
N9080C	6135	N517DW	2173	N34F	4790	N9848F	32867
N9081C	18910	N518DW	4813	N34FL	4790	N9849F	12813
N9082C	33140	N600D	1551	N35F(1)	13073	N9858F	20626
N9083C	12142	N666DG	2106	N35F(2)	6328	N9895F	26105
N9508C	26733	N730D	25888	N36F	12736 ?	N9896F	4223
N9516C	26263	N775D	11741	N37F	6343	N9897F	19238
N9518C	26093	N775DM	11741	N37FL	6343	N9935F	26423
N9519C	12555	N777DG	25634	N38F	4183	N9947F	34374
N9577C	13321	N805D		N39F	2191	N9959F	4865
N9881C	11928	N834D	43324	N40F	6319	N9973F	25483
		N843DD	34286	N40FN	4925	N9983F	19218
N2DD	6324	N943DJ	7313	N41F	2184	N9984F	19288
N10DC	4093	N983DC	12267	N42F	9531	N9985F	19975
N20DH	20401	N1030D	4810		see 33569	N9986F	13727
N23D	4986	N1800D	9028	N42FN	4842	N9988F	25282
N34D	4865	N1934D (DC-2)	1368	N44F	6208	N9989F	20562
N34DF	4865	N2000D	2264	N45F	9108	N9992F	4891
N39DT	4871	N2271D	33174	N47F	12726 ?	N9993F	9862
N49DE	34289	N2668D	10168	N47FE	19536	N9994F	9186
N49DF	34289	N2804D	12515	N47FJ	9053	N9997F	9510
N51D(1)	2108	N2815D	1945	N47FK	9700	N9999F	10101
N51D(2)	4550	N2816D	1946	N47FL	13087		
N62DA		N2817D	2054	N48F	2105	N3G	19662
N62DN	12830	N2818D(1)	2121	N48FN	4306	N8GR	25371
N69D	4363	N2818D(2)	3283	N49F	6325	N30G	4200
N77D	6338	N2841D	34193	N49FN	4179	N38G(1)	2243
N100DW	13643	N2883D	10048	N50F	9049	N38G(2)	4759
N102DH	20830	N2898D	12337	N51F	6095	N40G(1)	9075
N116DT	43307	N2899D	25944	N53FN	4319	N40G(2)	12386
N123D	19770	N6895D	13676	N70F(1)	9075	N42G	12853
N123DZ	12004	N6896D	33625	N70F(2)	12386	N44GH	43393
N128D	4815	N6897D	20008	N83FA	20698	N47GW	20079
N129D	11650	N6898D	20082	N85FA	25720	N59G	4988
N130D	19800	N6899D	20411	N86FA	9967	N73G	9042
N131D	2140	N8486D (DC-2)	1376	N87FA	26705	N91GA	12295
N132D	7328			N88FA	19239	N91GC	19822
N133D	1499	N8EQ		N99FS	12425	N92GA	13087
N134D	11731	N11EL	2105	N115FC	6208	N110G	43084
N135D	1547	N13E	12727	N131FS	32920	N170GP	33436
N136D	18925	N19E	12386	N132FS	25778	N207GB	26283
N137D	2249	N47E	13816	N133FS	27202	N208GB	33100
N138D	2245	N50E	11657	N134FS	33299	N210GB	33100
N139D(1)	2027	N50EB	11657	N135FS	20063	N211GB(1)	33201
N139D(2)	2165	N104E	9510	N136FS	10267	N211GB(2)	26133
N140D	2126	N124E	7393	N138FS	9967	N212GB	33216
N141D	1945	N162E	4926	N139FS	12357	N213GB	33232
N142D	1946	N163E	7394	N144FS	2216	N214GB	26388
N143D	2054	N166E	25567	N203FE	12853	N219GB	26273
N144D	3283	N225ES	4359	N211FF	12970	N220GB	4438
N145D	12048	N333EF	25778	(N212FF)	19227	N221GB	11859
N146D	9231	N340EL	4110	N219F	9894	N223GB	11928
N147D	12753	N405E	25409	N230F	9074	N224GB	12261
N147DC	19347	N625E	20427	N308FN	9700	N225GB	33251
N148D	6335	(N625EB)	20427	N395F	11651	N226GB	13004
N149D	4919	N688EA	12254	N464FS	4692	N227GB	33345
N150D(1)	20195	N700E(1)	4237	N480F	9719	N228GB	26093
N150D(2)	4463	N700E(2)	20401	N481F	26461	N229GB	26874
N151D	20171	N912E	19992	N482F	26423	N230GB	20443
N177DM	33053	N3433E	19458	N483F	4223	N231GB	26108
N191DM	2237	N4332E	32561	N484F	9470	N232GB	26268
N193DP	4433	N4990E	12007	N485F(1)	11654	N233GB	26283
N212DD	43386	N4991E	12106	N485F(2)	33042	N235GB	26558
N230D	4986	N4992E	12139	N486F	20214	N236GB	20743
N243DC	9247	N4993E	12440	N487F	19240	N237GB	26968
N259DC	25951	N4994E	12442	N488F	26105	N238GB	9526
N400D	1556	N4995E	12039	N489F	12269	N239GB	11808
N401D	1964	N4996E	12141	N612F	1960	N240GB	26713
N402D	1994	N4997E	12191	N715F	4129	N308G	26882
N403D	1995	N4998E	13559	N912F	1960	N321GR	43086
N404D	2107	N5000E	20475	N950FA	4306	N338G	2250
N405D	2211	N7164E	13087	N2271F	19252 ?	N343G	34351
N406D	2214	N8011E	4521	N2893F	26578	N407G	4095
N407D	2244	N8014E	3291	N3029F	25778	N437GB	19999
N408D	2247	N8187E	13840	N3139F	9635	N444G	19662
N409D	3277	N8694E	2250	N3149F	25572	N480G	4932
N410D	4970	N8695E	1911	N3261F	26209	N512GL	20016
N456D	6340			N4946F	20555	N513GL	26716

249

Registration	Number	Registration	Number	Registration	Number	Registration	Number
(N514GL)	4479	N3433H	43090	N172K	26880	N48ME	32935
N515GL	33052	N4458H	43360	N176K	2272	N65MK	13174
N516GL	33203	N4797H	25623	N200KC	11669	N70M	4912
(N519GL)	32814	(N8153H)	19394	N301K	3264	N77MM	9149
N541GA	34370	N9032H	6353	N302K	6097	N79MA	4089
N655GP	1911	N9033H	20228	N303K	9210	N80M	34378
N671G	11737	N9061H	19737	N310K	4843	N90M	25802
N705GB	13854	N9144H	12487	N343K	6148	N90ML	25802
N728G	4359	N9399H	4365	N346K	6148	N100M	19716
N759G	12853	N9562H	9028	N364K	20215	N100MA	20180
N792G	6314	N9835H (DC-2)	1246	N400KC	11719	N101MX	2102
N805GP	20875	N9922H	4662	N461K	2265	N118M	9026
N1021G	26725			N650K	13174	N147M	7313
N1047G	4812	N13JA	4082	N777K(1)	4174	N171MV	19627
N2312G	33216	N20JM	43082	N777K(2)	11693	N200MF(1)	9990
N2577G	43366	N26J	4862	N800KC	12055	N200MF(2)	4082
N2782G	26104	N38JB	4760	N843K	4733	N200MF(3)	9766
N3454G	33144	N70JC	26133	N1334K	43374	N200MX	4082
N3455G	26108	N109JB	33010	N1559K	4134	N203M	43082
N3458G	12261	N139JR	20550	(N1969K)	19227	N208MA	
N3630G	20422	N140JR	26815	N2141K	43397	N213M	
N3671G	26593	N141JR	19366	(N2273K)	19320	N213MA	7320
(N9271G)	20835	N142JR	32843	N2668K	33518	N217MA	2171
		N143JB	13757	N5590K	10000	N222MA	4114
N3HA	4138	N143JR	1995			N256M	2105
N7H	6062	N145JR	33144	N1L	4141	N258M(1)	2105
N10HB	25980	N146JR	27085	N7L	19751	N258M(2)	9555
N15HC	43080	(N150JD)	4463	N19LR	3283	N300M	2225
(N19HA)	25816	N155JM	4463	N47L	7313	N300MF	27121
N24H	43076	N163J	19402	N55L	26675	N300MR	2014
N25H	20054	N164J	12717	N55LT	10035	N301MF	4082
N26H	4871	N165J	12004	N76LP	6343	N353MM	11665
N30H	1964	N166J	12027	N117LR	43158	N355MJ	43076
N41HQ	2053	N255JB	1911	N121L	43084	N400MF	26877
N47HL	27203	N376JC	12550	N165LG	6314	N423MB	27079
N66HL	9247	N401JB	3299	N166LG	4138	N535M	20558
N69HA	25816	N403JB(1)	6318	N168LG	4089	N567M	43159
N79HA	25816	N403JB(2)	34202	N222LW	4114	N587MB	43312
N81HA(1)	13840	N502J	4484	N225LS	4359	N603MC	4932
N81HA(2)	19074	N574JB	20145	N264LC	10035	N701M	19716
N84H(1)	4795	N600JD	3291	N269LM	26054	N705M	11672
N84H(2)	19593	N678JC	19029	N271L	4110	N712MW	43086
N88HA	19691	N742J	7356	N272L	2263	N793MU	2189
N89HA	19603	N743J	1963	N292L	25923	N795M	2127
N90HA	12300	N800J	20806	N321L	43345	N795MU	2127
N92HA	4306	N818J	10168	N456L	6340	N822M	4200 ?
N93HA	34368	N2001J	12261	N456LF	6340	(N830M)	13105
N96H	19224	N2002J	26108	N503L	43075	N833M	33299
N97H	33613	N2003J	33251	N547LM	43369	N834M	26211
N98H	20061	N2004J	33216	N582LA	13070	N836M	25977
N99H	32588	N2005J	26268	N587LM	43369	N837M	12524
N98HA	25485	N2006J	26558	N683LS	43084	N838M	20448
N99HA	25964	(N2007J)	33232	N943L	19433	N839M	20166
N123H	12679	(N2009J)	4438	N993L	7319	N840M(1)	9670
N124H	43076	N2805J	20835	N2000L	4082	N840M(2)	25771
N125H	20054	N3906J	43344	N2290L	12289	N840MB	9670
N129H(1)	2108	N4471J	6187	N4565L	2108	N841M	18961
N129H(2)	4126	N4550J	6055	N8040L	34236	N841MB	18961
N136H	13658	N4948J	25418			N842M	19741
N137H	42965			N1M	2102	N842MB	19741
N138H	9904	N6K	9995	N3M	2119	N843M	34286
N139HH	4112	N22KN	26183	N3MJ	13840	N843MB(1)	34286
N142HD	2172	N44K	4918	N6M	3283	N843MB(2)	13228
N157H	4132	N45K	4918	N12MA	4908	N844M	34143
N177H	1920	N46K	2265	N13MA	26612	N844MB	34143
N222H	19999	N55KN	4936	N14MA	25347	N845MB	19685
N222HC	43159	N56KS	25769	N15M	1998	N846MB	33305
N257H	2173	N62K	34374	N15MA	19286	N848M	43378
N321HA	4519	N67K	7313	N18M	2200	N851M	43302
N333H	1911	N69K	43086	N26MA	2169	N877MG	20806
N335HH	20562	N73KW	2252	N28MA	11677	N886M	43378
N585H	19992	N74KW	7317	N29MA	2249	N919M	34133
N600HA	6318	N75KW	4861	N31MC	6148	N1039M	19126
(N667H)	12255	N76KW	9397	N31MS	11631	N1050M	20558
N734H	4727	N77KW	12299	N32MS	4978	N1075M	4877
N737H	6062	N84K(1)	2194	N33M(1)	19992	N1085M	4918
N770HB	19770	N84K(2)	9040	N33M(2)	2119	N1086M	4755
N791HH	33123	N84KB	9040	N33MS	9174	N1093M	7408
N932H	34368	N85K	4992	N33MW	4965	N1200M	4962
N950HA	19276	N95KT	6255	N34MS	20037	N1213M	4209
N1944H	34378	N101KC	11639	N36MK	20215	N1300M	2225
(N3269H)	43375	N115KW	4112	N43M	6262	N1310M	7375

Chapter 4: Commercial Operators of the DC-3, C-47, R4D, Dakota and Li-2

Registration	C/N	Registration	C/N	Registration	C/N	Registration	C/N
N1350M	26342	N9700N	12073	N22RB	4926	N20S	4998
N1561M	25443	N9796N	43375	N24RK	9149	N23SA	4903
N1605M	9519			N29R	33542	N26S	4862
N1659M	4764	N3PG	9700	N50R	19770	N32SC	2264
N1694M	25360	N4PG	4997	N60R	4877	N47SJ	25869
N1696M	20463	N5PG	20444	N65R	2145	N53ST	9380
N1699M	4363	N27PR	11776	N71R	4129	N56S	13757
N1821M	4727	N28PR	6323	N72R	26590	N59SC	12332
N1826M	19770	N29PR	3278	(N79RD)	9920	N60SA	1926
N1844M	19024	N30PB	2213	N80R	2008	N61SA(1)	2121
N1847M	34368	N31PB	2201	N81R	4979	N61SA(2)	11645
N1848M	20750	N32PB	4827	N82R	20438	N62SA	4976
N1944M	19394	N33PB	4944	N94R	2103	N63SA	7356
N1968M	26893	N34PB	2204	N100RW	11741	N64SA	4107
N2111M	4319	N35PB	2216	N104RP	12727	N65SA	4925
N2270M	10239	N38PB	2137	N117RR	43305	N66SA	11631
N2619M	32776	N40PB	2167	N145RD	20175	N67SA	7403
N2630M	19593	N43PB	1953	N146RD	32897	N68SA	7318
N4440M	4807	N67PA	32920	N147RD	9766	N69SA	4822
N5584M	43325	N129PC	9795	N148RD	27199	N70SA	4894
		N130PB	2213	N149RD	33552	N71SA	6352
N2N	6164	N136PB	1997	N154R	6156	N78SR	12680
N7NB	3299	N137PB	4128	N169RB	4939	N85SA	11637
N10NA	25771	N139PB	2239	N173RD	25313	N86SA	4951
N11ND	13439	N156PM	43193	N192RD	12115	N87SA	11628
N21ND	4430	N181PM	2191	N193RD	33375	N89SA	4978
N38N	6340	N206PP	19662	N194RD	32948	N90SA	11751
N39N	2218	N222PV	43087	N195RD	26439	N91SA	2179
N41N	6315	N233P	4944	N198RD	33024	N91SR	4218
N53NA	27202	N233PB	4944	N208R	19662	N92SA	2240
N54NA	19475	N331P	7323	N222RR	34368	N93SA	4106
N56NA	4979	N333PS		N223R	43159	N94SA	1963
N57NA	19560	(N333PV)	4209	N272R	13678	N95SA	11666
N58NA	12970	N412P	6315	N294R	2103	N96SA	42967
N59NA(1)	11750	N491P	43075	N305R(1)	4200	N100SD	12853
N59NA(2)	9043	N502PA	26744	N305R(2)	11741	N101SF	11674
N60NB	19029	N671P	11737	N330RD	25546	N110SU	2165
N60NR	11651	N747PG	19345	N332RD	33211	N111SA	43193
N103NA	9531	N777PG	25634	N395R	25449	N111ST	4661
	see 33569	N832PB	4827	N400RS	4979	N115SA	13310
N115NA	11625	N888PR	4093	N405RG	4816	N116SA	32855
N115NK	4134	N889P	11737	N447RS	4810	N123S	26114
N212NW	7403	N890P	20401	N456R	7369	N124SF	26111
N388N	6340	N912PS	19992	N471RF	11627	(N125SF)	6343
N391N	2218	N1385P	34371	N560R	4080	N127SF	
N423NA	25771	N3433P	4346	N561R	13063	N181SB	19039
N501NA	26787	N4241P	33224	N562R	20838	N195SP	12195
N510NR	9100	N4261P	26111	N569R	7390	N242SM	4877
(N600NA)	3291	N8059P	20875	"N569R"	4828	N258SW	
N622NU	12830	N9049P	26358	"N569R"	10100	N285SE	2177
N636NA	26787			N570R	20416	N286SE	2004
N638NA	25347	N1QJ	19476	N573R	2200	N287SE	1951
N722NR	43342	N8QE	4084	N578R	20416	N288SE	2222
N777N	6331	N50Q	4438	N582R	20838	N289SE	1963
N777NA	6331	N90Q	4147	N600RC	2193	N301SF	20698
N801NC	4200	N130Q(1)	25483	N686RP	2272	N302SF	26705
N817NA(1)	12287	N130Q(2)	11761	N700RC	11628	N303SF	9967
N817NA(2)	26787	N211Q	10202	N752R	4359	N304S	32624
N827NA	26787	N541Q	34370	N800RC	25449	(N305S)(1)	26595
N1051N	13887	N886Q	1970	N811RB	25509	N305S(2)	34400
N1268N	32542	N3100Q	12269	N2724R	25483	N305SF	6208
N1274N	20464	N3101Q	4911	N4421R	34291	N306SF	43393
N1280N	13364	N3102Q(1)	33042	(N5584R)	43382	N307SF	43345
N1369N	19217	N3102Q(2)	11654	N8538R	43393	N308SF	18984
N1388N	12377	N3161Q	26716	N8744R	20156	(N350SA)	43089
N1399N	26363	N3176Q	32814	N9025R	4998	(N351SA)	6085
N2270N	19831	N3177Q	33021	N9060R	19691	(N352SA)	33201
N2668N	11982	N3178Q	33143	N9081R	34272	(N353SA)	12857
N2782N	20847	N3179Q	33353	N9089R	4174	N393SW	2202
N3264N	12255	N3749Q	43082	N9097R	2232	N400S(1)	43080
N3753N	33604	N8194Q	32961	N9123R	12110	N400S(2)	11672
N4425N(1)	6341	N9983Q	33532	N9124R	12004	N430SF	4813
N4425N(2)	1963	N9984Q	18977	N9127R	34292	N467SP	32948
N4805N	4760	N9985Q	27215	N9184R	12027	N540S	43191
N4806N	4441	N9986Q	25810	N9308R	19792	N541S	43192
N4843N	1920	N9994Q	25966	N9310R	34373	N542S	43193
N4994N	25771			N9313R	2200	N560S	1926
(N5478N)	4891	N1R	4129	N9319R	9719	N561SV	20139
N5584N	43326	N12RB	20401	N9321R	11775	N564S	4107
N7043N	13816	N14RD	2145	N9351R	4939	N569S	4822
N7252N	9530	N16R	4644			N591S	2179
N9663N	43385	N21R	33305	N15SJ	33049	N592S	2240

Registration	S/N	Registration	S/N	Registration	S/N	Registration	S/N
N593S	4106	N5597T	43327	(N60V)	12555	N6067V	26888
N595S	11666	N7777T	2243	(N113VB)	2220		
N596S	42967	(N8241T)	32897	N125V	11815	N1W	43159
N625SL	13798	N8241T	33134	N161V	4644	N3W	9700
N625ST	2195	N9050T	12472	N163VW	11737	N4W	4997
N702S	13331			N164VW	20454	N5W	20444
N711SA	2014	N28U	7394	N245V	4219	N11W	20196
N711SE	2014	N48UC	6325	N502V	11815	N20W(1)	11761
N770SU	2252	N55U	20455	N583V	12369	N20W(2)	25483
N845S	25509	N56U	19394	N744V	4700	N23WT	11650
N873SN	43327	N57U	20454	N755VM	12196	N27W	43073
N906SA	11751	N58U(1)	9276	N777V	2195	N30W(1)	11759
N973SN	43347	(N58U)(2)	7354	N778V	2195	N30W(2)	4109
N1010S	6097	N59U	19433	N783V	4219	N45WT	4918
N1157S	6208	N60U	10189	N784V	11664	N47WG	19770
N1159S	2237	N77U	4219	N797V	4104	N62WS	12005
N2203S	25441	N78U	4994	N902VC	13074	N66W(1)	9380
N2204S	12798	N86U	13073	N1198V	6070	N66W(2)	11665
N2216S	12936	N90U	4936	N1430V	26479	N72WL	18978
N2217S	9589	N92U	2200	N1433V	9590	N75W(1)	9149
N2782S	4148	N94U	2127	N1472V	19662	N75W(2)	13840
N4039S	32974	N95U	2238	N1478V	19766	N75WA	13840
N4646S	4692	N96U	13331	N1499V	25409	N75WS	33564
N4658S	10131	N97U	4692	N1501V	19032	N78W(1)	4109
N4730S	25748	N98U	11653	N1511V	19830	N78W(2)	11759
N4731S	13074	N99U	4654	N1514V	11780	N85WE	4992
N4732S	19496	N141U	4433	N1526V	13452	N89WA	43312
N4792S	34149	N157U	4132	N1534V	9395	N130W	11759
N4793S	12556	N166U	1951	N1549V	13480	N156WC	43193
N7711S	4784	N189UM	6262	N1555V	19830	N175W	9149
N9101S	19961	N190UM	2119	N1592V	25802	N180W	2169
N9923S	25964	N207U	4984	N4618V	4392	N180WK	2169
		N315UT	4090	N4630V	4823	N182WC	20438
(N3TV)	2108	N391U	2218	N4642V	19649	N182WP	20438
N20TW	2236	N403UB	6318	N4660V	13296	N195W	20403
N22T	4784	N404U	26612	N4661V	26704	N293WM	13860
N30TN	43159	N404US	26612	N4662V	26906	N287W	20054
N32TN	43301	N793U	2189	N4663V	32588	N305WC	11741
N40TG	4095	N1230U	11742	N4668V	"5994"	N341W	13041
N46TE	4926	N1800U(1)	9028		see 26172	N349W	25944
N47TF	12317	N1800U(2)	19731	N4669V	32746	(N352WJ)	12352
N63T	9470	N1840U	19731	N4670V	26172	N356W	9858
N75T	see 12726	N2000U	3296	N4673V	4756	N427W	43073
N81T	25888	N2121U	43335	N4719V	4442	N456WL	43332
N87T	6148	N3433U	43087	N4720V	2145	N524W	43086
N95TM	6255	N4683U	10131	N4721V	34373	N525W	20054
N140T	12550	"N6059U"	33170	N4723V	see "33550"	(N607W)	20875
N169T	2180	N7506U	10217	N4724V	27098	(N720W)	33241
N175TD	43301			N4730V	see "33572"	N750WM	26167
N200TA	19998	N2VM	13757	N4731V	see "33573"	N977W	6352
N211TA	6342	N3VB	2220	N4733V	19246	N1000W	13643
N222TS	2120	N5V	9380	N4865V(1)	4497	N1234W(1)	20454
N300TX	26744	N7V	9700	N4865V(2)	9040	N1234W(2)	11651
N333TS	34342	N8V	4997	N4867V (DC-2)	1368	N1901W	2232
N343T	25615	N11VU	13439	N4868V	11883	N1902W	4369
N386T	20411	N21VU	4430	N4883V(1)	19452	N1981W	2232
N387T	20507	N24V	18978	N4884V	19313	N2270W	13387
N462T	13445	N24VL	18978	N4887V	4563	N2685W	33010
N502T	11815	N33VW	20401	N4892V	27069/a	N3239W	19677
N503T	43075	N40V	3287	N4893V	27069/b	(N3269W)	12428
N504T	4258	N41V	2227	N4908V	20193	N4504W	43365
N504TL	4258	N42V	42974	N4909V	see "34387"	N4957W	33282
N520TT	4842	N43V	42958	N4930V	25965 ?		
N711T(1)	4810	N44V(1)	9914	N4946V	20813	N1X	19029
N711T(2)	4784	N44V(2)	4545	N4947V	25687 ?	N1XP	4733
N711TD	12679	N45V	18984	N5086V	12736 ?	N2X	34326
N780T	20865	N46V	19402	N5089V	4352	N3X	26882
N781T	4306	N47V	20471	N5091V	9783	N3XW	34373
N782T	4382	N48V	13835	N5177V	33232	N72X	2220
N783T	4219	N49V	20002	N5178V	25627	N72XA	2220
N784T	6054	N50V	19288	N5250V	7319	N102X	2102
N786T	20238	N51V	19975	N5504V	34314	N514X	9380
N834TP	12590	N52V	19649	N5597V	43382	N717X	25356
N835TD	43321	N53V(1)	13041	N5602V	26818	N727XW	
N844TH	13070	N53V(2)	12717	N5606V	9456	N766X	11815
(N999TS)	25634	N54V	25443	N5631V	1955	N777X	1960
N1181T	25888	N55V	20447	N5644V	26690	N778X	4141
N3239T	19054	N56V(1)	4900	N5647V	34342	N1234X	20454
N4682T	13849	N56V(2)	33153	N5873V(1)	20054	N2071X	43354
N4696T	19809	N57V	4225	N5873V(2)	1551	N5106X	9058
N5156T	25509	N58V	9856	N5874V	7377	N5117X	6054
N5595T	20002	(N59V)	12555	N5900V	20244	N8042X	19041
						N8071X	12704
						N8190X	33478

N8502X	43376	N620Z	25234
N13YD	3266	N709Z	27182
N66Y	11654	N710Z	32914
N88Y	9995	N808Z	20731
N88YA	9995	N810Z	34143
N223Y (DC-1)	1137	N811Z	26508
N711Y	13658	N907Z	12300
N777YA	25634	N982Z	25485
N2123Y	43386		& see 4875
N2299Y	26283	N998Z	20145
N3433Y	43089	N999Z	4976
N3748Y	25368	N2270Z	13491
"N4443Y"	33170 ?	N2627Z	12476
N5467Y	33153	N2922Z	25611
N6326Y	25771	N3146Z	25802
N8071Y	25546	N4577Z	9795
N9002Y	4683	N8021Z	20444
N9049Y	34299	N8071Z	11746
N9060Y	19603	N8160Z	20472
		N8194Z	12166
N22Z	1977	N8502Z	43316
N74Z	25954	N9052Z	25956
N94Z	20442	N9053Z	10096
N100Z	20494	N9118Z	26133
N100ZZ	25485	N9119Z	26874
N101Z	4574	N9196Z	6173
N101ZG	20145	N9197Z	4436
N102Z	20560	N9445Z	25951
N102ZP	4661	N9457Z	26475
N115Z	33567	N9464Z	12733
N124Z	20533	N9465Z	9940
N125Z	9635	N9466Z	26373
N142Z	20494	(N9467Z)(1)	26724
N143Z	26542	N9467Z(2)	32810
N145Z	13110		
N145ZA	13110	NASA010	25771
N146Z	33567	NASA017	12287
N148Z	20422	NASA018	33110
N150Z	6156	NASA106	26367
N151Z	26408	NASA268	25771
N151ZE	26408	NASA501	26787
N151ZL	26408	NASA701	33110
N168Z	20850	NASA817	12287
(N168ZZ)	20850		
N200ZZ	25409	U.S.1 (DC-2)	1312
N203ZZ	6324	U.S.2 (DC-2)	1310
N234Z	4363	U.S.3 (DC-2)	1311
N300ZZ	9833 /	U.S.8 (DC-2)	1239
	later 25371	U.S.9 (DC-2)	1249
N510Z	12196	U.S.10 (DC-2)	1367

Notes:-

Considering the huge number of aircraft markings used in the USA, there are very few for which details are lacking, a mere 25. Some of these may be the result of mistakes in painting the mark on the aircraft or faulty observation. If any reader can identify any of the following aircraft the compiler would be pleased to hear. Several of the unknowns are believed to be aircraft used by the CIA or DEA and excluded from the register.

N44567 - A report in Lloyds List gives the owner as Peninsular Air Transport and states that it crashed on 6Feb47 - It has not appeared on any FAA card.

N91244 - This has been quoted with c/n 9724 but that aircraft was condemned as missing by the USAAF in 1945.

N7904A - The c/n is given as 1240. This could be the fuselage/line number or merely a corruption of the c/n or USAAF serial number.

N7713C and N7714C were noted at Bangkok on 25Nov79, possibly ex Thai Airways or AF, but nothing more has been heard of them.

Details would be most welcome of those listed above, together with:- N8037, N15219, N21351, N40160, N61696, N67178, N67422, N68459, N79062, N82103, N32AP, N62DA, N805D, N8EQ, N208MA, N213M, N333PS, N127SF, N258SW and N727XW.

URUGUAY - CX

PLUNA - Primeras Líneas Uruguayas de Navegación Aérea, Montevideo, bought two DC-2s in 1945 for use on scheduled services. They remained in use until 1951. DC-3s were added in 1946 and some of these survived until 1974 when they were transferred to the Air Force.

DC-2s:- CX-AEF; CX-AEG.
DC-3s:- CX-AFE; CX-AGD; CX-AGE; CX-AIJ; CX-AJZ; CX-AQC; CX-BDA; CX-BDB; CX-BDF; CX-BDG; CX-BDH.

TAMU - Transporte Aéreo Militar Uruguaya, Montevideo, was formed in 1974 by the Air Force, to take over PLUNA's domestic services and with them about eight DC-3s. The aircraft used were ex Air Force C-47s, bearing combined civil and military markings. One has been preserved at Montevideo.

CX-AFE; CX-AGD; CX-AIJ; CX-AQC; CX-BHO to CX-BHR incl; CX-BIN; CX-BJD; CX-BJG; CX-BJH; CX-BKH.

Index:-

CX-AEF (DC-2) c/n 1351		CX-BDG	19212
CX-AEG (DC-2)	1324	CX-BDH	12863
CX-AFE	32551	CX-BHO	13744
CX-AGD	13306	CX-BHP	25608
CX-AGE	12113	CX-BHQ	33431
CX-AIJ	4471	CX-BHR	19231
CX-AJZ	2266	CX-BIN	
CX-AQC	9226	CX-BJD	13744
CX-BDA	12083	CX-BJG	19021
CX-BDB	33392	CX-BJH	19301
CX-BDF	4400	CX-BKH	20604

VENEZUELA - YV

Douglas C-39s and DC-3s played an important part in helping to expand airline operations in Venezuela from 1944 onwards and the type still remains in service today. Identifying individual aircraft has proved more complicated than in many countries due to the use of three series of markings and the re-use of the same markings - sometimes twice. The earliest series was conventional and alphabetic, but later an intermediate letter was inserted, indicating the use to which the aircraft was put, e.g. YV-C-ACO, where C indicates Commercial use, P Petroleum companies and O Obras Publicas, ie Public Works. Finally a numbered system was introduced, with yet another series of functional letters, as suffixes, from 1975 on. C continues to indicate Commercial use with CP for Corporate or executive.

Aeroejecutivos, Miranda, started operations as early as 1983, using DC-3s as well as one or two other types. Operations continued into 2005, with three DC-3s.

YV-352CP; YV-475CP/YV-415C; YV-416C; YV-426C; YV-427C; YV-440C; YV-500C.

Aerotécnica SA, Ciudad Bolivar, has operated charter services since 1951, with a variety of types. DC-3s were introduced in about 1970, but are now out of use.

YV-C-GAF/YV-108C; YV-C-GAI; YV-C-GAJ/YV-109C; YV-C-GAK/YV-110C; YV-C-GAO/YV-115C; YV-C-GAP/YV-112C.

Aerovenca, Caracas, have used DC-3 YV-670C for general cargo work since 1992.

AVENSA - Aerovías Venezolanas SA, Caracas, was formed in May 1943 with help from Pan American. Domestic services started in May 1944, using Ford Trimotors and several C-39s. DC-3s arrived a year or so later and some remained until about 1970.

C-39s:- YV-AVG; YV-AVH; YV-AVJ(two) to YV-AVL incl.
DC-3s:- YV-AVA; YV-AVB; YV-AVF; YV-AVI; YV-AVN; YV-C-AVA to YV-C-AVG incl; YV-C-AVI; YV-C-AVJ(three); YV-C-AVK to YV-C-AVM incl; YV-C-AVO to YV-C-AVS incl; YV-C-AVU to YV-C-AVX incl; YV-AVY(two); YV-C-AVZ; YV-C-EVM; YV-C-EVO. YV-98C was acquired in 1989.

Caribbean Flights, Valencia, leased two DC-3s from L A Canedo of Bolivia. YV-912C remained in use in 2001, but YV-911C was stored.

Comeravia, Ciudad Bolivar, used DC-3 YV-184C in the late seventies.

LAV - Línea Aeropostal Venezolana, Caracas, bought DC-3s immediately after the war to replace the smaller Lockheed twins. In Jun57 further DC-3s were acquired with the take-over of TACA de Venezuela. The last few DC-3s were stored by 1978 and probably broken up.

YV-AGI; YV-AGU; YV-AHI; YV-AKA; YV-AKE; YV-AKU; YV-ALA; YV-ALE; YV-ALI; YV-ANA; YV-ANI; YV-C-ACO; YV-C-AFA; YV-C-AFE; YV-C-AFO; YV-C-AGI; YV-C-AHA; YV-C-AHI; YV-C-AHO; YV-C-AKA; YV-C-AKE; YV-C-AKO; YV-C-AKU; YV-C-ALA; YV-C-ALE/(YV-11C); YV-C-ALI; YV-C-ALO; YV-C-ALU; YV-C-AMD; YV-C-AMF; YV-C-AMG/YV-14C; YV-C-AMH; YV-C-AMO(two?); YV-C-AMP; YV-C-AMQ; YV-C-AMU; YV-C-ANA; YV-C-ANG/YV-13C; YV-C-ANH; YV-C-ANI; YV-C-ANQ; YV-C-ANR; YV-C-ANS; YV-C-AZA; YV-C-AZC; YV-C-AZF; YV-C-AZJ; YV-C-AZK/YV-12C; YV-C-AZO; YV-C-AZQ; YV-C-AZR/ YV-15C; YV-C-AZS; YV-C-AZT; YV-C-AZV; YV-C-AZX; YV-C-AZY.

Latin Carga - Latinamericana Aérea de Carga SA, Caracas, took over cargo operations from Tigres Voladores, using a DC-3 at first. This was replaced by C-46s.

YV-C-TGB/YV-144C.

LEBCA - Línea Expresa Bolivar CA, Caracas, operated cargo flights to Miami using various types, including DC-3s, between 1959 and 1969.

YV-C-LBC; YV-C-LBE; YV-C-LBF; YV-C-LBO.

Midas Commuter Airlines, Caracas-Maiquetia, operated DC-3 YV-506C in 1989 and R4D YV-505C between 1989 and 1992. An unidentified YV-507C was reported in 1993.

RANSA - Rutas Aéreas Nacionales SA, Caracas, was formed in 1948 to carry cargo and passengers. DC-3s were used until passenger services were given up in 1961 and C-46s were used.

YV-C-ARA; YV-C-ARB; YV-C-ARC; YV-C-ARF; YV-C-ARG; YV-C-ARJ; YV-C-ARM.

Rentavion, Caracas, was formed about 1990 with a Martin 404 and subsequently bought two DC-3s YV-146C and YV-147C, of which the last has been leased or sold to Servivensa.

RUTACA - Rutas Aéreos CA, Ciudad Bolivar, were using six DC-3s from 1978 on, one as a freighter. Four remained in store in 2003.

YV-214C; YV-215C; YV-216C; YV-218C; YV-222C; YV-224C; YV-225C; YV-226C; YV-227C.

Servivensa - Servicios AVENSA SA, a subsidiary of AVENSA has operated DC-3s since about 1991. Three were in use in 2003 and two were stored.

YV-147C; YV-609C; YV-610C; YV-611C; YV-761C; YV-769C; YV-822C, YV-2184C.

TACA de Venezuela, Caracas, started operations in January 1945, using two C-39s and about 20 DC-3s. Following financial difficulties in 1952 TACA was taken over by LAV in July 1957. [Note: Further TACA group entries will be found under Colombia, Costa Rica, El Salvador and Honduras]

C-39s:- YV-AZF; YV-AZI;
DC-3s:- YV-AZC; YV-AZD; YV-AZH to YV-AZR incl; YV-AZU; YV-C-AZA; YV-C-AZB; YV-C-AZC; YV-C-AZE; YV-C-AZF; YV-C-AZH to YV-C-AZK incl; YV-C-AZO to YV-C-AZV incl; YV-C-AZX; YV-C-AZY.

Tigres Voladores, Caracas, used a single DC-3, YV-TGB, on cargo services from 1963 until operations were taken over by Latin Carga.

Transporte Aéreo Transandino, Maracaibo, used a single DC-3, YV-C-AQC, until it was destroyed by fire in June 1948.

Transcarga - Transportes Aéreos de Carga, Caracas, was formed in 1968 to replace LEBCA on cargo operations. It took over some of the assets of the latter, but was wholly owned by VIASA. Two DC-3s were used during 1968/69.

YV-C-TCA/YV-C-TCC; YV-C-TCB.

Turismo de Oriente bought DC-3 YV-247C in 1976 and sold it in 1981.

Index:-

YV-C-ACO	c/n 19241	YV-C-AFE	26798
YV-P-AEI	13651	YV-C-AFO	13699
YV-P-AEK	12740	YV-AGI/YV-C-AGI	10111
YV-C-AFA	4525	YV-AGU	4205
YV-C-AHA		YV-AZI(2)/YV-C-AZI	34368
YV-AHI/YV-C-AHI	34254	YV-AZJ/YV-C-AZJ	19193
YV-C-AHO		YV-AZK/YV-C-AZK	19121
YV-AKA/YV-C-AKA	4449	YV-AZL	19222
YV-AKE/YV-C-AKE	4705	YV-AZM	19189
YV-C-AKO	9174	YV-AZN	9661
YV-AKU/YV-C-AKU	4581	YV-AZO/YV-C-AZO	19385
YV-ALA/YV-C-ALA	9750	YV-AZP/YV-C-AZP	20750
YV-ALE/YV-C-ALE	4537	YV-AZQ/YV-C-AZQ	19986
YV-ALI/YV-C-ALI	6210	YV-AZR/YV-C-AZR	9882
YV-C-ALO		YV-C-AZS	4773
YV-C-ALU	4791	YV-C-AZT	19141
YV-C-AMD	20037	YV-AZU	
YV-C-AMF	6115	YV-C-AZU	
YV-C-AMG	4458	YV-C-AZV	13449
YV-C-AMH	19783	YV-C-AZX	19411
YV-C-AMO(1)		YV-C-AZY	43077
YV-C-AMO(2)	13656	YV-P-BPF	13143
YV-C-AMP	19292	YV-O-BYS	4234
YV-C-AMQ	19053	YV-C-CAJ	
YV-C-AMU	9512	YV-C-CML	4269
YV-ANA/YV-C-ANA	12932	YV-P-CPY	43079
YV-C-ANG	11865	YV-C-DVL	4269
YV-C-ANH	20595	YV-P-EPE	20212
YV-ANI/YV-C-ANI	42960	YV-P-EPF	43085
YV-C-ANL		YV-P-EPO	12386
YV-C-ANQ	25264	YV-C-EVM	13372
YV-C-ANR	11687	YV-C-EVO	4240
YV-C-ANS	19000	YV-C-FAB	
YV-C-ANU		YV-C-FAC	
YV-P-APF	19593	YV-C-GAF	43079
YV-C-AQC	19126	YV-C-GAI	26613
YV-C-ARA	19871	YV-C-GAJ	13063
YV-C-ARB		YV-C-GAK	43078
YV-C-ARC	27098	YV-C-GAO	19000
YV-C-ARF(1)	2195	YV-C-GAP	19783
YV-C-ARF(2)	12957	YV-T-JTA	13651
YV-C-ARG	4522	YV-T-JTP	10111
YV-C-ARJ	2194	YV-T-JTV	9750
YV-C-ARM		YV-C-LBC	26888
YV-AVA/YV-C-AVA	20225	YV-C-LBE	4785
YV-AVB/YV-C-AVB	11620	YV-C-LBF	4202
YV-C-AVC	4958	YV-C-LBO	9061
YV-C-AVD	4955	YV-O-MAR-3	20595
YV-C-AVE	4179	YV-O-MAR-4	20212
YV-AVF/YV-C-AVF	6321	YV-O-MC	19335
YV-AVG (C-39)	2057	YV-MC-1	4234
YV-C-AVG	4764	YV-O-MC-1(1)	19335
YV-AVH (C-39)	2074	YV-O-MC-1(2)	4234
YV-AVI/YV-C-AVI	2195	YV-O-MC2	4234
YV-C-AVI(2)		YV-O-MC-3	4234
YV-AVJ(1) (C-39)	2060	YV-O-MOP-9	20595
YV-AVJ(2)	2057	YV-O-MOP-10	20212
YV-C-AVJ(1)	2194	YV-O-MTC-2	4234
YV-C-AVJ(2)	4202	YV-O-MTC-12	4234
YV-C-AVJ(3)	11649	YV-T-MTE	43079
YV-C-AVK	9049	YV-T-MTF	43078
YV-AVK (C-39)	2083	YV-T-MTH	19193
YV-C-AVL	4269	YV-T-MTY	4773
YV-AVL (C-39)	2084	YV-T-RTC	12386
YV-C-AVM	4086	YV-C-SAB	4522
YV-AVN	19984	YV-C-TAO	43078
YV-C-AVO	4863	YV-C-TAP	4773
YV-AVP/YV-C-AVP	3291	YV-C-TCA	4202
YV-C-AVQ	2232	YV-C-TCB	4785
YV-C-AVR	20558	YV-C-TCC	4202
YV-C-AVS	4372	YV-C-TGB	19411
YV-C-AVU	4432	(YV-11C)	4537
YV-C-AVV	"1160"	YV-12C	19121
YV-C-AVX	7391	YV-13C	11865
YV-C-AVY(1)	4785	YV-14C	4458
YV-C-AVY(2)	11772	YV-15C	9882
YV-C-AVZ	4551	YV-25CP	12476
YV-C-AZA	43079	YV-29CP	43085
YV-C-AZB		YV-32CP	13143
YV-AZC/YV-C-AZC	25278	YV-98C	43087
YV-AZD	11653	YV-108C	43079
YV-C-AZE		YV-109C	13063
YV-AZF (C-39)	2068	YV-110C	43078
YV-C-AZF	43078	YV-112C	19783
YV-AZH/YV-C-AZH	26267	YV-115C	19000
YV-AZI(1) (C-33)	1509	YV-144C	19411

CHAPTER 4: COMMERCIAL OPERATORS OF THE DC-3, C-47, R4D, DAKOTA AND LI-2

YV-146C	see 9392	YV-427C	4944
YV-147C	25278	YV-440C	2201
YV-184C	4269	YV-500C	6135
YV-214C	4269	YV-505C(1)	9894
YV-215C	19783	YV-505C(2)	43335
YV-216C	13063	YV-506C	1977
YV-218C	43079	YV-609C	43087
YV-222C	7386	YV-610C	9894
YV-224C	19055	YV-611C	1977
YV-225C	4537	YV-670C	13074
YV-226C	19121	YV-761C	12476
YV-227C	19000	YV-769C	19513
YV-247C	43085	YV-822C	9137
(YV-271CP)	4237	YV-911C	32761
YV-352CP	4237	YV-912C	25951
YV-389CP	11696	YV-475CP	43085
YV-415C	43085	YV-2183P	see 9392
YV-416C	4237	YV-2184P	25278
YV-426C	4093		

Note:-
YV-C-AZU was w/o 29Mar52, Cerro Grande Mt, 30km E of San Felipe.

VIETNAM - F-VN and XV and VN

Until 1951 Viêtnam was part of French Indo-China, and earlier airlines are recorded under that section heading. In December 1949 aircraft were registered in the F-VN.. section of the French register. The country was divided into North and South Viêtnam in 1954 and XV- was adopted by the South in 1959 on independence from France. The North was allocated 3W- but this remains unused. The country was reunified in 1976 following the fall of the South in the previous year. Aircraft that survived the Viêt Cong takeover were then given markings in the VN- sequence.

Air Viêtnam, Saigon, was formed in October 1951 to take over Air France's domestic services as well as those of SITA and Avions Taxis d'Indo-Chine. Services began with F-VNAF to 'H and the High Commission's F-BCYC which became XV-NIN in 1967. Four further DC-3s were added in 1956. Operations continued until the advancing North Vietnamese made them impossible. A few surviving DC-3s may have gone to Hang Khong Vietnam.

F-VNAF, F-VNAG, F-VNAH, F-VNBG, F-VNBM, F-VNBT, F-VNBU, XV-NIA to XV-NIE incl; XV-NIK to XV-NIO incl. Leased DC-3s included B-301; B-304; B-305; B-307; B-311; B-1531; F-BAOC; N7302; RP-C2122.

Hang Khong Viêtnam, Hanoi, took over all airline operations in Viêtnam in 1975 and initially used at least four captured DC-3s. These were all withdrawn from use at Saigon in February 1982, along with another 20 C-47s. Li 2s were also used.

VN-C502, VN-C503, VN-C512, VN-C514, VN-C533, VN-C585, VN-C680.

SILA - Service impérial de liaisons aériennes - was owned by the Vietnam Government and operated, sometimes on lease, some 9 DC-3s.

F-VNAC; F-VNAD; F-VNAE (two aircraft); F-VNAQ; F-VNAU; F-VNAV; F-VNBD; F-VNBL

Index:-

F-VNAC	c/n 20001	XV-NIC	20301
F-VNAD	9339	XV-NID	32822
F-VNAE(1)	12685	XV-NIE	26355
F-VNAE(2)	25591	XV-NIK	33323
F-VNAF	13256	XV-NIL	25248
F-VNAG	12832	XV-NIM	10247
F-VNAH	20301	XV-NIN	19071
F-VNAQ		XV-NIO	11717
F-VNAU	25275	VN-C502	
F-VNAV	11995	VN-C503	
F-VNBD	20114	VN-C508	26682
F-VNBG	19387	VN-C509	
F-VNBL	20184	VN-C512	
F-VNBM	32822	VN-C514	
F-VNBT	26355	VN-C533	
F-VNBU	25875	VN-C585	
XV-NIA	12832	VN-C680	
XV-NIB	19387		

Notes:-
Five DC-3s were re-registered from the F-VN series to XV-NIA to -NIE in 1959. F-BCYC became XV-NIN in Dec67.
F-BAOC was probably leased from Air France in 1960 during fleet overhaul.
N7302 of CASI was noted in Air Viêtnam colours in 1970 and RP-C2122 was leased in 1975.
VN-C503 is also reported as being a DC-4.

WESTERN SAMOA - 5W

Polynesian Airlines Ltd, Apia, W Samoa, used DC-3s on scheduled services from June 1963 until they were replaced by HS.748s in 1972.

Index:-

5W-FAA	c/n 32895	5W-FAH	33315
5W-FAB	25441	5W-FAI	33135
5W-FAC	34224		

YEMEN - North & South Yemen, Aden - VR-A and 7O; YE and 4W

Aden was a British colony until combining with the South Yemen Emirates to become South Arabia in 1963 and the bulk of the DC-3's operations were under the VR-A nationality mark. Upon independence in 1967 the name South Yemen was adopted (officially the Popular Democratic Republic of Yemen), and the nationality mark changed to 7O-. In the north, the Yemen Arab Republic used the YE- prefix, changing to 4W- in 1969. In 1990 South Yemen combined with the north to become the Republic of Yemen which now uses 7O- exclusively.

Aden Airways Ltd, Aden, was formed as a subsidiary of BOAC in November 1948, using DC-3s supplied by the latter and commencing operations with UK-registered aircraft on 01Oct49. Operations ceased in 1966 upon independence and Brothers Air Services took over services.

VR-AAA to VR-AAF incl; VR-AAI to VR-AAK incl; VR-AAM to VR-AAO incl; VR-AAZ; VR-ABJ.

Alyemda-Democratic Yemen Airlines, Aden, was formed on 11Mar71 to take over BASCO's operations and the latter's DC-3s. By 1984 the DC-3s were stored and either scrapped or put up for sale, and all seem to have been scrapped by 1993.

7O-ABE to 7O-ABH incl; 7O-ABP; 7O-ACB; 7O-ACE to 7O-ACH incl; G-BFPT.

BASCO - Brothers Air Services Co, Aden, took over Aden Airways' operations when the latter closed down in 1966, using newly acquired DC-3s. Operations were taken over by Alyemda in March 1971.

VR/7O-ABE to VR/7O-ABH incl.

Yemen Airways Corp, Sana'a, was formed as **Yemen Airlines** in 1954 and then became **Yemen Arab Airlines** in 1967, taking its current name in 1972. The first DC-3s were probably taken over from Yemenite Airlines, but information is lacking, as it is on most Yemeni DC-3s. Despite heavy attrition a few remained in 1982, though all had been withdrawn from use by 1984.

YE-AAB; YE-AAC/4W-AAC; YE-AAS/4W-AAS; YE-ABC/4W-ABC; 4W-ABD; 4W-ABE; 4W-ABG; 4W-ABH; 4W-ABI; 4W-ABK; 4W-ABR; 4W-ABS; 4W-ABT; 4W-ABW; 4W-ABX; 4W-ABY.

Yemenite Airlines was formed in North Yemen in 1948 or 1949 by the Milan-based Italian company Salpanavi Soc. di Navig. Aerea, which supplied three DC-3s. These were registered YE-AAA, YE-AAB and YE-AAC.

Index:-

VR-AAA	c/n 25586	VR-AAI	27215
VR-AAB	25806	VR-AAJ	12142
VR-AAC	25810	VR-AAK	13474
VR-AAD	26105	VR-AAM	26975
VR-AAE	26423	VR-AAN	4284
VR-AAF	26719	VR-AAO	33159

VR-AAZ	4495	
VR/7O-ABE	33331	
VR/7O-ABF	13475	
VR/7O-ABG	?	
VR/7O-ABH	26101	
VR-ABJ	33189	
7O-ABP	?	Cr 16Sep75. Remains at Aden in Nov85.
7O-ACB	26578	
7O-ACE	?	
7O-ACF	?	
7O-ACG	?	
7O-ACH	?	
YE-AAA	4329?	"Belges" ex Italy 1949
YE-AAB	4345	"Shiban" ex Italy.
YE-AAC	?	"Dhofar" ex Italy 1949
YE-AAS/4W-AAS	?	Ex HZ- Cr 19Mar69 at Taiz
YE-ABC/4W-ABC	13335	Wfu.
4W-ABD	?	Wfu.
4W-ABE	?	Regd 1969. wfu.
4W-ABF	?	Regd Apr69. Canx.
4W-ABG	1980	Wfu.
4W-ABH	13311	To Ethiopia
4W-ABI	9334	
4W-ABJ	?	Cr 01Nov72 at Beihan, Yemen
4W-ABK	?	Canx.
4W-ABR	12823	Cr 13Dec73 at Taiz.
4W-ABS	?	Regd Mar72 to 1980
4W-ABT	4607	
4W-ABW	12210	
4W-ABX	13584	Std Nov93 Sana'a
4W-ABY	13174	Regd Nov77, Dbr 14Nov78

Notes:-

7O-ABG derelict at Aden in Nov85. It had crashed 12Nov76 and has been suggested as ex AP-AJT c/n 26868.

7O-ACE to 7O-ACH originated in the UK and were delivered in 1978, ex Spanish AF surplus. (c/ns 12758, 19268, 25505 and 34357. tie-ups unknown).

YUGOSLAVIA - YU

Two airlines used the DC-3 or Li-2 in Yugoslavia, the Li-2s surviving only briefly.

Jugoslovenska Soviet Transport Aviaciga, Belgrade, was formed jointly with Russia in September 1947, to use Li-2s. Operations ceased in 1948 when the aircraft returned to Russia.

YU-BAA to YU-BAJ, YU-BAP, YU-BAR

JAT - Jugoslovenski Aerotransport, Belgrade, was formed in 1946 as a state owned airline with its origins in the pre-war Aeroput. DC-3s replaced Ju52/3ms on scheduled services in 1947, and were themselves retired in 1971 when DC-9s finally replaced them.

YU-ABA to YU-ABM incl; YU-ACA to YU-ACD incl.

OCZS - Obrazovni Centar Zracnog Saobracaja, Zagreb (Education Centre for Air Transport) registered YU-ABU, YU-ABV, YU-ABW in 1979 for sale to the USA.

Index:-

DC-3:
YU-ABA	c/n 12366	YU-ABK	33277
YU-ABB	13713	YU-ABL	?
YU-ABC	13254	YU-ABM	1980
YU-ABD	13311	YU-ABU	12704
YU-ABE	12381	YU-ABV	25546
YU-ABF	25294	YU-ABW	11746
YU-ABG	25480	YU-ACA	12210
YU-ABH	9488	YU-ACB	13367
YU-ABI	25453	YU-ACC	13014
YU-ABJ	12823	YU-ACD	9334

Li-2P:
YU-BAA	184 256 06	YU-BAC	184 270 04
YU-BAB	184 270 03	YU-BAD	184 270 09
YU-BAE	184 270 10	YU-BAI	184 270 08
YU-BAF	184 270 07	YU-BAJ	184 275 10
YU-BAG	184 275 09	YU-BAP	184 266 03
YU-BAH	184 275 03	YU-BAR	184 266 04

Notes:-
YU-ABL was an unidentified JRV aircraft used only in July/August 1951.
YU-ACA has been quoted as 42-9412 (12210) which was sold as 4W-ABW to Yemen. It was also reported as c/n 12381 but this is YU-ABE.

ZAIRE/DEMOCRATIC REPUBLIC OF CONGO - 9O and 9Q

After originally using OO-Cxx registrations within the Belgian register but with a separate CofR sequence, the former colony of the Belgian Congo became independent as the Democratic Republic of Congo in 1960 after a bloody civil war, taking up the prefix 9O-. The nationality mark had been quickly changed from 9O- to 9Q- in 1962 and this was retained when the name Zaire was adopted in 1971. By 1995 no DC-3s remained in service in Zaire. Again renamed the Democratic Republic of Congo in 1997, a few other DC-3s have recently appeared there, legally or otherwise.

Air Congo, Leopoldville/Kinshasa, was formed in June 1960 to take over Sabena's Congo operations. DC-3s were supplied for use on domestic services and used until they were replaced by F.27s from 1969 onwards. It is unlikely that any were in use when the airline's name was changed to Air Zaire, and most DC-3s passed to the Air Force. Air Congo used two ex-UN DC-3s for spares, UN-206 (20069) and UN-215 (2205).

9Q-CBB; 9Q-CBC; 9Q-CUD; 9Q-CUF; 9Q-CUH; 9Q-CUK to 9Q-CUP incl; 9Q-CUS. Most were earlier registered 9O-... .

Air Kasai, Ndolo, formerly **TAZ**(qv), have used 9Q-CTR, 9Q-CUK(2), 9Q-CYC and 9Q-CYE.

AMAZ - Agence de Messageries Aérienne du Zaire, Kinshasa, operated domestic and charter services throughout Zaire, using a fleet which included several DC-3s.

9Q-CKU; 9Q-COI; 9Q-CRL; 9Q-CUD; 9Q-CUK(1).

Elkivu operated DC-3 9Q-CSN.

Interfret Transport Aérien used various jet airliners and a single DC-3 9Q-CJM. It was merged with Air Charter Service. The DC-3 was used briefly in 1981and sold on to Safari Air and TAZ.

ITAB - International Trans Air Busin, Lubumbashi, had DC-3 9Q-CGW but this adopted Portuguese marks following refurbishment and was intended for operation by Airumbria in Italy.

Kinair-Cargo, Kinshasa, has a single DC-3 9Q-CNG in use, bought from Gabon. It was out of service by 1994.

Lukas-Lukim Aero Service, Kinshasa, used one DC-3 9Q-CAM along with DC-4 and DC-6 freighters, but it was withdrawn from service by 1983.

Safari Air are believed to have operated DC-3s 9Q-CFM and 9Q-CJM.

SNEL, Kinshasa, operated DC-3s 9Q-CIT and 9Q-CSL.

SOTEXKI, Kinshasa, had DC-3 9Q-CRL in service by 1989. Operations ceased in 1992.

TAZ - Transport Aérien Zairois, owned by L Britzelli and A Jannsson had DC-3s 9Q-CJM, 9Q-CKA, 9Q-CTR, 9Q-CUK(2), 9Q-CYC, 9Q-CYD and 9Q-CYE. The name changed to Transport Aérien Congo in 1996 and then to **Air Kasai** in mid-1999. 9Q-CYC now resides in Sweden.

Virunga Air Charter - VAC, Goma, used DC-3 9Q-CAM from at least 1992 until it was wfu by 2004.

Wimbi Dira Airways, Kinshasa, began operating domestic passenger and freight services on 13Aug03. One DC-3, 9Q-CWI, was acquired for a mixed fleet but it was written off in a landing accident on 19Jun05.

Index:-

9O/9Q-AED	c/n 7367	9Q-CAM	34409
9O/9Q-AEE	13348	9O/9Q-CBB	6339
9O/9Q-AEG	9938	9O/9Q-CBC	4144

9Q-CFM	?	9O/9Q-CUF	13486	
(9Q-CGC)?	26244	9O/9Q-CUH	19551	
9Q-CGW	26244	(9Q-CUI)	13457	
9Q-CHN	?	9O/9Q-CUK(1)	12734	
9Q-CIG	26974	9Q-CUK(2)	33445	
9Q-CIR	25925	9Q-CUL	42968	
9Q-CIT	32742	9O/9Q-CUM	42973	
9Q-CJJ	10110	9O/9Q-CUN	42977	
9Q-CJM	26457	9O/9Q-CUO	10129	
9Q-CKA	13348	9O/9Q-CUP	10063	
9Q-CKU	10129	9O/9Q-CUS	43092	
9Q-CNG	4335	(9O-CUW)	26297	
9Q-COI	?	(9O-CUX)	43088	
9Q-CRL	25399	9Q-CWI	33257	
9Q-CSL	19809	9Q-CYC	18977	
(9Q-CSN)(1)	25243	9Q-CYD	9010	
9Q-CSN(2)	25459	9Q-CYE	19771	
9Q-CTR	9452	9Q-CYI	11746	
9Q-CUD	9780			

Notes:-
9Q-CHN No details known.
9Q-COI of AMAZ was derelict at Kinshasa-Ndolo in April 1981.

ZAMBIA - 9J

Formerly Northern Rhodesia, using VP-Rxx until 1953, then VP-Yxx and again VP-Rxx in 1964, finally adopting 9J- as AZambia from 01Jan65. See Rhodesia/Zimbabwe below for VP- details.

Zambia Airways, Lusaka, was formed as a subsidiary of CAA in 1964, with two DC-3s. Two more were added later, but all had been replaced by HS.748s by 1970 and sold.

VP-YKH/9J-RFX; VP-YKL/9J-RFY; 9J-RGY; 9J-RDR.

Index:-

9J-DAK	c/n 32954	9J-RGY	32825
9J-RDR	25928	9J-RHZ	32656
9J-RFX	26994	9J-RIF	
9J-RFY	25805	9J-RIG	

Note:- 9J-RIF and 9J-RIG were both used in 1968 in Biafra. One was derelict at Libreville from 1970 until at least 2002. These have been connected with ex Zambian Air Force or Italian aircraft (such as c/n 4236), but the date does not fit known Italian disposals.

ZIMBABWE / RHODESIA / SOUTHERN RHODESIA
- VP-W, VP-Y and Z

Southern Rhodesia was first to use the British colonial sequence VP-Yxx from 1930 to Sep53 when it was joined by Northern Rhodesia and Nyasaland to become the Central African Federation, combining under VP-Yxx marks. The Federation dissolved on 31Dec63 and Southern Rhodesia declared independence as Rhodesia in Nov65; with VP-YYZ reached, VP-Wxx was adopted and used until, renamed as Zimbabwe, in 1980 the country took Z- as its new prefix.

Air Rhodesia, Salisbury, was formed on 01Sep67 to take over Rhodesia's share of CAA. Three DC-3s were then used and a fourth added later in the year. One was sold and three stored, but following the shooting down of two Viscounts by heat-seeking SAMs, the DC-3s were reinstated on the Victoria Falls route, fitted with modified exhausts to cut down heat emission. In 1980 Air Zimbabwe was formed and VP-YNH remained in use for a couple of years until it was sold to Zambia.

VP-WCG; VP-YKP; VP-YNH; VP-YUU.

Central African Airways Corp - CAA, Salisbury, acquired DC-3s in 1953 to replace Doves and Vikings on internal services, eight being used in all. Three passed to Air Rhodesia and the others to Air Malawi and Zambia Airways in 1964, when these operated as subsidiaries of CAA.

VP-YKH; VP-YKL to VP-YKP; VP-YNH; VP-YPB.

Hunting Clan African Airways Ltd, Salisbury, was formed in 1956 as an African subsidiary of Hunting Clan Air Transport. Two DC-3s were used on charter work until operations ceased in 1959.

VP-YNH; VP-YON.

Rhodesian Air Services (Pvt) Ltd, Salisbury, started charter operations in 1960, with DC-3s. These remained until about 1965.

VP-YRX; VP-YSK; VP-YTT; VP-YUU.

Spencer Airways, Victoria Falls, bought DC-3 VP-YFD in 1947, but it crashed at Croydon on delivery, killing the proprietor.

WENELA - See under Africair, South Africa.

Index:-

VP-WCG	c/n 32741	VP-YSK	12090
VP-YFD	19979	VP-YSL	26087
VP-YKH	26994	VP-YSM	33257
VP-YKL	25805	VP-YSN	32961
VP-YKM	32935	VP-YSO	26244
VP-YKN	32741	VP-YSP	26439
VP-YKO	26554	VP-YSR	33408
VP-YKP	26437	VP-YSY	11989
VP-YNH	32954	VP-YTT	9628
VP-YON	9131	VP-YUU	25928
VP-YPB	13018	VP-YXP	19484
VP-YRX	19351	Z-WRJ	11989
VP-YSJ	12066	Z-WRU	42963

One of the ongoing DC-3 mysteries involves the identities of various aircraft masquerading as RI-001, the original of which operated from Burma against the Dutch blockade of Indonesia prior to independence. This example is preserved at Taman Mini-Indonesia theme park, Djakarta. [Dave Partington]

COMMERCIAL OPERATORS - INDEX

This listing includes all the operators detailed above in Chapter Four listed by their company names, alternative or operating names and by initials or acronyms where relevant. In each case this is followed by the name of the country under which the relevant entry may be found.

A. Fecteau Transport Aérien Ltée - Canada
A.L.A. - Aerotransportes Litoral Argentina SA - Argentina
A.L.F.A. - Aviación del Litoral Fluvial Argentina - Argentina
A.Sorinao Air Cargo - Philippine Republic
A.V. Air Transport - South Africa
AAT Airlines - USA
AAXICO - USA
AB Aerotransport/Swedish Air Lines - Sweden
ABA - Sweden
Academy Airlines (Airline Aviation Academy Inc) - USA
ACASA - Costa Rica
Accelerated Charter Express - USA
ACE Air Cargo Express - USA
Adastra Aerial Surveys Pty Ltd - Australia
Aden Airways Ltd - Yemen
ADES - Aerolíneas del Este - Colombia
Admiral Air Service - USA
AECA - Ecuador
Aer Lingus Teoranta - Ireland
Aer Turas Teoranta - Ireland
Aéreo Panini - Mexico
Aereo Teseo SA (Orario Linee Aereo Teseo) - Italy
Aéreos El Venado Ltda - Colombia
Aéro Africaine - Algeria
Aero Air - South Africa
Aero California - Mexico
Aero Caribbean - Cuba
Aero Coach - USA
Aero Express - Guatemala
Aero Finance Corp - USA
Aero Freight Inc - USA
Aero Geral Ltda - Brazil
Aero Libertad SA - Mexico
Aero Maya - Mexico
Aero Mexico - Mexico
Aero Norte - Colombia
Aero Oy - Finnish Airlines / Finnair - Finland
Aero Pacifico - Mexico
Aero Perú - Peru
Aero Portuguesa Ltda - Portugal
Aero Retardant Inc - USA (see Pacific Alaska Airlines)
Aero Services Inc - USA
Aero Taxis Ecuatorianas SA - Ecuador
Aero Trades Western - Canada
Aero Transportes de España - Spain
Aero Transportes del Sureste SA - Mexico
Aero Transportes Ecuatorianas SA - Ecuador
Aero Transportes SA (also Aerovías Transportes) - Mexico
Aero Union Corp - USA
Aero Virgin Islands - Leeward Islands
Aero Virgin Islands Corp - USA
Aerocondor - Aerovías Condor de Colombia Ltda - Colombia
AeroDyne Airlines - USA
Aeroejecutivos - Venezuela
Aeroflete - Spain
AEROFLOT - Grazhdanskogo vozdushnago flota - Russia
Aero-Holland NV - Netherlands
Aerolíneas Abaroa - Bolivia
Aerolíneas Andinas SA - Colombia
Aerolineas Argentinas - Argentina
Aerolíneas California Pacifico - Mexico
Aerolíneas Condor - Bolivia
Aerolíneas de Guatemala Aviateca - Guatemala
Aerolíneas del Este - Colombia
Aerolíneas del Pacifico SA - Mexico
Aerolíneas El Salvador - El Salvador
Aerolíneas La Paz - Bolivia
Aerolíneas Mexicanas SA - Mexico
Aerolíneas Moxi - Mexico
Aerolíneas Nacionales del Ecuador SA - Ecuador
Aerolíneas Nacionales SA (ANSA) - Costa Rica
Aerolineas Peruanas SA - Peru
Aerolíneas TAO Ltda - Colombia
Aerolíneas Vega SA - Mexico
Aeromarket - Spain
Aeromaya SA - Mexico
Aero-Mitla - Mexico
Aeronautical Services - USA
Aeronaves Alimentadoras - Mexico
Aeronaves de Mexico SA - Mexico
Aeronaves Dodero - Argentina
AERONICA - Nicaragua
Aeronorte - Empresa de Transportes Aéreos Norte do Brasil SA - Brazil
Aeronorte SA - Peru

Aeroposta Argentina SA - Argentina
Aeroservicios de Sonora - Mexico
Aeroservicios Ecuatorianos - Ecuador
Aeroservicios Puntarenas SA, (APSA) - Costa Rica
Aerosucre Ltda - Colombia
Aerosun International - USA
AEROTAL - Aerovías Territoriales de Colombia - Colombia
Aerotaxi - Cuba
Aerotaxi de Calamar - Colombia
Aérotechnique SA - Algeria
Aerotécnica SA - Venezuela
Aero-Transit Inc - USA
Aerotransportes Litoral Argentina SA - Argentina
Aerovanguardia - Colombia
Aerovenca - Venezuela
Aerovias "Q" SA - Cuba
Aerovías Braniff SA - Mexico
Aerovias Brasil SA Empresa de Transportes - Brazil
Aerovías Cariari SA, (ACASA) - Costa Rica
Aerovías Coahuila - Mexico
Aerovías Colombianas Ltda - Colombia
Aerovías Condor de Colombia Ltda - Colombia
Aerovías Contreras - Mexico
Aerovías Cubanas Internacionales - Cuba
Aerovías del Norte Ltda - Colombia
Aerovías del Sur SA - Mexico
Aerovias Ecuatorianas - Ecuador
Aerovías Internaciónales - Mexico
Aerovías Internacionales de Mexico - Mexico
Aerovías Latino Americanas - ALASA - Mexico
Aerovias Latino Americanas SA - El Salvador
Aerovías Nacionales de Colombia SA - Colombia
Aerovías Nacionales de Honduras SA - Honduras
Aerovías Nacionales Quisqueyanas - Dominican Republic
Aerovías Oaxaquenas SA - Mexico
Aerovías Pilotos Asociados - Colombia
Aerovías Reforma SA - Mexico
Aerovías Rojas SA - Mexico
Aerovias SA - Brazil
Aerovías Territoriales de Colombia (AEROTAL) - Colombia
Aerovías Transcontinentales - Mexico
Aerovías Transportes - Mexico
Aerovías Urraca SA - Panama
Aerovías Venezolanas SA - Venezuela
Aerovilla - Colombia
AFRIC - Air France régie indo-chine - Indo-China
Africa Charter Airlines - South Africa
Africair - Sté. Algérienne de Constructions Aéronautiques - Algeria
Africair Ltd - South Africa
African Air Carriers - Mozambique
African Air Carriers (Pty) Ltd - South Africa
AFRYPESCA - Empresa de Aviación Refrigeración y Pesca - Colombia
Agence de Messageries Aérienne du Zaire - Zaire
Agencia Interamericana de Aviación Ltda - Colombia
AIDA - Agencia Interamericana de Aviación Ltda - Colombia
Aigle Azur - Indo-China
Aigle Azur d'Extrême Orient - Indo-China
Aigle Azur Indochine - Indo-China
Air Afrique - Ivory Coast
Air Algérie - Cie Généra le de Transports Aériens - Algeria
Air Algérie - Sté. Algérienne de Constructions Aéronautique - Algeria
Air America, Inc - USA
Air Americana - USA
Air Anglia - UK
Air Anguilla - Leeward Islands
Air Antilles - France
Air Asia Co Ltd - Taiwan
Air Atlantique / Atlantic Airways - UK
Air Atlas - Sté. Cherifienne de l'Air - Morocco
Air BC - Canada
Air Beni - Bolivia
Air Botswana (Pty) Ltd - Botswana
Air Brazeau - Canada
Air Burundi or STAB - Sté. de Transports Aériens du Burundi - Burundi
Air BVI - USA
Air BVI Ltd - Leeward Islands
Air Cambodge - Cambodia
Air Cameroun S/A des Avions Meyer et Cie - Cameroun
Air Cape (Pty) Ltd - South Africa
Air Caravane Inc - Canada
Air Cargo America - USA
Air Cargo Express Inc - USA (and see also Columbia A/L)
Air Cargo Express/ACE - USA
Air Cargo Transport Corp - USA
Air Caribbean - USA
Air Ceylon Ltd - Sri Lanka
Air Charter - UK
Air Charter - USA
Air Charter West - USA
Air Chicago Freight - USA
Air Colombia - Colombia
Air Commuter Express - Airgo Inc - USA

CHAPTER 4: COMMERCIAL OPERATORS INDEX

Air Comores SARL - Comores
Air Congo - Republic of Congo
Air Congo - Zaire
Air Congo/CFL - Belgium
Air Contractors Ltd - UK
Air Creebec - Canada
Air Dakota - France
Air Dauphine - France
Air Djibouti - Cie Territoriale de Transports Aériens de la Côte Française des Somalis - Somaliland (French)
Air East Inc - USA
Air Florida - USA
Air France - France
Air France régie indo-chine - Indo-China
Air Freight - New Zealand
Air Freight Inc - USA
Air Freight Ltd - UK
Air Fresh Sea Foods Inc - USA
Air Gaspé Inc - Canada
Air Gava Ltd - Canada
Air Gregory Ltd - UK
Air Guadeloupe (SATA) - France
Air Guinée - Guinea
Air Indiana - USA
Air Indies Corp - USA
Air Indonesia - Indonesia
Air Inter - France
Air Inuit - Canada
Air Ivoire - Ivory Coast
Air Jordan Co - Jordan
Air Jordan of the Holyland - Jordan
Air Kasai - Zaire
Air Katanga - Katanga
Air Kenya - Kenya
Air Kruise Ltd - UK
Air Laos SA - Laos
Air Liban - Cie Générale de Transports (CGT) - Lebanon
Air Liberia Inc - Liberia
Air Libya - Libya
Air Link International Airways - Philippine Republic
Air Links Ltd - UK
Air Lowveld - South Africa
Air Luton - UK
Air Malawi - Malawi
Air Mali - Mali
Air Manila Inc - Philippine Republic
Air Manitoba - Canada
Air Maroc - Sté. Marocaine de Construction Aéronautique - Morocco
Air Martinique (Satair) - Martinique
Air Mauritanie - Sté Nationale Air Mauritania - Mauritania
Air Miami - USA
Air Mid-America - USA
Air Molokai - USA
Air Nashua - USA
Air Nevada - USA
Air New England Inc - USA
Air Niger - Niger
Air Niugini - New Guinea
Air Normandie - France
Air North - Australia
Air North - USA
Air North Charter - Canada
Air Nova - Canada
Air O'Hare - USA
Air Oasis Airline - USA
Air Ontario - Canada
Air Outre-Mer - Indo-China
Air Pacific - Fiji
Air Pacific International Inc - USA
Air Puerto Rico - USA
Air Queensland - Australia
Air Rajneesh - USA
Air Rambler (Australia) Pty Ltd - Australia
Air Resorts Airlines - USA
Air Rhodesia - Zimbabwe
Air San Jose - USA
Air Sénégal - Cie Sénégalaise de Transports Aériens - Senegal
Air Service Co - Iran
Air Services Inc - USA
Air Services of India Ltd - India
Air Siesta - USA
Air South - USA
Air Sunshine - USA
Air Taos - USA
Air Tasmania Pty Ltd - Australia
Air Taxi - Sudan
Air Taxi Co - Iran
Air Taxi International - USA
Air Tchad - Tchad
Air Texana - USA
Air Transport Charter (C.I.) Ltd - UK
Air Ulster - UK

Air Vientiane Laos - Laos
Air Viêtnam - Vietnam
Air Zambezi - South Africa
Airborne Transport Inc - USA
Aircrafts Pty Ltd - Australia
Air-Dale Ltd - Canada
Airfast Indonesia - Indonesia
Airgo Air Freight - USA
Airgo Inc - USA
Air-India International Ltd - India
Air-India Ltd - India
Airline of the Virgin Islands - USA
Airline Transport Carriers Inc - USA
Airlines of New South Wales Pty Ltd - Australia
Airlines of South Australia Pty Ltd - Australia
Airnautic GECA - France
Airnews Inc - USA
Airplane Charter by Mercer Inc - USA
Airtaco AB - Sweden
Airways (India) Ltd - India
Airways Burma Ltd - Burma
Airwork Ltd - UK
Airworks India Ltd - India
Airworld - South Africa
Alamo Airways Inc - USA
Alas Chiricanas - Panama
Alas del Caribe - Dominican Republic
ALASA - Mexico
Alaska Aeronautical Industries Inc - USA
Alaska Airlines Inc - USA
Alaska Coastal - Ellis Airlines - USA
Alaska Island Air - USA
Alaskan Southern Airlines - USA
Alberta Northern Airlines Ltd - Canada
ALCOM - Colombia
ALIA - Royal Jordanian Airlines - Jordan
ALIANSA - Aerolíneas Andinas SA - Colombia
ALICOL - Colombia
ALITALIA - Linee Aeree Italiane - Italy
All Nippon Airways Co Ltd - Japan
All World Aviation - Libya
All-American Airways Inc - USA
Allegheny Air Cargo Inc - USA
Allegheny Airlines Inc - USA
Allied Air Carrier Corp - USA
Allied Air Freight - USA
Aloha Airlines Inc - USA
Alpa Aerotaxis - Peru
ALPAR - Schweizerische Luftverkehr AG - Switzerland
Alpena Flying Services Inc - USA
Alpha Airlines - USA
Alyemda-Democratic Yemen Airlines - Yemen
AMAZ - Agence de Messageries Aérienne du Zaire - Zaire
Ambica Air Lines Ltd - India
American Air Cargo - USA
American Air Export & Import Co - AAXICO - USA
American Air Transport Inc - USA
American Airlines Inc - USA
American Airways Charters - USA
American Flyers Airline Corp - USA
American Flyers Inc - USA
American International Airways - USA
American Overseas Airlines Inc - USA
ANDES - Aerolíneas Nacionales del Ecuador SA - Ecuador
Anglo-Vaal Air Transport - South Africa
Anguilla Airways - USA
ANHSA - Aerovías Nacionales de Honduras SA - Honduras
ANSA - Costa Rica
Ansett (P&NG) Pty Ltd - Australia
Ansett Airlines of Australia Pty Ltd - Australia
Ansett Airlines of Papua New Guinea Pty Ltd - Australia
Ansett Airlines of SA - Australia
Ansett Airways Pty Ltd - Australia
Ansett-ANA - Australia
Ansett-MAL - Australia
Ansett-Mandated Airlines Ltd - Australia
APEL Express SA - Colombia
Apollo Airlines - USA
Appalachian Flying Service Inc - USA
Apple Air Services Ltd - Ireland
APSA - Costa Rica
Arab Airways (Jerusalem) Ltd - Jordan
Arabian American Oil Co - ARAMCO - USA
ARAMCO - USA
Arax Airlines - Nigeria
ARCA - Aerovías Colombianas Ltda - Colombia
Arctic Air - Canada
Arctic Frontier Airways - USA
Arctic Pacific Inc - USA
Ardic - Senegal
AREA - Aerovias Ecuatorianas - Ecuador
Argonaut Airways Inc - USA

Argosy Air Lines Inc - USA
Ariana Afghan Airlines - Afghanistan
Arizona Airways Inc - USA
ARKIA - Israel Inland Airlines Ltd - Israel
Arnold Air Services Inc -USA
ARPA - Colombia
Arrow Airways Inc - USA
Asean Air Freight - Philippine Republic
Aspen Airways Inc -USA
Associated Airways Ltd - Canada
Astro Air Transport - Philippine Republic
Astro Airlines - Canada
Astro Airways - USA
ATAPSA - Peru
ATESA - Aero Taxis Ecuatorianas SA - Ecuador
Atkins Aviation - USA
Atlantic Air Cargo - USA
Atlantic Airways - UK
Atlantic Central Airlines - Canada
Atlantic Northern Airlines Inc - USA
Atlantic, Gulf & Midland Corp - USA
Atorie Air - USA
Audi Air Inc - USA
Austin Airways Ltd - Canada
Austral Líneas Aéreas - Argentina
Australian National Airways Pty Ltd - Australia
Austria-Flugdienst - Austria
Austrian Airlines (Osterreichische Luftverkehr AG) - Austria
Autair Ltd - UK
Avalon Air Transport Inc - USA
AVENSA - Aerovías Venezolanas SA - Venezuela
Avex Air - South Africa
Avia Air Charter - South Africa
Aviación del Litoral Fluvial Argentina - Argentina
Aviación y Comercio SA - Spain
AVIACO - Aviación y Comercio SA - Spain
AVIANCA - Aerovías Nacionales de Colombia SA - Colombia
AVIATECA - Aerolíneas de Guatemala Aviateca - Guatemala
Aviation Boréal - Canada
Aviation Corp. of Seattle - USA
Avio Linee Italiane - Flotte Riunite - Italy
Aviolinee Italiane - Italy
Avions Bleus - France
AVISPA - Aerovías Pilotos Asociados - Colombia
B Airways - USA
BAFIN - Bolivia
Bahamas Airways Ltd - Bahamas
Bahamasair - Bahamas
Balair AG - Switzerland
Ball Bros Inc - USA
Bar Harbor Airlines - USA
Baron Aviation Services Inc - USA
BASCO - Brothers Air Services Co - Yemen
Basler Flight Services Inc - USA
Bavaria Fluggesellschaft - Germany
Bayview Air Services Ltd - Canada
BBA Air Cargo Pty Ltd - Australia
BEAC - British European Airways Corp - UK
Beach Airways - Trinidad & Tobago
Bearskin Lake Airways - Canada
Bechuanaland National Airways (Pty) Ltd - Botswana
Belgian International Air Services - Belgium
Bergen Air Transport AS - Norway
Bharat Airways Ltd - India
Bharatair - India
BIAS - Belgian International Air Services - Belgium
Biman Bangladesh - Bangladesh
Bird & Sons, Inc - USA
Bixby Airlines - USA
BKS Air Transport Ltd - UK
Blatz Airlines Inc - USA
Blue-Line Airways Ltd - UK
BMA - UK
BOAC - British Overseas Airways Corp - UK
Bolivian Air Flying (BAFIN) - Bolivia
Bolivian Air Tourmen - Bolivia
Bonanza Air Lines Inc - USA
Borinquen Air - USA
Borneo Airways Ltd - Malaya
Bo-S-Aire Corp - USA
Botswana Airways - Botswana
Botswana National Airways (Pty) Ltd - Botswana
Bouraq Indonesia Airlines - Indonesia
Bowman Aviation - USA (see Bo-S-Aire Corp)
BRAATHENS - South American and Far East Air Transport AS (SAFE) - Norway
Bradley Air Services Ltd - Canada
Brain & Brown Airfreighters Pty Ltd - Australia
Braniff Airways Inc (Braniff International) - USA
Bretagne Air Services - France
British Caribbean Airways Ltd - Jamaica
British European Airways Corp - BEAC - UK

British Island Airways - UK
British Midland Airways Ltd (BMA) - UK
British Nederland Air Services Ltd - UK
British Overseas Airways Corp - UK
British United Airways Ltd (BUA) - UK
British United Island Airways Ltd (BUIA) - UK
British West Indian Airways - Trinidad & Tobago
British Westpoint Airlines Ltd - UK
Brooks Fuel - USA
Brothers Air Services Co - Yemen
Bruning Aviation Inc - USA
BUA - UK
Buckeye Air Freight - USA
Buffalo Airways - Canada
Buffalo Airways Ltd - Canada
BUIA - UK
Buker Airways - USA
Burke Air Transport - USA
Burma Airways Corp - Burma
Burma National Airways - Burma
Bush Pilots Airways Ltd - Australia
Business Air - USA
Butler Air Transport Pty Ltd - Australia
BWIA - British West Indian Airways - Trinidad & Tobago
C & M Airlines - USA
C N Shelton & Co - USA
CADET - Cooperativa Aérea de Transportes - Bolivia
Cal Aero Airways - USA
California Air Tours - USA
California Central Airlines - USA
California Growers Air Express Inc - USA
Calm Air - Canada
Cal-Neva Air Inc - USA
Cambodair - Cambodia
Cambodia Air Commercial - Cambodia
Cambodian Air Service - Cambodia
Cambrian Air Services - UK
Cambrian Airways Ltd - UK
Cameroons Air Transport Ltd - Cameroun
Canadian Colonial Airways - Canada
Canadian Colonial Airways Inc - USA
Canadian Pacific Airlines - Canada
Cape Smythe Air Service - USA
Capital Airlines Inc - USA
Capitol Airways Inc - USA
Caprivi Airways - South Africa
Carco Air Services Inc - USA
Carga Aerolíneas Dominicanas - Dominican Republic
Carib Air Cargo, t/a GMD Air - USA
CARIBAIR, Caribbean-Atlantic Airlines Inc - USA
Caribbean Air Services - CASAIR - USA
Caribbean Airlines - Costa Rica
Caribbean American Airlines Inc - USA
Caribbean Aviation Services - USA
Caribbean Express - USA
Caribbean Flights - Venezuela
Caribbean International Airlines - USA
Caribbean Island Airlines - USA
Caribbean-Atlantic Airlines Inc - USA
Caribe Air - USA
Caribe Airways - USA
Carib-West Airways Ltd - Barbados
Carriba Air - USA
Cascade Air - USA
Caspair Ltd - Kenya
CATA - Cie Algérien de Transports Aériens - Algeria
Catalina Airlines - USA (see Avalon Air Transport Inc)
Catalina Flying Boats - USA
Catalina Pacific Airlines - USA
CATC - China
Cathay Pacific Airways Ltd - Hong Kong
CATI - Cie de Transports Indochinois - Indo-China
CATI - Taiwan
Cayman Airways Ltd - Costa Rica
Cayman Brac Airways - Costa Rica
Central Aérea Ltda - Brazil
Central African Airways Corp - CAA - Zimbabwe
Central Air Transport Corp (CATC) - China
Central Airlines Inc - USA
Central American Airways Flying Services Inc - USA
Central Cargo Inc - USA
Central Iowa Airlines - USA
Central Mountain Air - Canada
Central Northern Airways Ltd - Canada
Century Airlines - USA
Ceskoslovenská letecká spolecnost - Czechoslovakia
Ceskoslovenske státní aerolinie - Czechoslovakia
Cessnyca Ltda - Colombia
Challenger Airlines Co - USA
Champlain Air - USA
Channel Airways Ltd - UK
Chaparal Air (Chaparal Charters Inc) - Canada

Chapter 4: Commercial Operators Index

Charter Airlines/Charter Air Center/Charterair - USA
Chesapeake Airways Inc - USA
Chicago and Southern Airlines Inc - USA
China Air Lines Ltd - Taiwan
China National Aviation Corp (CNAC) - China
China National Relief & Rehabilitation Administration (CNRRA) - China
China People's Airline Company (SKOGA) - China
Christler Flying Service - USA
Cia Aérea Trans-America Peru SA (ATAPSA) - Peru
Cia Argentina de Aeronavegación - t/a Aeronaves Dodero - Argentina
Cia Argentina de Cargas Aéreas Internas - Argentina
Cía Boliviana de Aviación - Bolivia
Cia Chitreana de Aviación SA - Panama
Cía Cubana de Aviación SA - Cuba
Cia de Aviación Aero Amazonas - Ecuador
Cia de Aviación Faucett SA - Peru
Cía Dominicana de Aviación C por A - Dominican Republic
Cia Interandina de Aviación - Colombia
Cia Mexicana de Aviación SA - Mexico
Cia Panamena de Aviación SA - Panama
Cia Sinuana de Transporte Aéreo Costa - Colombia
Cia Sudamericana C & S - Bolivia
Cia Tabasquena de Aviación SA - Mexico
Cia Trasandina de Aviación SA - Colombia
Cie Aérienne de Transports Indochinois (CATI) - Indo-China
Cie Air Transport - France
Cie Algérien de Transports Aériens - Algeria
Cie Autrex - Indo-China
Cie Belge de Transports Aériens - Belgium
Cie de Transports Aériens et de Commerce - Indo-China
Cie de Transports Aériens Intercontinentaux - France
Cie de Transports Indochinois - Indo-China
Cie Généra le de Transports Aériens - Algeria
Cie Générale de Transports (CGT) - Lebanon
Cie Générale Transaharienne - Algeria
Cie Haitienne de Transports Aériens - Haiti
Cie Nationale de Transports Aériens - Morocco
Cie Sénégalaise de Transports Aériens - Senegal
Cie Territoriale de Transports Aériens de la Côte Française des Somalis - Somaliland (French)
Ciro's Aviation Ltd - UK
Civil Aeronautics Admin/Federal Aviation Agency - USA
Civil Air Transport - Taiwan
Civil Air Transport Inc (CATI) - USA
Civil Aviation Administration of China (CAAC) - China
Classic Air - New Zealand
Classic Air - Switzerland
Classic Air - UK
Classic Express Airways - USA
CLS - Ceskoslovenská letecká spolecnost - Czechoslovakia
Clyden Airways - Ireland
CNAC - China
CNRRA Air Transport - Taiwan
Coastal Air Lines - USA
Coastal Airways Inc - USA
Coastal Cargo Co Inc - USA
COBETA - Cie Belge de Transports Aériens - Belgium
COHATA - Cie Haitienne de Transports Aériens - Haiti
Coker Air Freight Inc - USA
Colbnra Transport - Australia
Colinizadora e Consutoria Agrária - Brazil
Colonial Airlines Inc - USA
Columbia Air Cargo Inc - USA
Columbia Airlines - USA
Comair - Commercial Air Services (Pty) Ltd - South Africa
Comeravia - Venezuela
Commercial Air Lines Inc - Philippine Republic
Commercial Air Services (Pty) Ltd - South Africa
Commercial Air Transport Inc - Philippine Republic
Communicaciónes Aéreas de Veracruz SA - Mexico
Companhia de Transportes Aéreos - Portugal
Compañía de Carga - Dominican Republic
Comut-Aire - USA
CONAGRA - Colinizadora e Consutoria Agrária - Brazil
CONFISA - Dominican Republic
Connair Pty Ltd - Australia
Conner Airlines Inc - USA
Consolidated Air Transit Inc - USA
Consolidated Airlines - USA (also see Vance Intl A/W)
Consórcio Nacional de Transportes Aéreos - Brazil
Consumers Air Freight Corp - USA
Contact Airways - Canada
Continental Air Lines Inc - USA
Continental Air Services Inc (CASI) - USA
Continental Air Transport Ltd - UK
Continental Airways - Philippine Republic
Continental Charters Inc - USA
Continental Sky-Van Inc - USA
Cooperativa Aérea de Transportes - Bolivia
COPA - Cia Panamena de Aviación SA - Panama
CORAL - Coronado Aerolíneas - Colombia
Cordova Airlines Inc - USA
Coronado Aerolíneas - Colombia
Corporación Boliviano de Fomento - Bolivia
Corporate Express - USA
COSARA - Indo-China
COSTA - Cia Sinuana de Transporte Aéreo Costa - Colombia
Cotenair - Canada
Cranways Pty Ltd - Australia
Crescent Air Transport Ltd - Pakistan
Crewsair Ltd - UK
Crown Charter Services - Canada
Cruzeiro - Serviçios Aéreos Cruzeiro do Sul SA - Brazil
Cryderman Air Services Inc - USA
Crystal Shamrock Airlines - USA
CSA - Ceskoslovenske státní aerolinie - Czechoslovakia
CTA - Companhia de Transportes Aéreos - Portugal
CTAC - Cie de Transports Aériens et de Commerce - Indo-China
Cuba Aeropostal SA - Cuba
Currey Air Transport Ltd - USA
Cyprus Airways - Cyprus
Dai Nippon Airways (DNKKK) - Japan
Dakota Downunder - Australia
Dakota National Air - Australia
Dalmia-Jain Airways Ltd - India
Dan-Air Services Ltd - UK
Darbhanga Aviation - India
Davis Airways Inc - USA
DC-3 Queensland PL - Australia
DDL - Det Danske Luftfartsselskab A/S - Denmark
De Kroonduif - Nederlands New Guinea Luchtvaartmaatschappij "De Kroonduif" - Netherlands New Guinea
Deccan Airways Ltd - India
Delta Air Lines Inc - USA
Delta Air Transport - Belgium
Delta Airways - Philippine Republic
Democratic Yemen Airlines - Yemen
Derby Airways Ltd - UK
Derby Aviation Ltd - UK
Det Danske Luftfartsselskab A/S - Denmark
Det Norske Luftfartselskap AS - Norway
DETA - Direcção de Exploração dos Transportes Aéreos - Mozambique
Deutsche Lufthansa AG - Germany
Deutsche Lufttransport Gesellschaft mbH - Germany
DHL Island Airways - USA
DHY - Devlet Hava Yollari - Turkey
Diamond Leasing Co - Libya
Diaz Aviation Corp - USA (see Borinquen Air)
Dick Lang's Desert Air Safaris - Australia
Direcção de Exploração dos Transportes Aéreos - Angola
Direcção de Exploração dos Transportes Aéreos - Mozambique
Dirgantara Air Services - Indonesia
Discovery Air Tours - Australia
Discovery Airways - Australia
DNKKK - Japan
DNL - Det Norske Luftfartselskap AS - Norway
Dodson International Air - USA
Dominicana - Cía Dominicana de Aviación C por A - Dominican Republic
Don Everall (Aviation) Ltd - UK
DTA - Direcção de Exploração dos Transportes Aéreos - Angola
EAAC - Kenya
Eagle Air Freight Inc - USA
Eagle Airways Ltd - UK
Eagle Aviation Ltd - UK
East African Airways Corp (EAAC) - Kenya
East Anglian Flying Services Ltd - UK
East Coast Flying Services Inc - USA
Eastern Air Lines Inc - USA
Eastern Airways Ltd - UK
Eastern Express - USA
Eastern Provincial Airways Ltd - Canada
East-West Airlines Ltd - Australia
Economy Airways Inc - USA
Edde Airlines - USA
El Al Israel Airlines - Israel
El Venado - Colombia
Eldorado Aviation - Canada
Elkivu - Zaire
Emerald Airways - Ireland
Empire Air Lines Inc - USA
Empire Airlines - USA
Empresa Aerovías del Pacifico Ltda (ARPA) - Colombia
Empresa de Aviación Refrigeración y Pesca - Colombia
Empresa de Transporte Aéreo Brasileiro Ltda - Brazil
Empresa de Transportes Aéreos Norte do Brasil SA - Brazil
Enterprise Air - Canada
ERA Helicopters/Jet Alaska - USA
Essair - USA
Ethiopian Airlines Inc - Ethiopia
European Air Transport, SA - Luxembourg
Evergreen International Airlines - USA
Executive Air Transport Inc - USA
Executive Air Transport Ltd - UK
Executive Transport Corp - USA

Expreso Aéreo Inter Americano SA - Cuba
Expreso Aéreo Ltda - Colombia
Express Airways - USA
Eyethu Air Cargo - South Africa
Fairbanks Air Services - USA
Fairflight Charters Ltd - UK
FAIRWAYS - Filipinas Orient Airways - Philippine Republic
Fairways - Netherlands
Fairways Corp - USA
Falcon Airways Inc - USA
FAMA - Flota Aérea Mercante Argentina - Argentina
Far East Air Transport Corp - Taiwan
Far East Fur Trading Co Ltd - Mongolia
Far Eastern Air Transport Inc - Philippine Republic
Faroe Airways A/S - Denmark
FAST - Fleming Airways System Transport - Philippine Republic
Faucett - Cia de Aviación Faucett SA - Peru
Federal Aviation Agency - USA
Federal Express Corp - USA
Federated Air Lines Inc - USA
Fiji Airways - Fiji
Filipinas Orient Airways - Philippine Republic
Finnish Airlines / Finnair - Finland
Fireball Air Express - USA
First Air - Canada
First United Air - Philippine Republic
Flamenco Airways - USA
Flamingo Air Services Inc - USA
Flamingo Airlines - Bahamas
Fleet Air Services (Tasmania) Pty Ltd - Australia
Fleetwood Airlines - USA
Fleetwood Airways Inc - USA
Fleming Airways System Transport - Philippine Republic
Flight Australia - Australia
Flightways Corp - USA
Flite Services Inc - USA
Florida Air Cargo - USA
Florida Air Lines Inc, - USA
Florida Air Transport - USA
Florida Airways International - USA
Florida Commuter Airlines - USA
Florida Express - USA
Florida National Airways - USA
Florida-Fresh Air Express Inc - USA
Flota Aérea Mercante Argentina (FAMA) - Argentina
Flota Aérea Nicaraguense - Nicaragua
Flugfélag Islands hf - Icelandair - Iceland
Flugfélag Norðurlands sf - Iceland
Flugsyn - Iceland
Flying Tiger Lines - USA
Forrestair Pty Ltd - Australia
Foshing Airlines - Taiwan
Four Star Air Cargo/Four Star Aviation - USA
Fred Olsen's Flyselskap AS - Norway
Freight Air Inc - USA
Fretair - France
Friendship Air Alaska - USA
Frigorifico Cooperativo "Los Andes" SA - Bolivia
Frigorifico Reyes - Bolivia
Frigorifico Santa Rita - Bolivia
Fromhagen Aviation - USA
Frontier - USA
Frontier Air Service - Canada
Frontier Airlines Inc - USA
Frontier Flying Service - USA
Frontier Pacific Airlines - USA
Gallagher Brothers - USA
Gander Aviation Ltd - Canada
Garuda Indonesia Airways - Indonesia
Gateway Airlines Ltd - Canada
Gateway Aviation Ltd - Canada
Genavco Air Cargo - USA
General Administration of Civil Aviation of China - China
General Air Cargo Inc - USA
General Air Lines - USA
General Airways - USA
General Cargo Australia - Australia
Ghana Airways Ltd - Ghana
Gibair - UK
Gibraltar Airways Ltd - UK
Gilley Airways Corp - USA
Glade Air - USA
Global Airways Inc - USA
Globe Freight Airlines Inc - USA
Golden Eagle Airlines - Cambodia
Golden Gate Airways - USA
Golden Isles Air Inc - USA
Golden North Airways - USA
Golden State Airlines Inc - USA
Golden West Airways - Australia
Golden Wings Australia - Australia
Golfe Air Quebec Ltd - Canada

Grazhdanskogo vozdushnago flota (AEROFLOT) - Russia
Great China Aviation Corp - China
Great Circle Airways Inc - USA
Great Lakes Air Lines - Canada
Great Lakes Air Services Ltd - Canada
Great Lakes Airlines Inc - USA
Great Northern Airways Ltd - Canada
Great Northern Freight - Canada
Great Southern Airways - USA
Greater Japan Air Lines - Japan
Greek Railway Express - USA
Gregory Air Services - UK
Guinea Air Traders Ltd - Australia
Guinea Airways Pty Ltd - Australia
Gulf & Western Airlines Inc - USA
Gulf Air Taxi - USA
Gulf Aviation Co Ltd - Bahrain
Gulf Aviation Co Ltd - UK
Gulf Aviation Inc - Canada
Guyana Airways - Guyana (British Guiana)
Haiti Air Inter - Haiti
Haiti Air Transport - Haiti
Haiti Overseas Airways - Haiti
Hamiata - China/Russia
Hammond Forner Air Service - USA
Hang Khong Viêtnam - Vietnam
Hang Meas Airlines - Cambodia
Hankins Air Service - USA
Hankins Airways - USA
Harolds Air Service - USA
Harrington's Inc - USA
Harrison Airways Ltd - Canada
Havenstrite Aircraft Inc - USA
Hawaiian Airlines Ltd - USA
Hawkeye Airlines - USA
Hawkins and Powers Aviation - USA
Hawthorne Nevada Airlines - USA
Helda Air - Bahamas
Hellenic Air Transport Co Ltd - Greece
Hellenic Airlines SA - Greece
Hemet Exploration - France
Hemisphere Air Transport - USA
Heritage Air Tours - USA (see Viking Express)
Hiawatha Airways Inc - USA
Hibernian Airlines Ltd - Ireland
Himalayan Aviation Ltd - India
HoganAir - USA
Hollinger Ungava Transport Ltd - Canada
Holymans Airways Pty Ltd - Australia
Hong Kong Airways Ltd - Hong Kong
Hooker Air Services Ltd - Canada
Hoosier Air Freight - USA
Horizon Air - USA
Horizontes - Bolivia
Hornton Airways Ltd - UK
Hudson Bay Air Transport Ltd - Canada
Humber Airways Ltd - UK
Hunting Air Transport Ltd - UK
Hunting Clan African Airways Ltd - Zimbabwe
Hunting Clan Air Transport Ltd - UK
IBERIA - Líneas Aéreas de España - Spain
Icelandair - Iceland
Ilford-Riverton Airways Ltd - Canada
Imperial Airlines - USA
Indamer Co (Pvt) Ltd - India
Indian Airlines Corp - India
Indian National Airlines Ltd - India
Indian Overseas Airlines Ltd - India
Indonesian Airways - Indonesia
Inland Air Lines - USA
Inter-Air - South Africa
Interandes - Cia Interandina de Aviación - Colombia
Inter-Coastal Airways - USA
Intercontinental Air Transport Co Inc - USA
Interfret Transport Aérien - Zaire
Interior Airways Inc - USA
Intermountain Aviation Inc - USA
International Air Cargo - Egypt
International Air Freight Inc - USA
International Air Service - USA
International Airlines - USA
International Airports Inc - USA
International Aviation Development Corp - Libya
International Jet Air Ltd - Canada
Interstate Air Services Corp - USA
Interstate Airmotive Inc - USA
Interstate Parcel Express - Australia
Intra Airways Ltd - UK
IPEC (Interstate Parcel Express) - Australia
Iran National Airlines Corp - Iran
Iranair - Iran National Airlines Corp - Iran
Iranian Airways Co - Iran

Chapter 4: Commercial Operators Index

Iraqi Airways - Iraq
Irelfly Ltd - UK
Island Air Ferries - USA
Island Air Transfer - USA
Island Airlines - USA
Island Airlines Hawaii - USA
Island Traders - USA
Israel Inland Airlines Ltd - Israel
Israelair - Israel
ITAB - Zaire
ITAVIA - Societe di Navigazione Aerea SpA - Italy
Jamaica Air Services - Jamaica
Jamair Co (Pvt) Ltd - India
Japan Air Lines - Japan
Japan Domestic Airlines - Japan
Japan Helicopter and Aeroplane Transport Co (JHAT) - Japan
JARI Florestal - Brazil
JAT - Jugoslovenski Aerotransport - Yugoslavia
Jefferson State Airlines Inc - USA
Jersey Airlines - UK
Jersey European Airways - UK
Jersey Shore Air Freight - USA
Jet Air Charters - South Africa
Jet Alaska - USA
Jetair Australia Ltd - Australia
Jim Hankins Air Services Inc - USA
Jimsair Aviation Services - USA
JLR Air Transport Inc - USA
John Mahieu Aviation - Belgium
Johnson Flying Services Inc - USA
Jugoslovenska Soviet Transport Aviaciga - Yugoslavia
Jugoslovenski Aerotransport - Yugoslavia
Jupiter Airways Ltd - India
K & K Aircraft - USA
Kahila A/L - USA
Kahila Airlines - USA
Kalinga Air Lines (Pvt) Ltd - India
Kampuch Airways - Cambodia
Kansas City Southern Skyways Inc - USA
KAR-AIR Oy - Karhumaki Airways - Finland
Karhumaki Airways - Finland
Kearsley Airways Ltd - UK
Kelowna Flightcraft Charter - Canada
Kenn Borek Air Ltd - Canada
Kenting Atlas Aviation - Canada
Kenting Aviation Ltd - Canada
Kestrel Airways Ltd - UK
Key Brothers Flying Service - USA (see Meridan Air Cargo)
Key West Airlines - USA
Khmer Airlines - Cambodia
Khmer Akas (Reseau Aérien Interieur Cambodgien) - Cambodia
Khmer Hansa - Cambodia
Kinair-Cargo - Zaire
KLM - Koninklijke Luchtvaart Maatschappij NV - Netherlands
KLM (West Indies Divn.) - Netherlands West Indies
KLM Aerocarto - Netherlands
Knight Air Ltd - Canada
KNILM - Indonesia
Knox Air Service - Canada
Koninklijke Luchtvaart Maatschappij NV - Netherlands
Koninklijke Nederlandsch-Indische Luchtvaart Maatschappij NV - Netherlands
Koomeela Australia - Australia
Korean Air Lines - South Korea
Korean National Airlines - South Korea
Kuwait Airways - Kuwait
Kwin Air - Bahamas
Kwin Aircraft Corp - USA
LAAS - USA
LAB - Bolivia
Labrador Airways - Canada
LAC Colombia - Líneas Aéreas del Caribe - Colombia
LACAS - Líneas Aéreas Commerciales Al Sur - Argentina
LACOL - Líneas Aéreas Colombianas - Colombia
LACSA - Líneas Aéreas Costarricenses SA - Costa Rica
LADE - Líneas Aéreas del Estado - Argentina
LAGOSA - Mexico
LAI - Italy
LAICA - Líneas Aéreas Interiores de Catalina - Colombia
Lake Central Airlines Inc - USA
Lake Wales Air Services - USA
Lambair Ltd - Canada
LAMSA - Mexico
LANC - Líneas Aéreas del Norte de Colombia - Colombia
Lancashire Aircraft Corp. Ltd - UK
Lane Xang Airlines - Cambodia
Lane Xang Airlines - Laos
LANICA - Líneas Aéreas de Nicaragua SA - Nicaragua
LANSA - Líneas Aéreas Nacionales SA - Colombia
LANSA - Líneas Aéreas Nacionales SA - Dominican Republic
LANSA - Líneas Aéreas Nacionales SA - Honduras
Lao Airlines - Sté. Anon. de Transports Aériens - Laos

Laos Air Charter - Laos
LAOS Ltda - Líneas Aéreas Orientales Ltda - Colombia
LAPE - Líneas Aéreas Postales Españolas - Spain
LAPSA - Mexico
LAPSA Inc - USA
LARES - Liniile Aeriene Române Exploatate cu Statul - Romania
Latin Carga - Latinamericana Aérea de Carga SA - Venezuela
LATINA - Colombia
Latinamericana Aérea de Carga SA - Venezuela
LAUMSA - Mexico
Laurentian Air Services Ltd - Canada
LAUSA - Mexico
LAV - Línea Aeropostal Venezolana - Venezuela
Lebanese Air Transport (Charter) Co - Lebanon
LEBCA - Línea Expresa Bolivar CA - Venezuela
Leeward Islands Air Transport Services Ltd - Leeward Islands
Legend Airways of Colorado - USA
Legion Express - USA
Les Ailes du Nord Ltée - Canada
Lesotho Airways - Lesotho
Liberian International Airways - Liberia
Libyan Aviation - Libya
Libyan National Airways - Libya
Limitada Nacional de Servicio Aéreo - Colombia
Lina Congo - Republic of Congo
Linair - Belgium
Linair - Libyan National Airways - Libya
Línea Aeropostal Venezolana - Venezuela
Línea de Aviación "Condor" Ltda - Colombia
Línea Expresa Bolivar CA - Venezuela
Líneas Aérea Condor - Ecuador
Líneas Aéreas Canedo - Bolivia
Líneas Aéreas Colombianas - Colombia
Líneas Aéreas Commerciales Al Sur - Argentina
Líneas Aéreas Costarricenses SA - Costa Rica
Líneas Aéreas Darien Uraba - Colombia
Líneas Aéreas de España - Spain
Líneas Aéreas de Nicaragua SA - Nicaragua
Líneas Aéreas del Caribe - Colombia
Líneas Aéreas del Centro - Mexico
Líneas Aéreas del Estado - Argentina
Líneas Aéreas del Mar - Colombia
Líneas Aéreas del Norte de Colombia - Colombia
Líneas Aéreas del Pacifico SA - LAPSA - Mexico
Líneas Aéreas El Dorado - Colombia
Líneas Aéreas Guerrero-Oaxaca - LAGOSA - Mexico
Líneas Aéreas Interiores de Catalina - Colombia
Líneas Aéreas La Urraca - Colombia
Líneas Aéreas Mexicanas SA - LAMSA - Mexico
Líneas Aéreas Nacionales SA - Colombia
Líneas Aéreas Nacionales SA - Dominican Republic
Líneas Aéreas Nacionales SA - Honduras
Líneas Aéreas Orientales Ltda - Colombia
Lineas Aereas Paraguayas SA - Paraguay
Líneas Aéreas Petroleras - Colombia
Líneas Aéreas Postales Españolas - Spain
Líneas Aéreas TACA de Colombia - Colombia
Líneas Aéreas Taxader - Colombia
Líneas Aéreas Unidas Mexicanas (LAUMSA) - Mexico
Líneas Aéreas Unidas SA - LAUSA - Mexico
Linee Aeree Italiane SpA - LAI - Italy
l inha Aérea Transcontinental Brasileira SA - Brazil
Linhas Aéreas Brasileiras - Brazil
Linhas Aéreas da Guiné Bissau - Guiné Bissau
Linhas Aéreas Natal - Brazil
Linhas Aéreas Paulistas SA - Brazil
Liniile Aeriene Române Exploatate cu Statul - Romania
Linjeflyg AB - Sweden
Lloyd Aéreo Boliviano - LAB - Bolivia
Loadair - Sweden
Loftleiðir hf - Iceland
Loide Aéreo Nacional SA - Brazil
Lone Star Cargo Lines - USA
Los Angeles Air Services Inc (LAAS) - USA
LOT - Poland
Lucaya Air - Bahamas
Luchtvaartmaatschappij "De Kroonduif" - Netherlands New Guinea
Lukas-Lukim Aero Service - Zaire
Luxair - Luxembourg
Luxembourg Airlines - Luxembourg
Lynbird International - USA
Mabuhay Airways - Philippine Republic
Macair Air Charter Service - Australia
Macedonian Aviation Ltd - UK
Mackey Airlines Inc - USA
MacRobertson Miller Aviation Co Pty Ltd - Australia
Magic Carpet Transport Co - USA
Magnum Airlines - South Africa
Magyar Légiköziekedési Válialat - Hungary
Magyar-Szovjet Polgári Légiforgalmi Társaság - Hungary
Maine Air Cargo Express Inc - USA
Maine Air Transport Co Inc - USA

Majestic Air Cargo - USA
Majestic Airlines - USA
Malayan Airways Ltd - Malaya
Malaysian Airways Ltd - Malaya
Malaysia-Singapore Airlines - Malaya
MALÉV - Magyar Légiköziekedési Válialat - Hungary
Maluti Air Services - South Africa
Mandala Airlines - Indonesia
Mandated Airlines Ltd - Australia
Manila Air Transport System - Philippine Republic
Mannion Air Charter - USA
Manx Airlines Ltd - UK
Marian Air Service Inc - USA
Maritime Central Airways Ltd - Canada
Marshall Airways Pty Ltd - Australia
Martins Air Charter - Netherlands
Masling Commuter Services Pty Ltd - Australia
Massachusetts Air Industries (E Anthony & Sons Inc) - USA
MASZOVLET - Magyar-Szovjet Polgári Légiformgalmi Társaság - Hungary
Matane Air Services Ltd - Canada
May Air X-Press - USA
Maya Airways - Mexico
Maya Airways Ltd - British Honduras
McFerrin Air Express Inc - USA
McNeely Charter Services Inc - USA
Mercer Airlines - USA
Mercer Enterprises - USA
Mercury Airlines Inc - USA
Mercury Airlines Ltd - UK
Mercury Aviation Services (Pty) Ltd - South Africa
Meredith Air Transport Ltd - UK
Meridian Air Cargo Inc - USA
Merpati Nusantara Airlines - Indonesia
Meteor Air Transport Inc - USA
Methow Aviation - USA
Mey-Air AS - Norway
Miami Airlines Inc - USA
Miami Valley Aviation - USA
Michigan Central Airlines Inc - USA
Mid-America Airlines/Mid-America Air Transport - USA
Midas Commuter Airlines - Venezuela
Mid-Continent Airlines Inc - USA
Middle East Airlines Co - Lebanon
Midline Air Freight Inc - USA
Midstate Air Services - USA
Midwest Air Freighters - USA
Midwest Airlines Ltd - Canada
Midwest Airways Inc - USA
Midwest Aviation Inc - USA
Millardair Ltd - Canada
Mineral County Airlines - USA
Misrair SAE - Egypt
Missionair - USA
Missouri Airways Inc - USA
Mistri Airways - India
Modern Air Transport Inc - USA
Mohawk Airlines Inc - USA
Monarch - USA
Monarch Air Lines Inc - USA
Mongolian Air Transport Co - Mongolia
Monmouth Airlines - USA
Mont Laurier Aviation Co Ltd - Canada
Montauk-Caribbean Airways - USA
Montreal Air Services Ltd - Canada
Moormanair - Moorman Vliegtuigonderhoudsbedrijf, NV - Netherlands
Mor-Fresh Air Express Inc - USA
Morton Air Services Ltd - UK
Mount Cook & Southern Lakes Tourist Co - New Zealand
Mount Cook Airlines - New Zealand
Mountainwest Aviation - USA
Mt McKinley Air Freight Inc - USA
Nacional - Brazil
Nahanni Air Service - Canada
Nalanda Airways Ltd - India
Namib Air - Namibia
Namib Air - South Africa
Naples Airlines - USA
National Air Cargo Corp - USA
National Air Charter - Indonesia
National Air Express Co - USA
National Air Transport Co - USA
National Air Transportation Service (NATS) - USA
National Airways Corp, (Pty) Ltd - South Africa
National Greek Airlines - Greece
National Skyways Freight Corp - USA
Nationwide Air Transport Service Inc - USA
Nationwide Airlines Inc - USA
NATS - USA
Navegação Aérea Brasileira, SA - Brazil
Nederlands New Guinea Luchtvaartmaatschappij "De Kroonduif" - Netherlands New Guinea

Nenana Air Services - USA
Nevada Airlines Inc - USA
New England Air Express Inc - USA
New Holland Airways Pty Ltd - Australia
New Mexico Flying Service - USA
New Zealand National Airways Corp - New Zealand
Nigeria Airways - Nigeria
Nigeria Trade Wings Airways - Nigeria
Nihon Koku Yuso KK (NKYKK) - Japan
Nile Delta Air Services - Egypt
NKYKK - Japan
NOLI - Bolivia
Norcanair - North Canada Air Ltd - Canada
Nord Aviation - USA
Nordair Ltd - Canada
Nordseeflug Sylter Lufttransport - Germany
Nor-Fly - Norway
Normandie Air Services - France
Norseman Air Transport Inc - USA
North American Airlines - USA
North American Skyliners - USA
North Canada Air Ltd - Canada
North Cariboo Air - Canada
North Cay Airways Inc - USA
North Central Airlines Inc - USA
North Coast Air Services - Canada
North East Airlines - Australia
North Japan Airlines - Japan
Northeast Airlines Inc - USA
Northern Air Cargo - USA
Northern Airlines Inc - USA
Northern Airlines Ltd - Australia
Northern Airways - USA
Northern Consolidated Airlines - USA
Northern Pacific Transport - USA
Northern Thunderbird Air - Canada
Northern Wings Ltd (Les Ailes du Nord Ltée) - Canada
Northland Air Cargo Inc - USA
Northland Air Manitoba - Canada
Northland Airlines Ltd - Canada
North-South Airlines Ltd - UK
Northward Aviation - Canada
North-West Airlines (IOM) Ltd - UK
Northwest Airlines Inc - USA
Northwest Territorial Airways Ltd - Canada
Northwestern Air Lease - Canada
Norwegian Overseas Airways AS - Norway
Nucleo Ala Littoria - Italy
Nunasi Central Airlines - Canada
Nunasi-Northland Airlines - Canada
NZNAC - New Zealand
OASIS Inc - Orient Air Systems and Integrated Services Inc - Philippine Republic
Obrazovni Centar Zracnog Saobracaja - Yugoslavia
Ocean Reef Airways - USA (see Montauk-Caribbean A/W)
OCZS - Obrazovni Centar Zracnog Saobracaja - Yugoslavia
Old South Air Services - USA
Olympic Airways SA - Greece
Omega Aero Transportes - Mexico
Ontario Central Airlines Ltd - Canada
Onyx Aviation Inc - USA
Orario Linee Aereo Teseo - Italy
Orient Air Systems and Integrated Services Inc - Philippine Republic
Orient Airways Ltd - India
Orient Airways Ltd - Pakistan
Ortner Air Service - USA
Osterreichische Luftverkehr AG - Austria
Otis Spunkmeyer Air - USA (see Sentimental Journey)
Out Island - Bahamas
Overseas Airways - USA
Ozark Air Lines Inc - USA
PAA - USA
PAA-Africa - USA
PAB - Panair do Brasil SA - Brazil
Pacific Air Cargo Inc - USA
Pacific Air Lines Inc - USA
Pacific Airlines Inc - USA
Pacific Alaska Air Express Inc - USA
Pacific Alaska Airlines - USA
Pacific American Airlines - USA
Pacific Coast Airlines - USA
Pacific Coastal Airlines - Canada
Pacific National Air Express - USA
Pacific National Airways - USA
Pacific Northern Airlines - USA
Pacific Overseas Airlines (Siam) Ltd - Thailand
Pacific Southwest Airlines Inc - USA
Pacific Western Airlines Ltd - Canada
Page Airways Inc - USA
Pak-Air Ltd - Pakistan
Pakistan Airways Ltd - Pakistan
Pakistan International Airlines Corp - Pakistan

Chapter 4: Commercial Operators Index

PAL - Philippine Republic
Pan African Air Charter - Israel
Pan African Air Charter Ltd - South Africa
Pan American Airways Inc - USA
Pan American-Grace Airways Inc ('Panagra') - USA
Pan Malaysia Air - Malaya
Panagra - USA
Panair do Brasil SA - Brazil
Panama Cargo Three - Panama
Papuan Air Transport Ltd - Australia
Papuan Airlines Pty Ltd - Australia
Parachute Air Cargo - USA
Paradak Pty Ltd - Australia
Paradise Airlines - USA
Paraense Transportes Aéreos SA - Brazil
Parks Air Lines - USA
Patricia Air Transport Ltd - Canada
Payloads (Charter) Co Ltd - UK
PBA - USA
Peachbrand PL - Australia
Peacock Airlines - Burma
Pearson-Alaska Inc - USA
Peau Vav'u Air - Tonga
Pegasus Air Freight Corp - USA
Pem-Air Ltd - Canada
PENAS Cargo (Perusahaan Negara Areal Survey) - Indonesia
Peninsular Air Transport - USA
Pennsylvania-Central Airlines Corp - USA
People Express - USA
People's Aviation Corp of China (SKOGA) - China
Perimeter Airlines - Canada
Perle Air - Haiti
Perusahaan Negara Areal Survey - Indonesia
Philair - Philippine Republic
Philippine Airlines Inc (PAL) - Philippine Republic
Philippine Express Co - Philippine Republic
Philips Flying Service Inc - USA
Phoebus Apollo - South Africa
Phoenix Airlines - South Africa
Piedmont Air Cargo - USA
Piedmont Airlines - USA
Piedmont Aviation Inc - USA
Pilgrim Airlines - USA
Pinehurst Airlines Inc - USA
Pioneer Air Lines Inc - USA
Pipirite Air - Haiti
Plains Airways - USA
PLUNA - Primeras Líneas Uruguayas de Navegación Aérea - Uruguay
PMC Associated Co.Ltd - Thailand
PN Garuda Indonesia Airways - Indonesia
PN Merpati Nusantara Airlines - Indonesia
Points North Air Services - Canada
Polaris Air Transport AS - Norway
Polskie Linie Lotnicze "LOT" - Poland
Polynesian Airlines Ltd - Western Samoa
Pompano Airways - USA
Pretoria Air Services - South Africa
Primeras Líneas Uruguayas de Navegación Aérea - Uruguay
Pro Airlines Inc - USA
Pro-Air Services - USA
Professional Airways - South Africa
Projeto Rondon - Brazil
Pronto Air Services - USA
Pronto Aviation Services - USA
Protea Airways (Pty) Ltd - South Africa
Provincetown-Boston Airlines/Naples Airlines - USA
PT Air Indonesia - Indonesia
PT Airfast Indonesia - Indonesia
PT AOA Zamrud Aviation Corp - Indonesia
PT Bouraq Indonesia Airlines - Indonesia
PT Dirgantara Air Services - Indonesia
PT National Air Charter - Indonesia
PT Safari Air - Indonesia
PT Seulawah Air Service - Indonesia
Puerto Rico Air Transport - USA
Purdue Aeronautics Corp - USA
Purdue Airlines Inc - USA
Pyramid Airlines - Egypt
Qantas Empire Airways Ltd - Australia
Quaker City Airways Inc - USA
Quebecair Ltd - Canada
Queen Charlotte Airlines Ltd - Canada
Queensland Airlines Pty Ltd - Australia
Queensland Pacific Airways Ltd - Australia
Railway Air Services Ltd - UK
Rainbow Airlines Inc/ Rainbow Airlines of Honolulu - USA
Rainier Air Freight Lines Inc - USA
RANSA - Ruta Aérea Nacional SA - Costa Rica
RANSA - Rutas Aéreas Nacionales SA - Venezuela
Rapid Air - USA
RAPSA - Rutas Aéreas Panamenas SA - Panama
RCR Air Transport Inc - USA

Reading Aviation Services - USA
REAL - SA Transportes Aéreos - Brazil
REAL-Aerovias - Brazil
Rebel Air - Australia
Rebel Air Pty Ltd - Australia
Red Baron Air - USA
Red Carpet Airlines - USA
Red Carpet Flying Services Inc - USA
Redes Estaduais Aereas Ltda (REAL) - Brazil
Reeve Aleutian Airways Inc - USA
Refugee Relief Commission - Ethiopia
Regina Airlines/Imperial Airlines - USA
Regina Cargo Airlines Inc - USA
Regional Air - South Africa
Reindeer Air Services - Canada
Rennies Air (Transvaal) - South Africa
Rentavion - Venezuela
Reseau Aérien Interieur Cambodgien - Cambodia
Resort Airlines Inc - USA
Rhoades Aviation - USA
Rhoades International - USA
Rhodesian Air Services (Pvt) Ltd - Zimbabwe
RICO - Rondonia Importação, Exportação, Industria e Comércio - Brazil
Rig-Air Ltd - UK
Riis Flyrederei - Norway
Rimouski Airlines Ltd - Canada
Rio Airways - USA
Robinson Airlines Corp - USA
Roblex Aviation - USA
Rockdale Flying Service - USA
Rog-Air - Canada
Rondonia Importação, Exportação, Industria e Comércio (RICO) - Brazil
Rossair Executive Air Charter - South Africa
Rousseau Aviation - France
Royal Air Cambodge - Cambodia
Royal Air Lao - Laos
Royal Air Maroc - Cie Nationale de Transports Aériens - Morocco
Royal Air Services - USA
Royal Airlines Inc - USA
Royal Jordanian Airlines - Jordan
Royal Nepal Airline Corp, Ltd - Nepal
Royal Taxi Aéreo - Brazil
Royal West Airways - USA
Royalair Ltd - Canada
RRC - Refugee Relief Commission - Ethiopia
Ruta Aérea Nacional SA - Costa Rica
RUTACA - Rutas Aéreos CA - Venezuela
Rutas Aérea Mexicana SA - Mexico
Rutas Aéreas de Colombia Ltda - Colombia
Rutas Aéreas Nacionales SA - Venezuela
Rutas Aéreas Panamenas SA - Panama
Rutas Aéreas SAM Ltda - Colombia
Rutas Aéreos CA (RUTACA)- Venezuela
S A Air Nolis - France
S S W Inc - USA
S/A des Avions Meyer et Cie - Cameroun
SA Empresa de Viação Aérea Rio Grandense - Brazil
SA Medellin Consolidada - Colombia
SA Viacao Aérea Gaúcha - SAVAG - Brazil
SABENA - Sté. Anonyme Belge d'Exploitation de la Navigation Aérienne - Belgium
Saber Air Pte Ltd - Malaya
Saber Cargo Airlines - USA
Sabourin Lake Airways - Canada
SADELCA - Servicio Aérea del Caqueta - Colombia
SADIA SA Transportes Aéreos - Brazil
SAEP - Servicios Aéreos Petroleros - Colombia
SAESA - Servicios Aéreos Especiales SA - Mexico
SAETA - Sociedad Aérea de Tolima SA - Colombia
SAETA - Sociedad Ecuatoriana de Transportes Aéreos - Ecuador
Safari Air - Indonesia
Safari Air - Zaire
Safari Airways - India
Sahakol Air - Thailand
SAHSA - Servicio Aéreo de Honduras SA - Honduras
Salair - USA
Salpanavi, Societe di Navigazione Aerea - Italy
SAM - Sociedad Aeronáutica Medellin SA - Colombia
SAM - Societa Aerea Mediterranea - Italy
Samaki Peanich Airlines - Cambodia
Samoan Air Lines Inc - USA
SAN - Servicios Aéreos Nacionales - Ecuador
San Diego Sky Freight - USA
Sandriver Safaris - South Africa
SANSA - Servicios Aéreos Nacionales SA - Costa Rica
SANTA - Servicio Aéreos Nacionales de Territoriales Andes - Ecuador
Santa Fe Skyway Inc - USA
SARPA - Servicios Aéreos del Patumayo - Colombia
Saskair - Canada
Saskatchewan Government Airways (Saskair) - Canada
SATA - Soc. Açoriana de Transportes Aéreos Ltda - Portugal
SATA - Sté. Antillaise de Transports Aériens - France

SATAIR - Sté. Antillaise de Traitements Aériens - France
SATCO - Servicio Aéreo de Transporte Commerciales - Peru
SATENA - Servicio Aeronavegación a Teritorios Nacionales - Colombia
SATT - Sté. Africaine de Transports Tropicaux t/a Aéro Africaine - Algeria
Saudi Arabian Airlines - Saudi Arabia
SAVA - Serviçios do Aerotaxis e Abastecimento do Vale Amazônica - Brazil
Scala Taxi Aéreo - Brazil
SCAN Air Charter - Mozambique
SCANA - Sté Commerciale d'Aviation Nord Africaine - Morocco
Scandinavian Airlines System - Denmark/Norway/Sweden
Schreiner Aerocontractors NV - Netherlands
Schweizerische Luftverkehr AG - Switzerland
SCOLTA - Sociedad Colombiana de Transportes Aéreos Ltda - Colombia
Scottish Airlines Ltd - UK
SCS Air Transport - USA
Sea-Bear Air Transport - USA
Seaboard and Western Airlines Inc - USA
Seagreen Air Transport - Leeward Islands
Seattle Air Charter Inc - USA
SELVA - Colombia
Sempati Air Transport - Indonesia
Senaki Peanich Airlines - Thailand
Sentimental Journeys - USA
Service impérial de liaisons aériennes - Vietnam
Servicio Aérea del Caqueta - Colombia
Servicio Aéreo de Honduras SA - Honduras
Servicio Aéreo de Transporte Commerciales - Peru
Servicio Aéreo Gomez Mendez - Mexico
Servicio Aéreo Panini - Mexico
Servicio Aéreos Nacionales de Territoriales Andes - Ecuador
Servicio Aeronavegación a Teritorios Nacionales - Colombia
Servicios Aéreos - Mexico
Servicios Aéreos Cochabamba - Bolivia
Serviçios Aéreos Cruzeiro do Sul SA - Brazil
Servicios Aéreos del Patumayo - Colombia
Servicios Aéreos Especiales SA - SAESA - Mexico
Servicios Aéreos Nacionales - Ecuador
Servicios Aéreos Nacionales SA - Costa Rica
Servicios Aéreos Petroleros - Colombia
Servicios Aéreos Rio Negro - Argentina
Servicios Aéreos Santa Isabel - Argentina
Servicios Aéreos Virgen de Copacabana - Bolivia
Servicios AVENSA SA - Venezuela
Serviçios do Aerotaxis e Abastecimento do Vale Amazônica - Brazil
Serviços Aéreos Regionales SA (VOTEC) - Brazil
Servivensa - Servicios AVENSA SA - Venezuela
Setair - Australia
SETCO - Honduras
Seulawah Air Service - Indonesia
Shamrock Airlines - USA
Shawnee Airlines Inc - USA
Shorter Airlines - USA
Siamese Airways Co Ltd - Thailand
SILA - Service impérial de liaisons aériennes - Vietnam
SILA - Svensk Interkontinental Lufttrafik AB - Sweden
Silver City Airways Ltd - UK
Sioux Narrows Airways - Canada
SISA - Societa Italiane Servizi Aerei - Italy
Site Aviation Ltd - UK
Sivewright Airways Ltd - UK
Skandinaviska Aero AB - Sweden
SKOGA (or SKOAGA) - People's Aviation Corp of China - China
Sky of Siam Co Ltd - Thailand
Sky Tours Inc - Philippine Republic
Sky Train Air - USA
Skycraft Air Transport Inc - Canada
Skyfreight Airlines - USA
Skyfreight Airlines Inc - USA
Skyfreighters - Canada
Skyfreighters - USA
Skyline Inc - USA
Skyway Airlines - USA
Skyways (E Africa) Ltd - Kenya
Skyways Cargo Airline Ltd - UK
Skyways Coach-Air Ltd - UK
Skyways Ltd - UK
Slate Falls Airways - Canada
SMB Stage Line - USA
SNEL - Zaire
SOACO - Sté. Anon. de Constructions - Gabon
SOBELAIR - Sté Belge de Transports Aériens - Belgium
Soc. Açoriana de Transportes Aéreos Ltda - Portugal
Sociedad Aérea de Tolima SA - Colombia
Sociedad Aeronáutica Medellin SA - Colombia
Sociedad Colombiana de Transportes Aéreos Ltda - Colombia
Sociedad Ecuatoriana de Transportes Aéreos - Ecuador
Sociedad Transportes Aéreos Boyacenses - Colombia
Societa Aerea Mediterranea - Italy
Societa Italiane Servizi Aerei - Italy
Societe di Navigazione Aerea SpA - Italy

Somali Airlines - Somali Republic
SONATRA Air Sénégal - Senegal
Sorya Airlines - Cambodia
Sorya Airlines - Laos
SOTEXKI - Zaire
Soundair - Canada
Sourdough Air Transport - USA
South African Airways - South Africa
South American and Far East Air Transport AS (SAFE) - Norway
South Central Air - USA
South Coast Air Services Ltd - UK
South Coast Airways - UK
South East Airlines Inc - USA
South Pacific Airlines of N.Z - New Zealand
South Pacific Airmotive - Australia
South West Air Transport (Pty) Ltd - South Africa
South West Aviation Ltd - UK
Southampton Air Services Ltd - UK
Southeast Airlines Inc - USA
Southern Air Express - USA
Southern Air Transport - USA
Southern Airways Inc - USA
Southern Commercial Air Transport Inc - USA
Southern Flyer - USA
Southern Frontier Air Transport - Canada
Southern International Ltd - UK
Southwest Airlines - USA
Southwest Airways Co - USA
Southwind Airlines - USA
Southwind Aviation - USA
SPANTAX SA - Spain
Spencer Airways - Zimbabwe
SS Airways - USA
St Felicien Air Services Ltd - Canada
St Lucia Airways - St Lucia
STAB - Sté. de Transports Aériens du Burundi - Burundi
STAEO - Sté de Transports Aériens en Extrême Orient - Indo-China
Standard Air Cargo - USA
Standard Air Lines Inc - USA
Standard Airways Inc - USA
Starflite Inc - USA
Starways Ltd - UK
State Airlines Inc - USA
Sté Aérienne de Transports Alpes Provence - France
Ste Aéro Cargo - France
Sté Belge de Transports Aériens - Belgium
Sté Commerciale d'Aviation Nord Africaine - Morocco
Sté d'Etude du Transport Aérien - Belgium
Sté de Transports Aériens en Extrême Orient - Indo-China
Sté Khmer Aviation - Cambodia
Sté Transafricaine d'Aviation - Algeria
Sté Transafricaine d'Aviation - France
Sté. Africaine de Transports Tropicaux t/a Aéro Africaine - Algeria
Sté. Airtransivoire - Ivory Coast
Sté. Algérienne de Constructions Aéronautiques - Algeria
Sté. Anon. de Constructions - Gabon
Sté. Anon. de Transports Aériens - Laos
Sté. Anonyme Belge d'Exploitation de la Navigation Aérienne - Belgium
Sté. Cherifienne de l'Air - Morocco
Sté. de Transports Aériens Camerounais - Cameroun
Sté. de Transports Aériens du Burundi - Burundi
Sté. Marocaine de Construction Aéronautique - Morocco
Sté. Transatlantique Aérienne - France
Sté. Tunisienne de l'Air - Tunisia
Stellair - France
Stellar Air Freighter - Norway
Sterling Air Services - Canada
Stewart Air Service - USA
Strathair - UK
Strato Freight Inc - USA
Suburban Airlines - USA
Sudair Ltd - Canada
Sudan Airways - Sudan
Suidair International Airways Ltd - South Africa
Suidwes Lugdiens (Edms) Beperk - South Africa
Summit Airlines - USA
Summit Airways - USA
Sun Belt Airways - USA
Sun International Airways - USA
Sunbird Air Charter - Kenya
Sunland Air Transport Co - USA
Superior Airways Ltd - Canada
Surinam Airways - Surinam
Surrey Flying Services Ltd - UK
Survair Ltd - Canada
Svensk Flygjanst AB - Sweden
Svensk Interkontinental Lufttrafik AB - Sweden
Sverigeflyg AB - Sweden
Swazi Air Ltd - Swaziland
Swedair AB - Sweden
Swedish Air Lines - Sweden
Swift Delivery Air Freight - USA

Chapter 4: Commercial Operators Index

Swiftair Inc - Philippine Republic
Swissair - Schweizerische Luftverkehr AG - Switzerland
Syrian Airways Co - Syria
Syrian Arab Airlines Co - Syria
TAAG - Transportes Aéreos de Angola SARL - Angola
Tabors Luxury Airlines - USA
TABSO - Bulgarian Civil Air Transport - Bulgaria
TAC Air Services - South Africa
TACA - Colombia
TACA de Costa Rica SA - Costa Rica
TACA de El Salvador - El Salvador
TACA de Honduras - Honduras
TACA de Nicaragua - Nicaragua
TACA de Venezuela - Venezuela
TACATA - Taxi Aéreo Caqueta - Colombia
TAE - Greece
TAERCO - Taxi Aereo Colombiano - Colombia
TAI - Cie de Transports Aériens Intercontinentaux - France
Taino Air - Bahamas
Taino Airlines - Dominican Republic
TALA Ltda - Transportes Aéreos Latinamericanos - Colombia
TAM - Transportes Aéreos Militares - Peru
TAME - Transportes Aéreos Militar Ecuador - Ecuador
TAMSA - Mexico
TAMU - Transporte Aéreo Militar Uruguaya - Uruguay
TAN - Brazil
TAN - Transportes Aéreos Nacionales SA - Costa Rica
TANA - Transportes Aéreos Nacional - Colombia
TAO - Taxi Aéreo Opita - Colombia
TAP - Transportes Aéreos Portugueses SARL - Portugal
TAPSA - Transportes Aéreos Profesionales SA - Guatemala
TAROM - Transportuli Aeriene Române - Romania
TARS - Transporturi Aeriene Româno-Sovietice - Romania
TASSA - Trabajos Aéreos del Sahara SA - Spain
Tata Air Lines - India
TAXADER - Líneas Aéreas Taxader - Colombia
Taxi Aéreo "El Llanero" Ltda - Colombia
Taxi Aéreo Caqueta - Colombia
Taxi Aereo Colombiano - Colombia
Taxi Aereo de Santander - Colombia
Taxi Aéreo El Venado - Colombia
Taxi Aéreo Fortaleza - Brazil
Taxi Aéreo Lider Ltda - Brazil
Taxi Aéreo Opita - Ecuador
Taxi Aéreo Opita (TAO) - Colombia
Taxi Aéreo Selva - Peru
Taxis Aéreos Nacionales SA - Mexico
TAZ - Transport Aérien Zairois - Zaire
TBM Inc - USA
Technical & Aeronautical Exploitation Co Ltd (TAE) - Greece
Texas Airways - USA
Texas International - USA
Texoma Airways - USA (see Mid-America Airlines)
Thai Airways Co Ltd - Thailand
The Maine SeaFood Airlines - USA
THY - Türk Hava Yollari - Turkey
Tigres Voladores - Venezuela
Tol Air Services - USA
Topflight Ltd - UK
Torair AB - Sweden
Trabajos Aéreos del Sahara SA - Spain
Trans Air - USA
Trans Air Service - Philippine Republic
Trans American Airways - USA
Trans Asiatic Airlines Inc - Philippine Republic
Trans Australia Airlines - Australia
Trans Caribbean Air Cargo Lines Inc/Trans Caribbean A/w - USA
Trans Continental - USA
Trans Eastern Airlines - USA
Trans Europe Air - France
Trans Florida Airlines Inc - USA
Trans Gaspésian - Canada
Trans Global Airlines - USA
Trans Island Airways - USA
Trans Mar de Cortes SA - Mexico
Trans Marine Airways - USA
Trans National Airlines Inc - USA
Trans New England Airlines - USA
Trans North Air - Canada
Trans North Turbo Air - Canada
Trans Oriental Ltda - Bolivia
Trans Pacific - USA
Trans Provincial Airlines Ltd - Canada
Trans Sierra Airlines - USA
Trans South Airways - USA
Trans Tropic Airlines - USA
Trans West Air Express - USA
Trans World Airlines Inc (TWA) - USA
Transadriateca, Societe di Navigazione Aerea SpA - Italy
TRANSAER - Aéreos Terrestres y Maritimos - Argentina
Transaero Rotterdam - Netherlands
Trans-Air Hawaii Ltd - USA
Transair Inc - USA
Transair Ltd - Canada
Transair Ltd - UK
Transair Sweden AB - Sweden
Trans-Alaskan Airlines Inc - USA
Transamazonica - Colombia
Trans-Asiatic Airlines (Siam) Ltd - Thailand
Trans-Canada Air Lines - Canada
Transcarga - Transportes Aéreos de Carga - Venezuela
Transcontinental Air Express Corp - USA
Transcontinental and Western Air Inc (TWA) - USA
Transfair - Canada
Transgabon - Transports Aériens du Gabon - Gabon
Trans-Gaspesian - Canada
Trans-Jamaican Airlines - Jamaica
Trans-Labrador Airlines Ltd - Canada
Trans-Luxury Airlines Inc - USA
Transna Indonesia (Trans National Airways / Trans Nusantara Airways PT) - Indonesia
Transocean Air Lines - USA
Trans-Pacific Airlines Ltd - USA
Trans-Peruana de Aviación SA - Peru
Transport Aérien Congo - Zaire
Transport Aérien du Mali - Mali
Transport Aérien Sept- Iles - Canada
Transport Aérien Zairois - Zaire
Transporte Aereo Militar - Paraguay
Transporte Aéreo Militar Uruguaya - Uruguay
Transporte Aéreo Transandino - Venezuela
Transporte Carga Aérea SA - Brazil
Transportes Aéreos Acre - Bolivia
Transportes Aéreos Bandeirantes Ltda - Brazil
Transportes Aéreos Catarinense SA - Brazil
Transportes Aereos da Guinee-Bissau - Guiné Bissau
Transportes Aéreos de Angola SARL - Angola
Transportes Aéreos de Carga - Venezuela
Transportes Aéreos de Nayarit SA - Mexico
Transportes Aéreos Itanez - Bolivia
Transportes Aereos Jalisco - Mexico
Transportes Aéreos Latinamericanos - Colombia
Transportes Aéreos Ltda - Brazil
Transportes Aéreos Luwior - Bolivia
Transportes Aereos Mexicanos SA - TAMSA - Mexico
Transportes Aéreos Militar Ecuador - Ecuador
Transportes Aéreos Militares - Bolivia
Transportes Aéreos Militares - Peru
Transportes Aéreos Nacional - Colombia
Transportes Aéreos Nacional Ltda - TAN - Brazil
Transportes Aéreos Nacionales SA - Costa Rica
Transportes Aéreos Opita (TAO) - Colombia
Transportes Aéreos Orientales - Ecuador
Transportes Aéreos Portugueses SARL - Portugal
Transportes Aéreos Profesionales SA - Guatemala
Transportes Aéreos Salvador Ltda - Brazil
Transportes Aéreos San Antonio - Bolivia
Transportes Aéreos San Jorge - Bolivia
Transportes Aéreos San Miguel - Bolivia
Transportes Aéreos Sul Americanos SA - Brazil
Transportes Aéreos Tadeo - Bolivia
Transportes Aereos Tampico S de RL de CV - Mexico
Transportes Aéreos Tauro - Bolivia
Transportes Aéreos Virgen de Carmen - Bolivia
Transportes Carga Aérea - Brazil
Transports Aériens du Benin - Dahomey
Transports Aériens Réunis - France
Transporturi Aeriene Româno-Sovietice - Romania
Transporturile Aeriene Române - Romania
Trans-Texas Airways - USA
Transvalair, Air Charter Express - France
Transwest Air Express - USA
Travair - Australia
Travmar Holdings Pty Ltd - Australia
Trek Airways (Pty) Ltd - South Africa
Trent Valley Aviation Ltd - UK
Tricon International Airlines Inc - USA
Triple H Flying Service - USA
Triumph Airways Ltd - Canada
Tropic Air (Tropical Air Services) - Barbados
Tropic Airlines - USA
Tropic Airways (Pty) Ltd - South Africa
Tropical Air Services - Barbados
Tropics International Inc - USA
Tunis Air - Sté. Tunisienne de l'Air - Tunisia
Turismo de Oriente - Venezuela
Türk Hava Yollari - Turkey
Turks & Caicos National Airlines Ltd - Turks & Caicos Is
Turner Airlines - USA
TWA - USA
Twentieth Century Airlines - USA
Tyne Tees Air Charter Ltd - UK
Tyne Tees Airways Ltd - UK
UAT - Union Aéromaritime de Transport - France

Uganda Aviation Services Ltd - Uganda
UKAMPS - North Korea
Ulster Air Transport Ltd - UK
Uni-Air - France
Union Aéromaritime de Transport - France
Union Flights - USA
Union of Burma Airways - Burma
Union Southern Airlines - USA
United Air Lines Inc - USA
United Air Services (Pty) Ltd - South Africa
United Arab Airlines - Egypt
United Khmer Airlines - Cambodia
United Libyan Airlines - Libya
Universal Airlines Inc - USA
UODU Air - Australia
Up Over Down Under (UODU Air) - Australia
US Air Express - USA
US Airlines Inc - USA
US Forest Service - USA
VAC - Zaire
Vacation Airways - USA
Vance International Airways - USA
Vargas Aviation -France
VARIG - SA Empresa de Viação Aérea Rio Grandense - Brazil
VASP - Viação Aérea São Paulo SA - Brazil
Veljekset Karhumaki Oy - Finland
Vero Monmouth Airlines - USA
Veteran Airways Ltd - USA
Veteran's Air Express Co - USA
VIABRAS - Viação Aérea Brasil SA - Brazil
Viação Aérea Bahiana - Brazil
Viação Aérea Brasil SA - Brazil
Viação Aérea Santos Dumont SA - Brazil
Viação Aérea São Paulo SA - Brazil
VIARCO - Vías Aéreas Colombianas - Colombia
Vías Aéreas Colombianas - Colombia
Victoria Air Inc - Philippine Republic
Victorian Air Coach Services - Australia
Viking Air Transport Co Inc - USA
Viking Express - USA
Viking International Airfreight Inc - USA
Village Airways - Philippine Republic
Vintage Air Tours - USA
Vintage Airways - USA
Virgin Air - USA
Virgin Island Air Service Inc - USA
Virgin Islands International - USA
Virunga Air Charter - VAC - Zaire

VOTEC - Serviços Aéreos Regionales SA - Brazil
WAAC (Nigeria) Ltd - Nigeria
Waglisla Air (t/a Wagair) - Canada
Wallace Air Service Inc - USA
Waterman Airlines Inc - USA
WENELA - South Africa
Wenela Air Service - Botswana
West African Airways Corp (WAAC) - Nigeria
West Coast Airlines Inc - USA
Westair Transport - USA (see Avn Corp of Seattle)
Western Air Express - USA
Western Air Lines Inc - USA
Westland Airlines Inc - USA
Westminster Airways Ltd - UK
Westpoint Aviation Ltd - UK
Wheeler Airlines Ltd - Canada
Wideroe's Flyveselskap AS - Norway
Wien Air Alaska - USA
Wien Alaska Airlines Inc - USA
William Dempster Ltd - UK
Willis Air Services Inc - USA
Williston Lake Air Service - Canada
Winged Cargo Inc - USA
Winner Airways Co - Taiwan
Wisconsin Central Airlines Inc - USA
Witwatersrand Native Labour Association (WENELA) - South Africa
Wonderair - South Africa
Woods Air Fuel - USA
World Aviation Enterprises Inc - El Salvador
World Wide Airways Inc - Canada
Xiengkhouang Air Transport - Laos
Yakima Sky Chief - USA
Yellowbird Air - Canada
Yemen Airlines - Yemen
Yemen Airways Corp - Yemen
Yemen Arab Airlines - Yemen
Yemenite Airlines - Yemen
Yukon Air Service - USA
Yute Air Alaska - USA
Zambia Airways - Zambia
Zamrud Aviation Corp - Indonesia
Zantop Air Transport Inc - USA
Zonas Oeste y Norte de Aerolineas Argentinas Soc Mixta - Argentina
ZONDA - Zonas Oeste y Norte de Aerolineas Argentinas Soc Mixta - Argentina
Zoom Zoom Air - USA

Australia - *Featured on chapter heading pages in this book are the above pair of unidentified DC-3s in Ansett Airlines of Papua New Guinea titles.*
[Mervyn W Prime]

CHAPTER 4: COMMERCIAL OPERATORS OF THE DC-3, C-47, R4D, DAKOTA AND LI-2

Australia VH-EDD C-47A-30-DK c/n 25367 - Delivered to the RAAF in Aug44, this aircraft spent its whole life in Australia and the Far East. VH-EDD was the third registration it carried in QANTAS use, and is seen here at Melbourne-Essendon, VIC on 13Mar70. The C-47 was withdrawn in 1977 and subsequently used for fire practice at Cairns in Queensland. [J A Vella via Stephen Piercey collection]

Austria OE-LBN DC-3D c/n 42963 - Austrian Airlines used their DC-3s on local services for three years only, but had withdrawn them from use by the time this photo was taken at Vienna in 1968. The aircraft was sold to Comair in South Africa shortly afterwards, ending its life in Kenya where it survived in a damaged condition at Nairobi until Aug98. [P M Richter via P J Marson]

Belgium OO-AUZ DC-3C c/n 43090 - This aircraft was converted by Douglas from a surplus C-47A, retaining the forward half of the cargo door, while the rear part was sealed. The colour scheme dates from 1947, but OO-AUZ served with SABENA in Belgium and the Belgian Congo until 1966, when it went to Spantax as EC-BED. [via A Pearcy]

Bolivia *CP-1020 C-47-DL c/n 9028 - After transfer to the RFC in 1945, this aircraft was converted for executive use and after serving a number of companies was sold to the Instituto Linguistico de Verano in 1973. It is seen at Opa-Locka, FL in 1980 prior to its sale to JAARS in 1981. Note the 'maximiser' undercarriage doors.* [Stephen Piercey collection via P J Marson]

Brazil *PP-AVL C-47A-DL c/n 9886 awaiting overhauled engines at Sao Paulo-Congonhas in Aug60. REAL had taken over Aerovias Brasil already in 1954 and was in turn merged into VARIG in 1961. PP-AVL was lost in an accident at Videira, Brazil in Sep61.* [Peter Keating]

British Virgin Islands *VP-LVM Dakota III c/n 12195 - This former BEA 'Pionair' was exported to the British Virgin Islands in 1980 after use by a number of British charter airlines and was used on scheduled services in the Caribbean. This photo was taken at its Tortola base in Dec82 after being repainted in the airline's smart dark blue and white livery. The aircraft was stored in a derelict condition at San Juan, PR by 1989.*
[A J Brown via Stephen Piercey collection]

CHAPTER 4: COMMERCIAL OPERATORS OF THE DC-3, C-47, R4D, DAKOTA AND LI-2

Canada *CF-BZN C-47A-DK c/n 25290* in Canadian Pacific Airlines colours at Edmonton, Alta probably in the late 1940s. This aircraft spent ten years with CPA and remained in Canadian service with various operators until lost in an accident in 1989. *[Canadian Pacific Airlines]*

Canada *CF-CTD C-47A-30-DL c/n 9633* - This C-47 served with the USAF until 1961, when it was sold to the Aero American Corp from storage. Norcanair used it from 1972 to 1979, and it is seen here at Saskatoon, Sask in Apr77. It returned to the USA, but disappeared in the early 1980s.
[Stephen Piercey collection via P J Marson]

Colombia *HK-1340 C-53D c/n 11704* - Seen in the colours of one of the many small Colombian airlines that have operated C-47s/DC-3s over the years, this aircraft was civilianised as a DC-3A for Pan American, who later passed it on to AVIANCA. It is seen at Villavicencio, Colombia on an apron full of similar types in Apr80. It was sold to SADELCA two years later, but was written-off in a take-off crash in Jul85.
[Stephen Piercey collection via P J Marson]

Costa Rica *TI-ACC C-47-DL c/n 6215* - Aerovias Cariari SA operated up to four DC-3s between 1970 and 1979, based on San Jose, Costa Rica where this photograph was taken in Feb78 when the aircraft passed to RANSA and eventually to Nicaragua. [Karl Krämer]

Czechoslovakia *OK-AIB DC-2-115K c/n 1582* - CLS operated a mix of DC-2s and DC-3s out of Prague, Czechoslovakia, where this obviously posed photograph was taken a year before the airline was taken over by Germany and Lufthansa when the country was invaded in 1938. [Milan Janac]

Denmark *OY-DDY C-47A-80-DL c/n 19771* was operated by Danish Air Lines between its delivery in Apr47 and the airline's merger into SAS in 1948. It then flew for the Royal Swedish AF for 31 years, before transferring to Zaire. [A J Jackson collection]

CHAPTER 4: COMMERCIAL OPERATORS OF THE DC-3, C-47, R4D, DAKOTA AND LI-2

France F-BAXR C-47A-DL c/n 20100 - Rousseau Aviation operated this former Air France aircraft with 'maximiser' undercarriage door mods for ten years from 1963. It was photographed at Amsterdam, Netherlands on 15Jun69 whilst undertaking a charter assignment. The C-47 was broken up at Toulouse-Blagnac, France in the late 1970s.
[P J Marson collection]

French Indo-China had numerous DC-3 operators, including STAEO who used six of the type. F-BFGG c/n 19387 was registered in Mar49 and photographed at Kai Tak, Hong Kong in Dec53. It moved on to Vietnam in Apr56 and flew for Air Vietnam for many years as XV-NIB. [Peter Keating]

Germany D-CNSF C-47B-DK c/n 26977 was bought by Nordseeflug from the Luftwaffe in Aug66, but saw little service before it passed to Airwork in 1968 and then to The Sultan of Muscat and Oman AF, serialled 501. It spent its final years stored at East Midlands, UK during the mid-1970s.
[Brian Stainer/APN]

Ghana 9G-AAE Dakota III c/n 12054 - Ghana Airways operated this former BOAC aircraft and BEA 'Pionair' for ten years from 1960. The photo was taken prior to delivery at London (Heathrow) in Apr60. The Dakota was sold to Liberian Airways in 1970, but was written-off five years later.
[Brian Stainer via P J Marson]

Greece SX-BAL C-47B-DK c/n 25923 photographed at Athens, Greece in Apr53. TAE was formed in 1946 with support from TWA and this aircraft was acquired from the USAAF store at Payne Field, Cairo, Egypt ex-RAF. TAE merged with Hellenic to form National Greek Airlines in Jul51.
[via P J Marson]

Guinea-Bissau CR-GBS C-47A-DK c/n 25475 was a visitor to Tenerife in Nov78. Linhas Aereas da Guiné-Bissau had some half a dozen DC-3s, but their origins have proved difficult to trace. This particular example came from Air Senegal as 6V-ACA. Unusually there are vents above the windows to introduce fresh air.
[via Ulf Boie]

Chapter 4: Commercial Operators of the DC-3, C-47, R4D, Dakota and Li-2

Guyana 8R-GAS C-47A-DL c/n 19691 at Georgetown, Guyana on 22Oct73. This aircraft was a rebuild of VP-GAH after a major accident, and was later sold as N88HA to Hoganair.
[via Brian Stainer/APN]

Iran EP-AAK C-47A-DK c/n 13016 in Iranian Airways colours, probably after overhaul in the United Kingdom. Named 'Persepolis', it was acquired from US stocks at Payne Field in Egypt after service with the RAF as KG333.
[A J Jackson collection]

Ireland EI-ACE DC-3D c/n 42956 - One of the Aer Lingus fleet that was delivered new in 1946, this aircraft saw eighteen years' service with the airline before sale in Nepal in 1964, only to be written-off there five years later. This photo was taken at Southampton (Eastleigh), UK on 25Sep55.
[P J Marson collection]

Italy *I-TAVE* C-47A-DK c/n 12083 at Gatwick, UK in Feb64. This aircraft was traded in to Handley Page by Itavia in exchange for Heralds and went to Keegan Aviation who sold it on to Uruguay as CX-BDA in Jul64 where it was used only for spares. [Peter Keating]

Ivory Coast *TU-TIA* DC-3D c/n 42955 - This post-war example, built for Pacific Northern from uncompleted C-117D parts in 1946, passed to Air Ivoire in 1964 and was used by them until it fell into disrepair at Abidjan, Ivory Coast by mid-1977. [Bill Fisher]

Japan *JA5078* C-47-DL c/n 6173 at Haneda, Japan in Jul68. After over ten years' service in Colombia as HK-318 this aircraft travelled via the US as N9196Z to All Nippon in 1961 and then went to C Itoh Air Transport for geological survey work, for which some windows appeared to be blacked out and an extra square one fitted towards the rear. [Peter Keating]

CHAPTER 4: COMMERCIAL OPERATORS OF THE DC-3, C-47, R4D, DAKOTA AND LI-2

Jordan JY-ACJ C-47B-DK c/n 26057 at Beirut, Lebanon in Oct61. This aircraft was leased from MEA in 1961 soon after the merger of Air Jordan and Arab Airways. Jordan Airways operated as Jordanian and became Royal Jordanian in 1963, when this aircraft was returned to MEA. It crashed in Syria in 1964 but was repaired as VT-DUP.
[Peter Keating]

Korea (South) HL-05 C-47 c/n unknown at K-16 Seoul airport, Korea in Aug 53. Korea National Airways operated DC-3s between 1950 and Jun62 when Korean Airlines was formed. Little is known of the aircraft used.
[Charles Trask]

Malawi VP-YKM Dakota c/n 32935 of Air Malawi soon after the airline's formation in1964. This aircraft was sold in South Africa in 1970 and then progressed via a short spell in Germany and being impounded in Algeria as F-GILV before it took up 3C-JJN briefly in 1995 and then transferred to T9-ABC. As such it went to the Malta Aviation Museum at TaQali in Malta in Oct02.
[Aftel]

Malaysia *9M-ANF C-47A-DL c/n 20763* started commercial life with Cathay Pacific and then passed to Malayan Airways as VR-SCC before transfer to Borneo Airways as VR-OAJ. Later it was absorbed into Malaysia-Singapore Airlines as 9V-BAM and was last heard of derelict at Vientiane, Laos as XW-TDK. [Photavia]

Netherlands *PH-AKL DC-2-115E c/n 1358* at North Beach, CA doing engine runs before delivery to New York for shipment by sea to Fokker in Apr35. This aircraft was destroyed in a crash at Croydon, UK in Dec36, in which Juan de la Cierva was killed. [via A Pearcy]

Netherlands New Guinea *JZ-PDF Dakota c/n 13334* at Kai Tak, Hong Kong in May62. PH-DAT was transferred by KLM to New Guinea as JZ-PDF in Jan61 and two years later was taken over by Merpati Nusantara as PK-GDP. [Peter Keating via Dacre Watson]

CHAPTER 4: COMMERCIAL OPERATORS OF THE DC-3, C-47, R4D, DAKOTA AND LI-2

New Guinea *P2-ANT C-47-DL c/n 6108* - This aircraft started life with the 5th AF as 41-19465, named 'Cold Turkey' at one time. Its first civil marks were VH-AEU with QANTAS and TAA amongst others, before going to Air Niugini in 1973 and being re-registered twice before it was destroyed in a collision with a SOCATA TB-10 at Bankstown, NSW in 1982.
[Peter Keating]

New Zealand *c/n 34227 C-47B-45-DK ZK-APK* - It tends to be forgotten that New Zealand used the DC-3 for phosphate dressing to improve the grasslands for its sheep. This aircraft operated for the RNZAF before periods with New Zealand National Airways and Fiji Airways, until it joined Airland in Nov68 and Fieldair ten years later. It ended its days preserved first at a petrol station, and then as a restaurant, on New Zealand's North Island.
[Bill Fisher]

Nicaragua *YN-BVK C-47-DL c/n 6215* - This aircraft spent all its post-war life in Central & South America, having been exported to Colombia in 1945. LANICA bought the C-47 in 1979 and this photo taken at Managua, Nicaragua on 04Nov80 shows the airline's later colour-scheme. Note the radar nose and fleet name 'Pancasan'.
[Stephen Piercey collection via P J Marson]

Nigeria c/n 9874 C-47A-45-DL 5N-AAQ and c/n 25366 C-47A-30-DK 5N-AAK had both been operated by Nigeria Airways, but ended on opposite sides in the Biafran war. 5N-AAQ was taken over by the Federal Government and operated by the Nigerian AF as 'AAQ' until it was damaged in Nov69 by an MFI-9B raid at Escravos. 5N-AAK on the other hand was obtained for the Biafran side by a ruse recounted in Michael Draper's book 'Shadows', but was destroyed at Enugu, Nigeria in Sep67. [Bernard Clarkson via Bill Fisher]

Panama HP-86 C-47-DL c/n 6144 - Delivered to COPA as RX-86 in 1946, this DC-3 served with COPA for thirty-eight years until it was sold in 1986 as HK-3286. It is currently in service with SADELCA. Photograph probably taken at Panama City, Panama. [COPA via P J Marson]

Peru OB-XAD DC-3A-279A c/n 2192 - Acquired from PANAGRA, with whom it flew as NC25652, this aircraft passed through various branches of the Fuerza Aerea del Peru between 1950 and 1960 until it became derelict in about 1971. This photograph was taken between 1960 and 1964, at which time it became OB-R-537, still with SATCO. [via A Pearcy]

CHAPTER 4: COMMERCIAL OPERATORS OF THE DC-3, C-47, R4D, DAKOTA AND LI-2

Philippines *RP-C647* C-47A-35-DL c/n 9786 - Having been declared surplus in the USA in 1946, this C-47 was exported to the Philippines in 1965. Commercial Air Transport used it in its later years there, this photo being taken at Manila, Philippines on 23Apr79 where the aircraft was to become derelict a mere two years later. [A Wettstein via Stephen Piercey collection]

Poland *SP-ASL* DC-2-115F c/n 1378 - This Bristol Pegasus-powered DC-2 was photographed at North Beach, CA during test-flying in mid-1935. It was flown to Romania on its way to Britain to become G-AGAD but was taken over en route by the Romanian Government on 10Sep39 and became YR-GAD. [Pinnell via David Lucabaugh]

Polynesia *5W-FAH* Dakota 4 c/n 33315 in American Samoa in Feb70. This aircraft was ZK-BQK leased in 1969/70 by Polynesian Airlines. On its return to New Zealand it was preserved as NZ3544 and then re-painted in NZNAC colours as ZK-BQK. [via Peter Russell-Smith]

Portugal *CS-ADB C-47A-DL c/n 20012* - Aero Portuguesa operated this single DC-3 between Jun50 and Jul53 in a colour scheme resembling its former operator Air France, and is illustrated here at Lisbon, Portugal in 1951. [D Walsh]

Russia *URSS-M132 DC-3-196 c/n 1589* - The date on this photograph appears to be 01Apr38 at which time this aircraft, the first to be delivered to Russia in Nov36, had been in service with Aeroflot for nine months. [Harry Gann/Douglas]

South Africa *ZS-BRW Dakota 3 c/n 13468* - A fleet of DC-3s was operated out of Johannesburg, S Africa and were frequent visitors to the United Kingdom (and Israel) between 1947 and 1951. This aircraft became G-AMHJ with British United Airways and Morton Air Services, amongst others, before ending its life performing pollution control duties with Atlantic Air Transport in 2003. [MAP]

CHAPTER 4: COMMERCIAL OPERATORS OF THE DC-3, C-47, R4D, DAKOTA AND LI-2

South Yemen 7O-ABF Dakota 3 c/n 13475 - At one time this aircraft was registered G-AIWD with, amongst others, BEA and BKS, but it moved to Aden and BASCO, later Alyemda, in 1967, serving there for a further ten years, before crashing in 1977. [Peter Keating/APN]

Spain EC-AXS DC-3A-197 c/n 1984 - Spantax operated this DC-3 between 1964 and 1977, but it started life with United Air Lines as NC18112 in 1937. The windmills in the background confirm Palma, Majorca as the photograph location; by October 2003 the aircraft was stored devoid of its C9-ATG markings at Johannesburg-Rand, South Africa, after rebuild by Phoebus Apollo. [Javier Saez]

Switzerland HB-ISI DC-2-115D c/n 1331 - Probably taken in Jul35 taxying in on delivery, this aircraft visited Croydon, UK as X1331 in 1935. It was destroyed by bombing at Stuttgart, Germany in Aug44. [Swissair]

Syria *SR-AAD C-47B-DK c/n 26349* - Showing the 1947 Syrian prefix 'SR' this aircraft was supplied by Pan American via Scottish Aviation in that year. It was damaged in Nov55 and was sold unrepaired as N79004 to Lund Aviation, who sold it on to Eagle Aviation for rebuild at Manchester/Ringway, UK and then to the French AF. It was scrapped in 1970. [Scottish Aviation]

Turkey *TC-ETI Dakota III c/n 12319* - Purchased from surplus RAF stocks in 1946, this aircraft spent the whole of its civilian life with Turkish Airlines (DHY/THY). It is seen on a charter flight to London (Heathrow) in the mid-1950s. Note the fleet number '41' and lack of airline titling. It was written-off in a crash in Turkey in Feb64. [Stephen Piercey collection via P J Marson]

United Kingdom *G-AGHE Dakota c/n 9189* in immediate post-war BOAC colours, before sale to Malayan Airways in Aug48. It was delivered to BOAC by the RAF almost as soon as it reached the UK in May43, ex-FD827. [BOAC]

CHAPTER 4: COMMERCIAL OPERATORS OF THE DC-3, C-47, R4D, DAKOTA AND LI-2

United Kingdom *G-AGHO Dakota c/n 9862 was used by BOAC for five years and then sold to Scottish Aviation and in turn to North-West Airlines in Jun49 for cargo operations based on the Isle of Man. It was photographed at Manchester/Ringway, UK in 1950 before sale eventually to the RCAF in 1951.* [M J Hyde via R A Scholefield]

United Kingdom *In 1985 Air Atlantique painted one of its Dakotas specially for the 50th Anniversary celebration of the DC-3's first flight. G-AMSV (c/n 32820) is seen at Stansted, UK in Oct85 after visiting the RIAT show at Fairford, UK earlier that summer.* [M Massey-Gates]

United States *N15598 DC-3-201D c/n 2258 – After twelve years with Eastern Air Lines and sixteen with North Central, this aircraft finished its life with Aero Virgin Islands, who operated it until it crashed into the sea off Puerto Rico in Jan78. This photograph was taken at San Juan, PR in May77.* [Ulf Boie]

United States *N15567* DC-3-454 c/n 6342 was ordered originally by Delta Airlines but became a C-49J 43-1986 and served in the USA, partly with the Caribbean Wing ATC, before lease and later sale to Eastern Airlines. A series of smaller operators ended with damage in 1982, which probably resulted in its demise as a spares source. [Eastern Air Lines]

United States *N87FA* C-47D c/n 26705 - Falcon Airways operated a fleet of C-47s on cargo charter work in the mid-western and southern states of the USA from 1976 until 1980. The photo was taken at Addison, TX on an unknown date. The aircraft still exists, but is currently stored.
[Stephen Piercey collection via P J Marson]

United States *N9012* C-53 c/n 4936 - After wartime use with the 8th AF in the UK as the personal aircraft of General Miller for a time, this C-53 was sold as surplus to Transcontinental & Western Air in 1945 and subsequently operated with a large number of companies in the USA and Mexico before its use with the third-level airline Kwin Air in Florida. It was photographed at Nassau, Bahamas on 19Jul80 sporting a very individual colour-scheme, consisting basically of an orange cheat-line with a stylised, elongated dragon in multiple colours superimposed on it, and a multi-coloured bird feather design on the undersurfaces of the wings. The fate of the aircraft is unknown after its storage at Nassau. [R Klijn via Stephen Piercey collection]

CHAPTER 4: COMMERCIAL OPERATORS OF THE DC-3, C-47, R4D, DAKOTA AND LI-2

United States *NC50037 C-47-DL c/n 4307* - Lone Star Air Cargo Lines operated four C-47s briefly in 1946/47 for cargo work, but like many companies that started at that time they failed to survive and this aircraft was sold in Brazil where it flew for the next eighteen years. It moved on to Colombia, where its remains were dumped at Villavicencio in 2001, but like many DC-3s in this condition, it had become airborne again before the end of the year.
[William T Larkins]

United States *N19912 C-53D-DO c/n 11716* - This Pan American Airways DC-3 flew for some years with Pan American Grace, and was fitted with R-2000-D5s to cope with the high-altitude airfields in South America. It returned to Pan American Airways in the 1950s, dated by the colour scheme, and then flew with AVIANCA as HK-1341X from 1966 until it was destroyed in a mid-air collision with Hi-Per DC-3 HK-107 over Las Palomas, Colombia in Jul72.
[Warren P Shipp]

United States *N300ZZ C-47A-40-DL c/n 9833* - After service with the Royal Canadian AF, this C-47 was sold off in the early 1970s and purchased by Zoom Zoom Air in 1975 (hence the registration), being used on cargo charter work in the western states of the USA. The aircraft is seen in storage at Fort Lauderdale, FL on 19Oct80 after use with Transwest Air Express (who were connected with previous owners Zoom Zoom and Air Charter West). It was last reported stored at Port-au-Prince, Haiti in 1983.
[A Wettstein via Stephen Piercey collection]

Venezuela YV-C-AMD C-47A-DL c/n 20037 - Twenty years were spent with LAV until this aircraft returned to the USA, where this photograph was taken at Opa-Locka, FL in Aug67. [Peter Keating]

Zaire 9Q-CSN C-47A-30-DK c/n 25459 - Caught at Gatwick, UK this Oklahoma-built C-47 had been the personal aircraft (KG782) of Bomber Harris in WWII before being civilianised as G-ALBG in 1948. It then passed to the Armée de l'Air as 48198 before transferring to the Mauritanian AF with callsign 5TMAA. A period with Rousseau Aviation in France preceded its final employment, based at Kinshasa in Zaire during the 1970s. [Bill Fisher]

Zaire 9Q-CUM DC-3D c/n 42973 - This aircraft served with SABENA for many years in the Belgian Congo as OO-CUM and became 9O-CUM with Air Congo in 1961, being re-registered 9Q-CUM in 1962. The photograph was taken at Dakar, Senegal in Jun65, and shows the wider than normal passenger door. The aircraft was destroyed by fire at N'Djili, Zaire in 1968. [Roger Caratini]